Adaptive and personalized learning

W9-BPL-146

AN ADAPTIVE VOCABULARY AND GRAMMAR PRACTICE EXPERIENCE DESIGNED TO TRANSFORM THE WAY STUDENTS LEARN

More students earn **A's** and **B's** when they use McGraw-Hill Education **Adaptive** products.

LearnSmart®

Proven to help students study more efficiently and improve grades, LearnSmart is an adaptive learning program that provides each student a fully customized vocabulary and grammar practice experience. By identifying the student's strengths and weaknesses and responding with personalized instruction that guides the learner to understand and retain the foundational vocabulary and grammar of the language, LearnSmart helps the student learn and master this critical course content.

LearnSmart delivers—with target precision—the content needed, exactly when it's needed.

Fueled by the Proven and Adaptive LearnSmart Engine

LearnSmart Assignments (Experimental) (n=358)

Testbank Question Assignments (Control) (n=332)

0% 10% 20% 30% 40% 50% 60% 70% 80% 90% 100%

More students earn A's and B's when they use LearnSmart.

Over **8 billion questions** have been answered, making McGraw-Hill Education products more intelligent, reliable, and precise.

www.mheducation.com

CONÉCTATE

Introductory Spanish

CONÉCTATE

Introductory Spanish

Second Edition

Grant Goodall
University of California, San Diego

Darcy Lear
University of Chicago

Mc
Graw
Hill
Education

CONÉCTATE: INTRODUCTORY SPANISH, SECOND EDITION

Published by McGraw-Hill Education, 2 Penn Plaza, New York, NY 10121. Copyright © 2018 by McGraw-Hill Education. All rights reserved. Printed in the United States of America. Previous editions © 2016. No part of this publication may be reproduced or distributed in any form or by any means, or stored in a database or retrieval system, without the prior written consent of McGraw-Hill Education, including, but not limited to, in any network or other electronic storage or transmission, or broadcast for distance learning.

Some ancillaries, including electronic and print components, may not be available to customers outside the United States.

This book is printed on acid-free paper.

1 2 3 4 5 6 7 8 9 LWI 21 20 19 18 17

Student Edition
ISBN: 978-1-259-84585-7
MHID: 1-259-84585-0

Instructor's Edition (not for resale)
ISBN: 978-1-259-99392-3
MHID: 1-259-99392-2

Chief Product Officer, SVP Products & Markets: *G. Scott Virkler*
Vice President, General Manager, Products & Markets: *Michael Ryan*
Vice President, Content Design & Delivery: *Betsy Whalen*
Managing Director: *Katie Stevens*
Senior Brand Manager: *Kim Sallee*
Director, Product Development: *Meghan Campbell*
Product Developer: *Misha MacLaird*
Director, Marketing: *Craig Gill*
Marketing Manager: *Mike Ambrosino*
Executive Market Development Manager: *Helen Greelea*
Senior Faculty Development Manager: *Jorge Arbujas*
Senior Director of Digital Content: *Janet Banhidi*

Senior Digital Product Analyst: *Susan Pierre-Louis*
Product Development Coordinator: *Sean Costello*
Marketing Coordinator: *Jasmine Santana*
Director, Content Design & Delivery: *Terri Schiesl*
Program Manager: *Kelly Heinrichs*
Content Project Managers: *Erin Melloy / Amber Bettcher*
Buyer: *Susan K. Culbertson*
Design: *Matt Backhaus*
Content Licensing Specialists: *Carrie Burger / Beth Thole*
Cover Image: *© Alexander Rieser / Alamy Stock Photo*
Compositor: *Lumina Datamatics, Inc.*
Printer: *LSC Communications*

All credits appearing on page or at the end of the book are considered to be an extension of the copyright page.

Library of Congress Cataloging-in-Publication Data

Names: Goodall, Grant, author. | Lear, Darcy, author.
Title: Conbectate : introductory Spanish / Grant Goodall, Darcy Lear.
Description: Second edition. | New York, NY : McGraw-Hill Education, [2017]
   Includes bibliographical references and index.
Identifiers: LCCN 2016051459| ISBN 9781259845857 (Student Edition : alk. paper) | ISBN 1259845850 (Student Edition : alk. paper) |
   ISBN 9781259993923 (Instructor's Edition) | ISBN 1259993922 (Instructor's Edition)
Subjects: LCSH: Spanish language—Textbooks for foreign speakers—English. Spanish language--Grammar. | Spanish language—Spoken Spanish.
Classification: LCC PC4129.E5 G58 2017 | DDC 468.2/421—dc23
LC record available at https://lccn.loc.gov/2016051459

The Internet addresses listed in the text were accurate at the time of publication. The inclusion of a website does not indicate an endorsement by the authors or McGraw-Hill Education, and McGraw-Hill Education does not guarantee the accuracy of the information presented at these sites.

Dedications

For their patient support and encouragement, I thank el amor de mi vida, Armando Vargas Matus, and my parents, Frank and Lois Goodall. My father did not live to see the book in print, but he felt pride knowing that his son would be published by McGraw-Hill, the company that he devoted his professional life to for more than 30 years. This book is for him.
—Grant

To my two Nancys and my two Bills. I am because of them.
—Darcy

CONTENTS

	COMUNICACIÓN	VOCABULARIO

*See the **Instructors Manual** for more resources and information on integrating film and music into lessons.

---

*See the **Instructors Manual** for more resources and information on integrating film and music into lessons.

	COMUNICACIÓN	VOCABULARIO
Capítulo 7: Los recuerdos y la nostalgia 198	**Lo pasé bien.** Expressing *to have a good time* 199 **Felicitaciones/Felicidades/Enhorabuena** Congratulating someone 202	**¿Cómo se celebra?** Celebrations in the Spanish-speaking world 203
Capítulo 8: La ropa y la moda 226	**¡Qué padre!** Talking about how great something is 227 **Disculpe...** Using polite expressions in appropriate contexts 229	**¿Qué llevas?** Describing clothing 231 **El cuerpo humano** Parts of the body 233 **¿Cómo te queda?** Expressing how clothing fits 234
Capítulo 9: ¿Adónde te gustaría viajar? 259	**¿Te gustaría... ? / ¿Le gustaría... ?** Asking what people would like to do 260 **Favor de no fumar.** Expressing rules with infinitives 261	**Los mejores lugares turísticos** Travel and tourism 262 **¿Qué tiempo hace?** Talking about the weather 266

*See the **Instructors Manual** for more resources and information on integrating film and music into lessons.

	COMUNICACIÓN	VOCABULARIO
Capítulo 10: La vida profesional 292	**A sus órdenes** Expressions for professional contexts 293 **Quiero presentarle a...** Introducing people to each other 297	**Las profesiones y oficios** Professions and careers 299 **La tecnología en el lugar de trabajo** Technology in the workplace 302
Capítulo 11: ¡Estás en tu casa! 325	**¡Bienvenido!** Welcoming people 326 **Pasa.** Making polite invitations 328	**La casa y los muebles** Rooms and other parts of a home 330 **Los muebles y los electrodomésticos** Furniture and appliances 331
Capítulo 12: El deporte y el bienestar 356	**¡Suerte!** Wishing someone good luck 357 **Para mantenerse sano/a, hay que...** Giving advice on healthy living 359	**Los deportes y cómo mantenerse en forma** Sports and fitness 360 **La salud y el bienestar** Health and well-being 364

ESTRUCTURA

CONÉCTATE

PARA SABER MÁS

*See the **Instructors Manual** for more resources and information on integrating film and music into lessons.

COMUNICACIÓN

VOCABULARIO

ESTRUCTURA

CONÉCTATE

PARA SABER MÁS

*See the **Instructors Manual** for more resources and information on integrating film and music into lessons.

ESTRUCTURA

CONÉCTATE

*See the **Instructors Manual** for more resources and information on integrating film and music into lessons

PREFACE

The Story

Conéctate is a fresh approach in every way. With its focus on the most critical language for communication, its active presentation of vocabulary and grammar, and its inclusion of real-world culture throughout, the program provides a unique framework for the Introductory Spanish course, with two separate but complementary goals in mind: learning to use the language and appreciating the world that it comes from.

What makes *Conéctate* so unique?

- **A focused approach:** The tailored scope and sequence of *Conéctate* allows students to concentrate on what they can reasonably be expected to learn in an introductory course, allowing time for systematic review and recycling. This offers a solution to the Introductory Spanish programs that, in an effort to cover everything, include too much grammar and rush students through the curriculum without spending sufficient time for true learning or mastery.

- **Active learning:** *Conéctate* carefully balances a mix of inductive and explicit vocabulary and grammar presentations, applying the concept of desirable difficulty throughout. This leads students to discover and retain the language, and avoids the common type of presentations that only allow for passive learning.

- **Integration of culture:** Language is culture and culture is language. This central idea shapes the way culture is treated in *Conéctate*: not as something separate from the language acquisition process, but as something that is integral to the process. Students acquire cultural knowledge and understanding in a natural way as they learn how the language is used within the rich and diverse Spanish-speaking world.

Chapter Walkthrough

The **Chapter Opener** page offers a visual introduction to the chapter theme and regional focus, as well as a list of learning objectives that outline what a student "can do" upon completing the chapter.
Each chapter contains four main sections.

Comunicación

- Every chapter in *Conéctate* opens with the **Comunicación** section, which presents students with fixed expressions through the authentic, unscripted interviews in the *Conéctate* video series.

- In the videos, students see and hear Spanish as it is truly spoken by hundreds of native speakers representing a wide variety of Spanish-speaking countries. Our author team traveled and conducted unscripted person-on-the-street interviews, asking questions and capturing the spontaneous, authentic answers.

■ The result is a collection of unique and varied responses that showcase to students the many different ways to engage appropriately in key social interactions.

■ The activities that follow the video reinforce the high-frequency communicative expressions and allow students to begin communicating effectively in everyday situations. With these language chunks, students are empowered to complete tasks such as inviting and declining politely and responding to requests, even within the first semester.

A. ¿Por qué no? Empareja la Invitación con la justificación más lógica.

1. _____ ¿Tienes ganas de dar un paseo (*take a walk*) después de la cena?

2. _____ ¿Qué te parece ir al nuevo club con nosotros?

3. _____ ¿Te apetece tomar un café?

4. _____ ¿Quieres almorzar con nosotros el domingo?

a. No, gracias. Voy a viajar este fin de semana.

b. Gracias, pero no puedo. No me gusta hacer ejercicio después de comer.

c. No, gracias. No puedo consumir la cafeína.

d. Gracias, pero no puedo. No sé bailar.

■ Additional video support added in this second edition provides suggestions and notes to students and instructors to assist with the effective use of the video and its activities.

Vocabulario

■ The **Vocabulario** section is where students engage with the words that will become the building blocks of their language development.

■ Vocabulary presentations are embedded within active-learning activities that immediately get students interacting with the new words in a realistic way. Students are not simply memorizing words, but instead are able to develop associations with images or contexts that allow them to do much of their language processing in Spanish.

En la mesa
Eating at home and at restaurants

A. ¡Pongamos la mesa! (*Let's set the table!*)   El cubierto (*place setting*) consiste en varios elementos que se usan para comer. ¿Qué elementos del cubierto usas para cada cosa? **¡Atención!** Las bebidas y la sopa (*soup*) requieren el verbo **tomar.**

el vaso — la taza
el bol — la cuchara
el tenedor — el cuchillo
la servilleta — el plato

MODELO: Como el brócoli con un tenedor y un plato, pero tomo la sopa de brócoli con una cuchara y un bol.

1. la pasta
2. la ensalada
3. el café
4. la sopa
5. una torta de chocolate
6. el yogur
7. el agua
8. la carne

Here are some other words to describe food and its preparation.

a la plancha grilled
la salsa sauce
al ajillo fried with garlic
asado/a roasted

dulce sweet
frito/a fried
picante spicy
saludable healthy

When in a restaurant, you can use **pedir** to order food from the **camarero/a** (*server, waiter/waitress*). Ask for **la carta** (*menu*) to decide what you want to eat.

—**¿Sabes qué vas a pedir?**

Do you know what you are going to order?

—**No, es mi primera vez en este restaurante. Tengo que ver la carta.**

No, it's my first time at this restaurant. I have to see the menu.

—**Bueno, yo voy a pedir una hamburguesa.**

OK, well I'm going to order a hamburger.

Estructura

■ The **Estructura** section of each chapter allows students to put words together to express more complex ideas and to understand how the language works. Students learn by doing; they use new structures meaningfully and uncover the rules that underlie them. They do this through supportive activities that are fun and lead them to success.

■ Beginning in **Capítulo 3,** every grammar topic in the **Estructura** section opens with a **Reciclaje** activity to reinforce language learned earlier in the course that will be built upon in the subsequent activities.

■ After **Reciclaje,** each grammar topic has three parts. **Para empezar** guides students through an engaging activity where they are introduced to and use the target structure in a meaningful way. The **Actividades analíticas** help students disassemble the target structure and analyze how it works. The **Actividades prácticas** that follow allow students to use the structure to communicate with others and to express their own ideas. Throughout the entire **Estructura** section, the activities are carefully sequenced so that students truly learn the structure. In addition, thanks to the active-learning techniques that *Conéctate* incorporates, students are fully engaged throughout each lesson and see how to use the target structures to communicate with others and learn about the world.

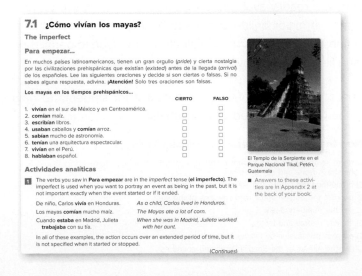

Conéctate

Each chapter closes with the **Conéctate** section, which includes activities that encourage students to "bring it all together." Here you'll find the **¡Leamos!, ¡Escuchemos!, ¡Escribamos!,** and **¡Hablemos!** features, ending with either a **Conéctate al cine** or **Conéctate a la música.** Each of these presents a process approach with *before, during,* and *after* activities that maximize students' engagement and learning. Strategies are offered with each task and help students to develop strong communication skills that are transferable to all of their academic and professional activities.

- **¡Leamos!** This feature provides students with authentic readings from the very beginning of their language studies. Activities ensure comprehension by supporting students' language abilities, enabling students to be successful at building their receptive skills.

- **¡Escuchemos!** Another video-based activity, this feature presents authentic language that incorporates many of the chapter's linguistic and cultural topics together into a cohesive activity that builds confidence and further promotes cultural exploration. Follow-up activities put students in the active-communicator role as they deliver similar information in spoken situations.

- **¡Escribamos!** This activity integrates a process approach to writing, in which students focus on real-life and academic writing tasks, such as developing an online profile or writing a descriptive paragraph. The process starts with a unique writing strategy in every chapter, followed by a brainstorming and drafting stage, and ending with a careful editing of student work using a peer-review system.

- **¡Hablemos!** This section pulls together the chapter theme, grammar, vocabulary, and culture, and encourages students to talk extensively in pairs or complete group-based activities. These fun, engaging, oral-based activities can be used for oral exams, in-class culminating conversations, and/or oral presentations.

- **Conéctate a la música / Conéctate al cine** In these sections that alternate chapters, students listen to a Spanish-language song or watch a scene from a Spanish-language film that relates to some cultural, thematic, and/or linguistic aspect of the chapter. Information on the artists, background information on the films, and vocabulary support are provided, as well as pre- and post-listening and viewing activities. All songs are readily available online through iTunes and/or YouTube. All films are available at major online and in-store video retailers, including Netflix (whose timestamps are provided for the selected clips). Due to permissions limitations, songs and films are not provided by McGraw-Hill Education.

Each chapter closes with an end-of-chapter checklist for students to gauge their progress against the Can Do-oriented chapter goals.

Now that I have completed the chapter, I can . . .

- ☐ greet someone, find out his/her name, how he/she is doing, where he/she is from, and say good-bye
- ☐ pronounce the letters and sounds of the alphabet
- ☐ express the date, months, and seasons of the year
- ☐ say the numbers 0–99
- ☐ identify people and things
- ☐ express possession by talking about the objects people have
- ☐ say the names of the Spanish-speaking countries

What's New?

- **Revised and integrated vocabulary:** This revision integrates the vocabulary box features from the first edition into the main content of the text. It includes several sections with revised illustrations and active vocabulary to make the activities and content more accessible to students, shifting content away from static vocabulary presentations towards a consistent active-learning approach.

- **More high-frequency vocabulary:** The vocabulary presentations and end-of-chapter vocabulary lists from the first edition were analyzed against a corpus of high frequency vocabulary items, drawn from spoken, fiction, and nonfiction texts from both Spain and Latin America. This same digital analysis was applied to all the readings. Based on this research, the useful vocabulary lists have been reworked to emphasize the key words that appear over and over in authentic texts such as newspapers, magazine articles, and literature. As a result, the active vocabulary in this edition ensures that students are learning the essential vocabulary they need to communicate.

- **More active learning:** Many vocabulary and grammar presentations from the previous edition have been revised to follow an active-learning approach more closely. Now, nearly every section in the book begins with an activity, having students actively engage with the new materials in Spanish before reading the explanations, rules, or English translations.

- **Conéctate al mundo profesional:** This new box feature encourages students to engage with the content of each chapter in a way that makes it applicable to their life beyond the university, especially their professional careers. It includes tips on how to use foreign-language and cross-cultural experiences to boost one's professional profile or make a good impression in a job interview. It presents cultural differences within the Spanish-speaking professional world, as well as ideas on how to seek opportunities to use Spanish in a volunteer or career environment.

- **Enhanced visual design:** For this edition, the font size has been increased in order to improve in-class use of the textbook. Feature boxes and sections have been redesigned in order to facilitate a more cohesive flow throughout the chapter.

- **English-Grammar Support Modules:** Assignable within Connect, these brief explanations and practice activities provide students with easy-to-access instruction on English grammar concepts.

- **Heritage-Speaker Support Modules:** Connect now includes assignable heritage-speaker practice modules to address the unique needs of heritage learners taking an introductory Spanish course.

VISUAL PRODUCT MAP

EBOOK

- Integrated textbook audio
  - Vocabulary audio
  - Listening comprehension activity audio
  - Recordings of select reading passages
- Embedded videos
- Textbook illustrations available for download

ASSIGNABLE CONTENT

- eBook activities
- Workbook / Laboratory Manual activities
- Connect-only activities
- Grammar Tutorial activities
- LearnSmart
- Create-your-own activities
- Writing assignments with optional peer review
- Testing Program
- *Diversidad del español* modules
- English-Grammar support modules
- Heritage-Speaker support modules

VIDEOS

- *Conéctate* video program
- *Diversidad del español* videos
- Grammar Tutorial videos
- Tegrity: Create-your-own videos

GRAMMAR TUTORIALS

- Grammar explanations with related activities

INSTRUCTOR RESOURCES

- Activities: Info Gap and more
- Connect User's Guide
- Grammar PowerPoints
- Instructor's Manual
- Integrated Performance Assessments
- Practice Spanish User's Guide
- Sample Lesson Plans
- Scripts: Audio & Video
- Testing Program & Audio
- Writing Prompts

LEARNSMART

- Adaptive vocabulary and grammar practice
- Adaptive countries and capitals practice

TESTING PROGRAM

- Assignable exam questions
- Tegrity Remote Proctoring

Note: Additional print and media resources are also available, including the *Workbook / Laboratory Manual, Testing Program,* and *DVD.*

Acknowledgements

We would like to thank the overwhelming number of friends and colleagues who served on boards of advisors or as consultants, completed reviews or surveys, and attended symposia or focus groups. Their feedback was indispensable in creating the *Conéctate* program. The appearance of their names in the following lists does not necessarily constitute their endorsement of the program or its methodology.

Professional Development Workshops

Pablo Arribas Bulnes, *Susquehanna University*

Yuly Asención-Delaney, *Northern Arizona University*

Theresa Baginski, *Jamestown Community College*

Fleming Bell, *Valdosta State University*

Ana Benito, *Indiana University—Purdue University Fort Wayne*

Ashley Bizzell, *Carteret Community College*

JoAnn Buehler, *Central Virginia Community College*

Rachel Butler, *Anderson University*

Esther Castro, *San Diego State University*

Carmelinda Chilelli, *Ohio University*

Kristin Connor, *University of Virginia*

Lilian Contreras-Silva, *Hendrix College*

Darren Crasto, *Houston Community College*

Angela Cresswell, *Holy Family University*

Stephanie Daffer, *Santa Clara University*

Luis Delgado, *Olive-Harvey College*

Agustin Díaz, *New England College*

Andrea DiBernardo, *Perimeter College—Georgia State University*

Conxita Domenech, *University of Wyoming—Laramie*

Jabier Elorrieta, *New York University*

Dulce Estévez, *Arizona State University*

Daniel Figueroa, *University of Dayton*

Williams Flores, *Christian Brothers University*

Frank Freeman, *High Point University*

Amy Fuglestad, *Valley City State University*

Wendy Gallagher, *Metropolitan State University of Denver*

Alicia Gignoux, *University of Montana*

John Gladstein, *Texarkana College*

Nydia Gregory, *University of Maryland—Eastern Shore*

Elizabeth Hayes, *Columbus State University*

Heather Hinds, *University of Arkansas*

Dianne Hobbs, *Texas Christian University*

Bobby Hobgood, *University of North Carolina at Charlotte*

Javier Ibañez, *Susquehanna University*

Becky Jaimes, *Austin Community College*

Karen Jones, *Santa Fe College*

Melissa Knosp, *Johnson C. Smith University*

Sandra Kornuc, *California State University—Channel Islands*

Susan Lauria, *State University of New York at Purchase*

Kathleen Leonard, *University of Nevada - Reno*

Lisha Duarte, *Cuesta College*

Frauke Loewensen, *California State University—Monterey Bay*

Soumaya Long, *Community College of Baltimore County*

Carmen López, *University of Tennessee at Martin*

Maria Mahaffey, *University of North Carolina at Charlotte*

Francisco Martínez, *Northwestern Oklahoma State University*

Kelley Melvin, *University of Missouri—Kansas City*

Ingrid Mendoza-Batista, *Wake Forest University*

Johnathan Mercer, *Chabot College*

Katherine Mickel, *Louisiana State University*

Donald Mueller, *Pellissippi State Community College*

Sandra Mulryan, *Community College of Baltimore County*

Sandy Oakley, *Palm Beach State College*

Martha Oregel, *Southwestern College*

Angela Palacios, *Oregon State University*

Michelle Petersen, *Arizona State University*

Carol Pettigrew, *Georgia Military College*

María Portal, *Hamilton College*

Alma Ramírez-Trujillo, *Emory & Henry College*

Marilyn Rivera, *Borough of Manhattan Community College*

Silvia Roca-Martínez, *The Citadel—The Military College of South Carolina*

Catherine B. Rossi, *Massachusetts Bay Community College*

Maria Rossi, *University of New Hampshire*

Laura Ruiz-Scott, *Scottsdale Community College*

Rachel Salerno, *Kutztown University of Pennsylvania*

Claudia Silvy, *Bowling Green State University*

Dawn Slack, *Kutztown University of Pennsylvania*

Bryant Smith, *Nicholls State College*

Juan-Manuel Soto, *El Centro College*

Irena Stefanova, *Santa Clara University*

Mariana Stoyanova, *Georgia College & State University*

Kori Swalls, *Indiana State University*

Julio Torres, *University of California—Irvine*

Robert Train, *Sonoma State University*

Amy Uribe, *Winona State University*

Imelda Vásquez, *Ivy Tech Community College*

Vangie Vélez-Cobb, *Palo Alto College*

Nancy Virumbrales, *Waubonsee Community College*

Sarah Vitale, *Loyola University of Maryland*

Kathi Wong, *University of Tennessee—Knoxville*

Claudia Young, *Northwestern Oklahoma State University*

Ekaterina Younger, *College of the Albemarle*

Symposia Attendees

Luz Álvarez, *Johnson County Community College*

Julie Alweheiby, *Coastline Community College*

Manuel Apodaca-Valdez, *University of Southern Indiana*

Maxi Armas, *Triton College*

Julian Arribas, *University of Alabama at Birmingham*

Ashlee Balena, *University of North Carolina—Wilmington*

Tracy Bishop, *University of Arkansas—Fayetteville*

Aymará Boggiano-Barbieri, *University of North Texas*

Óscar Cabrera, *Community College of Philadelphia*

Martin Camps, *University of the Pacific*

Irene Carrion-Upson, *West Valley College*

Sara Casler, *Sierra College*

An Chung Cheng, *University of Toledo*

Tanya Chroman, *California Polytechnic State University*

Chyi Chung, *Northwestern University*

Karina Clarke, *Metro Community College—Fort Omaha*

Christine Cotton, *University of Arkansas—Little Rock*

Laurie de González, *University of Oregon*

Christopher DiCapua, *Community College of Philadelphia*

Dorian Dorado, *Louisiana State University—Baton Rouge*

Mandy Faretta-Stutenberg, *Northern Illinois University*

Erin Finzer, *University of Arkansas—Little Rock*

Stephanie Gaillard, *Louisiana State University—Baton Rouge*

Inés García, *American River College*

Mari Carmen García, *Sacramento City College*

Amy George-Hirons, *Tulane University*

Ronald Gest, *Milwaukee Area Tech—Milwaukee*

Ana Hartig-Ferrer, *California Polythech State University*

Luis Hermosilla, *Kent State University—Kent*

Susana Hernández, *Savannah State University*

Ileana Hester, *Grand Canyon University*

Deborah Holmberg, *Azusa Pacific University*

Alfonso Illingworth-Rico, *Eastern Michigan University*

Franklin Inojosa, *Harold Washington College*

Natalia Jacovkis, *Xavier University*

Keith Johnson, *California State University—Fresno*

Anna Kalminskaia, *University of Nevada—Reno*

Alissa Keith, *Liberty University*

Anne Kelly-Glasoe, *South Puget Sound Community College*

Gioia Kerlin, *Rogers State University*

Melanie Kleeschulte, *Missouri State University*

Pedro Koo, *Missouri State University*

David Leavell, *College of Southern Nevada*

Eduardo León, *Columbus State University*

Dolores Lima, *University of Pittsburgh—Pittsburgh*

María Manni, *University of Maryland—Baltimore County*

Mariam Manzur, *University of Southern Florida-Tampa*

Silvia Marijuan, *California Polytech State University*

Dora Marin, *University of Delaware*

Melissa Massie, *Bellevue College*

David Migaj, *Wilbur Wright College*

Monica Millan, *Eastern Michigan University*

Linda Miller, *Tidewater Community College—Virginia Beach*

Gerardo Mireles, *Butte College*

Christina Nuñez, *Kutztown University of Pennsylvania*

Eva Nuñez, *Portland State University*

Milagros Ojermark, *Diablo Valley College*

Raquel Olivera, *Moorpark College*

Joyce Pauley, *Moberly Area Community College*

Marcelo Paz, *California State University—East Bay*

Carlos Pedroza, *Palomar College*

Elizabeth Petree, *Joliet Junior College*

Sylvain Poosson, *Thomas Nelson Community College*

Sayda Postiglione, *Sierra College*

Herlinda Ramírez-Barradas, *Purdue University Calumet—Hammond*

Norma Rivera-Hernández, *Millersville University*

Beatriz Robinson, *University of Nevada—Reno*

Judy Rodríguez, *California State University—Sacramento*

Teresa Roig-Torres, *University of Cincinnati—Blue Ash*

Norma Rosas Mayen, *University of Southern Indiana*

Brenda Ross, *University of Arkansas—Fort Smith*

Cristobal Sartori, *Indian River State College - Central*

Julie Sellers, *Benedictine College—Atchison*

Leslie Smith, *Missouri Southern State University*

Sam Sommerville, *Johnson County Community College*

Kerri Stephenson, *Johnson County Community College*

Octavian Stinga, *Dominican University*

Irina Tedrick, *Savannah State University*

Lucero Tonkinson, *Olive Harvey College*

Laura Valentin, *Kansas State University*

Alina Vega Franco, *Broward College Central*

Juanita Villena-Álvarez, *University of South Carolina—Beaufort*

Melanie Waters, *University of Illinois - Champaign*

Christina Wolff, *Johnson County Community College*

Jack Yeager, *Louisiana State University—Baton Rouge*

German Zarate-Sandez, *Western Michigan University—Kalamazoo*

Reviewers & Webinar Participants

Maria Akrabova, *Metropolitan State University of Denver*

Veronica Álvarez, *Mt. San Antonio College*

Barbara Avila-Shah, *The State University of New York–The University at Buffalo*

Geoffrey Barrow, *Purdue University Calumet—Hammond*

Sara Beaudrie, *Arizona State Univserity—Tempe*

Stephanie Blankenship, *Liberty University*

Amy Bomke, *Indiana University—Purdue University Indianapolis*

Alicia Bralove, *Bronx Community College*

Ruth Brown, *University of Kentucky*

Krista Chambless, *University of Alabama at Birmingham*

Heather Colburn, *Northwestern University*

Mayra Cortés-Torres, *Pima Community College*

Juliet Falce-Robinson, *University of California—Los Angeles*

Rafael Gómez, *California State University—Monterey Bay*

Yolanda González, *Valencia College—East Campus*

Donna Hodkinson, *Oklahoma City University*

Elias Jureidini, *Lamar State College—Orange*

Kajsa Larson, *Northern Kentucky University*

Juliana Luna-Freire, *Framingham State University*

Rob Martinsen, *Brigham Young University*

Janie McNutt, *Texas Tech University*

Joseph Menig, *Valencia College—West Campus*

Tanesha Parker, *Cape Fear Community College*

John Petrovsky, *College of Marin*

Anne Prucha, *University of Central Florida—Orlando*

Claire Reetz, *Florida State College at Jacksonville*

Sandra Reynolds, *Raritan Valley Community College*

Miguel Rincón, *Bellarmine University*

Eva Rodríguez González, *University of New Mexico—Albuquerque*

Bethany Sanio, *University of Nebraska—Lincoln*

Marcela Squires, *Bellarmine University*

Veronica Tempone, *Indian River State College*

Silvina Trica-Flores, *Nassau Community College*

Marianne Verlinden, *College of Charleston*

Amber Workman, *Arizona State University*

Gabriela C. Zapata, *Texas A & M University*

Author Acknowledgments

Conéctate would not be possible without the hard work of a hugely talented and creative group of people. I thank the entire editorial team at McGraw-Hill Education, especially Katie Crouch, who got us started, and Kim Sallee, Sadie Ray, and Misha MacLaird, who led us through to a successful completion; our wonderful video crew led by Hugo Krispyn, David Murray, Lamar Owen, and Rocío Barajas; my co-author, Darcy Lear, who has been a great friend and companion along this amazing journey; my own teachers Leonard Newmark and David Perlmutter, from whom I learned so much about education and language; and Alicia Muñoz Sánchez, Peggy Lott, Elke Riebeling, Françoise Santore, and the many other inspiring instructors and teaching assistants at UC San Diego whose influence is spread throughout these pages. Finally, my deepest gratitude to the hundreds of people in Spain and Latin America who spoke to us on camera for *Conéctate*. Hearing their stories and their perspectives on the world was an immense privilege and an unforgettable experience.

—Grant Goodall

First and foremost, I am grateful to Katie Crouch for bringing me on board this project with Grant Goodall, a terrific leading man for the textbook and its tale. Surely there are many people at McGraw-Hill Education who remain anonymous to me to whom I owe my gratitude for their role in *Conéctate,* but it has been a pleasure to know and work with those whose names I've learned over the course of the project: Kim Sallee, Chris Brown, Susan Blatty, Misha MacLaird, Allen Bernier, Pennie Nichols, Margaryta Bondarenko, and Sadie Ray. The international travel was truly a thrilling once-in-a-lifetime experience, thanks in a large part to our crew: Hugo Krispyn, David Murray, Lamar Owen, and Rocío Barajas. I owe my career in language education to some amazing mentors who always gently put me where I belonged, pushed me when I needed it, and told me the truth. They are all textbook authors themselves: the late Graciela Ascarrunz Gilman at UC Santa Barbara, Janice Macián and Donna Reseigh Long at The Ohio State University, and Glynis Cowell and Larry King at the University of North Carolina, Chapel Hill. My work at the University of Illinois brought me close Diane Musumeci—half of the *Avanti!* author team— who always offered good advice about everything textbook- and work-related.

—Darcy Lear

We would also like to gratefully acknowledge all of the people who worked tirelessly to produce the entire *Conéctate* program.

Contributing Writers
Student Edition: Maria Akrabova, Misha MacLaird
Workbook / Laboratory Manual: Maria Akrabova, Allen Bernier, Dorian Dorado, Gayle Fiedler-Vierma, Eileen Fancher, Kristina Gibby, Misha MacLaird, Nuria López Ortega, Pennie Nichols, Alfonso J. Quiñones-Rodriguez

Product Team
Editorial and Marketing: Jorge Arbujas, Janet Banhidi, Shaun Bauer, Allen Bernier, Susan Blatty, Margaryta Bondarenko, Sean Costello, Katie Crouch, Craig Gill, Lorena Gómez Mostajo, Helen Greenlea, Misha MacLaird, Pennie Nichols, Sadie Ray, Kim Sallee, Jasmine Santana, Katie Stevens, Melanie Kleeschulte, Maya Marquez, Verónica Esteban, Juan Sebastian Ospina Leon
Art, Design, and Production: Matt Backhaus, Amber Bettcher, Harry Briggs, Carrie Burger, Sue Culbertson, Danielle Havens, Kelly Heinrichs, Lynne Lemley, Erin Melloy, Ron Nelms, Terri Schiesl, Sandy Schnee, Preston Thomas, Beth Thole
Media Partners: Eastern Sky Studios, Lumina Datamatics, Truth-Function, SPI Global

ABOUT THE AUTHORS

Grant Goodall is Professor of Linguistics and Director of the Language Program at the University of California, San Diego, where he is also affiliated with the Center for Iberian and Latin American Studies. An internationally recognized scholar of Spanish syntax, he has a long-standing commitment to the development and implementation of highly effective, research-based practices in language teaching. He brings a rich international background to the *Conéctate* project: He was educated in both the United States and Mexico, has spent much of his life along the border between the two, and has taught or lectured in twenty countries.

Darcy Lear holds a Ph.D. in Foreign- and Second-Language Education from The Ohio State University. She has been the director of the Spanish basic-language program at the University of Illinois, Urbana-Champaign; the inaugural coordinator of the minor program in Spanish for the professions at the University of North Carolina at Chapel Hill; and, most recently, a lecturer at the University of Chicago. She devotes most of her professional time to career coaching, which includes workshops for foreign-language students navigating the campus-to-career transition.

En la clase

Estudiantes en la
Universidad Nacional
Autónoma de Honduras
(UNAH) en Tegucigalpa

Objetivos

When you finish this chapter, you will be able to:

- greet someone, find out his/her name, how he/she is doing, where he/she is from, and say good-bye
- pronounce the letters and sounds of the alphabet
- express the date, months, and seasons of the year
- say the numbers 0–99
- identify people and things
- express possession by talking about the objects people have
- say the names of the Spanish-speaking countries

connect

www.mhhe.com/connect

COMUNICACIÓN ~~LARIO~~ ~~UCTURA~~ ~~ATE~~

¡Hola!
Greeting people in Spanish

Introduction to *Comunicación:* This section presents students with high-frequency expressions that they can use to communicate from the very first day of class. Some activities include portions of video interviews with native speakers, which give students the opportunity to get accustomed to a variety of accents in real-life contexts. It is important to reassure students that they are not expected to understand every word, and that they will be listening only for specific information in each activity. As the book progresses and their listening skills develop, they will be watching and listening to longer segments and will be able to understand more and more.

Video track (Act. A): This video clip can be found on the DVD to accompany *Conéctate: Cap. 1,* Track 1.

Suggestion (Comunicación): As a general rule, have students watch the video 2 to 3 times. Have them read over the activity first. During the initial viewing, have them listen to the speakers, watch their body language, and take in the settings. During the second viewing, have them focus on the listening task. Students can check answers on the third viewing.

Videoscript (Act. A): 1. *Buenos días.* **2.** *Hola.* **3.** *Buen día.* **4.** *Buenas tardes.* **5.** *¿Cómo anda?* **6.** *Hola, muchachos.* **7.** *Hola, buenas tardes.* **8.** *¡Hola! Buenos días.*

A. A ver (*Let's see*): ¡Hola! Watch and listen as the following people say hello. Listen once without trying to complete the activity. The second time, pause between each speaker and indicate which greeting he or she uses. Listen a third time to check your answers. **¡Atención!** Some speakers use more than one greeting.

		BUENOS DÍAS / BUEN DÍA	BUENAS TARDES	¿CÓMO ANDA?	HOLA
1.	Adolfo, de México	☑	☐	☐	☐
2.	Marlén, de México	☐	☐	☐	☑
3.	Rodrigo, de Argentina	☑	☐	☐	☐
4.	Maritza, de la República Dominicana	☐	☑	☐	☐
5.	Manuel, de Cuba	☐	☐	☑	☐
6.	Mariana, de Costa Rica	☐	☐	☐	☑
7.	Esteban, de Costa Rica	☐	☑	☐	☑
8.	Keylin, de Costa Rica	☑	☐	☐	☑

To say hello to someone before noon, use **buenos días,** which translates as *good morning* (literally, *good days*). In the afternoon, use **buenas tardes,** which means *good afternoon* or *good evening*. After dark, use **buenas noches.** This means *good night*, and may be used to greet people or to wish them well as they turn in for the night.

B. ¡Buenos días!   Decide whether you would use **buenos días, buenas tardes,** or **buenas noches** in each of the following situations.

	BUENOS DÍAS	BUENAS TARDES	BUENAS NOCHES
1. as you walk into your first class of the morning	☑	☐	☐
2. at a 9 P.M. dinner	☐	☐	☑
3. in line for a cup of morning coffee	☑	☐	☐
4. on your way to the library for an all-nighter	☐	☐	☑
5. as you leave your last class of the afternoon	☐	☑	☐
6. just before bedtime	☐	☐	☑

C. Los saludos (*Greetings*)   Turn to the students on either side of you and greet each one with an expression you heard in the video in **Actividad (*Activity*) A**. Offer your hand to shake and smile.

CONÉCTATE (*CONNECT*) AL MUNDO (*WORLD*) PROFESIONAL

In professional contexts, body language matters. Practice in class where the stakes are low so you are comfortable later In high-stakes environments, such as job fairs, networking events, and interviews. When meeting new people, offer your hand to shake, smile, and make eye contact.

Spanish speakers often engage in a formal, physical greeting, such as a handshake combined with a slap on the back, or kisses on one or both cheeks.

Video track (Act. A, Paso 1): This video clip can be found on the DVD to accompany *Conéctate: Cap. 1,* Track 2.

Video track (Act. A, Paso 2): This video clip can be found on the DVD to accompany *Conéctate: Cap. 1,* Track 3.

Note (Act. A): Videoscripts for Tracks 2 and 3 are identical; however Track 3 (for **Paso 2**) includes the speakers' names onscreen.

Videoscript (Act. A): 1. *Yo me llamo Marlina Rodríguez.* **2.** *Mi nombre es Natalia López.* **3.** *Mi nombre es Pedro Alberto Jiménez Mancilla.* **4.** *Yo me llamo Paul Reid.* **5.** *Me llamo Víctor Rodrigo.* **6.** *Mi nombre es Bertha Lara.*

Note (En español): En español boxes point out some grammatical principles and vocabulary that students can use to communicate before they've formally learned the full grammar point.

¿Cómo te llamas? / ¿Cómo se llama?

Asking someone his/her name

A. A ver: ¿Cómo te llamas? / ¿Cómo se llama usted?

PASO 1. Watch and listen as Spanish speakers say their names. Then watch again with pauses and match each photo with the correct name.

1. _c_   2. _d_

3. _f_   4. _e_

5. _b_   6. _a_

a. Bertha Lara
b. Víctor Rodrigo
c. Marlina Rodríguez
d. Natalia López
e. Paul Reid
f. Pedro Alberto Jiménez Mancilla

Note (Act. A): In order to give students exposure to both *tú* and *Ud.*, interviewees who are college-aged or younger are addressed as *tú*; those who are older than college-aged are addressed as *Ud.*

PASO 2. Watch and listen again with pauses. Indicate which expression each person uses to say their name.

		(YO) ME LLAMO	MI NOMBRE ES
1.	Marlina Rodríguez	☑	☐
2.	Natalia López	☐	☑
3.	Pedro Alberto Jiménez Mancilla	☐	☑
4.	Paul Reid	☑	☐
5.	Víctor Rodrigo	☑	☐
6.	Bertha Lara	☐	☑

En español...

The use of **tú** and **usted** (Ud.) can vary from region to region, so when in doubt, use **usted**. The person you are addressing will usually invite you to use **tú** if it is appropriate.

To introduce yourself and ask someone's name, you could use the following expressions.

INFORMAL (**TÚ**)	FORMAL (**USTED**)
¡Hola! Me llamo Pablo.	**Buenas tardes. Me llamo Marta Campillos.**
¿Cómo te llamas?	**¿Cómo se llama?**

You can also introduce yourself in the following way.

¡Hola! Mi nombre es Pablo.	**Buenas tardes. Mi nombre es Marta Campillos.**

To ask *And you?*, simply add the question after you've introduced yourself.

¿Y tú?	**¿Y usted?**

One way to say *Nice to meet you* is **Mucho gusto,** to which you could reply **Igualmente** (*Likewise*).

INFORMAL (**TÚ**)	FORMAL (**USTED**)
—**¿Cómo te llamas?**	—**¿Cómo se llama usted?**
—**Me llamo Elena. ¿Y tú?**	—**Raúl Fuentes. ¿Y usted?**
—**Marina.**	—**Soy** (*I am*) **Ana Freire.**
—**Mucho gusto.**	—**Mucho gusto.**
—**Igualmente.**	—**Igualmente.**

En español...

The verb **llamarse** is used to give your name in Spanish. It literally means *to call oneself*. The question **¿Cómo te llamas?** means *What do you call yourself?* and the answer **Me llamo...** means *I call myself . . .*

To literally say *My name is . . .* in Spanish, use **Mi nombre es...**

—Hola, me llamo Jorge.
—Mucho gusto. Mi nombre es Iván.

B. ¿Cómo se llaman los otros estudiantes?

PASO 1. Walk around the room and greet at least five other students using appropriate expressions. Introduce yourself and find out their names.

PASO 2. Working in groups, see if you can remember and repeat your classmates' names. Follow the model as you point to the desk where each person is seated. **¡Atención!** With the pronouns **él** and **ella** in the **MODELO** below, you're getting a sneak peek at a grammar point that soon we'll present at length. For now, simply follow the model and see if you can detect the pattern. What might be the difference between the pronouns **él** and **ella**?

> **MODELO:** Él se llama Christopher. Ella se llama Miranda. Ella se llama Gloria. Él se llama Jason.

Suggestion (Act. B): Have students draw the classroom as it is laid out and write in the names of at least 4 students they know as a "pop quiz." Stress the importance of remembering names in academic and professional contexts.

Suggestion (Act. B, Paso 2): Break students into groups of 5–10, or do this **Paso** as a whole class.

Christopher

Miranda

Gloria

Jason

CONÉCTATE AL MUNDO PROFESIONAL

Knowing people's names is important. When starting out in professional contexts: find out names, remember names, and use names. People are impressed when you call them by name on a second or third encounter. It's also good to get comfortable saying: **Lo siento. Se me olvidó su nombre. Soy _____. ¿Cómo se llama usted?** (*I'm sorry, I've forgotten your name. I'm _____. What's your name again?*).

Un consejo (*Advice*)...

When learning a new language, it is easy to get caught up in translating and become frustrated when expressions do not translate literally. Remember that there is no master language from which all other languages are derived. You have to think of different languages as separate systems that have evolved over centuries—and continue to evolve as they come into contact with each other. In the **Comunicación** sections of each chapter you will learn Spanish expressions that you can use immediately to communicate successfully, but it is best to try to use them as fixed expressions without attempting to translate every nuance to English.

For example, in English you might say *What's up?* to which the literal answer would be *the sky* or *the ceiling,* yet it is understood as a common greeting. Likewise in Spanish, **¿Qué onda?** is the equivalent of *What's up?*, even though **onda** literally means *wave*.

C. ¿Cómo te llamas? ¿Cómo se llama usted? Read the following questions. Based on the question's level of formality, select the person who is being addressed appropriately.

1. ¿Cómo se llama usted?

a.

b.

2. ¿Cómo te llamas?

a.

b.

3. ¿Cómo te llamas?

a.

b.

4. ¿Cómo se llama usted?

a.

b.

Note (Conéctate al mundo hispano): **Conéctate al mundo hispano** boxes present information about Hispanic cultures. Indicate to students whether or not such cultural information will appear on their quizzes, chapter exams, and so on.

CONÉCTATE AL MUNDO HISPANO

Residents of Spain and most Latin American countries usually have two last names (**dos apellidos**): the first one is inherited from the father, and the second one from the mother. The first of these names, the paternal family name, is considered primary, and is the one passed on to future generations. For example, when we look at the name of Mexican actor Gael García Bernal we know that García is his father's family name (that is, inherited from his father), and Bernal is his mother's family name (that is, inherited from his mother). When Gael García Bernal and Argentine actress Dolores Fonzi had a son, they named him Lázaro García Fonzi. Their daughter is Libertad García Fonzi. What would your last name look like if you were to adopt this custom?

When moving to a country that doesn't practice this custom, some Spanish speakers choose to drop their mother's last name in order to avoid confusion. Others prefer to hyphenate the two last names to maintain this important part of their identity.

Suggestion (Conéctate al mundo hispano): In general, it is always the first *apellido* of the two parents that is given to the children. You may wish to share an example from your experience, or use the following example: If Hugo Morales López marries Isabel Martínez Flores, their child will be called David Morales Martínez.

D. Los apellidos

PASO 1. Based on what you read in the **Conéctate al mundo hispano** box about dual last names in Spanish, what would the last names be of the following children?

1. Father: Marco Ruiz Cortés   Mother: Josefa Martín González
   Son: Andrés _____ _____
2. Father: Alberto Esquivel Muñoz   Mother: Liliana Andrade Arbujas
   Daughter: Jana _____ _____
3. Mother: Emilia Barajas Bermúdez   Father: Alfonso Silva Arce
   Son: Enrique _____ _____

PASO 2. In groups, use the above pattern to introduce yourselves, saying what your last names would be if you used both your father's and mother's last names.

¿Cómo estás? / ¿Cómo está?

Asking people how they are

To find out how someone is doing, you might ask the following questions.

¿Cómo estás? for informal (**tú**) or **¿Cómo está usted?** for formal (**usted**)

When addressing someone informally, you can also use the Spanish equivalent of *How is it going?*: **¿Qué tal?**

In English, *How are you?* can be another way to just say *hello,* but in the Spanish-speaking world an answer is expected. Common responses for **¿Cómo está(s)?** include: **(Muy) Bien** ([*Very*] *Good*), **Más o menos** (*Okay*), **(Muy) Mal** ([*Very*] *Bad*).

When someone asks how you are, it is polite to say **gracias** after you answer. Return the question by asking, **¿y tú?** or **¿y usted?**

—**Buenos días. ¿Cómo estás?**   —**Buenas tardes. ¿Cómo está?**
—**Bien, gracias. ¿Y tú?**   —**Muy bien, gracias. ¿Y usted?**
—**Muy bien.**   —**Bien, gracias.**

If someone answers with anything less positive than **bien,** you can inquire further by asking *What's the matter?* using **¿Qué te pasa? (tú)** / **¿Qué le pasa? (usted)**

Hola, ¿cómo estás?

Script (Act. A): Read each sentence to students twice, pausing for them to jot down answers. **1.** *¿Cómo estás, Marlina?* **2.** *Buenos días, profesor. ¿Cómo está Ud.?* **3.** *Bien, gracias. ¿Y Ud.?* **4.** *Muy bien, gracias. ¿Y tú?* **5.** *Bien. Y tú, ¿qué tal?*

■ The audio files for in-text listening activities are available in the eBook, within Connect activities, and on the Online Learning Center.

Note (Act. B): Tell students that although there are general guidelines for interacting in the situations outlined in **Act. B,** there are no hard and fast rules. Possible answers include: **1.** *Buenos días. ¿Cómo está?* **2.** *Buenas tardes. ¿Cómo está?* **3.** *¿Cómo anda?* **4.** *¡Hola! ¿Qué tal?* **5.** *Buenos días. ¿Cómo está?*

 A. ¿Formal o informal?

    PASO 1. Indicate whether each expression you hear is formal (**usted**) or informal (**tú**).

	INFORMAL	FORMAL	
1.	☑	☐	_____
2.	☐	☑	_____
3.	☐	☑	_____
4.	☑	☐	_____
5.	☑	☐	_____

PASO 2. Listen a second time to the expressions in **Paso 1** and jot down the words that let you know if each expression is informal or formal.

B. ¿Cómo estás? How would you greet the following people and ask how they are? Write the appropriate answers next to the image of each person, then share your responses to check for accuracy.

MODELO: *¡Hola! ¿Cómo estás?*

Suggestions (Act. B):
· Share additional informal expressions that convey the English *How is it going?,* such as *¿Cómo anda? ¿Cómo te va?*
· Scenario-writing. **Paso 1:** Have students work in pairs to envision two scenarios of greeting, one informal and one formal. Write them down as scenarios a and b. For example: a) a student greets a classmate and b) a student

1.
2.
3.
4.
5.

greets her professor. **Paso 2:** Have each pair select either their scenario a or b for which to write an appropriate greeting in Spanish. For example: *¡Hola! ¿Qué tal?* **Paso 3:** Ask for volunteer pairs to read their two possible scenarios and then their one greeting to the class. The class, based solely on formality, will determine which it must be, scenario a or b. For example, given the above greeting, it has to be scenario a.

C. El desarrollo de la red de contactos *(Networking)* Using everything you've learned so far, greet as many classmates as you can in three minutes. You must use professional body language (shake hands, smile, and so on), ask each other's names, give **los dos apellidos** (*both last names*), and ask and answer how you are doing.

¿De dónde eres? / ¿De dónde es?

Asking where someone is from

Previewing (Act. A): Go over the names of the countries so students know how they're pronounced in Spanish before they watch the video.

Note (Act. A): Point out to students that the countries are listed in alphabetical order. Pause often during viewing so students have time to complete the activity (or remind them to do so at home if assigned for homework).

Video track (Act. A): This video clip can be found on the DVD to accompany *Conéctate: Cap. 1,* Track 4.

Videoscript (Act. A): 1. *Soy de España. / Soy de Colombia. / Soy de México. / Soy de Colombia. / Soy de Paraguay. / Soy de Perú. / Soy de Argentina. / Soy de Panamá.* **2.** *Soy de Venezuela. / Soy de Ecuador. / Yo soy de Honduras. / Soy de Colombia. / Soy de Chile. / Soy de San José, Costa Rica. / Soy de Nicaragua. / Yo soy de Bolivia.*

Note (Act. B): You may need to remind students that Mexico is part of North America. If there is any confusion, have students look at the map to see how Mexico forms part of the North American land mass.

A. A ver: ¿De dónde eres? / ¿De dónde es usted? Watch and listen at least three times, pausing as needed, as people from all over the Spanish-speaking world say where they are from. For each group of speakers, check the names of all the countries you hear.

1. ✓ Argentina   ✓ Panamá   2. ___ Argentina   ___ España
   ✓ Colombia   ✓ Paraguay   ✓ Bolivia   ✓ Honduras
   ___ Ecuador   ✓ Perú   ✓ Chile   ___ México
   ___ El Salvador ___ la República Dominicana   ✓ Colombia   ✓ Nicaragua
   ✓ España   ___ Uruguay   ✓ Costa Rica   ___ Panamá
   ✓ México   ___ Venezuela   ✓ Ecuador   ✓ Venezuela

To ask a person where he/she is from, use one of the following questions.

INFORMAL (**TÚ**)		FORMAL (**USTED**)
¿De dónde eres?	or	**¿De dónde es?**

To say *I am from . . .* in Spanish, say: **Soy de...**

—**Elena, ¿de dónde eres?**   —**¿De dónde es usted, señora Gallegos?**

—**Soy de México.**   —**Soy de El Salvador.**

If you want to know where someone currently lives, ask one of the following questions.

—**¿Dónde vives?**   —**¿Dónde vive usted?**
—**Vivo en Village Hall.**   —**Vivo en Puebla.**

B. Los orígenes y la geografía Read the following statements about people's origins. Then, using your knowledge of geography (and the map at the back of your book), select the country that each speaker could be from.

1. «Soy de Centroamérica.»
   a. Venezuela   (b.) Honduras   c. España

2. «Soy de Europa.»
   a. Ecuador   b. Guatemala   (c.) España

3. «Soy del Caribe.»
   (a.) Honduras   b. Argentina   c. Bolivia

4. «Somos de Norteamérica.»
   a. Nicaragua   (b.) México   c. Paraguay

5. «Somos de Sudamérica.»
   (a.) Chile   b. Panamá   c. Cuba

C. Soy de...   Circulate around the room asking **¿De dónde eres?** Can you find two classmates from different cities than you? Can you find a classmate from another state? Ask at least five classmates.

MODELOS: ESTUDIANTE 1: Hola, me llamo Gabriela y soy de Miami. ¿De dónde eres?

ESTUDIANTE 2: Hola, Gabriela. Me llamo Jason. Soy de Miami, también (*also*).

ESTUDIANTE 1: Hola, mi nombre es Gabriela y soy de Miami. ¿De dónde eres?

ESTUDIANTE 3: Buenos días, Gabriela. Me llamo Dana y soy de Atlanta.

¡Adiós!
Saying good-bye

Suggestion (Act. A): If students have a hard time keeping track of the different expressions, suggest that they use a tally to keep track of each one. The video is short, so it could be played six times with students listening for one expression each time they watch.

 A. A ver: ¡Adiós!   Watch and listen at least three times, with pauses as needed. How many times do you hear each expression? Which isn't used at all?

1. _4_ Adiós.
2. _1_ Chau chau.
3. _0_ Hasta mañana.
4. _1_ ¡Bye-bye!
5. _3_ Hasta luego.
6. _2_ Chau.

Video track (Act. A): This video clip can be found on the DVD to accompany *Conéctate: Cap. 1,* Track 5.

Videoscript (Act. A): 1. *Adiós. Adiós.* **2.** *Adiós.* **3.** *Hasta luego.* **4.** *Chau.* **5.** *¡Bye-bye!* **6.** *Chau chau.* **7.** *Hasta luego.* **8.** *Chau.* **9.** *Adiós.* **10.** *Hasta luego.*

There are several ways to say good-bye in Spanish.

Adiós is commonly used throughout the Spanish-speaking world.

Chau (or **chau chau**) is used more in Latin America than in Spain and is commonly used among people who address each other informally (as **tú**).

Hasta luego literally means *Until later* but conveys the sense of *See you later* or *Until we meet again.* If you know when you will see the person again, you can give a specific time instead of **luego**.

Hasta mañana.	*See you tomorrow.*
Hasta el jueves.	*See you (on) Thursday.*
Hasta pronto.	*See you soon.*

B. Presentaciones (*Introductions*)

PASO 1.   Make a short list of expressions you would use to do the following. **¡Atención!** Don't forget that there are often several ways to say the same thing!

... say *hello* in Spanish
... say what your name is
... ask another person what their name is
... express that you are pleased to meet someone
... ask someone how he or she is doing
... ask someone where he or she is from
... say where you are from
... say *good-bye* in Spanish

 PASO 2.   Find a classmate you haven't yet met or whom you don't know very well, and use your list to have a conversation and get to know one another better.

 PASO 3.   Act out your conversation for the class.

Dos amigos (*friends*) vestidos de Superhombre dicen (*say*) «¡Adiós!».

Expansion (Act. B): Give students a time limit of 3-4 minutes to jot down all expressions in Spanish they remember so far. Then, divide the class in pairs. Students will compare lists, and check off all expressions that are the same. In the follow-up, ask about the expressions they found on their partner's list, but were not included in their own.

COMUN VOCABULARIO UCTURA ATE

Suggestion (¿Cómo se escribe?):
· Start by modeling the pronunciation of the letters of the alphabet and their accompanying words.
· Write examples of words using c and g on the board and ask your students to pronounce them to practice the different sounds.

Note (¿Cómo se escribe?): There is more practice, including audio listening and pronunciation practice, on Connect.

¿Cómo se escribe?°

How do you spell . . . ?

The Spanish alphabet and campus vocabulary

(a)
el **a**ula

(be)
el **b**olígrafo

(ce)*
la **c**omputadora /
las **c**iencias

(de)
el **d**iccionario

(e)
el **e**scritorio

(efe)
la **f**ilosofía

(ge)*
la **g**raduación /
el **g**imnasio

(hache)
la **h**oja de papel

(i *or* i latina)
la **i**dea

(jota)
el **j**oven

(ka)
el **k**ilo

(ele)
el **l**ibro

(elle *or* doble ele)'
la **ll**ave

(eme)
la **m**ochila

(ene)
los **n**úmeros

(eñe)
el a**ñ**o

(o)
la **o**ficina

(pe)
la **p**uerta

(cu)
la **q**uímica

(ere)
el **r**eloj

(erre *or* doble erre)'
la piza**rr**a

(ese)
la **s**illa

(te)
la **t**area

(u)
la **u**niversidad

Note (¿Cómo se escribe?): Many letters have other variations not included here. You may wish to teach *be grande* and *be chica* for the letters *b* and *v*. Also note *ch, ll* and *rr* have been officially dropped from the Spanish alphabet and are considered digraphs (two letters making one sound). However, *ll* and *rr* are included here to point out their special pronunciation.

(uve)
la **v**entana

(doble ve)
la página **w**eb

(equis)
el e**x**amen

(i griega *or* ye)
el pro**y**ector

(zeta)
el lápi**z**

*The letters **c** and **g** each have two examples because they are pronounced differently depending on which letters follow them. When followed by a consonant or the vowels **a, o,** or **u,** these letters make hard **c** and **g** sounds. The soft **c** and **g** sounds are followed by the vowels **e** or **i**.
'The clusters **ll** and **rr** are not actually letters of the Spanish alphabet, but they are included here because of their unique pronunciation.

Here is more useful vocabulary for talking about campus life.

el amigo / la amiga *friend*	**la cosa** *thing*	**la página** *page*
la biblioteca *library*	**el cuaderno** *notebook*	**el profesor / la profesora** *professor*
el borrador *eraser*	**el hombre** *man*	**la residencia** *dormitory*
la clase *class*	**la librería** *bookstore*	
el compañero / la compañera	**la mesa** *table*	
(de clase) *classmate*	**la mujer** *woman*	

There are about 500 million Spanish speakers in twenty-one Spanish-speaking countries; different regions might use different words for the same thing. You should learn these common synonyms in Spanish that have to do with campus life.

el aula = **el salón de clase**	**el bolígrafo** = **la pluma**	**la oficina** = **el despacho**

A. El alfabeto español y las capitales
Each of the following sequences of letters spells the name of a capital city. Identify the city, then spell out its country's name. The map at the back of your book will help you.

MODELO: Ele - i - eme - a: Lima.
Lima es la capital de Perú: pe - e - ere - u con acento.

1. eme - a - de - ere - i - de
2. ese - a - ene - te - i - a - ge - o
3. be - o - ge - o - te - a con acento
4. ce - a - ere - a - ce - a - ese
5. eme - a - ene - a - ge - u - a

B. A ver: ¿Cómo se escribe?

PASO 1. Watch and listen at least three times, with pauses as needed, as the following people spell their names. Match each photo with the correct name. **¡Atención! Mi nombre se deletrea...** is another way to say **Mi nombre se escribe...**

1. __b__   2. __e__

3. __c__   4. __d__

5. __a__

a. Anlluly
b. Juan Andrés
c. Keylin*
d. Olman
e. William

PASO 2. Watch and listen multiple times as the following people spell their names. Write each name beside the corresponding photo.

¿Cómo se escribe tu nombre?

1.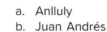
___ ___ ___ ___ ___ ___

2.
___ ___ ___ ___ ___ ___

3.
___ ___ ___ ___ ___ ___

4.
___ ___ ___ ___ ___

5.
___ ___ ___ ___ ___ ___ ___ ___ ___

(*Continues*)

*When Keylin spells her name, she distinguishes between **y griega** and **i latina**. Many people use the term **i latina** to make it clear they are talking about **i** and not **y** (**y griega**).

Note (¿Cómo se escribe?): While lexical variations will be presented throughout *Conéctate*, space constraints prevent detailed breakdowns of the regions and comprehensive lists of all variations. Please share with students your experiences with lexical variation and urge them to notice variants as they engage with Spanish speakers in this country and abroad.

Video track (Act. B, Paso 1): This video clip can be found on the DVD to accompany *Conéctate: Cap. 1,* Track 6.

En español...

Watch out for **amigos falsos** (*false cognates*)—words that have similar spellings but different meanings. For example, **el dormitorio** means *bedroom* for most Spanish speakers and a dorm(itory) building is usually **la residencia estudiantil** or **residencia** for short.

Videoscript (Act. B, Paso 1): **1.** *Mi nombre se deletrea así: Se deletrea J-u-a-n-A-n-d-r-e-s.* **2.** *W-i-l l-i-a-m* **3.** *¿Cómo se escribe? Se escribe K-e-y-l-i-n.* **4.** *O-l-m-a-n. Olman.* **5.** *Mi nombre se escribe A-n-l-l-u-l-y.*

Suggestion (Act. B, Paso 2): Have students work in pairs to practice spelling the names of famous people aloud as preparation for *Paso 2.* You may wish to read the names in *Paso 2* aloud to students before showing the video.

Video track (Act. B, Paso 2): This video clip can be found on the DVD to accompany *Conéctate: Cap. 1,* Track 7.

Act. B, Paso 2: **1.** A-l-l-a-n **2.** Y-e-n-a-r-o **3.** Z-u-l-a-y **4.** H-e-n-r-y **5.** A-l-e-x-a-n-d-e-r

PASO 3.   Working in small groups, take turns spelling your names out loud while the others write them down. Did everyone spell your name correctly?

MODELO: Mi nombre es Ana: a-ene-a, y mi apellido es Peña: pe-e-eñe-a.

PASO 4.   Working in small groups, spell out your email addresses (**direcciones de email**) for each other. (See the **Vocabulario** box below for spelling tips.) Be sure to write down your classmates' addresses so you can contact each other about homework and other assignments. **¡Atención!** If you need to include numbers, look ahead to their vocabulary presentation in this chapter. Also, note that common domain names such as *com* and *edu* are normally pronounced as words rather than spelled out.

MODELO: Mi dirección de email es ache - o - ele - a - arroba - gmail - punto - com.

> Some important words and phrases for sharing your email or web address in Spanish include:
>
> **arroba** = @
> **punto com** = .com
> **punto edu** = .edu
> **doble ve, doble ve, doble ve** (*or* **triple doble ve**) = www
>
> As in English, many Spanish speakers choose to eliminate the "www" when giving a web address because it is generally understood as part of the address.
>
> While the expression **email** is generally accepted by Spanish speakers (and pronounced mostly the same in Spanish), you will often hear the term **correo electrónico** (*electronic mail*) as well.

Suggestion (Act. C): Assign each pair or group of students one or more letters to work with. Allow 1–3 minutes for the entire activity.

Expansion (Act. C): Have a member of each group spell one of their words for the class.

Expansion (Act. C) Spell out classroom words for your students, have them write the letters you dictate, then check responses. For example:

1. s-i-l-l-a **2.** l-l-a-v-e **3.** m-o-c-h-i-l-a **4.** e-s-c-r-i-t-o-r-i-o **5.** p-i-z-a-r-r-a **6.** c-l-a-s-e

C. ¿Cómo se escribe... ?   Meet and greet a new partner (*Hello!, How are you?, What is your name?,* and so on). Your instructor will assign each pair one or more letters of the alphabet. Write as many Spanish words as you can that contain the assigned letter(s). Finally, take turns spelling the words aloud in Spanish.

CONÉCTATE AL MUNDO PROFESIONAL

Your ability to get and give accurate contact information—in any language—can be the difference between creating or losing an important professional opportunity. To ensure that you have complete, accurate names and emails, take control of the conversation using specific communication strategies.

Tengo el nombre; repita el apellido, por favor.
¿Se escribe con *ese* o con *zeta*?
Le voy a repetir la dirección de email:
   [...] ¿Es correcto?

I've got the first name; repeat the last name, please.
Is that spelled with an s or a z?
I'm going to repeat that email address back to you:
   [. . .] Is that correct?

Suggestion: Select 5-6 words that have noticeable spelling differences in Spanish (such as *diseño, química,* and *filosofía*), and ask students to spell them out for you while you write them on the board. Use *¿Cómo se escribe... ?* as a prompt.

Suggestion: Spell the words out loud, while one or several students write them on the board.

Suggestion: Write *difícil* and *fácil* as column heads on the board or on a transparecy, explaining the meaning of the adjectives. Then ask students to rate each subject area: *La biología, ¿es difícil o es fácil?* You may wish ask for full-sentence answers, expecting students to pronounce the academic subject as well: *La biología es fácil.*

Cognados (*Cognates*) are words that have similar spelling and meaning in Spanish and English. Can you figure out the English equivalents of the following **materias** (*academic subjects*)?

las ciencias políticas	el francés	la literatura
el diseño	la historia	la psicología
la filosofía	las humanidades	las relaciones
la física	el inglés	internacionales

D. ¿Qué estudias?

PASO 1. Based on what you know about cognates, pair each academic subject with the image that best represents it.

1. __a__ la arquitectura
2. __c__ la biología
3. __e__ las comunicaciones
4. __g__ la economía
5. __f__ la ingeniería
6. __b__ las matemáticas
7. __d__ la química

a.

b.

c.

d.

e.

f.

g.

 PASO 2 Ask at least four different classmates what they study and write the answers in the table below. If you don't know someone's name, be sure to ask in Spanish!

MODELO: ESTUDIANTE 1: ¿Cómo te llamas?
ESTUDIANTE 2: Me llamo Elena.
ESTUDIANTE 1: ¿Qué estudias?
ESTUDIANTE 2: La psicología. ¿Y tú?

¿CÓMO SE LLAMA?	¿QUÉ ESTUDIA?
Elena	la psicología

En español...

In Spanish, the months begin with a lower case letter, unlike English, where they begin with an upper case letter. You'll notice that this also applies to the days of the week and nationalities.

Suggestion (Conéctate al mundo hispano): Assign each student (or pair of students) a country and have them check the weather in the capital city (or several cities) on the Internet. Ask a few pairs to report back to the class on their findings.

Expansion (Act. B): Have students work with a partner, taking turns saying the letters of the alphabet. If there is a month that begins with that letter, the student will name it and then spell it out. Continue until all the months have been named.

Los meses y las estaciones
Months and seasons

Note (Act. A): Students may have slightly different answers based on where they live.

A. Los meses y las estaciones Match each month to the appropriate season, based on where you live.

| marzo | agosto | mayo | febrero | abril | octubre |
| septiembre | diciembre | junio | noviembre | julio | enero |

la primavera   el verano   el otoño   el invierno

B. Las estaciones en los dos hemisferios

Script (Act. B, Paso 1): 1. *enero* 2. *marzo* 3. *septiembre* 4. *julio* 5. *octubre* 6. *abril* 7. *junio* 8. *febrero*

PASO 1. You will hear the months of the year in Spanish. Write down the month and then add the appropriate season in the northern hemisphere: **primavera, verano, otoño, invierno.**

	MES	ESTACIÓN			MES	ESTACIÓN
1.	enero	invierno		5.	octubre	otoño
2.	marzo	primavera		6.	abril	primavera
3.	septiembre	otoño		7.	junio	verano
4.	julio	verano		8.	febrero	invierno

PASO 2. Now look at the months in **Paso 1** and say the corresponding season in the southern hemisphere. How would your daily life in those months be different if you lived in the southern hemisphere?

CONÉCTATE AL MUNDO HISPANO

About half of the world's Spanish-speaking countries are in the southern hemisphere (**el hemisferio sur**) and therefore have opposite seasons from the northern hemisphere (**el hemisferio norte**). For example, when it's summer in Mexico, it's winter in Argentina and Chile. This means that in many South American countries, great beach weather is likely to be in December, January and February, deciduous leaves will fall in April and May, and that a "white Christmas" is unlikely in most places that aren't at a very high altitude.

Answers (Act. C): 1. *N* **2.** *S* **3.** *N* **4.** *N* **5.** *N* **6.** *S*.

C. El hemisferio norte y el hemisferio sur For each of the following countries, indicate whether it is located in the northern (**N**) or southern (**S**) hemisphere. **¡Atención!** Remember that the equator divides the two hemispheres. Then say what season it is now in that country.

1. México (**N / S**)
2. Argentina (**N / S**)
3. Venezuela (**N / S**)
4. Costa Rica (**N / S**)
5. España (**N / S**)
6. Bolivia (**N / S**)

Script (Act. A, Paso 1): **1.** siete **2.** dieciocho **3.** trece **4.** veintiuno
5. cincuenta **6.** tres punto catorce (3.14 = π)

Los números y las fechas
Numbers and dates

ote (Los
úmeros y
s fechas):
umbers
00–9,999
e presented
Cap. 5.

A. Los números importantes

Paso 1.   You will hear some well-known numbers associated with luck, significant ages, or math. Circle each of the numbers you hear.

0 **cero**				
1 **uno**	11 **once**	21 (**veintiuno**)	31 **treinta y uno**	...
2 **dos**	12 **doce**	22 **veintidós**	32 **treinta y dos**	50 (**cincuenta**)
3 (**tres**)	13 (**trece**)	23 **veintitrés**	33 **treinta y tres**	60 **sesenta**
4 **cuatro**	14 (**catorce**)	24 **veinticuatro**	34 **treinta y cuatro**	70 **setenta**
5 **cinco**	15 **quince**	25 **veinticinco**	35 **treinta y cinco**	80 **ochenta**
6 **seis**	16 **dieciséis**	26 **veintiséis**	36 **treinta y seis**	90 **noventa**
7 (**siete**)	17 **diecisiete**	27 **veintisiete**	37 **treinta y siete**	
8 **ocho**	18 (**dieciocho**)	28 **veintiocho**	38 **treinta y ocho**	
9 **nueve**	19 **diecinueve**	29 **veintinueve**	39 **treinta y nueve**	
10 **diez**	20 **veinte**	30 **treinta**	40 **cuarenta**	

Use **y** (*and*) to build any number between 31 and 99: **cuarenta y uno, setenta y cuatro, noventa y seis.**

Script (Act. A, Paso 2): **1.** tres **2.** sesenta y ocho **3.** noventa y tres **4.** veintiocho **5.** setenta y dos **6.** trece **7.** cuarenta y siete **8.** treinta y nueve **9.** once **10.** cincuenta y cuatro

PASO 2.   Write the numerals as you hear them.

1. ___3___   3. ___93___   5. ___72___   7. ___47___   9. ___11___

2. ___68___   4. ___28___   6. ___13___   8. ___39___   10. ___54___

The word **hay** is a simple and easy way to express *there is* or *there are* in English.

Hay un escritorio.
There is one desk.

Hay tres sillas.
There are three chairs.

To say that something does not exist, just add **no** before **hay:**

No hay ventanas en el aula.
There are not any windows in the classroom.

To ask how many there are of something, say **¿Cuántos/as _____ hay?**

¿Cuántos libros hay?
How many books are there?

¿Cuántas sillas hay?
How many chairs are there?

En español...

When identifying the number of specific things, use **un** before something that ends with **-o** or **-os** (**un libro, treinta y un libros**) and **una** before something that ends with **-a** or **-as** (**una puerta, cuarenta y una sillas**). The reasons and variations for this will be explained in more detail in **Estructura 1.1.** Note the one-word form to indicate twenty-one of something (**veintiún meses, veintiuna semanas**).

Suggestion (Act. A, Paso 1): Follow up by having students tell you why these numbers might be significant.

Expansion (Act. B): To practice the numbers 0 to 29, pick various things from the classroom, such as books, pencils, chalk, pieces of paper, and students, and ask: *¿Cuántos libros hay? ¿Cuántas mesas hay?*

Expansion (Act. B): Ask students about different objects from the alphabet presentation (*¿Cómo se escribe?*) that appear or do not appear in your classroom to practice using *hay: ¿Hay estudiantes en el aula? ¿Sí? ¿Cuántos estudiantes hay en el aula?*

Expansion (Act. C):
- Ask students with January birthdays to raise their hands. Call on some to say their birthdays out loud. Then ask for a volunteer to count the raised hands and tell how many people have their birthdays in January: *Hay [x] personas en esta clase que tienen sus cumpleaños en enero.* Repeat for each month.
- Alternative version (if you have room in your classroom): Have students stand up, say their birthdays out loud, then sort themselves in order from Jan. 1 to Dec. 31. Once in order, have them say their birthdays out loud. Then do a show of hands for birthdays in each month; have a volunteer count them and tell how many there are, as explained above.
- Follow-up activity: Call out a season and have students with birthdays in that season step forward. Repeat with each season.

B. ¿Cuántos? Tell how many of the specified unit there are in each of the following things.

> **MODELO:** los días en septiembre:
>
> Hay treinta días en septiembre.

1. los días en diciembre
2. los días en junio
3. los días en mayo
4. los segundos en un minuto
5. los minutos en una hora
6. los días en una semana (*week*)
7. las semanas en un año (*year*)
8. las letras en tu nombre (¿y cómo se escribe?)

To ask today's date in Spanish, use:

> **¿Cuál es la fecha de hoy?**

To express the date, use this structure:

> **el** + *date* + **de** + *month*
>
> **Hoy es el cinco de noviembre.**
> *Today is November 5.*

To express *the first* of the month, use **el primero.**

> **Hoy es el primero de mayo.**
> *Today is May first.*

C. Las fechas In Spanish, the day and month are written left to right, as one would say them. For instance, 7/6 in Spanish is the 7th of June (**el siete de junio**). Based on this information, how would you write numerically the 6th of July? _6/7_

Look at the following images representative of important days and match them with their numerical date.

a. 17/3   b. 25/12   c. 14/2   d. 7/4   e. 4/7

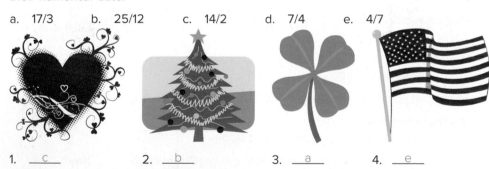

1. _c_   2. _b_   3. _a_   4. _e_

 D. Nuestro calendario Working in pairs, take turns consulting the course syllabus and asking about important dates. Write them down and check each other's answers. Be sure to plan your studying, projects, and travel for the semester.

> **MODELO:** ESTUDIANTE 1: ¿Cuál es la fecha del examen final?
> ESTUDIANTE 2: Es el 7 de diciembre.

¿Cuál es la fecha

1. ...del primer (*first*) examen?
2. ...del primer día festivo (*holiday*) del semestre?
3. ...del primer día de vacaciones?
4. ...del último (*last*) día de vacaciones durante el semestre?
5. ...del último día de clase?
6. ...del examen final?

E. Mi número de teléfono

Note (Act. E, Paso 1): Tell students that if they don't feel comfortable giving out their personal phone number, to use another number they know.

PASO 1. In groups, take turns introducing yourself and dictating your phone number. Write down the numbers of other group members.

MODELO: Buenos días. Me llamo Elena. Mi número de teléfono es el cuatro, cincuenta y seis, noventa y ocho, trece (456-9813).

PASO 2. Your instructor will give one group member a written phone number—this is the only person who can look at the number. The person with the number dictates it to a second person, the second to a third, and so on. The last person writes the number on the board. How many teams ended with the same number they started with?

Expansion (Act. E): Ask students to exchange contact information with 3 classmates. Provide the following models: *¿Cuál es tu número de teléfono? ¿Cuál es tu email?* This will allow students to communicate with each other instead of the instructor outside of class while also developing important skills for the workplace: independence, decision-making, problem-solving, resourcefulness.

F. Las tarjetas de presentación

Choose one of the identities shown on the business cards. Your partner will close his or her book while you introduce yourself, providing some of the information on your business card. When you've finished, check your partner's notes for accuracy, then switch roles.

MODELO: Me llamo Franklin Soto. Mi número de teléfono es el veinticinco - ochenta y seis - trece - setenta y nueve.

txt o llamar: 51-1-2586-1379

Franklin Soto

chofer profesional

vehículos de lujo

Helena Ruiz Guzmán
Producción multimedia

comerciales
documentales
televisión
noticias

hrg@prodmultimedia.com

★ Empanadas porteñas ★

Avenida Madero 431
Puerto Madero
Martha Cochet, dueña
54-11-1167-2385

horario: 11:00 - 22:00
empanadas.deliciosas@gmail.com

El Centro Latino
1240 Main St.
Springfield

Toni Martínez, directora
331-456-7962   t.martinez@hotmail.com

En español...

In Spanish it is most common to divide the seven digits of telephone numbers into four groups: the single first digit followed by three groups of two. Note that the article **el** may be used before the first number.

—¿Cuál es tu número de teléfono?
—Es el cinco, cincuenta y cinco, ochenta y siete, sesenta y dos. (5-55-87-62)

Similar strategies are used in countries where telephone numbers have more or fewer digits.

CONÉCTATE AL MUNDO PROFESIONAL

As a volunteer or intern at an organization with Spanish-speaking employees, clients, or vendors, you could serve as a gatekeeper who greets people as they enter. You could ask how they are, who they are, who they need to see, and how to spell names if necessary, and then literally point them in the right direction. In the right role, you don't need a lot of Spanish to use it in the workplace.

COMUN VOCABUL **ESTRUCTURA** TE

■ Answers to these activities are in Appendix 2 at the back of your book.

En español...

For most nouns, the gender is unrelated to the noun's meaning. That is, some words (such as **libro**) are masculine and others (such as **mesa**) are feminine even though there is nothing inherently masculine or feminine about a book or a table. With other nouns, however, the gender corresponds to the biological or natural gender (**género natural**) of the object being described. For example, **un hombre** is masculine and **una mujer** is feminine.

■ For more tips on determining the gender of nouns that end in letters other than **-o** or **-a**, see **Para saber más** (*To find out more*) **1.1** at the back of your book.

1.1   Un lápiz en la mochila

Singular nouns and articles

Para empezar (*To start*)...

Suggestion (Para empezar): Review the *¿Cómo se escribe?* vocabulary before starting *Estructura 1.1.*

Which of the following items might you expect to find in a backpack?

☑ **un** bolígrafo   ☐ **un** escritorio   ☐ **una** puerta

☑ **una** computadora   ☑ **un** libro   ☐ **una** silla

☑ **un** diccionario   ☐ **una** mesa

Actividades analíticas

1   Words such as **computadora, diccionario, libro,** and **mesa** are *nouns* (**sustantivos**). The words **un** and **una,** like the English words *a* and *an,* are *indefinite articles* (**artículos indefinidos**). Based on the pattern that you see in **Para empezar,** choose the appropriate indefinite article for each noun.

UN	UNA	
☐	☑	mochila
☑	☐	gimnasio
☑	☐	año
☐	☑	pizarra

2   Nouns in Spanish are classified by *gender* (**género**). Those that use **un** are called *masculine* (**masculino**), and those that use **una** are *feminine* (**femenino**). As a general rule of thumb, nouns that end in **-o** are masculine and those that end in **-a** are feminine. Do all the nouns in **Para empezar** obey this generalization?

Sí ☑   No ☐

3   More than 90% of the nouns that end in **-o** or **-a** have the gender that you would expect, but you will occasionally run into nouns that don't.

un día   *a day*   **una** mano   *a hand*

With nouns that end in letters other than **-o** or **-a**, some are masculine and some are feminine.

un reloj   *a clock*   **una** universidad   *a university*

The article or other surrounding words can tell you the gender of the noun.

4   Spanish also uses *definite articles* (**artículos definidos**), which function like English *the.* These also have a separate form for each gender.

	masculino	femenino
artículos definidos	el	la
	el libro *the book*	la mesa *the table*
artículos indefinidos	un	una
	un libro *a book*	una mesa *a table*

Note (Para saber más): *Para saber más 1.1 covers nouns ending in -tad, -dad, -ción, -sión, and -ma as well as singular feminine nouns that take the definite article el.*

Autoprueba

Give the indefinite article for each of the following words.

1. _____ escritorio
2. _____ llave
3. _____ oficina

Now give the definite article for the following words.

4. _____ reloj
5. _____ ventana
6. _____ clase

Respuestas (Answers): 1. un 2. una 3. una 4. el 5. la 6. la

Actividades prácticas

A. En la clase   Look at the image of the classroom and respond in complete sentences to the questions that follow.

> **MODELOS:** ¿Hay una puerta en el salón de clase?
> Sí, hay una puerta.
> ¿Hay un proyector en el salón de clase?
> No, no hay un proyector.

1. ¿Hay un reloj en el salón de clase?   Sí, hay un reloj.
2. ¿Hay un profesor en el salón de clase?   Sí, hay un profesor.
3. ¿Hay una pizarra en el salón de clase?   Sí, hay una pizarra.
4. ¿Hay una mesa en el salón de clase?   No, no hay una mesa.
5. ¿Hay una mochila en el salón de clase?   Sí, hay una mochila.
6. ¿Hay una puerta en el salón de clase?   Sí, hay una puerta.
7. ¿Hay un libro en el salón de clase?   No, no hay un libro.

¿Por qué?

Spanish and many other languages divide their nouns into different genders because, among other advantages, this makes it easier for our brains to process speech. As we listen to language spoken to us, our brains try to predict what the next word will be. When we hear an article with gender like **el** or **la**, this gives our brains an important clue about the upcoming word, which leads to quicker processing of the incoming message. This efficiency is a big advantage, and it helps explain why so many languages in the world have gender on nouns.

Suggestion (¿Por qué?): Give students a minute to read this box and then have them see for themselves how gender helps them predict the next word. Give them sentences like *En la mochila, hay un...*" and *"En la mochila, hay una..."* and have them give possible completions to the sentence.

Point out (Act. B): If students have questions about the gender of *universidad,* refer them to *Para saber más 1.1,* to explain that nouns ending in *-dad, -tad, -ción,* and *-sión* are feminine.

B. Categorías

PASO 1. Write the indefinite article (**un** or **una**) before each noun in column **A**.

A	**B**
1. _un_ número _d_	a. *Conéctate*
2. _un_ bolígrafo _g_	b. arquitectura
3. _una_ computadora _f_	c. enero
4. _un_ mes _c_	d. dieciséis
5. _una_ materia _b_	e. Yale
6. _una_ universidad _e_	f. Mac
7. _un_ libro _a_	g. Bic

PASO 2. Match each item in column **B** to the correct category in **A**.

C. Más categorías

PASO 1. Write the definite article (**el** or **la**) for each of the following nouns.

1. _el_ otoño
2. _la_ economía
3. _la_ primavera
4. _la_ historia
5. _el_ profesor de la clase
6. _el_ verano
7. _la_ profesora de la clase
8. _la_ química

PASO 2. Using **es** (*is*), say whether each of the above items is **una estación del año, un hombre, una materia,** or **una mujer.**

> **MODELO:** El otoño es una estación del año.

Suggestion (Act. D): Tell students to ask 5 questions each and to keep track of how many of their guesses are correct. If students do not have a backpack, then a purse (*el bolso*), messenger bag / briefcase (*el maletín*), or even their pocket (*el bolsillo*) will work.

D. ¡Adivina! (*Guess!*) Working with a partner, try to guess what is in his/her backpack using the vocabulary you learned in this chapter. How many of your guesses are correct?

> **MODELO:** ESTUDIANTE 1: ¿Hay un teléfono?
> ESTUDIANTE 2: ¡Sí!

1.2 Los estudiantes y la universidad

Plural nouns and articles

Para empezar...

Suggestion (Para empezar): To make sure students are doing this activity in Spanish, before beginning, call on students to say the numbers 0–5 and have them name the objects in the art.

How many of each of the following can you find in this picture?

■ Answers to these activities are in Appendix 2 at the back of your book.

1. _cinco_ libros
2. _dos_ mochilas
3. _dos_ borradores
4. _cuatro_ mujeres
5. _tres_ hombres
6. _dos_ relojes

Actividades analíticas

1 All of the nouns in **Para empezar** have a *plural ending* (**una terminación plural**): **-s** or **-es.** Place the singular form of each of these nouns into the appropriate column here, depending on which ending it takes.

-s	-es
hombre	borrador
libro	mujer
mochila	reloj

When you're finished, take a look at the two columns. How are the words in these two columns different? What pattern can you detect? See if you can formulate a hypothesis about pluralization before you read the next grammar segment, because you may be on the right track already.

2 There is a simple rule that determines which plural ending a noun takes: If the noun ends in a vowel (**una vocal**), it takes **-s,** and if it ends in any consonant (**una consonante**), it takes **-es.**

Use this rule to create the plural form of these nouns.

singular	plural
estudiante	estudiantes
mes	meses
universidad	universidades
bolígrafo	bolígrafos

3 For nouns that end in **-z,** change the **-z** to **-c** and add **-es.**

singular	plural
lápiz	lápices
luz (*light*)	luces

4 The definite and indefinite articles also come in both singular and plural forms.

	masculino	femenino
artículos definidos		
singular	el	la
plural	los	las
artículos indefinidos		
singular	un	una
plural	unos	unas

Which definite articles would you use for these words?

__el__ lápiz   __las__ computadoras   __los__ escritorios   __la__ mochila

Which indefinite articles would you use for these words?

__un__ gimnasio   __unas__ sillas   __una__ pizarra   __unos__ bolígrafos

Point out (Act. analíticas 3):
The accent remains when *lápiz* becomes plural (*lápices*). Note that some nouns follow the general rule for pluralization, but require a change in the accent mark;

estación → estaciones;
examen → exámenes.

En español...

The plural indefinite articles are equivalent to *some* in English.

unos estudiantes
some students
unas mochilas
some backpacks
unos relojes
some clocks/watches

Autoprueba

Make each of these nouns plural and add the appropriate plural definite article.

1. año: _____
2. mujer _____
3. puerta _____
4. hombre: _____
5. reloj: _____

Respuestas: 1. los años, **2.** las mujeres, **3.** las puertas, **4.** los hombres, **5.** los relojes

Actividades prácticas

Script (Act. A):
1. *pizarras* **2.** *mujeres*
3. *mochilas*
4. *profesores* **5.** *diccionarios*
6. *borradores* **7.** *puertas*
8. *mesas*

Suggestion (Act. A): If you prefer, you may substitute the given objects with other things in your classroom that are more visible or easier for students to count.

A. ¡Escucha bien! (*Listen up!*) Listen to the plural nouns and write down how many there are in your classroom. If there is only one, use **un** or **una** and change the noun to singular.

> **MODELOS:** You hear: *estudiantes*
> You write: *Hay veinticinco estudiantes.*
>
> You hear: *escritorios*
> You write: *Hay un escritorio.*

1. _____   5. _____

2. _____   6. _____

3. _____   7. _____

4. _____   8. _____

B. Categorías

PASO 1. Write the appropriate definite article (**los** or **las**) for the items in column **A**, then complete the lists in column **B**, if necessary. Finally, match the items in column **A** with the lists in column **B**.

A	**B**
1. _las_ estaciones del año en el hemisferio norte _d_	a. uno, dos, tres, _cuatro_, _cinco_
2. _los_ meses del verano en el hemisferio norte _e_	b. el gimnasio, la biblioteca, (answers will vary; these are examples) la residencia, la librería
3. _los_ números del uno al (*to*) cinco _a_	c. la biología, la física, la química
4. _los_ edificios (*buildings*) del campus _b_	d. la primavera, el verano, _el otoño_, el invierno
5. _las_ materias de ciencias _c_	e. junio, _julio_, _agosto_

PASO 2. Write the appropriate indefinite article (**un, una, unos,** or **unas**) for each category in **A**, then choose the item(s) in **B** that go with each category in **A**.

A	**B**
1. _unas_ mujeres: _a_, _g_	a. Salma Hayek
2. _un_ año: _e_	b. filosofía
3. _unos_ hombres: _c_, _i_	c. Mario Vargas Llosa
4. _una_ universidad: _d_	d. Notre Dame
5. _un_ número de teléfono: _j_	e. 1492
6. _unas_ materias: _b_, _f_, _h_	f. literatura
	g. Cristina Fernández de Kirchner
	h. química
	i. Diego Luna
	j. 735-394-9065

Diego Luna es un actor mexicano.

C. ¿Cuáles son las diferencias?   Working with a partner, create two lists. In one, write sentences saying what image A (**dibujo A**) and image B (**dibujo B**) have in common. In the other, write sentences saying how they are different. Begin your sentences with **hay** (*there is/are*), and mention these people and objects: **puerta(s), ventana(s), escritorio(s), estudiante(s), profesor(es), computadora(s), reloj(es), pizarra(s), hombre(s), mujer(es)**.

MODELOS: En dibujo A y dibujo B, hay un profesor.
En dibujo A, hay una pizarra, pero (*but*) en dibujo B, hay dos pizarras.

Dibujo A   Dibujo B

1.3   Son estudiantes. Tienen mochilas.

The verbs *ser* (to be) and *tener* (to have)

Para empezar...

Find the best ending for each incomplete sentence. The first is done for you.

1. Los estudiantes __e__
2. Un libro __f__
3. Juanes y Shakira __h__
4. Zoe Saldana y América Ferrera __b__
5. Enero __g__
6. Octubre __a__
7. Un año __c__
8. Los diccionarios __d__

a. **es** un mes de otoño.
b. **son** de los Estados Unidos (*United States*).
c. **tiene** doce meses.
d. **tienen** las definiciones de muchas palabras (*words*).
e. **tienen** mochilas, bolígrafos, libros y cuadernos.
f. **tiene** páginas.
g. **es** un mes de invierno en el hemisferio norte.
h. **son** de Colombia.

■ Answers to these activities are in Appendix 2 at the back of your book.

América Ferrera es de Los Ángeles.

En español...

In Latin America, the plural form of *you* is always **ustedes,** both for informal and formal uses. In *Conéctate*, you will be expected to know and use this form.

Latin America
¿De dónde son (ustedes)?
Where are you (plural) *from?*

In most of Spain, people use **vosotros/vosotras** for the informal plural and **ustedes** for the formal plural. While the **vosotros/vosotras** form appears in *Conéctate*, it is for recognition only.

Spain
¿De dónde sois (**vosotros**)?
Where are you (informal, plural) *from?*
¿De dónde son (**ustedes**)?
Where are you (formal, plural) *from?*

In any Spanish-speaking country, **tú** and **usted** refer only to a single individual.

In many parts of Latin America, (such as Argentina, Paraguay, Uruguay, and much of Central America) especially in spoken Spanish, the alternative form **vos** is used instead of the singular informal **tú.**

¿De dónde sos (vos)?
Where are you (informal, singular) *from?*

Actividades analíticas

1 In **Para empezar,** you saw some forms of the verbs **ser** (*to be*) and **tener** (*to have*). You may have noticed that the form of the verb changes depending on what the subject is. Use the forms from **Para empezar** to complete this chart.

Note (En español): *Vos* and the other pronouns are discussed in more detail in the *La diversidad del español* feature in the workbook.

	ser	tener
yo *I*	soy	tengo
tú *you* (informal, singular)	eres	tienes
él/ella, usted *he/she, you* (formal)	es	tiene
nosotros/nosotras *we* (masculine/feminine)	somos	tenemos
vosotros/vosotras* *you* (informal, plural, m./f.)	sois	tenéis
ellos/ellas, ustedes *they* (m./f.), *you* (formal, plural)	son	tienen

You will see that the conjugation of **ser** in particular shows many changes from form to form. Keep in mind that this verb has irregularities in English, as well: I *am*, You *are*, He/She *is*, and so on.

2 The conjugations in the chart above list the verb forms according to the pronoun (**el pronombre**) that corresponds to the subject. This pronoun is often not used, however, since the verb form itself frequently makes the subject clear.

Soy de los Estados Unidos.	*I am from the United States.*
¿Eres estudiante?	*Are you a student?*
Somos de Canadá.	*We are from Canada.*
Tengo un amigo de Venezuela.	*I have a friend from Venezuela.*
¿Tienes libros en la mochila?	*Do you have books in the backpack?*
Tenemos una profesora de Perú.	*We have a teacher from Peru.*

3 **Usted** uses the same verb form as do **él** and **ella.** If you were speaking to someone more formally, then, how would you say the following?

(INFORMAL, TÚ)

a. ¿De dónde eres?
   ¿Tienes un lápiz?

(FORMAL, USTED)

b. ¿De dónde __es__ usted?
   ¿__Tiene__ usted un lápiz?

Autoprueba

Here is a typical sentence in Spanish: **Soy de Guatemala.** What subject is implied by the form of the verb **ser** here? ____

What are the implied subject pronouns in each of the sample sentences in **Actividades analíticas 2**?

Respuestas: Yo; Yo, Tú, Nosotros/Nosotras, Yo, Tú, Nosotros/Nosotras

---

***Vosotros** and **vosotras** are informal plural forms of *you,* and are used only in Spain. Latin America uses **ustedes** for both formal and informal plural *you.*

Actividades prácticas

A. Preguntas y respuestas   For each question, choose the best answer and write its letter in the corresponding space. The first is done for you. **¡Atención!** Questions with **tú** are always addressed to a single person, while those with **ustedes** are to a group.

1. ¿Tienes amigos en la clase? _b_
2. ¿De dónde eres? _g_
3. ¿De dónde son Uds.? _e_
4. ¿Tienen un diccionario? _f_
5. ¿Tienes una computadora? _d_
6. ¿Penélope Cruz es de México? _c_
7. ¿Eres de Canadá? _a_

a. No, soy de los Estados Unidos.
b. Sí, tengo dos. Son Melissa y Steve.
c. No, es de España.
d. Sí, tengo una Mac.
e. Somos de Paraguay.
f. Sí, tenemos dos.
g. Soy de Costa Rica.

B. ¿De dónde eres?

PASO 1.   Ask as many of your classmates as possible where they're from. Keep track of the answers by writing down their names grouped according to the part of your city or country that they are from. If you don't know your classmates' names, you will need to ask them.

MODELO: ESTUDIANTE 1: ¿Cómo te llamas? ¿De dónde eres?
    or   ¿Cómo se llama? ¿De dónde es?
    ESTUDIANTE 2: Me llamo Marisa. Soy de Atlanta.

PASO 2.   Tell the class where your classmates are from.

MODELO: ESTUDIANTE 1: Yo soy de California. Mis compañeros son de Colorado y de Utah.
    ESTUDIANTE 2: Son de Atlanta. Yo soy de Athens.
    ESTUDIANTE 3: Somos de Nebraska.

Lionel Messi juega en el equipo nacional de su país (*country*). ¿Sabes (*Do you know*) de dónde es?

C. Gente famosa (*Famous people*)   How well do you know these Spanish-speaking celebrities? With a partner, alternate asking each other questions about where they are from. **¡Atención!** When asking about one person, use the singular form **es.** When asking about a group, use **son.** If you don't know the answer, say **no sé** (*I don't know*).

MODELO: ESTUDIANTE 1: ¿De dónde es Rafael Nadal?
    ESTUDIANTE 2: Es de España. (No sé.)

1. Javier Bardem y Penélope Cruz   España
2. Gael García Bernal y Salma Hayek   México
3. Lionel Messi   Argentina
4. Daddy Yankee   Puerto Rico
5. Juanes y Shakira   Colombia
6. Rosario Dawson y Jennifer López   los Estados Unidos

D. ¿Qué tienes?

PASO 1.   Check off those items in the list that you have with you in class today.

	YO	MI COMPAÑERO/A
1. un bolígrafo	☐	☐
2. una computadora	☐	☐
3. un cuaderno	☐	☐
4. un lápiz	☐	☐
5. un reloj	☐	☐
6. un teléfono	☐	☐

PASO 2.   Ask a partner whether he or she has each of these items, and complete the chart in **Paso 1.**

MODELO: ESTUDIANTE 1: ¿Tienes un bolígrafo?
    ESTUDIANTE 2: Sí, tengo un bolígrafo. (No, no tengo un bolígrafo.)

Suggestion (Act. B, Paso 1): Give students the areas/regions that they should use to organize the answers before they begin. If your students are mostly from the same city, choose different areas of the city for your class (for example, the east or west side, specific neighborhoods). If your students are from all over your state or country, choose different regions.

Expansion (Act. B, Paso 2): After students have completed *Paso 1,* ask them to tell you where their classmates are from: *¿De dónde son tus compañeros?* Write the names of the places they are from on the board. When each group has announced where they are from, ask them to say where all the other groups are from (for example, *Son de Massachusetts*). You may want to have students form groups based on where they are from and use the *nosotros* form to say where they are from.

Expansion (Act. C): Follow up by asking students to tell the class where some of the celebrities in the activity are from. Another option is to ask them where other celebrities or the students themselves are from.

Expansion (Act. D): Ask pairs to state what items they both have. Model an answer for them using *mi compañero/a y yo* or *los/las dos: Mi compañero/a y yo / Los/Las dos tenemos un bolígrafo.*

Puerto Rico **los Estados Unidos**

E. Cultura: La vida bilingüe en los Estados Unidos y Puerto Rico

PASO 1. Read the following text about the United States and Puerto Rico.

Puerto Rico... ¿Es un país[a]? ¿O es una parte de los Estados Unidos? En realidad Puerto Rico se llama «el Estado Libre Asociado de Puerto Rico». Es un territorio no incorporado de los Estados Unidos con estatus de autogobierno.[b]

Pero en los Estados Unidos, las personas hablan[c] inglés y en Puerto Rico hablan español, ¿no? La verdad[d] es que[e] en los dos países hay muchas personas bilingües y cada[f] día hay más. En los dos países, hay personas que hablan un idioma[g] en la casa y toman[h] clases para estudiar otro idioma.

Hay muchas palabras en el español de Puerto Rico que tienen influencia del inglés. Por ejemplo,[i] una persona puede decir[j] «No te panikees» for *Don't panic*. Otros anglicismos son **parquear** (*to park*), **gufear** (*to goof around*) y **hanguear** (*to hang out*). ¿Sabes[k] algunas palabras en inglés que son del español?

[a]*country* [b]*estatus... self-governing status* [c]*speak* [d]*truth* [e]*that* [f]*each* [g]*language* [h]*take* [i]*Por... For example* [j]*puede... can say* [k]*Do you know*

Expansion (Act. E, Paso 2): Have students correct the false statements.

PASO 2. Indicate whether the following statements are true (**cierto**) or false (**falso**), according to information presented in the reading.

	CIERTO	FALSO
1. Hay personas en los Estados Unidos que hablan español.	☑	☐
2. Hay muchas personas bilingües en Puerto Rico.	☑	☐
3. Cada día hay menos (*fewer*) personas bilingües en los Estados Unidos.	☐	☑
4. Puerto Rico es un estado de los Estados Unidos.	☐	☑
5. En Puerto Rico, los estudiantes toman clases de inglés.	☑	☐

PASO 3. With a partner, answer the following questions and discuss the ideas behind your responses.

1. ¿Por qué (*Why*) hablan inglés en los Estados Unidos y español en Puerto Rico?
2. ¿Cuáles son los cuatro idiomas europeos que ahora hablan más (*the most*) en América (*the Americas*)?
3. ¿Qué otras partes de los Estados Unidos fueron (*were*) colonias españolas? ¿Hay huellas (*traces*) de esto todavía (*still*)?

Suggestion (Act. E., Paso 3):
- Give students the words *Inglaterra* and *España*, and help them make the connection: *Los Estados Unidos fueron colonia de Inglaterra y Puerto Rico fue colonia de España*. You may also want to introduce *Canadá/Quebec* and *Francia*, so that students see the three biggest European powers that competed for control of North America.
- Help students with the names of the languages: *inglés, español, francés, portugués*. Point out that these four languages are the result of these four European countries conquering and dividing up the Americas.
- Students can answer with names of U.S. states. Most of the western U.S. and the southern coastline (including Florida) were formerly Spanish possessions. This is still seen in names of cities, architecture, and so on.

San Juan, la ciudad capital de Puerto Rico

1.4 Nuestra (*Our*) clase de español

Possessive adjectives

Para empezar...

Choose the appropriate response for each question, then provide the information needed to complete the answer.

Preguntas	Respuestas
1. __d__ ¿Cómo se llama **nuestra** universidad?	a. **Nuestro** libro de español se llama ____.
2. __b__ ¿Cómo se llama **nuestro** profesor / **nuestra** profesora de español?	b. **Nuestro** profesor / **Nuestra** profesora de español se llama ____.
3. __a__ ¿Cómo se llama **nuestro** libro de español?	c. **Mis** (*My*) otras clases son ____.
4. __c__ ¿Cuáles son **tus** (*your*) otras clases?	d. **Nuestra** universidad se llama ____.
5. __e__ ¿Cuál es **tu** clase favorita?	e. **Mi** clase favorita es ____.

■ Answers to these activities are in Appendix 2 at the back of your book.

Actividades analíticas

1 Possessive adjectives (**adjetivos posesivos**), such as **mi** and **nuestro**, show who possesses a noun. Using what you saw in **Para empezar**, complete this chart of possessive adjectives.

__mi__(s)	*my*	**nuestro(s)/**_nuestra_**(s)**	*our*
__tu__(s)	*your* (informal, singular)	**vuestro(s)/vuestra(s)**	*your* (informal, plural, Spain)
su(s)	*your* (formal, singular), *his/her*	**su(s)**	*your* (formal, plural), *their*

2 The ending **-s** is added to any possessive adjective when it is used with a plural noun.

mis amigos	*my friends*
tus teléfonos	*your* (informal, singular) *telephones*
sus bolígrafos	*his/her, your* (formal, singular and plural)*, their pens*

su casa   su casa

sus casas   sus casas

You may think of possessive adjectives as consisting of two parts: the beginning agrees with the owner, and the ending agrees with the possession.

(Continues)

En español...

The subject pronoun **tú** is spelled with an accent mark and the possessive adjective **tu** is not.

Tú eres mi amigo.
You are my friend.

Tu profesora es de Colombia.
Your teacher is from Colombia.

Similarly, the subject pronoun **él** is spelled with an accent mark, but the definite article **el** is not.

Él es mi compañero de clase.
He is my classmate.

Tengo **el** libro.
I have the book.

Autoprueba

Use what you now know about possessive adjectives to express the following in Spanish.

1. my books
2. my book
3. our professor (*male*)
4. our professors (*female*)
5. your (*inform. sing.*) desk
6. their house

Respuestas: 1. mis libros **2.** mi libro **3.** nuestro profesor **4.** nuestras profesoras **5.** tu escritorio **6.** su casa

Suggestion (Act. A, Paso 2): Using appropriate gestures, ask students who has books that weigh a lot (*¿Quién tiene libros que pesan mucho?*) and then do a quick check to see who has the heaviest books in the whole class (*Ella se llama Karen. ¡Sus libros pesan mucho!*).

Suggestion (Act. C): Tell students to ask their partners five questions and to keep track of how many they answer correctly.

Suggestion (Act. D): If you have a smaller class, you may wish to split your students into larger groups, or have the whole class participate together.

When using **nuestro(s)/nuestra(s)** and **vuestro(s)/vuestra(s),** the ending of the possessive must show agreement with the gender (masculine/feminine) and number (singular/plural) of the noun that follows it.

nuestros profesores	*our teachers*
nuestra clase	*our class*
vuestras mochilas	*your (informal, plural, Spain) backpacks*

Actividades prácticas

Suggestion (Act. A, Paso 1): Tell students that if they do not have one of the objects, write *No tengo* for that item.

A. Mis cosas

PASO 1. Check off all of the objects in the **yo** column that you have with you. If you have more than one of any item, add **-s** to the possessive and the noun. Then see how many objects your partner has and add **-s** where appropriate in the **mi compañero/a** column.

YO	MI COMPAÑERO/A
☐ mi____ computadora____	☐ su____ computadora____
☐ mi____ libro____	☐ su____ libro____
☐ mi____ llave____	☐ su____ llave____
☐ mi____ teléfono____	☐ su____ teléfono____

PASO 2. For each item that both you and your partner have, answer the question **¿Cuál pesa más?** (*Which weighs more?*) by comparing both, and then indicating the heavier one.

> **MODELO:** Mi computadora pesa más.

B. Nuestro salón de clase
Working with a partner, make a list of five objects that are an integral part of your classroom, preceding each with the correct form of **nuestro(s)/nuestra(s).** One item is partially done for you.

1. nuestr____ pizarra(s)
2. _____
3. _____
4. _____
5. _____

C. ¡Una prueba!
Give your partner a vocabulary quiz! Point to an object or objects in his or her possession and ask **¿Es tu ____?** for something singular or **¿Son tus ____?** for something plural. Use the wrong word sometimes and see if your partner can catch you.

> **MODELOS:** ESTUDIANTE 1: ¿Es tu lápiz?
> ESTUDIANTE 2: Sí, es mi lápiz.
>
> ESTUDIANTE 1: ¿Son tus libros?
> ESTUDIANTE 2: No, ¡son mis bolígrafos!

D. ¿De quién es?

PASO 1. Working in groups of five, give something that belongs to you, such as your backpack or your keys, to the person sitting next to you. Tell your neighbor what the object is. Now your neighbor will pass the item to another classmate, telling him/her who it belongs to and what it is.

> **MODELO:** ESTUDIANTE 1: Es mi mochila. / Son mis llaves.
> ESTUDIANTE 2: Es de Susan. Es su mochila. /
> Son de Susan. Son sus llaves.

PASO 2. Continue in this manner until your instructor says to stop. You should now be holding someone else's object(s). Go around the group and say who each object belongs to. Did the message get transmitted properly? Don't forget to return the objects to their owners!

¡Leamos!

¡Conéctate al mundo!

Antes de leer° *Before reading*

The following reading is an advertisement for **Universidad del Cerro - Puebla.**
Looking at the visual cues, what do you think the title **Conéctate al mundo** implies?

_____ It's important to be well connected. _____ College connects you to the world.

_____ Study abroad and connect to the world.

A leer° *Start reading*

Read the advertisement from **Universidad del Cerro - Puebla** and answer the
questions that follow.

¡CONÉCTATE AL MUNDO!

La **Universidad del Cerro - Puebla** (UCP) es una universidad
global que les prepara a sus estudiantes con la capacitación
necesaria para avanzar en un mercado de trabajo cada vez
más internacional. Aparte de su selección de cursos académicos,
ofrece preparación profesional a través de un programa de
prácticas y estudios en diferentes partes del mundo.

Licenciaturas:

Arquitectura	Física
Biología	Historia
Ciencias políticas	Ingeniería
Comunicaciones	Matemáticas
Economía	Psicología
Filosofía	Química
Finanzas	Relaciones internacionales

Maestrías:

Administración de empresa
Turismo sostenible

LA UNIVERSIDAD DEL CERRO - PUEBLA
Oficina de Programación Comunitaria y Profesional

Información detallada: 22-811-6510 o www.ucp.edu
Para programar una visita: 22-811-7349

■ Have you ever wondered what it would be like to study abroad and live with a host family? *Practice Spanish: Study Abroad* is an immersive, 3-D, virtual game in which you take on the role of a foreign exchange student in Colombia. You will interact in Spanish with your host family, local residents, and students from around the world while you problem-solve, communicate, and navigate through a variety of fun and engaging cultural scenarios and adventures. You might even forget you are practicing Spanish! Access the first Quest for free on Connect or at MHPractice.com.

Note: Supplemental activities for *Practice Spanish: Study Abroad* have been developed for use either in or out of your classroom and are available via Connect and MHPractice.com.

(Continues)

1. __a__ La UCP quiere atraer a (*wants to attract*)...
   a. estudiantes.   b. familias.   c. profesores.   d. turistas.

2. __c__ ¿Qué tipo de universidad es la UCP?
   a. científica   b. doméstica   c. global   d. psicológica

3. __c__ La estudiante en la foto quiere estudiar (*wants to study*) en...
   a. Buenos Aires.   b. Nueva York.   c. París.   d. Roma.

4. ¿En cuántas materias se ofrecen licenciaturas (*undergraduate degrees*) en la UCP? __14__

5. ¿Cuál es el número de teléfono que debemos llamar (*we should call*) para saber más (*to find out more*) sobre este programa? __22-811-6510__

6. ¿Cuál es la dirección de internet (URL) que debemos visitar para saber más sobre el programa? __www.ucp.edu__

En español...

American students often want to know how to say *What's your major?* in Spanish. While you can translate it directly as **¿Cuál es tu carrera?,** it is more common to ask **¿Qué estudias?** (*What do you study?*).

Después de leer°
After reading

PASO 1. Make a chart to say what you study, where you study for your classes, and where you would like to study abroad, if given the opportunity.

MODELO:

Nombre	¿Qué estudias?	¿Dónde estudias para tus clases?	Quiero viajar a (*I want to travel to*)...
Gustavo	ciencias políticas	la biblioteca, la residencia	Bolivia, Ecuador, Perú

 PASO 2. Pass your chart along to a classmate and, in turn, fill in your own information on your fellow students' sheets as they come your way. When your own chart comes back to you, read the information provided by all other students. If you think you have found someone with similar academic interests, study habits, and travel interests, find that person and stand up together. How many students found a match?

CONÉCTATE AL MUNDO HISPANO

Studying a foreign language gives you the chance to think of things from the perspective of other people. Americans often think of the word *immigrant,* for instance, as referring to people coming into the United States, but in the Spanish-speaking world, there have been many immigrants from Japan to Peru, or from Italy to Argentina. More recently, there have been many immigrants from China to Spain and from Honduras to Mexico. And just like many North American college students go abroad to study, students from all over the world go to the United States and Canada to study.

Suggestion (Después de leer): For *Paso 2,* divide the class in relatively large groups of 5-6 to complete the activity. This will help you with the timing.

Suggestion (Conéctate al mundo hispano): Have students research study-abroad programs offered through your school or one of the many study-abroad companies. Ask them to choose a program based on their major or country of interest, and then help promote interest in study-abroad programs by having them report to the class what they found.

¡Escuchemos!

¿De dónde son?

 ### Antes de escuchar°

listening

Work in pairs to make a list of all the Spanish-speaking countries you know. Then combine your list with that of another group. Together, see if you can sort the countries by the region of the world: **África, Centroamérica, el Caribe, Europa, Norteamérica, Sudamérica.** Finally, listen to the names of the various countries and write down the ones you missed.

 ### A escuchar

Watch and listen at least three times, pausing where necessary. Complete the sentences to tell which country each person is from.

1.

Juan Péndola ___es de Chile___.

2.

Santiago Mariscal ___es de Panamá___.

3.

Andrea Suárez ___es de España___.

4.

Sabrina Vélez ___es de Perú___.

5.

Hérley Alegría González ___es de Colombia___

Después de escuchar

Look at the map at the back of the book and name the capital of each country mentioned in **A escuchar.** Then say in which hemisphere (northern or southern) that country is located. What season is it there now?

MODELO: Juan Péndola es de Chile. Santiago es la capital de Chile. Chile está en el hemisferio sur. Ahora en Chile es... (*the season depends on time of year you respond to this question*).

Note (Antes de escuchar): While students are making their lists, quickly model the Spanish pronunciation of the names of the countries: *Argentina, Bolivia, Chile, Colombia, Costa Rica, Cuba, Ecuador, El Salvador, España, Guatemala, Guinea Ecuatorial, Honduras, México, Nicaragua, Panamá, Paraguay, Perú, Puerto Rico, la República Dominicana, Uruguay, Venezuela.*

Video track (A escuchar): This video clip can be found on the DVD to accompany *Conéctate: Cap. 1,* Track 8.

Note (A escuchar): Remind students to listen for the country each person is from. Listening for details like this will help them understand even when the speaker is fast.

Suggestion (A escuchar): Have students consult maps at the back of the book for spelling.

Videoscript (A escuchar):
1. Juan (Chile): *Yo soy Juan Péndola, soy chileno, vivo en Santiago de Chile.*
2. Santiago (Panamá) *Mi nombre es Santiago Mariscal. Soy de aquí de la ciudad de Panamá, del distrito capital de Panamá.* **3. Andrea (España)** *Me llamo Andrea Suárez, vivo en España.*
4. Sabrina (Perú) *Mi nombre es Sabrina Vélez. Soy de Lima, Perú.* **5. Hérley (Colombia)** *Mi nombre es Hérley Alegría González. Yo soy del país de Colombia.*

¡Escribamos!

La información de contacto

On the first day of class, you might have filled out an information card for your instructor. It's also a good idea to get some contact information from classmates so you can communicate outside of class.

Suggestion: Point out to students that their hours are probably different from the hours of their professors, and a classmate is probably more available to answer questions such as *What was the homework?* and *When is the test?* at night.

Antes de escribir°   *writing*

Use the images to help you write the questions you will have to ask to elicit the information needed to complete **A escribir.**

1. ¿ ___Cómo___ ___te___ ___llamas___?

2. ¿ Cuál es la ___fecha___ de tu cumpleaños (*birthday*)?

3. ¿Cuál es tu dirección de ___email___?

4. ¿Qué ___clases___ tomas (*do you take*)?

5. ¿Cuál es tu ___número___ ___de___ ___teléfono___?

A escribir

In small groups, ask and answer classmates' questions to complete the contact sheets provided. Don't peek at each other's sheet.

MODELO: ESTUDIANTE 1: ¿Cómo te llamas?
ESTUDIANTE 2: Me llamo Marcos.

ESTUDIANTE 1: ¿Cómo se escribe?
ESTUDIANTE 2: Eme - a - ere - ce - o - ese.

ESTUDIANTE 1: ¿Eme - a - ere - ce - o - ese?
ESTUDIANTE 2: ¡Sí!

	ESTUDIANTE 1	ESTUDIANTE 2	ESTUDIANTE 3
Nombre			
Número de teléfono			
Email			
Clases			
Cumpleaños			

ESTRATEGIA

Spelling

Spelling mistakes can alter the meaning of information in any language or context. If you spell a name wrong, you can't look up that person's contact information online. If you write one digit wrong on a phone number, you can't contact the person. One character off on an email address and you never know what happens—it may go to the wrong person or it may be lost forever.

To be sure to get complete and accurate information, try these strategies.

■ Ask for a repetition of just the name or number: **¿Puede usted / Puedes repetir el nombre / el número de teléfono?**

■ Ask how to spell a word: **¿Cómo se escribe?**

■ Ask for one number or letter at a time: **Un número / Una letra a la vez, por favor.**

■ To verify, read back the letters and numbers you have understood.

Después de escribir

In your groups, compare your contact lists and check your own contact information on your classmates' lists for accuracy. Are your first and last names spelled correctly? Are all necessary numbers, including area codes, included for the phone numbers? Is your email address correct and does it include the **arroba** and at least one **punto**?

☐ nombre correcto   ☐ la dirección de correo electrónico correcta

☐ número de teléfono correcto

¡Hablemos!

Una charla°   *A chat*

Antes de hablar°   *speaking*

In groups, make a list of all the questions you have learned so far. Use the vocabulary list at the end of the chapter if you need help coming up with more questions.

A hablar

Now, in the same groups, create the longest conversation you can with the expressions you have learned so far. One student should start by asking a question of the person on his or her left. That person should answer the question and then ask another question of the person to his or her left, continuing clockwise around the circle until the group is unable to come up with any more questions. Include as many of the expressions you learned in this chapter as possible. Have someone keep track of how many questions were asked in your group.

Después de hablar

Which group came up with the longest conversation? Try to recreate it for the rest of the class.

Conéctate a la música

Canción (*Song*): «Doce meses» (2010)
Artista: Pacifika (Canadá)

Pacifika es un trío de músicos. Ellos son de Vancouver, Canadá. La cantante (*singer*), Silvana Kane, es de Perú. La canción «Doce meses» es del álbum *Supermagique*.

Antes de escuchar

What do you associate with each season? Does it depend on the weather? Write whether each of the following items is a season or a month.

	¿ESTACIÓN O MES?
diciembre	_mes_
verano	estación
abril	_mes_
otoño	estación

A escuchar

First read through the phrases below, then listen to the song "**Doce meses**." You won't understand the meaning of every word, but pay attention to the names of seasons and months that you recognize. Match each month with the actions that occur in that month.

■ For copyright reasons, the songs referenced in **Conéctate a la música** have not been provided by the publisher. The video for this song can be found on YouTube, and it is available for purchase at the iTunes store.

1. enero __g__
2. febrero __f__
3. abril __b__
4. mayo, junio, julio __h__
5. septiembre __e__
6. octubre __c__
7. noviembre __a__
8. diciembre __d__

a. ...abrí (*I opened*) mi ventana...
b. ...cantan (*sing*) los pajaritos (*little birds*)...
c. ...mandaste (*you sent*) flores...
d. ...no estás en mi mente...
e. ...perdí la mente (*I lost my mind*)...
f. ...sentí (*I felt*) tus besos (*kisses*)...
g. ...te conocí (*I met you*) por el parque...
h. ...te perseguí (*I pursued you*)...

Después de escuchar

Which statement best summarizes the song?

a. __×__ Después de doce meses, la cantante está contenta (*happy*) porque está enamorada (*in love*).
b. ____ Después de doce meses, la cantante está triste (*sad*) porque perdió (*lost*) su amor (*love*).

VOCABULARIO

Now that I have completed the chapter, I can . . .

☐ greet someone, find out his/her name, how he/she is doing, where he/she is from, and say good-bye

☐ pronounce the letters and sounds of the alphabet

☐ express the date, months, and seasons of the year

☐ say the numbers 0–99

☐ identify people and things

☐ express possession by talking about the objects people have

☐ say the names of the Spanish-speaking countries

Comunicación

¡Hola!	Hello!
Buenos días. / Buen día.	Good morning.
Buenas tardes.	Good afternoon/ evening.
Buenas noches.	Good evening/night.
¿Cómo te llamas? /	What is your name?
¿Cómo se llama?	(informal/formal)
Me llamo /	My first/last
Mi nombre/apellido es...	name is . . .
Soy...	I am . . .
¿Y tú? / ¿Y usted?	And you?
	(informal/formal)
Mucho gusto.	Nice to meet you.
Igualmente.	Likewise.
¿Cómo estás? / ¿Cómo está?	How are you?
	(informal/formal)
¿Qué tal? / ¿Cómo anda?	How's it going?
¿Qué te pasa? /	What's happening
¿Qué le pasa?	with you? / What's the matter?
	(informal/formal)
(Muy) Bien.	(Very) Well.
Más o menos.	OK.
(Muy) Mal.	(Very) Bad.
Gracias.	Thank you.
¿De dónde eres? /	Where are you from?
¿De dónde es?	(informal/formal)
Soy de...	I am from . . .
¿Dónde vives? /	Where do you live?
¿Dónde vive?	(informal/formal)
Vivo en + place	I live in + place
¿Cómo se llama él/ella?	What is his/her name?
Se llama...	His/Her name is . . .

¡Adiós!	Good-bye!
Chau / Chau chau.	Good-bye.
Hasta luego.	See you later.
Hasta mañana / el jueves.	See you tomorrow / (on) Thursday.
Hasta pronto.	See you soon.

Los meses y las estaciones — The months and the seasons

el año	year
las estaciones	seasons
la primavera	spring
el verano	summer
el otoño	autumn, fall
el invierno	winter

los meses: enero, febrero, marzo, abril, mayo, junio, julio, agosto, septiembre, octubre, noviembre, diciembre

Los números y las fechas — Numbers and dates

cero, uno, dos, tres, cuatro, cinco, seis, siete, ocho, nueve, diez, once, doce, trece, catorce, quince, dieciséis, diecisiete, dieciocho, diecinueve, veinte, veintiuno, veintidós, veintitrés, veinticuatro, veinticinco, veintiséis, veintisiete, veintiocho, veintinueve, treinta, treinta y uno... , cuarenta, cuarenta y dos, cincuenta, sesenta, setenta, ochenta, noventa

¿Cuál es la fecha de hoy?	What is today's date?
el día	day
Hoy es...	Today is . . .
el primero de mayo.	the first of May.
el cinco de noviembre.	November fifth.

En la universidad — At the university

Spanish	English
el amigo / la amiga	friend
el aula	classroom
la biblioteca	library
el bolígrafo	pen
el borrador	eraser
la cosa	thing
el cuaderno	notebook
el despacho	office
el diccionario	dictionary
el escritorio	desk
el examen	exam, test
el gimnasio	gymnasium
la hoja de papel	sheet of paper
el hombre	man
el/la joven	young person
el lápiz (*pl.* lápices)	pencil
la librería	bookstore
el libro	book
la llave	key
la mesa	table
la mochila	backpack
la mujer	woman
la página web	web page
la pizarra	chalkboard; whiteboard
la pluma	pen
la puerta	door
el reloj	clock; watch
la residencia (estudiantil)	dormitory
el salón de clase	classroom
la silla	chair
la tarea	homework
la ventana	window

Los cognados: la clase, la computadora, el/la estudiante, la graduación, la idea, el kilo, la oficina, el profesor / la profesora, el proyector, la universidad

Las materias — Subjects

la arquitectura, la biología, las ciencias (políticas), las comunicaciones, el diseño, la economía, la filosofía, la física, el francés, la historia, las humanidades, la ingeniería, el inglés, las matemáticas, la psicología, la química, las relaciones internacionales

Para dar y pedir información — Giving and asking for information

Spanish	English
arroba	@ (at, *in an email address*)
¿Cómo se escribe... ?	How do you spell . . . ?
¿Cuál es tu... ?	What is your . . . ?
carrera	major
(dirección de) email	email (address)
número de teléfono	phone number
¿Cuántos/as... (hay)?	How many . . . (are there)?
doble ve, doble ve, doble ve / triple doble ve	www *in an email address*
punto com/edu	dot com /edu (*in an email address*)
¿Qué estudias?	What do you study? / What's your major?

Verbos — Verbs

Spanish	English
hay	there is, there are
ser (*irreg.*)	to be
soy, eres, es, somos, sois, son	
tener (*irreg.*)	to have
tengo, tienes, tiene, tenemos, tenéis, tienen	

Otras palabras y expresiones útiles — Other words and useful expressions

antes (de)	before
de	of; from
después (de)	after
diferente	different
el, la, los, las	the
en	in; on; at (a place)
más	more
mi(s)	my
no	no
o (u before **o-** or **ho-**)	or
nuestro/a(s)	our
un, una / unos, unas	a, an / some
sí	yes
su(s)	your (form.); his/her; their
también	also
tu(s)	your
vuestro/a(s)	your (*plural inform. Sp.*)
y (e before **i-** or **hi-**)	and

Mis amigos y yo

A estos jóvenes argentinos les gusta (*like*) el fútbol (*soccer*). Y a ti, ¿qué te gusta (*do you like*)?

Objetivos

When you finish this chapter, you will be able to:

- talk about your age
- say where you are going
- express likes and dislikes
- describe people, places, and things

2

www.mhhe.com/connect

COMUNICACIÓN LARIO UCTURA TE

Suggestion (Act. A): Urge students to use listening strategies that extend beyond pausing between each speaker. For example, have them watch the entire video once without looking at the activity. Then have students read all items in the activity before watching a second time and, during the second viewing, answer each item. Finally, check answers on a third viewing.

Video track (Act. A): This video clip can be found on the DVD to accompany *Conéctate: Cap. 2*, Track 1.

Suggestion (Act. A): Before viewing, review the following numbers aloud so students know what to listen for in the video: *nueve* versus *veintinueve, veinte* versus *veintiún, sesenta* versus *setenta*.

¿Cuántos años tienes? / ¿Cuántos años tiene Ud.?

Finding out someone's age

A. A ver: ¿Cuántos años tienes? / ¿Cuántos años tiene? Watch and listen at least twice, pausing as needed, as the following people say their age. Then choose the correct answer.

1. Tengo _b_ años.
   a. nueve
   b. diecinueve
   c. veintinueve

2. Tengo _a_ años.
   a. veinte
   b. veintiséis
   c. treinta

3. Tengo _a_ años.
   a. seis
   b. diecisiete
   c. sesenta

4. Tengo _c_ años.
   a. dieciocho
   b. diecinueve
   c. veinte

5. Tengo _b_ años.
   a. cuatro
   b. catorce
   c. cuarenta

6. Tengo _b_ años.
   a. quince
   b. once
   c. nueve

7. Tengo _a_ años.
   a. diecisiete
   b. veintisiete
   c. siete

8. Tengo _b_ años.
   a. dieciocho
   b. veintiún
   c. veinte

9. Tengo _b_ años.
   a. veinte
   b. veintitrés
   c. veintiséis

10. Tengo _a_ años.
    a. veinticinco
    b. cuarenta y siete
    c. sesenta y seis

11. Tengo _b_ años.
    a. veinte
    b. veintitrés
    c. veintiséis

12. Tengo _a_ años.
    a. treinta y tres
    b. cuarenta y tres
    c. cincuenta y tres

To ask someone's age in Spanish, you can say the following.

¿Cuántos años tienes? (*informal*)   **¿Cuántos años tiene (Ud.)?** (*formal*)

To answer that question, say: **Tengo _____ años.**

—Alicia, ¿cuántos años tienes?   —Señora Beltrán, ¿cuántos años tiene?
—Tengo 18 años.   —Tengo 40 años.

¡Atención! Before the word **años**, use **un** (instead of **uno**) for any age ending in *one* (*one, twenty-one, thirty-one,* and so on).

Tengo 21 (veintiún) años.
Tengo 61 (sesenta y un) años.

Videoscript (Act. A): 1. CAROLINA: *Tengo 19 años.* **2.** MAURICIO: *Tengo 20 años.* **3.** JOSÉ PABLO: *Tengo 6 años.* **4.** JUAN MANUEL: *Tengo 20 años.* **5.** DANIELA: *Bueno, yo tengo 14 años.* **6.** ABRIL: *Tengo 11 años.* **7.** MICHAEL: *Tengo 17 años.* **8.** BRENDA: *Tengo 21 años.* **9.** SEIJI: *Tengo 23 años.* **10.** EUGENIA: *Tengo 25 años.* **11.** MARLÉN: *Tengo 23 años.* **12.** SABRINA: *Tengo 33 años.*

B. ¿Cuántos años tienen (*How old are*) los estudiantes de la clase?

PASO 1.   In groups of four, take turns asking each other's ages. Individually complete the following form to note your age and the age of each group member. Then calculate the average (**el promedio**) for the group. Did you all get the same average? What is the average age for the whole class?

NOMBRE	EDAD (*AGE*)
yo	
Total:	

MODELO: ESTUDIANTE 1: ¿Cuántos años tienes?
ESTUDIANTE 2: Tengo 20 años.

Total de las edades ÷ el número de personas en el grupo = el promedio del grupo
El promedio de la clase es de _____ años.

PASO 2.   Who are the oldest and youngest members of your group? Share this information with the rest of the class. Based on the information provided by each group, who is the oldest in your class? Who is the youngest?

La persona mayor (*oldest*) del grupo / de la clase tiene (*is*) _____ años.
La persona menor (*youngest*) del grupo / de la clase tiene _____ años.

¿Adónde vas? / ¿Adónde va?

Finding out where someone is going

 A. A ver: ¿Adónde vas? / ¿Adónde va?

PASO 1.   Watch and listen as people say where they go on a typical weekday. Play the video again, pausing between each speaker to check the appropriate boxes.

		LAS CLASES	EL GIMNASIO (*GYM*)	LA OFICINA	EL TRABAJO (*WORK*)	LA UNIVERSIDAD
1.	Elisabeth	☐	☑	☐	☐	☐
2.	Enrique	☑	☐	☐	☐	☐
3.	Nuria	☐	☐	☑	☐	☐
4.	Cinthya	☐	☐	☐	☑	☐
5.	Esteban	☐	☐	☑	☐	☐
6.	Lourdes	☐	☐	☐	☐	☑
7.	Diego	☐	☑	☐	☐	☐

(*Continues*)

Suggestion (Act. B, Paso 2): Start by reminding students that *tiene* is the form for *él* and *ella*. As there are often many students of the same age in a class, have students who are the same age tell when their birthday is so they can accurately determine who's older and younger. You may want to write a model sentence on the board: *Yo soy la persona mayor de este grupo porque tengo ___ años y mi cumpleaños es el ___ de ___. Miguel también (also) tiene ___ años pero su cumpleaños es el ___ de ___.*

Video track (Act. A, Paso 1): This video clip can be found on the DVD to accompany *Conéctate: Cap. 2,* Track 2.

Suggestion (Act. A, Paso 1): Read all the places out loud so that students know how they are pronounced and have some familiarity with them before they watch the video.

Videoscript (Act. A, Paso 1): **1.** *Voy al gimnasio.* **2.** *Voy a las clases.* **3.** *Voy a la oficina.* **4.** *Voy a mi trabajo.* **5.** *El martes voy a la oficina.* **6.** *Voy a la universidad.* **7.** *Voy al gimnasio.*

Suggestion (Act. A, Paso 1): Instead of trying to understand everything these speakers say, encourage students to listen for key sounds. Are the final syllables *-dad* or *-cina*? If students can use that strategy to answer effectively, that is great! It will not be possible to understand everything, but context together with strategies can help communication in any situation.

En español...

Just like in English, where *picture* becomes *pic*, *refrigerator* becomes *fridge*, and *biography* becomes *bio*, in Spanish, long words also often get shortened. For example, people might say **el súper** instead of **el supermercado.** Other examples include **la uni** (**la universidad**), **la moto** (**la motocicleta**), **el/la profe** (**el profesor / la profesora**) and **la foto** (**la fotografía**).

Videoscript (Act. A, Paso 2): **1.** *Voy al súper.* **2.** *Voy al cine.* **3.** *Voy al gimnasio.* **4.** *Voy al supermercado.*

PASO 2.   Where do the following people say they go on a typical weekend?

1. Sabrina: «Voy al ___c___.»
2. Benjamín: «Voy al ___a___.»
3. María José: «Voy al ___b___.»
4. Angélica: «Voy al ___d___.»

a. cine (movies)
b. gimnasio
c. súper
d. supermercado

Video track (Act. A, Paso 2): This video clip can be found on the DVD to accompany *Conéctate: Cap. 2,* Track 3.

Follow-up (Act. A): As a transition to *Act. B,* ask students where the people from the video go on weekdays and weekends: *¿Adónde van las personas en un día típico? ¿Adónde van las personas en un fin de semana típico?*

Suggestion (Act. A, Paso 2): Refer students to the column heads in *Act. A, Paso 1* for assistance, and remind them that they are listening for weekend activities (that is, not *el trabajo, la oficina, las clases, la universidad*).

To ask where someone is going, use one of the following questions.

¿Adónde vas? (*informal*)   **¿Adónde va?** (*formal*)

To answer, say: **Voy a** + *name of place.*

Note the contraction **al (a + el): Voy a + el gimnasio = Voy al gimnasio.**

Voy al gimnasio.	I go to the gym.
Voy a la oficina.	I go to the office.

B. ¿Adónde vas en un día típico?

PASO 1.   Check all the places that you go on a typical day (**un día típico**) and all the places that you go on the weekend (**el fin de semana**).

	UN DÍA TÍPICO	EL FIN DE SEMANA
1. el cine	☐	☐
2. la clase	☐	☐
3. el gimnasio	☐	☐
4. la oficina	☐	☐
5. el supermercado	☐	☐
6. el trabajo	☐	☐
7. la universidad	☐	☐

PASO 2.   Now ask a classmate if what he or she does is the same or different from what you do.

MODELO: ESTUDIANTE 1: Yo voy al gimnasio en un día típico. ¿Y tú?
ESTUDIANTE 2: Yo no. Yo voy al gimnasio solo los (*only on*) fines de semana.

CONÉCTATE AL MUNDO PROFESIONAL

Listening is key to successful networking. It is important to find common interests in order to build relationships; you have to give as well as receive in any networking relationship.

Practice this on a small scale in your Spanish course. When talking about yourself, have clear, practiced, polished information, so you neither say too little nor ramble too much. Then ask others about themselves, listen closely to what they say, and ask follow-up questions. Start building your professional network now!

C. ¿Adónde van los otros estudiantes?

PASO 1. Write down one place where you go on a typical weekday and one place you go on the weekend. Then find out where three of your classmates go, and fill out the chart.

MODELO: ESTUDIANTE 1: En un día típico / un fin de semana típico, ¿adónde vas?
ESTUDIANTE 2: Voy al gimnasio.
ESTUDIANTE 1: Gracias.

NOMBRE	EN UN DÍA TÍPICO	EN UN FIN DE SEMANA TÍPICO
yo	voy a/al...	
	va a/al...	

PASO 2. If two or more people on your chart have a place in common, write it on the board. Answer the following questions based on the final list created by the class.

1. En un día típico, ¿adónde va la mayoría (*the majority*) de la clase?
2. En un fin de semana típico, ¿adónde va la mayoría de la clase?

Me gusta...
Expressing likes and dislikes

A. A ver: Me gusta...

PASO 1. Read the list of activities and check the ones that you enjoy.

- ☐ **andar** (correr) **en bicicleta** (*to ride a bike*)
- ☐ **hacer ejercicio** (*to exercise*)
- ☐ **ir a la playa** (*to go to the beach*)
- ☐ **ir al cine**
- ☐ **ir de compras** (*to go shopping*)
- ☐ **jugar** fútbol/bola (*to play soccer*)
- ☐ jugar los videojuegos (*to play video games*)
- ☐ montar a caballo (*to ride horses*)
- ☐ **nadar** (*to swim*)
- ☐ **tocar la guitarra** (*play the guitar*)

PASO 2. Now watch and listen. Then listen two more times with pauses where appropriate and check which activities each person likes.

	JULIÁN	NASLY	YENARO	HENRY
1. andar/correr en bicicleta	☐	☐	☑	☑
2. hacer ejercicio	☑	☐	☐	☐
3. ir a la playa	☐	☑	☐	☐
4. ir al cine	☐	☑	☐	☐
5. ir de compras	☐	☑	☐	☐
6. jugar fútbol/bola	☑	☐	☑	☑
7. jugar los videojuegos	☐	☐	☑	☐
8. montar a caballo	☑	☐	☐	☐
9. nadar	☐	☑	☐	☑
10. tocar la guitarra	☐	☐	☑	☐

Suggestion (Act. C, Paso 2): Have students look over the lists in groups and then ask individual students to report back their group's conclusions.

Video track (Act. A): This video clip can be found on the DVD to accompany *Conéctate: Cap. 2*, Track 4.

Videoscript (Act. A): JULIÁN: *En mi tiempo libre me gusta jugar fútbol, hacer ejercicio, montar a caballo.* NASLY: *Bueno, me gusta ir al cine, me gusta ir de shop... de compras, me gusta nadar, me gusta ir a la playa.* YENARO: *Me gusta pasar mi tiempo tocando la guitarra, jugando bola. Me gusta jugar los videojuegos. Me gusta andar en bicicleta.* HENRY: *Bueno, me gusta nadar, me gusta correr en bicicleta, me gusta fútbol, el soccer, no el fútbol americano y me gusta también explorar la montaña, salir de camping.*

Suggestion (Act. A): Point out to students that boldface words are new chapter vocabulary. Model the pronunciation of the activities for students before beginning.

To talk in Spanish about activities you like to do, use **me gusta** + *activity*.

Me gusta tocar la guitarra.   I like to play the guitar.

To say you don't like to do something, just add **no** to the beginning.

No me gusta jugar* los videojuegos.   I don't like to play video games.

To ask someone else about what activities he or she likes to do, use **te gusta** (*informal*) or **le gusta** (*formal*).

INFORMAL	FORMAL
¿Te gusta + *verb*?	**¿Le gusta** + *verb*?
Do you like to . . . ?	Do you like to . . . ?
—**¿Te gusta nadar?**	—**¿Le gusta ir al cine?**
Do you like to swim?	Do you like to go to the movies?
—**Sí, me gusta nadar.**	—**No, no me gusta ir al cine.**
Yes, I like to swim.	No, I don't like to go to the movies.

Suggestion (Act. B): Help students build their listening networking skills by brainstorming questions they could ask, using names of local shops, buildings and locations, or familiar products. *¿Te gusta jugar los videojuegos? ¿Te gusta hacer ejercicio en el gimnasio Miller? ¿Te gusta ir de compras en Westfield Mall?*

B. El tiempo libre (*Free time*)   At this point your vocabulary is still limited, but take a look at the phrases from **Act. A, Paso 1** and see if you can add a detail (with whom? where?) or an example to each of your answers.

MODELOS: Me gusta jugar los videojuegos, especialmente Halo.
Me gusta montar a caballo. Mi caballo se llama Silver.
Me gusta hacer ejercicio en el parque.
Me gusta ir de compras con mi mamá.

C. ¿Qué te gusta hacer (*to do*)?   Find a partner and take turns asking each other what you like to do. Use the list of activities in **Actividad A**. Does your partner have more in common with Julián, Nasly, Yenaro, or Henry?

MODELOS: ESTUDIANTE 1: ¿Te gusta hacer ejercicio?
ESTUDIANTE 2: Sí, me gusta hacer ejercicio.
ESTUDIANTE 1: ¿Te gusta ir de compras?
ESTUDIANTE 2: No, no me gusta ir de compras.
ESTUDIANTE 1: Entonces (*Well then*), tienes más en común con Julián.

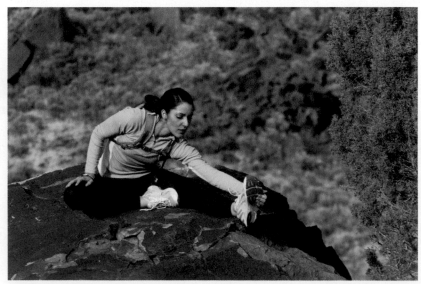

¿Te gusta hacer ejercicio?

---

*If you have studied Spanish before, you may have learned the construction **jugar a** + *sport/ activity*. Many native speakers of Spanish omit the **a,** as you will see and hear on the video.

COMUN **VOCABULARIO** UCTURA ATE

¿Cómo somos?°

What are we like?

Describing people, places, and things with adjectives and colors

Answers (Act. A): *alto/bajo, animado/reservada, contenta/ triste, débil/fuerte, delgada/gordo, grande/pequeño, joven/ vieja, lento/rápido, perezoso/trabajador, pobre/rica*

A. ¿Cómo somos?

PASO 1. Here are some common adjectives used to describe people, places, and things. Look at the images and match the pairs of opposites.

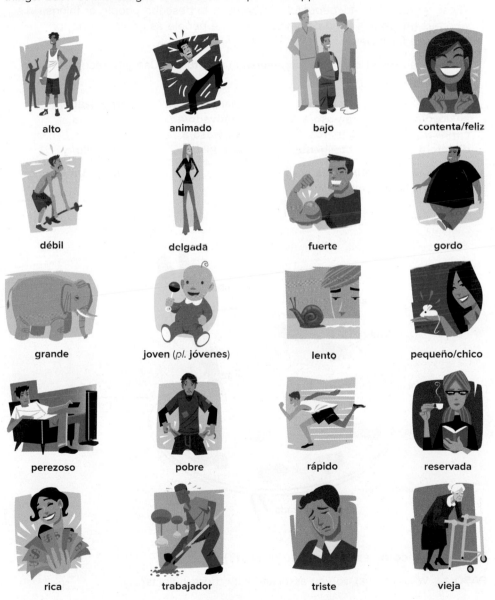

alto

animado

bajo

contenta/feliz

débil

delgada

fuerte

gordo

grande

joven (*pl.* jóvenes)

lento

pequeño/chico

perezoso

pobre

rápido

reservada

rica

trabajador

triste

vieja

En español...

You may have noticed by now that the endings of adjectives change according to whom or what they describe. We will come back to this and discuss it in detail in **Estructura 2.1**.

PASO 2. Select at least three of the adjectives from **Paso 1** and name a well-known person or fictional character who fits each one.

MODELO: rápido → Usain Bolt es rápido.
vieja → Betty White es vieja.
bajo → Bilbo Baggins es bajo.

Suggestion (Act. A, Paso 2): Give a list (or use a series of images) of well-known people and fictional characters, then ask students to match the person/character with the adjectives that best describe him or her.

Here are more opposites.

aburrido/a (*boring*) ≠ **interesante**
antipático/a (*disagreeable*) ≠
  simpático/a (*nice*)
barato/a (*cheap*) ≠ **caro/a** (*expensive*)
bonito/a (*pretty*) ≠ **feo/a** (*ugly*)
bueno/a (*good*) ≠ **malo/a** (*bad*)

corto/a (*short [length]*) ≠ **largo/a** (*long*)
difícil (*hard*) ≠ **fácil** (*easy*)
limpio/a (*clean*) ≠ **sucio/a** (*dirty*)
nuevo/a (*new*) ≠ viejo/a (*old*)
serio/a ≠ **gracioso/a** (*funny*)

As with any language, there are often many synonyms for a frequently used adjective. Here are a few examples in Spanish.

contento/a = feliz = alegre

bello/a = bonito/a = hermoso/a = lindo/a = precioso/a

These words for *pretty/beautiful* can be used to describe people or things, whereas **guapo/a** is used commonly describe people as *good-looking*, or *handsome* for males.

You learned about cognates (**cognados**) in **Capítulo 1**. Can you recognize these adjectives?

activo/a	**excelente**	**maravilloso/a**	**organizado/a**
ansioso/a	**famoso/a**	**motivado/a**	**pesimista**
curioso/a	**generoso/a**	**nervioso/a**	**popular**
directo/a	**inteligente**	**optimista**	**tranquilo/a**

¡Atención! Some adjectives are false cognates. For example, **blanco/a** means *white* and **largo/a** means *long*.

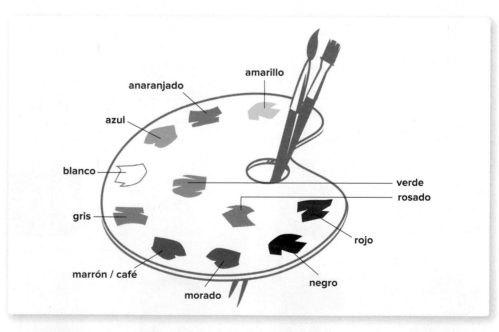

Expansion (Act. B, Paso 1):
Use classroom objects to ask
students ¿De qué color es... ?

B. ¿De qué color es? (*What color is it?*)

PASO 1.   What color(s) do you associate with these objects?

1. el amor
2. la bandera (*flag*) de este país (*this country*)
3. el café (*coffee*)
4. el equipo de fútbol americano de tu universidad o ciudad (*university or city football team*)
5. el mar (*sea*)
6. el otoño
7. la pizza
8. el sol (*sun*)
9. la rosa

PASO 2. In groups of three or four, take turns playing "I Spy" (**Yo veo**) based on colors. Look around the room and select an item, then give a hint, naming the color of the item. Your group will take turns trying to guess what it is.

> **MODELO:** ESTUDIANTE 1: Yo veo algo (*something*) blanco.
> ESTUDIANTE 2: ¿Es la pizarra?
> ESTUDIANTE 1: No, no es la pizarra.
> ESTUDIANTE 3: ¿Es tu libro?
> ESTUDIANTE 1: ¡Sí!

To talk about hair (**el pelo**) color, use a form of the verb **tener** with the following color adjectives.

castaño	*brown*	**rubio**	*blond*
moreno	*dark brown / black*	**trigueño**	*light brown*
negro	*black*		

Tengo el pelo castaño.   I have brown hair.
La niña tiene el pelo rubio.   The girl has blond hair.

Use these same words with **ser** to describe someone as *blond, dark-haired* (or *dark-skinned*), and so on; use **pelirrojo/a** for *redheaded*.

Marcela es rubia, Marcos es /   Marcela is (a) blond, Marcos is dark,
moreno y Dolores es   and Dolores is redheaded / a
pelirroja.   redhead.

For eye color, use **tener + los ojos +** *color* when describing someone or **ser +** *color* to describe or refer to their eye color

Tengo los ojos azules.   I have blue eyes.
—¿De qué color son los ojos de Ricardo?   What color are Ricardo's eyes?
—Son negros / de color negro.   They are black / dark.

C. ¿Quién es... ? Match each image with the description.

a.

b.

c.

d.

1. __b__ Paco tiene el pelo trigueño y los ojos verdes.
2. __d__ Anita tiene el pelo negro y los ojos negros.
3. __a__ Carmen es rubia: tiene el pelo rubio y largo.
4. __c__ Felipe es moreno: Tiene los ojos marrones y el pelo moreno y corto.

D. Ese Fulano de Tal (*Whatshisface*) Study the picture. Then for each item, indicate if the sentence you hear is describing **Fulano A** or **Fulano Z.**

	FULANO A	**FULANO Z**		**FULANO A**	**FULANO Z**
1.	☐	☑	7.	☐	☑
2.	☑	☐	8.	☑	☐
3.	☑	☐	9.	☑	☐
4.	☐	☑	10.	☐	☑
5.	☐	☑	11.	☑	☐
6.	☑	☐			

Fulano A   Fulano Z

Note (Vocabulario): In some varieties of Spanish, *moreno* is only used to describe skin color; in others it is used for either hair or skin color.

■ The audio files for in-text listening activities are available in the eBook, within Connect activities, and on the Online Learning Center.

Note: Act. D: Point out that *fulano* roughly translates as *guy, whatshisname,* or *so-and-so,* and can refer to any imaginary or indeterminate person. In some parts of the Spanish-speaking world, *fulano* can have a negative connotation, as in *fool*.

Script (Act. D): 1. *Es alto.* **2.** *Es bajo.* **3.** *Es delgado.* **4.** *Es gordo.* **5.** *Es gracioso.* **6.** *Es joven.* **7.** *Es moreno.* **8.** *Es rubio.* **9.** *Es serio.* **10.** *Tiene un diccionario pequeño.* **11.** *Tiene una mochila grande.*

Videoscript (Act. E, Paso 1):
1. Mi familia es un poco grande. Es feliz mi familia. 2. Tengo una familia grande. *3. Muy linda… una familia muy excelente, muy… 4. Somos una familia grande. 5. Eh, somos una familia pequeña. 6. Una familia grande. 7. Bueno, pues, nuestra familia es grande. 8. Tengo una familia muy bonita, muy bendecida.*

Notes (Act. E):
- Point out that in **Paso 1**, question 8 (Q8), Óscar also says *bendecida*, which means *blessed*.
- Point out that most adjectives that describe *familia* end in *-a*. Adjective agreement is covered in *Estructura 2.1*. Family—including relative family size—is covered in *Cap. 4*.

Video track (Act. E, Paso 1): This video clip can be found on the DVD to accompany *Conéctate: Cap. 2*, Track 5.

E. A ver: ¿Cómo es? (What's it like?)

PASO 1. Watch and listen, then repeat with pauses after each speaker: what adjective(s) does each person use to describe his or her family?

	BONITA	EXCELENTE	FELIZ	GRANDE	LINDA	PEQUEÑA
1. Juan Andrés	☐	☐	☑	☑	☐	☐
2. Andrea	☐	☐	☐	☑	☐	☐
3. Mayra	☐	☑	☐	☐	☑	☐
4. Delano	☐	☐	☐	☑	☐	☐
5. Tania	☐	☐	☐	☐	☐	☑
6. Ricardo	☐	☐	☐	☑	☐	☐
7. Lourdes	☐	☐	☐	☑	☐	☐
8. Óscar	☑	☐	☐	☐	☐	☐

PASO 2. In small groups, take turns describing your family using at least two adjectives, just as the speakers did in **Paso 1**.

MODELO: Mi familia es pequeña y feliz.

CONÉCTATE AL MUNDO HISPANO

You know that Spanish (**el español**) used as a noun can refer to the language or, as a plural noun (**los españoles**), to the people of Spain. But remember that when it is used as an adjective (**español[a]**), it refers exclusively to people, things, and traditions of Spain. Spanish people live in or are from the European country of Spain. Spanish food is very different from Mexican food, typical Spanish music is different from typical Argentine music, and traditional Spanish dances are very different from traditional Puerto Rican dances.

Additional Practice: To help students learn the meaning of the adjectives, write two sets of adjectives on the board or on a transparency. *Grupo A:* (1) *fuerte* (2) *pequeño* (3) *grande* (4) *lento* (5) *rápido* (6) *feo; Grupo B:* (1) *verde* (2) *blanco* (3) *rojo* (4) *aburrido* (5) *interesante* (6) *famoso*. Each adjective is given a number, corresponding to the side of a die. Ask students to form teams of 3–4 students each and give each team a die. Each team rolls the die twice and writes down the numbers without telling the rest of the class. The number on the first roll corresponds to the same number adjective from *Grupo A*, the number on the second roll to *Grupo B*. The team decides on something or someone that both adjectives describe and writes it down (for example, first roll = 1 [*fuerte*], second roll = 1 [*verde*]: *El Increíble Hulk*). Then each team takes turns telling the name of the thing or person to the class. The team that can guess the two numbers rolled wins a point. Allow students to provide nouns in English (or to ask you for help) if they don't know the words in Spanish.

F. Los países (countries), las nacionalidades y las banderas Escribe el adjetivo debajo de la bandera correspondiente.

paraguayo/a   guatemalteco/a   dominicano/a

nicaragüense   puertorriqueño/a   estadounidense

argentino/a
(Argentina)

boliviano/a
(Bolivia)

canadiense
(Canadá)

chileno/a
(Chile)

colombiano/a
(Colombia)

costarricense
(Costa Rica)

cubano/a
(Cuba)

dominicano/a
(la República
Dominicana)

ecuatoriano/a
(Ecuador)

español(a)
(España)

estadounidense
/norteamericano/a
(los Estados Unidos)

guatemalteco/a
(Guatemala)

hondureño/a
(Honduras)

mexicano/a
(México)

nicaragüense
(Nicaragua)

panameño/a
(Panamá)

paraguayo/a
(Paraguay)

peruano/a
(el Perú)

puertorriqueño/a
(Puerto Rico)

salvadoreño/a
(El Salvador)

uruguayo/a
(Uruguay)

venezolano/a
(Venezuela)

Suggestions (Act. F):
• Practice colors and nationalities. Ask students *¿Cuáles son los colores de la bandera _____?* You can include the distinction between a light and dark version of a color: *claro/oscuro.* Light blue would be *azul celeste.* You can also ask the question differently: *¿Qué banderas tienen los colores blanco, rojo y azul?* Insist that students repeat the formula *bandera* + nationality adjective in their answers: *la bandera costarricense, la bandera cubana, la bandera dominicana, también la bandera estadounidense,* and so on.
• Have students group the adjectives of nationality by ending so that they are aware of all the *-eco, -ense,* and *-ayo* endings.
• Using classroom projection of online images, have students match 4 commonly-known flags with their corresponding countries (for example, U.S., Canada, Mexico, Cuba).

Suggestion (Act. G, Paso 1): Direct students to use appropriate resources: classmates, photo caption on this page, images you provide that might trigger their memories, or Google if you allow devices in class.

Expansion (Act. G, Paso 2): Have students provide more questions. Get them started by asking if they know where some people (e.g., Shakira, Lionel Messi, Gael García Bernal, Sofia Vergara) are from.

G. Es peruano; son chilenas.

PASO 1. Match the following famous people with their nationality.

1. _b_ Julieta Venegas
2. _c_ Isabel Allende y Violeta Parra
3. _a_ Julio y Enrique Iglesias
4. _d_ Mario Vargas Llosa

a. españoles
b. mexicana
c. chilenas
d. peruano

PASO 2. In pairs, take turns reviewing **Paso 1** by saying where the people are from and responding with the correct nationality.

> **MODELO:** ESTUDIANTE 1: ¿De dónde es Isabel Allende?
> ESTUDIANTE 2: Es de Chile. Es chilena.

Mario Vargas Llosa, escritor peruano y ganador del Premio Nobel de la Literatura

COMUN VOCABU ESTRUCTURA ATE

■ Answers to these activities are in Appendix 2 at the back of your book.

2.1   Una estudiante alta

Adjectives

Para empezar...

Match each picture to the appropriate word or words.

1. _g_   2. _b_   3. _c_   4. _e_

a. altos
b. contenta
c. contentos, jóvenes, guapos
d. contento, viejo
e. alta
f. tristes
g. triste
h. alto

5. _d_   6. _f_   7. _a_   8. _h_

¿Por qué?

Spanish has two different plural endings, **-s** and **-es**, in order to make pronunciation smoother and easier. The ending **–s** is used with nouns and adjectives that end in a vowel, and **–es** is used with those that end in a consonant. The **e** of **–es** breaks up what would otherwise be a sequence of two consonants.

Note (¿Por qué?): Help students see this for themselves by writing a variety of nouns and adjectives on the board (e.g., *mujer, reloj, inteligente, niño, amarillo, joven, trabajador*), write an *s* after each one, and challenge students to pronounce the words. For those that are "difficult", add an *e*, resulting in an *–es* ending.

Note (Act. analítica 3): What is described here is the general pattern. There is one class of exceptions: Certain adjective suffixes (*-ador, -és, -ol, -ón*) that end in a consonant nonetheless take *-a* in the feminine form. For example: *trabajador/trabajadora, francés/francesa, español/española, cabezón/cabezona*. These few exceptions are unlikely to interfere with students' acquisition of the general case.

Actividades analíticas

1 Words such as **alto, triste,** and **joven** are *adjectives* (**los adjetivos**), and they describe nouns. In Spanish, adjectives often change their form to agree with the noun that they describe. What two other forms of **alto** do you see in **Para empezar?**

alto   altos   alta

2 Adjectives that end in **-o** like **alto** must agree with both the gender (masculine/feminine) and the number (singular/plural) of the noun. Masculine gender is indicated by **-o,** feminine by **-a,** and plural by **-s.** In Spanish, adjectives usually follow the noun that they modify.

	singular	plural
masculine	el hombre alt**o**	los hombres alt**os**
feminine	la mujer alt**a**	las mujeres alt**as**

3 Adjectives that end in **-e,** such as **triste,** or that end in a consonant, like **joven,** agree only with the number of the noun. The ending **-s** or **-es** is added to indicate plural, but the masculine and feminine forms are exactly the same.

	singular	plural
masculine	el hombre triste el hombre joven	los hombres triste**s** los hombres jóven**es***
feminine	la mujer triste la mujer joven	las mujeres triste**s** las mujeres jóven**es***

The rule for choosing between **-s** and **-es** is just like what you saw in **Estructura 1.2** for nouns: add **-s** if it ends in a vowel, and add **-es** if it ends in a consonant.

---

*Adding **–es** to make the adjective plural also adds an extra syllable, so a written accent mark is sometimes needed in order to preserve the stress in the right place, as is is seen here: **joven   jóvenes**.

Autoprueba

For each of the following phrases, adjust the adjective in parentheses as needed so that it agrees with the noun.

1. los libros _____ (nuevo)
2. las profesoras _____ (joven)
3. una mochila _____ (viejo)
4. la niña _____ (inteligente)

Respuestas: 1. nuevos **2.** jóvenes **3.** vieja **4.** inteligente

Note (Para saber más): *Para saber más 2.1* covers the placement of adjectives—including ordinal numbers—and the variation of meaning of *gran/grande, pobre,* and *viejo* based on placement before or after the noun they modify.

■ For more on the placement of adjectives in Spanish, see **Para saber más 2.1** at the back of your book.

Actividades prácticas

A. ¿Cómo son? (What are they like?)
Finish each sentence in column **A** with an item from column **B**.

A

1. El cálculo y la física son materias __h__.
2. Hillary Clinton y Oprah Winfrey son mujeres __a__.
3. La química avanzada (*advanced*) es una materia __b__.
4. Penélope Cruz y Rafael Nadal son personas __e__.
5. En general, un perro Chihuahua es __i__.
6. Barack Obama y Brad Pitt son hombres __g__.
7. La Universidad Nacional Autónoma de México es una universidad muy __f__.
8. Los Estados Unidos y Canadá son muy __d__.
9. En general, los teléfonos celulares son __c__.

B

a. famosas de los Estados Unidos
b. difícil (*difficult*)
c. pequeños
d. grandes
e. famosas de España
f. grande
g. famosos de los Estados Unidos
h. difíciles
i. pequeño

B. ¿Quién es?
Listen as your instructor describes various people in your class. Guess who they are and write down their names here.

1. _____
2. _____
3. _____
4. _____
5. _____
6. _____

C. Una comparación
Working in a group, create two lists: one of what everyone in your group has in common, and another of the ways in which you are different from each other. Use adjectives (pp. 41, 42) and colors (p. 42), including hair and eye color (p. 43).

MODELO: Somos inteligentes y jóvenes.
Yo tengo el pelo negro. Kathy y Mark tienen el pelo rubio.

D. Más listas
In each of the lists below, eliminate the item that doesn't belong. Then say what the remaining items have in common, using the correct form of the following adjectives. **¡Atención!** Make sure the adjective's ending matches the noun that it is describing.

académico/a   azul   electrónico/a   rojo/a
amarillo/a   blanco/a   famoso/a

MODELO: Shakira, ~~Mary Smith~~, Lady Gaga, Eva Longoria
Son mujeres *famosas*.

1. ~~La bandera (*flag*) española~~, la bandera guatemalteca, la bandera hondureña, la bandera nicaragüense
Son banderas ___azules___ y ___blancas___.

2. ~~Un bolígrafo~~, una computadora, un teléfono, un iPad
Son cosas ___electrónicas___.

3. Antonio Banderas, Javier Bardem, Penélope Cruz, ~~Gael García Bernal~~
Son españoles ___famosos___.

(*Continues*)

Típicamente, los perros Gran Danés son grandes y los perros Chihuahua son pequeños.

Note (Act. B): Describe people in the class with sentences such as *Es alta y tiene el pelo rubio* or *No es alto; es delgado y tiene el pelo negro.*

Note (Act. C): Before they start the activity, remind students that *y* becomes *e* when it is followed by a word beginning with the same sound (*i-* or *hi-*), and that *o* becomes *u* when followed by a word beginning with *o* or *ho-*. Model this change using adjectives that would follow this rule: *Carla es guapa e inteligente. ¿Mario es pesimista u optimista?*

Suggestion (Act. C): Have each group describe at least four things they have in common and four differences.

Note (Act. D): For Q1 and Q5, tell students to refer to the flags in Act. F of the *¿Cómo somos?* vocabulary section.

4. El café, el oso (*bear*) polar, una hoja de papel, la luna (*moon*)
   Son cosas ___blancas___.

5. La bandera colombiana, la bandera ecuatoriana, la bandera mexicana, la bandera venezolana
   Son banderas ___amarillas___, ___azules___ y ___rojas___.

6. La biología, la televisión, la literatura, la química
   Son materias ___académicas___.

Panamá

E. Cultura: La diversidad de Panamá

PASO 1. Read the following text about Panama.

¿Cómo son los panameños? No es fácil describirlos[a] porque son muy diversos. Las familias panameñas son de diferentes orígenes étnicos y nacionales. Este fenómeno tiene que ver[b] con dos eventos importantes en la historia de Panamá: la conquista de América y la construcción del canal.

En 1501 (mil quinientos uno), los primeros exploradores de España llegan[c] a Panamá. Durante ese siglo,[d] llegan muchos españoles y se mezclan[e] con los habitantes[f] indígenas. Varios siglos después, en 1850 (mil ochocientos cincuenta), empieza[g] la construcción del ferrocarril[h] y luego del canal. En este periodo llegan ingenieros[i] de Francia y trabajadores antillanos,[j] por ejemplo de Jamaica, Barbados y Cuba. Llegan trabajadores chinos, colombianos y eventualmente estadounidenses. A Panamá, durante los últimos[k] siglos, han llegado[l] inmigrantes de países árabes, como Líbano, Palestina y Siria, y también del sur de Asia, como la India y Paquistán.

[a]*to describe them* [b]*tiene… has to do* [c]*arrive* [d]*century* [e]*se… they mix* [f]*inhabitants* [g]*begins* [h]*railroad* [i]*engineers* [j]*West Indian (from the Antilles)* [k]*last* [l]*han… have arrived*

PASO 2. Using information from the reading, complete the list of nationalities and countries of origin.

1. franceses, de ___Francia___
2. jamaicanos, de ___Jamaica___
3. libaneses, de ___Líbano___
4. palestinos, de ___Palestina___
5. paquistanís, de ___Paquistán___

6. ___chinos___, de China
7. ___colombianos___, de Colombia
8. ___españoles___, de España
9. ___estadounidenses___, de los Estados Unidos
10. ___panameños___, de Panamá

Note (Act E, Paso 3): For Q1, students can give very simple answers in Spanish: *No tienen trabajo, No tienen dinero*, and so on. For Q2, list categories of people on the board (*personas europeas, personas africanas, personas indígenas, personas asiáticas*) and have students match these with how they got to Latin America (*colonia, inmigración, esclavitud, originarios*).

PASO 3. With a partner, answer the following questions and discuss the ideas behind your responses.

1. Los trabajadores que llegan a Panamá durante la construcción del canal enfrentan (*face*) muchos problemas: un viaje costoso (*costly trip*), un idioma (*language*) nuevo, la malaria, etcétera. ¿Por qué crees que lo hacen (*do you think that they do it*)?
2. Los latinoamericanos son de muchas razas (*races*) diferentes, igual que (*just like*) los norteamericanos. ¿Cómo pasó eso (*how did that happen*)?
3. Llegan muchos trabajadores a Panamá durante la construcción del canal entre 1881 y 1914. En tu país, ¿también hay mucha inmigración en este periodo? ¿Tu familia llega en este periodo?

Una de las esclusas (*locks*) del canal de Panamá.

2.2   ¿Estás triste?

The verbs *estar* (to be) and *ir* (to go)

Para empezar...

Note (Para empezar): Answers will vary somewhat. Allow students to justify different choices. Problems with **Estás** match solutions with **Vas**, while those with **Estamos** match **Vamos**.

Match each problem to the most likely solution. Some solutions can be used more than once since certain problems can have more than one solution.

1. __b__ **Estás** (*You are*) cansado/a (*tired*).
2. __f__ **Estamos** nerviosos/as.
3. __c__ **Estás** solo/a (*alone*).
4. __a__ **Estás** ansioso/a.
5. __e__ **Estamos** aburridos/as (*bored*).
6. __b, d__ **Estás** enfermo/a (*sick*).
7. __a, b, c__ **Estás** triste.

a. **Vas** a un consejero (*counselor*).
b. **Vas** a la cama (*bed*).
c. **Vas** a una fiesta (*party*) con amigos.
d. **Vas** a la farmacia.
e. **Vamos** al cine.
f. **Vamos** a una clase de yoga.

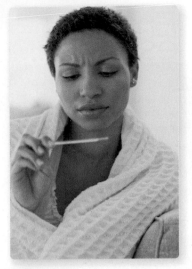

Estoy enferma.

Actividades analíticas

1   In **Para empezar,** you saw examples of two new verbs: **estar** (*to be*) and **ir** (*to go*). Use these examples to complete the conjugations here.

- Answers to these activities are in Appendix 2 at the back of your book.

	estar	ir
SINGULAR		
yo	estoy	voy
tú	estás	vas
él/ella, Ud.	está	va
PLURAL		
nosotros/as	estamos	vamos
vosotros/as	estáis	vais
ellos/ellas, Uds.	están	van

As with other verbs in Spanish, the subject is usually left unexpressed unless it is needed for clarification.

Estoy contenta.	*I'm happy.*
Están aburridos.	*They are bored.*
Vamos a la fiesta.	*We're going to the party.*
¿Vas a clase?	*Are you going to class?*

2   As you saw in **Estructura 1.3,** the form of the verb used to address someone formally (with **Ud.**) is different from the form used to address someone informally (with **tú**). Change the following questions from the **tú** form to the **Ud.** form.

¿Cómo estás?   →   ¿Cómo __está__ usted?

¿Vas a la fiesta?   →   ¿ __Va__ usted a la fiesta?

(*Continues*)

Autoprueba

For each sentence, decide between **estar** or **ir**, then conjugate the verb appropriately.

1. ¿Adónde ____ tus amigos?
2. Carmen ____ muy cansada.
3. Nosotros ____ contentos.
4. Yo ____ a la universidad hoy.

Respuestas: 1. van 2. está 3. estamos 4. voy

En español...

Like **estar**, the verb **tener** can also express states that are not necessarily lasting. For example, **tener hambre** (literally, *to have hunger*) means *to be hungry*.

Tengo hambre!	*I'm hungry!*
El perro tiene sed.	*The dog is thirsty.*
¿Tienes calor o frío?	*Are you hot or cold?*

■ To learn how to use the verb **tener** to express how you are feeling, see **Para saber más 2.2** at the back of your book.

Note (Para saber más): *Para saber más 2.2* covers expressions with the verb *tener*.

Suggestion (En español): Have students prepare a question for each of the question words. Then have them work with a partner, taking turns asking and answering their questions. Be sure to have them respond in complete sentences.

---

3 The verb **estar** expresses characteristics that are not necessarily lasting. For example, the state of being tired or being sick could change at any time, so you express this with **estar**.

Estamos cansados.	*We are tired.*
¿Estás enferma?	*Are you sick?*

Characteristics that are not likely to change are expressed with the verb **ser**, which you saw in **Estructura 1.3**.

Soy de Guatemala.	*I'm from Guatemala.*
UCLA **es** una universidad.	*UCLA is a university.*

You will learn more about the differences between **ser** and **estar** in **Estructura 4.4** and **5.3**.

Note (Act. A.): The word *casa* was introduced briefly in Cap. 1. Point out here that it literally means "house," but that *Voy a la casa* means "I'm going home."

Actividades prácticas

A. En orden The following sentences form a simple conversation, but they are out of order. Put them in an order that makes sense. The first one is done for you.

- _4_ Porque mañana tengo un examen.
- _1_ ¿Cómo estás?
- _6_ Buena idea. Voy. ¿Adónde vas tú?
- _3_ ¿Por qué?
- _2_ Ansioso.
- _5_ ¿Por qué no vas a la biblioteca a estudiar?
- _7_ Voy a la casa (*home*) a dormir (*to sleep*). Tengo sueño (*I'm sleepy*).

B. ¿*Estoy o soy*? Select the correct form to complete the sentences.

1. (<u>Estoy</u> / Soy) frustrado (*frustrated*).
2. (Estoy / <u>Soy</u>) de Panamá.
3. (Estoy / <u>Soy</u>) una mujer alta.
4. (<u>Estoy</u> / Soy) triste.
5. (Estoy / <u>Soy</u>) profesor.
6. (<u>Estoy</u> / Soy) cansada.

En español...

By now you have seen many ways of asking questions. Here are some useful question words.

Spanish / English		Spanish / English	
¿Qué?	What?	**¿Cómo?**	How?
¿Quién?	Who?	**¿Cuándo?**	When?
¿Cuál?	Which?	**¿Cuántos/as?**	How many?
¿Dónde?	Where?	**¿Por qué?**	Why?
¿Adónde?	(To) Where?		

Notice that **dónde** and **adónde** are both translated as *where* in English, but **dónde** is used to ask where you *are* and **adónde** to ask where you are *going*.

Questions with **por qué** are often answered with **porque** (*because*), which is spelled as one word and has no accent mark.

What do all of the above question words have in common?

What do you notice about the punctuation that is different from English?

C. Preguntas y respuestas Match each question with the appropriate answer.

1. _f_ ¿Cómo estás?
2. _g_ ¿Dónde estás?
3. _b_ ¿Adónde vas?
4. _i_ ¿Por qué van al cine?
5. _j_ ¿Adónde va Julia?
6. _h_ ¿Quién va a la biblioteca?
7. _a_ ¿Por qué vas a la farmacia?
8. _c_ ¿Por qué estás ansioso?
9. _e_ ¿Adónde van?
10. _d_ ¿Dónde están?

a. Porque estoy enferma.
b. Voy a una fiesta.
c. Porque voy a un examen.
d. Estamos en el gimnasio.
e. Vamos al cine.
f. Bien, gracias.
g. Estoy en el restaurante.
h. María Elena.
i. Porque estamos aburridos.
j. Va al gimnasio.

D. ¿Adónde vas?

PASO 1. Where do you go in the following situations? Choose one of the answers provided or think of an alternative and mark your answer with an X.

1. ¿Adónde vas cuando (*when*) estás enfermo/a?
   ☐ al médico (*doctor*)   ☐ a la clínica de la universidad   ☐ a la farmacia
   ☐ otra (*another*) respuesta: _____

2. ¿Adónde vas para estudiar?
   ☐ a la casa   ☐ a la biblioteca   ☐ a la casa de un amigo
   ☐ a un café   ☐ otra respuesta: _____

3. ¿Adónde vas cuando tienes hambre a mediodía (*at midday*)?
   ☐ a la casa   ☐ a un restaurante   ☐ al comedor (*dining area*) de la universidad
   ☐ otra respuesta: _____

4. ¿Adónde vas cuando estás triste?
   ☐ a un parque   ☐ a la casa   ☐ a una iglesia (*church*)
   ☐ otra respuesta: _____

Now, for each of the questions, circle the box next to the answer you think will be the most common among your classmates.

PASO 2. Your instructor will assign you one of the four questions. Interview as many of your classmates as you can, and keep a tally of the results (using the area to the left of each answer, if you wish). Some possible answers are given, but keep in mind that there may be others.

MODELO: ESTUDIANTE 1: ¿Adónde vas cuando estás triste?
ESTUDIANTE 2: Voy a la casa de una amiga.

PASO 3. Report your results to the class. **¡Atención!** If the answer you are reporting applies to you also, use the **nosotros/as** form of the verb: **Vamos a la biblioteca.** If the answer does not necessarily apply to you, use the **ellos/ellas** form of the verb: **Van a la casa.** If you wish to report a split response, use numbers: **Tres van a la biblioteca. Cinco van a la casa.**

Others will report their results, so you should now get a good picture of how the class answered each of the four questions. How good were your predictions from **Paso 1?**

Normalmente voy a la biblioteca para estudiar.

Suggestion (Act. E, Paso 1): You may wish to add other adjectives included in the *Vocabulario* section.

E. La clase de actuación

PASO 1.   Working in a team of three students, read through this list of adjectives and choose one that you will act out as a team in front of the class.

aburrido/a	cansado/a	enojado/a (*angry*)	serio/a
ansioso/a	contento/a	loco/a (*crazy*)	simpático/a
bueno/a	enfermo/a	malo/a	triste

Suggestion (Act. E, Paso 2): Here are some possible variations on this activity: 1) Assign each team an adjective from the list. 2) Have teams of two, and have each team member act out a different adjective simultaneously in front of the class. The class then has to guess the psychological state of each person separately. 3) Pair each team with one other team, and have each pair of teams do a few rounds of *Paso 2* on their own. 4) Same as variation 3, but have the teams rotate after each round of *Paso 2*.

PASO 2.   Act out your adjective as a team, while the other students try to describe your psychological state. **¡Atención!** As you watch other teams act, pay attention to the gender composition of the team in order to know which form of the adjective to use.

> **MODELO:**   ESTUDIANTE 1: ¿Están cansadas?
> ESTUDIANTE 2: No, no estamos cansadas.
> ESTUDIANTE 3: ¿Están enojadas?
> ESTUDIANTE 2: ¡Sí! Estamos enojadas.

2.3   ¿Te gusta la clase de español?

The verb *gustar*

Para empezar...

Note (Para empezar): If you wish, you can provide students with the term *pasatiempo(s) favorito(s)*.

PASO 1.   Below you see four people and what they like to do in their free time. Write the name of the person most likely to say each of the quotes that follow. **¡Atención!** One sentence doesn't belong to any of these four. Which is it?

Agustina, de Argentina
En el tiempo libre: música
metal progresivo

Javier, de España
En el tiempo libre: el cine (*film*)

Esther, de España
En el tiempo libre: novelas

Pedro, de México
En el tiempo libre: fútbol

Suggestion (Para empezar): Pronounce the word *hobbies* for students in Spanish (*jobis*) and help them pronounce it this way too. If they pronounce this word the English way, they may not be understood by many Spanish speakers.

Persona

Javier	1. «Me gustan las películas (*movies*).»
Agustina	2. «Me gusta la música.»
Pedro	3. «Me gustan los deportes (*sports*).»
nobody	4. «Me gusta la biología.»
Esther	5. «Me gustan los libros.»

PASO 2.   Now think about your interests and those of your classmates. Which of the above sentences apply to you? Can anyone in the class say that all of these sentences apply to them?

Actividades analíticas

1   In **Para empezar,** you saw examples of both **me gusta** and **me gustan.** They both mean *I like,* so what is the difference between the two? Read the statements from **Paso 1** again, then complete this chart with the things that follow **me gusta** and those that follow **me gustan.**

me gusta	me gustan
la música	las películas
la biología	los deportes
	los libros

What conclusion can you come to? In the table below, write the words **singular** and **plural** in the appropriate places.

me gusta	con un sustantivo (*noun*) <u>singular</u>
me gustan	con un sustantivo <u>plural</u>

2 **Te gusta** and **te gustan** work the same way as **me gusta** and **me gustan.** They both mean *you like,* but which form you use depends on whether the noun is singular or plural. Which would you use to ask if someone likes the following things?

¿<u>Te gustan</u> los deportes?   ¿<u>Te gusta</u> la historia?

3 **Le gusta** and **le gustan** mean *he/she likes* or *you* (formal) *like.* If you want to clarify who you are talking about, you may use **a** + *name or pronoun.*

¿A usted <u>le gustan</u> las novelas gráficas?

A Carolina no <u>le gusta</u> el chocolate.

Autoprueba

Use what you know about the verb **gustar** to fill in its correct forms below.

1. Me ____ la clase de español.
2. ¿Te ____ tus clases este semestre?
3. ¿Te ____ la filosofía?
4. A Sabrina le ____ el arte.
5. ¿A Ud. le ____ los deportes?

Respuestas: 1. gusta **2.** gustan **3.** gusta **4.** gusta **5.** gustan

Actividades prácticas

A. Preguntas y respuestas Match each question with the most logical answer.

1. <u>b</u> ¿Te gustan los deportes?
2. <u>e</u> ¿A usted le gusta el cine español?
3. <u>h</u> ¿Te gusta la música hip hop?
4. <u>f</u> ¿A Jerónimo le gusta la televisión?
5. <u>d</u> ¿A Ana le gusta el jazz?
6. <u>a</u> ¿Te gusta la música clásica?
7. <u>c</u> ¿A usted le gusta el café?
8. <u>i</u> ¿Te gusta nadar (*to swim*)?
9. <u>g</u> ¿A tu madre le gusta ir al gimnasio en su tiempo libre?

a. Sí, me gusta mucho Bach.
b. Sí, me gusta mucho el fútbol.
c. No, me gusta más el té (*tea*).
d. Sí, le gusta la música de Miles Davis.
e. Sí, me gustan las películas de Almodóvar.
f. No, le gustan más las películas.
g. No, no le gusta hacer ejercicio (*to exercise*).
h. Sí, me gusta Nicki Minaj.
i. No, no me gusta estar en el agua (*water*).

B. Las banderas Some people like certain flags because of their colors. Using the list of flags in **Actividad F** of the **¿Cómo somos?** vocabulary section, match each description with the appropriate flag(s). **¡Atención!** Notice whether the statements in the first column end in **me gusta** or **me gustan.**

<u>c</u> 1. Me gusta el color rojo. Me gusta...
<u>e</u> 2. Me gusta el color blanco. Me gustan...
<u>b</u> 3. Me gusta el color azul. Me gusta...
<u>a</u> 4. Me gusta el color verde. Me gustan...
<u>d</u> 5. Me gusta el color amarillo. Me gustan...

a. las banderas de Bolivia y México.
b. la bandera de Honduras.
c. la bandera del Perú.
d. las banderas de Ecuador y Venezuela.
e. las banderas de Chile y Costa Rica.

C. Tus clases

PASO 1. What classes are you taking this term and how do you feel about them? Create two sentences: one that lists classes you like, and another that lists any you don't like.

MODELO: Me gustan las clases de español y química. No me gusta la clase de historia.

 PASO 2. Ask a partner which classes he or she has (**¿Qué clases tienes?**). Then find out whether he or she likes each one.

MODELO: ESTUDIANTE 1: ¿Qué clases tienes?
ESTUDIANTE 2: Tengo clases de historia, español y biología.
ESTUDIANTE 1: ¿Te gusta la clase de español?
ESTUDIANTE 2: Sí, mucho.
ESTUDIANTE 1: A mí, también. (*I do, too.*) Es muy buena.

■ For more on how to say in Spanish what different people like or don't like, see **Para saber más 2.3** at the back of your book.

Note (Para saber más): *Para saber más 2.3* covers additional forms of the *gustar* construction, such as *nos gusta(n), os gusta(n),* and *les gusta(n).*

Me gusta el chocolate.

D. Una encuesta (survey) People often make assumptions about what students like, such as the items in the list below. Is there any truth to these stereotypes?

PASO 1. Circulate throughout the classroom and ask classmates **¿Qué te gusta?** (*What do you like?*). Your classmates should use the items in the list to respond.

> **MODELO:** ESTUDIANTE 1: ¿Qué te gusta?
> ESTUDIANTE 2: Me gustan el café, el chocolate y las películas de terror (*horror*).

___ el café	___ las computadoras	___ la música
___ la cerveza (*beer*)	___ las fiestas	___ las películas de terror
___ el chocolate	___ las hamburguesas	___ la pizza

PASO 2. Now present your results to the class! Who likes each of the items from **Paso 1?**

> **MODELO:** A Sarah le gusta el café. Pero a Jaime le gustan las computadoras y la música.

2.4 ¿Qué te gusta hacer? ¿Qué vas a hacer?

Infinitives with *gustar* and *ir*

Para empezar...

PASO 1. Here are some activities that many people enjoy doing. Rank them in order of preference (1–9) for you. Write an X for any activity that you do not like to do (**No me gusta...**).

Me gusta...   **No me gusta...**

___ bailar (*dance*)	___ dormir	___ leer (*read*)
___ comer (*eat*)	___ hablar (*talk*) por teléfono	___ nadar
___ correr (*run*)	___ hacer ejercicio	___ usar la computadora

PASO 2. Which of these activities are you going to do over the next eight hours? Write those verbs here.

Voy a _____

Actividades analíticas

1 In the examples in **Para empezar**, **me gusta** is followed by the infinitive (**el infinitivo**), the unconjugated form of the verb. Infinitives in Spanish always end in **-ar, -er,** or **-ir.** Find an example from **Para empezar** of each of these three types.

Infinitive ending	-ar	-er	-ir
Example	bailar, hablar, nadar, usar	comer, correr, hacer, leer	dormir

You will find out more about these three types of verbs in **Capítulo 3.**

2 **Gustar** is always in the singular form when used with one or more infinitives.

Me **gusta ir** al cine.   *I like to go to the movies.*

A José le **gusta escuchar** música y bailar.   *José likes to listen to music and dance.*

Suggestion (Para empezar): Ask (some) students to write their top-ranked activity on the board (for example, *Me gusta bailar*) and to write *sí* if they are going to do this today and *no* if they are not (*Vas a bailar hoy?*). Depending on what students write, ask them if they are *contento/a* or *triste*.

Suggestion (Act. analíticas 1): Point out that infinitives are easy to recognize in Spanish because they always end in *-r*.

■ Answers to these activities are in Appendix 2 at the back of your book.

3 Infinitives are also used after **ir a,** as a way of expressing a future event.

ir a + *infinitive*

Voy a estudiar.	*I am going to study.*
Van a nadar.	*They are going to swim.*
¿Vas a correr?	*Are you going to run?*
Ana **va a** usar la computadora.	*Ana is going to use the computer.*

Actividades prácticas

A. ¿Dónde estás? ¿Qué vas a hacer?   If you are in the place stated in column **A,** which activity in column **B** are you most likely going to do?

A

1. _f_ Estoy en la biblioteca.
2. _e_ Estoy en la cama (*bed*).
3. _h_ Estoy en un restaurante.
4. _g_ Estoy en un gimnasio.
5. _a_ Estoy en la clase de español.
6. _c_ Estoy en la playa.
7. _b_ Estoy en una discoteca.
8. _d_ Estoy en la universidad.

B

a. Voy a hablar español.
b. Voy a bailar.
c. Voy a nadar.
d. Voy a asistir a clase (*attend class*).
e. Voy a dormir.
f. Voy a leer.
g. Voy a hacer ejercicio.
h. Voy a comer.

B. ¿Dónde te gusta... ?   Do your classmates like to do things on campus, at home, or somewhere else? Think of three common activities and ask a partner where he/she likes to do them.

MODELO: ESTUDIANTE 1: ¿Dónde te gusta estudiar?
ESTUDIANTE 2: Me gusta estudiar en casa.

C. ¡Me gusta!

PASO 1. Complete each of these sentences with either **gusta** or **gustan.**

1. «Me _gusta_ ir al cine.»
2. «Me _gusta_ leer.»
3. «Me _gustan_ las películas norteamericanas.»
4. «Me _gustan_ los gimnasios.»
5. «Me _gusta_ la música de Juanes.»
6. «Me _gustan_ los libros de Carlos Ruiz Zafón.»
7. «Me _gusta_ ir a conciertos (*concerts*).»
8. «Me _gusta_ hacer ejercicio y bailar.»

PASO 2. Now look at the sentences in **Paso 1** and find the pairs that relate to the same topic and would likely have been spoken by the same person. Use the sentence numbers to identify the pairs of sentences that go together.

_1_ y _3_   _2_ y _6_   _4_ y _8_   _5_ y _7_

D. ¿Qué vas a hacer?

PASO 1. Ask as many classmates as possible what they are going to do this weekend (**este fin de semana**). Keep track of their answers. When another student asks you what you are going to do, name up to three activities.

MODELO: ESTUDIANTE 1: ¿Qué vas a hacer este fin de semana?
ESTUDIANTE 2: Voy a ir a una fiesta, hacer ejercicio y estudiar.

PASO 2. Now tally up the answers. What were the top three activities in your class?

Autoprueba

Complete each sentence logically, using **ir a** + *inf.* with one of the following verbs: **bailar, correr, estudiar, hacer ejercicio.**

1. Ernesto _____ en el parque.
2. ¿Tú _____ en la biblioteca?
3. Ana y Cecilia _____ en el gimnasio.
4. Yo _____ en una discoteca.

Respuestas: 1. va a correr
2. vas a estudiar
3. van a hacer ejercicio
4. voy a bailar

El niño (*boy*) está en la cama.

Suggestion (Act. B): When students are done, ask them what most people liked to do and what the most common place for doing each activity was: *la universidad, la casa u otro lugar.*

Note (Act. C): If students need help remembering the rule for *Me gusta + noun,* remind them to review *Estructura 2.3.*

¡Leamos!

¿Cómo son los profesionales?

Suggestion (Antes de leer): Encourage students to use adjectives presented earlier in the chapter.

Answers (Antes de leer, Paso 1): Answers may include: *fuerte, inteligente, interesante, optimista, organizado, simpático, trabajador.* You may want to give them the word *cano* or *canoso/a* for grey-haired.

Antes de leer

PASO 1. Write down a list of adjectives you might expect to see in an advertisement for the services offered by a group of people working at a small business.

> **MODELO:** Es un grupo *motivado* y *profesional*.

 PASO 2. In groups, take turns describing the individuals pictured in the ad (without using any names). Can the other members of the group name the person being described?

> **MODELO:** ESTUDIANTE 1: Es baja, delgada y tiene el pelo trigueño.
> ESTUDIANTE 2: ¿Es Heather Ramos?

Ortiz & Gutiérrez

Clínica Médica (919) 268-5439

1ERA CONSULTA = $0

HABLAMOS INGLÉS Y ESPAÑOL

Heather Ramos
asistente médica

Carlos Ortiz
doctor de medicina

Antonia Gutiérrez
doctora de medicina

Teresa Miller
asistente médica

18 Sacramento St.
www.ortizgutierrez.com

▶ SE ESPECIALIZA EN INSOMNIO   ▶ LOS ESTUDIANTES SON BIENVENIDOS

▶ SE ESPECIALIZA EN SICOLOGÍA   ▶ TRATAMIENTOS ECONÓMICOS

A leer

Examine the ad for a clinic run by two physicians, Ortiz & Gutiérrez, and answer the following questions.

1. ¿Cómo son los doctores?
2. ¿Cuánto cuesta una consulta?
3. ¿Qué tipo de asistente es Heather Ramos?
4. ¿Cuáles adjetivos describen a un(a) paciente antes de (*before*) visitar la clínica?

   activo/a   ansioso/a   cansado/a   contento/a   motivado/a

5. ¿Cuáles adjetivos describen a un(a) paciente después de (*after*) visitar la clínica?

   activo/a   ansioso/a   cansado/a   contento/a   motivado/a

Después de leer

Working in groups, use the nouns and adjectives below—plus any others you want to add—to prepare another ad for Ortiz & Gutiérrez. Take turns presenting your ads to the class. **¡Atención!** Make sure the adjectives agree with the nouns they describe in both gender and number.

En Ortiz & Gutiérrez...

el equipo (*team*)	las asistentes médicas	inteligente	organizado/a
la clínica	animado/a	limpio/a	simpático/a
los doctores	fuerte	motivado/a	trabajador(a)

CONÉCTATE AL MUNDO PROFESIONAL

When sharing with the class, take 30–60 seconds to practice and prepare what you are going to say so that you can stand up and deliver a quick, polished summary of the work you've done. Your audience will appreciate it! You're getting practice for the kind of brief but formal presentations you'll deliver at job fairs, networking events, and interviews. And this is the kind of verbal communication employers will want you to be prepared for when presenting in meetings, interacting with clients or colleagues, and representing the employer outside the workplace.

¡Escuchemos!

¿Cómo es tu familia?

Antes de escuchar

With a partner, use the following adjectives to describe your family and family members. **¡Atención!** Make sure the endings agree in gender and number.

alto/a   delgado/a   grande   maravilloso/a
bajo/a   gordo/a   hermoso/a   pequeño/a

1. Mi familia es...
2. Mi hermana (*sister*) es...
3. Mi hermano (*brother*) es...
4. Mi padre (*father*) es...
5. Mi madre (*mother*) es...
6. Mi hija (*daughter*) es una niña...
7. Mi hijo (*son*) es un niño...

(*Continues*)

Suggestion (Después de leer): Remind students that reading is much more than decoding words. You have to consider images, tone, headings, context, who wrote the text, where it appears. It's important to know that this reading is an advertisement—even though it's not labeled as such.

Suggestion (Después de leer): Remind students to form complete sentences using *ser* (e.g., *En Ortiz & Gutiérrez el equipo es maravilloso.*). Encourage them to be creative, adding subjects and adjectives of their own choosing.

Suggestion (Conéctate al mundo profesional): Consider making it the status quo to give students up to a minute to prepare practiced, polished responses when reporting back to the whole class after group work. That way no single student has to take the social risk of being the only person who prepares, and everyone will notice improvement in oral production, confidence in speaking, and workplace readiness.

Suggestion (A escuchar): Before moving on to *A escuchar*, have students review age by asking each other *¿Cúantos años tienes?* and colors by pointing at things and asking *¿De qué color es?*

En español...

You may notice that some speakers will add the diminutive suffix **-ito** or **-ita**, to the ends of adjectives used to describe their family members. This suffix adds the meaning "a little bit." For example, one speaker describes her mom as **"un poquito más bajita y más gordita."** She's not calling her mom short and fat, but rather "a little on the shorter side" and "a little chubbier" than the rest of the family, as a sort of term of endearment.

Videoscript (¡A escuchar!):
1. ÓSCAR: *Tengo un hijo de 17 años y una niña de 13 años.* 2. MARÍA LUZ: *Y mi hija también es muy hermosa. Ella tiene el cabello largo, los ojos verdes.* 3. ZULAY: *Bueno, el mayor tiene 21 años. Bueno, mi hijo es grande, alto, gordito.* 4. GUADALUPE: *Bueno, mi padre es alto, delgado y mi madre es un poquito más bajita y más gordita. Y mis hermanos son altos también y delgados.*

A escuchar

Video track (A escuchar): This video clip can be found on the DVD to accompany *Conéctate: Cap. 2,* Track 6.

Watch and listen to the video. Then watch again, pausing as needed, and fill in the descriptions of the following people's families.

Óscar

1. El hijo tiene ___17___ años.
La niña tiene ___13___ años.

María Luz

2. La hija es *hermosa*. Tiene el cabello (pelo) *largo* y los ojos *verdes*.

Zulay

3. Su hijo, Luis Miguel, tiene ___21___ años. Él es *grande*, *alto* y *gordito*.

Guadalupe

4. Su padre es *alto* y *delgado*. Su madre es *bajita* y *gordita*. Sus hermanos son *altos* y *delgados*.

Suggestion (A escuchar): Tell students that Óscar has teenage children (*hijos adolescentes*) and review the numbers 13–19 so that they are listening specifically for two numbers in the teens. This type of support makes the authentic speech more manageable for beginning students.

Después de escuchar

Suggestion (Después de escuchar): Ask some students to share their descriptions with the class.

Write sentences using other adjectives you have studied in this chapter. Pick three adjectives that you think best describe you and/or your personality and three that describe your siblings, parents, guardians, or children.

MODELO: Soy graciosa, simpática y alta. Mi madre es baja y trabajadora. Mis hermanitos son altos y delgados y muy animados.

Suggestion (Después de escuchar): Refer students to the end of chapter vocabulary list if they have trouble coming up with descriptions.

ESTRATEGIA

Audience. Audience is always important to consider, especially before posting content online for the world to see. For example, who is your audience for an online profile? Is it limited to a certain group of friends, family members, colleagues, or potential employers? If it is all of the above, you have to present yourself differently than if your audience is just one segment of your social life. Once you know your audience, be sure to keep your tone and information presented appropriate for them.

¡Escribamos!

El perfil electrónico°

Online profiles

Being able to present yourself succinctly in Spanish to others will be an invaluable skill as you get to know more native speakers, study, travel, work, and explore the Spanish-speaking world. An online profile is one way to do this, allowing you to connect with people who share your interests so you can develop personal or professional relationships.

Antes de escribir

PASO 1. To get started on your online profile (for Facebook, a blog, a networking site, or an online dating site) in Spanish, answer the following questions.

¿Cómo te llamas?

¿Cómo eres? (cinco adjetivos)

¿De dónde eres?

¿Cuántos años tienes?

¿Qué te gusta hacer (*to do*)? (¿esquiar? ¿leer?) (cuatro actividades)

PASO 2. Choose the audience for your profile.

☐ mi familia

☐ mis colegas de trabajo (*work*)

☐ todos (*all*) mis contactos

☐ todos mis amigos

☐ un grupo de amigos: _____

PASO 3. Look at the information you listed in **Paso 1** and cross off the items you wouldn't want to share with your selected audience.

> **MODELO:** (Audience: *todos mis contactos*)
> Soy ~~pesimista~~, trabajadora, ~~ansiosa~~,...
> Me gusta ir al gimnasio.
> ~~Me gusta ir a las fiestas todas las noches~~.
> Me gustan los videojuegos.

A escribir

Use the information you compiled in **Antes de escribir** to write a clear, simple, compelling profile that is appropriate for your selected audience. Use complete sentences, and add details where appropriate.

 Después de escribir

Check your own work, then exchange profiles with a classmate and use the following checklist to edit your classmate's work. (Proofreading your own work and that of your classmates is an important way to improve your language skills!)

☐ hay concordancia (*agreement*) de género (*gender*) entre los adjetivos y los sustantivos (*nouns*)

☐ hay concordancia de número (singular o plural) entre los adjetivos y los sustantivos

☐ ha usado (*he/she has used*) **soy** con adjetivos para describir la personalidad

☐ ha usado **me llamo** o **mi nombre es** para indicar el nombre

☐ ha usado **tengo** ____ **años** para indicar la edad (*age*)

☐ ha usado **me gusta** para nombrar los pasatiempos (*hobbies*)

When you are finished, make corrections to your own papers based on each other's feedback.

Suggestion (Después de escribir): Remind students that adjectives that end in consonants, such as *joven*, don't specify gender by adding *-o* or *-a: los/las jóvenes.*

¡Hablemos!

A conocernos°   *Getting to know each other*

Antes de hablar

Prepare a list of seven questions you can use to get to know your classmates better. Be strategic: Ask about personality traits and activities that they do not like as well as ones that they do like.

> **MODELO:** ¿Eres muy activo/a?
> ¿Te gusta + *activity*... ? / ¿Te gusta(n) + *noun(s)*... ?

 A hablar

Use your questions from **Antes de hablar** as a checklist to quickly interview three or more classmates. **¡Atención!** Don't forget to take notes on their responses.

Después de hablar

Use your notes from **A hablar** to find the person in the class with whom you have the most in common. Write a few sentences about that person and what you have in common. Share this with the class.

> **MODELO:** Tengo mucho en común con Alicia. Ella es muy activa y le gusta nadar y cantar. Yo también soy activa y me gusta nadar.

Suggestion (A hablar): If you have enough space in your classroom, have students line up in two rows directly across from one another. Once they've completed their first interview, have one line shift down so that everyone has a new partner to interview. Continue in this manner until students have interviewed 3–6 students, or as your time allows.

Suggestion (Después de hablar): Have students post their profiles from *¡Escribamos!* on an online forum so they can read through each other's work and decide whom they have the most in common with.

Conéctate al cine

Película: *El laberinto del fauno* (*Pan's Labyrinth*,
drama, México/España, 2006)
Director: Guillermo del Toro

Sinopsis:
Several years after the end of the Spanish Civil War, Ofelia and her mother arrive at the rural home of Captain Vidal, an officer loyal to Francisco Franco. Ofelia's mother is married to Captain Vidal and pregnant with his son. On arriving, the two meet Mercedes, the captain's head maid. Amid the cruelty and violence of her new home, where the captain kills and tortures members of the continuing resistance movement, Ofelia discovers a secret world of mythical creatures.

Escena (DVD, Scene 6, 00:24:50 to 00:29:14):
In the first of these three scenes, Captain Vidal orders Mercedes to clean some rabbits and taste his coffee. In the second scene, Ofelia's mother gives her a new dress to wear at a special dinner with the captain. In the third scene, Mercedes and the other maids see Ofelia in her new dress.

Antes de ver

El laberinto del fauno contrasts a world of magic with a world of harsh realities. It also contrasts very kind characters with very cruel characters. Read the following list of adjectives and circle the words you consider to be positive traits of a person. Underline the words you consider to be negative.

aburrido/a	feo/a	malo/a	simpático/a
antipático/a	gracioso/a	organizado/a	trabajador(a)
bueno/a	hermoso/a	serio/a	triste

Suggestion (A ver): Turn subtitles off, if possible. Students won't understand everything,
A ver   but they won't need to. Stop at the words *leche con miel.*

PASO 1.   Review the **Expresiones útiles,** then watch the film clip. Don't worry about understanding every word, but try to make guesses about what is happening in each scene based on the words you do understand and the actions and expressions of the characters.

PASO 2.   Complete the sentences with the correct form of the following adjectives.

castaño	fuerte	negro	trabajador
débil	joven	organizado	verde
estricto	largo	serio	viejo

1. El capitán Vidal es un hombre __estricto, serio, fuerte__ y __serio, estricto, fuerte__.
2. Mercedes dice (*says*) que los conejos son muy __jóvenes__ .
3. Dos de las mujeres que trabajan en la cocina son __viejas, trabajadoras__.
4. Mercedes y las otras mujeres son muy __trabajadoras__; ellas hacen muchas cosas.
5. La madre de Ofelia es __débil__ , pero su esposo (*husband*) es __fuerte__.
6. Mercedes maneja (*manages*) todas las actividades de la casa. Es muy __organizada, trabajadora__.
7. La madre de Ofelia tiene el pelo __largo__ y __castaño__.
8. El vestido de Ofelia es __verde__ y sus zapatos son __negros__.

Después de ver

Use your own adjectives to describe the following characters. **¡Atención!** Try not to repeat the adjectives used for each person in **A ver, Paso 2.**

MODELO: La madre de Ofelia es guapa y generosa.

1. Ofelia es _____.
2. El capitán Vidal es _____.
3. Mercedes es _____.
4. Las cocineras (*cooks*) son _____.

Expresiones útiles

conejos	rabbits
café	coffee
está quemado	is burnt
el vestido	dress
los zapatos	shoes
date prisa	hurry up (*you, informal*)
gallinas	hens
limpias	clean
leche con miel	milk and honey

■ For copyright reasons, the feature-film clips referenced in **Conéctate al cine** have not been provided by the publisher. Each of these films is readily available through retailers or online rental sites such as Amazon, iTunes, or Netflix.

VOCABULARIO

Now that I have completed the chapter, I can. . .

- ☐ talk about my age
- ☐ say where I am going
- ☐ express likes and dislikes
- ☐ describe people, places, and things

Comunicación

¿Cuántos años tienes? / ¿Cuántos años tiene?	How old are you (informal /formal)?
Tengo + number + años.	I'm + number + years old.
¿Adónde vas? / ¿Adónde va?	Where are you (informal/ formal) going?
Voy a/al + place	I'm going to . . .
Me gusta + infinitive(s)/noun	I like + infinitive(s)/ noun
Me gustan + nouns	I like + nouns
No me gusta + infinitive(s)/ noun	I don't like + infinitive(s)/noun
No me gustan + nouns	I don't like + nouns
¿Te gusta + activity?/ ¿Le gusta + activity?	Do you (informal/ formal) like + infinitive(s)?
¿Te gustan + nouns?/ ¿Le gustan + nouns?	Do you (informal/formal) like + nouns?

Las descripciones — Descriptions

aburrido/a	(with estar) bored; (with ser) boring
alto/a	tall
animado/a	lively
antipático/a	disagreeable
bajo/a	short
barato/a	cheap
bueno/a	good
cansado/a	tired
caro/a	expensive
corto/a	short (length)
débil	weak
difícil	difficult
enfermo/a	sick

enojado/a	angry
fácil	easy
feo/a	ugly
fuerte	strong
gordo/a	fat
gracioso/a	funny
grande	big
guapo/a	good-looking
joven (pl. jóvenes)	young
largo/a	long
lento/a	slow
limpio/a	clean
malo/a	bad
nuevo/a	new
perezoso/a	lazy
pobre	poor
rico/a	rich
serio/a	serious
simpático/a	nice
solo/a	alone
sucio/a	dirty
trabajador(a)	hard-working
triste	sad
viejo/a	old

Sinónimos

bello/a, bonito/a, hermoso/a, lindo/a, precioso/a	pretty
alegre, contento/a, feliz (pl. felices)	happy
delgado/a, flaco/a	thin
chico/a, pequeño/a	small

Cognados: activo/a, ansioso/a, curioso/a, directo/a, excelente, famoso/a, generoso/a, horrible, inteligente, interesante, maravilloso/a, motivado/a, nervioso/a, optimista, organizado/a, pesimista, popular, rápido/a, reservado/a, tranquilo/a

¿De qué color es? — What color is it?

amarillo/a, anaranjado/a, azul, blanco/a, café, gris, marrón, morado/a, negro/a, rojo/a, rosado/a, verde

los colores del pelo y de la piel

castaño/a	brown
moreno/a	dark brown
negro/a	black
rubio/a	blond
trigueño/a	light brown
pelirrojo/a	redhead(ed)

Las nacionalidades

argentino/a, boliviano/a, canadiense, chileno/a,
colombiano/a, costarricense, cubano/a, dominicano/a,
ecuatoriano/a, español(a), estadounidense /
norteamericano/a, guatemalteco/a, hondureño/a,
mexicano/a, nicaragüense, panameño/a, paraguayo/a,
peruano/a, puertorriqueño/a, salvadoreño/a,
uruguayo/a, venezolano/a

Los verbos

andar en bicicleta/bici	to ride a bike
bailar	to dance
dormir	to sleep
estar (*irreg.*)	to be
estudiar	to study
hablar	to speak
hacer (*irreg.*) ejercicio	to do exercise
ir (*irreg.*)	to go
ir a + *infinitive*	to be going to (*do something*)
ir de compras	to go shopping
jugar	to play
leer	to read
nadar	to swim
tocar la guitarra	to play the guitar

Los sustantivos — Nouns

la bandera	flag
la casa	house; home
el cine	movies; movie theater; film (*in general*)
el deporte	sport
la fiesta	party
la música	music
el/la niño/a	boy/girl
el país	country
la película	film
la playa	beach
el supermercado (el súper)	supermarket
el trabajo	work

Las palabras interrogativas

¿Adónde?	To where?
¿Cómo?	How?
¿Cuál?	Which?
¿Cuándo?	When?
¿Cuánto/a/os/as?	How much/many?
¿Dónde?	Where?
¿Por qué?	Why?
¿Qué?	What?
¿Quién(es)?	Who?

¿Qué hacesº?

do you do

Tomando el sol (*Sunbathing*) en la orilla (*shore*) del lago Villarrica en Chile

Objetivos

When you finish this chapter, you will be able to:

- ask and tell time
- say when events occur
- get someone's attention
- say what you do in your free time
- talk about daily schedules in the Spanish-speaking world

connect

www.mhhe.com/connect

COMUNICACIÓN LARIO UCTURA ATE

Videoscript (Act. A): 1. ALEXAN-
DER: *Son las seis de la tarde.*
2. VICTORINO: *Nueve y media.*
3. OLMAN: *Son las cuatro y
veinticinco minutos de la
tarde.* **4.** ÓSCAR: *Son las
cuatro y cincuenta y
cinco.* **5.** NOEL: *Doce
cincuenta y cinco
minutos.* **6.** JUAN
ANDRÉS: *Son las nueve y
treinta y dos de la mañana.*

Video track (Act. A): This
video clip can be found on
the DVD to accompany
Conéctate: Cap. 3, Track 1

Disculpa, ¿qué hora es?

Getting someone's attention, asking for the time

A. A ver: ¿Qué hora es?   Watch and listen, replaying and pausing as needed, as the following people say the time. Then choose the correct answer.

1. __b__ Alexander   a. 5:00   b. 6:00   c. 7:00   d. 8:00

2. __c__ Victorino   a. 9:00   b. 9:15   c. 9:30   d. 9:45

3. __d__ Olman   a. 4:00   b. 4:05   c. 4:15   d. 4:25

4. __a__ Óscar   a. 4:55   b. 5:00   c. 5:05   d. 5:15

5. __d__ Noel   a. 12:05   b. 12:15   c. 12:25   d. 12:55

6. __c__ Juan Andrés   a. 9:02   b. 9:22   c. 9:32   d. 9:42

Disculpe, ¿qué hora es?
Son las dos.

Oye, ¿qué hora es?
Son las seis y media.

If you want to get someone's attention before asking a question, use a form of the verb **disculpar** (*to excuse, pardon*) or **oír** (*to hear, listen*).

TÚ	UD.*
Disculpa or **Oye, ¿...?**	**Disculpe** or **Oiga, ¿...?**

If you address more than one person (**Uds.***), use **Disculpen** or **Oigan, ¿...?**

---

*The words **usted** and **ustedes** are abbreviated as **Ud.** and **Uds.**, respectively. You will see them appear with this abbreviation throughout *Conéctate.*

To ask the time in Spanish, say: **¿Qué hora es?**

> —**¿Qué hora es?**
> —**Son las cinco.**

To tell the time in Spanish, use the verb **ser.**

> **Es + la una.**
> **Son + las dos, las tres, las cuatro...**

INFORMAL (TÚ)

—**Disculpa, ¿qué hora es?**
—**Son las tres.**

FORMAL (USTED)

—**Disculpe, ¿qué hora es?**
—**Es la una.**

You can say *noon* in Spanish two ways.

> **Es mediodía.** or **Son las doce del día.**

You can also say *midnight* in Spanish two ways.

> **Es medianoche.** or **Son las doce de la noche.**

To say *half-past* or *thirty,* use either **y media** or **(y) treinta.**

> **Es la una y media.** = **Es la una (y) treinta.**

To say *quarter-past* or *fifteen,* use either **y cuarto** or **y quince.**

> **Son las dos y cuarto.** = **Son las dos (y) quince.**

For times after the half-hour, it is common to use **menos** or **para.**

> **Son las ocho y cincuenta.**
> **Son las nueve menos diez.**
> **Son diez para las nueve.**

Suggestion (Disculpa...): Practice formats of telling time past the half hour. Write the digital representation on the board, and bring a clock face to class, to show the *menos/para* concept visually: **1.** 9:35 (*Son las nueve y treinta y cinco. / Son las diez menos veinticinco. / Son veinticinco para las diez.*) **2.** 3:40 **3.** 8:45 **4.** 11:50 **5.** 6:55

En español...

In the Spanish-speaking world, times are often written using the 24-hour clock (or "military clock") instead of the 12-hour clock. For example, at a train station, 1:00 in the afternoon would be posted as 13:00.

B. Son las... Match each clock with the appropriate time.

1. _e_

2. _b_

a. Son las tres.
b. Son las cuatro y trece.
c. Son las seis y media.
d. Es medianoche. (Son las doce.)
e. Son las tres menos diez.
f. Es la una.

3. _f_

4. _a_

Suggestion (Act. B): Introduce other regional ways to ask the time, such as *¿Qué horas son?, ¿Me podría(s) dar la hora?, ¿Tiene(s) la hora?* Ask students to distinguish between *tú* and *Ud.* forms.

5. _c_

6. _d_

Recycle (Act. C): Review numbers by asking students, *¿Cuántos minutos hay en una hora?, ¿Cuántas horas hay en un día?,* and so on.

You can distinguish between A.M. and P.M. by using one of these expressions.

de la mañana	in the morning
de la noche	at night
de la tarde	in the afternoon/evening
de la madrugada	in the early morning hours

Son las siete y media de la mañana.

C. ¿Día o noche?   In pairs, take turns asking and answering questions about the time. When asked what the time is, pick randomly one of the pictures below, and give your partner the time shown on that picture. Can the student who asked for the time point to the correct clock?

MODELO: E1: ¿Qué hora es?
E2: Son las tres de la tarde.
[Estudiante 1 points to 3:00.]

1.

Es mediodía/ Son las doce del día.

2.

Son las seis y media/ treinta de la mañana.

3.

Son las ocho y cuarenta de la noche. / Son las nueve menos veinte de la noche. / Son veinte para las nueve de la noche.

4.

Son las siete y media/ treinta de la mañana.

5.

Son las diez y diez de la noche.

6.

7.

Son las dos y cinco de la tarde.

Son las doce y cinco de la noche.

¿A qué hora... ?

Asking at what time events occur

To ask at what time something happens, say: **¿A qué hora?**

Answer with **a: *a* la una, *a* las dos y media, *a* las tres menos cuarto, *a* las cuatro y cinco...**

—**¿A qué hora es la clase de español?**
—**Es a las diez.**

Other words to help you talk about what time and how often you do something include:

el horario	schedule
una vez / dos veces	once/twice
siempre	always

Video track (Act. B, p. 69): This video clip can be found on the DVD to accompany *Conéctate: Cap. 3,* Track 2.

Videoscript (Act. B, p. 69):
1. *Pues, me levanto a las 8 más o menos.* **2.** *Pues, me levanto a las 5 de la mañana.* **3.** *Me levanto a las 6 de la mañana.* **4.** *Me levanto a las 6:30.* **5.** *Me levanto a las 6 de la mañana.* **6.** *Normalmente me levanto a las 7 de la mañana.* **7.** *En un día típico, yo me levanto como a las 8 de la mañana.* **8.** *Normalmente, me levanto como a las 9 de la mañana.* **9.** *Generalmente, me levanto como a las 7 de la mañana.*

A. Preguntas sobre la hora

1.   Check all the possible answers to the question **¿Qué hora es?**
☑ Es medianoche.   ☑ Son las diez menos veinte.
☐ A las tres y media.   ☐ A las cinco de la tarde.

2.   Check all the possible answers to **¿A qué hora es la clase de español?**
☑ Es a mediodía.   ☐ Son las dos menos cinco.
☑ Es a las cinco de la tarde.   ☑ No sé. No tengo el horario (*schedule*).

3.   Now answer each question yourself: **¿Qué hora es? ¿A qué hora es la clase de español?**

B. A ver: ¿A qué hora se levantan? Watch and listen, replaying and pausing as needed. Then write the time each person gets up in the morning.

Video track (Act. C): This video clip can be found on the DVD to accompany *Conéctate: Cap. 3,* Track 3.

Videoscript (Act. C):
1. *Luego entro aquí en clase a las 8:30.* **2.** *Entro a la escuela a las 3 de la tarde.* **3.** *Empiezo clase a la 1.* **4.** *Salgo a las 11.* **5.** *Y entro a la escuela a las 8.* **6.** *Más o menos a las 8 de la mañana estoy en mi oficina ya.*

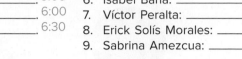

¿A qué hora te levantas?	**¿A qué hora se levanta Ud.?**
Me levanto a las…	Me levanto a las…

1. Belén: _____. 8:00
2. Diana: _____. 5:00
3. Marlén: _____. 6:00
4. Abril: _____. 6:30

5. Pudenciano: _____. 6:00
6. Isabel Baña: _____. 7:00
7. Víctor Peralta: _____. 8:00
8. Erick Solís Morales: _____ 9:00
9. Sabrina Amezcua: _____ 7:00

 C. A ver: ¿A qué hora… ? Watch and listen as various Spanish speakers from around the world describe their daily routines. Watch again, pausing between speakers to choose the correct time.

 1. __d__ Jorge entra en clase…
a. a las 6:00 de la mañana.
b. a las 7:30 de la mañana.
c. a las 8:00 de la mañana.
d. a las 8:30 de la mañana.

4. __a__ Eduardo sale (*leaves*) de la universidad…
a. a las 11:00 de la mañana.
b. a mediodía.
c. a la 1:00 de la tarde.
d. a las 2:00 de la tarde.

Expansion (Act. C): Use the questions from the video to ask students what time they go to class, wake up, and so on. They will learn to conjugate regular verbs in *Estructura 3.1* and *3.2,* so for now they should only be expected to give the time.

2. __c__ Javier entra a la escuela (*school*)…
a. a las 6:00 de la tarde.
b. a las 6:30 de la tarde.
c. a las 3:00 de la tarde.
d. a las 3:30 de la tarde.

 5. __c__ Abril entra a la escuela…
a. a las 6:00 de la mañana.
b. a las 7:30 de la mañana.
c. a las 8:00 de la mañana.
d. a las 8:30 de la mañana.

3. __c__ Carolina empieza (*starts*) las clases…
a. a las 11:00 de la mañana.
b. a mediodía.
c. a la 1:00 de la tarde.
d. a las 2:00 de la tarde.

6. __c__ Florencio Fernández Labrador está en su oficina…
a. a las 6:00 de la mañana.
b. a las 7:30 de la mañana
c. a las 8:00 de la mañana.
d. a las 8:30 de la mañana.

D. ¿A qué hora abre (*does it open*)… / cierra (*does it close*)… ?

PASO 1. In pairs, decide which of you will be **Estudiante 1,** and which will be **Estudiante 2.** Ask and respond to the questions about what time each business opens and closes, based only on your particular image. The image and questions for **Estudiante 2** are on page 70.

MODELO: E1: Oye. ¿A qué hora abre la panadería Los Cielos?
E2: A las seis y media.
E1: ¿A qué hora cierra?
E2: A las cinco.
E1: Gracias.

Estudiante 1 Ask your partner for the hours of operation of the establishments listed here. Then use the following image to answer your partner's questions about the hours of operation of the businesses pictured.

1. la peluquería (*hair salon / barber shop*)
2. el veterinario

3. el museo
4. la agencia de viajes (*travel agency*)

(*Continues*)

Suggestion (Act. D, Paso 1): Have students look at the museum's hours and point out that museums around the world are often closed on Mondays. Do any of the hours of operation reflect the traditional *siesta*? Point out that restaurants in parts of the Spanish-speaking world would not serve dinner as early as we are accustomed to eating dinner. Do the restaurant's hours (p. 69) reflect that?

Estudiante 2 Use the following image to answer your partner's questions about the hours of operation of the businesses pictured. Then ask your partner for the hours of operation of the establishments listed here.

1. la papelería
2. el restaurante
3. la farmacia
4. la biblioteca

Expansion (Act. D, Paso 2): Add some questions about locations on campus or in the community. For example: You want to get a late dinner at the student union (*centro estudantil*), you want to go shopping at the local mall (*centro comercial*), you want to get coffee before your earliest class.

PASO 2. Using the questions you learned in **Paso 1 (¿A qué hora abre? / ¿A qué hora cierra?)**, take turns formulating and answering questions based on the situations below.

> **MODELO:** You have a headache and need medicine, but it's getting late.
> E1: ¿A qué hora cierra la farmacia?
> E2: A las doce y media.

1. You want the first appointment to get your hair cut.
2. You have a long drive tomorrow and want to get some coffee and pastries for the trip as early as possible.
3. You would like to study at the library as late as possible this weekend.
4. Your have to pick up your dog from his medical procedure before the office closes.

CONÉCTATE AL MUNDO HISPANO

In parts of the Spanish-speaking world, the **siesta** is scheduled as part of the workday. Where the **siesta** is practiced, actual times may vary, but businesses often operate from 7:00 A.M. to 1:00 P.M. and then again from 3:00 or 4:00 P.M. to 7:00 P.M. This gives people time to go home for lunch, rest, and spend time with their families. While a nap might be part of **siesta,** it is not the definition of the practice.

CONÉCTATE AL MUNDO PROFESIONAL

Cultural knowledge is important to one's professional life in the 21st century globalized workplace. An understanding of the 24-hour clock (page 67) could be vital to setting up an international business meeting. This is just one example, so pay attention to subtle cultural differences that may give you an advantage in your future workplace.

¿Cómo es tu rutina diaria?

Your daily routine and the days of the week

A. ¿Qué haces?

PASO 1. Match each activity pictured with the appropriate description.

1. __c__   a. **mirar la televisión**
2. __h__   b. **asistir a** clase
3. __e__   c. **practicar el fútbol**
4. __g__   d. **leer el periódico** (*newspaper*)
5. __b__   e. **hablar por teléfono**
6. __f__   f. estudiar en la biblioteca
7. __a__   g. **trabajar** en una oficina
8. __i__   h. **comer** con mi familia
9. __d__   i. **cantar** en el coro (*choir*)

Note (Act. A): Remind students that new active vocabulary is indicated in the activity with boldface.

(*Continues*)

Suggestion (Act. A):
Divide the class into two teams. Give a new vocabulary word or phrase to one team member, who must then act out or draw it on the board. If the rest of the team can guess the word in under 1 minute *and* in 3 guesses or fewer, the team gets a point. If not, the other team gets one guess to get the point. Switch teams after each turn.

PASO 2.   Check all the activities you like to do on a regular basis, then compare activities with your partner.

MODELOS: E1: Solo me gusta desayunar los fines de semana (*on weekends*).
E2: A mí me gusta desayunar todos los días (*every day*).

E1: Me gusta cenar en casa.
E2: A mí me gusta cenar en la cafetería o en restaurantes. No me gusta cenar en casa.

_____ **desayunar**   _____ **almorzar / comer**   _____ **cenar**

_____ bailar   _____ ir a la playa   _____ ir al cine   _____ ir de compras / **comprar**

_____ **correr en el parque**   _____ hacer ejercicio _____ **practicar yoga**   _____ **montar a caballo** _____ **jugar básquetbol**   _____ nadar

_____ dormir   _____ **jugar los videojuegos**   _____ leer   _____ **usar la computadora / escribir un email**

B. Los estilos de vida de dos estudiantes

Tomás Teleadicto   Adela Atleta

En español...

Spanish uses the single verbs **desayunar, almorzar,** and **cenar** where English uses the multi-word expressions *to have breakfast, to have lunch,* and *to have dinner.* **Comer** may be used in a general sense to mean *to eat,* but in some places it is used more specifically to mean *to have lunch.* Meal times vary greatly across the Spanish-speaking world, although lunch and dinner often occur much later than is common in English-speaking countries.

PASO 1. Who is more likely to make each of the following statements, **Tomás Teleadicto** or **Adela Atleta?**

	TOMÁS TELEADICTO	ADELA ATLETA
1. Me gusta ir de compras en bicicleta (*bicycle*).	☐	☑
2. Me gusta usar la computadora para comprar.	☑	☐
3. Me gusta comer pizza.	☑	☐
4. Me gusta desayunar, almorzar y cenar comida saludable (*healthy food*).	☐	☑
5. Me gusta jugar videojuegos de básquetbol.	☑	☐
6. Me gusta comer la comida chatarra (*junk food*).	☑	☐

PASO 2. Identify each of the following activities and tell who probably likes to do each one, **Tomás Teleadicto** or **Adela Atleta.**

MODELO: A *Adela Atleta* le gusta *jugar fútbol.*

1.

2.

3.

Follow-up (Act. B): Take a quick survey of your students to find out whether they have more in common with *Tomás Teledicto* or *Adela Atleta.*

4.

5.

6.

Note (Act. C, Paso 1): Some answers for the general times for the activities may vary, as some speakers give a sequence of activities and not specific times.

Videoscript (Act. C, Paso 1):
1. ANDREA: *Pues me levanto por la mañana, eh... este año tengo clase por la tarde y entonces por la mañana, pues acudo al gimnasio o hago otras actividades y luego por la tarde, pues acudo a clase de 6 de la tarde a 10 de la noche, y luego ya, pues ceno en casa y ya me quedo en casa.* **2.** NICOLÁS: *Eh... me levanto temprano, vengo a clases o sea tomo el tren, agarro la bicicleta, me vengo a clases, salgo a la 1 del mediodía de clases y de ahí me voy al trabajo que entro a las 2 salgo a las 8, llego a mi casa, saco a pasear a mi perro, estudio y a dormir.* **3.** GUADALUPE: *De la casa... saliendo de la casa sí, voy al trabajo. Al campus de la universidad porque es donde está el centro de operaciones, digamos. De allí, vamos... voy a los jardines, visitamos los jardines. Y luego regresamos allá otra vez... digamos a las oficinas y ya después regreso a la casa otra vez entre 3 y 4 de la tarde.* **4.** NOEL: *Me levanto cinco y media porque tengo que alistarme, salir a coger el bus para viajar hacia la práctica, que viajo a las 7 de la mañana. De allí, la hora de... tomo media hora para desayunar. Ocho de la mañana empiezo la práctica. Después a las 12 sería el almuerzo, y a las 5 salgo del trabajo.*

Video track (Act. C): This video clip can be found on the DVD to accompany *Conéctate: Cap. 3,* Track 4.

To talk about the morning, afternoon, and evening in general, use:

por la mañana	in the morning
por la tarde	in the afternoon
por la noche	at night
Estudio por la tarde.	I study in the afternoon.

C. A ver: ¿Cómo es tu rutina diaria?

PASO 1.   Watch and listen as many times as needed as the following university students describe their daily routines. For each one, put the list of activities in the correct order. Then decide when each person does each activity: **por la mañana, por la tarde,** or **por la noche.**

			MAÑANA	TARDE	NOCHE
1.	_3_	Asistir a clase.	☐	☑	☐
	_4_	Cenar en casa.	☐	☐	☑
	_2_	Ir al gimnasio.	☑	☐	☐
Andrea	_1_	Levantarse (*To get up*).	☑	☐	☐
2.	_2_	Asistir a clase.	☑	☑	☐
	_5_	Dormir.	☐	☐	☑
	_4_	Estudiar.	☐	☐	☑
Nicolás	_1_	Levantarse.	☑	☐	☐
	_3_	Trabajar.	☐	☑	☐
3.	_2_	Ir a los jardines (*gardens*).	☑	☑	☐
	_3_	Ir a las oficinas.	☐	☑	☐
	_1_	Ir al trabajo.	☑	☐	☐
Guadalupe	_4_	Regresar (*To return*) a la casa.	☐	☑	☐
4.	_4_	Almorzar.	☐	☑	☐
	_3_	Empezar la práctica (*internship*).	☑	☐	☐
	_1_	Levantarse.	☑	☐	☐
Noel	_2_	Viajar hacia (*Travel to*) la práctica en bus.	☑	☐	☐

PASO 2.   Answer each question about the daily routines of the speakers in the video and your own routine.

1. a. ¿Se levanta temprano (*early*) o tarde (*late*) Noel?
   b. ¿A ti te gusta levantarte temprano o tarde?
2. a. ¿A Andrea qué le gusta hacer (*to do*) por la mañana?
   b. ¿Y a ti? ¿Qué te gusta hacer por la mañana?
3. a. ¿Qué tiene que (*have to*) hacer Nicolás entre las dos y las ocho de la tarde?
   b. ¿Y tú? ¿Qué tienes que hacer entre las dos y las ocho de la tarde normalmente?

Answers (Act. C, Paso 2):
1a. *temprano* **2a.** *acude/va al gimnasio o hace otras actividades* **3a.** *trabaja*

PASO 3.   Look again at the daily routines of the speakers in **Paso 1** and your own answers to **Paso 2.** With a partner, express whose routine is most like your own. Use porque to explain why.

> **MODELO:**   Mi horario es parecido (*similar*) al horario de ____ porque también me gusta...

Suggestion (Act. C, Paso 2): Tell students that they don't have to answer the questions in complete sentences. The objective is to gather information to be used in **Paso 3.**

D. Tu rutina   With a partner, take turns asking each other the general time of day that you prefer to do the following activities. Say **No lo hago** if you don't do the activity at all.

MODELO: E1: ¿Cuándo prefieres (*do you prefer*) trabajar?
   E2: Prefiero (*I prefer*) trabajar por la mañana. / No lo hago.

1. Asistir a clase.
2. Cenar con mi familia.
3. Comer en el comedor (*dining area*).
4. Correr en el parque.
5. Desayunar.

6. Estudiar en la biblioteca.
7. Escribir emails.
8. Leer el periódico.
9. Mirar la televisión.
10. Jugar básquetbol / los videojuegos.

The calendar week begins on Monday in the Spanish-speaking world. Starting with Monday, these are **los días de entre semana** (*weekdays*).

lunes   martes   miércoles   jueves   viernes

Here are the days that make up **el fin de semana.**

sábado   domingo

To express *on* a day, use **el** (no preposition).   This works for plurals, too.

el lunes = on Monday   **los lunes** = on Mondays

Tengo un examen **el** lunes.   Trabajo **los** lunes.

Remember that, like months, days of the week are not capitalized in Spanish.

 E. La rutina de Claudia   Listen to the description of Claudia's weekly routine. Then match the days with the appropriate places and activities.

1. __c__ Los lunes Claudia...
2. __e__ Los miércoles...
3. __d__ Los jueves...
4. __a__ Los viernes...
5. __b__ Los sábados...

a. hace ejercicio.
b. va a casa para pasar tiempo con su familia y comer juntos.
c. va de compras.
d. va a la universidad.
e. trabaja.

 F. La rutina diaria de tu compañero/a de clase

PASO 1.   With a partner, choose an activity you will plan to do together (**ir a bailar, ir al cine, ir de compras, ir al gimnasio, ir a jugar, ir a la playa...**).

MODELO: E1: ¿Vamos a bailar?
   E2: No me gusta bailar. ¿Vamos al cine?
   E1: Sí. Me gusta ir al cine.

PASO 2.   Now use your real schedules to find a day that you are both available. Once you have agreed on a day, find a time that works for the two of you, then report your findings to the class.

MODELO: E1: ¿El viernes?
   E2: No. ¿El jueves? (Sí, el viernes.)
   E1: ¿A las siete?
   E2: No. ¿A las nueve? (Sí, a las siete.)
   E1: Sí, está bien.

Script (Act. E): *Los lunes Claudia va al supermercado y a otras tiendas para tener todas las necesidades para la semana. Los martes y los jueves, va a sus clases y después estudia en la biblioteca. Los miércoles trabaja en el museo de la universidad. Los viernes, Claudia practica el fútbol o corre en el parque con sus amigos. Los sábados cena con toda su familia. Los domingos se queda en casa; no va a ningún lugar ni participa en ninguna actividad.*

Suggestion (Act. F, Paso 2): Point out to students that even though they are not communicating in complete sentences, they do have the necessary language to set up an appointment, which is a very important life skill.

Follow-up (Act. F): When students have finished, ask them follow-up questions, such as (to one pair) *¿Adónde van Uds.?* (*Vamos al cine.*) *¿Qué van a mirar? ¿A qué hora es?* (to another student) *Y tú, ¿vas al cine también?*, and so on.

Expansion (Act. F): Have two pairs of students form a group and try to find a time and activity that works for all members. Or form new groups to set up a time that they can all get together to study for this class.

COMUN VOCABU **ESTRUCTURA** ATE

Reciclaje: The *Reciclaje* activities appear at the beginning of all *Estructura* sections from this point on. *Reciclaje* reactivates students' previous knowledge and prepares them for the activities to follow. Frequent recycling of previously studied structures leads to better learning outcomes.

■ Answers to this activity are in Appendix 2 at the back of your book.

Reciclaje

Singular forms of **estar, ir, ser,** and **tener**

Complete the sentences in column **A** by choosing the best match in column **B**. Then complete column **B** by choosing one of the verbs given and writing the appropriate form of the verb in the blank.

estar   ir   ser   tener

A	**B**
1. Voy a clases porque __d__	a. __tiene__ una clase de física mañana a las siete y media de la mañana.
2. Ricky Martin __c__	b. ¿Tú __vas__ a la clase de inglés a las tres?
3. Mario se acuesta (*goes to bed*) temprano (*early*) porque __a__	c. __es__ de Puerto Rico.
4. Son las dos y media. __b__	d. __soy__ estudiante.
5. Paula bailó toda la noche (*danced all night long*). Ahora, ella __e__	e. __está__ muy cansada.

3.1 **Vivo en España**

Present indicative: Singular forms

Para empezar...

PASO 1.   Over the past decade, Gael García Bernal and Javier Bardem have become international movie stars. Based on the descriptions below, which statement could be uttered by which actor? Which could be uttered by both? **¡Atención!** For languages spoken, the names of some of their films will help you!

GAEL GARCÍA BERNAL

Es de México.

En las películas:

> *Y tu mamá también*
> *Diarios de motocicleta*
> *La science des rêves* (Francia)
> *No*
> *The Loneliest Planet*

JAVIER BARDEM

Es de España.

En las películas:

> *Mar adentro*
> *Before Night Falls*
> *No Country for Old Men*
> *Skyfall*

■ Answers to these activities are in Appendix 2 at the back of your book.

	GAEL GARCÍA BERNAL	JAVIER BARDEM
1. «**Soy** español.»	☐	☑
2. «**Soy** mexicano.»	☑	☐
3. «**Hablo** francés.»	☑	☐
4. «**Hablo** inglés.»	☑	☑
5. «**Vivo** en la Ciudad de México.»	☑	☐
6. «**Vivo** en Madrid.»	☐	☑
7. «**Trabajo** en el cine.»	☑	☑
8. «**Leo** muchos guiones (*screenplays*).»	☑	☑

PASO 2. Now answer the following questions about yourself. You can answer **sí** to at least one of them, but can anyone in the class answer **sí** to more than one?

¿Y TÚ?	SÍ	NO
1. **¿Eres** español?	☐	☐
2. **¿Eres** mexicano?	☐	☐
3. **¿Hablas** francés?	☐	☐
4. **¿Hablas** inglés?	☐	☐
5. **¿Vives** en la Ciudad de México?	☐	☐
6. **¿Vives** en Madrid?	☐	☐
7. **¿Trabajas** en el cine?	☐	☐
8. **¿Lees** muchos guiones?	☐	☐

Actividades analíticas

1 Using what you saw in **Para empezar,** complete these partial conjugations of **trabajar, leer,** and **vivir.**

	trabajar	leer	vivir
SINGULAR			
yo	trabajo	leo	vivo
tú	trabajas	lees	vives
él/ella, Ud.	trabaja	lee	vive

2 Verbs like these are known as *regular verbs* (**los verbos regulares**), because their conjugations follow a predictable pattern. For example, what ending do all of these regular **yo** forms have in common?

La forma **yo** siempre (*always*) termina en (*ends in*) ____-o____.

The rest of the verb form (the part without this ending) is known as the *root* or *stem* (**la raíz del verbo**). For the three verbs here, the stems are **trabaj-, le-, viv-.**

3 The ending for the **él/ella** and **Ud.** form is always a vowel (**una vocal**). For **-ar** verbs like **trabajar,** this vowel is **-a,** and for **-er** and **-ir** verbs like **leer** and **vivir,** it is **-e.** What single letter can you then add to this to create the **tú** form?

La forma **tú** siempre termina en ____-s____.

Actividades prácticas

A. Gael y Javier   Gael García Bernal and Javier Bardem know each other, and in fact, Gael has said that Javier is his favorite actor. Based on this and the information in **Para empezar,** write **G** for each sentence that Gael might say to Javier and **J** for each sentence that Javier might say to Gael. If it is something that they could both say, write **G/J.**

1. __J__ Vives en México.
2. __G__ Eres mi actor favorito.
3. __G/J__ Trabajo en el cine.
4. __J__ Vivo en España.
5. __G/J__ Trabajas en el cine.
6. __G__ Vivo en México.
7. __G__ Vives en España.

Note (Act. analíticas): This section presents the singular forms of the verb conjugations, and *Estructura 3.2* presents the plural forms. Presenting the singular and plural forms separately gives students the time they need to fully absorb them. Since subjects are often not expressed in Spanish, students must internalize these verb forms completely in order to participate in even simple conversations.

Suggestion (Act. analíticas 1): Point out that these three verbs represent the three verb classes: *-ar, -er,* and *-ir.* When these infinitive endings are removed, the stem is left. This stem forms the basis for the whole conjugation.

Suggestion (Act. analíticas 2): Show on the board how combining the stem plus the *-o* ending results in *trabajo, leo,* and *vivo.*

Expansion (Act. analíticas 2): Have students answer the questions in *Para empezar, Paso 2,* using complete sentences to practice *yo* forms.

Suggestion (Act. analíticas 3): Show on the board how adding *-s* to the *él/ella/* and *Ud.* form always gives you the *tú* form.

Autoprueba

Use what you know about the conjugation of regular verbs in the present indicative to conjugate the following verbs.

1. yo _____ (leer)
2. ella _____ (correr)
3. Ud. _____ (comprar)
4. tú _____ (usar)
5. yo _____ (cantar)
6. tú _____ (asistir)

Respuestas: 1. leo **2.** corre **3.** compra **4.** usas **5.** canto **6.** asistes

Expansion (Act. analíticas 3): Now have students use the sentences in *Para empezar, Paso 1* to practice third person conjugations. Have them write complete sentences to say which things each of the actors does. For example, *Javier Bardem vive en Madrid.*

Note (Act. A): Remind students to think about this activity from the point of view of Gael García Bernal and Javier Bardem.

Follow-up (Act. B): Have students partner up and ask each other the questions from *Act. B,* and make up their own answers. You may also wish to go around the class and ask these questions of individual students.

B. Preguntas y respuestas

Match the questions on the left with the most logical answer on the right.

1. ¿Estudias en la biblioteca? __h__
2. Escribes muchos mensajes de texto? __d__
3. ¿Tomas mucho café? __e__
4. ¿Trabajas? __f__
5. ¿Corres mucho? __g__
6. ¿Cantas? __a__
7. ¿Y tu amiga canta? __c__
8. ¿Tu amigo corre mucho? __b__

a. Sí canto, pero mal.
b. Sí, corre todos los días (*every day*).
c. Sí canta, pero mal.
d. Sí, escribo mensajes, pero también hablo por teléfono.
e. Tomo café de vez en cuando (*every once in a while*), pero no mucho.
f. Sí, trabajo en la biblioteca de la universidad.
g. Sí, corro todos los días.
h. No, estudio en casa.

C. Cuatro colombianos

Suggestion (Act. C): Poll students to see which Colombian has the most in common with the class.

PASO 1. With a partner, look at the chart about four well-known Colombians and some of the things they are known for. Ask your partner whether he or she does these activities and keep track of the answers in the column on the right.

> **MODELO:** E1: ¿Cantas?
> E2: Sí, canto. (No, no canto.)

	Juanes	Shakira	Camilo Villegas	Sofía Vergara	tu compañero/a
	CANTANTE DE MÚSICA ROCK	CANTANTE DE MÚSICA POP	JUGADOR DE GOLF	ACTRIZ	
Canta y escribe canciones.	☑	☑	☐	☐	☐
Baila mucho.	☐	☑	☐	☐	☐
Practica un deporte.	☑	☐	☑	☐	☐
Toca (*He/She plays*) la guitarra.	☑	☑	☐	☐	☐
Habla árabe.	☐	☑	☐	☐	☐
Practica el golf.	☐	☐	☑	☐	☐
Trabaja en la televisión.	☐	☐	☐	☑	☐
Lee mucho.	☑	☑	☐	☑	☐
Vive en Colombia.	☑	☐	☐	☐	☐
Vive en los Estados Unidos.	☐	☐	☑	☑	☐

PASO 2. By comparing check marks, with which person does your partner have the most in common? How many things does he or she have in common with this person?

_____ tiene _____ cosas en común con _____.

D. ¿Miras la televisión?

Suggestion (Act. D): Tell students they can use activities not on this list if they prefer.

PASO 1.   With a partner, take turns asking each other whether you do the activities listed below. Tell your partner whether you do them **todos los días, a veces** (*sometimes*), or **nunca** (*never*).

MODELO: E1: ¿Miras la televisión?
              E2: No, nunca miro la televisión.

caminar (*to walk*)	desayunar	ir al gimnasio
cocinar (*to cook*)	estudiar	mirar la televisión
comer comida (*food*) mexicana	hablar por teléfono	practicar un deporte
correr	ir al cine	trabajar

PASO 2.   Create two statements about your partner: one about what he or she does *every day* and another about what he or she *never* does.

MODELO: Mike cocina todos los días. Nunca baila.

Miro la televisión los fines de semana.

Reciclaje

Plural forms of *ser, tener, estar,* and *ir*

Complete each sentence using a verb from the following list that would make sense in the context. Then indicate whether each sentence is **cierto** (*true*) or **falso** (*false*).

estar   ir   ser   tener

		CIERTO	FALSO
1. Los españoles <u>son</u> de Asia.		☐	☑
2. Nosotros <u>somos</u> estudiantes.		☑	☐
3. Los profesores de español <u>van</u> a muchas clases de química.		☐	☑
4. Mis amigos <u>están</u> muy contentos hoy.		☑	☑
5. Las universidades <u>tienen</u> muchas clases.		☑	☐
6. Nosotros <u>vamos</u> a la clase de español los domingos.		☐	☑

■ Answers to this activity are in Appendix 2 at the back of your book.

3.2   Desayunamos a las siete.

Present indicative: Plural forms

Para empezar...

PASO 1.   In many cultures, the daily schedule of activities is organized around the schedule of meals. In Mexico, families typically have breakfast (**desayunar**) at around 7:00, eat their midday meal (**comer**) at around 2:00, and dinner (**cenar**) at around 8:00. Use this information to complete the following sentences about meals in Mexico and about your own personal habits.

Note (Para empezar): Point out that in Mexico, the meal at 2:00 is the main meal (*la comida principal*) of the day. Ask students which is the main (largest) meal for them, or for most people in the area where they are from.

En México en general...

1. **desayunan** a las __7__.
2. **comen** a las __2__.
3. **cenan** a las __8__.

Yo en general...

1. **desayuno** a las ____.
2. **como** a las ____.
3. **ceno** a las ____.

PASO 2.   What is the general schedule for meals for most people in your country?

En nuestro (*our*) país en general...

1. **desayunamos** a las ____.
2. **comemos / almorzamos** a las ____.
3. **cenamos** a las ____.

Actividades analíticas

1 Use the examples that you saw in **Para empezar,** as well as what you already know about verbs in Spanish, to complete the following conjugations.

■ Answers to these activities are Appendix 2 at the back of your book.

	cenar	comer	vivir
SINGULAR			
yo	ceno	como	vivo
tú	cenas	comes	vives
él/ella, Ud.	cena	come	vive
PLURAL			
nosotros/as	cenamos	comemos	vivimos
vosotros/as	cenáis	coméis	vivís
ellos/ellas, Uds.	cenan	comen	viven

2 In **Estructura 3.1** you saw the pattern for the singular forms of regular verbs.

		ENDINGS	EXAMPLES
yo		-o	trabajo leo vivo
tú	**-ar** verbs	-as	trabajas
	-er, -ir verbs	-es	lees vives
él/ella, Ud.	**-ar** verbs	-a	trabaja
	-er, -ir verbs	-e	lee vive

In the **tú** and the **él/ella** and **Ud.** forms, the vowel that is added to the stem is **-a** (for **-ar** verbs) or **-e** (for **-er** and **-ir** verbs).

Now complete this chart of endings for *plural* verb forms, basing your answers on the examples given.

		ENDINGS	EXAMPLES
nosotros/as	**-ar** verbs	-amos	cenamos
	-er verbs	-emos	comemos
	-ir verbs	-imos	vivimos
vosotros/as	**-ar** verbs	-áis	cenáis
	-er verbs	-éis	coméis
	-ir verbs	-ís	vivís
ellos/ellas, Uds.	**-ar** verbs	-an	cenan
	-er, -ir verbs	-en	comen viven

Suggestion (Act. analíticas 3):
It is not a coincidence that *-ar* verbs use the vowel *-a* and *-er* verbs use the vowel *-e* (plus *-mos, -is, -n*). Explain to students that they should take advantage of these regularities, rather than just memorizing the chart.

Point out (Act. analíticas 3):
Point out that for the *vosotros/as* forms, an accent mark is written on the vowel that is added to the stem. For *-ir* verbs, only one *i* vowel is written (for example, *vivís*, rather than *viviís*).

3 As you saw in the charts in **2,** verb endings vary slightly depending on whether the verb is of the **-ar, -er,** or **-ir** type. Despite these differences, what do the three **nosotros/as** endings all have in common?

La forma **nosotros/as** siempre termina en _-mos_.

What about the **vosotros/as** and **ellos/ellas/Uds.** endings?

La forma **vosotros/as** siempre termina en _-is_.

La forma **ellos/ellas/Uds.** siempre termina en _-n_.

4 You can now conjugate any regular verb in Spanish. Practice this by completing the conjugations for these regular verbs.

	bailar	**correr**	**asistir**
SINGULAR			
yo	bailo	corro	asisto
tú	bailas	corres	asistes
él/ella, Ud.	baila	corre	asiste
PLURAL			
nosotros/as	bailamos	corremos	asistimos
vosotros/as	bailáis	corréis	asistís
ellos/ellas, Uds.	bailan	corren	asisten

Expansion (Act. analíticas 4): Point out that the three stems here are *bail-, corr-,* and *asist-.* Then have students circle the *-a* that is added to the stem in all forms of *bailar* (except *bailo*), the *-e* that is added to the stem in all forms of *correr* (except *corro*), and the *-e* or *-i* that is added to the stem in all forms of *asistir* (except *asisto*).

Autoprueba

Write the correct form for these verbs.

1. Ellos _____ (*cocinar*).
2. Nosotras _____ (*practicar*) muchos deportes.
3. Nosotros _____ (*comer*) a la una.
4. Ellas _____ (*correr*) todos los días.
5. Ellos _____ (*vivir*) en El Salvador.

Respuestas: 1. cocinan **2.** practicamos **3.** comemos **4.** corren **5.** viven

Actividades prácticas

A. La vida (*life*) en nuestro país

PASO 1. When interacting with Spanish speakers, you may be asked what life is like in your country. Which of these statements do you think are true for most people in your country?

	CIERTO	FALSO
En general...		
1. Trabajamos de lunes a viernes.	☐	☐
2. Hablamos inglés.	☐	☐
3. Cenamos muy temprano (*early*).	☐	☐
4. Leemos muchos libros.	☐	☐
5. Bailamos muy bien.	☐	☐
6. Vivimos en casas.	☐	☐
7. Practicamos muchos deportes.	☐	☐
8. Cocinamos todos los días.	☐	☐
9. Caminamos mucho.	☐	☐

 PASO 2. Compare your answers with those of two classmates. Do you disagree about any of the statements? Report these disagreements to the class using **según** (*according to*).

MODELO: Según Mary, bailamos muy bien. Según yo, no bailamos muy bien.

En este país, ¿leemos muchos libros?

Suggestion (Act. A, Paso 2): Point out to students that to say *According to me...*, they must use the pronoun *yo*, not *mí*.

Answers (Act. B): Answers to Q4, Q6, and Q8 may differ depending on student's conclusions in *Para empezar*.

Nosotros...

B. Una mexicana habla Given what you saw in **Para empezar** about meal times, which of the following would be reasonable things for a Mexican woman to say when comparing her own country with this country? For each sentence, write **C** for **cierto** or **F** for **falso. ¡Atención!** Use the verb endings to know whether she is referring to people in her own country (**nosotros**) or to most people in this country (**los estadounidenses/canadienses**).

En general...

1. __C__ comemos a las dos.
2. __F__ comen a las dos.
3. __C__ cenamos a las ocho.
4. __F__ cenan a las ocho.
5. __F__ comemos a mediodía.
6. __C__ comen a mediodía.
7. __F__ cenamos a las seis.
8. __C__ cenan a las seis.

C. ¿Tomas café? (*Do you drink coffee?*)

PASO 1. In many parts of the world, coffee is a traditional part of the early morning routine, but does everyone drink it at that time, or at all? Ask as many classmates as possible whether they drink coffee, and if so, at what times. Use the table to keep track of the responses that you get.

MODELO: E1: ¿Tomas café?
E2: Sí.
E1: ¿Cuándo?
E2: A las ocho y media.

¿CUÁNDO?	NÚMERO DE PERSONAS
7:00–8:00	
8:00–10:00	
10:00–12:00	
12:00–15:00	
15:00–19:00	
19:00–	
todo el día	
nunca	

PASO 2. Now report to the class what you have found. What statements can you make about the habits of the people in your class?

MODELOS: Todos (*Everyone*) tomamos café.
Catorce personas toman café de las siete a las ocho.
Nadie (*No one*) toma café.
Nadie toma café por la noche.

D. ¿Qué hacen todos los estudiantes de la clase?

PASO 1. Working in groups, take five minutes to create as many sentences as possible using **todos** (*everyone; all of us*) to express what you think everyone in the class does every day (**todos los días**). Use the following list of activities to get you started, but you may think of others as well.

MODELO: Todos desayunamos todos los días.

asistir a clase	correr	hablar por teléfono
caminar	desayunar	leer
cenar	dormir	mirar la televisión
cocinar	escuchar música	practicar un deporte
comer	estudiar	trabajar

PASO 2. Now report your results from **Paso 1** to the class. Can any student in the class contradict your claims?

MODELO: Grupo 1: Todos desayunamos todos los días.
Grupo 2: ¡No es cierto! Cathy no desayuna.

E. Cultura: El café de Nicaragua y El Salvador

PASO 1. Read the text about coffee production in Nicaragua and El Salvador.

¿Tomas café cuando desayunas? ¿Tomas café antes de ir a tus clases? ¿Cuando estudias? ¿Después de cenar? A muchos de nosotros nos gusta tomar café. Es parte de la rutina diaria. Pero en varios países de Centroamérica, como en Nicaragua y El Salvador, cultivar, producir y exportar el café es la rutina diaria de muchas personas.

¿Cómo es la rutina diaria del agricultor de café? Él se levanta muy temprano, desayuna y toma su café. Va a los campos y recolecta[a] las bayas de café rojas. Descansa[b] para almorzar y entonces vuelve a[c] recolectar más bayas de café. Finalmente camina a la planta donde procesan el café y entrega[d] las bayas que tiene.

En la planta, el café tiene su propia[e] rutina. Los trabajadores lavan[f] el café. Entonces procesan las bayas para separar la pulpa de los granos. Dejan[g] el café en agua por un día y entonces secan[h] los granos. Procesan el café otra vez para quitarle la cáscara.[i] Entonces tienen que tostar el café y meterlo en costales.[j] Venden[k] el café a un distribuidor y el distribuidor exporta el café a otros países.

[a]he picks [b]He rests [c]vuelve... he goes back to [d]he delivers [e]own [f]wash [g]They leave [h]they dry [i]quitarle... remove the shell [j]meterlo... put it into sacks [k]They sell

PASO 2. Number the first set of sentences from 1–5 to show a coffee farmer's daily routine. Then, number the second set of sentences from 1–8 to show the process for preparing raw coffee beans once they arrive at the processing plant.

La rutina del agricultor

_4_ Almuerza y luego recolecta más café.

_5_ Camina a la planta para entregar su café.

_3_ Recolecta el café toda la mañana.

_1_ Se levanta y desayuna.

_2_ Va a los campos de café.

El proceso del café en la planta

_3_ Dejan los granos en agua durante un día.

_8_ El distribuidor exporta el café a muchos países.

_1_ Primero (*First*), lavan las bayas.

_2_ Procesan las bayas para separar la pulpa de los granos.

_5_ Procesan los granos de café para quitar la cáscara.

_4_ Secan el café.

_6_ Tuestan el café y lo meten en costales.

_7_ Venden el café al distribuidor.

Nicaragua

El Salvador

Vocabulario útil	
el agricultor / la agricultora	farmer
las bayas	coffee berries/ cherries
el campo	field
los granos	coffee beans
tostar (o → ue)	to roast

Unas bayas de café

PASO 3. With a partner, answer the following questions and discuss the ideas behind your responses.

1. El arbusto (*bush*) del café necesita lluvia (*rain*) todo el año y temperaturas moderadas o altas. Además de (*In addition to*) El Salvador y Nicaragua, ¿en qué países hispanos crees (*do you think*) que cultivan el café?
2. En el mundo hispano, hay países relativamente ricos y países relativamente pobres. Muchos de los países donde cultivan el café son relativamente pobres. ¿Por qué crees?
3. Cultivan el café comercialmente en solo un estado (*state*) de los Estados Unidos. ¿Qué estado es? ¿Por qué crees que es muy caro el café de ese estado?

Answers/Notes (Act. E, Paso 3): 1. Coffee is grown commercially in tropical climates, ranging from southern Mexico and the Caribbean in the north, to Paraguay in the south. 2. Help students express their ideas in simple Spanish: *Los trabajadores del café no ganan mucho dinero.* 3. Coffee is grown in the state of Hawaii.

■ Answers to this activity are in Appendix 2 at the back of your book.

Answers (Reciclaje): B/C/O answers depend on student's preferences.

↻ Reciclaje

Infinitives

Complete each verb with its infinitive ending: **-ar, -er,** or **-ir.** Then indicate whether you prefer to do the activity **en la biblioteca (B), en la casa (C),** or **en otro lugar (O)** (*in another place*).

	B / C / O			B / C / O
1. almorz_ar_	_____	7. estudi_ar_	_____
2. cen_ar_	_____	8. le_er_	_____
3. corr_er_	_____	9. mir_ar_ la televisión	_____
4. desayun_ar_	_____	10. nad_ar_	_____
5. dorm_ir_	_____	11. tom_ar_ café	_____
6. hac_er_ ejercicio	_____	12. jug_ar_ videojuegos	_____

3.3 Podemos nadar.

Stem-changing verbs: *o → ue*

Para empezar...

The daily lives of university students in the Spanish-speaking world are sometimes different than those of students in this country. University students in the Spanish-speaking world typically do not live on campus, and beginning in their first year of studies they typically focus on a specialized area, such as law, pharmacy, or dentistry.

PASO 1. The following is a list of things that students can do on the campus of the **Universidad de Panamá,** but one item on the list is incorrect. Basing your answer on the information in the paragraph above, select the things that students can most likely do.

EN LA UNIVERSIDAD DE PANAMÁ...

☑ **pueden** (*they can*) tomar café. ☑ **pueden** leer en la biblioteca.
☑ **pueden** estudiar medicina. ☐ **pueden** vivir en la universidad.
☑ **pueden** nadar.

PASO 2. Now compare what you just saw for the **Universidad de Panamá** with your own university. Which of these things can you do? Can you do all of these things? Any of them?

EN NUESTRA UNIVERSIDAD...

☐ **podemos** (*we can*) tomar café. ☐ **podemos** leer en la biblioteca.
☐ **podemos** estudiar medicina. ☐ **podemos** vivir en la universidad.
☐ **podemos** nadar.

■ Answers to these activities are in Appendix 2 at the back of your book.

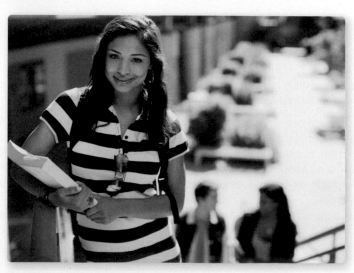

En la universidad, podemos aprender mucho.

Suggestion (¿Por qué?): Have students review the entire conjugation for *poder* and verify that *ue* is always stressed and that *o* is always unstressed.

Actividades analíticas

1 Use the verb forms that you saw in **Para empezar** to complete the conjugation of **poder** (*can, to be able to*).

	poder (o → ue)
SINGULAR	
yo	**pue**do
tú	**pue**des
él/ella, Ud.	**pue**de
PLURAL	
nosotros/as	podemos
vosotros/as	podéis
ellos/ellas, Uds.	pueden

Note (¿Por qué?): A "stressed syllable" is *una sílaba acentuada* or *una sílaba tónica* in Spanish. (The same adjectives are also used when describing a vowel, *una vocal*.) Whichever term you use, you may want to write it on the board and make clear that it is equivalent to "stressed."

Poder is typically followed by a verb in the infinitive form.

A veces **puedo** estudiar en la biblioteca.	*Sometimes I can study in the library.*
¿**Puedes** llegar a las once?	*Can you arrive at 11:00?*
Graciela **puede** correr muy rápido.	*Graciela can run very fast.*

2 The endings that you see in the conjugation of **poder** are exactly what you would expect of an **-er** verb. The *stem*, on the other hand, is sometimes **pod-** and sometimes **pued-**. Complete the following list of the three instances where the stem is **pod-**, and write the conjugated form of **poder** associated with each.

1. el infinitivo: **poder**
2. la forma _nosotros/as_: _podemos_
3. la forma **vosotros/as**: _podéis_

In all other instances, the stem is **pued-**.

3 **Poder** is a *stem-changing verb* (**un verbo que cambia de raíz**). In this particular type of stem-changing verb, the vowel **o** of the stem changes to **ue** in all forms except **nosotros/as** and **vosotros/as.** Some other verbs of this type in Spanish are **almorzar, dormir,** and **soñar** (*to dream*).

José **almuerza** a la una.	*José has lunch at 1:00.*
¿Cuántas horas **duermes**?	*How many hours do you sleep?*
¿**Sueñas** todas las noches?	*Do you dream every night?*

Following the pattern with **poder,** write the **yo** and the **nosotros/as** forms for these verbs here.

	almorzar (o → ue)	dormir (o → ue)	soñar (o → ue)
yo	almuerzo	duermo	sueño
nosotros/as	almorzamos	dormimos	soñamos

Verbs of this type belong to the **o → ue** family of stem-changing verbs; you will see some other families of stem-changing verbs in **Capítulo 4.**

¿Por qué?

The stem vowel in **poder** does not change randomly, but follows a clear pattern. When the syllable containing the stem vowel is stressed, the **o** it is pronounced **ue** (as in **PUE-do**), and when it is not stressed, it remains as **o** (as in **po-DE-mos**). This is characteristic of this entire family of verbs; the **o → ue** change occurs when the stem syllable is stressed. In languages around the world, vowels often change their pronunciation when stressed, just as you see here in Spanish.

■ For additional **o → ue** stem-changing verbs, see **Para saber más 3.3** at the back of your book.

Note (Para saber más): *Para saber más 3.3* covers the stem-changing verbs *contar, costar, encontrar, jugar, mostrar, recordar, soler,* and *volver.*

Autoprueba

Complete these sentences with the correct form of the verb.

1. Ellos _____ (soñar) por la noche.
2. ¿Tú _____ (almorzar) en tu casa?
3. Nosotros _____ (dormir) mucho todas las noches.
4. Ellas _____ (poder) estudiar con nosotros.

Respuestas: 1. sueñan **2.** almuerzas **3.** dormimos **4.** pueden

Suggestion (Act. A): When students are done, ask for examples of those who can do each of the activities. For example, ¿Quién puede correr cuatro millas?

Un consejo...

You will recognize cognates more easily in Spanish if you keep in mind that the **o → ue** change happens in many words, not just in verbs. English doesn't have this change, so it typically has just the **o** (sometimes in combination with other letters). Here are some examples.

ac<u>ue</u>rdo *acc<u>o</u>rd, agreement*
esc<u>ue</u>la *sch<u>oo</u>l*
f<u>ue</u>nte *f<u>o</u>untain*
f<u>ue</u>rza *f<u>o</u>rce*
p<u>ue</u>rco *p<u>o</u>rk, pig*
p<u>ue</u>rto *p<u>o</u>rt*

Remember this **o → ue** change when you encounter new words with **ue** in Spanish.

Actividades prácticas

A. ¿Qué puedes hacer? Write the correct form of the verb **poder** next to activities that you are able to do. Then ask others in the class whether they can do the remaining activities (**¿Puedes... ?**). Write the name of the person who can do each activity along with the correct form of **poder**.

MODELO: _____ hablar francés.
Puedo hablar francés. (**Stephanie puede** hablar francés.)

¿QUIÉN PUEDE?	¿QUÉ PUEDE HACER?
1. _____	correr cuatro millas (*miles*).
2. _____	cocinar comida china.
3. _____	dormir bien en una silla en la biblioteca.
4. _____	hablar dos o más idiomas (*languages*).
5. _____	leer en el autobús (*bus*).
6. _____	mirar la televisión y estudiar al mismo tiempo (*at the same time*).
7. _____	nadar estilo mariposa (*butterfly*).
8. _____	tocar la guitarra, cantar y bailar.

B. ¿Durante (*During*) el día o por la noche? When do you usually do each of the following activities, during the day or at night? Or never? Place each activity in the appropriate category. **Expansion (Act. B):** Ask students to add at least five other verbs that they learned earlier in the chapter.

Actividades: almuerzo, sueño, duermo, juego los videojuegos

DURANTE EL DÍA: _____ _____ _____ _____
POR LA NOCHE: _____ _____ _____ _____
NUNCA: _____ _____ _____ _____

C. ¿Cuántas horas duermes?

PASO 1. In a group of three or four, find out how many hours each of you sleeps on a normal night and on a night when circumstances are ideal (that is, with a quiet environment, no alarm clock, and so on). Keep track of each person's answer.

MODELO: ¿Cuántas horas duermes en una noche normal?
¿Cuántas horas duermes en una noche ideal?

PASO 2. Calculate the average for your group for the normal night and for the ideal night. Report your results in two separate sentences and state whether the situation is good (**bien**) or bad (**mal**).

MODELO: En una noche normal, dormimos 5,6 (cinco coma seis) horas. (La situación) Está muy mal.
En una noche ideal, dormimos 9,5 (nueve coma cinco) horas.

Suggestion (Act. C, Paso 2): Point out that decimal points are often expressed with a comma in Spanish and expressed as, for example, *siete coma seis horas* (instead of *siete punto seis horas*).

D. ¿A qué hora... ? In small groups, ask your classmates when they usually do the following activities. Then use the **nosotros/as** form to say whether you do the activity at the same time or at different times. **¡Atención!** All of these verbs belong to the **o → ue** family.

almorzar   **dormir**   **volver a casa** (*return home*)

MODELO: E1: ¿A qué hora almuerzas?
E2: Almuerzo a las doce y media.
E1: Yo también. Almorzamos a la misma (*same*) hora. (Yo almuerzo a la una. Almorzamos a horas diferentes.)

↻ Reciclaje

Gender and definite articles

Note (Reciclaje): This activity refreshes students' memory of gender, which they will need in learning about demonstrative adjectives.

Write the correct article (**el** or **la**) for each word. Then circle the words related to *time*.

1. _el_ teléfono
2. _la_ (noche)
3. _el_ (día)
4. _el_ (mes)
5. _el_ deporte
6. _la_ televisión
7. _la_ (semana)
8. _el_ parque
9. _el_ profesor
10. _la_ (hora)
11. _la_ (mañana)
12. _la_ biblioteca

■ Answers to this activity are in Appendix 2 at the back of your book.

3.4 ¿A qué hora es esa clase?

Demonstrative adjectives

Para empezar...

In many countries, university students choose a specialized major from the beginning of their studies and all students in that major take the same classes. Here, for example, you see a class schedule for first-semester pharmacy students at the **Universidad Central de Venezuela.** Use this schedule to complete the sentences that follow.

HORA	LUNES	MARTES	MIÉRCOLES	JUEVES	VIERNES
7–8 A.M.	Física Prof. Michael Mijares		Química General Profa. Carmen Chirinos	Física Prof. Michael Mijares	Química General Profa. Carmen Chirinos
8–9 A.M.		Salud (*Health*) Pública Prof. Jaime Charris			
9–10 A.M.	Formación General Prof. Carlos Ayala		Química Orgánica I Profa. Ingrid Merchán		Química Orgánica I Profa. Ingrid Merchán
10–11 A.M.					
11–12 A.M.	Prácticas (*Laboratory*)	Prácticas		Prácticas	Prácticas
12–1 P.M.					
1–2 P.M.					
2–3 P.M.		Talleres (*Workshops*)		Química Orgánica I Profa. Ingrid Merchán	

1. Tienen una clase a las siete de la mañana los lunes. **Esa** (*That*) clase se llama ___Física___.
2. Uno de los profesores se llama Jaime Charris. Tienen la clase con **ese** profesor los ___martes___.
3. Los martes, no tienen muchas clases. **Ese** día, solo tienen la clase de ___Salud Pública___.

(*Continues*)

■ Answers to these activities are in Appendix 2 at the back of your book.

4. Los miércoles tienen dos clases. **Esas** clases son <u>Química General</u> y <u>Química Orgánica</u> |

5. Los lunes y jueves tienen la clase de Física a las siete. También tienen la clase de <u>Química General</u> a **esa** hora los miércoles y viernes.

6. Dos de los profesores son Michael Mijares y Carlos Ayala. Tienen clases con **esos** profesores los <u>lunes</u> y <u>jueves</u>.

Actividades analíticas

1 **Este, esta, estos,** and **estas** are *demonstrative adjectives* (**los adjetivos demostrativos**). They indicate that something is close or nearby, in the same way you would use English *this* or *these*. **Ese, esa, esos,** and **esas** are also demonstrative adjectives, but they refer to something that is farther away, similar to English *that* or *those*.

Esta mochila es vieja, pero me gusta.	*This backpack is old, but I like it.*
Este libro es muy bueno.	*This book is very good.*
Me gustan **esas revistas.**	*I like those magazines.*

Note (Para saber más): *Para saber más 3.4* covers demonstrative adjectives *aquel/aquella/aquellos/aquellas* as well as the demonstrative pronouns.

■ For more on demonstrative adjectives and demonstrative pronouns, see **Para saber más 3.4** at the back of your book.

Suggestion (Act. analíticas 2): Point out that the masculine singular form (*este, ese*) ends in *-e*, not *-o*.

2 Demonstrative adjectives, like other adjectives in Spanish, agree with the noun that they modify in both number and gender. Complete the following chart by correctly writing the demonstrative adjectives in the chart.

	DEMONSTRATIVE ADJECTIVES			
	SINGULAR		**PLURAL**	
MASCULINE	**este** libro	*this book*	**estos** libros	*these books*
	<u>ese</u> libro	*that book*	<u>esos</u> libros	*those books*
FEMININE	**esta** clase	*this class*	**estas** clases	*these classes*
	<u>esa</u> clase	*that class*	<u>esas</u> clases	*those classes*

3 Choose the correct demonstrative adjective for these nouns, assuming that they are close to you.

<u>este</u> bolígrafo   <u>estas</u> señoras   <u>estos</u> niños   <u>esta</u> mochila

Autoprueba

Write the correct demonstrative adjectives for these nouns, assuming that they are *far* from you.

1. _____ señor
2. _____ relojes
3. _____ universidades
4. _____ persona

Respuestas: 1. ese **2.** esos **3.** esas **4.** esa

Actividades prácticas

A. ¿Cierto o falso?   Listen to the sentences and write **C** for **cierto** or **F** for **falso**.

1. _F_   2. _C_   3. _F_   4. _C_   5. _C_   6. _F_   7. _F_   8. _C_

B. Preguntas   For each of the following items, first answer the question in (a), then provide the correct form of **ese, esa, esos,** or **esas.** Finally, answer the question in (b).

RESPUESTAS

1. a. ¿Cómo se llama el actor favorito de Gael García Bernal?   _Javier Bardem_
   b. ¿De qué país es _ese_ actor?   _España_
2. a. ¿Cuántos colombianos hay en la **Actividad práctica C** de **3.1**?   _cuatro_
   b. ¿De qué país son _esas_ personas?   _Colombia_
3. a. ¿Cómo se llama el país al norte (*north*) de Guatemala?   _México_
   b. ¿A qué hora comen en _ese_ país?   _A las dos_
4. a. ¿Cómo se dice *to work* en español?   _trabajar_
   b. ¿Cuál es la forma *yo* de _ese_ verbo?   _trabajo_
5. a. ¿Cuál es la palabra para *five* en español?   _cinco_
   b. ¿Cuántas letras tiene _esa_ palabra?   _cinco_
6. a. ¿Cuántos bolígrafos tienes en tu mochila?   _____
   b. ¿De qué color son _esos_ bolígrafos?   _____

C. En la sala de computación   Imagine that you are the student in the doorway. What is nearest him is nearest you, and what is far from him is far from you. With a partner, write four sentences comparing and contrasting what you see in the lab.

MODELO: Esta chica tiene el pelo castaño, pero esa chica tiene el pelo rubio.

D. Las cosas de la clase   Create five sentences, some true and some false, about objects in the classroom. Choose some objects that are in your possession (such as **este libro**) and others that are far away (such as **ese libro**). Read the sentences to a partner and point to the objects you're talking about. Ask him/her to reply **cierto** or **falso** to each one.

MODELOS: Estos bolígrafos son rojos.
Esos libros son de Mary.
Esa mochila es muy grande.

■ The audio files for in-text listening activities are available in the eBook, within Connect activities, and on the Online Learning Center.

Script (Act. A): 1. (holding this book) *Este libro es de matemáticas.* **2.** (pointing to student across the room) *Esa persona se llama* ___ (give real name). **3.** *Esta noche todos vamos a bailar.* **4.** (pointing to this book on a student's desk) *Ese libro es de esta clase.* **5.** (pointing to student across the room) *Ese/ Esa estudiante estudia español.* **6.** (pointing to student across room) *Ese hombre / Esa mujer se llama* ___ (give false name). **7.** (pointing to backpack near you) *Esta mochila es* ___ (give wrong color). **8.** (picking up one student's pen) *Este bolígrafo es de* ___ (name of student).

¡Leamos!

Un día en la vida° de la presidenta   *life*

Suggestion (Antes de leer): Print and cut out the six items in the list and have groups of students put them in order as if it were a puzzle.

Note (Antes de leer, Paso 2): Possible answers depend on your student body. For some of them, the answers might be the same as those of a professional. For more "traditional" students, they might come up with activities such as *comer con amigos / el compañero de cuarto, reunirse con estudiantes de la misma clase, and reunirse con estudiantes de otras universidades.*

Antes de leer

PASO 1. You're going to read about the work schedule of Cristina Fernández de Kirchner, the president of Argentina from 2007 to 2015. First, read the following elements of a typical work day and put them in the order you would expect from a president.

____ comer con la familia

____ hacer ejercicio

____ informarse de las noticias (*to find out about news*)

____ reunirse con (*to meet with*) colegas

____ reunirse con representantes de otras (*other*) organizaciones

____ trabajar en el despacho (la oficina)

PASO 2. The activities in **Paso 1** come from a professional's work schedule. For each element in that schedule, write on a separate piece of paper an equivalent for the life of a student.

> **MODELO:** Para una persona profesional, **trabajar en el despacho** es como (*is like*) **estudiar en la biblioteca** para un(a) estudiante.

1. comer con la familia
2. hacer ejercicio
3. informarse de las noticias
4. reunirse con colegas
5. reunirse con representantes de otras organizaciones

A leer

Read the article about the daily activities of the former President of Argentina, Cristina Fernández de Kirchner and answer the questions that follow.

Un día en la vida de la presidenta

La presidenta, Cristina Fernández de Kirchner, comienza[a] su día en la Quinta de Olivos, donde vive. [...]

Su primera actividad de la mañana es leer los diarios[b] y hacer algo de ejercicio antes de tomar el helicóptero que la traerá[c] a su despacho en la Casa Rosada. ...

Normalmente su actividad empieza[d] con reuniones[e] internas junto al Secretario General u otros miembros del Gabinete.[f]

A media mañana es habitual que la presidenta participe de algún acto[g] en el Salón Blanco o en distintas localidades del país. Habitualmente se trata de firma de acuerdos,[h] inauguraciones o anuncios de obras[i] que el gobierno lleva adelante.[j]

Siempre que[k] puede, vuelve[l] a la residencia de Olivos para almorzar junto a su familia. Después regresa a su despacho para seguir[m] con la actividad de gobierno.

Durante la tarde suele[n] tener reuniones en su despacho y otras actividades públicas. ...

También es frecuente que la presidenta viaje a otros países para participar en encuentros[ñ] internacionales o reunirse con otros gobernantes y firmar acuerdos entre naciones o simplemente estrechar vínculos.[o] ...

Tanto cuando viaja como[p] en Buenos Aires, su actividad suele terminar tarde por la noche.

Muchos fines de semana se traslada[q] a su provincia, Santa Cruz, donde descansa junto a su familia en (la provincia de) Río Gallegos...

[a]*begins* [b]*periódicos* [c]*la... will take her* [d]*comienza* [e]*meetings* [f]*Cabinet* [g]*participe... participates in some activity some* [h]*firma... signing agreements* [i]*public works projects* [j]*lleva... takes forward* [k]*Siempre... As often as* [l]*she returns* [m]*continue* [n]*she tends* [ñ]*conferences* [o]*estrechar... strengthen connections* [p]*Tanto... Both when she travels and when she's* [q]*se... she goes*

1. ¿Cómo se llama la casa de la presidenta de Argentina?   Quinta de Olivos
2. ¿Qué hace la presidenta antes de (*before*) trabajar?   lee los diarios, hace ejercicio
3. ¿Cómo llega (*does she arrive*) al trabajo?   toma el helicóptero
4. ¿Dónde está la oficina de la presidenta?   en la Casa Rosada
5. Indica las actividades que hace la presidenta.

    ☑ anuncia obras del gobierno   ☑ tiene reuniones con sus empleados
    ☑ asiste a inauguraciones   ☑ participa de actos públicos
    ☐ escribe las leyes (*writes laws*)   ☑ tiene reuniones con líderes de otros
       del país   países
    ☑ firma acuerdos   ☑ viaja a otros países

6. ¿Cuándo termina el día de trabajo?   tarde por la noche

Después de leer

PASO 1.   Look again at the activities you put in order in **Antes de leer, Paso 1**. This time, order them according to what you just read about Fernández de Kirchner's schedule and compare the lists. Does the president's schedule differ from how you envisioned a typical work day? If so, how?

Answers (Después de leer, Paso 1): 4, 2, 1, 3, 5, 6

 PASO 2.   Now work in pairs to interview each other about your own daily routines following the model from the reading.

1. ¿Cuál es tu primera actividad de la mañana?
2. ¿Cómo empiezan las actividades del trabajo o de la universidad?
3. ¿Qué haces a media mañana?
4. ¿Qué haces para almorzar?
5. Normalmente, ¿cuándo termina el día?
6. ¿Qué haces los fines de semana?

PASO 3.   Prepare a presentation of your classmate's day using format and structures from the reading as models. **¡Atención!** Deliver a prepared, practiced, and professional presentation.

> **MODELO:**   (*Nombre*) comienza su día en... Normalmente su actividad empieza con...
>
>   A media mañana...
>   Para almorzar...
>   Su día termina...
>   Los fines de semana...

Suggestion (Después de leer, Paso 3): Have students work in groups of four, taking turns to present their partner's day. Ask for one or two volunteers to present to the whole class.

CONÉCTATE AL MUNDO PROFESIONAL

Comparing and contrasting daily routines with others is a great way to make cross-cultural connections while traveling or studying abroad. It is also excellent practice for professional networking. Successful networking is about building mutually beneficial relationships. The starting point is always finding out what you have in common (by listening attentively to what others say), then using those commonalities in future communications. At some point you may be able to do the other person a favor, and vice versa.

¡Escuchemos!

El horario para comer

En español...

In many parts of the Spanish-speaking world, **la comida** and **el almuerzo** refer to the same midday meal, but that isn't true everywhere. In Mexico, for instance, **el almuerzo** is a morning meal. As you may notice in the video, in Argentina, as in many other Spanish-speaking countries, some people eat **la merienda**

regularly between lunch and dinner.

CONÉCTATE AL MUNDO HISPANO

The schedules of the people in the video represent common patterns in the Spanish-speaking world, where a large family meal is often eaten at midday and a light supper is eaten later in the evening. But be careful not to jump to conclusions about a whole country based on one person—schedules vary widely and Isabel, Claudia, Roberto, and María are just four individuals. Think of your schedule at college, which is probably quite different than your parents' schedule; neither one can be said to represent all of this country's culture.

Suggestion (A escuchar): Tell students to expect some answers to be a range of times such as *de tres a seis;* in Roberto's case, he is the owner of a restaurant so he is giving the range of hours when each meal is served at the restaurant.

Antes de escuchar

Fill in the first row of the table below with the times you typically eat. Then ask three of your classmates when they tend to eat, and include their information in the table.

MODELO: E1: ¿A qué hora desayunas?
E2: A las nueve y media. ¿Y tú?
E1: A las ocho.

A escuchar

Video track (A escuchar): This video clip can be found on the DVD to accompany *Conéctate: Cap. 3,* Track 5.

Now watch the video of Isabel, Claudia, Roberto, and María, replaying and pausing as necessary. Fill in the times they say they eat.

NOMBRE	EL DESAYUNO	EL ALMUERZO/ LA COMIDA	LA CENA
yo			
Isabel (México)	9 A.M.	2 o 3 P.M.	9 P.M.
Claudia (Argentina)	7:00–7:30 A.M.	12:30–1 P.M.	9 P.M.
Roberto (Costa Rica)	6–11 A.M.	11 A.M.–3 P.M.	6–10 P.M.
María (España)	7:30–8:30 A.M.	2:30 P.M.	10:00 P.M.

Después de escuchar

PASO 1. Compare the schedules of Isabel, Claudia, Roberto, and María and say whether they are **muy diferentes, similares** or **iguales.**

1. Los horarios de desayunar de Isabel, Claudia, Roberto y María son...

2. Los horarios de comer/almorzar de Isabel, Claudia, Roberto y María son...

3. Los horarios de cenar de Isabel, Claudia, Roberto y María son...

PASO 2. Now compare your schedule and those of your classmates to the schedules of the people in the video. Present your conclusions to the class.

MODELO: Mi horario y el horario de Isabel son iguales porque desayunamos a las nueve, comemos a las dos y cenamos a las nueve.
Los horarios de cenar de los estudiantes de esta clase y los de Isabel y María son muy diferentes porque nosotros cenamos a las seis de la tarde y ellas cenan a las nueve o diez de la noche.

Videoscript (A escuchar): ISABEL: *Por lo regular aquí se desayuna por decir a las 9 de la mañana, es un desayuno completo ¿no? En eso, como a las 2 o 3 de la tarde, y la cena, pues ya, se juntan todos y venimos cenando como a las 9 de la noche.* CLAUDIA: *El horario de comidas es... el desayuno es a las 7 de la mañana, entre 7 y 7:30 de la mañana, el almuerzo alrededor de las 12:30 a u... 12:30, 13 horas, la merienda alrededor de las 17:30 y cenamos a las 21. Ese es el horario.* ROBERTO: *Seis de la mañana a las 11 es el desayuno y 11 a 3, almuerzo. De 3 a 6, eh, café, y de 6 a 10 de la noche, cena.* MARÍA: *Pues, desayuno temprano sobre la, depende del día, eso, a partir de 7:30 y 8:30 suelo desayunar... la comida sobre las 2:30, que comemos aquí y la cena sobre las 10.*

¡Escribamos!

Las rutinas diarias

When you interact with people as you travel or study abroad, you may find that you have activities in common, and can plan to do them together, allowing you to meet new people and experience the culture from a more intimate perspective. Or, you may find that your routines are very different, which provides an opportunity to learn and try new things.

You've worked a lot in this chapter with your own schedule, so for this activity you'll focus on the schedule of someone who is not a student.

Timelines

When writing text in which time sequences are important, a timeline can help you sort your ideas so that readers can easily follow the sequential flow of what you have written. Whether recounting historical events, a person's lifetime, or a daily routine, try to set up a timeline as a pre-writing strategy.

Antes de escribir

Prepare a timeline of at least four activities in a family member's routine on a typical day. (Ideally, select someone who is not a student.)

> **MODELO:** mi madre
>
> | 6:30 | 7:00 | 8:00 | | 3:00 |
> desayunar | ir a la oficina | trabajar | | comer

A escribir

PASO 1. Use the timeline to guide you as you convert these isolated activities into at least four complete sentences.

> **MODELO:** Mi madre desayuna a las seis y media de la mañana.
> A las siete de la mañana, ella va a la oficina.

PASO 2. Next, flesh out each sentence by adding more description to help turn them into a more cohesive paragraph. Try to anticipate questions your readers might have (such as **¿dónde?** and **¿con quién?**), and incorporate the answers into your paragraph.

> **MODELO:** Todos los días a las seis y media de la mañana, mi madre desayuna cereal en casa (*at home*) con mi hermanito. Los días de entre semana, él va en autobús (*bus*) a la escuela y ella va en coche (*car*) a la oficina.

 ## Después de escribir

PASO 1. Check your own work, then exchange paragraphs with a classmate. Read the content of your classmate's essay carefully. Are there any important pieces of information missing? If so, be sure to point that out.

PASO 2. Read the essay again, using the following checklist to edit the grammar. Verifica que (*Check that*)...

☐ hay concordancia (*agreement*) de género (*gender*) entre los adjetivos y lo que describen (*what they describe*)

☐ hay concordancia de número (singular o plural) entre los adjetivos y lo que describen

☐ hay concordancia entre los sustantivos (*nouns*) y verbos

☐ los verbos con cambio de raíz tienen los cambios correctos

When you are finished, return the paper to your classmate and make corrections to your own, based on your classmate's feedback.

Suggestion (Después de escribir): To motivate students to edit their own work as well as their classmates' carefully, occasionally grade their editing instead of their writing.

Suggestion (Antes de hablar): First review the *En español* box with students, then model explanations as to why some items will be logical and other will not. For example, the first item *No es lógico porque Jaime no corre por la mañana. Ignacio corre por la mañana.* Item 4 has the right person running, but at exactly the time he is eating lunch with his family.

¡Hablemos!

La rutina de la familia Ramírez

Antes de hablar

Based on the illustrations of this family's daily routine, indicate which of the invitations below would make sense (**Es lógico**) and which would not (**No es lógico**). Can you explain why?

En español...

Just as you might say *Joe, are we going running at 2:00?* as a way to invite someone to do something or to confirm plans, you can also use present tense to invite in Spanish.

Carmen, ¿vamos al comedor a las seis y media?
Carmen, do you want to go to the cafeteria at 6:30?
(Carmen, we're going to the cafeteria at 6:30, right?)

	ES LÓGICO	NO ES LÓGICO
1. Jaime, ¿corremos a las siete y media de la mañana?	☐	☑
2. Elena, ¿vamos de compras a las diez de la mañana?	☑	☐
3. Marisol, ¿montamos a caballo por la tarde?	☑	☐
4. Ignacio, ¿corremos a las dos de la tarde?	☐	☑
5. Marisol, ¿jugamos fútbol a las nueve de la noche?	☐	☑

 ### A hablar

Make plans with at least two different classmates to do some of the activities the family pictured does.

MODELO: E1: Claire, ¿montamos a caballo a las cinco?
E2: No puedo. Tengo clase hasta las seis. ¿Montamos a caballo mañana a las diez de la mañana?
E1: Sí.

 ### Después de hablar

In groups, take turns describing something from the pictures without naming the item. Can the others guess what you are describing? **¡Atención!** Use vocabulary from **Capítulos 1** and **2.**

MODELO: E1: Es pequeño y es blanco y negro. Tiene números.
E2: ¿Es el reloj?
E1: ¡Sí!

Expansion (A hablar): Have students narrate the pictures in a game similar to the memory game of "I'm going on a trip and I'm going to take . . . ". Start with everyone in the class standing. Students take turns telling the story of the pictured family's day, adding one new element each time it is their turn. If a student can't remember all the items previously listed or add anything he/she has to sit down. The winner is the last person standing. Remind students to talk about the time of day, say at what time people do things and talk about the things the family members probably do in between the times pictured.

Conéctate a la música

Canción: «Ella tiene fuego (*fire*)» (2010)
Artistas: Celia Cruz (Cuba) y El General (Panamá)

Celia Cruz (1925–2003) era (*was*) una cantante muy famosa de Cuba. Era muy conocida (*well known*) en Cuba y en los Estados Unidos. La canción «Ella tiene fuego» es del álbum *Regalo del alma* (*Gift from the Soul*). Es el último (*last*) álbum de estudio que ella hizo antes de su muerte (*made before her death*) en 2003. La canción (*song*) incluye la voz (*voice*) del cantante panameño El General, quien es conocido por su música reggae.

Antes de escuchar

PASO 1.   Music is a very important aspect of Cuban culture. **Tiene fuego** is a slang expression to describe someone who is dancing. What do you think it could mean?

PASO 2.   Circle the verbs that you associate with music.

almorzar	comer	mover (*to move*)
bailar	escuchar	tocar la guitarra
cantar	jugar los videojuegos	viajar

 A escuchar   Suggestion (A escuchar): Briefly review the *Expresiones útiles* with students before having them listen to the song.

Read the text below, then listen once to the song all the way through. Then listen again, paying attention to the chorus. Fill in the blanks with the correct form of the verb **tener, ser,** or **mover** (*to move,* o → ue).

> **Expresiones útiles**
>
> **las caderas** hips   **la fiesta** party
> **el ciclón** cyclone   **todo el mundo** everyone
> **las piernas** legs   **pregunta de qué está hecha** asks what she is made of

La cantante cubana, Celia Cruz

■ For copyright reasons, the songs referenced in **Conéctate a la música** have not been provided by the publisher. The video for this song can be found on YouTube, and it is available for purchase from the iTunes store.

Ella _tiene_ fuego cuando _mueve_ las caderas.
Ella _tiene_ fuego; _tiene_ un ciclón en las piernas.
Ella _tiene_ fuego; _es_ la atracción de la fiesta.
Ella _tiene_ fuego y todo el mundo pregunta de qué está hecha.

Después de escuchar

PASO 1.   ¿Cierto o falso? Indicate whether the following statements are true or false.

	CIERTO	FALSO
1. La mujer de la canción no puede bailar bien.		X
2. A ella le gusta bailar.	X	
3. Se mueve lentamente (*slowly*) cuando baila.		X
4. Ella atrae (*attracts*) mucha atención en las fiestas.	X	

PASO 2.   Work with a partner to ask and answer the following questions. Be sure to use complete sentences in your answers.

¿A ti te gustan las fiestas? ¿Te gusta bailar? ¿Bailas bien? ¿Tus amigos «tienen fuego» cuando ellos bailan? ¿Qué otras actividades haces (*do you do*) en las fiestas? (¿Comes? ¿Tocas la guitarra? ¿Hablas con amigos? ¿Juegas videojuegos? ¿ ?)

VOCABULARIO

Now that I have completed the chapter, I can . . .

- ☐ ask and tell time
- ☐ say when events occur
- ☐ get someone's attention
- ☐ say what I do in my free time
- ☐ talk about daily schedules in the Spanish-speaking world

Comunicación

Disculpa... / Disculpe... / Disculpen...	Excuse me . . . (*inform. / form. / pl.*)
Oye... / Oiga... / Oigan...	Listen . . . (*inform. / form. / pl.*)
¿Qué hora es?	What time is it?
Es la una.	It's 1:00.
Es la una y media/treinta.	It's 1:30.
Son las dos y cuarto/quince.	It's 2:15.
Son diez para las nueve. / Son las nueve menos diez. / Son las ocho y cincuenta.	It's 8:50.
Es mediodía. / Son las doce del día.	It's noon.
Es medianoche. / Son las doce de la noche.	It's midnight.
¿A qué hora... ?	At what time . . . ?
Es a la/las...	It's at . . .
de la mañana	in the morning
de la tarde	in the afternoon/ evening
de la noche	at night
de la madrugada	in the early morning

Los días de la semana — The days of the week

los días de entre semana lunes, martes, miércoles, jueves, viernes	weekdays
el fin de semana sábado, domingo	weekend

Los sustantivos

la comida	food; (midday) meal
la escuela	school
el horario	schedule
la vez (*pl.* veces)	time; instance
una vez	once
dos veces	twice

La rutina diaria — The daily routine

almorzar (ue)	to eat lunch
asistir (a)	to attend
caminar	to walk
cantar	to sing
cenar	to eat dinner
cocinar	to cook
comer (comida mexicana)	to eat (Mexican food)
comprar	to buy
correr (en el parque)	to run (in the park)
desayunar	to eat breakfast
escribir (un email)	to write (an email)
escuchar	to listen (to)
hablar (por teléfono)	to talk (on the phone)
ir (*irreg.*) al gimnasio	to go to the gym
jugar (ue) básquetbol	to play basketball
leer (el periódico)	to read (the paper)
mirar (la televisión)	to watch (television)
montar a caballo	to go horseback riding
nadar	to swim
poder (ue)	can, to be able to
practicar...	to practice/do/play . . .
un deporte	a sport
yoga	yoga
soñar (ue)	to dream
tomar	to take; to drink
trabajar	to work
usar (la computadora)	to use (the computer)
viajar	to travel
vivir	to live
volver (ue)	to return

Los adjetivos demostrativos — Demonstrative adjectives

ese/esa, esos/esas	that, those
este/esta, estos/estas	this, these

Expresiones útiles

a veces	sometimes
nunca	never
por la mañana	in the morning
por la tarde	in the afternoon/ evening
por la noche	at night
siempre	always
todo/a; todos/as	all; everyone; all of us /them/you
todo el día / toda la noche	all day/night
todos los días / todas las noches	every day/night

¡Qué bonita familia!°

What a beautiful family!

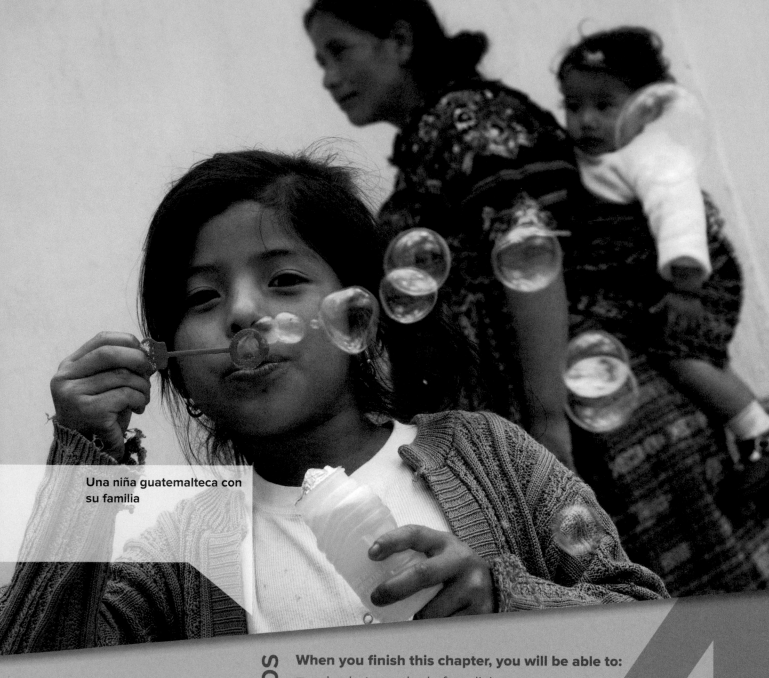

Una niña guatemalteca con su familia

¡Qué bonita familia!°

Objetivos

When you finish this chapter, you will be able to:

- ask what people do for a living
- comment on things and compliment people
- talk about your family members and their activities
- compare and contrast people and things
- talk about what you want or plan to do

COMUNICACIÓN ~~ARIO~~ ~~UCTURA~~ ~~ATE~~

Video track (Act. A): This video clip can be found on the DVD to accompany *Conéctate: Cap. 4, Track 1.*

¿A qué te dedicas? / ¿A qué se dedica?

Asking what people do for a living   Suggestion (Act. A): Play the video twice. The first time, students should just listen. The second time, pause the video after each person speaks to allow students time to fill in the information on the chart. Urge students to try

A. A ver: Introducciones   to listen for first names, but let them know not to expect stereo typical names such as María and José. If the

PASO 1. First, work in pairs to ask and answer the questions that you will hear answered in the video clips.   names are too hard, provide a list of first names for

MODELO: E1: ¿Cómo te llamas?   students to fill in the same way as professions are provided in

E2: Mónica.   the box on the next page.

¿Cómo te llamas?   ¿De dónde eres?   ¿Cuántos años tienes?

PASO 2. Watch and listen as Spanish speakers introduce themselves. Replay and pause as needed, then complete the chart.

En español...

profesión es guía naturalista. **7.** Me llamo Carmen. Tengo 30 años. Soy de Madrid, España, y trabajo en banca privada.

Just as English speakers use fillers such as *uh, um,* and *OK* in spontaneous speech, Spanish speakers use expressions such as **pues, bueno, eh,** and **OK.** Almost all the speakers in this video use one of those fillers when they begin to speak.

Videoscript (Act. A, Paso 2): 1. *Mi nombre es Óscar Alberto Chavarría Mora. Soy de San José, Costa Rica, y vivo en ciudad Colón, fuera de la capital. Tengo 38 años y me dedico al transporte. Soy chofer.* **2.** *Me llamo Charo Sánchez López, eh... soy de Salamanca, de España y... soy periodista.* **3.** *Yo soy Víctor Peralta, nací aquí en la Ciudad de México, y soy pintor.* **4.** *Tengo 29 años. Me llamo Kadín Eliecer Morán, trabajo en la Policía Nacional.* **5.** *Mi nombre es Yasmín Lyons, eh... soy socióloga eh... egresada de la Universidad de Panamá, actualmente estoy estudiando Infor... eh... la carrera de Informática Aplicada en la Facultad de Informática, Electrónica y Comunicación.* **6.** *Bueno, mi nombre es Henry Sequeira Chávez. Yo vivo acá en Monteverde. Tengo 36 años y mi*

¿QUIÉN ES?	¿CÓMO SE LLAMA?	¿CUÁNTOS AÑOS TIENE?	¿DE DÓNDE ES?	¿A QUÉ SE DEDICA?
1.	<u>Óscar Alberto</u> Chavarría Mora	38 años	San José, Costa Rica	chofer
2.	Charo Sánchez López	X	Salamanca, España	periodista
3.	Víctor Peralta	X	la Ciudad de México	pintor
4.	Kadín Eliecer Morán	29 años	Panamá	policía
5.	Yazmín Lyons	X	Panamá	socióloga, estudiante
6.	<u>Henry</u> Sequeira Chávez	36 años	<u>Monteverde</u>, Costa Rica	guía naturalista
7.	Carmen	30 años	Madrid, España	trabaja en banca privada

Expansion (Act. A, Paso 2): Have students write descriptions of the people they saw on the video using the vocabulary they studied in *Cap. 2.*

Note (¿A qué te dedicas?):
Professions are covered in
Capítulo 10. Materias are covered in *Cap. 1.* Help students
with the professions related to
the *materias: arquitecto/a* for
arquitectura, and so on.

**Suggestion (¿A qué te
dedicas?):** Remind students
that the question *¿A qué se
dedica?* can be answered with
any verb; they don't have to
use *dedicar.*

You have learned how to introduce yourself and respond to the following
questions.

¿Cómo te llamas? / ¿Cómo se llama?
¿De dónde eres? / ¿De dónde es?
¿Cuántos años tienes? / ¿Cuántos años tiene?

An additional piece of information that people may offer when introducing
themselves is the answer to these questions.

¿Cuál es tu profesión? / ¿Cuál es su profesión? ⎤ What do you do
¿A qué te dedicas? / ¿A qué se dedica? ⎦ (for a living)?

—**Mavi, ¿a qué te dedicas?**   —**Señora Serna, ¿cuál es su profesión?**
—**Estudio ciencias políticas.**   —**Soy ingeniera** (*engineer*).

Here are some common professions. Can you figure out all the cognates?

el/la abogado/a	attorney	**el/la pintor(a)**	painter
el/la chofer		**el/la policía**	
el/la doctor(a) / médico/a		**el/la psicólogo/a**	
el/la guía naturalista		**el/la sociólogo/a**	
el/la periodista	journalist		

Expansion (Act. B): Have students work in teams to think of
other people they know of with
the same professions as those
presented in the video. Which
team has the most? *Otros perio-
distas son... , Otros pintores
son...*

Note (Act. B): An explanation
of *saber* and *conocer* can be
found in the *Para saber más*
section in *Cap. 5.*

B. ¿A quién conoces? (*Whom do you know?*)   Draw a grid with nine cells,
like tic-tac-toe: three columns of three rows each. Fill each cell with a profession
you know how to say in Spanish. For each cell in the table, try to find a classmate
who knows someone who practices that profession and circle it. When you have
three circles in a row, sit down.

MODELO: E1: ¿Conoces a (*Do you know*) un policía?
                    E2: No. ¿Conoces a un ingeniero?
                    E1: ¡Mi padre es ingeniero!

¡Qué lindo!
Commenting on things and complimenting people

To express the equivalent of *How* + adjective! or *What a* + noun! use: **¡Qué... !**

¡Qué + adjective!
    ¡Qué guapo/a!   How handsome/pretty

¡Qué + noun!
    ¡Qué lío!   What a mess!
    ¡Qué frío/calor!   It's so cold/hot!

¡Atención! Remember, whenever you use an adjective, it must agree in
number and gender with the noun it refers to.

Suggestion (Act. A):
Remind students that
adjectives were
covered in *Cap. 2.*

A. No estamos de acuerdo. (*We don't agree.*)   Work in pairs, using the list
of adjectives as a starting point. For each word your partner gives, say the opposite. How many more adjectives can you add to the list?

MODELOS: E1: ¡Qué bueno!
                    E2: ¡Qué malo!

                    E1: ¡Qué feo!
                    E2: ¡Qué lindo!

alto/a bajo/a bello/a
débil delgado/a feo/a frío/a
gordo/a gracioso/a guapo/a
joven lento/a lindo/a
pequeño/a rápido/a

B. Las reacciones   For each image, indicate if the expression using **¡Qué... !** is logical (**es lógico**) or illogical (**no es lógico**). If it's not logical, suggest a reaction that would be logical.

Script (Act. B): **1.** *¡Qué frío!* **2.** *¡Qué gorda!* **3.** *¡Qué bello!* **4.** *¡Qué alto!* **5.** *¡Qué lindo!* **6.** *¡Qué rápido!*

MODELO:

You hear: ¡Qué triste! *You say:* Es lógico.

■ The audio files for in-text listening activities are available in the eBook, within Connect activities, and on the Online Learning Center.

1.

Es lógico.

2.

No es lógico.

3.

Es lógico.

4.

Es lógico.

5.

No es lógico.

6.

No es lógico.

En español...

Here are more expressions that use **¡Qué... !**

¡Qué cara (tiene)!
What nerve!

¡Qué coraje! / ¡Qué rabia!
How frustrating/annoying!

¡Qué feo/a!
How ugly! / How horrible! (*weather, behavior, situation, and so on*)

¡Qué pesado!
What a pain! / How annoying!

¡Qué rico/a!
How delicious!

C. ¡Qué bueno!

PASO 1.   Write an example of each of the following. Try to include examples from the Spanish-speaking world.

1. el nombre de un actor
2. el nombre de una actriz
3. el título de una película
4. el título de un libro
5. el nombre de un grupo musical
6. el título de una canción (*song*)
7. el nombre de un restaurante
8. el nombre de un curso
9. el nombre de una ciudad
10. el nombre de una universidad

 PASO 2.   Now express your opinions! Working in pairs, take turns naming things from your list. Your partner will react using **¡Qué... !** expressions.

MODELO: E1: La clase de biología.
E2: ¡Qué aburrida! ¡Qué pesada! *or* ¿La biología? ¡Qué interesante!

COMUN **VOCABULARIO** UCTURA ATE

¿Cómo es la familia de Camila?

Describing family members

A. La familia de Camila

PASO 1.   Use the family tree to provide the missing names of Camila's family members.

El **padre (papá)** de Camila se llama <u>Antonio.</u> <u>María</u> es **la madre (mamá)** de Camila.
Camila es **hija única:** Ella no tiene **hermanos.**
El tío de Camila se llama Jaime. Él es soltero (no tiene **esposa/mujer**).
<u>Aurelia</u> es **la tía** de Camila. Su **esposo/marido** se llama Gustavo.
Jaime tiene otra **sobrina** además de (*in addition to*) Camila: Isabel.
Aurelia y Gustavo tienen dos **hijos: un hijo,** Sebastián, y **una hija,** Isabel.
La abuela de Camila se llama <u>Carmen</u>; <u>Ricardo</u> es **el abuelo** de Camila.
Sebastián es **el nieto** de Carmen y Ricardo.
Camila tiene **un perro,** <u>Chispa</u>, y **una gata,** <u>Reina</u>.
Sebastián (**el primo** de Camila) e Isabel (**la prima** de Camila) tienen **un pez,** <u>Hernán</u>.
La familia tiene tres **mascotas** en total: un perro, un gato y un pez.

Relatives are **los familiares** or **los parientes**. *Parents* are **los padres** or **los papás**. Here are some more family relationship terms.

el/la bisabuelo/a	great-grandfather/great-grandmother
el/la cuñado/a	brother-in-law/sister-in-law
el/la esposo/a	husband/wife, spouse
la nuera	daughter-in-law
el/la suegro/a	father-in-law/mother-in-law
el yerno	son-in-law
el/la novio/a	boyfriend/girlfriend

Step-relationships use the suffix **-astro/a.**

el/la hermanastro/a	stepbrother/stepsister
el/la hijastro/a	stepson/stepdaughter
la madrastra	stepmother
el padrastro	stepfather

PASO 2. Answer the following questions about Camila's family tree.

1. ¿Quiénes son **los padres** de Camila? Antonio y María
2. ¿Cuántos **cuñados** tiene Jaime? dos
3. ¿Cómo se llaman **los hijos** de Aurelia y Gustavo? Sebastián e Isabel
4. ¿Cómo se llaman las dos **sobrinas** de Jaime? Camila e Isabel
5. ¿Cuántos años tiene **la suegra** de Antonio? setenta y dos
6. ¿Quiénes son **los abuelos** de Camila? Carmen y Ricardo
7. ¿Cuántos **nietos** tienen Carmen y Ricardo? tres
8. ¿Quién es **el nieto** de Carmen y Ricardo? Sebastián
9. ¿Cómo se llaman los dos **yernos** de Ricardo y Carmen? Antonio y Gustavo
10. ¿Cuántas **mascotas** hay en la familia? tres

B. Definiciones Provide the family term that corresponds to each definition.

1. La hermana de mi madre es mi... tía
2. El hijo de mi hijo es mi... nieto
3. La hija de mi hermano es mi... sobrina
4. La esposa de mi padre es mi... madre
5. La esposa de mi padre, que no es mi madre, es mi... madrastra
6. El marido de mi abuela es mi... abuelo
7. Los hijos de mi tía son mis... primos
8. La madre de mi sobrina es mi... hermana/cuñada
9. El padre de mi nieto es mi... hijo/yerno
10. El hijo de mi esposo y su ex esposa es mi... hijastro

Suggestion (Vocabulario): Follow the pattern used in Activity B (**Definiciones**). Give students more definitions, and ask them to match the definition to the correct relative. Sample definitions: **1.** *Es el padre de mi abuelo.* (*bisabuelo*) **2.** *Es el esposo de mi hermana.* (*cuñado*) **3.** *Es la mujer de mi hijo.* (*nuera*) **4.** *Es el padre de mi marido.* (*suegro*) **5.** *Es el marido de mi hija.* (*yerno*) **6.** *Es la esposa de mi padre, pero no es mi madre.* (*madrastra*) **7.** *Es el hijo de mi padrastro e hijastro de mi madre.* (*hermanastro*). Then ask students to provide definitions for the following relatives. **1.** *la bisabuela* **2.** *la cuñada* **3.** *el marido* **4** *la esposa* **5.** *la suegra* **6.** *el padrastro* **7.** *la hermanastra* **8.** *el yerno*

Suggestion (Act. A): Have students refer to the family tree to draw their own family tree, filling in the real names of their relatives. Suggest that they make up a family if they don't feel comfortable using their own.

Suggestion (Act. A or B): Make the activity a chalkboard race with two teams. Which team can send a representative to write the correct answer to each question first?

Note (Act. B): Tell students that matching definitions and words is a much better way to learn and study new vocabulary than with English–Spanish flashcards because it allows you to work 100% in Spanish, without translating.

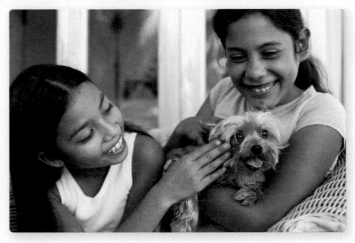

¿Tienen una nueva mascota? ¡Qué bueno!

C. Noticias sobre mi familia

PASO 1. Read the following statements about the speaker's family and react accordingly using the **¡Qué... !** structure. The following words will help you.

bueno	horrible	terrible
emocionante (*exciting*)	interesante	triste (*sad*)
fabuloso	malo	
fantástico	maravilloso	

MODELO: Mi primo ganó una beca (*won a scholarship*) para asistir a la universidad. → ¡Qué maravilloso!

1. Mi padre perdió (*lost*) su trabajo.
2. Mi tía está embarazada (*pregnant*).
3. Mi prima tiene 16 años y quiere casarse con (*marry*) su novio.
4. Mi hermana acaba de empezar su propio negocio (*own business*).
5. Mis abuelos están de vacaciones en Puerto Rico.
6. Mi hermano está enfermo (*sick*).

PASO 2. Now share at least two pieces of news about your own family (or be creative and invent news) with a partner. Your partner will react using the **¡Qué... !** structure.

D. A ver: Los miembros de la familia

Video track (Act. D): This video clip can be found on the DVD to accompany *Conéctate: Cap. 4,* Track 2.

PASO 1. Watch and listen at least twice, pausing as needed, as the following people describe their families. For each family member they mention, there are two terms provided. Circle the one used in the video.

Videoscript (Act. D, Paso 1):
1. FRANCISCO: *Mi papá, mi mamá y una hermana. Después tengo de verdad una familia bastante grande, de abuelos, tengo 7 tíos.*
2. ANGÉLICA: *Mi familia, bueno yo vivo con mis papás, este... con mis 2 hermanas. Mi mamá me cuida a mi hija. Una... mi otra hermana vive aparte.*
3. MICHAEL: *Mi mamá, mi papá, mis abuelos, todos los hermanos de mi mamá y mi hermana.* **4.** GUADALUPE: *Mi padre, mi madre y tengo 3 hermanos y 4 sobrinos.*

Expansion (Act. D, Paso 2): After students list all of their own family relationships, have them work in groups to compare their lists: ¿Quién tiene más tíos (primos, sobrinos, cuñados, hermanastros, etcétera)? Have each person count how many vocabulary terms related to family relationships he/she used. Who used the most?

1. Francisco
   a. padre (papá)
   b. madre (mamá)
   c. hermano (hermana)
   d. abuelo (abuelos)
   e. (tíos) hermanos de mi mamá

2. Angélica
   a. padres (papás)
   b. (hermanas) hermanos
   c. madre (mamá)
   d. (hija) hijo

3. Michael
   a. madre (mamá)
   b. padre (papá)
   c. abuelo (abuelos)
   d. tíos (hermanos de mi mamá)
   e. hermano (hermana)

4. Guadalupe
   a. (padre) papá
   b. (madre) mamá
   c. hermanas (hermanos)
   d. sobrino (sobrinos)

Expansion (Act. D): Give students a copy of your family tree with only a few names filled in. Ask students to complete the tree as you describe your family. If you want to make the activity more challenging, ask students to listen for additional information, such as ages and professions.

PASO 2. Make a list of your family members, indicating a) those you see most often and b) those you see only once in a while. Try to use two ways of describing each relative (for example, **madre/mamá; tía / hermana de mi mamá,** and so on). Are there occasions that usually bring your whole family together? What are they?

E. ¿Cómo es la familia de Pedro y Manuela?

PASO 1.   Work in pairs to complete Pedro and Manuela's family tree. One partner should consult only the family tree labeled **Estudiante 1,** while the other should consult only the family tree labeled **Estudiante 2.**

MODELO: E1: ¿Cómo se llama la esposa de Pedro?
E2: Manuela.

E2: ¿Cuántos años tiene?
E1: 65 años.

PASO 2.   Compare your finished products. Do you both have the same family tree and correct ages?

Para Estudiante 1

(*Continues*)

Suggestion (Act. E): Ask students about Pedro and Manuela's family: *¿Elena es la madre de quién? ¿Cuántos años tiene Marisol? ¿José Manuel es el hermano de quién? ¿Cómo se llama la esposa de Ignacio? ¿Cómo se llaman los nietos de Pedro y Manuela?*

Expansion (Act. E): Ask students to bring a picture of their immediate family to class or to draw a rough sketch. Have them show it to a partner who will ask questions in order to find out as much as he/she can about the family. Encourage students to show interest in what their partner is saying by following up with a compliment and/or another question: *¡Qué alto! ¿Qué hace?*

CONÉCTATE AL MUNDO PROFESIONAL

In many Spanish-speaking countries, it's common to include a head shot, as well as your age and marital status, on resumes. In the United States, it's illegal to ask job applicants for that information.

Observe as you interact with others from around the world to know when it's appropriate to talk about family and personal lives in professional contexts.

En español...

In Spanish, *godmother* and *godfather* are **la madrina** and **el padrino** (*godparents* = **los padrinos**). The *godchild* is **el ahijado** or **la ahijada**.

Comadre and **compadre** are terms that parents use to refer to the godmother and godfather of their child. There's usually a close relationship between parents and their **comadre** and **compadre**.

Elena es mi comadre; es la madrina de mi hijo.

Fernando y yo somos compadres.

Compadres can also sometimes just be close family friends.

Pedro
70 años

Manuela
— años

—— años

Elena
45 años

—— años

José Manuel
39 años

—— años

Jorge
22 años

25 años

F. ¡Qué bonita familia!

PASO 1.   Work in pairs to interview each other and find out more about your family members and pets. (You can make up an imaginary family if you prefer.) Draw your partner's family tree as you go and react to what you find out about your partner using **¡Qué... familia!**

Sample questions:
¿Con quién vives?
¿Cómo se llaman los padres de tu mamá/papá?
¿Tienes hermanos? ¿Cuántos? ¿Cómo se llaman? ¿Cómo son?
¿Quién es tu pariente favorito? ¿Por qué?
¿Tienes primos?

PASO 2.   Report to the class your reaction about your partner's family. Use the family tree you created and any other details you learned during your interview to support your reaction.

> **MODELO:**   ¡Qué pequeña familia tiene Joe! Es hijo único. Vive con su mamá y papá y no tiene mascotas.

COMUN VOCAB **ESTRUCTURA** CTATE

⟳ Reciclaje

Adjectives

Expansion (Reciclaje): Ask students how their answers would be different if there were also a brother.

The Grammy award–winning Mexican singer Julieta Venegas has an identical twin sister Yvonne, an accomplished and very successful photographer whose work has been exhibited at several major museums. Given this information, and given the photo here, how would you describe the two sisters? Choose from the adjectives provided. **¡Atención!** Be sure to make the adjectives agree!

> bonito/a   delgado/a   feo/a   gordo/a
> joven   pobre   rico/a   viejo/a

Las hermanas Venegas son...

bonitas____ , delgadas____ ,
jóvenes____ y ricas____ .

■ Answers to this activity are in Appendix 2 at the back of your book.

4.1 Es más alto que su padre

Comparatives

Para empezar...

As in some other European countries with monarchies, Spain's **familia real** (*royal family*) has played a prominent but mainly ceremonial role in the country. Members of the family include **el rey** (*king*) Felipe VI, **la reina** (*queen*) Letizia, and the king's parents **el rey** Juan Carlos I and **la reina** Sofía.* King Felipe and Queen Letizia have two daughters, **la princesa** Leonor and **la princesa** Sofía. Match each of the statements below to a member of the royal family. **¡Atención!** Some items have more than one possible answer.

■ Answers to these activities are in Appendix 2 at the back of your book.

	LA REINA LETIZIA	EL REY FELIPE	EL REY JUAN CARLOS	LA REINA SOFÍA	LA PRINCESA SOFÍA	LA PRINCESA LEONOR
1. Es más (*more*) alto que su padre.	☐	☑	☐	☐	☐	☐
2. Es más delgada que su esposo.	☑	☐	☐	☑	☐	☐
3. Es más bajo que su hijo.	☐	☐	☑	☐	☐	☐
4. Es más alta que sus nietas.	☐	☐	☐	☑	☐	☐
5. Es más alto que su esposa.	☐	☑	☑	☐	☐	☐
6. Es más baja que su mamá.	☐	☐	☐	☐	☑	☑

*With King Juan Carlos' abdication of the throne in 2014, **el príncipe** (*prince*) Felipe became king and his wife became queen. The former king and queen retain their titles for life.

José es más alto que Antonio.

Point out: You may want to point out that *más* has an accent mark to differentiate it from *mas,* a synonym of the more common word *pero,* which means *but.*

■ For more on expressing comparisons and superlatives in Spanish, see **Para saber más 4.1** at the back of your book.

Suggestion Act. Analítica 3: Bring 4–6 images of well-known people, and ask the class to compare pairs of images. *¿Quién es mejor (actor/cantante/atleta)? ¿Quién es peor (actor/cantante/atleta)? ¿Quién es mayor? ¿Quién es menor?*

Suggestion (Act. Analítica 4): Point out to students that when not referring to someone's age, *más/menos viejo* is used: *Este libro es más viejo que ese libro.*

Script (Act. A): Select two students who are sitting where everyone can see them (reseat them if necessary). Suggested sentences: **1.** _____ *es más alto/a que* _____. **2.** _____ *tiene el pelo más rubio que* _____. **3.** _____ *es mayor que* _____. **4.** _____ *es menos alto/a que* _____. **5.** _____ *tiene más libros que* _____. **6.** _____ *tiene una mochila más grande que* _____.

Sofía Vergara, actriz colombiana

Actividades analíticas

1 In English, to make comparisons in which one person has *more* of a given quality, *-er* may be added to the adjective: *Mary is taller than Catherine.*

The word *more* may also be used: *Mary is more intelligent than Catherine.*

What word is used to make these comparisons in Spanish? __más__

Where English uses the word *than*, Spanish uses **que.**

José es **más** alto **que** Antonio.	*José is taller than Antonio.*
Mónica y Julia son **más** delgadas **que** José	*Mónica and Julia are thinner than José.*

You can see in these comparisons that the adjective agrees with the subject, just as it would in any other sentence.

2 To express a comparison in which one person has *less* of a given quality than the other, use **menos.**

Antonio es **menos** alto **que** José.	*Antonio is less tall than (not as tall as) José.*

Now try converting the following statements with **más** into ones with **menos. ¡Atención!** Be sure the adjective agrees with the subject.

María es más rica que Celia. → Celia es __menos rica__ que María.

Juan es más alto que Marisela. → Marisela es __menos alta__ que Juan.

Patricia es más alta que los niños. → Los niños son __menos altos__ que Patricia.

3 For the adjectives **bueno** and **malo,** there are special comparative forms.

mejor	*better*	Mi hermano es **mejor** jugador de fútbol que yo.
		My brother is a better soccer player than I am.
peor	*worse*	El lunes es **peor** que el martes.
		Monday is worse than Tuesday.

4 When comparing people's ages, it is common to use **mayor** (*older*) and **menor** (*younger*).

Arturo es **mayor** que su hermana.	*Arturo is older than his sister.*
Yo soy **menor** que tú.	*I'm younger than you.*
Nosotros somos **menores** que nuestros amigos.	*We're younger than our friends.*

Note that these comparative forms do not change based on gender, but they do show number agreement: **mejores, peores, mayores, menores.**

Note (Para saber más): *Para saber más 4.1* covers *más de* with numerals, comparatives of equality, and superlatives.

Autoprueba

Use the adjectives given to create comparisons with **más.** Be sure to make the adjective agree with the subject and be aware of adjectives that have special comparative forms.

1. Arturo y Beatriz son _____ que Ernesto. (*fuerte*)
2. Elena está _____ que Javier. (*contento*)
3. Tus padres son muy viejos. Son _____ que mis abuelos. (*mayor*)
4. El coche de mi hermano es _____ que el coche de mi primo. (*bueno*)

Respuestas: 1. más fuertes **2.** más contenta **3.** mayores **4.** mejor

Actividades prácticas

 A. ¿Cómo son mis compañeros/as? Listen as your instructor compares two of your classmates. For each statement, write **C** for **cierto** or **F** for **falso.**

1. ____　2. ____　3. ____　4. ____　5. ____　6. ____

B. ¿Quién es más famoso?   Which Spanish-speaking celebrities are famous in your country? Are some better known than others? Complete each of the following sentences with **más famoso/a** or **menos famoso/a**.

En mi país...

1. Juanes es _____ que Shakira.
2. Penélope Cruz es _____ que Javier Bardem.
3. Antonio Banderas es _____ que Diego Luna.
4. Julieta Venegas es _____ que Gael García Bernal.
5. Daddy Yankee es _____ que Plácido Domingo.
6. Salma Hayek es _____ que Sofía Vergara.

 C. ¿Qué te dice una foto?

PASO 1.   In pairs, look at the photos and read the descriptions of each person. Then write a statement comparing each person to someone else.

MODELO: Angélica es menos seria que Carolina.
Diego es más estudioso que Ignacio y Erick.

Denise, de Argentina

Estudia teatro. Canta y baila mucho.

Carolina, de Colombia

Estudia cine. Lee mucho, ve películas y viaja (*travels*).

Angélica, de Costa Rica

Trabaja en un hotel. Cocina y pasa tiempo con la familia y con amigos.

Diego, de México

Estudia derecho (*law*). Va a fiestas con amigos y baila.

Erick, de Nicaragua

Trabaja en un parque nacional. Sale a comer con amigos y va al cine.

Ignacio, de España

Trabaja en un banco. Viaja mucho a otros países.

PASO 2.   Now match up people who you think have something in common, such as classes, activities, or interests. Share your answers with the class.

MODELOS: Carolina e Ignacio tienen mucho en común porque los dos (*both of them*) viajan.

D. Una clasificación

PASO 1.   With a partner, rank the items in each list from 1 to 4 (1 = **máximo,** 4 = **mínimo**), according to the criterion given.

CARO/A (*expensive*)	DIFÍCIL	PEOR
____ un Ford	____ un curso de español	____ un examen de matemáticas
____ un Kia	____ un curso de historia	____ una cita (*appointment*) con el dentista
____ un Mercedes	____ un curso de matemáticas	____ un día sin (*without*) hablar con amigos
____ un Rolls-Royce	____ un curso de química	____ una noche sin dormir

(*Continues*)

Suggestion (Act. B): Have teams of students research and do mini reports on the celebrities. They should be able to present name, age, country of origin, a basic physical description, and profession, all in Spanish.

Note (Act. B): There are no correct answers to this exercise. What matters (and what can be interesting) is who students perceive to be more famous and whether everyone's perceptions are the same.

Expansion (Act. B): Have students rank all of these people, from most famous to least, with a series of statements such as *X es más famoso que Y* and *Y es más famoso que Z.*

Note (Act. C): Certain preferred words for describing men and women vary by region. You may want to suggest which words they use (for example, *guapo* for men and *bonita* for women), or you may leave it as their choice.

Suggestion (Act. C): Have students recycle "mejor". Ask separately about the men and women: *Entre Denise e Ignacio, ¿quién es mejor actor o actriz? Entre Diego y Erick, ¿quién es mejor bailador?*

Suggestion (Act. C, Paso 1): Write each name on the board as headings and have students contribute statements about two people, writing them under the appropriate name.

Suggestion (Act. D): Write each adjective as a heading on the board and ask one student from each pair to write a sentence under one of the headings. Lead a class discussion of each heading to see if there are any interesting differences of opinion.

DIVERTIDO/A	MAYOR	MEJOR
_____ un concierto	_____ un abuelo	_____ una película de acción
_____ un examen	_____ un padre	_____ una película cómica
_____ una noche con la familia	_____ un hijo	_____ una película romántica
_____ una película	_____ un bisabuelo	_____ una película de terror

PASO 2.   For each category, create a statement that compares the top-ranked member (number 1) with the lowest ranked member (number 4).

> **MODELO:**   Una película romántica es mejor que una película de terror.

E. La familia de tu compañero/a

Interview a classmate about his/her family. Select four family members (for example, **abuelo/a, tío/a, hermano/a, primo/a**) and then find out how they compare. In addition to the obvious information (who is older, younger, taller, or shorter), find out more interesting information as well (such as, who is more intelligent, who is funnier, and so on). Take good notes so you can share your findings with the class!

F. Cultura: La planificación (*planning*) familiar en Guatemala

PASO 1.   Read the following text about Guatemala.

En ciertas comunidades del altiplano[a] guatemalteco, las familias son muy grandes. En esta región, la tasa de fertilidad[b] es muy alta. Muchas veces las madres tienen hasta[c] diez u once hijos.

Hay organizaciones internacionales que se dedican a ofrecerles alternativas a estas familias. Los trabajadores de estas organizaciones están preocupados por[d] las familias, en particular por la salud[e] de las madres y sus hijos. Las mujeres pueden tener problemas de salud porque sus cuerpos[f] no tienen mucho tiempo para descansar entre cada embarazo.[g] Otro problema en las familias con muchos hijos es que todos necesitan comer. Muchas veces los padres no tienen suficiente dinero y los hijos sufren hambre[h] o malnutrición.

Sin embargo,[i] no todas las mujeres del altiplano quieren[j] usar contraceptivos para limitar el número de hijos que tienen. La mayoría de las familias son mayas católicas. Según sus tradiciones culturales y religiosas, no es normal controlar o planificar[k] el número de hijos en una familia. En algunos[l] casos, las mujeres sí quieren usar contraceptivos, pero sus maridos no están de acuerdo.[m] Las organizaciones de salud continúan ofreciendo a las mujeres programas educativos sobre[n] la salud femenina y la planificación familiar.

[a]*high plains* [b]*tasa... fertility rate* [c]*up to* [d]*preocupados... worried about* [e]*health* [f]*bodies* [g]*entre... between pregnancies* [h]*sufren... suffer from hunger* [i]*Sin... However* [j]*want* [k]*to plan* [l]*some* [m]*no... don't agree* [n]*about*

PASO 2.   Complete the sentences with **más... que** or **menos... que** to create logical comparisons according to the information found in the reading.

1. El altiplano de Guatemala tiene una tasa de fertilidad ____más____ alta ____que____ la tasa de fertilidad de otros países.
2. Las familias de otras partes de Latinoamérica son ____menos____ grandes ____que____ las familias del altiplano guatemalteco.
3. La malnutrición es ____más____ frecuente en las familias grandes ____que____ en las familias pequeñas.
4. La planificación familiar es ____menos____ común en las familias mayas católicas ____que____ en familias de otras tradiciones culturales y religiosas.

PASO 3.   With a partner, answer the following questions and discuss the ideas behind your responses.

1. En algunos países hispanos, hay mujeres que quieren tener muchos hijos por razones (*reasons*) prácticas. ¿Puedes pensar en una de esas razones prácticas?
2. En Guatemala y en muchos otros países, en general las mujeres en las áreas urbanas tienen menos hijos que las mujeres en las áreas rurales. ¿Por qué crees (do you think that is so)?
3. En Guatemala, las mujeres con más acceso a la educación tienen menos hijos. ¿Es así en los Estados Unidos también?

Suggestion (Act. E): Tell students to use the rankings in the previous activity as a model. You may want to provide them with 3-4 adjectives to serve as a base for comparison. When they are done, ask some to come to the board, list the family members, and explain how they compare on a certain quality.

Guatemala

Una mujer guatemalteca

Note/Answers (Act. F, Paso 3): 1. Help students express some ideas in simple Spanish: *Los hijos pueden trabajar y ayudar a la familia económicamente; Los hijos pueden ayudar a los padres en su vejez,* and so on. 2. Help students express ideas: *En las áreas urbanas, las mujeres pueden trabajar fuera de la casa, van a la universidad,* and so on. 3. This is true in the U.S., as it is around the world.

Reciclaje

Present indicative

Categorize these activities into those that you do with your family together (**juntos**), those that you do alone (**solo/a**), and those that you don't do at all.

almorzar	cocinar	jugar al fútbol
cantar	correr	mirar la televisión
cenar	desayunar	nadar

MODELO: Mis amigos y yo cenamos juntos. Almuerzo sola y no desayuno.

Suggestion (Reciclaje): Do a quick poll of the class to find out what people do together with their families (or have students write their answers on the board) and look for any trends in the answers.

Note (Para empezar): The words here are these people's real answers. Remind students that there are several ways to answer the telephone in Spanish, and that each region has its own preferred way. Share with students how you answer the phone in Spanish, or give them other ways of answering not listed here, and remind them that they will be understood regardless of which term they use.

4.2 ¿Qué dices para contestar el teléfono?

Stem-changing verbs: e → i

Para empezar...

When you answer the phone (**contestar el teléfono**), what do you say? Here is what people from around the Spanish-speaking world say.

Nadia Angélica, de México:
Decimos «bueno».

Luis, de Nicaragua:
Decimos «hola».

María, de Argentina:
Decimos «hola».

Mario, de España:
Decimos «diga».

Edgardo, de Venezuela:
Decimos «aló».

Now complete the following sentences, then say how you answer the telephone.

1. Los argentinos **dicen** (*say*) __«hola»__ para contestar el teléfono.
2. Los españoles **dicen** __«diga»__ para contestar el teléfono.
3. Los mexicanos **dicen** __«bueno»__ para contestar el teléfono.
4. Los nicaragüenses **dicen** __«hola»__ para contestar el teléfono.
5. Los venezolanos **dicen** __«aló»__ para contestar el teléfono.
6. En mi país, **decimos** _____ para contestar el teléfono.

Actividades analíticas

1 In the **Para empezar** activity, you saw two forms of the verb **decir** (*to say*). Use these forms and what you know about verb endings in general to complete the conjugation in the chart.

You may notice that the **yo** form (**digo**) has a **g**, which might seem unexpected. This is because **decir** has an irregular **yo** form, a trait we will discuss in depth in **Capítulo 5**. For now, we'll focus on the other forms.

decir (e → i)	
SINGULAR	
yo	digo
tú	dices
él/ella, Ud.	dice
PLURAL	
nosotros/as	decimos
vosotros/as	decís
ellos/ellas, Uds.	dicen

- Answers to these activities are in Appendix 2 at the back of your book.

Suggestion (Act. analíticas 1):
- If students struggle with the *tú* form, remind them that they simply need to add an -s to the *él/ella, Ud.* form.
- Remind students that the infinitive form (*hablar, comer, decir*) is made up of two parts: the stem and the ending. The ending is the last two letters, the -ar, -er, or -ir part of the verb. The stem is the rest of the verb: *habl-, com-, dec-*. When we talk about stem-changing verbs, we are referring to changes to the last vowel of the stem. With *decir*, for example, the stem is *dec-*, so the change happens in the e.

(*Continues*)

2 The endings on the verb forms of **decir** are completely regular, but the stem vowel (**la vocal de la raíz**) changes: sometimes it is **e** (as in **decir**) and sometimes it is **i** (as in **dice**). The stem vowel **e** is used in the infinitive **decir** and in the **nosotros/as** and **vosotros/as** forms. In all other forms, the stem vowel changes to **i**.

3 There are other verbs that behave in a similar way. Two examples are **servir** (*to serve*) and **pedir** (*to ask for*). These verbs have an **e** in the infinitive and the **nosotros/as** and **vosotros/as** forms, and this vowel becomes **i** in all other forms. Use this information to complete the conjugations of these verbs.

	servir (e → i)	pedir (e → i)
SINGULAR		
yo	sirvo	pido
tú	sirves	pides
él/ella, Ud.	sirve	pide
PLURAL		
nosotros/as	servimos	pedimos
vosotros/as	servís	pedís
ellos/ellas, Uds.	sirven	piden

Both of these verbs are very common in everyday Spanish.

Sirven desayuno en ese restaurante.   *They serve breakfast at that restaurant.*

¿**Pedimos** café?   *Shall we ask for coffee?*

Servir is often used in the sense of *to work* (as in whether something functions or not) or, with **para,** to express *to be good* at/for *doing* something.

¿Tu computadora **sirve?**   *Does your computer work?*

No **sirvo para** jugar al fútbol.   *I'm no good at playing soccer.*

The rest of this chapter will concentrate on **decir, servir,** and **pedir,** but now that you know how these verbs work, you can conjugate any member of this family of verbs. Some other common verbs in this family are **repetir** (*to repeat*) and **seguir** (*to follow*).

Repito las palabras difíciles.   *I repeat the difficult words.*

Paula siempre **sigue** las instrucciones.   *Paula always follows the instructions.*

Note (Para saber más): *Para saber más 4.2* covers the verbs *conseguir, reír,* and *sonreír.*

■ For additional **e → i** stem-changing verbs, see **Para saber más 4.2** at the back of your book.

Autoprueba

Use what you now know about verbs with the **e → i** stem change to provide these forms for **repetir** and **seguir.**

repetir (e → i)
1. yo _____
2. tú _____
3. nosotras _____

seguir (e → i)
4. Uds. _____
5. nosotros _____
6. ella _____

Respuestas: 1. repito **2.** repites **3.** repetimos **4.** siguen **5.** seguimos **6.** sigue

Actividades prácticas

A. ¿Para qué sirve?   A family, like any group, is a mix of people with varying strengths and weaknesses. Think of those things that individuals in your own family are *not* especially good at and complete the following sentences, adding or subtracting family members as needed.

1. No sirvo para _____
2. Mi padre no sirve para _____
3. Mi madre no sirve para _____
4. Mi hermano/a no sirve para _____
5. _____ no sirve para _____
6. En general en mi familia, no servimos para _____

B. ¿Qué piden para tomar?   You have probably observed that in some families, everyone is remarkably alike, whereas in others, each family member is very different from the others. In your family, what does everyone order to drink when you go out to eat? Using the following list of beverages, state what your family's preferences are. Do you all ask for the same thing (**lo mismo**) or for different things (**cosas diferentes**)? Answer using complete sentences.

> **MODELOS:**   En mi familia, todos pedimos lo mismo.
> Pedimos leche.
> Pedimos cosas diferentes. Mi papá pide cerveza, mi mamá pide jugo, mis hermanas piden soda y yo pido leche.

café   cerveza
jugo (*juice*)   leche (*milk*)
soda   té (*tea*)
vino (*wine*)

C. Saludar a los padres de los amigos   How do you greet a parent of one of your friends? When you say *hi* or *hello* to him/her, do you add anything else, such as *sir/ma'am, Mr./Mrs.*, or use a first name? What do you think people generally say in Spanish? For each sentence, in the first blank write the correct form of **decir,** then on the second line write the greeting you would say. **¡Atención!** In cases where you don't say anything, mark an X.

Para saludar a uno de los padres de un amigo o una amiga, ...

1. yo __digo__ (decir), «*Hello/Hi,* _____».
2. otros __dicen__ (decir), «*Hello/Hi,* _____».
3. en general, en nuestro país nosotros __decimos__ (decir), «*Hello/Hi,* _____».
4. en general, los hispanohablantes (*Spanish speakers*) __dicen__ (decir), «*Hola,* _____».

Expansion (Act. A): Use *servir para* as an opportunity to recycle classroom vocabulary. Give students the names of several classroom items (pens, backpacks, calculators, the internet, and so on) and have them explain what each one is good for. (e.g., *Las mochilas sirven para llevar los libros y otras cosas.*)

Suggestion (Act. B): Add other items to this list that are popular among your students, or lexical variants that you are more comfortable with (e.g., *zumo, refresco*).

Suggestion (Act. B): Have students briefly write out family members' names and their preferred beverages before answering the questions.

Note (Act. C): Individuals will vary in their responses, but in circumstances like this, English-speakers generally say *hello* without anything else, whereas many Spanish speakers would consider it odd not to add *señor* or *señora* (usually without the last name). There is much regional variation on this point, however, and you may want to share your own usage with students.

Suggestion (Act. C): Create two columns on the board labeled *En inglés decimos* and *En español dicen*. As students give you their answers, write them under the first column. Then put *señor/señora* under the second column, and point out that is nearly obligatory for many Spanish speakers. You may also want to give other options in addition to (or instead of) *hola.*

Note (Act. D): This type of activity gives students practice with **decir**, but it also helps develop their "transcultural competence" (their ability to view their own culture and language the way an outsider might).

Suggestion (Act. D):
• Point out that *¡salud!* is more common in Latin America and *¡Jesús!* is more common in Spain. Other points of variation include *madre/mamá/mami/mamita* and *padre/papá/papi/papito,* and the various ways of answering the phone. Emphasize the main point: Spanish and English are alike in offering several ways of saying the same thing.
• To save time, divide the class into three groups and assign each group one case.

Suggestion (Act. D, Paso 2): Have students work in small groups with others who chose or were assigned the same case. Advise students to use words like *muchos* and *algunos* in their statements. For example, *Muchos decimos* «mom» *y algunos dicen* «mother». Write the three cases as headings on the board and have each group write their statement under the appropriate heading.

D. ¿Qué dices?   You have already seen examples where there is more than one way to say something in Spanish. The same phenomenon occurs in English. Here are three well-known cases, as they might be described in a textbook for Spanish speakers learning English.

■ Para decir **¡salud!** o **¡Jesús!** cuando una persona estornuda (*sneezes*), dicen *bless you* o *gesundheit,* o no dicen nada.
■ Para decir **mamá** (cuando hablan con ella), dicen *Mom, Mommy, Momma, Mother* o *Ma*.
■ Para decir **papá** (cuando hablan con él), dicen *Dad, Daddy, Pop, Father* o *Pa*.

PASO 1.   Are these statements about English accurate? To find out, choose one of these cases, ask at least five classmates what they say, and keep track of the results.

> **MODELO:**   Para decir **mamá** en inglés, ¿qué dices tú?

PASO 2.   If a Spanish speaker who was learning English asked you about one of these cases, what would you say? Use the information you gathered in **Paso 1** to create a statement describing which words your classmates actually say. **¡Atención!** If your statement includes yourself, use **decimos.** If it does not include you, use **dicen.**

Suggestion (Act. E): Create three columns on the board: *Nosotros/Nosotras, Los hijos, El empleado / La empleada.* Ask some pairs of students to write their answers to *Paso 2* on the board.

E. El trabajo de la casa

PASO 1.   In many parts of Latin America, middle-class families often employ full-time domestic help, which means that multiple people are available to do any household chore: the parent(s), the children, or the employee (**el empleado / la empleada**). Imagine that you are the head of a household in Latin America and you need to make a list of who is going to do which task. Place each task in the list below under the appropriate heading, keeping in mind that no single person can do everything. **¡Atención!** You will need to conjugate each verb according to who is doing that task.

lavar la ropa (*wash clothes*)   **preparar el desayuno**   **servir el café /**
lavar los platos (*dishes*)   **preparar la cena**   **la leche por la mañana**
limpiar (*clean*) **la casa**   **servir el almuerzo**   **servir el desayuno**
preparar el almuerzo   **servir la cena**

YO	MIS HIJOS	EL EMPLEADO / LA EMPLEADA

PASO 2.   Now compare your answers with those of a classmate. Do the two of you have anything in common in your choices? Report this to the class. Is there anything that the whole class has in common?

> **MODELO:**   Lavamos la ropa y servimos el almuerzo. Los hijos preparan la cena.
> La empleada sirve la cena.

⟳ Reciclaje

The infinitive of the verb

For many people, the weekends are when they have the most free time, but even then, it's difficult to squeeze in everything they want to do. Make two lists: one with what you *are* able to get done on weekends (**Puedo...**) and one with what you generally are *not* able to get done on weekends (**No puedo...**).

4.3 ¿Adónde quieren ir?

Stem-changing verbs: e → ie

Para empezar...

Some friends are visiting from out of town, and you need to find out what they want to do. For each question that you ask them from column **A,** choose an answer that makes sense from column **B.**

A	**B**
1. __c__ ¿**Quieren** (*do you* [*pl.*] *want*) comer en un restaurante?	a. Sí, **queremos** ver una película de terror.
2. __d__ ¿Adónde **quieren** ir?	b. Sí, ¡vamos a la playa!
3. __e__ ¿**Quieren** ver la universidad?	c. No, no tenemos hambre.
4. __b__ ¿**Quieren** ir a nadar?	d. **Queremos** ir al parque.
5. __a__ ¿**Quieren** ir al cine?	e. Sí, **queremos** ver dónde estudias.

- Answers to these activities are in Appendix 2 at the back of your book.

Actividades analíticas

1 In **Para empezar**, you saw two forms of the verb **querer** (*to want*). Add these forms to the conjugation below.

querer (e → ie)	
SINGULAR	
yo	qu**ie**ro
tú	qu**ie**res
él/ella, Ud.	qu**ie**re
PLURAL	
nosotros/as	queremos
vosotros/as	queréis
ellos/ellas, Uds.	quieren

2 In the infinitive of **querer**, the stem vowel is **e**, as it is also in the **nosotros/as** and **vosotros/as** forms. In all of the other conjugated forms, this vowel changes to **ie**. Everything else about the conjugation of **querer** is completely regular.

| ¡**Quiero** dormir! | *I want to sleep!* |
| Mañana **queremos** jugar fútbol. | *We want to play soccer tomorrow.* |

Note (**Para saber más**): *Para saber más 4.3* covers the verbs *cerrar, comenzar, entender, perder,* and *preferir.*

- For additional **e → ie** stem-changing verbs, see **Para saber más 4.3** at the back of your book.

(Continues)

Autoprueba

See if you can give the forms of verbs in each of the three stem-changing families (o → ue, e → i, e → ie).

dormir
1. yo _____
2. tú _____
3. nosotros _____

pedir
4. nosotras _____
5. él _____
6. yo _____

pensar
7. ella _____
8. Uds. _____
9. nosotros _____

Respuestas: 1. duermo 2. duermes 3. dormimos 4. pedimos 5. pide 6. pido 7. piensa 8. piensan 9. pensamos

En español...

Many of the verbs that we see in this section are often followed by an infinitive.

Juan **quiere andar** en bicicleta.
Juan wants to ride bikes.
Angélica **piensa comprar** un coche.
Angélica is thinking about / planning to buy a car.

Some verbs are followed by another word and then the infinitive.

To express that somebody starts an action, use

empezar a + *inf.*
Los niños **empiezan a comer** a las dos.
The children begin to eat at 2:00.

To use **tener** to express that someone *has to do something,* you will need to add **que.**

tener que + *inf.*
Tenemos que leer ese libro.
We have to read that book.

There is a whole family of verbs that behave like **querer,** including **empezar** (*to begin*) and **pensar** (*to think, to plan*).

Nuestra clase **empieza** a las once.   *Our class begins at 11:00.*

¿**Piensas** ir a la biblioteca esta noche?   *Are you planning to go to the library tonight?*

Following the pattern with **querer,** complete the conjugations for **empezar** and **pensar.**

	empezar (e → ie)	pensar (e → ie)
SINGULAR		
yo	empiezo	pienso
tú	empiezas	piensas
él/ella, Ud.	empieza	piensa
PLURAL		
nosotros/as	empezamos	pensamos
vosotros/as	empezáis	pensáis
ellos/ellas, Uds.	empiezan	piensan

The verb **tener,** which you already know, is also a member of this family.

¿**Tienes** un diccionario?   *Do you have a dictionary?*

Tenemos un examen el martes.   *We have a test on Tuesday.*

3 We have now seen three families of verbs in which the vowel in the stem changes.

	o → ue	e → i	e → ie
Ejemplos:	**poder**	**decir**	**querer**
	dormir	**servir**	**pensar**
	almorzar	**pedir**	**empezar**

Expansion (Act. analíticas 3): Review here the fact that all 3 families follow the same simple principle: The vowel in the stem changes when it is stressed (*La vocal de la raíz cambia cuando está acentuada / es tónica*).

The vowel change that occurs is different in each family, but the change always occurs in the same forms: everywhere except the infinitive and the **nosotros/as** and **vosotros/as** forms.

Actividades prácticas

A. Empiezas a vivir

Suggestion (Act. A, Paso 1): Emphasize that students should answer based on what they think is true for *most people* in their country. Their own personal experience may have been different.

PASO 1. Working with a partner, place the following events on a timeline based on the age at which they occur for *most people* in your country. Then, report your results to the class. Can you all reach a consensus on what is typical for most people in your country?

MODELO: A los 28 años, quieres empezar a tener hijos.

1. Quieres empezar a tener hijos.
2. Empiezas a pensar que tus padres no son perfectos.
3. Empiezas a vivir fuera (*away*) de la casa de tus padres.
4. Empiezas a salir con chicos/chicas y tener citas (*dates*).
5. Quieres casarte (*get married*).
6. Piensas que eres más inteligente que tus padres.

Suggestion (Act. A, Paso 1): Draw a timeline on the board, and then go through each event on the list, asking students to tell you when each occurs. Alternatively, give each pair of students an event, and ask them to place that event on the timeline on the board.

PASO 2. In many parts of the Spanish-speaking world, and especially in Latin America, children typically live with their parents until they get married, which for many people means until at least their late 20s. Select the answer below to compare this to what your class put on its timeline.

En general, los latinoamericanos empiezan a vivir fuera de la casa de sus padres...

a. más tarde que nosotros.
b. más temprano que nosotros.
c. a la misma edad (*age*) que nosotros.

Note (Act. A, Paso 2): This activity gives students exposure to this family of stem-changing verbs, but it also helps develop their transcultural competence by allowing them to see that their culture's way of organizing one's life is one possibility, but not the only way.

B. Unos consejos   Parents are known for giving lots of advice to their children, and Spanish-speaking parents are no exception. Match the information in the two columns to create sensible advice (and commands disguised as advice!).

1. __c__ Si (*If*) quieres sacar (*get*) buenas notas (*grades*),...
2. __f__ Si piensas comprar un auto,...
3. __d__ Si no quieres ser tan (*so*) delgado/a,...
4. __e__ Si quieres ir al cine con tus amigos,...
5. __g__ Si pensamos comprar una casa,...
6. __h__ Si tus amigos quieren sacar buenas notas,...
7. __b__ Si empezamos a limpiar todos,...
8. __a__ Si empiezas a estudiar hoy,...

a. vas a estar listo/a (*ready*) para el examen mañana.
b. podemos tener la casa muy limpia.
c. tienes que estudiar mucho.
d. tienes que comer más.
e. primero (*first*) tienes que limpiar la casa.
f. tienes que empezar a ahorrar (*save*) más.
g. tenemos que empezar a ahorrar más.
h. tienen que estudiar mucho.

C. ¿Qué tienes que hacer? ¿Qué quieres hacer?

PASO 1.   Time is precious and responsibilities often take precedence over things we want to do . . . and vice versa! Think about your average weekend. What do you have to do? What do you want to do? What about your family members? What do they have to do and want to do? What can you normally get done?

> **MODELO:**   Los fines de semana tengo que estudiar y trabajar, pero quiero dormir y ver películas (*movies*).
> Mi padre quiere mirar la televisión los fines de semana, pero tiene que hacer ejercicio.
> Normalmente puedo dormir y también estudiar, pero no puedo mirar muchas películas.

 PASO 2.   With a classmate, compare weekends. Whose do you prefer?

Suggestion (Act. D): Give students a couple of minutes to read through and answer these questions. Then divide them in groups of 4 or 5, and have them ask each other the questions. Give them a time limit for Paso 2 and make it clear that they need to stay focused on the task.

D. Tu vida en el futuro

PASO 1.   We all have ideas of how we would like to live in the future, but do we all think the same? First, ask yourself the following questions about your life over the next several years and write your answers on a separate piece of paper.

1. ¿Quieres tener hijos? (¿Ya (*already*) tienes hijos?) ¿Cuántos?
2. ¿Quieres vivir en la ciudad o en el campo (*countryside*)?
3. ¿Piensas estudiar más para sacar la maestría (*master's*) o el doctorado (*doctorate*)?
4. ¿Quieres tener un perro o un gato?

PASO 2.   Now ask three or four of your classmates the same questions and keep track of their answers, then share your findings with the class. Did anyone answer two of the questions the same as you? Three of the questions? All four?

Expansion (Act. D, Paso 2): Ask students to create statements on their findings for the class. For example: *Mark, Brittany y yo tenemos tres cosas en común. Queremos tener tres hijos, queremos vivir en la ciudad y no pensamos estudiar más.*

Suggestion (Act. A, Paso 2): Share experiences on this topic from your own life or from that of family members or friends. Students will do more with this information in the *Leamos* section at the end of the chapter.

Si quieres ir a la fiesta, tienes que hacer la tarea.

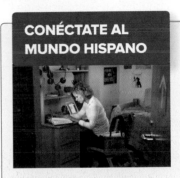

CONÉCTATE AL MUNDO HISPANO

Latin Americans and Spaniards are often surprised to hear that North Americans traditionally move away from their parents' home to attend university. In many countries, this would be considered a needless extravagance, unless there were some very good reason for it (such as, to pursue a major not offered at your local university). In addition, many universities in the Spanish-speaking world do not have housing for students, and off-campus housing is sometimes difficult to find or very expensive. For these reasons, it is more common for students to live with their parents and attend a university in their area.

Suggestion (Act. D): If you are at a community college, add *licenciatura* (*bachelor's*) to the list of ways to *estudiar más* in **Q3**.

Expansion (Act. E): Ask students to use examples of their own and their partner's plans to answer a bigger question: *En nuestro país, ¿hacemos mucho con nuestras familias?* For purposes of comparison, add personal experiences of family life in the Spanish-speaking world.

Expansion (Reciclaje): Ask students to identify the infinitive of the verb in each sentence and to explain why *ser* or *estar* is used. In all of the examples here, *ser* expresses origin, and *estar* expresses a condition subject to change.

E. Tu familia y el fin de semana   Many Spanish speakers have the idea that North Americans are not very close to their families and don't interact with them much. To what extent is this true? In this spirit, ask your partner what he/she plans to do this weekend (or on the next school break) that involves his/her family (parents, siblings, spouse, children, and so on).

> **MODELO:**   E1: ¿Qué piensas hacer con tu familia este fin de semana / durante (*during*) las vacaciones?
>
> E2: Pienso cenar con mis padres el sábado. El domingo, quiero jugar fútbol con mi hermano.

↻ Reciclaje

The verbs *ser* and *estar*

Read through these statements and check off those that are true for you. Then, talk to a classmate and find out which statements are true for him/her.

> **MODELO:** ¿Eres de los Estados Unidos?

	YO	MI COMPAÑERO/A
1. Soy de los Estados Unidos.	☐	☐
2. Soy de Canadá.	☐	☐
3. Soy de otro país.	☐	☐
4. Mi madre es de otro país.	☐	☐
5. Mi padre es de otro país.	☐	☐
6. Estoy contento/a hoy (*today*).	☐	☐
7. Estoy muy ansioso/a hoy.	☐	☐

La actriz Cecilia Roth y el músico Fito Páez

■ Answers to these activities are in Appendix 2 at the back of your book.

4.4   Es su mamá; está en Argentina.

Ser and *estar* for identity and location

Para empezar...

Cecilia Roth is an Argentinian actress, partly raised in Spain, who now works in both countries. Her mother and brother are also well-known entertainers, but all three have adopted stage names (**nombres artísticos**) so you might not know that they are related. Choose the right ending for each of these sentences. **¡Atención!** In Spanish, everyone has both **un apellido paterno** and **un apellido materno** and women often continue to use their birth name after marriage.

1. Cecilia Roth **es** __c__.
2. Dina Rot **es** __b__ y __f__.
3. Ariel Rot **es** __d__ y __e__.
4. Martín Páez Rotenberg **es** __a__.
5. Fito Páez **es** __h__.
6. Dina Rot **está** __k__.
7. Fito Páez **está** __g__.
8. Cecilia Roth trabaja mucho en España pero sus padres **están** __l__ y viven en diferentes países.
9. Cecilia Roth, Dina Rot y Ariel Rot **son** __i__, pero **están** __j__.

a. el hijo de Cecilia Roth y Fito Páez
b. el nombre artístico de Dina Gutkin, la cantante
c. el nombre artístico de Cecilia Rotenberg Gutkin
d. el nombre artístico del músico español Ariel Rotenberg Gutkin
e. el hermano de Cecilia Roth
f. la madre de Cecilia Roth
g. muy orgulloso de su ex esposa
h. un músico argentino y el ex esposo de Cecilia Roth
i. familiares
j. en diferentes países
k. muy orgullosa de su hija
l. divorciados

Actividades analíticas

1 In **Para empezar,** you saw these forms of the verbs **ser** and **estar.**

ⓔⓢ   está   están   ⓢⓞⓝ

Circle those that are forms of **ser**; underline those that are forms of **estar.**

2 Often, a form of **estar** is followed by a phrase indicating location (**ubicación**). Find an example of this in **Para empezar.** ...están en diferentes países.

3 The forms of **ser** in **Para empezar** are always followed by a person, thing, or nationality.

Es el hermano de Cecilia Roth.   **Es** un músico argentino.

Son familiares.

This use of **ser** indicates the identity (**identidad**) of the subject.

4 This chart summarizes everything that you have seen so far about **ser** and **estar,** including the information from **Capítulos 1** and **2.**

ser	estar
Origin	Location
Soy de Los Ángeles.	Los hijos **están** en casa.
Identity	Characteristic that could change
Ese señor **es** mi papá.	**Estamos** cansados.

Now for each of the following sentences, identify the infinitive of the verb and say which of these four uses it exemplifies.

	VERB	USE
a. Argentina está en Sudamérica.	estar	location
b. Los niños están tristes.	estar	characteristic that could change
c. Mario es de Venezuela.	ser	origin
d. María y Vicente son estudiantes.	ser	identity

¿Por qué?

You may have noticed that the **yo** forms of **ser, estar,** and **ir** end in **-oy,** rather than the usual **-o.**

Soy estudiante.   **Estoy** en la universidad.   **Voy** a la biblioteca.

The verb **dar** (*to give*) behaves the same way: the **yo** form is **doy.** These verb forms might seem like an irregularity, but in fact there is a simple rule behind them. When the present tense **-o** ending is stressed, it is pronounced **-oy.** This is one more example of what you saw earlier with the **o → ue, e → i,** and **e → ie** families of verbs. In all of these cases, Spanish does what many languages around the world do: It changes the pronunciation of the vowel when it is stressed.

Suggestion (¿Por qué?): Write a table on the board with two columns (*Vocal no acentuada* and *Vocal acentuada*) and four rows (Row 1: _____ and *voy.* Row 2: *podemos* and _____. Row 3: _____ and *dice.* Row 4: *pensamos* and _____). Ask students to fill in blanks with an example of a verb form in which the underlined syllable is (un)stressed. Possible answers: *hablo, puede, decir, piensa.*

Suggestion (Act. analítica 4): Reproduce this chart on the board in Spanish (using VERBO and USO for the categories and *Origen, Identidad, Cambio* and *Ubicación* for the specific uses), Make sure students understand the noncognates *cambio* and *ubicación.*

Autoprueba

Use **ser** or **estar,** as appropriate, in each of the following sentences.

1. Mi mamá _____ muy contenta esta semana.
2. Mis primas _____ estudiantes en la universidad.
3. Jorge _____ de Canadá.
4. Mi hermano _____ en el trabajo.

Respuestas: 1. está **2.** son **3.** es **4.** está

Buenos Aires, Argentina

Actividades prácticas

A. ¡Adivinanzas! (*Riddles*)

PASO 1.   Work with a partner or small group to see if you can solve these riddles about cities or countries in the Spanish-speaking world. **¡Atención!** The four photos below provide clues to solving the riddles. If necessary, you can also consult the maps at the back of the book.

Hay hermosas playas en El Salvador.

El cerro Santa Ana es un barrio bonito de Guayaquil.

La Casa Milà de Antoni Gaudí está en Barcelona.

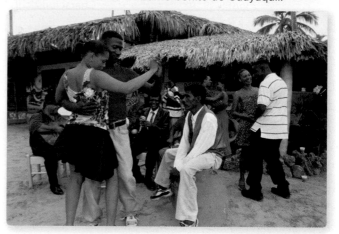

Se baila mucha bachata en la República Dominicana.

1. Estoy en un país.
   Es uno de los países de América Central.
   Está en la costa del Pacífico.
   Tiene frontera (*border*) con Guatemala y Honduras.
   ¿En qué país estoy? _____ El Salvador _____

2. Estoy en una ciudad.
   Está en Ecuador, pero no es la capital.
   Es más grande que la capital.
   Está en la costa del Pacífico.
   ¿En qué ciudad estoy? _____ Guayaquil _____

3. Estoy en una ciudad.
   No es la capital, pero es muy grande.
   Está en la costa del Mediterráneo.
   Está en España, muy cerca (*close*) de la frontera con Francia.
   ¿En qué ciudad estoy? _____ Barcelona _____

4. Estoy en un país.
   El país está en una isla (*island*).
   La isla está en el Caribe.
   El país tiene frontera con Haití.
   ¿En qué país estoy? _ la República Dominicana _

PASO 2. Pick a recognizable location on your school's campus and write four clues similar to those in **Paso 1** so your partner can guess it. Be sure to include at least one use of **ser** and one use of **estar**. The following phrases will help you describe the location.

Suggestion (Act. A, Paso 2): If your class is fully online, have students name a place in your town, rather than campus.

al lado de (*beside*)   **estar lejos de** (*to be far from*)

el edificio (*building*)   **un lugar** (*a place*)

estar cerca de (to be close to)

> **MODELO:** E1: Es un edificio viejo.
>   Está cerca de la librería.
>   Está lejos del gimnasio.
>   Es un lugar donde podemos estudiar.
>   E2: ¿Es la biblioteca?
>   E1: ¡Sí!

B. Cuatro hispanos de los Estados Unidos

There are many very famous Hispanics in the United States, but many people don't know what their family origins are (that is, whether they are Mexican-American, Cuban-American, and so on). Here you will find out about a few.

PASO 1. The following are descriptions of four different people. Fill in each blank with a form of **ser** or **estar**.

1. Sus padres _son_ de la República Dominicana.
   _Es_ actriz (*actress*) en las películas de *Star Trek* y *Guardians of the Galaxy*.

2. Su padre _es_ de Puerto Rico.
   _Es_ jugador de básquetbol.
   Su equipo (*team*) _está_ en Nueva York.

3. Sus padres _son_ de Cuba.
   _Es_ cantante (*singer*) de reggaetón y hip hop.
   Está en un video musical con Jennifer López.

4. Sus abuelos _son_ de México.
   _Es_ astronauta.
   Su casa _está_ en Houston.

PASO 2. Match each person to the corresponding description.

Armando Pérez (Pitbull) _3_   Ellen Ochoa _4_

Zoe Saldaña _1_   Carmelo Anthony _2_

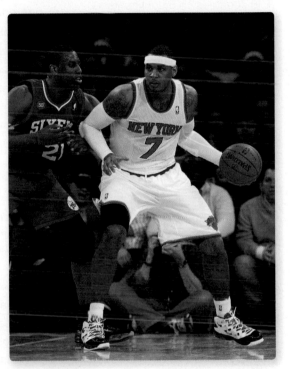

El padre de Carmelo Anthony es puertorriqueño.

 C. ¿Dónde están tus familiares? Another impression that Spanish speakers often have of North Americans is that our families are very dispersed, with many family members living very far from their birthplace and very far from each other. Is there any truth to this? To explore this question, interview a classmate about his/her family (parents, uncles and aunts, grandparents) and find out where each one is from (**¿De dónde es?**) and where each one is now (**¿Dónde está?**).

Expansion (Act. C): Ask students to share general statements about their classmate's family (for example, *Los padres de John son de Corea. Ahora están en Los Ángeles.*)

> **MODELO:** E1: ¿Tienes tíos?
>   E2: Sí, tengo una tía y un tío.
>   E1: ¿De dónde es tu tía?
>   E2: Es de Minnesota.
>   E1: ¿Y ahora dónde está?
>   E2: Está en Nueva York.

D. ¡Más adivinanzas! Create a riddle about a famous person using **Actividad B** as a model, then try it out on your classmates. Be sure to give enough facts that the other person will be able to guess whom you're talking about.

Suggestion (Act. D): Give students 3 minutes to create their riddle, then divide the class in groups, and ask each person to share their riddle with the group.

¡Leamos!

La edad dorada°: de 25 a 34   *golden*

Follow-up (A leer): Tell students that this was an international survey that included 18 countries on 5 continents (specific countries and continents were not reported in this article). Discuss how, even so, results may vary from country to country and subculture to subculture within a given country.

Antes de leer

Answer the questions about the ideal age to embark on different aspects of adulthood.

¿A qué edad (*age*)...

piensas viajar sin (*without*) tus padres? _____

quieres irte de (*leave*) la casa de tus padres? _____

quieres comprar un coche (*car*)? _____

empiezas a disponer de una tarjeta de crédito propia (*have your own credit card*)? _____

empiezas a ahorrar para la jubilación (*save for retirement*)? _____

quieres comprar una casa? _____

piensas convertirte en (*to become*) padre/madre? _____

Suggestion (A leer): Tell students that if they do not agree, they should write down the age that they consider ideal for that action.

A leer

Read the results of **un sondeo** (*survey*) **internacional** about the ideal age to embark on different aspects of adulthood. For each item, indicate whether you agree (**Estoy de acuerdo**) with the survey results or not.

VIVIR A LOS...

19 La edad escogida para comenzar a viajar sin los padres.

22 La edad perfecta para irse de casa, emanciparse de los padres y comprarse un coche.

23 Un buen momento para empezar a disponer de una tarjeta de crédito propia.

26 Ideal para disfrutar del amor, y también el momento de empezar a ahorrar para la jubilación.

27 La etapa idónea para lanzarse a la compra de una casa y también para convertirse en padres.

	ESTOY DE ACUERDO	NO ESTOY DE ACUERDO
Viajar sin los padres:	☐	☐
Irse de la casa de los padres:	☐	☐
Comprar un coche:	☐	☐
Disponer de una tarjeta de crédito propia:	☐	☐
Ahorrar para la jubilación:	☐	☐
Comprar una casa:	☐	☐
Convertirse en padre/madre:	☐	☐

Después de leer

PASO 1. Write three comparisons between your ideal ages and those in the survey (**sondeo**) in **A leer**.

MODELO: Para mí, la edad ideal para ahorrar para la jubilación es mayor que la edad del sondeo, pero la edad ideal para irse de la casa de los padres es menor que la edad del sondeo.

PASO 2. Compare your answers to **Paso 1** with those of at least three other classmates and decide which of the following statements is most true for you. Then see if the whole class agrees.

_____ En general, la edad ideal para nosotros es menor que la edad del sondeo.

_____ En general, estamos de acuerdo con el sondeo.

_____ En general, la edad ideal para nosotros es mayor que la edad del sondeo.

¡Escuchemos!

¿De dónde son sus antepasados°?

ancestors

Antes de escuchar

Where are your ancestors from? Check all the places that apply.

- ☐ África
- ☐ Japón
- ☐ América
- ☐ México
- ☐ Asia
- ☐ otro: _____
- ☐ Europa

 A escuchar

Lourdes and Abigaíl are sisters from Mexico. Lourdes will describe their large family, then Abigaíl will speak about their ethnic heritage.

PASO 1. Watch the video several times, pausing as necessary. Then answer the questions.

1. ¿Es grande o pequeña la familia de Lourdes y Abigaíl?   grande
2. ¿Cuántos abuelos vivos (*alive*) tienen?   tres
3. ¿Cuántas hermanas tiene su mamá?   tres
4. ¿Cuántos primos tienen?   cinco
5. ¿Cuántas tías viven en los Estados Unidos?   una

PASO 2. Lourdes and Abigaíl have a rich ethnic past. Out of four great-grandparents Abigaíl mentions, one is **indígena** (*indigenous*). What are the nationalities or ethnic origins each one?

1. El bisabuelo materno (de parte de la mamá) es ___ japonés ___.
2. La bisabuela materna es ___ mexicana ___.
3. El bisabuelo paterno (de parte del papá) es ___ español ___.
4. La bisabuela paterna es ___ indígena ___.

 Después de escuchar

Working with a classmate, take turns using **¡Qué... familia!** to comment on Lourdes and Abigaíl's family. Use adjectives such as: **grande, interesante, diverso/a, divertido/a, internacional, típico/a, a típico,** and so on. Make sure you use the correct gender/number. Can you think of more adjectives?

Abigaíl y Lourdes

Video track (A escuchar, Paso 1): This video clip can be found on the DVD to accompany *Conéctate: Cap. 4,* Track 3.

Videoscript (A escuchar, Paso 1): LOURDES: *Bueno pues, nuestra familia es grande, tenemos todavía tres abuelos. Tenemos dos abuelos de parte de mi mamá, mi abuela de parte de mi papá. Tenemos, mi mamá tiene tres hermanas, ¡eh! y tenemos... uno, dos, tres, cuatro, cinco primos, cinco primos de parte de mi mamá. Una tía de nosotros vive en Estados Unidos y las, las otras tres hermanas de mi mamá, dos hermanas perdón, viven aquí en México y nosotros vivimos en Guadalajara.*

Suggestion (A escuchar): Remind students that they probably won't understand every word, but should listen for the main idea on one viewing and the key words to complete the activity on another viewing (which are all basic adjectives, numbers, and nationalities)

Video track (A escuchar, Paso 2): This video clip can be found on the DVD to accompany *Conéctate: Cap. 4,* Track 4.

Videoscript (A escuchar, Paso 2): ABIGAÍL: *Mi bisabuelo de parte de mi mamá es japonés. Se casó con una mexicana y él, mi bisabuelo de parte de mi papá, se casó con, era español y se casó con una indígena.*

Note (A escuchar, Paso 2): Most adjectives of nationality are covered in *Cap. 2.* You may want to teach the forms of *japonés/japonesa.* Use *portugués/portuguesa, danés/danesa* and *irlandés/irlandesa* to show examples of nationalities with similar endings.

CONÉCTATE AL MUNDO HISPANO

Did you know that the Mexican actress, Salma Hayek, has Lebanese ancestors? And that the large influx of Italian immigrants to Argentina in the early twentieth century is still evident in the many Italian restaurants and pizzerias there? Because of this immigration, there is no one "look" for Spanish speakers from any country. Throughout this book you will see Spanish speakers in the video from many countries with ancestors from all over the world.

ESTRATEGIA

Brainstorming

Brainstorming is a great way to come up with several ideas so that you can then evaluate each one to choose the best topic before you start your writing assignments. This process allows your mind to explore and play, so that creativity can open up new possibilities, and then your analytical mind can hone in to select and develop the strongest option.

Un consejo...

Some basic concepts challenge Spanish students during the first several years of language study. It's a great strategy to check your work for very specific (and very common) mistakes. As with so many things in life, you'll learn more from your mistakes than anything else!

¡Escribamos!

Una familia famosa

Suggestion (Antes de escribir): If you let students use electronic devices in class, this is a good time for them to use technology to search for famous families—a quick online search will trigger a lot of ideas.

In this activity, you will write a description of a family without naming it. Can your instructor and classmates figure out which family you are describing?

Suggestion (Estrategia): Remind students to deploy strategies they learned in other chapters. In this case, have them review adjectives and character traits from *Cap. 2*. Encourage students

Antes de escribir

Brainstorm a list of famous families that you can describe. They can be historical, political, or from literature, film, television, or pop culture. Choose the best one to write about. List the nationality, each person's age, profession, and adjectives that describe each person. Include both physical and personality descriptions.

to use many adjectives in addition to establishing family relationships in their writing.

> **MODELO:** familia: los Bush
> descripción: una familia norteamericana; el padre es político (ex presidente) y es conservador, la madre es bibliotecaria, el abuelo es político (ex presidente), una hija es rubia, otra hija tiene el pelo castaño.

 ### A escribir

Suggestion (Antes de escribir): Encourage students to think of Latino families, if they can.

Write a description of the family you chose. Don't mention any names, but include the number of family members, their relationships to each other, their ages, what they do, and comparisons of their appearances and personalities. Use complete sentences.

Después de escribir

 PASO 1. Check your own work, then exchange descriptions with a classmate and check each other's work using the following list. Then share your edited description with the class to see if they can guess who it is.

☐ hay concordancia (*agreement*) de género (*gender*) entre los artículos y los sustantivos

☐ hay concordancia de número (singular o plural) entre los adjetivos y lo que describen

☐ los verbos que cambian de raíz tienen los cambios correctos

☐ hay comparaciones con **más/menos... que** (o **mayor/menor... que**)

PASO 2. In groups, share your descriptions. Can everyone identify the families that are described?

Suggestion (Después de escribir): Have students underline every adjective in their classmate's essay. Then have them circle the nouns those adjectives describe and draw a line connecting the two. This should make the agreement items from the checklist obvious. Can they find each other's mistakes?

¡Hablemos!

¡Esta es mi familia!

Antes de hablar

Note (Antes de hablar): The materials for this activity are in the online *Instructor Resources, Activities: Info-Gap and More, Cap. 4*.

What if you were trying to locate family members and only had a few pieces of information? Your instructor will give you information about an imaginary person (such as, **nombre, estado civil** [*marital status*], **lugar de origen, profesión**). Read the information and prepare to talk to others about your new identity.

A hablar

Circulate around the room to ask and answer questions in Spanish and find the other members of your imaginary family. Then sit down as a group.

Después de hablar

Be prepared to introduce your family member(s) to the rest of the class.

Conéctate al cine

Película: *Cautiva* (*Captive,* drama, Argentina, 2005)
Director: Gastón Biraben

Sinopsis:

Cristina is in high school when a judge tells her that the parents she knows adopted her illegally when she was a baby. This was a common practice in Argentina's Dirty War (1976–1983), when babies were born to political prisoners, taken away, and then placed with families supportive of the military dictatorship. The judge introduces Cristina to Elisa, the mother of her biological mother, Leticia.

Escena (Netflix 00:32:34 to 00:34:34):

Cristina and Elisa have just recently met. Cristina is still very confused about who her parents are. Elisa shows Cristina photos of her biological parents (Leticia and her husband, Agustín) and tells her stories about them. She explains that they disappeared during the military dictatorship.

Cautiva

A WHOLE LIFE AHEAD. A WHOLE PAST TO FACE.

Antes de ver

In *Cautiva,* Cristina learns that her name at birth was not Cristina, but Sofía. How would you feel if you found out news that changed your identity? Write at least three adjectives.

Estaría (*I would be*) _____ y _____. Probablemente estaría _____, también.

Note (A ver): Even if you choose to show the clip with subtitles, review the *Expresiones útiles* to reinforce students' word recognition as they listen to the dialogue.

 A ver

Use the film summary to begin to make a list of the relationships between the characters in *Cautiva*. Then read over the **Expresiones útiles** and watch the clip, adding more names and relationships to the list. Finally, complete the sentences with the family relationship. Include the definite article (**el/la/los/las**).

■ For copyright reasons, the feature film clips referenced in **Conéctate al cine** have not been provided by the publisher. Each of these films is readily available through retailers or online rental sites such as Amazon, iTunes, or Netflix.

Expresiones útiles	
recién empezaban a salir	they had just started dating
un asado en casa	a barbeque at home
no decía nada	he didn't talk
era muy tímido	he was very shy
habían elegido los nombres	they had picked out names
varón	boy/male
nena	(baby) girl
desaparecieron	they disappeared
no supimos nada más de ellos	we never heard from them again
déjame sola	leave me alone

1. Agustín y Leticia son <u>los padres</u> biológicos de Cristina.
2. Cristina es <u>la nieta</u> de Elisa.
3. Leticia es <u>la hija</u> de Elisa y Beto.
4. Beto es <u>el marido</u> de Elisa.
5. Leticia es <u>la esposa</u> de Agustín.
6. Beto y Elisa son <u>los suegros</u> de Agustín.

Expansion (A ver): Ask for a volunteer to draw Cristina's family tree on the board.

 ## Después de ver

Use the following questions to discuss your own family with a classmate.

¿Eres similar a tus padres o eres muy diferente? ¿Físicamente eres más similar a tu madre o a tu padre? En cuanto a (*Regarding*) tu personalidad, ¿con cuál de tus padres tienes más en común? ¿Ellos forman una parte importante de tu identidad? Explica.

VOCABULARIO

Now that I have completed the chapter, I can . . .

- ☐ ask what people do for a living
- ☐ comment on things and compliment people
- ☐ talk about my family members and their activities
- ☐ compare and contrast people and things
- ☐ talk about what I want or plan to do

Comunicación

¿A qué te dedicas? / ¿A qué se dedica?	What do you do (occupation)?
¿Cuál es tu/su profesión?	What is your profession?
Las profesiones	**Professions**
el/la abogado/a	attorney
el/la guía naturalista	nature guide
el/la médico/a	doctor
el/la periodista	journalist

Cognados: el/la chofer, el/la doctor(a), el/la ingeniero/a, el/la pintor(a), el/la policía, el/la psicólogo/a, el/la sociólogo/a

¡Qué + adj.!	
¡Qué feo/a!	How ugly! / How horrible!
¡Qué guapo/a!	How handsome/ pretty!
¡Qué lindo/a!	How cute/pretty!
¡Qué + n.!	
¡Qué calor!	It's so hot!
¡Qué frío/a!	It's so cold!
¡Qué lío!	What a mess!
¡Qué + adj. + n.!	
¡Qué bonita familia!	What a beautiful family!

La familia

el/la abuelo/a	grandfather/grandmother
el/la bisabuelo/a	great-grandfather/ great-grandmother
el/la cuñado/a	brother-in-law/ sister-in-law
el/la esposo/a	husband/wife
los familiares	relatives
el/la gato/a	cat
el/la hermanastro/a	stepbrother/stepsister
el/la hermano/a	brother/sister
el/la hijastro/a	stepson/stepdaughter
el/la hijo/a	son/daughter
el/la hijo/a único/a	only child
la madrastra	stepmother
la madre/mamá	mother
el marido	husband
la mascota	pet
la mujer	woman; wife
el/la nieto/a	grandson/granddaughter
el/la novio/a	boyfriend/girlfriend
la nuera	daughter-in-law
el padrastro	stepfather
el padre/papá	father
los padres/papás	parents
los parientes	relatives
el/la perro/a	dog
el pez (pl. peces)	fish
el/la primo/a	cousin
el/la sobrino/a	nephew/niece
el/la suegro/a	father-in-law/ mother-in-law
el/la tío/a	uncle/aunt
el yerno	son-in-law

Los verbos

decir (i) (g)	to say; to tell
empezar (ie)	to begin
empezar a + inf.	to begin (to do something)
lavar	to wash
los platos / la ropa	the dishes/clothes
limpiar	to clean
pedir (i)	to ask for
pensar (ie)	to think; to plan
preparar	to prepare
el desayuno / el almuerzo / la cena	breakfast/lunch/dinner
querer (ie)	to want
querer + inf.	to want (to do something)
repetir (i)	to repeat
seguir (i)	to follow
servir (i)	to serve; to be useful; to work
servir para + inf.	to be good at/for (doing something)
tener (ie) (g) que + inf.	to have (to do something)

Las comparaciones

más/menos + *adj.* + que	more/less (-er) (+ *adj.*) than
más alto que	taller than
menos alto que	less tall than
mayor	older
mejor	better
menor	younger
peor	worse

Por la ciudad°

El tráfico en la avenida
**18 de Julio, Montevideo,
Uruguay**

Objetivos

When you finish this chapter, you will be able to:

- express gratitude
- ask for and give directions
- describe cities and towns
- compare urban and rural life
- use numbers from 100–9,999
- talk about your daily routine
- describe people and places
- express negation and indefinite
  quantities of people and things

McGraw Hill Education **connect**®

Video track (Act. A, Paso 1): This video clip can be found on the DVD to accompany *Conéctate: Cap. 5,* Track 1.

Muchas gracias
Expressing gratitude

Videoscript (Act. A, Paso 1): 1. *Gracias.* **2.** *Gracias.* **3.** *Muchas gracias.* **4.** *Gracias.* **5.** *Bueno, gracias.* **6.** *Gracias.* **7.** *Muchísimas gracias.* **8.** *Muchas gracias.*

Video track (Act. A, Paso 2): This video clip can be found on the DVD to accompany *Conéctate: Cap. 5,* Track 2.

A. A ver: ¡Gracias!

PASO 1. Mira y escucha el video. Luego mira otra vez con pausas e indica la expresión que cada (*each*) persona dice. Mira una tercera vez para verificar (*check*) tus respuestas.

	GRACIAS	MUCHAS GRACIAS	MUCHÍSIMAS GRACIAS			GRACIAS	MUCHAS GRACIAS	MUCHÍSIMAS GRACIAS
1.	☑	☐	☐		5.	☑	☐	☐
2.	☑	☐	☐		6.	☑	☐	☐
3.	☐	☑	☐		7.	☐	☐	☑
4.	☑	☐	☐		8.	☐	☑	☐

PASO 2. Ahora mira y escucha otro video. Luego mira otra vez con pausas, emparejando (*matching*) la persona que habla con lo que dice (*what he or she says*).

1. __b__   3. __c__

2. __d__   4. __a__

a. Bueno, yo les agradezco por ponernos atención.
b. Muchísimas gracias, gracias por entrevistarme. Es un honor.
c. Pues, muchas gracias por este tiempo.
d. Bueno, muchas gracias por la entrevista, muchas gracias por venir, ustedes aquí con nosotros. Muy agradecida de parte mía (*I am very grateful*).

Videoscript (Act. A, Paso 2): **1.** *Muchísimas gracias, gracias por entrevistarme. Es un honor.* **2.** *Bueno, muchas gracias por la entrevista, muchas gracias por venir, ustedes aquí con nosotros. Muy agradecida de parte mía.* **3.** *Pues, muchas gracias por este tiempo.* **4.** *Bueno, les agradezco por ponernos atención.*

Suggestion (Act. A, Paso 2): Remind students that getting the main idea (instead of understanding every word) is one important communication strategy.

Note (Muchas gracias): Tell students this is not a comprehensive list. They are likely to hear things like *Estoy agradecido/a por...* , *Doy gracias por...* and *Le doy las gracias por...*

To thank someone in Spanish, you can use one of these expressions.

Gracias. — Thank you.
Muchas/Muchísimas gracias. — Thank you very much.
Gracias por + *noun/infinitive*.
  Gracias por la entrevista. — Thank you for the interview.
  Gracias por venir. — Thank you for coming.
Te/Le/Les agradezco por... — I appreciate that you . . . / I thank you for . . .

¡Atención! To say *Yes, please* in Spanish, say **Sí, gracias.** To say *You're welcome,* use **De nada** or **No hay de qué.**

Suggestion (Act. B): Tell students that *No, gracias* is also an option for answers 1 and 3. The purpose of the exercise is to distinguish between the English equivalents *Thank you* and *Yes, please.*

B. Sí, gracias. Para cada situación, escoge (*choose*) la expresión adecuada (*appropriate*).

	MUCHAS GRACIAS.	SÍ, GRACIAS.
1. ¿Quieres un café?	☐	☑
2. Tu profesor te ayuda (*helps you*) con el proyecto.	☑	☐
3. Estás perdido/a (*lost*) en una ciudad nueva. Una persona te pregunta: «¿Necesita ayuda?»	☐	☑
4. Un amigo te da (*gives you*) un regalo (*gift*).	☑	☐
5. Una persona te da información sobre la ciudad que visitas.	☑	☐

C. ¡Gracias! En parejas (*With a partner*), túrnense (*take turns*) para regalarse (*giving each other*) las siguientes (*following*) cosas y darse las gracias (*thanking each other*) usando las expresiones en la página 129.

> **MODELO:** E1: Muchas gracias por el reloj.
> E2: ¡De nada! (No hay de qué.)

CONÉCTATE AL MUNDO PROFESIONAL

Thank-you notes are important in professional contexts, especially after an interview or an important networking encounter. It's OK to send thanks by email, but do personalize the message to each individual.

1.

2.

3.

4.

5.

6.

D. ¿Quieres... ? Circula por el salón de clase, pídeles y ofréceles algo (*something*) de la lista a cinco compañeros. Agradéceles (*Thank*) a tus compañeros por lo que te ofrecen a ti.

algo de comer	una curita (*band-aid*)	hojas de papel
un bolígrafo	un diccionario	el libro de texto
chicle (*gum*)	gel antibacterial	una soda

> **MODELOS:** E1: ¿Quieres ayuda con la tarea?
> E2: No, gracias. (Sí, gracias.)
>
> E1: ¿Tienes un lápiz?
> E2: Sí. (No.)
> E1: Gracias por el lápiz. (Gracias de todas maneras. [*Thanks anyway.*])
> E2: No hay de qué.

Note (Act. D): It's important that students learn the various ways to say *thank you* as fixed expressions. By learning the phrase *Gracias por...* , students will avoid making mistakes with *por* and *para* even without having studied it. Make sure they also recognize other ways to express gratitude so that they don't expect to only ever hear and use *gracias.*

¿Dónde está... ?

Asking for and giving directions

To ask where something is located, use **¿Dónde está... ?** or **¿Dónde queda... ?**

¿Dónde está / queda el supermercado?	Where is the supermarket?

To say *here* and *there*, use **aquí** and **allí**.

De aquí no está muy lejos.	From here, it's not very far.
Allí está el mercado.	The market is over there.

To give directions, you can use **Siga** (*Go / Keep going / Continue*).

Siga derecho/recto ____ cuadras.	Keep going straight (for) ____ blocks.

For long distances, you can add references to intersections.

Siga hasta llegar a la esquina de ____ y ____.	Continue until you get to the corner of ____ and ____.

These are more expressions you might need when giving directions.

Doble/Gire...	Turn...
a la derecha/izquierda.	(to the) right/left.
Suba/Baje...	Go up / Go down . . .
por esta calle.	this street.
hasta llegar al parque.	until you get to the park.
Está/Queda...	It's . . .
a la derecha/izquierda.	on/to the right/left.
enfrente de ____.	across from ____.
detrás de ____.	behind ____.
al lado de ____.	next to ____.

To say *block(s)* in Spanish, use **cuadra(s)**.

—**Perdone, ¿dónde está el gimnasio?**
—**Siga derecho dos cuadras, doble a la izquierda y siga una cuadra. El gimnasio está a la derecha, en la esquina de la calle San Martín y la avenida 18 de Septiembre.**
—**Gracias.**

Note that the formal **Ud.** is used in all of these examples because asking for directions often involves talking to someone you don't know and therefore would not want to treat informally.

En español...

The expressions presented in **¿Dónde está?** will be understood anywhere in the Spanish-speaking world, but you may hear other expressions as well when people are giving directions. For instance, instead of the verbs **doblar** or **girar** for *to turn,* some people use **dar la vuelta** or **virar**. In Spain and some South American countries, the word **manzana** is used for *block.*

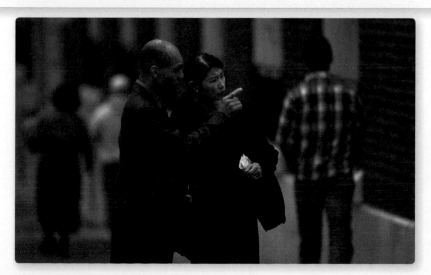

«Siga todo derecho por tres cuadras... »

A. Cómo llegar

PASO 1. Escoge (*Choose*) la respuesta que mejor describe cada imagen.
¡Atención! En cada una, la equis (**X**) marca tu punto de partida (*starting point*).

1. ___a___

   a. Siga recto tres cuadras.
   b. Siga recto una cuadra, gire a la izquierda y siga recto tres cuadras.
   c. Siga recto una cuadra, gire a la derecha y siga recto tres cuadras.

2. ___c___

   a. Siga derecho una cuadra, doble a la derecha y siga derecho dos cuadras.
   b. Siga derecho tres cuadras, doble a la derecha y siga derecho una cuadra.
   c. Siga derecho una cuadra, doble a la derecha y siga derecho tres cuadras.

3. ___c___

   a. Siga recto una cuadra, doble a la derecha y siga recto una cuadra.
   b. Doble a la derecha y siga recto una cuadra.
   c. Siga recto una cuadra, doble a la izquierda y siga recto una cuadra.

4. ___a___

   a. Siga derecho dos cuadras, gire a la izquierda y siga derecho dos cuadras.
   b. Siga derecho dos cuadras, gire a la derecha y siga derecho dos cuadras.
   c. Siga derecho dos cuadras, gire a la derecha y siga derecho tres cuadras.

5. ___b___

   a. Siga recto tres cuadras, doble a la derecha y siga recto una cuadra.
   b. Siga recto tres cuadras, doble a la izquierda y siga recto una cuadra.
   c. Siga recto una cuadra, doble a la derecha y siga recto tres cuadras.

PASO 2. Ahora dibuja (*draw*) una imagen para cada descripción.

1. Siga recto una cuadra, doble a la derecha y siga recto una cuadra.
2. Siga derecho cuatro cuadras.
3. Siga derecho dos cuadras, gire a la izquierda y siga derecho tres cuadras.
4. Siga derecho una cuadra, doble a la derecha y siga derecho una cuadra. Doble a la izquierda y siga derecho tres cuadras.

[a]Me... *They are watching me!*

B. De vacaciones en Ushuaia   En parejas (*With a partner*), imaginen que están en Ushuaia, una ciudad en la región de Patagonia, al sur (*south*) de Argentina. Están en la equis (**X**) y quieren llegar a los lugares (*places*) de las listas. **Estudiante 1** debe consultar **Mapa 1** y **Estudiante 2** debe consultar **Mapa 2**. No mires el mapa de tu pareja.

MODELO: E1: Perdone, ¿dónde está la Casa de Gobierno?
E2: Siga recto cinco cuadras hasta llegar a Comodoro Augusto Lasserre. Doble a la derecha en Lasserre. Siga recto una cuadra y media y la Casa de Gobierno está a la izquierda.
E1: Muchas gracias.

Estudiante 1 (le pregunta a **Estudiante 2**)
Pregúntale a tu pareja cómo llegar a los siguientes lugares que no están en tu mapa. Luego marca en el mapa dónde está cada lugar.

1. el Museo Marítimo
2. la oficina de correos (*post office*)
3. el Museo del Fin del Mundo
4. el Restaurante Kaupé
5. el Hotel Austral

Expansion (Act. B): To show that there are many possible ways to ask for directions, give students examples such as *¿Dónde está... ? ¿Cómo llego a... ? ¿Estoy cerca de... ?*

Suggestion (Act. B): Project the map onto the board or screen at the front of the room and have one student draw with chalk or fingers as other students give directions. You can set this up like a game of telephone where each teammate takes turn giving a single direction. How many teams get lost? How many give good directions?

MAPA 1

(Continues)

Suggestion (Act. B): Print copies of (or project) a map of your town for your students. Pick a few points of interest (such as *la oficina de correos, la biblioteca, el supermercado, el museo,* and *la estación de trenes/autobuses*), and have students give directions from one place to another.

Estudiante 2 (le pregunta a **Estudiante** 1)

Pregúntale a tu pareja cómo llegar a los siguientes lugares que no están en tu mapa. Luego marca en el mapa dónde está cada lugar.

1. la Oficina de Información Turística
2. la Antigua Legislatura
3. el Pub Restaurante Naútico
4. el Hostal Los Calafates
5. la Agencia de Turismo Rumbo Sur

MAPA 2

Restaurante Kaupé

Museo Marítimo

Museo del Fin del Mundo

Hotel Austral

Casa de Gobierno

Oficina de correos

C. ¿Cómo llego?   En parejas, túrnense para describir un lugar en su universidad o ciudad sin mencionar el nombre. Tu pareja primero (*first*) tiene que adivinar (*guess*) el lugar y luego darte (*give you*) direcciones. ¿Pueden decir cómo llegar a cada lugar?

MODELO: E1: ¿Cómo llego al lugar donde puedo estudiar y buscar libros?
E2: ¿A la biblioteca? ¿A la librería?
E1: A la biblioteca.
E2: De aquí gire a la derecha, siga recto hasta llegar al centro estudiantil. Luego doble a la izquierda y la biblioteca está enfrente.

COMUN **VOCABULARIO** CTURA ATE

Paisajes urbanos
Urban landscapes

To talk about types of communities, use these words.

la ciudad	city
el campo	countryside; rural area
las afueras	suburbs; outskirts

The American concept of *suburbs* does not exist in most of the Spanish-speaking world. If you are an American from the suburbs, you can use **las afueras** to talk about where you live.

Vivo en las afueras de Phoenix.   I live in the suburbs of Phoenix.

A. Más vocabulario: En la ciudad

PASO 1. Mira los siguientes dibujos (*drawings*) y lee los párrafos. Escoge el párrafo que mejor (*best*) describe cada dibujo y llena (*fill in*) los espacios en blanco con la palabra más lógica de la lista, según (*according to*) el dibujo.

1. d

2. a

3. c

4. b

(Continues)

Note (Act. A): Students will use information from this activity to work with numbers 100+ in the next section.

Suggestions (Act. A)
- To make the images easier for students to interpret, provide them with some cultural background or have them do an online search for topics such as: *names of famous department stores in Spain, Gaudí landmarks in Barcelona,* and *famous landmarks in Buenos Aires.*
- Point out that compound nouns that end in *-s* can be singular or plural: *el rascacielos, los rascacielos; el cumpleaños, los cumpleaños; el lavaplatos, los lavaplatos; el abrelatas, los abrelatas.*

apartamentos	jardín (*garden*)	museo	tráfico
banco	mercado	restaurantes	
cine	metro	taxis	

a. En Barcelona, hay muchas construcciones del famoso arquitecto Antoni Gaudí, como La Sagrada Familia, una **iglesia** muy grande y **moderna** que ha estado en construcción (*has been under construction*) desde 1882. Si (*If*) quieres un poco de **tranquilidad,** puedes visitar el **parque** Güell, también diseñado por Gaudí. Aquí hay un ___jardín___ lleno de flores, **árboles** y esculturas (*sculptures*) decoradas con mosaicos coloridos. Además de (*Besides*) la arquitectura, se puede ir de compras en los grandes **almacenes** y comer en los varios ___restaurantes___ sofisticados de esta ciudad. Si se necesita sacar dinero, es fácil encontrar un cajero automático (*ATM*) de un ___banco___ international.

b. Buenos Aires es la **capital** de Argentina. Entre sus **lugares** famosos están el **Teatro** Colón (1908); el ___Museo___ de Arte Latinoamericano de Buenos Aires (MALBA), construido (*built*) en 2001; y la **avenida** 9 de Julio, nombrada por el día de independencia del país en el año 1816. Al igual que (*Just like*) muchas ciudades grandes, la cantidad (*quantity*) de **coches,** ___taxis___ y **autobuses** resulta en mucho ___tráfico___, lo cual (*which*) produce ___contaminación___ del aire y mucho **ruido** por los sonidos de todos los motores.

c. En el **centro moderno** de la ciudad de Panamá, muchas personas viven en **edificios** de ___apartamentos___ muy altos (llamados **rascacielos**) como la **Torre** Vitri, construida en 2012. Hay un ___cine___ para el entretenimiento de los aficionados a (*fans of*) las películas, **escuelas** para estudiar desde el primer grado (*first grade*) hasta la universidad, **tiendas** para comprar todo tipo de cosas —incluso la famosa **librería** Exedra donde se venden (*sell*) libros de todo el mundo. Si cruzas (*you cross*) el Canal de Panamá por el **Puente** de las Américas, puedes viajar por la **carretera** Panamericana para visitar el **campo** y otros **pueblos** del país.

d. Santo Domingo es una de las ciudades más viejas de las Américas, pero tiene una mezcla (*mixture*) de lo moderno y lo **antiguo.** Por ejemplo, el tren subterráneo (es decir, el ___metro___) fue completado en 2009 y es uno de los principales **transportes públicos** de la ciudad; y la primera **catedral** del Nuevo Mundo (*World*), conocida como la Catedral Primada de América, fue construida en 1541. Junto a la catedral está la **plaza** central, que en 1887 cambió su nombre a parque Colón (*Columbus*). En una de las calles centrales hay un ___mercado___ con **carnicerías, fruterías** y otros **puestos** en los que (*in which*) se puede comprar de todo.

PASO 2. En grupos, analicen los cuatro destinos apuntando (*writing down*) las ventajas y desventajas (*advantages and disadvantages*) de cada ciudad. Luego hagan (*make*) una lista de los cuatro destinos en orden de más deseable (*desirable*) a menos deseable para visitar.

■ The audio files for in-text listening activities are available in the eBook, within Connect activities, and on the Online Learning Center.

B. ¿Qué es? Escucha las descripciones e indica qué describe cada una.

1. ___el almacén___
2. ___el rascacielos___
3. ___el coche___
4. ___el cine___
5. ___el puesto___
6. ___el puente___
7. ___el parque___
8. ___el metro___

Script (Act. B): 1. Es una tienda en un edificio grande donde se venden ropa y muchas otras cosas. 2. Es un edificio muy alto con muchos pisos.
3. Generalmente es transporte personal, pero si se usa como taxi, se considera transporte público. 4. Es el edificio adónde vas para ver una película. 5. Es una tienda pequeña y no permanente; se especializa en vender algo como frutas o carnes. 6. Lo usas para cruzar un río en un vehículo, como en un coche o un autobús. 7. Es un lugar tranquilo con muchos árboles y jardines. 8. Es una forma de transporte público que no pasa por las calles de una ciudad.

C. ¿Dónde vive tu familia? En grupos de tres personas, hagan y contesten las siguientes preguntas. Según las respuestas de sus compañeros, adivinen (*guess*) si cada uno es de la ciudad, el campo o las afueras.

¿Tu familia...

1. vive en un apartamento?
2. viaja más de un kilómetro (0,6 millas) para ir de compras?
3. vive en un lugar donde los niños caminan a las escuelas?
4. viaja más de diez minutos para ir a un museo?
5. vive en un lugar donde los niños van al parque para jugar?
6. viaja en transporte público por lo menos una vez (*time*) a la semana?

Creo que eres de la ciudad / el campo / las afueras. ¿Tengo razón? (*Am I right?*)

Suggestion (Act. C): Help students organize their work. Propose that they fill out a chart, containing the following columns: *Preguntas, E1 [nombre], E2 [nombre]*. The number of rows will correspond to the number of questions. You can draw the chart on the board or give a copy to each student as a handout. Hint that in each group one person can start by interviewing both classmates together by adding *¿Y tu familia?* to the other classmate after each question. Then another group member can ask the interviewer the questions.

 D. A ver: ¿Dónde estamos en este momento?

PASO 1. Mira las imágenes en el video, con pausas entre cada una. Según lo que ves (*what you see*), decide dónde está cada persona. ¿Por qué crees (*do you think*) que la persona está en ese lugar?

 1. __c__ Abril está en...
a. un almacén.
b. una iglesia.
c. un parque.

 2. __a__ Aníbal está en...
a. una ciudad.
b. un jardín.
c. un parque.

 3. __a__ Antonio está en...
a. un mercado.
b. un restaurante.
c. una tienda.

 4. __b__ Jama está en...
a. un mercado.
b. una galería de arte.
c. una plaza.

5. __c__ José Manuel está en...
a. un campo.
b. una plaza.
c. un parque.

6. __c__ María está en...
a. un museo.
b. una iglesia.
c. una plaza.

7. __b__ Roberto está en...
a. un mercado.
b. un restaurante.
c. una tienda.

La Plaza de la Constitución (mejor conocida como «el Zócalo») en la Ciudad de México.

Video track (Act. D, Paso 1): This video clip can be found on the DVD to accompany *Conéctate: Cap. 5*, Track 3.

Note (Act. D): *Paso 2* includes the audio for the slide show. *Paso 1* is set up as a slide show without sound to emphasize the importance of using visual clues.

Video track (Act. D, Paso 2): This video clip can be found on the DVD to accompany *Conéctate: Cap. 5*, Track 4.

PASO 2. Mira y escucha. Luego mira otra vez con pausas, emparejando la descripción con el lugar que se describe. Mira una tercera (*third*) vez para verificar tus respuestas.

__e__ 1. la Plaza Francia
__c__ 2. la parte antigua de la ciudad
__a__ 3. Buenos Aires
__d__ 4. la galería de arte
__b__ 5. el Jardín Borda
__f__ 6. la Plaza Manuel Belgrano
__g__ 7. El Mirador

a. la capital de Argentina
b. el Centro Cultural de Morelos, México
c. la Ciudad de Panamá
d. la calle Ocho en Miami
e. un parque en Argentina
f. una plaza principal en Argentina
g. un restaurante en Costa Rica con vistas muy bonitas

E. ¿Dónde están ahora? Nombra por lo menos tres de tus seres queridos (*loved ones*) y di (*say*) dónde están ahora.

MODELO: Mi novio está en el supermercado ahora.

Videoscript (Act. D, Paso 2). 1. ABRIL: *Estamos en Plaza Francia... eh... eh... en un parque.* **2.** ANÍBAL: *¡Sí! Estamos en la parte antigua de la Ciudad de Panamá.* **3.** ANTONIO: *Estamos en Buenos Aires, la capital argentina, en América del Sur.* **4.** JAMA: *Bueno, estamos en una galería recién abierta en la calle Ocho del South West de la ciudad de Miami, Florida* **5.** JOSÉ MANUEL: *Bueno, aquí están en el Centro Cultural de, de Morelos... este... se llama Jardín Borda.* **6.** MARÍA: *Esta es la plaza principal, eh... Manuel Belgrano, se llama.* **7.** ROBERTO: *Básicamente, este es un restaurán. El restaurante se llama El Mirador y hay una vista de todo, todo. Casi como medio Costa Rica: San José, Alajuela, Heredia, se ve tres volcanes, se ve el mar. Es una vista muy, muy bonita.*

Los números del 100 al 9.999

Numbers from 100 to 9,999

Suggestions (Los números del 100 al 9.999):
- Point out that for 200–900 the hundreds number agrees in gender with the noun it refers to: *novecientos siete libros* but *doscientas diez personas.*
- Give students the month and year of your birth and ask them to figure out how old you are. Continue with the years they, their parents, siblings, and friends were born. To review, have students give their full date of birth: *el doce de febrero de mil novecientos noventa y seis.*

100 cien/ciento	1.000 mil
200 doscientos/as	2.000 dos mil
300 trescientos/as	3.000 tres mil
400 cuatrocientos/as	4.000 cuatro mil
500 quinientos/as	5.000 cinco mil
600 seiscientos/as	6.000 seis mil
700 setecientos/as	7.000 siete mil
800 ochocientos/as	8.000 ocho mil
900 novecientos/as	9.000 nueve mil

By itself, the number 100 is **cien**. When any other number follows it, use **ciento**.

101 ciento uno
199 ciento noventa y nueve

Do not use **y** immediately after **ciento, cientos,** or **mil**.

178 ciento setenta y ocho
235 doscientos treinta y cinco
1.315 mil trescientos quince

To say the year in Spanish, say the whole four-digit number.

1492 = mil cuatrocientos noventa y dos
1988 = mil novecientos ochenta y ocho
2015 = dos mil quince

When written in Spanish, numerals in the thousands place are usually separated from the hundreds by a period, but they can be written in other ways as well. You might see one thousand (**mil**) represented as any one of the following:

1.000   1,000   1 000   1000

Script (Act. A): 1. *Se presentan 450 propuestas para el diseño del Museo de Arte Latinoamericano en Buenos Aires. Ahora el edificio exhibe y conserva aproximadamente 400 obras de arte.* **2.** *El Puente de las Américas mide 1.654 metros. Está a 36 kilómetros de la ciudad de Panamá.* **3.** *En el año 2012, 8.738 empleados trabajan en el Corté Inglés de Barcelona.* **4.** *Por 360 pesos, puedes comprar una tarjeta de 20 viajes en el Metro de Santo Domingo. Cuesta 40 peso más si no compras tarjeta.*

A. ¿Cuánto(s)... ? Escucha las oraciones y escribe el número correcto para completar cada frase.

1. El número de arquitectos que querían diseñar el Museo de Arte Latinoamericano en Buenos Aires: __450__ .
2. El Puente de las Américas mide __1654__ metros.
3. El número de empleados del Corté Inglés Barcelona: __8738__ .
4. Con una tarjeta, 20 viajes en el Metro de Santo Domingo cuesta __360__ pesos.

B. ¿Cuántos años tiene? Usa las imágenes y las descripciones de la **Actividad A** en las páginas 135–136 para contestar las siguientes preguntas.

1. ¿Cuántos años tiene el Teatro Colón? current year minus 1908
2. ¿Cuántos años tiene el metro de Santo Domingo? current year minus 2009
3. ¿Cuántos años tiene la iglesia La Sagrada Familia? current year minus 1882
4. ¿Cuántos años tiene la Catedral Primada de América? current year minus 1541
5. ¿Cuál es el día de la independencia de Argentina? 9 de julio de 1816
6. ¿Cuánto tiempo hace que (*How long since*) la plaza central de Santo Domingo se llama «parque Colón»? current year minus 1887
7. ¿En qué año se construyó (*was built*) la Torre Vitri? 2012

Script (Act. C): 1. *La construcción del Teatro Colón empieza en 1890 y dura 18 años. ¿En qué año termina la construcción?* **2.** *La construcción del metro de Santo Domingo empieza en 2005 y dura 4 años. ¿En qué año termina la construcción?* **3.** *La construcción del canal de Panamá empieza en 1881 y dura 33 años. ¿En qué año termina la construcción?* **4.** *La construcción del parque Güell empieza en 1900 y abre como parque municipal 26 años después. ¿En qué año abre?*

C. ¿Cuánto tiempo dura (*lasts*) la construcción? Escucha la historia de la construcción de cada lugar y apunta el año en que termina cada uno.

1. __1908__ 2. __2009__ 3. __1914__ 4. __1926__

Expansion (Act. C): Have students calculate the current age of the places mentioned.

⟳ Reciclaje

The verbs *estar, ir, ser,* and *tener*

Escribe la forma **yo** de uno de los siguientes verbos en cada oración. Luego indica si la persona habla de **la ciudad** o **del campo.**

estar   ir   ser   tener

	CIUDAD	CAMPO
1. «_Soy_ de Buenos Aires.»	☑	☐
2. «_Voy_ a la casa de mi abuelo, donde tiene muchas gallinas (*chickens*).»	☐	☑
3. «_Soy_ de una zona rural.»	☐	☑
4. «_Estoy_ en una estación del metro.»	☑	☐
5. «_Tengo_ tres caballos (*horses*).»	☐	☑
6. «_Estoy_ en la capital del país.»	☑	☐

Mi abuelo cría (*raises*) gallinas en su finca (*farm*).

■ Answers to this activity are in Appendix 2 at the back of your book.

5.1 Traigo el mapa del metro.

Verbs with irregular *yo* forms

Para empezar...

Las siguientes oraciones (*sentences*) hablan de la vida (*life*) en el campo y en la ciudad. Selecciona de la lista para completar las oraciones de una manera lógica. Los verbos **oír** (*to hear; to listen to*), **salir** (*to leave; to go out*) y **traer** (*to bring; to carry*) son nuevos. **¡Atención!** La respuesta **d** se usa dos veces.

Suggestion (Para empezar): Point out that *hago* is from the verb *hacer*, which they already know from *hacer ejercicio* and *¿qué te gusta hacer?*

EN EL CAMPO

1. «Cuando **salgo** de mi casa, **oigo** _f_ y _h_.»
2. «Cuando camino por (*through/along*) _a_, siempre **traigo** _i_.»
3. «Cuando voy al campo para descansar, no **hago** _d_.»

EN LA CIUDAD

4. «Cuando **salgo** de mi apartamento, **oigo** _c_ y _e_.»
5. «Cuando camino por _g_, siempre **traigo** _b_.»
6. «Cuando corro por las calles, **hago** _d_.»

a. los campos
b. el mapa del metro
c. los coches
d. mucho ejercicio
e. los autobuses
f. los caballos
g. el centro
h. las gallinas
i. un bastón (*stick*) para caminar

■ Answers to these activities are in Appendix 2 at the back of your book.

¿Por qué?

There is a reason why so many verbs add a -**g**- in the **yo** form. This form ends in the vowel -**o**, which is pronounced with the tongue positioned in the back of the mouth. The -**g**-, which is also pronounced with the tongue in the back of the mouth, smooths the transition between the verb stem and the -**o** and makes the verb easier to pronounce.

Suggestion (¿Por qué?): Have students pronounce exaggerated versions of the vowels e and o, so that they can see how the tongue is in the front of the mouth for e and in the back of the mouth for o. Have them do the same for the consonant g.

Autoprueba

Complete the sentences below with the correct form of the verb in parentheses.

1. Yo _____ (venir) de una ciudad grande.
2. ¿Tú _____ (oír) eso?
3. Yo siempre _____ (salir) los fines de semana.
4. Yo _____ (poner) mi mochila en la mesa.
5. ¿De dónde _____ (venir) Uds.?
6. Yo no _____ (oír) nada.

Respuestas: 1. vengo 2. oyes 3. salgo 4. pongo 5. vienen 6. oigo

Actividades analíticas

1 Use what you saw in **Para empezar** to complete this set of conjugations.

	hacer	**poner**	**traer**	**salir**
yo	hago	pongo	traigo	salgo
tú	haces	pones	traes	sales
él/ella, Ud.	hace	pone	trae	sale
nosotros/as	hacemos	ponemos	traemos	salimos
vosotros/as	hacéis	ponéis	traéis	salís
ellos/ellas, Uds.	hacen	ponen	traen	salen

In the present tense, these verbs are irregular only in the **yo** form. They are otherwise completely regular.

¿Dónde **pongo** mi tarjeta de metro?　*Where do I put my metro pass?*

Ponen sus libros en la mesa.　*They put their books on the table.*

2 Some stem-changing verbs also add **g** in the **yo** form. **Tener** and **venir** (*to come*) belong to the **e → ie** family, and **decir** belongs to **e → i** family. Complete their conjugations here.

	tener (e → ie)	**venir (e → ie)**	**decir (e → i)**
yo	tengo	vengo	digo
tú	tienes	vienes	dices
él/ella, Ud.	tiene	viene	dice
nosotros/as	tenemos	venimos	decimos
vosotros/as	tenéis	venís	decís
ellos/ellas, Uds.	tienen	vienen	dicen

Vengo de Nicaragua.　*I come from Nicaragua.*

¿**Vienes** a la fiesta el sábado?　*Are you coming to the party on Saturday?*

3 **Oír** is another common verb with **g** in the **yo** form. It makes some spelling adjustments in the other forms: the **i** is accented in **oír**, **oímos**, and **oís**, and the **i** changes to **y** when between two vowels (**oyes**, **oye**, **oyen**).

	oír (y)
yo	oigo
tú	oyes
él/ella, Ud.	oye
nosotros/as	oímos
vosotros/as	oís
ellos/ellas, Uds.	oyen

Oigo el tráfico de mi casa.　*I hear the traffic from my house.*

¿Ud. **oye** mucha música clásica?　*Do you listen to a lot of classical music?*

4 The verbs **saber** (*to know [a fact]*) and **conocer** (*to know, be familiar with*) are two important verbs with irregular **yo** forms. With **saber**, the **yo** form is **sé**, and with **conocer**, it is **conozco**. The present tense of these verbs is completely regular otherwise.

Saber and **conocer** can both be translated as *to know*, but they are not the same. **Saber** means to know a fact or to know how to do something.

Sé que vives en el centro.	*I know that you live downtown.*
Sabemos que Miami está en Florida.	*We know that Miami is in Florida.*
—¿**Sabes** dónde está la biblioteca?	*Do you know where the library is?*
—Sí, **sé** dónde está.	*Yes, I know where it is.*
Está detrás del gimnasio.	*It's behind the gym.*
Ella **sabe** nadar.	*She knows how to swim.*

Conocer, on the other hand, means *to be familiar or acquainted with something or someone.*

Conozco muy bien mi universidad.	*I know my university very well.*
Juan **conoce** Boston.	*Juan knows (is familiar with) Boston.*
¿**Conoces** a mi hermano?	*Do you know my brother?*

Actividades prácticas

A. Preguntas y respuestas
Empareja cada pregunta con la respuesta más lógica.

1. _c_ ¿Tienes un lápiz?
2. _g_ ¿Por qué estás cansado?
3. _f_ ¿Qué tipo de música te gusta?
4. _d_ ¿Qué haces los sábados?
5. _a_ ¿Qué haces cuando tienes mucho sueño en el trabajo?
6. _b_ ¿Conoces Chicago?
7. _e_ ¿Cuál es la capital de la Guinea Ecuatorial?

a. Pongo la cabeza (*head*) en el escritorio y duermo.
b. ¡Claro! Vengo de allí.
c. No, pero traigo un bolígrafo en mi mochila.
d. Salgo a bailar con mis amigos.
e. No sé.
f. Oigo mucho rock en español.
g. Vengo del gimnasio.

B. Una conversación entre dos estudiantes
Las siguientes oraciones vienen de una conversación entre dos estudiantes que se encuentran (*who meet*) en la calle. Ponlas en orden (*Put them in order*).

_1_ —¡Hola! ¿Por qué no contestas el teléfono?

_6_ —No, no conozco ese lugar, pero dicen que es muy bueno. Oye, ¿pongo mi mochila aquí en tu coche?

_4_ —¡Sí, puedo! ¿Adónde quieren ir? ¿Conoces un lugar bueno?

_7_ —Sí, está bien. ¿Viene Silvia también?

_9_ —Sí traigo, pero no mucho.

_3_ —Pues, te llamo para saber si puedes salir a comer con mi compañero de cuarto y yo.

_5_ —Sí. ¿Conoces el restaurante La Buena Vida? Cuando salgo con mis compañeros del trabajo, vamos allí, y me gusta mucho.

_8_ —No sé. Sé que tiene un examen mañana y tiene que estudiar. Oye, ¿traes dinero?

_2_ —¡Ay, perdón! Vengo de mi clase de historia, y tengo el teléfono apagado (*turned off*).

■ For more on **saber** and **conocer,** as well as more irregular verbs ending in **-zco,** see **Para saber más 5.1** at the back of your book.

Note (Para saber más): *Para saber más 5.1* includes further explanation of *saber* and *conocer,* as well as the *yo* forms of *agradecer, aparecer, conducir, favorecer, merecer, ofrecer, parecer, pertenecer, reconocer,* and *traducir.*

Point out (Act. A): *El español es uno de los idiomas oficiales de la Guinea Ecuatorial. La capital es Malabo.*

Suggestion (Act. A): Have students do this activity in pairs, taking turns asking and answering the questions.

Note (Act. B): With all irregular verb forms, students need plenty of input before they can produce the forms naturally. This activity is challenging, but it gives them the kind of meaningful input that they need.

Suggestion (Act. B): After students have finished the activity, ask for two volunteers to act out the dialogue in front of the class (*¡con emoción!*), while everyone else checks to see if they have the correct order.

Expansion (Act. C): After students have done the activity for themselves, have them work with a partner and ask each other questions based on these items, for example: *¿Tú sabes cuál es la capital de México?* Then have students report any differences with their partner to the class: *Amy sabe hacer yoga, pero yo no.*

C. ¿Saber o conocer?   Escribe la forma **yo** de **saber** o **conocer** en cada una de las siguientes oraciones. Luego decide si la oración es **cierta (C)** o **falsa (F)** para ti.

		¿Cierto o falso?
1. _____Sé_____ cuál es la capital de México.		C F
2. ___Conozco___ Bolivia.		C F
3. _____Sé_____ quién es Beto Cuevas.		C F
4. _____Sé_____ hacer yoga.		C F
5. ___Conozco___ la comida italiana.		C F
6. _____Sé_____ preparar una pizza.		C F
7. ___Conozco___ a la mejor amiga de mi abuela.		C F
8. _____Sé_____ cómo se llama el presidente de nuestra universidad.		C F

Note (Act. D): Rastafari is a religious movement, originally from Jamaica, that is often associated with reggae music. It is popular in several Latin American countries, especially in the Caribbean.

D. Los extranjeros en la ciudad   En las grandes ciudades de España y Latinoamérica, hay muchos extranjeros (*foreigners*) de muchos países diferentes. Estos son algunos ejemplos.

	Benjamín	Elena	Miguel
PAÍS	Bélgica	Rumania	Portugal
TRABAJO	turismo	camarera (*waitress*)	promoción de eventos de surf y eventos rastafari
CIUDAD DONDE VIVE Y TRABAJA	Ciudad de México	Madrid	Panamá

Completa cada una de las siguientes oraciones con la forma **yo** de los verbos de la lista. Luego escribe el nombre de la persona de la tabla que probablemente dice la oración.

conocer   oír   saber   salir   tener   venir

1. ___Elena___ dice: «___Salgo___ de mi casa para ir al restaurante.»
2. ___Benjamín___ dice: «_Tengo/Conozco_ una agencia de viajes.»
3. ___Elena___ dice: «_Salgo/Vengo_ del trabajo a las tres de la mañana.»
4. ___Miguel___ dice: «___Vengo___ de Lisboa.»
5. ___Miguel___ dice: «___Oigo___ música reggae cuando estoy en el trabajo.»
6. ___Benjamín___ dice: «___Conozco___ muchas partes de México. Es un país fascinante.»
7. ___Benjamín___ dice: «___Sé___ que hay muchas películas belgas muy buenas.»
8. ___Elena___ dice: «___Vengo___ de Rumania.»
9. ___Miguel___ dice: «___Conozco___ muchas playas de muchas partes del mundo, y puedo decir que las playas de Panamá son excelentes.»

Expansion (Act. E, Paso 1): Have students create sentences contrasting their own habits with those of their partner. For example: *John sale con amigos, pero yo salgo con mi novia.* Ask a few students to share their comparisons with the class.

E. ¿Sales los sábados?

PASO 1. En general, ¿sales los sábados por la noche? Si sales, ¿a qué hora? ¿Con quién? ¿Adónde van? Entrevista (*Interview*) a un compañero / una compañera y completa las primeras dos líneas de la tabla.

Suggestion (Act. E): Have students write a complete sentence for each cell in the table.

¿QUIÉN?	¿SALE(N) LOS SÁBADOS?	¿A QUÉ HORA?	¿CON QUIÉN?	¿ADÓNDE?
yo				
mi compañero/a: _____				
Estudiantes de <u>aquí</u>				
Estudiantes de <u>Madrid</u>				

PASO 2. Con tu compañero/a, decide qué hace la mayoría de los estudiantes en su universidad. Luego lee la información sobre los estudiantes de Madrid y completa el resto de la tabla.

> En general en España, los estudiantes salen a las diez o a las once de la noche. Álvaro, un estudiante de Madrid, dice: «Todo el mundo (*Everybody*) sale... con sus amigos, con la gente de clase».
>
> Andrea, también estudiante en Madrid, dice: «Salen a bailar y van a los bares».

F. ¿Qué hace tu compañero/a?

PASO 1. En parejas, pregúntense si hacen estas actividades **siempre, casi** (*almost*) **siempre, a veces, casi nunca** o **nunca.**

escuchar música en español

poner la computadora en la mochila

traer una mochila a clase

venir a clase tarde (*late*) / temprano (*early*)

venir a la universidad a pie (*on foot*)

> **MODELO:** E1: ¿Vienes a la universidad a pie?
> E2: Sí, a veces vengo a pie. ¿Y tú?
> E1: No, casi nunca vengo a pie. Siempre vengo en autobús/bicicleta/coche/taxi.

PASO 2. En parejas, miren las actividades del **Paso 1** y escriban cuatro oraciones que resumen (*summarize*) lo que (*what*) hacen Uds. Si los/las dos hacen lo mismo (*the same thing*), usen **los/las dos** (*the two of us*) y la forma **nosotros/as.** Si hay una diferencia, describan qué hace cada uno/a. Luego compartan (*share*) sus respuestas con la clase para ver qué cosas tienen en común.

> **MODELOS:** Los dos escuchamos música en español a veces.
> Yo nunca traigo una mochila, pero Kevin casi siempre trae una mochila.

Expansion (Act. E, Paso 2): Have students create sentences contrasting the habits of the majority with their own. Give them models such as *Muchos salen a las 8, pero yo salgo a las 9.* or *Muchos salen los sábados, pero yo no salgo.*

Suggestion (Act. E, Paso 2): As a class, look for interesting differences between the students in Madrid and in this country and speculate why these differences might exist.

Expansion (Act. E): As a follow-up, ask the pairs to decide whose Saturdays are the most fun: *¿Quién tiene los mejores sábados?* Do a quick, whole-class check to see if the different pairs agree: *¿Están de acuerdo?*

CONÉCTATE AL MUNDO HISPANO

Los **bares** en España no son iguales a los *bars* en los Estados Unidos y Canadá. En España, los bares son el centro de la vida (*life*) social para mucha gente y no abren solo por la noche. Además de (*In addition to*) bebidas (*beverages*) alcohólicas, sirven las famosas tapas y comidas (*meals*). Muchas personas van al bar por la mañana para charlar (*chat*) con los amigos y tomar café y pan tostado (*toast*).

↻ Reciclaje

The verb *llamarse*

En la siguiente conversación, escribe las formas más lógicas del verbo **llamarse.**

ELENA: Hola! ¿Cómo _____te llamas_____[1]?
RAFAEL: _____Me llamo_____[2] Rafael.
ELENA: ¿Conozco a tu hermano? ¿Cómo _____se llama_____[3]?
RAFAEL: _____Se llama_____[4] Jorge. Y tú, ¿cómo _____te llamas_____[5]?
ELENA: _____Me llamo_____[6] Elena.

■ Answers to this activity are in Appendix 2 at the back of your book.

Note (Para empezar): For most Latin American speakers, *bañarse* is a general term for bathing, whether in a bathtub or shower or by other means, whereas *ducharse* refers specifically to showering. For many speakers from Spain, *bañarse* refers only to bathing in a bathtub.

Note (Para saber más): *Para saber más 5.2* covers the meaning of the verbs *alegrarse, atreverse (a), encontrarse, imaginarse, preguntarse, quedarse,* and *referirse (a).* It also covers the reciprocal meaning of reflexive verbs and the use of an infinitive after a preposition.

■ Answers to these activities are in Appendix 2 at the back of your book.

Answers (Para empezar):
Biblioteca: dormirse, sentarse. Gimnasio: any four: *afeitarse, bañarse, ducharse, maquillarse, peinarse, vestirse. Hotel:* any four.

■ For additional reflexive verbs, see **Para saber más 5.2** at the back of your book.

Suggestion (Act. analíticas 1): Point out that in English one often omits the reflexive pronoun and says simply *to shave* or *to bathe.*

5.2 Me ducho en el gimnasio.

Reflexive verbs

Para empezar...

Usa la siguiente lista para escribir algunas (*some*) actividades que son comunes en cada lugar.

despertar**se**   maquillar**se**   duchar**se**/bañar**se**   peinar**se**   afeitar**se**

vestir**se**   sentar**se**   bañar**se**   acostar**se**   dormir**se**

LUGARES	EJEMPLOS DE ACTIVIDADES COMUNES			
En una biblioteca	_____	_____		
En un gimnasio	_____	_____	_____	_____
En un hotel	_____	_____	_____	_____

Actividades analíticas

1 The verbs in **Para empezar** are all infinitives, but they have an additional ending that other infinitives don't have. What is this ending? ____-se____

This ending is a *reflexive pronoun* (**pronombre reflexivo**) and verbs that have it are called *reflexive verbs* (**verbos reflexivos**). Reflexive verbs often, but not always, indicate an action that one does to oneself: **afeitarse** (*to shave* [*oneself*]), **bañarse** (*to bathe* [*oneself*]).

2 Reflexive verbs are conjugated just like other verbs, but when conjugated, the reflexive pronoun is placed *before* the verb. The form of the reflexive pronoun depends on the subject.

SUJETO	PRONOMBRE REFLEXIVO	EJEMPLO	
yo	me	Yo **me peino** después de hacer ejercicio.	*I comb my hair after exercising.*
tú	te	¿A qué hora **te duermes**?	*At what time do you fall asleep?*
él/ella, Ud.	se	Marisa **se baña** por la mañana.	*Marisa bathes in the morning.*
nosotros/as	nos	Julieta y yo **nos acostamos** temprano.	*Julieta and I go to bed early.*
vosotros/as	os	**¿Os afeitáis** cada día?	*Do you shave every day?*
ellos/ellas, Uds.	se	Esos estudiantes **se duchan** en el gimnasio.	*Those students shower at the gym.*

Now complete the conjugations of these reflexive verbs.

	afeitarse	bañarse	peinarse
yo	me afeito	me baño	me peino
tú	te afeitas	te bañas	te peinas
él/ella, Ud.	se afeita	se baña	se peina
nosotros/as	nos afeitamos	nos bañamos	nos peinamos
vosotros/as	os afeitáis	os bañáis	os peináis
ellos/ellas, Uds.	se afeitan	se bañan	se peinan

3 Some reflexive verbs have stem changes.

FAMILIA	VERBO		
o → ue	acostarse	**Me acuesto** a las once.	*I go to bed at 11:00.*
	dormirse	A veces **me duermo** en el autobús.	*Sometimes I fall asleep on the bus.*
e → ie	despertarse	**Me despierto** a las siete.	*I wake up at 7:00*
	sentarse	**Me siento** para cenar con mi familia.	*I sit down to eat dinner with my family.*
e → i	vestirse	**Me visto** en tres minutos.	*I get dressed in three minutes.*

(*Continues*)

Mi hermano mayor y yo nos cepillamos los dientes.

Suggestion (Act. analíticas 4, p. 146): Point out that not all reflexive verbs refer to an action that one does to oneself. *Acordarse* and *irse* do not, for instance, and there are many others. Also point out that *lavarse los dientes* is very common and is equivalent to *cepillarse los dientes*.

Expansion (Act. analíticas 4): Contrast *irse,* which emphasizes the initial part of the action of going (that is, leaving, departing, setting off), with *ir,* which emphasizes the final part (that is, arriving at the destination). *Irse* is thus more natural in *¿A qué hora te vas?* while *ir* is more natural in *¿Adónde vas?* This distinction is subtle, so don't expect students to master it now, but *irse* is extremely common in the input and they should begin paying attention to it.

Autoprueba

Use what you know about reflexive verbs to conjugate the following.

1. **ducharse**
   yo _____
   tú _____
   él/ella, Ud. _____
   nosotros/as _____
   vosotros/as _____
   ellos/ellas, Uds.

   _____

2. **vestirse (e → i)**
   yo _____
   tú _____
   él/ella, Ud. _____
   nosotros/as _____
   vosotros/as _____
   ellos/ellas, Uds.

   _____

3. **despertarse (e → ie)**
   yo _____
   tú _____
   él/ella, Ud. _____
   nosotros/as _____
   vosotros/as _____
   ellos/ellas, Uds.

   _____

4 Reflexive verbs are very common in Spanish. In fact, one of the first verbs you learned is a reflexive verb. **Me llamo Miguel** literally means *I call myself Miguel.* Here are some other common reflexive verbs.

acordarse (ue) de	*to remember*
Me acuerdo muy bien **de** mis abuelos.	*I remember my grandparents very well.*
cepillarse los dientes	*to brush one's teeth*
Me cepillo los dientes cada noche antes de dormir.	*I brush my teeth every night before bed.*
irse	*to leave; to go away*
¿A qué hora **te vas**?	*At what time are you leaving?*
lavarse (las manos / la cara)	*to wash one's hands/face*
Me lavo la cara antes de salir para el trabajo.	*I wash my face before leaving for work.*
levantarse	*to get up; to stand up*
Me levanto muy tarde.	*I get up very late.*
ponerse (g) (los lentes / los lentes de contacto)	*to put on (glasses / contact lenses)*
Me pongo los lentes cuando me levanto.	*I put on my glasses when I get up.*
quedarse	*to stay*
Siempre **se queda** con su tía en Miami.	*He always stays with his aunt in Miami.*

5 When reflexive verbs are in their infinitive form, the reflexive pronoun may be attached to the end of the infinitive.

¿A qué hora **vas a acostarte**? / ¿A qué hora **te vas a acostar?**   *What time are you going to sleep?*

No tengo que ducharme antes de ir a la fiesta. / **No me tengo que duchar** antes de ir a la fiesta.   *I don't have to shower before going to the party.*

Actividades prácticas

A. Tu rutina   Usa números para indicar el orden (*order*) en que haces las siguientes actividades. Si hay una actividad que no haces, indícala con una **X**.

____ Me acuesto.   ____ Me baño.   ____ Me duermo.   _____ Me maquillo.

____ Me afeito.   ____ Me despierto.   ____ Me levanto.   ____ Me peino.

B. Preguntas y respuestas   Empareja cada pregunta con la respuesta más lógica.

1. __b__ ¿Te acuerdas dónde queda la oficina de correo?

2. __e__ ¿Nos vamos inmediatamente después de la clase?

3. __g__ ¿A qué hora se despiertan los niños?

4. __c__ ¿Te maquillas todos los días?

5. __d__ ¿Te quedas o te vas con nosotros?

6. __a__ ¿Me pongo estos zapatos (*shoes*) negros?

7. __f__ ¿A qué hora se acuesta Abril?

a. Mejor no. Vamos al gimnasio, ¿por qué no te pones los tenis (*tennis shoes*)?

b. Sé que está en esta calle.

c. Sí, por supuesto (*of course*). No me pongo maquillaje solo cuando hago ejercicio.

d. Me quedo. No puedo salir todavía (*yet*), y ya conozco ese museo.

e. Sí, está bien. Tengo que llegar a casa temprano.

f. Ella dice que se acuesta a las doce.

g. Normalmente, a las siete.

Respuestas: 1. me ducho, te duchas, se ducha, nos duchamos, os ducháis, se duchan **2.** me visto, te vistes, se viste, nos vestimos, os vestís, se visten **3.** me despierto, te despiertas, se despierta, nos despertamos, os despertáis, se despiertan

Suggestion (Act. B): Have students do this activity in pairs, taking turns asking and answering the questions.

Suggestion (Act. A): Have students compare their answers in groups. Or, list the activities along the left edge of the board and have each student (or as many as possible) create a column with his/her name at the top and their results (numbers) below. Then have the groups or the class make comparisons and answer questions, such as: *¿Los hombres se afeitan antes de bañarse o después? ¿Las mujeres se maquillan antes de peinarse o después? ¿Alguien se levanta antes de despertarse?*

C. Tus hábitos Usa la imagen para completar cada pregunta. Luego en parejas, túrnense para hacer y contestar las preguntas.

> **MODELO:** ¿A qué hora _____ los domingos?
> E1: ¿A qué hora te acuestas los domingos?
> E2: Me acuesto a las once de la noche los domingos.

Suggestion (Act. C): Have students stand up, ask each other Q1 about weekdays, and arrange themselves in a line from the earliest riser to the latest. Then have them arrange themselves in groups according to their answer to Q3. If your class is too large for this to be manageable, split them into two groups first.

te despiertas

te bañas

1. ¿A qué hora _____ los días de entre semana? ¿Y los fines de semana?

2. ¿Normalmente _____ por la mañana o por la noche?

te cepillas los dientes

te lavas el pelo

3. ¿Cuántas veces _____ al día?

4. ¿Con qué frecuencia _____? ¿Todos los días? ¿Una vez a la semana?

D. ¿Qué hace Pudenciano?

PASO 1. Pudenciano es un maestro de secundaria (*high school teacher*) en México. Vas a escuchar lo que (*what*) dice Pudenciano sobre (*about*) su rutina de la mañana. Escucha y apunta (*take notes on*) lo que hace. **¡Atención!** Tienes que cambiar el verbo a la forma **él.**

¿Qué hace Pudenciano?

Se levanta a las ___seis___[1] de la mañana. ___Se baña___,[2] ___desayuna___[3] y ___se va___[4] en su auto hacia (*toward*) su trabajo. Su trabajo es en una escuela telesecundaria.

¿A qué hora se levanta Pudenciano?

PASO 2. En una hoja de papel, usa la oración de Pudenciano como modelo para describir lo que tú haces por la mañana. Luego crea (*create*) una oración para decir qué tienes en común con Pudenciano, y otra oración en que dices una diferencia entre Pudenciano y tú.

> **MODELO:** **Mi rutina:** Me levanto a las ocho de la mañana. Desayuno, me baño, me visto y a las nueve y media me voy en autobús a clase.
> **Comparación:** Los dos desayunamos. Prudenciano se baña antes de desayunar, pero yo me baño después de desayunar.

Script (Act. D, Paso 1): *Todos los días me levanto a las 6 de la mañana... me baño, desayuno y me voy en mi auto hacia mi trabajo; es una escuela telesecundaria.*

Suggestion (Act. E):
Have one pair come to the front of the class. Read the time and have them say and act out what they are doing at that time. Repeat this with additional pairs of students.

E. ¡Una crisis por la mañana! En parejas, lean la situación. Luego usen la lista de posibles actividades para escribir qué hacen Uds. en esta situación y a qué hora. **¡Atención!** No hay tiempo para hacerlo todo. ¡Tienen que negociar!

Situación: Tú y tu compañero/a viven en la misma casa. Se despiertan. Son las siete menos un minuto. Hoy hay muchísimo tráfico y tienen que salir a las siete y cuarto para llegar a la universidad a tiempo. Solo hay un baño (*bathroom*) en la casa.

| afeitarse | cepillarse los dientes | maquillarse | ponerse los lentes (de contacto) |
| bañarse | desayunar | peinarse | vestirse |

	YO	**MI COMPAÑERO/A**
6:59	Me despierto.	Se despierta.
7:04	_____	_____
7:08	_____	_____
7:12	_____	_____
7:15	Nos vamos juntos/as.	

Suggestion (Act. F, Paso 2):
Ask students to present their *resumen* to the class, orally or on the board. Is there any item that everyone remembers, or that no one does? Ask if anyone remembers all 5 items (*¿Alguien se acuerda de los nombres de los cinco lugares y personas?*) and ask one or more of them to name all 5 places/people. Does anyone have any of these items in common?

F. ¿Te acuerdas?

PASO 1. Pregúntales a cuatro de tus compañeros si se acuerdan de cómo se llaman los siguientes lugares o personas.

> **MODELO:** ¿Te acuerdas de cómo se llama tu escuela primaria?

1. tu escuela primaria (*elementary school*)
2. tu maestro/a (*teacher*) de primer año (*first grade*) en la escuela primaria
3. tu profesor(a) de tu primera clase en la universidad
4. el nombre de tu primera mascota
5. tu mejor amigo/a en la escuela primaria

PASO 2. Crea un resumen (*summary*) de los resultados y compártelo (*share it*) con la clase.

> **MODELO:** De cuatro estudiantes, tres se acuerdan de cómo se llama su escuela primaria.

⟳ Reciclaje

The verbs *ser* and *estar*

Empareja cada sujeto con la descripción más lógica. Luego completa cada oración con la forma correcta de **ser** o **estar**.

1. __d__ nosotros
2. __a__ Shakira
3. __e__ el banco nacional y la biblioteca nacional
4. __c__ Rafael Nadal y Javier Bardem
5. __b__ el árbol

a. __Es__ de Colombia.
b. __Está__ en el parque.
c. __Son__ de España.
d. __Somos__ estudiantes.
e. __Están__ en el centro de la capital.

■ Answers to this activity are in Appendix 2 at the back of your book.

5.3   ¿Cómo es? ¿Cómo está?

Ser and *estar* with adjectives

Para empezar...

En la calle

En el Banco Mundial (*World Bank*)

En un teatro

Shakira es una cantante de Colombia, pero también trabaja en varias organizaciones como la Fundación Pies Descalzos (*Bare Feet*) y ALAS (la Fundación América Latina en Acción Solidaria [*Supportive*]), que ayudan a niños pobres. Mira las fotos y decide si las siguientes oraciones son ciertas o falsas.

■ Answers to these activities are in Appendix 2 at the back of your book.

	CIERTO	FALSO
1. **Es** famosa.	☑	☐
2. En la foto del teatro, **está** triste.	☐	☑
3. **Es** pobre.	☐	☑
4. En la foto de la calle, **está** contenta.	☑	☐
5. **Es** vieja.	☐	☑

	CIERTO	FALSO
6. En la foto de la calle, **está** enojada.	☐	☑
7. **Es** fea.	☐	☑
8. En la foto del banco, **está** seria.	☑	☐
9. **Es** delgada.	☑	☐
10. En la foto de la calle, **está** bonita.	☑	☐

Actividades analíticas

1 In **Capítulo 4,** you saw that the verb **ser** is used to express origin or identity.

| Mis padres **son** de Honduras. | *My parents are from Honduras.* |
| Maritza **es** estudiante. | *Maritza is a student.* |

You also saw that the verb **estar** may express location.

| Mario **está** en el parque. | *Mario is at the park.* |

In **Para empezar,** both **ser** and **estar** are used with adjectives to describe Shakira. Which type of description uses **ser,** and which uses **estar?**

¿SER O ESTAR?

___ser___ Shakira en general

___estar___ Shakira en la foto (en un momento específico)

■ For more comparison of **ser** and **estar**, see **Para saber más 5.3** at the back of your book.

Note (Para saber más): *Para saber más 5.3* contrasts *estar* for location of people and things and *ser* for location of events.

(*Continues*)

Autoprueba

Decide whether you would use **es (ser)** or **está (estar)** for expressing the following ideas in Spanish.

1. The library is downtown. _____
2. Marta is a biology student. _____
3. Your little brother is really tall now! _____
4. San Salvador is in El Salvador. _____
5. That teacher is from the Engineering Department. _____
6. The coastline in Chile is beautiful.

_____

Respuestas: 1. está **2.** es **3.** está **4.** está **5.** es **6.** es

Note (Act. analíticas 3): Compare *Jorge es muy alto* (which focuses on the fact that Jorge is tall, which is unlikely to change) and *Jorge está muy alto* (which focuses on the fact that there has been a change). The latter sentence would make sense when exclaiming how tall a child has grown, for instance.

---

2 The sentences in **Para empezar** are good examples of the basic difference between **ser** and **estar** when used with adjectives.

	CONCEPTO	EJEMPLOS
ser + *adjective*	intrinsic quality (unlikely to change suddenly)	Shakira **es** famosa. Estos libros **son** interesantes. Bill Gates **es** rico.
estar + *adjective*	quality subject to change or resulting from change	Shakira **está** contenta. Jorge **está** muy triste. ¿**Estás** enojado?

3 The same adjective can often be used with either **ser** or **estar,** but the overall meaning of the sentence will be different.

Shakira **es** muy bonita.	*Shakira is very pretty.*
Shakira **está** muy bonita en la foto.	*Shakira looks very pretty in the photo.*
Víctor **es** muy viejo.	*Víctor is very old.*
¡Víctor **está** muy viejo!	*Víctor is very old (compared to when I last saw him)!*
María **es** muy limpia.	*María is a very clean and tidy person.*
María **está** muy limpia.	*María is all cleaned up.*

The sentences with **ser** describe lasting qualities or properties of the people that are not likely to change suddenly. The sentences with **estar** describe qualities or properties that could change or that are the result of change: Shakira looks pretty in this particular photo, but in another less flattering photo she may not, and Víctor didn't appear old before, but now he does. María was dirty before, but now she is clean (or she looks particularly clean).

Notice that expressing the meaning of **estar** in English often involves the use of additional words, such as *look* or *appear*.

4 Here is a summary of all the uses of **ser** and **estar** that you have seen.

ser		estar	
origin	Shakira **es** de Colombia.	**location**	Shakira **está** en el parque.
identity	Shakira **es** cantante.	**subject to change or resulting from change**	Shakira **está** bonita en la foto.
intrinsic quality	Shakira **es** famosa.		

Suggestion (Act. analíticas 4): Reproduce this chart on the board in Spanish, using *origen, identidad, propiedad intrínsica, ubicación,* and *cambio.* Have students use these Spanish terms in identifying the uses in the sentences.

Which of these uses does each of the following sentences exemplify?

a. Tegucigalpa está en Honduras. _____location_____
b. Estoy muy enojado. _____change_____
c. Tegucigalpa es la capital de Honduras. _____identity_____
d. Jorge es muy alto. _identity intrinsic quality_
e. Ésther es de La Ceiba, una ciudad en el norte de Honduras. _____origin_____

Note (Act. analíticas): If students have the idea that *estar* is used only for temporary properties, show them sentences like *Juan está muerto* or *María está casada.* These are clearly not temporary situations, but they use *estar* because they are highlighting the result of a change.

La Catedral San Miguel Arcángel está en la Plaza Morazán, Tegucigalpa.

5 Estar may be followed by a verb form that ends in **-ndo** to indicate an action that is taking place at the moment, and therefore is subject to change or that is the result of change. This structure is easy to recognize.

Guillermo Anderson **está cantando** en este momento.

Guillermo Anderson is singing at this moment.

Ahora **estoy trabajando** en el museo.

I'm working at the museum right now.

Por el momento, **estamos viviendo** en un apartamento.

For right now, we're living in an apartment.

This use of **estar** with a verb ending in **-ndo** is known as the present progressive tense. It is less frequent than its counterpart in English (with *-ing*) and is sometimes overused by English speakers learning Spanish. It will be treated in more detail in **Estructura 11.3**.

Actividades prácticas

A. Español e inglés   Gracias al uso de **ser** y **estar**, el español puede expresar ideas muy complejas (*complex*) con muy pocas (*few*) palabras. Empareja cada oración en español con la traducción adecuada.

1. _c_ Eres malo.
2. _e_ Estoy muy fea.
3. _f_ Son bastante (*quite*) serios.
4. _a_ ¡Qué delgado estás!
5. _g_ Soy muy fea.
6. _b_ Están muy serios.
7. _h_ Estás malo.
8. _d_ Eres muy delgado.

a. You've really slimmed down!
b. They look like they're in a very serious mood.
c. You are a bad person.
d. You are very thin.
e. I look like a mess.
f. They are pretty serious people.
g. I'm very ugly.
h. You are sick / not doing well.

B. Diferentes lugares en la ciudad   Escoge el verbo más lógico para completar cada oración. Luego contesta la pregunta, usando una de estas opciones.

En un parque.   En un museo.   En un hospital.   En un banco.

1. [Soy / Estoy] una persona muy tranquila en general, pero en este momento [soy / estoy] enojada y triste porque dicen que no tengo dinero en mi cuenta (*account*). ¿Dónde [soy / estoy]? _En un banco_

2. [Soy / Estoy] muy aburrida porque no me gusta el arte, y este edificio tiene puro (*only*) arte. A mi amigo le gusta mucho el arte, y él [es / está] fascinado (*fascinated*). ¿Dónde [soy / estoy]? _En un museo_

3. [Soy / Estoy] muy contenta porque [soy / estoy] en un lugar muy tranquilo. También [es / está] un lugar muy bonito, porque hay muchos árboles y flores (*flowers*). ¿Dónde [soy / estoy]? _En un parque_

4. [Soy / Estoy] aquí porque [soy / estoy] malo. No [soy / estoy] médico (*doctor*), pero dicen que los médicos aquí [son / están] muy buenos. ¿Dónde [soy / estoy]? _En un hospital_

C. Reacciones   Si una persona te dice una de las siguientes oraciones, ¿cómo reaccionas? Para cada una, escoge la reacción (una pregunta) más lógica y complétala con la forma **tú** de **ser** o de **estar**.

MODELO: Estoy estudiando.
¿Eres estudiante?

1. _e_ Estoy viviendo con mi mamá en Bogotá.
2. _a_ Estoy trabajando con los pacientes (*patients*).
3. _b_ Estoy cantando y estoy bailando. Es parte de mi trabajo.
4. _f_ Estoy hablando, pero no sé qué estoy diciendo.
5. _c_ Estoy en una fiesta con Luisa, pero no estoy hablando con ella.
6. _d_ Estoy saliendo de la oficina del presidente en la Casa Blanca.

a. ¿ _Eres_ un médico / una médica?
b. ¿ _Estás_ en el teatro?
c. ¿ _Estás_ enojado con ella?
d. ¿ _Eres_ importante?
e. ¿ _Estás_ de Colombia?
f. ¿ _Estás_ muy cansado/a?

En español...

One common way to express the idea of to *become* in Spanish is with the reflexive verb **ponerse** followed by an adjective.

***Me pongo* contenta cuando estoy en el parque.**
I become/get happy when I'm at the park.

Se ponen muy divertidos en las fiestas.
They become lots of fun at parties.

Se pone muy serio en el trabajo.
He becomes/gets very serious at work.

Note (En español): The verb ponerse is a useful complement to students' developing knowledge of *ser* and *estar*. In addition, it refreshes their ability to use reflexive verbs, seen in *Estructura 5.2.*

D. Se ponen...

PASO 1. Completa cada oración en la primera columna con la terminación más lógica en la segunda columna. Usa cada terminación solo una vez (*time*).

1. Julia se pone bastante enojada cuando ___d___
2. Me pongo muy triste cuando ___f___
3. Nos ponemos muy cansados y aburridos cuando ___b___
4. Me pongo muy gordo cuando ___c___
5. Los jardines y los parques se ponen muy bonitos ___g___
6. Los estudiantes se ponen bastante serios cuando ___a___
7. Los estudiantes se ponen muy contentos cuando ___e___

a. hablan con el maestro.
b. tenemos que estudiar mucho.
c. como mucho.
d. no puede usar la computadora.
e. sacan buenas notas.
f. saco mala nota en una clase.
g. en primavera.

 PASO 2. En parejas, digan cómo se ponen Uds. en las siguientes situaciones. Pueden usar las palabras de esta lista u otras.

asustado/a (*scared*)   contento/a   nervioso/a
cansado/a   enojado/a   triste

MODELO: Pierdes (*You miss*) el autobús.
Cuando pierdo el autobús, me pongo frustrado/a.

1. Tienes un examen.
2. Tus amigos no dejan de enviarte (*won't stop sending you*) mensajes de texto.
3. Ves una película de terror.
4. Haces mucho ejercicio.
5. No ves a tu familia por mucho tiempo.

 E. ¿Estás de acuerdo? ¿Somos así? Muchos norteamericanos viven y trabajan en las grandes ciudades de Latinoamérica y España, y muchos van de turistas también. ¿Qué fama (*reputation*) tienen? En grupos, lean las opiniones de estas personas y para cada persona, contesten las preguntas.

- **Jorge, Panamá:** «Son muy trabajadores, y son muy buenos para la tecnología.»
- **Lourdes, México:** «Son personas amables (*nice*). Los jóvenes que vienen a Cancún no son tan (*so*) amables, a lo mejor (*probably*), pero los que viven allá sí son amables.»
- **María, Argentina:** «Tengo compañeros norteamericanos en el trabajo, y son muy buenas personas. Son quizá (*perhaps*) más nacionalistas que nosotros.»
- **Eric, México:** «A lo mejor quieren ser dominantes y superiores a los otros países.»
- **Jimena, México:** «Van mucho a fiestas y son muy divertidos.»

1. ¿Están Uds. de acuerdo con esta persona?
2. ¿Las personas de este país son así (*like that*)?
3. ¿Uds. son así?

Point out (Act. E): Point out to students that if they are from this country, they should say *somos.* Otherwise, they should say *son.*

MODELO: Estoy de acuerdo con Jorge. En general, somos muy trabajadores en este país, pero yo no soy así.

¿Cómo te pones cuando pierdes el autobús?

F. La personalidad de tu compañero/a

PASO 1. En parejas, pregúntense y contesten las siguientes preguntas.

¿Cómo eres en general? ¿Cómo estás hoy? ¿En qué momentos te pones muy contento/a (triste, enojado/a...)?

PASO 2. Haz (*Make*) una oración para describir a tu compañero/a. Luego haz otra oración que explica si Uds. dos son parecidos/as o diferentes, y por qué. Después, comparte la información con la clase.

> **MODELO:** Mi compañero es simpático, divertido y trabajador; se pone muy contento cuando está con sus amigos. Somos parecidos porque yo soy simpática y divertida y me pongo muy contenta cuando estoy con mis amigos, pero somos diferentes porque yo no soy muy trabajadora.

Suggestion (Act. F): Ask several students to share their sentences with the class. Survey the class to see how everyone is doing today or to find out what things make them happy/sad/angry.

G. Cultura: Asunción, la capital de Paraguay

PASO 1. Lee el texto sobre Asunción, la capital de Paraguay.

Asunción fue[a] una de las primeras ciudades en ser fundada[b] cuando los españoles llegaron[c] a Sudamérica. Es la ciudad más grande de Paraguay y está situada en la región suroeste[d] del país, cerca de la frontera con Argentina. La zona metropolitana se llama «Gran Asunción».

Aunque[e] Paraguay es un país interior (no tiene acceso al mar), la capital es un puerto[f] industrial muy importante en esta región. El río[g] Paraguay, que forma una de las fronteras naturales con Argentina, permite que los barcos entren y salgan de[h] esta ciudad portuaria.[i] La economía de Paraguay está creciendo[j] mucho en estos años y varias corporaciones tienen sus oficinas en las afueras de Asunción.

Una de las calles más antiguas y más conocidas[k] de Asunción es la calle Palma. Comienza en la Plaza de los Héroes, donde se encuentra[l] el histórico monumento llamado el Panteón Nacional de los Héroes. La calle Palma sigue hacia el noroeste[m] y termina a unas cuadras del puerto. A lo largo de[n] la historia de Asunción, esta avenida ha sido[ñ] un importante espacio público para los habitantes, lleno de[o] tiendas, boticas (antiguas farmacias) y grandes librerías. Hoy en día las personas que visitan Asunción pueden encontrar tiendas y puestos[p] con productos locales, restaurantes con comida típica y bellas casas históricas.

[a]*was* [b]*en... to be founded* [c]*arrived* [d]*southwest* [e]*Although* [f]*port* [g]*River* [h]*barcos... ships enter and leave* [i]*port (adj.)* [j]*growing* [k]*más... most well-known* [l]*se... is located* [m]*northwest* [n]*A... Throughout* [ñ]*ha... has been* [o]*lleno... filled with* [p]*stands*

Paraguay

La ciudad de Asunción y el río Paraguay

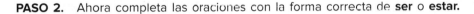

PASO 2. Ahora completa las oraciones con la forma correcta de **ser** o **estar.**

1. Asunción <u>está</u> en Paraguay.
2. Argentina <u>está</u> al sur (*south*) del país.
3. Asunción <u>es</u> una ciudad portuaria que <u>está</u> en el río Paraguay.
4. Asunción <u>es</u> una de las ciudades en la zona metropolitana Gran Asunción.
5. Las oficinas de las grandes corporaciones <u>están</u> en las afueras de la ciudad.
6. Asunción <u>es</u> grande y antigua.
7. La calle Palma y el Panteón Nacional de los Héroes <u>son</u> sitios importantes en la historia de Asunción.
8. Últimamente (*Lately*) muchos paraguayos <u>están</u> contentos porque su economía está creciendo.

PASO 3. En parejas, contesten las preguntas y explíquense (*explain to each other*) sus respuestas.

1. Muchas ciudades portuarias, como Asunción, tienen una población muy grande. ¿Por qué crees que es así?
2. ¿Hay otras ciudades grandes en el mundo hispano que son puertos? ¿Y hay ciudades grandes que no tienen puerto?
3. En tu país, ¿hay ciudades grandes que son portuarias? ¿Hay otras ciudades grandes que no tienen puerto?

Suggestion (Act. G, Paso 3): For item 1, help students express their ideas in Spanish: *Hay mucho trabajo en los puertos, y por eso llega mucha gente a vivir allí*. For item 2, point out that there are many examples of large cities with ports (e.g., Buenos Aires, Sevilla, Barcelona) and some that are large despite not having a port (e.g., Mexico City, Madrid). For item 3, point out that in the U.S., most large cities are ports (e.g., New York, Chicago, Los Angeles), but some are not (e.g., Denver).]

Reciclaje

Demonstrative adjectives

Escribe la terminación de género y número para cada adjetivo demostrativo. Luego completa cada oración con la expresión adecuada.

est__ muchacho   est__ catedral   est__ edificios

est__ chicas   est__ tienda

1. _____Estos edificios_____ son más altos que los otros.
2. _____Esta tienda_____ tiene mejores precios que la otra.
3. _____Este muchacho_____ es más fuerte que el otro.
4. _____Estas chicas_____ son más bonitas que las otras.
5. _____Esta catedral_____ es más alta que la otra.

■ Answers to this activity are in Appendix 2 at the back of your book.

5.4 Hay algo interesante en Tegucigalpa.

Indefinite and negative expressions

Para empezar...

Mira el mapa del centro de Tegucigalpa, la capital de Honduras. Usando la información en este mapa, decide si cada oración es cierta o falsa.

■ Answers to these activities are in Appendix 2 at the back of your book.

En este mapa...

	CIERTO	FALSO
1. **algunos** hoteles están cerca de (*close to*) la avenida República de Chile.	☑	☐
2. no hay **ningún** parque en Tegucigalpa.	☐	☑
3. hay **algo** interesante en la calle Bolívar, si te gusta el arte.	☑	☐
4. **ninguna** librería está en la avenida Máximo Jerez.	☑	☐
5. hay **algunas** tiendas en la avenida Miguel Cervantes.	☑	☐
6. no hay **ningún** cine en el paseo Casamata.	☐	☑
7. **algunos** hospitales están en la calle Morelos.	☐	☑
8. **ningún** museo está en la calle Los Dolores.	☑	☐
9. hay **algunos** edificios del gobierno (*government*) en la calle Bolívar.	☑	☐
10. no hay **nada** interesante en el centro de Tegucigalpa.	☐	☑

Actividades analíticas

1 In **Para empezar,** you see some words in **boldface** type. Write those words in the appropriate position in the chart here. When there are two forms of the same word, write both next to the same English translation.

algo something	_algunos_ _algunas_ some	
nada nothing	_ningún_ _ninguna_ no (not one/any)	

2 Given what you know about Spanish adjectives, you should not be surprised to see that **algún** and **ningún** change their form to agree with the gender and number of the noun that follows them. Circle the correct form to complete the sentences here.

a. Hay algunos / **algunas** casas en la avenida Cervantes.
b. Tengo **algunos** / algunas libros en mi mochila.
c. No hay **ningún** / ninguna parque en esta parte de la ciudad.
d. No conozco ningún / **ninguna** galería de arte en esa calle.

For **algunos/algunas**, the plural forms are the most common, though singular forms do exist (**algún/alguna**). For **ningún/ninguna**, it is the singular forms that are the most common, though plural forms also exist (**ningunos/ningunas**).

3 The verb must be preceded by **no** when negative expressions such as **ningún/ninguna** or **nada** come after the verb. Unlike English, double negatives are common in Spanish.

No hay **ningún** cine en el paseo Casamata. — There isn't any / There is no movie theater on Paseo Casamata.

No tengo **nada** en mi mochila. — I don't have anything / I have nothing in my backpack.

4 **Algo** and **nada** both refer to things. To talk about people, use **alguien** (someone) and **nadie** (no one). These words are invariable; that is, there are no separate masculine/feminine or singular/plural forms.

Hay **alguien** en esa tienda. — There is someone in that store.

Nadie vive en esa casa. — No one lives in that house.

When **alguien** and **nadie** are objects of the verb, they are preceded by **a.**

¿Conoces **a alguien** en Tegucigalpa? — Do you know anyone / someone in Tegucigalpa?

No conozco **a nadie** en ese banco. — I don't know anyone / I know no one in that bank.

5 A common negative expression for time is **nunca** (never).

Nunca llego tarde a mi clase. — I never arrive late to my class.

No voy al campo **nunca.** — I never go to the countryside.

The opposite of **nunca** is **siempre** (always).

Siempre voy al parque los domingos. — I always go to the park on Sundays.

Expansion (Act. analíticas): You may wish to point out that when the masculine singular forms algún and ningún are used as pronouns (i.e., when there is no following noun), the forms are alguno and ninguno. Examples: —Busco un hotel. ¿Hay alguno en esta calle? —No, no hay ninguno.

Suggestion (Act. analíticas 2–5): Go over the sample sentences with students and have them change each expression to its opposite. For example, they should change Hay alguien en esa tienda. to No hay nadie en esa tienda. You can do this orally as a class or have students do it in writing or in pairs.

Suggestions (Act. A):
• Point out that when filling in the blanks for items 4–7, students should look to the same item in the adjacent column to determine what they are commenting on.
• Remind students that algunos/as is usually used as plural while ningún/ninguna is usually used as singular.
• If you live in a large city, you may find it more interesting to restrict this activity to a particular part of el centro or el campus so that students are not able to choose (a) for everything. Alternatively, you may ask students to respond based on their hometown.
• Have students do this in groups of 3 or 4, and see if they all agree on the answers.
• Ask for volunteers to give their answers. When they choose the affirmative options, require them to justify their answers with examples. ¿Sí? ¿Hay algunas galerías de arte? Da un ejemplo, por favor.

Actividades prácticas

A. El centro de tu ciudad
¿Cómo es el centro de tu ciudad? ¿Qué hay y qué no hay? Completa las oraciones que tienen un espacio en blanco. Luego escoge **a** o **b** como la mejor descripción del centro de tu ciudad.

1. ____ a. Hay algunos lugares buenos para bailar. b. No hay ningún lugar bueno para bailar.
2. ____ a. Algunas veces hay conciertos. b. Nunca hay conciertos.
3. ____ a. Hay algunos museos buenos. b. No hay ningún museo bueno.
4. ____ a. Hay algunas galerías de arte. b. No hay <u>ninguna galería de arte.</u>
5. ____ a. Hay algunos cines. b. No hay <u>ningún cine</u>.
6. ____ a. Hay <u>algunos parques bonitos</u>. b. No hay ningún parque bonito.
7. ____ a. Hay <u>algunos teatros</u>. b. No hay ningún teatro.

Eduardo José Cabra Martínez, Ileana Cabra Joglar y René Pérez Joglar del grupo Calle 13

B. Los miembros de Calle 13
Calle 13 es un grupo musical de Puerto Rico. Sus miembros son los hermanastros René Pérez Joglar y Eduardo José Cabra Martínez, conocidos como (*known as*) «Residente» y «Visitante» y su media hermana, Ileana Cabra Joglar, conocida como «PG-13». Completa las oraciones usando la siguiente lista. Cada palabra se usa solo una vez. **¡Atención!** Dos de las oraciones son falsas. ¿Cuáles son?

alguien   algunas   algunos   nada   nadie   ningún   nunca

	CIERTO	FALSO
1. <u>Algunas</u> personas dicen que el estilo de su música es reggaetón, pero ellos dicen que es «música urbana».	☑	☐
2. En su música, siempre canta <u>alguien</u>. Casi siempre son los dos hermanastros, pero a veces es su media hermana, Ileana.	☑	☐
3. Reciben (*They receive*) <u>algunos</u> premios (*awards*) Grammy casi cada año entre 2006 y 2015.	☑	☐
4. <u>Nadie</u> compra sus canciones nunca.	☐	☑
5. Como muchos músicos latinoamericanos, no tienen <u>ningún</u> problema (*m.*) en mezclar (*mixing*) la música con la política.	☑	☐
6. <u>Nunca</u> pierden (*miss*) la oportunidad de colaborar con otros artistas, como Nelly Furtado o Café Tacuba.	☑	☐
7. Los miembros de este grupo musical no tienen <u>nada</u> de importancia en la vida (*life*) cultural de Puerto Rico.	☐	☑

C. Algunas ciudades
Primero, indica si conoces a alguien en cada una de las siguientes ciudades. Luego, si no conoces a nadie en alguna ciudad, pregúntales a varios (*several*) compañeros si conocen a alguien allí. Apunta el nombre de la persona que conoce a alguien en esa ciudad.

> **MODELO:** E1: ¿Conoces a alguien en Atlanta?
> E2: No, no conozco a nadie allí. (Sí, conozco a alguien allí.)

☐ Atlanta _____   ☐ Lima _____   ☐ Panamá _____

☐ Boston _____   ☐ Madrid _____   ☐ Portland _____

☐ Buenos Aires _____   ☐ Medellín _____   ☐ Vancouver _____

D. ¿Qué hacen los estudiantes en la clase?

PASO 1. ¿Qué hace un estudiante bueno en nuestra clase? ¿Hay cosas que nunca hace? Crea tres respuestas con **siempre** y tres respuestas con **nunca**.

> **MODELOS:** Un estudiante bueno siempre habla español en la clase.
> Los estudiantes buenos nunca hablan inglés en la clase.

PASO 2. Indica las respuestas que son ciertas para tu clase.
1. «Siempre nos sentamos bien.» ☐
2. «Nunca tomamos café o refrescos (*soft drinks*) en la clase.» ☐
3. «No dormimos nunca en la clase.» ☐

Suggestion (Act. B): Point out that the word *reggaetón* is sometimes spelled *reguetón*, in accordance with Spanish spelling rules.

Suggestion (Act. C): If needed, modify the list of cities to fit your local circumstances. There should be some cities where it is very likely that students know someone, and others where it is less likely. When students are done, ask them about the results. *¿Hay alguna ciudad donde nadie conoce a nadie? ¿Alguna ciudad donde todos conocen a alguien?*

Follow-up (Act. C): Have students tell the rest of the class in which cities they or their classmates know someone. *No conozco a nadie en Lima, pero Sarah sí conoce a alguien.*

Suggestion (Act. D, Paso 2): Demonstrate that *sentarse bien* means sitting up straight with the feet on the floor. Add observations from your own experience about differences in classroom behavior between North American universities and Spanish-speaking ones.

¡Leamos!

«¿Padre, hijo o caballo°?», por don Juan Manuel   *horse*

Antes de leer

PASO 1. Indica si cada palabra se refiere a la ciudad, al campo o a los dos.

1. la tranquilidad
2. los edificios
3. los caballos

4. el silencio
5. la metrópoli
6. el monumento histórico

7. el taxi
8. el estrés (*stress*)
9. la soledad (*solitude*)

10. los mercados y las tiendas

 PASO 2. En grupos de tres o cuatro personas, ¿cuántos otros lugares, cosas o personas que se asocian con la ciudad y el campo pueden apuntar (*write down*) en una lista en dos minutos? Comparen con los otros grupos.

A leer

PASO 1. Mientras (*While*) lees el cuento (*story*), empareja cada párrafo con el dibujo que mejor lo acompañe.

«¿Padre, hijo o caballo?»
                                                                por don Juan Manuel

—Hoy es día de mercado; vamos al pueblo para comprar unas cuantas[a] cosas que necesitamos

1 Deciden llevar con ellos un caballo para transportar sus compras. Parten[b] por la mañana muy temprano para el mercado: el caballo sin carga,[c] ellos a pie.[d]

2 Por el camino[e] se topan con[f] unos hombres que regresan del pueblo. Dichos[g] señores dicen entonces que ni el padre ni[h] el hijo parecen muy cuerdos[i] pues ambos[j] van a pie cuando el caballo va sin carga. Al oír esto, el padre le pide opinión a su hijo. Este admite que los hombres tienen razón,[k] y que, como el caballo no tiene carga, uno de ellos debe montarlo. Así pues, el padre manda[l] montar a su hijo y siguen adelante.[m]

3 Un poco más tarde, topan con otro grupo de hombres que regresa del pueblo. Estos hombres declaran que el padre está loco pues, viejo y cansado, va a pie mientras que su hijo, tan joven y robusto, va montado a caballo. El padre pide consejo[n] a su hijo y este declara que, en efecto, los hombres tienen razón. Así es que el hijo baja[ñ] del caballo y el padre se monta.

4 Algunos minutos más tarde, otros hombres que regresan del mercado critican al padre: según ellos, un joven tan[o] delicado no debe ir a pie. Por eso[p] el padre hace montar a su hijo en su caballo y ninguno de los dos va entonces a pie.

Más adelante se topan con otros hombres que también regresan del pueblo y estos critican tanto al padre como[q] al hijo. Dicen:

—¿Cómo va a poder cargar un caballo tan flaco a dos hombres tan grandes y pesados[r]?

5 El padre le pregunta al hijo qué deben hacer para no ser reprochados[s] ya más y al fin[t] llegan a la conclusión de que lo único que les resta[u] es cargar con el caballo. Padre e hijo llegan al mercado, pues, con el caballo en sus hombros[v] pero, a pesar de[w] esto, muchos se lo critican.

[a]unas... *a few* [b]*They depart* [c]sin... *without a load* [d]a... *on foot* [e]Por... *On the road* [f]se... *they run into* [g]*These* [h]ni... *neither the father nor* [i]*sane*
[j]pues... *since both* [k]tienen... *are right* [l]*orders* [m]*ahead, forward* [n]*advice* [ñ]*gets down* [o]*so* [p]Por... *For that reason* [q]tanto... *both father and* [r]*heavy*
[s]*criticized* [t]al... *in the end* [u]lo... *the only option that remains* [v]*shoulders* [w]a... *in spite of*

a. _4_   b. _1_   c. _3_   d. _5_   e. _2_

(Continues)

PASO 2. Indica si cada oración es cierta o falsa. Corrige (*Correct*) las oraciones falsas.

	CIERTO	FALSO
1. El padre y su hijo viven en la ciudad.	☐	☑
2. El padre y su hijo van al pueblo para comprar un coche.	☐	☑
3. El padre y su hijo llevan el caballo para transportar sus cosas.	☑	☐
4. El padre y su hijo escuchan los consejos de los hombres que ven (*they see*) durante el viaje.	☑	☐
5. Después de mucha crítica, el padre y su hijo deciden llevar (*carry*) el caballo en sus hombros.	☑	☐

Después de leer

PASO 1. Contesta las preguntas según lo que leíste (*what you read*) en el cuento.

1. ¿Cómo es el padre? ¿Cómo es el hijo?
2. ¿Dónde están ellos? ¿Adónde van?
3. ¿Cómo se pone el padre cuando lo critican los hombres del pueblo?
4. ¿Cómo se ponen los hombres del pueblo al ver a dos hombres llevando un caballo?
5. ¿Cómo crees que se sienten (*feel*) el padre y su hijo después de llevar el caballo?

PASO 2. Escoge la mejor moraleja del cuento para ti.

☐ No debes escuchar los consejos de otras personas.
☐ Es importante explicar las razones por las que haces algo.
☐ Es importante entender por qué haces algo.
☐ Es imposible evitar (*avoid*) la crítica.
☐ Es importante pensar por uno mismo (*oneself*).

Suggestion (Después de leer, Paso 2): Put students into groups according to which moral of the story they chose and have each group explain their choice.

Expansion (Después de leer): Have students work in groups to act out the story.

¡Escuchemos!

¿Cómo llego al Ranario?

Note (Antes de escuchar): Point out to students that most of the antonyms will be used in the videos.

Note (A escuchar, Paso 1): Students may notice that Yenaro uses *tú*, not *Ud.*, to give directions. If students ask about this, remind them that the use of *tú* and *Ud.* varies from country to country.

Video track (A escuchar, Paso 1): This video clip can be found on the DVD to accompany *Conéctate: Cap.* 5, Track 5.

Antes de escuchar

Empareja cada palabra con su antónimo.

1. __d__ bajar
2. __c__ la derecha
3. __a__ doblar
4. __b__ salir

a. continuar sin desviarte (seguir derecho)
b. entrar
c. la izquierda
d. subir

A escuchar

PASO 1. El Ranario (*Frog Pond*) es una atracción popular en Monteverde, Costa Rica. Mira y escucha por lo menos tres veces mientras Yenaro explica cómo se llega del Ranario a otros lugares de Monteverde. Mientras escuchas, completa las indicaciones (*directions*) con la información que falta (*that is missing*).

1. Tomas la calle a la _____. Bajas. Llegas a la intersección. De la _____, doblas hacia la _____. Subes un poco. Después del supermercado, SuperCompro, doblas a la _____, caminas unos veinticinco metros y llegas al restaurante Tree House.

2. Al Hotel Montaña, okay, _____ esta dirección, hacia arriba. Continúas sin _____, o desviarte, como un kilómetro. Después del Hotel Establo, a mano derecha _____ perfectamente al Hotel Montaña.

PASO 2. Mira y escucha mientras otros explican cómo se llega al Ranario de sus lugares de trabajo. Luego contesta las preguntas con un compañero / una compañera.

Expresiones útiles

el cruce	intersection
la curva	curve

1. ¿En qué restaurante está Erick? El Restaurante Morphos
2. ¿Cuántos metros hay que viajar para llegar al Ranario?
3. ¿Subes o bajas para llegar al Ranario? Subes

4. ¿Dónde está Anlluly? El Hotel Montaña
5. ¿Cuántos metros hay que viajar para llegar al Ranario? 600 metros
6. ¿Vas a la izquierda o a la derecha para llegar al Ranario? izquierda

Después de escuchar

Mira el mapa y escoge un punto de partida (*starting point*) y un destino final en el pueblo. Luego dile (*tell*) a un compañero / una compañera dónde tiene que empezar (pero no su destino final) y dale (*give him/her*) instrucciones para ir de un lugar al otro.

Video track (A escuchar, Paso 2): This video clip can be found on the DVD to accompany *Conéctate: Cap. 5,* Track 6.

Videoscript (A escuchar, Paso 1): 1. *Tomas la calle a la izquierda. Bajas. Llegas a la intersección. De la intersección, doblas hacia la derecha. Subes un poco. Después del supermercado, SuperCompro, doblas a la izquierda, caminas unos 25 metros y llegas al restaurante Tree House.* **2.** *Al Hotel Montaña, okay, tomas esta dirección, hacia arriba. Continúas sin doblar, o desviarte, como un kilómetro. Después del Hotel Establo, a mano derecha llegas perfectamente al Hotel Montaña.*

Note (A escuchar, Paso 2): Tell students they will have to do some addition to get the answers to questions 2 and 5.

Videoscript (A escuchar, Paso 2): 1. ERICK: *Salimos del resta..., agarramos a la derecha aproximadamente 200 metros. Llegamos al cruce y agarramos a la izquierda unos 300 metros subiendo.* **2.** ANLLULY: *Saliendo, okay, saliendo del hotel, coge a mano izquierda. Son como unos 400 metros. Después hay una intersección; igual, coge a mano der... a mano izquierda y de ahí son unos 200 metros. El edificio está a mano izquierda.*

¡Escribamos!

Un lugar que conozco

Es importante poder escribir una descripción de un lugar que conoces para el uso de un turista de visita en ese lugar.

Antes de escribir

Haz (*Make*) una lista de las ciudades que conoces bien. De esas ciudades, decide qué ciudad conoces mejor y piensa en todas las cosas que se pueden hacer allí.

Dibuja una rueda (*wheel*) de todas las categorías de atracciones de la ciudad y da por lo menos un ejemplo para cada una. El modelo te puede ayudar.

MODELO: Chicago, ~~Ocean City, Philadel-phia~~

A escribir

Ahora usa la información de tu dibujo para formar un párrafo sobre la ciudad que escogiste (*you chose*). Escribe oraciones completas para dar una descripción amplia de la ciudad. ¿Cuáles son los mejores lugares para visitar y por qué? ¿Qué se puede hacer en una visita de un día o un fin de semana?

Después de escribir

Revisa (*Check over*) tu ensayo. Luego intercambia (*exchange*) ensayos con un compañero / una compañera. Lee el ensayo de tu compañero/a y determina si falta (*it lacks*) información necesaria. Lee de nuevo (*again*) el ensayo de tu compañero/a con cuidado (*carefully*) para revisar los siguientes puntos de gramática.

☐ usa **ser** y **estar** de manera correcta (es decir, describe dónde **están** los mejores lugares para visitar y cómo **son** esos lugares)

☐ usa comparaciones correctas (**más... que, menos... que**)

☐ hay concordancia (*agreement*) entre los sustantivos (*nouns*) y verbos

☐ hay concordancia de género (*gender*) entre los adjetivos y lo que describen

☐ tiene la ortografía (*spelling*) correcta

Después de revisar el ensayo de tu compañero/a, devuélveselo (*return it to him/her*). Mira tu propio (*own*) ensayo para ver los cambios que tu compañero/a recomienda y haz las revisiones necesarias.

Diagrama (rueda)

Chicago

Arte
- National Museum of Mexican Art
- ver el arte de Carlos Cortez y Leopoldo Méndez

Música
- escuchar música jazz

Monumentos
- subir la torre Sears
- hacer un tour de la arquitectura
- tomar el tren «L» por la ciudad

Atracciones naturales
- la playa
- el río
- el parque Humboldt

Comida
- comer en los restaurantes puertorriqueños
- comer una salchicha (*hot dog*) «Chicago-style»

De compras
- Macy's en la calle State
- caminar por The Magnificent Mile

Deportes
- ver un partido de béisbol en Wrigley Field

Vida nocturna
(*Nightlife*)
- bailar en los clubes

ESTRATEGIA

Drawing

For some writing assignments, the best way to organize your ideas is by using drawings—a wheel with ideas radiating off the spokes, a flow chart, or a series of quote bubbles. Drawing can help you visualize your thoughts for better coverage, organization, and flow.

Suggestions (Después de leer):
- To motivate students to edit their own work as well as their classmates' carefully, occasionally grade their editing instead of their writing.
- Have students circle all examples of *ser* and underline all examples of *estar* in their classmates' essays. Then have them identify the corresponding subjects. Does each verb agree with its subject?

¡Hablemos!

Hagamos un viaje°   *Let's take a trip*

Antes de hablar

Primero escoge un destino de la lista. Luego piensa en las respuestas a las preguntas que siguen.

- el barrio (*neighborhood*) favorito de tu ciudad
- el mejor parque que conoces
- una ciudad grande de este país
- el mejor lugar para ir de compras

- la mejor atracción cultural
- tu lugar natural favorito (un lago [*lake*], una montaña, una playa, etcétera)

1. ¿Dónde está el lugar?
2. ¿Cómo es el lugar?
3. ¿Cuál es la mejor manera de viajar al destino? (¿A pie, en autobús, en avión, en coche, en metro o en taxi?) Explica cómo llegar, paso por paso (*step by step*).
4. ¿Cuál es la mejor manera de viajar una vez llegado/a (*once you've arrived*) al destino?
5. ¿Cuánto cuesta(n)...

- el viaje?
- el transporte en el destino?
- las entradas (*tickets*)?

- el alojamiento (*lodging*)?
- la comida y las bebidas *(drinks)*?

6. ¿Cuáles son los monumentos y/o edificios famosos?

A hablar

Usa las preguntas de **Antes de hablar** para entrevistar a tres compañeros de clase para saber más sobre sus destinos y apunta sus respuestas. ¡No te olvides de agradecerles (*thank*) a tus compañeros por sus recomendaciones!

COMPAÑERO/A	DESTINO	TRANSPORTE LOCAL	PRECIOS	MONUMENTOS FAMOSOS
1.				
2.				
3.				

Después de hablar

De los lugares que han descrito (*have described*) tus compañeros, ¿adónde quieres ir? ¿Por qué? Justifica tu decisión. ¿Cuál es el lugar más popular entre tus compañeros de clase?

CONÉCTATE AL MUNDO PROFESIONAL

Employers often want employees who are willing to travel and who can independently navigate a new city, learn to use public transportation, and deal with unexpected delays and outages—all while making the employers look good by arriving on time to meetings and representing them well. Studying abroad can provide you with a lot of these important professional skills.

Conéctate a la música

Canción: «No hay nadie como tú» (2008)
Artistas: Calle 13 (Puerto Rico) con Café Tacuba (México)

Calle 13 es un grupo puertorriqueño que consiste en los hermanastros «Residente» (René Pérez Joglar) y «Visitante» (Eduardo José Cabra Martínez), y a veces su media hermana «PG-13» (Ileana Cabra Joglar). Calle 13 hace música urbana y alternativa, con influencias fuertes de hip hop y reggaetón. En esta canción, también participa el grupo mexicano Café Tacuba.

Note (Conéctate a la música): Be advised that the lyrics for this song contain the words *prostituta* and *sexo*, though these words play no role in the activities here.

Antes de escuchar

Esta canción habla de muchos opuestos (*opposites*) en el mundo. Para empezar, piensa en un opuesto de cada uno de los siguientes conceptos.

1. ciudad ____campo____

Expansion (A escuchar): Ask students to write down other words that they hear in the song. Watching the video makes this task much more manageable.

2. silencio ____ruido____
3. mujer ____hombre____
4. ricos ____pobres____

Note (A escuchar): The video that was released with this song is particularly good for students, since it gives clear visual cues to the meaning of many of the words. Be aware that it contains some sexual images.

A escuchar

PASO 1. Escucha y contesta las siguientes preguntas.

La primera estrofa (*verse*)

Dicen que hay micrófonos y altoparlantes (*loudspeakers*), y que el mundo tiene ____seis mil____ millones de habitantes (*inhabitants*).

El estribillo (*chorus*)

El estribillo es muy sencillo (*simple*). ¿Qué dice?
No hay nadie como tú. No hay nadie como tú, mi amor.

Según la canción, ¿cuál es la idea opuesta (*opposite*) de cada una de las siguientes cosas?

La segunda estrofa

a. vegetarianos: ____carnicerías____
b. enfermedades (*diseases*): ____medicinas____
c. capitalismo: ____comunismo____

La tercera estrofa

d. muchas preguntas: ____pocas respuestas____

PASO 2. En tu opinión, ¿cuál es el mensaje principal de esta canción?

MODELO: Pienso que el mensaje principal es que...

Después de escuchar

PASO 1. Escribe por lo menos cinco oraciones para describirte. Piensa en tus intereses, tus talentos, tu familia, tu hogar (*home*), tu educación, tus esperanzas (*hopes*) y tus planes.

PASO 2. Ahora comparte tu descripción con dos o tres compañeros de clase. Tacha (*Cross out*) cualquier parte de tu descripción que también aparezca (*that also appears*) en la descripción de uno de los miembros de tu grupo, y reemplázala con algo único (*replace it with something unique*). Al terminar, comparte las cinco maneras en que no hay nadie como tú.

MODELO: Me llamo Silvia Pérez y soy hija única. Vivo en Austin, pero soy de Baltimore. Me gusta jugar fútbol y soy bastante rápida: Puedo correr cinco kilómetros en menos de veintidós minutos. Un día quiero participar en los Juegos Olímpicos. ~~Estudio terapia física en la universidad.~~ Me levanto todos los días a las cinco de la mañana y hago ejercicio con mi equipo.

Residente y Visitante, dos miembros del grupo Calle 13

■ For copyright reasons, the songs referenced in **Conéctate a la música** have not been provided by the publisher. The video for this song can be found on YouTube, and it is available for purchase from the iTunes store.

Expansion (A escuchar, Paso 2): Ask students to give the grammatical reason for why the title of the song contains the word *no* (that is, why there is a double negative).

VOCABULARIO

Now that I have completed the chapter, I can . . .

- ☐ express gratitude
- ☐ ask for and give directions
- ☐ describe cities and towns
- ☐ compare urban and rural life
- ☐ use numbers from 100 to 9,999
- ☐ talk about my daily routine
- ☐ describe people and places
- ☐ express negation and indefinite quantities of people and things

Comunicación

Gracias por + *noun/infinitive.*	Thank you for . . .
(Muchas/Muchísimas) gracias.	Thank you (very much).
Sí, gracias.	Yes, please.
Te/Le/Les agradezco por	I appreciate that you/ I thank you for
De nada. / No hay de qué.	You're welcome.
¿Dónde está / queda... ?	Where is . . . ?
aquí/allí	here/there
Siga	Go / Keep going
derecho/recto	straight
hasta llegar a	until you arrive at
Doble/Gire	Turn
a la derecha/izquierda	(to the) right/left
Suba/Baje	Go up/Go down
por esta calle	this street
Está/Queda	It's
a la derecha/izquierda	on/to the right/left
al lado de	next to
detrás de	behind
enfrente de	across from
en la esquina de... y	on the corner of . . . and

Los paisajes urbanos y rurales / Urban and rural landscapes

las afueras	outskirts, suburbs
el almacén	department store
el árbol	tree
el autobús	bus
la calle	street
el campo	countryside / rural area
la carnicería	butcher shop
la carretera	highway
el centro	downtown

el cine	(movie) theater, movie
la ciudad	city
el coche	car
la contaminación	pollution
la cuadra	block
el edificio	building
la escuela	school
la frutería	fruit store
la iglesia	church
el jardín	garden
el lugar	place
el pueblo	town
el puente	bridge
el puesto	stand
el rascacielos	skyscraper
el ruido	noise
la tienda	store
la torre	tower

Cognados: el apartamento, la avenida, el banco, la capital, la catedral, el hospital, el mercado, el metro, el museo, el parque, la plaza, el restaurante, el taxi, el teatro, el tráfico, la tranquilidad, el transporte público

Los verbos

acordarse (ue) (de)	to remember
acostarse (ue)	to go to bed
afeitarse	to shave
bañarse	to bathe (oneself)
cepillarse los dientes	to brush one's teeth
conocer (zc)	to know; to be familiar with
despertarse (ie)	to wake up
dormirse (ue)	to go to sleep
ducharse	to shower
hacer (*irreg.*)	to make; to do
irse (*irreg.*)	to leave; to go away
lavarse	to wash (oneself)
la cara	to wash one's face
las manos	to wash one's hands
levantarse	to get up; to stand up
llegar	to arrive
maquillarse	to apply make-up
oír (*irreg.*)	to hear; to listen to
peinarse	to comb (one's hair)
poner (*irreg.*)	to put
ponerse (*irreg.*)	to put on; to become
contento/a	to become happy
los lentes / los lentes de contacto	to put on glasses/ contacts
quedarse	to stay
saber (*irreg.*)	to know (*a fact*)
salir (*irreg.*)	to leave; to go out
sentarse (ie)	to sit down
traer (*irreg.*)	to bring; to carry
venir (*irreg.*)	to come
vestirse (i)	to get dressed

Los adjetivos y los adverbios

antiguo/a	ancient; former; old
Cognados: moderno/a, rural, urbano/a	
bastante	quite, enough
muy	very

Las expresiones indefinidas y negativas

algo	something
alguien	someone
algunos/as	some
nada	nothing
nadie	no one
ningún/ninguna	none, not any, no

Los números del 100 al 9.999

cien/ciento	one hundred
doscientos/as	two hundred
trescientos/as	three hundred
cuatrocientos/as	four hundred
quinientos/as	five hundred
seiscientos/as	six hundred
setecientos/as	seven hundred
ochocientos/as	eight hundred
novecientos/as	nine hundred
mil	one thousand
dos mil	two thousand
tres mil	three thousand
cuatro mil	four thousand
cinco mil	five thousand
seis mil	six thousand
siete mil	seven thousand
ocho mil	eight thousand
nueve mil	nine thousand

¡A comer!°

Let's eat!

Un camarero (*waiter*)
guatemalteco nos presenta
los postres (*desserts*) del día.

Objetivos

When you finish this chapter, you will be able to:

- respond affirmatively to a request
- give and decline invitations politely
- describe meals, table settings, and foods
- talk about the past
- use pronouns to avoid repetition
- discuss meals and foods in the Spanish-speaking world

Mc Graw Hill Education **connect**
www.mhhe.com/connect

6

COMUNICACIÓN LARIO UCTURA TE

Video track (Act. A): This video clip can be found on the DVD to accompany *Conéctate: Cap. 6*, Track 1.

Videoscript (Act A): 1. *Por supuesto.* **2.** *¡Claro que sí!* **3.** *¡Cómo no! ¡Cómo no!* **4.** *Ya por supuesto.* **5.** *Con mucho gusto.* **6.** *Por supuesto.* **7.** *Sí, cómo no.* **8.** *¡Cómo no!*

¡Cómo no!
Responding to requests

A. A ver: ¡Cómo no! Mira y escucha. Luego mira otra vez con pausas e indica la expresión usada para contestar cada pregunta. Mira una tercera vez para verificar tus respuestas.

		¡CLARO QUE SÍ!	¡CÓMO NO!	CON MUCHO GUSTO.	¡POR SUPUESTO!
1.	¿Quieres vivir en otro país?	☐	☐	☐	☑
2.	¿Es importante poder hablar inglés?	☑	☐	☐	☐
3.	¿Ud. tiene un sueño (*dream*) en la vida?	☐	☑	☐	☐
4.	¿Quiere mandarles un saludo (*send a greeting*) a los estudiantes de español?	☐	☐	☐	☑
5.	¿Nos hace el favor de presentarse?	☐	☐	☑	☐
6.	¿Nos hace el favor de describir el propósito (*purpose*) del viaje a Madrid?	☐	☐	☐	☑
7.	¿Quiere mandarles un saludo a los estudiantes de español?	☐	☑	☐	☐
8.	¿Nos hace el favor de presentarse?	☐	☑	☐	☐

If someone invites you to do something or offers you something, here's what you might say if you want to accept.

Sí, gracias.   Yes, please.
Si no es molestia.   If it's not a bother.

¡Atención! Remember, in Spanish, **gracias** is used in instances where North Americans might say *please*.

—**¿Quieres un café?**
—**Sí, gracias.**

You can also use any of these expressions, which convey the English *Sure!*, *No problem,* and *Of course,* to respond in the affirmative.

¡Claro que sí!   **Con mucho gusto.**
¡Cómo no!   **Por supuesto.**

—**¿Me traes un café, por favor?**
—**Sí. ¡Cómo no!**
—**Gracias.**

¡Atención! The expression **¡Cómo no!** means *Of course!,* but **como no...** followed by a verb means *since/because + negative statement.*

Como no tenemos tiempo, no   Since we don't have time, we're not
**   vamos a tener la prueba hoy.**   going to have the quiz today.

B. ¡Por supuesto!

PASO 1. Para cada pregunta, escoge la respuesta más adecuada para ti y luego termina la frase para dar una explicación.

1. ¿Quieres vivir en otro país?
   ☐ No, quiero vivir aquí, porque...
   ☐ Por supuesto. Quiero vivir en...

2. ¿Es importante poder hablar español?
   ☐ No. Es útil (*useful*), pero no es importante, porque...
   ☐ ¡Claro que sí! Es importante porque...

3. ¿Tienes un sueño (*dream*) en la vida?
   ☐ No, no soy ambicioso/a. Solo quiero...
   ☐ Por supuesto. Quiero...

4. ¿Quieres cenar en mi casa esta noche?
   ☐ No, gracias. Ya (*Already*) tengo planes. Voy a...
   ☐ ¡Claro que sí! Yo puedo llevar...

5. ¿Nos haces el favor de presentarte (*introduce yourself*) a la clase?
   ☐ Lo siento. No puedo. Soy muy introvertido/a y no me gusta...
   ☐ ¡Cómo no! ¡Hola! Me llamo...

6. Quieres ir al campo conmigo este fin de semana?
   ☐ Lo siento. No puedo. Este fin de semana...
   ☐ ¡Cómo no! Podemos...

PASO 2. En parejas, practiquen las expresiones, pidiéndole algo a su compañero/a.

MODELO: E1: ¿Puedo sentarme aquí?
             E2: Por supuesto. ¿Me prestas (*Can you lend me*) el diccionario?
             E1: ¡Claro que sí!

Tengo muchas ganas de vivir en Guanajuato, México, el año que viene.

—¿Quieres... ? —No, gracias.
Inviting and declining politely

To ask someone if they want something, you can use **querer.**

TÚ	**UD.**
¿Quieres + *noun*?	**¿Quiere (Ud.)** + *noun*?
¿Quieres un café?	**¿Quiere Ud. un sándwich?**

There are many ways to invite someone to do something.

TÚ

¿Quieres + *infinitive*?
   ¿Quieres ir al restaurante?

¿Tienes ganas de + *noun/infinitive*?
   ¿Tienes ganas de pizza?
   ¿Tienes ganas de pedir una pizza?

¿Qué te parece + *noun/infinitive*?
   ¿Qué te parece una hamburguesa?
   ¿Qué te parece cenar en casa?

¿Te apetece + *noun/infinitive*?
   ¿Te apetece un café?
   ¿Te apetece tomar un café?

UD.

¿Quiere (Ud.) + *infinitive*?
   ¿Quiere Ud. ir al restaurante?

¿Tiene (Ud.) ganas de + *noun/infinitive*?
   ¿Tiene Ud. ganas de una cerveza?
   ¿Tiene ganas de tomar algo?

¿Qué le parece + *noun/infinitive*?
   ¿Qué le parece un mango?
   ¿Qué le parece pedir un café?

¿Le apetece + *noun/infinitive*?
   ¿Le apetece un café?
   ¿Le apetece salir a comer?

In some cultures it is polite to decline an invitation to eat or drink something the first time and then accept when it's been offered for a second or third time. To decline politely say: **No, gracias.**

If you really want to decline, it's nice to add a reason the second (and maybe third) time you decline.

No puedo...	I can't . . .
Debo + *infinitive.*	I should (do something)
Debo regresar a casa.	I should go back home.

Note (No, gracias): When used with a noun, *apetecer* is almost always used for food. On the other hand, the usage is more flexible when used with an infinitive. For example, *¿Te apetece ir al cine?*

Suggestion (Act. A): Have students work in pairs and come up with their own reasons why they can't do each activity.

A. ¿Por qué no?   Empareja la invitación con la justificación más lógica.

1. __b__ ¿Tienes ganas de dar un paseo (*take a walk*) después de la cena?
2. __d__ ¿Qué te parece ir al nuevo club con nosotros?
3. __c__ ¿Te apetece tomar un café?
4. __a__ ¿Quieres almorzar con nosotros el domingo?

a. No, gracias. Voy a viajar este fin de semana.
b. Gracias, pero no puedo. No me gusta hacer ejercicio después de comer.
c. No, gracias. No puedo consumir la cafeína.
d. Gracias, pero no puedo. No sé bailar.

B. Gracias, pero...

Expansion (Act. B, Paso 2): Ask a few students to report the plans they have made with classmates to the entire class.

PASO 1.   Haz una lista de cinco actividades que normalmente haces y cuándo piensas hacerlas (*plan to do them*).

MODELO:

ACTIVIDAD	¿CUÁNDO?
correr en el parque	mañana a las tres de la tarde
estudiar en la biblioteca	hoy, después de almorzar
tomar un café en el Café Turrón	el sábado a las diez de la mañana

PASO 2.   Circula por la clase e invita a otros compañeros a participar en algunas de tus actividades. Responde a las invitaciones que recibes, ofreciendo una justificación si la respuesta es «no».

MODELO: E1: ¿Quieres ir al Café Turrón a tomar un café el sábado a las diez de la mañana?
   E2: No, gracias. No puedo. Debo visitar a mis padres.

C. ¿Dónde quieres comer?

PASO 1. Consulta la publicidad de estos tres restaurantes. En parejas, decidan dónde quieren ir a comer. **¡Atención!** Los precios están en dólares estadounidenses.

MODELO: E1: ¿Qué te parece comer en El Mirasol?

E2: No me gusta mucho la carne (*meat*). ¿Quieres comer en Las Mañanitas?

E1: Pues, es muy caro. ¿Vamos al restaurante cubano Versailles?

E2: ¡Cómo no!

Las Mañanitas (Cuernavaca, México)

Ambiente: terrazas y áreas de comedor (*dining room*) rodeado de (*surrounded by*) un maravilloso jardín entre aves (*birds*) exóticas y obras (*works*) de arte.

Especialidades de la casa: tradicionales platillos (*main courses*) de comida mexicana hasta exquisitos platillos de la cocina (*cuisine*) internacional.

Rango de precios: de $19 a $39

El Mirasol (Buenos Aires, Argentina)

Ambiente: un excelente salón con las mejores vistas a la ciudad, un lugar para relajarse y comer sin apuro (*without being rushed*) con vista al puerto.

Especialidades de la casa: clásica comida argentina: empanadas de carne (*pastry stuffed with beef*) y carne a la parrilla (*grill*)— bifes (*steaks*), asados (*roasts*) y lomo (*loin*).

Rango de precios: de $25 a $50

Versailles (Miami, Estados Unidos)

Ambiente: uno de los mejores restaurantes cubanos de Miami, ubicado en la Pequeña Habana, con precios moderados (*moderate*). Aquí se reúnen (*meet*) muchos cubanos a disfrutar de (*to enjoy*) un café y discutir (*discuss*) sobre la política de Cuba.

Especialidades de la casa: comida típica cubana, arroz (*rice*) con frijoles (*beans*) y ropa vieja (*shredded beef in tomato sauce*).

Rango de precios: de $6 a $12

PASO 2. Ahora comparen sus respuestas con las de (*those of*) otras parejas. ¿Adónde van a comer ellos y por qué?

MODELO: Vamos a comer en el restaurante cubano Versailles porque tienen precios muy económicos para una comida buena. ¿Y Uds.?

En español...

To say *Enjoy your meal*, use **¡Buen provecho!**

English doesn't have an exact equivalent for **¡Buen provecho!** The closest thing in English is *Bon appétit!*, borrowed from French. In the Spanish-speaking world it would be rude to come across anyone eating and not say **¡Buen provecho!**

COMUN **VOCABULARIO** UCTURA ATE

Suggestion (Act. A): Tell students that a sandwich would probably be made with sliced bread, but that regional variations are quite different than what they might think of as a sandwich. In Mexico, a *torta* is made with a sort of oval-shaped hard roll called a *telera* and often includes refried beans and avocado in addition to meat and cheese. In Spain, a *bocadillo* is made with baguette-style bread and might contain anchovies, Manchego cheese, chorizo sausage or a traditional egg and potato tortilla (to name just a few possibilities).

Point out (Act. A): The correct term for red wine is *vino tinto*.

Suggestion (Act. A): Tell students that *pez* refers to the animal and *pescado* refers to the food.

A comprar la comida

Food and where to buy it

A. De compras

Imagina que vas a la página web del supermercado para comprar toda la comida que necesitas para la semana. Mira la selección de comidas y bebidas. Luego usa la tabla en la siguiente página para hacer una lista de lo que vas a comprar.

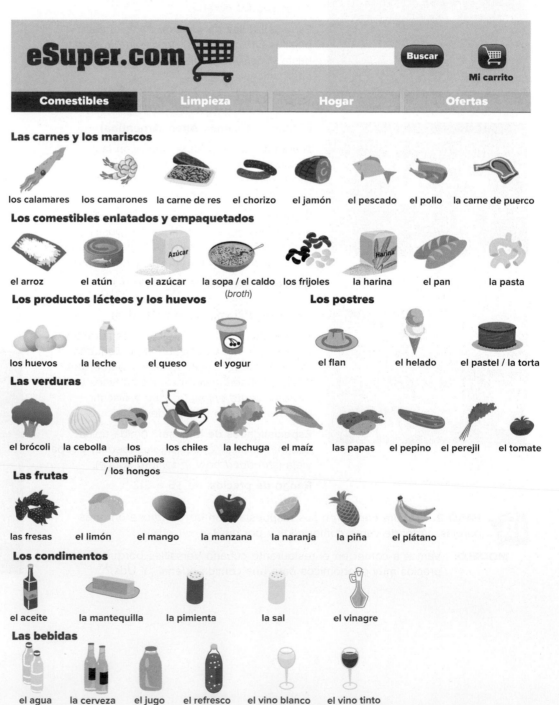

eSuper.com   Buscar   Mi carrito

| Comestibles | Limpieza | Hogar | Ofertas |

Las carnes y los mariscos

los calamares   los camarones   la carne de res   el chorizo   el jamón   el pescado   el pollo   la carne de puerco

Los comestibles enlatados y empaquetados

el arroz   el atún   el azúcar   la sopa / el caldo *(broth)*   los frijoles   la harina   el pan   la pasta

Los productos lácteos y los huevos   **Los postres**

los huevos   la leche   el queso   el yogur   el flan   el helado   el pastel / la torta

Las verduras

el brócoli   la cebolla   los champiñones / los hongos   los chiles   la lechuga   el maíz   las papas   el pepino   el perejil   el tomate

Las frutas

las fresas   el limón   el mango   la manzana   la naranja   la piña   el plátano

Los condimentos

el aceite   la mantequilla   la pimienta   la sal   el vinagre

Las bebidas

el agua   la cerveza   el jugo   el refresco   el vino blanco   el vino tinto

LOS DESAYUNOS	LOS SÁNDWICHES	LAS ENSALADAS	LA CENA	MERIENDAS (SNACKS)	LAS BEBIDAS	LOS POSTRES

Supermercados (*grocery stores*) and even **hipermercados** (*warehouse stores, such as Sam's Club or Costco*) are increasingly common in large cities in the Spanish-speaking world. However, in smaller towns, there are often locally owned stores that specialize in selling one type of food product. Here are some examples.

La carnicería vende carne de todos los animales.

La frutería vende fruta.

La panadería vende pan y pasteles.

La pescadería vende pescado y mariscos.

La verdulería vende verduras.

En español...

The names of different fruits and vegetables vary from region to region. Here are some examples. The more common word appears first.

fresa / frutilla (*Arg.*)	strawberry
chile / pimiento (*Sp.*)	pepper
plátano / banana (*Sp.*) / **guineo** (*D.R.*)	banana
papa / patata (*Sp.*)	potato
tomate / jitomate (*Mex.*)	tomato

B. ¡Qué rico! (*How delicious!*)   Escucha las descripciones y escribe el número al lado del plato correspondiente.

_8_ el banana split   _6_ el espagueti   _7_ el sándwich
_3_ la ensalada   _4_ el omelet   _5_ la sopa
_1_ la hamburguesa   _2_ la quesadilla

Script (Act. B): **1.** *carne de res encima de pan con lechuga, tomate y condimentos como mostaza y salsa de tomate* **2.** *queso entre dos tortillas de harina; a veces incluye pollo o verdura* **3.** *lechuga con tomates, pepino y champiñones con un aderezo de aceite y vinagre* **4.** *huevos con queso, champiñones, tomate u otras verduras adentro* **5.** *un caldo con carne, verduras y pasta o arroz* **6.** *pasta con una salsa de tomate hecha de tomates con cebolla, sal, pimienta y a veces chorizo u otra carne* **7.** *jamón y queso entre dos rebanadas de pan* **8.** *helado con plátano, salsa de fresa, salsa de piña y salsa de chocolate*

Suggestion (En español): Tell students that the examples in the *En español* box are just a few of many examples. Other examples are cucumber = *pepino / cohombro* (*P.R.*), lemon = *limón / lima* (*Mex.*), lime = *lima / limón* (*Mex.*), peach = *durazno / melocotón* (*Sp.*). Share with them other examples from your experience. Make sure they understand that the important thing is to expect lexical variation—especially with things like fruits and vegetables that vary from region to region in their availability and use.

■ The audio files for in-text listening activities are available in the eBook, within Connect activities, and on the Online Learning Center.

Point out (Vocabulario): Let students know that *salsa* is any kind of sauce, not just the "salsa" they see at Mexican restaurants in this country.

Suggestion (Act. C, Paso 1): In order to save time, split the class into groups. Have students poll their group and then have each group report its findings.

Note (Act. C, Paso 1): Students learned how to express time in *Cap. 3: Comunicación.*

C. Las comidas

PASO 1. ¿Cuántas veces comes al día? Apunta a qué horas comes durante el día. Luego haz un sondeo del resto de la clase y llena (*fill in*) la tabla. Sigue el modelo y usa la lista de **comidas** y **verbos.**

Comidas	Verbos
el desayuno	desayunar
el almuerzo	almorzar
la comida	comer
la merienda	merendar
la cena	cenar

MODELO: Desayuno a las ocho de la mañana, almuerzo a la una de la tarde y ceno a las siete de la noche. ¿Y tú? ¿Cuántas veces comes al día?

	2 VECES	3 VECES	4 VECES	5 VECES
Número de estudiantes				

PASO 2. Ahora, usa las siguientes preguntas (o inventa otras) para saber más detalles sobre las comidas que tus compañeros de clase comen. ¿Uds. tienen algo en común? Presenta un resumen (*summary*) que incluye por lo menos una diferencia entre tú y alguno/a de tus compañeros.

- ¿Te sientas para desayunar o comes algo en el camino (*on the way*) a la universidad / al trabajo?
- ¿Normalmente traes tu almuerzo o compras comida en el comedor?
- ¿Qué comidas son tus favoritas para merendar?
- ¿Con quién cenas usualmente?
- ¿Sabes cocinar? ¿Qué te gusta cocinar?
- ¿Prefieres la comida saludable (*healthy*) o la comida basura (*junk food*)?

Suggestion (Act. D): Have students work in groups. Give each group a different type of store and have them make a list of the items that can be bought there.

Answers (Act. D): 1. *Para comprar pan, puedo ir a la panadería.* **2.** *Para comprar pescado, puedo ir a la pescadería.* **3.** *Para comprar ajo, puedo ir a la verdulería.* **4.** *Para comprar naranjas, puedo ir a la frutería.* **5.** *Para comprar jamón, puedo ir a la carnicería.* **6.** *Para comprar aceite de oliva, puedo ir al supermercado.*

D. Vamos de compras

Mira las siguientes imágenes, identifica la comida y di (*say*) adónde puedes ir para comprar cada una.

MODELO: Para comprar camarones, puedo ir a la pescadería.

1.

2.

3.

4.

5.

6.

E. A ver: Las horas de comer
Mira y escucha por lo menos dos veces con pausas. Luego escribe las palabras que usa cada persona para las distintas comidas.

¿Cómo es el horario de comidas en su país?

Selene de México dice:

«En México es el ___desayuno___¹ primero que nada, y es un café. Después sigue el ___almuerzo___² que ya es un... la comida fuerte que son huevos, cereal, algo así por el estilo. Después como a eso de la una y media, dos de la tarde, que ya es la ___comida___³ es una comida fuerte. Después sigue la ___merienda___⁴ que es el café, un pastel o algo por el estilo, y ya por la noche la ___cena___,⁵ que por lo tradicional son los antojitos mexicanos o tacos.»

María de Argentina dice:

«Bueno, empezamos con ___desayuno___⁶ que es a las siete u ocho según a la hora que uno se levanta, y después a las doce que yo les doy (I give them) el ___almuerzo___⁷ a mis hijos, y después tiene la ___merienda___⁸ que es a las cinco de la tarde, nada más. Y después la ___cena___⁹ a la noche.»

Víctor de España dice:

«Como algo muy suave porque aquí en España se hace ___desayuno___¹⁰ en casa, eh... luego ___comida___¹¹ a las 14:30, una ensalada, un postre, un poco de pasta habitualmente y luego por la noche, ___cena___¹² en casa más fuerte, de la comida más fuerte.»

Carolina de Costa Rica dice:

«Aquí dan desayunos de seis de la mañana a las nueve de la mañana, se puede tomar el ___desayuno___.¹³ Un ___almuerzo___¹⁴ casi siempre empieza al mediodía o a la una de la tarde. Tenemos algo muy típico que es la hora del ___café___¹⁵ o depende del área de la provincia que es la hora del aguadulce que es una bebida muy nacional. Y después tenemos la ___cena___¹⁶ que ya sería como algo también como parecido a lo que se sirve en el almuerzo en algunas familias como entre las siete de la noche a las nueve de la noche.»

¡Buen provecho!

Video track (Act. E): This video clip can be found on the DVD to accompany *Conéctate: Cap. 6,* Track 2.

Suggestions (Act. E):
- Remind students that they do not need to understand everything, but that they should listen for the key words (the names of the meals). Students will likely need to watch this video more than once in order to fill in all the blanks.
- In her hurry to describe the mealtimes in Mexico, Selene says, *de las una y media, dos de la tarde.* If students pick up on this use of *las una,* remind them that even native speakers get nervous and make mistakes!

Expansion (Act. E): Ask students *¿Cómo se llama la comida que se come por la mañana?* (el desayuno). *Dos palabras para la comida que se come por la tarde son...;* (el almuerzo, la comida). *En Argentina y en México, ¿qué tienen después del almuerzo y antes de la cena?* (la merienda). *¿Y en Costa Rica?* (la hora del café). *¿Cómo se llama la comida que se come por la noche?* (la cena)

Suggestion (¡Pongamos la mesa!):
- Have students describe how to set the table. *¿Cómo se pone la mesa? ¿Qué pones a la izquierda del plato? ¿Qué pones a la derecha del plato?* Demonstrate with gestures.
- Bring in a set of tableware to practice the vocabulary. Students take turns being servers, preparing a place setting, leaving out one or two items. Then other students must point out the missing item to the server: *Perdone, ¿me trae... , por favor?*

Answers (Act. A): 1. *Como la pasta con un tenedor / una cuchara / un plato.* **2.** *Como la ensalada con un tenedor/bol/ plato.* **3.** *Tomo/Bebo el café con una taza.* **4.** *Tomo la sopa con un bol / una cuchara.* **5.** *Como una torta de chocolate con un tenedor/plato.* **6.** *Como el yogur con una cuchara / un bol.* **7.** *Tomo/Bebo el agua con un vaso.* **8.** *Como la carne con un tenedor/cuchillo/plato.*

En la mesa
Eating at home and at restaurants

A. ¡Pongamos la mesa! (*Let's set the table!*)   El cubierto (*place setting*) consiste en varios elementos que se usan para comer. ¿Qué elementos del cubierto usas para cada cosa? **¡Atención!** Las bebidas y la sopa (*soup*) requieren el verbo **tomar.**

el vaso — la taza — la cuchara — el cuchillo — el plato — el bol — el tenedor — la servilleta

MODELO: Como el brócoli con un tenedor y un plato, pero tomo la sopa de brócoli con una cuchara y un bol.

1. la pasta
2. la ensalada
3. el café
4. la sopa
5. una torta de chocolate
6. el yogur
7. el agua
8. la carne

Here are some other words to describe food and its preparation.

a la plancha grilled
la salsa sauce
al ajillo fried with garlic
asado/a roasted

dulce sweet
frito/a fried
picante spicy
saludable healthy

When in a restaurant, you can use **pedir** to order food from the **camarero/a** (*server, waiter/waitress*). Ask for **la carta** (*menu*) to decide what you want to eat.

—**¿Sabes qué vas a pedir?**

Do you know what you are going to order?

—**No, es mi primera vez en este restaurante. Tengo que ver la carta.**

No, it's my first time at this restaurant. I have to see the menu.

—**Bueno, yo voy a pedir una hamburguesa.**

OK, well I'm going to order a hamburger.

B. Tus platos favoritos

En grupos, describan sus platos favoritos en casa con sus familias y sus platos favoritos de un restaurante en su ciudad. Comparen y contrasten los dos platos.

MODELO: En casa mi plato favorito es la pasta con pollo y brócoli. Aquí mi plato favorito es la pizza de Frisky's. La pasta es más saludable, pero me encanta la pizza...

C. ¿Para pedir o para evitar (avoid)? Las siguientes personas van a comer en el Restaurante Piña. En parejas, miren la carta y decidan qué platos y/o bebidas cada uno va a pedir y qué va a evitar.

Suggestion (Act. C): To save time, assign one or more of the situations to each pair of students and have them share their answers with the class.

Note (Act. C): The prices on the menu are in Costa Rican colones. One U.S. dollar is roughly equivalent to 500 colones.

Restaurante Piña

Aperitivos

coctel de camarón	₡2,500
empanada de jamón y queso	₡1,750
empanada de verdura	₡1,500
melón con jamón	₡3,500

Primero

ensalada mixta	₡2,750
ensalada rusa (de patatas)	₡2,500
sopa de champiñones	₡2,500
sopa de pollo con fideos (pasta)	₡2,750

Segundo

filete de carne "la Piña"	₡6,000
pescado del día	₡5,000
salmón asado	₡5,750
ravioles de queso	₡4,500
ravioles de verdura	₡4,500

Acompañamientos

arroz	₡1,000
champiñones al ajillo	₡1,500
frijoles negros	₡1,500
papas fritas	₡1,000
puré de papas	₡1,000

Postres

flan	₡750
fruta fresca	₡1,000
helado de piña	₡1,000
torta de chocolate	₡1,200

Bebidas

agua	₡750
café	₡950
cerveza	₡2,000
vino	₡2,500

Restaurante Piña 8494 Paseo Colón, San José, Costa Rica

CONÉCTATE AL MUNDO HISPANO

En muchos países hispanos, **el menú del día** (o **menú**) se refiere a una comida especial compuesta de **sopa** u otro **primer plato** (first course), **un plato principal / segundo plato** (main course) y **postre** con **pan** y **una bebida**. En algunos restaurantes se ofrecen varias posibilidades para cada plato y se paga **un precio fijo** (fixed). Si no quieres el menú del día, debes pedir **la carta** y seleccionar un plato **y un acompañamiento** (side order).

Como en el inglés, hay muchas palabras para decir appetizers; por ejemplo, **aperitivos, entradas, botanas** o **tapas**. Estas palabras varían de región en región.

MODELO: E1: Teresa está a dieta.
E2: Ella pide una ensalada mixta y el pescado del día a la plancha. Evita los postres.

1. Ronaldo no tiene hambre.
2. Pablo y Javier tienen hambre.
3. Sara es vegetariana.
4. Elena y Tomás van al gimnasio después de la comida.
5. Olga no toma alcohol.
6. Ricardo tiene prisa (is in a hurry).
7. A Margarita no le gustan los mariscos.
8. Franco no come carbohidratos.

D. Nunca como...

PASO 1. Consulta la carta del Restaurante Piña y haz una lista de cinco alimentos (*foods*) o bebidas que nunca comes o tomas.

NUNCA COMO...	NUNCA TOMO...
salmón	*vino*

Suggestion (Act. D, Paso 2): Model an example if students need help with *nosotros: Elizabeth y yo nunca comemos salmón.* You may want to point out that the definite article is usually omitted in negative statements, as when saying *I never eat meat. / Nunca como carne.*

Suggestion (Act. E, Paso 2): Ask students to write down their partners' orders. Remind the "waiters" to ask what the "customer" wants to eat and drink for each course.

Expansion (Act. E, Paso 2): Divide the class into two groups: a larger group of *clientes* and a smaller group of *camareros*. Begin with the clients standing at the front of the room. The servers should greet them, find out how many are in the party, show them to a table (rearranged desks) and give them menus (copies of the text opened to this page). When food arrives, the servers must remember to say *¡Buen provecho!* The instructor should play the role of *gerente* (*manager*) to work out any problems that arise.

PASO 2. En parejas, entrevístense para determinar si evitan las mismas (*same*) comidas y bebidas. Luego presenten lo que tienen en común al resto de la clase.

MODELO: E1: Nunca como salmón. ¿Y tú?
E2: Me gusta el salmón. Nunca como carne. ¿Y tú?
E1: ¡Yo tampoco! (*Me neither!*)

E. ¡A pedir!

PASO 1. Usando la carta del Restaurante Piña, completa el diálogo entre el camarero (*waiter, server*) y un cliente alérgico a los productos lácteos y a quien no le gustan ni (*neither*) el pescado ni (*nor*) los mariscos. **¡Atención!** Al servir la comida, usa: **¡Buen provecho!**

EL CAMARERO: ¿Está listo para pedir?

EL CLIENTE: Para mi primer plato, quiero _____

EL CAMARERO: ¿Y para el segundo plato?

EL CLIENTE: _____

EL CAMARERO: ¿Y para tomar?

EL CLIENTE: _____

EL CAMARERO: ¿Algo más?

EL CLIENTE: _____

EL CAMARERO: ¿Está listo para pedir postre?

EL CLIENTE: _____

PASO 2. En grupos, túrnense para ser camarero/a mientras los otros piden comida de la carta. Es importante usar el trato formal (**Ud.**).

MODELO: E1: ¿Está listo/a para pedir?
E2: Para primer plato, la ensalada mixta, por favor.
E1: ¿Y para segundo?

CONÉCTATE AL MUNDO PROFESIONAL

Culinary adventurousness can help you succeed in a globalized workplace. Even if you're not fluent in a language, try to be aware of a few cultural customs and be willing to try new foods as you encounter them in other cultures. This can make you stand out against the competition.

COMUN VOCABUL **ESTRUCTURA** ATE

⟲ Reciclaje
The present indicative

¿Eres igual a un cocinero (*chef*) profesional? Escribe cada verbo en tiempo presente y así di cómo es un cocinero profesional y cómo eres tú. ¡Usa **no** si es necesario!

Un cocinero profesional   Yo

cocinar	___Cocina___ muy bien.	_(No) Cocino_ muy bien.
escribir	___Escribe___ libros de cocina.	_(No) Escribo_ libros de cocina.
trabajar	___Trabaja___ en un restaurante.	_(No) Trabajo_ en un restaurante.
aprender	___Aprende___ a cocinar cosas nuevas de vez en cuando.	_(No) Aprendo_ a cocinar cosas nuevas de vez en cuando.

Según tus respuestas, ¿qué tienes en común con un cocinero profesional? Si no tienen nada en común, escribe eso.
Los dos _____.

Suggestions (Reciclaje):
• Remind students that they do not need to write *yo* in each sentence in the right column. The verb already contains this information.
• Remind students that when talking about a group of people that includes yourself, you use the *nosotros/as* form, so *los dos* here should be followed by this form of the verb.

■ Answers to this activity are in Appendix 2 at the back of your book.

Suggestion (Para empezar):
Your students may be interested in watching the documentary *El Bulli: Cooking in Progress* (2011).

6.1   Empezó a trabajar como cocinero.

The preterite: Regular verbs

Para empezar...

Según muchos, Ferran Adrià es el mejor cocinero (*chef*) del mundo y su restaurante **El Bulli,** en el noreste de España, fue (*was*) uno de los más famosos del mundo. Adrià es conocido (*known*) por el uso de nuevas técnicas (*techniques*) en la cocina que cambian la textura y el aspecto de los alimentos (*foods*) para hacer algo inesperado (*unexpected*). Por ejemplo, una de sus técnicas más conocidas es hacer espuma (*foam*) de cosas como el café, los champiñones (hongos) o la carne. Ahora Adrià es director de *elBulliFoundation,* un centro de innovación culinaria.

PASO 1. Usa la introducción y tu sentido (*sense*) común para emparejar cada evento en la vida de Ferran Adrià con el año correspondiente. Dos ya están hechos.

Ferran Adrià, director de elBulliFoundation

AÑO		EVENTO
1. _i_ 1962	a.	**Escribió** el libro *Cocinar en 10 minutos con Ferran Adrià.*
2. _f_ 1980	b.	**Empezó** a trabajar en El Bulli.
3. _h_ 1981	c.	**Cocinó** con espuma por primera vez (*for the first time*) en El Bulli.
4. _b_ 1984	d.	**Ganó** por primera vez el premio al mejor restaurante del mundo.
5. _c_ 1988	e.	**Abrió** su nuevo centro culinario, elBulliFoundation.
6. _a_ 1998	f.	**Trabajó** como lavaplatos (*dishwasher*) en un hotel. **Aprendió** a cocinar.
7. _d_ 2002	g.	**Cerró** su restaurante El Bulli para concentrarse en la gastronomía creativa.
8. _g_ 2011	h.	**Empezó** a trabajar como cocinero en el servicio militar.
9. _e_ 2013	i.	**Nació** (*He was born*) en la región de Barcelona, España.

Note (Para empezar, Paso 1): Students will need to rely on logic to put these events in order. Because this is an active-learning activity that introduces new content, allow students more time than usual to complete **Paso 1:** about twice as long as you would allow in regular practice activities.

(*Continues*)

■ Answers to these activities are in Appendix 2 at the back of your book.

PASO 2. Ahora que sabes más sobre la vida de Ferran Adrià, haz tu propia (*own*) minibiografía. Para cada pregunta, escoge la respuesta adecuada y escribe la información que falta (*is missing*). Si es necesario, puedes empezar tu respuesta con **nunca** (por ejemplo, «Nunca aprendí a cocinar»).

1. __b__ ¿En qué año **naciste**?
2. __d__ ¿Dónde **naciste**?
3. __f__ ¿Dónde **estudiaste** primaria?
4. __a__ ¿En qué año **empezaste** a estudiar en la universidad?
5. __c__ ¿En qué año **trabajaste** como lavaplatos?
6. __e__ ¿En qué año **aprendiste** a cocinar una cena completa?

a. **Empecé** a estudiar en la universidad en el año _____.
b. **Nací** en el año _____.
c. **Trabajé** como lavaplatos en el año _____.
d. **Nací** en _____.
e. **Aprendí** a cocinar una cena completa en el año _____.
f. **Estudié** primaria en _____.

Actividades analíticas

1 The verbs in **Para empezar** are in the *preterite tense* (**el tiempo pretérito**). This tense is used when you want to portray an event as happening at a specific point in the past. Use the verb forms from **Para empezar** to complete these conjugations of **trabajar, aprender,** and **escribir** in the preterite.

	trabajar	**aprender**	**escribir**
yo	trabaj**é**	aprend**í**	escrib**í**
tú	trabaj**aste**	aprend**iste**	escrib**iste**
él/ella, Ud.	trabaj**ó**	aprend**ió**	escrib**ió**
nosotros/as	trabaj**amos**	aprend**imos**	escrib**imos**
vosotros/as	trabaj**asteis**	aprend**isteis**	escrib**isteis**
ellos/ellas, Uds.	trabaj**aron**	aprend**ieron**	escrib**ieron**

2 Complete this chart of endings for **-ar, -er,** and **-ir** verbs in the preterite. Note that the endings for **-er** and **-ir** verbs are the same.

	-ar		**-er / -ir**	
yo	_-é_ trabaj**é**		_-í_ aprend**í**	escrib**í**
tú	_-aste_ trabaj**aste**		_-iste_ aprend**iste**	escrib**iste**
él/ella, Ud.	_-ó_ trabaj**ó**		_-ió_ aprend**ió**	escrib**ió**
nosotros/as	_-amos_ trabaj**amos**		_-imos_ aprend**imos**	escrib**imos**
vosotros/as	_-asteis_ trabaj**asteis**		_-isteis_ aprend**isteis**	escrib**isteis**
ellos/ellas, Uds.	_-aron_ trabaj**aron**		_-ieron_ aprend**ieron**	escrib**ieron**

Suggestion (Act. analíticas 2): If students have a hard time grasping the preterite conjugation, have them compare the two sets of endings (that is, the endings for -*ar* and -*er*/-*ir* verbs) and circle what they have in common (-*ste*, -*ó*, -*mos*, -*steis*, -*ron*). Point out that most of the endings for the -*ar* verbs have an -*a*, and that most of the endings for the -*er* and -*ir* verb have an -*i*.

Expansion (Act. analíticas 2): As a class, compare a verb such as *trabajar* in both the preterite and the present. Have students circle what the endings in the plural forms have in common (-*amos*, -*is*, -*n*). Point out that the *nosotros/as* form *hablamos* is identical in the preterite and the present (as are -*ir* forms, such as *escribimos*).

■ For more verbs in the preterite, see **Para saber más 6.1** at the back of your book.

Note (Para saber más): *Para saber más 6.1 presents leer, creer, oír, ver,* and *dar* in the preterite.

3 The preterite is often used with specific time expressions such as **ayer** (*yesterday*) and **anoche** (*last night*).

¿Aprendiste algo **ayer**?	*Did you learn something yesterday?*
Anoche cené a las ocho.	*I had dinner at 8:00 last night.*

To express the idea of *ago*, use the word **hace** followed by the period of time that has passed.

Trabajé en el restaurante **hace cinco años.**	*I worked in the restaurant five years ago.*
Comimos **hace dos minutos.**	*We ate two minutes ago.*

4 For **-ar** verbs with stems that end in **-g-** (such as **jugar** and **llegar**), add a **-u-** to the **yo** form to preserve the hard **g** sound before the **-é** ending. This change is not needed when the ending begins with **a** or **o.**

Llegué ayer en la tarde.	*I arrived yesterday in the evening.*
¿**Llegaste** a tiempo?	*Did you arrive on time?*

Similarly, for **-ar** verbs whose stems end in **-c-** (such as **practicar**), change the **-c-** to **-qu-** in the **yo** form to preserve the hard [k] sound of the **-c-** when followed by the **-é** ending. For verbs whose stems end in **-z-** (such as **empezar**), change the **-z-** to **-c-.** These changes are not needed when the ending begins with **-a** or **-o.**

Ayer no **practiqué** tenis.	*I didn't practice tennis yesterday.*
¿Tú sí **practicaste**?	*Did you practice?*
Empecé a estudiar matemáticas el año pasado.	*I started studying math last year.*
¿Cuando **empezaste** tú?	*When did you start?*

Actividades prácticas

A. Preguntas y respuestas Empareja cada pregunta con una respuesta adecuada.

1. __c__ ¿A qué hora cenaron anoche?
2. __i__ ¿Estudiaste mucho ayer?
3. __e__ ¿Cuándo empezaste a bailar salsa?
4. __f__ ¿Quién cocinó ayer?
5. __a__ ¿A qué hora cenaste anoche?
6. __g__ ¿Dónde vivieron el año pasado?
7. __h__ ¿Estudiaron mucho para el examen?
8. __d__ ¿Cuándo empezaron a cocinar?
9. __b__ ¿Dónde vivió Ud. en 2012?

a. Cené a las nueve.
b. Viví en la casa de mi madre.
c. Cenamos a las siete.
d. Empezamos hace diez minutos.
e. Empecé hace cuatro meses.
f. Cociné yo.
g. Vivimos en la universidad.
h. Sí, estudiamos mucho.
i. Sí, estudié mucho.

Suggestion (Act. analíticas 4): You may want to delay discussion of this point until students have had a little more experience with using the preterite (such as after they have done some of the *Actividades prácticas*).

Autoprueba

How would you express these ideas in Spanish?

1. I studied last night. _____

2. Julieta lived in Chile three years ago. _____

3. Did you cook yesterday? _____

4. I bought a bicycle one week ago. _____

Respuestas: 1. (Yo) Estudié anoche. **2.** Julieta vivió en Chile hace tres años. **3.** ¿Cocinaste ayer? **4.** (Yo) Compré una bicicleta hace una semana.

B. Entrevistas   Lee las entrevistas con Gonzalo, Isabel, María y Pilar sobre qué comieron y cuándo comieron. Usa la siguiente información para completar las entrevistas.

- Los argentinos tienen fama (*reputation*) de comer mucha carne.
- Los argentinos y los españoles tienen fama de cenar a las diez o más tarde.
- Los mexicanos tienen fama de desayunar y comer (almorzar) mucho, pero cenar poco.

Gonzalo

María y Pilar

Isabel

Gonzalo (Argentina)
— _d_ ¹
—Desayuné a las seis y media.
—¿Y qué desayunaste?
— _l_ ²
—¿A qué hora cenaste ayer?
— _e_ ³
—¿Qué cenaste?
— _h_ ⁴

María y Pilar (España)
— _b_ ⁵
—Cenamos anoche a las diez.
—¿Qué cenaron?
— _j_ ⁶

Isabel (México)
— _k_ ⁷
—Desayuné a las ocho.
—¿Y qué desayunó?
— _f_ ⁸
—¿A qué hora comió?
— _i_ ⁹
— _g_ ¹⁰
—Comí una sopa, arroz, un guisado (*stew*) y un postre.
—¿A qué hora cenó?
— _a_ ¹¹
—¿Qué cenó?
— _c_ ¹²

a. Cené a las nueve.
b. ¿A qué hora cenaron anoche?
c. Cené muy ligero (*light*): un pan y un vaso con leche.
d. ¿A qué hora desayunaste esta mañana?
e. Cené anoche a las diez.
f. Desayuné huevo, frijoles, pan de dulce y fruta.
g. ¿Y qué comió?
h. Cené carne y una ensalada.
i. Comí a las tres.
j. Cenamos pescado.
k. ¿A qué hora desayunó Ud. esta mañana?
l. Desayuné una medialuna (*croissant*) con un café.

Suggestion (Act. B): Tell students to pay attention to whether the interviewer is using *tú* or *Ud.*, since this will help them find the right answers. You may want to point out that Isabel is being addressed as *Ud.* because she is being interviewed at her workplace, where she holds a position of responsibility.

Suggestion (Act. C): Before students begin, give them a minute to think and jot down how many portions of each item they had. As they do their surveys, write the 8 items on the board as headings. When they are done, ask each group to compute the average (*el promedio*) of their results and write it on the board under the appropriate heading.

Suggestion (Act. D, Paso 1): Have some students report to the class about themselves and their partners.

Expansion (Act. D): Ask students to contrast what they did last Sunday with what they do in general on Sundays. Example: *El domingo pasado desayuné con mis padres, pero en general, los domingos desayuno solo.*

La comida del domingo

C. ¿Cómo comen los estudiantes?   ¿Tus compañeros comen de una manera balanceada (*balanced*)? Escoge uno de los siguientes tipos de comida o bebida y pregúntales a tres compañeros cuántas veces comieron o tomaron cada una durante las últimas (*last*) veinticuatro horas. Apunta los resultados.

MODELO: E1: ¿Cuántas veces comiste carne en las últimas veinticuatro horas?
E2: Comí carne dos veces.

1. agua
2. carne
3. frijoles
4. fruta
5. granos integrales (*whole grains*)
6. leche
7. pescado
8. verduras

D. ¡A juntarse!

PASO 1.   En muchos países hispanos, es muy común juntarse (*to get together*) con toda la familia los domingos para comer. ¿Es así (*like that*) para tus compañeros también? En parejas, pregúntense con quién desayunaron, con quién almorzaron y con quién cenaron el domingo pasado.

MODELO: E1: ¿Con quién desayunaste el domingo pasado?
E2: Desayuné solo.

PASO 2.   ¿Cuándo fue (*was*) la última vez que se juntó tu familia? En parejas, túrnense para describir la reunión y den (*give*) muchos detalles. (¿Celebraron Uds. algo específico? ¿Cuántas personas asistieron [*attended*]? ¿Dónde fue el evento? ¿Quién preparó la comida? ¿Cocinaste tú alguna comida especial? ¿Qué comieron Uds.? ¿A qué hora terminó la reunión?)

⟳ Reciclaje

Verbs with irregular **yo** forms

Completa cada oración usando uno de los siguientes verbos en la forma **yo** del presente.

decir   hacer   ir   poner   ser

1. ____Soy____ una persona perfecta.
2. Cada mañana, ____hago____ un desayuno muy rico para todos mis amigos.
3. ____Digo____ «¡Buen provecho!» antes de empezar a comer.
4. ____Voy____ al súper cada día para comprar la comida más fresca.
5. Siempre ____pongo____ las cosas en el lugar correcto.

6.2   ¿Hice algo mal en la cena?

The preterite: Some common irregular verbs

Para empezar...

Uno de tus amigos está en Buenos Aires y la semana pasada lo invitaron (*they invited him*) a una cena. **Fue** (*He went*), pero ahora tiene la impresión de que **hizo** (*he did*) algo mal en la cena. Según él, estas son las cosas que **hizo**. ¿Qué **estuvo** (*was*) bien, y qué **estuvo** mal? Primero lee **Conéctate al mundo hispano.** Luego haz la actividad. **¡Atención!** ¡Tu amigo solo **hizo** dos cosas bien!

CONÉCTATE AL MUNDO HISPANO

Muchos aspectos de **una cena latinoamericana** son similares a las costumbres en este país, pero hay algunas diferencias importantes.

- Al llegar (*Upon arriving*) es normal darse la mano o darle un beso a cada persona presente.
- En general, la cena empieza más tarde.
- Debes tener las manos sobre (*on top of*) la mesa durante la comida, no debajo de (*under*) la mesa.
- La conversación en la mesa (conocida como **la sobremesa**) es animada y puede durar (*last*) hasta mucho después de terminar (*end*) la cena.

Puede haber diferencias en ciertos lugares, pero estas características se aplican en la mayoría de los países hispanos.

LAS COSAS QUE YO HICE (*I DID*)	ESTUVO BIEN	ESTUVO MAL
1. Primero **fui** (*I went*) a la casa equivocada (*wrong*).	☐	☑
2. Llegué a la casa de mis amigos a las seis y media.	☐	☑
3. **Fui** (*I was*) muy educado (*polite*). Les di la mano a todos los invitados.	☑	☐
4. **Hice** un brindis (*a toast*) con un vaso de agua.	☐	☑
5. Antes de empezar a comer, **dije**: «¡Qué rara comida!»	☐	☑
6. **Puse** (*I put*) las manos debajo (*under*) de la mesa.	☐	☑
7. Tomé mucho vino y **me puse** muy borracho (*drunk*).	☐	☑
8. Después de cenar, **dije**: «**Estuvo** muy rica la cena. ¡Gracias!»	☑	☐
9. Me levanté y **me fui** inmediatamente después de cenar.	☐	☑

Note (Reciclaje): This activity refreshes students' memory of the meanings of these five verbs and the irregular forms of these verbs in the present tense. They will learn the preterite forms of these verbs here in *Estructura 6.2.*

- Answers to this activity are in Appendix 2 at the back of your book.

Suggestions (Para empezar):
- Point out that sentence #9 shows the verb *irse* (*to leave*) in the preterite.
- Ask students to justify their answers, relying on the *Conéctate al mundo hispano* box and their common sense. You may want to highlight some cultural points: 2: Arriving at 6:30 would be way too early for a typical dinner in Buenos Aires. 4: Most Spanish speakers would consider it very strange (or even offensive) to toast someone with something as inconsequential as water. 7: Drinking until you are drunk at dinner is considered bad form in many parts of the world.

Expansion (Act. analíticas 1): Give students additional examples and have them identify the verb as *ir* or *ser*: *Ayer fue un día muy bonito*. (ser) / *Fuimos a la playa el sábado*. (ir) / *¿A qué hora fuiste a casa?* (ir) / *El sábado fue el primer día del mes.* (ser)

■ Answers to these activities are in Appendix 2 at the back of your book.

Actividades analíticas

1 In **Para empezar** you saw some new verb forms in the preterite tense. One of these verb forms, **fui**, has two meanings. Write out the sentence from **Para empezar** that illustrates each of the meanings listed here.

EXAMPLE

fui = *I went*   Primero fui a la casa equivocada (Q1)

fui = *I was*   *Fui muy educado (Q3)*

The reason that **fui** has two meanings is that the verbs **ir** (*to go*) and **ser** (*to be*) are conjugated in exactly the same way in the preterite.

	ir/ser
yo	fui
tú	fuiste
él/ella, Ud.	fue
nosotros/as	fuimos
vosotros/as	fuisteis
ellos/ellas, Uds.	fueron

The context generally makes it clear which meaning (**ir** or **ser**) is intended.

¿Adónde **fueron** Uds.? *Where did you* (pl.) *go?*

Fuimos al supermercado. *We went to the supermarket.*

Alberto Fujimori **fue** presidente de Perú. *Alberto Fujimori was president of Peru.*

La fiesta **fue** en casa de Ana. *The party was at Ana's house.*

2 Use the other verbs forms that you saw in **Para empezar** to complete these conjugations.

	decir	estar	hacer	poner
yo	dije	estuve	hice	puse
tú	dijiste	estuviste	hiciste	pusiste
él/ella, Ud.	dijo	estuvo	hizo	puso
nosotros/as	dijimos	estuvimos	hicimos	pusimos
vosotros/as	dijisteis	estuvisteis	hicisteis	pusisteis
ellos/ellas, Uds.	dijeron	estuvieron	hicieron	pusieron

«Hice sopa de tortilla para la comida. ¡Buen provecho!»

Suggestion (Act. analíticas 2): Point out that *hizo* has a spelling change. The *z* before *o* preserves the pronunciation of *c* before *i* or *e*.

Suggestion (Act. analíticas 2): Reassure students that it is easy to see why *dijeron* has a special ending (and to remember that it does), since the *-ieron* ending would be more difficult to pronounce with the stem *dij-*.

These verbs use a special stem in the preterite (**dij-, estuv-, hic-, pus-**). Despite their irregular stems, the endings of these verbs all follow the same pattern. The only exception to this pattern is **dijeron** (and other irregular preterite verbs whose stems end in **-j-**, such as **traer [trajeron]**), in which **i** of the **-ieron** ending is dropped, making the ending **-eron**. Use the examples to complete the chart on page 182.

(Continues)

Expansion (Act. analíticas 2): Have students compare the preterite endings of *poner* with those of the regular *-er* verb *comer*. They should be able to find many similarities and a few differences. Point out that, unlike endings for regular verbs, which have accent marks on the *yo* and *él/ella, Ud.* forms, the endings for irregular verbs have no accent marks: *estuve, dijo*.

Terminaciones del pretérito: Verbos de raíz irregular			
yo	-e	No **dije** nada.	*I didn't say anything.*
tú	-iste	¿**Estuviste** en la fiesta?	*Were you at the party?*
él/ella, Ud.	-o	¿Qué **hizo** Mario?	*What did Mario do?*
nosotros/as	-imos	**Pusimos** la comida allí.	*We put the food there.*
vosotros/as	-isteis	¿**Estuvisteis** contentos ayer?	*Were you happy yesterday?*
ellos/ellas, Uds.	-ieron	**Hicieron** sopa para todos.	*They made soup for everyone.*

3 Here is a list of the most common verbs with irregular stems in the preterite, including the four just seen.

Verbos de raíz irregular en el pretérito		
INFINITIVO	**RAÍZ**	**EJEMPLO**
decir	dij-	¿Qué **dijo** tu amigo? — *What did your friend say?*
estar	estuv-	Eva no **estuvo** en la cena. — *Eva was not at the dinner.*
hacer	hic-	**Hicieron** una paella muy rica. — *They made a delicious paella.*
poder	pud-	**Pude** llegar a la clase a tiempo. — *I was able to arrive to class on time.*
poner	pus-	¿Dónde **pusiste** las peras? — *Where did you put the pears?*
tener	tuv-	Ayer **tuvimos** un día muy bonito. — *We had a very nice day yesterday.*
traer	traj-	¿**Trajeron** Uds. la comida? — *Did you bring the food?*

Actividades prácticas

Suggestion (Act. A): Have students work on this in pairs or small groups. Those who know how to cook will find it easier to figure out the most reasonable order.

A. ¡Arepas! Las arepas son una comida tradicional de Colombia y Venezuela hecha (*made*) de harina de maíz. Hay comidas parecidas en otros países, como **las pupusas** de El Salvador y **las gorditas** de México. Las siguientes oraciones describen lo que hicieron Bárbara y Mari para preparar arepas, pero las oraciones están desordenadas (*in the wrong order*). Ponlas (*Put them*) en orden, ¡y aprende a hacer arepas!

CÓMO HICIMOS AREPAS

a. __4__ Separamos la masa en bolas (*balls*).
b. __7__ Comimos las arepas.
c. __2__ Pusimos la harina de maíz en agua, con un poco de sal.
d. __6__ Pusimos las arepas en aceite caliente.
e. __3__ Mezclamos (*We mixed*) todo, y así hicimos la masa (*dough*).
f. __1__ Tuvimos que salir a comprar harina de maíz.
g. __5__ Pusimos queso entre (*between*) dos bolas y las aplastamos (*we flattened them*) en forma de arepa.
h. __8__ ¡Estuvieron muy ricas!

Expansion (Act. analíticas 3): Have students do a complete conjugation in the preterite for *poder, tener,* or *traer,* or ask them to make up their own sentences using the different forms of the verbs.

Autoprueba

Use the preterite form of each verb to complete the sentence.

1. ¿Tú _____ (poder) comprar las manzanas?
2. ¿Quién _____ (traer) la ensalada de fruta?
3. Mis hermanos _____ (tener) una comida muy rica.
4. Mi mamá _____ (hacer) unas enchiladas de queso.
5. Yo _____ (decir) que desayuno muy poco.

Respuestas: 1. pudiste **2.** trajo **3.** tuvieron **4.** hizo **5.** dije

La preparación de arepas

¿Por qué?

With regular verbs, the preterite endings for **yo** and **él/ella** are stressed and thus written with an accent mark (**hablé, habló**). So why are these endings not accented for verbs with special stems in the preterite (for example, **dije, dijo**)? The answer is that the stem itself is enough to signal that the verb is in the preterite in these cases, and the special stressed ending is not necessary.

Suggestion (¿Por qué?):
Have students do complete conjugations of comer (regular) and *poner* (irregular) in the preterite and identify the ways in which the endings are different.

Suggestion (Act. C):
Create 5 columns on the board (*Persona, Fecha, Restaurante, Comida, ¿Cómo estuvo?*) and have as many students as possible write their partner's responses there.

Suggestion (Act. D, Paso 2):
Ask some or all of the groups to write their sentences from *Paso 2* on the board, and then go over them as a class to find any unexpected or amusing responses (and to correct any grammatical problems). Confirm that the responses are correct and ask for elaboration.

Suggestion (Act. D, Paso 3):
Model possible questions for students: *¿Probaste una comida nueva este año? ¿Cuál fue? ¿Te gustó? ¿Comiste en un restaurante nuevo este año? ¿Dónde? ¿Te gustó? ¿Cocinaste una cena especial recientemente? ¿Por qué? ¿Qué preparaste?*

B. Completar la oración

PASO 1. Completa cada oración con el verbo adecuado.

dijeron   estuvimos   fue   fuimos   hicieron   pudieron   trajo   tuviste

1. Araceli _____fue_____ la mejor estudiante de la clase ayer.
2. Beto y yo _____fuimos_____ a la biblioteca para estudiar.
3. Edgar _____trajo_____ un perro a nuestra clase.
4. Los cocineros _____hicieron_____ una paella exquisita.
5. ¿_____Tuviste_____ un examen de matemáticas?
6. Brenda y Gustavo no _____pudieron_____ hacer la tarea.
7. ¡_____Estuvimos_____ en la biblioteca por cuatro horas ayer!
8. _____Dijeron_____ que el español es muy bonito.

PASO 2. Cambia cada oración del **Paso 1** a la forma **yo** e indica si hiciste eso ayer.

¿HICISTE ESO AYER?

SÍ   NO

1. Fui el/la mejor estudiante de la clase. ☐ ☐
2. Fui a la biblioteca para estudiar. ☐ ☐
3. Traje un perro a nuestra clase. ☐ ☐
4. Hice una paella exquisita. ☐ ☐
5. ¿Tuve un examen de matemáticas? ☐ ☐
6. No pude hacer la tarea. / No hice la tarea. ☐ ☐
7. Estuve en la biblioteca por cuatro horas ayer. ☐ ☐
8. Dije que el español es muy bonito. ☐ ☐

C. ¿Adónde fuiste a comer?

PASO 1. Pregúntale a tu compañero/a cuándo fue la última vez que salió a comer. ¿Adónde fue? ¿Qué comió? ¿Cómo estuvo la comida? Apunta sus respuestas.

PASO 2. Ahora comparte con la clase las experiencias de tu compañero/a.

MODELO: Kristen salió a comer anoche. Fue a Dino's Restaurante Italiano y comió pasta con verduras. ¡La comida estuvo muy rica!

D. ¿Qué hicieron?

PASO 1. En grupos, pregúntense si hicieron alguna de estas acciones en los últimos doce meses, y apunten los resultados.

MODELO: E1: ¿Quién dijo «bon appétit» en una comida?
E2: Yo dije eso muchas veces.

¿Quién hizo esto?

1. decir «bon appétit» en una comida
2. hacer comida mexicana en casa
3. hacer un brindis (*a toast*) en una comida
4. ir a un restaurante peruano
5. tener una cena especial en Año Nuevo (*New Year's*)
6. traer comida para una clase

PASO 2. Creen (*Create*) un resumen de lo que hicieron.

MODELO: Chris dijo «bon appétit» en una comida.
Kathy y Sean hicieron comida mexicana en casa.
Nadie hizo un brindis en una comida.

PASO 3. En sus grupos, hablen de otras experiencias culinarias que han tenido Uds. (*you have had*) recientemente. Pueden ayudarlos/las (*help you*) las siguientes palabras.

cocinar   comer   ir   probar (*to try; to taste*)   tener

Reciclaje

Definite articles

Para cada sustantivo, escribe el artículo definido (**el, la, los, las**) correcto. Cinco de estos sustantivos son cosas que no se puede comer. ¿Cuáles son?

1. _el_ aceite
2. _la_ carne
3. _la_ cebolla
4. _el_ chile
5. _la_ cuchara
6. _el_ cuchillo
7. _las_ fresas
8. _los_ frijoles
9. _la_ leche
10. _la_ lechuga
11. _el_ maíz
12. _el_ pan
13. _las_ papas
14. _los_ pollos
15. _la_ servilleta
16. _las_ tazas
17. _el_ tenedor
18. _los_ tomates
19. _la_ vainilla
20. _el_ yogur

Note (Reciclaje): This activity reactivates students' memory of the four definite article forms, which with the exception of *el*, are identical to the direct object pronouns that they are about to learn. The activity also refreshes their memory of some of the crucial vocabulary from this chapter.

■ Answers to this activity are in Appendix 2 at the back of your book.

Suggestion (Para empezar): If students seem to have trouble understanding, write *lo, la = it* on the board.

6.3 Lo encontraron en México

Direct objects and direct object pronouns

Para empezar...

¿Qué tienen en común el chile, la papa, el tomate y la vainilla? Todos son originarios (*natives*) de América. En la siguiente lista de oraciones, escribe **C** si se trata (*it's about*) del chile, **P** si se trata de la papa, **T** si se trata del tomate y **V** si se trata de la vainilla. **¡Atención!** Para entender las oraciones mejor, acuérdate que **chile** y **tomate** son sustantivos masculinos, y **papa** y **vainilla** son sustantivos femeninos.

1. _P_ **La** domesticaron en la región de los Andes. Los españoles **la** llevaron a Europa y ahora **la** usan mucho en la cocina alemana e irlandesa, por ejemplo.
2. _C_ En Sudamérica y en el Caribe, **lo** conocen como «ají». **Lo** usan para hacer más picante la comida.
3. _V_ **La** usan mucho en los postres.
4. _C_ En España, **lo** conocen como «pimiento».
5. _T_ En el centro y el sur de México, **lo** conocen como «jitomate».
6. _C_ Los españoles **lo** encontraron en varias partes de América y **lo** llevaron a Europa y Asia en tiempos coloniales. Ahora **lo** usan mucho en la cocina tailandesa, china y coreana.
7. _P_ En España, **la** llaman «patata».
8. _T_ Los españoles **lo** encontraron en México y **lo** llevaron a Europa. Desde entonces (*since then*) es un ingrediente muy importante en la cocina española e italiana (en la pizza, por ejemplo).

Actividades analíticas

1 In the examples in **Para empezar, lo** and **la** are *pronouns* (**pronombres**) like *it, him,* or *her* in English. They are used to avoid repetition and replace the full name of a person or thing. **Lo** and **la** specifically replace the *direct object* (**el objeto directo**) of the sentence. The direct object is the person or thing upon which the action of the verb is performed. Circle the direct object in each sentence, then note how it is replaced by **lo** or **la.** The first is done for you.

a. Los españoles encontraron (el chile) en México.
→ Los españoles **lo** encontraron en México.

b. Los españoles llevaron (la papa) a Europa.
→ Los españoles **la** llevaron a Europa.

c. Veo (a mi hermano) todos los días.
→ **Lo** veo todos los días.

d. Gustavo conoce muy bien (a Marisela.)
→ Gustavo **la** conoce muy bien.

(*Continues*)

el chile (C)

la papa (P)

el tomate (T)

la vainilla (V)

Expansion (Para empezar): Of the four food items discussed here, ask students *¿Cuáles tres son de la misma familia biológica?* Answer: *el chile, la papa, el tomate.* (All are members of the nightshade family; vanilla is from the orchid family.) Some students may know what the plants look like, and they will be able to see the family resemblance.

Autoprueba

In each sentence, find the direct object and change it to a pronoun.

1. Juan hizo las tortillas.

_____

2. Mi mamá conoce a Ana y Mario.

_____

3. Llevé la fruta a la cocina.

_____

4. Pusimos el arroz en los platos.

_____

5. No necesito las tazas.

_____

Respuestas: 1. Juan las hizo **2.** Mi mamá los conoce. **3.** La llevé a la cocina. **4.** Lo pusimos en los platos **5.** No las necesito

■ Answers to these activities are in Appendix 2 at the back of your book.

Point out (Act. analíticas 4): Point out that **os** is only used in regions where **vosotros** is used (though it is understood everywhere).

2 Circle the direct object of each sentence, then rewrite the sentence, replacing the direct object with **lo** or **la**. The first is done for you.

a. Encontré ⟨este libro⟩ en la biblioteca. → Lo encontré en la biblioteca.
b. Ana toma ⟨café⟩ por la mañana. → Ana lo toma por la mañana.
c. Julián compró ⟨la fruta⟩ ayer. → Julián la compró ayer.

3 If the direct object is plural, the pronouns **los** or **las** are used.

Necesito **los libros**. → **Los** necesito.

Mi amiga conoce **a Ana y Luisa**. → Mi amiga **las** conoce.

The other direct object pronouns (**me, te, nos,** and **os**) are already familiar to you, because they look exactly the same as the reflexive pronouns (**Estructura 5.2**). The full set is given here.

PRONOMBRES DE OBJETO DIRECTO			
singular		**plural**	
me	*me*	**nos**	*us*
te	*you* (inform.)	**os**	*you* (inform., Sp.)
lo	*him/it* (m.)	**los**	*them* (m.)
	you (m., form.)		*you* (m., form.)
la	*her/it* (f.)	**las**	*them* (f.)
	you (f., form.)		*you* (f.)

¿**Me** conoces?   *Do you know me?*
Perdón, no **te** oí.   *I'm sorry, I didn't hear you.*
Marta **nos** invitó a una fiesta.   *Marta invited us to a party.*

4 Direct object pronouns are usually placed before the conjugated verb. If the conjugated verb is immediately followed by an infinitive, the pronoun can instead be attached to the end of the infinitive.

Puedo encontrar **el libro** en la biblioteca. → { **Lo** puedo encontrar en la biblioteca.
                                                   Puedo encontrar**lo** en la biblioteca. }

You will explore the placement of the pronoun in more detail in **Estructura 8.3**.

5 In addition to being used to mean *it* (m. and f.) and *him/her/them,* the pronouns **lo, la, los,** and **las** may be used to refer to people that you are addressing as **Ud.** or **Uds.** (*you*).

Mi madre **la** conoce.   *My mother knows you* (f. sing., form.). / *My mother knows her.*

Los invité a la cena.   *I invited you* (m. pl.) *to the dinner.* / *I invited them to the dinner.*

The following sentences are addressing the person as **tú**. Change them to address the person as **Ud.**

a. Te invito a desayunar con nosotros. → Lo invito a desayunar con nosotros.
                                           (addressing a male)

b. Te llevamos (*take*) a la fiesta. → La llevamos a la fiesta.
                                         (addressing a female)

Actividades prácticas

A. El maíz y las tortillas   De las siguientes oraciones, ¿cuáles se refieren (*refer*) al maíz y cuáles se refieren a las tortillas? Además (*In addition*), hay dos oraciones falsas, una sobre el maíz y una sobre las tortillas. ¿Cuáles son?

¿El maíz o las tortillas?

Note (Act. A): Students should be able to figure out most of the answers to the true/false portion of this activity just using their general knowledge and critical thinking. If they have ever eaten tortillas, for instance, they can probably guess that they are not made with sugar.

		CIERTO	FALSO
1. _el maíz_	Lo domesticaron en América.	☑	☐
2. _las tortillas_	Los españoles las llevaron a Europa, y desde entonces las comen mucho los españoles y los italianos.	☐	☑
3. _las tortillas_	Las comen en México, Guatemala y El Salvador.	☑	☐
4. _el maíz_	Lo ponen en agua con cal (*lime [mineral]*) para hacer la masa para las tortillas.	☑	☐
5. _el maíz_	Lo ponen en agua con azúcar para hacer la masa para las tortillas.	☐	☑
6. _las tortillas_	Tradicionalmente las hacen de maíz.	☑	☐
7. _el maíz_	Los españoles lo llevaron a Europa y al resto del mundo.	☑	☐
8. _el maíz_	En muchos países lo llaman «choclo».	☑	☐
9. _las tortillas_	En el norte de México, donde tradicionalmente no hay mucho maíz, las hacen de harina.	☑	☐

CONÉCTATE AL MUNDO HISPANO

La tortilla es importante a la gastronomía mexicana, centroamericana y española. Pero, ¿sabes que hay varios tipos de tortillas?

Tortillas de maíz

En el norte de México, se puede encontrar tortillas de harina. Estas suelen ser (*tend to be*) más grandes y se usan para hacer los burritos. En el centro y el sur de México y en Centroamérica se encuentran tortillas de maíz. Son hechas con harina de maíz, y normalmente son más pequeñas. Se usan para hacer los tacos o enchiladas, o para acompañar algún plato.

En España, la tortilla tradicional es totalmente distinta. Está hecha de huevo y papa y es un tipo de «omelette».

Una tortilla española

B. Preguntas y respuestas   Vas a escuchar ocho preguntas. Escoge la respuesta más lógica para cada una.

1. _g_
2. _f_
3. _b_
4. _d_
5. _a_
6. _c_
7. _e_
8. _h_

a. ¿No me conoces? Soy Mari, la amiga de Jorge.
b. La tiré (*threw out*).
c. Las puse en la cocina.
d. Porque no nos invitaron a la fiesta.
e. Sí, está bien. Te veo allí.
f. ¿No lo conoces? Es el amigo de Ana.
g. Lo puse en la cocina.
h. Los tiré.

Script (Act. B): 1. ¿Dónde pusiste el pescado? **2.** ¿Quién es ese hombre? **3.** ¿Dónde está la naranja? **4.** ¿Por qué estás enojado con ellos? **5.** Perdon, ¿quién eres? **6.** ¿Dónde pusiste las manzanas? **7.** ¿Te veo mañana en la biblioteca? **8.** ¿Dónde están los plátanos?

Suggestion (Act. C):
This works well as a either a pair or small group activity. Ask students to state (*no*) *lo/la/los/las tienen* for each item, depending on whether it is available in local restaurants. Depending on local circumstances, add in other dishes that you think some students might be familiar with.

Expansion (Act. D): Write on the board: *Lo/La/Los/Las como con las manos* and *Lo/La/Los/Las como con tenedor y cuchillo.* Read each of the following food items and have students say how they eat it: *la carne, la manzana, la naranja, el pescado, el plátano, los champiñones, las fresas.* Point out that in most restaurants in Spanish-speaking countries, all of these items would normally be eaten with a knife and fork.

Note (Act. D): In the American style, the fork is in the left hand and the knife in the right for cutting. After cutting, the knife is placed on the plate, and the fork switches from the left hand to the right to bring the food to the mouth. In the European style, the fork is in the left hand (tines down) and the knife is in the right. After cutting, the fork stays in the left hand as food is brought to the mouth. The European style is the most common in the Spanish-speaking world.

Suggestion (Act. E):
Ask several students who they see outside of class and where. *¿A quién ves? ¿Dónde y cuándo lo/la ves?* Remind students to use the direct object pronoun to answer the second question.

C. La comida mexicana en tu país   De toda la comida hispana, la mexicana es la más conocida en este país. Pero, ¿tú la conoces bien? En esta lista de platillos (*dishes*) mexicanos, ¿cuáles conoces? ¿Cuáles tienen en restaurantes donde tú vives? En parejas, comparen sus experiencias. **¡Atención!** El número y género de cada platillo es diferente.

> **MODELO:**   E1: ¿Conoces el arroz con leche?
> E2: No, no lo conozco, pero lo tienen en restaurantes aquí.

ALGUNOS PLATILLOS MEXICANOS

1. el arroz con leche
2. la birria (carne de chivo [*goat*])
3. las carnitas
4. los chilaquiles (trozos [*pieces*] de tortilla de maíz con huevo y salsa picante)
5. la crema de espárragos (*cream of asparagus soup*)
6. la sopa de tortilla
7. los huevos motuleños (tortilla de maíz con huevos, frijoles negros y queso)
8. los nopalitos (*cactus pads*)
9. la sopa de lima (de pollo con jugo de lima [*lime*])
10. los tamales dulces

D. El tenedor y el cuchillo   Hay dos maneras de cortar (*to cut*) la comida con el tenedor y el cuchillo en el mundo: «el estilo norteamericano» y «el estilo europeo». Lee las siguientes descripciones, y trata de identificar cuál es el estilo norteamericano y cuál es el estilo europeo. Luego cambia la expresión subrayada (*underlined*) a un pronombre y escribe la descripción en el espacio correcto.

> **MODELO:**   Tengo <u>el tenedor</u> en la mano izquierda (*left hand*). →
> Lo tengo en la mano izquierda.

El estilo A:

1. Tengo <u>el tenedor</u> en la mano izquierda. Después de cortar algo, cambio <u>el tenedor</u> de la mano izquierda a la mano derecha (*right*) para comer.
2. Tengo <u>el cuchillo</u> en la mano derecha. Después de cortar algo, pongo <u>el cuchillo</u> en el plato.

El estilo B:

1. Tengo <u>el tenedor</u> en la mano izquierda. Después de cortar algo, dejo (*I leave*) <u>el tenedor</u> en esa mano para comer.
2. Tengo <u>el cuchillo</u> en la mano derecha. Después de cortar algo, dejo <u>el cuchillo</u> en esa mano.

Estilo __B__ es el estilo europeo.

El tenedor: _____

El cuchillo: _____

Estilo __A__ es el estilo norteamericano.

El tenedor: _____

El cuchillo: _____

E. ¿A quién ves fuera de la clase?   Haz una lista de los compañeros de tu clase que ves fuera de la clase de vez en cuando. En parejas, explíquense dónde y cúando ven a cada persona en su lista.

> **MODELO:**   *Tú:* Te veo en mi clase de biología los martes y jueves.
> *Steve:* Lo veo en la residencia todos los días.
> *Alycia y Karen:* Las veo en el trabajo de vez en cuando.

Answers (Act. D): *ESTILO «B» ES EL ESTILO EUROPEO,* **El tenedor:** *Lo tengo en la mano izquierda. Después de cortar algo, lo dejo en esa mano para comer.* **El cuchillo:** *Lo tengo en la mano derecha. Después de cortar algo, lo dejo en esa mano. ESTILO «A» ES EL ESTILO NORTEAMERICANO,* **El tenedor:** *Lo tengo en la mano izquierda. Después de cortar algo, lo cambio de la mano izquierda a la mano derecha para comer.* **El cuchillo:** *Lo tengo en la mano derecha. Después de cortar algo, lo pongo en el plato.*

F. Cultura: Los productos agrícolas (*agricultural*) en Chile

PASO 1.   Lee el texto sobre Chile.

Chile

¿Conoces la comida chilena? Aunque no conozcas[a] todos los platillos tradicionales, sin duda[b] conoces los ingredientes. Chile produce y exporta mucha comida que llega a las mesas de familias en otros países. Por ejemplo, se cultivan muchas frutas y verduras. Chile es el primer exportador de manzanas, uvas, duraznos y ciruelas[c] en el mundo. También produce muchos aguacates, fresas, peras y espárragos.

Por tener una costa tan larga, claro que otra comida que se exporta de Chile es el pescado. Después de Noruega, Chile es el segundo exportador en todo el mundo de salmón y trucha.[d] Un dato interesante es que en los Estados Unidos y Canadá, el pez que se pesca en los océanos entre Patagonia y Antártida, y que antes se conocía como *Patagonian toothfish,* es ahora mejor conocido como *Chilean sea bass,* el nombre que inventó un vendedor de pescado.* Chile produce otros pescados y varios mariscos también, como mejillones, vieiras, ostras y abulón.[e]

Y una mesa de comida chilena no está lista hasta tener una botella (o tal vez, una caja[†]) de vino chileno. Chile es el quinto[f] exportador de vino en todo el mundo. Los vinos que más produce son los Cabernet Sauvignon y los Merlot. El valle de Maipo es una de las regiones más reconocidas por la producción de vino chileno excelente.

El pescado es un producto económico importante de Chile.

[a]Aunque... *Even if you aren't familiar with*   [b]*doubt*   [c]*uvas... grapes, peaches, and plums*   [d]*trout*
[e]*mejillones... mussels, scallops, oysters and abalone,*   [f]*fifth*

PASO 2.   Ahora empareja cada producto chileno con la oración que lo describe usando un pronombre de objeto directo.

 _a_ 1. Chile la exporta al resto del mundo.
 _d_ 2. Los niños de los Estados Unidos las traen en sus almuerzos.
 _c_ 3. Chile los exporta junto (*along*) con sus pescados.
 _b_ 4. Incluso los franceses y los italianos lo beben durante la cena.
 _f_ 5. Los sirven en los restaurantes vegetarianos en todo el mundo.
 _e_ 6. Los noruegos (*Norwegians*) casi no lo comen porque tienen un producto nacional similar.

a. la fruta chilena
b. el vino chileno
c. los mariscos chilenos
d. las manzanas chilenas
e. el salmón chileno
f. los espárragos chilenos

PASO 3.   En parejas, contesten las preguntas y explíquense sus respuestas.

1. Chile es uno de los pocos países hispanos que exporta grandes cantidades (*quantities*) de vino al resto del mundo (los otros son Argentina y España). ¿Por qué produce tanto (*so much*) vino Chile, y no países como Colombia o Guatemala?
2. En comparación al resto de Latinoamérica, Chile es un país relativamente rico y tiene una economía fuerte. ¿Ves una relación entre eso y la producción de vino en Chile?
3. En tu país, ¿dónde producen vino y dónde no? En general, ¿las zonas donde producen vino son más ricas que otras partes del país?

Note (Act. F, Paso 3): Chile has several regions with the right climate for wine, and this has been an advantage for its economic development. Few other Latin American countries have this.

Expansion (Act. F, Paso 3): Ask students to consider whether it is better for a country to export something like wine or something like bananas. What advantages are there to exporting wine?

*Este pez, que tiene el nombre científico de *Dissostichus eleginoides,* se conoce como «bacalao de profundidad» (*deep-water cod*) en Chile y «merluza (*hake*) negra» en Argentina.
†En Chile algunos de los vinos más sabrosos (*best-tasting*) se venden en caja (a box).

¡Leamos!

El huitlacoche

Antes de leer

PASO 1. Indica tus gustos en cuanto a (*with regard to*) la comida mexicana.

	ME GUSTA(N)	NO ME GUSTA(N)	NO HE PROBADO (*I HAVEN'T TRIED*)...
1. los chiles asados	☐	☐	☐
2. la pechuga (*breast*) de pollo rellena (*stuffed*) de hongos (champiñones)	☐	☐	☐
3. las quesadillas	☐	☐	☐
4. los tamales	☐	☐	☐
5. las tortillas de harina	☐	☐	☐
6. las tortillas de maíz	☐	☐	☐

PASO 2. Ahora contesta las preguntas.

1. ¿Eres atrevido/a (*daring*) cuando pruebas (*you try*) comida? ¿Te gusta probar comidas nuevas?
2. ¿Cuál fue la última (*last*) comida nueva que probaste? ¿Te gustó?
3. ¿Te gustan los hongos?
4. Nombra dos platos que normalmente tienen hongos.
5. ¿Conoces el huitlacoche?

Suggestion (A leer): Tell students that the word *huitlacoche* is from the Nahuatl language, which was used by the Aztecs. The most common term in English for *huitlacoche* is *corn smut* or *common smut;* it is principally viewed as an agricultural parasite and pest in this country.

A leer

Lee el artículo sobre el hongo huitlacoche y contesta las preguntas.

El huitlacoche

¡Todas las mazorcas[a] de maíz de esta cosecha[b] están arruinadas[c]! Atacadas por hongos que crecen dentro de la chala,[d] hasta abrirla.[e] Qué desastre, ¿no?

¡No! Porque estos hongos que atacan el maíz son muy nutritivos, deliciosos y, para el agricultor[f] de maíz, no son desastrosos porque los hongos se venden en el mercado a un precio mucho más alto que el maíz.

Estos hongos se llaman «huitlacoche» o «cuitlacoche», un nombre que viene de dos palabras indígenas: *cuitlatl* (*excremento*) y *cochi* (*dormir*).

Según los científicos de la alimentación,[g] estos parásitos del maíz ofrecen una generosa cantidad[h] de proteínas, minerales y propiedades nutritivas.

El «ataque» de estas bolitas hongosas[i] resulta en un proceso metabólico dentro de la mazorca que produce nutrientes nuevos y más robustos. Uno de los minerales derivados de este hongo es la lisina.[j] Prácticamente ausente en el maíz, la lisina abunda en el huitlacoche. La lisina as un aminoácido fundamental para nuestra salud que el organismo no reproduce por sí mismo.[k] Combate infecciones, fortifica el esqueleto y es

[a] *ears cobs*   [b] *crops*   [c] *ruined*   [d] *crecen... grow inside the husk*   [e] *hasta... until it opens it*   [f] *farmer*   [g] *científicos... nutrition scientists*   [h] *quantity*   [i] *bolitas... mushroom balls*   [j] *lysine*   [k] *por... on its own*

popular entre los fisicoculturistas y los esteticistas[l] para aumentar los músculos y rejuvenecer la piel.[m]

No tienes que tomar una pastilla[n] para recibir los beneficios del huitlacoche. Pero sí tienes que cenar en restaurantes exclusivos, como la James Beard House de Nueva York, donde periódicamente este hongo indígena luce[ñ] en el menú. Saboréalo[o] también en el platillo de pechuga de pollo rellena de huitlacoche en La Cocina Michoacana de Cedar Park, Texas, en las quesadillas de Tú y Yo en Boston o en los tamales de La Casita Mexicana de Los Ángeles.

Steve Sando —dueño de Rancho Gordo en el Valle de Napa— diría: «¡Olvídate del valor nutritivo[p]! El sabor[q] es espectacular». Sando viajó a México para obtener el hongo. Probó el huitlacoche en una feria culinaria con su amiga Ruth Alegría, una chef mexicana. En la feria, comieron quesadillas de maíz rellenas de huitlacoche, cebollas y granos de maíz y otros platos con el hongo. Son platos como este que inspiran su compañía, Rancho Gordo, donde cultiva[r] productos únicos y exclusivos como el huitlacoche y otros cultivos indígenas.

[l]fisicoculturistas... *bodybuilders and aestheticians* [m]aumentar... *build muscle and rejuvenate skin* [n]*pill* [ñ]*is featured* [o]*Taste it* [p]valor... *nutritional value* [q]*flavor* [r]*cultivates*

1. ¿Qué es el huitlacoche? Hongo de maíz / parásito del maíz
2. Según estudios, ¿qué propiedades nutritivas tiene el huitlacoche? Tiene proteínas, minerales y lisina
3. ¿Cuál **no** es un beneficio de la lisina?
   a. ayuda a sacar músculos   b. combate infecciones   (c.) protege los órganos internos
4. ¿Cómo es el sabor del huitlacoche? Es espectacular.
5. Describe el negocio de Steve Sando: ¿Qué es? ¿Dónde está? ¿Por qué visitó México? Menciona pechuga de pollo rellena de huitlacoche, quesadillas

   Steve Sando tiene un rancho en Napa Valley. Cultiva huitlacoche y otros productos indígenas del Nuevo Mundo. Visitó México para explorar la posibilidad de agregar el huitlacoche a la línea de productos que vende en el norte de California.
6. ¿Qué platos hechos con huitlacoche menciona el artículo? de huitlacoche y tamales.
7. En este país se puede comer huitlacoche en...
   (a.) algunos de los mejores restaurantes.   c. exclusivamente en los restaurantes
   b. todos los restaurantes Tex-Mex.   de baja calidad.

 Después de leer

En grupos, contesten las preguntas.

1. ¿Qué comidas te parecen raras, extrañas o asquerosas (*disgusting*)? ¿Por qué?
2. ¿Hay comidas que se comen en este país que pueden ser raras para gente de otros países? Expliquen.
3. ¿Te gustaría (*Would you like*) probar el huitlacoche? ¿Por qué sí o por qué no?

En español...

A number of foods originating from the Americas take their name from words in Nahuatl, the language spoken in the Aztec Empire and most commonly spoken indigenous language in Mexico today. The influence of Nahuatl can be seen in both Spanish and English food names.

NAHUATL	SPANISH
ahuacatl	**aguacate**
chocolatl	**chocolate**
colanto	**cilantro**
chilli	**chile**
xitomatl	**(ji)tomate**

Note (Después de leer): Students should understand that *huitlacoche* is really like any other mushroom. Q2 is designed to show that, like with almost all cultural practices, "normal" food can always seem "weird" when viewed from an outsider perspective. The names we give things can bias us for or against them by either disguising what they really are or making them sound gross (as in *corn smut*).

¡Escuchemos!

La cocina tradicional

Antes de escuchar

Video track (A escuchar):
This video clip can be found
on the DVD to accompany
Conéctate: Cap. 6, Track 3.

En grupos, describan platos típicos de sus países, estados o familias. Cada
estudiante debe añadir (*add*) detalles. Describan por lo menos cuatro platos típicos.

> **MODELO:** E1: La hamburguesa es como un sándwich de carne con pan.
> E2: Generalmente lleva (*it comes with*) lechuga, tomate, queso y salsa
> de tomate.
> E3: Normalmente lleva papas fritas como acompañamiento.

A escuchar

Mira y escucha las descripciones de platos tradicionales que se comen en varias
partes del mundo hispano. Luego mira otra vez con pausas y completa las recetas
con los ingredientes que corresponden a cada plato.

El ceviche (de Perú y otros países costeros de América)

LISTA DE INGREDIENTES

las cebollas rojas   el limón
el culantro (*cilantro*)   el pescado

PREPARACIÓN

Tenemos el ceviche que es ____pescado____ crudo que lo maceramos (*marinate*) con
____limón____ y __cebollas rojas__ y ____culantro____.

El gallo pinto (de Costa Rica)

LISTA DE INGREDIENTES

el arroz   el chile   la mantequilla
la cebolla   los frijoles

PREPARACIÓN

Bueno, gallo pinto son especias como ____cebolla____, ____chile____ picado, luego
se le pone _la mantequilla_, y ya le pone ____arroz____, ____frijoles____ y se mezcla.
Sí, es el plato típico.

El gazpacho (de España)

LISTA DE INGREDIENTES

el aceite   el pan   el pimiento (*bell pepper*)   el tomate
la cebolla   el pepino   la sal   el vinagre

PREPARACIÓN

¿El gazpacho? Pues es ____pepino____, ____pimiento____, ____cebolla____ y
____tomate____, y ____pan____ mojado (*wet*)... Se pasa por la batidora
(*blender*), se le echa (*add*) ____sal____, ____aceite____ y ____vinagre____
y luego se cuela (*strain*) y se bebe líquido como si fuera, pues yo que sé...
como un zumo (*jugo*).

El pico de gallo (de Nicaragua)

LISTA DE INGREDIENTES

la cebolla   la pimienta   la sal   el tomate

PREPARACIÓN

Pico de gallo es tomate picado con ____cebolla____ y todo eso mezclado. Es como una salsita, pero de ____tomate____ picado en cuadritos más cebolla y ____sal____ y ____pimienta____.

El pabellón criollo (de Venezuela)

LISTA DE INGREDIENTES

el arroz   los frijoles   el huevo   el plátano

PREPARACIÓN

El pabellón criollo es un plato a base de ____arroz____ negros y ____frijoles____. Luego lleva un ____huevo____ frito y ____plátano____ frito también.

Después de escuchar

En grupos, hablen de cuál(es) de los platos descritos quieren probar y por qué.

> **MODELO:** Quiero probar el ceviche porque me gustan los mariscos. No sé si quiero probar los plátanos fritos del pabellón criollo.

Videoscript (A escuchar):
1. Tenemos el ceviche que es pescado crudo que lo maceramos con limón y cebollas rojas y culantro. 2. Bueno, gallo pinto son especias como cebolla, chile picado, luego se le pone la mantequilla, y ya le pone arroz, frijoles y se mezcla. Sí, es el plato típico. 3. ¿El gazpacho? Pues es pepino, pimiento, cebolla y tomate y pan mojado... Se pasa por la batidora, se le echa sal, aceite y vinagre y luego se cuela y se bebe líquido como si fuera, pues yo qué sé... como un zumo, un... y está buenísimo. 4. Pico de gallo es tomate picado con cebolla y todo eso mezclado. Es como una salsita, pero de tomate picado en cuadritos más cebolla y sal y pimienta. 5. El pabellón criollo, es el plato más típico que se come en todo el país, que es un plato a base de frijoles, frijoles negros, arroz. Luego lleva un huevo frito y plátano frito también.

¡Escribamos!

Una celebración memorable

¿Recuerdas una celebración especial en la comida estuvo muy rica?

A. Antes de escribir

Piensa en una celebración a la que asististe y en la que estuvo muy rica la comida que sirvieron. Puede ser una fiesta, una celebración de cumpleaños o «todos los domingos en casa de mis padres». Prepara dos listas de vocabulario: todas las palabras en español relacionadas con el tema y las palabras que necesitas en español pero que no sabes.

> **MODELO:** *el primer cumpleaños de mi prima*

Vocabulario en español:	Vocabulario en inglés:
la ensalada	*candle*
la lechuga	*carrots*
el tomate	*gifts*
el helado	
la torta	

ESTRATEGIA

Vocabulary

It is often helpful to make sure you have all the vocabulary you will need in Spanish before you start writing your essay. Write a list of words that you associate with the topic and circle the ones that will be the most helpful for your piece. Then make a list in English of words you do not know, but will need; look them up before writing so that you can do all your writing entirely in Spanish.

A escribir

Escribe un ensayo de diez frases (mínimo) para describir la celebración. Explica qué celebraron Uds., qué comida sirvieron, quiénes estuvieron y por qué la recuerdas.

(Continues)

Suggestion (Después de leer): To motivate students to edit their own work as well as their classmates' carefully, occasionally grade their editing instead of their writing.

Después de escribir

Revisa tu ensayo. Luego intercambia ensayos con un compañero / una compañera. Lee el ensayo de tu compañero/a y determina si falta información necesaria. Lee de nuevo (*again*) el ensayo con cuidado para revisar los siguientes puntos de gramática.

☐ el ensayo está escrito en el pasado

☐ los verbos regulares tienen las terminaciones correctas en el pretérito

☐ los verbos irregulares tienen las conjugaciones correctas en el pretérito

☐ hay concordancia de sustantivos y adjetivos

☐ tiene la ortografía (*spelling*) correcta

Después de revisar el ensayo de tu compañero/a, devuélveselo (*return it to him/ her*). Mira tu propio (*own*) ensayo para ver los cambios que tu compañero/a recomienda y haz las revisiones necesarias.

¡Hablemos!

La fiesta de la clase

Suggestion (¡Hablemos!): Have students prepare before class by consulting web references to get ideas about the kind of foods they might prepare, but remind them that they should use resources from this chapter so that their classmates understand the menus when they have to decide which meals they'll eat in *Después de hablar.*

Antes de hablar

¡La clase va a hacer una fiesta! En grupos de tres o cuatro, hagan una lista de lo que van a servir en la fiesta (bebidas, aperitivos, postre [*appetizers*], etcétera).

A hablar

Cada grupo escoge un tipo de comida (argentina, china, cubana, española, italiana, mexicana...) para su menú y habla de lo que se va a servir para cada elemento de **Antes de hablar.** Decidan quién va a traer cada cosa. Mencionen una por una (*one by one*) las cosas de su lista y pidan voluntarios. **¡Atención!** Tengan cuidado (*Be careful*) con los pronombres de objeto directo.

> **MODELO:** E1: Para nuestra fiesta española, necesitamos una tortilla española.
> E2: Yo la traigo.
> E1: También necesitamos olivas.
> E3: Yo las traigo.

Después de hablar

Cada grupo presenta su menú e invita a la clase a asistir. Los otros grupos deben o aceptar o rechazar la invitación usando el vocabulario de este capítulo.

Conéctate al cine

Película: *Como agua para chocolate*
(comedia/drama, México, 1992)
Director: Alfonso Arau

Sinopsis:

Tita y sus hermanas, Gertrudis y Rosaura, viven con su madre en un rancho en México durante los años de la Revolución (1910 a 1920). El joven Pedro declara su amor por Tita, pero la madre de Tita prohíbe el matrimonio (*marriage*) porque Tita, la menor de las tres hermanas, tiene que cuidar a (*care for*) su madre el resto de su vida. Entonces Pedro se casa con (*marries*) Rosaura porque quiere vivir cerca de (*close to*) Tita. A Tita le gusta cocinar y ella prepara unos platillos tan sabrosos como (*both delicious and*) místicos para toda la familia.

Escena (Netflix, 00:15:46–00:21:38):

Tita está triste porque Pedro y Rosaura se casan y ella tiene que preparar la comida para la boda (*wedding*). Ella ayuda a Nacha, la cocinera de la familia, en la cocina y la madre de Tita las regaña (*scolds*). Luego en la boda, pasa algo misterioso cuando los invitados (*guests*) comen lo que Tita y Nacha prepararon.

Antes de ver

Tita y Nacha preparan la comida para la boda de Rosaura y Pedro. ¿Qué tipo de comida se sirve (*is served*) en las bodas de tu familia o de tus amigos? ¿Qué beben las personas en una boda? ¿Qué tipo de postre comen?

A ver
Suggestion (A ver): Students should be able to use the Expresiones útiles to answer all of the questions, but you may want to teach the verbs llorar and vomitar.

Lee las **Expresiones útiles** y mira la escena. Luego contesta las preguntas usando el pretérito.

1. ¿Qué ingrediente usaron Tita y Nacha para preparar el postre? usaron huevos
2. ¿Qué hizo Tita en la cocina porque estaba muy triste? Lloró/Chilló en la masa.
3. ¿Qué comieron los invitados en la boda? comieron pastel
4. ¿Qué bebieron los invitados en la boda? bebieron vino y champán
5. ¿Qué hicieron los invitados después de comer? lloraron/chillaron y vomitaron; participaron en una vomitona colectiva

Expresiones útiles

solo nos faltan	we only need . . . more
apúrense	hurry up
suelta tus lágrimas	let it all out
adivino	I (can) guess
las ollas	pots
los hervores	boiling (*n.*); ardor (*fig.*)
deja de chillar	stop crying
la masa	batter
logré	I managed to
anhelaba	I was longing for
no me engañes	don't try to fool me
el llanto	weeping
añorando	yearning for
se escapó del hechizo	escaped the spell
la vomitona colectiva	group vomiting

Después de ver

Con un compañero / una compañera, responde a las siguientes preguntas.

1. Explica en tus propias palabras qué pasó en la boda. ¿Por qué pasó?
2. Nacha le dice a Tita: «Solo las ollas saben los hervores de su caldo... ». ¿Qué puede significar este refrán (*saying*)?

Suggestion (A ver): Turn subtitles off, if possible. Students won't understand everything, but they won't need to. Stop after Tita finds Nacha dead, holding the photograph of her love.

■ For copyright reasons, the feature-film clips referenced in **Conéctate al cine** have not been provided by the publisher. Each of these films is readily available through retailers or online rental sites such as Amazon, iTunes, or Netflix.

VOCABULARIO

Now that I have completed the chapter, I can . . .

☐ respond affirmatively to a request

☐ give and decline invitations politely

☐ describe meals, table settings, and foods

☐ talk about the past

☐ use pronouns to avoid repetition

☐ discuss meals and foods in the Spanish-speaking world

Comunicación

¿Quieres/Quiere + *noun/inf.*?	Do you (*inform./form.*) want . . . ?
¿Tienes/Tiene ganas de + *noun/inf.*?	Do you (*inform./form.*) feel like . . . ?
¿Qué te/le parece + *noun/inf.*?	How about (*inform./form.*) . . . ?
¿Te/Le apetece + *noun/inf.*?	How about (*inform./form.*) . . . ?
Sí, gracias.	Yes, please.
Si no es molestia.	If it's not a bother.
No, gracias.	No, thank you.
Debo + *inf.*	I should (*do something*).
No puedo	I can't.
¡Cómo no! / ¡Claro que sí! / ¡Por supuesto!	Sure/No problem. / Of course!
¡Con mucho gusto!	With pleasure!

La comida — Food

el aceite	oil
el agua	water
el arroz	rice
el atún	tuna
el azúcar	sugar
la bebida	drink
los calamares	squid
el caldo	broth, clear soup
los camarones	shrimp
la carne	(red) meat
la carne de res	beef
la carne de puerco	pork
la cebolla	onion
la cerveza	beer
los champiñones/hongos	mushrooms
el chile	chili pepper
el chorizo	sausage
los comestibles...	groceries, food
empaquetados	packaged goods
enlatados	canned goods
la ensalada	salad
el flan	custard
la fresa	strawberry
los frijoles	beans
la harina	flour
el helado	ice cream
el huevo	egg
el jamón	ham
el jugo	juice
la leche	milk
la lechuga	lettuce
el limón	lemon; lime
el maíz	corn
la mantequilla	butter
la manzana	apple
los mariscos	seafood
la merienda	snack
la naranja	orange
el pan	bread
la papa	potato
el pastel	cake
el pepino	cucumber
el perejil	parsley
el pescado	fish
la pimienta	black pepper
la piña	pineapple
el plátano	banana
el pollo	chicken
el postre	dessert
los productos lácteos	dairy products
el puerco	pork
el queso	cheese
el refresco	soda
la sal	salt
la salsa	sauce
la sopa	soup
la torta	cake
la verdura	vegetable
el vino blanco/tinto	white/red wine

Cognados: el brócoli, el condimento, la fruta, el mango, la pasta, el sándwich, el tomate, el vinagre, el yogur

En la mesa — At the table

En la mesa	At the table
el bol	bowl
el/la camarero/a	waiter, server
la carta	menu
el cubierto	place setting
la cuchara	spoon
el cuchillo	knife
el plato	plate; dish; course
el primer plato	first course
el segundo plato / plato principal	main course
la servilleta	napkin
la taza	coffee cup; measuring cup
el tenedor	fork
el vaso	(drinking) glass

Las tiendas de comida — Food stores

Las tiendas de comida	Food stores
el hipermercado	large supermarket
el mercado	(outdoor) market
la panadería	bakery
la pescadería	fish market
el supermercado (el súper)	supermarket
la verdulería	vegetable market

Repaso: la carnicería, la frutería

Otros términos culinarios

Otros términos culinarios	
a la plancha	grilled
al ajillo	sauteed with garlic
asado/a	roasted
dulce	sweet
frito/a	fried
picante	spicy
saludable	healthy

Los verbos

Los verbos	
abrir	to open
aprender	to learn
cerrar (ie)	to close
evitar	to avoid
merendar (ie)	to have a snack
nacer (zc)	to be born
pedir (i)	to order (food); to ask for
poner (irreg.) la mesa	to set the table
probar (ue)	to try; to taste
ver (irreg.)	to see

Los pronombres de objeto directo

me, te, lo/la, nos, os, los/las

Los recuerdos° y la nostalgia

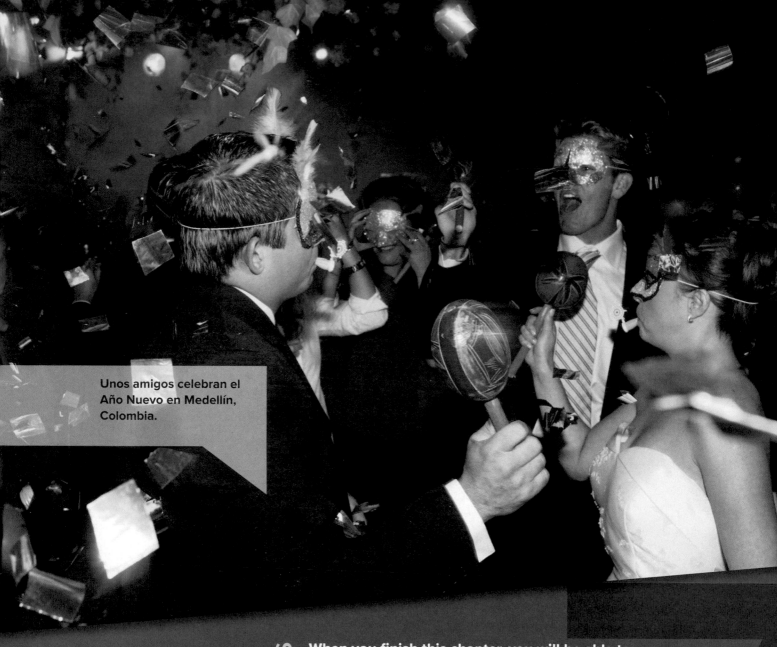

Unos amigos celebran el Año Nuevo en Medellín, Colombia.

Objetivos

When you finish this chapter, you will be able to:

- say you had a good time
- wish someone well and congratulate them
- talk about holidays and celebrations in the Spanish-speaking world
- talk about ongoing events in the past
- express to whom or for whom an action is performed

www.mhhe.com/connect

COMUNICACIÓN ~~LARIO~~ ~~UCTURA~~ ~~ATE~~

Lo pasé bien

Expressing *to have a good time*

Video track (Act. A): This video clip can be found on the DVD to accompany *Conéctate:* Cap. 7, Track 1.

Suggestion (Lo pasé bien): The use of *lo* or *la* in *Lo/La pasé bien* varies by region and sometimes by social class. Remind students that they will always have to pay attention to how language is really used in a given context.

A. A ver: ¿Cómo lo pasan bien los estudiantes?   Mira y escucha. Luego mira otra vez con pausas y completa las frases. Mira y escucha una tercera vez para verificar tus respuestas.

1. Según Adrián, los estudiantes van a ___la playa___ para pasarlo bien.

2. Ellos practican _mucho deporte_, usan _la computadora_ y salen ___al campo___.
   a la naturaleza

3. Según José Antonio y David, van de __fiesta__ y juegan mucho __fútbol__ para divertirse.

4. En España, los jóvenes se divierten en _los bares_ y en _las fiestas_.

5. A Aline le gusta ___bailar___ y pasársela bien.

6. A William le gusta _tocar guitarra_, _(ir a) caminar_, _andar en bici_ y _salir con amigos_ para divertirse.

7. Para pasarlo bien, a Keylin le gusta _ver películas_.

8. Para divertirse, a Esteban le gusta ___salir___, _ir (se) de fiesta_, _ir a algún bar_ e _ir a alguna disco_.

9. A Anlluly le gusta _ir a bailar_ para pasarlo bien.

10. A Ignacio le gusta divertirse, ___salir___, _estudiar/trabajar_ y _estar con la familia_.

Note (Act. A): Prepare students to listen for key words. As in any natural speech, people embellish their comments with details and include a lot of repetition. Students should focus on listening for places or activities enjoyed in free time.

Videoscript (Act. A):
1. ADRIÁN: *Eh... Como en Madrid no hay playa, pues normalmente se viaja a la costa para la playa, tomar el sol, eh... y pasarlo bien, y despejarse un poco de la ciudad.*
2. MAYRA: *Bueno, ellos los fines de semana practican mucho deporte, sí. Y les gusta mucho estar, bueno, en computación. Les gusta mucho usar la computadora. Les gusta mucho la recreación. Ellos salen al campo y les gusta mucho la naturaleza.*
3. JOSÉ ANTONIO: *De fiesta, fútbol, deportes... todo.* DAVID: *En mi caso, los fines de semana, lo que son los sábados yo salgo a jugar con el hotel que... donde yo trabajo y los domingos salgo a jugar con el equipo del pueblo. Y los sábados... los domingos vamos de fiesta a lo que es disco-club RadioEstablo. Así lo pasamos bien nosotros aquí.* **4.** VÍCTOR: *Ah, para divertirse, bueno aquí en España los jóvenes se divierten en los bares, tomando copas, en las fiestas.*
5. ALINE: *Este... bailar, me gusta bailar mucho, y pasármela bien, así en compañía de mis amigos o mi familia depende del momento ¿no?* **6.** WILLIAM: *Después, toco guitarra. Ir a caminar un rato, andar en bici, o salir con mis amigos.* **7.** KEYLIN: *Me gusta ver películas, pero no tenemos cine en Monteverde.*
8. ESTEBAN: *Simplemente salir, irme de fiesta, ir a algún bar, ir a alguna disco.* **9.** ANLLULY: *Me gusta mucho ir a bailar, sí. Normalmente salgo una vez a la semana.* **10.** IGNACIO: *Salir por la noche, divertirte, estudiar, trabajar, estar en la familia.*

To say you had a good time in Spanish, use **pasarlo/la bien** (*to have a good time*) or **divertirse** (*to have fun*).

—**Lo pasé muy bien de vacaciones. ¿Y tú?**   "I had a good time on vacation. And you?"
—**Sí, me divertí mucho en las montañas.**   "Yes, I had a lot of fun in the mountains.
  ¿Adónde fuiste tú?   Where did you go?"
—**A la playa.**   "To the beach."

¡Atención! There is no literal translation of the English *to have a good time*. You must use an expression like one of those presented here.

B. ¿Adónde van para divertirse?   Lee la cita (*quote*) de cada persona y luego selecciona la oración que mejor la resume (*summarizes*).

1. __b__ Nuria (de Madrid, España), dice: «El fin de semana pasado, mis amigos y yo nos divertimos tomando el sol y nadando en el mar».
   a. Fueron a las montañas.
   b. Fueron a la playa.
   c. Fueron al campo.
   d. Fueron al mercado.

2. __a__ Eduardo (de Panamá) dice: «Me gustan las películas de acción».
   a. Eduardo lo pasa bien en el cine.
   b. Eduardo lo pasa bien en la playa.
   c. Eduardo lo pasa bien en los mercados.
   d. Eduardo lo pasa bien en las fiestas.

3. __d__ Sara (de Colombia) dice: «El año pasado fui a Buenos Aires, Río de Janeiro, Tokio, Londres y Barcelona. Siempre me divierto».
   a. Sara lo pasa bien en la cocina.
   b. Sara lo pasa bien en la clase de música.
   c. Sara lo pasa bien en la oficina.
   d. Sara lo pasa bien en los viajes.

4. __a__ María (de México) dice: «Los jóvenes la pasan bien en los antros y discos».
   a. Se divierten en los clubes.
   b. Se divierten en la playa.
   c. Se divierten en la biblioteca.
   d. Se divierten en las pistas de fútbol.

5. __c__ Rodrigo (de Buenos Aires) dice: «Los fines de semana me divierto en las fiestas con mis amigos de la universidad».
   a. Rodrigo lo pasa bien en la biblioteca.
   b. Rodrigo lo pasa bien en los cafés.
   c. Rodrigo lo pasa bien en las casas de sus amigos.
   d. Rodrigo lo pasa bien en los salones de clase en la universidad.

El fin de semana pasado, me divertí con mis amigos en la costa de Alicante.

En español...

The word **antro** literally means *cave* or *cavern,* but in Mexico it's a very common term for *club*—a place to socialize, dance, and drink. **Discoteca** is the general word that is understood everywhere, but other words may be used locally. Part of the fun of meeting people from around the Spanish-speaking world is learning the local slang terms that they use.

C. ¿Te divertiste?

PASO 1. Para cada actividad que hiciste alguna vez, concluye con una de las siguientes expresiones, según tu experiencia.

(no) me divertí   (no) lo pasé bien

MODELO: Visité a mi familia y *lo pasé bien*.

1. Bailé en un club y _____.
2. Cené en un nuevo restaurante y _____.
3. Estudié en la biblioteca y _____.
4. Fui a la playa y _____.
5. Fui de compras y _____.
6. Hice la tarea y _____.
7. Limpié mi cuarto y _____.
8. Practiqué un deporte y _____.
9. Tomé un café en el centro estudiantil y _____.
10. Visité a mis abuelos y _____.

 PASO 2. Habla con tres personas para saber qué hicieron o adónde fueron el fin de semana pasado y si lo pasaron bien.

MODELOS: E1: ¿Qué hiciste el fin de semana pasado?
E2: Visité a mi familia, que vive en Chicago.
E1: ¿Lo pasaste bien?
E1: Sí, lo pasé muy bien. (No, lo pasé mal.)

E1: ¿Qué hiciste el sábado por el día?
E2: Fui a una fiesta para celebrar el cumpleaños de mi sobrina.
E1: ¿Te divertiste?
E2: Sí, me divertí mucho. (No, no me divertí nada.)

Mi sobrina lo pasó bien en su fiesta de cumpleaños con una piñata.

CONÉCTATE AL MUNDO PROFESIONAL

Networking should always be about building relationships, not asking for favors. Give as much as you get and make all networking mutually beneficial. One way to do this is to engage in genuine but light conversation. The **Comunicación** sections throughout the textbook provide you with fixed expressions that you can use immediately to build networking relationships in Spanish. Whatever language you use, you should be able to comfortably employ polite expressions, talk to people about activities they enjoy, and react appropriately.

Suggestions (Act. C, Paso 2):
- Encourage students to add details to their answers.
- Model an alternative to the negative response for the first MODELO: *No, no lo pasé nada bien.* Or: *No, no lo pasé bien para nada.*
- Give students the preterite forms *se divirtió / se divirtieron*, and point out the *e → i* change. Then ask them to share what they learned about their classmates with the rest of the class.

Felicitaciones/Felicidades/ Enhorabuena
Congratulating someone

To say *Congratulations* in Spanish, use **Felicitaciones, Felicidades,** or **Enhorabuena.**

—**Voy a graduarme de la universidad en mayo.**	"I'm going to graduate from the university in May."
—**¡Felicitaciones!**	"Congratulations!"

Sometimes this is expressed with the verb **felicitar** and a direct object pronoun.

—**En agosto empiezo a trabajar de psicólogo escolar.**	"In August, I will start working as a school psychologist."
—**Te felicito. / Te felicitamos.**	"I/We congratulate you."

Note: To express your condolences for something say **Lo siento** (*I'm sorry*).

A. ¿Bueno o malo?   Para cada cita, indica si es más lógico decir «**Felicitaciones**» o «**Lo siento**».

		FELICITACIONES.	LO SIENTO.
1.	Saqué mala nota en mi examen ayer.	☐	☑
2.	Mi hermana tuvo un bebé. ¡Soy tío!	☑	☐
3.	Estoy comprometida (*engaged*).	☑	☐
4.	Tengo malas noticias (*bad news*) de mis padres.	☐	☑
5.	Conseguí un trabajo.	☑	☐
6.	Recibí mi título (*degree*) de la universidad.	☑	☐
7.	¡Gané la lotería!	☑	☐
8.	No lo pasé bien en la fiesta anoche.	☐	☑

B. ¡Gracias!

PASO 1.   Escoge una de las siguientes situaciones y díselo (*tell it*) a tu compañero/a. Tu compañero/a debe responder de manera lógica y ofrecer una solución si es apropiado. Luego cambien de papeles (*roles*).

> **MODELO:**   E1: Tengo examen mañana y perdí mi libro.
> E2: Lo siento mucho. ¿Quieres usar mi libro?
> E1: ¡Gracias! Te lo agradezco.

1. Mi equipo de fútbol ganó el campeonato.
2. Estamos muy tristes; nuestro perro se murió (*died*).
3. Me voy a graduar de la universidad en mayo.
4. Me voy a casar (*get married*) este verano.
5. No me aceptaron en el máster (los estudios de posgrado).

PASO 2.   Siguiendo el modelo del **Paso 1**, dile a tu compañero/a tres cosas (muy buenas o muy malas) que hiciste la semana pasada. Tu compañero/a tiene que responder de una manera apropiada.

> **MODELO:**   E1: Salí mal en el último (*last*) examen de español.
> E2: Lo siento mucho. ¿Quieres estudiar conmigo (*with me*) para este examen?
> E1: ¡Con mucho gusto!

Suggestion (Act. B, Paso 1): Remind students to offer a solution to the negative situations such as *¿Quieres usar mi libro?* in the model. For the positive situations, they can offer to celebrate in some way: *¿Quieres celebrar con una fiesta/cena/cerveza?*

Suggestion (Act. B, Paso 2): Give students 1–2 minutes to write down three things so that they're ready to engage in conversation once they get into pairs.

COMUN **VOCABULARIO** CTURA ATE

¿Cómo se celebra?

Celebrations in the Spanish-speaking world

A. ¡Celebremos!

PASO 1. Empareja la imagen con la mejor descripción.

a. acción de ofrecer buenos deseos antes de beber
b. algo que una persona le da a otra persona
c. una celebración, puede ser por cualquier (*any*) razón
d. una celebración religiosa y fiesta para un bebé
e. una celebración de un viaje o una mudanza (*move*)
f. una celebración al recibir un título académico
g. una celebración o aniversario de un nacimiento (*birth*)
h. la celebración del casamiento (*marriage*) de una pareja

1. __a__ **el brindis**

2. __g__ **el cumpleaños**

3. __e__ **la despedida**

4. __c__ **la fiesta**

5. __b__ **el regalo**

6. __d__ **el bautizo**

7. __h__ **la boda**

8. __f__ **la graduación**

(*Continues*)

CONÉCTATE AL MUNDO HISPANO

En algunas partes del mundo hispano, un término para un fin de semana largo es **un puente** (*bridge*). Si el día festivo que se celebra es un jueves, hacen «un puente» de viernes para crear un fin de semana de cuatro días. Es parecido a la tradición en los Estados Unidos en que el viernes después del **Día de Acción de Gracias** (*Thanksgiving Day*) también es día festivo.

Videoscript (Act. F, p. 206): 1. CAITLIN: *Bueno, celebramos Nochebuena, y hacemos como el puerco y todo el 24 de diciembre.* **2.** ISABEL: *Pues la boda española... pues es... eh... bueno esta... esta boda es por la iglesia, entonces es una boda católica, tampoco somos muy católicos hoy en día en España, que hacemos un poco la tradición, pero luego no... no... no somos muy practicantes normalmente y esta boda es más o menos es así. Pero, pues vas a la ceremonia, ves a la novia llegar, que suele llegar tarde y después de la boda se suele ir a co... a hacer las fotos, esperas un tiempo, vas a al restaurante, comes y luego bailas y las, suele ser corto, suele ser hasta las 4 o 5 de la mañana y ya se retira uno, no son bodas muy largas, no...* **3.** CHARO: *Mi madrina, pues... es en el bautizo, cuando bautizamos a los niños, normalmente hay una madrina y un padrino que lo eligen los padres del niño.* **4.** ANLLULY: *Se hace un cumpleaños grande. La quinceañera va con su vestido muy bonito. Bailan el vals. Va toda su familia, sus amigos. Las fiestas, sí, son bonitas, son grandes. Hay música para bailar. Yo pienso que en todos los países es parecido los quinceaños lo que siempre es el queque, la comida para compartir con la familia o con los amigos.* **5.** GABRIEL: *Bueno, el 9 de julio es el Día de la Independencia argentina. Como el 4 de julio es en América, nosotros tenemos el 9 de julio. Ese es el Día de la Independencia.* **6.** RODRIGO: *Sí, eh... Por ejemplo, eh, mayormente, son fiestas de cumpleaños, o casamientos... eh, graduaciones, eh... despedidas. Lo que no me dedico a hacer, que es bastante tradicional... este... acá... son fiestas por ejemplo de 15 años, este, porque trabajar con chicos de esa edad, es bastante feo, eh, por la música que consumen, así que yo más que nada me dedico a trabajar, y disfruto mucho más, de trabajar con gente más grande, de un promedio de edad de 25 para arriba.**

CONÉCTATE AL
MUNDO HISPANO

La mayoría de los hispanos se identifica como **católica** o **cristiana**. Sin embargo, hay gente de varias religiones en el mundo hispano. Por ejemplo, hay grandes comunidades **judías** en Argentina y México, y hay comunidades **musulmanes** (*Muslim*) en España, Argentina, México y Venezuela. Se encuentran **budistas** en México, Costa Rica y especialmente en Perú, gracias a las grandes inmigraciones de japoneses y chinos al país en los siglos XIX y XX.

PASO 2. Empareja cada descripción en la próxima página con una de las siguientes imágenes.

a. **el Día de los Reyes Magos** (*Wise Men*)

b. **el Carnaval**

c. **la fiesta de quinceañera**

d. **la Semana Santa**

e. **el Día de la Independencia**

f. **el Día de Muertos**

g. **el Jánuca**

h. **la Nochebuena y la Navidad**

i. **la Nochevieja y el Año Nuevo**

Suggestions (Act. A):
- Point out that *el Día de los Reyes Magos* is the religious equivalent of the Christian Feast of the Epiphany, yet it is celebrated more like the cultural equivalent of Christmas in parts of the Spanish-speaking world, including being a day off from work/school for most and a day of giving/receiving presents.
- Tell students that *el Domingo de Pascua* is a quiet day of reflection, not a day of festive celebration.

En español...

The term **quinceañera** has made its way from Spanish into common usage in English, where it refers to a party for a girl turning 15 years old. However, in Spanish, **quinceañera** originally refers to the girl herself. The party is most often referred to as **la fiesta de quinceañera** or **la fiesta de quince años.**

1. __h__ Son dos días festivos que celebran el **nacimiento** del niño Jesús. Las familias cristianas tienen tradiciones especiales para **celebrar,** pero muchas cenan juntas e intercambian regalos.

2. __f__ El 1 y 2 de noviembre los mexicanos tienen la **costumbre** de honrar a sus parientes muertos (*dead*). Hacen altares con objetos personales de los muertos.

3. __g__ Es una fiesta judía (*Jewish*) de ocho noches. Cada noche se enciende (*light*) otra vela (*candle*) de la menorá. Se celebra mucho en Argentina, donde vive la población de judíos más grande del mundo hispano.

4. __c__ Cuando una niña **cumple** 15 años, muchas familias hispanas dan una gran fiesta para marcar la transición de niña a mujer. La niña lleva un vestido elegante y recibe muchos regalos, **flores** (*flowers*) y **tarjetas** (*cards*) con dinero.

5. __e__ Es una celebración del establecimiento de una nación independiente. Normalmente hay **desfiles**, es decir, procesiones en que las personas caminan, llevan banderas y tocan música. En muchos países se celebra con **fuegos artificiales** por la noche.

6. __a__ Esta celebración conmemora (*commemorates*) la visita de los tres reyes (*kings*) al niño Jesús. Muchos hispanos dan regalos en este día porque los reyes le llevaron regalos al bebé. Se celebra el 6 de enero con desfiles y reconstrucciones (*reenactments*) de la visita.

7. __i__ Es una celebración del fin de un año y la esperanza (*hope*) de un nuevo comienzo (*beginning*). La gente toma **champán** cuando el reloj marca la medianoche.

8. __d__ Esta es la semana más importante en la tradición cristiana. Empieza con el Domingo de Ramos (*Palm*) que recuerda la entrada de Jesús en Jerusalén y termina en el Domingo de **Pascua Florida** que celebra su resurrección.

9. __b__ Son tres días de fiesta antes de la Cuaresma (*Lent*) cristiana. La gente usa muchos **disfraces**, hay desfiles y se come y se bebe mucho.

B. Asociaciones

PASO 1. Para cada celebración, indica todos los elementos asociados.

	LAS BEBIDAS	UNA CENA	UNA CEREMONIA	UNA FIESTA	UN REGALO	UNA TARJETA
1. el Año Nuevo	☐	☐	☐	☐	☐	☐
2. la boda	☐	☐	☐	☐	☐	☐
3. el Carnaval	☐	☐	☐	☐	☐	☐
4. el cumpleaños	☐	☐	☐	☐	☐	☐
5. la graduación	☐	☐	☐	☐	☐	☐
6. el Jánuca	☐	☐	☐	☐	☐	☐
7. la Nochevieja	☐	☐	☐	☐	☐	☐

PASO 2. En grupos de dos o tres, digan en qué mes normalmente se celebra cada una de las celebraciones del **Paso 1**. Si es algo que celebran sus familias, digan qué hacen Uds. para conmemorarlo.

MODELO: El Año Nuevo se celebra en enero. Siempre celebro el Año Nuevo con mi familia de una manera muy tranquila, porque la noche anterior, la Nochevieja, siempre estoy con mis amigos en una gran fiesta hasta muy tarde. Nos despertamos tarde y miramos El Desfile de las Rosas en la televisión.

C. Vocabulario: ¿Qué le dices? En parejas, túrnense para dar la expresión más lógica para cada celebración o evento.

¡Buen viaje! (*Bon voyage!*)   ¡Enhorabuena!   ¡Feliz cumpleaños!
¡Buena suerte! (*Good luck!*)   ¡Feliz Año Nuevo!   ¡Feliz Navidad!

1. «Hoy cumplo 20 años.» ¡Feliz cumpleaños!
2. «Salgo para Hawái mañana.» ¡Buen viaje!
3. «Es el 25 de diciembre.» ¡Feliz Navidad!
4. «Hoy bautizan a mi ahijado (*godson*).» ¡Enhorabuena!
5. «Hoy tengo un examen.» ¡Buena suerte!
6. «Es el primero de enero.» ¡Feliz Año Nuevo!

D. ¿Para cuándo? Consulta el calendario y empareja cada elemento de la lista de quehaceres (*to-do list*) con la fecha más adecuada.

1. __h__ Celebrar la medianoche.
2. __g__ Celebrar el nacimiento del niño Jesús.
3. __e__ Llegar a la iglesia con media hora de anticipación (*early*).
4. __a__ Preparar lo que voy a decir sobre los novios para el brindis.
5. __c__ Salir a un restaurante elegante con mi esposo.
6. __d__ Encender las velas (*candles*) con los vecinos (*neighbors*).
7. __f__ Enviar (*Mail*) la tarjeta de cumpleaños.
8. __b__ Invitar a los compañeros de trabajo a la fiesta para Jaime.

a. el 3 de diciembre
b. el 7 de diciembre
c. el 9 de diciembre
d. el 12 de diciembre
e. el 13 de diciembre
f. el 15 de diciembre
g. el 25 de diciembre
h. el 31 de diciembre

Suggestion (Act. B, Paso 1): Allow students to do a brief online search for any celebrations that they don't know about.

Expansion (Act. C): Have students create their own situations that use the given expressions as responses. Students read their situations aloud to their partners (or to the class), who will respond with a logical expression.

Suggestion (Act. D): Point out that some of the chores have to be done in advance of an event, in which case students may have to use process of elimination to determine the correct answers.

Expansion (Conéctate al mundo hispano): Have students search the Internet for images of *el Día de Muertos, Las Posadas* and *el Día de los Reyes Magos.* What are the most common images for each holiday?

CONÉCTATE AL MUNDO HISPANO

Una procesión durante Las Posadas

En México se celebran **Las Posadas** (*The Inns*) del 16 al 24 de diciembre. Es una actuación de la búsqueda (*search*) de alojamiento (*lodging*) que hicieron José y la Virgen María antes del nacimiento del niño Jesús. Cada noche, una procesión va pidiendo posada (*lodging at the inn*) y en la tercera casa se aceptan todos los participantes para una fiesta.

Videoscript (Act. F): See page 203 for complete videoscript.

Variation (Act. G): Have students describe one of the celebrations in Act. G and have other students guess the holiday.

Expansion (Act. G): Ask students to use past tense to describe the last holiday party or dinner they went to.

E. Festividades típicas Antes de ver los videos, decide si cada afirmación describe algo típico o no.

	ES TÍPICO.	NO ES TÍPICO.
1. Se hace una fiesta con todos los amigos para celebrar el cumpleaños.	☑	☐
2. Se celebran los bautizos con fuegos artificiales.	☐	☑
3. Hay un DJ (*pronounced "DEE yay"*) en la Nochebuena en la iglesia.	☐	☑
4. Se celebra la boda en una iglesia.	☑	☐
5. En la Nochebuena y la Navidad hay mucha comida con toda la familia.	☑	☐
6. En la Nochevieja se hace un brindis con champán.	☑	☐
7. La fiesta de quinceañera celebra el paso de la niñez a la adolescencia.	☑	☐

F. A ver: Las celebraciones típicas

Video track (Act. F): This video clip can be found on the DVD to accompany *Conéctate:* Cap. 7, Track 2.

PASO 1. Mira y escucha. Luego mira otra vez con pausas y apunta de qué celebración o celebraciones habla cada uno. Mira y escucha una tercera vez para verificar tus respuestas.

1. Caitlin — la Nochebuena
2. Isabel — la boda
3. Charo — el bautizo
4. Anlluly — la fiesta de quinceañera
5. Gabriel — el Día de la Independencia
6. Rodrigo — los cumpleaños (las fiestas de quinceañera) las graduaciones, los casamientos (las bodas), las despedidas

PASO 2. Mira y escucha otra vez, luego contesta las preguntas.

1. ¿Qué comida preparan en la casa de Caitlin? puerco
2. ¿A qué hora termina la celebración que describe Isabel? a las cuatro o cinco de la mañana
3. Según Charo, ¿quiénes eligen (*choose*) la madrina (*godmother*)? los padres del niño
4. Según Anlluly, ¿cómo son las fiestas de quince años? bonitas y grandes, con música para bailar y comida
5. ¿Cuál es el Día de la Independencia argentina? el 9 de julio
6. ¿En qué tipo de evento *no* trabaja Rodrigo? las fiestas de quinceañera

G. Nuestras tradiciones ¿Qué tradiciones tiene tu familia? Escoge una de las siguientes celebraciones (u otra celebración especial) y describe la tradición familiar a tu compañero/a.

el Día de Acción de Gracias
el Día de la Independencia
el Día del de San Valentín

la Pascua Florida
el *Halloween*

COMUN VOCABU **ESTRUCTURA** ATE

↻ Reciclaje
Present indicative and preterite

¿Ayer fue un día típico para ti? Usa los verbos indicados para completar las oraciones sobre lo que haces **regularmente** (en tiempo presente) y lo que hiciste **ayer** (en tiempo pretérito) y añade (*add*) la información que falta.

regularmente		**ayer**	
hablar	<u>Hablo</u> estos idiomas (*languages*): _____.	<u>Hablé</u> estos idiomas: _____.
comer	<u>Como</u> ___ porciones de fruta.	<u>Comí</u> ___ porciones de fruta.
leer	Sí / No <u>leo</u> las noticias (*news*) en línea.	Sí / No <u>leí</u> las noticias en línea.
dormir	<u>Duermo</u> _____ horas.	<u>Dormí</u> _____ horas.
ir	Sí / No <u>voy</u> a clases.	Sí / No <u>fui</u> a clases

Note (Reciclaje): This activity reminds students of the two tenses that they already know (present and preterite) before they begin using the imperfect. Many of these verbs will be used in the imperfect in *Estructura 7.1.*

Expansion (Reciclaje): Tell students to think of (additional) ways in which yesterday was not a typical day for them, and have them use these patterns to create sentences contrasting what they do *regularmente* vs. *ayer.*

■ Answers to this activity are in Appendix 2 at the back of your book.

7.1 ¿Cómo vivían los mayas?

The imperfect

Para empezar... Note (Para empezar): Horses and rice were introduced into the Americas by the Spanish.
En muchos países latinoamericanos, tienen un gran orgullo (*pride*) y cierta nostalgia por las civilizaciones prehispánicas que existían (*existed*) antes de la llegada (*arrival*) de los españoles. Lee las siguientes oraciones y decide si son ciertas o falsas. Si no sabes alguna respuesta, adivina. **¡Atención!** Solo tres oraciones son falsas.

Los mayas en los tiempos prehispánicos...

	CIERTO	FALSO
1. **vivían** en el sur de México y en Centroamérica.	☑	☐
2. **comían** maíz.	☑	☐
3. **escribían** libros.	☑	☐
4. **usaban** caballos y **comían** arroz.	☐	☑
5. **sabían** mucho de astronomía.	☑	☐
6. **tenían** una arquitectura espectacular.	☑	☐
7. **vivían** en el Perú.	☐	☑
8. **hablaban** español.	☐	☑

El Templo de la Serpiente en el Parque Nacional Tikal, Petén, Guatemala

Actividades analíticas

1 The verbs you saw in **Para empezar** are in the *imperfect* tense (**el imperfecto**). The imperfect is used when you want to portray an event as being in the past, but it is not important exactly when the event started or if it ended.

De niño, Carlos **vivía** en Honduras.	*As a child, Carlos lived in Honduras.*
Los mayas **comían** mucho maíz.	*The Mayas ate a lot of corn.*
Cuando **estaba** en Madrid, Julieta **trabajaba** con su tía.	*When she was in Madrid, Julieta worked with her aunt.*

In all of these examples, the action occurs over an extended period of time, but it is not specified when it started or stopped.

■ Answers to these activities are in Appendix 2 at the back of your book.

(*Continues*)

Autoprueba

Now that you have the basic pattern for verb conjugation in the imperfect tense, you can apply it to any verb. Try it!

festejar (celebrar)
yo _____
tú _____
nosotros/as _____

envolver* (*to wrap*)
yo _____
tú _____
él/ella, Ud. _____
nosotros/as _____
ellos/ellas, Uds. _____

vestirse*
yo _____
él/ella, Ud. _____
ellos/ellas, Uds. _____

*Don't forget, most verbs are regular in the imperfect! There are no verbs with stem changes or spelling changes.

(rotated text) vestían, se vestíais, os vestíamos, nos vestía, se vestías, te ves-tía; me vestía envolvían, envolvíamos, vía, envolvías, envolvíais, festejaban; envol-festejabais, **Respuestas:** festejaba, feste-jabas, festejaba, festejábamos,

Expansion (Act. analíticas 4): Ask students if they can see why *ver* is considered irregular in the imperfect. (Answer: The stem is *ve-*, rather than the expected *v-*.)

Un estatua en las ruinas de Uxmal, antigua ciudad maya en México

---

2 Use the verb forms in **Para empezar** and the patterns you see here to complete these conjugations in the imperfect.

Expansion (Act. analíticas 2): Have students conjugate a single verb in the present, preterite, and imperfect tenses, and then have them compare the endings. They will find significant overlap, especially with the plural forms.

	hablar	comer	vivir
yo	hablaba	comía	vivía
tú	hablabas	comías	vivías
él/ella, Ud.	hablaba	comía	vivía
nosotros/as	hablábamos	comíamos	vivíamos
vosotros/as	hablabais	comíais	vivíais
ellos/ellas, Uds.	hablaban	comían	vivían

3 Complete this chart of endings for **-ar** and **-er/-ir** verbs in the imperfect.

	-ar	-er/-ir	
yo	_-aba_: habl**aba**	_-ía_: com**ía**	viv**ía**
tú	_-abas_: habl**abas**	_-ías_: com**ías**	viv**ías**
él/ella, Ud.	_-aba_: habl**aba**	_-ía_: com**ía**	viv**ía**
nosotros/as	_-ábamos_: habl**ábamos**	_-íamos_: com**íamos**	viv**íamos**
vosotros/as	_-abais_: habl**abais**	_-íais_: com**íais**	viv**íais**
ellos/ellas, Uds.	_-aban_: habl**aban**	_-ían_: com**ían**	viv**ían**

4 The verbs **ir, ser,** and **ver** are the only irregular verbs in the imperfect. There are no verbs with stem changes or spelling changes.

	ir	ser	ver
yo	iba	era	veía
tú	ibas	eras	veías
él/ella, Ud.	iba	era	veía
nosotros/as	íbamos	éramos	veíamos
vosotros/as	ibais	erais	veíais
ellos/ellas, Uds.	iban	eran	veían

The stems of these verbs are irregular in the imperfect, but the endings show similarities with those of regular verbs.

Íbamos a muchas fiestas cuando yo **era** niño.

We went to a lot of parties when I was a child.

¿**Veías** ese programa de televisión todos los días?

Did you watch that TV show every day?

5 The verb form **hay** becomes **había** in the imperfect.

Había un edificio maya en este lugar.

There was a Mayan building in this place.

Había cuatro niños en la fiesta.

There were four children at the party.

Actividades prácticas

A. Las tradiciones de mi familia   Las siguientes descripciones están basadas en la imagen de la vida tradicional norteamericana que se ve en el cine y en la televisión. Indica las que son ciertas en el caso de tu familia.

1. ☐ Íbamos a la playa en verano.
2. ☐ Cenábamos con mis abuelos el Día de Acción de Gracias.
3. ☐ Íbamos a la iglesia los domingos.
4. ☐ Celebrábamos mi cumpleaños cada año.
5. ☐ Comprábamos un árbol de Navidad cada año.
6. ☐ Veíamos los fuegos artificiales el Día de la Independencia.
7. ☐ Hacíamos una fiesta de Nochevieja en casa.
8. ☐ Jugábamos béisbol en la calle.
9. ☐ Mis amigos y yo íbamos a la escuela en un autobús amarillo.
10. ☐ Comíamos de vez en cuando en casa de mi abuela.

B. España y América antes de 1492   Las siguientes oraciones describen la vida en España y en América en los siglos (centuries) antes de la llegada de los españoles a América.

PASO 1.   Primero, escoge el verbo más lógico para cada oración y escríbelo en la forma **ellos** del imperfecto (por ejemplo, **trabajar** → **trabajaban**).

comer	ir	tener (x2)
hablar (x2)	ser	vivir

Antes de 1492...   **¿E, A o E/A?**

1. _comían_ tomates.   _A_
2. _tenían (vivían)_ caballos.   _E_
3. el calendario y los días festivos _eran_ muy importantes.   _E/A_
4. _hablaban_ español, árabe y otros idiomas (languages).   _E_
5. en algunas ciudades, _iban_ a las pirámides (pyramids) para hacer ritos religiosos.   _A_
6. _tenían_ ciudades muy grandes.   _E/A_
7. en algunas partes, los cristianos, los judíos y los musulmanes _vivían_ en armonía (harmony).   _E_
8. _hablaban_ náhuatl, quechua y otros idiomas.   _A_

PASO 2.   Ahora escribe **E** si la oración describe la vida en España antes del año 1492, **A** si describe la vida en América o **E/A** si describe los dos lugares.

La Piedra (Stone) del Sol (Sun) muestra (shows) los varios soles de la cosmología mexica de México.

Suggestion (Act. A): Poll students at the end to see how close they come to the "movie image" of North American life. If they find that their childhood reality was different from the movies, point out the basic lesson here: Not everyone lives the life you see in movies. They should keep this in mind when they see movies that portray life in other countries.

Note (Act. A): This type of activity helps develop students' "transcultural competence," their ability to think about how others see them.

Expansion (Act. B): Have students convert each statement to the *nosotros* present tense form (for example, *Comemos tomates*) and judge whether the statement is true or false for *nuestro país*.

¿Por qué?

As you know, Spanish has the preterite form to talk about the past, so why have a second past tense? The imperfect gives Spanish-speakers an easy and concise way of describing a past event or action at the point when it was still ongoing (that is, before it was completed or ended). In English it typically takes more words to describe this type of event or action, and it is less precise than in Spanish.

Suggestion (¿Por qué?): To help students see this point, ask them to try translating this sentence into English: *En 2015, yo vivía en San José.* One could say *In 2015, I lived in San Jose,* but to convey the full meaning of the Spanish sentence, one would have to say something like *In 2015, I lived (was living) in San Jose and continued living there for some time after that.*

Suggestion (Act. C): Point out that unlike Halloween, with which *Día de Muertos* is often confused, people do not traditionally have parties or dress up in costumes.

Expansion (Act. C): Have students choose a holiday that they celebrate that they know has changed over the years, and have them compare *cómo era antes* and *cómo es ahora*. You may also want to give an example from your own experience.

Una ofrenda para el Día de Muertos

Suggestion (Act. D): Have students jot down the answers and ask some of them to share the most interesting answer they received.

Suggestion (Act. E, Paso 1): Have students brainstorm additional questions and follow-up questions that they can ask. For example, *¿Dónde trabajaban?*, *¿Cuántos hijos tenían?*

Suggestion (Act. E, Paso 2): Ask students to share their examples of similarities and differences with the class, alternating between the two.

Variation (Act. E, Paso 2): Have students create sentences about themselves and their own parents.

C. El Día de Muertos   Una de las tradiciones mexicanas más conocidas es el Día de Muertos. Tradicionalmente, ese día la gente va a las tumbas (*graves*) de sus familiares difuntos (*deceased*), hacen altares y comen varios tipos de pan y dulces (*sweets*) especiales.

PASO 1.   En una entrevista en 1984, una mujer mexicana dijo cinco de las siguientes oraciones sobre las tradiciones en su familia para el Día de Muertos. De las ocho oraciones en total, ¿cuáles dijo y cuáles no?

	LO DIJO.	NO LO DIJO.
1. «Vamos al cementerio.»	☑	☐
2. «Limpiamos las tumbas (*graves*) y las decoramos con flores.»	☑	☐
3. «Hacemos un altar con una foto del difunto (*deceased*) y algunos de sus objetos favoritos.»	☑	☐
4. «Hacemos una fiesta y bailamos mucho.»	☐	☑
5. «Comemos pan de muerto—un pan dulce, a veces con figuras en forma de hueso (*bone*).»	☑	☐
6. «Vamos a una ceremonia especial en Buenos Aires.»	☐	☑
7. «Nos ponemos disfraces y vamos de casa en casa para pedir dulces.»	☐	☑
8. «Hacemos calaveras (*skulls*) de dulce.»	☑	☐

PASO 2.   Ahora usa las oraciones que dijo para hacer una descripción de lo que hacía esta familia el Día de Muertos en 1984. **¡Atención!** Usa la forma **ellos** del imperfecto.

MODELO: «Vamos al cementerio.» → *Iban* al cementerio.

D. ¿Qué hacías antes?   Por razones (*reasons*) sociales, emocionales o físicas, hay muchas cosas que hacíamos de niños que ya no (*no longer*) hacemos ahora. Pregúntales a tres compañeros qué hacían antes que ya no hacen. Usa una de las siguientes ideas o piensa en otra.

correr muy rápido	jugar todo el día
dormir mucho	recibir muchos regalos
ir a muchas fiestas de cumpleaños	ver televisión todo el día

MODELO: E1: ¿Qué hacías antes que no haces ahora?
  E2: Nadaba mucho, pero ya no nado.

E. Tus padres cuando tenían tu edad

PASO 1.   Entrevista a tu compañero/a para saber qué hace y qué hacían sus padres cuando tenían su edad (*age*). Apunta las respuestas.

■ ¿Dónde vives? ¿Dónde vivían tus padres cuando tenían tu edad?
■ ¿Qué haces? ¿Trabajas? ¿Estudias? ¿Ya tienes hijos? Y tus padres, ¿qué hacían cuando tenían tu edad? ¿Trabajaban?...

PASO 2.   Crea una oración con una semejanza (*similarity*) entre tu compañero/a y sus padres, y otra oración con una diferencia.

MODELO: Alex estudia. Cuando tenían su edad, sus padres también estudiaban.
  Alex tiene una hija. Cuando tenían su edad, sus padres no tenían hijos.

F. Cultura: El Carnaval en Uruguay

PASO 1. Lee el texto sobre Uruguay.

Uruguay

En general, los uruguayos tienen vidas largas. ¿A qué se debe?[a] Quizás[b] a la belleza de su país con su larga costa y bellas playas, o quizás a su espíritu positivo y fiestero que se ve, por ejemplo, cuando celebran el Carnaval. El Carnaval uruguayo, como en el resto del mundo, se caracteriza por música, baile, disfraces y másca-ras, desfiles y mucha diversión, pero en contraste con las costumbres del resto del mundo, el Carnaval en Uruguay es mucho más largo.

El Carnaval es una tradición de fiestas públicas que se observa en varios países europeos, caribe-ños[c] y latinoamericanos. Los orígenes del Carnaval vienen de Europa, donde las fiestas paganas del equinoccio de primavera se combinaron con tradicio-nes católicas. El Carnaval se celebra las semanas antes de la Cuaresma,[d] un periodo de solemnidad y ascetismo. Un elemento muy importante del Carna-val uruguayo es «la murga». Las murgas son cancio-nes interpretadas por un coro[e] de quince a veinte personas. Tienen influencia del teatro español y así usan las canciones para contar historias.[f]

Un tamboril es el tipo de tambor (*drum*) usado para la música candombe.

Otra cosa notable del Carnaval uruguayo es que una gran parte de su música viene de tradiciones afro-uruguayas. Estas tradiciones musicales se cono-cen como «candombe» y se practicaban entre[g] las comunidades de esclavos[h] en la época de la colonia. Durante el Carnaval, las comparsas[i] de candombe consisten en[j] muchos bailadores disfrazados y por lo menos cincuenta percusionistas que tocan ritmos africanos.

[a]¿A... *To what is this owed?* [b]*Perhaps* [c]*Caribbean* [d]*Lent* [e]*choir, chorus* [f]contar... *tell stories* [g]*among* [h]*slaves* [i]*musical groups* [j]consisten... *are made up of*

PASO 2. Indica si cada oración es lógica (**L**) o ilógica (**I**) según la información que leíste.

___ 1. Los esclavos afro-uruguayos cantaban murgas.
___ 2. Los primeros inmigrantes españoles a Uruguay tocaban música candombe.
___ 3. Para los primeros africanos que llegaron a Uruguay, era importante conser-
     var sus tradiciones musicales.
___ 4. Las fiestas paganas de Europa marcaban el fin (*end*) del invierno.
___ 5. Los católicos creían que era importante tener un periodo festivo en las
     semanas antes de la Cuaresma.

 PASO 3. En parejas, contesten las preguntas y explíquense sus respuestas.

1. La cultura afro-uruguaya existe porque en la época de la colonia llegaron muchos esclavos africanos, principalmente por la capital, Montevideo. ¿Qué rela-ción hay entre esto y la ubicación geográfica de Uruguay, y de Montevideo en particular?
2. Hoy en día, hay muchos descendientes de esclavos africanos en varios países de Latinoamérica, pero sobre todo en las islas del Caribe, en algunas zonas de Centroamérica, y en Colombia y Venezuela. ¿Por qué piensas que llegaron tantos esclavos a estos lugares en particular?
3. La cultura latinoamericana tiene mucha influencia africana. ¿La cultura de tu país es así también? ¿Hay más influencia africana en las zonas donde llegaron muchos esclavos en los tiempos de antes (*earlier*)?

Note (Act. F, Paso 3):
Montevideo was an important port in the slave trade, partly due to its closeness to Africa. In general, large populations of people of African heritage are seen today in areas that were easily accessible to the ships of slave-traders, includ-ing the United States. The presence of large groups with African ancestry had a huge influence on the culture (mu-sic, food, and so on), espe-cially in regions close to slave-trading ports.

⟳ Reciclaje

Direct object pronouns

Cuando eras niño/niña, ¿a quién veías? Completa las siguientes oraciones usando el pronombre de objeto directo (**me, la, lo, los** o **las**) correcto e indica si la oración es cierta o falsa para ti.

		CIERTO	FALSO
1. A mi abuela __la__ veía todos los días.		☐	☐
2. A mi abuelo __lo__ veía todos los días.		☐	☐
3. A los amigos de la escuela __los__ veía todos los días.		☐	☐
4. A las amigas de mi mamá __las__ veía todos los días.		☐	☐
5. A mí mis papás __me__ veían todos los días.		☐	☐

■ Answers to this activity are in Appendix 2 at the back of your book.

7.2   Le doy un abrazo

Indirect objects and indirect object pronouns

Para empezar...

PASO 1.   Cuando es tu cumpleaños, ¿cómo te felicitan? ¿Te dan la mano? ¿un beso? ¿un abrazo? Y cuando es el cumpleaños de alguien más, ¿cómo lo/la felicitas tú? Indica tus respuestas aquí.

	LA MANO	UN BESO	UN ABRAZO
El día de mi cumpleaños...			
mi papá **me** da:	☐	☐	☐
mi mamá **me** da:	☐	☐	☐
mis amigos **me** dan:	☐	☐	☐
mis amigas **me** dan:	☐	☐	☐
El día de su cumpleaños...			
a mi papá **le** doy (*I give*):	☐	☐	☐
a mi mamá **le** doy:	☐	☐	☐
a mis amigos **les** doy:	☐	☐	☐
a mis amigas **les** doy:	☐	☐	☐

PASO 2.   ¿Piensas que las respuestas serían (*would be*) diferentes en un país hispano? ¿Cómo?

Actividades analíticas

1 The words **me, le,** and **les** in **Para empezar** are *indirect object pronouns* (**pronombres de objeto indirecto**). Add these words to the chart of indirect object pronouns here.

Singular		Plural	
_me_	to me	**nos**	to us
te	to you (*inform.*)	**os**	to you (*inform.*)
_le_	to him/her/it; to you (*form.*)	_les_	to them; to you (*form.*)

Suggestion (Para empezar): Share your own experiences related to how cultures differ in how they congratulate people on their birthday. In many Spanish-speaking countries, *un abrazo* is nearly obligatory for a birthday, often accompanied by a kiss.

■ Answers to these activities are in Appendix 2 at the back of your book.

Suggestion (Para empezar): Point out that the *yo* form of *dar* is *doy*. Like other one-syllable verbs, such as *ser* (*soy*) and *ir* (*voy*) the ending for the yo form is -*oy*.

2 An indirect object is the person or thing that receives something from the action of the verb. In English, it is often indicated by the preposition *to*. For instance, in the sentence *Mary gave the book to John,* the indirect object is *John*. Underline the indirect object in these sentences.

Suggestion (Act. analíticas 2): Before explaining the indirect object, review the concept of direct object. Have students circle the direct object in the example sentences. (Answers: **a.** a letter **b.** the problem)

a. Bill sent a letter to his parents.

b. Diane explained the problem to her friends.

3 In Spanish, an indirect object is usually indicated by the preposition **a.** In general, an indirect object pronoun is used whenever there is an indirect object.

Le doy un abrazo **a mi papá.**	*I gave a hug to my dad.*
Mi mamá **les** da besos **a sus amigas.**	*My mom gives kisses to her friends.*

Indirect object pronouns differ in this way from direct object pronouns, which replace the direct object. Indirect object pronouns may also be used on their own, when the context makes it clear whom the pronoun refers to.

Ellos son mis vecinos. **Les** doy el periódico cada mañana.	*They are my neighbors. I give them the newspaper every morning.*
Mis amigos **me** dan un abrazo en mi cumpleaños.	*My friends give me a hug on my birthday.*

Me dio un abrazo y un beso.

Suggestion (Act. analíticas 4): Point out that indirect objects in English don't always include *to*. In *Miguel showed me his new house,* for instance, *me* is understood as the indirect object. You can also say *Miguel showed his new house to me,* though this is slightly less natural.

4 Indirect objects are very frequent with the verb **dar** and similar verbs expressing a similar action. They are also common with verbs of communication such as **decir, hablar, pedir,** and **preguntar,** as well as verbs such as **enseñar** (*to show; to teach*) and **regalar** (*to give [a present]*).

Te digo que es la verdad.	*I'm telling you that it's the truth.*
Nos habló de su viaje a Lima.	*He told us about his trip to Lima.*
Le pido un café.	*I ask him/her for a coffee.*
¿Les preguntaste dónde está la universidad?	*Did you ask them where the university is?*
Miguel **me enseñó** su nueva casa.	*Miguel showed me his new house.*
Nos regalaron un libro.	*They gave us a book.*

5 Just as you saw with direct object pronouns, indirect object pronouns can be placed before the main verb or be attached to the end of infinitives.

Le voy a preguntar algo. ⎫	*I am going to ask him/her/you* (form.)
Voy a preguntar**le** algo. ⎭	*something.*

You will explore the placement of object pronouns in more detail in **Estructura 8.3.**

En español...

The indirect object pronouns that you are studying here are the same as those used with the verb **gustar.**

Me gusta nadar en el mar.	*I like to swim in the ocean.* (Lit., *It is pleasing to me to swim in the ocean.*)
Le gusta ese tipo de películas.	*She likes that type of movie* (Lit., *That type of movie is pleasing to her*).
Nos gusta ir a fiestas.	*We like to go to parties.* (Lit., *Going to parties is pleasing to us.*)

Autoprueba

Identify the indirect objects and their pronouns in the following sentences.

1. Para el Día de San Valentín, siempre le regalaba flores a mi novia.
2. En la víspera del Día de Todos los Santos (*Halloween*) los vecinos les dan muchos dulces a los niños.
3. El Día de Acción de Gracias pasado, mi abuela le enseñó a mi padre a cortar el pavo (*carve the turkey*).

Respuestas: 1. mi novia, le **2.** los niños, les **3.** mi padre, le

Actividades prácticas

A. ¿Por qué no... ? (*Why don't you . . . ?*)
A veces las invitaciones y los regalos pueden causar situaciones difíciles. Pero cuando le explicas el problema a un amigo, casi siempre hay una solución. Empareja cada problema con la respuesta adecuada.

PROBLEMA

1. __e__ Quiero invitar a Silvia a la fiesta, pero no está aquí.
2. __b__ Ayer le compré un regalo a mi mamá, pero en realidad no me gusta.
3. __f__ No quiero ir a la fiesta de Juan.
4. __d__ ¿Te compro este lápiz por tu cumpleaños?
5. __a__ Paula y Jorge me invitaron su casa, pero no quiero ir.
6. __c__ No puedo ir con Uds. a la fiesta.

RESPUESTA

a. ¿Por qué no les dices que estás enfermo y que no puedes ir?
b. ¿Por qué no le buscas otra cosa?
c. ¿Por qué no nos acompañas a la cena antes de la fiesta?
d. ¿Por qué no me regalas algo mejor?
e. ¿Por qué no le hablas por teléfono?
f. ¿Por qué no le dices que estás enfermo y que no puedes ir?

Suggestion (Act. B): Have students create a sentence with each pair's general conclusion. For example: *En general, los padres les dan más regalos a los hijos.*

B. Los padres y los hijos
Los padres a veces les dan regalos a los hijos, y los hijos a veces les dan regalos a los padres. Pero, ¿quién lo hace más? Completa las dos frases sobre tu familia con el pronombre correcto.

> **Ejemplos:** el cumpleaños, el Día de las Madres / los Padres, el Jánuca, la Navidad, la Semana Santa

1. Mis padres _me_ dan regalos en las siguientes ocasiones: _____
2. Yo _les_ doy regalos a mis padres en las siguientes ocasiones: _____

Note (Act. B): If students don't have two parents at home as mentioned, tell them they should answer however they would with whoever is/was their primary caregiver(s).

Ahora pregúntale a tu compañero/a sobre su familia y completa las oraciones sobre ellos.

3. ¿En qué ocasiones tus padres _te_ dan regalos? _____
4. ¿En qué ocasiones tú _les_ das regalos a tus padres? _____

C. ¿A quién le pides ayuda?
Cuando tienes problemas, ¿a quién le pides ayuda (*help*)? Escoge un tipo de problema de la siguiente lista. Pregúntales a varios compañeros de clase a quién(es) le(s) piden ayuda en ese caso y apunta los resultados.

> **MODELO:** E1: Cuando tienes problemas de dinero, ¿a quién le pides ayuda?
> E2: Les pido ayuda a mis papás.

1. problemas de amor
2. problemas de dinero
3. problemas en una clase
4. problemas con tu coche

Suggestion (Act. C): Help the class brainstorm for possible people to go to for help: *amigo/a, compañero/a de cuarto/apartamento, papá/mamá, hermano/a, profesor(a)*, and so on. *No sé* is also a possible answer. Then, assign each student one of the four items, and give them a specific number of students they need to ask before they can sit down. Write the four types of problems as headers on the board and when students have the responses to their question, have them write the most common response under the appropriate header.

¿Quién me dio este regalo?

D. La Nochevieja   ¿Qué te gusta hacer para celebrar la Nochevieja? En parejas, comparen sus ideas y completen la tabla con lo que les gusta hacer.

YO	MI COMPAÑERO/A	LOS DOS

Suggestion (Act. D): Give students an example of what to write: *Me gusta ver una película en casa. A Michelle le gusta salir a los bares. A los dos nos gusta comer en un restaurante tailandés.* Divide the board into three parts and as students finish, ask them to write their answers there. Then ask the whole class to comment on which activities are most interesting or unique.

E. El problema de «Anónimo»

PASO 1.   Un chico anónimo le escribe al Doctor Amor (*Love*) para decirle su problema y proponer (*propose*) algunas posibles soluciones. Lee la carta (*letter*) al Doctor Amor. En la lista de ideas de la carta, encierra (*circle*) cada pronombre de objeto indirecto. Luego decide cuáles son las tres mejores ideas que tiene el chico que escribió la carta.

> Doctor Amor:
>
> Me gusta mucho una chica que trabaja en la universidad donde estudio. Me ve casi todos los días, pero parece que ni sabe que existo. ¿Qué hago? Quiero salir con ella, pero no sé qué hacer. Tengo algunas ideas, pero no sé si son buenas o no.
>
> MIS IDEAS
>
> 1. Preguntar(le) directamente si quiere salir conmigo (*with me*) el día de mi cumpleaños
> 2. Decir(le) que es muy bonita.
> 3. Enseñar(le) que traigo mucho dinero.
> 4. Hablar(le) de cosas triviales—por ejemplo, el clima, las películas, etcétera— y así puede ver que soy muy buena persona.
> 5. Preguntar(le) adónde (le) gusta salir. Va a ser más fácil hablar con ella en un club que en el sitio donde trabaja.
> 6. No prestar(le) atención (*pay attention*). Posiblemente así empieza a hablar(me) más.
> 7. Decir(le) que soy de otra ciudad, que no conozco a nadie y que me siento (*feel*) muy solo.
> 8. Decir(le) que solo (me) quedan (*remain*) seis meses de vida y no sé todavía qué es el amor.
>
> ¿Qué piensas? ¿Puedes ayudarme con este problema?
>
> Gracias,
>
> Anónimo

 PASO 2.   En grupos pequeños, piensen en otras cosas que podría hacer «Anónimo» (es decir, ideas que no están en la lista del **Paso 1**). Conversen, seleccionen las tres mejores y apúntenlas (*write them down*) para compartir con la clase. ¡Sean creativos!

Suggestion (Act. E, Paso 1): Have students work in small groups and put their conclusions on the board. Set up the groups as all-male and all-female so that at the end the class can see whether men and women came up with different conclusions. At the end, ask whether *Anónimo*'s problem is unique to the Spanish-speaking world or is more universal.

Expansion (Act. E, Paso 1): Ask students to choose the 2–3 worst ideas, in addition to the best.

↻ Reciclaje

Subject pronouns

Los vecinos van a tener una fiesta de cumpleaños para su hija y te invitan a ti. Empareja cada persona de la lista con la oración que le corresponde, y completa la oración con el pronombre adecuado.

las abuelas   el hermano   el hermano y yo   la mamá   el papá   los papás

¿Quién(es)?

los papás	1.	Ellos están organizando la fiesta.
la mamá	2.	Ella está muy contenta por el cumpleaños de su hija.
el hermano	3.	Él quiere jugar con los regalos de su hermana.
el papá	4.	Él está muy contento porque le compró una bicicleta a su hija.
el hermano y yo	5.	Nosotros le vamos a cantar una canción a la niña.
las abuelas	6.	Ellas quieren ir a la fiesta pero no pueden porque las dos (*both of them, female*) viven lejos.

■ Answers to this activity are in Appendix 2 at the back of your book.

■ Answers to these activities are in Appendix 2 at the back of your book.

Suggestion (Act. analíticas 2):
• Point out that in *A mí me llevaban a la playa...,* the indirect object pronoun *me* is required and the phrase *a mí* emphasizes that they took *me* (as opposed to someone else). The basic meaning would be the same without the prepositional phrase.
• Point out that *mí* takes an accent mark here to distinguish it from *mi.* Ask students if they recall how *mi* without an accent mark is used (to show possession) and to give an example (*mi casa*). Point out that *ti* does not requiere this distinction.

7.3   Un buen regalo para mí

Pronouns after prepositions

Para empezar...

Suggestion (Para empezar): Take a poll among the class and find out which was the most popular gift for oneself.

Cada persona tiene sus propios gustos (*tastes*), y no puedes darles el mismo regalo a todos. Compara los gustos de tu mamá, de tu papá, los tuyos y de alguien más (tu amigo/a, tu primo/a, etcétera). ¿Qué sería (*would be*) un buen regalo para cada uno?

	PARA MI MAMÁ	PARA MI PAPÁ	PARA MÍ	PARA ____
1. una bicicleta	☐	☐	☐	☐
2. una computadora	☐	☐	☐	☐
3. flores	☐	☐	☐	☐
4. un libro de historia	☐	☐	☐	☐
5. una planta	☐	☐	☐	☐
6. ropa	☐	☐	☐	☐
7. un teléfono	☐	☐	☐	☐
8. _____	☐	☐	☐	☐

Actividades analíticas

1 Based on what you saw in **Para empezar,** complete the following chart of singular pronouns after prepositions (that is, words such as **a, de, en, por,** and **para**).

para/de _mí_	*for me*
para/de ti	*for you* (sing., inform.)

2 The pronouns **mí** and **ti** may be thought of as specialized forms of **yo** and **tú.** They are only used when they are the object of a preposition (such as **a, de,** and **para**).

A mí me llevaban a la playa cada verano.	*They would take me to the beach every summer.*
Vamos a hablar **de ti.**	*We're going to talk about you (sing., inform.).*
Tengo un regalo **para ti.**	*I have a gift for you.*

All other pronouns (**él/ella, Ud., nosotros/as, vosotros/as, ellos/ellas, Uds.**) retain their regular form when used as the object of a preposition.

A él le dan un abrazo cuando lo ven.	*They give him a hug when they see him.*
¿Este libro es **de Ud.**?	*Is this book yours (sing., form.)?*
Ya escogieron un regalo **para nosotros.**	*They already chose a present for us.*
A ellas les gusta estudiar en la biblioteca.	*They like to study in the library.*

3 The preposition **con** has two special forms: **conmigo** (*with me*) and **contigo** (*with you* [sing., inform.]).

¿Quieres ir a la playa **conmigo**?	*Do you want to go to the beach with me?*
Vamos a comer **contigo.**	*We are going to eat with you.*

With other pronouns, **con** is used in the regular way, without any special form.

El profesor quiere hablar **con nosotros.**	*The teacher wants to speak with us.*
Vamos a comer **con Ud.**	*We are going to eat with you (sing., form.).*

4 Some other useful prepositions that are often followed by pronouns are **en** (*in, on*), **sin** (*without*), and **sobre** (*on, above; about*).

¿Crees **en** mí?	*Do you believe in me?*
¡No puedo vivir **sin** ti!	*I can't live without you!*
Van a hacer un libro **sobre** ella.	*They are going to make a book about her.*

The preposition **en** is especially common with the verb **pensar.** In English, you *think about* someone, but in Spanish, the equivalent expression is **pensar en.**

Cuando veía esa película, pensaba **en** ti.	*When I was watching that movie, I was thinking about you.*

En español...

The verb **gustar** generally takes an indirect object, and as you saw in **Estructura 7.2,** this is expressed by using an indirect object pronoun. The preposition **a** is sometimes used with a noun (such as a person's name) or a pronoun to specify or emphasize the indirect object.

A mí me gusta trabajar de noche.	*I like to work at night.*
A Teresa le gusta el fútbol.	*Teresa likes soccer.*

Some other verbs that behave like **gustar** are: **encantar** (*to delight*), **fascinar** (*to fascinate*), **importar** (*to matter; to be important to*), **interesar** (*to interest*), **molestar** (*to bother*), and **parecer** (*to seem*). They all use an indirect object pronoun, and they all allow further specification or emphasis with **a** + *noun/pronoun*.

A mí me encanta este libro.	*I love this book.*
A María le fascinan las películas viejas.	*María loves / is fascinated by old movies.*
¿**A ti** no **te importa**?	*Doesn't it matter to you?*

Note (Para saber más): *Para saber más 7.3* presents pronouns after prepositions such as *según, cerca de, lejos de, delante de, detrás de,* and *enfrente de.* It also includes a presentation of stressed possessives.

■ For more on the use of pronouns after prepositions, and to learn about stressed possessives, see **Para saber más 7.3,** at the back of your book.

Actividades prácticas

A. Completa la oración Completa las oraciones con una de las siguientes opciones. **¡Atención!** Cada opción se puede usar *solo una vez.*

1. ¿Quieres salir __d__? ¡Yo sí quiero salir __e__!
2. Magda, ¿__b__ te gusta correr en la calle?
3. ¿De quién hablan? ¿Hablan __g__?
4. ¿Sabes que __a__ me encanta salir a bailar los sábados?
5. ¿Y Marcos? ¿Ya le preguntaste __c__ si puede ir a la fiesta?
6. ¿Te gustan las flores? Espero que sí, porque estas flores son __h__.
7. Tus amigos van a salir a cenar este fin de semana. ¿Quieres ir __f__?

a. a mí
b. a ti
c. a él
d. conmigo
e. contigo
f. con ellos
g. de mí
h. para ti

Autoprueba

Using what you now know about pronouns, complete the sentences with **tú, ti** or **contigo.**

1. ¿A _____ te gustan los cumpleaños?
2. Todos piensan que _____ quieres tener una fiesta.
3. Tu hermano habla mucho de _____.
4. Quiero ir a la fiesta _____.

Respuestas: 1. ti 2. tú 3. ti 4. contigo

■ The audio files for in-text listening activities are available in the eBook, within Connect activities, and on the Online Learning Center.

Script (Act. B): 1. *Quiero conocer España y Portugal.* **2.** *Pienso que es muy divertido ver televisión con toda la familia.* **3.** *Pienso que las fiestas con mucha gente son maravillosas.* **4.** *Pienso que es muy aburrido ver televisión con toda la familia.* **5.** *Pienso que cuesta demasiado dinero ir al cine.* **6.** *Quiero ir a Ecuador y al Perú.* **7.** *Prefiero no ir a fiestas donde hay mucha gente.* **8.** *Me encanta ver películas.*

Suggestion (Act. C, Paso 3): Have students write their six sentences on a sheet of paper in random order and pass them to another group. That group should then read through and decide which of the sentences are appropriate messages for *el Día del Amor y la Amistad.*

Suggestion (Act. D): Divide the board into two sections and write one question on each side: *¿Qué les gusta hacer a los niños?* and *¿Qué les gusta hacer a Uds.?* Have each group write one answer on the board for each question. Model the type of answers they could give: *A los niños les gusta...* and *A nosotros nos gusta...*

Note (Act. D): Remind students that if they agree with what someone else likes, they should use *A mí también* when reacting to a sentence with *gustar* (rather than *yo también*) because *yo* is not the subject of the verb.

Suggestion (Act. E): Give students a fixed amount of time to work on this, and make it a contest to see which pair can come up with the most differences. Also, ask for nominations for the most interesting difference in the class.

B. ¿Le gusta o le molesta?   Escucha las descripciones de algunas personas y empareja cada descripción con una de las siguientes oraciones.

a. __3__ Le encantan las fiestas muy grandes.
b. __7__ No le gustan las fiestas muy grandes.
c. __8__ Le fascina el cine.
d. __5__ Le parece muy caro ir al cine.
e. __6__ Le interesa viajar a Sudamérica.
f. __1__ Le interesa viajar a Europa.
g. __2__ Le encanta ver televisión con la familia.
h. __4__ Le molesta ver televisión con la familia.

C. El Día del Amor y la Amistad (*Friendship*)   En muchos países el 14 de febrero se celebra el Día del Amor y la Amistad. Es común mandarle una tarjeta o un mensaje romántico a otra persona.

PASO 1.   En cada mensaje, escribe el pronombre más lógico: **yo, tú, mí** o **ti**.

1. ¿_Tú_ piensas en _mí_ de vez en cuando?
2. _Yo_ voy a escribir un poema sobre _ti_.
3. _Yo_ no quiero pasar el día sin _ti_.
4. Eres horrible. Cuando pienso en _ti_, me siento mal.
5. _Tú_ eres mi vida.
6. _Yo_ soy mucho más atractivo/a que tú.
7. ¿Quieres una foto de _mí_?

PASO 2.   Dos de los mensajes no son lógicos para el Día del Amor y la Amistad. ¿Cuáles son?   4 y 6

PASO 3.   En parejas, sigan el modelo del **Paso 1** y creen tres oraciones adecuadas para el Día del Amor y la Amistad y tres oraciones que no son adecuadas.

¡¿Para mí?!

D. Los cumpleaños

PASO 1.   En grupos pequeños, hablen de los siguientes temas.

1. A los niños, ¿qué les gusta hacer para el cumpleaños?
2. A ti, ¿qué te gustaba hacer para tu cumpleaños cuando eras niño/a?
3. ¿Qué te gusta hacer ahora para tu cumpleaños?

PASO 2.   Apunten sus conclusiones y compártanlas (*share them*) con la clase.

E. Las diferencias   Pregúntale a tu compañero/a qué le gusta hacer y compara sus respuestas con tus propios (*own*) intereses. Usen las actividades de la lista o inventen sus propias ideas. ¿Qué diferencias pueden encontrar?

bailar	jugar básquetbol	salir con mis amigos
cantar	nadar	viajar
cocinar	practicar yoga	visitar a mi familia

MODELO: A mí me gusta correr, pero a ella no. A ella le encanta ver películas viejas pero a mí no.

¡Leamos!

Los ritos y conjuros° de la Nochevieja

spells

Antes de leer

PASO 1. Contesta las siguientes preguntas.

1. ¿Cuáles son algunas de las costumbres que tenemos para celebrar la Nochevieja en este país? ¿Qué significado (*meaning*) tienen estas costumbres?

2. Nombra dos cosas que mucha gente espera (*expect*) del Año Nuevo.

3. ¿Qué haces tú para celebrar la Nochevieja?

PASO 2. Para entender mejor la lectura sobre los ritos de la Nochevieja en el mundo hispano, empareja las actividades con los resultados esperados (*desired results*).

ACTIVIDADES

Suggestion (Antes de leer, Paso 2): Direct students to pay attention to hints in the answer choices. They may need to use process of elimination for a couple answers.

1. __b__ comer doce uvas (*grapes*) a medianoche

2. __c__ comer las uvas apoyándose (*standing*) en la pierna (*leg*) izquierda

3. __e__ barrer (*sweep*) la casa de dentro a fuera (*from inside to out*)

4. __f__ quemar (*burn*) muebles (*furniture*) y ropa vieja

5. __d__ correr por la ciudad con las maletas (*luggage*)

6. __a__ usar ropa interior (*underwear*) de color amarillo

RESULTADOS ESPERADOS

a. atraer (*attract*) el amor
b. atraer la prosperidad y la buena suerte
c. empezar el Año Nuevo con el pie (*foot*) derecho para entrar mejor al porvenir (*future*)
d. hacer muchos viajes en el nuevo año
e. limpiar todas las impurezas (*impurities*)
f. purificarse de lo malo con el fuego (*fire*)

(*Continues*)

A leer

Lee el artículo de Carmen Domingo. Luego completa las oraciones con los lugares en donde se hace cada actividad.

«Los ritos y conjuros de la Nochevieja»

escrito por Carmen Domingo

La tradición de comer una uva con cada campana-da[a] a las doce de la noche el 31 de diciembre es originaria de España.

La última noche del año tiene siempre algo de mágico y se presta[b] a toda clase de conjuros y agüeros[c] que, aunque tienen diferentes manifestaciones, persiguen[d] el objetivo común de atraer la prosperidad y la buena suerte en los 365 días siguientes.

Millones de latinoamericanos siguen la tradición española de tomar las doce uvas al compás de las campanadas[e] de la medianoche del 31 de diciembre, aunque hay multitud de supersticiones acordes con[f] la idiosincrasia popular.

El ritual de las uvas se puede complicar un poco para aumentar[g] sus efectos y tomarlas de pie,[h] apoyándose solo en la pierna izquierda para entrar en el Año Nuevo con el pie derecho, por suponérsele más hábil[i] que el izquierdo en la caminata hacia el porvenir.[j]

Los mexicanos siguen ese rito al son[k] de las campanadas de la Catedral Metropolitana de la Ciudad de México, pero antes o después de tomar las uvas, barren la casa, de dentro a fuera, para dejarla limpia[l] de impurezas de todo tipo.

Otra forma de acabar con[m] lo malo es someterlo[n] al fuego purificador. Se queman muebles y ropas viejas en el Perú, Honduras y Ecuador. [...]

Pasear o correr con maletas en Nochevieja no es una prueba[ñ] de atletismo urbano. Se trata de un ritual para que el Año Nuevo traiga[o] muchos viajes, muy extendido en Colombia y seguido también por venezolanos, panameños, paraguayos, peruanos, chilenos, salvadoreños y costarricenses. [...]

En Argentina todos corren también, pero a abrir sus regalos después del brindis con champán o sidra[p] en la medianoche del 31 de diciembre. [...]

Comer una cucharada[q] de las lentejas[r] en Nochevieja es una tradición en Chile, donde también está muy extendido el uso de ropa interior de color amarillo para atraer el amor. [...]

Todos estos rituales ayudan a franquear el umbral[s] del nuevo año y hasta aquellos que se dicen más escépticos[t] siguen alguno... por si acaso.[u]

[a]*stroke of the clock* [b]*se... lends itself* [c]*omens* [d]*follow* [e]*al... to the rhythm of the bells tolling* [f]*acordes... in keeping with* [g]*increase* [h]*de... standing up* [i]*por... because one would suppose that it is more capable* [j]*caminata... journey toward the future* [k]*sound* [l]*dejarla... leave it clean* [m]*acabar... do away with* [n]*to subject it* [ñ]*test* [o]*para... so that the New Year might bring* [p]*hard cider* [q]*spoonful* [r]*lentils* [s]*franquear... clear the way* [t]*hasta... even those said to be more skeptical* [u]*por... just in case*

Domingo, Carmen, "Los ritos y conjuros de la Nochevieja," El Nuevo Herald, December 31, 2008. Copyright © 2008 by Miami Herald. All rights reserved. Used with permission.

Follow-up (A leer): Tell students that the list of countries mentioned in the article isn't necessarily complete. Some of these traditions exist in many countries. Share with students your own experiences.

PAÍS

1. Comen doce uvas en...   España, países latinoamericanos

2. Barren la casa en...   México

3. Queman muebles y ropa vieja en...   el Perú, Honduras, Ecuador

4. Corren con las maletas en...   Chile, Colombia, Costa Rica, El Salvador, Venezuela, Panamá, Paraguay, el Perú

5. Abren regalos en...   Argentina

6. Comen lentejas en...   Chile

7. Usan ropa interior de color amarillo en...   Chile

Después de leer

En grupos de tres o cuatro estudiantes, hablen de las tradiciones del mundo hispano que quieren adoptar y expliquen por qué. ¿Cuál les parece la idea más extraña (*strange*)? ¿Por qué?

MODELO: Me gusta la tradición de correr con las maletas porque me gusta viajar. La costumbre de llevar ropa interior de color amarillo para la Nochevieja me da risa (*makes me laugh*), pero como mi vida romántica no va muy bien, necesito la suerte, ¡así que la voy a probar!

¡Escuchemos!

Nuestros recuerdos°   *memories*

Antes de escuchar

Indica si tienes un buen recuerdo asociado con cada uno de los siguientes eventos o celebraciones. Apunta algunos detalles sobre los recuerdos para poder compartirlos con la clase.

¿Tienes buenos recuerdos...

		SÍ	NO			SÍ	NO
1.	del Año Nuevo?	☐	☐	5.	de la Navidad?	☐	☐
2.	del bautizo de un bebé?	☐	☐	6.	de la Nochevieja?	☐	☐
3.	de un juego infantil (*childhood game*)?	☐	☐	7.	de un viaje para visitar a tus tíos y primos?	☐	☐
4.	del nacimiento de un bebé?	☐	☐	8.	de una visita de tus tíos y primos?	☐	☐

A escuchar

Mira y escucha. Luego mira otra vez con pausas y empareja cada persona con el recuerdo feliz que describe. Mira y escucha una tercera vez para verificar tus respuestas.

Vídeo track (A escuchar): This video clip can be found on the DVD to accompany *Conéctate:* Cap. 7, Track 3.

a. la graduación
b. el nacimiento de primas
c. el nacimiento de perritos
d. el nacimiento de sus hijos
e. el regreso a su país después de vivir fuera (*away*)
f. un viaje a Guatemala
g. una visita a la casa de una persona famosa

1. __a__ Guadalupe, de Costa Rica

2. __e__ Henry, de Costa Rica

3. __c__ Catalina, de Colombia

4. __f__ Michael, de Guatemala

5. __d__ Anlluly, de Costa Rica

6. __g__ Olman, de Costa Rica

7. __b__ Zuly, de Colombia

Videoscript (A escuchar): 1. GUADALUPE: *Bueno, el momento más feliz de mi vida fue cuando yo me gradué de bachillerato porque me costó mucho.* **2.** HENRY: *El momento más feliz de mi vida ha sido cuando regresé después de cinco años de estar en Canadá.* **3.** CATALINA: *¿De mi vida? El día que mi perra tuvo ocho perritos... . y dio a luz en mi cuarto.* **4.** MICHAEL: *Pues el momento más feliz ha sido que... cuando fui a Guatemala y, eh, estaba mi abuelita, mi abuelito, toda mi familia reunida que hace... hace muchos años que no está mi familia junta. Y estaba mi mamá, mi papá, mis abuelos, todos los hermanos de mi mamá y mi hermana... Por cierto que ya se había casado y hace rato que nunca, nunca vamos con ella a Guatemala. Entonces la pasé muy bien allí. Yo puedo decir que sería mi momento más feliz.* **5.** ANLLULY: *Tengo tres, que son cuando nacieron mis hijos. Pero en especial cuando nació mi primer hijo, fue como... para mí fue el momento más, más feliz.* **6.** OLMAN: *Llegar a la casa del Bob Marley.* **7.** ZULY: *El momento más feliz de mi vida fue cuando nacieron mis primitas. Nunca tuve primos, pequeñitos o sobrinos no he tenido y era... son mellizas. Yo creo que ese fue el momento más bonito, el recuerdo más bonito que tengo.*

Note (Después de escuchar): Briefly review with students what they have learned about when to use the preterite and when to use the imperfect so that they are using it appropriately in this exercise. This distinction is covered in depth in *Cap. 8.*

Después de escuchar

Escoge una de las siguientes celebraciones y cuéntale a tu compañero/a un recuerdo feliz. ¿Qué año era? ¿Quiénes estaban? ¿Cómo se sentía la gente? ¿Qué hacía la gente para prepararse?

| un bautizo | un cumpleaños | una Navidad |
| una boda | una graduación | una Nochevieja |

Suggestion (Después de escuchar): Set up *Después de escuchar* as a "speed dating" activity by arranging the students in two rows facing each other (you can have them stand in two rows if it's too difficult to rearrange the classroom). The students in Row A get one minute to share their memories with the student across from them as Student B gives feedback and asks follow-up questions. Then, Row B has one minute to share their memories as Row A gives feedback and asks questions. After one cycle, students in Row B move over one place so that everyone has a new partner. Repeat as many times as you like. Students should retell the same story each time in order to refine and improve it with the feedback from their peers.

ESTRATEGIA

Question-asking for richer narration

When you have to explain something to someone who knows nothing about it, using the 5 Ws from journalism (*Who?, What?, When?, Where?, Why?* [and *How?*]) ensures that you are covering all the details from a perspective that will be understandable to someone who is unfamiliar with the subject. To organize your piece, jot down answers for each of these questions, then make sure to work in the responses as you write.

¡Escribamos!

Una entrada° en un blog   *entry*

Es muy común usar un blog para compartir información nueva y explicarle algo a un grupo que no sabe nada con respecto al tema presentado. ¿Puedes explicarle una tradición o celebración única a un grupo que no sabe nada de las costumbres asociadas con el evento?

Antes de escribir

En grupos, hagan una lista de algunas celebraciones de este país o región. ¿Qué hace la gente? ¿Cuáles son las costumbres y tradiciones? ¿Saben Uds. el origen de las costumbres? De su lista de celebraciones, ¿cuáles serían (*would be*) las más interesantes para personas de otros países?

A escribir

PASO 1. Escoge una celebración de la lista que hicieron en **Antes de escribir** y escribe una entrada en un blog sobre esa celebración. Tu entrada informativa debe contestar todas las preguntas: **¿quién?, ¿qué?, ¿cuándo?, ¿dónde?, ¿por qué?** y **¿cómo?**

> **MODELO:** la víspera del Día de Todos los Santos (*Halloween*)
> **¿quién?** los niños (menores de 13 años)
> **¿qué?** se ponen disfraces y van de casa en casa pidiendo dulces
> **¿cuándo?** el 31 de octubre por la noche
> **¿dónde?** en todos los estados de los Estados Unidos
> **¿por qué?** es una tradición relacionada con la cosecha (*harvest*) en otoño, los disfraces imitan y/o asustan a los espíritus malignos
> **¿cómo?** los jóvenes tocan a la puerta, dicen «*trick or treat*» y la gente (*people*) en la casa les da dulces

PASO 2. Escribe una descripción detallada para una persona que no sabe nada de la celebración. ¿Qué se celebra? ¿Qué hace la gente? ¿Cuáles son las costumbres/tradiciones? Describe la historia de la celebración. Usa oraciones completas e incluye todos los detalles del **Paso 1.**

Después de escribir

Revisa tu ensayo. Luego intercambia descripciones con un compañero / una compañera para evaluarlas. Lee el ensayo de tu compañero/a y determina si el ensayo explica la celebración para una persona que no sabe nada de ella o si falta información necesaria. Lee de nuevo (*again*) el ensayo con cuidado para revisar los siguientes puntos de gramática.

☐ usa el imperfecto para describir la historia de las costumbres
☐ hay concordancia entre sujetos y verbos
☐ hay concordancia entre sustantivos (*nouns*) y adjetivos
☐ la ortografía es correcta

Después de revisar el ensayo de tu compañero/a, devuélveselo (*return it to him/her*). Lee tu propio (*own*) ensayo para ver los cambios que tu compañero/a te recomienda y haz las revisiones necesarias.

Suggestion (Después de leer): To motivate students to edit their own work as well as their classmates' carefully, occasionally grade their editing instead of their writing.

CONÉCTATE AL MUNDO PROFESIONAL

Potential employers will almost certainly do an online search for your name as part of the screening process. When they do, you want them to see that you have useful tech skills and know how to apply them in the workplace context. Having designed a website or blog is one way to impress potential employers, as are having an online professional profile and evidence of using social media for marketing or other workplace purposes.

¡Hablemos!

Un regalo terrible

Antes de hablar

Cada año recibimos regalos en varias ocasiones (para el cumpleaños, la Navidad, la graduación) y la mayoría del tiempo los regalos son buenos. Pero, ¿recibiste alguna vez un regalo terrible? Haz (*Make*) dos listas: una de los peores regalos que recibiste en tu vida y otra de los regalos que querías recibir en su lugar (*in their place*).

Recibí...   Quería recibir...

 A hablar

Suggestion (A hablar): Model for students by sharing about a terrible gift that you received.

Habla con un compañero / una compañera sobre el peor regalo que recibiste. ¿Qué fue? ¿Quién te lo dio? ¿Por qué fue tan terrible? ¿Qué querías como regalo?

 Después de hablar

Compartan sus historias con la clase. ¿Quién de la clase recibió el peor regalo?

Suggestion (Antes de hablar): Encourage fictional accounts. Tell students they can make up their best and worst gift stories, then have their classmates guess if which stories are real and which are invented.

Conéctate a la música

Canción: «Tu Amor» (2006)
Artista: Luis Fonsi

Luis Alfonso Rodríguez López, conocido artísticamente como Luis Fonsi, es un cantante puertorriqueño de música pop. Desde los 10 años vive en la Florida, y estudió música en Florida State University.

Antes de escuchar

1. Según el título, ¿a quién le canta esta canción?

2. Generalmente, ¿de qué se tratan las canciones de amor? ¿Las canciones que hablan de un amor actual (*current*) son diferentes de las que hablan de un amor del pasado (*past*)? ¿De qué manera?

A escuchar

La canción «Tu amor» de Luis Fonsi tiene dos secciones principales. Las dos tratan de contestar la pregunta «¿Cómo era mi vida contigo?».

PASO 1. Lee las **Expresiones útiles** y escucha la canción. Luego empareja cada frase con lo que le sigue (*what follows it*) en la canción.

Expresiones útiles	
el alma	soul
alzar	to raise, lift up
la fuerza	force
la voz	voice

1. Contigo me sentía __d__
2. ...no me acordaba __a__
3. Contigo no había __b__
4. Contigo no morían (*weren't dying*) __e__ mis labios (*lips*)
5. Contigo una y otra vez quería __c__
6. Contigo el mundo parecía __g__
7. Contigo yo era __h__
8. ...porque al quererte (*when I loved you*), quería __f__

a. del pasado
b. un día gris ni noches frías antes de dormir
c. volver para salvarme (*save myself*)
d. bien
e. de hambre ni de sed
f. ser mejor
g. un lugar amable (*kind, nice*)
h. más que yo

PASO 2. Después del primer estribillo (*chorus*), el cantante usa los verbos **reírse** (*to laugh*) y **gustar** en tiempo imperfecto. Escribe la forma correcta de los verbos aquí.

Contigo __me reía__ (reírse) más porque la vida me __gustaba__ (gustar).

Después de escuchar

Televisión Española invitó a Luis Fonsi a presentar esta canción en su programa de Año Nuevo. ¿Por qué crees que a la gente le gusta este tipo de canciones (o esta canción en particular) para el Año Nuevo?

Un concierto de Luis Fonsi en Pasadena, California

For copyright reasons, the songs referenced in **Conéctate a la música** have not been provided by the publisher. The video for this song is available on YouTube or from the iTunes store.

Suggestion (Antes de escuchar): Prepare students for the song activity by expanding on the questions in item 2: *Esta canción habla de una relación terminada. Cuando una persona piensa en una relación romántica ya terminada, ¿cuál es la actitud más común? ¿Es que todo era perfecto y que le gustaba mucho su vida con esa persona? ¿o que su vida con esa persona era horrible? Según el título, ¿cómo piensas que va a ser la actitud del cantante?*

Suggestion (A escuchar, Paso 1): Have students try to guess the correct answers before listening to the song. They can then listen to check their answers.

Expansion (A escuchar):
- Have students give the infinitive form of each of the imperfect verbs in 1–8.
- Have students listen again and have them transcribe as much of the chorus (*el estribillo*) as they can. With the *Expresiones útiles,* they should be able to understand all of it.

VOCABULARIO

Now that I have completed the chapter, I can . . .

☐ say I had a good time

☐ wish someone well and congratulate them

☐ talk about holidays and celebrations in the Spanish-speaking world

☐ talk about ongoing events in the past

☐ express to whom or for whom an action is performed

Comunicación

Lo pasé bien/mal.	I had a good/bad time.
Lo siento.	I'm sorry. / My condolences.
Me divertí mucho.	I had a lot of fun.
¡Felicitaciones!/¡Felicidades!/ ¡Enhorabuena!	Congratulations!
Te felicito/felicitamos.	I/We congratulate you.

Los días festivos / Holidays

el Año Nuevo	New Year's
el bautizo	baptism
la boda	wedding
el brindis	toast (to a person)
el Carnaval	Carnival (the festivities in the days preceding Lent)
el champán	champagne
la costumbre	custom, habit
el cumpleaños	birthday
el desfile	parade
la despedida	farewell, good-bye
el Día de la Independencia	Independence Day
el Día de Muertos	Day of the Dead
el Día de los Reyes Magos	Three Kings' Day (Epiphany)
el disfraz (pl. los disfraces)	costume
la fiesta	party
la fiesta de quinceañera	girl's 15th birthday celebration
la flor	flower
los fuegos artificiales	fireworks
la graduación	graduation

el Jánuca	Hanukkah
el nacimiento	birth
la Navidad	Christmas
la Nochebuena	Christmas Eve
la Nochevieja	New Year's Eve
la Pascua (Florida / de Resurrección)	Easter
el regalo	gift
la Semana Santa	Holy Week
la tarjeta	card

Los verbos

celebrar	to celebrate
cumplir ____ años	to turn ____ years old
divertirse (ie, i)	to have fun
encantar	to delight
enseñar	to show; to teach
escoger (j)	to choose
fascinar	to fascinate
felicitar	to congratulate
importar	to matter; to be important to
interesar	to interest
invitar	to invite
molestar	to bother
parecer (zc)	to seem
preguntar	to ask
regalar	to give (a present)

Los pronombres de objeto indirecto

me, te, le, nos, os, les

Las preposiciones y los pronombres

con	with
conmigo	with me
contigo	with you
en	in, on; at (a place)
para	for
para mí	for me
para ti	for you
sin	without
sobre	on, above; about

La ropa° y la moda°

Clothes, fashion

En un desfile de moda en México, una modelo lleva un vestido (*dress*) de la diseñadora (*designer*) Lydia Lavin.

Objetivos

When you finish this chapter, you will be able to:

■ say how great something is
■ use polite expressions in appropriate contexts
■ talk about clothing and fashion
■ talk about the human body
■ express how clothing fits
■ express events in the past
■ discuss the fashion world and industry

8

connect®

www.mhhe.com/connect

COMUNICACIÓN ~~LARIO~~ ~~UCTURA~~ ~~ATE~~

¡Qué padre!

Talking about how great something is

A. A ver: ¿Cómo se dice «¡Qué bueno!» en su país? Mira y escucha. Luego mira otra vez con pausas para contestar. Mira una tercera vez para verificar tus respuestas.

1. Edgardo, de Venezuela, dice... _c_

2. Olga, de España, dice... _e_

3. Mirelle, de México, dice... _b_

4. Jordi, de España, dice... _a_

5. Nadia Angélica, de México, dice... _h_

6. Víctor, de México, dice... _g_

7. Luis, de Nicaragua, dice... _d_

8. Daniela, Ana Marcela y Estela, de Costa Rica, dicen... _f_

a. «Qué bien, qué chulo, qué guay...»
b. «Qué chido, está muy padre...»
c. «Qué bueno, ¡qué chévere!»
d. «¡Qué bárbaro!»
e. «¡Qué bien! ¡Estupendo! ¡Fenomenal!»
f. «¡Pura vida!»
g. «¡Está padre!»
h. «Qué padre, qué chido...»

Suggestion (Act. A): Before watching the video, have students work as a class or in small groups to guess what each person will say based on where they are from. Students should consult the list at the bottom of this page to see where the phrases are most commonly used.

Video track (Act. A): This video clip can be found on the DVD to accompany *Conéctate: Cap. 8,* Track 1.

To express *cool!* or *awesome!* in Spanish, use one of the following words.

bárbaro/a (*Arg., Chile, C.A.*)	**estupendo/a**
bien	**fenomenal**
chévere (*Carib., Andes*)	**guay** (*Sp.*)
chido/a (*Mex.*)	**padre** (*Mex.*)
chulo/a (*Sp., D.R.*)	**pura vida** (*C.R.*)

Except for **pura vida**, these expressions are often used as exclamations with **¡Qué... !**

—**Mira, compré un teléfono nuevo.**   *"Look, I bought a new phone."*
—**¡Qué chévere/chido/chulo/padre!**   *"Cool!"*

To say something is *not* cool or great, use one of these expressions.

¡Qué aburrido/a (*boring*)!	**¡Qué pesado/a** (*annoying*)!
¡Qué malo!	**¡Qué pésimo/a** (*awful*)!

En español...

In Costa Rica, people use the expresion **¡Pura vida!** for many things: it can mean **hola, adiós, ¿qué pasa?, perfecto, estoy satisfecho/a, la vida es bella** and more. This expression is used in other Spanish-speaking countries, but in Costa Rica it is so common that it has become the national motto.

Suggestion (Act. B): Have students do this activity in pairs. Students take turns saying what they're going to do, and the other reacts. For example, E1: *Voy a estudiar en la biblioteca.* E2: *¡Qué pesado!* Students can add their own activities and reactions to supplement the ones on the list.

B. ¿Chévere o pesado?   Indica tu reacción a cada actividad de la lista.

	¡QUÉ CHÉVERE!	¡QUÉ PESADO!
1. estudiar en la biblioteca	☐	☐
2. acampar (*go camping*) en las montañas	☐	☐
3. ir a la ópera	☐	☐
4. ir a la playa	☐	☐
5. ir a una entrevista de trabajo	☐	☐
6. ir de compras	☐	☐
7. jugar los videojuegos	☐	☐
8. preparar la cena	☐	☐
9. hacer una presentación en una clase	☐	☐
10. salir con los amigos	☐	☐

Expansion (Act. C, Paso 1): Once students have had the chance to discuss within their groups, bring the class back together and ask a few students to share their findings with the class.

C. Las marcas (*brands*) más chéveres

PASO 1.   En grupos, decidan si cada cosa es **chévere, pesado/a** o **pésimo/a. ¡Atención!** Usen también los sinónimos que ya saben.

> **MODELO:**   E1: ¿Qué piensas de la consola Wii?
> E2: ¡Qué aburrida!

1. un teléfono Droid
2. el iPad
3. la ropa de H&M
4. la marca Hollister
5. la marca Óscar de la Renta
6. los zapatos Nike

PASO 2.   Ahora, apunta tus cosas favoritas en cada una de las siguientes categorías: **marca de ropa, sitio web, marca de teléfono celular, videojuego.**

PASO 3.   Habla con tres compañeros de clase para saber si están de acuerdo contigo o no. ¿Qué piensan ellos de tus cosas favoritas? ¿Cuáles son sus cosas favoritas? Usa las expresiones de la página 227 para reaccionar.

> **MODELO:**   E1: Me gusta la marca Gap.
> E2: ¡Qué padre! ¡A mí también! ¿Qué piensas de... ?

El diseñador de modas Óscar de la Renta

Disculpe...

Using polite expressions in appropriate contexts

There are many ways to say *Excuse me,* most of which depend on the situation. (You've already seen some of these in **Capítulo 3.**)

Con permiso.	Excuse me.
Disculpa. / Disculpe. / Disculpen.	Excuse me. (*sing. inform./form.; pl. form.*)
Perdón.	Sorry. / Excuse me. / Pardon me.
Perdona. / Perdone. / Perdonen.	Sorry. / Excuse me. / Pardon me. (*sing. inform./form.; pl. form.*)
¿Puedo pasar?	Excuse me. (*Literally,* May I pass by? *or* May I enter?)

While any of these phrases can mean *Excuse me,* **Con permiso** is generally used when entering or leaving a room, to leave the table, or to get past someone. **Perdón** and the forms of the verbs **disculpar** and **perdonar** are usually used as apologies for an interruption or inconvenience.

To apologize for something, you can also say **Lo siento.** (*I'm sorry.*)

To respond politely to a request, use one of these expressions.

¡Claro (que sí)!	Of course!
¡Cómo no!	Sure!
Con mucho gusto.	With pleasure.
Gracias.	Thank you.
Gracias por...	Thank you for . . .
Sí, gracias. / No, gracias.	Yes, please. / No, thank you.
No puedo.	I can't.
Pasa. / Pase. / Pasen.	Come in. / Go ahead. (*inform./form.; pl. form.*)
Por supuesto.	Of course.

A. ¿Puedo pasar?   Escoge la mejor expresión para cada situación.

1. Estás en una cena y quieres ir al baño (*restroom*).
   - ☑ Con permiso.
   - ☐ Lo siento.
   - ☐ Con mucho gusto.

2. Estás en el transporte público con mucha gente y quieres bajar en la próxima parada (*get off at the next stop*).
   - ☐ ¡Claro que sí!
   - ☐ Sí, gracias.
   - ☑ ¿Puedo pasar?

(Continues)

Suggestion (Act. A): Have students create a dialogue using the vocabulary that they learned in *Act. A* and the *Disculpe...* presentation.

3. Chocas con (*bump into*) otra persona sin querer (*unintentionally*).
☐ Con permiso.
☑ Lo siento.
☐ ¡Cómo no!

4. Das una fiesta y tienes que dejar (*leave*) una conversación para darle la bienvenida a la persona que llega.
☑ Con permiso.
☐ ¿Puedo pasar?
☐ Pase.

5. Tienes que preguntarle algo a alguien, pero esta persona ya está hablando con otra persona. Decides interrumpir.
☐ Con mucho gusto.
☑ Disculpen.
☐ Por supuesto.

6. Quieres pedirle la hora a alguien en la calle.
☐ Con mucho gusto. ¿Qué hora es?
☑ Perdón. ¿Qué hora es?
☐ ¿Puedo pasar? ¿Qué hora es?

B. ¡Sí, gracias!

PASO 1. En parejas, den una reacción de aceptación o una de negación para cada oración.

MODELO: E1: ¿Quieres estudiar conmigo esta noche?
E2: Sí, como no. ¿A qué hora? *o* Lo siento, pero no puedo. Tengo que trabajar esta noche. ¿Tal vez (*Perhaps*) mañana?

¿Quieres un chicle?

1. ¿Quieres un chicle (*gum*)?
2. Tengo coche, así que te puedo llevar a la casa de tus padres este fin de semana.
3. Vamos al cine hoy a las diez. ¿Quieres ir?
4. ¿Me puedes ayudar con la tarea?
5. ¿Me puedes prestar (*lend*) cien dólares?
6. Vamos a tomar un café después de clase. ¿Quieres ir?

PASO 2. Escoge un lugar o una actividad e invita a tu compañero/a a ir contigo. Responde a las invitaciones que recibes con una expresión adecuada.

MODELO: E1: Después de clase, voy de compras en La Bella. ¿Quieres ir?
E2: No, gracias. No puedo. Tengo otra clase.

C. Perdón, ¿puedo usar el teléfono?
Circula por la clase y pídeles algo prestado (*ask to borrow*) a tus compañeros: el libro, el teléfono, el bolígrafo, etcétera. **¡Atención!** Usa expresiones como **Con permiso** y **¿Puedo pasar?** mientras circulas por la clase.

MODELO: E1: Perdón, ¿puedo usar tu teléfono?
E2: Lo siento. No tengo teléfono. *o* ¡Cómo no!
E1: Gracias.
E2: De nada.

Expansion (Act. B): To conclude *Act. B, Paso 2,* ask students about the plans that they made: *¿Quiénes hicieron planes? ¿Adónde van? ¿Qué van a hacer?*

Suggestion (Act. C): You may wish to mention the following items if you find that your students are having trouble coming up with their own: *el diccionario, una hoja de papel, los apuntes, la calculadora.*

¿Qué llevas?
Describing clothing

Suggestion (Act. A, p. 232): Create four separate stations in the classroom and label each for one occasion, then have groups of students move through the stations and identify or list clothing items that correspond to each occasion. For more practice or as an alternative, have students organize the vocabulary by season.

¡Luce perfecto para tu entrevista de trabajo!

la camisa
la corbata
la camiseta
la blusa
el cinturón
el traje
el bolso
el abrigo
la falda
el pantalón
el paraguas
los tacones
los zapatos
el gorro
la bufanda
la chaqueta
los guantes

¡La última moda para los niños y los jóvenes!

la gorra
la chaqueta
el suéter
el vestido
los jeans
los pantalones cortos
los calcetines
las sandalias
los tenis

el sombrero
los lentes
el traje de baño
¡Lo más caliente para el verano!

Ropa interior y pijamas

el reloj
la pulsera
los pendientes
el calzón
el sujetador
el anillo
el collar
el pijama

¡Las mejores tendencias en accesorios y complementos!

¡REBAJAS!
Conjuntos de snowboard y esquí
¡Hasta 50% de descuento!

A. ¿Qué llevas para cada ocasión? En grupos pequeños, organicen las prendas (*items*) de ropa en la página 231 según la ocasión: **un día en la playa, el primer día de la escuela, unas vacaciones de esquí, una entrevista de trabajo.**

- The audio files for in-text listening activities are available in the eBook, within Connect activities, and on the Online Learning Center.

B. ¿Cierto o falso? Escucha las frases sobre las prendas de ropa que aparecen en el anuncio en la página 231. Indica si cada frase es **cierta** o **falsa** y corrige las oraciones falsas. Script (Act. B): **1.** *La mujer lleva una blusa azul para su entrevista.* **2.** *Un niño lleva una camiseta anaranjada.* **3.** *El niño de arriba lleva pantalones cortos verdes.* **4.** *La chica joven lleva un suéter gris.* **5.** *El hombre lleva una corbata verde azul para su entrevista.* **6.** *Una niña lleva un traje de baño verde.* **7.** *La mujer lleva tacones negros para su entrevista.* **8.** *Un niño lleva una gorra azul.* **9.** *La chica joven lleva un bolso negro.*

	CIERTO	FALSO		CIERTO	FALSO		CIERTO	FALSO
1.	☐	☑	4.	☑	☐	7.	☑	☐
2.	☑	☐	5.	☑	☐	8.	☐	☑
3.	☑	☐	6.	☐	☑	9.	☐	☑

Recycle! (Act. C): Talking about clothes is a great way to review colors, which were presented in *Cap. 2.* You may wish to provide additional vocabulary so students can distinguish between light and dark shades of colors when describing: *claro/oscuro.* Note that when these adjectives are used, most speakers use only the masculine forms, the agreement being with the unspoken word *color: Lleva una camisa (color) amarillo claro y pantalones (color) verde oscuro.* You may wish to point out that light blue is *azul celeste* and navy blue is *azul marino.*

Expansion (Act. C): With music playing (or timing them for 10 seconds), have students walk around the room observing each other carefully. When the music stops (or time runs out), they form pairs with the person closest to them and then turn back to back. One student in the pair begins by stating one item (and an appropriate descriptive adjective, not just *Llevas pantalones!*) the other is wearing. If the other student verifies that the statement is correct, they continue to the next round. If, instead, the statement is incorrect, the student that described the clothing incorrectly sits down. *MODELO: E1: Llevas una gorra roja. E2: Sí, ¡es correcto! / No, no es correcto. Llevo una gorra, pero no es roja.*

C. ¿De qué color es la ropa?

PASO 1. En parejas, creen una tabla con los siguientes colores para categorizar las prendas de ropa del anuncio. Túrnense para hacerse preguntas sobre los colores y describir el color de cada prenda.

> **MODELO:** E1: ¿Hay alguna prenda rosada?
> E2: El traje de baño de la niña es rosado. También el calzón de mujer es rosado.

Suggestion (Act. C, Paso 2): Have students count off 1–4 or 1–5 to form groups, then as they move around the room to get in their numeric groups, require that they use the expressions from *Comunicación* to excuse themselves and comment on each other's clothes: *¡Qué lindo es tu collar!*

PASO 2. En grupos, túrnense para describir su propia ropa y añadan cada prenda a la lista debajo del (*below the*) color correspondiente.

> **MODELO:** Hoy llevo una camiseta roja y azul y unos pantalones cortos color caqui (*khaki*). También llevo calcetines blancos, los zapatos marrones y una gorra de los Red Sox.

D. A ver: ¿Qué llevas hoy?

PASO 1. Mira las fotos e indica todas las prendas que llevan Alexander, Carolina y David.

1.

☐ el anillo	☐ el cinturón	☐ los calcetines	☐ el reloj
☐ la camisa	☑ la gorra	☑ los jeans	☑ los zapatos
☑ la camiseta		☐ la falda	

2.

☑ la pulsera	☐ la camisa	☐ el cinturón	☐ el pantalón
☑ la blusa	☐ la gorra	☑ la falda	☑ el paraguas
☑ los lentes	☑ el collar	☑ el bolso	

En español...

The verb **llevar** has several meanings in Spanish. Two of the most common uses are to *wear* (**La niña lleva un vestido rosado.**) and to *bring* or *to carry* (**Llevo refrescos a la fiesta.**)

The verb **usar** can also be used to mean *to wear*: **Yo no uso lentes, pero mis padres sí los usan.**

3.

☑ la gorra   ☑ la camiseta   ☑ los calcetines   ☐ la pulsera
☐ el anillo   ☐ el cinturón   ☐ el pantalón   ☑ los tenis

PASO 2. Mira y escucha. Luego mira otra vez y apunta cada prenda y accesorio que mencionan Alexander, Carolina y David.

PASO 3. Escucha otra vez y apunta una descripción más detallada (*detailed*) de la ropa que describe cada una.

MODELO: Alexander lleva una camiseta gris.

El cuerpo humano
Parts of the body

A. Asociaciones

PASO 1. Empareja la parte del cuerpo con la ropa o accesorio que más se asocia con esa parte.

1. __a__ el torso   a. la camisa
2. __c__ la cabeza   b. la corbata
3. __d__ las manos   c. la gorra
4. __g__ las orejas   d. los guantes
5. __b__ el cuello   e. los calcetines
6. __e__ los pies   f. el pantalón
7. __f__ las piernas   g. los pendientes

PASO 2. Di qué parte del cuerpo se asocia más con cada verbo. **¡Atención!** A veces hay más de una posibilidad.

1. comer   5. pensar   9. ver
2. escribir   6. correr   10. hablar
3. saludar   7. escuchar
4. abrazar   8. sentarse

 B. ¿Qué es... ? En grupos, túrnense para describir la ropa y las partes del cuerpo mientras los otros miembros del grupo adivinan qué palabra describes.

MODELOS: E1: Llevamos estas prendas de ropa en los pies, sobre los calcetines.
E2: ¿Son los zapatos?
E1: ¡Exacto!

E3: Es la parte del cuerpo que usas para besar (*to kiss*).
E1: ¿Es la cabeza?
E3: No exactamente. Pero sí están en la cabeza.
E2: ¿Son los labios?
E3: ¡Correcto!

la cabeza
la oreja
la cara
la boca
el cuello
el hombro
la mano
el pecho
el torso
el codo
el brazo
la cadera
los dedos
el pelo
la rodilla
el ojo
la pierna
la nariz
los dientes
los labios
el pie

Answers (Act. D, Pasos 2 y 3):
1. ALEXANDER: los jeans (celestes), la gorra (negra), los zapatos (café), la camiseta (gris) **2.** CAROLINA: la blusa (celeste/turquesa), la enagua/falda (gris); el bolso (negro), la sombrilla / el paraguas (rosada), el anillo (de plata), el collar (celeste), los lentes (café) **3.** DAVID: los tenis (negros), las medias (blancas), los shorts (de cuadros), la camiseta (verde claro), la gorra, el piercing, las pulseras, los anillos

Expansion (Act. D, Paso 2): Have students react to the clothing in the video using *¡Qué... !* expressions from *Comunicación.*

Videoscript (Act. D):
1. ALEXANDER: *Eh, jeans celestes, gorra negra, zapatos café y camiseta gris.*
2. CAROLINA: *Bueno, esto le llamamos blusa en español, color celeste o turquesa — hay dos colores se pueden aprender. Presentamos que la enagua, como le decimos acá —la enagua o falda— lo mismo... enagua es de color gris. Y el bolso sería negro y la sombrilla rosada. También si hablamos de accesorios, tengo lo que es un anillo de plata, un collar también del mismo color celeste. Y unos lentes como en un tono café como mi pelo.* **3.** DAVID: *Ya y ahorita ando tenis negros como me pueden ver, medias blancas, mis shorts de cuadros... y una camisa verde. Bueno, verde claro. Eh, la gorra para lucir bien, obvio. Y el piercing para verse guapo. Pulseras y anillos.*

Note (Act. D): Remind students that they just have to listen for individual clothing items in *Paso 2.* They will be asked to listen for more details in *Paso 3.*

Expansion (Act. A): Play *Simón dice (Simon Says!)* with the class. Have everyone stand up, then start the game by saying "*Simón dice tóquense...* " and touching the related body part. If a student fails to touch the correct body part or if they touch when a body part was not preceded by the expression "*Simón dice...* ", he/she must sit down. To get more students out, touch the wrong body part to see how many follow you and how many get it right. If you wish, have a student take the role of Simón.

C. ¿Qué debo llevar? A veces es difícil saber qué ropa es apropiada para diferentes ocasiones. En parejas, túrnense para darse consejos sobre qué llevar en cada ocasión.

> **MODELO:** E1: ¿Qué debo llevar para conocer (*meet*) a los padres de mi novia en un restaurante?
>
> E2: Tienes que llevar un traje azul, con camisa y corbata. Y necesitas zapatos negros o marrones; no puedes usar tenis.

1. un concierto de música rock
2. una entrevista de trabajo
3. una cita a ciegas (*blind date*) en un restaurante elegante
4. un partido (*game*) de fútbol americano
5. la playa
6. las montañas de Colorado en enero
7. una fiesta con amigos
8. la boda de un buen amigo

¿Cómo te queda?
Expressing how clothing fits

Note (¿Cómo te queda?): Adjectives were first presented in *Cap. 2.*

The verb for *to try* (*something*) *on* is **probarse (ue).** To talk about how clothing fits, use the verb **quedar. Quedar** is conjugated in the same manner as **gustar.**

Me probé este vestido. Me queda bien. I tried on this dress. It fits me well.
Los pantalones de mi hermano le quedan mal. Están demasiado apretados. My brother's pants fit him poorly. They're too tight.

Here are other words to describe how clothing fits.

ancho/a	loose
apretado/a	tight
corto/a	short
grande	loose, big
largo/a	long
pequeño/a	small

¡Atención! Note that **largo** means *long*; use **grande** to say that something is *large.*

To talk about a particular size of clothing, use **el número** to refer to shoe size and **la talla** for clothing size.

Disculpe, señor. ¿Tiene este zapato en el número 9? Excuse me, sir. Do you have this shoe in a size 9?
Perdone, señorita, pero quisiera probarme la camisa en una talla más grande. Excuse me, miss, but I would like to try on the shirt in a larger size.

Here are some words you can use to talk about fashion in general.

el desfile de moda	fashion show
el/la diseñador(a)	designer
estar de moda	to be in fashion
estar pasado/a de moda	to be out of fashion
la marca	brand
de marca	brand-name (*adj.*)

A. Le quedan largos.   Empareja las oraciones con la persona que mejor describen, según el dibujo.

1. __f__ Le queda apretado.

5. __e__ Le quedan grandes.

2. __a__ Le quedan apretados.

6. __b__ Le quedan largos.

3. __c__ Le queda corta.

7. __d__ Le queda pequeña.

4. __g__ Le queda grande.

B. No me queda bien.   Escucha las descripciones. Luego empareja cada descripción con la reacción más lógica.

1. __e__

2. __c__

3. __f__

4. __d__

5. __b__

6. __a__

a. Debes usar una talla más grande.
b. Está de moda.
c. Está pasado de moda.
d. Son marcas de diseñadores famosos.
e. Te quedan grandes.
f. Te quedan pequeños.

Script (Act B): 1. *Normalmente uso número 6, pero los zapatos que me gustan solo los tienen en el número 7. 2. Mi padre siempre lleva el suéter que le regalé en 1999. 3. Normalmente uso número 8, pero los zapatos que me gustan solo los tienen en el número 6. 4. Prefiero llevar ropa de Ralph Lauren. Mi hermano mayor prefiere la ropa de Calvin Klein. 5. Me gusta mucho el nuevo vestido que mi prima compró en la tienda Zara. 6. Toda mi ropa me queda apretada.*

Reciclaje

Note: The preterite is first covered in *Estructura 6.1.*

The preterite

PASO 1. Estos cinco panameños dicen qué hicieron el fin de semana pasado. Subraya todos los verbos que están en el tiempo pretérito.

 Kathyuska, 19 años, estudiante: «Pasé el fin de semana en la casa de una amiga. Después, regresé a la casa y terminé de hacer mis quehaceres (*chores*).»

 Graciela, 47 años, ingeniera (*engineer*) y gerente de una empresa (*business manager*): «Estuve en la playa con mi familia.»

 Marco Antonio, 48 años, trabaja en el sistema de bibliotecas de la Universidad de Panamá: «Les ayudé a unos muchachos de la escuela secundaria a estudiar.»

 Mauricio, 20 años, estudiante: «Fui a una fiesta en la playa. La pasamos muy bien. Hicimos una fogata (*bonfire*), comimos y bailamos.»

 Ricardo, 32 años, gerente de una cadena (*chain*) de tiendas: «Trabajé.»

PASO 2. Da un ejemplo de dos personas que hicieron cosas parecidas.

Nombres: ___Graciela___ y ___Mauricio___
¿Qué hicieron? _Fueron a la playa._

Ahora da un ejemplo de dos personas que hicieron cosas distintas.

Nombre: ___Marco Antonio___   ¿Qué hizo? _Ayudó a unos muchachos._
Nombre: ___Ricardo___   ¿Qué hizo? ___Trabajó.___

¿Y tú? ¿Hiciste lo mismo que una de estas personas?
El fin de semana pasado, ___Ricardo___ y yo ___trabajamos___.

 PASO 3. En grupos de tres, hablen de lo que hicieron Uds. el fin de semana pasado. Cada persona debe nombrar por lo menos tres cosas. Mientras conversan, apunten las actividades para poder compartir la información con la clase.

Reciclaje (Paso 2): Answers will vary.

■ Answers to this activity are in Appendix 2 at the back of your book.

8.1   Balenciaga vistió a la familia real española

More irregular preterite forms

Para empezar...

Cristóbal Balenciaga y Carolina Herrera son grandes figuras en el mundo de la moda. Tres de las siguientes oraciones describen a Balenciaga y cuatro a Carolina Herrera. Indica cuáles se refieren a Balenciaga con **B** y cuáles a Herrera con **H.**

Cristóbal Balenciaga, español, 1895–1972

Carolina Herrera, venezolana, 1939–

1. ___B___ **Nació** en el País Vasco (*Basque Country*).
2. ___H___ **Vistió** (*He/She dressed*) a Jacqueline Kennedy Onassis en los últimos años de su vida. Ahora viste a Oprah Winfrey, a Michelle Obama y a Hillary Clinton.
3. ___H___ **Asistió** a un desfile de moda de Balenciaga a los trece años (*at age thirteen*).
4. ___B___ **Murió** en 1972.
5. ___H___ Le **pidió** ayuda a su hija Carolina Adriana para crear una línea de perfumes.
6. ___H___ **Nació** en Caracas.
7. ___B___ Una exposición (*exhibition*) en el Metropolitan Museum of Art en 1973 **sirvió** como reconocimiento (*recognition*) de su importancia después de su muerte (*death*).

Actividades analíticas

1 Complete these conjugations in the preterite using the verbs you saw in **Para empezar** and following the pattern that you see here. **¡Atención!** Pay close attention to the stems of these verbs and note where they do and do not change. They share a pattern!

	pedir (i, i)	seguir (i, i)	servir (i, i)	vestir (i, i)
yo	pedí	seguí	serví	vestí
tú	pediste	seguiste	serviste	vestiste
él/ella, Ud.	pidió	siguió	sirvió	vistió
nosotros/as	pedimos	seguimos	servimos	vestimos
vosotros/as	pedisteis	seguisteis	servisteis	vestisteis
ellos/ellas, Uds.	pidieron	siguieron	sirvieron	vistieron

Remember that the verb **vestir** is often used in its reflexive form (**vestirse**) with the sense of *to dress oneself* or *to get dressed*.

Carlos **se vistió** bien para la entrevista.	*Carlos dressed well for the interview.*
Ayer **me vestí** después de desayunar.	*Yesterday I got dressed after having breakfast.*

(*Continues*)

Note (Para empezar): Remind students that *el País Vasco* is in Spain.

Suggestion (Para empezar): Point out to students that they should be able to figure out answers using the information in the photo captions (and a bit of logical guessing).

■ Answers to these activities are in Appendix 2 at the back of your book.

■ **NOTE:** The letters in parentheses following stem-changing verbs such as **dormir (ue, u)** and **pedir (i, i)** will help you know what type of change(s) to expect when those verbs appear in different tenses. When there is one set of vowels in parentheses (such as for **despertar [ie]** and **probar [ue]**), it refers to the stem change that occurs in the present tense in all forms but **nosotros/as** and **vosotros/as: despiert-, prueb-.** When there are two sets of vowels in parentheses (such as for **dormir [ue, u]** and **pedir [i, i]**), the first item in parentheses refers to the stem change that occurs in the present tense and the second is the change that occurs in the preterite: **durmió, durmieron; pidió, pidieron.**

■ For additional irregular verbs in the preterite, see **Para saber más 8.1** at the back of your book.

Note (Para saber más): *Para saber más 8.1 presents the preterite forms of the verbs divertirse, mentir, preferir, reírse, repetir, sentirse, sonreír,* and *sugerir.*

2 The verbs **pedir, seguir, servir,** and **vestir** are all **-ir** verbs with an **e** in the stem. In the **él/ella, Ud.** and **ellos/ellas, Uds.** preterite forms of this type of verb, the stem vowel **e** becomes **i.** Circle these verb forms in the conjugation.

¡Atención! Recall that these verbs also change their stem vowel in the present tense: **pedir, seguir, servir,** and **vestir** all belong to the **e → i** family in the present tense, though the pattern of stem changes there is slightly different.

3 Use the verbs in **Para empezar** once again, as well as the general pattern that you see here, to complete the conjugations of these verbs.

	dormir (ue, u)	morir (ue, u)
yo	dormí	morí
tú	dormiste	moriste
él/ella, Ud.	durmió	murió
nosotros/as	dormimos	morimos
vosotros/as	dormisteis	moristeis
ellos/ellas, Uds.	durmieron	murieron

4 With the verbs **dormir** and **morir,** the stem vowel **o** becomes **u** in the **él/ella, Ud.** and **ellos/ellas, Uds.** forms of the preterite. Circle the verb forms in the chart where this vowel change occurs.

¡Atención! Recall that these verbs also change their stem vowel in the present tense: **dormir** and **morir** both belong to the **o → ue** family in the present tense.

Suggestion (Act. analíticas 4): Have students conjugate one of these verbs in both the present and the preterite, and have them indicate where the change occurs in each tense. (Answer: In the present tense, the change occurs in all of the forms except *nosotros/as* and *vosotros/as.* In the preterite tense, the change occurs only in the *él/ella, Ud.* and ellos/ ellas, Uds. forms.)

Suggestion (Act. A): Go over the verbs to make sure students understand the forms and meanings before they complete the activity.

Actividades prácticas

A. Completa las oraciones   Usa los verbos para completar las siguientes oraciones. **¡Atención!** Debes usar uno de los verbos dos veces.

durmió   murió   pidió   siguió   sirvió   vistió

1. ¿A quién le ___pidió___ dinero Jorge?
2. A causa del examen que tiene ahora, Marisela ___durmió___ muy poco anoche.
3. Parece que Santiago se levantó y se ___vistió___ en treinta segundos.
4. Eva ___siguió___ el mismo camino (*path*).
5. Paco ___sirvió___ una cena exquisita. Él lo preparó todo.
6. Iván está triste porque su perro ___murió___ hace unos días.
7. María Elena tenía mucho sueño y ___durmió___ por mucho tiempo.

B. Preguntas y respuestas   Empareja cada pregunta con la respuesta más lógica.

1. _d_ ¿Quién durmió más anoche? ¿Guillermo o Pedro?
2. _f_ ¿Ya se vistieron los niños?
3. _a_ Después de las elecciones, ¿Villegas siguió (*continued*) como presidente?
4. _g_ ¿Por qué te pidieron cinco dólares?
5. _c_ ¿Sirvió ese teléfono desechable (*disposable*) que compraste?
6. _b_ ¿Seguiste las instrucciones?
7. _e_ ¿En qué año murió tu abuelo?

a. No, perdió las elecciones presidenciales.
b. Yo sí, pero no las siguió Elena.
c. No, no muy bien.
d. Pedro. Durmió diez horas.
e. En 2011.
f. Sí. Ya salieron a jugar.
g. Porque quieren comprar algo.

Autoprueba

Complete each sentence using the preterite of the verb in parentheses.

1. Mariana ____ (vestirse) rápido.
2. Los niños no ____ (seguir) las instrucciones.
3. Ese teléfono viejo no ____ (servir).
4. ¡Mi hermano ____ (dormir) diez horas anoche!
5. Después de bañarme esta mañana, yo ____ (vestirse).

Respuestas: 1. se vistió **2.** siguieron **3.** sirvió **4.** durmió **5.** me vestí

C. Poner las acciones en orden

PASO 1. Mira la lista de las cosas que hizo Angélica esta mañana. Pon las oraciones en el orden más lógico.

a. __5__ «Antes de ir al trabajo, fui a un café.»
b. __2__ «Me levanté temprano.»
c. __8__ «Tomé el café solo.»
d. __4__ «Me puse los zapatos.»
e. __7__ «Me sirvieron un café solo (*black*) por equivocación (*by mistake*).»
f. __1__ «Dormí.»
g. __9__ «Fui al trabajo.»
h. __6__ «Pedí un café con leche.»
i. __3__ «Me vestí.»

PASO 2. Ahora, en parejas, usa la lista de lo que hizo Angélica esta mañana para crear una narración del día de ella. **¡Atención!** Para una narración más natural, usa expresiones de tiempo: **primero, entonces** (*then*), **luego** (*later, then*), **después** (*next, afterwards*), **al final** (*in the end*), **finalmente / por fin** (*finally, at last*).

MODELO: E1: Primero, Angélica durmió.
E2: Luego...

PASO 3. En parejas, túrnense para explicar cuáles de las actividades del **Paso 1** hicieron Uds. esta mañana. ¿Alguien hizo todas las cosas? ¿Alguien no hizo ninguna?

MODELO: Dormí. Me levanté a las diez; no me levanté temprano.

D. Cuatro preguntas

PASO 1. Pregúntales a cuatro compañeros una de las siguientes preguntas y apunta las respuestas. **Note (Act. D):** *Hugo Chávez murió el 5 de marzo de 2013.*

1. ¿En qué año murió el presidente venezolano Hugo Chávez? (Si no lo sabes, ¡adivina!)
2. La última vez que comiste en un restaurante, ¿qué pediste de tomar?
3. ¿Cuántas horas dormiste anoche?
4. ¿En cuánto tiempo te vestiste esta mañana?

PASO 2. Presenta tus resultados del **Paso 1** a la clase.

MODELO: Dos personas dicen que Hugo Chavez murió en el año _____, una persona dice...

Hugo Rafael Chávez Frías, presidente venezolano

Answers (Act. C, Paso 2):
Durmió. Se levantó temprano. Se vistió. Se puso los zapatos. Antes de ir al trabajo, fue a un café. Pidió un café con leche. Le sirvieron un café solo por equivocación. Tomó el café solo. Fue al trabajo.

Suggestion (Act. C, Paso 3): Have students present their morning routine to the class, or have one student present the morning routine of his/her partner.

Suggestion (Act. D): To ensure that all of the questions get asked, divide the class into 4 groups and assign each one of the questions. Ask for volunteers to report their findings back to the class.

CONÉCTATE AL MUNDO HISPANO

Hugo Chávez fue presidente de Venezuela durante catorce años. Una figura muy polémica (*controversial*), por un lado Chávez es conocido por sus grandes reformas sociales que ayudaron a mejorar el nivel de vida (*standard of living*) de muchos venezolanos. Por otro lado, también fue criticado por las divisiones que creó dentro del país y entre Venezuela y otros países. Murió al principio de su cuarto periodo presidencial, tras (*following*) una lucha (*fight*) contra el cáncer.

Expansion (Reciclaje): Have students interview each other using these questions. When students are done, poll them on their answers, focusing on the last three in particular. Are there any surprising answers?

Note (Reciclaje): The imperfect is first covered in *Estructura 7.1.*

■ Answers to this activity are in Appendix 2 at the back of your book.

Expansion (Para empezar): As preparation for the *Act. analíticas,* have students look at the true/false sentences that follow the timeline and circle verbs in the preterite and underline verbs in the imperfect.

Javier Bardem y Penélope Cruz

■ For more comparisons of preterite and imperfect, see **Para saber más 8.2** at the back of your book.

Note (Para saber más): *Para saber más 8.2* presents further explanation of the preterite and imperfect and includes the different meanings of *conocer, saber, poder,* and *querer* in these tenses.

Reciclaje

The imperfect

¿Cómo te vestías de niño o de niña? Usa el verbo entre paréntesis para completar las preguntas en el imperfecto. Luego contesta cada pregunta.

1. ¿Qué tipo de ropa ___llevabas___ (llevar)? _____
2. ¿Qué tipo de zapatos ___tenías___ (tener)? _____
3. ¿Quién te ___escogía___ (escoger) la ropa? _____
4. ¿Te ___gustaba___ (gustar) la ropa que te escogían? _____
5. ¿Quién te ___lavaba___ (lavar) la ropa? _____

8.2 Él modelaba y ella lo vio

The preterite and imperfect together

Para empezar...

Las carreras (*careers*) artísticas de los actores españoles Penélope Cruz y Javier Bardem se han cruzado (*have crossed*) en más de una ocasión. Basándote en la información de la tabla, indica cuáles de las siguientes oraciones son ciertas y cuáles son falsas.

	PENÉLOPE CRUZ	JAVIER BARDEM
1969		Nace el primero de marzo en las Islas Canarias.
1974	Nace el 28 de abril en Madrid.	
1975		Empieza a trabajar como actor.
1989	Empieza a trabajar como actriz.	
1992	Tiene su primer gran éxito con *Jamón, jamón,* una película sobre un modelo de ropa interior masculina.	Tiene su primer gran éxito con *Jamón, jamón,* una película sobre un modelo de ropa interior masculina.
2001	Empieza a salir con Tom Cruise.	
2004	Termina su relación con Tom Cruise.	Sale (*Appears*) en *Mar Adentro*.
2006	Sale en *Volver*.	
2007	Empieza una relación con Javier Bardem. Recibe la nominación para el Premio Óscar a la mejor actriz para *Volver*.	Empieza una relación con Penélope Cruz. Sale en *No Country for Old Men*. Gana un Premio Óscar.
2008	Sale en *Vicky Cristina Barcelona*. Gana un Premio Óscar.	Sale en *Vicky Cristina Barcelona*.
2010	Se casa con Javier Bardem.	Se casa con Penélope Cruz.
2011	Da a luz (*Gives birth*) a su hijo, Leonardo.	Nace su hijo, Leonardo.
2012		Sale en *Skyfall*.
2013	Da a luz a su hija, Luna.	Nace su hija, Luna.

		CIERTO	FALSO
1.	Cuando **nació** Penélope, Javier ya **tenía** cinco años.	☑	☐
2.	En 1982, Javier **trabajaba** como actor y Penélope como actriz.	☐	☑
3.	En 1992, los dos **tuvieron** su primer gran éxito, en la película *Jamón, jamón*.	☑	☐
4.	De 2001 a 2004, Penélope **tuvo** una relación romántica con Tom Cruise.	☑	☐
5.	Mientras **tenía** la relación con Tom Cruise, Penélope **salió** en *Volver*.	☐	☑
6.	Javier ya **tenía** una relación romántica con Penélope cuando **salió** en *No Country for Old Men*.	☑	☐
7.	Penélope y Javier **empezaron** a tener una relación en 2007 y **salieron** juntos en *Vicky Cristina Barcelona* en 2008.	☑	☐
8.	Penélope y Javier ya **estaban** casados (*were already married*) cuando ella **ganó** el Premio Óscar.	☐	☑
9.	Penélope y Javier **se casaron** en 2010 y su hijo Leo **nació** dos años después.	☐	☑
10.	Javier solo **tenía** un hijo cuando **salió** en *Skyfall*.	☑	☐

Actividades analíticas

1 You have seen the imperfect tense used to portray an event as happening over a period of time, where the exact starting and ending points don't matter.

Javier **tenía** una relación con Penélope.   *Javier was in a relationship with Penelope.*

You have seen that the preterite tense, in contrast, is used to portray an event as being completed at a specific point in time.

Javier **salió** en esa película en 2007.   *Javier appeared in that movie in 2007.*

These same basic principles apply when the two tenses are in the same sentence.

Javier ya **tenía** una relación con Penélope cuando **salió** en esa película.   *Javier was already in a relationship with Penelope when he appeared in that movie.*

The verb **tenía** is in the imperfect because it refers to the time period when they are already in the relationship. It is not important here when it started or if it ever ended. The verb **salió** is in the preterite because it portrays that action as being completed. The implication is that Javier was in the relationship first, and then while still in it, he appeared in the movie.

2 Here is one way the use of the preterite and imperfect tenses together can be visualized.

The imperfect verb portrays an ongoing action happening in the background, while the preterite verb portrays an action that "interrupts" it, something that happens and is completed while the background action is still going on. Here are some examples of this type.

Enrique **buscaba** una camisa en la tienda cuando María Elena lo **vio**.   *Enrique was looking for a shirt at the store when María Elena saw him.*

Cuando Pilar **vivía** en Caracas, **consiguió** su primer trabajo en Zara.   *When Pilar was living in Caracas, she got her first job at Zara.*

(Continues)

Suggestion (¿Por qué?): Give students the following "mini-stories" in Spanish: 1. *Juan caminaba. Gritaba.* 2. *Juan caminó. Gritó.* 3. *Juan caminaba. Gritó.* Have them express these ideas in English, so they can see how English tends to use more words to capture the same idea. Sample translations: 1. *Juan was walking. He was shouting.* 2. *Juan walked. Then he shouted.* 3. *Juan was walking. He shouted.* In both languages, of course, people typically elaborate stories with more words, but Spanish can clearly express a lot with very little.

■ Answers to these activities are in Appendix 2 at the back of your book.

¿Por qué?

In all cultures, talking about the past is important, whether you're discussing what you had for breakfast or what your ancestors did hundreds of years ago. So it makes sense that languages provide ways to make it easier to convey the details. Many languages are like Spanish and use verb tenses to make it clear whether two actions happened simultaneously, one after another, or with one action interrupting the other. These are important distinctions, and although all languages can express them in one way or another, Spanish does so in a particularly concise and helpful way.

Suggestion (Act. analíticas 2): Use the visual to help portray the meaning of these additional sentences, or create more sentences and have students apply them to the visual.

Suggestion (Act. analíticas 3, 4):
Contrast the two forms of *hablar* in *Act. analíticas 3* and *4:* With the preterite (*habló*), Enrique had already looked for a shirt when he started talking with María Elena. With the imperfect (*hablaba*), he is looking for a shirt and talking with María Elena at the same time (and it doesn't matter which he started doing first).

Expansion (Act. analíticas 4): Ask students if they can figure out why item 4 in *Para empezar* uses *tuvo* while item 5 uses *tenía*, even though they are talking about the same event (Answer: Item 4 portrays the relationship as being completed/finished, while item 5 leaves this open, because it is looking at a stage in the relationship when it was still ongoing.).

Autoprueba

Using what you now know about the preterite and the imperfect, tell which you would use for the verbs in the following situations.

1. two instantaneous actions that happened at the exact same moment: a person sneezing once just as another person entered the room
2. one action is happening and another interrupts it: we were shopping when you called
3. two actions, one that follows the other, and each has a definite end: she got dressed and went to the party
4. two actions that were taking place at the same time, their start and finish times are not relevant: he was trying on sweaters while she was looking at shoes

Fuimos a la playa porque **hacía** mucho calor.   *We went to the beach because it was really hot.*

Which sentences in **Para empezar** are also of this type, containing one verb in the imperfect and another in the preterite? _____ 1, 5, 6, 8, 10

3 When both verbs in a sentence are in the imperfect, it means that the two events happened at the same time, or at least overlapped.

Enrique **buscaba** una camisa en la tienda y **hablaba** con María Elena.   *Enrique was looking for a shirt at the store and talking with María Elena (at the same time).*

Cuando Pilar **vivía** en Caracas, **trabajaba** en Zara.   *When Pilar was living in Caracas, she worked at Zara. (Whether she continued working for the company afterwards is not relevant.)*

This can be visualized in the following way.

4 When both verbs in a sentence are preterite, it means that both events were completed, usually one after the other.

Enrique **buscó** una camisa y luego **habló** con María Elena.   *Enrique looked for a shirt and then spoke with María Elena.*

Pilar **fue** a Caracas y **trabajó** en Zara.   *Pilar went to Caracas and worked at Zara.*

Sequential actions in the past can be visualized like this.

Which sentences in **Para empezar** are an example of this? _____ 7, 9

Dana encontró los zapatos perfectos para la fiesta mientras paseaba por la avenida con sus amigas.

Respuestas: 1. preterite (sneezed), preterite (entered). **2.** imperfect (were shopping), preterite (called) **3.** preterite (got dressed), preterite (went to the party) **4.** imperfect (was trying on sweaters), imperfect (was looking at shoes)

El pretérito versus el imperfecto

THE PRETERITE: To show that an action was completed

Enrique **habló** con María Elena ayer en la tienda.	*Enrique spoke with María Elena yesterday at the store.*
Angélica **fue** estudiante en la Escuela Argentina de Moda en 2009.	*Angélica was a student at the Argentina School of Design in 2009 (but not after).*

THE IMPERFECT: To show that an action was ongoing (when beginning and end points are not important)

De niño, Enrique **hablaba** mucho con María Elena.	*As a child, Enrique spoke a lot with María Elena.*
Angélica **era** estudiante en la Escuela Argentina de Moda en 2009.	*Angélica was a student at the Argentina School of Design in 2009 (and possibly before/after).*

Para expresar dos acciones en el pasado

IMPERFECT AND PRETERITE TOGETHER: Imperfect shows ongoing action occurring in background. Preterite shows "interruption," something that happened while background was going on.

Enrique **buscaba** una camisa en la tienda cuando María Elena **lo vio.**	*Enrique was looking for a shirt at the store when María Elena saw him.*
Cuando Pilar **vivía** en Caracas, **consiguió** su primer trabajo en Zara.	*When Pilar was living in Caracas, she got her first job at Zara.*
Fuimos a la playa porque **hacía** mucho calor.	*We went to the beach because it was really hot.*

BOTH IMPERFECT: The actions are simultaneous (or overlapping).

Enrique **buscaba** una camisa mientras (*while*) **hablaba** con María Elena.	*Enrique was looking for a shirt while he was talking with María Elena. (at the same time)*
Cuando Angélica **era** estudiante, **trabajaba** en la universidad.	*When Angélica was a student, she worked at the university.*

BOTH PRETERITE: Two actions occur one after another.

Enrique **buscó** una camisa y luego **habló** con María Elena.	*Enrique looked for a shirt and then spoke with María Elena.*
Angélica primero **fue** estudiante y después **trabajó** en la misma universidad.	*Angélica first was a student and then she worked at the same university.*

¿Encontró la camisa que buscaba?

Expansion (Act. A): Ask students to explain why the *eventos históricos* are in the preterite and the descriptions of *la moda* are in the imperfect (Answer: The *eventos* are completed by the date given, while the descriptions of *la moda* are ongoing both before and after that date.)

Actividades prácticas

A. La historia y la moda Para cada año, escribe las letras que corresponden a lo que pasó y pasaba en el mundo hispano en ese año. **¡Atención!** Las imágenes te pueden ayudar.

AÑO	¿QUÉ PASÓ EN LA HISTORIA?	¿QUÉ PASABA EN EL MUNDO DE LA MODA?
1. 1492	b	e

2. 1821	f	g

3. 1939	h	c

4. 1973	d	a

a. Las mujeres usaban minifaldas (*miniskirts*) y trajes de pantalón. Los hombres (y también las mujeres) usaban pantalones de campana (*bell*). Los dos sexos llevaban zapatos de plataforma.

b. Los primeros españoles llegaron a América.

c. Las mujeres usaban faldas que iban hasta debajo (*below*) de las rodillas. También era muy común usar guantes. Los hombres llevaban trajes con corbatas anchas y sombreros Fedora.

d. El comandante Augusto Pinochet derrocó (*overthrew*) al gobierno de Salvador Allende en Chile, y empezó una dictadura (*dictatorship*) que duró (*lasted*) hasta 1990.

e. Las mujeres usaban vestidos largos con mangas (*sleeves*). Los hombres usaban camisas, pero no usaban pantalones. Llevaban medias (*stockings*) que llegaban hasta la cadera.

f. Simón Bolívar ganó la Batalla de Carabobo. Venezuela se independizó (*became independent*) de España.

g. Las mujeres llevaban corsés (*corsets*) con sus vestidos cónicos (*conical*) con mangas muy voluminosas (*bulky*). Los hombres usaban corsés con pantalón que llegaba hasta la rodilla y chaqueta, y también sombreros de dos picos (*two-cornered*).

h. Terminó la Guerra (*War*) Civil española y empezó la Segunda Guerra Mundial (*World*).

B. Más sobre Penélope Basándote en la información de la tabla, escoge el tiempo del verbo más adecuado en cada caso.

ALGUNOS EVENTOS EN LA VIDA DE PENÉLOPE CRUZ

1974 Nace en Madrid.

1980 Empieza a estudiar danza.

1989 Deja (*leaves*) la danza; empieza a trabajar como actriz.

1999 Sale en *Todo sobre mi madre,* su primera película con el director Pedro Almodóvar.

2000 Se hace vegetariana.

2005 Empieza una relación con Matthew McConaughey.

2006 Sale en *Volver;* termina la relación con Matthew McConaughey.

2007 Empieza una relación con Javier Bardem.

2008 Gana un Premio Óscar por su interpretación en *Vicky Cristina Barcelona.*

2010 Se casa con Javier Bardem.

2011 Nace su primer hijo, Leo.

1. En 1974, Penélope nació / nacía en Madrid.
2. En 1981, cuando Javier salió / salía en una película, Penélope estudió / estudiaba danza.
3. Estudió / Estudiaba danza por nueve años, y después empezó / empezaba a trabajar como actriz.
4. Primero salió / salía en *Todo sobre mi madre,* y luego se hizo / se hacía vegetariana.
5. Mientras estuvo / estaba en una relación con McConaughey, salió / salía en *Volver.*
6. Tuvo / Tenía una relación con Javier Bardem cuando ganó / ganaba el Premio Óscar.

C. La clase de actuación

PASO 1. En las siguientes oraciones, subraya los verbos que aparecen en el pretérito y encierra (*circle*) los verbos que aparecen en el imperfecto.

SITUACIÓN 1

a. Una persona se ponía los zapatos y la otra escribía una carta.
b. Mientras (*While*) una persona se ponía los zapatos, la otra escribió una carta.
c. Una persona se puso los zapatos mientras la otra escribía una carta.
d. Una persona se puso los zapatos y luego la otra escribió una carta.

SITUACIÓN 2

a. Una persona se ponía la corbata mientras la otra cantaba una canción.
b. Mientras una persona se ponía la corbata, la otra cantó una canción.
c. Una persona se puso la corbata mientas la otra cantaba una canción.
d. Una persona se puso la corbata y luego la otra cantó una canción.

SITUACIÓN 3

a. Una persona se probaba la chaqueta y la otra se lavaba los dientes.
b. Mientras una persona se probaba la chaqueta, la otra se lavó los dientes.
c. Una persona se probó la chaqueta mientras la otra se lavaba los dientes.
d. Una persona se probó la chaqueta y luego la otra se lavó los dientes.

 PASO 2. En parejas, escojan una oración y actúen lo que dice que pasó. Sus compañeros de clase tienen que adivinar qué oración escogieron y decidir si las acciones eran (1) simultáneas, (2) consecutivas o (3) si una acción interrumpió a la otra.

 PASO 3. En parejas, usen el modelo del **Paso 1** para crear cuatro oraciones nuevas. Las oraciones deben (*should*) tener los mismos (*same*) dos verbos en diferentes combinaciones del pretérito y el imperfecto.

Note (Act. C): You may wish to assign sentences to pairs of students in order to ensure that there will be a good variety of sentences "performed" when it comes time to act them out.

Suggestion (Act. C, Paso 2): Remind students to read their chosen sentence very carefully to make sure they understand it before deciding how to act it out.

Expansion (Act. C, Paso 3): Have students act out their situations in front of the class.

Note (Act. D): Item 7 is false. Despite his great fortune, Ortega lives in a simple apartment in A Coruña.

D. Amancio Ortega y Zara

Amancio Ortega es el presidente de Zara, una compañía española que tiene más de 1800 tiendas de ropa en más de setenta países del mundo. Ortega vive en A Coruña, una ciudad en el noroeste de España. Completa las siguientes oraciones con el tiempo (pretérito o imperfecto) más adecuado de los verbos entre paréntesis. Además, una oración es falsa. ¿Cuál piensas que es?

1. Amancio Ortega __llegó__ (llegar) a A Coruña cuando __tenía__ (tener) 14 años y su padre __trabajaba__ (trabajar) en los ferrocarriles.
2. En 1975, __abrió__ (abrir) en A Coruña su primera tienda, Zara. Esta tienda __se hizo__ (hacerse) muy popular porque __tenía__ (tener) versiones más económicas de ropa de diseñador.
3. A finales (*At the end*) de los años 80, la compañía Zara ya __tenía__ (tener) más de ochenta tiendas en España.
4. En 1988, Ortega __abrió__ (abrir) la primera tienda en el extranjero (*abroad*), en Portugal.
5. Ortega __creó__ (crear) un sistema en que pueden diseñar un producto nuevo y tenerlo en las tiendas en menos de quince días.

Amancio Ortega con la reina Letizia

6. En 1989, __entró__ (entrar) al mercado norteamericano, pero su presencia en Europa y Latinoamérica sigue siendo (*continues to be*) mucho más fuerte.
7. En 2010, Amancio Ortega __compró__ (comprar) una de las casas más grandes de Madrid.
8. En 2013, la revista Forbes __anunció__ (anunciar) que Amancio Ortega __era__ (ser) el tercer (*third*) hombre más rico del mundo, después de Carlos Slim Helu y Bill Gates.

Suggestion, (Act. E): Put students in groups of 3-4. Have each student write his/her own sentence and then read it to the rest of the group. The group then picks the best or funniest excuse and writes it on the board. Number these sentences on the board, and have the class vote on which is the best. Emphasize to students that they can follow the model closely.

E. Una excusa

¿Te gusta inventar excusas? Haz varias excusas para explicar por qué no pudiste terminar las siguientes actividades y compártelas con un compañero / una compañera. Tu excusa no tiene que ser verdadera (*truthful*), ¡pero sí tiene que ser creativa!

estudiar para el examen   hacer la tarea   lavar los platos   limpiar la casa

MODELO: Hacía mi tarea anoche, pero perdí mi lápiz y mientras lo buscaba, mi perro comió todas las hojas de tarea, entonces no pude terminar.

F. Un cuento de cuando era niño/a

Cuéntale a tu compañero/a algún evento verdadero o falso de cuando eras niño o niña, y luego pregúntale si piensa que es cierto o no. Usa la siguiente estructura en tu cuento.

- ¿Cuántos años tenías?
- ¿Dónde vivías?
- ¿Dónde estabas y qué ropa llevabas?
- ¿Qué pasó?

MODELO: Tenía 10 años y vivía en Nueva York con mis papás. Estaba en el parque y llevaba una camiseta y pantalones cortos porque era verano y hacía calor. Entonces vi que Rihanna caminaba cerca de mí. ¿Cierto o falso?

G. Cultura: Los modistas (*fashion designers*) de la República Dominicana y Cuba

PASO 1. Lee el texto sobre la República Dominicana y Cuba.

la República Dominicana　　**Cuba**

Cuando piensas en la ropa del Caribe, sin duda[a] viene a la mente la guayabera, una camisa tradicional para hombres, generalmente con cuatro bolsillos[b] y muchos pliegues[c] verticales. Pero los países caribeños como Cuba y República Dominicana han contribuido[d] mucho más al mundo de la moda. Un gran número de influyentes diseñadores de alta costura[e] son de esta región y ahora trabajan en los centros urbanos de moda en los Estados Unidos, Canadá, Europa, Asia y Latinoamérica. Adolfo Sardina y Óscar de la Renta son dos ejemplos.

El diseñador Adolfo Sardina

Adolfo Sardina nació en la provincia de Matanzas, Cuba, en 1933. Su madre murió en el parto[f] y por eso, durante su niñez Adolfo vivía con una tía. Ellos solían viajar[g] juntos y en un viaje a Europa, Adolfo conoció a la famosa diseñadora Coco Chanel. Inspirado por ese encuentro, Adolfo salió de Cuba y se fue a vivir a Nueva York, donde trabajaba como sombrerero.[h] En 1955, empezó a trabajar con telas[i] para diseñar vestidos elegantes. Entre sus clientes estaban la diseñadora Gloria Vanderbilt y la Duquesa de Windsor. Luego conoció a la primera dama Nancy Reagan y durante muchos años la vistió con sus trajes.

Óscar de la Renta nació en Santo Domingo en 1932. Cuando tenía 18 años, decidió ir a estudiar arte en Madrid. Allí se dio cuenta de[j] su interés en la moda y empezó a trabajar con varios diseñadores conocidos. En 1963, fue a Nueva York para colaborar con Elizabeth Arden y dos años después creó una empresa[k] de moda con su propio nombre. A lo largo de[l] su carrera, recibió muchos premios[m] por sus diseños. En 1977, lanzó[n] Óscar, un perfume para mujeres. En los años 80 y 90, lanzó varias otras fragancias, incluso para hombres.

[a]sin... *without doubt* [b]*pockets* [c]*pleats* [d]han... *have contributed* [e]alta... *haute couture* [f]*childbirth* [g]solían... *usually traveled* [h]*hat maker* [i]*fabrics* [j]se... *became aware of* [k]*company* [l]A... *Throughout* [m]*awards* [n]*launched*

PASO 2. Completa las oraciones con la forma apropiada del verbo en el pretérito o el imperfecto.

1. Cuando Adolfo ___nació___ (nacer) en Cuba, Óscar ___tenía___ (tener) 7 meses de edad y su familia ___vivía___ (vivir) en Santo Domingo.
2. Cuando ___estaba___ (estar) en Nueva York, Adolfo ___consiguió___ (conseguir* [*to get*]) su primer trabajo como sombrerero.
3. ___Era___ (Ser) el año 1955 cuando Adolfo ___decidió___ (decidir) diseñar vestidos.
4. Óscar ___fue___ (ir) a estudiar en España cuando ___tenía___ (tener) 18 años.
5. La Duquesa de Windsor y Gloria Vanderbilt ya (*already*) ___eran___ (ser) clientes de Adolfo cuando Nancy Reagan le ___pidió___ (pedir) diseñar un vestido para ella.
6. Mientras Adolfo ___trabajaba___ (trabajar) como sombrerero en Nueva York, Óscar y varios diseñadores ___colaboraban___ (colaborar) en Europa.
7. Ya ___existía___ (existir) el perfume Óscar para mujeres cuando el diseñador ___lanzó___ (lanzar) la colonia para hombres.

PASO 3. En parejas, contesten las preguntas y explíquense las respuestas.

1. Cuando gente talentosa como Adolfo Sardina y Óscar de la Renta se va de su país para vivir en otro, se llama «fuga de cerebros» (*brain drain*) y es un fenómeno muy común en muchos países. En el caso de Sardina y de la Renta, ¿por qué crees que se fueron?
2. ¿Qué piensas que siente (*feel*) la gente que se ha ido (*have left*) de su país natal (*native*)?
3. La fuga de cerebros no es siempre hacia (*toward*) los Estados Unidos, Canadá o Europa. En los últimos años, mucha gente joven de todas partes del mundo se ha ido a vivir a la Ciudad de México, por las oportunidades económicas y culturales que ofrece (*offers*). ¿A ti te interesa vivir en otro país por razones (*reasons*) profesionales o económicas? ¿Por qué sí o por qué no?

*Conseguir follows the same pattern as **seguir.**

Suggestions (Act. G, Paso 1):
- Bring in a *guayabera* shirt or a photo of one for students who might no know it by name.
- Point out that *trajes* in this context refers to formal gowns.

⟳ Reciclaje

Direct and indirect object pronouns

Empareja cada palabra con la definición lógica. Luego completa la definición con el pronombre **lo, la, los** o **le**.

1. __d__ el abrigo
2. __e__ el anillo
3. __f__ la camisa
4. __b__ los guantes
5. __a__ el pantalón
6. __c__ el sombrero

a. __Lo__ usas en la parte inferior del cuerpo.
b. __Los__ usas para proteger (*protect*) las manos.
c. __Lo__ pones en la cabeza.
d. __Lo__ usas para protegerte contra (*against*) el frío.
e. __Le__ das esto a tu novio/a cuando te casas.
f. __La__ usas para tapar la parte superior del cuerpo.

■ Answers to this activity are in Appendix 2 at the back of your book.

Note (Para saber más): An explanation of double-object pronoun usage, as well as *lo* + *adjective,* may be found in the *Para saber más 8.3.*

■ For additional uses and placement of object pronouns, see **Para saber más 8.3** at the back of your book.

■ Answers to these activities are in Appendix 2 at the back of your book.

Autoprueba

Using what you now know about the placement of direct and indirect object pronouns with infinitives, determine what object pronoun would be used for the following sentences, then express each sentence using the two possible placements of the object pronoun.

1. Quiero comprar estas botas.
2. Necesitamos ver los guantes de cerca (*up close*).
3. ¿Vas a llevar tu chaqueta nueva?

llevar? ¿Vas a llevarla?
de cerca. **3.** la: ¿La vas a
de cerca. Necesitamos verlos
2. los: Los necesitamos ver
comprar. Quiero comprarlas.
Respuestas: 1. las: Las quiero

8.3   ¡Lo voy a comprar!

Object pronoun placement with infinitives

Para empezar...

Empareja a cada persona con su reacción al ver (*after seeing*) la ropa mencionada.

PERSONA Y ROPA

1. __e__ Un muchacho de 15 años: una corbata muy seria, pero barata
2. __b__ Un joven de 25 años en su primer trabajo profesional: un traje
3. __a__ Una muchacha de 17 años: un anillo y un collar
4. __d__ Una estudiante de 20 años: unas sandalias
5. __c__ Un estudiante de 22 años: unos zapatos de Zara

REACCIONES

a. «No **los** necesito, pero **los** voy a comprar.»
b. «No **lo** quiero, pero **lo** tengo que comprar.»
c. «**Los** quiero tener y **los** voy a comprar. Como (*Since*) son negros, ahora necesito calcetines negros también.»
d. «**Las** tengo que comprar, porque voy a la playa y allí no quiero usar zapatos.»
e. «**La** puedo comprar, pero ¿para qué **la** quiero?»

Actividades analíticas

1 As you saw in **Estructura 6.3** and **7.2,** direct and indirect object pronouns generally appear before verbs that are conjugated, whether the verbs are in the present, preterite, or imperfect tense. The object pronoun in these cases is written as a separate word.

Lo quiero.   *I want it.*

Le di el libro ayer.   *I gave the book to him/her yesterday.*

2 Object pronouns can appear after infinitive verb forms; in this case, the infinitive and the object pronoun are written as a single word.

Es importante leer**lo**.   *It's important to read it.*

Es necesario dar**le** el libro.   *It's necessary to give the book to him/her.*

3 When a conjugated verb is followed by an infinitive, the object pronoun may be placed either before the conjugated verb or after the infinitive: **¿Las camisas? Las queremos ver. / Queremos verlas.** Use the sentences in **Para empezar** to find examples of the following expressions, and write the expressions and pronouns here.

a. **voy a** + *infinitive*   Los voy a comprar.
b. **quiero** + *infinitive*   Los quiero tener.
c. **tengo que** + *infinitive*   Lo/Las tengo que comprar.
d. **puedo** + *infinitive*   La puedo comprar.

4   Now write these same expressions, but with the pronoun placed after and attached to the infinitive verb.

a. **voy a** + *infinitive*   Voy a comprarlos.
b. **quiero** + *infinitive*   Quiero comprarlos.
c. **tengo que** + *infinitive* Tengo que comprarlo/las.
d. **puedo** + *infinitive*   Puedo comprarla.

Actividades prácticas

A. Corbatas, sombreros y zapatos

Para cada oración, escribe **C** si se trata de (*it has to do with*) corbatas, **S** si se trata de sombreros y **Z** si se trata de zapatos. Hay dos oraciones que no se tratan de ninguno de estos objetos. En esos casos, escribe **N. ¡Atención!** Presta (*Pay*) atención a los pronombres de objeto directo e indirecto.

1. __Z__ En los restaurantes, casi siempre los tienes que usar.
2. __C__ No es común usarlas cuando haces deporte.
3. __Z__ Es común comprarlos en tiendas especializadas que se llaman zapaterías.
4. __N__ Es muy común usarlas cuando vas a la playa.
5. __S__ No los puedes comprar en muchas tiendas de ropa, porque mucha gente no los usa.
6. __Z__ Los tienes que usar para hacer casi cualquier (*any*) tipo de deporte. En ese caso, se llaman «tenis» o «zapatillas».
7. __C__ Los hombres las tienen que usar en muchos tipos de eventos formales.
8. __C__ Es común comprarlas en los grandes almacenes.
9. __S__ Tradicionalmente, los caballeros (*gentlemen*) no pueden llevarlos puestos (*put on*) dentro (*inside*) de un edificio.
10. __N__ Los puedes comprar en las bibliotecas.

Tengo muchas corbatas. Me las pongo para ir al trabajo.

B. Preguntas y respuestas

Escucha las preguntas y escoge la respuesta más adecuada para cada una.

a. __5__ No, pero me van a regalar algo mañana.
b. __2__ No, pero lo tengo que comprar para mañana.
c. __4__ No, pero la tenemos que comprar para mañana.
d. __7__ Las voy a poner en el coche.
e. __6__ No. La puedo hacer mañana.
f. __1__ No, pero voy a regalarle un collar esta noche.
g. __3__ Están en el coche todavía, pero los vamos a poner en la habitación (*room*).

Script (Act. B): 1. *¿Ya le regalaste algo a Josefina?* **2.** *¿Ya compraste el anillo?* **3.** *¿Dónde están los trajes que compraron?* **4.** *¿Compraron la falda?* **5.** *¿Te regalaron algo en el trabajo?* **6.** *¿Ya hiciste la tarea?* **7.** *¿Dónde vas a poner las corbatas?*

C. Ya no sirve

¿Qué puede hacer una persona con objetos que ya no necesita? ¿Venderlos (*Sell them*)? ¿Guardarlos (*Save them*)? ¿Donarlos (*Donate them*)? ¿Tirarlos (*Throw them away*)? ¿Reciclarlos? ¿Algo más? En parejas, túrnense para escoger un objeto de la lista y pregúntense qué va a hacer con cada uno. Apunten sus respuestas.

- este libro
- tu teléfono
- tus lentes, si usas lentes
- tu computadora
- tus zapatos
- tu cepillo de dientes

MODELO: E1: ¿Qué vas a hacer con este libro?
E2: Voy a guardarlo.
E1: Yo no. Yo voy a venderlo. *o* Yo también, pero Alicia lo va a reciclar.

D. ¿Cómo puedes usar este libro?

Obviamente puedes usar este libro para estudiar, pero, ¿para qué más? ¿Y cómo puedes usar tu mochila y tus zapatos? En parejas, piensen en otras maneras de usarlos.

MODELO: Este libro: Puedo usarlo para protegerme (*protect myself*) contra los criminales.
Mi mochila: Puedo usarla como sombrero.

Este libro: _____

Mi mochila: _____

Mis zapatos: _____

Suggestion (Act. C): Assign students an object and a fixed number of classmates they need to ask, and tell them to sit down when they are done. Create a chart on the board with the 6 objects as headings for columns and ask some students to write the most popular answer (e.g., *Guardarlo, Venderlos, Reciclarla,* and so on) to their question under the appropriate heading. Are there any interesting differences among the six objects?

Suggestion, Act. D: Create 3 columns on the board (for *este libro, mi mochila,* and *mis zapatos*). Tell students to choose their best answer out of the 3 and write it on the board in the appropriate column. Then go over all the sentences in each column, asking students to choose the most creative one.

Suggestion, Act. D: If students need more vocabulary in order to describe how they would use their objects, remind them to use "*¿Cómo se dice... ?*" to ask for help.

¡Leamos!

Conceptos que cautivan°   *captivate*

Antes de leer

En grupos de dos o tres, conversen sobre las siguientes preguntas.

Suggestion (Antes de leer): Have groups choose 1 or 2 questions to answer, then have them present their answers to the class. Remind them to practice and prepare for these in-class presentations as if they were the brief but professional presentations they'll have to do frequently in meetings once in the workforce.

1. Describe tu estilo de vestirte. ¿Es un estilo formal o informal? ¿Es profesional o relajado? ¿cómodo (*comfortable*) o lujoso (*luxurious*)? ¿de moda? ¿diseñador? ¿único (*unique*)?

2. ¿Cuáles factores consideras al comprar (*when buying*) ropa? ¿Consideras la talla / el número? ¿Piensas en cómo te queda? ¿en la marca? ¿el color? ¿la tela (*fabric*)? ¿el precio? ¿otros factores? De ellos, ¿cuáles son los tres factores que te importan más?

3. ¿Cuáles diseñadores de ropa puedes nombrar?

4. ¿Qué factores crees que les importan más a los diseñadores al crear ropa para el público?

5. ¿Dónde crees que encuentran la inspiración los diseñadores?

A leer

Lee el artículo sobre **Ángel Sánchez**, un diseñador venezolano. Luego decide si cada una de las frases se refiere a Ángel Sánchez o a la actriz y activista, **Eva Longoria**.

Conceptos que cautivan

¿Moda arquitectónica[a]? ¿Vestidos construidos? ¿Prendas conceptualizadas? ¿Conceptos a medida[b]? Pues, claro.

La energía y el brío[c] de los diseños[d] de Ángel Sánchez fascinan a las más famosas, como Taylor Swift, Eva Longoria, Beyoncé, Brooke Shields y Sandra Bullock.

Estas y muchas más estrellas empezaron a cautivarse por las creaciones del modista venezolano cuando se estableció en Nueva York en 1997. El ingenio de sus diseños brota[e] de sus experiencias en la casa de su niñez, de sus estudios y carrera en la arquitectura y de una cierta chispa creativa regalada del cielo.[f]

Sánchez nació en Valera, Venezuela, donde se crió en la modistería[g] de su madre. Desde muy temprano, el mundo del diseño impregnó[h] su mundo e imaginación, pero siguió una carrera en arquitectura. En los años 90, volvió al mundo de su juventud, el diseño. Pero no dejó atrás[i] su formación y sus destrezas[j] arquitectónicas.

Como la conceptualización de los edificios[k] de una comunidad, las colecciones de Sánchez se estructuran alrededor[l] de un concepto unificador.[m] «Concepto es la palabra más clara que define cómo yo asumo[n] mi trabajo. A mí me gusta no solo hacer el vestido bonito, sino que[ñ] el vestido te diga[o] algo. Todo tiene su explicación, su concepto, técnicamente y creativamente hablando.» Cada prenda de sus colecciones tiene un principio y un final,[p] y se relaciona con las otras prendas de la colección.

Pero el diseñador no se limita a sus colecciones. Sandra Bullock lo buscó para diseñar su vestido de boda y otras lo han buscado con el deseo de lucir[q] una de sus creaciones en la alfombra[r]

Eva Longoria en un diseño de Sánchez en los premios ALMA

[a]*architectural* [b]*a... custom-made* [c]*spirit* [d]*designs* [e]*springs, flows* [f]*chispa... God-sent creative spark* [g]*dress shop* [h]*impregnated, imbued* [i]*behind* [j]*skills* [k]*buildings* [l]*around* [m]*unifying* [n]*take on, approach* [ñ]*sino... but rather* [o]*te... tell you* [p]*principio... beginning and an end*

Ángel Sánchez

roja u otra ocasión especial, ¿De dónde vienen los conceptos para estos vestidos a medida? De las clientas mismas.ˢ Sánchez primero escucha a sus clientas para entender su personalidad y sus gustos.ᵗ

El concepto de su última colección se inspiró en la arenaᵘ y en el desierto. En muchos aspectos, el diseñador salió de su elemento. Sánchez es famoso por sus elegantes y suntuosos trajes de noche y vestidos de novia, pero esta colección es más casual, «prendas que no necesiten una ocasión para ser usadas, que puedan estar en el clóset listasᵛ para salir». Además, la arquitectura de esta colección se basó en una tela más ruda:ʷ el lino. Sánchez quiso retarse,ˣ explorar materiales desconocidosʸ y crecer como artista.

ᵃto wear, show off ʳcarpet ˢthemselves ᵗtaste ᵘsand ᵛready
ʷtela... course cloth ˣchallenge himself ʸunfamiliar

	Ángel Sánchez	Eva Longoria
1. Luce (*wears, shows off*) un elegante vestido en los Emmys.	☐	☑
2. Es de Venezuela, pero vive en Nueva York.	☑	☐
3. Crea vestidos y otra ropa.	☑	☐
4. Quiere llevar ropa única en eventos especiales.	☐	☑
5. Su preparación en la arquitectura forma la base de su trabajo actual (*current*).	☑	☐
6. Cada traje de su colección tiene algo en común con los otros trajes de la misma colección.	☑	☐
7. Le inspiran el desierto, la playa y la arena.	☑	☐

Después de leer

Contesta las siguientes preguntas según lo que leíste en la lectura.

1. __d__ Las creaciones de Ángel Sánchez son resultado de:
   a. su formación académica
   b. su niñez en la modistería de su madre
   c. su talento creativo
   d. todas las respuestas son correctas

2. __b__ ¿Cuál es la mejor descripción de las colecciones de Ángel Sánchez?
   a. Las colecciones son como los planes arquitectónicos para una ciudad entera.
   b. Todos los elementos de una colección se relacionan.
   c. Primero que nada, los vestidos son bonitos.
   d. Todas las colecciones tienen un principio y un final.

3. Según Sánchez, ¿cuál es la palabra que mejor describe sus colecciones? ¿Por qué usa esa palabra? concepto; porque cuentan una historia

4. Además de sus colecciones, ¿qué tipo de ropa diseña?
   vestidos de boda, vestidos para llevar en la alfombra roja u otra ocasión especial.

5. Si Sánchez diseña algo especial para una de sus clientas famosas, ¿de dónde vienen las ideas para sus vestidos? ¿por qué? de las clientas mismas; porque quiere diseñar algo que refleje la personalidad y los gustos de cada una

6. ¿Cómo es diferente su nueva colección de lo típico de Sánchez?
   Es más casual, usa lino y la ropa es para cualquier ocasión y no una ocasión especial.

7. ¿Cuáles son los elementos inspiradores de la nueva colección?
   la arena y el desierto

¡Escuchemos!

Lo tradicional y lo moderno de los indios kuna

Antes de escuchar

PASO 1. Vas a escuchar a Marlina hablar de las molas, una artesanía (*handicraft*) típica de Panamá. Primero, empareja lo que dice Marlina con su explicación más adecuada.

Note (Conéctate al mundo hispano): In order to conform to the phonological requirements of the native Kuna language, the *k* was dropped from their alphabet and replaced with *g* in 2011, changing the spelling to *Guna*. However, most resources still use the spelling *Kuna* and the spelling remains inconsistent even within the Kuna communities.

MARLINA DICE

1. __d__ «Nosotros tenemos tres tipos de molas.»

2. __e__ «Las antiguas son de dos telas (*fabrics*) y son puras figuras geométricas.»

3. __b__ «Las tradicionales vienen de diferentes capas (*layers*). Pueden tener hasta cinco capas: se van cortando (*cutting*) para que la otra capa vaya saliendo y saliendo... »

4. __c__ «La nueva mola comercial que ha salido (*has come out*) es cosida (*sewed*) a mano, pero no se corta la capa: uno le pone la figura para ir cosiéndola encima (*on top*) de la tela negra.»

5. __a__ «Mi mamá no puede usar esta clase de mola para su vestuario (ropa) porque no tienen los diseños ni los colores tradicionales.»

EXPLICACIÓN

a. Marlina dice que el vestuario tradicional Kuna usa la mola con colores y diseños (*designs*) tradicionales; las molas que venden a los turistas son diferentes.

b. Marlina explica cómo se hace la mola tradicional de varias capas.

c. Marlina dice que la mola comercial no tiene varias capas.

d. Marlina va a describir diferentes tipos de molas.

e. Marlina dice que no hay animales ni flores en las molas antiguas.

CONÉCTATE AL MUNDO HISPANO

Marlina es de la comarca (región) **Kuna Yala,** también conocida como San Blas, una comunidad indígena (*indigenous*) de Panamá. La gente Kuna Yala tiene sus propias costumbres, tradiciones, cultura e idioma, pero también tiene éxito comercializando sus productos. Uno de los productos es la **mola,** un textil tradicional que se usa para la ropa femenina. Cada mola tiene varias capas (*layers*) de tela (*fabric*) colorida cosida (*sewn*) y cortada (*cut*) para revelar muchos colores y figuras.

Note (Antes de escuchar): Spanish is not Marlina's native language, and she is inconsistent in her choice of gender for *mola* (sometimes treating it as masculine and other times as feminine). Beginning students are unlikely to notice this. You may want to point out, though, that there are hundreds of thousands of Latin Americans like Marlina who speak an indigenous language as their first language and learned Spanish later.

PASO 2. Ahora lee las citas (*quotes*) de Marlina y decide si cada cita se refiere a una **tradición** cultural o a la **comercialización** de sus productos.

1. «Estas [molas] son tradicionales, ellas vienen de diferentes capas. Tienen... Pueden tener hasta cinco capas, se van cortando y se van, para que la otra capa vaya saliendo y saliendo... »
   ☑ tradición   ☐ comercialización

2. «[La nueva mola comercial] es cosida a mano, pero no es elaborada por corte: [...] [U]no le va poniendo la figura para ir cosiéndola encima de la tela negra.»
   ☐ tradición   ☑ comercialización

3. «Siempre son estos y estos colores que representan más el vestuario Kuna.»
   ☑ tradición   ☐ comercialización

A escuchar

Mira y escucha las veces que sea necesario. Luego contesta las preguntas.

Video track (A escuchar): This video clip can be found on the DVD to accompany *Conéctate: Cap. 8,* Track 3.

1. __b__ Las molas antiguas son...
   a. de diferentes capas —hasta cinco capas en total.
   b. dos telas con figuras geométricas.
   c. una tela negra con una figura cosida a mano encima.

2. __a__ Las molas tradicionales para los vestuarios son...
   a. de diferentes capas —hasta cinco capas en total.
   b. dos telas con figuras geométricas.
   c. una tela negra con una figura cosida a mano encima.

Marlina y su primo nos enseñan sus molas.

3. __c__ ¿Cuáles son los colores principales de la mola tradicional que muestra Marlina?
   a. negro, morado, rosado y verde
   b. negro, rojo oscuro y anaranjado
   c. rojo oscuro, anaranjado y verde
   d. rojo oscuro, morado y rosado

Suggestion (A escuchar): Remind students that excerpts straight from the video appeared in the **Antes de escuchar** activities to provide background information before listening to this challenging video clip. At this point, they should be able to pick up just enough information to answer the 7 questions—*if* they listen various times and with pauses. They should not be expected to understand every word Marlina says. Encourage them to try to get the gist and main ideas rather than every word.

4. __c__ Las nuevas molas comerciales son...
   a. de diferentes capas —hasta cinco capas en total.
   b. dos telas con figuras geométricas.
   c. una tela negra con una figura cosida a mano encima.

5. __a__ ¿Cuáles son los colores principales de la mola comercial que muestra Marlina?
   a. negro, morado, rosado y verde
   b. negro, rojo oscuro y anaranjado
   c. rojo oscuro, anaranjado y verde
   d. rojo oscuro, morado y rosado

6. De los tres tipos de molas, ¿cuáles son hechas a mano? todas

7. ¿Qué tipo de mola *no* muestra Marlina: la antigua, la tradicional, o la comercial? No muestra la mola antigua.

Después de escuchar

En grupos, hagan un plan para popularizar la mola (u otro producto cultural que conocen) en su país. ¿Qué hacen con la mola? ¿Cómo la van a presentar al público? ¿Cómo la van a explicar? ¿Dónde la van a vender? Compartan sus ideas con el resto de la clase para ver quiénes tienen el mejor plan.

MODELO: Vamos a poner la mola en la pared de nuestros dormitorios y así se populariza la mola entre los estudiantes universitarios.

Videoscript (A escuchar): MARLINA: *Nosotros tenemos tres tipos de molas: Unos que son bastantes antiguos que son como de dos telas, solamente coses dos telas y son puras figuras geométricas, ahora, segundo tenemos esta mola, ellas usan el vest... para vestuario, y son todas... estas son tradicionales, ellas vienen de diferentes capas. Tiene... Puede tener hasta cinco capas, se van cortando y se van, para que la otra capa vaya saliendo y saliendo. Y ahora la última tenemos esta, está igual es cosida a mano, pero no es elaborada por corte, esta es cosida encima, como usted lo ve, la tela negra es el que está abajo y arriba vienen las telas estas, que solo uno le va poniendo la figura para ir cosiéndola encima de la tela negra. Igual, esta no, esta se tiene que ir cortando, cortando, para que la otra tela de abajo vaya saliendo, vaya saliendo. Por eso esta es la nueva mola que ha salido comercial. La... Igual la gente lo compra porque es todo hecho a mano, pero el que sí tiene significado... Mi mamá no puede usar esta... esta clase de mola como pa' su vestuario, no, ¿por qué? Porque nunca se ha visto eso, siempre son estos y estos colores que representan más el vestuario Kuna.*

¡Escribamos!

Ser testigo°   *witness*

En la vida diaria, especialmente al leer y escribir, es importante ser buen observador / buena observadora. Para ayudarte a practicar esta habilidad, en esta actividad vas a ser testigo de un robo imaginario. Vas a observar todos los detalles que puedas sobre «los sospechosos» (*suspects*) y luego usar esa información para formar una descripción detallada para las autoridades.

ESTRATEGIA

Background description and details

Background descriptions help to set the scene for the action, allowing readers to better understand the environment and appreciate the significance of highlighted events. The details can help readers paint a more nuanced mental picture of the piece they are reading, bringing the scene to life and making it easier to remember.

Antes de escribir

Primero, a escondidas (*secretly*), observa la ropa que llevan tres compañeros de clase. Luego inventa una descripción de lo que hacía cada uno antes de que empezara la clase (*before class started*). **¡Atención!** Incluye detalles sobre el color de la ropa y los accesorios que llevan.

Nombre	Ropa que lleva	¿Qué hacía? / ¿Qué pasaba en el salón de clase?
Gladys	*los jeans azules; una camiseta verde; un suéter gris; los pendientes verdes...*	*Ponía su mochila debajo del escritorio mientras escribía un text a una amiga...*

A escribir

Imagínate que alguien le robó un diccionario de español del salón de clase antes de clase. Inventa una historia: describe «el lugar del crimen» y los estudiantes que observaste cerca del diccionario. Usando la información de **Antes de escribir,** escribe dos párrafos. En el primer párrafo describe el escenario.

- ¿Qué pasaba en el salón de clase?   ■ ¿Qué ropa llevaban los sospechosos?

En el segundo párrafo, describe las acciones que viste.

- ¿Qué hizo cada uno de los sospechosos y cuándo?

Termina tu historia con una conclusión. Por ejemplo: **Creo que _____ robó el diccionario porque...**

Suggestion (Después de leer): If group dynamics of your class allow, ask volunteers to read their essays out loud. Do they frame their classmates (or the instructor)? If so, who do they think is the robber?

Después de escribir

Revisa tu ensayo. Luego intercambia ensayos con un compañero / una compañera para evaluarlos. Lee el ensayo de tu compañero/a y determina si falta información necesaria. Lee de nuevo el ensayo con cuidado, subrayando todos los verbos conjugados en el imperfecto y encerrando todos los verbos conjugados en el pretérito. Verifica que...

- ☐ usa el imperfecto para describir en el pasado.
- ☐ usa el pretérito para hablar de las acciones que ocurrieron en el pasado.
- ☐ hay concordancia entre sujetos y verbos.
- ☐ se puede entender qué ropa se describe en el ensayo.
- ☐ usa adjetivos descriptivos para describir la ropa.
- ☐ hay concordancia entre sustantivos y adjetivos (género y número).

Después de revisar el ensayo de tu compañero/a, devuélveselo. Mira tu propio ensayo para ver los cambios que tu compañero/a te recomienda y haz las revisiones necesarias.

👥📹 ¡Hablemos!

Un pase de modelos°

fashion runway

Antes de hablar

En grupos, practiquen como si presentaran (*as if you were presenting*) un desfile de moda. Cada persona debe describir la ropa de otro miembro del grupo. Cambien de papeles (*Change roles*) hasta que todos hayan sido (*have been*) modelos y presentadores.

A hablar

Ahora, escojan a una persona de cada grupo para ser el/la modelo y otra para ser el presentador / la presentadora en un pase de modelos de la clase. El/La modelo debe tener ropa variada y complementos.

Los modelos salen del salón de clase y esperan en el pasillo. Un(a) modelo entra a la vez. Cada presentador(a) presenta el/la modelo de **otro** equipo. Los otros estudiantes son reporteros y deben tomar apuntes. Después del desfile, en grupos de pequeños, escriban un resumen lo que vieron.

- ¿Qué describe el presentador / la presentadora?
- ¿Falta algo (*Is something missing*)? ¿Qué?
- ¿Incluye detalles además de nombrar las prendas de ropa?

Después de hablar

De toda la clase, ¿quién fue el/la mejor modelo? ¿el mejor presentador / la mejor presentadora? Defiende tu opinión con detalles de los apuntes que tomaste para la sección de **A hablar.**

Suggestion (¡Hablemos!): If your students don't feel comfortable being "models" for this activity, choose photos of famous Hispanics to show to the class or have students bring in photos of people to describe.

Note (Antes de hablar): Encourage students to use expressions with *¡Qué… !* including the expressions from the *Comunicación* section in this chapter and in *Cap. 4.*

Suggestion (A hablar): Require students to practice, prepare and polish these presentations so that they are both brief and engaging. Assign a presentation grade if possible.

CONÉCTATE AL MUNDO PROFESIONAL

Public speaking in your professional life will probably include succinct, articulate summaries during meetings or brief professional phone calls to give and obtain information. Employers will be looking for candidates who possess these skills. Language classes are a great opportunity to practice for that kind of presentation. Practice, prepare, and polish before reporting back from group work!

Conéctate al cine

Película: *Volver* (drama, España, 2006)
Director: Pedro Almodóvar

Sinopsis:
Sisters Raimunda (Penélope Cruz) and Sole (Lola Dueñas) have a strained relationship, but they are united by grief over their mother's death a few years earlier, and now they must deal with the death of their Aunt Paula. To make matters worse, Raimunda has a corpse in the freezer that she must somehow dispose of. These circumstances result in a film that is an unlikely mix of comedy, mystery, and touching drama. Penélope Cruz was nominated for an Academy Award for her performance as Raimunda.

Escena (54:10–58:54):
Suggestion (Escena): Turn subtitles off. Stop the film when the screen goes black.
Raimunda and her daughter stop by Sole's apartment to use the bathroom. Sole's odd behavior and an unexpected smell make Raimunda suspicious, and she begins snooping around the apartment. She is surprised by what she finds and accuses Sole of taking their late aunt's possessions for her own use.

Expresiones útiles

lavabo	bathroom
me meo	I've gotta pee!
olor a pedo	the smell of passed gas
peyéndose a culo lleno	passing a huge amount of gas
la bata	bathrobe
los muertos	the dead
maleta/maletilla	suitcase / small suitcase
joyero	jewelry box
¡Qué poca vergüenza!	What little shame (you have)!
¡No pienses mal!	Don't think badly (of me)!
¡No te vayas así!	Don't go like that!

Suggestion (Antes de ver): If students have trouble coming up with ideas, some possibilities are: *la vendo, la tiro a la basura, la regalo, la guardo siempre,* and so on.

■ For copyright reasons, the feature film clips referenced in **Conéctate al cine** have have not been provided by the publisher. Each of these films is readily available through retailers or online rental sites such as Amazon, iTunes, or Netflix.

Antes de ver

La ropa que usamos es algo tan ligado (*bound*) a nuestra identidad que es difícil saber qué hacer con esa ropa cuando ya no nos queda. ¿Qué haces tú con la ropa que ya no necesitas?

A ver

Lee las **Expresiones útiles** y mira la escena. Luego contesta las preguntas.

1. El cinturón y los zapatos de la hija, y el bolso de Raimunda son todos del mismo color. ¿De qué color son?
   anaranjados/rojos

2. ¿Qué le dice Sole a la hija de Raimunda?
   Dice: «Te voy a cortar un poquito ___el pelo___».

3. Raimunda encuentra ropa de su madre sobre la cama. ¿Qué tipo de ropa dice que es?
   a. una bata   b. una falda   c. un vestido

4. Según Raimunda, ¿qué hay que hacer con la ropa de los muertos?
   Raimunda dijo: «Hay que ___regalarla___».

5. Cuando Raimunda ve el joyero, ¿qué le pregunta a Sole?
   ¿Qué pensabas hacer con esto?

6. Según Sole, ¿ella trajo la maleta de la tía a la casa? ____no____

7. Sole empieza a dar una explicación (*explanation*), pero no termina. ¿Qué dice?
   «Cuando ___llegué a casa de la tía Paula...___»

Después de ver

Esta escena de la película trata (*treats*) varios temas un poco delicados: el funcionamiento (*functioning*) del cuerpo humano, las pertenencias (*belongings*) de los muertos y los conflictos entre dos hermanas. En tu país, ¿las películas tratan estos temas de la misma manera? Explica tu respuesta y da ejemplos.

Expansion (A ver): Q1: Ask students why they think the director used the same color for these three objects, and why he chose this particular color. **Q3:** The word *bata* is often used to mean *bathrobe,* but the clothing seen here doesn't look like a bathrobe. Ask students what it looks like to them. When do you think the mother wore this? Note that in many countries, women traditionally wear a kind of smock to do work around the house. **Q5–7:** When students answer item 5, have them explain why Raimunda uses the imperfect. When answering items 6 and 7, have them explain why Sole uses the preterite.

VOCABULARIO

Now that I have completed the chapter, I can . . .

☐ say how great something is
☐ use polite expressions in appropriate contexts
☐ talk about clothing and fashion
☐ talk about the human body
☐ express how clothing fits
☐ express events in the past
☐ discuss the fashion world and industry

Comunicación

¡Qué bárbaro/bien/ chévere/chido/chulo/ estupendo/fenomenal/ guay/padre!	How cool/awesome!
¡Qué...!	How . . . !
aburrido	How boring!
malo	That's terrible!
pesado	How annoying!
pésimo	That's awful!
Repaso: Lo siento.	
Con permiso.	Excuse me.
Disculpa/Disculpe/ Disculpen...	Excuse me . . .
Perdón/Perdona/ Perdone/Perdonen.	Sorry. / Excuse me. / Pardon me.
¿Puedo pasar?	Excuse me. (May I pass by/enter?)
¡Claro (que sí)!	Of course!
¡Cómo no!	Sure!
Con mucho gusto.	With pleasure.
Por supuesto.	Of course.
Sí, gracias.	Yes, please.
Gracias (por + noun/verb).	Thank you (for . . .).
Sí/No, gracias.	Yes/No, thank you.
Pasa/Pase/Pasen.	Come in.; Go ahead.
¡Pura vida!	Cool! /Awesome!
Repaso: No puedo.	

¿Qué llevas?	What are you wearing?
el abrigo	coat
el anillo	ring
el bolso	purse
la bufanda	scarf
los calcetines	socks
el calzón (pl. los calzones)	underwear
la camisa	shirt
la camiseta	t-shirt
el cinturón	belt
el collar	necklace
la corbata	tie
el desfile de moda	fashion show
el/la diseñador(a)	designer
la falda	skirt
la gorra	(baseball) cap
el gorro	knitted hat
los guantes	gloves
los lentes	(eye)glasses
la marca	brand
de marca	brand-name
el número	number; size (shoes)
el pantalón	pants
los pantalones cortos	shorts
el paraguas	umbrella
los pendientes	earrings
la prenda (de ropa)	item (of clothing)
la pulsera	bracelet
la rebaja	sale, price reduction
el reloj	watch
la ropa interior	undergarments
las sandalias	sandals
el sombrero	hat
el sujetador	bra
los tacones	high-heeled shoes
la talla	size (clothing)
los tenis	tennis shoes
el traje	suit; formal gown
el traje de baño	bathing suit
el vestido	dress
los zapatos	shoes

Cognados: los accesorios, la blusa, la chaqueta, el descuento, los jeans, el pijama, el suéter

El cuerpo humano / The human body

El cuerpo humano	The human body
la boca	mouth
el brazo	arm
la cabeza	head
la cadera	hip
la cara	face
el codo	elbow
el cuello	neck
el dedo	finger
los dientes	teeth
el hombro	shoulder
los labios	lips
la mano	hand
la nariz	nose
el ojo	eye
la oreja	ear
el pecho	chest; breast
el pelo	hair
el pie	foot
la pierna	leg
la rodilla	knee

Cognado: el torso

¿Cómo te queda? / How does it fit?

¿Cómo te queda?	How does it fit?
ancho/a	loose
apretado/a	tight
corto/a	short
largo/a	long

Repaso: grande, pequeño/a

Los verbos

Los verbos	
buscar (q)	to look for
estar (*irreg.*) (pasado/a) de moda	to be (un)fashionable
guardar	to save
llevar	to wear; to bring; to carry
morir (ue, u)	to die
probarse (ue)	to try on
quedarle + *adj./adv.*	to fit
tirar	to throw (away)
usar	to use; to wear

¿Adónde te gustaría° viajar?

M0-M1-M2-M3 ↓ **Portes**
Gates
Puertas **01** to a **39**

tida
out
da

    ↓ **Informació Trànsits**
Transits Information
Información Tránsitos

Recollida d'equipatges
Baggage claim
Recogida equipajes **B**

**Viajeros (_Travelers_)
caminan por el aeropuerto
en Barcelona, España.**

Objetivos

When you finish this chapter, you will be able to:

■ say what you would like to do
■ use infinitives to express rules
■ talk about travel and the weather
■ talk about destinations, travel routes, and modes of transportation
■ talk about what people do customarily
■ talk about travel in the Spanish-speaking world

9

 connect®
www.mhhe.com/connect

COMUNICACIÓN LARIO UCTURA TE

Video track (Act. A): This video clip can be found on the DVD to accompany *Conéctate: Cap. 9,* Track 1.

Videoscript (Act. A): 1. CHARO: *Me gustaría mucho ir a Australia.*
2. JUAN: *Sí, me gustaría comprarme un campo en Argentina y mudarme ahí y vivir con mi esposa, mi hija y más hijos.* **3.** MIRELLE: *Me gustaría poner restaurantes mexicanos en otros países.*
4. ISABEL: *Pues, me gustaría vivir en el extranjero algún día, en alguna ciudad de Europa, especialmente de Alemania.*
5. ISRAEL: *Me gustaría alguna vez coger un coche y viajar por toda Europa, toda Asia, Australia, entrar a América por el sur y hacerme todo, recorrer todo el mundo en coche.* **6.** DANIEL: *Me gustaría ver el Tour de France en Francia.*

¿Te gustaría... ? / ¿Le gustaría... ?
Asking what people would like to do

A. A ver: ¿Qué le gustaría hacer algún día?   Mira y escucha. Luego mira otra vez con pausas y empareja la persona con la actividad más lógica. Mira y escucha una tercera vez para verificar tus respuestas.

1.
A Charo... _e_

4.
A Isabel... _d_

2.
A Juan... _c_

5.
A Israel... _f_

3.
A Mirelle... _a_

6.
A Daniel... _b_

a. le gustaría estudiar administración de restaurantes.
b. le gustaría participar en el ciclismo.
c. le gustaría vivir con su familia en Argentina.
d. le gustaría vivir en un país europeo.
e. le gustaría ver canguros y koalas en su hábitat.
f. le gustaría visitar todos los países del mundo.

To ask someone if he or she would like to do something, use
¿Te/Le gustaría + *infinitive***?**

TÚ	UD.
—**¿Te gustaría ir a la playa?**	—**¿Le gustaría viajar** (*travel*) **a Costa Rica?**
—**¡Claro que sí!**	—**Sí, y me gustaría ir a Panamá también.**

Suggestion (Act. B, Paso 1): Have students share their answers and determine *¿Quién es el más aventurero o la más aventurera de la clase?*

B. ¿Cuáles son tus preferencias?

PASO 1.   Indica si te gustaría hacer las siguientes actividades.

ME GUSTARÍA	NO ME GUSTARÍA	NO SÉ SI ME GUSTARÍA	
☐	☐	☐	1. pasar las vacaciones de primavera (*spring break*) en la playa
☐	☐	☐	2. viajar por toda Europa
☐	☐	☐	3. trabajar en otro país
☐	☐	☐	4. vivir en Alemania (*Germany*)
☐	☐	☐	5. viajar por toda Sudamérica
☐	☐	☐	6. ver las pirámides en Egipto
☐	☐	☐	7. ir al Caribe
☐	☐	☐	8. mudarme (*move*) a Costa Rica
☐	☐	☐	9. viajar por el mundo en un crucero (*cruise ship*)
☐	☐	☐	10. ver el Tour de France

PASO 2.   Pon tus preferencias en orden de más (1) a menos (5).

a. ____ Me gustaría mudarme a otro país para estudiar.

b. ____ Me gustaría mudarme a otro país para vivir y trabajar.

c. ____ Me gustaría viajar a un destino y pasar dos o tres semanas allí.

d. ____ Me gustaría viajar para un acontecimiento (*event*) especial (como una boda, una feria, etcétera).

e. ____ Me gustaría viajar a muchos lugares diferentes durante las vacaciones.

 PASO 3.   Ahora pregúntale a tu compañero/a si le gustaría hacer las actividades del video (u otras actividades) y por qué sí (o por qué no). Puedes usar las opciones de los **Pasos 1** y **2** u otras actividades para crear las preguntas.

MODELO: E1: ¿Te gustaría trabajar en el extranjero?
E2: ¡Sí, claro! (No, creo que no.)
E1: ¿Por qué? (¿Por qué no?)
E2: Porque me gusta aprender sobre otras culturas. (Porque no me gusta viajar en avión.)

Favor de no fumar.
Expressing rules with infinitives

The infinitive can be used to express rules and regulations that are often posted as signs. You may see them on buses, trains, and taxis, and in streets, parks, and restaurants as you travel.

Empujar.	Push.
Jalar.	Pull.
No beber y conducir.	Don't drink and drive.
No dar de comer.	Don't feed (the animals).
No doblar. / No girar.	Do not turn.
No entrar. / No pasar.	Do not enter.
No estacionar.	No parking.
No fumar.	No smoking.
No pisar.	Stay off. (*Lit.,* Do not step on.)
No tirar basura.	No littering. (*Lit.,* Do not throw trash.)

En español...

- In some countries, the word **aparcar** is used instead of **estacionar**.
- In Spain, the word **tirar** is used in place of **jalar**.

A. No...   Empareja la regla (*rule*) con la señal correspondiente.

1. _a_ No estacionar.
2. _c_ No pisar el césped (*grass*).
3. _g_ No beber y conducir.
4. _f_ No entrar.
5. _b_ No dar de comer.
6. _e_ No tirar basura.
7. _d_ No doblar.
8. _h_ No fumar.

a.   b.   c.

d.   e.   f.

g.   h.

 B. Las reglas de la universidad   En grupos, usen el infinitivo para inventar cinco reglas para la universidad donde estudian o para otro lugar de la comunidad.

MODELO: No andar en bicicleta en la plaza central de la universidad.

Suggestion (Act. B): Give each group a different location to make rules for, such as *la clase de español, la casa, el autobús,* and so on, or have them make a list of rules for a "mystery place" so other students can guess the location based on the context of the rules.

Variation (Act. B): Have students draw signs for the rules, then other groups have to guess what the rule is. Remind students to use the infinitive when guessing the rules.

COMUN **VOCABULARIO** UCTURA TE

Los mejores lugares turísticos
Travel and tourism

A. ¿Adónde fueron de viaje?

PASO 1.   Empareja cada escena con la tarjeta postal (*postcard*) más adecuada.
Luego completa la tarjeta postal con las palabras que faltan (*are missing*).

<u>c</u> 1.   DE VIAJE (*ON A TRIP*) EN SEVILLA, ESPAÑA

EL VUELO INTERNACIONAL

la seguridad

MADRID: VUELO 237

el avión

abordar el avión

AEROPUERTO

recoger el equipaje /
la recogida de equipaje

SEVILLA

el tren

<u>a</u> 2.   LA PLAYA BOCA CHICA,
REPÚBLICA DOMINICANA

el hotel

tomar el sol

el mar

la playa

el bloqueador solar

el ascensor

la recepción

registrarse

<u>d</u> 3.   ¡COSTA RICA ES UN PARAÍSO!

el bosque
tropical

la naturaleza

la catarata

el ecoturismo

UN RECORRIDO/TOUR
DE LAS ATRACCIONES:
el bosque tropical
las cataratas
el volcán

las artesanías

la guía

el guía

_b_ 4. **AVENTURAS EN LA PAZ, BOLIVIA**

la montaña

hacer las maletas

ir de viaje

TURISMO DE AVENTURA

hacer ciclismo de montaña

la bicicleta de montaña

escalar

Answers (Act. A, Paso 1):
1. _mar_ 2. _bloqueador de sol_
3. _aventura_ 4. _escalar_ 5. _avión_
6. _el equipaje_ 7. _naturaleza_
8. _bosque tropical_

a.

El hotel de lujo (_luxury_) tiene un **servicio** excelente. Después de registrarnos, nadamos en el _____¹ y nos relajamos en la playa todo el día. Un problema: no usé _____² y tengo **una quemadura de sol** (_sunburn_)!

c.

Ayer fue mi primer viaje **al extranjero** y mi primer **vuelo** internacional. **La vista** de la ciudad desde arriba era increíble. Llegamos en _____⁵ al **aeropuerto** de Madrid, recogimos _____⁶ y tomamos el tren conocido como el AVE (Alta Velocidad Española) para llegar a Sevilla en menos de tres horas.

b.

Este **viaje** es espectacular. Si te gustan las vacaciones activas, **el turismo de** _____³ es para ti. En las montañas, puedes _____⁴ o hacer ciclismo de montaña.

d.

¡Las flores, las plantas tropicales, los animales exóticos! La _____⁷ aquí es increíble. Ayer hicimos **un recorrido** con un guía de un _____ _____,⁸ lleno de espectaculares árboles. También vimos varias cataratas. ¡Quiero estar de viaje aquí para siempre!

(Continues)

PASO 2. Empareja cada destino con la(s) actividad(es) correspondiente(s) según el **Paso 1.**

<u>c</u> 1. Bolivia
<u>a</u> 2. Costa Rica
<u>d</u> 3. España
<u>b</u> 4. la República Dominicana

a. hacer un recorrido de un bosque tropical
b. relajarse en la playa y nadar en el mar
c. turismo de aventura: hacer ciclismo de montaña y escalar
d. visitar museos y disfrutar de las vistas bonitas

 PASO 3. Con tres compañeros, pregúntense adónde quieren ir, escogiendo entre (*choosing among*) los cuatro destinos del **Paso 2**. En sus respuestas, expliquen por qué.

MODELO: E1: ¿Adónde quieres ir?

E2: A la República Dominicana porque me gustar relajarme en la playa más que hacer recorridos turísticos. ¿Y tú?

Here are more useful travel words.

hacer escala	to have a layover
visitar	to visit
el boleto	ticket
el paisaje	scenery; landscape
el pasaporte	passport
el recuerdo	souvenir
la visita	visit
cerca (de)	close, near (to)
lejos (de)	far (from)

B. Las preparaciones para las vacaciones Pon las siguientes acciones en el orden más lógico.

<u>5</u> abordar el avión
<u>4</u> esperar el vuelo
<u>1</u> hacer las maletas
<u>2</u> ir al aeropuerto
<u>7</u> ir al hotel en taxi

<u>3</u> pasar por la seguridad
<u>6</u> recoger el equipaje
<u>8</u> registrarse en la recepción
<u>9</u> subir al cuarto en el ascensor
<u>10</u> usar las llaves para entrar en la habitación (*room*)

C. Viajes a lugares turísticos Empareja el lugar turístico con la actividad más adecuada.

1. <u>e</u> Un hotel de lujo en Cancún o Puerto Vallarta con vista al mar
2. <u>f</u> Madrid, Barcelona u otra ciudad grande
3. <u>b</u> El Parque Nacional Torres del Paine en Patagonia, Chile
4. <u>c</u> La Reserva Natural Tambopata en la Amazonia del Perú
5. <u>a</u> El mercado de Chichicastenango, Guatemala, con sus muchos productos hechos a mano
6. <u>d</u> San Carlos de Bariloche, Argentina, u otro lugar frío con montañas

a. comprar artesanías
b. acampar en la naturaleza
c. aprender sobre la flora y fauna del bosque
d. esquiar
e. ir a la playa
f. tomar taxi para visitar museos famosos

 D. El sitio ideal En parejas, pregúntense adónde van o adónde les gustaría ir (por ejemplo, a la playa, a las montañas, al bosque tropical) para hacer las siguientes actividades.

disfrutar del paisaje tropical
escalar

esquiar
hacer ciclismo de montaña

ir de viaje
participar en el ecoturismo
tomar el sol

CONÉCTATE AL MUNDO PROFESIONAL

Social media is the 21st-century equivalent of a postcard, except that your Instagram photos and captions are available to the whole world instead of just select recipients. As you craft your professional digital identity, be sure to control as much of the content as you can with an abundance of positive, professional posts. Put yourself in the place of future employers and imagine what their reaction might be to your content. It's fine to use social media for social purposes; just be conscious of your message to the world beyond your close friends.

En español...

The word **autobús** is understood everywhere, but in many places other words are used to refer to this form of transportation.

camión (México)
colectivo (Argentina)
guagua (Caribe, Islas Canarias)
micro (varios países)

E. A ver: ¿Adónde les gustaría viajar?

PASO 1. Mira y escucha. Luego mira otra vez con pausas y contesta las preguntas.

1. __c__ A Olman le gustaría viajar a...
   a. Alemania b. Chile c. Italia d. Nicaragua

2. __d__ A Mariana le gustaría viajar a los países...
   a. balcánicos b. centroamericanos c. del Cono Sur d. medio orientales (*Middle Eastern*) y europeos

3. __a__ A Henry le gustaría viajar a...
   a. África b. Alemania c. Antártida d. Asia

4. __a__ A Aline le gustaría viajar a...
   a. África o el Medio Oriente (*Middle East*) b. Sudamérica c. Australia y Nueva Zelanda d. España

5. __c__ A Yenaro le gustaría viajar a...
   a. Asia b. España c. Europa d. Inglaterra

6. __b__ A Selene le gustaría viajar a...
   a. Asia b. España c. Europa d. Inglaterra

Video track (Act. E): This video clip can be found on the DVD to accompany *Conéctate: Cap. 9*, Track 2.

Suggestion (Act. E., Paso 2): Put a table on the board with the column headings: *Italia, España, África, Europa* and have students add names as they listen. Then practice *le gustaría* and *les gustaría* structures after listening for names of places each person would like to go to.

Note (Act. E, Paso 2): Point out to students that they might have to know what continents specific countries are in; for example, Egypt and Morocco are in Africa. Model the *gustaría* structure for students if they need the support: *A _____ le gustaría... .*

PASO 2. Mira y escucha otra vez con pausas. Luego contesta las preguntas.

1. ¿A quiénes les gustaría viajar a Europa? A Olman, a Mariana, a Yenaro y a Selene les gustaría viajar a Europa.
2. ¿A quiénes les gustaría viajar a África? A Mariana, a Henry y a Aline les gustaría viajar a África.
3. ¿A quién le gustaría ir de safari? A Henry le gustaría ir de safari.
4. ¿A quién le gustaría viajar a Italia? A Olman le gustaría viajar a Italia.
5. ¿A quién le gustaría conocer culturas diferentes? A Mariana y a Yenaro les gustaría conocer culturas diferentes.
6. ¿A quién le gustaría viajar a España? A Selene le gustaría viajar a España.

F. ¿Adónde van Uds.?

PASO 1. Circula por el salón de clase para preguntarles a tus compañeros adónde les gustaría viajar y qué les gustaría hacer allí.

MODELO: E1: ¿Adónde te gustaría viajar?
E2: Me gustaría viajar a Canadá y esquiar en las Montañas Rocosas canadienses. ¿Y a ti?
E1: Me gustaría viajar a Argentina. Allí me gustaría visitar las cataratas del Iguazú.

PASO 2. Organícense según las regiones geográficas del mundo adonde les gustaría viajar. Hagan un informe (*report*) para decir adónde quieren ir los miembros del grupo y por qué. ¿Cuál es la región más popular? ¿La actividad más popular? ¿Cuál es el grupo con los planes más aventureros? ¿Más relajantes?

MODELO: Nos gustaría ir a África porque queremos ir de safari. A Lisa y a James les gustaría visitar Sudáfrica para ver pingüinos. A Karen le gustaría ir a Egipto para caminar por las pirámides y a mí. . .

Suggestion (Act. F): If students need help with the names of the continents, write *América, África, Antártida, Asia, Oceania (Australia e islas cercanas),* and *Europa,* on the board. Point out that in most Spanish-speaking countries, *América* refers to North, South, and Central America as one continent. Students can instead organize themselves by country if there are enough students.

Videoscript (Act. E): 1. OLMAN: *Mi próximo viaje, si pudiera ir, sería a las cataratas del Iguazú o a Italia.* **2.** MARIANA: *Me gustaría viajar a los países orientales y europeos porque la cultura es bastante... bastante diferente, creo que los paisajes son muy diferentes y sería una experiencia bastante bonita. Y entre los países orientales, me gustaría visitar Egipto o Marruecos.* **3.** HENRY: *Si pudiera viajar a cualquier parte del mundo... África porque tiene los animales más grandes del mundo, porque tiene una diversidad increíble y es un continente fuera de este mundo.* **4.** ALINE: *Quisiera viajar, y mi sueño es viajar hacia África o Medio Oriente.* **5.** YENARO: *Si pudiera viajar en... cualquier lugar. No sé. Viajaría a Europa a conocer cosas que nunca se pueden ver aquí en Costa Rica. Sudamérica, cerca.* **6.** SELENE: *Sí, viajar a España.*

Variation (Act. G): Split students into three groups and have each group list criteria for using one mode of transportation.

CONÉCTATE AL MUNDO HISPANO

Fuera de los Estados Unidos, se usa más la escala centígrada (*centigrade/Celsius*) que la escala Fahrenheit para hablar de la temperatura. Para entender el pronóstico del tiempo, es más importante entender la escala centígrada que saber las palabras para describir el tiempo. Por ejemplo, si no sabes que hace mucho calor a 35 grados centígrados, no va a importar si entiendes español o no.

Para tener una idea de la temperatura, solo tienes que recordar algunos ejemplos.

grados centígrados	grados Fahrenheit
0	32
15	59
30	86
35	95

Suggestion (Conéctate al mundo hispano): To practice the centigrade scale, give students centigrade temperatures and have them provide a corresponding weather expression. For example *¿Qué tiempo hace a los 40 grados?* (*Hace mucho calor.*) *¿A los 20 grados?* (*Hace buen tiempo.*) *¿A los 5 grados bajo cero?* (*Hace frío.*)

G. El mejor transporte En parejas, decidan los criterios para usar cada modo de transporte. Luego comparen con otra pareja. ¿Tienen los mismos criterios?

MODELO: Viajas en avión si...
- es un viaje largo
- el viaje cruza el mar
- tienes suficiente dinero (porque es caro viajar en avión)
- tienes un modo de transporte al llegar (*upon arrival*)

1. Viajas en taxi si...
2. Viajas en tren si...
3. Viajas en autobús si...
4. Viajas en bicicleta si...
5. Viajas a pie (*on foot*) si...
6. Viajas en coche alquilado (*rented*) si...

¿Qué tiempo hace?
Talking about the weather

Suggestion (Act. A): Refer students to Cap. 1 for the seasons of the year vocabulary.

A. El tiempo y las estaciones Mira los dibujos y lee las expresiones. Luego escribe la estación correspondiente en el hemisferio norte.

Hace (muy) buen tiempo.
The weather's (very) good.

1. la primavera

Hace (muy) mal tiempo.
The weather's (very) bad.

2. el invierno

Hace (mucho) calor.
It's (very) hot.

3. el verano

Hace (mucho) frío.
It's (very) cold.

4. el invierno

Hace (mucho) sol.
It's (very) sunny.

5. el verano

Hace (mucho) viento.
It's (very) windy.

6. el otoño

You can use the verb **estar** to describe some types of weather.

Está despejado.	The skies are clear.
Está (muy) nublado.	It's (very) cloudy.

To talk about precipitation, use the verb **llover (o → ue)** (*to rain*) or **nevar (e → ie)** (*to snow*).

Está lloviendo. / Llueve mucho.	It's raining. / It rains a lot.
Está nevando. / Nieva mucho.	It's snowing. / It snows a lot.

B. ¿Qué tiempo hace?   Para cada situación que escuchas, indica el tiempo más típico donde vives.

1. ☑ Hace calor.   ☐ Hace frío.   ☐ Llueve.
2. ☐ Hace calor.   ☑ Hace frío.   ☐ Llueve.
3. ☑ Hace buen tiempo. ☐ Hace mal tiempo.   ☐ Nieva.
4. ☐ Hace calor.   ☑ Hace viento.   ☐ Nieva.
5. ☐ Hace calor.   ☑ Hace frío.   ☐ Llueve.
6. ☑ Hace calor.   ☐ Hace frío.   ☐ Hace viento.
7. ☐ Hace calor.   ☐ Hace frío.   ☑ Llueve.

■ The audio files for in-text listening activities are available in the eBook, within Connect activities, and on the Online Learning Center.

Script (Act. B): 1. *En el mes de julio...* **2.** *En enero...* **3.** *Durante la primavera...* **4.** *En el otoño muchas veces...* **5.** *Si llevas abrigo, guantes, gorra y bufanda, es porque...* **6.** *Si llevas traje de baño, probablemente...* **7.** *Si traes paraguas, es porque...*

Expansion (Act. B): Have students do Q1–Q2 again, as if they were in the southern hemisphere. Answers: **1.** *Hace frío.* **2.** *Hace calor.*

Note (Act. B): Answers will vary depending on your geographical region.

C. ¿Qué tiempo hace en estos lugares?   Empareja cada imagen con el lugar más lógico. Luego completa la oración con una descripción del tiempo en cada lugar.

a.

b.

b 1. En el bosque tropical ___llueve___ todos los días.
c 2. En las montañas más altas del mundo probablemente _está nevando_ ahora.

D. ¿Qué estación es? ¿Qué tiempo hace?   Mira las siguientes fotos y di lo más que puedas (*as much as you can*) sobre cada una. ¿Qué estación es? ¿Qué tiempo hace? ¿Qué ropa debes llevar? ¿Cuáles son algunas actividades que puedes hacer en esta estación?

Suggestion (Act. D): Reinforce that these are formal in-class presentations and can be practice for the brief but professional presentations they'll have to do once in the workforce. You may want to give a presentation grade.

MODELO:

Hace viento, pero puede hacer viento en todas las estaciones. Cuando hace viento y también frío, es necesario llevar una chaqueta. No debes usar un paraguas ni (*nor*) un sombrero cuando hace viento. Es divertido volar una cometa (*kite*) cuando hace viento.

1.

2.

3.

4.

COMUN VOCABU ESTRUCTURA ATE

Suggestion (Reciclaje):

• Remind students that names like *México* and *Guatemala* may refer to the countries or the cities, depending on the context. In this context, clearly, they refer to Mexico City and Guatemala City.

• Before students begin, have them identify the country that each of the cities is in, using the maps at the end of the book. Note that since the focus here is on major airports, *Guadalajara* and *Santiago* refer to the cities in Mexico and Chile, respectively (though there are also cities with that name in other countries).

■ Answers to this activity are in Appendix 2 at the back of your book.

Note (Reciclaje): This activity focuses students' attention on the prepositions *de* and *a*. This is not a difficult topic for English speakers, but it is good background before looking more closely at *por* and *para*.

Suggestion (Para empezar): If you are doing this activity in class, divide students into 3 or 4 teams and have them work through the activity. Then go over the answers "game show style": Have each team write **A** on one sheet of paper and **B** on another. As you ask each question, a representative for the team should hold up the correct answer. Assign a point for each correct answer (keep track on the board).

Reciclaje

The prepositions *de* and *a*

El aeropuerto internacional de la Ciudad de México, conocido oficialmente como el Aeropuerto Internacional Benito Juárez, ofrece vuelos a más de cien destinos en todo el mundo y es el aeropuerto más grande de Latinoamérica. ¿Cuánto crees que duran los vuelos de México a otras ciudades? Empareja cada ciudad con la duración del vuelo, describiendo el vuelo con las preposiciones **de** y **a.** Usa los mapas al final del libro si necesitas ayuda.

Bogotá   Guatemala   Madrid   Nueva York   Santiago   Guadalajara

Duración del vuelo	**¿De México a qué otra ciudad?**
1. 1 hora 20 minutos	De México a Guadalajara
2. 2 horas	De México a Guatemala
3. 4 horas 30 minutos	De México a Bogotá
4. 5 horas	De México a Nueva York
5. 8 horas 25 minutos	De México a Santiago
6. 10 horas 50 minutos	De México a Madrid

9.1 Salimos para Machu Picchu

The prepositions *por* and *para*

Para empezar...

¿Te gustaría ir al Perú? Las ciudades de Lima y Cusco tienen mucho que ofrecer, pero la atracción turística número uno del país es la zona arqueológica de Machu Picchu. Cada día visitan las ruinas 2.500 personas, o casi un millón por año. Las ruinas quedan a cuatro horas de Cusco. Usando el mapa y tu sentido (*sense*) común, escoge la respuesta adecuada para cada oración. Si no estás seguro/a, ¡adivina (*guess*)!

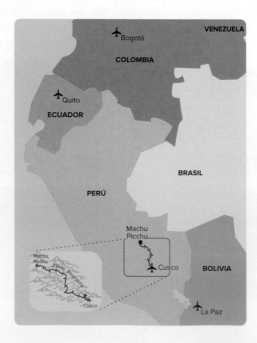

1. __b__ **Para** ir a Machu Picchu, primero tienes que llegar a...
   a. Bogotá   b. Cusco
2. __b__ De allí a Machu Picchu, puedes ir...
   a. **por** avión   b. **por** tren
3. __a__ Hay salidas **para** Machu Picchu...
   a. cuatro veces al día   b. veinte veces al día
4. __b__ Cuando vas, pasas...
   a. **por** Quito   b. **por** el Valle Sagrado (*Sacred Valley*)
5. __a__ Si quieres prepararte **para** tu viaje, es recomendable leer un libro como...
   a. *La vida de los incas*   b. *La vida de los mayas*
6. __a__ **Para** evitar (*avoid*) los grandes grupos de turistas, es aconsejable (*advisable*) ya estar en la zona de las ruinas...
   a. **para** las ocho   b. **para** la una
7. __a__ Si quieres comprar recuerdos **para** tus amigos o **para** tu familia, es más barato hacerlo...
   a. en Cusco   b. en Machu Picchu
8. __b__ Algunos piensan que el futuro de Machu Picchu está en peligro (*danger*)...
   a. **por** los animales que llegan de noche
   b. **por** la gran cantidad de turistas que llegan todos los días

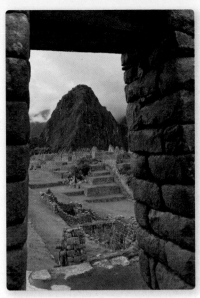

En las ruinas de Machu Picchu

- Answers to these activities are in Appendix 2 at the back of your book.

Actividades analíticas

1 The core meaning of the preposition **para** is *aiming toward*. You may aim toward a place, a time (as in a deadline), or an outcome that you desire, or your action may be intended for, or benefiting, someone or something.

PARA	IDEA CENTRAL: *AIMING TOWARD*
A PLACE	Mañana salimos **para** España. *Tomorrow we're departing for (toward) Spain.*
A DEADLINE	Tenemos que estar en el aeropuerto **para** las seis. *We have to be at the airport by 6:00.*
A DESIRED OUTCOME (with infinitive verb)	Vamos a España **para** ver a mi tía. *We are going to Spain (in order) to see my aunt.*
A PERSON OR THING THAT BENEFITS	¡Compré este regalo **para** ti! *I bought this present for you (intended for you)!* Esta tarea es **para** mi clase de química. *This homework is for (intended for) my chemistry class.*

2 Find one example of each of these uses of **para** in the numbered items of **Para empezar** and write each example beside its corresponding **para** usage listed below. In some cases, more than one example is available.

Aiming toward . . .
a. a place   *para Machu Picchu*
b. a time deadline   *para las ocho*
c. a desired outcome   *para ir a Machu Picchu, para evitar los grandes grupos de turistas*
d. a person/thing that will benefit   *para tus amigos, para tu familia, para tu viaje*

3 The core meaning of the preposition **por** is *passing through*. You may pass through a place or a time period, or **por** may indicate the means that you used ("passed through") in order to achieve an end. This core meaning of *passing through* may also be extended to include what *caused* you to undergo ("pass through") some experience.

Suggestion (Act. analíticas 2): Reproduce this chart on the board in Spanish (*un lugar, un tiempo límite, un resultado, una persona o una cosa*). Alternatively, write the chart in English, and point to each item when you refer to it in Spanish. This allows you to keep the discussion in Spanish, while making sure the meaning is clear.

(*Continues*)

Suggestion (Act. analítica 3): Here again, write this chart on the board in Spanish (*un lugar, un período de tiempo, un medio [para lograr un fin], una causa*), or write it in English and point to each item when you refer to it in Spanish.

Autoprueba

Now that you've read about the different uses of **para** and **por,** see if you can identify which would be used in each of the following sentences. Notice how you cannot consistently substitute a particular Spanish word for a particular English word, but rather you have to think about the "aiming toward" versus "passing through" meaning of each sentence.

1. On Saturday we leave <u>for</u> Panama.
2. We picked Panama <u>because</u> of its interesting history.
3. Tomorrow I'm staying home <u>to</u> pack.
4. <u>Throughout</u> the morning I'll be getting ready, but you can reach me <u>by</u> phone.
5. I don't need to go to the bank <u>to</u> change currency, because they use both the Panamanian balboa and the U.S. dollar there.
6. We're going to the airport <u>by</u> bus, so I have to be ready <u>by</u> 9 o'clock.
7. Don't worry, I'll buy a souvenir <u>for</u> you!

Respuestas: 1. por **2.** para **3.** para **4.** Por, por **5.** para **6.** por, para **7.** para

■ For more on the uses of **por** and **para,** see **Para saber más 9.1** at the back of your book.

POR	IDEA CENTRAL: *PASSING THROUGH*
A PLACE	Cuando vamos a España tenemos que pasar **por** Francia. *When we go to Spain we have to pass through France.* El año pasado viajamos **por** todo Chile. *We traveled throughout all of Chile last year.*
A TIME PERIOD	Siempre estudio **por** la noche. *I always study at night (during the night).*
A MEANS (noun) TO DO SOMETHING	Llegué **por** avión. *I arrived by plane.* Vamos a hablar **por** teléfono. *We're going to speak by phone.*
A CAUSE	**Por** el calor, me siento muy cansado. *Because of the heat, I feel very tired.* Decidí vivir en Honduras **por** las playas. *I decided to live in Honduras because of the beaches.*

4 Now find one example of each of these uses of **por** in the numbered items of **Para empezar** and write each example beside its corresponding **por** usage listed below.

Passing through . . .

a. a place
b. a time period
c. a means to an end
d. What caused you to have an experience

por el Valle Sagrado _____
por la mañana _____
por tren _____

por la gran cantidad de turistas _____

En español...

Although both **para** or **por** can be translated as *for,* there are many English equivalents. Rather than learning these words by translation, focus on the simple core meaning of each. Visualizing this meaning may help.

Since **para** can be thought of as *aiming towards,* think of an arrow pointing at the object of **para.**

 Vamos al hotel **para** dormir.
We're going to the hotel (in order) to sleep.

 No me gusta estudiar **para** los exámenes.
I don't like to study for exams.

Since **por,** on the other hand, often can be thought of as *passing through,* think of the arrow as passing through the object of **por.**

 Vamos al hotel **por autobús**.
We're going to the hotel by (means of) bus.

 No me gusta estudiar **por la mañana**.
I don't like to study in/during the morning.

Note (Para saber más): *Para saber más 9.1* covers further uses of *para* (place of employment, point of comparison) and *por* (to express a rate, picking something or someone up).

Actividades prácticas

A. La agenda

PASO 1. Mira la agenda de Susana, una estudiante universitaria. Luego lee las oraciones y decide cuáles son ciertas y cuáles son falsas.

	LUNES	MARTES	MIÉRCOLES	JUEVES	VIERNES
9:00	sociología	ciencias políticas	sociología: examen	ciencias políticas	
10:00					
11:00	economía	historia	economía	historia	
12:00					
13:00					13:15 salir al aeropuerto
14:00		trabajo		trabajo	
15:00	hacer ejercicio		hacer ejercicio		15:30 vuelo
16:00			tarea: ciencias políticas		
17:00		tarea: historia			

	CIERTO	FALSO
1. Asiste a clase todos los días por la mañana.	☐	☑
2. Trabaja el martes y jueves por la tarde.	☑	☐
3. El martes, tiene que entregar la tarea de historia para las diez.	☐	☑
4. Probablemente va a revisar (*review*) el libro de sociología el martes por la noche.	☑	☐
5. Para el jueves tiene que estar lista (*ready*) para el examen de sociología.	☐	☑
6. Para el miércoles a las diez, tiene que entregar (*turn in*) la tarea de ciencias políticas.	☐	☑
7. El viernes, tiene que hacer la maleta para las nueve.	☐	☑
8. El viernes por la tarde, va a salir de la ciudad.	☑	☐
9. Tiene que salir para el aeropuerto para la una y cuarto.	☑	☐
10. Tiene que estar en el aeropuerto para las tres cuarenta y cinco.	☐	☑

PASO 2. En general, ¿qué hace Susana por la mañana? ¿Y qué hace por la tarde? ¿Crees que ella tiene una vida equilibrada (*balanced*)?

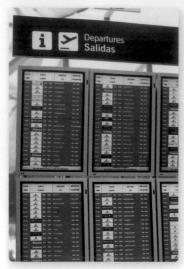

La lista de salidas en el
Aeropuerto de Madrid-Barajas

B. Itinerarios

Suggestion (Act. B): Quiz students on the cities in Act. B before they begin the activity so they have an easier time answering the questions.

PASO 1. En los viajes largos, es común hacer escala en otra ciudad. Empareja cada itinerario con la mejor descripción. Usa los mapas al final del libro si necesitas ayuda.

ITINERARIO	DESCRIPCIÓN
1. __f__ París → Madrid → Lisboa	a. Van para Uruguay.
2. __d__ Londres → París → Madrid	b. Van para Puerto Rico.
3. __e__ Nueva York → Montreal → La Habana	c. Van por Colombia.
4. __c__ Cartagena → Medellín → Bogotá → Cali	d. Van para España.
5. __b__ Dallas → Miami → San Juan	e. Van por Canadá.
6. __a__ Bogotá → Caracas → Buenos Aires → Montevideo	f. Van por España.

PASO 2. Ahora completa la descripción de cada itinerario con **por** o **para**.

ITINERARIO	DESCRIPCIÓN
1. Oaxaca → Ciudad de México → Durango → El Paso	Van _para_ los Estados Unidos.
2. Guatemala → San Salvador → Tegucigalpa → Managua	Van _por_ Centroamérica.
3. Los Ángeles → Ciudad de México → Managua	Van _para_ Centroamérica.
4. Caracas → Miami → Lisboa	Van _por_ los Estados Unidos.
5. Lima → San Salvador → Santo Domingo	Van _por_ Centroamérica.

C. Los viajes

PASO 1. En parejas, háganse las preguntas usando **por** o **para** y las palabras de la lista para completar cada oración.

MODELO: E1: ¿Se quedan muchos estudiantes en albergues (*hostels*)? (los precios bajos)
E2: Sí, muchos estudiantes se quedan en albergues por los precios bajos.

avión	mi madre	tomar el sol
comprar un boleto	la mañana	ver el Canal
la lluvia	las oportunidades de escalar	

1. ¿Cómo se llega a Argentina?   Se llega a Argentina por avión.
2. ¿Por qué te gusta pasar tiempo en las montañas?   Me gusta pasar tiempo en las montañas por las oportunidades de escalar.
3. ¿Para qué tienes dinero?   Tengo dinero para comprar un boleto.
4. ¿Por qué cancelaron el vuelo?   Cancelaron el vuelo por la lluvia.
5. ¿Compras recuerdos cuando estás de viaje?   Sí, siempre compro recuerdos para mi madre.
6. ¿Cuándo tienes clases?   Tengo clases por la mañana.
7. ¿Por qué quieres ir a Panamá?   Quiero ir a Panamá para ver el Canal.
8. ¿Por qué vas a la playa?   Voy a la playa para tomar el sol.

Answers (Act. C, Paso 2): 1. *un medio (para lograr un fin)* 2. *una causa* 3. *un resultado* 4. *una causa* 5. *una persona que se beneficia* 6. *un período de tiempo* 7. *un resultado* 8. *un resultado*

PASO 2. Ahora, indiquen por qué se usa **por** o **para** en cada circunstancia. Compartan sus respuestas con el resto de la clase. ¿Tienen todos las mismas respuestas?

Suggestion (Act. C, Paso 2): To help students keep the discussion in Spanish, write the uses of these prepositions in Spanish: PARA → *un lugar, un tiempo límite, un resultado, una persona o una cosa que se beneficia*; POR → *un lugar, un período de tiempo, un medio (para lograr un fin), una causa.*

D. Tu agenda

¿Cuáles son las fechas límites (*deadlines*) que tienes en las próximas (*upcoming*) semanas? Escribe una lista, usando la agenda de Susana en la **Actividad A** como modelo. En parejas, compárenlas y decidan entre los dos quién tiene el horario más difícil.

MODELO: Para mañana, tengo que estar listo para el examen de historia. Para el próximo lunes, tengo que terminar un proyecto para mi clase de inglés.

Suggestion (Act. D): When students are done, ask for nominations for the person in the class who has the easiest or most difficult schedule in the upcoming weeks.

E. Tu itinerario Usando el mapa y siguiendo el ejemplo de la **Actividad B,** escribe un itinerario de vuelos de múltiples <u>ciudades</u> y dáselo a un compañero / una compañera. Tu compañero/a va a describir tu viaje en términos (*terms*) de <u>países</u> usando **por** y **para**.

Suggestion (Act. E): If students need help with countries, have them refer to the maps in the back of the book. Let students know how many itineraries they should make up and present to their partners, or tell them to keep doing it until you tell them to stop.

MODELO: E1: Los Ángeles a la Ciudad de México, y de la Ciudad de México a Managua.

E2: ¡Vas para Nicaragua y vas por México!

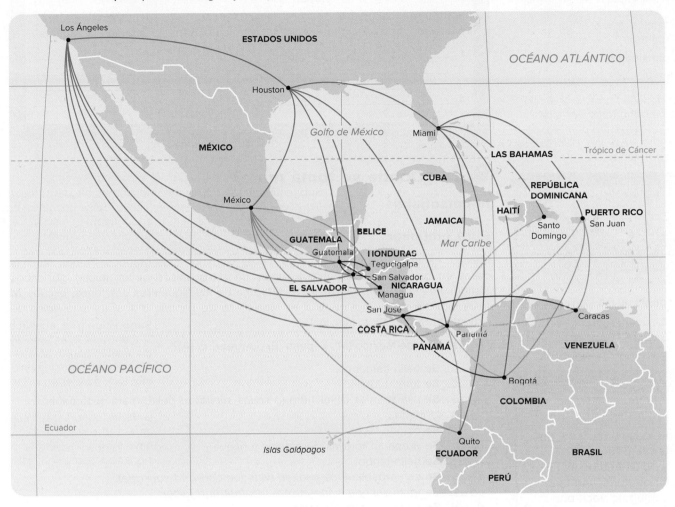

Answers (Reciclaje): (any order) *me acuesto, me afeito, me baño, me estiro, me lavo la cara, me lavo los dientes, me peino, me quito los zapatos*

Note (Reciclaje): Tell students that if *afeitarse* or *estirarse* is not something they normally do, they should simply put it in last place in their list of priorities.

Expansion (Reciclaje): Have students work with a partner or small group to create a sentence based on a comparison of their #1 priority. For example, *Yo me estiro primero, pero Heather se peina y Marissa se quita los zapatos.*

Un grupo de mariachis, México

■ Answers to these activities are in Appendix 2 at the back of your book.

Reciclaje

Note (Reciclaje): Reflexive verbs were presented in *Estructura 5.2.*

Reflexive verbs

Cuando pasas toda la noche viajando por autobús o avión, ¿qué haces primero cuando llegas a tu destino? Pon las siguientes actividades en orden de prioridad, conjugando cada verbo en la forma **yo** del tiempo presente.

acostarse	bañarse	lavarse la cara	peinarse
afeitarse	estirarse (*stretch*)	lavarse los dientes	quitarse los zapatos

1. _____   5. _____
2. _____   6. _____
3. _____   7. _____
4. _____   8. _____

9.2   ¿Dónde se toma mate?

Impersonal *se*

Para empezar...

Suggestion (Para empezar): Emphasize to students that these are activities that are considered typical of these countries, but that does not necessarily mean that they are unheard of elsewhere. *Paella,* for instance, is known and enjoyed by many in Argentina and Mexico, but it is not considered typical in those places.

México, España y Argentina son los países hispanos más grandes. Tienen muchas cosas en común, pero la gente y cultura de estos países varían mucho. ¿Tú sabes distinguirlos (*tell them apart*)? Para cada una de las siguientes oraciones, escribe **M** si es algo típico de México, **E** si es algo típico de España o **A** si es algo típico de Argentina. Si no sabes, ¡adivina!

¿Es típico de México (M), España (E) o Argentina (A)?

1. __E__ **Se** baila flamenco.
2. __M__ **Se** toma tequila.
3. __A__ **Se** usa la salsa chimichurri (*a sauce similar to pesto*) para acompañar la carne.
4. __M__ **Se** comen tacos.
5. __E__ **Se** preparan tortillas de patatas y huevo.
6. __A__ **Se** baila tango.
7. __E__ **Se** come paella (*rice cooked with seafood and sausage*).
8. __E__ **Se** toma sangría (*wine mixed with fruit and juice*).
9. __M__ **Se** hacen tortillas de maíz.
10. __A__ **Se** come más carne que en ningún otro país del mundo.
11. __M__ **Se** escucha música mariachi.
12. __A__ **Se** toma mate (*a hot herbal drink*).

Suggestion (Act. analíticas 1): If your students live in an area where there are many Spanish-speaking businesses, ask them to think of signs that they have seen with se (such as *se habla español, se vende auto,* and so on). You may also wish to have them take pictures of such signs as a homework assignment.

Actividades analíticas

1 You have seen **se** used for reflexive verbs (see **Estructura 5.2**), but the sentences in **Para empezar** show a different use of **se,** often referred to as *impersonal se* (**el se impersonal**). This usage means that the action indicated is something that people in general do, without referring to a specific person.

En España **se** baila flamenco.   *People dance flamenco in Spain.*

Aquí **se** habla español.   *Spanish is spoken here.*

2 In most sentences with impersonal **se,** the verb is in the third-person singular (**él/ella, Ud.**) form, but sometimes it is in the third-person plural (**ellos/ellas, Uds.**) form. Which three sentences in **Para empezar** use this plural form? __4__, __5__, __9__

Why do you think the verb is plural in these sentences but not in the others?
<u>The noun is plural.</u>

Autoprueba

In the following sentences about Peru, determine whether the verb should be singular or plural, and then conjugate each one accordingly.

En Perú...

1. se _____ (comer) papas a la huancaína, un plato de papas, crema y huevos.
2. también se _____ (comer) ají de gallina, un plato picante de pollo.
3. se _____ (tomar) pisco, una bebida alcohólica hecha de uvas.

Respuestas: 1. comen **2.** come **3.** toma

Expansion (Act. analíticas 2): Give students the following sentences and have them provide the correct impersonal se form. If there is a plural noun, they will need to make the verb plural. **1.** (*enseñar*) muchas materias en la universidad. **2.** En una librería, vender) libros. **3.** (*comer*) bien en México.

Note (Act. analíticas, p. 274): Scholars traditionally distinguish between impersonal *se*, in which the verb is always singular and the actor is understood as "people in general," and passive *se*, in which the verb

Estructura 275

CONÉCTATE AL MUNDO HISPANO

Las cosas típicas de un país muchas veces vienen de una sola región del país. Por ejemplo, **el flamenco** viene de Andalucía en el sur de España, **el mariachi** es de Jalisco en el oeste de México y **el tango** tiene su origen en Buenos Aires, la capital de Argentina. ¿Hay cosas que se consideran típicas de tu país, pero que en realidad son de una región en particular?

Actividades prácticas

A. Tres países chicos

En **Para empezar,** aprendiste información sobre tres países muy grandes. Aquí vas a leer algo sobre tres países chicos: Nicaragua, Paraguay y Uruguay. Lee la descripción de cada país y luego escribe **N** para Nicaragua, **P** para Paraguay o **U** para Uruguay.

- **Nicaragua** es un país centroamericano que tiene volcanes, lagos y playas. Todavía (*Still*) hay mucha influencia de las antiguas civilizaciones mesoamericanas (las culturas indígenas de la región).
- **Paraguay** tiene fronteras con Brasil, Argentina y Bolivia pero no tiene costa. Hay mucha influencia indígena.
- **Uruguay** está ubicado entre Brasil y Argentina. Tuvo mucha inmigración europea a principios (*beginning*) del siglo (*century*) XX, sobre todo de Italia.

¿Se refiere a Nicaragua (N), Paraguay (P) o Uruguay (U)?

1. __N__ En los volcanes, se puede esquiar sobre arena (*sand*).
2. __U__ Se comen muchos tipos de pasta y de pizza.
3. __P__ Se hablan español y guaraní (una lengua indígena de Sudamérica).
4. __N__ En la costa del Caribe, se habla inglés criollo (*creole*).
5. __P__ Se hace «sopa paraguaya», pero no es una sopa normal. Es sólida, y se hace con huevos, queso y harina de maíz.
6. __U__ Se toma «grappamiel», un licor con miel (*honey*) que trajeron los inmigrantes europeos.
7. __N__ En las playas del Pacífico, se hace muchísimo surf.
8. __N__ Se come «gallo pinto», un plato de arroz y frijoles que se come con tortillas de maíz.
9. __P__ No hay mar y no hay mucho turismo, pero sí se hace «turismo rural». Los turistas se quedan en estancias (*ranches*) y disfrutan del campo y de la naturaleza.
10. __P, U__ Se toma mate.

¿Por qué?

You have seen that **se** is sometimes used to indicate a reflexive verb and sometimes used to indicate an impersonal action (that is, one that is performed by people in general).

Reflexive verb:
Marta **se** despierta a las siete.   *Marta wakes up at 7:00.*

Impersonal:
Se habla portugués en Brasil.   *Portuguese is spoken in Brazil.*

Why is this same pronoun used for such different functions? The answer is that **se** is a kind of "catch-all" pronoun, used in a variety of situations where no other pronoun can do the job. If Spanish did not have **se,** it would have to have a much larger collection of pronouns, each specialized for a very particular function. Spanish avoids this situation by allowing the single pronoun **se** to perform many functions in the language.

agrees with the noun and the actor is understood as "some unspecified individual(s)." For most speakers, though, this distinction collapses when the noun is plural, so the verb shows agreement even with the "people in general" meaning. This is the variety of Spanish we present here. For beginning students, a discussion of the impersonal vs. passive contrast is not recommended; the main point they need to grasp is that *se* is often used when you do not mention who is doing the action.

Raúl, de Uruguay, muestra su mate.

Expansion (Conéctate al mundo hispano): Discuss this question with students: Is there anything that is popular in one region that people consider typical of the country as a whole? Some possibilities: bluegrass/country music; baseball, basketball, football, barbecue, grits, clam chowder (for United States), maple syrup, hockey, poutine (for Canada).

Note (Act. A): Students can deduce most of the answers using the descriptions of the countries given here and their common sense.

Expansion (¿Por qué?): Give students sentences to identify as either reflexive or impersonal. Examples: *Se usa el libro en clase. Mario se va mañana.*

Se ven papagayos y otros pájaros en los bosques tropicales.

Note (Act. B, Paso 2):
Turismo sostenible is also known as *turismo alternativo, turismo responsable,* and *ecoturismo.*

Suggestion (Act. B, Paso 3):
While students work in pairs, write the questions on the board or project them for students to see. Call on volunteers to write one or two of their answers next to each question, trying to get as many different answers as possible; use the answers as a way to initiate class discussion.

Variation (Act. B, Paso 3):
Divide the class into four groups and give each group one of the four questions to answer with as many examples as they can come up with. Have a volunteer from each group present selected answers; use the answers as a way to initiate class discussion.

Variation (Act. C, Paso 1):
Have students create statements about the campus rather than their city or region.

Variation (Act. C, Paso 2):
Rather than sharing with the entire class, put the pairs in larger groups and have each pair of students read their sentences to the group. Follow up by asking a few pairs to share their sentences with the class.

B. El turismo sostenible   Cuando viajas, ¿piensas en los efectos de tu viaje en el medio ambiente (*environment*) y en la gente del lugar? El «turismo sostenible (*sustainable*)» tiene el propósito de evitar los efectos negativos y de crear así una alternativa al turismo tradicional.

PASO 1.   Para cada oración, cambia el verbo a la forma correcta del **se** impersonal.

1. **aprender:** _Se aprende_ mucho sobre la vida de la gente del lugar.
2. **usar:** _Se usan_ muchísimos recursos (*resources*) naturales, como el agua y la electricidad.
3. **gastar** (*to spend*): _Se gasta_ dinero en pequeñas empresas (*enterprises*) locales.
4. **aprender:** _Se aprende_ muy poco sobre la vida de la gente del lugar.
5. **hacer:** No _se hace_ nada a beneficio de (*to benefit*) la gente del lugar.
6. **minimizar:** _Se minimiza_ el uso de recursos naturales.
7. **donar:** _Se donan_ cosas que la gente de la comunidad necesita.
8. **gastar:** _Se gasta_ mucho dinero en los grandes hoteles y otros negocios grandes.

PASO 2.   En parejas, decidan si cada oración del **Paso 1** tiene que ver con (*has to do with*) el turismo tradicional o el turismo sostenible. Escriban el número de la oración en la posición correcta en la tabla según la categoría.

CATEGORÍA	EL TURISMO TRADICIONAL	EL TURISMO SOSTENIBLE
el bienestar (*well-being*) **de la gente del lugar**	5	7
el dinero	8	3
la educación	4	1
los recursos naturales	2	6

PASO 3.   En parejas, contesten las preguntas.

1. ¿Cómo se puede gastar dinero en pequeñas empresas locales?
2. ¿Cómo se puede aprender algo sobre la vida de la gente del lugar?
3. ¿Cómo se puede minimizar el uso de recursos naturales?
4. ¿Cómo se puede saber qué necesita la gente del lugar?

C. Tu ciudad o tu región

PASO 1.   En parejas, creen tres oraciones ciertas y una falsa para explicarle a un turista extranjero lo que se hace en la ciudad o región de Uds. Usen la **Actividad A** como modelo. **¡Atención!** Acuérdense que una de sus oraciones tiene que ser falsa.

PASO 2.   Ahora compartan sus oraciones con la clase. ¿Sus compañeros pueden decir cuál oración es falsa?

D. ¡Adivinanzas!   Piensa en un lugar en tu universidad o en tu ciudad, y dile a tu compañero/a qué se hace en ese lugar sin decirle el nombre. ¿Tu compañero/a puede adivinar en qué lugar estás pensando?

> **MODELO:**   E1: Aquí se come, se habla con amigos y se estudia.
> E2: ¿Es el centro estudiantil?
> E1: No, es otro lugar.
> E2: ¿La cafetería?
> E1: ¡Sí!

Costa Rica

E. Cultura: El ecoturismo en Costa Rica

PASO 1. Lee el texto sobre Costa Rica.

Costa Rica es uno de los grandes destinos en el mundo para el ecoturismo. Fue uno de los primeros países en desarrollar[a] esa industria. ¿Cómo es diferente el ecoturismo del turismo convencional? El ecoturismo tiene como objetivo dejar[b] un impacto mínimo sobre los lugares que se visitan y sobre el planeta en general. Además, una parte del dinero que se genera en el ecoturismo se dirige hacia[c] la conservación de la naturaleza. Los ecoturistas pueden hacer actividades muy divertidas y emocionantes,[d] disfrutar de la flora y la fauna del país y a la vez[e] ayudar a conservarlas.

La geografía de Costa Rica es ideal para el ecoturismo porque ya se ofrecen muchas actividades distintas. Se puede ir a la playa para nadar en las aguas tibias[f] del Caribe o rentar una tabla[g] para surfear en el Pacífico. Para observar animales como monos, pájaros y perezosos,[h] se puede viajar por los canales del Parque Nacional Tortuguero. En el Parque Nacional Arenal, donde se encuentra el gran volcán Arenal, los turistas más tranquilos pueden simplemente dar un paseo mientras que los más aventureros pueden hacer una visita al bosque y bajar en tirolina.[i]

Los turistas son bienvenidos[j] en Costa Rica y muchas de las personas que trabajan en el turismo son bilingües o trilingües para poder hablar con los extranjeros. El ecoturismo es importante para los costarricenses no solo porque genera ingresos[k] y crea empleos, sino también porque a ellos les da la oportunidad de compartir[l] la espectacular naturaleza y biodiversidad con el resto del mundo. Estas cosas se consideran importantes y la actitud de Costa Rica frente a[m] la conservación sirve como ejemplo para otros países.

[a]en... to develop [b]to leave [c]se... is directed toward [d]exciting [e]a... at the same time [f]tepid
[g]board [h]monos... monkeys, birds, and sloths [i]bajar... go ziplining [j]welcome [k]income [l]share [m]frente... toward

PASO 2. Completa las oraciones con los verbos de la lista usando el **se** impersonal. **¡Atención!** Cada verbo se usa solo una vez.

alquilar (to rent)	hablar	poder	valorar (to value)
dar	ofrecer	usar	ver

1. En las playas de Costa Rica _se alquilan_ tablas de surf.
2. Durante el día _se usa_ mucho bloqueador solar.
3. En todo el país _se valoran_ la naturaleza y la biodiversidad.
4. _Se dan_ paseos en los volcanes.
5. Para ver monos, _se ofrecen_ viajes por los canales de Tortuguero.
6. _Se ve_ una variedad de pájaros en los bosques tropicales.
7. _Se puede_ visitar el bosque y bajar en tirolina.
8. En muchos hoteles y tiendas _se habla_ inglés.

PASO 3. En parejas, contesten las preguntas y explíquense las respuestas.

1. Costa Rica tiene un nivel (level) de desigualdad (inequality) económica relativamente baja y un sistema político estable. ¿Piensas que hay una relación entre estos dos factores? ¿Y piensas que estos factores ayudan a crear un ambiente (atmosphere) atractivo para los turistas?
2. Además del turismo, la economía de Costa Rica depende de la agricultura (principalmente los plátanos y el café) y la manufactura de componentes electrónicos. ¿Piensas que es mejor tener una economía variada de este tipo o especializarse en una sola cosa?
3. ¿Hay mucho turismo donde tú vives? ¿Por qué sí o por qué no? Si lo hay, ¿puedes ver efectos positivos y negativos?

Un ecoturista escala un árbol en una reserva natural de Costa Rica.

Notes (Act. E, Paso 3):
- For item 1, the two factors are almost certainly related. Low income inequality means that conflicts across social groups are more easily managed within the political framework, and when the political system works, the interests of different socioeconomic levels are represented, creating a more egalitarian society. Costa Rica has a level of income inequality similar to the United States, Argentina, or Mexico, but lower than many other Latin American countries.
- For item 2, a more varied economy is usually better than one that depends on a single sector.

Note (Reciclaje): This activity refreshes students' memory of indirect object pronouns with impersonal verbs like *gustar*, first introduced in *Cap. 2*. Verbal expressions such as *se me antoja* (the topic of *Estructura 9.3*) are the same, except that the verb is reflexive.

Answers (Reciclaje): (The verb selected will vary.)
1. *Me encantan...* **2.** *Me molesta...* **3.** *Me fascinan...* **4.** *Me gusta...* **5.** *Me encanta...* **6.** *Me gustan...*

Suggestion (Reciclaje): Point out that *fascinar* is slightly stronger than *encantar* in expressing how much you like something.

Expansion (Reciclaje): Have students work with a partner and see if they can find any interesting differences among them. For example: *A mí me molesta hacer nuevos amigos en los aviones, pero a Raymond le gusta.*

↻ Reciclaje

Verbs like **gustar**

Usa uno de estos verbos para describir tu reacción a las siguientes actividades. ¿Te encantan, te fascinan, te gustan o te molestan?

encantar   fascinar   gustar   molestar

1. los viajes en autobús: _____
2. llevar una maleta muy pesada: _____
3. los viajes en avión: _____
4. hacer nuevos amigos en los aviones o autobuses: _____
5. la playa: _____
6. los trenes: _____

9.3 Se me olvidó el nombre del hotel

Se for unplanned events

Para empezar...

Las oraciones en la página 279 describen un día horrible en el aeropuerto, pero están desordenadas. Usa los dibujos (*drawings*) para poner las oraciones en el orden más adecuado.

1.

2.

3.

4.

5.

6.

7.

8.

9.

Mi día horrible

__7__ **se me cayó** (*I dropped*) el teléfono y...

__5__ Luego iba a registrarme para el vuelo, pero **se me olvidó** (*I forgot*) la tarjeta de identificación.

__2__ Llegué muy temprano, y **se me antojó** (*I felt like*) un café.

__1__ Fui al aeropuerto para ir a San Salvador.

__9__ Cancelaron mi vuelo, y por eso regresé a casa.

__8__ **se me rompió** (*I accidentally broke it*).

__6__ Iba a llamar a mi amigo para traérmela (*bring it to me*), pero...

__4__ **Se me mancharon** (*I accidentally stained*) el chaleco (*vest*) y los pantalones.

__3__ Compré un café, pero **se me cayó.**

Actividades analíticas

■ Answers to these activities are in Appendix 2 at the back of your book.

1 What nouns agree with the verbs in the bold-faced expressions in **Para empezar**?

se me cayó	el teléfono; un café
se me olvidó	la tarjeta de identificación
se me antojó	un café
se me rompió	el teléfono
se me mancharon	el chaleco y los pantalones

All these verbs use **se** because they are reflexive (see **Estructura 5.2**). Like many reflexive verbs, these indicate an action that occurs without anyone intentionally doing it. **Caerse**, for instance, means *to fall down,* an action that does not occur intentionally. The indirect object pronoun **me** indicates who is affected by this unintentional action (see **Estructura 7.2**). This can be the person who owns the object that underwent the action, such as the owner of the phone in **Se me cayó el teléfono** or the person who is experiencing the mental state, such as the person who experienced a craving in **Se me antojó un café.**

2 Most of these verbs may be used with or without the indirect object pronoun. The meaning of each verb is constant in Spanish, but adding the indirect object pronoun sometimes requires a different way of expressing the idea in English. In the following chart, use the pattern that you see to add the two missing sentences.

VERBO	SIN OBJETO INDIRECTO	CON OBJETO INDIRECTO
acabarse *to end, run out*	**Se acabó** el dinero. *The money ran out.*	**Se me acabó** el dinero *I ran out of money.*
caerse *to fall down*	**Se cayó** el teléfono. *The phone fell down.*	**Se me cayó** el teléfono. *I dropped the phone. /* *My phone fell down.*
mancharse *to get stained*	**Se manchó** la camisa. *The shirt got stained.*	**Se me manchó** la camisa. *I (accidentally) stained the shirt. /* *My shirt got stained.*
romperse *to break* *(get broken)*	**Se rompió** el lápiz. *The pencil broke.*	Se me rompió el lápiz. *I (accidentally) broke the pencil. /* *My pencil broke.*
perderse *to get lost*	**Se perdió** el pasaporte. *The passport got lost.*	Se me perdió el pasaporte *I lost my passport.*

With **antojarse** (*to feel like, have a craving for, be in the mood for*), the indirect object pronoun is almost always included.

—¿**Se te antoja** un helado?

"Are you in the mood for (Do you feel like) an ice cream?"

—No, gracias. Pero sí **se me antojan** estos caramelos.

"No, thank you. But I do have a craving for these candies."

■ For more on **se** for un-planned events, see **Para saber más 9.3** at the back of your book.

Note (Para saber más): *Para saber más 9.3 covers the verbs irse, notarse, quebrarse, quedarse, and hacerse.*

Note (Act. prácticas): *These activities emphasize me and te (e.g., se me olvidó, se te olvidó), as this is the first step in learning how to use this complex construction.*

Autoprueba

For each of the following situations, select the most logical verb and form an appropriate expression with **se** and an indirect object pronoun, based on the context clues.

acabarse
caerse
olvidarse
perderse

1. _____ los lentes. No los puedo encontrar.
2. ¿Estás en el aeropuerto y _____ el pasaporte? No te preocupes, te lo llevo ahora mismo.
3. Creo que _____ las tarjetas de embarque (*boarding passes*) en el baño (*restroom*). Voy a regresar para ver si todavía están en el suelo (*floor*).
4. ¿Estuviste en la playa y _____ el bloqueador solar (*sunscreen*)? ¿Fuiste a comprar más?

---

3 Any of the indirect object pronouns may be used with these verbs in order to express who is affected by the action. To clarify further who this person is, use the preposition **a.**

Se **te** cayó el café.	*You dropped the coffee.*
Se **le** rompió el teléfono.	*His/Her/Your (form.) telephone broke.*
Se **nos** antojó un café.	*We felt like a coffee.*
A mis amigos se **les** olvidó la fecha.	*My friends forgot the date.*

Actividades prácticas

A. ¿Qué pasó? Completa cada oración con la expresión más lógica. **¡Atención!** Tienes que usar cada expresión dos veces.

se me antoja   se me cayeron   se me cayó   se me olvidó   se me rompió

1. <u>Se me olvidó</u> tu número de teléfono.
2. <u>Se me antoja</u> ir al cine esta noche contigo. ¿A qué hora vamos?
3. La computadora <u>se me cayó</u>, pero por suerte (*luckily*) no <u>se me rompió</u>.
4. No <u>se me antoja</u> salir a bailar hoy. Tengo que limpiar el apartamento.
5. ¡<u>Se me cayeron</u> de mi bolso los pases de abordar! ¿Dónde están?
6. <u>Se me cayó</u> el plato y <u>se me rompió</u> en pedacitos (*little pieces*).
7. <u>Se me olvidó</u> cómo se llama nuestro libro. ¿Recuerdas tú el nombre?
8. ¡Perdón! <u>Se me cayeron</u> los libros en el piso.

B. Reacciones Completa cada oración o pregunta usando la persona indicada entre paréntesis. Luego empareja la oración o pregunta con la respuesta más lógica.

<u>d</u> 1. ¿Qué se <u>te</u> antoja hacer? (tú)
<u>f</u> 2. Se <u>me</u> olvidó decirte que tuviste una A en el examen. (yo)
<u>c</u> 3. A tu primo, ¿qué se <u>le</u> antoja comer? (él)
<u>b</u> 4. ¡Se <u>te</u> olvidó nuestro aniversario! (tú)
<u>g</u> 5. ¿Se <u>te</u> cayó algo? (tú)
<u>a</u> 6. ¿A quién se <u>le</u> cayó este lápiz? (él/ella)
<u>h</u> 7. ¿Se <u>te</u> olvidaron las llaves? (tú)
<u>e</u> 8. ¿Cuándo se <u>le</u> rompió el brazo a tu hermano? (él)

a. ¡A mí!
b. ¿No es mañana?
c. Le gustan las hamburguesas.
d. No quiero hacer nada.
e. El martes, cuando fue a esquiar (*ski*).
f. ¡Qué bueno! ¡Gracias!
g. Sí, mi teléfono, pero no le pasó nada.
h. No, no las necesito.

 C. ¿Qué se te olvida llevar? En grupos de tres o cuatro compañeros, túrnense para saber qué es lo que a sus compañeros más se les olvida llevar cuando van de viaje. ¿El cargador (*charger*) del teléfono? ¿El pasaporte? ¿El traje de baño? Apunten los resultados y compartan los a la clase.

MODELO: E1: ¿Qué se les olvida llevar cuando van de viaje?
E2: A mí siempre se me olvida llevar el cargador del teléfono.
E3: ¡A mí no! Pero a mí sí se me olvida el cepillo de dientes con frecuencia.

Suggestion (Act. C): *Give each group a different travel destination/situation so they will have different items to talk about: a la playa, a las montañas, a un hotel de lujo (luxury), a otro país, a casa de tus padres u otros familiares, al campo (countryside), en un crucero (cruise), con amigos, solo/a. Ask each group what their forgotten items are and tally them up to see what the most forgotten item is.*

D. Historias En parejas, escojan tres de las siguientes imágenes e inventen historias para explicar qué pasó. Creen situaciones lógicas y creativas. Para cada una, escriban por lo menos tres frases.

Los siguientes verbos les pueden ayudar.

acabarse   caerse   olvidarse   romperse

MODELO:

Tenía mucha prisa esta mañana porque me desperté tarde y tenía que estar en la estación de tren a las diez. Estaba muy nerviosa porque no quería llegar tarde. Hice mi maleta y salí de la casa con prisa, pero mientras corría, se me rompió el zapato, me caí y se me cayó el contenido de mi bolso en el suelo.

1.

2.

3.

4.

5.

E. ¿Adónde se te antoja ir?

PASO 1. En parejas, túrnense para entrevistarse, preguntándole a su compañero/a adónde se le antoja ir para sus próximas vacaciones, qué se le antoja hacer y qué se le antoja ver. Apunten las respuestas. **¡Atención!** Para hacer las preguntas en forma de **tú,** tienen que cambiar el pronombre **le** a **te** y el adjetivo posesivo **sus** a **tus.**

> **MODELO:** E1: ¿Adónde se te antoja ir para tus próximas vacaciones?
> E2: Se me antoja ir a una playa. ¿Y a ti?
> E1: Se me antoja ir a una ciudad vieja e histórica.

A tu compañero/a...

¿adónde se le antoja ir para sus próximas vacaciones?

☐ a una ciudad grande
☐ a un lugar histórico o antiguo
☐ a las montañas

☐ a una playa
☐ a un rancho o una granja (*farm*)
☐ a otro lugar: _____

¿qué se le antoja hacer?

☐ dormir, leer libros y pensar
☐ escuchar música y bailar
☐ hacer deportes de invierno

☐ hacer turismo de aventura
☐ observar animales
☐ otra cosa: _____

¿qué se le antoja ver?

☐ artesanías típicas
☐ una cultura indígena
☐ edificios coloniales

☐ el mar
☐ montañas o volcanes
☐ otra cosa: _____

Expansion (Act. E, Paso 2):
- Do a poll of the class to find out which vacation spots were the most popular. Ask some students to justify their choice.
- Have students work in small groups for a few minutes to create a radio/TV ad for one of the tourist destinations using as many instances of *se me/te antoja* as they can, and then have each group perform their ad for the class.

PASO 2. Lee la siguiente información sobre cuatro destinos turísticos muy populares y piensa en las respuestas de tu compañero/a a las preguntas del **Paso 1.** ¿Qué lugar recomiendas tú para tu compañero/a? Dile tu recomendación y pregúntale si está de acuerdo (*if he or she agrees*).

Antigua, Guatemala: Una ciudad fundada (*founded*) por los españoles en el siglo (*century*) dieciséis, con calles muy bonitas, edificios hermosos y mucha artesanía indígena. Está rodeada de (*surrounded by*) volcanes activos.

Bariloche, Argentina: También conocida como San Carlos de Bariloche, es una ciudad a un lado de la cordillera (*mountain range*) de los Andes. Tiene lagos, bosques y montañas, y es un centro importante de esquí.

Islas Galápagos, Ecuador: En las famosas islas que le encantaron a Carlos Darwin, hay mucho que ver a pie (*by foot*) —como las famosas tortugas gigantes— pero también se puede explorar en kayak.

Samaná, República Dominicana: En esta península, hay hermosas playas y lugares para ver ballenas (*whales*). Como en toda la República Dominicana, la música es buenísima y hay muchos lugares para bailar si te gustan la salsa y el merengue.

¡Leamos!

Vacaciones en Tequila

Follow-up (Antes de leer): After students have completed *Paso 2,* ask them to guess: *¿Qué piensan? ¿En esta clase hay más estudiantes aventureros o cautelosos?* Then ask for a show of hands: *Según sus respuestas al Paso 2, levanten la mano los estudiantes que son aventureros.* (count hands) *Ahora levanten la mano los que son cautelosos.* (count hands) *¿En esta clase hay más estudiantes aventureros o cautelosos?*

Antes de leer

PASO 1. Para cada actividad a continuación, escribe una **A** si le gustaría (*would like*) a una persona aventurera o una **C** si le gustaría a una persona cautelosa (*cautious*). **¡Atención!** Hay algunas actividades que les interesarían a ambos.

_____ 1. aprender cómo se hace el tequila
_____ 2. conocer los museos
_____ 3. aprender de la historia
_____ 4. explorar cavernas
_____ 5. hacer camping
_____ 6. andar en bicicleta
_____ 7. escalar
_____ 8. hacer turismo de aventura
_____ 9. nadar debajo de las cataratas
_____ 10. montar a caballo
_____ 11. caminar
_____ 12. visitar ruinas arqueológicas

PASO 2. Ahora haz una lista de las actividades del **Paso 1** que te gustaría hacer y otra de las actividades que no te gustaría hacer. ¿Eres una persona aventurera o cautelosa?

Suggestion (A leer): Have students skim each of the paragraphs and indicate whether each one refers to *el tequila, otras actividades* or *los dos.*

A leer

Lee el artículo y contesta las preguntas a continuación.

Vacaciones en Tequila

En 2006, UNESCO designó como Patrimonio de la Humanidad el paisaje entre el volcán Tequila y el Valle del Río Grande. La «Ruta del Tequila», un programa establecido al final del siglo XX,[a] promociona el turismo en esa zona tequilera. No se limita al pueblo Santiago de Tequila, sino que[b] el tren Tequila Express hace giras[c] por todo el valle. El turista puede degustar[d] tequila en las destilerías y haciendas de todo el valle.

Agave tequilana en Guadalajara, Jalisco, México

El inmenso valle azul-esmeralda[e] de las plantaciones de agave —la planta que nos brinda el «vino de mezcal[f]»— por sí solo proporciona[g] oportunidades de recorridos hermosos de mucha historia, pero más allá de las enormes plantaciones, Ruta del Tequila ofrece una variedad seductora[h] de turismos.

Unas vacaciones en Tequila pueden saciar a diversos gustos[i] e intereses. Los *agroturistas* van a estar muy a gusto[j] con una estadía[k] en una de las grandes haciendas tequileras. En las haciendas, el turista puede visitar destilerías, presenciar muestras[l] de los procesos, visitar museos y probar las especialidades (tequilas y comidas) de la casa.

Los *histoturistas* y *arqueoturistas* disfrutarán[m] de una visita a las ruinas de las pirámides circulares en Guachimontones. Las ruinas quedan al oeste de Guadalajara en el estado de Jalisco, y datan de 300 aC.[n]

[a]siglo... *twentieth century* [b]sino... *but rather* [c]*tours, excursions* [d]*taste* [e]*emerald-blue* [f]*mescal* [g]por... *in and of itself provides* [h]*alluring* [i]saciar... *satiate a variety of tastes (preferences)* [j]estar... *feel very comfortable* [k]*stay (n.)* [l]presenciar... *witness demonstrations* [m]*will enjoy* [n]datan... *date from 300 B.C.*

(Continues)

La Ruta del Tequila también complace[ñ] a todos los turistas que prefieren pasar sus vacaciones al aire libre.[o] Los *excurturistas* pueden dar caminatas[p] en las faldas[q] del Volcán Tequila, o hacer ciclismo o montar a caballo por los senderos[r] que serpentean[s] la rica vegetación hasta la Barranca de Tequila y la Cascada de los Azules. En la barranca,[t] los *ecoturistas* pueden acampar cerca de las cataratas y relajarse en las aguas azul-turquesas de los estanques.[u] Los *aventuristas* pueden practicar el rápel en los precipicios o la espeleología[v] en las cavernas cerca de las cataratas.

En Tequila, todos pueden degustar los mejores tequilas del mundo, la excelente cocina de la región y una variedad de platos especiales preparados con tequila.

¿Vacaciones en Tequila? ¡Cómo no!

[ñ]*pleases*   [o]*al... outdoors*   [p]*dar... take hikes*   [q]*foothills*   [r]*trails, paths*   [s]*wind*   [t]*ravine*   [u]*pools*   [v]*spelunking*

1. __c__ ¿Cuál **no** es un lugar que se puede visitar en la Ruta del Tequila?
   a. las cataratas
   b. las destilerías que fabrican el tequila
   c. las playas tropicales
   d. las ruinas arqueológicas

2. __d__ ¿Cuál es el enfoque de los atractivos turísticos en el Valle del Río Grande?
   a. el aventurismo
   b. la cerveza
   c. la naturaleza
   d. el tequila

3. __b__ ¿Cuál **no** es un campo profesional relacionado con los atractivos que se mencionan?
   a. la arqueología
   b. la astronomía
   c. la destilería
   d. la historia

4. __d__ ¿Cuántas destilerías hay en Jalisco?
   a. cero
   b. una
   c. dos
   d. varias

5. __d__ ¿Cómo se puede hacer un recorrido de la Ruta del Tequila?
   a. a caballo
   b. a pie
   c. en bicicleta
   d. todas las anteriores

6. __b__ ¿Cuál es la actividad que **no** menciona el artículo?
   a. el camping
   b. el fútbol
   c. las degustaciones
   d. la exploración de cavernas

7. __b__ ¿Qué se ofrece en todos los restaurantes de la región?
   a. la comida hecha de las hojas de la planta agave
   b. degustaciones de diferentes tequilas
   c. degustaciones de diferentes vinos
   d. los postres más ricos de México

8. __c__ ¿Cuál **no** es una atracción además del tequila?
   a. el rápel
   b. el ciclismo
   c. el vino
   d. la historia

Después de leer

PASO 1. En grupos, usen la información de la lectura para planear un fin de semana largo en Tequila. ¿Qué actividades les gustan? ¿Qué actividades no les gustan? ¿Por qué? ¿Cuándo van a participar todos en grupo y cuándo se van a separar? Hagan un itinerario para mostrar qué van a hacer cada día por la mañana, por la tarde y por la noche.

PASO 2. En grupos, repasen todas las actividades que se pueden hacer en estas excursiones y piensen en por lo menos cinco reglas que los organizadores de las excursiones Ruta del Tequila probablemente tienen para los turistas.

MODELOS: Tener cuidado al subirse y bajarse de sus caballos.
No pisar las plantas de agave.

¡Escuchemos!

Los viajes ideales

Script (Antes de escuchar): **1.** *Vamos a pasar las vacaciones y disfrutar un poco del tiempo libre.* **2.** *No me gusta pasar las vacaciones en las playas turísticas con tanta gente, con todo el calor del sol; siempre me quedo con una quemadura.* **3.** *Prefiero no volar en avión pero mi esposo siempre ha querido cruzar el Atlántico y pues, aquí estamos, pero no estoy contenta.* **4.** *El problema es que nos cancelaron el hotel sin avisar, la aerolínea perdió el equipaje y los dos nos enfermamos después de la primera cena aquí.* **5.** *Bueno, en realidad es un viaje soñado, tenía muchas ganas de hacer este viaje, es un paseo muy soñado.* **6.** *Estoy muy contenta de vacaciones aquí en la playa. No tengo que trabajar, no tengo que hacer nada. Me puedo relajar y tomar el sol todo el día.* **7.** *Prefiero lugares interesantes, a lo mejor coloniales, pueblos chicos pero que tengan mucha artesanía, que tengan museos y que haya cosas culturales. No me gusta este viaje a la playa.*

Antes de escuchar

Vas a escuchar las opiniones de varias personas sobre sus vacaciones. Decide si esa persona describe vacaciones buenas o malas.

	VACACIONES BUENAS	VACACIONES MALAS
1.	☑	☐
2.	☐	☑
3.	☐	☑
4.	☐	☑
5.	☑	☐
6.	☑	☐
7.	☐	☑

Follow up (Antes de escuchar): Ask students if they agree with the personal opinions expressed in **Antes de escuchar**.

Video track (A escuchar): This video clip can be found on the DVD to accompany *Conéctate: Cap. 9*, Track 3.

Suggestion (A escuchar): Before showing the clip, have students go over the speaker names and places so they will be able to do the matching while viewing.

A escuchar

PASO 1. Mira y escucha las descripciones de las vacaciones. Mira otra vez con pausas y empareja la persona con los lugares que menciona.

1. __a__ Adrián, de México

2. __b__ Juan Andrés, de Costa Rica

3. __e__ Magdalena, de Argentina

4. __d__ Erick, de Nicaragua

5. __g__ Olman, de Costa Rica

6. __f__ Natalia, de Argentina

7. __c__ Víctor, de México

a. Cancún y Puerto Vallarta
b. Colombia y Miami
c. Europa, los Estados Unidos y Canadá
d. las playas del Pacífico, como Guanacaste
e. Ushuaia, Argentina
f. varios ciudades grandes y estados de los Estados Unidos
g. varios países en varios continentes

Videoscript (A escuchar): **1.** ADRIÁN: *Bueno, este, la mayoría de los que estamos aquí, pues tratamos de ir a playas, que en México las playas son muy buenas, y pues tratamos de... de, visitar las playas como Cancún, este... Puerto Vallarta, no sé... Bueno, Cancún por ejemplo, es una playa, pues... yo creo que de las mejores que hay aquí en México, y es muy el, el clima es muy cálido, este el... también la gente que... te atiende en los hoteles así es, muy... te atiende muy bien, muy cálida así con todos los mexicanos y extranjeros que vienen de otros países, es muy buena.* **2.** JUAN ANDRÉS: *Es curioso. Pero, en Costa Rica la mayor gente que pase... que va a pasear de Costa Rica, gente de Costa Rica, ellos van a pasear a otros lados fuera de Costa Rica. Ellos no conocen el país e ignoran toda la belleza que tenemos. Por eso, ellos viajan a lugares como Colombia, San Andrés —a lugares más conocidos, más... un poco más famosos como Miami, San Andrés, a estos lugares. Ellos todavía no conocen Costa Rica.* **3.** MAGDALENA: *Mi ciudad natal es Ushuaia, está en Tierra del Fuego, es, eh... se dice que es la ciudad más austral del mundo, es, es... no es muy grande, tendrá 60.000 habitantes y es muy linda. Tiene una bahía muy grande y montañas. Y la atracción más grande creo que es la naturaleza y el paisaje eh... hay un parque nacional eh... muy grande a un lado. En invierno hay centros de esquí. En verano hay, bueno... hay... hay muchísimos... eh... ¿cómo se dice? viajes de turismo aventura y todo ese tipo de cosas para escalar por... por... por las paredes de la montaña para hacer paseos.* **4.** ERICK: *Okay, los que vivimos aquí generalmente como es montaña vamos mucho a la playa. Casi siempre nosotros preferimos las playas aquí del... de Guanacaste que son muy, muy buenas. El clima es un clima excelente, muy agradable, muy cálido. No es como el del Atlántico. Las playas del Pacífico son con un clima más cálido. El Atlántico es un clima un poco más húmedo, entonces es un poco más diferente. Es más agradable ir a las playas del Pacífico que a las playas del Caribe.* **5.** OLMAN: *El ser una persona abierta me dio mucha oportunidad de conocer el mundo, casi el mundo entero. Conozco muchos países y... Australia, Fiji, Nueva Zelanda, Guam, Japón, los Estados Unidos, México, Jamaica... todo Centroamérica.* **6.** NATALIA: *Bueno, fue un intercambio cultural... este, viajé dos meses, primero a Nueva York y a Washington, fuimos a hoteles, y después a Atlanta y a Colorado, estuvimos en casas de familia, eh... éramos un grupo de 30 que se dividió en dos, y bueno, 15 fuimos a Atlanta y a Colorado. Y bueno, ahí estuvimos en casa de familia, y, la verdad, estuvo buenísimo, para mí.* **7.** VÍCTOR: *Para las vacaciones, mucha gente va a las playas, a mí no me gusta ir a playas, yo prefiero lugares más interesantes, a lo mejor coloniales, pueblos chicos pero que tengan, mucha, mucha artesanía que tengan museos, y que haya cosas culturales, y cuando puedo, bueno... yo viajo... he ido a Europa a diferentes partes de Europa, Estados Unidos, que también he visitado mucho a Estados Unidos, y hasta Canadá, es lo que yo hago.*

(Continues)

PASO 2. Mira y escucha otra vez, indicando las tres atracciones que menciona cada uno.

	ADRIÁN	ERICK	NATALIA	VÍCTOR
1. un clima cálido	☑	☑	☐	☐
2. hoteles	☑	☐	☑	☐
3. un intercambio cultural	☐	☐	☑	☐
4. un lugar agradable	☐	☑	☐	☐
5. playas muy buenas	☑	☑	☐	☐
6. viajar a los Estados Unidos	☐	☐	☑	☑
7. viajar a Europa	☐	☐	☐	☑
8. visitar pueblos chicos con mucha cultura	☐	☐	☐	☑

Después de escuchar

PASO 1. En grupos, decidan si a cada persona del video le gustan o no las siguientes cosas y expliquen por qué.

Suggestion (Después de escuchar): Assign one person from the video to each group and then have each group report to the class on the person that they talked about.

> **MODELO:** A Víctor le gustan los museos porque va a las ciudades más grandes de Europa, pero no le gustan las playas.

las ciudades grandes   la naturaleza   los pueblos chicos

los hoteles excelentes   el paisaje   los viajes internacionales

los museos   las playas

PASO 2. Comparen sus propios (*your own*) gustos con los de las personas del video.

> **MODELO:** Me gustan las playas más que a Víctor porque prefiero pasar las vacaciones en las playas más que en las ciudades grandes. No me gustan mucho los museos.

CONÉCTATE AL MUNDO PROFESIONAL

Although not all negative vacation experiences are appropariate in the workplace, there are some that may reveal important details about your skill set and character. Tales of getting lost and finding your way back, overcoming challenges and hardships, or simply acclimating to new environments can make great answers to tough job interview questions, such as *What are your weaknesses?, Tell me about a challenge you overcame,* or *Why should we hire you?* Your response can include an interesting story, what you learned from it, how you now apply the skills and experiences gained, and how this will impact the organization if they hire you.

Traveling can help you develop skills like resourcefulness, problem-solving, and decision-making. Demonstrating those skills in the workplace can lead to great opportunities: new teams and projects, travel, and representing your organization outside the office.

¡Escribamos!

Las mejores y peores vacaciones

Algunas vacaciones son mejores que otras. ¿Puedes describir dos vacaciones muy diferentes? Si no tienes la experiencia de haber tenido (*having had*) unas vacaciones excelentes y otras desastrosas, describe viajes de amigos o familiares.

Antes de escribir

Piensa en el peor viaje y el mejor viaje de tu vida y llena la tabla. Puedes inventar tus respuestas si quieres.

	EL MEJOR VIAJE	**EL PEOR VIAJE**
¿Adónde fuiste?		
¿Cuándo fuiste?		
¿Con quién(es) fuiste?		
¿Por qué fuiste?		
¿Qué hiciste?		
¿Se te olvidó algo?		

A escribir

Usando la información de **Antes de escribir,** escribe dos párrafos —el primero para describir el peor viaje de tu vida y el segundo para describir el mejor.

> **MODELO:** Esta es la historia de dos viajes... El año pasado, fui a Chile con mis padres. Fue mi primer viaje fuera del país y por eso se me olvidó el pasaporte. Regresé a casa para recogerlo, pero luego perdí (*I missed*) el vuelo. El próximo vuelo no salió hasta el próximo día y por eso...

Después de escribir

Revisa tu ensayo. Luego intercambia ensayos con un compañero / una compañera para evaluarlos. Lee el ensayo de tu compañero/a y determina si cuenta una historia completa sobre el mejor y el peor viaje o si falta información necesaria. Lee de nuevo (*again*) el ensayo con cuidado para revisar los siguientes puntos de gramática.

☐ usa el imperfecto para describir el pasado
☐ usa el pretérito para hablar de las acciones que ocurrieron en el pasado
☐ usa **se + me/te/le(s)/nos** correctamente
☐ hay concordancia entre sustantivos y adjetivos (género y número)
☐ tiene la ortografía correcta

Después de revisar el ensayo de tu compañero/a, devuélveselo. Mira tu propio ensayo para ver los cambios que tu compañero/a recomienda y haz las revisiones necesarias.

ESTRATEGIA

Cause and effect

With the benefit of hindsight, it is almost always possible to trace a chain reaction that makes an extreme experience either a very positive one or a very negative one. When describing the best and worst travel experiences, for example, think of one event or piece of background information that set the cause-and-effect chain in motion and then describe what came of each action. Was it forgetting something? An illness? (Not) Making a list? (Not) Packing ahead of time? Then, use these sequences to carry the narrative thread throughout your descriptive paragraphs logically.

Suggestion (Después de leer): To motivate students to edit their own work as well as their classmates' carefully, occasionally grade their editing instead of their writing.

¡Hablemos!

¿Adónde vamos?

Expansion (Después de hablar): Have students split into 3–5 groups for a travel agent conference, where the travel agents come up with ideal vacation spots and activities for different types of travelers: *aventureros, cautelosos, solteros, novios, familias con niños jóvenes,* and so on.

Antes de hablar

Haz una lista de por lo menos cinco criterios para tus vacaciones ideales. Por ejemplo, ¿prefieres vacaciones activas o prefieres relajarte? ¿Prefieres el calor o el frío? ¿Quieres comer en los mejores restaurantes? ¿Quieres ir a muchos museos?

> **MODELO:** Me encanta la playa, pero no quiero gastar mucho dinero...

A hablar

En parejas, túrnense para hacer el papel de agente de viajes (*travel agent*) y el/la cliente que quiere ir de vacaciones pero no sabe adónde ir. El/La agente de viajes tiene que hacerle por lo menos siete preguntas al / a la cliente y luego recomendarle un lugar para sus vacaciones ideales. Pueden usar los lugares del capítulo u otros destinos que conocen.

> **MODELO:** E1: ¿A Ud. le gustaría ir de vacaciones durante el invierno o el verano?
> E2: Me gustaría ir de vacaciones durante el verano.
> E1: Bueno, y ¿le gustaría estar en la playa o en las montañas?
> E2: ...

Después de hablar

¿Quiénes están de acuerdo con las recomendaciones del / de la «agente de viajes» con quien hablaron en la sección **A hablar**? ¿Quiénes no están de acuerdo? Expliquen al resto de la clase por qué están de acuerdo o no.

Conéctate a la música

Canción: «Me voy» (2006)
Artista: Julieta Venegas (México)

Julieta Venegas es una cantante mexicana de Tijuana, Baja California. Es una de las más reconocidas cantantes de pop de los últimos años y ha tenido (*has had*) muchísimo éxito (*success*) en Latinoamérica, Norteamérica y Europa.

Antes de escuchar

Cuando uno sale de viaje, es muy común usar expresiones como **me voy, adiós** y **me despido** (*I say good-bye*). Pero además de lo que se dice, ¿qué es lo que se hace en estas circunstancias? ¿Qué tipo de acción o gesto es común?

Posibles respuestas: se llora, se abraza, se besa, se da la mano

> **A escuchar** Suggestion (A escuchar): Before playing the song, point out the *Expresiones útiles* and go over the questions in *A escuchar* to ensure students understand them.
>
> Escucha la canción, luego contesta las preguntas.

1. ¿Por qué se va? (Escoge cuatro respuestas.)

   a. Porque su pareja (*partner*) no sabe entender a su corazón.
   b. Porque ella quiere viajar por muchos países del mundo.
   c. Porque su pareja no tiene el valor (*courage*) de ver quién es ella.
   d. Porque su pareja no escucha lo que está tan cerca de él.
   e. Porque ella tiene que estar en Canadá para la próxima semana.
   f. Porque ella sabe que le espera (*awaits*) algo mejor.

   Note (A escuchar): The music video for this song can be found on the Internet. It is very amusing and contains many visuals for travel- and weather-related vocabulary.

2. ¿Va a llorar la cantante?   No.

3. Según la cantante, ¿es probable que merezca (*she deserves*) esta situación?   Es probable que sí.

4. ¿La cantante quiere quedarse con su pareja? ¿Qué hace?   No. Se va.

Después de escuchar

Cuando una persona termina una relación romántica, ¿qué hace típicamente? ¿Se queda en casa a llorar? ¿Sale de viaje? ¿Qué más se puede hacer? En grupos, hagan una lista de por lo menos cinco cosas que se puede hacer al terminar una relación romántica.

Suggestion (Después de escuchar): Ask each group for suggestions and create a list on the board.

La cantante mexicana Julieta Venegas toca el acordeón durante un concierto.

Expresiones útiles

merezco I deserve
(merecer)

qué lástima what a pity

■ For copyright reasons, the songs referenced in **Conéctate a la música** have not been provided by the publisher. The video for this song can be found on YouTube, and it is available for purchase from the iTunes store.

VOCABULARIO

Now that I have completed the chapter, I can . . .

☐ say what I would like to do

☐ use infinitives to express rules

☐ talk about travel and the weather

☐ talk about destinations, travel routes, and modes of transportation

☐ talk about what people do customarily

☐ talk about travel in the Spanish-speaking world

Comunicación

Me gustaría + *inf.*	I would like (*to do something*).
¿Te/Le gustaría + *inf.*?	Would you (*inform./ form.*) like (*to do something*)?
Favor de no fumar.	Please don't smoke.
Empujar.	Push.
Jalar.	Pull.
No beber y conducir.	Don't drink and drive.
No dar de comer.	Don't feed (the animals).
No doblar. / No girar.	Do not turn.
No entrar. / No pasar.	Do not enter.
No estacionar.	No parking.
No fumar.	No smoking.
No pisar (el césped).	Stay off / Do not walk on (the grass).
No tirar basura.	No littering. (*Lit.*, Do not throw trash.)

Las vacaciones

el aeropuerto	airport
la artesanía	craft(s)
el ascensor	elevator
el avión	airplane
la bicicleta de montaña	mountain bike
el bloqueador solar	sunscreen
el boleto	ticket
el bosque tropical	rainforest
la catarata	waterfall
el equipaje	baggage
la escala	layover

el/la guía	guide (*person*)
la maleta	suitcase
el mar	sea
la naturaleza	nature
el paisaje	scenery; landscape
un paseo	a walk/trip
la quemadura de sol	sunburn
la recogida de equipaje	baggage claim
el recorrido	trip/tour
el recuerdo	souvenir
la regla	rule
el sol	sun
el tren	train
el turismo de aventura	adventure tourism
el viaje	trip
la vista	view
el vuelo	flight

Cognados: la atracción, el ecoturismo, el hotel, la montaña, el pasaporte, la recepción, la seguridad, el servicio, el tour, el turismo, la visita

El tiempo — Weather

¿Qué tiempo hace?	What's the weather like?
Está despejado/nublado.	It's clear/cloudy.
Hace (muy) buen/ mal tiempo.	The weather is (very) good/bad.
Hace (mucho) calor/frío/ sol/viento.	It's (very) hot/cold/ sunny/windy.
llover (ue)	to rain
Llueve. / Está lloviendo.	It rains. / It's raining.
nevar (ie)	to snow
Nieva. / Está nevando.	It snows. / It's snowing.

Los adjetivos

agradable	pleasant
cálido/a	warm, hot
próximo/a	next; upcoming

Los adverbios

al extranjero	abroad
cerca (de)	close, near (to)
lejos (de)	far (from)

Los verbos

abordar	to board
acabarse	to end, run out
antojarse + *inf.*	to feel like (*doing something*)
antojarse + *n.*	to have a craving for (*something*)
caerse (*irreg.*)	to fall down
dar (*irreg.*) un paseo	to go for a walk
disfrutar de + *n.*	to enjoy (*something*)
escalar	to go rock climbing; to climb
esperar	to wait (for)
gastar	to spend
hacer (*irreg.*)...	
ciclismo de montaña	to go mountain biking
escala	to have a layover
la maleta	to pack a suitcase
un recorrido	to take a trip / go on a tour

ir de viaje	to go on a trip
mancharse	to stain
olvidarse	to forget
pasar por	to pass/go through
perder (ie)	to miss (*a bus/flight/ event*); to lose
perderse (ie)	to get lost
recoger (j)	to pick up
registrarse	to check in
romperse	to break
tomar el sol	to sunbathe
visitar	to visit

La vida profesional

Una doctora atiende a un paciente en La Guaira, Venezuela.

I Congreso Nacio
por la **Salud** y la **Vi**
Caracas, 12 al 14 de Marzo
INSTALACIÓN: Teatro Municipal
MESAS DE TRABAJO: Par

Objetivos

When you finish this chapter, you will be able to:

- conduct yourself professionally on the phone
- introduce people to each other
- talk about professions and technology used in the workplace
- give more detailed descriptions of a person, place, or thing
- make requests, invitations, and commands
- talk about work and professions in the Spanish-speaking world

10

www.mhhe.com/connect

COMUNICACIÓN ~~LARIO~~ ~~UCTURA~~ ~~ATE~~

A sus órdenes

Expressions for professional contexts

 A. A ver: A sus órdenes Mira y escucha. Luego mira otra vez con pausas e indica la expresión (o expresiones) que usa cada persona. Mira una tercera vez para verificar tus respuestas.

1. _e_ Angélica

2. _a_ Alexis

3. _f, c_ Eva

4. _a_ Guadalupe

5. _d_ Seiji

6. _d_ Felicitas

7. _b_ Ana

8. _a_ Mayra

9. _e_ Eduardo

10. _d_ Olman

a. Con mucho gusto.
b. Es un placer.
c. Estoy a sus órdenes.
d. Fue un placer.
e. Ha sido un placer.
f. Para servirle(s).

Video track (Act. A): This video clip can be found on the DVD to accompany *Conéctate: Cap. 10,* Track 1.

Videoscript (Act. A):
1. ANGÉLICA: *Ha sido un placer.* **2.** ALEXIS: *Con mucho gusto.* **3.** EVA: *Para servirles. Estoy a sus órdenes.* **4.** GUADALUPE: *Con mucho gusto.* **5.** SEIJI: *Claro, pues. Fue un placer haber contribuido para esta obra.* **6.** FELICITAS: *Fue un placer hacerlo. Hasta luego.* **7.** ANA: *Para mí es un placer compartir con Uds.* **8.** MAYRA: *Con mucho gusto.* **9.** EDUARDO: *Ha sido un placer.* **10.** OLMAN: *Fue un placer.*

To ask politely to do something, use: **Quisiera** + *infinitive.*

> **Quisiera hablar con la directora.**

To ask *How can I help you?,* say: **¿En qué puedo servirle(s)?**
When someone thanks you for your assistance, respond with one of the following expressions.

Para servirle. ⎫ **A sus órdenes.** ⎭	*At your service.*
Es / Fue / Ha sido un placer.	*It's / It was / It has been a pleasure.*
Con mucho gusto.	*My pleasure. / With pleasure.*

B. ¿En qué puedo servirle? Escoge la frase adecuada para cada situación.

1. _b_ En el banco
   a. La cuenta (*bill*), por favor.
   b. Quisiera cambiar (*cash*) un cheque.
   c. Perdone. Busco las manzanas.
   d. Quisiera enviar (*send*) estas cartas (*letters*).

2. _b_ En la librería
   a. Dos entradas (*tickets*), por favor.
   b. Perdone. ¿Dónde están los diccionarios?
   c. Quisiera cambiar un cheque.
   d. Quisiera hablar con el director.

Follow-up (Act. B): Point out that it is common to request something just by naming that item and following it with *por favor,* such as *La cuenta, por favor* or *Más café, por favor.*

(Continues)

3. __c__ En el mercado
   a. Quisiera hablar con el director.
   b. ¿Me trae un tenedor, por favor?
   c. Perdone. Busco las manzanas.
   d. Quisiera enviar estas cartas.

4. __a__ En el museo
   a. Dos entradas, por favor.
   b. Quisiera comprar estampillas (*stamps*).
   c. Quisiera cambiar el cheque.
   d. Perdone. Busco los tomates.

5. __d__ En la oficina de correos
   a. ¿Me trae un refresco, por favor?
   b. Perdone, ¿dónde están las novelas de detectives?
   c. ¿Me trae un tenedor, por favor?
   d. Quisiera enviar estas cartas.

6. __b__ En el restaurante
   a. Dos entradas, por favor.
   b. La cuenta, por favor.
   c. Disculpe. ¿Me puede decir dónde están los diccionarios?
   d. Quisiera hablar con el director.

C. ¿Qué se hace?

PASO 1. En parejas, hagan una lista de dos o tres actividades que se hacen en cada lugar.

> **MODELO:** en el banco: se depositan cheques, se cobran (*cash*) cheques, se saca dinero

1. en la librería
2. en el mercado
3. en el museo
4. en la oficina de correos
5. en el restaurante

PASO 2. Ahora pónganse en dos filas, cara a cara. Los estudiantes de una fila son los clientes; los estudiantes de la otra son los empleados (*employees*) de los lugares de la lista. Debes tener una conversación completa con la persona delante de (*in front of*) ti. Luego todos los estudiantes de una fila deben tomar un pasito (*small step*) a la izquierda para empezar de nuevo con otra pareja en una situación nueva.

> **MODELO:** E1: Buenas tardes. ¿En qué puedo servirle?
> E2: Quisiera depositar un cheque y cambiar (*exchange*) dinero.
> E1: ¡Cómo no!
> E2: Gracias.
> E1: Para servirle.

1. el banco
2. la librería
3. el mercado
4. el museo
5. la oficina de correos
6. el restaurante

Note (Act. C, Paso 2): The student at the left end of the line that steps to the left and is without a partner should move to the beginning of the line. If you don't have enough room for students to make two long lines, have them split up into groups and work through the exercise, switching partners and roles part way through.

Suggestion (Act. C, Paso 2): Repeat *Paso 2* up to six times, switching the roles (client and employee) of the two lines half way through.

Quisera cambiar dinero.

Note (En español): At this level of listening comprehension, students should be able to take an accurate message from a native Spanish speaker that includes a correctly spelled name and a complete phone number so that a more fluent Spanish-speaker could call back. Taking a more detailed message is intermediate or higher. See *Conéctate al mundo profesional* on p. 12 for similar communication strategies.

En español...

Telephone interactions are more challenging than face-to-face interactions, in part because there are no visual cues. Often it is important to be able to get just the most basic information, such as a name and telephone number, so that a fluent speaker can return the call. Here are a few sentences that can help you take control of the conversation and successfully acquire the most basic information.

MAKING THE CALL

Buenos días. / Buenas tardes.	Good morning/afternoon. This is
Habla ____, de la compañía ____.	____, from ____ (*company*) speaking.
¿Puedo hablar / Me puede comunicar con + *name of person*?	May I speak / Can you connect me with ____?
¿Está / Se encuentra + *name of person*?	Is ____ there?
¿Puedo dejarle un mensaje?	May I leave him/her a message?
Más despacio, por favor.	Slower, please.
Gracias, muy amable. Adiós.	Thank you, you've been very kind. Good-bye.

ANSWERING THE TELEPHONE

Buenos días. / Buenas tardes. + *name of company*	
¿De parte de quién?	Who's calling?
Un momento, por favor.	Just a moment, please.
No está en este momento.	He's/She's not here right now.
¿Le quiere dejar un mensaje?	Would you like to leave a message for him/her?
¿Cuál es su nombre y su número de teléfono?	What is your name and telephone number?
Número por número, por favor.	One number at a time, please.
Letra por letra, por favor.	One letter at a time, please.
¿Cómo se escribe?	How do you spell that?
Alguien lo/la volverá a llamar.	Someone will call you back.
Gracias por llamar. Adiós.	Thank you for calling. Good-bye.

These simple phrases can lead to a clear and successful telephone interaction that will be a lot less frustrating for both parties than a conversation full of requests for general repetitions such as **¿Cómo?** or **¿Qué?**

Script (Act. D): 1. *Buenos días. Soy Daniel Castro, vendedor para la empresa Instalaciones Interiores. Quisiera hablar con el licenciado Miguel Antonio Marcos. Mi número de teléfono es el 918-304-5720.* **2.** *Buenas tardes. Mi nombre es José María López García y represento la compañía Casa Química. Mi número de teléfono es el 673-910-4593. Quisiera hablar con el ingeniero Alberto Sáenz.* **3.** *Buenas tardes. Me llamo Leticia Fonseca Valladares y mi número de teléfono es el 971-725-6419. Quisiera conectarme con la presidenta de la compañía, la doctora Elisabet Maldonado Pereira.* **4.** *Buenos días. Soy María Luisa García Méndez y llamo del periódico nacional El Tiempo. Quisiera hablar con un representante de relaciones públicas. Mi número de teléfono es el 926-372-1674.* **5.** *Buenas tardes. Mi nombre es Ignacio Ordóñez Cienfuegos y mi número de teléfono es el 0011-1-663-290-2763, extensión 765. Espero su llamada.* **6.** *Buenos días. Me llamo Elena Amador. Trabajo para la firma de abogados Reyes, Amador y Morales. Quisiera hablar con la licenciada Adelaida Flores. Mi número de teléfono es el 823-746-3992.*

■ The audio files for in-text listening activities are available in the eBook, within Connect activities, and on the Online Learning Center.

D. «No está. ¿Le quiere dejar un mensaje?» Escucha los mensajes y apunta con quién quieren hablar, los nombres y apellidos de las personas que llaman y sus números de teléfono.

	MENSAJE PARA...	NOMBRE(S)	APELLIDO(S)	NÚMERO DE TELÉFONO
1.	Lic. Miguel Antonio Marcos	Daniel	Castro	918-304-5720
2.	Ing. Alberto Sáenz	José María	López García	673-910-4593
3.	Dra. Elisabet Maldonado Pereira	Leticia	Fonseca Valladares	971-725-6419
4.	representante de relaciones públicas	María Luisa	García Méndez	926-372-1674
5.	—	Ignacio	Ordóñez Cienfuegos	0011-1-663-290-2763 ext. 765
6.	Lic. Adelaida Flores	Elena	Amador	823-746-3992

Suggestion (Act. D): As an alternative to a whole-class activity, divide the class into groups. Give a different message to each group member and have them read their message to their group, who will transcribe them, asking for clarification as needed. After all groups have finished, have students write the essential information on the board and have the class check for accuracy.

Note (Act. D): If you are reading the script, encourage students to follow up with specific requests or questions such as *Número por número, por favor; ¿Fonseca es nombre o apellido?* Only allow global requests for repetition of the entire message if you are using recorded audio.

Suggestions (Act. E):
- In order to provide more realistic practice, you may wish to give students the option of using their phones to actually call students from the other side of the room, the hallway, or outside.
- To add more challenge to this activity, you may wish to have students state the reason for the call.

E. ¡Rin, rin!

PASO 1. En parejas, pónganse espalda con espalda (*back to back*) y túrnense para apuntar un mensaje telefónico. Cada mensaje debe incluir: la fecha y la hora de la llamada, el nombre de la persona que debe recibir el mensaje, el nombre de la persona que llama y su número de teléfono.

MODELO: E1: ¡Rin, rin!

E2: Buenos días, oficina de Suzy.

E1: ¿Está Suzy?

E2: No está en este momento. ¿Le quiere dejar un mensaje?

E1: Sí, gracias.

E2: ¿Cuál es su nombre, apellido y número de teléfono?

E1: Mi nombre es...

PASO 2.   Ahora, verifiquen los mensajes usando la siguiente lista.

- ¿El mensaje tiene correcto el nombre de la persona que debe recibir el mensaje?
- ¿El mensaje tiene correctas la fecha y hora de la llamada?
- ¿Tiene el nombre completo (nombre y apellido) de la persona que llama?
- ¿Tiene el número correcto?

Suggestion (Conéctate al mundo profesional): For a more complete discussion of job interviews, refer students back to the *Conéctate al mundo profesional* box in the Cap. 9 *¡Escuchemos!* section. Ask them what other types of experiences they would talk about in a job interview.

CONÉCTATE AL MUNDO PROFESIONAL

Your experiences studying languages can provide you with a lot of great topics for professional-school essays and anecdotes for job interviews. For example, medical school applications usually ask candidates to describe how they will interact with patients from a culture different than their own. Your own experiences of being different as you learn a new language and culture, as well as the communication strategies you develop, will help you to write a thoughtful answer. Similarly, you can use a situation of cross-cultural misunderstanding to answer job interview questions about weaknesses or overcoming difficulty.

Quiero presentarle a...

Introducing people to each other

To introduce people to each other, address by name the person with the highest status or whom you know less well and say: **Quiero presentarte/le a...**

—**Sara, quiero presentarte a mi hermano, Juan.**

—**Señor Olivares, quiero presentarle a mi amiga Sara.**

To introduce someone to more than one person, you can say: **Quiero presentarles a...**

—**Niños, quiero presentarles al nuevo estudiante, Antonio.**

To reply with something along the lines of *Nice to meet you* or *It's a pleasure,* use one of these expressions.

Mucho gusto.
Encantado/a.
Es un placer.

As you learned in **Capítulo 1,** if someone says *Nice to meet you* first, you can respond with **Igualmente,** which means *Likewise.*

—**Mario, quiero presentarte a mi amiga Anita.**

—**Mucho gusto, Anita.**

—**Igualmente, Mario.**

—**Profesora Alemán, quiero presentarle a mi madre, Magda Ordóñez Gil.**

—**Encantada, señora Ordóñez.**

—**Igualmente, profesora Alemán.**

A. A presentar   Pon la siguiente conversación en orden (de 1 al 5).

_5_ Adiós.

_1_ Buenas tardes, Juan Andrés. Quiero presentarte a mi novia, Elena.

_3_ Igualmente.

_2_ Mucho gusto, Elena.

_4_ Tengo clase en cinco minutos. Hasta luego.

Fernando, quiero presentarte a mi amiga Maribel.

Suggestion (Act. B, Paso 1):
For items 1, 2, 4, and 5, ask students what is inappropriate about each of the incorrect answers.

B. Quiero presentar...

PASO 1. Indica la mejor manera de presentar a las personas.

1. _b_ A tu amigo y tu profesor de inglés
   a. Efra, quiero presentarte a mi profesor de inglés, Adam White.
   b. Profesor White, quiero presentarle a mi amigo Efra.
   c. Los dos están bien.
   d. Ninguno de los dos está bien.

2. _b_ A una amiga de la universidad y tus padres
   a. Mariela, te presento a mis padres, Ernesto y Liliana.
   b. Mamá, papá, quiero presentarles a mi amiga Mariela.
   c. Los dos están bien.
   d. Ninguno de los dos está bien.

3. _c_ A dos amigos tuyos
   a. Héctor, quiero presentarte a Juan.
   b. Juan, quiero presentarte a Héctor.
   c. Los dos están bien.
   d. Ninguno de los dos está bien.

4. _d_ A la nueva gerente (*manager*) y el presidente de la compañía
   a. Estefanía Guzmán Torres, quiero presentarte al presidente, José Antonio López Gómez.
   b. Presidente López, quiero presentarte a la nueva gerente, Estefanía Guzmán.
   c. Los dos están bien.
   d. Ninguno de los dos está bien.

5. _b_ Al nuevo estudiante y la maestra
   a. Diego, quiero presentarte a la maestra, señora Maldonado.
   b. Señora Maldonado, quiero presentarle al nuevo estudiante, Diego.
   c. Los dos están bien.
   d. Ninguno de los dos está bien.

PASO 2. En parejas, túrnense para presentarles su amiga Elena a las siguientes personas. Hagan la presentación de dos maneras si se puede.

> **MODELO:** tus hermanos (Esteban y Manolo) → Esteban, Manolo, quiero presentarles a mi amiga Elena.
> o Elena, quiero presentarte a mis hermanos, Esteban y Manolo.

1. tu mejor amigo/a Quiero presentarte a Elena. / Elena, quiero presentarte a mi mejor amigo/a, _____.
2. el profesor de inglés Quiero presentarle a Elena.
3. los miembros de tu equipo (*team*) Quiero presentarles a Elena. / Elena, quiero presentarte a los miembros de mi equipo.
4. el gerente de una compañía Quiero presentarle a Elena.
5. la directora de marketing de una compañía Quiero presentarle a Elena.
6. el vecino Quiero presentarle/te a Elena.
7. tus padres Quiero presentarles a Elena.

Variation (Act. C):
Assign each student an identity (using names of famous people, if you like). They have to introduce themselves to as many people as possible in 3 minutes, then have 3 more minutes to introduce as many people to each other as they can. The student(s) who recall the most names correctly win.

C. A conocernos...
En grupos de cuatro o cinco, túrnense para presentarle un(a) estudiante a otro/a.

> **MODELO:** E1: Chelsea, quiero presentarte a mi amiga Leslie.
> E2: Encantada, Leslie.
> E3: Igualmente. Chelsea, ¿conoces a... ?

Las profesiones y los oficios
Professions and careers

A. Somos profesionales ¿Dónde se practica cada profesión? Completa las oraciones en la página 300 con la profesión que se describe.

el fotógrafo
el jefe
la ingeniera
la directora de marketing
la programadora
la diseñadora gráfica
el bloguero
la dueña
la ejecutiva
el empleado
la agente de seguros
la arquitecta
el gerente
el asistente administrativo / secretario
el agente de bienes raíces
el cajero
la jueza
la maestra /profesora
el bombero
la cosmetóloga
la abogada
la mujer policía
el estudiante
la trabajadora social
el dentista
el enfermero
el cirujano
la médica

Expansion (Conéctate al mundo profesional): Direct students to websites such as Indeed, Monster, Craigslist, and Idealist to conduct job searches, or ask them to share with the class names of online job-search sites for international, national, or local listings. Assign as homework that students search for entry-level jobs in 4–5 different fields and have students present their findings in class. As a follow-up, use the new vocabulary to ask about sites specific to certain fields: ¿Dónde se busca un trabajo de diseñador(a) gráfico/a? ¿de trabajador(a) social? ¿de programador(a)? ¿de asistente administrativo/a o ejecutivo/a?

(Continues)

CONÉCTATE AL MUNDO PROFESIONAL

How do you look for career options in which your Spanish-language skills would be considered a strong advantage? You might start by looking at job websites and searching for *Spanish* as a keyword. Which professional fields come up? What are the specific jobs and their required skills? Do any surprise you?

Another idea is to choose a company that you might like to work for in the future. Look at their job listings (on their own website or through another job portal) for any positions that require bilingual skills. Also, try reading the company's "About Us" page for ideas. It may be an architectural firm that has designed buildings in Spanish-speaking countries, a radio station that broadcasts to Hispanic communities, an online multimedia platform that localizes its content for Spanish-language users, or a fashion line that is manufactured and/or sold overseas. Figure out how your skills and career interests connect to the company's business profile and you might just discover the dream job you never knew existed!

Note (Act. A): The following professions were previously introduced: (*Cap. 1*) *profesor(a)*; (*Cap. 4*) *abogado/a, chofer, doctor(a), guía naturalista, ingeniero/a, médico/a, periodista, pintor(a), policía, psicólogo/a, sociólogo/a*; (*Cap. 6*) *camarero/a*; (*Cap. 8*) *diseñador(a)*; (*Cap. 9*) *guía*.

Suggestion (Act. A): Allow students to argue different answers than those provided, even if the answers seem odd to you.

1. _____El/La fotógrafo/a_____ saca fotos en bodas y otras celebraciones.
2. _____El/La asistente administrativo/a;_____ organiza reuniones, toma mensajes y
   _____El/La secretario/a_____ ayuda a los empleados de un negocio.
3. _____El/La arquitecto/a_____ diseña edificios, pero solo supervisa la construcción de ellos.
4. _____El/La agente de bienes raíces_____ ayuda a gente que quiere vender o comprar una casa.
5. _____El policía / La mujer policía_____ trabaja en la comunidad para asegurar la seguridad pública.
6. _____El/La profesor(a); El/La maestro/a_____ trabaja en una escuela donde enseña a los estudiantes.
7. _____El/La abogado/a_____ ofrece su argumento delante del juez / de la jueza en un tribunal.
8. _____El/La juez(a)_____ toma decisiones importantes dentro de una sala de justicia.
9. _____El/La cosmetólogo(a)_____ trabaja en una peluquería o salón de belleza.
10. _____El/La cirujano/a_____ trabaja en el quirófano (*operating room*) operando a los pacientes.
11. _____El/La médico/a; El/La enfermero/a; El/La doctor(a)_____ trabaja en una clínica médica u hospital.
12. _____El/La dentista_____ trabaja en una clínica dental.

Here are some useful verbs that have to do with work.

conseguir (i, i) (un puesto de trabajo)	to get (a job/position)
contratar	to hire
entrevistar	to interview
estar dispuesto/a	to be ready/willing
preparar un currículum	to prepare a resume/CV
solicitar empleo/trabajo	to apply for work/a job

El empleado le muestra el informe (*report*) a su gerente.

B. La jerarquía (*hierarchy*) en el lugar de trabajo

PASO 1. Para cada grupo, pon los profesionales en orden de la persona más alta en la jerarquía (1) a la menos alta (3).

1. _2_ el/la gerente
   _1_ el/la ejecutivo/a
   _3_ el/la secretario/a

2. _3_ el/la asistente médico/a
   _1_ el/la cirujano/a
   _2_ el/la enfermero/a

3. _3_ el/la cajero/a
   _1_ el/la dueño/a
   _2_ el jefe / la jefa

PASO 2. En parejas, decidan cuál de las profesiones del **Paso 1** es la que más se aplica a cada palabra y cuál es la que menos se aplica. Compartan sus decisiones con la clase y expliquen sus razones.

1. prestigioso
2. peligroso
3. interesante
4. divertido
5. lucrativo
6. fácil

C. ¿Qué hacen para el trabajo? Indica si cada frase es lógica o no para la persona de la profesión que se menciona.

	ES LÓGICA.	NO ES LÓGICA.
1. Un agente de seguros usa un libro de texto.	☐	☑
2. Una asistente administrativa usa mucho el teléfono.	☑	☐
3. Los estudiantes y profesores crean las leyes (*laws*).	☐	☑
4. Un fotógrafo usa una cámara.	☑	☐
5. Un ingeniero usa un bisturí (*scalpel*).	☐	☑
6. Los estudiantes y profesores usan los libros de texto.	☑	☐
7. Una cosmetóloga usa un horno (*oven*)	☐	☑
8. Un cirujano usa un bisturí.	☑	☐
9. Una diseñadora de multimedia y un escritor usan las computadoras.	☑	☐
10. Una cosmetóloga usa las tijeras (*scissors*).	☑	☐
11. Un abogado usa las leyes.	☑	☐

D. A ver: Las profesiones Mira y escucha. Luego mira otra vez con pausas y apunta la profesión de cada persona. Mira una tercera vez para verificar tus respuestas.

NOMBRE	PROFESIÓN
1. Catalina Haayen	profesora de colegio, instructora de yoga
2. Juan Asconapé	abogado (y trabaja para una universidad)
3. Lourdes Díaz	cosmetóloga
4. Zuly Viera	asistente administrativa
5. Pedro Vera	policía
6. Mario Lageire	agente de seguros
7. Néstor Olivera	ingeniero (en computación)
8. María Jesús Madrigal	profesora (de español)
9. Juan Francisco Funer Rodríguez	médico (cirujano)
10. Vanessa Anaya Loera	estudiante (de administración de empresas)
11. Juan Sol	estudiante
12. Andrea Suárez	estudiante (de marketing)

E. ¿Quién es? En grupos, túrnense para describir una profesión de la lista de vocabulario sin mencionar el nombre de la profesión. Los otros miembros del grupo deben hacer preguntas sobre la profesión hasta adivinar qué es.

MODELO: E1: Esta persona enseña a otras personas.
E2: ¿Es un juez?
E1: No, esta persona tiene una clase de estudiantes.
E3: ¿Es un profesor o una profesora?
E1: ¡Acertaste (*You guessed correctly*)!

F. ¿Qué profesiones te interesan? Mira de nuevo la lista de profesiones y decide cuáles son las tres que más te interesan. Nómbralas y explícale a un compañero / una compañera de clase por qué te interesan estas tres profesiones. ¿Qué destrezas (*skills*) requieren? ¿Las tienes tú? ¿Qué profesión de la lista te interesa menos? ¿Por qué?

Video track (Act. D): This video clip can be found on the DVD to accompany *Conéctate: Cap. 10*, Track 2.

Videoscript (Act. D):
1. *Me llamo Catalina Haayen. Eh… Soy de Colombia eh… Nací en Medellín, est… Vivo en Miami. Soy una profesora de colegio y enseño yoga.*
2. *Me llamo Juan Asconapé. Originalmente soy argentino pero nacionalizado norteamericano. Eh… Soy abogado y trabajo para una universidad en Miami.* **3.** *Mi nombre es Lourdes. Eh… Soy cosmetóloga y soy nacida en Cuba. Resido aquí en Miami.*
4. *Mi nombre es Zuly Viera. Tengo 30 años. Hoy es mi cumpleaños. Eh… Trabajo de asistente administrativa en una compañía de… planeación financiera aquí en Miami. Y soy de Cali, Colombia.*
5. *Mi nombre es Pedro Vera. Yo soy cubano. Mi edad es 34 años y mi profesión es policía para la ciudad de Miami. Yo monto a caballo.* **6.** *Bueno, mi nombre es Mario Lageire, yo vivo en Choele Choel, Río Negro, Patagonia Argentina. Eh… Soy agente de seguros.*
7. *Mi nombre es Néstor. Eh… Soy de la Patagonia, de Neuquén, y soy ingeniero en computación, trabajo acá en Buenos Aires.* **8.** *Vale, me llamo María Jesús. Eh… Vivo en Alcalá de Henares pero soy de… nací en un pueblo muy cerquita de Alcalá, que se llama Sigüenza, está a como a una hora de… de viaje en coche, y soy profesora de español en la Universidad de Alcalá de Henares.* **9.** *Mi nombre es Juan Francisco Funer Rodríguez. Eh… Yo nací y he vivido en San Francisco del Rincón, Guanajuato, trabajo en la ciudad de León, Guanajuato en México. Mi profesión*

es médico cirujano y la especialidad cirugía general. **10.** *Mi nombre es Vanessa, yo estudio administración de empresas, tengo 23 años y soy de Cuernavaca.* **11.** *Bueno, mi nombre es Juan. Juan Sol me llamo. Y… tengo 20 años, nací acá en Buenos Aires, Argentina y bueno, vi… vivo acá y… mi… mi profesión es estudiante.* **12.** *Me llamo Andrea Suárez. Eh… Vivo en España. Eh… Soy estudiante, estudio marketing.*

Suggestion (En español): Have students read these words aloud, encouraging them to have fun exaggerating the Spanish pronunciation (*u-ese-be*) and syllable stress (*el mon-i-TOR*). This will help them to move away from pronouncing the words as they do in English. You may want to ask them to recall the rules of accent marks that apply to *escáner* and *láptop* when written in Spanish.

La tecnología en el lugar de trabajo
Technology in the workplace

A. Escribir un email profesional Revisa las palabras que se asocian con la computación y la tecnología. Luego empareja cada palabra con su ejemplo más adecuado o descripción más adecuada.

la (computadora) portátil/láptop

el correo electrónico / el email / el mensaje

el saludo

adjuntar / el anexo

la despedida

la impresora

el escáner

la tableta

Para dra.rodriguez@abc.org
Asunto: Reporte Final
Estimada Dra. Rodriguez,
Aquí *adjunto* el reporte final. Espero sus comentarios.
Atentamente,
Kathy Bauer
Reporte_Final.docx (27 K)
Enviar

el escáner

la pantalla

el teclado

En español...

In the technological realm, there are a lot of cognates or borrowed words that change spelling or accentuation to match pronunciation. Here are a few examples.

el blog
el email
el escáner
la láptop
la web
el WiFi
el monitor
el (teléfono) celular/móvil
USB
chatear
hacer clic

1. __c__ el anexo   a. «Atentamente»
2. __e__ el asunto   b. lo que usas para imprimir documentos, mensajes o anexos
3. __a__ la despedida   c. un documento que quieres enviar con un correo electrónico
4. __b__ la impresora   d. «Estimados Profesores»
5. __d__ el saludo   e. «Reunión lunes a las 14:00»
6. __f__ la tableta   f. lo que usas para escribir un email cuando no puedes sentarte frente a la computadora

---

To talk about *uploading* or *downloading* in Spanish, use **subir** and **bajar**. Use **conectarse** to say *to get online*.

¿**Subiste** los documentos al servidor?   *Did you upload the files to the server?*

Voy a **bajar** la nueva canción de Calle 13.   *I'm going to download the new Calle 13 song.*

Voy a **conectarme** para chatear con una amiga.   *I'm going to get online so I can chat with a friend.*

B. Cómo escribir un correo electrónico profesional Sigue las instrucciones para escribir un mensaje a tu profesor(a) para decirle que necesitas recuperar (*make up*) un examen que perdiste (*you missed*).

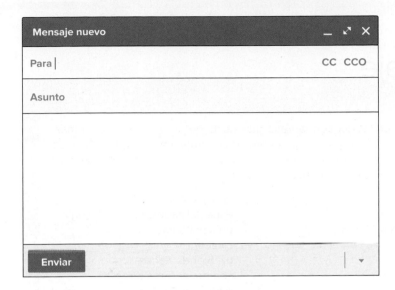

1. Usa la línea de **asunto.** El recipiente debe entender de qué se trata el mensaje basándose en esta frase.
2. Empieza con un saludo profesional, el título adecuado (**Profesor[a]** o **Doctor[a]**) y el apellido.
3. Incluye respuestas a estas preguntas.
    - ¿qué? (*el examen que perdiste*)
    - ¿quién? (*tú lo perdiste*)
    - ¿dónde? (*un lugar conveniente para el/la instructor[a]*)
    - ¿cuándo? (*un día y una hora apropiados*)
    - ¿por qué? (*explica tu situación*)
4. Termina con una despedida adecuada y profesional.

Suggestion (Act. B): I have students send the emails to you. Share the best ones with the class.

CONÉCTATE AL MUNDO HISPANO

¿Sabías que en México se instituyó (*established*) el sistema de educación de clases televisadas llamado Telesecundaria en 1968, mucho antes de surgir (*arose*) cualquier forma de educación a distancia en los Estados Unidos? Desde hace muchos años, la educación a distancia por televisión ha ampliado (*increased*) los niveles de educación de las poblaciones rurales por todo el mundo.

Más reciente, los teléfonos celulares han hecho (*have made*) posible mejor contacto con lugares donde no llegan los cables de los teléfonos tradicionales. **La conectividad** que nos da la tecnología no solo nos conecta socialmente, sino que ha aportado (*has offered*) opciones donde antes no existían.

COMÚN VOCABUL **ESTRUCTURA** TE

Reciclaje

Adjectives

Suggestion (Reciclaje): Tell students to pay attention to the article of each noun as a clue to its gender.

Note (Reciclaje): This *Reciclaje* activates students' knowledge of the fact that modifiers are placed *after* the noun in Spanish, whether it is an adjective or a prepositional phrase. In **10.1,** they will see that adjective clauses follow this pattern as well.

■ Answers to this activity are in Appendix 2 at the back of your book.

Empareja cada profesión con la frase que describe su especialización más común, modificando el número y género de los adjetivos cuando sea necesario. Luego escribe cada término (*term*) nuevo bajo el nombre del sector de la economía donde pertenece (*it belongs*).

los arquitectos	civil y estructural
una profesora	especializado/a en cardiología
los ingenieros	universitario/a
un médico	clínico/a
un policía	de bienes raíces
las psicólogas	comercial y residencial
una agente	motorizado/a (*on a motorcyle*)

EDIFICIOS / INFRAESTRUCTURA	EDUCACIÓN	SALUD (*HEALTH*)	SEGURIDAD
los arquitectos comerciales y residenciales	una profesora universitaria	un médico especializado en cardiología	un policía motorizado
los ingenieros civiles y estructurales		las psicólogas clínicas	
una agente de bienes raíces			

10.1 El arquitecto que diseñó este puente

The relative pronoun *que*

Para empezar...

Santiago Calatrava: Arquitecto de edificios y puentes; nació en Valencia, España, en 1951.

Santiago Calatrava y Carlos Slim son dos de los profesionales más destacados (*noteworthy*) y los dos son de países hispanos. Lee las oraciones e indica con una **C** las que describen a Calatrava y con una **S** las que describen a Slim. **¡Atención!** Hay dos oraciones que no tienen que ver ni con Calatrava ni con Slim. Usa **X** para estas oraciones.

1. __C__ Muchos lo comparan con Antoni Gaudí, un arquitecto español **que** hizo muchos edificios muy famosos en Barcelona.
2. __S__ Tiene varias compañías **que** administran sus hijos Carlos, Marco Antonio y Patrick.
3. __S__ Es el dueño de Telmex, una compañía **que** tiene el noventa por ciento de las líneas telefónicas en México.
4. __S__ Es uno de los dueños de un periódico **que** se llama el *New York Times*.
5. __C__ Diseñó la Ciudad de las Artes y las Ciencias, un complejo (*complex*) de museos **que** se encuentra en Valencia, España.
6. __X__ Es cocinero en un restaurante mexicano **que** está en Los Angeles.
7. __C__ Uno de sus edificios nuevos es el centro de transporte del World Trade Center, **que** se abrió en Nueva York en el 2016.
8. __S__ Es el dueño de Telcel y de América Móvil, las dos compañías **que** dominan el mercado de teléfonos celulares en México y el resto de Latinoamérica.
9. __X__ Su novela *El enlace,* **que** escribió en 1971, es de ciencia ficción.
10. __S__ Es un hombre **que** aparece en las listas de las personas más ricas del mundo.

Carlos Slim Helú: Dueño de compañías e inversionista (*investor*) en telecomunicaciones y otras industrias; nació en la Ciudad de México en 1940.

Actividades analíticas

1 The relative pronoun **que** is used to give additional information about a noun. You can easily make your sentences more informative by adding a clause with **que.**

La señora vive en esa casa.	The woman lives in that house.
La señora **que trabaja en el banco** vive en esa casa.	The woman who works at the bank lives in that house.

The additional information (here, **que trabaja en el banco**) is called a *relative clause* (**una cláusula relativa**). The relative pronoun **que** introduces the relative clause. Its equivalent in English is *that, which,* or *who,* depending on the context.

In sentence 1 in **Para empezar,** what is the relative clause that describes **un arquitecto español?** que hizo muchos edificios muy famosos en Barcelona

2 If a relative clause has an expressed subject, this subject may appear either before or after the verb.

El libro $\begin{Bmatrix} \text{que Ana leyó} \\ \text{que leyó Ana} \end{Bmatrix}$ es muy bueno.   The book that Ana read is very good.

In this case, **Ana** may appear either before or after the verb **leyó** and the basic meaning is the same. With this in mind, who manages the companies described in sentence 2 of **Para empezar?** sus hijos Carlos, Marco Antonio y Patrick

Actividades prácticas

A. Beto Cuevas Lee el párrafo sobre Beto Cuevas, un músico, cantante y compositor chileno. Luego empareja cada oración con la terminación adecuada. **¡Atención!** Hay una terminación que no se usa. ¿Cuál es?

Beto Cuevas nació en Santiago de Chile en 1967. Su familia se mudó a Montreal, Canadá, en los años setenta para escapar de la dictadura de Augusto Pinochet. Es allí donde Beto empezó su carrera musical. En 1987, se hizo cantante de La Ley, un grupo de rock muy popular en Latinoamérica. El grupo ganó un Grammy Latino por su álbum *La Ley MTV Unplugged* en 2001. En 2008, Beto lanzó (*released*) su primer álbum solista. El cantante tiene dos hijos, Martina y Diego, y vive ahora en Los Ángeles.

La Ley, con su premio gramófono de los Grammy Latino 2001

1. __i__ Nació en Chile, pero se crió (*was raised*) en Canadá, un país...
2. __d__ Su familia es de Chile, un país...
3. __b__ Su familia salió de Chile por la dictadura de Pinochet, un militar...
4. __g__ Fue vocalista en la banda chilena La Ley, un grupo...
5. __f__ Además del español, habla francés e inglés...
6. __c__ Ahora vive en Los Ángeles, una ciudad...
7. __h__ Empezó como solista en 2008 e hizo una gira (*tour*)...
8. __a__ Tiene dos hijos...

a. que se llaman Martina y Diego.
b. que estuvo veintisiete años en el poder (*power*).
c. que es conocida como el centro de la industria musical.
d. que está en el suroeste (*southwest*) de Sudamérica.
e. que está en el suroeste de Centroamérica.
f. que son los dos idiomas que se hablan más en Montreal, donde creció (*grew up*).
g. que fue uno de los más importantes en el mundo del rock en español entre 1987 y 2005.
h. que lo llevó a muchas ciudades de los Estados Unidos y Latinoamérica.
i. que recibió a miles de exiliados (*exiles*) chilenos después del golpe de estado (*coup d'état*) dirigido (*directed*) por Augusto Pinochet en 1973.

Expansion (Act. analíticas 1): Have students work with a partner to take turns pointing out the relative clauses in the rest of the sentences in *Para empezar.*

■ Answers to these activities are in Appendix 2 at the back of your book.

Suggestion (Act. analíticas 2): Ask students how they would say sentence 2 of *Para empezar* in English. Do this not as a translation exercise, but as a way to make sure students really understand what the sentence means. Also, point out that subjects in Spanish can generally appear either before or after the verb in any environment, but that this can be especially confusing for English speakers in relative clauses.

■ For more on the relative pronoun **que,** see **Para saber más 10.1,** at the back of your book.

Note (Para saber más): *Para saber más 10.1* provides more information about the relative pronoun *que,* and covers the relative pronouns *quien* and *quienes* and the expression *lo que.*

Autoprueba

Complete each sentence with an appropriate relative clause based on information from a previous chapter. Look back at the chapter if you need to refresh your memory.

1. En el **Capítulo 5,** leímos sobre la vida de Shakira, una cantante que ____.
2. En el **Capítulo 6,** aprendimos sobre El Bulli, un restaurante catalán que ____.
3. También leímos sobre el huitlacoche, un hongo que ____.
4. En el **Capítulo 8,** leímos sobre las molas, una artesanía que ____.
5. En el **Capítulo 9,** aprendimos sobre la Ruta del Tequila, unas excursiones mexicanas que ____.

En español...

The word **carrera** can mean professional *career* as well as *major* or *course of study* in a college or university context.

Note (Act. B, Paso 1): Point out that *licenciado/*a can also refer to someone who has graduate from a college or university, having received their *licenciatura*.

Suggestion (Act. B, Paso 2): Create a table on the board, with *Este país* and *Otros países* as rows, and *Ventajas* and *Desventajas* as columns. After students have had a few minutes for discussion with their partners, ask for suggestions on how to fill in the table.

Suggestion (Act. C): When students have completed their survey, have them work in pairs to summarize their findings. Offer a model sentence and have them write out their answers in complete sentences using a subordinate clause with *que: Para nosotros, la página web que usamos más es Facebook.*

Variation (Act. C): Have students poll their classmates. Assign one question to each student and tell them how many people they need to ask. Write the topic of the each of these questions as headings on the board, and as students finish, have them write their results under the appropriate heading. You and the students can then look over the results and see what is interesting or surprising.

B. Los profesionales

PASO 1. La educación y el trabajo de los profesionales son parecidos en los distintos países, pero no son siempre idénticos. En parejas, usen lo que ya saben de este tema para encontrar una terminación adecuada para cada oración. **¡Atención!** Hay una terminación que tienen que usar dos veces.

LOS ABOGADOS

1. _h_ Los abogados son las personas...
2. _g_ Para ser abogado en en este país, primero tienes que graduarte de una escuela de derecho (*law*), una escuela especializada...
3. _e_ Para ser abogado en la mayoría de los demás países, tienes que graduarte de una facultad (*school*) de derecho, una escuela especializada...
4. _b_ En algunos países, «licenciado» es una palabra...

LOS MÉDICOS

5. _i_ Un médico es un profesional...
6. _a_ Los médicos son profesionales...
7. _g_ Para ser médico en este país, primero tienes que graduarte de una escuela de medicina, una escuela especializada...
8. _c_ Para ser médico en muchos otros países, primero tienes que graduarte de una facultad de medicina, una escuela especializada...

LOS TRABAJADORES SOCIALES

9. _f_ Un trabajador social es un profesional...
10. _d_ Los trabajadores sociales son profesionales...

TERMINACIONES

a. que trabajan en hospitales, clínicas y otros lugares.
b. que usan también para decir «abogado».
c. que sigue después de la escuela secundaria y que también ofrece carreras en enfermería (*nursing*), nutrición y tecnología médica.
d. que ayudan a encontrar soluciones a los problemas sociales.
e. que ofrece la licenciatura (*bachelor's degree*) en Derecho.
f. que tiene la licenciatura en Trabajo Social.
g. que sigue después de la licenciatura.
h. que defienden los intereses del cliente en cuestiones jurídicas (*legal*).
i. que se dedica al tratamiento (*treatment*) y prevención de las enfermedades (*illnesses*).

PASO 2. Como ya vieron, en muchos países es común obtener una licenciatura en Medicina o en Derecho, mientras en este país, normalmente se requiere estudios de posgrado (*postgraduate*). En parejas, hagan una comparación entre el sistema que usan en este país y el sistema que usan en otros países. ¿Cuáles son las ventajas y desventajas de cada sistema?

C. Una encuesta sobre la tecnología

Circula por tu salón de clase para hacerles a tus compañeros dos de las siguientes preguntas. **¡Atención!** Todos deben responder con oraciones completas que usen el pronombre relativo **que.**

> **MODELO:** E1: ¿Cuál es el tipo de blog que te gusta más?
> E2: Los blogs que me gustan más son los blogs culinarios.

1. ¿Cuál es la página web que usas más?
2. ¿Cuál es la marca de teléfono que te parece mejor?
3. ¿Cuál es el navegador web (*browser*) que usas más?
4. ¿Cuál es el aparato que usas más: el teléfono, la portátil, la tableta u otra cosa?
5. ¿Cuál es el tipo de computadora que te gusta más: las PC o las Mac?
6. ¿Cuál es la aplicación o programa que te gusta más?

D. ¿Cómo se llama?   ¿Sabes bien cómo se llaman los demás estudiantes en tu clase? Pregúntale a un compañero / una compañera cómo se llaman varias personas de la clase, sin mirarlas directamente ni señalar (*nor pointing*).

MODELO: ¿Cómo se llama la persona que está a la izquierda de Erica y que tiene el pelo negro?

E. Cultura: El empleo en el Perú

PASO 1.   Lee el texto sobre el Perú.

el Perú

Si un país quiere que su economía crezca,[a] es importante tener trabajadores talentosos y bien formados[b] en las industrias que más van a expandirse. Los expertos dicen que en el Perú en los próximos años va a subir[c] la inversión,[d] en particular en la infraestructura (calles y carreteras, puentes, edificios, servicios públicos, etcétera) y en la minería.[e] En estos dos campos[f] se requieren personas con experiencia en ingeniería y en construcción.

Igual que el resto del mundo, los campos tecnológicos también necesitan más gente calificada, como por ejemplo personas que sepan[g] crear páginas web o manejar bases de datos. Hay un gran número de trabajos que emplean la tecnología en el sector financiero, que también está expandiéndose mucho. Y en esta época de la globalización, es cada vez más[h] importante saber hablar varios idiomas para tratar con[i] empresas internacionales.

A pesar de la expansión, la tasa[j] de desempleo y el número de personas en el Perú que trabajan sin beneficios siguen siendo altos. Una de las razones[k] es que no hay suficientes personas con experiencia y formación adecuada para ocupar los puestos en el sector

Unos ingenieros peruanos

formal. En ese sentido, es importante poner énfasis en la educación. Además, es necesario que los estudiantes que se especializan en las áreas de ingeniería, minería, tecnología, administración de negocios y relaciones internacionales se mantengan al tanto de[l] los avances recientes de sus disciplinas. Y por esa razón, siempre va a haber vacantes[m] en el sector de la educación, particularmente para profesores con un buen conocimiento de estos campos laborales.

[a]quiere... *wants its economy to grow* [b]*trained* [c]*increase* [d]*investment* [e]*mining* [f]*fields* [g]*know how* [h]cada... *increasingly* [i]tratar... *deal with* [j]*rate* [k]*reasons* [l]se... *keep themselves up-to-date on* [m]*vacancies*

PASO 2.   Ahora empareja las frases para crear oraciones completas.

1. Las personas ___d___ no reciben beneficios.
2. Los alumnos peruanos ___c___ encuentran trabajos en empresas internacionales.
3. En una facultad de informática hay mucha gente ___a___.
4. Los trabajadores ___f___ consiguen empleo en la construcción de puentes y carreteras.
5. El Perú es un país ___e___.
6. El sector financiero es un campo ___b___.

a. que sabe manejar bases de datos
b. que está creciendo (*growing*) mucho
c. que estudian inglés o chino
d. que trabajan en el sector informal
e. que quiere expandir su economía
f. que tienen experiencia en ingeniería

PASO 3.   En parejas, contesten las preguntas y explíquense las respuestas.

1. El Perú no es un país muy pobre, pero no tiene los recursos (*resources*) de un país rico como Canadá o los Estados Unidos. ¿Cómo piensas que debería gastar su dinero para crecer? ¿En qué orden de prioridad pones la educación, el ejército (*army*), la salud, el sistema judicial y el transporte, por ejemplo?

2. Las universidades son necesarias para el desarrollo económico, pero implican muchos gastos (*expenses*): las bibliotecas, las computadoras, los edificios, los profesores, servicios para los estudiantes, etcétera. Para un país sin muchos recursos, ¿en qué orden de prioridad pones estos gastos?

3. En tu país, ¿ves una relación entre las universidades y el desarrollo económico? ¿En las regiones donde hay buenas universidades, también hay un alto nivel económico?

Note (Act. E, Paso 3):
For item 2, you may want to share your own experiences about differences between universities in this country and in other countries. In many countries, money for elaborate student unions, recreation centers, and so on, would be considered an unnecessary and irresponsible expense, given other societal needs.

Suggestion (*Reciclaje*): Discourage students from using the pronoun *tú* (e.g., *Tú apagas*) in this impersonal usage, as it is redundant in this context.

⟳ Reciclaje

Present indicative: *tú* forms

Usa los verbos de la lista en la forma **tú** del tiempo presente para completar las siguientes oraciones. Luego empareja la profesión con la actividad que se hace.

aceptar	cuidar (*to take care of*)	dar	hacer	tomar
apagar (*to put out*)	cortar		escribir	llevar

Si eres...   **¿Qué haces?**

1. _g_ bombero
2. _e_ cajero
3. _b_ cirujano
4. _f_ enfermero
5. _a_ escritor

6. _d_ estilista
7. _c_ fotógrafo
8. _h_ taxista

a. _Escribes_ artículos o libros.
b. _Haces_ operaciones para curar las enfermedades.
c. _Tomas_ fotos de personas u objetos.
d. _Cortas_ el pelo de tus clientes.
e. _Aceptas_ el dinero de los clientes y les _das_ cambio.
f. _Cuidas_ la salud de la gente.
g. _Apagas_ incendios (*fires*).
h. _Llevas_ a la gente de un lugar a otro en un coche.

■ Answers to this activity are in Appendix 2 at the back of your book.

10.2 Pide ayuda para revisar tu currículum

Informal (*tú*) commands

Para empezar...

Alguna vez en la vida, casi todos tenemos que buscar trabajo. Aquí hay doce consejos (*pieces of advice*) que te pueden ayudar en ese proceso, ¡pero uno no es un buen consejo! Decide cuál es y táchalo (*cross it out*).

1. **Busca** el tipo de trabajo que quieres.
2. **Pide** ayuda para revisar tu currículum.
3. **Evita** *(Avoid)* cualquier tipo de error ortográfico en tu currículum.
4. **Piensa** bien si estás dispuesto/a (*willing*) a cambiarte de ciudad.
5. **Usa** todos los medios (*means*) posibles para buscar trabajo: el Internet, los contactos personales, tu universidad, etcétera.
6. **Vístete** bien para la entrevista. ¡Las primeras impresiones sí cuentan!
7. ~~**No te bañes** el día de tu entrevista. ¡Eso te da buena suerte (*luck*)!~~
8. **No hables** demasiado *(too much),* pero **no te quedes** callado/a (*silent*) tampoco.
9. **Aprende** los nombres de las personas que te entrevistan.
10. **No hables** mal de los lugares donde trabajaste antes.
11. **No comas** durante la entrevista.
12. **Escribe** una nota de agradecimiento (*thank-you note*) después de la entrevista.

■ Answers to these activities are in Appendix 2 at the back of your book.

CONÉCTATE AL MUNDO HISPANO

Al presentarse para puestos de trabajo en los países hispanohablantes, es común incluir varios **elementos demográficos** en el currículum, como por ejemplo, la fecha de nacimiento, el estado civil y una foto. Muchos consideran que estos datos ayudan a dar una imagen más completa del candidato como ser humano. En los Estados Unidos, en cambio, no es común incluir este tipo de información, por temor (*fear*) a que fomente (*encourages*) la discriminación laboral.

Actividades analíticas

1 The command form of the verb (**el mandato**) expresses what you want another person to do. Commands are used to give advice, to offer invitations, and to give orders. The verb forms in bold in **Para empezar** are *informal commands* (**los mandatos informales**), used when you address the person you're speaking to as **tú**. You will see other types of commands in **Estructura 10.3**.

Using as examples the boldfaced words in **Para empezar**, determine the informal command form of each of the following verbs.

MANDATOS INFORMALES (TÚ)		
pensar	**aprender**	**pedir**
POSITIVE piensa	aprende	pide

This form is exactly the same as which form of the verb in the present tense? **él/ella, Ud.** form (third person singular of the present indicative)

2 The examples in **Actividades analíticas 1** are all *positive commands,* which means that they invite the other person *to do* something. When you want the other person *not* to do something, you use a *negative command*.

Complete the following chart using examples that you find in **Para empezar.**

MANDATOS INFORMALES (TÚ)		
hablar	**comer**	**escribir**
POSITIVE habla	come	escribe
NEGATIVE no hables	no comas	no escribas

The negative informal command is the same as the **tú** form of the present tense, but with the "opposite" vowel in the ending: **-es** for **-ar** verbs and **-as** for **-er** and **-ir** verbs.

3 Verbs with stem changes in the present tense also show this change in negative informal commands.

e → ie   pensar → piensas → no pienses

o → ue   dormir → duermes → no duermas

e → i   pedir → pides → no pidas

Verbs ending in **-car, -gar,** and **-zar** have a spelling change in negative informal commands to preserve the **-c-, -g-,** and **-z-** sounds.

c → qu   buscar → no busques

g → gu   pagar (*to pay*) → no pagues

z → c   empezar → no empieces

(Continues)

Suggestions (Act. analíticas 1):
- Point out that while the verb forms are the same as the *él/ella, Ud.* form of the present tense, obviously the reflexive pronoun must be *te* for informal commands: *báñate, vístete, quédate.*
- Tell students to look only at positive (affirmative) command forms, that is, the commands that are not preceded by *no.*
- Point out to students that informal commands are used in the instructions to most activities in the book. Have them find three examples of this in previous chapters.

Autoprueba

Use the pattern you just learned to give the positive (+) and negative (−) informal commands for the following verbs.

1. **trabajar**
   + _____
   − no _____

2. **correr**
   + _____
   − no _____

3. **dormir**
   + _____
   − no _____

Respuestas: 1. trabaja, **2** corre, corras **3.** duerme, duermas

Notes (Act. analíticas 3):
- If students need to refresh their knowledge on stem-changing verbs, direct them to *Estructura 3.3* (o → ue), *4.2* (e → i), and *4.3* (e → ie).
- Remind students that they saw the same spelling changes in the presentation of the preterite, in *Estructura 6.1.*

Suggestions (Act. analíticas 2):
- Reproduce this table on the board and circle the "unexpected" vowel in the negative forms.
- You may wish to point out that the reflexive pronouns must be *te* for both positive and negative informal commands: *no te bañes, no te vistas, no te quedes.*
- Give students various -ar verbs (e.g., *bailar, cantar, cenar, cocinar, desayunar, estudiar, nadar, usar*) and have them give you the present tense *tú* form, followed by the positive and negative commands. **MODELO:** *hablar → tú hablas, habla tú, no hables tú.* Then give them various regular -er and -ir verbs (e.g., *abrir, asistir, correr, cumplir, dormir, pedir, subir, vivir*) and have them do the same. **MODELO:** *comer → tú comes, come tú, no comas tú; asistir → tú asistes, asiste tú, no asistas tú)*

Suggestion (Act. analíticas 4):
Point out that the spelling
change in *haz* preserves the
pronunciation of the stem, but
this spelling change should
not obscure the fact that *haz* is
simply the stem of *hacer*.

4 Some common irregular verbs have a special positive informal command form.

VERBO	MANDATO POSITIVO INFORMAL (TÚ)	EJEMPLO	
decir	**di**	**Di** «por favor».	*Say "please."*
hacer	**haz**	**¡Haz** la tarea!	*Do your homework!*
ir	**ve**	**Ve** a la biblioteca.	*Go to the library.*
poner	**pon**	**Pon** los libros aquí.	*Put the books here.*
salir	**sal**	**¡Sal** a la calle!	*Go out on the street!*
ser	**sé**	**Sé** buen niño.	*Be a good boy.*
tener	**ten**	**Ten** esto.	*Have (Take) this.*
venir	**ven**	**Ven** a mi casa.	*Come to my house.*

Many of these positive command forms are easy to remember, because they are simply the stem of the infinitive without any ending (-**ar**, -**er**, or -**ir**). Circle those forms that are of this type.

Note that **ve** is the positive command form of both **ir** and verb **ver.** The context makes it clear which is intended.

Ve a tu casa.   *Go to your house.*

Ve la dirección de esa casa.   *Look at / See the address of that house.*

5 Verbs that use a -**g**- in the stem of the **yo** form in the present tense, such as **decir** (**digo**) and **hacer** (**hago**), use this same stem with a -**g**- in the negative informal command.

VERBO	MANDATO NEGATIVO INFORMAL (TÚ)	EJEMPLO	
decir	no **digas**	No **digas** nada.	*Don't say anything.*
hacer	no **hagas**	No **hagas** eso.	*Don't do that.*
poner	no **pongas**	No **pongas** los pies allí.	*Don't put your feet there.*
salir	no **salgas**	No **salgas** a la calle.	*Don't go out on the street.*
tener	no **tengas**	No **tengas** miedo.	*Don't be afraid* (lit., *have fear*).
venir	no **vengas**	No **vengas** tan temprano.	*Don't come so early.*

All of these are -**er** and -**ir** verbs, so they all take the ending with the "opposite" vowel (-**as**).

Suggestions (Act. analíticas 5):
• Ask students to think of another verb that has a special form for *yo* in the present
  tense, and have them form the negative command based on this. Some possibilities:
  oír, traer, conocer, ver, nacer.
• Have students work in pairs. With the list in front of them, have them give the present
  tense *yo* form of each of the verbs in the list, followed by the negative *tú* command:
  *decir → yo digo, no digas tú; hacer → yo hago, no hagas tú; poner → yo pongo, no
  pongas tú; salir → yo salgo, no salgas tú; tener → yo tengo, no tengas tú; venir → yo
  vengo, no vengas tú.*

6 The verbs **ir, ser,** and **ver** have irregular forms when they are negative informal commands.

VERBO	MANDATO NEGATIVO INFORMAL (TÚ)	EJEMPLO	
ir	no vayas	No vayas a la playa.	*Don't go to the beach.*
ser	no seas	No seas así.	*Don't be like that.*
ver	no veas	No veas la película.	*Don't watch the movie.*

7 Object pronouns are attached to the <u>end</u> of positive commands, and written as a single word together with the verb. After the object pronouns are attached, a written accent mark is added if needed in order to keep the stress on the original stressed syllable.

| ¡Haz**lo**! | *Do it!* |
| ¡Levánta**te**! | *Get up!* |

Find one example of a positive command with an object pronoun in **Para empezar.** <u>vístete</u> With negative commands, object pronouns are always written before the verb.

| ¡No **lo** hagas! | *Don't do it!* |
| ¡No **te** levantes! | *Don't get up!* |

Find at least one example of this in **Para empezar.** <u>no te bañes, no te quedes</u>

En español...

All of the commands shown here are used when you are addressing people as **tú.** Because **tú** is strictly singular, these commands are only used for addressing one person. To give a command to more than one person in most of the Spanish-speaking world, you would use an **Uds.** command, which you will learn more about in **Estructura 10.3.**

In Spain, you would likely use **vosotros** commands to a group of people you would address as **tú.** Positive **vosotros** commands are just like the infinitive form, but with the final **-r** replaced by a **-d.**

hablar → ¡Hablad (vosotros)!
comer → Comed ahora.
escribir → Escribid la tarea.

Negative **vosotros** commands are like the negative **tú** commands in that they use "opposite" vowels in their endings: **-éis** for **-ar** verbs and **-áis** for **-er** and **-ir** verbs.

no hables → ¡No habléis!
no comas → No comáis ahora.
no escribas → No escribáis con lápiz.

Expansion (Act. analíticas 7): Ask students to explain why *levántate* takes an accent mark, when *levanta* and *no te levantes* do not.

¡Siéntate!

Autoprueba

Using what you now know about informal command formation and the different positions of object pronouns, write the positive (+) and negative (−) commands for the following reflexive verbs. **¡Atención!** One of the verbs has a stem change.

1. **bañarse**
   + _____ − _____

2. **ducharse**
   + _____ − _____

3. **dormirse**
   + _____ − _____

The verb **apurarse** (*to hurry*) is a new verb to you, but since it is regular and you know the pattern to form informal commands, you have the tools to form its positive and negative commands. Try it!

4. **apurarse**
   + _____ − _____

Respuestas: 1. Báñate, No te bañes. **2.** Dúchate, No te duches. **3.** Duérmete, No te duermas. **4.** Apúrate, No te apures.

Expansion (Act. A): Ask students to find every command in these sentences and to give the infinitive for each one. (Hint: There are 15 commands, including «*haz una lista*» in item h.)

Expansion (Act. A): Ask students to use commands to give additional ideas on how to organize their time.

¿Por qué?

When Spanish switches to the "opposite" vowel in negative commands, this is a simple and efficient way of signaling that the verb has a different function. Spanish only has five vowels to choose from, and of these, only **a, e,** and **o** are possible in unstressed verb endings. For **-ar** verbs, **-a** and **-o** are already used for the present tense (**habla, hablo**), so if negative commands are going to be different, the only possibility is **-e** (**no hables**). For the same reason, **-er** and **-ir** verbs switch to **-a** (**no comas, no duermas**); that is the only vowel available. What might seem strange and quirky is thus actually a very reasonable way to signal the verb's new function.

Suggestion (¿Por qué?): Give students a variety of verb roots (*corr-, viv-, trabaj-,* etc.) and have them identify the resulting verb form when *-a, -e,* and *-o* are added.

Suggestion (Act. C): Have each pair of students create at least one idea of their own beyond the ideas given here.

Suggestion (Act. D): Give students a few minutes to create their commands before finding a partner.

Actividades prácticas

A. Organiza tu día. ¿Cómo podemos usar mejor el tiempo? Las siguientes oraciones te dicen, paso por paso, cómo organizar un día de trabajo, pero están desordenadas. Ponlas en orden: La primera y la tercera ya están hechas.

a. __7__ Al final del día, revisa tu lista y tacha (*cross out*) todo lo que ya hiciste. Usa las cosas que quedan pendientes (*pending*) para empezar una nueva lista para mañana.

b. __2__ Haz una lista de todo lo que tienes que hacer.

c. __6__ Empieza a hacer las cosas que aparecen en tu lista. Ten en mente (*Keep in mind*) el orden de prioridad que hiciste y el tiempo en que trabajas mejor.

d. __5 (4)__ Revisa (*Review*) tu lista y pon las cosas en orden de prioridad.

e. __8__ ¡Vete a la casa!

f. __1__ Al llegar al trabajo, siéntate en tu escritorio.

g. __4 (5)__ Divide tu día en segmentos. Cada persona es distinta, así que si trabajas mejor por la mañana, usa ese tiempo para hacer los proyectos más difíciles de tu lista.

h. __3__ Pon absolutamente todo en la lista: desde las cosas más triviales hasta las cosas más importantes. ¡No tengas miedo! Si quieres, ¡puedes poner «haz una lista» en tu lista!

 B. Consejos buenos y consejos malos Como probablemente ya sabes, no todos los consejos son buenos. Escucha los consejos sobre la preparación para una entrevista profesional e indica si son buenos o malos.

	UN CONSEJO BUENO	UN CONSEJO MALO
1.	☑	☐
2.	☐	☑
3.	☑	☐
4.	☑	☐
5.	☐	☑
6.	☑	☐
7.	☐	☑
8.	☑	☐
9.	☐	☑
10.	☐	☑

Script (Act. B): 1. *Lee sobre la compañía para estar informado o informada.* **2.** *No duermas nada la noche anterior.* **3.** *Desayuna bien.* **4.** *Piensa en preguntas sobre la compañía.* **5.** *No lleves un traje. Lleva tu pijama para estar más cómodo o cómoda.* **6.** *Lleva tu currículum.* **7.** *Pon tus pies sobre la mesa durante la entrevista.* **8.** *Prepara una lista de referencias profesionales.* **9.** *Dales a todos un abrazo cariñoso; no les des la mano.* **10.** *No mires a los ojos a los entrevistadores.*

Vístete con ropa profesional.

 C. ¿Qué hacer con tantos emails? En muchos trabajos, la cantidad de correos electrónicos es increíble y no es posible dejarlos a un lado. En parejas, creen consejos sobre qué hacer con este problema tan común. Usen las ideas de abajo o hagan sus propios consejos. Luego compártanlos con la clase. **¡Atención!** Usen mandatos para crear los consejos.

IDEAS

contestar inmediatamente

indicar los mensajes que tienes que contestar todavía

borrar (*delete*) sin leer los mensajes que son correo basura (*junk*)

no dejar nada para otro día

no leer el correo electrónico antes de acostarte

no leer el correo electrónico si no tienes tiempo para contestar en ese momento

MODELO: IDEA: leer los emails

CONSEJO: Lee solamente los emails que tienen que ver (*have something to do*) con el trabajo.

D. ¡Hazme caso! Crea cinco mandatos y léelos uno por uno a un compañero / una compañera para que los haga. ¡Entre más creativo, mejor! Si quieres, puedes usar expresiones como **al mismo tiempo,** o **primero... , después... .**

MODELO: Levántate.

Baila y canta al mismo tiempo.

⟳ Reciclaje

Present indicative: *Ud.* forms

En las oficinas y otros lugares de trabajo, es común usar las formas correspondientes a **Ud.** cuando hablas. Practícalo con estas oraciones, cambiándolas de **tú** a **Ud.**

TÚ	UD.
1. ¿Necesitas ayuda?	¿Necesita ayuda?
2. Eres el nuevo gerente de la tienda.	Es el nuevo gerente de la tienda.
3. ¿Sabes cómo hacer esto?	¿Sabe cómo hacer esto?
4. ¿Dónde pones los documentos?	¿Dónde pone los documentos?
5. ¿Me puedes ayudar en algo, por favor?	¿Me puede ayudar en algo, por favor?
6. ¿En qué te puedo ayudar?	¿En qué le puedo ayudar?
7. Te voy a dejar el documento en tu escritorio.	Le voy a dejar el documento en su escritorio.
8. ¿Te vas después de la reunión (*meeting*)?	¿Se va después de la reunión?

Suggestion: Remind students of rules of thumb for when to use *Ud.*: when they don't know the person, when the person is one generation above them (i.e., old enough to be their parents), and when the person is working in some official capacity (e.g., a waiter, a police officer, an office worker).

■ Answers to this activity are in Appendix 2 at the back of your book.

10.3   Ponga el documento sobre el cristal.

Formal (*Ud./Uds.*) commands

Para empezar...

Las siguientes oraciones vienen de instrucciones para el uso de diferentes aparatos. Empareja cada oración con el aparato apropiado.

INSTRUCCIONES

1. __d__ **No lo use** dentro del restaurante.
2. __h__ **Ponga** el documento sobre el cristal (*glass*).
3. __c__ **Ponga** más tinta (*ink*) negra.
4. __a__ **Conecte** el monitor antes de usarla.
5. __a__ **Use** «control c» para copiar y «control v» para pegar (*paste*).
6. __d__ **Oprima** (*Press*) este botón para tomar una foto de sus amigos.
7. __c__ **Indique** el tamaño del papel que va a usar: A4 o 8½ × 11.
8. __a__ Si la va a usar mucho, **cómprela** con una pantalla grande.

APARATOS

a. una computadora
b. un escáner
c. una impresora
d. un teléfono móvil

Suggestion (Para empezar): Point out to students that written instructions are typically (though not always) done in the *Ud.* form.

■ Answers to these activities are in Appendix 2 at the back of your book.

Actividades analíticas

1 *Formal commands* (**los mandatos formales**) are used with people that you address as **Ud.** or **Uds.*** Unlike singular informal commands, the form of the verb is the same for both positive and negative formal commands (**compre Ud., no compre Ud.**). Use the examples that you saw in **Para empezar** to complete the following chart of formal command forms for **Ud.**

Suggestion (Act. analíticas 1): If students need help, review the construction of negative informal commands with regular and irregular verbs in *Estructura 10.2.*

MANDATOS FORMALES (UD.)		
usar	**comer**	**oprimir**
POSITIVE (AND NEGATIVE) (no) use	(no) coma	(no) oprima

(*Continues*)

---

*Remember that you use formal **Ud.** with strangers, people who are considerably older than you, and anyone you treat with respect (such as your professor, doctor, or boss). In most places outside of Spain you'd use **Uds.** as plural *you,* so it's the plural of both **tú** and **Ud.**

Suggestion (Act. analíticas 2): Ask students to find examples of plural commands in the instructions to activities that they have already done.

Expansion (Act. analíticas 2): Have students write out the *Ud.* and *Uds.* forms of *usar* in present, preterite, and imperfect tenses: *usa(n), usó/usaron, usaba(n).* Ask: In which of these tenses is *-n* added to the *Ud.* form to create the *Uds.* form? Answer: Present and imperfect.

Autoprueba

Use the patterns you just learned to give the positive and negative formal commands for the following verbs. Replace any direct objects you see with direct object pronouns and place them correctly. Watch out for irregular stems and spelling changes!

1. **preparar (Ud.)**
   + _____ – _____

2. **salir (Ud.)**
   + _____ – _____

3. **pagar la cuenta (Ud.)**
   + _____ – _____

4. **copiar las instrucciones (Uds.)**
   + _____ – _____

5. **hacer los cambios (Uds.)**
   + _____ – _____

6. **entregar el reporte (Uds.)**
   + _____ – _____

Respuestas: 1. Prepare, No prepare 2. Salga, No salga 3. Páguela, No la pague 4. Cópielas, No las copien 5. Háganlos, No los hagan 6. Entréguenlo, No lo entreguen

As you saw with negative informal commands in **Estructura 10.2**, formal commands consist of the verb stem plus the "opposite" vowel, that is **-ar** verbs use the **-e** ending, and **-er** and **-ir** verbs use the **-a** ending. Verbs with a stem change in the present (e → ie, o → ue, e → i) also have this change in the formal command. Verbs that use a stem with **-g-** in the **yo** form of the present tense, such as **poner** (**pongo**), use the same stem here (**ponga**).

Change the commands from **Para empezar** into their infinitive forms and write them in the correct column below. Don't repeat any verbs.

-ar VERBS	-er VERBS	-ir VERBS
usar indicar	poner	oprimir
conectar comprar		

As with negative informal commands, the verbs **ir, ser,** and **ver** have special forms: **vaya, sea,** and **vea.**

2 When addressing a group of people as **Uds.**, the command form of the verb is just like the **Ud.** command form except that **-n** is added to the end. Use this information to complete this chart.

MANDATOS FORMALES (UDS.)		
usar	**comer**	**oprimir**
(no) usen	(no) coman	(no) opriman

POSITIVE (AND NEGATIVE)

3 As you saw with informal commands, the placement of object pronouns changes depending on whether the formal command is positive or negative. Complete the chart by writing whether the object pronouns for the formal commands appear *before the verb* or *after and attached to the verb*, then give an example of each case from **Para empezar**.

TIPO DE MANDATO	LOS PRONOMBRES DE OBJETO SE COLOCAN...	EJEMPLO
POSITIVE FORMAL (UD./UDS.)	after and attached to the verb	cómprela
NEGATIVE FORMAL (UD./UDS.)	before the verb	no lo use

En español...

The forms for the formal commands (**Ud.** and **Uds.**) should remind you of the negative informal (**tú**) commands seen in **Estructura 10.2**.

INFORMAL (**TÚ**) COMMAND, NEGATIVE:	¡No **pongas** el documento allí!	*Don't put* (inform. sing.) *the document there!*
FORMAL COMMAND (**UD.**):	¡**Ponga** el documento allí!	*Put* (form. sing.) *the document there!*
FORMAL COMMAND (**UDS.**):	¡**Pongan** el documento allí!	*Put* (pl.) *the document there!*

These three command forms have much in common: They all use a stem with **-g-** (if the verb uses **-g-** in the **yo** form of the present tense) and they all change the stem vowel (if the verb belongs to one of the stem-changing families [e → ie, o → ue, e → i]). In addition, they all use the same sound-preserving spelling changes (c → qu in **-car** verbs, g → gu in **-gar** verbs, and z → c in **-zar** verbs). These forms have so much in common because they are all derived from the present subjunctive form. You will begin to explore the subjunctive in **Capítulo 12**.

Actividades prácticas

Note (Act. prácticas): Formal commands, like the related subjunctive construction, are not acquired until well beyond the first year, so the activities here emphasize comprehension rather than production. Act. B, D, and E do require some output, but not spontaneous production.

A. Problemas y soluciones

Empareja cada problema con una posible solución para ofrecerles consejos a varios estudiantes universitarios.

1. __d__ No tenemos el libro.
2. __e__ Siempre estamos cansados.
3. __h__ No tenemos suficiente dinero.
4. __g__ Llegamos tarde a la primera clase.
5. __b__ Tenemos hambre.
6. __c__ Tenemos un examen.
7. __a__ Tenemos sed.
8. __f__ Es viernes y ya no tenemos nada que hacer aquí.

a. Tomen un vaso de agua fría.
b. Coman algo. ¿Desean unos sándwiches?
c. Estudien mucho.
d. Pues, vayan a la librería a comprarlo.
e. ¡Duerman más!
f. ¡Váyanse a la casa!
g. ¡Levántense más temprano!
h. Pidan más horas en el trabajo.

B. Deseos

El arquitecto español Santiago Calatrava, el inversionista mexicano Carlos Slim (ejecutivo de América Móvil) y el empresario español Amancio Ortega (dueño de Zara) son personas de mucha influencia en el mundo de los negocios. Por cierto (*Indeed*), Slim y Ortega están entre las personas más ricas del mundo.

PASO 1. Las siguientes oraciones son deseos (*wishes*) que podrías (*you could*) pedir de estos tres hombres. Completa cada deseo (si es necesario) para hacerlo más a tu gusto (*to your taste*) e indica a quién le corresponde.

Suggestion (Act. B, Paso 1): Before beginning, review basic facts about these three men: Calatrava is the famous architect, known for his signature cantilever spar cable spans and spectacular public buildings. Ortega is the very private principal stockholder and former chairman of the corporation best known for the retail clothing chain Zara. He is the richest man in Spain and among the top 5 wealthiest in the world. Slim is the head of Latin American telecomunications company América Móvil and a major investor in the New York Times, and one of the top 5 richest men in the world. For more information on Amancio Ortega, see Estructura 8.3, and for more on Slim and Calatrava, see Estructura 10.1.

SANTIAGO CALATRAVA	CARLOS SLIM	AMANCIO ORTEGA	
☐	☐	☑	1. Haga más ropa de color _____ .
☐	☑	☐	2. Invíteme a su casa en México.
☑	☐	☐	3. Diseñe un edificio para la ciudad de _____.
☐	☑	☐	4. Deme un trabajo como _____ en América Móvil.
☑	☐	☐	5. Haga un puente en el río _____ (o entre _____ y _____).
☐	☐	☑	6. Ponga una tienda Zara en _____.
☐	☑	☐	7. Regáleme un plan de servicio telefónico.
☐	☐	☑	8. Deme un trabajo como _____ en Zara.
☑	☐	☐	9. Diseñe un(a) _____ para el campus de mi universidad.

PASO 2. ¿Qué industria te interesa más: la de la moda, de las telecomunicaciones o de la arquitectura? Formen grupos según sus intereses y hagan por lo menos tres recomendaciones (en forma de mandato) para el hombre del **Paso 1** (Calatrava, Slim o Ortega) que corresponde al interés del grupo.

MODELO: Haga faldas largas para la colección del otoño.

C. Descripciones y consejos

Para cada una de las profesiones en la tabla, escoge **una descripción** de lo que hace una persona con mucha experiencia. Luego escoge el mandato formal para darle **un consejo** a una persona que apenas (*barely*) empieza en ese trabajo.

Suggestion (Act. C): Let students work in pairs or small groups to collaborate. Have students first identify the verb and its infinitive in each sentence before deciding if it is in present tense or a command.

Expansion (Act. C): Give students names of other professions and have students create descriptions and advice for these.

	UNA DESCRIPCIÓN	UN CONSEJO
1. una abogada	e	c
2. una enfermera	g	b
3. un policía	a	f
4. un profesor de yoga	d	h

(Continues)

a. Piensa en la seguridad (*security*) del público.
b. Cuide a sus pacientes.
c. Defienda los derechos (*rights*) de su cliente.
d. Tiene mucha paciencia cuando da la clase.

e. Defiende los derechos (*rights*) de su cliente.
f. Piense en la seguridad del público.
g. Cuida a sus pacientes.
h. Tenga mucha paciencia cuando da la clase.

Suggestion (Act. D, Paso 1): Create a chart on the board where each group can write their choices of the three best and the three worst for subsequent class discussion. Lead a discussion of the results. You may wish to have students form all-male and all-female groups only; then students can compare responses based on the sex of the respondents.

Expansion (Act. D, Paso 1): Have students give the infinitive form of each verb in bold.

D. Amor en la oficina

PASO 1. Lee la carta al Doctor Amor. Luego, en grupos, decidan cuáles son las tres mejores y las tres peores sugerencias (*suggestions*). ¿Hay alguna en la lista de las mejores respuestas de un grupo y también en la lista de las peores respuestas de otro grupo?

Para: Doctor@amor.com
De: Anónimo
Asunto: Problemas del amor

Doctor Amor:

Somos amigos de muchos años, y desde hace un mes, trabajamos en la misma compañía. El problema que tenemos es que estamos enamorados (*in love*) de la misma mujer. Los tres somos arquitectos y trabajamos juntos en la misma oficina, pero ella lleva mucho más tiempo en este trabajo que nosotros y tiene un puesto (*position*) más alto. ¡Ayúdenos! ¿Qué hacemos? Ella no sabe nada de esto.

—Dos amigos anónimos

---

1. **Hablen** con ella y **explíquenle** cómo es la situación. **Pídanle** su opinión.
2. **Regresen** al trabajo y ya no **piensen** en eso.
3. **Salgan** juntos a cenar y a bailar con ella, y a ver qué pasa.
4. **Olvídenla** y **busquen** trabajo en otra compañía.
5. **Busquen** novias en otra parte, fuera del trabajo.
6. **Túrnense.** Si ella está de acuerdo, uno de Uds. puede salir con ella un fin de semana y el otro el siguiente fin de semana.
7. **Explíquenles** la situación a todos sus compañeros del trabajo y **pídanles** su opinión.
8. **Cálmense** (*Calm down*) y **esperen** un mes. Si para ese entonces todavía tienen el mismo problema, **escríbanme** de nuevo.
9. **Pónganse** a pelear (*fight*) allí en la oficina. El ganador (*winner*) puede preguntarle a ella si quiere salir con él.
10. No le **digan** nada. **Pongan** todo su tiempo y energía en el trabajo, y van a ver que este problema va a desaparecer (*disappear*).

Suggestion (Act. D, Paso 2): Have groups write their two sentences on the board in random order and then have the class as a whole decide which are *buenos consejos* and which are *malos consejos*.

PASO 2. Ahora creen dos consejos más, uno bueno y uno malo y compártanlos con la clase.

E. ¿Qué les dices a los nuevos? A los nuevos estudiantes que llegan a tu universidad por primera vez, ¿qué les puedes aconsejar sobre dónde comer, dónde estudiar, dónde vivir y qué clases tomar? En grupos, creen una lista de tres o cuatro consejos para cada una de estas categorías. Pongan su mejor sugerencia para cada categoría en la pizarra.

dónde comer   dónde estudiar   dónde vivir   qué clases tomar

MODELO: Coman (Uds.) en el restaurante Mi Rancho Grande. Allí tienen la mejor comida de la ciudad a los mejores precios.

¡Leamos!

Puestos y placeres

Antes de leer

Suggestion (Antes de leer): Have students tell why they would or would not like the jobs from *Antes de leer, Paso 2,* so that they begin to brainstorm the advantages and disadvantages they will have to present in *Después de leer.*

PASO 1. En parejas, describan el trabajo «ideal». ¿En qué consiste? ¿Qué beneficios (*benefits*) hay? ¿Cómo es el sueldo (*salary*)? ¿Dónde trabaja la persona que ocupa este puesto ideal? ¿Están de acuerdo Uds. o tienen trabajos ideales muy distintas? Prepárense para compartir sus ideas con la clase.

PASO 2. Todos sabemos de los puestos «normales» que hay en el mundo profesional, pero también hay muchos trabajos raros. Empareja cada puesto de trabajo con la descripción apropiada. Luego indica cuáles de los trabajos te gustaría hacer y cuáles no.

	ME GUSTARÍA	NO ME GUSTARÍA
1. __b__ catador (*taster*) de helados	☐	☐
2. __a__ cuidador (*caretaker*) de isla paradisíaca	☐	☐
3. __d__ diseñador de los vestidos de Barbie	☐	☐
4. __f__ diseñador de nuevos videojuegos	☐	☐
5. __e__ enfermo (*sick person*) imaginario	☐	☐
6. __c__ probador (*tester*) / crítico de aire	☐	☐

a. cuidar de la isla de Hamilton, situada en la Gran Barrera de Coral (*Great Barrier Reef*) de Australia
b. probar los sabores (*flavors*) hasta encontrar el resultado más satisfactorio para ser lanzado (*launched*) al mercado
c. viajar en los vuelos de los competidores para saber qué ofrecen
d. desarrollar (*develop*) ropa para la compañía Mattel
e. fingir (*pretend*) que tiene una enfermedad (*illness*) para que los alumnos de medicina se entrenen haciendo diagnósticos
f. desarrollar ideas o conceptos y crear niveles (*levels*) para los juegos en desarrollo

A leer

Lee el artículo sobre los puestos ideales. Luego escribe el puesto de trabajo que corresponde a cada sueldo.

Puestos y placeres

por Soraya Almendros

Entrevistamos sobre su futuro a más de cien alumnos recién graduados de la universidad. Un tema que salió en todas las entrevistas fue querer conseguir un puesto divertido, bien remunerado[a]... ideal. Le pedimos a los entrevistados que describieran[b] el puesto de sus sueños, pero las respuestas nos decepcionaron.[c] ¡Qué aburridas!

[a] bien... *well paid*   [b] que... *to describe*   [c] *disappointed*

(Continues)

Este resultado nos hizo preguntarnos: «¿Cuál es el puesto ideal? ¿Existe?» A partir de esto, realizamos más entrevistas y este artículo.

LUCILA: Soy crítica de aire. Estudié idiomas porque me gustaba viajar. Después de tres puestos agobiadores,[d] conseguí este con la aerolínea. No soy pilota o azafata.[e] Hago viajes todo el año, en primera clase, en vuelos de la competencia,[f] a ciudades grandes y a algunos destinos exóticos.

TOMÁS: Bueno, en la universidad era muy quejón[g] y me hacía el enfermo[h] para no ir a clase. Ahora tengo el puesto de enfermo imaginario. Trabajo en un hospital docente[i] donde me quejo[j] de mis síntomas. Hoy tengo la gripe.

ALBERTO: Cuando mi esposa y yo nos casamos, fuimos de luna de miel[k] a Australia. Allí supimos que se solicitaba un cuidador para la isla Hamilton. La visitamos y, como mi esposa es escritora y puede trabajar dondequiera,[l] solicité el puesto.

MONA: Hay algo de revancha[m] en mí, por todos esos años que mis padres me regañaban[n]: «Basta ya[ñ] de los videojuegos» o mi favorito: «¡Te pierdes la vida jugando esa basura!» Sigo perdiéndome la vida jugando videojuegos, pero ahora los diseño.

RAÚL: Me gradué en moda y diseño. Trabajé con dos compañías antes de conseguir este puesto, el más divertido y gratificante. En este puesto —mis amigos se divierten con esto— diseño ropa para la muñeca[o] Barbie.

LOLA: Soy catadora de helados. Mi puesto en dos palabras: ¡Como helado!

Para los que piensan que estos puestos pagan poco, a ver si estos datos desvanecen[p] sus dudas. Al volver de sus viajes, el jefe de Lucila le paga 2.400 dólares al mes por sus informes sobre la competencia. Por cada mes que pasa haciéndose el enfermo, le pagan a Tomás 1.440 dólares. Alberto y Susan no solo viven en un paraíso donde pasan los días buceando y disfrutando de[q] las playas, sino que Alberto también recibe 16.000 dólares al mes por cuidar la isla. Por cada juego que Mona diseña, le pagan 2.000 dólares. Raúl gana 5.000 dólares mensuales[r] por diseñar vestidos chiquititos[s] para Barbie. Y finalmente, Lola gana 4.600 dólares al mes por degustar[t] helados y determinar el sabor más satisfactorio.

Dedicamos este informe a los alumnos recién graduados en busca del puesto ideal.

[d]*exhausting* [e]*flight attendant* [f]*competition* [g]*muy... a big complainer* [h]*me... I pretended to be sick* [i]*teaching (adj.)* [j]*me... I complain* [k]*luna... honeymoon* [l]*wherever* [m]*vengeance* [n]*scolded* [ñ]*Basta... Enough already* [o]*doll* [p]*dispel* [q]*disfrutando... enjoying* [r]*monthly* [s]*tiny* [t]*tasting*

Expansion (A leer): Have students put the six jobs in order from the one they would like the most to the one they would like to do the least. Then have them put the salaries next to each one. Does anyone change their mind? Have them imagine that they have the job and ask what they do. For example, what flavors do they propose for ice cream?, what garments do they design for Barbie?, what games do they design?, what diseases do they pretend to have?

El enfermo imaginario. Porque tiene que fingir que tiene una enfermedad para que los estudiantes de medicina lo diagnostiquen.

Expansion (Después de leer, Paso 3): Ask students if the results of their investigations make them question the salaries mentioned in the article.

1. 1.440 dólares al mes
   <u>enfermo imaginario</u>

2. 2 mil dólares por producto
   <u>diseñador de nuevos videojuegos</u>

3. 2.400 dólares al mes
   <u>probador/crítico de aire</u>

4. 4.600 dólares mensuales
   <u>catador de helados</u>

5. 5 mil dólares al mes
   <u>diseñador de los vestidos de Barbie</u>

6. 16 mil dólares al mes
   <u>cuidador de isla paradisíaca</u>

De los seis, ¿cuál es el trabajo que paga mejor? cuidador de isla paradisíaca

Después de leer

PASO 1. Contesta las siguientes preguntas.

1. Según el título, ¿por qué son ideales los empleos que describe el autor?
   Porque «trabajar es un placer».
2. ¿Cuál puesto de trabajo requiere los talentos de un actor? ¿Por qué?

3. De los trabajos descritos en el artículo, ¿cuál es el mejor pagado? ¿Y el peor pagado?
   Cuidador de una isla paradisíaca; enfermo imaginario
4. Si trabajas como crítico de aire para Southwest, ¿vas a viajar mucho en vuelos de Southwest como parte de tu trabajo? Explica por qué.
   No. Porque el trabajo es viajar en los vuelos de la competencia.

PASO 2. De los trabajos mencionados en el artículo, ¿cuál prefieres tú? Explica tu decisión.

 PASO 3. En grupos, escojan uno de los trabajos del artículo y preparen una descripción para presentar al resto de la clase. Usen la información del artículo y sus propias ideas o busquen en Internet para poder hablar de estos aspectos del puesto de trabajo.

■ los requisitos   ■ las ventajas   ■ las desventajas

¡Escuchemos!

La tecnología en el lugar de trabajo

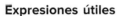 **Antes de escuchar**

Suggestion (Antes de escuchar): After students have finished, have a few students describe different objects for the class and have the class guess what they've described.

En parejas, apunten una lista de los elementos tecnológicos que usan más en sus estudios y/o trabajos. Luego pónganlos en orden de más a menos importante.

A escuchar

Video track (A escuchar): This video clip can be found on the DVD to accompany *Conéctate: Cap. 10*, Track 3.

Mira y escucha el video. Luego mira otra vez con pausas y escribe los números de 1 a 6 para indicar el orden en que menciona Esteban los elementos tecnológicos.

Expresiones útiles	
las facturas	bills
los recibos	receipts
los dispositivos	devices
los parlantes	speakers
el almacenamiento	storage
los audífonos	headphones

_6_ la cámara de video para Skype

_4_ la computadora

_5_ DVD, CD y video

_2_ el escáner

_3_ las impresoras

_1_ el teléfono

Suggestion (A escuchar): Remind students that putting the major technological elements in order requires listening for keywords. They won't need to understand everything Esteban says to complete this task successfully.

Después de escuchar

Haz un sondeo (*survey*) de la frecuencia con que usan los elementos tecnológicos varios compañeros de clase y escribe los resultados en la tabla. Basándote en los resultados, ¿cuál es el elemento tecnológico que más se usa? ¿Están de acuerdo muchos?

MODELO: E1: ¿Con qué frecuencia usas la impresora?
E2: La uso de vez en cuando.

	NUNCA	DE VEZ EN CUANDO	UNA VEZ AL DÍA	VARIAS VECES CADA DÍA
el correo electrónico				
un DVD				
el escáner				
la impresora				
la láptop				
la memoria USB				
el teléfono celular				
la web				
el WiFi				

Suggestion (Después de escuchar): Compare the most-used technologies to those deemed most important in *Antes de escuchar:* Are they the same? Or do we frequently use technologies that we don't necessarily value?

Expansion (Después de escuchar): Ask students to come up with a list of rules for using technology responsibly. For example, if you have pictures on a social network of yourself drinking, you probably should limit access so potential employers can't see the images.

Suggestion (Después de escuchar): Point out that if students want to learn more vocabulary related to technology, they can change their social media or phone language settings to Spanish!

Variation (Antes de escuchar): Have students write down 4 technological elements they value, each on a separate scrap of paper. Then have everyone choose the least important item and throw it away, then the least important of the remaining 3, and so on. What device is each student left with? Are there any surprises?

Videoscript (A escuchar): *Básicamente en una oficina hay... o en una oficina generalmente los elementos que más se utilizan son... el teléfono, ¿verdad?, algunas todavía tienen fax, aunque el fax es algo que se está perdiendo porque ya la gente prefiere usar Internet y entonces tiene un escáner. Entonces escanean las facturas o los recibos y las mandan a través de Internet por correo electrónico. Entonces, también hay escáner y hay impresoras, que muchas de las veces es el mismo... la misma consola, la misma máquina que hace ambas cosas y también a veces le añaden la función de fotocopias. Entonces, después está el monitor, que es el monitor de la computadora... la pantalla siempre hay una computadora que es la torre, digamos, donde se conecta ahí todos los demás dispositivos que son los parlantes, el teclado, el mouse (es como lo decimos, ¿verdad?). Y también tiene los accesos para conectar dispositivos de almacenamiento masivo como USBs, las tarjetas de memoria USBs, o si quiere conectar la impresora se conecta ahí, también tiene la unidad de DVD y de CD, entonces también eso es parte de la computadora. Y también tiene algunas aliadas como para sacar a veces videos por ahí a través de... digamos, de cables o a través de también como conectores de audífonos o micrófonos... Eso se usa más también como para hacer videollamadas por Internet. Entonces uno conecta la cámara de video allí a la computadora y el micrófono y el audífono y puede, digamos, usar Skype y hablar con alguien más.*

¡Escribamos!

La carrera de mis sueños

Para conseguir un puesto de trabajo, tienes que explicar por qué eres el/la mejor candidato/a, ofreciendo justificaciones y ejemplos de tu experiencia. ¿Puedes describir la carrera profesional ideal para ti?

Antes de escribir

Escribe la información apropiada para la carrera de tus sueños.

- el campo (*field*) y el puesto de trabajo
- las responsabilidades
- la experiencia necesaria para el puesto
- la tecnología u otras destrezas (*skills*) necesarias

A escribir

En tres párrafos, describe la carrera de tus sueños. En la primera frase, describe la carrera ideal. En el resto del primer párrafo, explica por qué te interesa el campo (o cómo te interesó). En el segundo párrafo, describe con más detalle el puesto ideal para ti, qué experiencia requiere el puesto y luego explica si tienes esa experiencia o si la vas a tener en el futuro. Termina el ensayo con un párrafo sobre qué tipo de tecnología se requiere, cómo tiene que usarse y si hay otras destrezas necesarias que tienes que te pueden ayudar en este campo.

MODELO: La carrera de mis sueños es la medicina. Mis padres son doctores en una zona rural. Desde una edad joven, entendí la importancia del cuidado médico básico. En el colegio, disfruté de mis cursos de ciencia y siempre sacaba buenas notas (*grades*). El verano pasado hice una práctica en una clínica en mi pueblo.

El puesto ideal para mí es ser doctor familiar. En los Estados Unidos hay muchos especialistas, pero no hay muchos doctores familiares (o doctores de atención primaria)...

Después de escribir

Revisa tu ensayo. Luego intercambia ensayos con un compañero / una compañera para evaluarlos. Lee el ensayo con cuidado para revisar los siguientes puntos.

☐ empieza con una descripción breve y clara de la carrera ideal

☐ explica la historia de su interés en el campo

☐ usa detalles para describir el puesto ideal

☐ describe la experiencia necesaria para el puesto

☐ explica el papel de la tecnología en su trabajo futuro

☐ usa el imperfecto para describir en el pasado

☐ usa el pretérito para hablar de las acciones que ocurrieron en el pasado

☐ hay concordancia entre sujetos y verbos

☐ hay concordancia entre sustantivos y adjetivos

☐ tiene la ortografía correcta

Después de revisar el ensayo de tu compañero/a, devuélveselo. Mira tu propio ensayo para ver los cambios que tu compañero/a te recomienda y haz las revisiones necesarias.

ESTRATEGIA

Supporting details

A solid thesis statement to open a paragraph should assert something, then the rest of the paragraph should explicitly support that assertion. Good supporting details include facts, statistics, examples, background information, descriptive adjectives, and brief anecdotes.

Suggestion (Después de escribir): Instead of grading the writing assignment, occasionally grade the corrections students do of their peers' work. This will help students take editing more seriously and do a more thorough job of reading their classmates' assignments.

¡Hablemos!

¿Le puedo dar un mensaje?

Antes de hablar

Suggestion (Antes de hablar): Have students use the call log on their phone to trigger their memories of recent calls.

En parejas, hablen de las llamadas telefónicas más profesionales que han hecho (*made*) o recibido (*received*). Pueden ser llamadas para hablar del producto o servicio de una compañía, un mensaje recordatorio sobre una cita médica, llamadas en el lugar de trabajo, entrevistas por teléfono —cualquier contexto que no sea personal (entre amigos).

- ¿Cuándo fue?
- ¿Llamaste tú o te llamaron?
- ¿Con quién(es) hablaste?
- ¿Por qué?

Suggestions (A hablar):
- Give students time to review phone call strategies from the *Comunicación* section of this chapter.
- Start by giving a slip of paper to a volunteer "caller" and complete the phone call as a model for the whole class before all the pairs try to complete a successful telephone interaction.
- Remind students that those who receive the calls should not know in advance what they are being called about.

A hablar

En parejas, túrnense para hacer las llamadas telefónicas en que le pides a tu compañero/a la información específica que tu profesor(a) le dará (*will give*).

MODELO: *Instrucciones para E1: Quieres el número de servicio al cliente.*
E1: ¡Rin, rin!
E2: ¿Aló? (¿Bueno?, ¿Diga?, ¿Dígame?)
E1: Buenas tardes. Soy ___. Busco el número de teléfono de servicio al cliente.
E2: Claro. Es 3-52-60 70.
E1: Gracias.
E2: De nada.

Suggestion (Después de hablar): Remind students that the ability to successfully communicate by telephone in a second language can be an important professional qualification. Employers say they want new employees who can communicate verbally with people inside and outside the organization. And since many companies increasingly want to expand their businesses into international markets, verbal communication in Spanish is an added qualification that could make a candidate stand out.

Después de hablar

En grupos, hablen de las llamadas telefónicas. ¿Entendieron lo que querían las personas que llamaron? ¿Consiguieron lo que querían? ¿Cuáles fueron los retos (*challenges*) y los triunfos? Presenten los resultados al resto de la clase.

Note (A hablar): Give each student a slip of paper listing one of the following tasks. **1.** *Quieres saber cuánto cuesta el libro de texto para este curso.* **2.** *Quieres la información de contacto del instructor / de la instructora de este curso.* **3.** *Quieres la dirección de casa de la persona a quien llamas para entregarle unos documentos importantes.* **4.** *Quieres el nombre completo de todas las personas que viven en la casa adonde llamas.* **5.** *Quieres organizar (el lugar, el día y la hora) una reunión (meeting)* **6.** *Quieres organizar (el lugar, el día y la hora) un almuerzo.* **7.** *Quieres organizar (el lugar, el día y la hora) una entrevista con este/a empleado/a, porque piensas contratarlo/la.* **8.** *Quieres organizar (el lugar, el día y la hora) una cita para arreglar la impresora rota.* **9.** *Quieres saber el mejor lugar para ir al médico aquí.*

Conéctate al cine

Película: *Los lunes al sol* (drama, España, 2002)
Director: Fernando León de Aranoa

Suggestion (Al ver, Paso 1):
Turn subtitles off, if possible. Students won't understand everything, but they won't need to. Stop at the words *ni idea*.

Sinopsis:
Santa, José y Lino son amigos. Ninguno de ellos tiene empleo desde que la fábrica donde trabajaban eliminó muchos trabajos. Pasan tiempo juntos hablando y tomando alcohol, muchas veces en el bar de otro amigo, Rico. Cada uno de ellos tiene una actitud diferente frente a estos tiempos difíciles.

Escena (DVD, 00:02:30 to 0:05:50):
José y Lino están en el transbordador (*ferry*) cuando sube Santa, sin boleto (*ticket*). Lino tiene un periódico con un anuncio de empleo. Santa y José le hacen preguntas sobre el trabajo.

Antes de ver

Lino va a una entrevista de trabajo. ¿Qué debe tener un candidato para tener éxito (*success*) en una entrevista profesional? Pon estos en orden del 1 al 6, de más importante (1) a menos importante (6).

____ un buen aspecto   ____ una edad apropiada

____ una buena actitud   ____ experiencia previa

____ conocimiento de la industria   ____ un vehículo propio

A ver

PASO 1. Lee las **Expresiones útiles** y mira la escena. No trates de entender cada palabra, pero escucha con atención cuando los amigos hablan del anuncio de trabajo.

PASO 2. Lee las preguntas y posibles respuestas. Luego mira la escena otra vez y escucha con atención para encontrar las respuestas correctas.

Expresiones útiles

tiene buena pinta	it looks promising
pagas	payments
vehículo propio	one's own vehicle
conocimientos de informática	knowledge of computers
posibilidades de ascenso	opportunities for promotion
edad	age
me echa a mí la culpa	puts the blame on me
canas	gray hair(s)
tener buen aspecto	to look presentable
ya veremos	we'll see
ni idea	(I have) no idea

■ For copyright reasons, the feature-film clips referenced in **Conéctate al cine** have not been provided by the publisher. Each of these films is readily available through retailers or online rental sites such as Amazon, iTunes, or Netflix.

1. __c__ ¿A qué hora es la entrevista?
   a. a las doce   b. a las dos   c. a las diez

2. __a__ Según el anuncio, ¿qué ofrece el trabajo?
   a. 14 pagas   b. 40 pagas   c. 120 pagas

3. __b__ ¿Qué límite de edad tiene el trabajo?
   a. 25 años   b. 35 años   c. 45 años

4. __c__ ¿Cómo va a conseguir Lino un vehículo propio?
   a. Su esposa se lo compra.   b. Su hijo se lo compra.   c. Él mismo (*himself*) se lo compra.

5. __b__ Según Santa, ¿qué debe tener el candidato?
   a. una buena actitud   b. un buen aspecto   c. un buen vehículo

6. __a__ ¿De qué se preocupa Lino?
   a. sus canas   b. su ropa   c. su vehículo

7. __a__ ¿Cómo va a aprender Lino las cosas necesarias para el trabajo?
   a. Su hijo se las enseña.   b. Va a tomar un curso.   c. Va a comprar libros.

Después de ver

En parejas, contesten las siguientes preguntas.

¿Alguna vez hiciste una entrevista de empleo? ¿Estabas nervioso/a? ¿Qué te preguntaron durante la entrevista? ¿Cómo respondiste a las preguntas? Al final, ¿te contrataron? ¿Por qué crees que (no) te contrataron?

VOCABULARIO

Now that I have completed the chapter, I can . . .

☐ conduct myself professionally on the phone

☐ introduce people to each other

☐ talk about professions and technology used in the workplace

☐ give more detailed descriptions of a person, place, or thing

☐ make requests, invitations, and commands

☐ talk about work and professions in the Spanish-speaking world

Comunicación

Quisiera + *Inf.*	I'd like to . . .
A sus órdenes.	At your (*form.*) service. (*Lit.,* At your orders.)
¿En qué puedo servirle(s)?	How may I help you (*form. s./pl.*)?
Es / Fue / Ha sido un placer.	It's / It was / It has been a pleasure.
Para servirle.	At your (*form.*) service. (*Lit.,* [I'm here] To serve you.)
Quiero presentarle(s) a...	I'd like you (*form. s./pl.*) to meet . . .
Quiero presentarte a...	I'd like you (*inform. s.*) to meet . . .
Encantado/a.	Nice to meet you. (*Lit.,* Enchanted.)
Es un placer.	Nice to meet you. (*Lit.,* It's a pleasure.)

Repaso: Con mucho gusto., Mucho gusto.

Las profesiones y los oficios / Professions and Trades

el/la agente de bienes raíces	real estate agent
el/la agente de seguros	insurance agent
el/la bloguero/a	blogger
el bombero / la mujer bombero	firefighter
el/la cajero/a	cashier
el/la cirujano/a	surgeon

el currículum	resume, curriculum vitae (CV)
el/la diseñador(a) gráfico/a	graphic designer
el/la dueño/a	owner
el/la ejecutivo/a	executive
el/la empleado/a	employee
el/la empresario/a	businessperson
el/la enfermero/a	nurse
la entrevista	interview
el/la escritor(a)	writer
el/la gerente	manager
el jefe / la jefa	boss
el/la juez(a)	judge
el/la maestro/a	teacher
el/la programador(a)	programmer
el puesto	job/position
la sala de justicia	courtroom
el/la trabajador(a) social	social worker
el tribunal	court

Cognados: el/la arquitecto, el/la asistente administrativo/a, el/la cosmetólogo/a, el/la dentista, el/la director(a) de marketing, el/la fotógrafo/a, el/la secretario/a

Repaso: el/la abogado/a, el/la camarero/a, el/la chofer, el/la doctor(a), el/la estudiante, el/la guía (naturalista), el/la ingeniero/a, el/la médico/a, el/la periodista, el/la pintor(a), el policía / la mujer policía, el/la profesor(a), el/la psicólogo/a, el/la sociólogo/a

La tecnología

el anexo	attachment
el asunto	subject
la (computadora) portátil	laptop computer
el correo electrónico	email
la despedida	closing (*in a letter*)
la impresora	printer
el mensaje	message
la pantalla	screen
el saludo	greeting
el teclado	keyboard

Cognados: la computadora, la (computadora) láptop, el email, el escáner, la tableta

Los verbos

adjuntar	to attach
bajar	to download
conectarse	to get online
conseguir (i, i) (un puesto de trabajo)	to get (a job/position)
contratar	to hire
entrevistar	to interview
enviar (í)	to send
estar (*irreg.*) dispuesto/a	to be ready/willing
mandar	to send
preparar un currículum	to prepare a resumé/CV
solicitar (empleo / un trabajo)	to apply for (work / a job)
subir	to upload

Un email profesional

Estimado/a...	Dear . . .
Atentamente	Sincerely

¡Estás en tu casa!

En Quechualla, Perú, una mujer regresa a casa.

Objetivos

When you finish this chapter, you will be able to:

- welcome people to your home or country
- make polite invitations
- describe homes and furnishings
- talk about what you have done
- talk about what you are currently doing
- discuss housing in the Spanish-speaking world and its cost

Mc Graw Hill Education **connect**

www.mhhe.com/connect

COMUNICACIÓN LARIO UCTURA ATE

Video track (Act. A): This video clip can be found on the *DVD to accompany Conéctate: Cap. 11*, Track 1.

¡Bienvenido!
Welcoming people

Videoscript (Act. A): 1. *Le damos la bienvenida siempre.* **2.** *Os doy la bienvenida.* **3.** *Aquí siempre van a ser bienvenidos.* **4.** *Son bienvenidos acá en Costa Rica cuando quieran venir.* **5.** *Acá son bienvenidos.* **6.** *Aquí siempre son bienvenidos.* **7.** *Si pueden venir, ¡bienvenidos!* **8.** *Todo el mundo es bienvenido.* **9.** *Bienvenidos siempre a mi país.*

A. A ver: ¡Bienvenidos! ¿Qué les dicen estos hispanos a los estudiantes que piensan visitar sus países? Mira y escucha. Luego mira otra vez con pausas y escoge la mejor respuesta.

1. Aníbal, de Panamá
   a. Le damos la bienvenida siempre.
   b. Os doy la bienvenida.
   c. Siempre van a ser bienvenidos.
   d. Son bienvenidos.

2. Guillermo, de España
   a. Le damos la bienvenida.
   b. Os doy la bienvenida.
   c. Siempre van a ser bienvenidos.
   d. Son bienvenidos.

3. Pedro, de México
   a. Si pueden venir, ¡bienvenidos!
   b. Siempre van a ser bienvenidos.
   c. Son bienvenidos.
   d. Todo el mundo es bienvenido.

4. Allan, de Costa Rica
   a. Si pueden venir, ¡bienvenidos!
   b. Siempre van a ser bienvenidos.
   c. Son bienvenidos.
   d. Todo el mundo es bienvenido.

5. Vilma, de Colombia
   a. Bienvenidos siempre.
   b. Le damos la bienvenida.
   c. Son bienvenidos.
   d. Todo el mundo es bienvenido.

6. Alexis, de Costa Rica
   a. Le damos la bienvenida.
   b. Os doy la bienvenida.
   c. Siempre son bienvenidos.
   d. Todo el mundo es bienvenido.

7. Sylvia, de Argentina
   a. Si pueden venir, ¡bienvenidos!
   b. Siempre van a ser bienvenidos.
   c. Son bienvenidos.
   d. Todo el mundo es bienvenido.

8. Víctor, de México
   a. Bienvenidos siempre.
   b. Le damos la bienvenida.
   c. Son bienvenidos.
   d. Todo el mundo es bienvenido.

9. Mauricio, de Costa Rica
   a. Si pueden venir, ¡bienvenidos!
   b. Bienvenidos siempre.
   c. Siempre van a ser bienvenidos.
   d. Todo el mundo es bienvenido.

Suggestion (Act. A): Remind students to read the multiple choice options before watching the video (or to pause between each clip). They are more likely to recognize the speech and be able to match it to the best answer if their minds have been activated by looking at all the possible choices.

To say *Welcome!*, use **¡Bienvenido(s)!** or **¡Bienvenida(s)!**

To specify who is welcome, use this construction: *subject* + **ser** + **bienvenido/a/os/as.**

Los estudiantes siempre son bienvenidos aquí.	Students are always welcome here.

To use the equivalent of the verb *to welcome,* use this construction: *indirect object pronoun* + **dar** + **la bienvenida a** + *noun.*

Les damos la bienvenida a los estudiantes.	We welcome students. (*Lit.,* We give welcome to the students.)

B. ¡Bienvenidos! Mira las imágenes y decide qué saludo de bienvenida debes usar para cada una.

MODELO:

¡Bienvenida, señora!

En español...

To address people whose names you do not know, it is common to use these words.

señor(es) for men (*sir; sirs* or *gentlemen* in English)
señora(s) for older women and a married woman (*Mrs./ ma'am; ladies*)
joven/jóvenes for younger males, from adolescence to their early 20s (*young man; young men*)
señorita(s) for younger, unmarried women (*Miss, ladies*)

These are all commonly used in the Spanish-speaking world, and you may come across as slightly rude or abrupt if you leave them out.

1.

Bienvenido, señor.

2.

Bienvenidos (Bienvenidos, jóvenes.)

3.

¡Bienvenidas

4.

¡Bienvenida, señorita!

Pasa.
Making polite invitations

> Here are some commands that can be used as polite invitations. Adding **por favor** to these commands will soften them even more, ensuring that your audience receives them as friendly, not bossy.
>
> | TÚ | UD. | UDS. | |
> |----|-----|------|---|
> | **Come más.** | **Coma más.** | **Coman más.** | Have some more (food). |
> | **¡Diviértete!** | **¡Diviértase!** | **¡Diviértanse!** | Have fun! |
> | **Pasa.** | **Pase.** | **Pasen.** | Come in. |
> | **Siéntate.** | **Siéntese.** | **Siéntense.** | Have a seat. |
> | **¡Sírvete!** | **¡Sírvase!** | **¡Sírvanse!** | Help yourself! |

A. Pase Ud.

PASO 1. Empareja cada imagen con la mejor invitación. **¡Atención!** Usa cada invitación solo una vez.

1. __b__

2. __d__

3. __e__

4. __a__

5. __c__

a. Diviértanse.
b. Pase.
c. Pasen.
d. Siéntese.
e. Sírvanse.

CONÉCTATE AL MUNDO PROFESIONAL

As you see in **Actividad A**, in professional contexts, it's best to defer to the formal register, **usted(es)**, at least at first. Then observe your surroundings carefully: Do people tell you it's okay to use the informal **tú**? Are you the only person using the formal register? Is there a difference related to job titles or seniority? This model of deferring to the most formal approach first can be applied to a lot of workplace culture: use of mobile devices, breaks, written correspondence, language use, and so on.

PASO 2. Para cada imagen, indica qué mandato debes usar.

1.

- ☑ Siéntate.
- ☐ Siéntese.
- ☐ Siéntense.

2.

- ☐ Pasa.
- ☐ Pase.
- ☑ Pasen.

3.

- ☑ Pasa.
- ☐ Pase.
- ☐ Pasen.

4.

- ☐ Siéntate.
- ☐ Siéntese.
- ☑ Siéntense.

5.

- ☐ Sírvete.
- ☐ Sírvase.
- ☑ Sírvanse.

6.

- ☐ Come más.
- ☐ Coma más.
- ☑ Coman más.

PASO 3. En parejas, inventen por lo menos dos mandatos más para cada imagen en el **Paso 2. ¡Atención!** No se olviden de mantener el nivel de formalidad apropiado.

MODELO: (Imagen 1) ¡Juega un videojuego conmigo! Cuéntame de tu día. No te olvides de llamar a tu mamá.

B. Las invitaciones en la clase En parejas, practiquen «las visitas». Un(a) estudiante llega, toca a (*knocks on*) la puerta y el otro / la otra lo/la invita a entrar, a sentarse y a comer algo. Luego practiquen con otra pareja para usar la forma de **Uds.**

MODELO: E1: (*Toca a la puerta.*)
E2: ¡Hola! Pasa. Bienvenido/a.
E1: ¿Qué pasa?
E2: Tenemos pizza. Sírvete, por favor.

Suggestion (Act. B): If class time allows, have one or more groups present their dialogue for the class.

Suggestion (Act. B): If you ever use candy (*dulces*) for prizes in class, bring some for students to offer to each other in *Act. B*.

COMUN **VOCABULARIO** CTURA TE

La casa y los muebles
Rooms and other parts of a home

Note (Act. A, Paso 1): Point out that *piso* can mean *floor* or *ground, story* (of a building), or *apartment* (in Spain). Also point out that *planta* is another word for the floor or story of a building; in the Spanish-speaking world, the *planta baja* is the ground floor and *la primera planta* or *el primer piso* is one floor up from street level.

A. Un piso en Madrid

PASO 1.   Usa el vocabulario de los dibujos para completar la descripción de un apartamento en Madrid.

En español...

You already know the first ordinal numbers in Spanish, **primer(a), segundo/a** and **tercer(a).** The ordinal numbers for 4–10 are as follows:

4th = **cuarto/a**

5th = **quinto/a**

6th = **sexto/a**

7th = **séptimo/a**

8th = **octavo/a**

9th = **noveno/a**

10th = **décimo/a**

apartamento   ascensor   escalera   jardín   pasillo   tendedero

Vivo en un <u>apartamento</u> (o «piso», como decimos aquí en España) en un **edificio** moderno en Madrid. Para subir a **la tercera planta,** tienes que usar el <u>ascensor</u> o, si prefieres hacer más ejercicio, la <u>escalera</u>. Al entrar en nuestro piso, hay dos **dormitorios** y entre los dos hay **un cuarto de baño.** Luego si pasas por el <u>pasillo</u>, hay **cocina** a la derecha y **un salón** a la izquierda. Si cruzas el salón, vas a ver **la terraza** con plantas, hierbas y flores. ¡Tenemos nuestro propio <u>jardín</u> en la terraza! Tenemos una mesa para comer y relajarnos allí. La vista es bellísima. Además, tenemos el <u>tendedero</u> para colgar la ropa limpia para secarse al aire.

PASO 2.   Contesta las siguientes preguntas sobre el lugar donde vives.

1. ¿Cuántas plantas tiene tu casa o apartamento?
2. ¿Hay ascensor en tu edificio?
3. ¿Tienes tu propio dormitorio o lo compartes con otra(s) persona(s)?
4. ¿Cuántas personas comparten el cuarto de baño donde vives? ¿Quién normalmente lo limpia?
5. Si hay una cocina donde vives, ¿cómo es? ¿Es grande? ¿moderna? Si no hay cocina, ¿echas de menos (*miss*) tener una cocina?

Los muebles y los electrodomésticos
Furniture and appliances

A. ¿Cúal no se encuentra (*isn't found*) en... ? Lee las siguientes preguntas y para cada una, selecciona la respuesta más lógica.

1. ¿Cuál de las siguientes cosas no se encuentra en una cocina normalmente?

   a. **un sofá**   b. **un fregadero**   c. **una estufa**   d. **un refrigerador**

2. ¿Cuál de las siguientes cosas no se encuentra en un cuarto de baño?

   a. **una bañera**   b. **un lavabo**   c. **una cama**   d. **un espejo**

3. ¿Cuál de las siguientes cosas no se encuentra en un dormitorio / una habitación?

   a. **un armario**   b. **una mesita de noche**   c. **una lámpara**   d. **un lavaplatos**

4. ¿Cuál de las siguientes cosas no se encuentra en el salón?

   a. **un sillón**   b. **un estante**   c. **una ducha**   d. **un televisor**

5. ¿Cuál de las siguientes cosas no requiere la electricidad para funcionar?

   a. **la aspiradora**   b. **el inodoro**   c. **la lavadora**   d. **el microondas**

To talk about household chores (**los quehaceres domésticos**) in Spanish, the following vocabulary is useful.

barrer (el piso)	to sweep (the floor)
hacer la cama	to make the bed
lavar (los platos, el suelo)	to wash/clean (the dishes, the floor)
limpiar	to clean
pasar la aspiradora	to vacuum
sacar la basura	to take out the trash
sacudir	to dust

B. ¿Cómo son las partes de la casa?   Empareja las partes de la casa con su mejor descripción.

1. __g__ la parte subterránea
2. __c__ el cuarto (*room*) que se usa para dormir durante la noche
3. __e__ una parte exterior con plantas y flores
4. __d__ la parte donde se aparca el coche
5. __a__ el cuarto que tiene mesa y sillas y que se usa para cenar
6. __f__ la parte que conecta un cuarto a otro
7. __b__ el cuarto que se usa para ducharse

a. el comedor
b. el cuarto de baño
c. el dormitorio
d. el garaje
e. el jardín
f. el pasillo
g. el sótano

C. ¿Qué haces en cada cuarto?

PASO 1.   Indica si cada oración describe una acción lógica o no.

	LÓGICA	NO ES LÓGICA
1. Me afeito en el garaje.	☐	☑
2. Me baño en la cocina.	☐	☑
3. Me lavo los dientes en el cuarto de baño.	☑	☐
4. Cocino en el dormitorio.	☐	☑
5. Como en el comedor.	☑	☐
6. Descanso (*I rest*) en la terraza.	☑	☐
7. Duermo en el cuarto de baño.	☐	☑
8. Me ducho en el pasillo.	☐	☑
9. Escucho música en el salón.	☑	☐
10. Lavo la ropa en el sótano.	☑	☐
11. Me lavo las manos en el salón.	☐	☑
12. Leo en el dormitorio.	☑	☐
13. Tomo el sol en el jardín.	☑	☐
14. Veo la televisión en el salón.	☑	☐

PASO 2.   Ahora, en parejas, túrnense para cambiar todas las acciones ilógicas a acciones lógicas para Uds.

Expansion (Act. C): Have students work in groups to build a story about their daily chores and activities in chronological order. One student starts, and then each group member follows, adding another chore/activity, with the goal of creating the longest chain possible. The chain should keep going around until students run out of things to add to the list or repeat an item already mentioned. Which group can come up with the most chores without repeating an item? Have some groups share their lists with the class.

CONÉCTATE AL MUNDO HISPANO

Antoni Gaudí i Cornet fue un famoso arquitecto español que nació en Cataluña, España, en 1852 y murió en 1926. Cuando diseñaba casas y otras estructuras, prefería trabajar con modelos tridimensionales en vez de con modelos planos (*flat*), y siempre improvisaba e incorporaba otros trabajos artesanales hechos de madera, cerámica, metal, vidrio y otros materiales. Su estilo, orgánico e innovador para esa época, ha sido reconocido mundialmente. A Gaudí le gustaba mucho la naturaleza y sus obras fueron inspiradas por ella. Entre sus mejores obras destacan (*stand out*) tres que están en Barcelona: la Casa Milà (en la página 120 de este libro), de paredes ondulantes (*wavy*); el Parque Güell, cubierto de mosaicos multicolores; y el Templo de la Sagrada Familia, una basílica que todavía está en construcción.

Note (Act. D): The images on page 330 are based on Jordi and Elena's home.

D. A ver: En casa de Jordi y Elena

PASO 1. Mira el video varias veces e indica las partes de la casa mencionadas por Jordi.

- ☑ la cocina
- ☐ el cuarto de baño
- ☑ la despensa (*pantry*)

- ☐ el dormitorio
- ☐ el garaje
- ☐ el jardín

- ☑ el salón
- ☐ el sótano
- ☑ la terraza

¿Qué electrodoméstico *no* menciona Jordi?

- ☑ la batidora (*mixer*)
- ☐ el horno (*oven*)

- ☐ el lavavajillas (lavaplatos)
- ☐ el microondas

- ☐ la nevera (*freezer*)
- ☐ la placa (*cooktop*)

PASO 2. Mientras miras el video otra vez, indica tres verbos que usa Jordi en cada parte de su apartamento. Luego contesta la pregunta.

1. En el salón
   - ☑ comer
   - ☑ descansar
   - ☑ dormir
   - ☐ lavar

2. En la terraza
   - ☐ comer
   - ☑ descansar
   - ☑ estar
   - ☑ preparar

3. En la cocina
   - ☑ cocinar
   - ☐ descansar
   - ☑ lavar
   - ☑ preparar

Según Jordi, ¿cuál es la cosa que no puede faltar en ninguna cocina española?
el aceite de oliva

E. El juego de las veinte preguntas

Formen grupos de por lo menos tres personas. Un miembro del grupo debe seleccionar un cuarto, un mueble o un aparato electrodoméstico. Los otros miembros deben hacerle preguntas de sí o no hasta adivinar la palabra correcta.

MODELO: (E1 selecciona la palabra «fregadero» sin decírsela a los otros estudiantes)

E2: ¿Es un mueble?
E1: No.
E2: ¿Está en el salón?
E1: No.
E3: ¿Está en la cocina?
E1: ¡Sí!
E2: ¿Se usa para cocinar?...

Expansion (Act. E): Play *En mi casa hay...*, in which each student has to add an item to the list of things that you might find in a room, repeating all the items already said by other students. For example, if the room is *salón*, by the fifth student it might be *En mi casa hay un salón con un sofá, un sillón, una mesita, un televisor, el equipo de música... española. Esto es la placa vitrocerámica donde cocinamos, nuestra campana y, bueno... los distintos muebles como tiene cualquier cocina típica española. Y si me perdonáis, os tengo que dejar porque le dije a Elena que le iba a preparar un café y vamos a preparárselo.*

Video track (Act. D): This video clip can be found on the *DVD to accompany Conéctate: Cap. 11*, Track 2.

Videoscript (Act. D): *Hola Elena, ya estoy en casa. Um... Hola chicos, este es mi salón, es donde pasamos parte de nuestra vida. Aquí está el sofá, que es donde normalmente dormimos la siesta y descansamos —que es una costumbre muy típica española— y donde solemos ver la televisión. Esta es la mesa donde normalmente solemos comer, las sillas donde nos sentamos a comer, y este es nuestro equipo de música, que es donde normalmente escuchamos la música para relajarnos, y aquí está mi terraza, donde está mi mujer. Vamos a conocerla. Esta es mi terraza, que es mi sitio de relajación donde normalmente venimos a descansar después de trabajar. Eh... Tenemos muchas plantas, hay rosas, rosales, claveles, pensamientos, hierba buena, mucho tipo de plantas, y la verdad que estamos encantados de estar aquí. Y ahora Elena, me voy a preparar un café, ¿quieres uno? (—Sí, gracias. —Ahora vengo.)*

Bueno chicos, antes de prepararle el café a Elena, voy a enseñaros mi cocina. Esta es la cocina típica española. Aquí tenemos el microondas, aquí tenemos el horno que es donde hacemos nuestros asados, este es el fregadero, y aquí tenemos la nevera y la despensa. La despensa es muy típico en España, eh... donde tenemos sobre todo muchas especias, cocinamos bastante especiado, con ajo, tomillo, romero, orégano, donde tenemos la leche, bueno..., cervezas, Coca-Colas y demás cosas. Esto es el lavavajillas, aquí tenemos platos, tenedores, cuchillos donde los lavamos y este es el aceite típico español, el aceite de oliva, no puede faltar en ninguna cocina

Suggestion (Act. F): Instead of a single room, have students describe their homes and the various rooms in it.

F. ¿Cómo son nuestras casas?

PASO 1. Piensa en un cuarto de tu casa, residencia o apartamento. Apunta todos los detalles que puedes recordar sobre el cuarto. ¿Qué cuarto es? ¿Qué muebles y otras cosas hay en el cuarto? ¿Dónde se encuentran (*are they located*)? ¿Qué haces en el cuarto?) Para explicar bien la ubicación (*location*) de cada mueble, usa estas expresiones.

a la derecha/izquierda de	detrás de
al lado de	en medio de (*in the middle of*)
cerca/lejos de	encima de (*on top of*)
debajo de (*below*)	enfrente de

Expansion (Act. F, Paso 2): Have volunteers describe a room they've drawn to the entire class, and have students draw what they hear. The volunteers then show the class the room they're describing. Which student has the most accurate drawing for each description? Does the drawing reflect what the describing student's partner had originally described?

PASO 2. En parejas, túrnense para describir sus cuartos. Mientras una persona describe el cuarto, la otra debe dibujar el plano (*floor plan*) con todas las cosas que escucha. Luego intercambien (*exchange*) dibujos. ¿Es parecido el dibujo de tu pareja al cuarto que describiste?

G. ¿Cómo viven los estudiantes?

PASO 1. En grupos, túrnense para contestar las preguntas sobre el lugar donde vive cada uno ahora.

¿Cómo es el edificio? ¿Cúantos pisos hay? ¿Hay ascensor en el edificio? ¿Hay cocina compartida (*shared*)?

¿Cuántos dormitorios hay? ¿Cuántos cuartos de baño?

Si hay cocina, ¿es moderna o anticuada? ¿Cuáles son los electrodomésticos en la cocina?

¿Cuántos televisores hay? ¿Dónde están? ¿Hay equipo de música? ¿Dónde?

¿Hay lavadora y secadora? ¿Dónde están?

¿Hay garaje? ¿sótano? ¿escaleras? ¿jardín?

Suggestion (Act. G): Compile the information from *Pasos 1* and *2* to find out the most common living situation for students in your class. If your students are uncomfortable sharing this information, have them describe their dream houses instead.

PASO 2. Basándose en la información del **Paso 1,** ¿quiénes viven en un apartamento, quiénes en una residencia estudiantil y quiénes en una casa? ¿Cuáles son algunas otras diferencias en los lugares donde viven tus compañeros?

¿Qué dormitorio es más similar al tuyo?

COMUN VOCABUL ESTRUCTURA ATE

↻ Reciclaje
Present, preterite, and imperfect tenses

¿Quién hace los siguientes quehaceres en tu casa regularmente? ¿Quién los hizo ayer? ¿Y quién los hacía cuando eras niño/a? Dibuja la siguiente tabla y complétala con esta información, usando los verbos indicados. Y si la respuesta es **nadie,** escribe eso, pero con el verbo.

	Regularmente...	Ayer...	Cuando era niño/a...
1. preparar el desayuno			
2. pasar la aspiradora			
3. limpiar la casa			
4. hacer la cama			
5. lavar la ropa			
6. sacudir los muebles			

Note (Reciclaje): Answers will vary by student. The tense/mood used should be consistent in each column: *Regularmente...* → present indicative, *Ayer...*→ preterite, *Cuando era niño/a....* → imperfect.

Suggestion (Reciclaje): Create three columns on the board (*Regularmente, Ayer, Cuando era niño/a*) and assign each row from the table to two or three different students, who will write their answers for that row on the board. When everyone is done, have the class inspect the answers for any grammatical errors or for any interesting (or amusing) results.

11.1 He limpiado mi cuarto cinco veces.

The present perfect

Para empezar...

Muchos profesionales en los países hispanos dicen que se vive mejor en su país que en los Estados Unidos o Canadá. Una razón es que es relativamente barato contratar a alguien para hacer los quehaceres domésticos y ayudar con los niños. Esto les deja mucho tiempo que pueden pasar (*spend*) con los amigos y con la familia, y por eso la vida en general es más relajada.

Y para ti, ¿cómo es la vida? ¿Tienes que hacer muchos quehaceres domésticos? ¿Tienes tiempo para relajarte con los amigos y la familia? Para explorar este tema, completa las siguientes oraciones con un número (usa el cero si es necesario). Marca **vez** o **veces** según sea necesario.

Los quehaceres domésticos

En la semana pasada... ,

1. **he preparado** (*I have prepared*) la cena _____ vez / veces.
2. **he lavado** los platos _____ vez / veces.
3. **he pasado** la aspiradora _____ vez / veces.
4. **he sacudido** los muebles _____ vez / veces.
5. **he limpiado** mi cuarto _____ vez / veces.
6. **he hecho** (*made*) la cama _____ vez / veces.

Note (Para empezar): This activity develops students' "transcultural competence," the ability to view and analyze their own culture from the perspective of others. Stress that it is not a matter of one culture being better or worse than the other; they both have advantages and disadvantages.

(Continues)

He lavado los platos.

Expansion (Para empezar): Select a few statements of interest in the first two sections and have students tell you how many times they have done the activity. Then poll students on their answers to the last two questions (that is, the third section of the questionnaire). Ask them if they think they are typical of the general adult population for the area. Ask: *¿Quién hace la mayoría* (most) *de los quehaceres domésticos en el lugar donde vives: tú, tu compañero/a de cuarto/casa o un miembro de la familia?* If you have lived in a Spanish-speaking country, you may want to compare your own experiences with what students report about their own lives.

■ Answers to these activities are in Appendix 2 at the back of your book.

El tiempo con los amigos y la familia

En la semana pasada... ,

1. mis amigos y yo **hemos comido** juntos _____ vez / veces.
2. mis amigos y yo **hemos tomado** un café o un refresco juntos _____ vez / veces.
3. **he visto** (*seen*) una película en el cine _____ vez / veces.
4. **he salido** a bailar _____ vez / veces.

Ahora, ¿cuáles son tus conclusiones?

1. En general, hago _____ quehaceres domésticos.
   a. muchos   b. algunos   c. pocos
2. En general, paso _____ tiempo con mis amigos y mi familia.
   a. mucho   b. algún   c. poco

Actividades analíticas

1 The verbs in first two sections of the **Para empezar** questionnaire are in the *present perfect* (**el presente perfecto**). The use of this verb form is similar in both Spanish and English.

He preparado la cena cinco veces.   *I have prepared dinner five times.*

The present perfect consists of two words: the *auxiliary verb* (**el verbo auxiliar**) **haber** in the present tense and the *past participle* (**el participio pasado**). To make a statement negative, just add **no** in front of the auxiliary verb.

No he preparado la cena todavía.   *I haven't prepared dinner yet.*

Based on what you saw in **Para empezar,** complete the following conjugation of the auxiliary verb **haber** and provide an example of its use.

EL VERBO AUXILIAR *haber*			
yo	he		
tú	has	¿**Has hecho** la cama?	*Have you made the bed?*
él/ella, Ud.	ha	Javier **ha lavado** los platos.	*Javier has washed the dishes.*
nosotros/as	hemos		
vosotros/as	habéis	¿**Habéis comido**?	*Have you eaten?*
ellos/ellas, Uds.	han	Ya **han salido.**	*They have already left.*

2 Use the forms in **Para empezar** to complete this chart of past participles.

	INFINITIVO	PARTICIPIO PASADO
-ar VERBS	lavar	lavado
-er VERBS	comer	comido
-ir VERBS	salir	salido

Autoprueba

Conjugate the verb **salir** in the present perfect.

salir
yo _____
tú _____
él/ella, Ud. _____
nosotros/as _____
ellos/ellas, Uds. _____

Respuestas: he salido, has salido, ha salido, hemos salido, han salido

The rule for forming regular past participles is very simple. For **-ar** verbs, add **-ado** to the stem (for example, **preparar → prepar- + -ado**), and for **-er** and **-ir** verbs, add **-ido** to the stem (for example, **sacudir → sacud- + -ido**). Note that when regular past participles are used as part of the present perfect verb tense, they can only end in **-ado** or **-ido**; they do not change to agree with the subject. Form the past participle for these verbs.

INFINITIVO	PARTICIPIO PASADO
trabajar	trabajado
aprender	aprendido
vivir	vivido

Autoprueba

Use the pattern you just learned to form the past participles of these regular verbs.

lavar: _____

barrer: _____

sacudir: _____

Respuestas: lavado, barrido, sacudido

3 A few verbs have irregular past participles. Use what you saw in **Para empezar** to complete this table of the most common irregular past participles and examples of how they are used.

INFINITIVO	PARTICIPIO PASADO		
decir	dicho	He **dicho** eso muchas veces.	*I have said that many times.*
escribir	escrito	Ella **ha escrito** cinco libros.	*She has written five books.*
hacer	hecho	He **hecho** la cama.	*I have made the bed.*
morir	muerto	El rey **ha muerto.**	*The king has died.*
poner	puesto	¿Dónde **has puesto** la llave?	*Where have you put the key?*
ver	visto	He **visto** una película.	*I have seen a movie.*

■ For more on past participles in Spanish, see **Para saber más 11.1** at the back of your book.

4 You know that **hay,** from the verb **haber,** expresses the idea of *there is* or *there are* in the present tense.

Hay un cambio en nuestros planes.	*There is a change in our plans.*
Hay muchos rumores sobre el nuevo celular.	*There are many rumors about the new cell phone.*

To express this idea in the present perfect (*there has been* or *there have been*), use the auxiliary **ha** and the past participle **habido.**

Ha habido un cambio en el horario.	*There has been a change in the schedule.*
Ha habido muchos rumores sobre la nueva láptop.	*There have been a lot of rumors about the new laptop.*

Notice that just as you saw with **hay,** which has one form for *there is* and *there are,* the singular form **ha habido** is used even when you are talking about something plural, such as **rumores.**

Note (Para saber más): *Para saber más 11.1* covers the irregular past participles of the verbs *abrir, cubrir, romper,* and *volver;* using past participles as adjectives; using past participles to form the passive voice; and using past participles to form the past perfect.

Note (Act. analíticas 4): In standard written language, only the singular *ha habido* is used in these cases, but in the spoken language, one occasionally hears *han habido* with a plural noun: *Han habido rumores.*

En español...

In general, the use of the present perfect in Spanish parallels its use in English. In both languages, the present perfect describes events that happened in the past but that are still relevant to the current moment.

> **Han cancelado** el vuelo. ¿Ahora qué hago?   *They've canceled the flight. Now what do I do?*

For many speakers from Spain, however, the present perfect is also used to describe events that happened very recently.

> **He comido** a la una.   *I ate at 1:00.*

For Latin American speakers, and for some from Spain as well, the simple preterite is used in these cases.

> **Comí** a la una.   *I ate at 1:00.*

Actividades prácticas

A. Preguntas y respuestas   Empareja cada pregunta con la respuesta apropiada.

1. __f__ ¿Qué han dicho los médicos?
2. __d__ ¿Dónde has puesto la aspiradora?
3. __b__ ¿Qué has hecho últimamente (*lately*)?
4. __e__ No me acuerdo. ¿Hemos visto esa película?
5. __h__ ¿Ya ha muerto el arquitecto que diseñó ese hotel?
6. __a__ ¿Ya has escrito la composición para mañana?
7. __g__ ¿Han ido a Ecuador?
8. __c__ ¿Les ha gustado esa casa?

a. No, pero me voy a levantar mañana muy temprano para escribirla.
b. Ayer fui al cine y hoy en la mañana ayudé a mi abuela a sacudir la casa.
c. Sí, más o menos. Es pequeña, pero tiene muy bonita terraza.
d. Creo que la dejé en el pasillo.
e. ¡Claro que sí! El DVD está allí (*over there*) en el salón.
f. Dicen que tu abuelo está muy bien.
g. No, pero tenemos muchas ganas de ir a conocerlo.
h. Sí. Se murió hace tres años.

B. Los quehaceres que hemos hecho esta semana   Lee la lista de quehaceres domésticos y marca los que has hecho esta semana. Luego forma oraciones completas para decir cuáles has hecho y cuáles no.

> **MODELO:**   lavar la ropa → He lavado la ropa esta semana.
>   barrer el piso → No he barrido el piso.

1. ☐ pasar la aspiradora
2. ☐ hacer la cama
3. ☐ pagar una cuenta (*bill*)
4. ☐ lavar los platos
5. ☐ limpiar el cuarto de baño
6. ☐ sacudir los muebles
7. ☐ sacar la basura
8. ☐ sacar el reciclaje

C. De África y Asia a América

¿Te has cambiado de casa alguna vez en tu vida? ¿Te has ido a vivir en otro continente? En la historia de la humanidad, muchos sí lo han hecho, y la población actual de Latinoamérica es prueba (*proof*) de eso. La mayoría es de origen indígena y europeo, pero muchos también tienen sangre (*blood*) africana o asiática. ¿Cómo es eso? Las siguientes oraciones lo explican. Primero indica si la información tiene que ver con los inmigrantes africanos o asiáticos. Luego completa la oración con el verbo más lógico en el espacio en blanco. **¡Atención!** Cada verbo se usa dos veces.

Suggestion (Act. C): Point out that the same factors that led to Africans and Asians moving to Latin America occurred in North America also. In some parts of Latin America, the African and Asian populations became so mixed with everyone else that they are now barely visible, whereas in other parts, they have maintained distinct communities.

Epsy Campbell Barr es una política costarricense. Su abuela era jamaicana.

Jorge Miyagui es un artista peruano, de ascendencia japonesa.

han emigrado (*emigrated*)   **ha habido**   **ha sido**   **han tenido**   **han vivido**

AFRICANOS	ASIÁTICOS	
☐	☑	1. Los filipinos ___han tenido___ una presencia en Latinoamérica desde los primeros años de la colonia de Nueva España (lo que hoy es México) en el siglo (*century*) XVI, cuando llegaron marineros (*sailors*) de Manila en barcos (*ships*) españoles.
☐	☑	2. Los chinos y los japoneses ___han vivido___ en Latinoamérica desde las últimas décadas (*decades*) del siglo XIX. Sus descendientes viven ahora en todos los países de Latinoamérica, pero sobre todo en Argentina, México y el Perú.
☑	☐	3. Desde los primeros años de la colonia, la influencia africana en Latinoamérica ___ha sido___ muy importante. Algunos africanos llegaron con los españoles como marineros y exploradores, y muchos otros llegaron después como esclavos (*slaves*).
☐	☑	4. ___Ha habido___ muchos que son famosos: el astronauta costarricense Franklin Chang-Díaz, la actriz mexicana/uruguaya Bárbara Mori y el ex presidente peruano Alberto Fujimori.
☑	☐	5. Muchos inmigrantes de Jamaica y otras islas del Caribe ___han vivido___ en Panamá desde los tiempos de la construcción del Canal de Panamá, cuando muchos llegaron para buscar trabajo.
☑	☐	6. Por siglos, la presencia africana ___ha sido___ muy notable en el Caribe, Centroamérica, Colombia y Venezuela, pero los afrolatinos ___han tenido___ influencia en todos los países latinoamericanos, desde México hasta Chile.
☑	☐	7. ___Ha habido___ muchísimos que son muy famosos: la cantante cubana Celia Cruz, el beisbolista dominicano Robinson Canó y el futbolista mexicano Giovani Dos Santos.
☐	☑	8. Muchos ___han emigrado___ a los Estados Unidos y a Canadá por razones económicas, y algunos de origen japonés ___han emigrado___ a Japón.

CONÉCTATE AL MUNDO HISPANO

La santería es una creencia religiosa típica del Caribe que mezcla elementos católicos con elementos de la cultura yoruba, o lucumí, del oeste de África. La base de la santería es el culto a los muertos y la creencia en que hay un solo Dios y varias deidades menores llamadas «orishás». La santería surgió (*emerged*) porque los esclavos (*slaves*) africanos no tenían permiso para practicar sus creencias (*beliefs*) religiosas cuando llegaron a América. Por eso, tuvieron que enmascarar (*disguise*) sus tradiciones, como por ejemplo dándole el nombre de un santo católico a cada orishá. Así, Changó, dios del trueno (*thunder*), es Santa Bárbara. Y Eleguá, el protector de los viajeros, es el Santo Niño de Atocha. Se practica la santería en casas privadas por falta de templos. El Caribe es la región donde más se practica la santería.

Suggestion (Act. D, Paso 1): Write a list on the board of the things that students should ask about: *países, ciudades, casas, universidades, habitaciones.* When students have completed their interviews, choose one or two items of interest and poll students on the results they obtained. Also ask some to give a summary and justification of their conclusions for the person they interviewed.

Suggestion (Act. D, Paso 2): Tell students that many speakers of Spanish have the impression that North Americans lead relatively unstable lives filled with many changes. Discuss as a class whether this might be true, based on their results.

Suggestion (Act. E): When students are done, find out if there is any activity that no one in the class has done. For some of the more obscure activities that people have done, find out who has done them and ask for more details (e.g., *¿Dónde tomaste mate? ¿Te gustó?*, and so on).

Expansion (Act E): Have students research one of the activities that they have not done and report back to the class about it.

Suggestion (Act. F): When students finish *Paso 2*, ask them to compare similarities and differences in what they have done and in their goals for the future. For example, *Yo he viajado a muchos países pero Megan no ha salido del país. Megan y yo queremos viajar a Argentina.*

D. Los cambios en la vida

PASO 1. En parejas, entrevístense sobre los cambios importantes en sus vidas. Pregúntale a tu compañero/a en cuántos países, en cuántas ciudades y en cuántas casas ha vivido. ¿En cuántas universidades ha estudiado? En la casa donde vive su familia ahora, ¿siempre ha dormido en la misma habitación? Apunta los resultados.

> **MODELO:** E1: ¿En cuántos países has vivido?
> E2: He vivido en dos países: en Canadá y en los Estados Unidos.

PASO 2. Según los resultados, ¿crees que tu compañero/a ha llevado una vida relativamente estable (*stable*) o una con muchos cambios? ¿Piensas que este caso es típico de tu país? Prepara para compartir los resultados con la clase.

E. Una encuesta

PASO 1. ¿Quién en tu clase ha hecho las siguientes actividades? Pregúntales a tus compañeros y apunta por lo menos una persona que ha hecho cada actividad. Si nadie ha hecho una, escribe «nadie». **¡Atención!** Los verbos **hacer** y **ver** tienen participios pasados irregulares.

> **MODELO:** E1: ¿Has bailado tango?
> E2: No, nunca he bailado tango.
> E1: Yo tampoco. ¿Has probado comida española?

1. bailar tango
2. probar comida española
3. probar comida salvadoreña
4. escuchar la música de Aleks Syntek
5. hablar en español con alguien fuera de la clase
6. hacer surf
7. tomar horchata (*drink made with nuts and/or rice*)
8. tomar mate (un té que se bebe en Argentina, Uruguay y Paraguay)
9. ver en persona a un actor famoso / una actriz famosa
10. viajar a México

PASO 2. En grupos, hagan oraciones para decir lo que han hecho todos del grupo, lo que no ha hecho nadie y lo que han hecho solo algunos.

> **MODELO:** Todos hemos bailado tango y todos hemos tomado horchata.
> Nadie ha hecho surf, nadie ha tomado mate y nadie ha viajado a México.
> Chris y Mary han probado comida española.

PASO 3. Inventa por lo menos tres preguntas originales para saber qué más han hecho los otros miembros de tu grupo. ¡Sé creativo/a! Luego haz las preguntas a tus compañeros y contesta las suyas (*theirs*).

> **MODELO:** ¿Han visto una película española? ¿Han ido a un partido (*game*) de fútbol? ¿Han estudiado otro idioma?

F. ¿Qué has hecho? ¿Qué quieres hacer todavía (*still*)?

PASO 1. Haz una lista de cuatro cosas significativas (*significant*) que has hecho en tu vida y cuatro cosas que quieres hacer todavía.

> **MODELOS:** He escalado el monte Katadihn en Maine y todavía quiero escalar el Gran Teton en Wyoming.
> He viajado a siete estados. Todavía quiero viajar a Alaska.

PASO 2. Basándote en tu lista de actividades del **Paso 1**, entrevista a un compañero o una compañera para saber qué cosas significativas ha hecho y qué quiere hacer en la vida. ¿Uds. dos han hecho cosas parecidas o diferentes? ¿Tienen metas (*goals*) parecidas o diferentes?

México

El multifamiliar Presidente Miguel Alemán en la Ciudad de México

G. Cultura: Mario Pani y la arquitectura moderna en México

PASO 1. Lee el texto sobre México.

México es un país tanto cosmopolita como rico[a] en cultura propia,[b] una característica que le ofrece complejidad a su expresión artística. En todo el mundo es conocido por sus grandes artistas, como los muralistas Diego Rivera y José Clemente Orozco. En paralelo a los movimientos artísticos del siglo XX, México produjo varias generaciones de arquitectos que ahora son conocidos en todo el mundo. Por ejemplo, María Luisa Dehesa fue la primera mujer latinoamericana en recibir su título[c] en arquitectura. El modernista Luis Barragán es conocido por las casas que construyó, por pintar las paredes con colores vibrantes que eran autóctonos[d] de México y por usar ventanas y tragaluces[e] para controlar de manera muy creativa el movimiento de la luz y la sombra. El arquitecto Juan O'Gorman, quien diseñó la casa-estudio de Diego Rivera y Frida Kahlo, también era pintor y tenía vínculos[f] fuertes con los otros artistas de su época. Y la hija de Rivera, Ruth Rivera Marín, es una arquitecta reconocida por su colaboración en la construcción del Museo de Arte Moderno en México.

Para los mexicanos, y sobre todo para los de la capital, el arquitecto Mario Pani es quizás[g] el más emblemático del urbanismo y la arquitectura moderna en México. La gran tarea[h] de Pani fue aplicar los conceptos del funcionalismo del famoso arquitecto suizo Le Corbusier a los aspectos particulares de la vida urbana en México. Logró[i] integrar los estilos de la arquitectura internacional con los detalles coloniales y precolombinos[j] que ya eran intrínsecos a los espacios domésticos en México.

Uno de los edificios más destacados de Pani es el multifamiliar[k] Presidente Alemán, la primera residencia multifamiliar de América Latina, construida en 1948. Este complejo cuenta con nueve edificios de trece pisos y seis edificios de tres pisos, con un total de 1.080 departamentos.[l] El terreno del multifamiliar es bastante grande, pero estos edificios altos solo ocupan un 25 por ciento del espacio y el otro 75 por ciento queda para áreas verdes, como parques y jardines. Era importante para Pani que el multifamiliar fuera[m] no solo una residencia grande, sino una comunidad, como un pueblo chico dentro de una ciudad monstruosa. Por eso el diseño incorporó espacios para los servicios que los habitantes necesitaban todos los días: tiendas, una guardería,[ñ] una oficina de correos, una lavandería y lugares para deportes, como una piscina semiolímpica.

[a]tanto... both cosmopolitan and rich [b](its) own [c]degree [d]native [e]skylights [f]ties, connections [g]perhaps [h]task [i]He succeeded in [j]pre-Columbian [k]multifamily apartment complex [l]apartments (Mex.) [m]A... In spite [n]be [ñ]daycare center

PASO 2. Completa las oraciones con los participios pasados de los verbos de la lista. **¡Atención!** Cada verbo se usa solo una vez.

decir   haber   producir   seguir   ser   tener

1. México ha <u>producido</u> varios artistas importantes.
2. Las culturas precolombinas siempre han <u>tenido</u> una influencia sobre la arquitectura mexicana.
3. Las familias de los multifamiliares han <u>sido</u> participantes en un gran experimento social.
4. Desde que se construyó, siempre ha <u>habido</u> muchos espacios verdes en el Multifamiliar Presidente Alemán.
5. Muchas personas han <u>dicho</u> que la arquitectura es lo más fascinante de la historia de México.
6. Los arquitectos de hoy han <u>seguido</u> con el estilo moderno que Mario Pani estableció en México en el siglo XX.

PASO 3. En parejas, contesten las preguntas y explíquense las respuestas.

1. México tiene una población muy grande y en comparación con otros países, su economía es fuerte. ¿Ves una relación entre eso y la gran tradición de arquitectura que tiene?
2. En las zonas residenciales más elegantes de las ciudades grandes en México, muchas de las casas tienen un estilo muy contemporáneo. ¿Por qué crees que es así? ¿Piensas que los habitantes son conscientes de la tradición de arquitectura moderna en el país?
3. ¿En tu país, cómo son las casas? ¿En su mayoría, tienen un estilo contemporáneo o un estilo más tradicional (por ejemplo, un estilo colonial o «ranch»)? ¿Por qué crees que es así?

Note (Act. G, Paso 3): Mexico's large population and economy mean that there is a lot of construction, and many opportunities for architecture to shine. For residential architecture, have students do an image search on the Internet for "Mexican residential architecture" and "residential architecture in the United States and Canada"; the difference in styles is striking. There may be many reasons for this difference, including esthetic sense, cost of construction, climate, restrictive zoning laws, the role of the front yard, and so on.

Expansion (Act G): Have students research other examples of Pani's work or of the other architects mentioned in the reading and report on them to the class.

Suggestion (Reciclaje):
Remind students that object
pronouns are placed before
conjugated verbs or after and
attached to infinitives.

Suggestion (Reciclaje):
Choose one or two of the
items and poll students to see
how many put *es cierto* for
that item, how many do it the
more common way instead,
and how many do it some
third way.

↻ Reciclaje

Direct objects and direct object pronouns

¿Tus hábitos en la casa son comunes o son diferentes a los de otras personas?
Completa las siguientes oraciones con el pronombre de objeto directo
correcto y luego indica si la oración es cierta para ti.

¿CIERTO PARA TI?

1. La televisión: __La__ veo en la cocina. Es más común ver__la__ en el salón. ☐
2. Los libros: __Los__ leo en la cama. Es más común leer __los__ en el sofá. ☐
3. Las sábanas (*sheets*): __Las__ lavo cada dos meses. Es más común lavar__las__ cada dos semanas. ☐
4. El comedor: __Lo__ uso para estudiar. Es más común usar__lo__ para cenar. ☐
5. La habitación: __La__ uso para hacer ejercicio. Es más común usar__la__ para dormir. ☐

■ Answers to this activity
are in Appendix 2 at the
back of your book.

11.2 ¡No te sientes allí!

Commands with object and reflexive pronouns

Para empezar...

Los siguientes mandatos son comunes en casi cualquier casa, pero ¿en qué cuarto
se oyen, generalmente? Para cada mandato, indica el lugar donde típicamente se
escucharía (*you would hear it*): el cuarto de baño (**B**), la cocina o el comedor (**C**) o el
dormitorio (**D**). Algunos mandatos pueden tener más de una respuesta.

1. __D__ **Duérmete,** hijo. Ya es tarde.
2. __C__ **Sírvele** el cereal a tu hermanito. **No le pongas** demasiado (*too much*) azúcar.
3. __C__ **No te sirvas** mucho, papi. Ya sabes que no puedes comer todo.
4. __B/C__ **Lávate** las manos. Están sucias.
5. __C__ **¡No te sientes** allí! Es para nuestro invitado.
6. __B__ **Báñate.** La fiesta es en dos horas.
7. __D__ **¡Despiértate!**
8. __D__ **Levántate.** Vas a llegar tarde a la escuela.
9. __C/B__ Si te quitas los zapatos, **no los dejes** aquí. **Ponlos** en tu dormitorio.
10. __B/D__ **Mírate** en el espejo, porque me parece que no te peinaste.
11. __D__ **Ponte** el pijama verde; el rojo está sucio.
12. __C__ Si los platos están sucios, **lávalos.**

■ Answers to these
activities are in
Appendix 2 at the back
of your book.

Actividades analíticas

Expansion (Act. analíticas 1):
Have students convert the
examples in the chart to
formal commands. *Pónga(n)-
los; Pónga(n)le; Pónga(n)se.*

1 As you saw in **Capítulo 10,** object and reflexive pronouns are attached to the end
of positive informal and formal commands. Use the examples of positive informal
commands with the verb **poner** in **Para empezar** to complete the following chart.

	EJEMPLO CON MANDATO POSITIVO INFORMAL
Direct Object Pronoun	Ponlos en tu dormitorio.
Indirect Object Pronoun	Ponle más azúcar al café.
Reflexive Pronoun	Ponte el pijama verde.

Answers (Act. analíticas 1):
*duérmete, sírvele, lávate,
báñate, despiértate, levántate,
mírate, lávalos.*

When needed, a written accent mark is added to keep the stress on the same syllable after the pronoun is attached. Can you find examples of this in **Para empezar?**

2 With negative commands, whether informal or formal, object and reflexive pronouns are written as a separate word before the verb. With this in mind, take the examples from the chart in **Actividades analíticas 1** and convert them to negative commands in the chart below.

	EJEMPLO CON MANDATO NEGATIVO INFORMAL
Direct Object Pronoun	No los pongas en tu dormitorio.
Indirect Object Pronoun	No le pongas más azúcar al café.
Reflexive Pronoun	No te pongas el pijama verde.

3 The general rule seen here is that object and reflexive pronouns appear after and are attached to positive commands and come before negative commands. This holds true for all command forms. Use this rule to complete this chart of commands with **limpiar** and the direct object pronoun **lo.**

	POSITIVO	NEGATIVO
tú	límpialo	no lo limpies
Ud.	límpielo	no lo limpie
vosotros/as	limpiadlo	no lo limpiéis
Uds.	límpienlo	no lo limpien

Actividades prácticas

A. Objetos y mandatos

PASO 1. Empareja cada objeto con el mandato más lógico. ¡Atención! Cada mandato solo se puede usar una vez.

1. __d__ la aspiradora
2. __f__ la cama
3. __e__ el equipo de música
4. __g__ el fregadero
5. __h__ el lavaplatos
6. __a__ la mesa
7. __c__ el horno y el microondas
8. __b__ el refrigerador

a. Sacúdela.
b. Límpialo por dentro (*inside*).
c. Límpialos por dentro.
d. Pásala.
e. Sacúdelo.
f. Hazla.
g. Llénalo (*Fill it*) con agua y lava bien las papas.
h. Ponle los platos sucios.

PASO 2. Ahora, en parejas, túrnense para cambiar los mandatos informales del **Paso 1** en mandatos formales (Ud.).

¡Ponte los tenis!

Expansion (Act. analíticas 2):
Have students convert the examples in the chart to *formal* commands: *No los ponga(n); No le ponga(n); No se ponga(n).*

Expansion (Act. analíticas 3):
Have students create this same type of chart for a reflexive verb, such as *levantarse.*

■ To learn how to say *Let's do something!* in Spanish, see **Para saber más 11.2** at the back of your book.

Note (Para saber más):
Para saber más 11.2 covers *nosotros* commands.

Autoprueba

Create positive and negative informal (**tú**) commands for these verbs by following the pattern you just learned for object pronoun placement.

1. sacudir los muebles
   + _____
   − _____

2. barrer el piso
   + _____
   − _____

3. lavar la camisa
   + _____
   − _____

Respuestas: 1. Sacúdelos, No los sacudas. **2.** Bárrelo, No lo barras. **3.** Lávala, No la laves.

Answers (Act. A, Paso 2):
a. *Sacúdala.* b. *Límpielo...*
c. *Límpielos...* d. *Pásela.*
e. *Sacúdalo...* f. *Hágala.*
g. *Llénelo...* h. *Póngale...*

Note (Act. B): Answers will vary by student.

Suggestion (Act. B): Poll students on the answers that they gave; in cases where there is some disagreement, have students explain/justify their answers.

Expansion (Act. B):
• Have students rephrase their answers using the verb *guardar.*
• If students have suggested not to throw out an item, have them give a command—including the appropriate object pronoun—for what to do with it.

Suggestion (Act. C): Create areas on the board for the 8 cases (situations 1–4, advice from angel and devil), and have each pair write their *consejos* in the appropriate area. If space is an issue, have each pair give just their best *consejo* for each case.

Note (Act C): Students will inevitably use many reflexive verbs in this activity: *despiértate, quédate, no te levantes,* and so on.

Expansion (Act. C): Have students change informal commands into singular formal commands.

Note (Act. D, Paso 2): By doing this activity in groups of 3, students can help each other with the *Uds.* commands, and shyer students will feel less self-conscious when it is time to act.

B. ¡Limpia tu cuarto! Cuando limpias un cuarto, una de las cosas más difíciles es decidir qué tirar (*throw out*) y qué guardar (*keep*). ¿Qué consejos das en cuanto a (*with regard to*) los siguientes objetos?

Consejos: Tíralo/la/los/las.
No lo/la/los/las tires.

1. <u>Tírala. / No la tires.</u> una pizza de hace un mes
2. <u>Tíralas. / No las tires.</u> unas revistas del año pasado
3. <u>Tíralos. / No los tires.</u> unos cupones para comprar pizza con un descuento de setenta y cinco por ciento (*percent*)
4. <u>Tíralo. / No lo tires.</u> el libro de tu clase de español
5. <u>Tíralos. / No los tires.</u> los exámenes de tus clases del año pasado
6. <u>Tíralas. / No las tires.</u> las llaves de tu coche
7. <u>Tíralo. / No lo tires.</u> un periódico del mes pasado
8. <u>Tíralos. / No los tires.</u> los DVDs de las películas en que salen juntos Penélope Cruz y Javier Bardem
9. <u>Tírala. / No la tires.</u> una foto de tu abuelo cuando era niño
10. <u>Tírala. / No la tires.</u> una foto de tu ex novio/a

C. Tu «ángel» y tu «demonio» Cuando tienes que tomar una decisión, ¿qué dicen tu «ángel» (tu lado bueno) y tu «demonio» (tu lado malo)? En parejas, creen por lo menos un consejo de tu «ángel» y otro de tu «demonio» para cada situación. **¡Atención!** Usa mandatos informales para dar los consejos.

MODELO: **Situación:** Sabes que tu amigo tiene un examen a las nueve. Son las ocho y media y está dormido todavía.
«Ángel»: Despiértalo y dile qué hora es.
«Demonio»: Déjalo dormir. No es tu problema.

SITUACIONES

1. Son las seis y media de la mañana y estás en la cama. Tu primera clase empieza a las ocho.
2. Son las once de la noche. Estás en una fiesta con unos amigos y estás muy contento. Mañana tienes un examen a las ocho.
3. A un compañero en tu clase se le cae un billete de veinte dólares. Tú lo ves pero él no.
4. Un compañero de clase se va al cuarto de baño y deja un sándwich en su escritorio. Tienes mucha hambre.

D. Actuación (*Acting*) en la casa y en el jardín

PASO 1. En grupos de tres o cuatro estudiantes, usen los verbos de la lista para decir cosas que se pueden hacer en la casa o en el jardín y exprésenlas en forma del mandato de **Uds.**

MODELO: barrer el piso → ¡Bárranlo!

bañarse ¡Báñense!

despertarse ¡Despiértense!

lavar (los platos) ¡Lávenlos!

levantarse ¡Levántense!

planchar (la ropa) ¡Plánchenla!

preparar (la comida) ¡Prepárenla!

PASO 2. Lean sus mandatos a otro grupo. El otro grupo tiene que decir en qué parte de la casa (o en el jardín) se hace cada uno y luego actuarlo.

MODELO: ¡Acuéstense! → Se hace en el dormitorio. (*El grupo actúa el mandato.*)

↻ Reciclaje

Ser and *estar*

¿Cómo es el lugar donde vives? ¿Y en qué condiciones está en este momento? Completa las oraciones con **es** o **está,** e indica si son ciertas o falsas para ti.

	CIERTO	FALSO
1. _Es_ una casa.	☐	☐
2. _Es_ una habitación en una residencia estudiantil.	☐	☐
3. La ropa limpia _está_ guardada (*put away*).	☐	☐
4. La ropa sucia _está_ en el piso.	☐	☐
5. _Está_ en la universidad.	☐	☐
6. La cama _es_ grande.	☐	☐
7. _Es_ buen lugar para estudiar.	☐	☐
8. _Está_ muy limpio hoy.	☐	☐
9. _Es_ un apartamento.	☐	☐
10. El coche en el garaje _es_ de Japón.	☐	☐

■ Answers to this activity are in Appendix 2 at the back of your book.

11.3   Estoy ayudando a mi mamá en la casa

The present progressive

Para empezar...

Alicia, una estudiante mexicana, tuitea (*tweets*) varias veces durante el día. Mira las fotos de su día y luego empareja cada una con el tuit que mandó a esa hora.

1. _c_ 5:45   2. _j_ 6:10   3. _g_ 9:22   4. _e_ 13:12   5. _d_ 14:03

6. _a_ 14:54   7. _h_ 16:12   8. _b_ 18:26   9. _f_ 20:10   10. _i_ 20:45

Los tuits de Alicia

a. «Mi mamá y yo **estamos comiendo.**»
b. «**Estoy haciendo** la tarea.»
c. «**Estoy desayunando.**»
d. «**Estoy ayudando** a mi mamá en la casa.»
e. «**Estoy llegando** a casa.»
f. «**Estoy cenando.**»
g. «Mis amigos y yo nos **estamos tomando** una foto en la universidad.»
h. «**Estoy bebiendo** refrescos con mis amigos. ¡Jorge **está bailando** en el pasillo!»
i. «Mi mamá y yo **estamos viendo** televisión.»
j. «**Estoy esperando** el autobús para ir a la universidad.»

Note (Reciclaje): Ser was taught in **Estructura 1.3; estar** was taught in **Estructura 2.2. Ser** vs. **estar: Estructura 4.4, 5.3.**

Expansion (Reciclaje): On the board, list the 3 uses of *ser* from *Estructura 5.3* (*origen, identidad, propiedad intrínsica*) and the 2 uses of *estar* (*ubicación, cambio*). Have students place each of the examples here into one of these categories. (Answers: *Origen:* 10. *Identidad:* 1, 2, 9. *Propiedad intrínsica:* 6, 7. *Ubicación:* 4, 5. *Cambio:* 3, 8.)

Point out (Para empezar): Remind students that in most areas, the verb *comer* is often used to mean *eating lunch.*

Expansion (Para empezar): Ask students to point out what aspects of Alicia's schedule would be unexpected in a North American context.

■ Answers to these activities are in Appendix 2 at the back of your book.

Note (Act. analíticas 2):
• Remind students that *-ir* verbs with an *e* in the stem syllable that precedes the infinitive ending will change the *e* to *i* in the preterite; *-ir* verbs with an *o* change to *u* when the ending contains a stressed *e* or *o*, such as in *durmió* and *murieron* but not *dormí* or *morimos*. The same process happens in the present participle.
• This spelling change for *leer, oír,* and *traer* occurs simply to avoid having three vowels in a row. The forms would otherwise be **leiendo* and **oiendo*.

Actividades analíticas

1 The verb forms in **Para empezar** are in the *present progressive* (**el presente progresivo**). The present progressive consists of the *auxiliary verb* (**el verbo auxiliar**) **estar** in the present tense, followed by the *present participle* (**el participio presente**), a verb with an **-ndo** ending. Find the present participles in the following sentences and write their infinitives in the column on the right.

		INFINITIVO
Estoy cenando.	*I am having dinner.*	cenar
Están estudiando.	*They are studying.*	estudiar
Mari **está escribiendo** una carta.	*Mari is writing a letter.*	escribir

As you saw in **Estructura 5.3**, **-ar** verbs add **-ando** to the stem, and **-er** and **-ir** verbs add **-iendo**. Given this information, what is the present participle (**-ndo** form) of each of these verbs?

	EL PARTICIPIO PRESENTE (-ndo)
comer	comiendo
salir	saliendo
ayudar	ayudando
ver	viendo

2 **-Ir** verbs with **e** as the final vowel in the stem (such as **decir, pedir, seguir,** and **servir**) change this vowel to **i** in the present participle: **diciendo, pidiendo, siguiendo, sirviendo.**

-Ir verbs with **o** in the stem (only **dormir** and **morir**) change this vowel to **u** in the present participle: **durmiendo, muriendo.** These changes are similar to the vowel changes that you saw for the preterite in **8.1.**

¿Qué estás d<u>i</u>ciendo?	*What are you saying?*
Estamos p<u>i</u>diendo tu ayuda.	*We are asking for your help.*
Estoy s<u>i</u>guiendo tu ejemplo.	*I am following your example.*
¡Ya están s<u>i</u>rviendo la cena!	*They're already serving dinner!*
Las plantas están m<u>u</u>riendo porque no ha llovido.	*The plants are dying because it hasn't rained.*
Los niños están d<u>u</u>rmiendo.	*The children are sleeping.*

The verbs **leer, oír,** and **traer** (and other **-er** and **-ir** verbs whose stem ends in a vowel) have a spelling change in the present participle form. The ending for these verbs is **-yendo** rather than **-iendo.**

¿Estás le<u>y</u>endo?	*Are you reading?*
Estamos o<u>y</u>endo la música.	*We're listening to the music.*

3 The present progressive describes an action in progress and is very similar in meaning to its counterpart in English with *-ing*. The present progressive is used less frequently in Spanish than it is in English, however. This is partly because the simple present in Spanish is often used for actions that are currently underway, whereas English has to use *-ing* in these cases.

Voy a la biblioteca.	*I am going to the library.*

In addition, *-ing* is often used in English to refer to future events, but the Spanish present progressive is not used in this way. The present indicative is used instead.

Mañana **hablo** con ella.	*I am speaking with her tomorrow.*

Autoprueba

Form the present progressive for the following situations by using the pattern you just learned.

1. Nosotros _____ (preparar) la cena.
2. Los chicos _____ (poner) la mesa.

This next one includes a verb that is probably new to you (**batir** [*to beat, stir, whip*]), but since it's regular and follows the rule, you can do it!

3. Mi padre _____ los ingredientes.

Now try an **-ir** verb with a stem change. Again, this is a new verb to you (**hervir [ie, i]** [*to boil*]), but you know the pattern for **-ir** verbs with **e** in the stem, so try it!

4. El agua _____ (hervir).

Respuestas: 1. estamos preparando **2.** están poniendo, **3.** está batiendo **4.** está hirviendo

4 The **–ndo** form may also be used with **ir, andar** (*to walk*), and **seguir** (*to continue*) in place of **estar**. **Andar** gives the sense of doing the action while moving around, and **seguir** gives the sense of continuing the action.

Manuel **va/anda buscando** una casa.	*Manuel is looking for a house.*
¿Qué **andas haciendo** aquí?	*What are you doing here?*
¿**Sigues barriendo** el pasillo?	*Are you still sweeping the hallway?*

¿Por qué?

You saw in **Estructura 5.3** that **estar** is used with adjectives to describe a state that is subject to change or is the result of a change.

Estamos contentos.	We are happy.

In the present progressive, the verb **estar** plays the same role with respect to verbs. It shows that the action described by the verb is subject to change or is the result of change.

Estamos trabajando.	We are working.

Just as **estamos contentos** conveys the idea that we haven't necessarily always been happy, **estamos trabajando** suggests that we are working right at the moment, but that this wasn't necessarily true in the past and might not be in the future either.

Actividades prácticas

A. ¿Qué estás haciendo? Empareja cada pregunta con la respuesta más lógica.

1. __f__ ¿Qué estás comiendo?
2. __h__ ¿Sigues buscando un coche?
3. __d__ ¿Qué están leyendo en esa clase?
4. __e__ ¿Qué andas diciendo de mí?
5. __b__ ¿Están pidiendo mi consejo?
6. __g__ ¿Por qué hay tanto ruido?
7. __a__ ¿Dónde está tu hermano?
8. __c__ ¿Estás haciendo la cama cada mañana como te dije?

a. Está en la cocina lavando platos.
b. Sí. No sabemos qué hacer.
c. No. Sí quiero, pero se me olvida.
d. Una novela de detectives.
e. ¡Que eres muy inteligente!
f. Pan con chocolate. ¿Quieres?
g. Están pasando la aspiradora.
h. Sí, todavía necesito uno.

B. ¿Dónde estoy? Escucha las oraciones e indica en qué lugar normalmente pasa ese tipo de acción.

	LA COCINA	EL COMEDOR	EL DORMITORIO	EL JARDÍN
1.	☐	☑	☐	☐
2.	☑	☐	☐	☐
3.	☐	☐	☑	☐
4.	☐	☐	☐	☑
5.	☑	☐	☐	☐
6.	☐	☐	☐	☑
7.	☐	☑	☐	☐
8.	☑	☐	☐	☐

Script (Act. B): 1. *Estoy cenando.* **2.** *Estoy haciendo arroz con pollo.* **3.** *Estoy haciendo la cama.* **4.** *Estoy mirando las plantas.* **5.** *Estoy limpiando el horno.* **6.** *Estoy plantando flores.* **7.** *Estoy poniendo la mesa.* **8.** *Estoy preparando el desayuno.*

■ To learn how to say in Spanish what you were doing in a past moment, see **Para saber más 11.3** at the back of your book.

Note (Para saber más): *Para saber más 11.3* covers the past progressive.

Expansion (¿Por qué?): Ask students to compare *contentos* and *trabajando* in the sentences here. Which one shows gender? Which one shows number? Students should be able to demonstrate that an adjective (like *contentos*) agrees with the subject, but a participle (like *trabajando*) is invariant.

Estoy trabajando en el jardín.

■ The audio files for in-text listening activities are available in the eBook, within Connect activities, and on the Online Learning Center.

Suggestion (Act. C): Put the times on the board and have several groups write their answers there. The entire class can then look for any interesting commonalities or differences.

Expansion (Act. C): Ask students: *Para un estudiante de Latinoamérica o de España, ¿cómo sería diferente el horario?*

C. Un día típico para un estudiante típico

PASO 1. Si un estudiante típico de tu universidad tuiteara (*tweeted*) en cada uno de los siguientes momentos, ¿qué diría (*would he/she say*) que está haciendo? Escribe el tuit más probable, según tu criterio.

> **MODELO:** 7:00 Estoy desayunando.

	Mensaje
7:00	_____
9:00	_____
12:00	_____
16:00	_____
18:00	_____
22:00	_____

PASO 2. Compara tus respuestas con las de un compañero o una compañera. ¿Pueden llegar a un acuerdo entre los dos sobre los tuits más probables?

D. ¿Qué están haciendo?

PASO 1. Piensa en por lo menos tres de tus seres queridos (*loved ones*) y en qué están haciendo probablemente en este momento. Comparte tus ideas con un compañero / una compañera de clase.

> **MODELOS:** Mi perro probablemente está durmiendo en el sofá.
> Mis padres probablemente están trabajando en su restaurante.

PASO 2. Ahora, túrnense para nombrar a por lo menos cuatro personas famosas (por ejemplo, el papa (*pope*), el presidente, tu estrella (*star*) de cine favorita, tu atleta favorito) e imaginar qué es lo que probablemente están haciendo en este momento.

Suggestions (Act. E):
• Before doing this activity, act out some activities yourself and have students write down what they think you are doing. Some possibilities: 1. *Está(s) lavando platos.* 2. *Está(s) jugando básquetbol.* 3. *Está(s) leyendo un libro.* 4. *Está(s) mirando una película.* 5. *Está(s) haciendo la cama.*
• To keep students on task, have them keep track of each action performed in their group by writing it down (using the present progressive) right after it is performed. Then have at least one student from each group write the actions on the board.

Variation (Act. E): Do this as a whole-class activity with only some students doing the acting.

E. ¡Actúen!

Escoge una acción de la lista o inventa tu propia acción. En grupos pequeños, actúala para tus compañeros. ¿Pueden adivinar qué estás haciendo?

barrer

sacar la basura

hacer la cama

lavar (la ropa, el coche, los platos, el suelo)

pasar la aspiradora

sacudir

¡Leamos!

Casas para el siglo XXI: Pequeñas, flexibles y mutables°   *changeable*

Antes de leer

PASO 1. Empareja cada tipo de casa con la descripción más lógica.

1. _a_ una casa innovadora del siglo XXI

2. _c_ una casa estática

3. _b_ una casa tradicional/convencional

a. Tiene un cilindro giratorio (*revolving*) dentro del cuarto principal.

b. Tiene cuatro paredes permanentes.

c. No se mueve.

PASO 2. Lee el título del artículo en **A leer**. ¿En cuál programa de televisión podrías (*could you*) ver las casas que se describen en el artículo?
a. *Fixer Upper*   b. *Sell This House*   c. *Tiny House Hunters*   d. *Property Brothers*

A leer

PASO 1. Mira las ilustraciones en la página 350 de una casa giratoria (como la de Luigi Colani) y una casa minimalista (como Casa PACO). Mientras lees el artículo, completa las ilustraciones con las palabras de la lista.

Casas para el siglo XXI: Pequeñas, flexibles y mutables

En esta primera década del siglo XXI, la arquitectura ha expuesto,[a] además de innovadoras[b] soluciones formales, proyectos que presentan nuevos tipos de alojamiento,[c] derivados de las exigencias[d] de la vida contemporánea, con sus nuevos artefactos tecnológicos, medios de comunicación y transporte.

¿Así van a ser las casas del futuro?

El modelo de vivienda[e] «tradicional» confinado entre cuatro sólidas y estáticas paredes ha sido uno de los primeros en presentar cambios sustanciales, ya que para los nuevos parámetros de vida que se experimentan[f] en muchos lugares del planeta, ya resulta ineficaz.[g] Debido a ello,[h] algunos arquitectos han comenzado[i] a estudiar soluciones diferentes a las convencionales. [...]

Un proyecto notable es el prototipo de vivienda prefabricada, diseñado por Luigi Colani para la empresa[j] Hanse Hause, que en tan solo treinta y seis metros cuadrados,[k] resuelve[l] una casa con habitaciones giratorias que cubre todas las funciones necesarias para vivir cómodamente.[m]

El objetivo del diseñador fue expandir al máximo el espacio de la vivienda, reduciendo al mínimo el cascarón[n] (solamente de 6m x 6m) y las circulaciones,[ñ] e insertando un cilindro giratorio dentro de un espacio o habitación principal.

El cilindro contiene los diferentes programas[o] de la casa. Un rotor hace girar[p] la gran pieza cilíndrica que contiene las diferentes áreas: recámara, baño, cocina, etcétera. El cilindro puede girar a la derecha o a la izquierda, dejando a la vista[q] la parte que el usuario[r] necesite, y que se conecta directamente con el cuarto principal, el que contiene al cilindro. Es importante mencionar que el movimiento de la casa puede llevarse a cabo mediante[s] el uso de un control remoto.

Todavía[t] más pequeña, pero igual de[u] funcional que la casa giratoria es la denominada[v] Casa PACO, resuelta en tan solo nueve metros cuadrados. En su interior la casa, diseñada por el joven arquitecto de origen

[a]*brought to light* [b]*innovative* [c]*lodging* [d]*demands* [e]*housing* [f]*se... one experiences* [g]*inefficient* [h]*Debido... Due to this fact* [i]*begun* [j]*firm* [k]*square*
[l]*achieves* [m]*comfortably* [n]*shell* [ñ]*hallways* [o]*áreas* [p]*turn* [q]*dejando... leaving within view* [r]*user* [s]*llevarse... be carried out through* [t]*Even* [u]*igual... just as*
[v]*called*

(Continues)

japonés Jo Nagasaka y la oficina de arquitectura Schemanta, contiene los elementos y servicios básicos para una vivienda: baño, cama, escritorio, cocina, comedor y estancia.[w] La estructura es de madera[x] con un acabado impermeable[y] en todos sus frentes.[z] La parte superior es abatible[aa] para iluminación[bb] y ventilación.

[w]*living room* [x]*de... made of wood* [y]*acabado... waterproof finish* [z]*faces* [aa]*moveable* [bb]*lighting*

el baño   la cama   la cocina   el comedor   la recámara   la sala (el cuarto principal)

UNA CASA GIRATORIA   **UNA CASA MINIMALISTA**

Suggestion (Después de leer, Paso 1): As a class, list important innovations described in the article: small, flexible, efficient, near public transit, careful use of light and ventilation, meets all needs but maybe not all wants, and so on.

Suggestion (Después de leer): Based on the two houses described in the reading and the results of *Pasos 1* and *2*, have students draw a plan for the ideal house of the future. Then have them describe their houses to each other in small groups and choose the best house design.

Expansion (Después de leer): Have groups research other examples of innovative housing solutions and present the unique features to the rest of the class.

PASO 2. Ahora indica si cada frase describe una casa giratoria (**CG**), una casa minimalista (**CM**), o las dos (**CG/CM**). Luego escribe los dos elementos que más te gustan de cada casa.

1. __CG__ Un control remoto puede mover el cilindro central de la casa.

2. __CM__ El cuarto principal contiene todo lo que se necesita.

3. __CG__ Cuando estás en el cuarto principal, tienes que escoger el otro cuarto que quieres ver.

4. _CG/CM_ Se construyó pensando en las necesidades tecnológicas y de transporte.

5. __CM__ La intención del diseño es ser lo más sencillo (*simple*) posible.

6. __CG__ El diseñador se inspiró en los círculos y las curvas.

7. _CG/CM_ Es eficaz y flexible.

8. __CG__ Es prefabricada.

9. __CM__ No tiene ventanas; la ventilación viene del techo.

10. _CG/CM_ Tiene lo que requiere la gente en el siglo XXI.

De la casa giratoria, me gusta(n) _____

De la casa minimalista, me gusta(n) _____

Después de leer

En grupos pequeños, hablen de por qué son importantes las innovaciones descritas en el artículo. En el futuro, ¿les gustaría vivir en una casa así? ¿Por qué sí o por qué no? ¿Qué más necesitan Uds. para vivir cómodamente?

¡Escuchemos!

¿Cuánto cuesta vivir aquí?

Suggestion (Antes de escuchar): Students should come up with a range of options, including living with parents, in university dorms, sorority and fraternity houses, off-campus apartments, and off-campus houses. Have them compare in groups their rankings from cheapest to most expensive.

 Antes de escuchar

En grupos, hagan una lista de los lugares en que pueden vivir los estudiantes de su universidad. Luego pongan los lugares en orden de más barato a más caro. **¡Atención!** Recuerda que la palabra para *dorm* en español es **residencia estudiantil.**

Video track (A escuchar): This video clip can be found on the *DVD to accompany Conéctate: Cap. 11,* Track 3.

 A escuchar

Mira y escucha. Luego mira otra vez con pausas e indica las respuestas a las preguntas.

1. Según Abigaíl, ¿cuánto cuesta un apartamento en una zona residencial de la Ciudad de México que tenga electricidad y servicios sanitarios?
   a. 2.000 pesos
   b. 4.000 pesos
   c. 6.000 pesos
   d. 8.000 pesos

2. Según Óscar, ¿cuánto cuesta un apartamento en una zona «cultural» en México?
   a. de 3.000 a 4.000 pesos
   b. de 5.000 a 6.000 pesos
   c. de 7.000 a 8.000 pesos
   d. de 10.000 a 12.000 pesos

3. Según Óscar, ¿dónde en México pagas entre 5.000 y 6.000 pesos mensuales (*monthly*)?
   a. en una colonia cultural
   b. en el centro de la ciudad
   c. en colonias no tan buenas
   d. en apartamentos exclusivos

4. Según Armon, ¿cuánto es el alquiler en el centro de Madrid?
   a. entre 200 y 300 euros
   b. entre 300 y 400 euros
   c. entre 400 y 500 euros
   d. entre 500 y 600 euros

5. Según Armon, ¿cuánto es el alquiler en las afueras de Madrid?
   a. entre 200 y 300 euros
   b. entre 300 y 400 euros
   c. entre 400 y 500 euros
   d. entre 500 y 600 euros

6. Según Liliana, ¿cuánto es un alquiler económico (*affordable*) en Panamá?
   a. 500
   b. 1.000
   c. 1.500
   d. 2.000

(*Continues*)

En español...

Words for talking about the cost of living vary from region to region. For example, in the video, Abigaíl and Óscar, from Mexico, say **el departamento, la colonia, los pesos (mexicanos), la renta;** Armon, from Spain, says **el piso, el barrio, los euros, el alquiler;** Liliana, from Panama, says **el apartamento, el barrio, los dólares, el alquiler;** and Eugenia and Carina, from Argentina, say **el departamento, el barrio, los pesos (argentinos), el alquiler.**

Videoscript (A escuchar): 1. ABIGAÍL: *Depende de la colonia... so... puedes... O sea si vives en una colonia donde tienes, donde es... bueno... es una área bien, quiere decir que tenga electricidad, este, servicios sanitarios y una zona residencial, como se dice aquí en México, puede costar, no sé, ¿4.000 pesos?, de 4.000 a 3.000 pesos y si es una zona alejada de la ciudad y no tan buen, no es una zona residencial, pues, puedes pagar como unos 1000 pesos, más o menos.* **2.** ÓSCAR: *Tiene que ver mucho la colonia. Por ejemplo, esta colonia, que es, cultural... que es buena colonia, anda pagando unos 10.000, 12.000 pesos, más o menos de... de renta, hay, hay colonias pegadas a esta que no son tan buenas, y paga uno, 5.000, 6.000 pesos, o sea no, sí varía mucho dependiendo la colonia, se dispara mucho la renta.* **3.** ARMON: *En Madrid, Madrid es el sitio más caro de España para alquilar y la media suele estar entre los 400, 500 euros, en el centro. Si te vas luego a las afueras, ya es un poquitín más barato, igual 300, 400, pero en el centro sí que es caro. Yo, el año pasado que estuve... pagaba 400 euros al mes, más los gastos de comunidad, de luz, o sea se ponía en 450 más o menos.* **4.** LILIANA: *Apartamentos depende de la... del área donde se ubique... Un apartamento, el más económico, podría estar como en 500 dólares... eh... de alquiler mensual, y ya este lo más alto sería, este, 2.000 dólares mensuales más o menos de alquiler.* **5.** EUGENIA Y CARINA: *700, 800 pesos de un solo dormitorio. Nosotras alquilamos un departamento de un solo dormitorio y nos sale 500 solamente alquiler, más impuestos, se nos va a 700 pesos, sí. Eso, en el centro. Si vos te vas a las afueras del centro, los alquileres varían, vas a encontrar cosas de 500 pesos pero están así para arriba.*

7. Según Liliana, ¿cuánto es un alquiler caro en Panamá?
   a. 500
   b. 1.000
   c. 1.500
   d. 2.000

8. Según Eugenia y Carina, ¿cuánto cuesta un apartamento con un dormitorio en el centro de Buenos Aires?
   a. entre 600 y 700 pesos
   b. entre 700 y 800 pesos
   c. entre 800 y 900 pesos
   d. entre 900 y 1.000 pesos

Suggestion (Después de escuchar): Remind students to talk about proximity of friends, travel time to school and shopping, availability of cultural venues, traffic and crowding, and so on.

 Después de escuchar

En grupos, hablen de las ventajas y desventajas de vivir en diferentes comunidades (las comunidades urbanas, rurales, en las afueras, ciudades grandes / de tamaño medio / pequeñas). Sin hablar de los costos específicos, hablen de sus propias experiencias. ¿Dónde prefiere vivir la mayoría? ¿Por qué?

¡Escribamos!

Un día típico en casa

Cuando compartimos con otras personas nuestras experiencias de la infancia (*childhood*), muchas veces tenemos más en común de lo que pensábamos. En esta actividad vas a describir tu rutina diaria cuando eras más joven. Antes de escribir, vas a comparar tus ideas con un compañero / una compañera.

ESTRATEGIA

Brainstorm with a partner

Hearing someone else's ideas can help trigger your own or help you consider things from a different perspective. Therefore, it is often worthwhile to pair up and discuss writing assignments with a partner while you are in the initial planning stages. Take time to present your ideas, ask each other questions, seek more details, and then give each other feedback concerning the most interesting aspects of what was shared. Is there anything missing? Are there pieces either of you could eliminate? Aim to suggest at least one way your partner could improve his or her plan.

 Antes de escribir

Vas a describir los fines de semana cuando eras niño/a o adolescente. Primero completa las primeras dos columnas de la tabla con los miembros de tu familia y las actividades (los quehaceres y/o las actividades divertidas) en que participaba cada uno. Luego intercambia tablas con un compañero / una compañera de clase. Lee su tabla y dale comentarios o hazle preguntas a tu compañero/a. Apunta los comentarios de la otra persona en la tercera columna.

MODELO: E1: Veo que todos los sábados por la mañana ibas a un café con

LOS MIEMBROS DE MI FAMILIA	LO QUE HACÍAN ESTAS PERSONAS	COMENTARIOS Y PREGUNTAS
yo		

tu padre y él leía el periódico. Luego Uds. iban al parque. ¿Qué hacían Uds. en el parque? ¿Jugaban algún deporte?

E2: Nuestro tiempo en el parque era lo más interesante de mi infancia. Mi padre es biólogo y me enseñaba los nombres científicos de diferentes plantas, animales, insectos y cosas así. Luego jugábamos para ver si yo podía recordar los nombres.

A escribir

Ahora escribe tres párrafos para describir tu rutina; trata de (*try to*) incorporar las sugerencias de tu compañero/a de clase para fortalecer (*strengthen*) tu descripción. En el primer párrafo, escribe una introducción en la que presentas el tema de la composición y la información que vas a detallar en los siguientes párrafos. En el segundo párrafo, describe el lugar donde vivías cuando eras niño/a. Luego describe qué hacías tú y/o los miembros de tu familia allí.

Después de escribir

Revisa tu ensayo. Luego intercambia ensayos con un compañero / una compañera para evaluarlos.

☐ Lee la introducción. ¿Sabes qué esperar (*to expect*) en el resto del ensayo?

☐ Subraya todos los verbos en el segundo párrafo.
   a. ¿Tienen concordancia los sujetos y los verbos subrayados?
   b. ¿Controla el pretérito e imperfecto?

☐ Después de leer toda la composición, lee de nuevo la introducción. ¿Describe lo que va a presentar en los siguientes párrafos en el orden en que se presenta en el resto del ensayo?

Después de revisar el ensayo de tu compañero/a, devuélveselo. Mira tu propio ensayo para ver los cambios que tu compañero/a recomienda y haz las revisiones necesarias.

¡Hablemos!

Andamos buscando un apartamento

Antes de hablar

1. ¿Has alquilado un apartamento o comprado una casa? ¿Cómo fue la experiencia? ¿Qué aprendiste?
2. ¿Qué hacen los agentes de bienes raíces? ¿Has trabajado con uno/a? ¿Para qué?
3. ¿Cuáles son las preguntas que normalmente le hacen los clientes a los agentes de bienes raíces?
4. ¿Cuáles son las cosas más importantes para investigar al ver un apartamento por primera vez?

 Suggestion (A hablar): Remind your students that the real estate agent is trying hard to rent the apartment. They can find creative ways to make sure someone agrees to rent, like giving a bonus, lowering the price on the rent, or other options.

A hablar

En grupos de tres, creen un diálogo en el que uno o una de Uds. va a hacer el papel de agente de bienes raíces que debe darles un tour de un apartamento disponible (*available*) a los otros miembros del grupo, que andan buscando un apartamento para alquilar. Primero el/la agente debe darles la bienvenida a los clientes (los otros estudiantes). Luego debe invitarlos a entrar y darles un tour de un apartamento. El apartamento puede ser perfecto para ellos o absolutamente terrible. Lo importante es que el/la agente mantenga (*maintains*) un tono cortés (*polite*) y una actitud profesional.

 Después de hablar **Suggestion (Después de hablar):** Have students act out the dialogues in front of the class.

Ahora ensayen (*rehearse*) su diálogo y prepárense para presentarlo al resto de la clase.

Suggestion (Después de leer): To motivate students to edit their own work as well as their classmates' carefully, occasionally grade their editing instead of their writing.

CONÉCTATE AL MUNDO PROFESIONAL

If you plan to use Spanish in professional contexts in the United States, you'll have a lot of options. Here are a few.
- Real estate, where Hispanic families represent at least 40% of households formed in the United States each year
- Banking, where the Spanish bank Santander has branches in the United States as well as ownership interest in many U.S. banks
- Medicine, where many of the world's top medical experts live and practice in Spanish-speaking countries and your Spanish would allow you to attend Spanish-language sessions and speak directly to the experts at international conferences

No matter what your profession is, there will be opportunities to speak Spanish with clients, colleagues, vendors, managers, and owners. Your ability to rise through the ranks could be tied to your Spanish skills!

Conéctate a la música

Canción: «Loca» (2009)
Artista: Aleks Syntek (México)

Aleks Syntek (Raúl Alejandro Escajadillo Peña) es cantante y compositor de música pop, a veces conocido como «el rey del pop mexicano».

Suggestion (Artista): Explain that the name *Syntek* comes from *un apodo* (nickname) that friends gave him when he asked to borrow a keyboard (*un teclado*): *Sin teclados* became *Syntek*. This is a good example of the very rich tradition of *apodos* in many Spanish-speaking countries.

Antes de escuchar

En general, decir que una persona está loca (*crazy*) es un comentario bastante negativo, pero a veces sí tiene un significado más positivo. ¿Cuáles de las siguientes palabras podrían ser equivalentes de **loco** en su sentido positivo?

☐ aburrido   ☑ divertido   ☐ serio

☑ alegre   ☑ espontáneo   ☐ trabajador

Expansion (A escuchar, Paso 1): The first two commands are positive and the third is negative. Ask students to make the first two negative and the third positive. (Answers: *no te acerques, no me beses, sé.*) For further practice, ask students to change the forms to *Ud.* (Answers: *acérquese, béseme, no sea.*)

 A escuchar

Expresiones útiles	
me encanta cuando provocas	I love it when you provoke (me)
voy a sacarte el instinto animal	I'm going to bring out your animal instinct

PASO 1. El cantante usa los siguientes verbos en forma de mandato. Lee las **Expresiones útiles** y escucha la canción. Luego escribe la forma exacta que él usa, incluyendo los pronombres y **no,** cuando los usa.

acercarse (*to approach*): _____acércate_____

besar: _____bésame_____

ser: _____no seas_____

PASO 2. El cantante usa el participio presente de cuatro verbos. Apúntalos aquí y escribe el infinitivo de cada verbo.

PARTICIPIO PRESENTE	INFINITIVO
bailando	bailar
soñando	soñar
pensando	pensar
peleando	pelear (*to fight*)

Después de escuchar

Todos tenemos un lado (*side*) loco de nuestra personalidad. En general, ¿piensas que en tu vida diaria deberías (*you should*) ser un poco más serio/a o un poco más loco/a? ¿Por qué?

Aleks Syntek, cantante mexicano

■ For copyright reasons, the songs referenced in **Conéctate a la música** have not been provided by the publisher. The video for this song can be found on YouTube, and it is available for purchase from the iTunes store.

Expansion (A escuchar, Paso 2):
• Ask students: *¿Por qué los cuatro verbos son de tipo -ar? ¿Por qué no usa también algunos verbos -er o -ir?* (Answer: *Porque para hacer rima, los cuatro verbos tienen que ser del mismo tipo.*)
• Ask students: *De las actividades en el Paso 2, ¿cuáles han hecho este semestre/mes/año? (¿Han bailado/soñado/pensado/peleado?)*

Suggestion (Después de escuchar): Have students discuss this and compare answers in small groups. Require each group to come up with a concrete report: how many think they should be *más serios* and how many *más locos.*

Variation (Después de escuchar): Ask students instead: *¿Piensan que los estudiantes de esta universidad deberían ser un poco más serios o un poco más locos?*

VOCABULARIO

Now that I have completed the chapter, I can . . .

- ☐ welcome people to my home or country
- ☐ make polite invitations
- ☐ describe homes and furnishings
- ☐ talk about what I have done
- ☐ talk about what I am currently doing
- ☐ discuss housing in the Spanish-speaking world and its cost

Comunicación

¡Bienvenido/a/os/as!	Welcome!
subject + **ser** + **bienvenido/ a/os/as.**	_____ is/are welcome.
Ud. es (siempre) bienvenido/a.	You are (always) welcome.
indirect object pronoun + **dar** + **la bienvenida.**	*subject* + welcome(s) + *direct object.*
¡Le damos la bienvenida a Ud.!	We welcome you!
¡Come/Coma(n) más!	Have some more!
¡Diviértete!/¡Diviérta(n)se!	Have fun!
¡Siéntate!/¡Siénte(n)se!	Have a seat!
¡Sírvete!/¡Sírva(n)se!	Help yourself!
Repaso: ¡Pasa!/¡Pase(n)!	

La casa y los muebles / House and furniture

el armario	armoire, closet
la aspiradora	vacuum cleaner
el balcón	balcony
la bañera	bathtub
la cama	bed
la cocina	kitchen
el comedor	dining room
el (cuarto de) baño	bathroom
la despensa	pantry
el dormitorio / la habitación	bedroom
la ducha	shower
el edificio (de apartamentos)	(apartment) building
el electrodoméstico	appliance
la escalera	stairs
el espejo	mirror

el estante	bookshelf
la estufa	stove
el fregadero	kitchen sink
el horno	oven
el inodoro	toilet
el jardín	yard; garden
la lámpara	lamp
el lavabo	bathroom sink
la lavadora	washing machine
el lavaplatos	dishwasher
la mesita de noche	nightstand
el microondas	microwave
la pared	wall
el pasillo	hallway
la piscina	pool
el piso	floor, story; apartment (*Sp.*)
el primer (segundo, tercer) piso	first (second, third) floor
la planta baja	ground floor
la primera (segunda, tercera) planta	first (second, third) floor
los quehaceres (domésticos)	(household) chores
el salón	living room
el sillón	armchair
el sofá	sofa, couch
el sótano	basement
el techo	roof
el televisor	television (set)
el tendedero	clothesline
la terraza	terrace

Cognados: el apartamento, el garaje, el refrigerador
Repaso: el ascensor, la mesa, la silla

Los verbos

barrer	to sweep
descansar	to rest
hacer (*irreg.*) la cama	to make the bed
lavar (los platos, el suelo)	to wash/clean (the dishes, the floor)
limpiar	to clean
pasar la aspiradora	to vacuum
sacar (qu) la basura	to take out the trash
sacudir	to dust

Otras palabras y expresiones útiles

en medio de	in the middle of
encima de	on top of
debajo de	below

El deporte y el bienestar° *well-being*

El equipo (*team*) de la República Dominicana celebra después de ganar (*winning*) el Clásico Mundial (*World*) de Béisbol en 2013.

Objetivos

When you finish this chapter, you will be able to:

- wish someone well
- say what needs to be done
- talk about sports, wellness, and injuries
- say what you would like to happen
- talk about sports and health in the Spanish-speaking world

www.mhhe.com/connect

12

COMUNICACIÓN LARIO UCTURA ATE

Videoscript (Act. A): 1. ROGELIO: *Suerte. Que les vaya bien.* **2.** SONIA: *Suerte.* **3.** OLMAN: *Adelante.* **4.** DELANO: *Mucha suerte.* **5.** MARTA: *Bueno, les deseo muchísima suerte.* **6.** ERICK: *Espero que les vaya muy bien.* **7.** ANLLULY: *Sí, se puede.* **8.** RAMÓN: *Mucha suerte.* **9.** DARÍO: *Buena suerte.* **10.** JUAN: *Muchísima suerte.* **11.** FRANCISCO: *Bueno, les deseo muchísima suerte.* **12.** MAURICIO: *Así que, que les vaya bien.*

¡Suerte!
Wishing someone good luck

 A. A ver: ¿Qué dicen?   ¿Qué les dicen estas personas a sus amigos que se preparan para correr un maratón? Mira y escucha. Luego mira otra vez con pausas y escoge la respuesta que corresponde a lo que dice cada persona.

Video track (Act. A): This video clip can be found on the DVD to accompany *Conéctate: Cap. 12*, Track 1.

1. Rogelio, de México
   a. Ánimo.
   b. Que les vaya bien.
   c. Suerte.
   (d.) Las respuestas **b** y **c** están bien.

2. Sonia, de España
   a. Ánimo.
   b. Que les vaya bien.
   (c.) Suerte.
   d. Las respuestas **b** y **c** están bien.

3. Olman, de Costa Rica
   (a.) Adelante.
   b. Ánimo.
   c. Suerte.
   d. Las respuestas **b** y **c** están bien.

4. Delano, de Argentina
   a. Les deseo mucha suerte.
   (b.) Mucha suerte.
   c. Que les vaya bien.
   d. Suerte.

5. Marta, de Argentina
   a. Ánimo.
   b. Buena suerte.
   (c.) Les deseo muchísima suerte.
   d. Las respuestas **a** y **b** están bien.

6. Erick, de Nicaragua
   (a.) Espero que les vaya muy bien.
   b. Les deseo mucha suerte.
   c. Sí, se puede.
   d. Suerte.

7. Anlluly, de Costa Rica
   a. Espero que les vaya muy bien.
   b. Les deseo mucha suerte.
   c. Suerte.
   (d.) Sí, se puede.

8. Ramón, de Argentina
   a. Ánimo.
   b. Les deseo mucha suerte.
   (c.) Mucha suerte.
   d. Que les vaya bien.

9. Darío, de Argentina
   a. Les deseo mucha suerte.
   (b.) Buena suerte.
   c. Que les vaya bien.
   d. Suerte.

10. Juan, de Argentina
    a. Ánimo.
    (b.) Muchísima suerte.
    c. Que les vaya bien.
    d. Que sigan adelante.

11. Francisco, de Colombia
    (a.) Les deseo muchísima suerte.
    b. Mucha suerte.
    c. Que les vaya bien.
    d. Suerte.

12. Mauricio, de Panamá
    a. Ánimo.
    b. Les deseo muchísima suerte.
    (c.) Que les vaya bien.
    d. Las respuestas **b** y **c** están bien.

To wish someone good luck in Spanish, you can use one of these expressions.

Buena suerte.	Good luck.
Suerte (con todo).	Good luck (with everything).
Mucha suerte.	Best of luck.
Le(s) deseo mucha suerte.	I wish you well. / I wish you lots of luck.

To give someone extra encouragement with something difficult (such as during a competition or before an exam or interview), you can use one of these.

¡Ánimo!	Keep your spirits high! / Give it all you've got! / Don't give up!
¡Adelante!	Go for it! / Let's go! / You can do it!
¡Sí se puede!	Yes you/we can! (*Lit.,* Yes, it can be done!)

To wish someone well in Spanish when you are saying good-bye, use one of these expressions.

Que te/le(s) vaya bien.	Have a good one. / I hope things go well for you.
Que tenga(s) un(a) buen(a) + *period of time*	Have a good . . .
Que tenga(s) un buen día / fin de semana / verano.	Have a good day/weekend/summer.
Que tenga(s) una buena tarde.	Have a good afternoon.

B. Que te vaya bien.   Imagínate que un amigo o una amiga te dice las siguientes cosas. ¿Qué le contestas? Indica la mejor expresión para responder.

1. —Me voy al médico a hacerme unas pruebas (*tests*). No sé qué me van a decir.
   a. —Adiós.   b. —Que tengas una buena tarde.   ©. —Suerte.

2. —Mi equipo perdió ayer y estoy destrozado (*devastated*).
   ⓐ. —¡Ánimo!   b. —¡Que te vaya bien!   c. —¡Suerte!

3. —Me voy al gimnasio a hacer ejercicio. Nos vemos más tarde.
   ⓐ. —Adiós.   b. —Ánimo.   c. —Mucha suerte con todo.

4. —Me voy a la biblioteca; tengo un examen de biología mañana. Hasta luego.
   a. —Adiós.   ⓑ. —Buena suerte.   c. —Que tengas un buen fin de semana.

5. —Hace semanas que estoy entrenando (*training*), pero no estoy lista (*ready*) para correr el maratón el sábado.
   a. —Adiós.   ⓑ. —Ánimo.   c. —Que tengas una buena tarde.

6. —Y con esto terminamos la tarea para hoy. Hasta el lunes.
   a. —Ánimo.   b. —Muy buena suerte.   ©. —Que tengas un buen fin de semana.

C. Después de clase   Pregúntale a un compañero / una compañera qué va a hacer hoy después de clase, hoy por la noche y este fin de semana. Luego despídete de él/ella usando una de las expresiones que acabas de aprender (*you just learned*).

MODELO: E1: ¿Qué vas a hacer después de clase?
E2: Voy a estudiar para mi examen de biología.
E1: ¿Y esta noche?
E2: Voy a acostarme temprano. El examen es a las ocho de la mañana.
E1: ¡Suerte en tu examen!

Para mantenerse sano/a,° hay que...

stay healthy

Giving advice on healthy living

> To say *You (don't) have to* (do something), use: **(No) Hay que** + *infinitive*. This can also be translated as *It's (not) necessary to* (do something).
>
> **Para mantenerse sano/a, hay que comer bien. Para bajar de peso, hay que hacer ejercicio.**
> To stay healthy, one has to (it's necessary to) eat well. To lose weight, one has to exercise.
>
> **No hay que levantar pesas para mantenerse en forma.**
> People/You don't have to lift weights to stay in shape.

A. Para llevar una vida (*life*) más sana...

PASO 1. Indica si estás de acuerdo o no con cada afirmación que escuchas.

	ESTOY DE ACUERDO	NO ESTOY DE ACUERDO
1.	☐	☐
2.	☐	☐
3.	☐	☐
4.	☐	☐
5.	☐	☐
6.	☐	☐
7.	☐	☐
8.	☐	☐

PASO 2. En parejas, completen cada frase de dos maneras: con algo que hay que hacer y también con algo que *no* hay que hacer. No repitan la información del **Paso 1.**

MODELO: Para participar en deportes, no hay que tener talento. Hay que querer jugar.

1. Para llevar una vida más activa...
2. Para comer mejor...
3. Para bajar de peso...
4. Para conocer a otras personas sanas...
5. Para participar en deportes...

B. ¿Qué hay que hacer para mantenerse o ponerse más sano/a?

PASO 1. Escribe tres oraciones sobre lo que debes hacer tú para ponerte más sano/a.

MODELO: Para vivir una vida más sana, debo inscribirme (*sign myself up*) en un gimnasio. También debo comer más verduras y menos azúcar. Debo preparar la comida en casa en vez de ir a restaurantes.

PASO 2. En grupos, compartan lo que quieren hacer para vivir más sano. Decidan cuáles son los dos puntos más importantes y preséntenlos a la clase. Empiecen su resumen (*summary*) con: **Según nuestro grupo...**

MODELO: Según nuestro grupo, para vivir una vida sana hay que comer muchas verduras y dormir ocho horas cada noche.

Script (Act. A, Paso 1): 1. *Para tener una vida más activa, hay que mirar menos la televisión.* **2.** *Para comer mejor, no hay que consultar con un especialista en nutrición.* **3.** *Para participar en deportes, hay que tener talento.* **4.** *Para conocer a otras personas sanas, hay que ser miembro de un gimnasio.* **5.** *Para vivir una vida más sana, hay que comer más en restaurantes.* **6.** *Para bajar de peso, no hay que hacer ejercicio.* **7.** *Para ponerse más sano, hay que dormir once horas cada día.* **8.** *Para vivir una vida más sana, hay que tomar ocho vasos de agua cada día.*

■ The audio files for in-text listening activities are available in the eBook, within Connect activities, and on the Online Learning Center.

Suggestion (Act. A, Paso 2): Have students include some absurd statements (such as, *Para llevar una vida más activa, hay que ver videos en YouTube ocho horas al día*). Ask volunteers to read their statements to the class. When students hear a statement that offers questionable advice, they should offer healthier suggestions (such as: *Para llevar una vida más activa, hay que ver videos en YouTube menos de dos horas al día*).

Los deportes y cómo mantenerse en forma

Sports and fitness

A. ¿Eres sedentario/a o activo/a? Completa la encuesta para saber si eres una persona sedentaria o activa.

PASO 1. ¿Con qué frecuencia haces las siguientes actividades?

1. ___ Veo películas y series en Internet...
   a. menos de una hora al día.
   b. de una a tres horas al día.
   c. más de tres horas al día.

2. ___ Viajo en coche o transporte público...
   a. menos de treinta minutos al día.
   b. de treinta a noventa minutos al día.
   c. más de noventa minutos al día.

3. ___ Camino... (Hago caminatas [*hikes*]... / Voy a la universidad a pie...)
   a. más de cuarenta y cinco minutos al día.
   b. de veinte a cuarenta y cinco minutos al día.
   c. menos de veinte minutos al día.

4. ___ Practico un deporte o hago una actividad física...
   a. más de cuatro horas a la semana.
   b. de dos a cuatro horas a la semana.
   c. menos de dos horas a la semana.

5. ___ Tomo siestas largas...
   a. muy raras veces.
   b. de vez en cuando.
   c. todos los días.

6. ___ Uso la computadora...
   a. menos de dos horas al día.
   b. de dos a cuatro horas al día.
   c. más de cuatro horas al día.

NÚMERO TOTAL DE CADA RESPUESTA

   a. _____
   b. _____
   c. _____

En español...

Mantenerse contains the verb **tener** and therefore is conjugated the same way.

Ella se mantiene en forma usando una She stays in shape using a
combinación de ejercicio y dieta. combination of exercise and diet.

You'll find the same pattern with other verbs you will come across that contain the verb **tener,** such as **contener** (*to contain*), **detener** (*to stop; to detain*), **obtener** (*to get, obtain*), **retener** (*to retain*), and **sostener** (*to sustain; to hold, support*).

PASO 2. Ahora, indica todos los deportes y otras actividades físicas que haces con frecuencia.

Note (Act A, Paso 2): Point out to students that words in bold (here and in Act. B) are new active vocabulary. Refer them to the *Vocabulario* section at the end of the chapter for the full list of new words. Additional sports vocabulary was introduced in previous chapters: (*Cap. 3*) *correr (en el parque), ir al gimnasio, jugar básquetbol/ fútbol, montar a caballo, nadar, practicar (un deporte, yoga)*; (*Cap. 8*) *la gorra, los tenis*; (*Cap. 9*) *la bicicleta de montaña, hacer ciclismo de montaña, escalar.*

☐ **andar en bicicleta**

☐ **hacer alpinismo**

☐ **jugar voleibol**

☐ **andar en patineta**

☐ **jugar béisbol**

☐ **levantar pesas**

☐ **boxear,** el boxeo

☐ **jugar fútbol americano**

☐ **patinar sobre hielo,** el patinaje

☐ **esquiar,** el esquí

☐ **jugar tenis**

☐ **surfear,** el surf

☐ bailar
☐ correr
☐ dar paseos largos

☐ hacer ejercicio aeróbico
☐ jugar básquetbol
☐ jugar fútbol

☐ montar a caballo
☐ **nadar, la natación**
☐ practicar yoga

☐ otro: _____

¿Cuántas actividades físicas marcaste? _____

PASO 3. Ahora, calcula los resultados.

En el **Paso 1,** todas las respuestas **a** valen 10 puntos; las **b** valen 5 puntos y las **c** valen 0 puntos. Para calcular los resultados de la encuesta, suma tus respuestas de **Paso 1** (máximo: 60). Luego suma el número total de deportes y actividades del **Paso 2** (máximo: 18) y agrega (*add*) este total a los resultados del **Paso 1.**

0–25: Tienes una vida muy sedentaria. No te gusta mucho la actividad física o no tienes tiempo en tu horario para hacerlo. Piensa en maneras en que puedes incorporar más actividad en tu vida. El trabajo es importante, pero mantenerte en buena salud también es importante.

26–45: Participas con frecuencia en actividades físicas y tal vez has encontrado un buen equilibrio entre el trabajo y el ejercicio. ¡Felicidades! Si también comes bien y duermes lo suficiente, vas hacia (*toward*) una vida muy sana.

46+: Eres una persona muy activa. Te gusta moverte y te molesta quedarte tranquilo/a. ¡Lo que puedes hacer ahora es explorar y probar otras actividades físicas para buscar aún (*even*) más aventuras!

Expansion (Act. B): Have groups of students compete to see which can come up with the longest list of sports in Spanish that use a ball, then a list of those that use a net (*una red*), a pool, and so on. Assist with vocabulary in Spanish when necessary.

Suggestion (Act. B): Have students review formal commands by stating rules and safety guidelines related to different sports (for example, *Lleve un casco para andar en bicicleta. No use las manos para jugar fútbol.*).

Videoscript (Act. C): 1. ADRIÁN: *Este sí, hago pesas y, este... también practico fútbol americano.* ZARYN: *República Dominicana es un lugar de mucho deporte, jugábamos mucho voleibol, béisbol es una cosa grande, Sammy Sosa, y tenemos mucho pelotero... ahm... ¿qué más? Voleibol más o menos, fútbol no tanto, pero básicamente desde que tú eres niño todo el mundo te, te empuja para jugar béisbol porque es el deporte nacional.* EDUARDO: *Sí, ¡eh! patino en hielo, soy patinador sobre hielo artístico.* MARCO ANTONIO: *Deportes, pues también es, todo lo que es fútbol, eh, pesas, básquetbol, voleibol, muchas, son muchas cosas, muchas actividades, las que tenemos aquí.* ISABEL: *No soy muy buena en deportes, pero sí intento ir al gimnasio y hacer algo de, de gimnasia para mantenerme en forma.* JUAN: *A mí me gusta, me gusta estar afuera. Me gusta ir a la playa, como dije, andar en bicicleta, eh... hacer deportes, jugar al fútbol, al básquet, eh... así actividades deportivas.* **2.** MORAVIA Y GISELA: *—¡Me encanta el fútbol americano! —A mí también, ¡je, je! —Sí, a las dos. —Soy cien por ciento Acereros de Pittsburg. —Y yo, Patriota de Nueva Inglaterra, ¡ja, ja, ja!* PAULA: *Eh, me, eh, gusta ver el fútbol y los Juegos Olímpicos.* HENRY: *Me gusta el fútbol, me gusta mirarlo cuando me, eh, queda tiempo. Me gusta el equipo Barcelona de España. Aquí en Costa Rica la liga*

B. ¿Para qué se usa?

PASO 1. En parejas, túrnense para decidir para qué deporte(s) puede servir cada uno de los siguientes elementos.

1. la bicicleta   2. **el casco**   3. las manos   4. **la raqueta**

5. **la patineta**   6. **la pelota**   7. **las pesas**   8. los pies

9. **la piscina**   10. los tenis

PASO 2. En parejas, túrnense para pensar en un deporte y —sin decir el nombre del deporte— nombrar todo el equipo (*equipment*) que se necesita para jugarlo. Tu compañero/a debe adivinarlo (*guess it*).

> **MODELO:** E1: Este deporte requiere una piscina, un traje de baño, un gorro...
> E2: ¡Es la natación!

C. A ver: El deporte en los países hispanos

Video track (Act. C): This video clip can be found on the DVD to accompany *Conéctate: Cap. 12,* Track 2.

PASO 1. Mira y escucha. Luego mira otra vez con pausas y contesta las siguientes preguntas.

1. ¿Qué deporte(s) o actividad(es) menciona cada persona?

Adrián, de México
hacer/levantar pesas, fútbol americano.

Zaryn, de la República Dominicana el voleibol, el béisbol, el fútbol

Eduardo, de México patinar en/sobre hielo

Marco Antonio, de México
el fútbol, las pesas, el básquetbol, el voleibol

Isabel, de España
ir al gimnasio

Juan, de Argentina
andar en bicicleta, el fútbol, el básquet(bol)

Continued, Videoscript (Act. C):

deportiva Alajuelense, per[o] también a veces observo e[l] fútbol americano. Me gus-tan varios equipos, pero m[e] gustan más los Steelers. Bueno aquí, normalmente se conocen así, pero sí los conocemos como los Acer-eros. ADRIÁN: *Eh, yo prac-tico el fútbol sala, eh, es el fútbol en cinco contra cinc[o] eh, luego también practico tenis habitualmente y me gusta ver en la tele sobre todo pues fútbol, eh... teni[s] baloncesto, cualquier de-porte menos la natación, verdad... porque no me gusta mucho la natación.*

2. ¿Qué deporte(s) les gusta ver en la televisión?

Moravia y Gisela,
de México
el fútbol americano

Paula, de México
el fútbol, los
Juegos Olímpicos

Henry, de Costa Rica
el fútbol, el fútbol
americano

Adrián, de España
el fútbol, el tenis,
el baloncesto

PASO 2.   Mira y escucha otra vez con pausas. Luego contesta las preguntas.

1. Según Zaryn, ¿cuál es el deporte nacional de la República Dominicana?   el béisbol
2. ¿Qué tipo de patinaje sobre hielo practica Eduardo?   el patinaje sobre hielo artístico
3. ¿Es atlética Isabel? ¿Qué hace ella para mantenerse en forma?   no, va al gimnasio
4. ¿A Juan le gustaría hacer ejercicio en un gimnasio? ¿Por qué sí o por qué no?   no; le gusta estar afuera
5. ¿Cuáles son los dos equipos de la NFL que mencionan Moravia y Gisela?   los Acereros de Pittsburg, los Patriotas de
6. ¿Cuál es el deporte que a Adrián (de España) no le gusta ver en la televisión?   Nueva Inglaterra
   la natación

 PASO 3.   En parejas, contesten las preguntas del video (¿Qué deportes practican?, ¿Qué deporte les gusta ver en la televisión?) según sus propios (*own*) intereses. ¿Tienen algo en común las respuestas de Uds. con las respuestas de las personas del video?

Suggestion (Act. C, Paso 3): Tally student answers on the board to see which sports are the most popular to participate in and which most students watch on TV.

CONÉCTATE AL MUNDO HISPANO

Algunos atletas famosos del mundo hispano incluyen a **Kilian Jornet Burgada**, atleta de élite español. Es corredor de larga distancia, esquiador, alpinista (*mountaineer*) y ciclista de montaña. En los meses fríos del invierno, Jornet cambia sus zapatos por los esquís. Ha ganado más de ochenta carreras y competencias (*competitions*) de esquí.

   Fernanda González es una de las mejores nadadoras de dorso (*backstroke*) del mundo. La mexicana ganó tres bronces en los Juegos Panamericanos de 2011 y compitió en los Juegos Olímpicos de verano en 2008 y 2012.

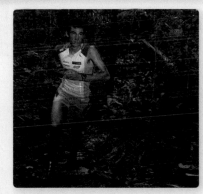

Kilian Jornet Burgada

D. Como ser atleta de élite

 PASO 1.   En parejas, hagan una lista de tres actividades que hay que hacer y tres hábitos que hay que tener para mantenerse en forma y tener éxito (*be successful*) como atleta de élite en cada uno de estos deportes: **la carrera** (*racing*) **de montaña, el esquí, el alpinismo, la natación.**

 PASO 2.   Formen un grupo de cuatro con otra pareja y pongan en orden los elementos de las dos listas, de lo más importante a lo menos importante para mantenerse en forma para cada deporte. ¿Cuáles de estos hábitos y actividades se aplican a varios deportes? ¿Cuáles se aplican a una vida sana en general?

Suggestion (Act. D, Paso 1): Remind students that beyond sporting activities, they should also include general lifestyle habits such as diet, sleep, travel, regular health checks, and so on.

Follow-up (Act. D, Paso 2): Ask for volunteers to share their lists with the class. Are most groups in agreement?

La salud y el bienestar
Health and well-being

Note (Act. A, Paso 1): You may need to help students to associate *la altura* with *alto/a*; they may have to use the process of elimination to learn that **peso** means weight. The other items are close cognates.

A. Medir (*Measuring*) la salud

PASO 1. Para cada imagen, escribe la cosa que se mide (*is measured*).

la altura   **el peso**   **la presión**   **la temperatura**

1. ____la presión____

2. ____el peso____

3. ____la temperatura____

4. ____la altura____

PASO 2. ¿Quién hizo qué? Mira las imágenes y luego contesta las preguntas.

enfermarse / no encontrarse bien

mejorarse

1. ¿Quién bajó de peso? _____Felipe_____
2. ¿Quién mide al paciente? _la enfermera_
3. ¿Quién se enfermó? ___Nayelly___

4. ¿Quién se mejoró? ___Roberto___
5. ¿Quién subió de peso? ____Susana____

To talk about *illness* (**la enfermedad**), *symptoms* (**los síntomas**), *complaints* (**las quejas**), and *pain* (**el dolor**), use the verb **doler** (*to ache, to hurt*).

The verb **doler** functions like **gustar**.

—**¿Te duele la cabeza?**   Does your head hurt?
—**No, pero me duele mucho**   No, but my stomach hurts a lot.
  el estómago.

—**¿Le duelen a Ud. los pies?**   Do your feet hurt?
—**Sí, me duelen los pies**   Yes, my feet and legs hurt.
  y las piernas.

There are many cognates in the medical field: **las alergias, el asma, la depresión, la infección, el insomnio.**

Here are more useful words to talk about ailments and illnesses.

el cambio	change
la fiebre	fever
la sangre	blood
la tos	cough
cambiar	to change
quejarse	to complain
sufrir de	to suffer from
tomar los datos / las medidas	to get someone's information/ measurements

En español...

In most of the Spanish-speaking world, weight is measured in kilograms (**kilogramos** o **kilos**) and height is measured in meters (**metros**) or centimeters (**centímetros**). To convert your weight from pounds (**libras**) to **kilos**, divide by 2.2.

150 lbs = 66.18 kg

To convert your height from feet (**pies**) and inches (**pulgadas**) to centimeters or meters, change to inches then multiply by 2.54.

5 ft. 6 in. = 66 in. = 167.64 cm = 1.68 m

Script (Act B): 1. Ud. subió de peso 2 libras. **2.** No me encuentro bien. Me duele la cabeza y sufro de insomnio. **3.** Tengo tos desde hace 3 semanas. **4.** Su temperatura está a 99 grados; es normal, no tiene fiebre. **5.** Me duelen los pies y tengo un dolor agudo en la rodilla izquierda. **6.** Su presión es normal. **7.** Tengo fiebre y me duele todo el cuerpo. **8.** El niño mide 3 pies, 9 pulgadas.

Suggestion (Act. C, Paso 2): You may want to give students mock information, including temperatures and blood pressure for the nurses to report, and height, weight and complaints/changes for the patients to disclose.

Expansion (Act. C, Paso 2): Have students form new pairs so that the patients will now be doctors. The nurses report to the doctors everything they learned about their patients in the intake. Make sure all partners switch so that no doctors were patients of the same nurse in original activity.

B. ¿Dolor o dato? Escucha y decide si cada persona habla de **un síntoma/dolor** o **un dato / una medida.**

1. <u>dato/medida</u>   3. <u>síntoma/dolor</u>   5. <u>síntoma/dolor</u>   7. <u>síntoma/dolor</u>

2. <u>síntoma/dolor</u>   4. <u>dato/medida</u>   6. <u>dato/medida</u>   8. <u>dato/medida</u>

C. La historia médica

PASO 1. Empareja cada pregunta o comentario con la reacción más lógica.

<u>c</u> 1. ¿Cuánto mide Ud.?
<u>e</u> 2. ¿Hay algún cambio en su historia médica?
<u>b</u> 3. ¿Cómo está su presión?
<u>a</u> 4. Estoy comiendo menos.
<u>d</u> 5. ¿Tengo fiebre?

a. Muy bien. Bajó de peso dos libras.
b. Me preocupa (*It worries me*). Subió desde la última cita (*appointment*).
c. Cinco pies, siete pulgadas.
d. No. Su temperatura es normal. Noventa y ocho coma seis.
e. Sí, estoy tomando una nueva medicina para el asma.

PASO 2. En parejas, túrnense para ser paciente o enfermero/a que le toma los datos. Inventen todos los detalles.

Temperatura normal: 98,6   Presión normal: 120/80 (**de 120 sobre 80**)

ENFERMERO/A	DATOS DEL (DE LA) PACIENTE
¿Cuánto pesa Ud.?	
¿Cuánto mide?	
¿Hay algún cambio en la historia médica?	
¿Por qué está Ud. aquí hoy?	
Le tomo la temperatura. Es...	
Le tomo la presión. Es...	

D. Los dolores más comunes

 PASO 1. Las personas que practican los mismos deportes generalmente sufren de los mismos dolores, por los movimientos repetidos y los riesgos (*risks*) del deporte. En parejas, adivinen los dolores de los atletas que practican estos deportes.

MODELO: el tenis → Al jugador de tenis le duele el codo.

el alpinismo	el esquí
el béisbol	el fútbol americano
el boxeo	la natación
el ciclismo	el patinaje

PASO 2. ¿Qué pueden hacer los atletas que participan en los deportes del **Paso 1** para protegerse mejor y no sufrir de tantos dolores? Menciona la parte del cuerpo, la prevención y el tratamiento.

MODELO: Para el jugador de tenis con dolor del codo, una prevención es levantar pesas y un tratamiento es hacer terapia física.

Expresiones útiles

estirarse	stretch
hacer calentamientos	warm-ups
hacer terapia física	
tomar medicina	
tomar mucha agua	
usar casco	
usar rodilleras y coderas	to use knee pads and elbow pads

CONÉCTATE AL MUNDO PROFESIONAL

Any level of Spanish can be useful in a medical profession. A volunteer with a basic knowledge of Spanish could be a greeter who works in the waiting area and interacts with children while their parents have medical appointments. A medical assistant who has learned the intake script as practiced in **Actividad C** could use it everyday at work. With special qualifications or a high level of fluency, a medical interpreter can work in a variety of contexts and a bilingual doctor could work with an international organization such as Doctors Without Borders (**Médicos Sin Fronteras**).

Suggestion (Conéctate al mundo profesional): Tell students that medical intakes follow a script that is easy to become fluent in, but exam rooms require a much higher level of communicative competence, as well as highly specific vocabulary. Remind aspiring medical professionals that learning how to communicate and developing strategies for improving communication will be more important throughout their careers than memorizing lists of medical terms.

E. ¿Qué deben hacer?

PASO 1. En parejas, túrnense para explicar la situación médica y ofrecer consejos.

> **MODELO:** E1: Necesito hacer más ejercicio pero me duelen las rodillas.
> E2: Debes practicar la natación. Y no uses tenis viejos para hacer ejercicio.

1. Me duele la cabeza.
2. Mi doctor me dijo que tengo que perder diez libras.
3. Quiero mantenerme en forma, pero no soy muy bueno/a en deportes.
4. Sufro de insomnio.
5. Necesito hacer más ejercicio y prefiero jugar en un equipo.
6. Me siento muy débil (*weak*) y quiero tener músculos más grandes.
7. Hace tres semanas que tengo tos.

PASO 2. En parejas, representen el papel de un entrenador (*coach/trainer*) personal y su cliente. Usen mandatos para preparar un plan de entrenamiento (*training*) para mejorar la salud de los siguientes clientes.

Suggestions (Act. E, Paso 2):
- Tell students that their training plan should include at least 2 positive and 1 negative command for each scenario.
- Have volunteers present their fitness plan to the class for evaluation.

Variation (Act. E, Paso 2):
Divide the class into 4 groups and assign one scenario to each group. They should come up with at least 5 commands: 3 positive and 2 negative. Have groups share their plans with the class, who will compare and critique the plans.

Expansion (Act. E, Paso 2):
Before pairs/groups present their fitness plans to the class, help the class decide on criteria for evaluating the plans. (Some possibilities: [*no*] *demasiado fácil/difícil*, [*no*] *muy drástico*, [*no*] *muy razonable* [realistic], [*no*] *consume demasiado tiempo*, [*no*] *permite que la persona haga un cambio gradual de estilo de vida*.) Have the class compare and evaluate plans, then debate which group has the best plans.

1.

Un hombre de 45 años que trabaja en una oficina de cincuenta a setenta horas a la semana. Come comida rápida por lo menos una vez al día, toma algunas cervezas después del trabajo todos los días y fuma veinte cigarrillos cada día.

2.

Un ama de casa (*homemaker*) de 37 años que pesa (*weighs*) 225 libras, pasa dos o tres horas diarias llevando a sus dos hijos a sus varias actividades; camina dos millas (*miles*) tres veces cada semana con otras señoras de su comunidad. En su tiempo libre (*free*) limpia la casa, cultiva el jardín y mira la televisión.

3.

Un estudiante universitario que no duerme lo suficiente, no tiene tiempo para comer bien y toma muchas bebidas con cafeína cada día. Pasa todo su tiempo estudiando y trabajando en una tienda.

4.

Una señora de 70 años con artritis que come mucha comida grasosa (*greasy*) y no hace ningún tipo de ejercicio.

COMUN VOCABU **ESTRUCTURA** ATE

⟳ Reciclaje
The present perfect

Note (Reciclaje): The present perfect was first presented in *Estructura 11.1*.

Dicen que es bueno para la salud hacer las siguientes actividades todos los días. Para cada actividad, crea una oración para decir cuántas veces has hecho esa actividad en las últimas cuarenta y ocho horas. Usa **no** si no has hecho la actividad.

1. caminar por más de veinte minutos
2. comer frutas o verduras
3. meditar o practicar yoga

4. dormir una noche completa (de ocho horas)
5. hacer media hora de ejercicio aeróbico
6. tomar agua

En las últimas cuarenta y ocho horas...
1. _____(no) he caminado..._____
2. _____(no) he comido..._____
3. _(no) he meditado/practicado yoga ..._

4. _____(no) he dormido..._____
5. _____(no) he hecho..._____
6. _____(no) he tomado..._____

■ Answers to this activity are in Appendix 2 at the back of your book.

12.1 Sofía lo ha ganado
The present perfect with object pronouns

Para empezar...

Sofía Mulánovich es una surfista peruana que ha ganado muchos premios (*awards*), incluyendo el título de Campeona Mundial (*World Champion*) de Surf de la Asociación de Surfistas Profesionales. En las siguientes oraciones, vas a aprender un poco más sobre su carrera como deportista. Empareja cada oración con el objeto directo adecuado.

Sofía Mulánovich se desliza sobre (*rides*) una ola.

1. __a__ **Lo ha practicado** desde que tenía 9 años, porque vivía cerca de la playa.
2. __f__ **Lo han considerado** desde hace tiempo como uno de los mejores lugares para surfear en Latinoamérica.
3. __b__ Sofía es la primera latinoamericana que **lo ha ganado.**
4. __g__ **Los han tomado** más en serio desde que Sofía Mulánovich empezó a tener tanto éxito.
5. __e__ **Las ha tenido** desde muy chica.
6. __c__ **La han introducido** al Salón de la Fama (*Hall of Fame*) del Surf.
7. __h__ **Los ha usado** para estar en contacto con los aficionados (*fans*).
8. __d__ **Lo ha sabido** hacer desde que tenía 3 años, cuando empezó a tomar clases.

a. el surf
b. el Campeonato Mundial de Surf
c. Sofía Mulánovich
d. nadar
e. ganas de ganar
f. el Perú
g. los surfistas latinoamericanos
h. su página web y su blog

■ Answers to these activities are in Appendix 2 at the back of your book.

Actividades analíticas

1 As you saw in **Estructura 6.3,** object pronouns (**pronombres de objeto**) appear before conjugated verbs.

Sofía **lo ganó.** *Sofía won it.*

It's no different in the present perfect tense, where object pronouns appear before the auxiliary verb **haber,** because it is the conjugated verb.

Sofía **lo ha** ganado. *Sofía has won it.*

In this example, the object pronoun (**lo**) is a direct object pronoun. What type of pronoun do you see in the following sentences: direct object, indirect object, or reflexive?

___reflexive___ Sofía **se** ha despertado temprano. *Sofía has woken up early.*

___indirect object___ Sofía **le** ha escrito una carta. *Sofía has written a letter to him/her/you* (form.).

Note (Act. analítica 2): Keep in mind that the goal here is to check to see if students are understanding these sentences, not to produce polished translations.

2 You also saw in **Estructura 6.3** that when a conjugated verb is followed by an infinitive, the object pronoun may appear either before the conjugated verb or after and attached to the infinitive.

Sofía **lo quiere** ganar.
Sofía quiere **ganarlo.** } *Sofía wants to win it.*

The same is true when a present perfect verb form is followed by an infinitive. The object pronoun may appear either before the conjugated form of **haber** or after and attached to the infinitive. The meaning is the same regardless of the placement of the object pronoun.

Sofía **lo ha** querido ganar.
Sofía ha querido **ganarlo.** } *Sofía has wanted to win it.*

The present perfect follows the same pattern of object pronoun placement as other verb tenses, but English speakers sometimes find these sentences difficult to understand. Check your comprehension by translating the following sentences into English.

Lo he tenido que hacer. ___I have had to do/make it.___

¿Le has podido contestar su pregunta? ___Have you been able to answer his/her question (for him/her)?___

La hemos querido comprar por mucho tiempo. ___We have wanted to buy it for a long time.___

Actividades prácticas

A. Los deportes y el mundo hispano Empareja cada oración con el deporte o premio que le corresponde.

1. __a__ Argentina, España y Uruguay son los únicos países hispanos que **la han ganado.**
2. __d__ El panameño Roberto Durán **lo ha practicado** desde 1968 y es reconocido (*recognized*) como uno de los mejores en toda la historia de este «deporte de los guantes».
3. __e__ El español Ricky Rubio **lo ha practicado** a nivel (*level*) profesional desde los 14 años. Ahora lo juega en la NBA de los Estados Unidos.
4. __b__ España es el único país hispano que **la ha ganado** en esquí alpino.
5. __c__ La República Dominicana **les ha mandado** a más de 400 jugadores a las Grandes Ligas de este deporte.
6. __f__ El argentino Lionel Messi **lo ha practicado** desde los cuatro años y es considerado por muchos como el mejor jugador de todos los tiempos.

a. la Copa Mundial de Fútbol
b. la medalla de oro en los Juegos Olímpicos de invierno
c. el béisbol
d. el boxeo
e. el básquetbol
f. el fútbol

Autoprueba

Using what you know about object pronoun use and placement, how would you respond affirmatively to the following questions?

1. ¿Has traído los cascos para los jugadores?

2. ¿El equipo ha preparado su plan para el partido?

3. ¿Han comprado los padres las bebidas?

4. ¿Han podido conseguir boletos Uds.?

Respuestas: 1. Sí, los he traído. **2.** Sí, lo ha preparado. **3.** Sí, las han comprado. **4.** Sí, los hemos podido conseguir / Sí, hemos podido conseguirlos.

Suggestion (Act. A): Have students do this in groups of 3–4, so they can pool their knowledge. A little knowledge of sports will help, but is not necessary. Students should be able to use the object pronouns to help determine answers they are unsure of.

B. El deporte en tu país

PASO 1. Para cada deporte en la tabla, escribe cuántas veces lo has visto (en televisión o en persona) y cuántas veces lo has practicado este año.

Número de veces que...	LO/LA HE VISTO	LO/LA HE PRACTICADO
1. el básquetbol	_____	_____
2. el béisbol	_____	_____
3. la escalada	_____	_____
4. el esquí (esquiar)	_____	_____
5. el fútbol	_____	_____
6. el fútbol americano	_____	_____
7. la natación (nadar)	_____	_____
8. el tenis	_____	_____
9. el voleibol	_____	_____
10. el yoga	_____	_____

PASO 2. En grupos, comparen sus respuestas. Para cada deporte, ¿quién lo ha visto más y quién lo ha practicado más? ¿Hay algún deporte que todos han visto o han practicado?

C. Compras para el deporte
Escoge una de las cuatro respuestas posibles para responder a las siguientes preguntas. Completa cada respuesta con el pronombre de objeto directo o indirecto correcto y escríbela en el espacio indicado.

Respuestas posibles: Sí, _____ he comprado.
Sí, _____ hemos comprado.
Sí, _____ he comprado una raqueta.
Sí, _____ hemos comprado una raqueta.

PREGUNTAS	RESPUESTAS
1. ¿Has comprado el casco?	Sí, lo he comprado.
2. ¿Han comprado las revistas de deporte que les recomendé?	Sí, las hemos comprado.
3. ¿Has comprado las bicicletas?	Sí, las he comprado.
4. ¿Le han comprado algo a Victoria?	Sí, le hemos comprado una raqueta.
5. ¿Han comprado los boletos para el partido?	Sí, los hemos comprado.
6. ¿Has comprado la raqueta de tenis que querías?	Sí, la he comprado.
7. ¿Le has comprado algo a Gerardo?	Sí, le he comprado una raqueta.

D. ¿Qué te ha funcionado?

PASO 1. Todos hemos empezado algún hábito bueno y después no lo continuamos. Pero alguna vez has empezado algo bueno para tu salud y lo has podido continuar? En parejas, hablen de este tema y creen una lista de cosas que han funcionado para Uds.

HÁBITO/ACTIVIDAD	¿POR CUÁNTO TIEMPO LO HAS HECHO?
correr por la mañana	Lo he hecho por dos años.
_____	_____
_____	_____
_____	_____

PASO 2. Ahora, crea dos mandatos informales para tu compañero/a y justifica tus recomendaciones con tu propia experiencia.

MODELO: Corre. Lo he hecho por dos años ya y me siento más fuerte.

Suggestions (Act. B):
• Recreate this chart on the board. Ask each group to total their responses for each item and write this on the chart (your chart will need to be large enough for each group to write a number in each cell). It should now be possible to see at a glance which sport is the most popular to watch on TV and which is the most popular to actually do. You and the class together can look for any surprises or interesting trends, and you can make comparisons with the Spanish-speaking world.
• Insist that students refer to soccer as *fútbol* and to American football as *fútbol americano*. They need to understand that they will be misunderstood if they refer to American football as *fútbol* without any further explanation.

Note (Act. C): This activity focuses learners' attention on the fact that the object pronoun and the auxiliary verb (*haber*) vary independently.

Colombia **Venezuela**

El ciclista colombiano Nairo Quintana en el Giro d'Italia de 2014

E. Cultura: Los deportes en Colombia y Venezuela

PASO 1. Lee el texto sobre Colombia y Venezuela.

Si preguntas a los sudamericanos cuál es el deporte más importante para su país, muchos van a mencionar el fútbol. Este es el caso de Colombia, donde la selección nacional ha participado cinco veces en la Copa Mundial de fútbol y en 2001 ganó la Copa América. Por otro lado, su nación vecina Venezuela no ha podido generar tanto entusiasmo alrededor del fútbol y, de hecho,[a] es el único país sudamericano que nunca ha participado en la Copa Mundial. Sin embargo, los venezolanos sí tienen mucho orgullo y mucho éxito en su deporte nacional: el béisbol. Se ve evidencia de esto en el gran número de beisbolistas —¡más de 300!— que participaron en las Grandes Ligas desde la primera edición en 1939.

Entonces, ¿el fútbol es el deporte nacional de Colombia? Para nada. El deporte nacional se llama «el tejo», un juego que se originó en la época prehispánica. El jugador tiene que lanzar[b] un disco de metal a una distancia de dieciocho metros al centro de una cancha de arcilla.[c] Lo divertido es que cuando el disco cae exactamente en el centro, hace ruido y saca chispas[d] porque allí hay unos pequeños paquetes de pólvora.[e] Y aparte del fútbol y el tejo, los colombianos son ciclistas excelentes. El ciclista Nairo Quintana ganó el Giro d'Italia de 2014 y consiguió el segundo lugar en el Tour de Francia de 2013 y 2015.

En Venezuela, no todos los deportistas están satisfechos con el ritmo lento de un partido de béisbol. De hecho, el país es conocido por la naturaleza espectacular que ofrece lugares tanto bellos como peligrosos, ideales para los deportes extremos. En la zona alrededor de Mérida, se puede hacer alpinismo en varios picos, los dos más altos de casi 5.000 metros. Los más atrevidos[f] pueden bajar volando, haciendo parapente,[g] un deporte muy popular. ¿Y en qué otro deporte participan los más atrevidos (o los más locos)? Hacen salto[h] B.A.S.E. de la catarata[i] más alta del mundo, el Salto Ángel, ubicada en el Parque Nacional Canaima.

[a]de... in fact   [b]toss   [c]clay   [d]saca... makes sparks   [e]gunpowder   [f]daring   [g]paragliding   [h]jumping   [i]waterfall

PASO 2. Usa la lectura para identificar a lo que se refieren los pronombres de objeto directo subrayados (*underlined*).

1. La selección nacional de fútbol de Colombia la ha ganado. ___la Copa América___
2. Venezuela los ha mandado a las Grandes Ligas más de 300 veces. ___los beisbolistas___
3. Los colombianos lo han jugado desde los tiempos prehispánicos. ___el tejo___
4. Las genera el disco de tejo cuando cae en el centro de la cancha. ___las chispas___
5. Lo ha ganado en 2014 el ciclista Nairo Quintana. ___el Giro de Italia___
6. Los que hacen parapente en Venezuela la pueden admirar porque es espectacular. ___la naturaleza___
7. Los deportistas más atrevidos de Venezuela lo han hecho. ___hacer salto B.A.S.E. del Salto Ángel___

Note (Act. E, Paso 3): Baseball spread quickly to countries that were in close maritime contact with the United States (shipping being the main mode of international transportation at the time). Venezuela, with its large population near the Caribbean coast, was more subject to this influence than Colombia, with a smaller Caribbean coastline and a larger Andean population. Baseball is still very popular today in the Caribbean (Cuba, Dominican Republic, Puerto Rico), much of Central America, and Mexico.

PASO 3. En parejas, contesten las preguntas y explíquense las respuestas.

1. El béisbol empezó en los Estados Unidos en el siglo XIX y ganó mucha popularidad en países que tenían mucho contacto con los Estados Unidos. Considerando la ubicación geográfica de Colombia y de Venezuela, ¿por qué crees que el béisbol se hizo mucho más popular en Venezuela que en Colombia?
2. Basándote de nuevo en la geografía, ¿en qué otros países hispanos piensas que es muy popular el béisbol?
3. ¿Cómo se comparan el béisbol y el fútbol en tu país? ¿Cuál se juega más? ¿Cuál es más popular en la televisión?

⟳ Reciclaje

The present progressive

Note (Reciclaje): The present progressive was first presented in *Estructura 5.3*, and then was detailed in *Estructura 11.3*.

¿Qué están haciendo en los siguientes dibujos? Usa el presente progresivo para describir la acción de cada imagen.

1. Están corriendo.

2. Están caminando.

3. Está nadando.

4. Están boxeando.

5. Está levantando pesas.

6. Está surfeando.

7. Está jugando tenis.

8. Está esquiando.

■ Answers to this activity are in Appendix 2 at the back of your book.

Rafael Nadal en el Abierto de Francia

Note (Para empezar): The dates in this activity are accurate. The times are approximate.

Suggestion (Para empezar): Reassure students that they can complete this activity just by using common sense and by paying attention to the object pronoun used. They don't need to know anything about tennis or Rafael Nadal. Suggest that they use the object pronoun first to narrow down the possible answers for each item.

■ Answers to these activities are in Appendix 2 at the back of your book.

Autoprueba

Use what you now know about placement of object pronouns with the present progressive to answer the following questions affirmatively in two different ways.

1. ¿Están mirando el partido Uds.?
2. ¿Los jugadores están siguiendo las reglas del partido?
3. ¿El entrenador está organizando la alineación (*lineup*) de jugadores?

Respuestas: **1.** Sí, lo estamos mirando. Sí, estamos mirándolo. **2.** Sí, las están siguiendo. Sí, están siguiéndolas. **3.** Sí, la está organizando. Sí, está organizándola.

■ For more on the use of object pronouns with the present progressive, see **Para saber más 12.2** at the back of your book.

12.2 Lo está ganando.

The present progressive with object pronouns

Para empezar...

Estos son algunos momentos clave (*key*) en la vida del tenista español Rafael Nadal. Él es de Mallorca, una isla en el Mediterráneo, y se considera uno de los mejores jugadores de la historia del tenis. Empareja cada hora, fecha y tema con lo que está haciendo Nadal en ese momento.

HORA	FECHA	TEMA
a. 16:32	23 de mayo, 2005	El Abierto (*Open*) de Francia
b. 11:08	13 de febrero, 2008	La Fundación Rafa Nadal
c. 19:28	6 de julio, 2008	Roger Federer
d. 10:35	12 de julio, 2008	El asteroide 128036
e. 14:42	16 de agosto, 2008	La medalla de oro en los Juegos Olímpicos
f. 20:35	24 de octubre, 2008	El premio Príncipe de Asturias
g. 10:48	8 de enero, 2010	Un video con Shakira, la cantante colombiana
h. 12:36	12 de agosto, 2016	La medalla de oro en los Juegos Olímpicos

1. __e__ **La está recibiendo** en Pekín (*Beijing*).
2. __b__ **La está anunciando** como una fundación de asistencia social.
3. __a__ **Lo está ganando** por primera vez, y con eso **se está haciendo** muy famoso en todo el mundo.
4. __g__ **Lo está filmando** en Barcelona.
5. __h__ **La está recibiendo** por segunda vez en Río de Janeiro.
6. __d__ La Unión Astronómica Internacional **le está dando** el nombre «Rafaelnadal» en honor a «uno de los mejores tenistas de todos los tiempos».
7. __f__ **Lo está recibiendo** del Príncipe Felipe en una ceremonia en Oviedo.
8. __c__ **Lo está venciendo** (*beating*) en Wimbledon. Según muchos, es el mejor partido en la historia del tenis.

Actividades analíticas

1 As you saw in **Estructura 11.3,** the present progressive consists of the auxiliary verb **estar** followed by the present participle of the main verb. Object pronouns can appear before **estar,** since it is the conjugated verb of the form.

Nadal **lo está** ganando.   *Nadal is winning it.*

In this example, the pronoun **lo** is a direct object pronoun. In **Para empezar,** find one example each of an indirect object pronoun and a reflexive pronoun, and write the pronoun and complete verb form here.

With indirect object pronoun: _____ le está dando _____

With reflexive pronoun: _____ se está haciendo _____

2 Object pronouns may instead appear after and attached to the present participle of the verb, just as you've seen with infinitives (see **Estructura 8.3**).

Nadal está **ganándolo.**   *Nadal is winning it.*

If you attach the object or reflexive pronoun to the end of a present participle, you'll need to write an accent mark in order to keep the stress on the right vowel: on the **a** of **-ando** for **-ar** verbs, and on the **e** of the **-iendo** for **-er** and **-ir** verbs. Whether you place the object/reflexive pronoun before the conjugated verb or attach it to the end of the present participle, the meaning is the same.

Take the verb phrases that you wrote in **Actividad analítica 1** and move the object/reflexive pronoun to the end of the present participle. Don't forget the accent marks!

Indirect object: _____ está dándole _____

Reflexive: _____ está haciéndose _____

Note (Para saber más): *Para saber más 12.2* covers the present progressive with multiple object pronouns.

Actividades prácticas

A. ¡Qué mala excusa!

PASO 1. Si invitas a un amigo o una amiga a hacer ejercicio contigo y te da una de las siguientes excusas, ¿cuáles son buenas y cuáles son ridículas?

No puedo hacer ejercicio contigo porque...	BUENA	RIDÍCULA
1. ya me estoy acostando. Tengo que levantarme muy temprano mañana.	☑	☐
2. me interesa más la televisión. La estoy viendo y cuando cambio el canal (*channel*), eso es muy buen ejercicio.	☐	☑
3. me estoy lavando los dientes.	☐	☑
4. encontré un libro en la basura y lo estoy leyendo.	☐	☑
5. tengo que presentar este libro mañana en mi clase de literatura y apenas (*barely*) lo estoy empezando a leer.	☑	☐
6. no encuentro mi computadora y la ando buscando.	☑	☐

PASO 2. Ahora, en parejas, creen dos excusas buenas y dos excusas ridículas para decir por qué no pueden hacer ejercicio en este momento. ¿Qué están haciendo que no les permite hacer ejercicio?

B. ¿Qué está haciendo? En parejas, para cada foto, túrnense para contestar la pregunta «¿Qué está(n) haciendo?»

1. Mateo   2. Luis   3. El padre y su hija   4. Yo

5. Gloria   6. Francisco   7. Elena   8. Amaya y Marlén

C. Dos contra dos En dos parejas, túrnense para actuar para la otra pareja algunas de las siguientes acciones, pero sin hablar. ¿La otra pareja puede adivinar qué están haciendo?

MODELO: ¿Lo/La estás ayudando a practicar yoga? (¿Estás ayudándolo/la a practicar yoga?)

ayudarlo/la a ponerse un casco	invitarlo/la a nadar
ayudarlo/la a practicar yoga	pasarle la pelota en un partido de fútbol
darle una raqueta	saludarlo/la
decirle que es muy buen(a) futbolista	seguirlo/la

Suggestion (Act. A, Paso 2): Have pairs write their excuses and turn them in. Read each aloud and have the class determine whether the excuse is *buena o ridícula*. When all have been read, ask: ¿*Cúal es la mejor excusa? ¿Cuál es la más ridícula?*

Suggestion (Act. B): After finishing *Act. B,* each student can stay with his/her partner for *Act. C.*

Answers (Act. B): 1. *Se está vistiendo (poniendo la corbata) / Está vistiéndose (poniéndose la corbata).* **2.** *Se está duchando. / Está duchándose.* **3.** *Se están lavando/cepillando los dientes. / Están lavándose/cepillándose los dientes.* **4.** *Me estoy poniendo los lentes de contacto. / Estoy poniéndome los lentes de contacto.* **5.** *Se está levantando. / Está levantándose* **6.** *Se está afeitando (la cara). / Está afeitándose (la cara).* **7.** *Se está bañando. / Está bañándose.* **8.** *Se están maquillando. (Se están poniendo el maquillaje.) / Están maquillándose. (Están poniéndose el maquillaje.)*

Suggestions (Act. C):
• To increase student success in using pronouns with the present progressive, have them refer to the list while trying to guess the other pair's activity.
• Encourage students to act as well as they can even when they might not be able to do the action in real life (as for *hablar francés*) and they can't use words (making *hablar francés* even more challenging!); this makes the activity more fun.

Alternative (Act. C): Have each 2-person team act in front of the entire class.

Note (Act. C): Even though both members of the pair will be acting, only one will be performing the action listed, so the guess should be in the *tú* form.

↻ Reciclaje

Commands

Usando las recomendaciones de la lista, crea consejos en forma de mandatos para tus compañeros que tienen los problemas mencionados. Cada recomendación se puede usar solo una vez. **¡Atención!** Algunos de los mandatos tienen que estar en forma singular (**tú**) y otros en plural (**Uds.**).

comer menos y hacer más ejercicio	dormir más	practicar yoga
correr	levantar pesas	tomar agua

PROBLEMA	CONSEJO
1. Tenemos sed.	Tomen agua.
2. Quiero tener más flexibilidad.	Practica yoga.
3. Queremos tener más músculo.	Levanten pesas.
4. Siempre tengo sueño.	Duerme más.
5. Quiero bajar de peso.	Come menos y haz más ejercicio.
6. Queremos tener mejor condición cardiovascular.	Corran.

Note (Reciclaje): Informal (*tú*) commands were presented in *Estructura 10.2*, vosotros commands were presented in an *En español* box there, and formal (*Ud.* and *Uds.*) commands were presented in *Estructura 10.3*.

■ Answers to this activity are in Appendix 2 at the back of your book.

12.3   Te recomiendo que comas chocolate

The subjunctive: Volition with regular verbs

Para empezar...

Lee las siguientes preguntas sobre la salud y las respuestas del Doctor América. Él te recomienda (*recommends*) puros productos autóctonos (*native*) de América para ayudarte con los problemas de salud. Pero, ¡cuidado! Una de sus recomendaciones es falsa.

1. Quiero bajar (*lower*) mi colesterol. ¿Qué hago?
   Doctor América dice: «Yo te recomiendo que **comas** mucho aguacate».

2. ¿Qué me recomienda para aumentar (*increase*) mi consumo (*consumption*) de antioxidantes? Doctor América dice: «Te recomiendo que **comas** o **tomes** mucho chocolate. El chocolate tiene un nivel muy alto de antioxidantes».

3. No me gusta el jugo de naranja. ¿Qué puedo hacer para tener suficiente vitamina C? Doctor América dice: «Te recomiendo que **comas** chiles. Los chiles contienen muchísima vitamina C».

4. Soy vegetariano. ¿Qué me recomienda para comer suficiente proteína?
   Doctor América dice: «Te recomiendo que **busques** quinua. Es de los Andes (sobre todo Bolivia) y tiene muchísima proteína. Se usa en forma de harina para hacer pan».

Una planta de quinua roja

5. A veces tengo problemas digestivos. ¿Qué me recomienda?
   Doctor América dice: «Te recomiendo que **compres** papaya. Ayuda mucho a la digestión y tiene muchas vitaminas y antioxidantes».

Note (Para empezar): Recommendation 7: Vanilla is native to Mexico but is not known to have any effect on male pattern baldness. For all the others, there is some evidence that they have the benefit indicated.

6. Sé que tengo que comer más verduras, pero no me gustan. ¿Qué hago?
   Doctor América dice: «Te recomiendo que le **des** una oportunidad al maíz. ¿Lo has probado (*tried*) en verano? Con sal y mantequilla (o chile, ¿por qué no?), es muy rico».

7. Me estoy quedando calvo (*bald*) y no sé qué hacer. ¿Ud. me puede recomendar algo? Doctor América dice: «Te recomiendo que **vivas** una vida muy tranquila, que **duermas** mucho y que **tomes** agua con vainilla todas las noches antes de acostarte. En poco tiempo vas a tener mucho pelo de nuevo (*once again*)».

8. ¿Ud. me puede recomendar alguna fruta o verdura para ayudar a prevenir (*prevent*) el cáncer?
   Doctor América dice: «Yo te recomiendo que **comas** mucho tomate. Su color rojo es por la presencia de licopeno (*lycopene*), un antioxidante importante».

■ Answers to these activities are in Appendix 2 at the back of your book.

La recomendación falsa es la del número __7__.

Actividades analíticas

1 The verbs in bold in **Para empezar** are all in the **tú** form of the *present subjunctive* (**el presente de subjuntivo**). The subjunctive is used in a variety of situations, and here it is used to express a recommendation, a piece of advice, or a desire.

Write the subjunctive forms in bold from **Para empezar** in the right-hand column of this chart. Then write the **tú** form for the *present indicative* (**el presente de indicativo**), the grammatical name for the simple present tense.

INFINITIVO	PRESENTE DE INDICATIVO	PRESENTE DE SUBJUNTIVO
	tú	tú
buscar	buscas	busques
comer	comes	comas
comprar	compras	compres
dar	das	des
dormir	duermes	duermas
tomar	tomas	tomes
vivir	vives	vivas

2 You can identify subjunctive forms by the vowel (**vocal**) in the ending. Just as in the formal commands and negative informal commands, both **-ar** and **-er/-ir** verbs use the "opposite" vowel. Use the examples given to complete the following chart.

	La vocal en el presente de indicativo	La vocal en el presente de subjuntivo
-ar verbs	-a-	-e-
Example	Tom**a**s chocolate.	...que tom**e**s chocolate.
-er/-ir verbs	-e-	-a-
Example	Com**e**s chocolate.	...que com**a**s chocolate.

3 Apart from the change in vowel that you just saw in **Actividades analíticas 2**, the endings in the present subjunctive are similar to those of the present indicative. Complete the following chart to see the entire conjugation.

	tomar	comer	vivir
yo	tome	coma	viva
tú	tomes	comas	vivas
él/ella, Ud.	tome	coma	viva
nosotros/as	tomemos	comamos	vivamos
vosotros/as	toméis	comáis	viváis
ellos/ellas, Uds.	tomen	coman	vivan

Note that the **yo** form and the **él/ella, Ud.** form are identical in the subjunctive. Context will help to determine which subject is intended, or the subject pronoun may be used.

(Continues)

Suggestion (Act. analíticas 1): You may wish to point out that verbs that end in **-car**, like *buscar*, change the final *-c-* of the stem to *qu* in the subjunctive in order to preserve the hard *c* sound of the stem. Similarly with a verb that ends in **-gar**, like *llegar*, a *-u-* is inserted in order to preserve the hard *g* sound when the *-e-* is added. You may wish to ask students in which verb tense they've seen similar changes (preterite [**Estructura 6.1**]).

Expansion (Act. analíticas 3): Have students compare these conjugations to the present indicative. Help them see that apart from the changed vowel, the endings are strikingly similar.

Suggestion (Act. analítica 4):
Explain that *ojalá* is a fixed
expression which is derived
from the Arabic *Inshallah*. It is
not conjugated and can be
used with or without the word
que. It always means *I hope /
Hopefully.*

■ For more expressions of
volition, see **Para saber
más 12.3** at the back of
your book.

Note (Para saber más): *Para
saber más 12.3* covers the
following expressions of
volition: *aconsejar, exigir,
insistir en, mandar, permitir,
preferir, prohibir, ser
importante, ser mejor,* and
sugerir.

4 You saw in **Para empezar** that **recomendar que** is followed by the subjunctive.
Here are some other expressions that do the same.

Se usa el subjuntivo después de...	Ejemplo
esperar (*to hope*) **que**	**Espero** que **puedas** venir a la fiesta. *I hope that you can come to the party.*
ojalá (que) (*I hope*)	**Ojalá** que **puedas** venir a la fiesta. *I hope that you can come to the party.*
pedir que	**Están pidiendo** que **trabajemos** en Bolivia. *They're asking us to work in Bolivia.*
querer que	**Quiero** que **lleguen** temprano mañana. *I want them to arrive early tomorrow.*
ser necesario que	**Es necesario** que tu papá **coma** más fruta. *It's necessary for your father to eat more fruit.*

These expressions trigger the use of subjunctive after **que** because they convey a
recommendation, a piece of advice, or a desire.

5 **Decir que** sometimes expresses a recommendation, in which case it is followed by the
subjunctive. When **decir que** is used simply to state information, it is followed by the
indicative.

EL SUBJUNTIVO Y EL INDICATIVO DESPUÉS DE *decir que*	
Subjunctive (Recommendation)	Los médicos **dicen** que **tomes** mucho chocolate. *The doctors say that you should / tell you to drink a lot of hot chocolate.*
Indicative (Statement)	Los médicos **dicen** que **tomas** mucho chocolate. *The doctors say that you drink a lot of hot chocolate.*

Verbs such as **pensar** and **creer** never express a recommendation, so they are
followed by the indicative.

Pienso que mi hijo **toma** mucho chocolate.   *I think my son drinks a lot of hot chocolate.*

Note (Act. analítica 5): The
fact that *pensar* and *creer* are
followed by the subjunctive
when they are negative will be
discussed in *Estructura 13.2.*

Autoprueba

Use what you've just learned to conjugate the following verbs in the present
subjunctive.

1. hablar (yo) _____
2. correr (tú) _____
3. sufrir (nosotros/as) _____
4. poder (ella) _____
5. cerrar (Uds.) _____

Respuestas: 1. hable **2.** corras **3.** suframos **4.** pueda **5.** cierren

Actividades prácticas

A. ¿Pensar o querer? Escoge **pienso** o **quiero** para completar cada oración. **¡Atención!** Presta atención al verbo que sigue después de **que**. ¿Está en el indicativo o el subjuntivo?

1. **Pienso / Quiero** que Pepe está en el gimnasio.   Pienso
2. **Pienso / Quiero** que Martina trabaja en San José.   Pienso
3. **Pienso / Quiero** que gane Nadal.   Quiero
4. **Pienso / Quiero** que van a limpiar la piscina al mediodía.   Pienso
5. **Pienso / Quiero** que llueva mañana.   Quiero
6. **Pienso / Quiero** que va a ganar Nadal.   Pienso
7. **Pienso / Quiero** que esté muy limpia la casa.   Quiero
8. **Pienso / Quiero** que corramos todos juntos en el parque mañana.   Quiero

> **Suggestion (Act. A):** Remind students that *querer que* is followed by the subjunctive because it expresses a desire. The verb *pensar* is followed by the indicative because it expresses a belief.

B. En otras palabras En el español, como en el inglés, a veces hay más de una manera de decir las cosas. Empareja cada oración con la oración en el subjuntivo con el mismo sentido (*meaning*).

1. __e__ Llámame antes del partido, por favor.
2. __b__ ¿Por qué no hablan tus padres con el entrenador? Creo que sería buena idea.
3. __f__ Diles a tus padres que tienen que hablar con el entrenador.
4. __g__ ¡Por favor! ¡Come más fruta!
5. __h__ Los atletas tienen que practicar. Es obligatorio.
6. __a__ Tienes que cooperar (*cooperate*) con el resto del equipo. No hay otra opción.
7. __d__ Si trabajas bien con el resto del equipo, voy a estar muy contento.
8. __c__ Si ganas en la competencia, voy a estar muy contento.

a. Es necesario que trabajes bien con ellos.
b. Recomiendo que tus padres hablen con el entrenador.
c. Espero que ganes en la competencia.
d. Ojalá que trabajes bien con ellos.
e. Te estoy pidiendo que me llames antes del partido.
f. Quiero que tus padres hablen con el entrenador.
g. Te estoy pidiendo que comas más manzanas, naranjas, plátanos, etcétera.
h. Es necesario que los atletas practiquen.

¿Por qué?

Why does the subjunctive look so similar to formal commands (and negative **tú** commands)? The reason is that their meaning is almost the same. Commands express what you want to happen, and the subjunctive does something similar: it expresses what the subject of the main verb wants to happen. These commands and the subjunctive both use the "opposite" vowel in their endings, and as you saw in **10.2**, this makes sense. Spanish only uses **a**, **e**, and **o** in unstressed endings, and since **o** is reserved for the **yo** ending of the present indicative, the simplest way to distinguish the subjunctive from the indicative is to "switch" the vowels **a** and **e**.

> **Expansion (¿Por qué?):** Give students two verbs (e.g., *trabajar* and *comer*), then have them add the three vowels discussed here (*a, e, o*) to the root and identify the result (e.g., *trabaja, trabaje, trabajo,* and *coma, come, como*).

Suggestion (Act. C): Before students begin, remind them that *decir* sometimes just describes or reports something (in which case it takes the indicative) and sometimes makes a recommendation (in which case it takes the subjunctive). In this activity, they see both uses. The "wrong" answers are not technically wrong, just extremely unlikely given the context.

C. Lo que dice la gente

Para cada oración, decide si lo que se dice es una recomendación o una declaración (*statement*). Luego indica el verbo adecuado.

1. Mi mamá siempre me está diciendo que **come / coma** más frutas y verduras para estar más sana.   coma
2. Este artículo en el Internet dice que Nadal **juega / juegue** tenis.   juega
3. Gloria dice que muchos estudiantes en su universidad **nadan / naden** todos los días.   nadan
4. La maestra dice que **escribimos / escribamos** una carta en español como tarea para mañana.   escribamos
5. Las instrucciones dicen que **nos acostamos / nos acostemos** después de tomar la pastilla (*pill*).   nos acostemos
6. Marcos dice que sus papás **viven / vivan** en el Perú.   viven
7. La televisión dice que el presidente **está / esté** viajando esta semana.   está
8. Para poder ganar la competencia, dicen que **estamos / estemos** presentes en todos los entrenamientos.   estemos

D. ¿Qué nos recomiendan los médicos?

PASO 1. En cada una de las siguientes oraciones, usa el verbo entre paréntesis en su forma **nosotros/as.** Luego, indica si la oración es **cierta** o **falsa.**

Los médicos nos recomiendan...

	CIERTO	FALSO
1. que (consultar) __consultemos__ con un doctor antes de empezar un programa de ejercicio fuerte.	☑	☐
2. que (comer) __comamos__ mucho azúcar para tener los dientes muy bonitos.	☐	☑
3. que (tomar) __tomemos__ jugo de papaya para poder nadar más rápido.	☐	☑
4. que (usar) __usemos__ bloqueador solar cuando estamos expuestos (*exposed*) al sol.	☑	☐
5. que (escuchar) __escuchemos__ música en español una hora al día.	☐	☑
6. que (evitar) __evitemos__ el estrés si es posible.	☑	☐
7. que (lavarse) __nos lavemos__ los dientes por lo menos dos veces al día.	☑	☐
8. que le (dar) __demos__ muchos regalos a nuestro médico favorito.	☐	☑

PASO 2. Ahora Uds. son los médicos. En grupos, creen seis recomendaciones para sus pacientes que tienen gripe (*the flu*). Usen las sugerencias de la lista o inventen otras.

beber muchos líquidos	descansar
comer caldo de pollo	sonarse (ue) (*to blow*) la nariz
comprar jarabe (*syrup*) para la tos	tomar unas aspirinas

MODELO: Les recomendamos que Uds. se queden en casa.

E. El espíritu deportivo (*Good sportsmanship*)

En parejas, creen tres recomendaciones para un(a) atleta que quiere ser un(a) ganador(a) cortés y no un perdedor resentido / una perdedora resentida (*sore loser*).

Te recomiendo que...   Ojalá que...   Es necesario que...

MODELO: Te recomiendo que no insultes a nadie.

¡Leamos!

Trancos° de gratitud en la 21K   *Strides*

Antes de leer

Contesta las siguientes preguntas sobre un deporte popular: carreras de fondo (*long-distance running*).

1. Para cada distancia, completa la tabla con el nombre de la carrera y los tiempos típicos para completar cada una.

   maratón   ultramaratón   1–3 horas   24 horas o más
   medio maratón   2–8 horas

DISTANCIA	NOMBRE DE LA CARRERA	TIEMPO TÍPICO
21 kilómetros	medio maratón	1–3 horas
42 kilómetros	maratón	2–8 horas
100 kilómetros	ultramaratón	24 horas o más

2. En general, ¿qué pisan (*step on*) los corredores?
   (a.) asfalto   b. flores   c. agua

3. En general, ¿para qué participan los mejores atletas?
   (a.) el espíritu de la competencia   b. el viaje   c. los premios

4. ¿Qué tipo de zapatos llevan la mayoría de los participantes en las carreras de fondo?
   a. Corren descalzos.   (b.) Llevan tenis.   c. Llevan sandalias.

5. ¿Qué tipo de ropa llevan los participantes?
   (a.) cómoda y ligera   b. fuerte y tradicional   c. larga y elegante

6. ¿Cuál no es un requisito para participar en una carrera de fondo?
   a. el entrenamiento   (b.) la predisposición genética
   c. la resistencia (*endurance*) física

A leer

Lee la siguiente lectura sobre un grupo de corredores indígenas. Mientras lee, pon el resumen del artículo en orden de 1 a 6. Luego contesta las preguntas que siguen.

   __2__ La antigua tradición indígena tiene raíces religiosas.

   __3__ Hay una carrera que mezcla un juego de pelota con una carrera de fondo.

   __6__ Un corredor tarahumara corre en muchas carreras de fondo, incluso los ultramaratones.

   __5__ Los indígenas modernos participan en maratones alrededor del mundo.

   __1__ Hay muchas razones por las cuales la gente corre.

   __4__ La religión tarahumara reconoce la tierra, el sol y la luna.

(*Continues*)

Trancos de gratitud en la 21K

por Santino Ayala

Saltillo, Coahuila, México — Mañana, nuestras calles se atestarán de[a] participantes en la Gran Carrera de México, la 21K de Coahuila. ¡A correr!

Las motivaciones para correr son tan variadas como las personas que corren: el buen estado físico, los beneficios cardíacos y aeróbicos, el alivio[b] del estrés y el deseo de competir. Y claro, a veces corremos por el peligro[c] o el miedo.

En la Sierra[d] Tarahumara del estado de Chihuahua, los tarahumaras corren por motivaciones muy disímiles[e] de las que típicamente influyen en que nosotros salgamos con tenis a correr unos kilómetros por el vecindario[f] o el parque.

Correr es la tradición más antigua de los tarahumaras. Históricamente, corrían, descalzos[g] o con huaraches,[h] para cazar,[i] para comunicarse y para expresar su devoción y agradecimiento[j] a Dios por su existencia. Rarámuri, el nombre de los tarahumaras en su idioma, significa *pie corredor.*[k]

Una de las carreras más importantes de su comunidad es el *rarajípari* o carrera de bolas.[l] Es una carrera que puede durar[m] unas horas o un par[n] de días. En esta carrera comunitaria, dos equipos de corredores lanzan[ñ] una bola entre sí hasta llegar a la meta,[o] que puede ser de unos metros o hasta 200 kilómetros. Para las carreras más largas, la comunidad corre con los equipos. Las mujeres participan con aros y palitos[p] y otros miembros corren al lado de los equipos, proveyéndoles[q] comida y bebida y, durante la noche, luz para iluminar el paso.

Según un miembro de la comunidad tarahumara, los rarámuris corren «para alegrar[r] al corazón de la

Un rarámuri expresa su devoción

Madre Tierra, al mismo Sol que es nuestro dios y nuestra Madre Luna[s]».

Aunque por muchas décadas esta comunidad vivía muy aislada del mundo moderno, ahora participan en carreras más allá de[t] la Sierra. Corren en maratones en las ciudades más grandes de México y también en maratones en el extranjero, en lugares como Colorado, Nevada y California.

Este año, un grupo de diez tarahumaras de Tatahuichi vuelve a Saltillo para participar en la Gran Carrera de México, la 21K de Coahuila. Entre ellos, Martín Roberto Ramírez dice que ha participado en esta carrera por cuatro años seguidos.[u] ¿Le será difícil? Dudable.[v] Más de una vez, Martín se puso los huaraches y corrió 100 millas seguidas en ultramaratones de los Estados Unidos.

Mientras Martín y sus compañeros expresan su gratitud y devoción durante la carrera, nosotros también queremos expresar nuestro agradecimiento a su comunidad y a esta gran comunidad de corredores que llega a nuestro estado todos los veranos —¡algunos por veinte años seguidos!— para correr. A todos les deseamos suerte y una buena carrera.

[a]*se... will be filled with* [b]*relief* [c]*danger* [d]*Mountains* [e]*unlike* [f]*neighborhood* [g]*barefoot* [h]*sandals* [i]*hunt* [j]*thankfulness* [k]*running* [l]*balls* [m]*last* [n]*couple* [ñ]*equipos... running teams throw* [o]*finish line* [p]*aros... hoops and sticks* [q]*providing them with* [r]*fill with joy* [s]*Moon* [t]*más... beyond* [u]*in a row* [v]*Doubtful*

Answers (A leer): 1. 21K
2. Porque para ellos es algo espiritual. Se hace para alegrar a los dioses e, históricamente, para cazar y comunicarse.
3. Las mujeres corren en la si erra con un aro y con un palito; los hombres corren mientras manejan una pelota de madera con los pies.
4. en ultramaratones
5. huaraches (o nada)

1. ¿Cuántos kilómetros corren los participantes en la carrera de Saltillo, en México?
2. ¿Por qué tienen un significado especial las carreras para los tarahumaras?
3. ¿Cómo corren los hombres y las mujeres tarahumaras en la sierra? ¿Qué cosas llevan?
4. ¿En qué tipo de carrera han participado los tarahumaras en los Estados Unidos?
5. ¿Qué llevan en los pies para correr los tarahumaras?
6. ¿Cómo son los tarahumaras como (*like*) los corredores / las corredoras de maratones de tu país? ¿Cómo son diferentes? Explica.

Después de leer

En parejas, lean las siguientes situaciones y den una felicitación, una reacción o una sugerencia para cada una. **¡Atención!** Pueden usar las expresiones en la página 358 y las recomendaciones en **Estructura 12.3.**

1. tu amigo está por correr su primera carrera 5K
2. tu amiga ha corrido la mitad de (*half of*) su carrera y está cansada, pero quiere seguir
3. a tus amigos solo les queda una milla más (*only one mile left*) por correr en el maratón
4. tu amiga no sabe qué llevar para correr una carrera de larga distancia
5. un corredor tarahumara está por correr por veinticuatro horas seguidas

¡Escuchemos!

El sueño° de ser deportista   *dream*

Antes de escuchar

PASO 1.   Completa cada una de las siguientes oraciones con tres posibilidades.

MODELO: De niña, quería trabajar como guía naturalista, periodista o veterinaria.

1. De niño/a, esperaba trabajar como...
2. Soy aficionado/a (*fan*) de los siguientes equipos deportistas: ...
3. Los miembros de mi familia son aficionados de los siguientes equipos deportistas: ...
4. Según mi opinión, los deportes más populares en el mundo hispano son...

 PASO 2.   En grupos pequeños, comparen sus respuestas al **Paso 1** y luego contesten las siguientes preguntas.

1. ¿Quiénes del grupo aún (*still*) quieren hacer el mismo trabajo que querían hacer en su niñez?
2. ¿Qué hacen los aficionados de los varios equipos deportistas que apuntaron en el **Paso 1** para demostrar (*show*) su pasión por el deporte o el equipo? ¿Cuál es la tradición más extraña?
3. ¿Quién(es) conoce(n) a alguien que haya tenido éxito como atleta profesional?
4. Según la mayoría, ¿cuál es el deporte más popular en el mundo hispano?

 A escuchar

Video track (A escuchar): This video clip can be found on the DVD to accompany *Conéctate: Cap. 12*, Track 3.

PASO 1.   Mira y escucha el video. Mira otra vez con pausas y marca los trabajos que mencionan los entrevistados.

bailador(a)	corredor(a)	(guitarrista)	tenista
beisbolista	(futbolista)	nadador(a)	torero/a (*bullfighter*)

Note: Students will have to listen carefully, as only 2 speakers mention jobs.

PASO 2.   Escucha otra vez con pausas y empareja cada equipo con su mejor descripción.

1. __a__ un equipo profesional de fútbol de Madrid
2. __c__ un equipo profesional de fútbol de la capital de México, el Distrito Federal
3. __b__ el equipo representativo del país en los partidos nacionales

a. Real Madrid
b. La selección de fútbol de Paraguay
c. Cruz Azul

Videoscript (A escuchar): 1. LAURA: *Y bueno, luego el fútbol que también es un deporte aquí, el deporte Rey, claro.* **2.** LUDMILA Y PAULA: *El deporte nacional que define a la cultura argentina es el fútbol.* **3.** VÍCTOR: *Y por la tarde me fui al fútbol, a ver el fútbol aquí en el Estadio Santiago Bernabéu, a ver el Real Madrid, pues, con un equipo de una provincia de España que se llama Almería.* **4.** MARIANO: *En el futuro quiero ser un futbolista y jugar en mi selección paraguaya... sí... ese es mi... mayor sueño que tengo.* **5.** PEDRO: *Bueno, a mí me gusta mucho lo que es el fútbol soccer. Mi sueño era ser profesional... Bueno, yo tuve una ilusión a los 15 años de ser profesional. Estuve en Cruz Azul, en La Noria... lo que es el Distrito Federal; estuve un año entrenando profesionalmente. Desgraciadamente los recursos económicos no nos dieron para más y entonces tomé la decisión de fútbol o estudiar una carrera, me incliné por lo segundo que es una, una carrera, yo creo que fue lo más viable.* **6.** DAVID: *Me gustaría, bueno, sacar la carrera sobre futbolista. Me gusta mucho el fútbol.* **7.** WILLIAM: *¿Sueño? Ser un gran guitarrista. Y si no puedo, futbolista. Y si no, trabajar.*

(*Continues*)

Después de escuchar

PASO 1. Mira y escucha otra vez con pausas. Luego contesta las preguntas.

LOS AFICIONADOS

1. Según Laura, ¿cuál es el deporte nacional de España?   el fútbol

2. Según Ludmila y Paula, ¿cuál es el deporte nacional de Argentina?   el fútbol

3. ¿Qué hizo Víctor el sábado por la tarde? fue a un partido de fútbol

4. ¿Qué término usan Mariano, David y William para decir «jugador de fútbol»?   futbolista

El futbolista portugués Cristiano Ronaldo, del Real Madrid Club de Fútbol

EL SUEÑO DE MUCHOS NIÑOS

1. Describe el sueño de Mariano.   ser futbolista

2. Describe el sueño de Pedro. ¿Por cuánto tiempo entrenó profesionalmente? ¿Por qué dejó de entrenar profesionalmente?   ser futbolista profesional; un año; fue caro entrenar

3. ¿Qué carrera quiere seguir Dávid?   futbolista

4. ¿Qué sueño tiene William?   guitarrista o futbolista

PASO 2. En parejas, contesten las siguientes preguntas sobre lo que escucharon.

1. Laura dice que el fútbol es «el deporte Rey». ¿Qué significa? ¿Cuál es «el deporte Rey» donde viven Uds.?

2. ¿Por qué puede costar mucho dinero cumplir el sueño de ser atleta profesional? ¿No ganan mucho dinero los atletas profesionales?

Suggestion (Conéctate al mundo hispano): Have students look for soccer commentary from an exciting game. Ask for volunteers to read the narration in the voice of a soccer commentator.

CONÉCTATE AL MUNDO HISPANO

Los buenos **comentaristas del fútbol** tienen un estilo de narrar los partidos para que cada patada (*kick*) de la pelota parezca emocionante (*seems exciting*). Tienen fama de gritar (*yell*) y cantar el «¡GOOOOOOOOOOOOOOLLLLLL!» como en ningún otro deporte. Imagínate la siguiente escena emocionante en un partido entre dos gran rivales.

COMENTARISTA: ¡La pelota pasa con rapidez entre los jugadores de los dos equipos: Barcelona y Manchester United! El entrenador Martínez grita, pero nadie lo oye porque los aficionados en el estadio hacen un ruido tremendo. Ninguno de los dos equipos ha marcado (*scored*) un gol y ahora —en los últimos segundos del partido— el nuevo jugador joven está por meter un gol: patea (*he kicks*) la pelota hacia el hombro izquierdo del portero (*goalkeeper*) inglés, pero el portero salta y agarra (*jumps and grabs*) la pelota con las manos. ¡Y así el partido termina en un empate (*tie*): 0–0!

¡Escribamos!

Cómo nos mantenemos en forma

Le vas a ofrecer consejos a alguien que, debido (*due*) a un cambio de circunstancias, busca nuevo equilibrio.

Antes de escribir

Lee las descripciones de la salud y los hábitos de Mila, Félix y Elena e indica las partes tal vez problemáticas. Para cada descripción, apunta algunas cosas que debe hacer esta persona para mejorar su salud.

ESTRATEGIA

Persuasive paragraph

Words can be powerful, even when up against strong convictions, tightly held beliefs, or deeply engrained habits. Being able to write a persuasive paragraph is therefore an invaluable skill to have. This involves being able to argue a point and strengthen your case by bringing in supporting statements, using solid reasoning, and anticipating the counterpoints to your argument and preemptively responding to them.

MILA: Estoy en clase toda la mañana de lunes a viernes. Luego por las tardes estudio y trabajo en la oficina de seguridad pública de la universidad. Como en la cafetería tres veces al día y no he subido de peso, pero siempre me siento cansada y sé que soy más débil que hace un año cuando hacía mucho más ejercicio con los equipos deportivos de mi colegio.

FÉLIX: Recientemente me hice socio (*member*) del nuevo gimnasio al lado de mi oficina. Voy los cinco días de la semana, pero no he perdido ni un kilo. Con todo el ejercicio, tengo ganas de comer más de lo normal para mí. Además de las comidas normales, como un sándwich y unas papas fritas en la tarde y algún postre después de la cena.

ELENA: Antes iba al gimnasio cinco veces a la semana pero ahora con un trabajo de tiempo completo y dos hijos no tengo tiempo. Seguir una dieta equilibrada es muy importante para mí y más o menos sigo comiendo lo que siempre he comido.

A escribir

Escoge una de las tres personas y escribe un ensayo para ayudarla a mejorar su salud. Escribe un párrafo para describir lo que está haciendo mal y un párrafo en que le ofreces recomendaciones de lo que debe hacer para mejorar su salud. Explica por qué cada acción sugerida (*suggested*) es beneficiosa. Trata de anticipar las respuestas de la persona y responde también a ellas.

> **MODELO:** No coma el sándwich y las papas fritas extras.
>
> (Reacción anticipada: ¡Pero tengo hambre por hacer tanto ejercicio!) En vez de comer el sándwich y las papas fritas, los nutricionistas recomiendan que la gente coma fruta y un puñado (*handful*) de nueces (*nuts*); así no va a tener hambre, pero va a poder bajar de peso. Estas comidas son mejores que su merienda típica porque la fruta tiene muchas vitaminas y poca grasa (*fat*), y las nueces son altas en proteína.

(Continues)

Suggestion (Después de leer): To motivate students to edit their own work as well as their classmates' carefully, occasionally grade their editing instead of their writing.

Después de escribir

Revisa tu ensayo. Luego intercambia ensayos con un compañero / una compañera para evaluarlos.

☐ Lee la introducción. ¿Explica lo que está haciendo mal la persona?

☐ ¿Tiene un párrafo en el que le ofrece consejos usando el subjuntivo o unos mandatos?

☐ Subraya todos los adjetivos en el ensayo. ¿Tienen concordancia los adjetivos y los sustantivos que describen?

☐ Hazle una recomendación a tu compañero/a: *Recomiendo / Es necesario que...*

☐ Dile a tu compañero/a qué hay que hacer para recibir una A en el ensayo: *Para recibir una A, hay que...*

Después de revisar el ensayo de tu compañero/a, devuélveselo. Revisa tu propio ensayo para ver los cambios que tu compañero/a recomienda y haz las revisiones necesarias.

¡Hablemos!

Somos entrenadores

Expresiones útiles

coger	to catch
doblar	to bend
lanzar	to throw
mover (ue)	to move
patear	to kick
pegar	to hit
rebotar	to bounce
saltar	to jump
usar rodilleras y coderas	to wear knee pads and elbow pads

Expansion (Después de hablar): Have each group of students give instructions on the proper use of a piece of sporting gear mentioned in this chapter. Have them consider safety as well as the rules of the game.

Antes de hablar

Haz una lista de seis o más pasos básicos que hay que seguir para practicar un aspecto de tu deporte favorito o actividad física favorita.

> **MODELO:** dar un paseo → ponerse los calcetines y los tenis, levantarse, levantar el pie derecho, dar un paso, levantar el pie izquierdo, dar un paso, repetir más rápidamente...

Suggestion (A hablar): After most students have led a fitness program, have the groups nominate the best "coaches" to lead the whole class.

A hablar

En grupos de tres o cuatro estudiantes, túrnense en el papel de entrenador(a) para enseñarles a los otros estudiantes cómo hacer el deporte o la actividad. Los otros miembros del grupo deben intentar seguir las instrucciones del entrenador o la entrenadora. Presten atención y anoten si a los líderes se les olvida algún paso importante. **¡Atención!** Usen mandatos de **Uds.** para dar instrucciones a más de una persona.

> **MODELO:** dar un paseo → Pónganse los calcetines y los tenis. Ahora levántense. Levanten el pie derecho y den un paso. Levanten el pie izquierdo y den otro paso. Repitan más rápidamente...

Después de hablar

En parejas, comenten las siguientes preguntas.

1. ¿Hay alguna instrucción importante que los otros entrenadores / las otras entrenadoras en tu grupo hayan olvidado (*have forgotten*) incluir? Añadan por lo menos una instrucción más a cada una de sus presentaciones.

2. ¿Cuáles son las instrucciones más comunes que dieron los entrenadores / las entrenadoras?

Conéctate al cine

Película: *Hermano* (drama, Venezuela, 2010)
Director: Marcel Rasquín

Sinopsis:

Julio, un niño, y su madre encuentran a un bebé abandonado en la calle, llorando como un gato. La madre lo adopta y Julio y Daniel crecen como hermanos. Julio le da a Daniel el apodo (*nickname*) «Gato». A los dos hermanos les encanta jugar fútbol y son muy competitivos entre sí (*with each other*). Llega la oportunidad de ir a las pruebas (*tryouts*) de un equipo profesional, el Caracas Fútbol Club. Sin embargo, sucede una tragedia que les complica la vida.

Escena (Netflix, 00:03:40 to 00:08:52):

Julio y Daniel/Gato están jugando en un partido importante. Después del partido, un cazatalentos (*talent scout*) del Caracas Fútbol Club quiere hablar con ellos.

Antes de ver

Julio y Daniel son hermanos que juegan en el mismo equipo. ¿Puedes imaginar cómo sería (*would be like*) la interacción entre dos hermanos en un campo (*field*) de fútbol? Indica qué se dirían (*they would say to each other*). Luego explica tu respuesta.

____ ¡Ánimo!   ____ ¡Lo hiciste mal!

____ ¡Bien hecho!   ____ ¡No hagas eso!

____ ¡Corre más rápido!

Suggestion (A ver): Turn subtitles off, if possible. Students won't understand everything, but they won't need to. Stop at the words *capaz vives tu sueño.*

A ver

PASO 1. Lee las **Expresiones útiles** y mira la escena. No trates de entender cada palabra, pero escucha con atención.

PASO 2. Indica si cada declaración es cierta (**C**) o falsa (**F**).

Expresiones útiles

la (tarjeta) roja	red card
quieto	quiet, calm
canchita	small, neighborhood field
el pase	pass
¡Qué golazo!	What a great goal!
licorería	liquor store
¡Qué juegazo!	What a great game!
la generación de relevo	incoming team/players
unos mesecitos	just a few short months
el más chamo (*Ven.*)	the youngest
humillar	humiliate

		C	F
1.	Julio le sugiere al portero que se quede quieto.	☑	☐
2.	El entrenador les dice a los jugadores que metan (*score*) dos goles más.	☐	☑
3.	Daniel (Gato) le dice a Julio que suba y espere el pase.	☐	☑
4.	La mamá desea que el equipo vaya a las finales.	☑	☐
5.	Daniel le pide a su amiga que deje a su novio por él.	☑	☐
6.	El entrenador aconseja a los hermanos que no hablen con el cazatalentos.	☐	☑
7.	El cazatalentos recomienda a los hermanos que vayan a las pruebas.	☑	☐
8.	Daniel no quiere que Julio juegue en Caracas Fútbol Club con él.	☐	☑

Después de ver

En parejas, túrnense para hacerse las siguientes preguntas y contestarlas.

¿Has practicado algún deporte? ¿Lo sigues haciendo? ¿Eres/Eras competitivo/a o juegas/jugabas para divertirte? ¿Tienes/Tenías sueños de ser deportista profesional? ¿Qué es lo más importante que has aprendido de practicar ese deporte?

■ For copyright reasons, the feature-film clips referenced in **Conéctate al cine** have not been provided by the publisher. Each of these films is readily available through retailers or online rental sites such as Amazon, iTunes, or Netflix.

VOCABULARIO

Now that I have completed the chapter, I can . . .

☐ wish someone well

☐ say what needs to be done

☐ talk about sports, wellness, and injuries

☐ say what I would like to happen

☐ talk about sports and health in the Spanish-speaking world

Comunicación

¡Adelante!	Go for it! / Let's go! / You can do it!
¡Ánimo!	Keep your spirits high! / Give it all you've got! / Don't give up!
(No) Hay que + *inf.*	You (*don't*) have to / It's (*not*) necessary to (*do something*)
Que te/le(s) vaya bien.	Have a good one. / I hope things go well for you.
Que tenga(s) un(a) buen(a)…	Have a good . . .
¡Que tengas un buen día!	Have a good day!
Sí, se puede.	Yes, you/we can! (It can be done!)
¡Suerte (con todo)!	Good luck (*with everything*)!
¡(Buena/Mucha) Suerte!	Good luck! / Best of luck!
Le(s) deseo mucha suerte.	I wish you (*sing./pl.*) well. I wish you (*sing./pl.*) lots of luck.

Los deportes — Sports

la carrera	race
el casco	helmet
la competencia	competition
el/la entrenador(a)	coach; trainer
el equipo	team; equipment
el esquí	skiing
el estadio	the stadium
el fútbol americano	(American) football
los Juegos Olímpicos	Olympic Games
el/la jugador(a)	player
la natación	swimming
el partido	game, match
los patines	skates
el patinaje	skating
la patineta	skateboard
la pelota	ball
las pesas	weights
la piscina	(*swimming*) pool

Cognados: el/la atleta, el béisbol, la raqueta, el tenis, el voleibol

La salud y el bienestar — Health and Wellbeing

la altura	height
el cambio	change
el dato	(piece of) information
el dolor	pain
la enfermedad	illness
la fiebre	fever
la medida	measurement
el peso	weight
la presión	(*blood*) pressure
la queja	complaint
la sangre	blood
el síntoma	symptom
la tos	cough
bajar/subir de peso	to lose/gain weight
cambiar	to change
doler (ue)	to hurt, to ache
(no) encontrarse (ue) bien	to (*not*) feel well
enfermarse	to get sick
medir (i, i)	to measure
mejorarse	to get better
quejarse	to complain
sufrir (de)	to suffer (from)
tener (*irreg.*) alergia a	to be allergic to
tomar los datos	to take down information (*medical intake*)

Cognados: las alergias, el asma (*f.*), la depresión, la infección, el insomnio, la temperatura

Los verbos

andar (*irreg.*) en patineta	to skateboard
boxear	to box
esperar	to hope; to wait (for)
esquiar (í)	to ski
ganar	to win
hacer (*irreg.*) alpinismo	to do/go mountaineering (mountain climbing)
jugar (ue) (gu)...	to play . . .
béisbol	baseball
fútbol americano	football
tenis	tennis
voleibol	volleyball
levantar pesas	to lift weights
mantenerse (*irreg.*) / ponerse (*irreg.*) en forma	to stay/get in shape
mantenerse (*irreg.*) sano	to stay healthy
patinar sobre hielo	to ice skate
recomendar (ie)	to recommend
surfear	to surf
tener (*irreg.*) éxito	to be successful

Otras palabras y expresiones útiles

ojalá (que)	I hope that

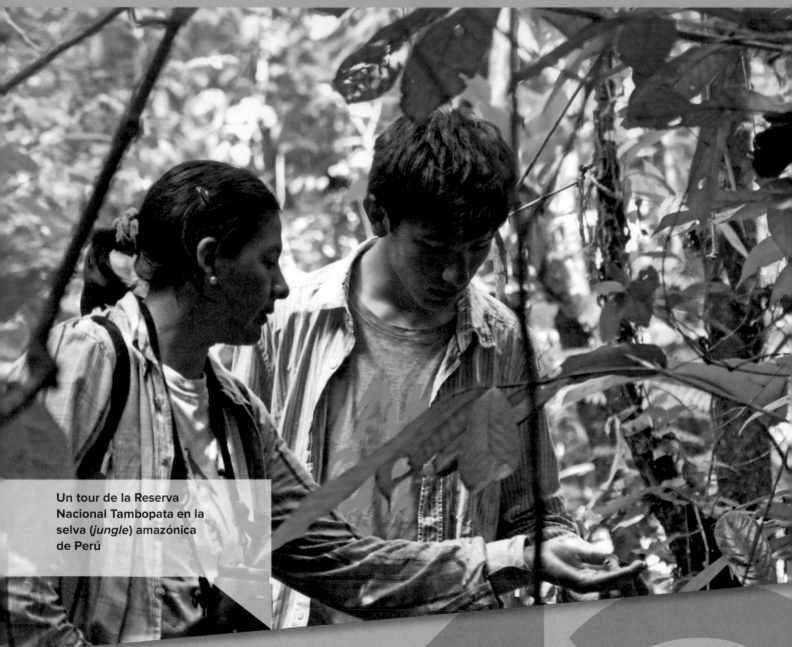

La naturaleza y el medio ambiente°

°environment

Un tour de la Reserva Nacional Tambopata en la selva (*jungle*) amazónica de Perú

Objetivos

When you finish this chapter, you will be able to:

- say what you think should happen
- say how long something has been going on
- talk about nature and the environment
- express what someone wants to happen
- express what someone thinks may not be true
- discuss nature and the environment in the Spanish-speaking world

13

www.mhhe.com/connect

COMUNICACIÓN ~~LARIO~~ ~~UCTURA~~ ~~ATE~~

Debería...

Talking about what you think someone should do

A. A ver: ¿Qué deberíamos hacer para mejorar el mundo?

PASO 1. Empareja cada frase con la palabra que describe.

1. __a__ Todos deberíamos cuidar (*take care of*) el planeta.   a. el ecologismo
2. __c__ Todos deberían ayudarse (*help each other*) y entenderse. b. el ecoturismo
3. __b__ Deberían visitar la naturaleza bonita.   c. el humanitarismo

PASO 2. Mira y escucha. Luego mira otra vez con pausas e indica si cada persona habla del **ecologismo,** del **ecoturismo** o del **humanitarismo.**

		ECOLOGISMO	ECOTURISMO	HUMANITARISMO
1.	Nelly habla del...	☐	☐	☑
2.	Yenaro habla del...	☑	☐	☐
3.	Juan Andrés habla del...	☐	☑	☐
4.	María Emilia habla del...	☑	☐	☐
5.	Enrique habla del...	☑	☐	☐
6.	Mayra habla del...	☐	☐	☑

PASO 3. Mira y escucha otra vez con pausas. Luego indica qué sugiere cada uno. Mira otra vez para verificar tus respuestas.

1. __a__ Nelly dice que todos deberíamos...
2. __f__ Yenaro dice que todos deberíamos...
3. __d__ Juan Andrés dice que todos deberíamos...
4. __b__ Maria Emilia dice que todos deberíamos...
5. __c__ Enrique dice que todos deberíamos...
6. __e__ Mayra dice que todos deberíamos...

a. ayudarnos los unos a los otros.
b. cuidar el agua y poner la basura en el lugar apropiado.
c. cuidar el planeta.
d. hacer el turismo sin dañar el medio ambiente (*environment*).
e. servirle a la humanidad y servirles a las personas.
f. tratar de no contaminar más el medio ambiente.

llevar una vida más... una vida más sana, una vida más... más progresiva. Que... que no pierdan el tiempo en... con cosas que no tienen que perderlas. Que sigan adelante con sus estudios y que se preparen mucho para que lleguen a ser grandes profesionales, no por ganar dinero, sino por servirle a la humanidad y servirles a las personas.

Video track (Act. A): This video clip can be found on the DVD to accompany *Conéctate: Cap. 13*, Track 1.

Videoscript (Act. A): 1. NELLY: *Así debería de ser el mundo, que cada uno nos ayudáramos los unos a los otros, y el mundo pues, no estaría tan malo.* **2.** YENARO: *Deberíamos, eh, tratar de no contaminar más el medio ambiente, tratar de no deforestarlo más de lo que está, eh, tratar de educar a los jóvenes, a los niños, cómo preservarlo. Sí. No destruir el hábitat y no matar las especies de animales.* **3.** JUAN ANDRÉS: *Ecoturismo es el turismo con el cual se tiene... se tiene relación con el medio ambiente, pero sin dañarlo. Es venir acá a lo que es el bosque, observar el bosque, aprender del bosque, pero sin tener ningún impacto en lo que es el medio ambiente.* **4.** MARÍA EMILIA: *Deberíamos como cuidar mucho la basura —en qué lugar se va a poner la basura. Y luego el agua. Debemos cuidar mucho el agua, no ensuciar ríos. A parte de eso como siempre que no vamos a usar el agua, cerrarla para que no... o sea, para siempre tener agua, debemos hacer eso, pienso.* **5.** ENRIQUE: *Pues la verdad creo que la ecología debería ser un gran valor, cuidar el planeta porque no tenemos otra barca donde estar todos.* **6.** MAYRA: *Que sigan avanzando en el estudio y que ahora el que no estudia, no progresa porque el estudio es una base fundamental para... para*

To talk about what you think you or someone else should or should not do, use a form of **(no) debería** + *infinitive*.

Debería andar en bicicleta en vez de coche.	I should ride my bike instead of driving.
Deberíamos reciclar.	We ought to recycle.
No deberías contaminar.	You shouldn't pollute.
Deberían cuidar el planeta.	They should take care of the planet.

Note (Act. B): Grammar references sometimes say that *debería de* + *infinitive* should be used to talk about future possibility or probability (not what should happen), but many native speakers use *debería de* synonymously with *debería,* as we hear Nelly do in the video.

B. ¿Qué deberíamos hacer? Empareja la imagen con la cita (*quote*) más adecuada.

1. __a__ «Deberíamos ahorrar (*save*) agua.»
2. __d__ «Deberíamos evitar (*avoid*) el uso excesivo de electricidad.»
3. __b__ «Deberíamos hacer abono (*fertilizer*) con los desechos (*waste*) orgánicos.»
4. __e__ «Deberíamos proteger (*protect*) el mar.»
5. __c__ «Deberíamos reciclar.»
6. __f__ «Deberíamos usar menos los coches.»

a.　　　　　b.　　　　　c.

d.　　　　　e.　　　　　f.

Suggestion (Act. C): Have students share their suggestions with the class; make a list of the different ideas on the board or on an overhead. Ask: *¿Qué sugerencias son particulares a un campus universitario? ¿Cuáles se aplican a cualquier (any) lugar?*

C. ¿Qué deberían hacer los nuevos estudiantes? En parejas, decidan qué deberían hacer los nuevos estudiantes que quieren participar en diversas actividades. Luego compartan sus respuestas con la clase.

¿Qué debería hacer un nuevo estudiante o una nueva estudiante que quiere...

1. comprar productos de bajo impacto ambiental (*low environmental impact*)?
2. ahorrar (*save*) agua?
3. hacer abono con los desechos orgánicos de la cafetería y los restaurantes de la universidad?
4. reciclar el papel y los plásticos del campus?

Expansion (Act C): Have students use *Debería...* to make more general suggestions for new students adapting to campus life. Where should they study, eat, work out, go off campus, and so on?

¿Cuánto tiempo hace que... ?

Expressing how long you've been doing something

To ask someone how long they have been doing something, use one of these expressions. Recall that you learned the present participle (the **-ndo** forms) with the present progressive in **Estructura 11.3.**

¿Cuánto tiempo lleva(s) + *present participle*?
¿Cuánto tiempo hace que + *present tense*?

¿Cuánto tiempo llevas reciclando?
¿Cuánto tiempo hace que reciclas? } How long have you been recycling?

To respond, you can use one of these expressions.

Llevo + *time expression* + *present participle*.
Hace + *time expression* + *present tense*.

Llevo tres años reciclando.
Hace tres años que reciclo. } I've been recycling for three years.

To express that something *hasn't* happened for a certain period of time, you can use one of these.

Llevo + *time expression* + **sin** + *infinitive*.
Hace + *time expression* + **que no** + *present tense*.

Llevo tres años sin usar bolsas de plástico.
Hace tres años que no uso bolsas de plástico. } I haven't used plastic bags for three years. / It's been three years since I've used plastic bags.

Here are some useful time expressions.

toda la vida — all my (your/his/her) life; all our (your/their/our) lives

mucho tiempo — a long time

A. La historia de la ecología
Lee las siguientes oraciones. Luego completa las oraciones para decir cuántos años hace (*how many years it's been*) que pasan estas cosas. **¡Atención!** ¡Vas a tener que hacer un poco de matemática!

1. En 1962, la Fundación Charles Darwin estableció una estación de investigación (*research*) en las islas Galápagos.
   Hace _____ años que los científicos (*scientists*) de la Fundación Charles Darwin estudian los animales de las islas Galápagos.

2. En 1977, el presidente Jimmy Carter instaló los primeros paneles solares en la Casa Blanca de los Estados Unidos.
   Hace _____ años que se usan paneles solares en la Casa Blanca.

3. En 1996, se fundó la organización Amazon Watch para proteger los bosques tropicales de Colombia, Ecuador, Perú y Brasil.
   La organización Amazon Watch **lleva _____ años trabajando** para proteger los bosques tropicales.

4. En 2005, la Universidad de Puerto Rico en Humacao empezó su programa de reciclaje (*recycling*).
   Los estudiantes de la Universidad de Puerto Rico en Humacao **llevan _____ años reciclando.**

5. En 2011, la energía eólica (*wind*) se convirtió en la principal industria enérgica en España.
   Hace _____ años que la energía eólica es la fuente (*source*) de energía más usada en España.

Answers (Act. A): **1.** current year minus 1962 **2.** current year minus 1977 **3.** current year minus 1996 **4.** current year minus 2005 **5.** current year minus 2011

CONÉCTATE AL MUNDO PROFESIONAL

Numbers are basic, but challenging to manipulate in any language other than your first. Everyday life provides a lot of opportunities to practice working with numbers in Spanish, such as calculating tips, prices per share, shares purchasable with a given amount to invest, workout data, distance to travel, and miles per gallon.

CONÉCTATE AL MUNDO HISPANO

El lago Enriquillo en la República Dominicana siempre ha sido el lago más grande del Caribe. Pero últimamente le pasa algo muy raro: se está haciendo más grande todavía. En 2004, el lago cubría (*covered*) 164 kilómetros cuadrados (102 millas cuadradas), pero diez años después, se había duplicado el tamaño: hasta 350 kilómetros cuadrados (217 millas cuadradas). El lago tenía tres islas, pero dos de ellas ya desaparecieron bajo el agua. Nadie sabe cuál es la causa, pero parece que el cambio climático es uno de los factores. El agua del mar Caribe se ha calentado (*gotten warmer*), y eso ha provocado un aumento (*increase*) en la cantidad de lluvia. Muchos campos (*fields*) agrícolas se han inundado (*flooded*) y miles de familias han sido desplazadas (*displaced*).

Expansion (Act. B):
- After students have completed *Paso 3,* ask for a show of hands to see who does each activity in *Paso 1.* Then ask for volunteers to tell you why they started doing the activities. For example, do they ride bikes because they're on a college campus and have no car or out of concern for the environment?
- Have each student make a list of 5 things they do (such as *jugar tenis, estudiar español, vivir en una residencia estudiantil*). Then, for each item on the list, have them ask around to find another classmate that does the same: *¿Juegas tenis?* When they find someone who does the

B. Actividades a favor del medio ambiente

PASO 1.   Indica todas las actividades ecológicas en que participas.

☐ comer comidas orgánicas
☐ comprar productos de bajo impacto ambiental
☐ conducir un auto eléctrico o híbrido
☐ ahorrar agua
☐ evitar el uso excesivo de electricidad
☐ hacer abono de los desechos orgánicos de la cocina
☐ llevar bolsas (*bags*) reusables al supermercado

☐ reciclar (el papel, las botellas, el cartón [*cardboard*], las latas [*cans*], etcétera)
☐ trabajar con organizaciones ecologistas
☐ transportarse en bicicleta en lugar de en coche

PASO 2.   Para cada actividad del **Paso 1** en que participas, di cuánto tiempo llevas haciéndola.

1. ¿Cuánto tiempo hace que comes comidas orgánicas? ____
2. ¿Cuánto tiempo llevas comprando productos de bajo impacto ambiental? ____
3. ¿Cuánto tiempo hace que conduces un auto eléctrico o híbrido? ____
4. ¿Cuánto tiempo hace que intentas ahorrar agua? ____
5. ¿Cuánto tiempo llevas ahorrando electricidad? ____
6. ¿Cuánto tiempo llevas guardando los desechos orgánicos en el jardín? ____
7. ¿Cuánto tiempo hace que usas bolsas reusables para tus compras? ____
8. ¿Cuánto tiempo hace que vas y vienes en bicicleta? ____
9. ¿Cuánto tiempo hace que reciclas? ____
10. ¿Cuánto tiempo llevas trabajando con una organización ecologista? ____

PASO 3.   En parejas, túrnense para hacer y contestar preguntas sobre su participación en las actividades del **Paso 1.** Si no participas en una actividad, debes decirlo.

MODELO: E1: ¿Cuánto tiempo hace que reciclas? / ¿Cuánto tiempo llevas reciclando?
E2: Hace cinco años que reciclo. / Llevo cinco años reciclando. / Nunca reciclo.

C. Todos somos ecologistas
Contesta las preguntas para decir cuántos años estas personas llevan haciendo cosas que benefician al medio ambiente.

MODELO: ¿La ciudad tiene un programa de reciclaje? (1990)
Hace ____ años que la ciudad tiene un programa de reciclaje.

1. ¿Cuántos años lleva Teresa usando transporte público en vez de conducir? (2013)

    _____

2. ¿Cuánto tiempo hace que tu tío conduce un auto híbrido? (2003)

    _____

3. ¿Cuánto tiempo llevan participando en el club de ecologistas? (2009)

    _____

4. ¿Hace mucho tiempo que tu familia usa abono natural en su jardín? (1998)

    Sí, _____

5. ¿Las tiendas de tu barrio todavía ofrecen bolsas de plástico a sus clientes? (2012: no ofrecer)

    No, _____

same thing, they should ask how long they have been doing it (*¿Cuánto tiempo hace que... ?* or *¿Cuánto tiempo llevas... ?*). Have them take notes on who does the same things they do so they can report back to the class something that they and another classmate do and how long they've been doing it.

La naturaleza y el medio ambiente

Nature and the environment

A. Nuestro medio ambiente Lee las siguientes descripciones y emparéjalas con la imagen que mejor corresponde a cada una.

1. Hay varias causas de la **deforestación.**

   <u>b</u> El descuido (*carelessness*) de una persona con un cigarrillo puede **causar** la quema (*burning*) de **bosques** enteros, matando (*killing*) muchos árboles y **animales.**

   <u>a</u> La agricultura y la ganadería (*ranching*) ocupan mucha **tierra**, lo cual requiere la **tala de árboles** y la **destrucción** de bosques. **La consecuencia**: bosques como la **selva** amazónica están en **peligro** (*danger*).

   <u>c</u> Al **destruir** tantos árboles, la cadena alimenticia (*food chain*) sufre porque muchos animales dependen de los árboles para comer.

   <u>d</u> **El daño** (*damage*) a los árboles puede causar gran efecto sobre todo tipo de animales y plantas que puede llegar hasta la **extinción** de **las especies.**

a. b.

c. d.

2. El **planeta Tierra** está en peligro.

   <u>d</u> La **contaminación** del **aire** y la **atmósfera** lleva (*leads*) al **calentamiento global**; es decir, la temperatura del planeta sube y **el clima** cambia.

   <u>c</u> Las temperaturas del agua del mar están subiendo también, **una situación** relacionada con el derretimiento (*melting*) de los icebergs.

   <u>b</u> El cambio climático puede causar otros problemas **ecológicos** graves, como **la sequía** (cuando no llueve por mucho tiempo).

   <u>a</u> También puede causar **las tormentas** muy fuertes como **huracanes*** que muchas veces causan **inundaciones*** (un exceso de agua que pone calles, coches y casas bajo el agua).

a. b.

c. d.

3. Hay que **cuidar** la Tierra.

   <u>c</u> Varios grupos de **activistas** luchan para **proteger** el medio ambiente, **prohibir** la contaminación y **salvar** los animales.

   <u>d</u> Algunos activistas quieren **conservar** las plantas y los animales **marinos**, que sufren a causa de los productos químicos y la basura que ponemos en el mar.

   <u>a</u> La **ecología** del mar es un **sistema** complejo: un mundo entero existe dentro de un **arrecife** (*reef*): corales, plantas y peces.

   <u>b</u> Los humanos pueden **participar** en la **protección** del mar si asumen la **responsabilidad** de la basura que producen en vez de tirarla al mar.

a. b.

c. d.

(*Continues*)

*La forma singular de **huracanes** es **huracán** y la forma singular de **inundaciones** es **inundación.**

a.

b.

c.

d.

4. A mucha gente le gusta visitar los parques nacionales y reservas naturales.

    _c_ Allí tienen vistas panorámicas de las montañas, el mar o el desierto, y los animales **salvajes** que viven allí.

    _a_ Sin embargo, la **disminución** de importantes **recursos naturales** como el agua, la madera y el petróleo pone en peligro estos paisajes bonitos y el planeta entero.

    _b_ Si los grandes países y sus industrias **explotan** los recursos naturales sin **una obligación** correspondiente de conservar, vamos a ver el **agotamiento** de los bosques y el agua dulce (*fresh*), y sin árboles y agua no podemos vivir.

    _d_ Dependemos de la naturaleza, la tierra y el agua del planeta. Por eso, deberíamos buscar soluciones **sostenibles** para mantener el planeta verde y saludable.

Suggestion (Act. B): Name animals from the list and have students mention problems from the *Vocabulario* presentation (*La naturaleza y el medio ambiente*), or other problems they can verbalize, that might affect each one.

Script (Act. C): 1. Participar en un programa de reciclaje es una manera de conservar el medio ambiente. **2.** El turismo ecológico apoya la economía y conserva los recursos naturales. **3.** Los animales salvajes viven en casas con familias. **4.** La protección de los recursos naturales causa la contaminación. **5.** La conservación de los bosques es importante para una atmósfera limpia. **6.** Los animales marinos son la causa de muchos problemas ecológicos.

B. Las especies en peligro de extinción.   ¿Reconoces estos animales?

Escribe el nombre del animal que corresponde a cada foto, basándote en su nombre en inglés.

el delfín   el mono   el pingüino

el león marino   el perezoso   la tortuga

el loro (el pájaro)   el mono   **el oso**

el perezoso   **el sapo**   la tortuga

la ballena   el delfín   el león marino   el pingüino

C. ¿Es lógica o no?   Escucha cada afirmación e indica si es lógica (L) o ilógica (I).

1. _L_   3. _I_   5. _L_

2. _L_   4. _I_   6. _I_

D. A ver: Los temas más importantes

PASO 1. Algunas personas van a presentar sus ideas sobre los problemas medioambientales más graves. Mira el video. Luego mira otra vez con pausas y completa cada frase con la mejor expresión.

1. __b__ Para Óscar, de Costa Rica, la causa medioambiental más importante es...

   a. la conservación de los arrecifes.
   b. la conservación del ecosistema.
   c. la protección del mar y la playa.

2. __c__ Para Cinthya, de Costa Rica, es importante...

   a. la conservación de los bosques.
   b. la protección de las especies en peligro de extinción.
   c. el reciclaje.

3. __b__ Para Yenaro, de Costa Rica, es importante...

   a. la conservación de los bosques.
   b. la protección de las especies en peligro de extinción.
   c. el reciclaje.

4. __c__ Para Andrea, de México, la causa medioambiental más importante es...

   a. el calentamiento global.
   b. la explotación de los recursos naturales.
   c. la protección del medio ambiente.

5. __c__ Luis, de Panamá, está preocupado por...

   a. el calentamiento global.
   b. la enseñanza sobre el medio ambiente.
   c. la explotación de un recurso natural en particular: la naturaleza.

6. __b__ Para Magdalena, de Argentina, es importante...

   a. la conservación de los arrecifes.
   b. la conservación de la naturaleza y el paisaje.
   c. la protección del mar y la playa.

7. __c__ Para Victorino, de Costa Rica, es importante...

   a. la conservación de los bosques.
   b. la protección del medio ambiente.
   c. el reciclaje.

8. __b__ Para Henry, de Costa Rica, es importante...

   a. el calentamiento global.
   b. la enseñanza sobre el medio ambiente.
   c. la explotación de los recursos naturales.

PASO 2. Mira el video otra vez con pausas. Según sus intereses, ¿qué debería hacer cada persona del video?

1. __f (d)__ Óscar debería...
2. __d__ Cinthya debería...
3. __g__ Yenaro debería...
4. __b__ Andrea debería...
5. __c__ Luis debería...
6. __h__ Magdalena debería...
7. __e (d)__ Victorino debería...
8. __a__ Henry debería...

a. empezar un programa sobre la diversidad de los bosques y la protección del medio ambiente.
b. fundar una compañía que proteja el mundo ecológico.
c. participar en el turismo ecológico de alguna manera.
d. participar en un programa que promueva el reciclaje para contaminar menos con basura.
e. promover (*promote*) el uso de menos plástico.
f. sembrar (*plant*) árboles.
g. trabajar en un lugar que proteja las especies en peligro de extinción.
h. trabajar para el sistema de parques nacionales.

que también ha causado un poco el medio ambiente; por ejemplo, el calentamiento global ha afectado a este bosque que es uno de los bosques más increíbles que hay en el mundo.

(Continues)

Video track (Act. D): This video clip can be found on the DVD to accompany *Conéctate: Cap. 13,* Track 2.

Videoscript (Act. D, Paso 1):
1. ÓSCAR: *Entonces estamos con muchos programas de reciclaje, siembra de árboles. Lo bueno es que es un país muy protegido en zonas de bosques porque aquí, aunque sea privado, el gobierno les paga para que no hagan nada... conservar el ecosistema. Entonces eso para mí es muy importante porque, sí, escuché una vez que Costa Rica es un filtro de aire en Centroamérica.*
2. CINTHYA: *Sí, como cada cosa que se pueda reciclar, mucho mejor, porque hay menos contaminación con basura.* **3.** YENARO: *Hay muchos que están en peligro de extinción. Por ejemplo, de eso se trata este lugar —de tratar de reproducir más las especies y tratar de reintroducirlas otra vez al bosque nuevamente.*
4. ANDREA: *Pues sí, creo que me gustaría, lo que más me gustaría hacer es eh... ser, estar en algún tipo de compañía que protege el medio ambiente, que es lo que más me gusta, y pues realmente poder viajar por el mundo y estar protegiendo, pues animales y ballenas y realmente todo el mundo ecológico, es lo que más me gustaría.* **5.** LUIS: *En Costa Rica están más enfocado al, la, el turismo ecológico, y aparte de que en Costa Rica tienen años en explotar ese recurso, la naturaleza y todo lo demás.* **6.** MAGDALENA: *Y la atracción más grande creo que es la naturaleza y el paisaje eh... hay un parque nacional.* **7.** VICTORINO: *Monteverde está con la idea de impulsar el reciclaje. Entonces, por ejemplo, en mi casa usamos poco plástico. Poco.* **8.** HENRY: *Acá para nosotros lo más importante es enseñar a la gente lo que significa la diversidad de Costa Rica y también la naturaleza en sí que se tiene que cuidar. Y la problemática*

PASO 3. Explícale a un compañero / una compañera con quién del video tienes más en común y por qué. Usa la información del **Paso 1** para formar tus respuestas.

MODELO: Tengo más en común con ____ porque los/las dos (ninguno de los/las dos)...

E. A cuidar y disfrutar del planeta

PASO 1. De las siguientes actividades, ¿cuáles te gustaría hacer?

Me gustaría...

☐ cuidar las playas y el mar
☐ disfrutar de la naturaleza
☐ participar en el turismo ecológico
☐ pasar tiempo al aire libre
☐ proteger los animales salvajes

☐ trabajar en una compañía que proteja el medio ambiente
☐ trabajar de voluntario/a para cuidar el planeta
☐ ver el paisaje de un parque nacional

PASO 2. En grupos, dense consejos sobre qué deberían hacer para impulsar sus metas medioambientales personales. Usen la estructura **debería** + *infinitivo*.

MODELO: Si a ti te gustaría trabajar de voluntario/a para cuidar el planeta, entonces *deberías ponerte* en contacto con una organización local para limpiar parques en tu comunidad.

F. El medio ambiente en las noticias

PASO 1. Lee los siguientes titulares (*headlines*) de varios periódicos y revistas. En grupos, hagan una lista de por lo menos diez palabras del **Vocabulario** que esperarían (*you would expect*) leer en cada artículo. Luego comparen sus listas con otro grupo.

1. **Huracanes amenazan° la costa** — *threaten*

2. **La tala masiva de árboles sigue en las selvas**

3. **Grupo estudiantil recauda fondos° para la protección de las especies** — *raises funds*

4. **Nueva ley protege la naturaleza del país**

5. **El turismo: ¿ayuda o daña al medio ambiente?**

6. **¿Estamos reciclando? Nuevo estudio pone en duda la mayoría de los programas de reciclaje**

7. La explotación de recursos naturales a nivel mundial sigue en aumento

8. **Nuevo estudio científico dice que están muriendo los arrecifes a un ritmo alarmante**

PASO 2. En parejas, escojan uno de los titulares del **Paso 1** y escriban el primer párrafo del artículo. Intenten usar todas las palabras de la lista que su grupo formó para ese titular. Cuando leen el artículo a los otros estudiantes, ¿pueden identificar el titular del **Paso 1**?

PASO 3. En parejas, piensen en un tema medioambiental que les importe mucho y escriban un titular para un artículo sobre el tema. Luego consideren las siguientes preguntas y escriban el primer párrafo del artículo.

¿Por qué se considera «noticia» este tema? ¿Por qué es un problema esta situación? ¿Cuáles son los datos más importantes que deben incluir? ¿Cuáles son los factores que contribuyen al problema?

Possible Answers (Act. F, Paso 1): **1.** *el calentamiento global, el clima, el daño, la especie, la inundación, el mar, el peligro; medioambiental* **2.** *el agotamiento, el bosque, el calentamiento global, el clima, el daño, la deforestación, la ecología, el medio ambiente, la tierra; conservar, cuidar, explotar, proteger* **3.** *el/la activista, la ecología, el ecoturismo, la extinción, el planeta, los recursos naturales, la selva; LOS ANIMALES: el pájaro, la ballena, el delfín, el león marino, el loro, el mono, el sapo, la tortuga; ayudar, conservar, cuidar, proteger* **4.** *el bosque, la contaminación, el daño, la deforestación, la disminución, el ecoturismo, la especie, la extinción, el medio ambiente, el peligro, la selva, la tala de árboles; ayudar, conservar, cuidar, proteger* **5.** *la contaminación, el daño, la disminución, la ecología, el ecoturismo, la especie, el medio ambiente, los recursos naturales; ahorrar, ayudar, conservar, cuidar, explotar, proteger; ecológico, medioambiental, sostenible* **6.** *el agotamiento, el reciclaje, los recursos naturales; ayudar, conservar, cuidar, proteger, reciclar; sostenible* **7.** *el agotamiento, la contaminación, el daño, la deforestación, la disminución, la ecología, el medio ambiente, la naturaleza, el planeta; ahorrar, ayudar, conservar, cuidar, explotar, proteger, reciclar; ecológico, sostenible* **8.** *el agotamiento, el calentamiento global, el clima, la contaminación, el daño, la disminución, la especie, la extinción; ayudar, cuidar, proteger*

Follow-up (Act. E, Paso 2): Ask students what environment-related activities they participate in already. Then ask how long they've been doing them, using *¿Cuánto tiempo llevas... ?* and *¿Cuánto tiempo hace que... ?*

Suggestion (Act. F): Assign each group a few *titulares* to ensure that they all get covered.

Suggestion (Act. F): Have students do Internet searches for these headlines or similar ones and read the first paragraph as models for writing.

⟳ Reciclaje

Present indicative: Verbs with irregular **yo** forms

Note (Reciclaje): Verbs with irregular yo forms (*conocer, decir, hacer, oír, poner, saber, salir, tener, traer,* and *venir*) were first presented in *Estructura 5.1.*

Usa la forma **yo** del presente de indicativo del verbo más lógico para completar cada oración. Luego indica si es algo que diría (*would say*) un **jaguar,** un **pájaro** o una **tortuga** si pudiera (*if it could*) hablar. Cada verbo se puede usar solo una vez. El primer verbo ya está hecho.

decir · ir · ser
estar · poner · tener
hacer · salir · traer

	JAGUAR	PÁJARO	TORTUGA
1. «A veces _voy_ a los lagos y a los ríos a cazar (*hunt*) animales que están tomando agua.»	☑	☐	☐
2. «_Hago_ nidos (*nests*) en los árboles.»	☐	☑	☐
3. «_Tengo_ una concha (*shell*) muy dura.»	☐	☐	☑
4. «_Soy_ reptil.»	☐	☐	☑
5. «_Salgo_ de noche a cazar animales grandes y chicos.»	☑	☐	☐
6. «_Traigo_ comida al nido para los bebés.»	☐	☑	☐
7. «En la selva, _estoy_ en el punto más alto de la cadena alimenticia.»	☑	☐	☐
8. «_Digo_ pío, pío, pío.»	☐	☑	☐
9. «_Pongo_ los huevos en la arena (*sand*).»	☐	☐	☑

■ Answers to this activity are in Appendix 2 at the back of your book.

13.1 Le pedimos que no salga de los senderos° *paths*

The subjunctive: Irregular verbs

Para empezar...

El Parque Nacional Tikal es la reserva natural y cultural más famosa de Guatemala y la zona arqueológica más importante de la antigua civilización maya. Aquí hay una lista de reglas (*rules*) para los visitantes del parque, pero ¡no todas son de verdad! Indica si cada regla es **cierta** o **falsa.**

Durante su estancia (*stay*) en el Parque Nacional Tikal, le pedimos que...

	CIERTO	FALSO
1. no **haga** ningún tipo de fuego.	☑	☐
2. no **salga** de los senderos.	☑	☐
3. **sea** respetuoso con las reglas del parque.	☑	☐
4. **se vaya** inmediatamente y nunca **vuelva.**	☐	☑
5. **tenga** mucho cuidado al momento de escalar los monumentos.	☑	☐
6. **ponga** comida para los animales en los senderos.	☐	☑
7. no **haga** fotos o videos con propósitos (*purposes*) comerciales sin la autorización adecuada.	☑	☐
8. **traiga** basura de su casa y que la **deje** en el parque.	☐	☑
9. **ponga** atención a la hora. Se apaga (*turn off*) la energía eléctrica a las 21:30. Por eso, pedimos que **esté** en su hotel antes de esa hora.	☑	☐

Las ruinas del Parque Nacional Tikal, Guatemala

■ Answers to these activities are in Appendix 2 at the back of your book.

¿Por qué?

Many verbs add a **-g-** to the stem whenever the ending begins with **-o**, as in the yo form of the present indicative (such as, **pongo, salgo, tengo**), or with **-a**, as in all of the subjunctive forms (such as, **ponga, salga, tenga**). These two vowels are pronounced with the tongue in the back of the mouth. The **-g-** is also, so it smooths the transition between the stem (**pon-, sal-, ten-**) and the vowel. The vowels **-e** and **-i** are pronounced in the front of the mouth, so the **-g-** is not inserted when these vowels are added to the stem (so you have **pone, salimos, tenemos,** and so on).

Autoprueba

Provide the correct subjunctive form for these verbs.

1. traer (tú) _____
2. tener (ellos) _____
3. ir (Uds.) _____
4. ser (ella) _____
5. salir (nosotros) _____

Respuestas: **1.** traigas **2.** tengan **3.** vayan **4.** sea **5.** salgamos

■ For more verbs in the subjunctive, see **Para saber más 13.1** at the back of your book.

Una iguana en las islas Galápagos

Actividades analíticas

1 The verbs in bold in **Para empezar** are in the present subjunctive form. Use this information, as well as what you know about how the present subjunctive is formed, to conjugate these verbs.

	hacer	poner	salir	tener	traer
yo	haga	ponga	salga	tenga	traiga
tú	hagas	pongas	salgas	tengas	traigas
él/ella, Ud.	haga	ponga	salga	tenga	traiga
nosotros/as	hagamos	pongamos	salgamos	tengamos	traigamos
vosotros/as	hagáis	pongáis	salgáis	tengáis	traigáis
ellos/ellas, Uds.	hagan	pongan	salgan	tengan	traigan

2 For all of these verbs, the stem in the subjunctive contains a **-g-** that is not present in the infinitive: **hag-, pong-, salg-, teng-** and **traig-**. This stem is the same as that used in the **yo** form of the present indicative: **hago, pongo, salgo, tengo** and **traigo.** The verb **decir** (**digo** in the **yo** form of the present indicative) also forms its subjunctive in this way.

Quiero que me **digas** la verdad.   *I want you to tell me the truth.*

Es necesario que **digan** si van a pasar la noche en el parque.   *It's necessary for you (plur.) to say if you are going to spend the night in the park.*

3 Two other common irregular verbs in the subjunctive are **ir** and **ser.** Use the forms that you saw in **Para empezar** to complete these conjugations.

Suggestion (¿Por qué?): Have students insert a finger into their mouths and pronounce the vowels o/a, then e/i. With e/i, their tongue will touch their finger, but not with o/a because the tongue has moved into the back of the mouth. The g is also pronounced there, so it eases the transition to o/a.

	ir	ser
yo	vaya	sea
tú	vayas	seas
él/ella, Ud.	vaya	sea
nosotros/as	vayamos	seamos
vosotros/as	vayáis	seáis
ellos/ellas, Uds.	vayan	sean

Note (Para saber más): *Para saber más 13.1* covers more stem-changing and irregular verbs in the present subjunctive. It also explains the present perfect subjunctive.

Actividades prácticas

A. Voluntarios en las islas Galápagos   Cientos de voluntarios van a las islas Galápagos cada año para ayudar en el trabajo de conservación e investigación (*research*). Pon en orden los elementos de la siguiente conversación entre María, una coordinadora de voluntarios en la conservación, y Alicia, una voluntaria que acaba de llegar (*has just arrived*).

a. __1__ MARÍA: ¡Qué bueno que estés aquí en las islas Galápagos! ¿Estás contenta?

b. __5__ MARÍA: ¡Ah, sí! Les voy a pedir también que hagan un conteo (*count*) de las iguanas marinas que se encuentran en la isla Genovesa. Parece que ahora hay menos y estamos un poco preocupados.

c. __4__ ALICIA: Está bien. Vamos a la isla Genovesa, entonces. Ayer mencionaste algo de las iguanas en esa isla, ¿no?

d. __6__ ALICIA: Bueno, vamos a hacer el conteo. El viernes viene otro grupo de voluntarios de Quito. ¿Quieres que traigan algo en especial?

e. __3__ MARÍA: Quiero que salgan a inspeccionar los senderos en la isla Genovesa. Ha habido muchísimos turistas allí últimamente y hacen mucho daño.

f. __2__ ALICIA: ¡Muy contenta! Mañana empezamos a trabajar todos los voluntarios de mi grupo. ¿Qué quieres que hagamos?

g. __7__ MARÍA: Sí. ¿Pueden traer más folletos (*brochures*) para los turistas sobre los problemas medioambientales que tenemos aquí?

h. __8__ ALICIA: ¡Claro! Les voy a decir que los traigan.

B. Los parques nacionales

PASO 1. Primero, indica con un círculo el verbo más adecuado para completar cada oración.

1. __d__ Muchos dicen que este parque ((es) / sea) uno de los lugares más impresionantes del mundo. Las cataratas son enormes y se encuentran cerca de la triple frontera (*border*) entre Paraguay, Brasil y Argentina.

2. __b__ Para ir a este lugar, al norte de Brasil, te recomiendan que (vas / (vayas)) en un coche que está en muy buena condición, que (traes / (traigas)) una cámara y que (sacas / (saques)) fotos del famoso Salto Ángel.

3. __c__ En este lugar, es necesario que (se ponen / (se pongan)) ropa caliente en algunos meses, por el intenso frío que hace. Hay cientos de glaciares en este parque en los Andes, a ocho horas al norte de Lima.

4. __f__ ((Dicen) / Digan) que los jaguares en este lugar, en la costa caribeña de este país centroamericano, solo ((salen) / salgan) de noche.

5. __g__ Si ((tienes) / tengas) ganas de ver muchos loros y colibríes (*hummingbirds*), puedes ir a este parque, en el extremo este de la isla.

6. __e__ Si te gustan las cataratas, los jaguares y las orquídeas, te recomiendo que (vas / (vayas)) aquí. Por su ubicación entre los Andes y la zona amazónica, tiene una gran diversidad de hábitats, desde selvas hasta sabanas (*savannahs*).

7. __a__ Si quieres que tus próximas vacaciones (son / (sean)) muy interesantes, considera un viaje a este parque en la Isla de Pascua, donde puedes encontrar cráteres volcánicos y estatuas creadas por los antiguos habitantes (*inhabitants*).

PASO 2. Ahora, escoge el parque nacional que corresponde a cada descripción en el **Paso 1.** Las pistas (*clues*) geográficas y los mapas (que se encuentran después del **Appendix 2** de este libro) te pueden ayudar.

Parques Nacionales

a. Parque Nacional Rapa Nui (Chile)
b. Parque Nacional de Canaima (Venezuela)
c. Parque Nacional Huascarán (el Perú)
d. Parque Nacional de Iguazú (Argentina)
e. Parque Nacional Noel Kempff Mercado (Bolivia)

f. Reserva de la Biosfera de Río Plátano (Honduras)
g. Parque Nacional Alejandro de Humboldt (Cuba)

El Salto Ángel en el Parque Nacional de Canaima

El Parque Nacional Rapa Nui en la isla de Pascua

C. Tus prioridades para tu comunidad

PASO 1. ¿Qué quieres que haga la gente de tu comunidad para mejorar el medio ambiente? Escoge las tres ideas más importantes para ti y crea tres oraciones que expresen lo que tú quieres.

> **MODELO:** hacer más esfuerzo (*effort*) para usar el transporte público →
> Quiero que la gente haga más esfuerzo para usar el transporte público.

1. decirles a los niños que es importante cuidar el medio ambiente
2. ir al trabajo o a la escuela a pie cuando es posible
3. poner más atención al reciclaje
4. salir más a la naturaleza

5. ser más conscientes (*aware*) del impacto que tienen sobre el medio ambiente
6. tener más conocimiento sobre el turismo sostenible
7. traer botellas de agua de metal, y no de plástico

PASO 2. Ahora, en parejas, comparen sus prioridades. ¿Pueden llegar a un acuerdo sobre cuál es la máxima (*top*) prioridad para mejorar el medio ambiente?

Variation (Act. C, Paso 1): Have students do this in pairs (using *queremos* instead of *quiero*), and have each pair write the sentence for their top choice on the board. Go over the sentences as a class, looking both for grammatical form and for commonalities in answers across the class.

Expansion (Act. C): Have students work in small groups to create a list titled *Queremos que...*. They should write additional things that can be done to improve the environment.

■ Answers to this activity are in Appendix 2 at the back of your book.

Un sapo dorado

■ Answers to these activities are in Appendix 2 at the back of your book.

CONÉCTATE AL MUNDO HISPANO

El lobo (*wolf*) **mexicano** es uno de los animales del hemisferio occidental (*western*) en más peligro de extinción. Su hábitat original se extendía del norte de México hasta Arizona, Nuevo México y Texas en los Estados Unidos. Sin embargo, el lobo fue casi totalmente exterminado en el siglo veinte. En las últimas décadas, los científicos han tratado de salvar al lobo mexicano y establecerlo de nuevo en las zonas donde vivía antes. Poco a poco, lo están logrando (*achieving*). Ahora hay lobos salvajes en Arizona y Nuevo México y en 2014, anunciaron dos grandes eventos: nació la primera camada (*litter*) de lobos en libertad en México y nació la primera camada por inseminación artificial en el Zoológico de Chapultepec, en la Ciudad de México.

Note (Act. analíticas): The clause following **esperar** expresses something that, in the mind of the speaker, is probably not presently true, so it is similar to **es posible,** but it also expresses something that the speaker would like to be true, so it is similar to verbs like **querer** and **recomendar** discussed in **12.3.**

↻ Reciclaje

Meanings of **creer, esperar, pensar,** and **saber**

Empareja cada expresión con su sinónimo.

1. _d_ Creo que sí.
2. _a_ No sé.
3. _f_ Espero que no.
4. _b_ Sé que sí.
5. _c_ Espero que sí.
6. _e_ Pienso que no.

a. No tengo idea.
b. Estoy muy seguro que sí.
c. No sé si es así, pero quiero que sea así.
d. Pienso que sí.
e. No creo.
f. No sé si es así, pero no quiero que sea así.

13.2 No creen que exista ya el sapo dorado° *golden*

The subjunctive: Disbelief and uncertainty

Para empezar...

El sapo dorado vivió en el bosque de Monteverde en Costa Rica. Lo descubrieron por primera vez en 1966, pero no lo han visto desde 1989 y lo declararon extinto (*extinct*) en 2004. ¿Qué dicen los expertos de esto? Lee las siguientes oraciones: ocho son ciertas y dos son falsas. Indica cuáles son **ciertas** y cuáles son **falsas**. ¡Atención! Solo hay dos oraciones falsas.

Los expertos...

	CIERTO	FALSO
1. creen que los machos (*males*) tenían un color dorado fluorescente.	☑	☐
2. creen que las hembras (*females*) eran de un color verde oliva con manchas (*spots*) rojas.	☑	☐
3. no creen que nadie **pueda** encontrar un sapo dorado hoy día.	☑	☐
4. piensan que vivían bajo tierra la mayor parte del año.	☑	☐
5. no piensan que las demás especies de sapos y ranas (*frogs*) **estén** fuera de peligro (*out of danger*).	☑	☐
6. esperan que no **pase** lo mismo a las otras especies de ranas y sapos.	☑	☐
7. dicen que es posible que el cambio climático **sea** un factor en la extinción de los sapos y ranas.	☑	☐
8. saben que hay sapos dorados en Wyoming.	☐	☑
9. esperan que **aprendamos** algo de esta triste historia.	☑	☐
10. esperan que otras especies **tengan** el mismo futuro que el sapo dorado.	☐	☑

Expansion (Act. analíticas 1): For each of the subjunctive verb forms in *Para empezar,* ask students to say what indicates that it is subjunctive. (*Answer:* The "opposite" vowel of *pueda, estén, pase, aprendamos;* that plus the irregular stem of *sea, tengan.*)

Actividades analíticas

1 As you saw in **Estructura 12.3** with expressions of volition, certain verbs and expressions require the verb that follows to be in the subjunctive form. Based on what you saw in **Para empezar,** indicate which of the following expressions require the subjunctive.

☐ creer que...   ☑ esperar que...   ☐ saber que...
☑ no creer que...   ☐ pensar que...
☑ es posible que...   ☑ no pensar que...

2 What do the expressions that you selected in **Actividades analíticas 1** all have in common?

☐ They all express the idea that what follows is (at least in the mind of the speaker) likely true.
☑ They all express the idea that what follows may not be true.

There are many more expressions that indicate uncertainty in Spanish, including **No es obvio** (*obvious*) **que...** and **Es improbable que...**

3 Similarly, expressions such as **Es imposible que…** , **No es cierto que…** , and **No es verdad que…** also require the subjunctive because what follows them is (at least in the mind of the speaker) not true.

No es cierto que puedas ver el sapo dorado en Costa Rica.

It is not true that you can see the golden toad in Costa Rica.

Antonio piensa que **no es verdad que seas** estudiante.

Antonio thinks that it's not true that you're a student.

The expressions **Es cierto que…** , **Es verdad que…** , and **Es obvio que…** are followed by an indicative form, since they express something thought to be true.

Es cierto que eres muy buen estudiante.   *It is true that you are a very good student.*

Actividades prácticas

A. ¿De acuerdo?

PASO 1. Escucha las oraciones e indica si estás de acuerdo (**DA**) o no (**NDA**) con lo que dice.

1. ____   2. ____   3. ____   4. ____
5. ____   6. ____   7. ____   8. ____

PASO 2. Ahora explica a la clase por qué no estás de acuerdo con ciertas declaraciones.

Script (Act. A, Paso 1): 1. Creo que debemos reciclar más. 2. No pienso que el plástico sea reciclable. 3. No creo que hagamos todo lo que podamos para proteger el planeta. 4. Sé que a muchas personas les importan mucho las plantas y los animales. 5. No es posible que las tortugas y los peces vivan en agua contaminada. 6. No creo que los estudiantes deban conducir sus coches todos los días. 7. Espero que las nuevas generaciones puedan usar el transporte público más. 8. Espero que no corten todos los árboles del planeta.

B. El oso hormiguero (anteater) ¿Cuánto sabes del oso hormiguero? Indica si cada oración debe comenzar con «**Es cierto que…** » o «**No es cierto que…** ». ¡Atención! Presta atención a la forma del verbo. ¿Es indicativo o subjuntivo?

ES CIERTO QUE…	NO ES CIERTO QUE…	
☑	☐	1. come hormigas (ants) y termitas.
☑	☐	2. tiene una lengua muy larga.
☐	☑	3. sea un tipo de oso.
☐	☑	4. viva en África.
☑	☐	5. es pariente de los perezosos.
☐	☑	6. use su cola (tail) para matar hormigas.
☐	☑	7. duerma bajo el agua.
☑	☐	8. varias especies del oso hormiguero están amenazadas (threatened) por la destrucción de su hábitat.
☐	☑	9. coma pájaros.
☑	☐	10. vive solo en América.

El oso hormiguero

Note (Para saber más): *Para saber más 13.2* covers the subjunctive in adjective clauses with nonexistent or indefinite antecedents, as well as uses of the subjunctive to express emotion.

■ To learn how to use the subjunctive to describe things that don't exist, or to express how you feel about something, see **Para saber más 13.2** at the back of your book.

■ The audio files for in-text listening activities are available in the eBook, within Connect activities, and on the Online Learning Center.

Autoprueba

When you come across a new expression, consider if it implies that what follows is true or thought to be true (+), is uncertain or doubtful (?), or is not true or thought to be not true (−). This will help you know whether it is followed by the indicative (+) or the subjunctive (? and −). Try it here with these expressions. Does each one trigger the indicative or the subjunctive?

1. Estoy seguro/a de que…
2. No estoy seguro/a de que…
3. Es una mentira (a lie) que…
4. Creemos que…
5. No pensamos que…
6. Es imposible que…
7. No es probable que…

Respuestas: 1. indicative **2.** subjunctive **3.** subjunctive **4.** indicative **5.** subjunctive **6.** subjunctive **7.** subjunctive

Suggestions (Act. C, Paso 1):

- Let students make their conjectures about these animals using *Creo que* and *No creo que* based on what they know. If they are interested, you can then give them some additional facts that are not obvious: *El quetzal come insectos. El tapir tiene pelo, come plantas y pasa mucho tiempo en el agua.*
- Have students work on this in small groups (perhaps having each group work on just one animal), and then discuss the answers as a class.

Note (Act. C): Point out the symbolic importance of the quetzal in Central America, especially in Guatemala. As it can't live when caged, it's a symbol of freedom and independence. The name is used for the national currency of Guatemala and the image appears on the country's flag.

Creo que los pingüinos son lindos.

Note (Act. D): Answers will vary but likely answers include the following: **1.** *No creo que haya...* **2.** *Creo que viven...* **3.** *No creo que vivan...* **4.** *No creo que vayan...* **5.** *No creo que trabajen...* **6.** *Espero que tengan...* **7.** *Sé que comen...* **8.** *Espero que tengan...*

Suggestion (Act. D): Break students into groups and assign each group one of the other animals from this chapter (such as *el oso, la tortuga,* or *la ballena*). Have the groups create sentences for their animal using the expressions *creo que, no creo que, espero que,* and *sé que.* Then, have the groups research their animal online to find the answers and report back to the class.

C. Cuatro especies

PASO 1. Las siguientes cuatro especies son muy interesantes, pero no son muy conocidas fuera de su región. En parejas, crean oraciones usando **Creo que** y **No creo que** y las seis frases que siguen para comentar sobre los animales.

El cóndor andino
Distribución: Cordillera de los Andes
Estado de conservación: No amenazado

El quetzal
Distribución: México, Centroamérica
Estado de conservación: Amenazado

El lince (*lynx*) **ibérico**
Distribución: España
Estado de conservación: En peligro de extinción

El tapir
Distribución: Centroamérica, Sudamérica
Estado de conservación: Amenazado

> **MODELO:** vuela / vuele →
> E1: No creo que el tapir vuele.
> E2: Yo tampoco, pero creo que el quetzal vuela.

1. pasa / pase mucho tiempo en el agua
2. come / coma carne
3. vive / viva en Europa
4. pone / ponga huevos
5. tiene / tenga pelo
6. vuela / vuele

PASO 2. Piensa en un animal del que sabes mucho. Dile a un compañero / una compañera dos oraciones ciertas y dos oraciones falsas sobre el animal. Tu compañero/a debe decir **Es cierto que...** o **No es cierto que...** para cada oración. Si no está seguro/a, puede decir **Es posible que...**

> **MODELO:** E1: Los conejos (*rabbits*) comen carne.
> E2: No es cierto que los conejos coman carne.
> E1: Los conejos tienen el pelo muy suave.
> E2: Es cierto que los conejos tienen el pelo muy suave.

D. Los pingüinos

Crea ocho oraciones sobre los pingüinos usando las siguientes expresiones y las oraciones que siguen. **¡Atención!** En algunos casos, tienes que cambiar el verbo al subjuntivo.

> Sé que...   Creo que...   Espero que...   No creo que...

> **MODELO:** Los pingüinos son pájaros. → Sé que los pingüinos son pájaros.

1. Hay pingüinos azules y rojos.
2. Viven en Argentina, Chile, el Perú y las islas Galápagos.
3. Viven en Bolivia y en el Polo Norte.
4. Van a México durante el verano.
5. Trabajan en restaurantes como camareros.
6. Tienen una vida muy feliz.
7. Comen mucho pescado.
8. Tienen un futuro seguro.

Ecuador   Bolivia

E. Cultura: Las luchas (*struggles*) ecológicas en Ecuador y Bolivia

PASO 1.   Lee el texto sobre Ecuador y Bolivia.

Los países de Ecuador y Bolivia tienen mucho en común. Los dos tienen sitios naturales espectaculares y diversos, como las islas Galápagos y los altiplanos[a] en Ecuador, y en Bolivia el lago Titicaca, la Laguna Verde y el salar[b] de Uyuni. En los dos países hay selvas amazónicas. Los dos países también cuentan con[c] grandes poblaciones indígenas que hablan una variedad de lenguas. Pero lamentablemente, desde la época de la Conquista española hasta hoy en día, los habitantes de los dos países han tenido que luchar en contra del imperialismo. El imperialismo del último siglo no solo es una conquista de la cultura autóctona,[d] sino[e] también del medio ambiente y los recursos naturales.

Desde 1971 hasta 1992, la gran empresa petrolera[f] transnacional Texaco se juntó[g] con el gobierno de Ecuador para extraer petróleo de la región amazónica y construir el Oleoducto[h] Transecuatoriano. Ahora este proyecto es conocido por muchos como «el peor desastre petrolero del mundo». Según algunas fuentes,[i] la empresa contaminó las aguas de la zona con casi 20 mil millones[j] de galones de residuo[k] tóxico. Además, del oleoducto se derramaron[l] casi 17 millones de galones de petróleo crudo. Como resultado, en las comunidades afectadas por la contaminación se aumentó drásticamente el número de casos de cáncer, enfermedades dermatológicas, problemas reproductivos y defectos de nacimiento.[m]

Los problemas medioambientales en Bolivia también se conectan con el agua, pero de otra forma. A finales de los años 90, el gobierno boliviano (siguiendo los requisitos[n] del Banco Mundial[ñ]) firmó dos tratos[o] para privatizar el suministro y saneamiento[p] del agua. Les vendió a corporaciones transnacionales los sistemas de agua municipales de La Paz y de Cochabamba. Como resultado, el precio del agua subió[q] bastante y la gente pobre perdió el acceso natural que tenían a diferentes fuentes de agua potable. En 2000, hubo protestas violentas en la ciudad de Cochabamba.* En 2006, el nuevo presidente Evo Morales declaró que «El agua no puede ser un negocio privado porque [...] se estaría[r] violando los derechos[s] humanos».

[a]*high plateaus* [b]*salt flat* [c]*cuentan... have* [d]*native* [e]*but* [f]*empresa... oil company* [g]*se... joined up with* [h]*Pipeline* [i]*sources* [j]*mil... billions* [k]*waste* [l]*se... spilled* [m]*birth* [n]*requirements* [ñ]*World* [o]*firmó... signed two accords* [p]*suministro... supply and sanitation* [q]*went up* [r]*se... it would be* [s]*rights*

El lago Titicaca, Bolivia

Note (Act. E, Paso 1): The events discussed here are complex and there are many differing accounts of what happened and why. Encourage students to research these topics more deeply and reach their own conclusions.

PASO 2.   Ahora lee cada declaración y selecciona la frase adecuada para indicar si estás de acuerdo o no. Luego completa la oración con la forma correcta del indicativo o el subjuntivo del verbo entre paréntesis.

1. (Creo / No creo) que las empresas petroleras _deben/deban_ (deber) extraer petróleo de las zonas amazónicas.
2. (Pienso / No pienso) que Texaco-Chevron _es/sea_ (ser) el responsable del desastre petrolero.
3. (Es cierto / No es cierto) que la contaminación del agua con residuo tóxico _causa/cause_ (causar) problemas de la salud entre los habitantes.
4. (Es verdad / No es verdad) que las corporaciones transnacionales _quieren/quieran_ (querer) explotar la mano de obra (*workforce*) y los recursos naturales de los países más pobres.
5. (Estoy seguro/a / No estoy seguro/a) que limitar el acceso que una comunidad tiene al agua _viola/viole_ (violar) los derechos humanos de esa comunidad.
6. (Es verdad / No es verdad) que Ecuador y Bolivia _tienen/tengan_ (tener) que luchar para proteger su naturaleza y su herencia (*heritage*) cultural.

PASO 3.   En parejas, contesten las preguntas y explíquense las respuestas.

1. Muchas veces, los países que aceptan que las grandes empresas transnacionales trabajen en zonas ecológicamente delicadas son países de pocos recursos (*resources*) económicos, como Bolivia y Ecuador. ¿Por qué crees que es así?
2. Los residentes de Bolivia y Ecuador causan mucho menos daño al planeta que los residentes de países como los Estados Unidos o Canadá. Por ejemplo, tienen una huella (*footprint*) de carbono muy baja. ¿Por qué crees que es así?
3. En tu país, ¿los grandes proyectos que pueden hacer daño al medio ambiente, como las minas o la extracción petrolera, también ocurren frecuentemente en zonas relativamente pobres?

Note (Act. E, Paso 3): Economically disadvantaged countries, or regions of a country, are often the ones that accept projects that are environmentally risky, because they have a great need for outside investment and such offers are very tempting.

*Estas protestas son el trasfondo (*background*) de la película *También la lluvia*, que vas a ver en la sección **Conéctate al cine** del **Capítulo 14.**

⟳ Reciclaje

Para and *por*

Empareja las frases para hacer oraciones completas lógicas, completándolas con **para** o **por**.

_c_ 1. Reciclamos papel...
_e_ 2. Ahorramos agua...
_d_ 3. Mantenemos los parques...
_f_ 4. Va a haber cambios climáticos...
_a_ 5. El huracán Mitch pasó...
_b_ 6. La contaminación causa muchos problemas...

a. _por_ Honduras en 1998.
b. _para_ los bosques.
c. _para_ no tener que cortar tantos árboles.
d. _para_ conservar la diversidad de zonas ecológicas.
e. _por_ la sequía en los últimos años.
f. _por_ el calentamiento global.

■ Answers to this activity are in Appendix 2 at the back of your book.

Una tortuga marina en Costa Rica

■ Answers to these activities are in Appendix 2 at the back of your book.

13.3 **Para que las tortugas puedan sobrevir°** *survive*

The subjunctive: Purpose and contingency

Para empezar...

Todas las especies de tortugas marinas están en peligro de extinción. Un grupo de biólogos (*biologists*) en Costa Rica ha tomado varias medidas (*measures*) para tratar de prevenir (*prevent*) la extinción de estas tortugas. Empareja cada medida con el objetivo más lógico. **¡Atención!** Cada objetivo solo se puede usar una vez.

MEDIDA	OBJETIVO
1. _b_ No usan luz en la playa de noche...	a. para que **entren** al mar.
2. _d_ Cuando las tortugas ponen huevos en la arena (*sand*), los conservacionistas los sacan...	b. para que las tortugas **lleguen** a la playa sin miedo (*without fear*) a poner los huevos en la arena.
3. _g_ Guardan los huevos en un lugar de temperatura controlada...	c. para que las tortugas **tengan** playas sin gente para poner sus huevos.
4. _a_ Cuando los bebés salen del huevo, los ponen en la playa...	d. para que los perros no los **coman.**
5. _c_ Tratan de limitar el uso turístico de la costa...	e. para que no **usen** los huevos de las tortugas como alimento.
6. _e_ Tratan de educar a la gente...	f. para que las tortugas **puedan** sobrevivir en el futuro.
7. _f_ Hacen todo esto...	g. para que **se desarrollen** (*develop*) bien.

Actividades analíticas

1 Based on what you saw in **Para empezar,** which form of the verb is used after **para que** (*so that*)?

☐ indicative ☑ subjunctive

Para que expresses what you want to happen as a result of your action.

Voy a hablar muy despacio **para que** me **entiendas.**   *I'm going to speak very slowly so that you understand me.*

In this example, you speak slowly because you want the other person to understand you. The meaning of **para que** is thus similar to that of **querer:** both express what you want to happen. As you saw in **12.3, querer que...** is always followed by the subjunctive, so it is not surprising that **para que** behaves the same.

Quiero que me **entiendas.**   *I want you to understand me.*

2 Another common expression that is followed by the subjunctive is **en caso de que** (*in case, in the event that*).

En caso de que llueva mañana, llámame.	*In the event that it rains tomorrow, call me.*
En caso de que no encuentres el parque, búscalo en el mapa.	*In case you don't find the park, look for it on the map.*

En caso de que expresses what might happen, when it is not at all certain that it will. Its meaning is thus similar to expressions like **Es posible que... ,** and both are typically followed by the subjunctive.

Es posible que llueva mañana.	*It's possible that it will rain tomorrow (but I don't know for sure).*

3 Expressions that simply introduce a fact (rather than something that you *want* to happen or something that *might* happen) are followed by an indicative verb form. For example, **porque** is generally followed by the indicative.

Voy a hablar muy despacio, **porque** a veces no me **entiendes.**	*I'm going to speak very slowly, because sometimes you don't understand me.*
Llámame, **porque va** a llover mañana.	*Call me, because it's going to rain tomorrow.*

4 The indicative and subjunctive moods each have their own core meaning. The indicative expresses what is *thought* to be true (such as, **Ellos saben que estudiamos todas las noches**). The subjunctive, on the other hand, expresses what someone *wants* to be true, but isn't yet (such as, **Quiero que estudiemos esta noche.**), or what is false or possibly not true (such as, **No es cierto que estudiemos todas las noches** and **Es posible que estudiemos esta noche**).

Resumen (*Summary*) de los usos del indicativo y del subjuntivo	
Indicativo	**Subjuntivo**
To indicate a fact, something thought to be true (Estructura 13.2)	**To indicate a desire, something that you want to be true (Estructura 12.3, 13.3)**
Sé que las tortugas **están** bien. *I know that the turtles are fine.*	Quiero que las tortugas **estén** bien. *I want the turtles to be fine.*
Pienso que **ahorras** agua. *I think that you save water.*	Te recomiendo que **ahorres** agua. *I recommend that you save water.*
Te voy a invitar a la playa porque **eres** mi amigo. *I'm going to invite you to the beach because you are my friend.*	Te voy a invitar a la playa para que **seas** mi amigo. *I'm going to invite you to the beach so that you'll be my friend.*
	To indicate something that may not be true (Estructura 13.2, 13.3)
	No creo que los bosques **estén** en buenas condiciones. *I don't think that the forests are in good condition.*
	Es posible que ese pájaro **sea** un cóndor. *It's possible that that bird is a condor.*
	En caso de que **veas** un oso, dime. *In the event that you see a bear, tell me.*

Note (Act. analítica 2): Both *en caso de que* and *es posible que* sometimes take the indicative when the speaker does not want to suggest that what follows might be false. For example, *en caso de que eres mujer* (when writing to someone whose gender is not known) or *es posible que tienes que arreglar tu computadora* (when suggesting possible solutions to a problem). These uses are not presented in activities here, but they fit in with the general message: the subjunctive expresses certain meanings, so whether it is used or not depends on what the speaker wants to say.

■ To see how to use the subjunctive to express situations that haven't happened yet or that will only happen under certain conditions, see **Para saber más 13.3** at the back of your book.

Note (Para saber más): *Para saber más 13.3* covers the subjunctive with adverbial clauses of time and more phrases that express contingency.

Autoprueba

Say whether these expressions should be followed by the indicative (I) or the subjunctive (S).

1. ____ Te voy a pedir que...
2. ____ Es imposible que...
3. ____ Sabemos que..
4. ____ Te voy a dar agua para que...
5. ____ Quiero ir al parque porque...
6. ____ Es cierto que...

Respuestas: 1. S 2. S 3. I
4. S 5. I 6. I

Actividades prácticas

A. ¿Qué hacemos para ayudar?   Empareja la primera parte de cada oración con la terminación más lógica. ¡**Atención!** Presta atención a los verbos en las terminaciones. ¿Están en subjuntivo o indicativo?

1. _e_ Uso bicicleta para moverme por la ciudad para que...
2. _b_ Uso bicicleta para moverme por la ciudad porque...
3. _h_ Pongo los productos reciclables en los contenedores de reciclaje para que...
4. _f_ No pido una bolsa cuando compro algo en una tienda porque...
5. _d_ Trato de usar muy poca agua para que...
6. _a_ Compro frutas y verduras orgánicas porque...
7. _g_ Compro frutas y verduras orgánicas para que...
8. _c_ Trato de minimizar el uso del papel para que...

a. no quiero que mi comida tenga pesticidas.
b. me gusta saber que no uso tanta gasolina.
c. no hagamos más daño a los bosques.
d. tengan suficiente en el futuro.
e. no esté tan sucio el aire de nuestra ciudad.
f. no la necesito y no quiero generar más basura.
g. no usen tanto pesticida en el campo.
h. puedan usarlos para producir otros productos.

B. Una casa ecológica   Imagínate que planeas la construcción de una casa ecológica. Completa cada oración con una conclusión lógica, usando las frases de la lista y conjugando el verbo en su forma más adecuada.

darme dinero   poder trabajar   visitarme en la nueva casa
no molestarse   ser totalmente ecológica   ya estar viviendo allí en verano
no tener ningún defecto

1. Primero, debo conseguir el permiso de la ciudad para que los obreros (*workers*) _puedan trabajar_.
2. Tengo que pedir un préstamo (*loan*) para que el banco _me dé dinero_.
3. Voy a avisar a los vecinos (*let the neighbors know*) para que _no se molesten_.
4. Luego voy a escoger puros materiales reciclados para la casa para que _sea totalmente ecológica_.
5. Les voy a pedir a los obreros que trabajen con mucho cuidado para que la casa _no tenga ningún defecto_.
6. Quiero que la casa esté lista para julio para que mi familia _ya esté viviendo allí en verano_.
7. Voy a invitar a todos mis amigos para que _me visiten en la nueva casa_.

C. ¡Está preparado/a!   Dile a un compañero / una compañera qué hay que llevar **en caso de que** pase una de las siguientes situaciones. Tu compañero/a debe decidir si lo que dices es lógico o no.

MODELO: E1: En caso de que llueva, hay que llevar un bolígrafo.
E2: ¡No es lógico!

En caso de que...

1. poder andar en las montañas
2. hacer mucho calor
3. ir a la playa
4. tener tiempo para relajarse
5. querer explorar el río
6. hacer mucho frío

Hay que llevar...

un abrigo

mucha agua

una balsa (*raft*)

botas de montaña

una gorra

un libro

un traje de baño

D. ¿Qué hacer en el peor de los casos?   Pasar tiempo en la naturaleza puede ser una experiencia muy bonita, pero también puede ser un poco peligroso. Pregúntale a un compañero / una compañera qué haces en caso de que te pase uno de los siguientes problemas. Tu compañero/a debe escoger la solución más lógica de la lista.

MODELO: picar (*to sting*) los mosquitos / ¡Aplástalos (*Squash them*) y ponte más repelente!
E1: ¿Qué hago en caso de que me piquen los mosquitos?
E2: ¡Aplástalos y ponte más repelente!

PROBLEMAS (EN CASO DE QUE...)

1. atacar un oso
2. picar una viuda (*widow*) negra
3. querer morder (*bite*) un jaguar
4. picar una medusa (*jellyfish*)
5. cagar (*poop*) un pájaro
6. ir a comer las pirañas

SOLUCIONES

a. ¡Grita, mueve los brazos y trata de asustarlo!
b. ¡Usa agua y una servilleta para limpiarte!
c. ¡Salte (*Get out*) del río inmediatamente!
d. ¡Vete al hospital, porque el veneno (*poison*) de este animal es muy peligroso!
e. ¡Salte del mar y lávate la zona afectada con vinagre o agua salada (*salt water*)!
f. ¡Ponte en posición fetal, cubre la cabeza con los brazos y no te muevas!

Answers (Act. D):
1. *¿Qué hago en caso de que me ataque un oso?* (l) **2.** *¿Qué hago en caso de que me pique una viuda negra?* (d) **3.** *¿Qué hago en caso de que me quiera morder un jaguar?* (a) **4.** *¿Qué hago en caso de que me pique una medusa?* (e) **5.** *¿Qué hago en caso de que me cague un pájaro?* (b) **6.** *¿Qué hago en caso de que vayan a comerme las pirañas?* (c)

Suggestion (Act. D):
• Point out that in order to maintain the right sound, some verbs will adjust their spelling. Remind them that when followed by *e* or *i*, *c*- changes to *qu*-, *g*- changes to *gu*-, and *z*- changes to *c*-.
• Point out that piranhas live in many rivers in South America, and they are frequently eaten by locals. You'll often find people swimming in rivers alongside piranhas and, despite their image in the movies, the fish do not usually attack humans.

CONÉCTATE AL MUNDO PROFESIONAL

Ecology and "green" activities have become important to many industries for both public relations and bottom line purposes. Most big companies engage in Corporate Social Responsibility (CSR) and a lot of new office buildings have LEED certifications prominently displayed at the entrance. Globalization expands the possibilities and increases the need for employees with industry expertise, ecological awareness, and the ability to communicate across languages and cultures.

¡Leamos!

La aventura y el ecoturismo en el Perú

Antes de leer

PASO 1. Decide si cada actividad es **sostenible** (S) o **no sostenible** (NS).

1. _S_ acampar
2. _NS_ viajar en vehículo motorizado
3. _S_ una caminata (*hike*)
4. _NS_ viajar en avión

5. _S_ viajar en bote de remos (*rowboat*)
6. _S_ observar flora y fauna
7. _S_ un proyecto ecológico
8. _S_ un centro etnobotánico

PASO 2. Escoge dos actividades del **Paso 1** y escribe una oración completa para explicar tus respuestas.

> **MODELO:** Acampar es sostenible porque no usa muchos recursos naturales y no destruye la naturaleza.

1. _____
2. _____

A leer

Lee el itinerario de «La aventura y el ecoturismo en el Perú» y contesta las preguntas.

La aventura y el ecoturismo en el Perú

PAÍS: Perú
LOCALIZACIÓN: Recorrido por Perú: Cusco, Camino Inca,[a] Parque de Tambopata
MODALIDAD DE VIAJE: Viaje de ecoturismo y aventura, turismo de naturaleza

¿Qué viaje vas a vivir?

Un viaje sostenible especialmente diseñado[b] para los amantes[c] del ecoturismo y la aventura. Conoceremos[d] algunos de los principales atractivos del Perú, pero, sobre todo, disfrutaremos del Camino Inca, de una impresionante estancia[e] en la Posada[f] Amazonas y de un espectacular recorrido en rafting. Una oportunidad sin igual para avistar[g] nutrias[h] gigantes, guacamayos,[i] monos, etcétera. Un viaje para conocer un mundo muy distinto al nuestro.

[...]

DÍA 2: Lima / Paracas / Ica / Islas Ballestas

Las islas Ballestas son formaciones rocosas[j] las cuales albergan[k] a leones marinos, pingüinos de Humboldt, gatos marinos,[l] delfines y una gran variedad de aves[m] residentes y migratorias... Navegando hacia[n] las islas Ballestas, en el camino se puede apreciar El Candelabro, que es un geoglifo[ñ] de grandes dimensiones que sirve de faro[o] a los navegantes.

El Candelabro de Paracas

[a]*Camino... Inca Trail* [b]*designed* [c]*lovers* [d]*We'll get to know* [e]*stay* [f]*Lodge* [g]*view* [h]*a large freshwater mammal* [i]*macaws* [j]*rocky* [k]*house* [l]*gatos... sea otters* [m]*pájaros* [n]*toward* [ñ]*large rock art; drawings on the ground designed to be seen from above* [o]*lighthouse*

DÍA 5: Camino Inca: Cusco / Huayllabamba

Nuestro vehículo nos llevará hasta el punto de inicio de nuestra caminata. El camino sigue [el banco oeste] del río Urubamba, donde apreciamos hermosas vistas de la montaña Verónica (5850m); después del almuerzo continuaremos nuestra caminata al valle de Huayllabamba para acampar cerca de la comunidad del mismo nombre.

[...]

DÍA 11: Cusco / Puerto Maldonado

A hora oportuna traslado[p] al aeropuerto para tomar el vuelo con destino a Puerto Maldonado. Recepción en el aeropuerto y traslado al puerto de donde seguimos en bote hacia la Posada Amazonas. Durante nuestro viaje podemos observar diferente flora y fauna en las orillas.[q] Si nos queda tiempo, visitamos una granja[r] de los nativos. Después de la cena se mostrará[s] un video sobre el parque nacional de Tambopata.

El río Urubamba con vista de la montaña Verónica

[...]

DÍA 13: Posada Amazonas

Después del desayuno visitamos una pequeña collpa.[t] Desde una plataforma escondida[u] cerca de la collpa podemos observar como decenas[v] de loros y guacamayos congregan aquí para alimentarse. En días soleados[w] se juntan[x] en este lugar decenas hasta a veces centenares[y] de loros para comer arcilla.[z] Después del almuerzo visitamos el Centro EtnoBotánico de una comunidad nativa, aprendiendo más sobre la cultura local y su interacción con la selva. Regresamos [a la posada] para la cena.

Una collpa con loros y guacamayos

[p]*transportation* [q]*shorelines* [r]*farm* [s]*se... will be shown* [t]*clay lick used by birds to neutralize toxins in their diet* [u]*hidden* [v]*scores* [w]*con mucho sol* [x]*se... gather* [y]*hundreds* [z]*clay*

1. ¿Qué tipo de viaje describe el artículo?
2. ¿Cuáles son cuatro atractivos del viaje?
3. ¿Qué atractivos ofrecen las islas Ballestas?
4. ¿Qué ven los turistas en la caminata del Camino Inca?
5. ¿Dónde pasan la noche los turistas en el Camino Inca?
6. ¿Cómo llegan los turistas a la Posada Amazonas el día once?
7. ¿Qué tipo de información reciben los turistas en la Posada Amazonas?
8. El último día, ¿qué hacen los turistas por la mañana? ¿Y por la tarde?
9. ¿Te gustaría participar en este viaje? Explica por qué sí o por qué no. ¿En cuáles actividades te gustaría participar y en cuáles no?

Después de leer

En grupos, diseñen un viaje ecológico en su comunidad. Para organizar el viaje, primero contesten las siguientes preguntas. Luego organicen la presentación del viaje en la forma de un anuncio en la televisión y preséntenlo al resto de la clase.

1. ¿Adónde van a ir los turistas?
2. ¿Qué lugares de interés van a conocer? Describe cada uno.
3. ¿Cómo van a llegar los turistas a cada lugar?
4. ¿Qué van a hacer en cada lugar?
5. ¿Dónde se van a quedar?
6. ¿Qué van a aprender?

Suggestions (Después de leer):
- Rather than focusing on their own community, have students plan an ecotour in a Spanish-speaking country.
- Have students vote on which trip sounds the most exciting, the most earth-friendly, the most adventurous, the most/least expensive, and so on.

Expansion (Después de leer): Have students design brochures or posters in Spanish to promote their trips.

Videoscript (A escuchar):
1. EDUARDO: *Los bosques se están reduciendo, los bosques que existen en las selvas tropicales, se están reduciendo, lo que es peligroso para nosotros y se están viendo también en los mismos cambios en el clima aquí en Panamá. La temporada lluviosa aquí en Panamá, no tenemos cuatro estaciones como lo tienen en las zonas templadas, aquí tenemos una estación lluviosa que dura la mayor parte del tiempo y una estación seca, y ya se está viendo alterado ese... ese equilibrio también, al igual que se están viendo desequilibrios en las estaciones en otros países. Es un mensaje también importante, que tiene que tener conciencia la gente, que el daño que se está causando es en todo el mundo.* **2.** ANLLULY: *Ayer justamente estaba hablando con un cliente sobre el cambio de clima que hemos tenido en Costa Rica, en Monteverde especialmente. Hace diez años solamente teníamos dos meses de verano. El resto del tiempo pasaba con mucho viento, mucha lluvia. Ahora es todo lo contrario. Ahora son... a veces son solo dos meses de invierno que tenemos lluvia y muchos animales se van. Es difícil. Pero es falta de educación también porque mucha gente contamina, no le importa tirar la basura en el bosque o tirarla en la calle. Hay mucha gente que corta muchos árboles. Es difícil, es difícil, pero yo pienso que sí, se puede. Si todos nos ponemos la mano en el corazón va a ser más fácil.* **3.** VÍCTOR: *Bueno, el calentamiento global lo que ha hecho, es que ha hecho más fuerte, por ejemplo las lluvias, antes sabíamos que había huracanes, había ondas frías y afectaban a la ciudad ahora son más fuertes, ahora se inundan ciudades, se inundan pueblos, se inundan lugares donde antes no se inundaba, ahora se inundan, antes estaban muy marcadas las estaciones veintiuno de marzo empezaba primavera y así, ahora empiezan en cualquier momento nunca sabes cuando va a terminar ahorita la lluvia empezó tres semanas tarde y entonces va a terminar tres semanas después y entonces se va a juntar con el invierno, entonces estamos ahorita teniendo época de frío con época de lluvia y eso produce granizo, que es muy raro verlo en algunos lugares de aquí de México, como estamos viendo granizo, incluso de tamaño de pelotas de golf y es por ese, esos cambios y es lo que antes no veíamos, pero ahora el cambio climático nos está trayendo esos problemas.* (Script continues next page.)

¡Escuchemos!

Algunas amenazas a nuestro planeta

Antes de escuchar

Suggestion (Antes de escuchar): Before reading the script, read the topics aloud and make sure students have a basic understanding of what they are.

Para cada frase que escuchas, indica a qué tema ecológico se refiere: **el calentamiento global (CG), la contaminación del mar (CM), la deforestación (D)** o **la escasez** (*shortage*) **de agua (EA).**

1. _D_   3. _CM_   5. _D_   7. _CM_

2. _CG_   4. _D_   6. _EA_

Script (Antes de escuchar): 1. *los bosques se están reduciendo* **2.** *el cambio climático* **3.** *le echan todo al mar* **4.** *se está perdiendo el pulmón del país* (Note: Demonstrate *pulmón* by pointing to both sides of your chest and breathing deeply) **5.** *las selvas tropicales* **6.** *la sequía* **7.** *cada año hay menos ballenas*

A escuchar

Mira y escucha mientras los participantes hablan sobre algunos problemas medioambientales. Escucha otra vez con pausas e indica cada expresión que oyes. **¡Atención!** En cada caso, hay tres respuestas. Mira una tercera vez para verificar tus respuestas.

Video track (A escuchar): This video clip can be found on the DVD to accompany *Conéctate: Cap. 13*, Track 3.

1. Eduardo, de Panamá
   - ☑ cambios en el clima
   - ☐ la contaminación
   - ☑ desequilibrio (*imbalance*) en las estaciones
   - ☐ medios de transporte
   - ☐ problemas ecológicos
   - ☑ las selvas tropicales

2. Anlluly, de Costa Rica
   - ☑ el cambio de clima
   - ☑ gente que corta muchos árboles
   - ☐ problemas medio ambientales
   - ☐ el pulmón (*lung*) del país
   - ☐ recursos naturales
   - ☑ tirar la basura en el bosque

3. Víctor, de México
   - ☑ el calentamiento global
   - ☑ el cambio climático
   - ☐ la contaminación
   - ☐ la destrucción de nuestro planeta
   - ☑ se inundan ciudades, se inundan pueblos
   - ☐ reciclar las bolsas plásticas

4. Guadalupe, de Costa Rica
   - ☐ el cambio climático
   - ☑ cortando árboles
   - ☐ la destrucción de nuestro planeta
   - ☐ se inundan ciudades, se inundan pueblos
   - ☑ mucha gente está conservando
   - ☑ protegiendo los bosques

5. Diego, de Argentina
   - ☐ el cambio climático
   - ☑ deforestación
   - ☐ problemas medio ambientales
   - ☑ el pulmón (*lung*) del país
   - ☐ recursos naturales
   - ☑ la selva

6. Andrea, de México
   - ☐ el cambio climático
   - ☑ cuánto daño le estamos haciendo
   - ☐ la destrucción de nuestro planeta
   - ☑ le echan todo al mar
   - ☑ el mar va a estar todo contaminado
   - ☐ el pulmón del país

7. Juan Andrés, de Costa Rica
   - ☑ la contaminación
   - ☐ desequilibrios en estaciones
   - ☑ medios de transporte
   - ☐ problemas ecológicos
   - ☑ reciclar las bolsas plásticas
   - ☐ las selvas tropicales

(Cont'd): **4.** GUADALUPE: *Sí, últimamente sí ha sido un problema porque hay muchas personas que están, este, cortando árboles para obtener madera y así. Pero en general yo pienso que Costa Rica es un país, este, privilegiado porque mucha gente, este, le está conservando, está protegiendo los bosques.* **5.** DIEGO: *Y... es triste, quizás, la parte... de la selva, porque hay mucha... deforestación, muchísima. Quizás... el gobierno que está a cargo... no se maneja para nada en este momento, son muy... muy egoístas en ese sentido, o sea, no, no... Y, se está deforestando mucho, se está perdiendo mucho lo que es, el pulmón quizás, el pulmón del país, quizás, porque es el lugar donde... hay... donde existe más diversidad de fauna, flora... eh, de todo, ¿no?* **6.** ANDREA: *En cuanto al medio ambiente, yo creo que el mar, yo creo que nadie, nadie se está dando cuenta de cuánto daño le estamos haciendo, y ahorita nos estamos enfocando más en las cuestiones del ozono y todo, y cuando menos nos demos cuenta pues el mar va a estar todo contaminado y ya no va a haber nada de animales, nada de ballenas, es*

Después de escuchar

Lee las siguientes preguntas y luego mira el video de nuevo. En parejas, contesten las preguntas usando oraciones completas.

1. Según Eduardo, ¿qué pasa con los bosques?
2. Según Eduardo, ¿qué pasa con el clima?
3. Según Anlluly, ¿qué hace la gente que es malo para el medio ambiente?
4. Según Víctor, ¿cuáles son algunos problemas que trae el cambio climático?
5. Según Guadalupe, ¿para qué están cortando árboles muchas personas?
6. ¿De qué habla Diego?
7. Según Andrea, ¿a qué deberíamos prestar más atención? Si no le prestamos más atención, ¿qué pasará?
8. ¿Qué sugerencias ofrece Juan Andrés para mejor cuidar el medio ambiente?

como un mundo que no conocemos y pues le echan todo al mar, todo lo que no nos sirve o no podemos usarlo, está en el mar, entonces yo creo que es una de las cuestiones más importantes. **7.** JUAN ANDRÉS: *El problema, el problema se puede mejorar creando medios de transporte que no contaminen tanto. Por ejemplo, los trenes eléctricos. Tal vez, podemos, este mejorar, reciclar las bolsas plásticas. Usar bolsas... cada vez que vamos al supermercado, las mismas bolsas. Pienso que eso puede mejorar mucho con la contaminación.*

¡Escribamos!

El problema medioambiental más grave°   serious

En esta actividad, vas a describir un problema medioambiental, explicar tu opinión en cuanto al asunto (*concerning the matter*) y luego ofrecer sugerencias para una posible solución.

Antes de escribir

Escoge uno de los temas presentados en **¡Escuchemos!** y apunta información siguiendo el modelo.

MODELO: I. El problema: *la contaminación del mar*

    A. la tesis del video: *no prestamos atención al mar*
       1. detalle: *echamos basura al mar*
       2. detalle: *dañamos los animales marinos*
       3. detalle: *enfocamos en otros problemas (el aire, los bosques)*

    B. Mi opinión: _____
       1. detalle: _____
       2. detalle: _____
       3. detalle: _____

    C. Posible solución: _____
       1. sugerencia: _____
       2. sugerencia: _____
       3. sugerencia: _____

A escribir

Usa tu bosquejo (*outline*) para ayudarte a escribir un ensayo de tres párrafos. Primero, describe el problema y resume lo que dice la persona en el video. Luego añade tu propia opinión y más detalles. Escribe una conclusión en la cual ofreces algunas sugerencias para una solución.

(Continues)

ESTRATEGIA

Outlining

Preparing an outline can help you to include more details than you might otherwise, which is especially important in a situation in which you are trying to urge others to action. Outlines also ensure that you organize your writing in the most logical way possible without proceeding out of order. The visual nature of the outline allows you to see where your assignment may be lacking in details, helping you address each key point equally.

Answers (Después de escuchar) **1.** *se están reduciendo* **2.** *hay un desequilibrio entre la estación seca y la estación lluviosa* **3.** *contamina: tira la basura en el bosque o en la calle y corta muchos árboles* **4.** *huracanes más fuertes, inundaciones, cambios en las estaciones, granizos del tamaño de pelotas de golf* **5.** *para obtener madera* **6.** *de la deforestación de la selva* **7.** *el mar; no va a haber nada de animales ni de ballenas en el mar* **8.** *medios de transporte que no contaminen y el reciclaje de las bolsas plásticas*

Después de escribir

Revisa tu ensayo. Luego intercambia ensayos con un compañero / una compañera para evaluarlos. Lee el ensayo de tu compañero/a y decide si falta información necesaria. ¿Se ha desarrollado (*developed*) bien cada párrafo? ¿Hay sugerencias apropiadas para una solución en la conclusión? Lee de nuevo (*again*) el ensayo con cuidado para revisar los siguientes puntos de gramática.

☐ hay concordancia entre los sujetos los verbos

☐ hay uso correcto del y subjuntivo

☐ hay concordancia entre los sustantivos y los adjetivos

Después de revisar el ensayo de tu compañero/a, devuélveselo. Mira tu propio ensayo para ver los cambios que tu compañero/a recomienda y haz las revisiones necesarias.

¡Hablemos!

¿A quién le gusta más la naturaleza?

Suggestion (Antes de hablar): This activity helps students use descriptions when they don't know the exact word. Allow them to work through the details of each image before giving them the words or phrases in Spanish.

Antes de hablar

Mira los dibujos y di a qué actividad se refiere. Si no sabes la palabra exacta para cada actividad, usa las palabras que sí sabes para explicársela.

MODELO: hacer camping *or* dormir fuera de la casa, en el bosque o en las montañas

1.   2.   3.

4.   5.   6.

A hablar

En parejas, túrnense para decir qué tienen que llevar o cómo tienen que preparar para hacer las actividades que identificaron en **Antes de hablar.** Expliquen para qué lo tienen que hacer o en qué situación va a ser necesario.

MODELOS: Deberíamos comprar un colchón inflable (*air mattress*) *para que* no tengamos que dormir en el suelo. / Debería llevar un traje de baño *en caso de que* haya un buen lugar para tomar el sol.

Después de hablar

Ahora, júntense con otra pareja y decidan cuál de las actividades prefieren hacer para este fin de semana.

Conéctate a la música

Canción: «Ojalá que llueva café» (1989)
Artista: Juan Luis Guerra (República Dominicana)

Juan Luis Guerra nació en Santo Domingo en 1957. Es cantautor (*singer-songwriter*), compositor y músico conocido en todo el mundo, en particular por sus canciones de merengue y salsa. Ha ganado veinte Grammys y ha recibido muchas nominaciones. Se han vendido más de 30 millones de copias de sus discos.

Antes de escuchar

En la canción «Ojalá que llueva café», el cantante quiere que varias cosas caigan (*fall*) del cielo. ¿Cuáles son las cosas que muchas personas probablemente esperan que caigan del cielo? ¿Por qué?

 A escuchar

Expresiones útiles			
aguacero	downpour	**en vez**	instead
batata	sweet potato	**hojas secas**	dry leaves
		jarina	sprinkling
berro	watercress	**llanura**	prairie
cerro	hill	**mapuey**	yam
colina	hill	**miel**	honey
cosecha	harvest	**trigo**	wheat

Juan Luis Guerra inició su gira (*tour*) de 2008 con un concierto en Miami.

■ For copyright reasons, the songs referenced in **Conéctate a la música** have not been provided by the publisher. The video for this song can be found on YouTube, and it is available for purchase from the iTunes store.

Lee las **Expresiones útiles** y las siguientes frases. Luego escucha la canción y escribe los números 1 a 7 al lado de las frases según el orden en que las oyes.

  <u>6</u> en vez de hojas secas, [...] una cosecha de pitisalé.*
  <u>5</u> la colina de arroz graneado
  <u>1</u> un aguacero de yuca y té
  <u>4</u> un alto cerro de trigo y mapuey
  <u>2</u> una jarina de queso blanco
  <u>7</u> una llanura de batata y fresas
  <u>3</u> una montaña de berro y miel'

Después de escuchar

Lee de nuevo la lista de cosas que el cantante pide. ¿Qué tipo de cosas son? ¿Por qué crees tú que él quiere que caigan del cielo? ¿De qué se trata (*is* [*it*] *about*) esta canción? Busca pistas (*clues*) en la canción para apoyar (*support*) tus ideas.

---

*petit-salé, un tipo de tocino (*bacon*)
'El berro y la miel se combinan en muchos remedios caseros (*home*) para curar una tos o gripe.

VOCABULARIO

Now that I have completed the chapter, I can . . .

☐ say what I think should happen

☐ say how long something has been going on

☐ talk about nature and the environment

☐ express what someone wants to happen

☐ express what someone thinks may not be true

☐ discuss nature and the environment in the Spanish-speaking world

Comunicación

(no) debería + *inf.*	should (not) (*do something*)
¿Cuánto tiempo lleva(s) + -ndo *form?*	How long have you (*form./inform.*) (*done / been doing something*)?
Llevo + *time expression* + -ndo *form.*	I've been (*doing something*) for + *time.*
Llevo + *time expression* + sin + *inf.*	I haven't (*done something*) for + *time.*
¿Cuánto tiempo hace que + *present tense?*	How long have you (*done / been doing something*)?
Hace + *time expression* + que + *present tense.*	I've been (*doing something*) for + *time.*
Hace + *time expression* + que no + *present tense.*	It's been + *time* + since I've (*done something*).
mucho tiempo	a long time
toda la vida	all my (your/his/her) life; all our (your/ their) lives

El medio ambiente	The environment
el agotamiento	depletion; exhaustion
el arrecife	reef
el bosque	forest
el calentamiento global	global warming
el clima	climate
la contaminación	pollution
el daño	damage
la disminución	decrease

la especie	species; kind
el huracán (*pl.* huracanes)	hurricane
la inundación (*pl.* inundaciones)	flood
el peligro	danger
el planeta (Tierra)	planet (Earth)
el reciclaje	recycling
los recursos naturales	natural resources
la selva	jungle
la sequía	drought
la tala de árboles	tree cutting
la tierra	earth; soil
la tormenta	storm

Cognados: el/la activista, el aire, el animal, la atmósfera, la causa, la consecuencia, la deforestación, la ecología, el ecologismo, el ecoturismo, la extinción, la fauna, la flora, el humanitarismo, la obligación, la protección, la responsabilidad, el sistema, la situación

Los animales

la ballena	whale
el delfín	dolphin
el león marino	sea lion
el loro	parrot
el mono	monkey
el oso	bear
el pájaro	bird
el perezoso	sloth
el pingüino	penguin
el sapo	toad
la tortuga	turtle

Los verbos

ahorrar (agua, electricidad, dinero)	to save (water, electricity, money)
ayudar	to help
causar	to cause
conservar	to preserve; to conserve; to keep
contaminar	to pollute
cuidar	to take care of
destruir (y)	to destroy
explotar	to exploit; to develop
participar	to participate
prohibir (prohíbo)	to prohibit
proteger (j)	to protect
reciclar	to recycle
salvar	to save

Los adjetivos

ecológico/a	ecological
marino/a	marine, sea
medioambiental	environmental
salvaje	wild
sostenible	sustainable

La cultura y la diversión°

fun

El taller (*studio*) de un pintor en La Habana, Cuba

When you finish this chapter, you will be able to:

- express uncertainty
- say what you and others would like or hope to do
- talk about what cultural activities you enjoy
- express desires in the past
- express future plans
- express speculation
- discuss cultural activities and entertainment in the Spanish-speaking world

connect

www.mhhe.com/connect

COMUNICACIÓN LARIO CTURA TE

Quizás. No sé. Tal vez...

Expressing uncertainty

A. A ver: ¿Cuáles son sus preferencias?

PASO 1. Mira y escucha. Luego mira otra vez con pausas e indica los géneros (*genres*) de cine de que habla cada persona. **¡Atención!** Algunas personas hablan de más de un género de cine. Indícalos todos.

1. __b, d__ Mariana, de Costa Rica
2. __f, h__ Brenda, de México
3. __a, b, g__ Víctor, de España
4. __c__ Denise, de Argentina
5. __g__ Cinthya, de Costa Rica

a. acción
b. comedia
c. comedia musical
d. drama
e. infantil
f. romance
g. suspenso/misterio
h. terror

PASO 2. Mira y escucha otra vez con pausas. ¿Qué expresión usa cada persona para expresar certeza (*certainty*) o duda?

	SÍ	CREO	TAL VEZ	QUIZÁ(S)	NO SÉ
1. MARIANA: «____ que me gusta la comedia... »	☐	☑	☐	☐	☐
2. BRENDA: «...bueno de género así de terror, ____... »	☐	☐	☑	☐	☐
3. VÍCTOR: «...que tengan algún valor y sobre todo ____ también... »	☐	☐	☐	☑	☐
4. DENISE: «...con Julio Bocca que, ____ lo conocen... »	☐	☐	☐	☑	☐
5. CINTHYA: «Me gusta el suspenso, pero ____... »	☐	☐	☐	☐	☑

PASO 3. Contesta las preguntas sobre lo que dijo la gente del video.

1. ¿Qué género no le gusta a Mariana? ¿Por qué no? el miedo/terror, porque ella es miedosa
2. ¿Cuáles películas le gustan a Brenda? *El exorcista* y *Titanic*
3. ¿Qué tipo de películas le gustan a Víctor más que las otras? las películas que tengan un mensaje social
4. ¿Quién es Julio Bocca? un bailarín clásico que hace comedia musical
5. ¿Ha visto Cinthya la película de suspenso, *Infección*? no
6. ¿Qué género de película del **Paso 1** no menciona nadie? ¿A ti te gusta este género? infantil

Video track (Act. A): This video clip can be found on the DVD to accompany *Conéctate: Cap. 14,* Track 1.

Videoscript (Act. A): 1.
MARIANA: *Creo que me gusta la comedia. La comedia creo que es siempre lo hace uno reír, pasar un buen rato. Pero, también disfruto del drama. No me gusta el miedo, no. Soy muy miedosa.* **2.** BRENDA: *¡Mmm!, pues es que son muchas, de, bueno de género así de terror, tal vez, El exorcista, ¡esa! Nada más como... Y pues de las de amor, de romance todas esas, a lo mejor Titanic.* **3.** VÍCTOR: *Películas de... de acción, de... de misterio, de,.. también me gustan las comedias pero películas de acción, con cierto concepto misterio, que tenga algún valor y sobre todo quizás también, películas que tengan un mensaje social, también es importante.* **4.** DENISE: *Bueno, acá estoy haciendo dirección de cine, acá en esta facultad y comedia musical con Julio Bocca que... quizá lo conocen... es conocido en el mundo, es un bailarín clásico... eh... y estoy haciendo con él comedia musical.* **5.** CINTHYA: *Me gusta el suspenso. Pero no sé esa que está saliendo nueva ahora que es de... se llama Infección. Es como suspenso pero no la he llegado a ver todavía. Entonces, no sé.*

To say *maybe* or *perhaps,* you can use **quizá/quizás** or **tal vez.**

—**¿Cuál es tu película favorita?**	"What's your favorite movie?"
—**No sé, tal vez** *Casablanca.*	"I don't know. Maybe *Casablanca.*
O quizá(s) *El padrino.*	Or perhaps *The Godfather.*"

To say that you're sure of how you feel about something, you can say: **Sin duda (alguna).**

—**¿Cuál es tu película favorita?**	"What's your favorite movie?"
—**Sin duda alguna, mi película favorita**	"Without a doubt, my favorite movie
es *El ciudadano Kane.*	is *Citizen Kane.*"

B. ¿Cuáles son tus preferencias?

PASO 1.   Apunta por lo menos dos personas, obras (*works*) o otras cosas que asocias con cada categoría.

> **MODELO:**   literatura: el autor Gabriel García Márquez; *Cien años de soledad*
>
> arte
> baile (*dance*)
> cine
> literatura
> música
> ópera
> teatro

Suggestions (Act. B, Paso 2):
- Before having students pair up, model a brief conversation with a student, using the expressions provided.
- Walk around and listen to the conversations. To keep students engaged, stop and ask a pair of students if they agree with what a student in another pair has said (*¡Qué interesante/maravilloso/aburrido/triste! ¿Están Uds. de acuerdo con John?*), asking the student to repeat his statement to the other pair (*John, repite lo que has dicho, por favor.*)

PASO 2.   En parejas, túrnense para hacer preguntas sobre cada categoría para aprender sus preferencias. Usen las expresiones de la siguiente escala.

para nada (*not at all*)		tal vez		sin duda alguna

> **MODELO:**   E1: *¿Cien años de soledad* es tu libro favorito de García Márquez?
> E2: Sin duda alguna es mi libro favorito. ¿Es el tuyo?
> E1: No sé. Tal vez. Pero también me gusta *El amor en los tiempos del cólera.*

CONÉCTATE AL MUNDO HISPANO

Durante décadas, las películas más famosas de Hollywood han entretenido a los públicos (*audiences*) en todo el mundo. En algunos países hispanohablantes, **el doblaje** (*dubbing*) es una parte importante de la industria de cine. Antes de que una película se estrene (*premieres*), doblan (*they dub*) los diálogos al español. En otras partes del mundo ponen **subtítulos.** El uso ubicuo de subtítulos hace que inglés goce de (*enjoys*) una presencia cultural incluso en los países donde no es un idioma oficial. Preocupadas por la preservación de la cultura hispana, algunas personas prefieren el doblaje, porque así los públicos escuchan la película en su propia lengua. Sin embargo, en países con su propia producción cinematográfica (*film*), muchas personas prefieren que las películas de los Estados Unidos tengan subtítulos porque las películas subtituladas presentan menos competencia para las películas locales.

Quisiera...

Talking about what you would like to do

El actor peruano Bernie Paz

A. ¿Qué quisieran hacer estas personas famosas?

Empareja cada persona famosa con la cita más lógica.

1. __e__ Bernie Paz es un actor peruano que trabaja en telenovelas (*soap operas*).
2. __c__ Pilar Bustos es una pintora de Ecuador.
3. __b__ Giovanna Rivero es una escritora boliviana de libros de ficción.
4. __a__ José Carreras es un cantante de ópera español.
5. __d__ Los Pájaros es un grupo de rock argentino.

a. «Quisiera cantar en el Teatro Colón en Buenos Aires.»
b. «Quisiera ganar otro premio para uno de mis libros.»
c. «Quisiera presentar una exposición en el Museo de Arte Moderno.»
d. «Quisiéramos hacer una gira mundial (*world tour*) de conciertos.»
e. «Quisiera trabajar en cine de arte.»

To talk about what you or someone else would like or hope to do, use a form of **quisiera** + *infinitive:* **(yo) quisiera, (tú) quisieras, (él/ella, Ud.) quisiera, (nosotros/as) quisiéramos, (vosotros/as) quisierais, (ellos/ellas, Uds.) quisieran.**

Quisiera ser una actriz famosa.
Quisieran asistir a clases de baile.

I would like to be a famous actress.
They would like to attend dance classes.

 B. Los aficionados   En grupos, digan algo que las siguientes personas probablemente quisieran hacer.

> **MODELO:**   una persona a quien le gusta la ópera →
> E1: Esta persona quisiera asistir a una ópera famosa.
> E2: Tal vez quisiera ver *Carmen* o *La flauta mágica*.

1. un aficionado al ballet
2. una estudiante de arte
3. alguien a quien le gusta escuchar música clásica
4. una profesora de la historia del arte
5. una persona a quien le gusta el cine
6. una joven a quien le encantan las obras (*works*) de Cervantes y Shakespeare
7. una persona que quiere ser actor
8. una chica que quiere aprender a tocar música rock

C. ¿Qué quisieras hacer tú?

PASO 1.   Escribe por lo menos tres frases con **quisiera** y la **Expresiones útiles** para decir qué quisieras hacer en el mundo del arte.

> **MODELO:**   Quisiera aprender a tocar el piano.

 PASO 2.   Ahora, hazles preguntas a otras personas en tu clase sobre sus aspiraciones. ¿Qué tienen en común las aspiraciones de Uds.? ¿Cómo son diferentes?

> **MODELO:**   E1: Quisiera tocar la guitarra acústica. ¿Y tú?
> E2: Yo quisiera tocar la guitarra eléctrica en una banda de rock.
> E1: Yo no, para nada; prefiero la música folclórica.

Suggestion (Act. C, Paso 2): Ask for volunteers to give information about classmates with interests similar to theirs. Ask: *¿Qué tienen en común las aspiraciones de Uds.? ¿Cómo son diferentes?*

Expresiones útiles

actuar

dibujar

pintar

bailar

escribir un guion (*screenplay*) / una novela

ser fotógrafo/a

cantar

escribir poesía / un poema

tocar la guitarra / el piano

El cine, el teatro, el museo
Movies, theater, and museums

A. El nuevo centro cultural El nuevo centro cultural en tu ciudad quiere saber cómo atraer al público. Responde al siguiente sondeo (*survey*).

ACTIVIDADES PARA ESPECTADORES (*spectators*) EN EL NUEVO CENTRO CULTURAL

	1–2 VECES AL MES	1–2 VECES AL AÑO	NUNCA
En general, me gusta ver...			
bailes	❑	❑	❑
conciertos (música en vivo)	❑	❑	❑
obras de arte	❑	❑	❑
películas	❑	❑	❑
obras de teatro (*plays*)	❑	❑	❑
Me gustaría ver conciertos de música...			
alternativa	❑	❑	❑
clásica	❑	❑	❑
electrónica	❑	❑	❑
folclórica	❑	❑	❑
de ópera	❑	❑	❑
pop	❑	❑	❑
rock	❑	❑	❑

En mi opinión, tres de los mejores **cantantes** son:

_____

En mi opinión, tres de los mejores grupos/**bandas** son:

_____

	1–2 VECES AL MES	1–2 VECES AL AÑO	NUNCA
Me gustaría ver espectáculos de baile...			
clásico/ballet	❑	❑	❑
cumbia	❑	❑	❑
flamenco	❑	❑	❑
folclórico	❑	❑	❑
merengue	❑	❑	❑
salsa	❑	❑	❑
tango	❑	❑	❑
Me gustaría ver exposiciones en la galería de...			
escultura	❑	❑	❑
pintura	❑	❑	❑
Me gustaría oír/ver presentaciones de...			
literatura	❑	❑	❑
obras de **artistas, pintores,** o cineastas (*filmmakers*) famosos	❑	❑	❑
poesía	❑	❑	❑

Me interesa participar en un taller (*workshop*) de...

☐ **arte**   ☐ **dirección (dirigir)**

☐ **danza**   ☐ escritura de novelas

☐ actuación (**actuar**)   ☐ producción de cine **alternativo**

Here are some common words used to talk about artists and the arts in Spanish.

el/la escritor(a)	writer
la estrella (de cine)	(movie) star
el personaje	character; celebrity, well-known person
el/la pintor(a)	painter
el/la protagonista	main character, protagonist
el público	audience
interpretar (un papel)	to play (a role or part)

—¿**La estrella** de cine Salma Hayek fue nominada a los Premios Óscar?

—Sí, por su actuación en *Frida*. Ella **interpretó el papel** de **la protagonista,** Frida Kahlo.

—Claro. **Los personajes** de esa película incluyen muchos artistas importantes del siglo XX.

B. ¿Qué hace cada uno?

PASO 1.   Empareja cada verbo con su mejor descripción.

1. __g__ actuar o interpretar un papel
2. __f__ dirigir
3. __a__ producir
4. __c__ pintar
5. __d__ tocar música
6. __b__ componer (*compose*) música
7. __h__ esculpir (*sculpt*)
8. __e__ dibujar (*draw*)

a. hacer los preparativos y arreglarlo todo (*arrange everything*)
b. arreglar y producir obras musicales originales
c. aplicar pintura a un lienzo (*canvas*)
d. interpretar una canción con un instrumento musical
e. usar lápiz o pluma para crear una imagen en una superficie con líneas y colores
f. es lo que hace la persona que da instrucciones a los actores
g. es lo que hacen los actores para hacer verosímil (*realistic*) el personaje
h. hacer una obra en piedra, madera o metal

> **Expresiones útiles**
>
> **el cuerpo**
> **la historia**   story
> **la voz**   voice
> **contar**   to tell
> **explicar**

PASO 2.   En parejas, describan las siguientes artes. Pueden usar el **Paso 1** como modelo. Para más ayuda, vean también la lista de **Expresiones útiles.**

1. cantar   2. bailar   3. escribir

C. Las estrellas y sus papeles

PASO 1.   Haz una lista de tres o cuatro estrellas de cine y un personaje que ha interpretado cada uno.

MODELO:	**ESTRELLA**	**PERSONAJE**
	Adrien Brody	Salvador Dalí
	Salma Hayek	Frida Kahlo
	Joaquin Phoenix	Johnny Cash
	Daniel Radcliffe	Harry Potter

PASO 2.   Ahora, en parejas, túrnense para compartir los pares de nombres de tu lista. Digan cuál es el **personaje** y cuál es la **estrella.** Digan también si la estrella es **actor** o **actriz** y cómo se llama la película.

MODELO: E1: Salvador Dalí y Adrien Brody
E2: El personaje es Salvador Dalí. La estrella es el actor Adrien Brody. ¡La película es *Medianoche en París*!

Note (Act. C): If students are having trouble coming up with combinations, here are some you can give them, listed as Actor / Character (*Film/Series*): Jennifer Lawrence / Katniss Everdeen (*Los juegos del hambre*), Chris Evans / Steve Rogers (*Capitán América*), Denzel Washington / Malcolm X (*Malcolm X*), Daniel Craig / James Bond (*James Bond*), Emma Watson / Hermione Granger (*Harry Potter*), Ewan McGregor / Obi-Wan Kenobi (*La guerra de las galaxias*), Carrie Fisher / Princess Leia (*La guerra de las galaxias*), Johnny Depp / Jack Sparrow (*Piratas del Caribe*), Meryl Streep / Margaret Thatcher (*La dama de hierro*), Harrison Ford / Indiana Jones (*En busca del arca perdida*), Matthew Morrison / Will Schuester (*Glee*), Christian Bale / Batman (*El caballero oscuro*), Jon Hamm / Don Draper (*Mad Men*), Jamie Foxx / Ray Charles (*Ray*).

Video track (Act. D, Paso 1): This video clip can be found on the DVD to accompany *Conéctate: Cap. 14*, Track 2.

D. A ver: ¿Qué actividades culturales prefieren?

PASO 1. Mira y escucha. Luego mira otra vez con pausas e indica todos los elementos culturales que menciona cada persona.

¿Qué tipo de actividades culturales hay aquí?

	ARTE	BAILE	LITERATURA	MUSEOS	MÚSICA	PINTURA	TEATRO
1. Andrea, de México	☑	☑	☐	☑	☐	☐	☑
2. Carlos, de México	☑	☑	☑	☐	☐	☑	☑
3. Ángela, de España	☐	☐	☑	☐	☑	☑	☐
4. Alejandro, de Argentina	☑	☐	☐	☑	☑	☐	☑

Point out (Act. D, Paso 2): The actual music genre is not always mentioned; students will have to listen to the description and determine the genre.

Videoscript: (Act. D, Paso 1):
1. ANDREA: *Eh, van al teatro. Hay muchísimos teatros aquí, muchísimas cuestiones de danza, de teatro, o sea el arte, van a muchos museos, son muy cultos.* **2.** CARLOS: *La Casa de Cultura Jesús Reyes Heroles, en esta casa se dan este, talleres, eh... de diferentes disciplinas artísticas, como pintura, ballet, teatro, danza, poesía, etcétera.* **3.** ÁNGELA: *En la cultura, no solo está la literatura, sino la pintura, la música, todo lo demás.* **4.** ALEJANDRO: *Hay muchos conciertos, vienen muchas bandas a nivel internacional... hay mucho teatro, hay mucho arte, hay mucha cultura en Buenos Aires... bueno acabamos de salir del Museo Nacional de Buenos Aires y ahora vamos al museo, al MALBA, al Museo de Arte Latinoamericano.*

PASO 2. Ahora mira y escucha otro video. Apunta el género (o los géneros) de música que menciona cada persona.

GÉNEROS DE MÚSICA

Video track (Act. D, Paso 2): This video clip can be found on the DVD to accompany *Conéctate: Cap. 14*, Track 3.

1. _d, h, k_ Rodrigo, de Argentina
2. _k_ Federico, de Nicaragua
3. _c_ Agustina, de Argentina
4. _f, j_ Carlos, del Perú
5. _a, g, h, k_ Isabel, de España

a. flamenco
b. música alternativa
c. música clásica
d. música disco
e. música hip hop
f. música latina
g. música moderna
h. música pop
i. música rap
j. música reggae
k. música rock

Note (Act. D, Paso 3): Students learned *la guitarra* in *Cap. 3*. In the video, Agustina mentions (*el*) *piano* and (*la*) *orquesta*, and Carlos mentions *salsa* and *merengue* music.

PASO 3. En parejas, contesten las siguientes preguntas sobre sus preferencias en música.

1. ¿Qué género de música te gusta a ti? ¿Qué género de música no te gusta para nada?
2. ¿Qué instrumentos musicales son populares en la música que te gusta?
3. ¿Te gusta la música electrónica o prefieres la música acústica?
4. ¿Bailas o cantas cuando escuchas música? ¿A qué género de música prefieres bailar? ¿A qué género te gusta cantar?
5. ¿Qué género de música escuchan las personas mayores donde vives tú? ¿Te gusta esa música también? ¿Qué instrumentos musicales son populares en esa música?

Videoscript (Act. D, Paso 2):
1. RODRIGO: *Por ejemplo, gente de 25 para arriba disfruta mucho más de, eh, de clásicos de, de música disco de los años 70, de música rock de los años 50, de los años 60, como Los Beatles, o como Chuck Berry, o como... Little Richard, o música para bailar... Em... o... mucho... mucha música... pop de los años 80, como Madonna, Michael Jackson... eh... B52, eh, puede ser muy larga la lista.* **2.** FEDERICO: *Eh... me gusta mucho ir a conciertos a ver los grupos en vivo. Soy mucho de rock, o sea... todos los conciertos a que voy son de grupos de rock.* **3.** AGUSTINA: *A mí, me gustaría también dar conciertos de piano con orquesta pero, bueno, hay que estudiar mucho para eso.* **4.** CARLOS: *Porque en el lugar donde trabajo hay música en vivo, hay bandas, y siempre tocan salsa, merengue, reggae y entonces es muy alegre, ¿no?* **5.** ISABEL: *Me gusta la música moderna, eh... tipo pop y rock, no me gusta mucho el flamenco.*

En español...

Here are names of some additional musical instruments in Spanish. As you see, many of them are cognates.

el acordeón	la flauta	el sintetizador/el
la armónica	el órgano	teclado (*keyboard*)
el arpa	la pandereta	la trompeta
el bajo (*bass*)	(*tambourine*)	el violín
la batería (*drum set*)	el piano	
el clarinete	el saxofón	

E. Entrevistas: Preferencias culturales

 PASO 1. Primero, apunta tus respuestas a estas preguntas. Luego, en parejas, túrnense para entrevistarse con las mismas preguntas.

1. En tu universidad, ¿qué hacen los estudiantes para divertirse?
2. ¿Te gustaría hacer algo en tu carrera (*career*) profesional relacionado con la cultura e identidad de una región o nación? ¿Por qué sí o no?
3. ¿Qué hay en la cultura norteamericana que les interesaría a los estudiantes de otros países? ¿Qué aspecto de la cultura de otro país te interesa a ti?
4. ¿De qué tipo de música u otra forma de arte de otro país (como, por ejemplo, la música salsa, la arquitectura de Gaudí, las novelas de Gabriel García Márquez, el baile folclórico o las películas de Guillermo del Toro) te gustaría aprender más?

 PASO 2. En grupos pequeños, hablen de sus preferencias en cuanto a la música. Pueden usar las siguientes preguntas como guía.

■ ¿Te gusta asistir a conciertos de música? ¿Cuál fue el primer concierto al que asististe? ¿Y cuál fue el último? ¿Qué género de música prefieres ver en vivo?
■ ¿Has bajado música del Internet? ¿Cuál fue la última canción que bajaste? ¿Qué sitio usas para bajar música? Si no bajas música del Internet, ¿dónde consigues la música que escuchas?
■ ¿Has asistido a una ópera o has visto una en la televisión? ¿Qué ópera viste? ¿Te gustó? Si no has visto una ópera, ¿te gustaría ver una? ¿Por qué sí o no?
■ ¿Has asistido a un ballet? ¿Qué ballet viste? ¿Dónde lo viste? Si no has visto un ballet, ¿te gustaría ver uno? ¿Por qué sí o no?

F. ¿Qué quisieras hacer?

PASO 1. Haz una lista de por lo menos tres actividades culturales que no haces, pero en las que quisieras participar algún día.

> **MODELO:** Quisiera ir a más museos de arte.
> También quisiera... y...

 PASO 2. En parejas, túrnense para expresar qué quisieran hacer. Luego cada uno debe decirle a su compañero/a qué debería hacer él o ella para realizar sus deseos.

> **MODELO:** E1: Quisiera ir a más museos de arte.
> E2: Deberías viajar a Washington, DC, para ver el Museo Nacional.

Suggestion (Act. F, Paso 2): Do this as a *Firma aquí* activity in which students mingle and converse until they find someone else with whom they have the first activity in common, then get that signature. Repeat the process to have students find additional cultural activities in common.

Note (Act. F, Paso 2): *Debería + inf.* was covered in *Comunicación* in *Cap. 13*.

Suggestion (Act. E, Paso 1): Assign one question to each pair, then have students report their answers to the class.

Suggestion (Act. E, Paso 2): Ask for 3 volunteers sit in front of the class and take turns spontaneously answering the questions as you ask them. Then have the rest of the class say who they have more in common with and why.

Expansion (Act. F): Have students work in groups if you have classroom Internet access, or work individually at home, and research the cultural activities of a Spanish-speaking city of their choice. Have them present three cultural activities in class, then say which they would like to do and why: *En Santiago de Chile hay el Centro Cultural Gabriel Mistral con salas para la danza, la música y el teatro. En el Museo Nacional de Bellas Artes hay muchas exposiciones con pinturas famosas. Quisiera ir a un concierto en el centro cultural porque me encanta la música.*

COMUN VOCABUL **ESTRUCTURA** TE

Note (Reciclaje): The subjunctive to express volition was presented in *Estructura 12.3*. The subjunctive to express disbelief and uncertainty was presented in *Estructura 13.2* and to express purpose and contingency in *Estructura 13.3*.

C Reciclaje

The present subjunctive

En todas partes (*Everywhere*), hay gente que está a favor de fomentar (*promote*) el arte y gente a quien no le da mucha importancia. Primero, completa cada oración con la forma correcta del verbo. Luego indica qué oraciones diría (*would say*) una persona a favor del arte. **¡Atención!** Algunos verbos tienen que estar en el subjuntivo y otros en el indicativo.

¿A FAVOR DEL ARTE?

- ☐ 1. «Espero que los músicos no __hagan__ (hacer) muchos conciertos este año.»
- ☑ 2. «Creo que la cultura __es__ (ser) importante para nuestra ciudad.»
- ☐ 3. «Quiero que los dueños __cierren__ (cerrar) las galerías de arte.»
- ☑ 4. «Tenemos que hacer algo para que la ciudad __tenga__ (tener) una vida cultural más activa.»
- ☑ 5. «Es muy importante que todos los ciudadanos (*citizens*) __participen__ (participar) en la vida cultural del país.»
- ☐ 6. «Siempre digo que para mí, la cultura no __tiene__ (tener) mucha importancia.»

■ Answers to this activity are in Appendix 2 at the back of your book.

14.1 Querían que la música fuera para todos

The past subjunctive

Para empezar...

El Sistema Nacional de las Orquestas Juveniles (*Youth*) e Infantiles (*Children's*) de Venezuela, conocido simplemente como «El Sistema», es un programa de educación musical y desarrollo (*development*) social que lleva la música a todos los sectores de la sociedad en todo el país. Desde su creación en 1975, ha sido un modelo para programas de música en muchos otros países, incluso los Estados Unidos y Canadá. La orquesta más conocida de El Sistema, la Sinfónica de la Juventud Venezolana Simón Bolívar, ha realizado giras (*tours*) en Europa, Asia y los Estados Unidos.

    ¿Qué querían los organizadores de El Sistema cuando lo crearon? Indica si cada una de las siguientes oraciones es cierta o falsa. **¡Atención!** Solo hay dos oraciones falsas.

La Sinfónica de la Juventud Venezolana Simón Bolívar

	CIERTO	FALSO
1. Querían que los jóvenes músicos venezolanos **tuvieran** la oportunidad de tocar en grupo.	☑	☐
2. Querían que la música **estuviera** al alcance (*reach*) de todas las clases sociales.	☑	☐
3. Recomendaban que **pusieran** orquestas juveniles solo en Caracas.	☐	☑
4. Era muy importante que los jóvenes de todo el país **pudieran** estudiar música.	☑	☐
5. Pedían que los profesores **pusieran** mucha pasión en sus clases.	☑	☐
6. Era necesario que el gobierno venezolano **diera** dinero para apoyar (*support*) El Sistema.	☑	☐
7. Pidieron que los profesores **hablaran** con los padres sobre la importancia de la educación musical.	☑	☐
8. Querían que los jóvenes **aprendieran** algo sobre la música clásica y la música tradicional venezolana.	☑	☐
9. Querían que los jóvenes **pudieran** estudiar música en un lugar seguro, alegre y divertido.	☑	☐
10. Esperaban que la música clásica **fuera** solo para los ricos.	☐	☑

Actividades analíticas

1 The verbs in bold in **Para empezar** are in the *past subjunctive* (**el imperfecto de subjuntivo**). Use what you saw there and what you know about Spanish verbs to complete the following conjugations.

	hablar	aprender	vivir
yo	habl**ara**	aprend**iera**	viviera
tú	hablaras	aprendieras	viv**ieras**
él/ella, Ud.	hablara	aprend**iera**	viv**iera**
nosotros/as	habl**áramos**	aprend**iéramos**	viviéramos
vosotros/as	habl**arais**	aprend**ierais**	viv**ierais**
ellos/ellas, Uds.	hablaran	aprendieran	viv**ieran**

2 The past subjunctive is formed with the stem of the verb (**habl-, aprend-, viv-**) plus one of the endings from the following chart. Use what you saw in **Actividades analíticas 1** to complete this chart.

TERMINACIONES DEL IMPERFECTO DE SUBJUNTIVO		
	-ar verbs	**-er / -ir** verbs
yo	-ara	-iera
tú	-aras	-ieras
él/ella, Ud.	-ara	-iera
nosotros/as	-áramos	-iéramos
vosotros/as	-arais	-ierais
ellos/ellas, Uds.	-aran	-ieran

3 Verbs that have an irregular stem in the preterite use this same stem in the past subjunctive, together with the endings for **-er / -ir** verbs.

verbo	raíz irregular	pretérito (yo)	imperfecto de subjuntivo (yo)
estar	estuv-	estuve	estuviera
poder	pud-	pude	pudiera
poner	pus-	puse	pusiera
tener	tuv-	tuve	tuviera

As in the preterite, **dar** is conjugated with the endings for **-er / -ir** verbs.

Yo quería que me **dieras** un libro.   *I wanted you to give me a book.*

The verbs **ir** and **ser** share the same irregular form, **fuera.** As with the preterite, the context will help you know whether **ir** or **ser** is intended.

Te recomendé que **fueras** al cine.   *I recommended that you go to the movies.*

No creían que **fuéramos** músicos.   *They didn't believe that we were musicians.*

(Continues)

Expansion (Act. analíticas 2): Write the verbs *hablar, aprender,* and *vivir* at the left side of the board with columns to the right headed with *presente, imperfecto, presente de subjuntivo,* and *imperfecto de subjuntivo.* Have volunteers conjugate one verb in each of the tenses. When the chart has been completed, ask for volunteers to circle the endings that are common to a subject across all verb tenses (*-s* for *tú, -mos* for *nosotros/as, -is* for *vosotros/as,* and *-n* for *ellos/ellas, Uds.*). It is important for students to see this pattern, since these endings are found in almost all tenses.

■ Answers to these activities are in Appendix 2 at the back of your book.

Autoprueba

Give the past subjunctive forms of the following verbs.

1. actuar (nosotros/as)
    _____
2. salir (yo) _____
3. comer (tú)
    _____

Respuestas: 1. actuáramos **2.** saliera **3.** comieras

Note (Act. 3): If you prefer, teach the past subjunctive forms as being based on the 3rd-person plural (*ellos/ellas*) form of the preterite with the final *-on* removed. *Estuvieron,* for instance, becomes *estuvier-,* to which *-a* (or *-as, -amos, -ais, -an*) is then added.

■ For more information and examples of irregular past subjunctive forms, as well as the past perfect subjunctive, see **Para saber más 14.1** at the back of your book.

Note (Para saber más): *Para saber más 14.1* covers irregular past subjunctive forms of *decir, dormir, hacer, mentir, morir, pedir, seguir, servir* and *traer.* It also covers the past perfect subjunctive.

4 The past subjunctive is used in the same environments as the present subjunctive when the main verb is in the past (whether preterite or imperfect), as seen in these examples.

PRESENTE DE SUBJUNTIVO	IMPERFECTO DE SUBJUNTIVO
To indicate a desire, something that you want to be true	
Piden que **hablemos** en la reunión. *They ask that we speak at the. meeting.*	**Pidieron** que **habláramos** en la reunión. *They asked that we speak at the meeting.*
Quiero que **estudies** conmigo. esta noche. *I want you to study with me tonight.*	**Quería** que **estudiaras** conmigo esta noche. *I wanted you to study with me tonight.*
To indicate something that may not be true	
No **creo** que **sea** muy buena idea. *I don't think it is a good idea.*	No **creía** que **fuera** muy buena idea. *I didn't think it was a good idea.*
Es imposible que **gane** el premio este año. *It's impossible for him/her to win the prize this year.*	**Era imposible** que **ganara** el premio este año. *It was impossible for him/her to win the prize this year.*

Actividades prácticas

A. Dos cineastas importantes　Luis Buñuel (España/México, 1900–1983) y Pedro Almodóvar (España, 1949–) son figuras muy importantes en el cine mundial. En las siguientes descripciones, hay cuatro posibles terminaciones, pero una es falsa. Primero, usa el tiempo del verbo (presente o imperfecto de subjuntivo) para emparejar las terminaciones con la descripción. Luego, para cada director de cine, adivina cuál es la terminación falsa y táchala (*cross it out*).

Suggestion (Act. A): Point out that the main verb in Q1 (*quería*) is in the imperfect, so it will be followed by the past subjunctive, while the main verb in sentence 2 (*quiere*) is in the present, so it will be followed by the present subjunctive.

1. Luis Buñuel quería que sus películas: __a__, __c__, __d__ y __h__.
2. Pedro Almodóvar quiere que sus películas: __b__, __e__, __f__ y __g__.

a. criticaran la religión en algunos casos
b. ~~critiquen el uso del violín en las orquestas sinfónicas~~
c. fueran fáciles de editar
d. mostraran una visión surrealista del mundo
e. muestren escenas escandalosas (*scandalous*)
f. sean a veces humorísticas (*humorous*)
g. tengan colores muy vivos y contrastantes (*contrasting*)
h. ~~tuvieran mucho éxito en Netflix.~~

Luis Buñuel

Pedro Almodóvar

B. Gustavo Dudamel   Gustavo Dudamel es un joven director de orquesta y un ex alumno de El Sistema en Venezuela. Empezó a dirigir orquestas en Venezuela en 1996, y en 2004 ganó el premio Gustav Mahler en Alemania. En 2009 lo designaron director de la Orquesta Filarmónica de Los Ángeles, cuando tenía solo 28 años. En octubre de ese año, hizo su primer concierto como director de la orquesta.

Escucha cada oración. Luego escribe **D** si se trata de lo que **Dudamel** quería durante su primera noche como director de la Filarmónica y **O** si se trata de lo que la **orquesta** quería. Escribe **X** si es **falsa** para los dos. Hay dos oraciones falsas.

1. __O__   3. __D__   5. __D__   7. __X__
2. __X__   4. __O__   6. __D__   8. __O__

Gustavo Dudamel, el director de la Orquesta Filarmónica de Los Ángeles

C. Diego Rivera y los deseos de los demás

PASO 1.   Diego Rivera fue uno de los artistas más famosos en la historia de Latinoamérica. Nació en México en 1886 y vivió en Europa entre 1907 y 1921. Desde su regreso a México hasta su muerte en 1957, fue una figura muy importante en el movimiento muralista mexicano. También es muy conocido por su matrimonio con la artista mexicana Frida Kahlo.

Completa cada oración con un verbo de la lista en su forma correcta. Luego adivina si Diego Rivera hizo lo que las personas mencionadas querían. **¡Atención!** Rivera hizo lo que querían en solo cinco de los ocho casos.

cambiar	estudiar	pintar	recrear (to recreate)
divorciarse	ir	quedarse	regresar

■ The audio files for in-text listening activities are available in the eBook, within Connect activities, and on the Online Learning Center.

Suggestion (Act. C, Paso 1): Have students work in pairs so that they can pool their knowledge. Encourage them to choose the verbs first and then decide what Rivera did and did not do, reminding them that he only did 5 of the activities listed.

¿Y LO HIZO?

	SÍ	NO

1. 1899: Su papá quería que ___estudiara___ en una escuela militar por muchos años. □ ☑
2. 1906: Su maestro de arte en México quería que ___fuera___ a Europa a estudiar. ☑ □
3. 1921: Sus amigos europeos querían que ___se quedara___ en Europa para siempre. □ ☑
4. 1921: El gobierno mexicano quería que ___regresara___ a su tierra natal (home country) a pintar murales. ☑ □
5. 1932: La familia Rockefeller le pidió que ___pintara___ un mural en el Rockefeller Center de Nueva York. ☑ □
6. 1933: La familia Rockefeller le pidió que ___cambiara___ el mural porque tenía un retrato (portrait) de Lenin, el revolucionario ruso (Russian). □ ☑
7. 1940: El gobierno mexicano le pidió que ___recreara___ el mismo mural con el retrato de Lenin en el Palacio de Bellas Artes en México. ☑ □
8. 1940: Frida Kahlo le pidió que ___se divorciaran___, pero volvieron a casarse unos meses después. ☑ □

Diego Rivera, muralista mexicano

PASO 2.   Siguiendo el modelo del **Paso 1,** completa las siguientes frases con lo que querían los demás que tú hicieras. Luego di si lo hiciste o no.

¿Y LO HICISTE?

	SÍ	NO

1. Cuando me gradué de la escuela secundaria, mis padres querían que yo _____ □ □
2. Cuando me gradué de la escuela secundaria, mis amigos esperaban que yo _____ □ □
3. Cuando empecé a estudiar en la universidad, mi familia quería que _____ □ □
4. Cuando empecé a estudiar en la universidad, mis profesores me recomendaron que _____ □ □

Suggestion (Act. C, Paso 2): Give students a few minutes to create their sentences, then have them exchange their work with a partner who can check to make sure the sentences make sense. Ask for volunteers to share one of their answers with the class and explain why they did or didn't do what was recommended.

Script (Act. B): 1. *Quería que Dudamel trabajara bien con todos los músicos.* **2.** *Prefería que el público empezara a dormirse en el concierto.* **3.** *Esperaba que la orquesta lo tomara en serio, a pesar de su edad.* **4.** *Quería que Dudamel les diera a los músicos suficiente tiempo para ensayar (es decir, practicar tocar sus instrumentos).* **5.** *Quería que los críticos escribieran cosas buenas de él.* **6.** *Esperaba que el público lo aceptara bien como persona y como director de la orquesta.* **7.** *Insistía en que la orquesta llegara tarde al concierto.* **8.** *Necesitaba que Dudamel entendiera el estilo de cada músico.*

D. Antes y ahora

PASO 1. En el pasado, ¿qué tenía uno que hacer para empezar una carrera artística? En parejas, completen las oraciones con uno de los consejos de la lista. **¡Atención!** Tienen que conjugar el verbo del consejo.

> **MODELO:** Si querías ser un buen director de cine, era necesario que tuvieras experiencia con la actuación para entender el proceso de hacer cine.

__a__ 1. Si querías ser una buena guitarrista de rock, era necesario que...

_____

__c__ 2. Si querías ser un buen cantante de ópera, era recomendable que...

_____

__d__ 3. Si querías ser una buena directora de orquesta, era importante que...

_____

__b__ 4. Si querías ser un actor famoso, era fundamental que...

_____

__e__ 5. Si querías ser una buena bailarina, era esencial que...

_____

__g__ 6. Si querías ser un buen fotógrafo, era vital que...

_____

__f__ 7. Si querías ser una buena pintora, era primordial (*fundamental*) que...

_____

CONSEJOS:

a. tomar clases de guitarra clásica para entender mejor su instrumento
b. poder bailar y cantar al mismo tiempo
c. cantar otro tipo de música de vez en cuando para relajar la voz
d. tocar algún instrumento para entender la orquesta mejor
e. estudiar danza clásica para entender mejor la historia del baile
f. aprender a dibujar para poder pintar mejor
g. ir a una escuela de fotografía para entender mejor la técnica de la fotografía

PASO 2. Hoy en día, ¿siguen siendo válidos estos consejos? En parejas, cambien las oraciones que escribieron en el **Paso 1** al tiempo presente y decidan si cada consejo es válido todavía.

> **MODELO:** Si quieres ser un buen director de cine, es necesario que tengas experiencia con la actuación para entender el proceso de hacer cine.
> Sí, es válido todavía.

CONÉCTATE AL MUNDO HISPANO

La Escuela Internacional de Cine y TV (EICTV) empezó en 1986 en una zona rural de Cuba llamada San Antonio de los Baños con el propósito de preparar cineastas de todas partes del mundo en estilos *no* hollywoodenses. Cuando la EICTV se estableció, era estrictamente para alumnos de Asia, África y Latinoamérica y ofrecían becas (*scholarships*) a los alumnos. La diversidad multinacional forma una parte integral de la escuela. Los profesores son cineastas internacionales con muchísima experiencia y éxito y a la vez los estudiantes tienen muchas oportunidades de participar en todos los papeles clave (*key*) del proceso creativo: actor, camarógrafo, director, editor, guionista o productor.

↻ Reciclaje

The infinitive

Aquí hay una conversación entre dos amigos, pero las oraciones están desordenadas. Primero, escribe la terminación correcta para cada infinitivo (**-ar, -er, -ir**). Luego pon las oraciones en un orden lógico. La primera y la última ya están hechas.

__3__ a. ¡Me encantan Los Amigos Invisibles! ¿Por qué no vamos a compr__ar__ ropa nueva para llevar al concierto?

__6__ b. ¡Perfecto! A ver si podemos com__er__ algo rápido antes de lleg__ar__ también. No me gusta asist__ir__ a los conciertos con hambre.

__1__ c. ¿Va a hab__er__ un concierto en el Teatro Nacional esta noche?

__7__ d. Me parece muy bien. ¡Va a s__er__ una noche de maravilla!

__5__ e. Sí, no te preocupes. El concierto va a empez__ar__ a las nueve.

__4__ f. ¡Qué buena idea! Pero si vamos primero a las tiendas, ¿vamos a lleg__ar__ al teatro a tiempo?

__2__ g. ¡Sí! Van a toc__ar__ Los Amigos Invisibles y quiero ir, pero no sé qué ropa us__ar__.

Note (Reciclaje): This activity focuses students' attention on the endings of the infinitive. It will be useful for them to have this fresh in mind as they begin to work on the future tense in *Estructura 14.2*.

■ Answers to this activity are in Appendix 2 at the back of your book.

14.2   ¿Qué será el «arte cinético»?

The future

Para empezar...

El arte cinético es un movimiento artístico que ha tenido una importancia especial en Sudamérica. El artista Carlos Cruz-Diez es uno de sus exponentes más distinguidos. Para aprender más sobre este arte y este artista, escoge la respuesta más adecuada para cada pregunta en la lista.

■ Answers to these activities are in Appendix 2 at the back of your book.

PREGUNTAS

1. __e__ ¿Qué **será** el «arte cinético»?
2. __h__ ¿Quién **será** Carlos Cruz-Diez?
3. __g__ ¿De dónde **será**?
4. __a__ ¿Dónde **vivirá**?
5. __d__ ¿Qué tipo de arte **hará**?
6. __f__ ¿Qué ciudades **tendrán** obras de él?
7. __b__ ¿Dónde **estará** el Museo Carlos Cruz-Diez?
8. __c__ ¿Por qué **será** tan importante Venezuela en el mundo del arte cinético?

RESPUESTAS

a. Vive en París.
b. Está en Caracas.
c. Porque hay varios artistas cinéticos importantes que son de Venezuela.
d. Hace pintura, escultura y arquitectura en que el color cambia según la posición del espectador.
e. Se refiere al arte que tiene movimiento o que parece tener movimiento.
f. Algunas de las ciudades que tienen obras de él son Caracas, Houston, Londres, Madrid y París.
g. Es de Venezuela.
h. Es un artista venezolano que hace arte cinético.

Una instalación cinética de Carlos Cruz-Diez en el piso de un aeropuerto

Actividades analíticas

1 The verbs in bold in **Para empezar** are in the *future* tense (**el futuro**). Despite its name, this tense is commonly used to express conjectures about what might be true in the present.

Jaime no ha llegado. **Estará** dormido.   *Jaime hasn't arrived. He might be asleep.*

The future is particularly common in questions, when one has little idea what the answer is.

¿Dónde **estarán**?	*Where could they be?*
¿Cómo **se llamará** ese hombre?	*What is that man's name? (I really have no idea.)*
¿De dónde **será** Pedro Almodóvar?	*Where on earth is Pedro Almodóvar from?*

The future is also used to express future actions, especially in the written language.

Mañana **tendrán** el nuevo libro de Isabel Allende.	*They will have the new book by Isabel Allende tomorrow.*
El director del museo **hablará** en la universidad el próximo año.	*The director of the museum will speak at the university next year.*

As you saw in **Estructura 2.4**, the future is also expressed with **ir + a** + *infinitive*.

Vamos a visitar el museo.   *We're going to visit the museum.*

2 Use the forms you saw in **Para empezar** and the patterns you see here to complete the following conjugations.

	estar	ser	vivir
yo	estaré	seré	viviré
tú	estarás	serás	vivirás
él/ella, Ud.	estará	será	vivirá
nosotros/as	estaremos	seremos	viviremos
vosotros/as	estaréis	seréis	viviréis
ellos/ellas, Uds.	estarán	serán	vivirán

3 The stem for the future consists of the entire infinitive form (in the above chart, **estar-**, **ser-** and **vivir-**), to which one of the following endings is added.

TERMINACIONES DEL FUTURO	
yo	-é
tú	-ás
él/ella, Ud.	-á
nosotros/as	-emos
vosotros/as	-éis
ellos/ellas, Uds.	-án

4 Several verbs have an irregular stem in the future, but they continue to use the above endings.

¿Por qué?

Future meaning is expressed easily in Spanish with **ir + a** + *infinitive*, so the future tense itself is used much less for that function. As a result, it has taken on the job of expressing conjecture and speculation. This is typical of what happens in languages. As two forms compete for the same meaning, each begins to take on a more specialized usage. **Ir + a** + *infinitive* has become the main way to express the future, and the future tense is used more to express conjecture.

Suggestion (¿Por qué?): Have students convert these sentences with **ir** to the future tense: *Mañana voy a estar en mi casa. Juan va a trabajar esta noche. El concierto va a ser muy bueno.* Then have them convert sentences in the future tense to use **ir**: *Tendremos que llegar temprano. Muchas películas saldrán este verano. ¿Vendrás a la clase mañana?*

Expansion (Act. analíticas 3): Have students circle those parts of the future tense endings that are common to almost all tenses (*-s, -mos, -is, -n*). To make this clearer, have them do a side-by-side conjugation of these same verbs in the present and future tenses.

VERBO	RAÍZ	EJEMPLO	
decir	**dir-**	¿Qué **dirá** tu mamá?	*What will your mom say?*
haber	**habr-**	¿**Habrá** un museo en la universidad?	*Do you suppose there's a museum at the university?*
hacer	**har-**	**Haremos** lo que te prometimos.	*We will do what we promised you.*
poder	**podr-**	¿**Podrás** cantar también?	*Do you think you'll be able to sing, too?*
poner	**pondr-**	Claro que puedes tomar prestado mi libro. Lo **pondré** en tu escritorio.	*Sure you can borrow my book. I'll put it on your desk.*
salir	**saldr-**	¿Cuándo **saldrá** el nuevo disco?	*When will the new record come out?*
tener	**tendr-**	¿**Tendrán** escultura en ese museo?	*Might they have sculpture art at that museum?*
venir	**vendr-**	¿**Vendrá** el pianista también?	*Will the pianist come too?*

■ For more examples of irregular future forms and a look at the future perfect tense, see **Para saber más 14.2** at the back of your book.

Note (Para saber más): *Para saber más 14.2* covers the irregular future forms of *querer, saber,* and *valer,* as well as the formation and use of the future perfect.

Actividades prácticas

A. ¿Qué pasará?   Empareja cada pregunta con la respuesta más lógica.

1. __h__ ¿Llegaré al concierto?
2. __e__ ¿Cuándo saldrá la nueva película de Almodóvar?
3. __f__ ¿A tus papás les gustará la pintura que hice?
4. __g__ ¿Cantarán los niños en el concierto?
5. __c__ ¿Tendrán algo interesante en la galería del centro?
6. __a__ ¿Visitaremos el museo de arte moderno mañana?
7. __b__ ¿No habrá otra obra de teatro? Esa no me gusta.
8. __d__ ¿Podremos pasar un día en Cusco?

a. ¡Sí, lo vamos a visitar!
b. No, es la única que hay esta noche.
c. Me imagino que sí, porque siempre tienen cosas interesantes.
d. ¡Claro que sí! Vamos a estar un mes en el Perú. ¡Será fabuloso!
e. Me parece que sale en noviembre.
f. Lo siento, pero sinceramente no creo que les guste.
g. Van a estar allí pero no van a cantar.
h. Sí, no hay tráfico.

 B. Los países y la cultura   En parejas, emparejen cada pregunta con un país o países de la lista.

Argentina	Cuba	México	Puerto Rico
Bolivia/Chile	España	Perú	la República Dominicana

1. ¿En qué país estará el Museo Larco (un museo de arte prehispánico andino)? ___el Perú___
2. ¿De qué país vendrá el «mambo» (una forma musical que se hizo popular en La Habana en los años treinta)? ___Cuba___
3. ¿De dónde serán los padres del actor y compositor Lin-Manuel Miranda? ___Puerto Rico___
4. ¿De dónde vendrá la música merengue? ___la República Dominicana___
5. ¿En qué país estará el Teatro Colón (un teatro de ópera)? ___Argentina___
6. Entre los países hispanos, ¿qué país tendrá más películas ganadoras (*winners*) en toda la historia de los premios Óscar? ___España___
7. ¿En qué países bailarán «la cueca»? ___Bolivia/Chile___
8. ¿En qué país dirán que el cantante Juan Gabriel fue «un ícono de nuestra música»? ___México___

Autoprueba

Use what you've just learned to conjugate the following verbs in the future. **¡Atención!** Be careful of the verb with the irregular stem!

1. **ir**
   yo _____
   tú _____
   él/ella, Ud. _____
   nosotros/as _____
   vosotros/as _____
   ellos/ellas, Uds. _____

2. **interpretar**
   ellos/ellas, Uds. _____

3. **tener**
   yo _____

Respuestas: 1. iré, irás, irá, iremos, iréis, irán 2. interpretarán 3. tendré

Suggestion (Act. B): Tell students that the future is often used in cases where one answers with one's best guess, and that is the case here. They will have to use their critical thinking skills and strategies (including process of elimination and intelligent guessing) to choose the best answer.

Suggestion (Act. C, Paso 1): Write 1–10 on the board and have each group write their answers (*C* or *F*) there. As a class, look over the results and see where there is consensus and where there is disagreement.

Suggestion (Act. C, Paso 3): Have each group choose a single area (*música, baile,* etc.) and write their predictions about that. Then, have them choose their top prediction and have them write it on the board for class discussion.

Suggestion (Act. D): Write each category on the board and have each group choose two of their sentences and write them in the appropriate category. Have students use the results to judge which categories are more in people's minds than others and how optimistic or pessimistic people are about the future. Alternatively, assign one group to each category.

C. La cultura en el año 2025

PASO 1. ¿Cómo será el mundo en 2025? En grupos, lean la siguiente lista de oraciones e indiquen si piensan que es **cierta** o **falsa** cada una. **¡Atención!** No hay respuestas correctas o incorrectas. Todo depende de la opinión del grupo.

	CIERTO	FALSO
1. Podremos ir al cine para ver, sentir y oler (*smell*) una película.	☐	☐
2. Comeremos en restaurantes siempre. No comeremos en casa nunca.	☐	☐
3. Solo leeremos libros electrónicos.	☐	☐
4. Iremos a museos y galerías de arte con más frecuencia.	☐	☐
5. Los músicos ya no usarán instrumentos. La música será electrónica.	☐	☐
6. Toda la música estará en inglés.	☐	☐
7. Todas las películas serán de los Estados Unidos.	☐	☐
8. Todavía habrá clases de historia de arte en las universidades.	☐	☐
9. Ya no habrá pinturas tradicionales. Los artistas harán todo en la computadora.	☐	☐
10. Iremos al teatro con más frecuencia.	☐	☐

PASO 2. ¿Cómo será el mundo según tu grupo? Cambien las oraciones falsas para que sean ciertas.

PASO 3. ¿Qué otras predicciones tienen Uds. para las artes en el futuro? Consideren la música, las artes plásticas, el baile, el teatro, el cine, la literatura, la poesía, etcétera. En sus grupos, hagan por lo menos cuatro predicciones más.

D. El futuro de tu país

En grupos, creen una predicción sobre la vida en este país en 2050 relacionada con cada categoría de la lista. Según tu grupo, ¿cómo será el futuro de este país?

la cultura   la educación   el medio ambiente   la política
la sociedad   la tecnología

E. Cultura: El cine de Argentina

PASO 1. Lee el texto sobre Argentina.

Argentina

La directora argentina Lucrecia Martel

Junto con México y Brasil, Argentina ha tenido una de las industrias cinematográficas[a] más fuertes de Latinoamérica desde finales del siglo XIX. De allí se lanzaron[b] las carreras de algunas de las estrellas más glamurosas del cine hispanohablante. Pero la turbulenta historia política de Argentina tuvo un impacto sobre el cine en varios momentos, no solo en la producción sino en las historias que las películas contaban.

A partir de la década de los 30, cuando empezó la producción de cine sonoro,[c] se produjeron en Argentina grandes películas musicales, comedias y dramas. Libertad Lamarque es, quizás, la actriz más conocida de esta época. En los años 40, bajo la presidencia de Juan Perón, se incrementó bastante la censura.[d] Esto, combinado con la importación de las películas de Hollywood, tuvo un impacto negativo sobre la industria de cine. A partir de los años 1960, se empezó un movimiento de cine de fuerte compromiso[e] político, el que luego se conoció como «el Tercer Cine». Los directores de este movimiento declaraban que en Latinoamérica se debía de reconocer sus condiciones de «tercer mundo» y hacer películas que reflejaban su propia realidad. La película emblemática del movimiento es *La hora de los hornos*[f] (1968), dirigida por Octavio Getino y Fernando Solanas, y funcionaba como un manifiesto audiovisual en contra del imperialismo cultural de los Estados Unidos y Europa.

Después de que terminó la dictadura militar y se disminuyó[g] la censura, se produjo un gran número de películas que contaba las historias traumáticas de aquellos años. Películas como *La historia oficial* (1985) y *La noche de los lápices* (1986) hicieron que los eventos políticos de los años 70 se conocieran en todo el mundo. A partir de los años 90, el cine argentino se transformó, en cierta manera rechazando[h] tantos años de cine político. Los jóvenes cineastas querían contar historias sobre la vida cotidiana,[i] con una cámara que observaba a sus personajes en vez de juzgarlos.[j] Esta nueva tradición, conocida como «el Nuevo Cine Argentino», ha atraído la atención de públicos en todo el mundo, en particular en festivales internacionales. Directores como Lucrecia Martel (*La niña santa, La mujer sin cabeza*) y Pablo Trapero (*El bonaerense, El clan*) están entre los más representativos de esta generación. Sus películas se caracterizan por su realismo, con observaciones agudas[k] sobre el estado de la sociedad argentina en los tiempos actuales.[l]

[a]*film (adj.)* [b]*se... were launched* [c]*sound (adj.)* [d]*censorship* [e]*engagement, commitment* [f]*furnaces* [g]*decreased* [h]*rejecting* [i]*daily* [j]*en... instead of judging them* [k]*sharp, acute* [l]*current, present-day*

PASO 2. Completa las oraciones con la forma correcta del futuro usando los verbos de la lista. Luego indica las oraciones probables según la lectura y lo que sabes.

haber   ir   obtener   poder   poner   tener   ver   volver

Durante los próximos diez años...   **¿ES PROBABLE?**

1. los argentinos __verán__ más películas chinas que norteamericanas.   ☐
2. los directores argentinos __obtendrán__ muchos premios (*awards*) más en los festivales internacionales.   ☐
3. la censura __volverá__ a controlar los medios de comunicación del país.   ☐
4. cualquier argentino __podrá__ hacer una película, sin mucho dinero, con solo un teléfono celular y una computadora portátil.   ☐
5. las películas __pondrán__ más énfasis en los efectos especiales que en sus historias.   ☐
6. los actores argentinos __tendrán__ los salarios más altos de todo el mundo.   ☐
7. mis amigos y yo __iremos__ al cine para ver una película del Nuevo Cine Argentino.   ☐
8. __Habrá__ un homenaje a Libertad Lamarque durante la presentación de los Premios Óscar en los Estados Unidos.   ☐

PASO 3. En parejas, contesten las preguntas y explíquense las respuestas.

1. Entre los países hispanos, Argentina, España y México son de los más ricos. ¿Qué relación ves entre eso y el hecho de que también son los países hispanos que tienen la industria cinematográfica más fuerte?
2. Para los países hispanos que son chicos y no tienen muchos recursos, es difícil crear una industria cinematográfica y competir contra países como Argentina. ¿Qué países piensas que están en esa situación?
3. La industria cinematográfica en los Estados Unidos es grandísima y es difícil que películas de otros países penetren el mercado norteamericano. Sin embargo, ¿hay películas de países hispanos que lo han podido hacer?

Note (Act. E, Paso 3): Almost all Spanish-speaking countries have some film industry, but many of the smaller countries, such as those of Central America, only rarely produce films that are seen internationally.

CONÉCTATE AL MUNDO PROFESIONAL

To see how international the U.S. television and movie industries are behind the scenes, look at the credits of some of your favorite shows and movies. How many international names do you see contributing to the productions? Filming the *Conéctate* videos required bilingual producers from around the world who could communicate with both the English-speaking film crew and the Spanish-speaking permit agencies, equipment vendors, and service providers for each location. Openness to and understanding of language and cultures can uncover professional opportunities in some aspect of almost any industry.

¡Leamos!

«La princesa azul» por Juan Luis Sánchez

La actriz Zoe Saldana

Suggestion (Antes de leer, Paso 2): Explain that movie titles often are not direct translations; for example: *Star Wars* is *La guerra de las galaxias* in Spanish, *The Dark Knight* was *El caballero de la noche* in Mexico, *All about Eve* was *Eva al desnudo* in Spain. The same is true of film titles translated into English: the Mexican film *El laberinto del fauno* became *Pan's Labyrinth* in the United States and the Spanish film *Abre los ojos* was named *Vanilla Sky* for its Hollywood remake.

Antes de leer

PASO 1. Zoe Saldana es una estrella de cine bilingüe que nació en Nueva Jersey de un padre dominicano y una madre puertorriqueña. Es conocida por su sus papeles en películas como *Star Trek, Avatar* y *Guardianes de la galaxia*. Vas a leer un artículo sobre Saldana, pero primero, trata de poner los datos de su vida en orden cronológico (del 1 a 5).

a. __2__ A los nueve años, se mudó a la República Dominicana.

b. __4__ La reclutó (*recruited*) una agencia de talentos.

c. __1__ Nació en Nueva Jersey en 1978.

d. __3__ Participó en un programa para jóvenes interesados por la interpretación.

e. __5__ Se hizo estrella con el papel de Neytiri en *Avatar*.

PASO 2. A veces las traducciones (*translations*) de los títulos de las películas parecen mucho a los títulos originales, pero otras veces usan juegos de palabras (*plays on words*) que no se traducen bien a otro idioma. Por eso, tienen que cambiarlos un poco (o por completo) para presentar la película en otro país. Empareja el título de cada película de Zoe Saldana en español con el título correspondiente en inglés.

1. __c__ *Adivina quién*
2. __h__ *Lazos de sangre*
3. __b__ *Un funeral de muerte*
4. __f__ *Ladrones* (Thieves)
5. __d__ *El ladrón de palabras*
6. __e__ *Piratas del Caribe*
7. __a__ *El ritmo del éxito* (success)
8. __g__ *En el punto de mira*

a. *Center Stage*
b. *Death at a Funeral*
c. *Guess Who*
d. *The Words*
e. *Pirates of the Caribbean*
f. *Takers*
g. *Vantage Point*
h. *Blood Ties*

PASO 3. En grupos, describan qué pasa en una o más de las películas de Zoe Saldana y expliquen el papel de la actriz. Usen las películas de la siguiente lista o las de los **Pasos 1** y **2.** Luego compartan la información con el resto de la clase.

Burning Palms
Crossroads
Los perdedores

Piratas del Caribe: La maldición de la Perla Negra
Star Trek: Más allá (Beyond)

A leer

Lee el artículo sobre la actriz Zoe Saldana y contesta las preguntas.

La princesa azul

No deja de[a] resultar paradójico que la protagonista de la película más taquillera[b] de la historia no se haya convertido en la gran megaestrella del momento. Pero nadie pudo ver en *Avatar* su rostro[c] porque su interpretación de la princesa azul Na'vi Neytiri fue digitalizada y retocada[d] por ordenador.[e] Aun así, Zoe Saldana empieza a ser reconocida, y se perfila[f] como una de las grandes para los próximos años. Extremadamente atractiva, transmite sencillez y simpatía.

Zoe Yadira Saldaña Nazario nació el 19 de junio de 1978, en Nueva Jersey (Estados Unidos), pero su madre era puertorriqueña y su padre dominicano. Cuando tenía 9 años, su progenitor[g] falleció[h] en accidente de tráfico, y su madre decidió trasladarse a la República Dominicana con Zoe y sus hermanas. [...]

En la República Dominicana, Zoe Saldaña se apuntó[i] a clases de danza. Al regresar a los Estados Unidos a los 17 años, decidió participar en un programa llamado *Face Theater,* para jóvenes interesados por la interpretación, y descubrió que no se le daba nada mal.[j] Junto con sus compañeros, representaba obras para concienciar[k] a los adolescentes de los riesgos del uso de las drogas y otros temas de interés, pero ella demostraba un talento fuera de lo común. De hecho, antes de acabar fue reclutada por una agencia de talentos, que le consiguió un pequeño papel en un episodio de *Ley y orden.*

Poco después, aprovechó sus dotes[l] para la danza para hacerse con el papel de la talentosa ballarina Eva, una de las protagonistas de *El ritmo del éxito.* Desde entonces no le ha faltado trabajo en títulos como *Crossroads (hasta el final)*, protagonizada por Britney Spears, aunque llamó especialmente la atención como la pirata Anamaría, en *Piratas del Caribe. La maldición de la Perla Negra,* donde le daba una bofetada[m] a Jack Sparrow, el personaje interpretado por Johnny Depp. Su apellido artístico es Saldana, no Saldaña, para no confundir a los angloparlantes.[n]

«Mi madre y yo éramos muy aficionadas al cine cuando yo era pequeña. Siempre veíamos películas de grandes directores como Spielberg, que para mí era muy lejano. Nunca soñé que trabajaría con él», me confesaba en la entrevista Saldana. La actriz aún no acaba de creerse los elogios[ñ] que le dedicó Steven Spielberg, muy satisfecho con su trabajo, tras reclutarla para interpretar a la agente de aduanas Dolores Torres, que le niega continuamente el permiso para pasar al personaje de Tom Hanks, en *La terminal.*

Tras sus trabajos en la comedia *Adivina quién* y el thriller *En el punto de mira,* a Saldana le llegó una gran oportunidad de la mano de J.J. Abrams, que necesitaba a una joven actriz para interpretar a Uhura, una de las protagonistas de *Star Trek* [...].

El film fue un gran éxito, pero no tanto como *Avatar,* de James Cameron, un auténtico fenómeno de masas en el que Saldana interpretaba a la protagonista, la Na'vi que encandilaba[o] al personaje de Sam Worthington. Aunque preparó su papel durante seis meses, y la voz es la suya, sus movimientos fueron digitalizados, y su personaje recreado por ordenador.

Ahora que empieza a convertirse en una estrella, el futuro de Zoe Saldana no puede ser más prometedor.[p] Tras interpretar a la chica que le da una droga a su novio por error, en el remake americano de *Un funeral de muerte,* ha protagonizado la cinta de acción *Los perdedores,* la comedia dramática *Burning Palms,* y el thriller *Ladrones.* No tardarán en caer también las secuelas[q] de *Avatar* y *Star Trek.*

[d]*deja... to stop* [b]*box office success* [c]*face* [d]*retouched* [e]*computer* [f]*se... is shaping up* [g]*father* [h]*died* [i]*se... enrolled* [j]*no... she didn't find it at all bad* [k]*to make aware* [l]*talents* [m]*a slap* [n]*English-speakers* [ñ]*praises* [o]*dazzled* [p]*promising* [q]*sequels*

1. ¿Por qué no vio nadie la cara de Zoe Saldana en la película *Avatar*?

2. ¿De dónde son los padres de Zoe Saldana?

3. ¿Por qué se mudó (*move*) a la República Dominicana?

4. ¿Cuál fue la primera pasión artística de Zoe Saldana?

5. ¿En qué año volvió a vivir en los Estados Unidos?

6. ¿Cuál fue su primer papel después de ser reclutada por una agencia de talentos?

7. ¿Por qué usa el apellido artístico «Saldana» en vez de su apellido verdadero, «Saldaña»?

8. Describe la relación entre Zoe Saldana y Stephen Spielberg.

9. Además de Stephen Spielberg, ¿con quiénes ha trabajado Zoe Saldana?

Después de leer

En parejas, hagan predicciones sobre el futuro de Zoe Saldana. ¿Cuál es la mejor predicción?

MODELO: Será la estrella de *Avatar 3, 4* y *5.* Tendrá mucho éxito y ganará un Premio Óscar.

¡Escuchemos!

La cultura que nos rodea°   *nos... surrounds us*

Antes de escuchar

Haz una lista de cuatro o cinco lugares culturales destacados (*renowned*) de tu ciudad o país. Luego escoge uno de los lugares de la lista y prepara una descripción del lugar para un turista de habla hispana. Describe el lugar y lo que lo hace famoso y haz una recomendación para el turista.

MODELO: El museo Smithsonian es un museo de historia natural grande y famoso. Está en una zona de muchos museos en la ciudad capital de los Estados Unidos, Wáshington, D.C. Recomiendo que visites la colección de joyería (*jewelry*) y, en especial, el diamante Hope.

A escuchar

Video track (A escuchar): This video clip can be found on the DVD to accompany *Conéctate: Cap. 14,* Track 4.

PASO 1. Mira y escucha mientras las personas describen algunos lugares famosos de sus países. Mira otra vez con pausas y empareja cada persona con el lugar que describe.

1. __e__
Benedicto, de Costa Rica

2. __c__
Paul, de Panamá

3. __a__
Jorge, de Argentina

4. __d__
Almudena, de España

5. __b__
José Manuel, de México

a. La Casa Rosada
b. El Centro Cultural de Morelos
c. El Centro de Visitantes del Canal de Panamá
d. El Museo del Prado
e. El parque Zarcero

PASO 2. Contesta las preguntas.

1. ¿Qué era el parque Zarcero antes de ser parque?   la plaza de deportes, para jugar fútbol
2. ¿Cuándo fue inaugurado el Centro de Visitantes del Canal de Panamá?   2004
3. ¿Cuál es la función de la Casa Rosada en Buenos Aires?   Es la casa de gobierno.
4. ¿Qué tipo de museo es el Museo del Prado?   Es un museo de arte.
5. ¿Cómo se llama el Centro Cultural de Morelos?   Jardín Borda

Después de escuchar

En grupos pequeños, escojan un lugar del video que quisieran visitar y expliquen por qué. Luego describan el lugar que escogieron al resto de la clase.

Videoscript (A escuchar):
1. BENEDICTO: *Parque Zarcero. Esto... este parque, o este lugar aquí pertenece a la iglesia también. Un señor —ya murió hace muchísimos años— regaló esto. Aquí era la plaza de deportes. Donde jugaba fútbol, o soccer. Fútbol. Después vino la idea de la municipalidad de hacer un parque.* **2.** PAUL: *Bueno, el edificio detrás de mi persona es el centro de visitantes que fue inaugurado en el año 2004 y es la ventana a través del cual, de la cual el público ve el canal.* **3.** JORGE: *Estamos en la Plaza de Mayo, en Microcentro, acá en Buenos Aires, en el centro de... en la capital de Argentina... parados frente a la Casa Rosada, la casa de gobierno.* **4.** ALMUDENA: *Estamos en el Museo del Prado. Es eh... pues uno, un museo de arte de Madrid, uno de los más importantes a nivel nacional en España, y donde están obras de Velázquez, de Goya,...* **5.** JOSÉ MANUEL: *Bueno, aquí están en el Centro Cultural de, de Morelos, este se llama Jardín Borda... y aquí día a día hacemos, tratamos de que se conserve, la antigüedad.*

Expansion (Después de escuchar): Have students (or groups of students) each select one of the places described in the video to research, then present a 3–5 minute talk encouraging other students to visit the location.

¡Escribamos!

Dos lugares famosos

Una manera excelente de entender un lugar que no conoces es por medio de una comparación con un lugar que ya conoces bien. Para describir un lugar que conoces bien en tu propio país vas a necesitar nuevo vocabulario en español.

Antes de escribir

Escoge un lugar mencionado en **¡Escuchemos!** (u otro lugar del cual has leído hasta ahora en *Conéctate*) y un lugar de tu país. Apunta información de los dos lugares en la tabla. Haz una lista del vocabulario que vas a buscar en un diccionario.

	Un lugar de ¡Escuchemos!	Un lugar de mi país
¿Qué es?	La Casa Rosada, casa de gobierno	la Casa Blanca, casa de ____
¿Dónde está?		
¿Cómo es?		
¿Qué se puede hacer allí?		
Una recomendación/ sugerencia		
Vocabulario nuevo que necesito		president, obelisk, diplomats

A escribir

Usando la información de la tabla, escribe tres párrafos. En el primero, describe los dos lugares. Luego describe lo que tienen en común y las diferencias entre los dos lugares. Termina con un párrafo que describe la visita que hará un turista que va a un lugar de tu país.

Después de escribir

Revisa tu ensayo. Luego intercambia ensayos con un compañero / una compañera para evaluarlos.

- ☐ ¿Ha usado tu compañero/a el diccionario bien para buscar e incorporar palabras? (Busca en un diccionario español cualquier palabra que te sea nueva. ¿Se entiende la palabra que ha escrito tu compañero/a?)
- ☐ ¿Hay concordancia de género y de número entre sustantivos y adjetivos?
- ☐ ¿Están bien escritas las comparaciones?
- ☐ ¿Hay concordancia entre sujetos y verbos?
- ☐ ¿Están bien escritos los usos del futuro? ¿Usa bien los verbos regulares y también los irregulares?

Después de revisar el ensayo de tu compañero/a, devuélveselo. Mira tu propio ensayo para ver los cambios que tu compañero/a te recomienda y haz las revisiones necesarias.

ESTRATEGIA

Using dictionaries to find the right word

When seeking a word in Spanish, pay attention to a lot more than the first word that appears in the dictionary entry. Is it a noun, adjective, or verb? If it's a verb, how will you conjugate it when you use it? You may want to cross-check it by looking it up in Spanish (either in a Spanish-definition or a Spanish-to-English dictionary) to make sure it is the right word and right part of speech. Is there a sample sentence so you can check the context? This will help you avoid the pitfall of poor dictionary use that causes people to mix up a baseball bat and the flying creature called bat, sports fans and electric devices that blow air, and the verb *to fly* and the insect.

Suggestion (Después de leer): To motivate students to edit their own work as well as their classmates' carefully, occasionally grade their editing instead of their writing.

¡Hablemos!

Nuestros gustos musicales

Antes de hablar

PASO 1. Nombra todos los géneros de música que puedas. Luego toma unos minutos para pensar en un(a) artista o una banda que representa cada tipo de música que nombraste.

PASO 2. En grupos pequeños, compartan sus ejemplos de música y músicos conocidos. ¿Pensaron Uds. en los mismos géneros y artistas? **¡Atención!** Si resulta que el resto del grupo no reconoce uno de los artistas que nombraste, explícale quién es, dándole todos los detalles que puedas.

A hablar

En sus grupos, respondan a las siguientes preguntas.

1. De todos los géneros de música, ¿cuáles son los que más les gustan a Uds.? ¿Por qué? ¿Qué tipo de música no les gusta? ¿Por qué? ¿Cuáles son sus grupos preferidos? ¿Y sus cantantes o músicos preferidos?

2. ¿Han cambiado sus preferencias musicales desde cuando eran más jóvenes? ¿Cuáles eran los grupos de música que más escuchaban Uds. de niños? Cuando eran adolescentes, ¿permitían sus padres que Uds. compraran la música que les gustaba?
   ¿O insistían ellos en que Uds. la escucharan gratis (*free*) en la radio o en Internet? ¿Cómo compraban sus padres u otros parientes su propia música?

3. ¿Cómo escuchan Uds. su música preferida hoy en día? ¿La compran? Si usan un sitio web para escuchar la música, ¿qué sitio es? ¿Por qué prefieren ese sitio?

4. ¿Tienen Uds. discos compactos? ¿Tienen discos (*records*)? ¿casetes? ¿canciones digitales que bajaron del Internet? ¿Qué formato prefieren y por qué?

Después de hablar

Ahora que han hablado de cómo el consumo (*consumption*) de música y las preferencias de Uds. han cambiado durante su vida, compartan sus predicciones para el futuro. ¿Todavía se venderán los discos compactos en el año 2025? ¿Cómo compraremos la música? ¿Qué tipos de música serán populares? ¿Cómo escucharemos la música?

CONÉCTATE AL MUNDO HISPANO

La música salsa tiene una larga tradición, pero el término «salsa» es de origen relativamente reciente. Se empezó a usar en Nueva York en los años setenta para referirse a la música afrocubana, un género que incorpora el mambo, el chachachá, la rumba y otros estilos. Se caracteriza por un ritmo muy bailable y el uso de instrumentos como el piano, el bajo (*bass*), la trompeta, la conga, las claves y las maracas. La música salsa se ha hecho famosa en el mundo entero, gracias a la cubana Celia Cruz, el panameño Rubén Blades y los norteamericanos Tito Puente y Marc Anthony (los dos de padres puertorriqueños), entre muchos otros. En general, se distingue entre la salsa, con sus raíces afrocubanas, y otros estilos bailables, como el merengue, de origen dominicano, y la cumbia, de origen colombiano. Aunque cada estilo es asociado a una región en particular, todos son populares en todo el mundo hispano.

Conéctate al cine

Película: *También la lluvia* (drama, Bolivia/España/México/Francia, 2010)
Directora: Icíar Bollaín

Sinopsis:

Sebastián es un director de cine mexicano y Costa es su productor español. Los dos van a Cochabamba, Bolivia, acompañados por un equipo técnico (*production crew*), para filmar una película sobre la llegada (*arrival*) de Cristóbal Colón a América y el inicio (*beginning*) de la Conquista española de las civilizaciones prehispánicas. Sin embargo, su rodaje (*film shoot*) se complica cuando se encuentran en medio de unas violentas protestas políticas en contra de (*against*) la privatización del agua en Bolivia.

Escena (Netflix, 00:40:50 to 00:47:42):

Mientras que el equipo técnico va en camino (*is on its way*) al lugar del rodaje, Sebastián lee el guion e imagina la escena que van a rodar. Luego Sebastián y el actor Daniel, cuyo (*whose*) personaje se llama Hatuey, tratan de (*try to*) explicar una escena difícil a las actrices.

Antes de ver

Para ti, ¿qué sería (*would be*) lo más difícil de hacer una película? Indica las tres cosas más difíciles y explica por qué.

____ construir la escenografía (*set*)   ____ conseguir dinero

____ dirigir a los actores   ____ encontrar un equipo

____ editar la película   ____ escribir la historia

Suggestion (A ver): Turn subtitles off, if possible. Students won't understand everything, but they won't need to. Stop at the words *la siguiente escena*.

▶ A ver

Lee las **Expresiones útiles** y las oraciones. Luego mira la escena y completa las oraciones con las palabras de la lista. Conjuga los verbos y usa el artículo definido cuando sea necesario.

| equipo técnico | género | interpretar | protagonista |
| filmar | guion | papel | tener |

1. Daniel __interpreta__ el papel de Hatuey, el líder de la rebeldía en contra de los conquistadores en la isla La Española.

2. __El guion__ que escribió Sebastián está basado en hechos reales.

3. __El género__ de la película de Sebastián es ficción histórica.

4. __El equipo técnico__ espera mientras que Daniel y Sebastián les explican la escena a las actrices.

5. En esta escena se entiende que no es fácil dirigir una película; es necesario que __tengas__ mucha paciencia y que puedas comunicarte bien con los actores.

6. Aunque Cristóbal Colón es __el protagonista__ de la película, la gente indígena que resistió la Conquista tiene un __papel__ igual de importante en la historia.

7. Sebastián no puede __filmar__ la toma que planeó porque las madres bolivianas no quieren simular el acto de ahogar a sus hijos.

Expresiones útiles

desgarradora	heartbreaking
soportar	to stand; to bear
todas juntas	all together
justamente	precisely
sumergen	submerge
ahogan	drown
la primera toma	the first shot
la cintura	waist
paramos	we stop
los muñecos	dolls
intercambiamos	we switch
seguro	safe
mojar	to get wet
lograr que lo hagan	get them to do it

■ For copyright reasons, the feature-film clips referenced in **Conéctate al cine** have not been provided by the publisher. Each of these films is readily available through retailers or online rental sites such as Amazon, iTunes, or Netflix.

Expansion (Después de ver): Show the class other scenes from the film, especially those related to the issues of water privatization. Then direct students back to **Act. E.** (*Cultura: Las luchas ecológicas en Ecuador y Bolivia*) in *Estructura 13.2.* Reread the last paragraph of the text together and ask students what they think about President Evo Morales's statement. Ask them if they see a connection between privatization of natural resources and the conquest of the Americas in the 1500s.

Después de ver

En parejas, túrnense para hacerse y responder a las siguientes preguntas.

¿Por qué sentimos emociones al ver una película aunque sabemos que no es real? ¿Qué género de películas te provoca más emoción? ¿Qué tipo de emoción? ¿Por qué crees que te afecta tanto? ¿Crees que las emociones que un buen actor o una buena actriz siente durante su actuación son iguales o similares a lo que una persona de la vida real siente en las mismas circunstancias? ¿Por qué sí o por qué no?

VOCABULARIO

Now that I have completed the chapter, I can . . .

☐ express uncertainty
☐ say what I and others would like or hope to do
☐ talk about what cultural activities I enjoy
☐ express desires in the past
☐ express future plans
☐ express speculation
☐ discuss cultural activities and entertainment in the Spanish-speaking world

Comunicación

para nada	not at all
quizá(s)	maybe, perhaps
sin duda (alguna)	without (any) doubt
tal vez	maybe, perhaps
Quisiera + *inf.*	I would like (*to do something*)

Los sustantivos

el actor / la actriz	actor/actress
el arte (*but* las artes)	art
el/la artista	artist
el bailarín / la bailarina	dancer
el baile	dance
la canción	song

el/la cantante	singer
la danza	dance
el/la escritor(a)	writer
la escultura	sculpture
la estrella	star
el género	genre, type
la música en vivo	live music
la obra	piece; work
la obra de arte	piece/work of art
la obra de teatro	play
el papel	role, part (*in a movie or play*)
el personaje	character (*in a movie, play or novel*); celebrity, well-known person
el/la pintor(a)	painter
la pintura	painting
la poesía	poetry
el/la protagonista	main character, protagonist
el público	audience

Cognados: el ballet, la banda, el concierto, el/la fotógrafo/a, la literatura, la ópera, la orquesta

Los adjetivos

Cognados: alternativo/a, clásico/a, electrónico/a, folclórico/a, pop, rock

Los verbos

actuar (actúo)	to act
componer (like poner)	to compose
dirigir (j)	to direct
interpretar (un papel)	to play (a role/part)

Si la vida fuera° diferente...

were

Los miembros del Tribunal Supremo Electoral en El Salvador empiezan a recontar los votos en una elección federal.

TSE TRIBUNAL SUPREMO ELECTORAL
PAPELETAS
ELECCIÓN
PRESIDENCIAL
2014

Objetivos

When you finish this chapter, you will be able to:

- express your opinions and beliefs
- talk about what you and others know and don't know
- discuss important social issues
- describe hypothetical situations
- explore social issues from Latin American and Spanish perspectives

15

www.mhhe.com/connect

Videoscript (Act. A, Paso 2):
1. MARLÉN: *Yo creo que como país, eh, lo que... lo que nos hace falta es la unión, ya que el problema que yo veo más fuerte en México es la corrupción y eso es lo que no permite que salgamos adelante.* **2.** FELICITAS: *En mi opinión, eh, la educación es un tema bastante que está... bueno, que preocupa el país y que desencadena muchas cosas.* **3.** JUAN ANDRÉS: *El problema que tenemos es que a veces, eh, contaminamos mucho y no tenemos conciencia con el medio ambiente. Ahora con estos programas de ecoturismo, con estos programas de reciclaje, estamos tratando de cambiar eso.* **4.** PAMELA: *Ehm... Creo que hay... no... no se combate la pobreza que es lo peor en nuestro país, el hambre.* **5.** BERTHA: *El terrorismo es la cosa más importante en este momento que yo creo que nos preocupa a todos.* **6.** DANIEL: *Bueno, yo tengo una preocupación; yo, en lo personal, que en Miami se acaba el agua. Puede ser una cosa fuera de lo normal pero mucha construcción y no suficiente agua para un futuro. Creo que eventualmente se va a pagar más para agua que para gasolina.* **7.** MARIANA: *Pero el principal sería... problema tal vez de seguridad, verdad. Que siempre es algo que en Centroamérica está presente. No es la misma seguridad que había antes en Costa Rica. Y eso es algo que se escucha mucho decir de las personas más mayores que antes podían salir a jugar tranquilos y era todo más seguro. Ahora la gente tiene que andar con más precaución.*

En mi opinión...
Expressing opinions

A. A ver: Los problemas más graves

PASO 1. Pon los siguientes temas en orden de más importante (1) a menos importante (7), según tus opiniones.

_____ los conflictos y la seguridad internacionales

_____ la contaminación del medio ambiente

_____ la corrupción de los políticos

_____ la educación

_____ la falta (*lack*) de recursos naturales

_____ la pobreza (*poverty*) y el hambre (*hunger*)

_____ el terrorismo

Video track (Act. A, Paso 2):
This video clip can be found on the DVD to accompany *Conéctate: Cap. 15,* Track 1.

PASO 2. Mira y escucha las respuestas a la pregunta «¿Cuál sería (*would/might be*) el problema más grave (*serious*) que enfrenta su país?» Escucha otra vez con pausas. Luego empareja cada frase con la persona que la diría (*would say*).

1. __b__ Marlén, de México

2. __a__ Felicitas, de Argentina

3. __e__ Juan Andrés, de Costa Rica

4. __g__ Pamela, de Argentina

5. __c__ Bertha, de Miami

6. __d__ Daniel, de Perú

7. __f__ Mariana, de Costa Rica

a. «Para mí, sin educación universal, la sociedad no puede progresar.»

b. «En mi opinión, con los políticos corruptos, es difícil tener un gobierno funcional.»

c. «Para mí, el terrorismo es el problema más grave al que nos enfrentamos porque es un problema internacional.»

d. «Creo que la falta de recursos naturales es el problema más fuerte porque afecta a todos los humanos.»

e. «Estoy de acuerdo con los activistas ecológicos. Ellos dicen que si no tenemos conciencia del medio ambiente, vamos a destruir nuestro planeta.»

f. «Para mí, si no hay seguridad, siempre se tiene que andar con precaución y no se puede estar tranquilo en su propia casa.»

g. «Creo que lo peor (*the worst thing*) es ver a la gente que sufre del hambre a causa de la pobreza.»

PASO 3. Mira y escucha otra vez. Según las opiniones de las personas que hablan, ¿por qué es importante resolver los problemas que describen?

1. __f__ Sin resolver el problema de la corrupción política... ,

2. __a__ Sin mejorar (*improving*) la educación... ,

3. __c__ Sin programas de ecoturismo y reciclaje... ,

4. __d__ Sin resolver el problema de la pobreza... ,

5. __b__ Sin resolver el problema del terrorismo... ,

6. __g__ Sin resolver el problema del uso excesivo del agua... ,

7. __e__ Sin resolver el problema de la seguridad... ,

a. las futuras generaciones no podrán aprender a mejorar su situación.

b. la gente siempre estará muy preocupada.

c. habrá muchísima contaminación del medio ambiente.

d. habrá muchísima más hambre.

e. los niños no podrán salir a jugar tranquilos.

f. el país no va a poder salir adelante.

g. va a costar más el agua que la gasolina.

To express your beliefs and opinions, you can use the following phrases.

Para mí...	For me (personally) . . .
En mi opinión...	In my opinion . . .
Creo que...	I believe (that) . . .
Para mí, el medio ambiente es importante.	For me, the environment is important.
En mi opinión, el terrorismo es el problema más grave del mundo.	In my opinion, terrorism is the most serious problem in the world today.
Creo que muchos políticos son corruptos.	I think many politicians are corrupt.

B. Los asuntos actuales (*Current issues*)   Indica la categoría que mejor describe cada elemento de la lista.

	LOS ASUNTOS SOCIALES	LOS ASUNTOS POLÍTICOS	EL MEDIO AMBIENTE
1. el activismo ecológico	☐	☐	☐
2. la contaminación	☐	☐	☐
3. la corrupción	☐	☐	☐
4. el ecoturismo	☐	☐	☐
5. la educación	☐	☐	☐
6. las elecciones democráticas	☐	☐	☐
7. la falta de recursos naturales, incluso el agua limpia	☐	☐	☐
8. el hambre	☐	☐	☐
9. la pobreza	☐	☐	☐
10. la seguridad	☐	☐	☐
11. el seguro médico	☐	☐	☐
12. el terrorismo	☐	☐	☐

C. Los asuntos más importantes para ti

PASO 1. Haz una lista de los tres asuntos de la lista en la **Actividad B** que son los más importantes para ti.

_____   _____   _____

PASO 2. Busca a un compañero o una compañera que esté de acuerdo contigo en un mínimo de dos de los tres asuntos que apuntaste en el **Paso 1.**

MODELO: E1: Para mí, la corrupción política, la educación y la pobreza son los asuntos más importantes.

   E2: Yo también creo que la corrupción política es un asunto importante. Pero a diferencia de lo que piensas tú, yo no creo que la educación y la pobreza sean tan importantes. En mi opinión, el terrorismo y la seguridad global son más importantes.

PASO 3. En parejas o en grupos pequeños, preparen una breve presentación para la clase sobre por qué estos asuntos les importan a los dos.

D. Algunos problemas sociales y nuestras predicciones   Completa las siguientes oraciones con sus propias predicciones. Luego, en parejas, compartan sus respuestas y comparen sus predicciones.

MODELO: Creo que si no nos dedicamos a reciclar más... , → será terrible porque los basureros se llenarán de tanta basura

1. En mi opinión, si no reducimos nuestra dependencia de los combustibles (*fuels*) fósiles... ,

(Continues)

Variation (Act. E, Paso 2):
Have students write their answers to turn in or share with members of other groups.

2. Para mí, si no paramos (*stop*) la tala de árboles en las selvas y en el campo... ,
3. Creo que si el seguro (*insurance*) médico no está disponible (*available*) para todos... ,
4. En mi opinión, si no exploramos maneras diferentes de cultivar y producir la comida... ,
5. Pienso que si todos continuamos a conducir nuestros coches en vez de usar el transporte público... ,

E. Entrevistas: El problema más grave de este país

PASO 1. En grupos de cuatro o cinco, entrevístense para saber cuál es el problema más grande de este país, según su opinión. Cada uno debe explicar su respuesta.

> **MODELO:** E1: Para ti, ¿cuál es el problema más grave que nos enfrentamos?
> E2: Creo que la pobreza es el problema más grave. Hay muchos problemas económicos.

PASO 2. Responde a las siguientes preguntas basándote en las respuestas que dieron tus compañeros de clase en el **Paso 1.**

Según la mayoría, ¿cuál es el problema más grave hoy en día? ¿Estás de acuerdo con ellos? ¿Por qué sí o no? ¿Te sorprenden las ideas de tus compañeros de clase?

F. ¿Cuál es tu opinión en cuanto a las noticias (*news*)?

PASO 1. ¿Lees o ves las noticias en Internet, en el periódico de la universidad, en la radio, en la televisión o en otras fuentes (*sources*)? ¿Cuáles son los eventos más importantes y comentados de las últimas semanas? Lee la lista de noticias típicas y luego apunta un ejemplo específico que has escuchado o leído de dos a cinco de ellas.

- un escándalo entre políticos
- un debate sobre el presupuesto (*budget*) en el Congreso
- una celebridad o un(a) atleta con problemas personales
- una nueva ley de tu ciudad, estado o país
- protestas contra el gobierno en este país o en otro
- un nuevo descubrimiento científico
- un desastre natural que ocurrió o va a ocurrir

Un basurero (*dump*) típico

Suggestion (Act. F, Paso 1):
Have students look up news in Spanish by searching key terms such as *bbcmundo*, *elnuevoherald*, *univisión*, *prensa escrita*. If you don't want students online during class, either assign this as homework and do the activity the following day, or prepare headlines plus the first paragraph of each news item and bring them to class.

Suggestion (Act. F, Paso 2):
Refer students to the *Comunicación sections in Caps. 4* and *8* to review expressions with *qué* + adj.

Variation (Act. F, Paso 2):
Have each group split into two subgroups that will debate the "news," where the subgroup member responding to the first statement has to disagree with that opinion: *Para mí, no es problema grave. Yo creo que también son seres humanos...* , then a member of the first group needs to counter the argument.

PASO 2. En grupos, túrnense para describir una noticia que apuntaron en el **Paso 1.** Soliciten las opiniones de los otros miembros del grupo.

> **MODELO:** E1: ¿Sabes que hay un nuevo escándalo político en Washington? ¿Cuál es tu opinión del escándalo del político ___?
> E2: ¡Qué pésimo! Creo que ese político debe renunciar a (*resign from*) su puesto.
> E3: No creo que sea nada grave. Para mí, es importante que tengamos confianza en nuestros representantes elegidos.

¿Qué sé yo?
Expressing what you know and don't know

To talk about what you and others know and what you don't know, you can use one of the following expressions.

dejarle saber	to let someone know
¿Qué sé yo? / ¿Yo qué sé?	What do I know?, Beats me!
Que yo sepa...	That I know of . . . / As far as I know . . .
¿Quién sabe?	Who knows?
sin saber	without knowing/realizing
el/la sabelotodo	know-it-all
Ve tú / Vaya Ud. a saber.	Your guess is as good as mine.

¡Ay, lo siento! Lo hice **sin saber** lo que hacía.	*I'm so sorry! I did it without knowing/ realizing what I was doing.*
Que yo sepa Miguel no ha regresado de su viaje.	*As far as I know Miguel hasn't returned from his trip.*
Déjame saber si te puedo ayudar en algo.	*Let me know if I can help you with something.*

A. ¿Qué sé yo?   Empareja cada pregunta u oración con la reacción más lógica.

____d____ 1. ¿Ha llegado el paquete que esperaba?

____a____ 2. Le mencioné a Anita la fiesta de Roberto, pero a ella no la invitaron. ¡Qué pena!

____e____ 3. No está la profesora. ¿Qué le pasará?

____b____ 4. Roberto va a hacer una fiesta, pero que yo sepa, todavía no tiene fecha.

____c____ 5. Ella siempre me ofrece consejos, pero muchas veces está equivocada (*wrong*).

a. No te preocupes; fue sin saber.

b. Pues, me encantaría ir. Déjame saber en cuanto la sepas.

c. No le hagas caso (*Pay her no mind*); es una sabelotodo.

d. ¿Qué sé yo? Nunca recojo el correo.

e. Ve tú a saber.

B. ¿De qué habla?   Escribe la expresión de la lista que corresponde a cada descripción que escuchas.

le dejo saber	¿Quién sabe?	sin saber	¿Yo qué sé?
que yo sepa	sabelotodo	vaya Ud. a saber	

1. _____¿Quién sabe?_____

2. _____sabelotodo_____

3. _____le dejo saber_____

4. ¿Yo qué sé? / vaya Ud. a saber

5. vaya Ud. a saber / ¿Yo qué sé?

6. _____que yo sepa_____

7. _____sin saber_____

C. ¿Quién sabe?

PASO 1.   Para cada tema, indica si es algo que ocurre **sin saber** o **a propósito** (*on purpose*).

OCURRE(N)...	SIN SABER	A PROPÓSITO
1. los conflictos armados internacionales	☐	☑
2. la contaminación del medio ambiente	☑	☑
3. la educación universal	☐	☑
4. las elecciones democráticas	☐	☑
5. la falta de agua limpia	☑	☐
6. el hambre	☑	☐
7. el precio de la gasolina	☐	☑
8. el terrorismo	☐	☑

Suggestion (Act. C, Paso 2): Allow students 6–9 minutes to ask their partners about 5 topics.

PASO 2.   En parejas, entrevístense para saber cuánto saben Uds. de cinco temas globales. Pueden escoger entre los temas del **Paso 1** y los de la lista que sigue. ¿Quién sabe más del tema? ¿Hay algún tema del que no tiene tu compañero/a el menor interés?

TEMAS ADICIONALES: el analfabetismo (*illiteracy*), la corrupción política, la crisis económica, la deuda (*debt*) externa, la pobreza, los problemas sociales relacionados con el racismo, el sistema penal (de prisiones), las violaciones de los derechos (*rights*) humanos

MODELO: E1: ¿Cuánto sabes de la participación de este país en los conflictos armados internacionales?

E2: **Que yo sepa**, el país participa menos y menos en conflictos armados internacionales.

Suggestion (Act. C, Paso 2): To ensure a diversity of topics is covered, assign pairs of students topics or have students use the same current event topics that they used in Act. F in the previous section on opinions.

CONÉCTATE AL MUNDO PROFESIONAL

As a volunteer or intern at an organization with Spanish-speaking employees, clients, or vendors, you could hold a position in which you greet people as they enter, ask who they are and whom they need to see, and write down their names if necessary. Then you can literally point them in the right direction or say that you'll let the person in the organization know that they have arrived: *Le dejo saber a _____ que Ud. está aquí.* For the right role, you don't need a lot of Spanish to use it in the workplace.

Script (Act. B): 1. *Es lo que dices cuando tú no sabes algo y tampoco sabes quién sabrá.* 2. *Es una persona que siempre tiene una respuesta.* 3. *Lo dices cuando no sabes algo pero le vas a dar información a alguien en cuanto la sepas tú.* 4. *Es una manera de decir que no sabes más que la persona que te pregunta algo.* 5. *Es una expresión que usas cuando no sabes la respuesta.* 6. *Es una manera de decir que no estás seguro o segura de que la información que tienes sea correcta o corriente.* 7. *Es cuando hiciste algo pero no estabas consciente de lo que hacías.*

Suggestion (Act. C, Paso 1): Answers may vary, so ask students to justify their answers. For example, *Un país tiene que declarar la guerra para montar un conflicto armado; ¡es algo que ocurre a propósito!*

Los problemas sociales, económicos y políticos

Social, economic, and political issues

A. ¿Qué quieren hacer las organizaciones sin fines de lucro (*nonprofit*)?

PASO 1. Empareja las citas (*quotes*) de los directores de varias organizaciones con las misiones correspondientes.

1. __b__ Queremos pasar de **la corrupción** política del pasado a **la democracia.** La gente tiene que participar en **el proceso político.** Es importante tener la oportunidad de **votar** en **las elecciones** democráticas y tener elecciones **justas** (*fair*).

2. __d__ Para ayudar a la gente más pobre y sin trabajo, trabajamos al **nivel** (*level*) «micro»: microfinanzas, microempresas y microproductos. Así vamos a cambiar la base del sistema económico para no depender del dinero de otros países.

3. __f__ Las organizaciones tradicionales como la Cruz Roja le dan provisiones a la gente necesitada; nosotros queremos colaborar con la gente en las zonas afectadas para que use los materiales donados para **desarrollar** (*develop*) **la infraestructura** sostenible a largo plazo (*over the long-term*).

4. __c__ La falta de educación es el mayor factor en **la violencia** a nivel mundial. En vez de (*Instead of*) participar en **el crimen** (como, por ejemplo, **el narcotráfico**) los jóvenes deben estar en la escuela.

5. __a__ Debemos combatir **los problemas sociales** relacionados con **el racismo** contra los obreros mal pagados que salen de su propio país para hacer los trabajos más **peligrosos** (*dangerous*) en otro país.

6. __e__ Queremos acabar con **la guerra** (conflicto armado) entre estados y entre grupos dentro del mismo país, y también queremos proteger los **derechos humanos** más básicos.

La misión es:

a. **Acabar con** (*Put an end to*) **la discriminación** contra **los indígenas** e **inmigrantes** que cruzan **las fronteras** (*borders*) internacionales para trabajar.

b. Acabar con **la tiranía** y **la dictadura** (*dictatorship*) a través de un proceso democrático.

c. Combatir **el analfabetismo, la esclavitud infantil** (*child slavery*) y la violencia a través de (*by way of*) **la alfabetización** universal para que todos los niños del mundo sepan leer y escribir.

d. **Mejorar** (*Improve*) la situación internacional de **la pobreza, el desempleo** (*unemployment*) y **la desigualdad** (*inequality*) **económica** a través de programas de microfinanzas y al hacer esto evitar **la deuda externa** y **una crisis económica.**

e. Promover (*Promote*) **la paz** (*peace*) en todas sus formas.

f. Proveer (*Provide*) ayuda sostenible que desarrolle infraestructuras para protegernos de **un desastre natural** como, por ejemplo, una inundación de agua como resultado de un huracán.

PASO 2. Ahora, empareja cada término con su antónimo.

1. __h__ la alfabetización
2. __b__ **el hambre**
3. __d__ **la igualdad**
4. __e__ **la libertad**
5. __c__ **la oferta**
6. __f__ la paz
7. __a__ la riqueza
8. __g__ **la seguridad**

a. la pobreza
b. comer en exceso
c. **la demanda**
d. la desigualdad
e. la esclavitud
f. la guerra
g. **el peligro** (danger)
h. el analfabetismo

Video track (Act. B): This video clip can be found on the DVD to accompany *Conéctate: Cap. 15, Track 2.*

B. A ver: Cada país tiene sus problemas

PASO 1. Mira y escucha el video. Luego mira otra vez con pausas e indica todos los tipos de problemas que le preocupan a cada persona.

		POLÍTICOS	ECONÓMICOS	SOCIALES
1.	Jama, de Cuba	☐	☑	☑
2.	Perla, de Argentina	☐	☑	☐
3.	Juan, de Argentina	☑	☑	☐
4.	Mayra, de Costa Rica	☐	☐	☑
5.	Gabriel, de Argentina	☑	☐	☑
6.	Eduardo, de España	☑	☑	☑
7.	Benedicto, de Costa Rica	☐	☐	☑

Note (Act. B, Paso 2): The interview with Eduardo was conducted in fall of 2007, when the economy of Spain was very strong, which is why he refers to *"esta época boyante."*

PASO 2. Mira y escucha otra vez. Luego, basándote en lo que dice cada persona, escoge el término al que **no** se refiere ni se puede inferir.

1. Jama
   ☐ la pobreza ☑ la crisis económica ☐ los problemas sociales
2. Perla
   ☐ la crisis económica ☐ la desigualdad económica ☑ el narcotráfico
3. Juan
   ☑ el analfabetismo ☐ la desigualdad económica ☐ la situación política
4. Mayra
   ☑ la contaminación ☐ la delincuencia ☐ la paz
5. Gabriel
   ☑ la deuda externa ☐ la pobreza infantil ☐ el hambre
6. Eduardo
   ☑ el analfabetismo ☐ los problemas económicos ☐ los problemas políticos
7. Benedicto
   ☐ la contaminación ☑ el hambre ☐ la inseguridad

Note (Act. B, Paso 1): The answers to this activity will vary depending on how students understand the issues. You may want to start by listing a few of the terms from *Paso 2* on the board (*el hambre, la pobreza, la seguridad*) and ask students to classify them and explain their reasoning.

Videoscript (Act. B): 1. JAMA: *Hay mucha pobreza y mucha esclavitud infantil y muchos problemas sociales.* **2.** PERLA: *Bueno, creo que... Latinoamérica está pasando por un momento de muchísima... problemática económica.*
3. JUAN: *Eh... también me preocupa, eh, la situación política en Latinoamérica, eh, que es un poco insegura. Eh, también la situación económica en Estados Unidos y en Latinoamérica también.* **4.** MAYRA: *Tal vez este... ehm... que tal vez ya no se vive con esa seguridad que vivíamos antes. Que podíamos andar por las calles, que podíamos caminar sin miedo —ya ahora tenemos que andarnos cuidando mucho. Es, más que todo, la delincuencia que nos ha venido a robar mucho la paz.* **5.** GABRIEL: *El problema político que me preocupa, es que lamentablemente los los que dirigen nuestros países no piensan en la gente pobre, lamentablemente. Piensan más en su...en su núcleo, en su política que en la... que en los pequeños niños que no tienen de comer.* **6.** EDUARDO: *Todos conocemos como está, sobre todo lo que es América del Sur y América Latina, los problemas económicos que tiene, los problemas políticos y sociales que tiene América y ellos, muchos han optado por volver. Hoy en día, España es un punto de referencia en cuanto a la inmigración, debido a esta ... esta época boyante que estamos viviendo, económicamente hablando, claro.* **7.** BENEDICTO: *Ahora la inseguridad que hay aquí... no aquí, en todo el mundo. Después la contaminación que hay.*

Script (Act. C): *1. La esclavitud infantil puede resultar de la pobreza extrema. 2. Después de 2008, no ha habido muchos problemas económicos en el mundo. 3. Los problemas de seguridad de que hablan Mayra y Benedicto tratan del crimen y la violencia. 4. El hecho de que narcotraficantes pasan cada vez más por Costa Rica probablemente no influye en la falta de seguridad de que hablan Mayra y Benedicto. 5. El calentamiento global, la deforestación y la contaminación son ejemplos de problemas políticos. 6. Según Gabriel, el egoísmo entre los políticos causa problemas sociales porque están preocupados por ellos mismos y no por asuntos sociales como el hambre. 7. Una situación política insegura puede afectar la democracia.*

C. ¿De qué se trata? Escucha las oraciones sobre los asuntos de la **Actividad B** y decide si son ciertas (**C**) o falsas (**F**).

1. _C_   3. _C_   5. _F_   7. _C_
2. _F_   4. _F_   6. _C_

Suggestion (Act. C): If students don't agree with the answers, give them an opportunity to discuss. For example, can they make a case for environmental problems being political issues because politicians have the ability to an enact laws to address them?

D. ¿Cuál sería (*would be*) el problema?

PASO 1. En parejas, indiquen cuáles serían los problemas que llevan a (*lead to*) las siguientes conclusiones. Luego comparen sus respuestas con otra pareja. ¿Están de acuerdo?

> **MODELO:** «En nuestra comunidad, necesitamos más escuelas y maestros cualificados.»
> El problema sería el analfabetismo. (Los problemas serían el analfabetismo y la falta de educación.)

1. «En nuestra comunidad necesitamos atraer o desarrollar una industria que nos provea de puestos de trabajo.»
2. «En mi opinión, es muy importante tener elecciones justas.»
3. «Para mí, hay que mejorar las relaciones entre los habitantes locales y los recién llegados (*newcomers*).»
4. «En este país necesitamos renovar el sistema bancario.»
5. «Nos gustaría ver menos armas y más paz.»

PASO 2. Escoge uno de los problemas mencionados en el **Paso 1** y describe los detalles específicos en el contexto de tu universidad, tu ciudad o pueblo o el estado donde vives. Luego, en parejas, intercambien ideas y ofrezcan por lo menos una posible solución al problema. **Suggestion (Act D, Paso 2):** If students need more information to present details of local issues, either show them examples or have them research online—and in Spanish, if possible.

E. Los problemas sociales

PASO 1. En grupos de tres, hagan una lista de por lo menos tres problemas (en orden de importancia) a los que cada uno de los siguientes grupos sociales se enfrenta.

> **MODELO:** Muchos ancianos (*elderly people*) no pueden conducir su propio coche.

1. los ancianos
2. los estudiantes
3. los inmigrantes
4. las mujeres
5. los padres
6. los recién titulados/graduados

Answers (Act. D, Paso 1): *Posibles respuestas: 1. el desempleo, la pobreza 2. la corrupción, la tiranía, la dictadura 3. la discriminación, el racismo 4. la crisis económica, la deuda externa 5. la violencia y la guerra*

PASO 2. En sus grupos, escojan uno de los grupos sociales del **Paso 1** y elaboren un mínimo de tres soluciones para empezar a resolver uno de los problemas al que se enfrenta ese grupo.

> **MODELO:** Muchos ancianos no pueden conducir su propio coche.

1. Debemos asegurar (*ensure*) que haya transporte público disponible.
2. Es importante tener transporte especial para llevar a los ancianos a sus citas médicas.
3. Hay que construir comunidades para ancianos cerca del centro de las ciudades.

¿Cuáles son los problemas a los que los ancianos se enfrentan? ¿Y las soluciones?

La alfabetización es la enseñanza (*teaching*) de la lectura y la escritura.

Reciclaje

The future

Aquí hay una lista de metas (*goals*) de diferentes organizaciones. Complétalas usando uno de los siguientes verbos en la forma **nosotros** del tiempo futuro, y luego empareja la meta con el campo (*field*) de actividad que le corresponde.

acabar   conseguir   erradicar   hacer   mejorar   resolver

METAS	CAMPOS
_b_ 1. <u>Erradicaremos</u> el analfabetismo.	a. desarrollo (*development*) económico
_e_ 2. ___<u>Haremos</u>___ un esfuerzo para parar la violencia en la frontera.	b. educación
_f_ 3. <u>Resolveremos</u> los conflictos entre los dos países.	c. medicina
_a_ 4. ___<u>Acabaremos</u>___ con la pobreza.	d. derechos de los indígenas
_d_ 5. ___<u>Mejoraremos</u>___ las condiciones de las mujeres indígenas.	e. derechos de los inmigrantes
_c_ 6. <u>Conseguiremos</u> una solución al problema de la malaria.	f. diplomacia internacional

■ Answers to this activity are in Appendix 2 at the back of your book.

15.1 Hablaría con los indígenas en Chihuahua

The conditional

Para empezar...

En muchas partes de Latinoamérica, la población indígena tiene una presencia muy notable. A veces hay relaciones muy buenas entre el grupo indígena y el resto de la población y a veces no. Si hicieras un viaje de norte a sur para conocer mejor la situación de los indígenas en Latinoamérica, ¿en qué orden harías (*would you do*) las siguientes actividades? Escribe la letra de la actividad en el lugar correcto en el mapa. **¡Atención!** Dos de las siguientes actividades serían (*would be*) físicamente imposibles. Indica cuáles son.

a. **Pasaría** unos días en la ciudad de Oaxaca, hacia el oeste del istmo (*isthmus*) de Tehuantepec, la parte estrecha (*narrow*) de México, para conocer mejor a los mixtecos y los zapotecos.

b. **Haría** la última parte del viaje en el sur de Chile, donde viven los mapuches.

c. De allí **tendría** que ir a las islas donde viven los kunas en Panamá.

d. De Ecuador **saldría** para Perú y Bolivia, donde muchas personas hablan quechua.

e. Después me **encantaría** ir a Guatemala para saber más del pueblo quiché, otro grupo maya.

f. De allí **caminaría** a la Isla de Pascua, donde muchos habitantes son de origen polinesio y hablan rapanui.

g. Primero, me **iría** a Chihuahua en el norte de México para hablar con los rarámuri, también conocidos como tarahumaras.

h. De allí, **nadaría** al estado de Chiapas en el sur de México porque allí viven los tzotziles, uno de los grupos mayas más grandes del país.

i. **Podría** conocer después a los quichuas en los Andes ecuatorianos.

Un consejo...

Relating a tense (**un tiempo verbal**) in Spanish to how you would say it in English can be helpful, but be cautious. The conditional, for instance, is almost always translated into English with *would,* as in the examples in **Actividades analíticas 1.** The reverse, however, is not always true: When *would* is used to describe a repeated past state or event (meaning *used to*), the imperfect is used in Spanish.

Mario **caminaría** a la escuela contigo pero no tiene suficiente tiempo.
Mario would walk to school with you but he doesn't have enough time.

De niño, Mario **caminaba** a la escuela.
As a child, Mario would (used to) walk to school.

■ Answers to these activities are in Appendix 2 at the back of your book.

Actividades analíticas

1 The verbs in bold in **Para empezar** are in the *conditional tense* (**el condicional**). The conditional is used to express what one *would* do under certain circumstances.

Para ayudarlos, yo **donaría** dinero.   *To help them, I would donate money.*

En un mundo ideal, todos **trabajaríamos** juntos.   *In an ideal world, we all would work together.*

2 Use the forms you saw in **Para empezar** and the patterns you see here to complete the chart.

	pasar	ser	ir
yo	pasaría	**sería**	iría
tú	pasarías	serías	**irías**
él/ella, Ud.	pasaría	sería	iría
nosotros/as	pasaríamos	seríamos	**iríamos**
vosotros/as	pasaríais	**seríais**	iríais
ellos/ellas, Uds.	pasarían	serían	**irían**

3 Just as you saw for the future tense in **Estructura 14.2,** the stem for the conditional consists of the entire infinitive form, to which one of the following endings is added.

TERMINACIONES DEL CONDICIONAL

yo	-ía	**nosotros/as**	-íamos
tú	-ías	**vosotros/as**	-íais
él/ella, Ud.	-ía	**ellos/ellas, Uds.**	-ían

Expansion (Act. analíticas 3): Have students circle those parts of the conditional tense endings that are common to almost all tenses (*-s, -mos, -is, -n*). To make this clearer, have them do side-by-side conjugations of the same verb in two different tenses.

4 Those verbs that have irregular stems in the future tense use this same stem in the conditional. As with the future, there are no irregular endings in the conditional tense.

VERBO	RAÍZ	EJEMPLO	
decir	**dir-**	Yo **diría** que la situación está mejor ahora.	*I would say that the situation is now better.*
haber	**habr-**	Con ese plan, **habría** menos pobreza.	*With that plan, there would be less poverty.*
hacer	**har-**	**Haría** un gran esfuerzo para ayudarte.	*I would make a great effort to help you.*
poder	**podr-**	¿**Podría** hablar con Ud.?	*Could I speak with you?*
poner	**pondr-**	**Pondríamos** fin al problema, pero no tenemos suficientes recursos.	*We would put an end to the problem, but we don't have enough resources.*
salir	**saldr-**	**Saldrían** del país, pero no está permitido.	*They would leave the country, but it's not permitted.*
tener	**tendr-**	Para entendernos mejor, **tendríamos** que hablar más.	*To understand each other better, we would have to talk more.*
venir	**vendr-**	Mi hermano **vendría** también, pero no puede.	*My brother would come too, but he can't.*

Note that **habría** here is the conditional of **hay** (**haber**). As with **hay**, **habría** is always used in the singular to express existence.

Habría un problema	*There would be a problem.*
Habría muchos problemas.	*There would be many problems.*

Actividades prácticas

A. ¿Qué harías?

Suggestion (Act. A, Paso 1): Have students go through the list of solutions, underline all of the conditional forms and identify the infinitive of each.

PASO 1. ¿Qué harías tú para solucionar los siguientes problemas? Empareja cada problema con una solución razonable. **¡Atención!** Los problemas indicados con (*) tienen más de una solución.

PROBLEMAS

1. _e, f_ Hay mucha pobreza.*
2. _g_ Hay mucho analfabe-tismo.
3. _d_ Hay mucha corrupción.
4. _a_ Hay mucha violencia en las calles.
5. _h_ No hay suficiente comunicación entre mi país y Latinoamérica.
6. _b, c_ No conozco bien la realidad del mundo hispano.*

¿QUÉ HARÍAS?

a. Haría un esfuerzo para tener más policías.
b. Viajaría a España o a Latinoamérica.
c. Leería más artículos sobre la situación en los países hispanos.
d. Les daría salarios decentes a los empleados del gobierno.
e. Ayudaría a crear microempresas en las comunidades pobres.
f. Crearía más trabajos.
g. Tendría más escuelas para toda la población.
h. Crearía clases de español para todos en mi país.

PASO 2. En parejas, escojan las tres soluciones de máxima prioridad para Uds. del **Paso 1** y supongan que tienen dinero ilimitado para implementar-las. ¿Qué harían Uds. bajo estas condiciones? ¿Por qué?

MODELO: Haríamos un esfuerzo para crear más trabajos, porque si la gente no tiene trabajo, hay más pobreza y más violencia.

B. ¿Cómo somos y qué haríamos?

Escucha las oraciones y decide si es algo que haría una persona consciente (*self-aware*) y/o bien informada (**C**) o si es algo que haría una persona poco consciente (**PC**) y/o de mente cerrada (*closed-minded*). **Suggestion (Act. B):** As you review answers, have students change the items marked *PC* to say what an aware and open-minded person would do.

1. _PC_
2. _C_
3. _C_
4. _PC_
5. _PC_
6. _C_
7. _PC_

Script (Act. B): 1. *Diría que las clases de historia son una pérdida de tiempo.* **2.** *Leería las noticias internacionales.* **3.** *Trataría de entender la situación antes de opinar.* **4.** *Preferiría pelear para resolver los problemas.* **5.** *Tendría su opinión ya formada antes de entender la situación.* **6.** *Sería crítico o crítica de los estereotipos y su uso en los medios de comunicación.* **7.** *Opinaría que su país no forma parte de los problemas internacionales como el narcotráfico y los conflictos armados.*

C. Prioridades para la comunidad local y global

PASO 1. En grupos pequeños, usen el vocabulario que ya aprendieron para crear una lista de tres cosas que harían Uds. para mejorar su propia comunidad o su universidad. Pueden usar la lista de abajo o hacer sus propias sugerencias.

- bajar el costo de la matrícula (*tuition*)
- comprar más libros para la biblioteca
- crear más lugares de estacionamiento (*parking spaces*)
- construir edificios nuevos
- mejorar los salarios de los maestros/profesores
- tener más computadoras accesibles a los estudiantes
- tener mejores opciones de transporte público para llegar a la universidad

(Continues)

- For more conditional forms, see **Para saber más 15.1** at the back of your book.

Note (Para saber más): *Para saber más 15.1 covers the conditional forms of the verbs querer, saber,* and *valer* as well as the conditional perfect.

Autoprueba

Use what you've just learned to provide the appropriate conditional forms of the following verbs.

1. **conseguir**
   yo _____
   tú _____
   él/ella, Ud. _____
   nosotros/as _____
   ellos/ellas, Uds. _____

2. **resolver**
   nosotros/as _____

3. **mejorar**
   yo _____

Respuestas: 1. conseguiría, conseguirías, conseguiría, conseguiríamos, conseguirían **2.** resolveríamos **3.** mejoraría

- The audio files for in-text listening activities are available in the eBook, within Connect Plus activities, and on the Online Learning Center.

Suggestion (Act. C): Have students work on this in groups of 3 or 4, and then have each group write their top choice from *Paso 1* and their top choice from *Paso 2* on the board. The class as a whole can then look for signs of consensus or disagreement.

PASO 2.　Ahora creen una lista de tres cosas que harían Uds. para mejorar la comunidad global.

> **MODELO:**　Ayudaríamos a otras personas a conservar el agua.

D. Tu vida ideal

PASO 1.　En tu vida ideal, ¿qué harías? ¿Y qué *no* harías? Crea una lista de lo que harías y una lista de lo que no harías. **¡Atención!** Debes tener diez oraciones en total entre las dos listas.

PASO 2.　Compara tus listas con las de un compañero / una compañera. ¿Tienen algo en común?

↻ Reciclaje

The past subjunctive

Siempre ha habido gente que quiere mejorar la sociedad en la que vive. Mira la siguiente lista de afirmaciones sobre nuestra sociedad. ¿Qué crees que la gente de antes quería y qué no quería? Escribe cada afirmación bajo la categoría **Querían que...** o **No querían que... ¡Atención!** Hay que cambiar el verbo al imperfecto (pasado) de subjuntivo.

Querían que...	No querían que...
los niños pudieran asistir a la escuela sin pagar.	creciera la desigualdad económica.
la esclavitud ya no existiera.	hubiera guerras.
las mujeres tuvieran el derecho de votar.	la corrupción estuviera presente en el sistema jurídico.
los trabajadores descansaran dos días a la semana.	
toda la gente tuviera la libertad de practicar su religión.	

Crece la desigualdad económica.
Los niños pueden asistir a la escuela sin pagar.
Hay guerras.
La esclavitud ya no existe.
Las mujeres tienen el derecho de votar.

La corrupción está presente en el sistema jurídico (*judicial*).
Los trabajadores descansan dos días a la semana.
Toda la gente tiene la libertad de practicar su religión.

■ Answers to this activity are in Appendix 2 at the back of your book.

Suggestion (Para empezar): Point out that students should not overgeneralize. Not all Americans use drugs, not all regions of Latin America are directly affected by the drug trade, and not all democratic institutions have been "bought" by drug traffickers.

■ Answers to these activities are in Appendix 2 at the back of your book.

15.2　**Si nadie usara drogas, la vida sería más tranquila**

Si clauses

Para empezar...

PASO 1.　Dicen que cada acción tiene sus consecuencias, que esas consecuencias tienen otras consecuencias, etcétera. Usa números para poner las siguientes oraciones en orden según una «cadena (*chain*) de consecuencias». La primera ya está hecha.

a. ___4___ Si los narcotraficantes (*drug traffickers*) no **ganaran** tanto dinero, no **podrían** «comprar» a los políticos y a los jueces latinoamericanos.

b. ___2___ Si no **fuera** un buen negocio vender drogas en los Estados Unidos, los narcotraficantes no las **importarían** al país.

c. ___6___ Si el sistema político y judicial **funcionara** mejor, los latinoamericanos **tendrían** una vida mejor.

d. ___5___ Si los narcotraficantes no **pudieran** «comprar» a los políticos y a los jueces, el sistema político y judicial **funcionaría** mejor en los países latinoamericanos.

e. __1__ Si nadie **usara** drogas en los Estados Unidos, no **sería** un buen negocio venderlas.

f. __3__ Si no **importara** drogas a los Estados Unidos, el crimen organizado en los países latinoamericanos no **ganaría** tanto dinero.

PASO 2.   Según esta cadena de consecuencias, ¿es cierta o falsa la siguiente oración?

Cierto Si nadie **usara** drogas en los Estados Unidos, muchos latinoamericanos **tendrían** una vida mejor.

Actividades analíticas

1   Each of the sentences in **Para empezar** consists of an *if* (**si**) clause and a consequence (**consecuencia**). Write the verb form that appears in each part of these sentences here.

	SI... ,	CONSECUENCIA		SI...,	CONSECUENCIA
a.	ganaran	podrían	d.	pudieran	funcionaría
b.	fuera	importarían	e.	usara	sería
c.	funcionara	tendrían	f.	importara	ganaría

2   What is the name of the verb tense that appears in each of these two parts?

Si... : past subjunctive / imperfecto (pasado) de subjuntivo

Consecuencia: conditional/condicional

The past subjunctive forms were presented in **Estructura 14.1**.

As in English, the **si** clause and the consequence may come in either order.

Si tuviera un millón de dólares, lo **donaría** a una organización sin fines de lucro.

If I had a million dollars, I would donate it to a nonprofit organization.

Donaría un millón de dólares a una organización sin fines de lucro **si** lo **tuviera.**

I would donate a million dollars to a nonprofit organization if I had it.

3   The pattern seen here with **si** + *past subjunctive* + *conditional* is used only when the *if* (**si**) clause describes a situation that is contrary to fact.

Si Guatemala **estuviera** en Europa, no **tendría** selvas tan bonitas.

If Guatemala were in Europe, it would not have such beautiful jungles.

Compraría una casa si yo **tuviera** el dinero.

I would buy a house if I had the money.

In these cases, the speaker knows that Guatemala is actually not in Europe and that he or she does not have a lot of money. The past subjunctive signals this contrary-to-fact status of the **si** clause. If the **si** clause describes a situation that is not contrary to fact (that is, it could be true or could happen), use an indicative tense such as present, preterite, or imperfect.

Si mañana **tengo** tiempo, **voy a pasar** por tu casa.

If I have time tomorrow, I'll stop by your house.

Si no **estudiaste**, no te **va a ir** bien en el examen.

If you didn't study, it's not going to go well for you on the test.

En esos tiempos, si **había** un conflicto entre dos países, **se convertía** en guerra.

In those days, if there was a conflict between two countries, it would turn into a war.

To summarize, the **si** clause can be in the past subjunctive or an indicative tense. It is never in the present subjunctive.

(Continues)

¿Por qué?

Spanish speakers distinguish clearly between statements that are thought to be true, using the indicative, and those that may not be true, using the subjunctive. Here you see a special case of the latter: *if* clauses that are contrary to fact. The speaker knows that these are not true, but is imagining what the world would be like if they were. These counterfactual (or hypothetical) statements are expressed with the past subjunctive. Distinguishing between what is thought to be true, what might not be true, and what is definitely not true is extremely important for human communication, so like many other languages, Spanish signals these distinctions by changing the ending on the verb.

Suggestion (¿Por qué?): Give students a simple statement to start with (*Hablan español.*) and have them modify the verb depending on whether it is thought to be true (*Sé que...*), may not be true (*Quiero/Quería que..., Es/Era posible que...*), or is hypothetical (*Si...*).

■ To find out how to use **si** clauses to express contrary-to-fact situations on the past, see **Para saber más 15.2** at the back of your book.

Note (Para saber más): *Para saber más 15.2 covers the past perfect subjunctive in si clauses.*

Autoprueba

Complete the hypothetical statements with the appropriate form of the conditional (to indicate the consequence) or the past subjunctive (to indicate the contrary-to-fact situation).

1. Si alguien _____ (querer) ayudar a eliminar el analfabetismo, _____ (poder) hacerse voluntario en la biblioteca.
2. Nosotros _____ (construir) un nuevo refugio (*shelter*) para las mujeres en nuestra comunidad si _____ (ganar) la lotería.
3. Si a ella le _____ (interesar) la política, _____ (buscar) oportunidades para trabajar en las elecciones.
4. Yo _____ (trabajar) en el comedor de beneficencia (*soup kitchen*) todos los días si _____ (tener) más tiempo libre.

Respuestas: 1. quisiera, podría **2.** construiríamos, ganáramos **3.** interesara, buscaría **4.** trabajaría, tuviera

SI CLAUSE	CONSEQUENCE
past subjunctive	*conditional*
a situation that is contrary to fact (that the speaker knows is not true)	
any indicative	*any indicative*
a situation that is not contrary to fact	

4 The word **hay** is **hubiera** in the past subjunctive, and it is very common in **si** clauses that express contrary-to-fact situations.

Yo estaría contento si **hubiera** menos pobreza en el mundo.

I would be happy if there were less poverty in the world.

En español...

The standard way of expressing contrary-to-fact situations in the written language is the pattern you've just seen: **si** + *past subjunctive*. It is common in the spoken language too, but you may also hear variants in some regions. For example, it is common to hear **yo que tú** with the meaning **si yo fuera tú.**

Si yo fuera tú, no lo haría.
Yo que tú, no lo haría.
If I were you, I wouldn't do it.

Actividades prácticas

Note (Act. A): The Human Development Index data here are based on the 2015 report. The Happiness Index is from the World Happiness Report 2016.

A. El desarrollo y la felicidad El Índice (*Index*) de Desarrollo Humano clasifica a los países según el nivel económico, el nivel de educación y la esperanza de vida (*life expectancy*). El Índice de Felicidad (*Happiness*) se calcula según las respuestas a varias encuestas. Basándote en la información en la tabla, indica si cada oración que sigue es cierta (**C**) o falsa (**F**).

	DESARROLLO HUMANO (%)	FELICIDAD
Argentina	muy alto (*high*) (84)	muy alto (67)
Bolivia	medio (66)	medio (58)
Canadá	muy alto (91)	muy alto (74)
Chile	muy alto (83)	muy alto (67)
Colombia	alto (72)	muy alto (65)
Costa Rica	alto (77)	muy alto (71)
España	muy alto (88)	alto (64)
Estados Unidos	muy alto (92)	muy alto (71)
México	alto (76)	muy alto (68)
Nicaragua	medio (63)	alto (60)
Paraguay	medio (68)	medio (55)

1. __C__ Si hubiera menos analfabetismo y más progreso económico en México, podrían tener un nivel de desarrollo más alto.

2. __F__ Si fuéramos de España, podríamos decir que nuestro país tiene un nivel de felicidad «muy alto».

3. __C__ Si los países tuvieran un nivel de educación más alto, tendrían un nivel de desarrollo más alto también.

4. __C__ Si Paraguay tuviera más desarrollo económico, podría estar en la lista de países con un nivel de desarrollo «alto».

5. __F__ Si yo fuera de Nicaragua, podría decir que mi país tiene el mismo nivel de desarrollo que Colombia.

6. __F__ Si Paraguay tuviera el mismo nivel de desarrollo que Argentina, sería uno de los países con un nivel de desarrollo «medio».

7. __C__ Si hubiera más felicidad en los Estados Unidos, los estadounidenses podrían tener un nivel de felicidad más alto que en Costa Rica.

8. __C__ Si todos los países pudieran tener como mínimo el mismo nivel de desarrollo que Colombia, el mundo sería mejor.

Expansion (Act. A): Ask students whether they agree or not with this statement, based on what they see in the chart: Si un país tiene un nivel de desarrollo alto, su índice de felicidad es alto.

B. Nuestras preferencias

PASO 1. Completa cada una de las siguientes oraciones, basándote en tus preferencias personales.

1. Si tuviera el dinero, viajaría a _____ por el fin de semana.
2. Si pudiera resolver solo un problema en mi país, sería el problema de _____.
3. Si pudiera resolver solo un problema en el mundo, sería el problema de

   _____.
4. Me iría a _____ si me dieran la oportunidad de vivir en otro país durante un año.
5. Cenaría con _____ si pudiera salir a cenar con cualquier persona del mundo hispano.
6. Me gustaría ser de _____ si yo pudiera ser de un país hispano.

PASO 2. Escoge una de las oraciones del **Paso 1,** cámbiala a una pregunta y pregúntasela a tres de tus compañeros. Apunta los resultados.

MODELO: Si tuvieras el dinero, ¿adónde viajarías?

Variation (Act. B, Paso 2): Have students work in pairs, forming questions from the Paso 1 statements to ask a partner, then following up each answer with one or more original questions. For example, E1: Si tuvieras el dinero, ¿adónde viajarías? E2: Viajaría a la Antártida. E1: ¿Qué harías allí? E1: Sacaría muchas fotos de los pingüinos y de los icebergs.

C. Si el mundo fuera diferente
En cada oración, decide si la cláusula con **si** expresa una situación que es contraria a la realidad. Luego escoge la forma correcta de los verbos.

1. Si Ecuador [está / estuviera] en Centroamérica, [es / sería] un país centroamericano.
2. Si la pobreza extrema [existe / existiera] en el mundo, [tenemos / tendríamos] que erradicarla.
3. Si [hay / hubiera] grandes diferencias económicas entre unos países y otros, [va a haber / habría] mucha inmigración de los países más pobres a los países más ricos.
4. Si Cristóbal Colón (Christopher Columbus) [está / estuviera] vivo, ¿qué [piensa / pensaría] de las Américas de hoy?
5. Si [hablan / hablaran] español en muchos países de Latinoamérica, eso no [significa / significaría] que las lenguas indígenas ya no existan.
6. Si no [hay / hubiera] ningún problema de desigualdad económica en el mundo, [podemos / podríamos] estar tranquilos.

D. Unas situaciones difíciles
En grupos de tres, creen una respuesta (una oración completa) a cada una de las siguientes preguntas.

1. Si vivieran en este país y no hablaran inglés, ¿qué trabajo podrían hacer?
2. Si fueran del norte de África y no pudieran encontrar trabajo allí, ¿a qué país se irían? ¿Por qué?
3. Si fueran líderes de un país y hubiera mucha desigualdad económica, ¿qué harían?
4. Si vivieran en un país no muy democrático, ¿qué podrían hacer para cambiar esta situación?

Suggestion (Act. D): As students are beginning to finish, assign each group one of these questions and have them write their answer to that question on the board.

CONÉCTATE AL MUNDO HISPANO

En el mundo entero, la gente busca lugares donde haya mucha oferta de trabajo y los salarios sean altos. Por eso, es común ver **flujos** (*flows*) **de migración laboral,** dentro de un solo país (de las áreas rurales hacia las grandes ciudades, por ejemplo) o de un país más pobre a otro país más rico. En el mundo hispano, por ejemplo, muchos africanos buscan trabajo en España, y por la misma razón, muchos guatemaltecos y hondureños se van a México y muchos bolivianos y paraguayos se van a Argentina o Chile. Todo este movimiento ocurre porque España, México, Argentina y Chile tienen economías relativamente grandes y fuertes.

De la misma manera (*way*), muchos salen del Caribe, de México o de Centroamérica a buscar trabajo en los Estados Unidos, un país con una de las economías más fuertes del mundo. Sin embargo (*However*), aun (*even*) este fenómeno tan conocido cambia según el estado de la economía. De 2009 a 2015, por ejemplo, el flujo migratorio entre los Estados Unidos y México cambió: la cantidad (*quantity*) de migrantes de México a los Estados Unidos era menos de la cantidad de los que iban de los Estados Unidos a México. Esto pasó por muchas razones, pero la recesión en los Estados Unidos y el crecimiento (*growth*) económico en México eran factores importantes. La mejoría (*improvement*) en la economía mexicana tuvo otro resultado interesante: la llegada de un gran número de inmigrantes de países lejanos (*distant*), como Argentina, Corea, España, Francia y Japón, todos buscando su futuro en México.

Honduras

Unos ciudadanos hondureños exigen (*demand*) el regreso (*return*) de Zelaya a la presidencia.

E. Cultura: La crisis constitucional en Honduras

PASO 1. Lee el texto sobre Honduras.

Honduras es una república constitucional y, según el censo de 2010, tiene una población de 8,2 millones de personas. Es uno de los países latinoamericanos con más desigualdad socioeconómica: el 10 por ciento más rico de la población controla un 42 por ciento de la riqueza del país.

A finales de 2008, el entonces presidente de Honduras, Manuel Zelaya, anunció su plan de hacer un referéndum en las próximas elecciones para determinar si había apoyo[a] popular para reescribir partes de la constitución federal. Dentro de los posibles cambios[b] se incluía la posibilidad de reelegir[c] un presidente, lo cual estaba prohibido en la constitución. En marzo de 2009, la Corte Suprema hondureña determinó que el referéndum no era legal, pero Zelaya siguió con su plan. El 28 de junio de 2009, el día del referéndum, un grupo de aproximadamente cien soldados[d] entraron a la fuerza en la casa del presidente y lo llevaron en avión a Costa Rica.

Este acto de quitar de su cargo[e] a un presidente democráticamente elegido usando fuerzas militares es considerado por muchos un golpe de estado[f]; el acto de llevarlo fuera del país es considerado un exilio forzado. Y el evento está rodeado de[g] mucha controversia. Por un lado, muchos piensan que Zelaya había violado la ley[h] cuando no reconoció la decisión de la Corte Suprema. Por otro lado, otros piensan que la decisión de la corte y el exilio de Zelaya eran estrategias de los grupos políticos conservadores de Honduras. Ellos temían[i] que la política de Zelaya fuera cada vez más para la izquierda, basándose en el apoyo que Zelaya tenía de los presidentes de Venezuela (Hugo Chávez), Cuba (Fidel Castro) y Nicaragua (Daniel Ortega). Además, Zelaya había hecho actos como subir el salario mínimo para tratar de mejorar[j] la situación de la pobreza extrema en Honduras y proteger a los trabajadores.

En los días después del exilio de Zelaya, el gobierno suspendió varias garantías constitucionales de los hondureños. En los primeros días, pusieron un toque de queda.[k] Cuando Zelaya regresó a Honduras el 22 de septiembre, el gobierno suspendió durante casi un mes la libertad personal, la libertad de expresión, la de tránsito,* de habeas corpus y de asamblea y asociación. El gobierno no dejó que Zelaya volviera a la presidencia y en las elecciones de enero de 2010, los hondureños eligieron a Porfirio Lobo como el nuevo presidente. Hubo elecciones generales en 2013, en las que Juan Orlando Hernández fue elegido como presidente.

[a]*support* [b]*changes* [c]*re-elect* [d]*soldiers* [e]*position* [f]*golpe... coup d'état* [g]*rodeado... surrounded by* [h]*law* [i]*feared* [j]*tratar... try to improve* [k]*toque... curfew*

*la libertad de viajar dentro y fuera del país

PASO 2. Completa las oraciones con tus propias opiniones.

1. Si yo fuera presidente/a de Honduras, _____.
2. Si la Corte Suprema no hubiera tomado su decisión en contra del referéndum, _____.
3. Sería justo hacer cambios a la constitución federal para permitir la reelección si _____.
4. Si Zelaya no tuviera el apoyo de otros presidentes latinoamericanos, _____.
5. Honduras sería un país más estable y próspero si _____.
6. Si el gobierno de este país suspendiera las libertades constitucionales de mis amigos y yo, _____.

 PASO 3. En parejas, contesten las preguntas y explíquense las respuestas.

1. En Honduras, como en muchos países tropicales, ha sido difícil establecer una economía fuerte, por el bajo (*low*) nivel de recursos naturales y terrenos cultivables, entre otros factores. Como resultado, hay mucho desempleo y mucha desigualdad económica. ¿Piensas que este tipo de dificultad económica puede causar la inestabilidad política?
2. ¿Piensas que la inestabilidad política puede causar problemas económicos?
3. Si vives en un país como Canadá o los Estados Unidos, ¿piensas que la economía fuerte ha contribuido a la estabilidad política? ¿Piensas que el sistema político podría entrar en peligro si hubiera problemas económicos muy fuertes?

¡Leamos!

«Malas y buenas noticias» por José Antonio Millán

Antes de leer

PASO 1. Vas a leer un texto sobre los libros digitales. Anticipando este tema, ¿a qué probablemente se refieren los siguientes términos?

_c_ 1. sagas vampíricas

_b_ 2. los aparatos/dispositivos (*devices*) lectores

_a_ 3. un buscador

_e_ 4. P2P

_d_ 5. la fórmula de negocio

a. Google o Bing

b. Kindle o iPad

c. la serie *Twilight*

d. el modelo que usa una empresa para ganar dinero

e. la conexión entre varias computadoras que se usa para compartir archivos

PASO 2. Indica si cada frase a continuación se consideraría **buena noticia** o **mala noticia** para las empresas que producen libros digitales.

	BUENA NOTICIA	MALA NOTICIA
1. Hay mucha demanda de libros digitales.	☑	☐
2. Hay pocos libros digitales disponibles (*available*).	☐	☑
3. Hay muchos dispositivos lectores como iPad y Kindle.	☑	☐
4. El contenido digital más popular está en sitios ilegales.	☐	☑
5. Es difícil comprar los libros digitales legalmente.	☐	☑
6. Es fácil conseguir libros digitales sin autorización.	☐	☑
7. Los jóvenes leen más que nunca.	☑	☐
8. Los jóvenes leen libros digitales descargados (*downloaded*) ilegalmente.	☐	☑

¿Cómo lees? ¿Dónde lees? ¿Leer es diferente con un libro digital?

A leer

Lee el artículo sobre los libros digitales escrito por José Antonio Millán, «Malas y buenas noticias», que apareció en el periódico español El País. Luego indica si cada frase que sigue es cierta (C) o falsa (F).

Malas y buenas noticias

Hagan una prueba: dejen a un puñado[a] de buenos lectores adolescentes un e-book y denles la oportunidad de bajarse[b] obras legalmente de los sitios web donde se comercializan. Al cabo[c] de unos meses comprobarán[d] que han leído vorazmente,[e] pero que las obras no provenían de descargas[f] autorizadas. Sencillamente, han buscado en las fuentes[g] legales los libros que querían leer y no los han encontrado. Y los han localizado «en Internet». Hay muchos libros en la red.[h] Quien quiera[i] probarlo solo tiene que escribir en un buscador el título de una obra. Y no se piense que para descargarla hay que entrar en las procelosas[j] aguas de los P2P. Basta llegar a una página web, y hacer clic en un enlace.[k]

Pues bien: en muchos casos estos archivos[l] para e-book no están disponibles[m] si uno trata de comprarlos legalmente. Y en Internet los encontramos: libros torpemente[n] escaneados, o archivos creados ad hoc, ¡a veces con la traducción de obras aún no aparecidas en el mercado hispanohablante! Sí: los fans seguidores[ñ] de sagas vampíricas no se caracterizan por su paciencia.

La oferta de libros digitales es muy inferior a la demanda que existe. Y esta seguirá creciendo, porque los dispositivos lectores han ido bajando de precio y han aparecido alternativas como el iPad. Estos son los hechos[o]: acceso a Internet muy extendido; buscadores que encuentran cualquier cosa y un montón[p] de aparatos lectores para los que falta[q] contenido.

¿Y esta situación puede cambiar? Por ejemplo: Supongamos que los editores se apresuran[r] a sacar en versión electrónica los libros más codiciados,[s] ¿dejarían de descargarse ilegalmente? Pero un momento, un momento: ¿a qué precio me han dicho que pondrían la descarga?

Precios bajos, o nuevas fórmulas de negocio: no parece haber otra solución. El año que viene, la empresa madrileña 24symbols intentará suministrar[t] libros electrónicos en dos modalidades:[u] gratis con anuncios o pagando una suscripción que permitirá leer los que se quiera. Es la fórmula que en música ha seguido Spotify, pero ¿querrán unirse a ella los editores de las obras que la gente realmente quiere leer? Se pueden pensar otras modalidades: hay empresas que patrocinan[v] ligas de fútbol o ciclos de conciertos: ¿no se animarían a patrocinar líneas editoriales[w] digitales?

¿No será que fallan[x] las alternativas de negocio? Cada vez que hay nuevos cálculos del acceso a obras sin autorización se habla de la «merma de negocio»,[y] y no es así (como se ha visto en el caso de la música): no toda obra descargada ilegalmente habría sido comprada, y menos a esos precios...

[a]handful [b]to download [c]Al... At the end [d]they will confirm [e]voraciously [f]downloads [g]sources [h]Web [i]Quien... Whoever wants [j]stormy [k]link [l]files [m]available [n]clumsily [ñ]followers [o]facts [p]ton [q]lack [r]se... hurry [s]coveted [t]deliver [u]ways [v]sponsor [w]publishing [x]are failing [y]merma... lost business

Millán, José Antonio, "Malas y buenas noticias," El País, November 3, 2010. Copyright © 2010 by El País. All rights reserved. Used with permission.

1. _F_ Los jóvenes parecen preferir los libros digitales disponibles legalmente en los sitios web que venden e-books.
2. _C_ Los libros que les interesan a los jóvenes están en Internet, pero muchos de ellos no están en sitios autorizados.
3. _C_ Las descargas ilegales de libros en Internet son fáciles de encontrar.
4. _F_ Las descargas ilegales de libros en Internet siempre son de muy buena calidad.
5. _C_ En cuanto a los libros digitales, la demanda es más alta que la oferta (supply).
6. _C_ Con más variedad de dispositivos lectores, los precios han bajado.
7. _F_ Según el autor, el precio de las descargas autorizadas de libros digitales no será muy importante.
8. _C_ Según el autor, hay dos soluciones posibles: precios bajos o nuevas fórmulas de negocio.
9. _C_ A los editores de los libros más populares no les van a gustar las nuevas fórmulas de negocio.
10. _F_ Todas las personas que descargan libros digitales ilegalmente pagarían si estuvieran disponibles legalmente las mismas obras.

(Continues)

Suggestion (A leer, Paso 2):
If students are having trouble coming up with examples, give them models such as Google or Facebook, Netflix, and Twitter or Spotify.

Expansion (Después de leer): Have students practice the future tense by giving their predictions about the future of books and electronic reading devices.

PASO 2. En grupos, hagan una lista de ejemplos de cada una de las tres fórmulas de negocio que menciona el texto.

- gratis con anuncios
- pagando una suscripción
- empresas patrocinadoras

Después de leer

PASO 1. Contesta las preguntas sobre tus hábitos como lector(a).

1. ¿Qué tipo de textos lees?

   ☐ biografías   ☐ literatura
   ☐ cómics   ☐ noticias
   ☐ libros de autoayuda (*self-help*)   ☐ reseñas (*reviews*) de películas y música
   ☐ libros de texto   ☐ revistas de moda

2. ¿Cuándo lees? ¿Dónde? En las situaciones en que tú lees, ¿cuál es el mejor formato para leer tus textos?

3. ¿Han cambiado en los últimos cinco o seis años tus prácticas como lector(a)? ¿Han cambiado los aparatos que usas para leer? ¿Cómo cambiaron y por qué?

4. ¿Tienes un aparato lector? ¿A ti te gusta leer con el aparato? ¿Por qué sí o no? ¿Conoces a alguien que use uno? ¿A esa persona le gusta leer con el aparato? ¿Por qué sí o no?

PASO 2. Ahora entrevista a un compañero / una compañera para saber sus criterios para comprar libros digitales. Luego escoge la conclusión que mejor describa la fórmula de negocio ideal para tu compañero/a y explícala.

> **MODELO:** E1: ¿Comprarías libros digitales si tuvieras que pagar más de diez dólares cada uno?
> E2: No. Sería demasiado caro para mí. Solo compraría libros digitales si costaran menos de tres dólares.

¿Comprarías libros digitales si...

1. ...primero tuvieras que mirar veinticinco segundos de anuncios de una empresa que patrocina a la editorial?

2. ...tuvieras que mirar anuncios en el margen de la pantalla?

3. ...tuvieras que pagar una suscripción de $15 al mes?

4. ...fuera necesario pagar una suscripción de $10 al mes?

5. ...fuera necesario pagar una suscripción de $5 al mes?

En conclusión:

Para mi compañero/a, la fórmula de negocio ideal es...

☐ gratis con anuncios porque _____.
☐ pagando una suscripción porque _____.
☐ empresas patrocinadoras porque _____.

¡Escuchemos!

¿Cómo cambiarían el mundo?

Antes de escuchar

PASO 1. Marlén, Javier, Enrique y Mariana van a hablar sobre cómo cambiarían el mundo si pudieran. Antes de escuchar la conversación, conversen en grupos pequeños sobre la siguiente pregunta: Si Uds. pudieran cambiar algo en el mundo, ¿qué harían?

PASO 2. Ahora, empareja cada cita que vas a escuchar en el video con dos explicaciones lógicas.

1. _a_ _h_ «Me gustaría darles a los niños pobres las herramientas (*tools*) necesarias con las cuales ellos, en algún momento de su vida, se puedan independizar por completo.»

2. _b_ _g_ «Creo que debemos establecer un organismo global para defender los derechos humanos.»

3. _c_ _f_ «En mi opinión, hay que participar si luego quieres tener voz (*a voice*).»

4. _d_ _e_ «Hay falta de vivienda barata y asequible (*cheap and affordable housing*).»

a. La ayuda para los niños pobres no solo mejora la calidad de vida en el momento actual, sino también lleva a la independencia en el futuro.
b. Es un comentario sobre las atrocidades cometidas en muchos países del mundo.
c. Es un comentario sobre la gente que no participa y luego protesta.
d. Gente de todos los estatus sociales con diversos niveles de educación no tiene dónde vivir.
e. Hay gente tirada (*thrown*) en las calles de muchas ciudades grandes.
f. Si quieres tener voz, tienes que ir a votar.
g. Si un grupo sufre en un país, no se puede recurrir a (*turn to*) ninguna entidad internacional para ayuda.
h. Tenemos que mejorar la vida de los ciudadanos más jóvenes para hacer los cambios sociales necesarios.

Video track (Act. A): This video clip can be found on the DVD to accompany *Conéctate: Cap. 15,* Track 3.

A escuchar

Mira y escucha las respuestas que dieron Marlén, Javier, Enrique y Mariana a la pregunta, «Si pudiera cambiar algo en el mundo, ¿qué haría Ud.?» Luego escucha otra vez con pausas y escoge la mejor conclusión para cada frase a continuación.

1. _c_ Cuando Marlén dice, «niños pobres», está hablando específicamente de...
   a. niños que no tienen acceso a las escuelas públicas.
   b. niños que viven por debajo del nivel de pobreza federal.
   c. niños de la calle.
   d. todos los niños.

2. _b_ Para Marlén, el cambio clave para realizar (*achieve*) un mundo mejor es...
   a. acabar con todos los conflictos armados internacionales.
   b. sacar a los niños de la pobreza de manera que se puedan independizar como adultos.
   c. proveer la educación universal a todos los niños entre los cinco y dieciséis años de edad.
   d. darles de comer a todos los niños que viven en la calle.

3. _d_ Para Javier si quieres tener voz... ,
   a. debes protestar.
   b. no tienes el derecho de participar.
   c. tienes que hablar en voz alta.
   d. tienes la obligación de votar.

4. _b_ Según Javier, si no vas a votar... ,
   a. no puedes matricularte (*enroll*) en los cursos universitarios.
   b. no tienes el derecho de protestar.
   c. no vas a tener éxito (*success*) profesional.
   d. no vas a ganar la elección.

Videoscript (Act. A): 1. MARLÉN: ... *Y bueno, en algún momento si llego a estar económicamente bien, o sea hacer asociaciones para... para... para niños pobres, para niños de la calle, en los cuales... eh, se pudiera, salir de la pobreza, para... para que... para darles las herramientas necesarias en las cuales... en los cuales ellos en algún momento de su vida se puedan independizar por completo y... y tengamos un país mejor y no solamente un país mejor sino un mundo mejor, yo creo que no... no solamente los países no hay que dividir países de tercer mundo, primer mundo, yo creo que si toda la humanidad fuera consciente tendríamos un mundo mejor, y un mundo más limpio.* **2.** JAVIER: *Yo creo que es importante, ¿no?, supongo que cada voto cuenta. El tema es que si... si tú quieres tener... quieres tener voz y quieres tener voto, tienes que ir a votar, eh... lo que no puedes hacer es prote.. si no vas a votar, luego a protestar porque no te gusta lo que pasa. ¿no? Hay que participar si luego quieres tener... tener... tener voz, por decirlo de alguna manera.*

(Continues)

(Videoscript Cont'd)

3. ENRIQUE: *Bueno, en este momento el sueño es que... la vivienda sea más barata y asequible a todo el mundo, que no haya gente tirada en la... en las calles de las ciudades europeas, aquí en concreto por ejemplo en Madrid que hay 14.000 indig..., personas que están viviendo en la calle, y no son precisamente indigentes, sino que son gente de todas las... eh... de todos los estatus sociales, con diversos niveles de de educación y esto creo que ya se debería de acabar en toda Europa, de hecho hay movimientos en este momento en Francia, en Italia, en Alemania, en Bélgica, en Inglaterra y... y aquí en España está empezando... empezando también.*

4. MARIANA: *Yo creo que empezaría con las leyes. Las leyes, tal vez, del país es lo que genera un poco de inseguridad en las mismas personas, verdad, y de delincuencia. Entonces, tal vez, con leyes y con mejor educación desde que los niños están bastante pequeños con algunos programas de, de... en donde las personas no dejen la escuela, tengan mejores oportunidades, podría tal vez mejorar un poco la situación del país.*

5. __b__ Para Enrique, el sueño (*dream, ideal*) es...
    a. un organismo internacional que defiende los derechos humanos.
    b. la vivienda asequible a todo el mundo.
    c. menos basura en las calles de las ciudades europeas.
    d. más gente tirada (*strewn about*) en las calles de las ciudades europeas.

6. __c__ En Madrid, ¿cuántas personas están viviendo en la calle?
    a. 1.400   b. 4.000   c. 14.000   d. 40.000

7. __a__ Según Enrique, ¿qué tipo de persona está viviendo en la calle?
    a. gente de todos los estatus sociales   c. gente con bajo nivel de educación
    b. gente con vivienda asequible   d. gente pobre

8. __c__ ¿Qué país **no** menciona Enrique?
    a. Francia   b. Italia   c. Portugal   d. Bélgica

9. __c__ Según Mariana, ¿qué es lo que genera la inseguridad?
    a. las elecciones   c. las leyes
    b. el analfabetismo   d. la pobreza

10. __a__ Cuando Mariana dice «mejor educación», se refiere a programas que...
    a. animan a los niños a que sigan con sus estudios para tener mejores oportunidades.
    b. acaban con el narcotráfico.
    c. acaban con todos los conflictos armados internacionales.
    d. sacan a los niños de la pobreza de manera que se puedan independizar como adultos.

Después de escuchar

PASO 1.   Lee otra vez las declaraciones de **Antes de escuchar, Paso 2.** Luego di si estás de acuerdo o no, y por qué.

1. _____
2. _____
3. _____
4. _____

PASO 2.   Busca a alguien que haya hecho cada una de las siguientes actividades. **¡Atención!** Para hacer las preguntas, tienes que cambiar los infinitivos al presente perfecto.

> **MODELO:**   E1: ¿Le has dado dinero, comida o ropa a una persona viviendo en la calle?
>
> E2: Sí, una vez en Denver le di mi bufanda a una señora sin hogar. Hacía mucho frío y ella no tenía ni una chaqueta.

1. ...hablar con un(a) representante del gobierno sobre un tema social que te importa.
2. ...organizar un grupo estudiantil o comunitario para mejorar la comunidad.
3. ...participar en una manifestación para protestar por una injusticia.
4. ...ganarte la vida (*to earn a living*) sin el apoyo (*support*) de tus padres.
5. ...votar.
6. ...formular un plan para lo que vas a hacer después de graduarte.
7. ...votar en una elección de mitad de período (*midterm* [*not presidential*] *elections*).
8. ...escribir una carta a un político / una política de Washington para protestar por algo.
9. ...empezar a ahorrar dinero para tu jubilación (*retirement*).
10. ...trabajar en un banco de alimentos (*food bank*) o participar un programa parecido (como, por ejemplo, Meals on Wheels).

PASO 3.   Según los resultados del **Paso 2,** ¿quiénes son las personas más activistas de la clase? ¿Quiénes son las más independientes? Explica tus respuestas.

¡Escribamos!

Si tuviera un millón de dólares...

Al ganar la lotería se dice que es una bendición (*blessing*) y una maldición (*curse*). En esta actividad, vas a escribir sobre lo bueno y lo malo de tener mucho dinero, qué harías para ti y tu familia, tus amigos y tu comunidad, y qué responsabilidades o problemas tendrías a causa de haber ganado la lotería.

Antes de escribir

Suggestion (Antes de escribir): Remind students to use *le* and *les* to talk about what they would do for others.

PASO 1. ¿Qué harías si tuvieras un millón de dólares? ¿Qué problemas tendrías? Considerando las siguientes preguntas, crea una lluvia de ideas y luego pon las ideas en orden lógico.

Si tuvieras un millón de dólares, ¿qué harías para ti, tu familia y tus amigos? (viajaría a... , me compraría... , viviría en... , tendría... , no tendría...) ¿Qué harías para la comunidad? ¿Qué responsabilidades o problemas tendrías?

MODELO: viajaría mucho _2_

necesitaría ayuda para manejar (*manage*) todo mi dinero _4_

me compraría una casa en la playa de Costa Rica y otra casa para mi familia _1_

viviría en la playa durante tres meses del año y en mi yate (*yacht*) el resto del año _3_

ayudaría a los demás también _6_

empezaría una fundación para ayudar a los niños enfermos _7_

contrataría a un contador / una contadora (*accountant*) _5_

A escribir

En un ensayo de cuatro párrafos, explica lo que harías con un millón de dólares. El primer párrafo debe incluir un breve resumen de lo que vas a decir en el resto de tu ensayo. En el primer párrafo, di también si crees que ganar la lotería sería una bendición o una maldición para ti y explica por qué. En el segundo párrafo, describe lo que harías para ti, tu familia y tus amigos si ganaras la lotería y explica por qué. En el tercer párrafo, habla de lo que harías para tu comunidad y explica por qué. Concluye con un párrafo sobre «las maldiciones» de tener tanto dinero, es decir, los nuevos problemas y responsabilidades que tendrías, y por qué.

Después de escribir

Revisa tu ensayo. Luego intercambia ensayos con un compañero / una compañera para evaluarlos. Lee el ensayo de tu compañero/a y determina si el ensayo tiene sentido. ¿Se ha desarrollado (*developed*) bien cada párrafo? Lee de nuevo el ensayo con cuidado para revisar los siguientes puntos.

☐ ¿Ha escrito tu compañero/a cuatro párrafos (uno de introducción, uno sobre sobre sí mismo y sus seres queridos, uno sobre su comunidad y el último sobre las dificultades y obligaciones asociadas con ganar la lotería)?

☐ ¿Siguen los párrafos el orden que nombró tu compañero/a en su introducción?

☐ Además de escribir una lista de lo que haría, ¿hay una explicación clara en cada párrafo?

☐ ¿Concuerdan los sujetos y los verbos?

☐ ¿Concuerdan los sustantivos y los adjetivos?

☐ ¿Ha usado bien el condicional?

☐ ¿Ha usado bien las cláusulas **si**?

Después de revisar el ensayo de tu compañero/a, devuélveselo. Mira tu propio ensayo para ver los cambios que tu compañero/a recomienda y haz las revisiones necesarias.

ESTRATEGIA

Flow

In a first draft, you will almost always write the ideas as they come to you, but that doesn't necessarily result in the most logical order. And sometimes you find that some back story is required to make sense of a particular action. It's important to edit your work so that if you say in your introduction you are going to talk about A, B, and C, you truly do write about those three things in that same order in the body of your writing. To help you do this, list all of your initial ideas first, then order them, and find the strongest, most logical flow. Eliminate anything that does not flow well.

¡Hablemos!

¿Crees que es buena idea o mala idea?

Antes de hablar

¿Crees que serían buena idea o mala idea los siguientes cambios en la política de tu universidad?

	BUENA IDEA	MALA IDEA
1. abolir (*abolish*) las notas (*grades*)	☐	☐
2. solo tener clases virtuales	☐	☐
3. requerir que los estudiantes que se especializan en idiomas estudien en el extranjero (*abroad*)	☐	☐
4. usar solo libros de texto electrónicos (en vez de impresos [*printed*])	☐	☐
5. tener el voluntariado (*volunteerism*) como requisito para la graduación	☐	☐
6. subir la matrícula para tener mejores profesores y programas	☐	☐
7. Otro: _____	☐	☐

A hablar

En grupos de cuatro, escojan uno de los temas de **Antes de hablar** y hagan un debate. Dos estudiantes tienen que estar a favor del asunto y dos en contra de ello. Presenten el debate al resto de la clase.

> **MODELO:** ¿Es buena idea abolir las notas?
> E1: Creo que no, porque sin notas, los estudiantes no participarían en las clases.
> E2: Yo creo que sí, porque así (*that way*) los estudiantes más interesados asistirían a las clases y la participación sería mayor.

Suggestion (Después de hablar): After each debate, give groups that did not present one minute to discuss before voting on the winner of the debate.

Después de hablar

¿Quién crees que gana cada debate? Voten para saber quiénes son los ganadores de cada debate.

CONÉCTATE AL MUNDO PROFESIONAL

If you think you'd like to study abroad at a university in another country, consider doing a professional internship at the same time. When you come back home, you can apply for jobs in partner businesses or branches of those same companies. Already having contacts and networks at headquarters abroad will help strengthen your potential career opportunities.

Conéctate a la música

Canción: «Volver a comenzar» (2007)
Artistas: Café Tacuba (México)

Café Tacuba (o Café Tacvba) es una banda mexicana conocida por sus combinaciones muy creativas del rock con elementos de la música folclórica. Fue uno de los grupos más importantes del boom de rock alternativo en el mundo hispano en los años 90 y sigue teniendo un gran renombre internacional.

Los miembros de Café Tacuba

Antes de escuchar

En esta canción, hablan de los errores que cometemos (*we commit*) en la vida. En tu opinión, ¿cuál es el error más grande que muchos cometemos en la vida *como individuos*? ¿Cuál es el error más grande que hemos cometido *como sociedad*?

A escuchar

En la canción hay oraciones hipotéticas que usan cláusulas con **si**. Mientras escuchas, completa las oraciones según lo que dice la canción. Puedes usar la lista de verbos si la necesitas. Luego empareja cada cláusula con **si** con su consecuencia. **¡Atención!** Una de las cláusulas no tiene consecuencia.

hacer   pedir   sobrevivir (*to survive, outlive*)   tener   volver

SI... ,

1. Si __hiciera__ una lista de mis errores, ___

2. Si __volviera__ a comenzar (*to begin*), __a__

3. Si __hiciera__ un viaje a mis adentros (*insides*) y __sobreviviera__ a los lamentos (*laments*), __b__

CONSECUENCIA

a. no __tendría__ tiempo de reparar (*to make amends*).

b. __pediría__ fuerzas (*ability*) para decir cuánto lo siento.

Después de escuchar

¿Qué significan estas oraciones de la última parte de la canción? Empareja cada una con el significado más lógico. **¡Atención!** Hay cuatro opciones, pero solo se necesitan dos.

1. __b__ «El agua derramada (*spilled*) está.»
2. __d__ «La sed que siento me sanará.»

a. Ya no puedo tomar agua.
b. He cometido muchos errores.
c. Cuando tengo sed, no me siento enfermo.
d. Lamento esos errores y eso es bueno.

Suggestion (Antes de escuchar): Have students work in small groups, with each group responsible for producing one answer to each of the questions. Have each group present their answers to the class (orally or on the board) and see if there is some consensus among the class.

■ For copyright reasons, the songs referenced in **Conéctate a la música** have not been provided by the publisher. The video for this song can be found on YouTube, and it is available for purchase from the iTunes store.

VOCABULARIO

Now that I have completed the chapter, I can . . .

☐ express my opinions and beliefs
☐ talk about what I and others know and don't know
☐ discuss important social issues
☐ describe hypothetical situations
☐ explore social issues from Latin American and Spanish perspectives

Comunicación

Creo que...	I think . . .
En mi opinión...	In my opinion . . .
Para mí...	For me (personally) . . .
dejarle saber	to let someone know
¿Qué sé yo? / ¿Yo qué sé?	What do I know?, Beats me!
Que yo sepa...	That I know of . . . / As far as I know . . .
¿Quién sabe?	Who knows?
sin saber	without knowing/ realizing (by coincidence or by accident)
el/la sabelotodo	know-it-all
Ve tú / Vaya Ud. a saber.	Your guess is as good as mine.

Los sustantivos

la alfabetización	literacy; teaching of literacy
el analfabetismo	illiteracy
el crimen	serious crime
el derecho humano	human right
el desarrollo	development
el desempleo	unemployment
la (des)igualdad	(in)equality

la deuda externa	foreign debt
la dictadura	dictatorship
la esclavitud infantil	child slavery
la frontera	border
la guerra	war
el hambre (f.)	hunger
el/la indígena	native (indigenous) person
la libertad	freedom
el narcotráfico	drug trafficking
las noticias	news
el nivel	level
la oferta	supply; offer
la organización sin fines de lucro	nonprofit organization
la paz	peace
el peligro	danger
la pobreza	poverty
el/la político/a	politician
la seguridad	safety; security

Cognados: la corrupción, la crisis, la demanda, la democracia, el desastre natural, la discriminación, la elección, la infraestructura, el/la inmigrante, el problema social, el proceso politico, el racism, la tiranía, la violencia

Los verbos

acabar con	to put an end to (a problem)
conseguir (i, i) (g)	to achieve, obtain
desarrollar	to develop
mejorar	to improve
resolver (ue)	to resolve

Cognados: erradicar, votar

Los adjetivos

grave	serious
justo/a	fair
peligroso/a	dangerous

Cognados: económico/a

La amistad° y el amor°

friendship, love

En La Paz, Bolivia, la familia de los novios los felicita después de la boda.

Objetivos

When you finish this chapter, you will be able to:

- discuss your marital status
- express sympathy and regret
- talk about personal relationships
- discuss personal relationships in the Spanish-speaking world

In this chapter you will review how to:

- talk about activities you do
- talk about activities you used to do
- use pronouns to avoid repetition
- express things that you want to happen

www.mhhe.com/connect

COMUNICACIÓN ~~LARIO~~ ~~CTURA~~ ~~TE~~

¿Eres soltero/a, casado/a o... ?

Describing your relationship status

Video track (Act. A):
This video clip can be found on the DVD to accompany *Conéctate: Cap. 16*, Track 1.

Videoscript (Act. A, Paso 1):
1. GERARDO: *Mi estado civil... Soy soltero.* **2.** ÓSCAR: *Mi estado civil... casado.* **3.** JORDI: *Mi estado civil... Yo estoy soltero. Mi estado civil es soltero.* **4.** JUAN ANDRÉS: *Yo soy soltero.*

Suggestion (Act. A): Point out that Spanish-speakers sometimes use *ser* with *casado/a* (for example, *soy casado*) and sometimes use *estar* (*estoy casado*). The use of *ser* reflects the idea of being married as part of one's identity, and the use of *estar* portrays marriage as the result of a change (from being single to being married).

Note (Act. A): Interviewees answered using the binary choices *casado* or *soltero*. For example, when a divorced person in a common-law relationship was asked the question, he answered: *soltero*. This is the case with Jordi, who you might remember from *Cap. 11* (*A ver: En casa de Jordi y Elena*).

Script (Act. A, Paso 2): 1. *no está casado y no tiene planes para casarse* **2.** *con planes para casarse* **3.** *ha experimentado la disolución legal de un matrimonio* **4.** *con esposo o esposa* **5.** *Una persona a quien se le ha muerto su esposo o esposa* **6.** *con novio/a, pero sin planes para casarse*

A. A ver: Los estados civiles

> To describe your relationship status, you can use the following expressions.
>
> | | | | |
> |---|---|---|---|
> | **casado/a** | married | **en una relación** | in a relationship |
> | **comprometido/a** | engaged; in a serious relationship | **soltero/a** | single |
> | | | **viudo/a** | widowed |
> | **divorciado/a** | divorced | | |

PASO 1. Mira y escucha. Luego mira otra vez con pausas e indica el estado civil de cada persona que habla.

1.   Gerardo, de España

☐ casado
☐ comprometido
☐ divorciado
☑ soltero
☐ viudo

3.   Jordi, de España

☐ casado
☐ comprometido
☐ divorciado
☑ soltero
☐ viudo

2.   Óscar, de Costa Rica

☑ casado
☐ comprometido
☐ divorciado
☐ soltero
☐ viudo

4.   Juan Andrés, de Costa Rica

☐ casado
☐ en una relación
☐ divorciado
☑ soltero
☐ viudo

PASO 2. Escucha cada descripción y apunta la palabra que corresponde.

casado/a   divorciado/a   viudo/a

comprometido/a   en una relación   soltero/a

1. _soltero/a_   4. _casado/a_
2. _comprometido/a_   5. _viudo/a_
3. _divorciado/a_   6. _en una relación_

PASO 3. Ahora en parejas, contesten las preguntas.

1. ¿Qué significa **estado civil**? ¿A qué se refiere?
2. ¿Cuál es la diferencia entre **ser casado/a** y **estar en una relación**?
3. ¿Cuál es la diferencia entre **ser soltero/a** y **ser divorciado/a**?

B. El estado civil de las personas famosas

PASO 1. Apunta una lista de personas famosas y el estado civil de cada una.

PERSONA FAMOSA	ESTADO CIVIL	PERSONA FAMOSA	ESTADO CIVIL
_____	_____	_____	_____
_____	_____	_____	_____
_____	_____	_____	_____

PASO 2. Formen grupos y hablen de los cambios en el estado civil de las personas famosas que apuntaron en el **Paso 1.**

MODELO: La cantante Gwen Stefani cambió su estado civil de casada a divorciada en 2016. Ella y su ex-esposo, el cantante Gavin Rossdale, estuvieron casados por trece años y tienen tres hijos.

Cuánto lo siento
Expressing sympathy and regret

Suggestion (Comunicación): Remind students that they learned to express good wishes in the *Comunicación* section of *Cap. 7.*

To express sympathy for a loss, especially the death of a loved one, you can use these expressions.

Lo siento mucho. / Cuánto lo siento.	I'm very sorry.
Mi/Nuestro más sentido pésame.	My/Our deepest condolences.
Te/Le/Les doy/damos el pésame.	My/Our condolences.
Te/Lo/La/Los/Las acompaño en el sentimiento/dolor.	You're in my thoughts. / I'm with you in your time of pain.
Te/Lo/La/Los/Las acompañamos en el sentimiento/dolor.	You're in our thoughts. / We're with you in your time of pain.

A. ¿Celebración o sufrimiento?

PASO 1. ¿Con qué expresión asocias cada uno de los siguientes términos?

	¡FELICITACIONES!	LO SIENTO MUCHO.
1. la alegría	☑	☐
2. la angustia	☐	☑
3. la desesperación	☐	☑
4. la diversión	☑	☐
5. el dolor	☐	☑
6. la felicidad	☑	☐
7. la pena	☐	☑
8. la risa (*laughter*)	☑	☐
9. el sufrimiento	☐	☑
10. la tristeza	☐	☑

Note (Act. A, Paso 1): Before starting **Paso 1**, help students use clues to guess the meaning for words they don't know. Remind them that they know other forms of many of the items (*alegre*, *triste*, *divertirse*) and that others are cognates.

PASO 2. Primero pon las siguientes circunstancias en orden de lo que sería la mejor (1) a la peor (5) para ti. Luego indica una expresión lógica para usar con una persona que se encuentra en esa circunstancia.

PON EN ORDEN	EXPRESIÓN APROPIADA
____ romper (*breaking up*) con el novio / la novia	_____
____ el nacimiento de un bebé	_____
____ la adquisición de un nuevo coche	_____
____ la muerte (*death*) de un pariente	_____
____ casarte con (*getting married to*) la pareja de tus sueños	_____

 B. ¿Qué te pasa? En parejas, imagínense que son dos viejos amigos (viejas amigas) que no se han visto desde hace mucho tiempo. Tienen que decirse qué les ha pasado en los últimos años —los mejores y peores momentos (pueden inventar momentos falsos también)— y reaccionar.

MODELO: E1: Mi abuela se murió en junio. Estaba muy enferma, así que no nos sorprendió su muerte, pero estamos muy tristes.
E2: Te acompaño en el sentimiento.

CONÉCTATE AL MUNDO HISPANO

En los países donde se habla español, es casi un requisito (*requirement*) expresar **el pésame** a todos los miembros (incluso la pareja, los padres, los hijos y los hermanos) de una familia en la cual alguien se ha muerto. Si es posible, se debe ofrecer el pésame en persona, en un servicio religioso por la persona muerta o en una visita a la casa de la familia. Si no es posible ver a los familiares, una llamada telefónica o una tarjeta escrita a mano son aceptables. Incluso los jóvenes tienen la obligación de buscar la oportunidad de ofrecer el pésame.

Esa actitud representa un contraste con las costumbres estadounidenses. En los Estados Unidos, es más común evitar el tema de la muerte porque puede sentirse incómodo mencionar un tema que parece delicado. El escritor mexicano y ganador del Premio Nobel de Literatura, Octavio Paz, escribió sobre el contraste entre la perspectiva mexicana y la perspectiva estadounidense hacia la muerte en su obra *El laberinto de la soledad*. Paz asegura que las dos culturas se obsesionan con la muerte, pero se manifiesta de dos maneras muy distintas. En una cultura la muerte es una presencia constante y en otra se evita constantemente la realidad de la muerte.

COMUN **VOCABULARIO** UCTURA ATE

En español...

La pareja is grammatically feminine, but it may refer to either a man or woman when used to mean *partner* and to two men, women, or a mixed couple when used to mean *couple*. The terms **novio** and **novia** can refer to a serious *boyfriend/ girlfriend,* an engaged *fiancé/fiancée,* or even an about-to-be-married or recently married *groom/ bride*. In general it is easy to recognize the meaning of *groom/bride* because the context of a wedding is usually very clear.

Suggestion (En español): Refer students to numbers 3 and 7 in *Act. A* for examples of the different contexts in which *novio* and *novia* are used.

Suggestion (Act. A): For Q4, highlight that the prepositions used with *enamorarse* (*de*) and *casarse* (*con*) are not what students might expect if they translate the expressions from English. Suggest that they study the prepositions with the verb so they use the correct preposition.

La amistad y el amor
Personal relationships

A. El amor en línea

PASO 1. Imagínate que has visitado un portal de citas (*dating website*) por Internet en español. Contesta las siguientes preguntas que encuentras en el sitio.

1. **Estado civil**
   - ☐ **casado/a**
   - ☐ **comprometido/a**
   - ☐ **divorciado/a**
   - ☐ **en una relación**
   - ☐ **soltero/a**
   - ☐ **viudo/a**

2. La **pareja** ideal debe ser...
   - ☐ **abierta**
   - ☐ **cariñosa** (muestra afecto)
   - ☐ **celosa** (tiene envidia)
   - ☐ **comprensiva** (se comprenden / se entienden)
   - ☐ **tolerante**

3. La edad (*age*) ideal para...
   - un **noviazgo** (relación romántica) serio entre dos personas que pasan de ser amigos a ser **novios** es a los _____ años.
   - **emanciparse** (**independizarse**) del **nido familiar** (es decir, de sus padres) y **responsabilizarse** es a los _____ años.
   - el **matrimonio** (*marriage*) es a los _____ años.

4. Con respecto al acto de **enamorarse de** (*falling in love with*) otra persona, creo...
   - ☐ en el amor a primera vista.
   - ☐ que, después de muy poco tiempo, uno sabe si está **enamorado** de otra persona.
   - ☐ que el amor crece de una **amistad** (un período de ser amigos) larga.
   - ☐ que **casarse con** el amor de su vida es la expresión mayor del **amor** (*love*).

5. La primera **cita** (*date*) debe ser...
   - ☐ una **cita a ciegas** (*blind date*).
   - ☐ después de salir varias veces con un grupo de amigos.
   - ☐ después de pasar tiempo como amigos.
   - ☐ en el momento en que se conocen.

6. ¿Cuánto tiempo debe pasar entre...
   - **conocerse** por primera vez y decir esas palabras mágicas: «**te quiero**» o «**te amo**»? _____
   - ser novios y **comprometerse** (hacer planes para hacerse esposos)? _____
   - comprometerse y **casarse** (hacerse esposos)? _____

7. La **boda** ideal es...
   - ☐ grande, cara, en una iglesia y con más de cien personas invitadas.
   - ☐ pequeña, en una iglesia y con solo la familia y los amigos más íntimos.
   - ☐ los dos novios en un lugar exótico.
   - ☐ una boda civil (es decir, no religiosa y con poca ceremonia).

8. Si una persona **rompe con** su esposo/a y el matrimonio termina en **divorcio...** ,
   - ☐ uno de los esposos debe **mudarse** (irse) de la casa.
   - ☐ las dos personas deben seguir viviendo en el **hogar** familiar (la casa de la familia).
   - ☐ la persona que cuida más a los hijos debe quedarse en la casa.

PASO 2. Rellena la tabla con la letra adecuada para describir la ventaja y desventaja de cada uno de los siguientes estados civiles.

a. Después de estar casado/a durante un período de tiempo, vuelves a la vida de un(a) soltero/a.
b. te has enamorado/a y estás en un momento optimista con planes para casarte y compartir tu futuro con tu pareja perfecta.
c. Has sufrido el fracaso (*failure*) de tu matrimonio.
d. No tienes con quien compartir los gastos, las responsabilidades, la vida.
e. No tienes que coordinar y colaborar con otro en casi todo.
f. Tienes con quien compartir los gastos, las responsabilidades, la vida.
g. Tienes que coordinar y colaborar con otro en casi todo.
h. Tienes que manejar toda la logística y los gastos de hacer planes para una boda.

ESTADO CIVIL	VENTAJA	DESVENTAJA
casado/a	f	g
comprometido/a	b	h
divorciado/a	a	c
soltero/a	e	d

Suggestion (Act. C): Have students concentrate on Q3–Q8, since that is where there are likely to be differences of opinion.

B. ¿Cómo ocurre una relación? Pon los elementos de una relación en orden cronológico de 1 a 5.

___5___ Casarse en una boda y contraer matrimonio con la pareja ideal.
___4___ Comprometerse y hacer los planes para una boda.
___1___ Conocer a otra persona soltera que es comprensiva y tolerante.
___3___ Enamorarse y entrar en un noviazgo.
___2___ Salir en una primera cita.

Video track (Act. D, Paso 1): This video clip can be found on the DVD to accompany *Conéctate: Cap. 16*, Track 2.

C. ¿Qué piensan los demás? En grupos pequeños, hablen de sus reacciones al **Paso 1** de la **Actividad A**. Expliquen sus respuestas.

MODELO: E1: Para ti, ¿cómo es una boda ideal?
E2: Personalmente quiero una boda muy grande, con muchos familiares y todos mis amigos.
E1: Yo prefiero algo más íntimo, con mi familia y mis amigos más íntimos.
E3: No soy religioso/a, así que (*so*) no quiero casarme en la iglesia. Una ceremonia civil sería ideal para mí.

Suggestion (Act. D, Paso 1): Before showing the video clip, have students quickly read over the items they will be answering while watching.

D. A ver: La pareja ideal Mira y escucha. Luego mira otra vez con pausas y completa la información que falta.

PASO 1. Para cada persona que habla, ¿cuál es la edad ideal para casarse?

1.   Sabrina, de México
Más de __30__ años

2. Héctor, de México
De __28__ a __30__ años

3.   Noelia, de España
De __25__ a __26__ años

4.   Nadia Angélica, de México
Más o menos a los __30__ años

5. Olman, de Costa Rica
Más de __30__ años

6.   María Luz, de Perú
De __22__ a __27__ años

Videoscript (Act. D, Paso 1):
1. SABRINA: *Yo creo que una buena edad ya para saber que te estás casando y lo que eso significa, pues después de los 30.*
2. HÉCTOR: *Yo creo que unos 28, o 29, o 30 años más o menos porque ya, salió uno de la carrera ya trabajó, y disfrutó, su trabajo y, ya está uno más responsable de lo que significa tener una familia.*
3. NOELIA: *25 a 26.* **4.** NADIA ANGÉLICA: *¡Ja, ja, ja! No, yo no estoy casada. No estamos casadas. No estamos casadas, ¡jej, y este... pues... sí me gustaría formar una familia, a un futuro pero, después de mucho tiempo, no sé, a los 30 años, algo así. ¡Je, je!* **5.** OLMAN: *De 30 años en adelante.* **6.** MARÍA LUZ: *Yo diría que a los... entre los 22 y los 27 porque cuando uno está más joven, no tiene la madurez para tener un matrimonio que dure.*

Suggestion (Act. D, Paso 2):
Before showing the video clip, have students quickly read over the items they will be answering while watching.

Note (Act. E, Paso 1): Remind students that they will have to modify questions when conducting their surveys. For example, ¿Cuál es *tu* estado civil? In order to be less abrupt and more conversational, students should use expressions like *Para ti* or *En tu opinión* as is illustrated in the model.

En español...

There are many terms of endearment used throughout the Spanish-speaking world. Here are a few you might come across.

mi amor	my love
cariño	(my) dear (*lit.*, affection)
cielo	(my) angel (*lit.*, heaven)
corazón	(my) love (*lit.*, heart)
gordito/a	honey (*lit.*, fatty)
mi media naranja	my better half (*lit.*, my half orange)
mi vida	my life
viejo/a	old man/ woman

Some of these terms of endearment may seem negative, but they truly are used affectionately among couples in the Spanish-speaking world. While there can be some negative connotation to calling your spouse *old man* or *old lady* in English, this is not necessarily true for the Spanish **viejo/a.** Note also that these words are not necessarily descriptive: someone very thin might be called **gordito** by his partner, and a young woman might be called **vieja.**

PASO 2. Según cada persona que habla, ¿cómo es la pareja ideal? Escucha por lo menos dos veces con pausas y marca todas las respuestas que mencionan.

1. Mirelle, de México

Video track (Act. D, Paso 2): This video clip can be found on the DVD to accompany *Conéctate: Cap. 16,* Track 3.

☑ Es cariñosa.
☑ Es comprensiva.
☑ No es celosa.
☑ Quiere a la otra persona.

2. Suny, de Panamá

☑ Es comprensiva.
☑ Es una persona abierta.
☐ No es celosa.
☑ Tiene buena comunicación.

3. Víctor, de México

☐ Es una persona abierta.
☑ Hay respeto mutuo.
☑ Te deja ser independiente.
☐ Tiene buena relación.

4. Noelia, de España

☑ Es cariñosa.
☐ Es comprensiva.
☑ Quiere a la otra persona.
☐ Se comunica bien.

5. Sabrina, de México

☑ Acepta a la otra persona.
☐ Es cariñosa.
☑ Es tolerante.
☐ Te deja ser independiente.

6. Anlluly, de Costa Rica

☑ Es cariñosa.
☑ Es comprensiva.
☑ Es honrada.
☑ Es sincera.

E. El momento pefecto y la persona ideal

PASO 1. En grupos de cuatro personas, entrevístense para saber sus ideas sobre casarse y la pareja ideal. Luego completa la tabla.

Nombre de mi compañero/a	¿Cuál es su estado civil?	¿Cuál es la edad ideal para casarse?	¿Cómo es la pareja ideal?

MODELO: E1: En tu opinión, ¿cuál es la edad ideal para casarse?
E2: Yo creo que entre los 28 y 30 años sería ideal.

PASO 2. Ahora, dividan su grupo en dos. Cada persona debe hablar con su compañero/a sobre sus opiniones de la pareja perfecta. **(¿Cuáles son sus pasatiempos? ¿Cómo es la personalidad? ¿Cómo es físicamente? ¿Cómo le trata a la pareja?)** Hablen también de la pareja ideal que sus compañeros solteros describieron en el **Paso 1.** ¿A quién conocen Uds. que sería una pareja buena (¡o perfecta!) para ellos? (Si no conocen a nadie, piensen en una persona famosa o de ficción que sería ideal.)

Videoscript (Act. D, Paso 2): 1. MIRELLE: *Muy cariñoso, muy comprensivo, detallista, que no sea celoso... ¡mm! trabajador, y... pues que me quiera muchísimo.* **2.** SUNY: *Cuando además de quererse son amigos. Cuando tienen una buena relación, una buena comunicación. Se comparten todo... lo bueno, lo malo. Cuando no hay secretos. Cuando son man... bien abiertos, comprensivos.* **3.** VÍCTOR: *La pareja ideal es una persona que... que te deje ser libre, que te deje ser lo que tú quieres ser y que te deje hacer lo que tú quieras hacer y que tú también la... la respetes a ella y entre los dos cada quien tenga su independencia.* **4.** NOELIA: *Pues, un chico que me quiera, que me dé cariño. No sé, lo que todo el mundo pide.* **5.** SABRINA: Pues yo creo que la pareja ideal es lo que cada quién trae en la cabeza ¿no? Pero, pues difícilmente se encuentra a la pareja ideal, hay que tener mucha tolerancia, y hay que aceptar a las personas como son, o sea no hay tanto pareja ideal, ¿y encontrarla? ¡Je, je, je! Pero hay que trabajar con uno mismo, para aceptar a tu pareja ¿no? y tal cual es.* **6.** ANLLULY: *Para mí la pareja ideal sería alguien muy cariñoso, comprensivo, honrado y muy sincero.*

↻ Reciclaje

Review: The present indicative and the infinitive

Completa las conjugaciones del presente de indicativo de los siguientes verbos.

caminar	camino	caminas	camin_a_	caminamos	camináis	camin_an_
correr	corr_o_	corr_es_	corr_e_	corr_emos_	corréis	corren
sacudir	sacudo	sacud_es_	sacude	sacud _imos_	sacudís	sacud_en_
volver	vuelvo	_vuelv_es	_vuelv_e	_volv_emos	_volv_éis	_vuelv_en
ped_ir_	_pid_o	pides	_pid_e	_ped_imos	_ped_ís	_pid_en
pens_ar_	_piens_o	piensas	_piens_a	_pens_amos	_pens_áis	_piens_an
ser	s_oy_	_ere_ s	es	_so_mos	_so_is	son
sal_ir_	sal_go_	sales	sal_e_	salimos	salís	sal_en_
casarse	me caso	_te_ cas_as_	_se_ cas_a_	nos casamos	os casáis	_se_ cas_an_

16.1 Los novios no quieren casarse en junio.

Review: The present indicative and the infinitive

Actividades prácticas

A. ¿Eres romántico/a o práctico/a?

PASO 1. Primero completa las siguientes oraciones con la forma correcta de los verbos entre paréntesis. Usa el presente de indicativo (la forma **tú** para la pregunta y la forma **yo** para las respuestas) o el infinitivo, según el contexto.

PREGUNTA

Cuando _te despiertas_ (despertarse) en la mañana, ¿qué es lo primero que ___piensas___ (pensar)?

RESPUESTAS ROMÁNTICAS

a. ___Quiero___ (Querer) mucho a mi novio/a.
b. ___Amo___ (Amar) mucho a mi esposo/a.
c. ___Necesito___ (Necesitar) un novio / una novia.

RESPUESTAS PRÁCTICAS

d. ___Quiero___ (Querer) ___ir___ (ir) al baño.
e. ___Tengo___ (Tener) hambre.
f. Esta noche ___voy___ (ir) a ___acostarme___ (acostarse) más temprano.

Ahora, contesta las preguntas.
¿Cuál es la mejor respuesta para ti? _____
¿Es una respuesta romántica o práctica? _____

PASO 2. En grupos, conversen sobre los primeros pensamientos de Uds. al despertarse. Comparen sus respuestas y escriban un resumen (*summary*) de lo que dicen. En general, ¿Uds. son románticos o son prácticos en sus pensamientos al comienzo del día? **¡Atención!** Acuérdate que si eres parte del grupo, usa la forma **nosotros/as**, pero si no eres parte del grupo, usa la forma **ellos/ellas.**

> **MODELO:** En general, somos prácticos. Tres de nosotros pensamos que tenemos hambre y solo uno piensa en cuánto ama a su novia.

■ Answers to this activity are in Appendix 2 at the back of your book.

Note (Reciclaje): This section reviews the patterns that occur across many verbs in the present tense, including stem changes, the use of *g* in the *yo* form, and reflexive verbs. The present tense was introduced in the following *Estructura* sections: 1.3 The verbs *ser* (*to be*) and *tener* (*to have*); 2.2 The verbs *estar* (*to be*) and *ir* (*to go*); 2.4 Infinitives with *gustar* and *ir;* 3.1 Present indicative: Singular forms; 3.2 Present indicative: Plural forms; 3.3 Stem-changing verbs: o → ue; 4.2 Stem-changing verbs: e → i; 4.3 Stem-changing verbs: e → ie; 5.1 Verbs with irregular *yo* forms; 5.2 Reflexive verbs.

Suggestion (Act. A, Paso 2): Have students do this in all-male and all-female groups. The class can then compare whether men and women are different in their answers.

Suggestion (Act. C): Have students do this in small groups. For discussion when they are done, choose one of the women in the list and ask for groups to vote on who is the best match for her. Ask groups to provide justification for their choice. Then repeat the procedure with one of the men on the list.

Expansion (Act. C): Have all students write a short profile of themselves using the cases here as models. If you have a comfortable rapport with your students, pick one male and one female student in your class to write their profiles on the board, and then ask students to choose a match for each of these two using the profiles here.

B. ¿Un rechazo (*rejection*) o no? Cuando uno emprende (*initiates*) una amistad (¡o algo más!) con alguien, siempre existe la posibilidad de rechazo. En esta actividad, vas a ver algunas formas de empezar a hablar con alguien y algunas respuestas posibles.

PASO 1. Para cada pregunta o exclamación en la primera columna, escoge la mejor respuesta en la segunda columna y complétala usando el verbo entre paréntesis.

PREGUNTAS/EXCLAMACIONES

1. __e__ ¿Quieres ir al cine?
2. __f__ ¿Me das tu número de teléfono?
3. __d__ ¿Dónde vives?
4. __a__ ¿Qué vas a hacer este fin de semana?
5. __b__ ¿Estás en mi clase de español?
6. __c__ ¡Qué guapo eres!

RESPUESTAS

a. No sé. ¿ __Tienes__ (Tener) planes tú?
b. No, no __soy__ (ser) estudiante. ¿Tú sí?
c. ¡Gracias! Mira, te __presento__ (presentar) a mi novia.
d. ¡Muy lejos de ti, __espero__ (esperar)!
e. Sí. Me __encanta / encantaría__ (encantar) ir al cine.
f. No. Lo __siento__ (sentir), pero no __quiero__ (querer) que me llames.

PASO 2. ¿Cuáles son las respuestas en la segunda columna que se pueden considerar como rechazos? *Rechazos:* c, d, f.

C. A encontrar la pareja perfecta Lee los siguientes perfiles (*profiles*) de jóvenes españoles y latinoamericanos. ¿Quién sería buena pareja para quién? ¿Por qué?

MUJERES

Andrea
España

Estudia marketing.
«Me gusta estar con amigos, leer y practicar deporte. Practico gimnasia y pádel, que es un deporte muy parecido al tenis.»

Ximena
Argentina

Trabaja en una agencia de prensa y estudia.
«Me gusta mucho leer y en Buenos Aires hay mucha oferta cultural. Hay mucho cine, exposiciones, recitales... Me gusta mucho reunirme (*get together*) con amigos.»

Laura
Colombia

Estudia artes visuales.
«Pinto. Soy artista y me gusta pintar.»

Nadia Angélica
México

Estudia relaciones internacionales.
«Practico natación, salgo con mis amigos, voy al cine, leo, escucho música y voy a bailar.»

HOMBRES

Adrián
España

Estudia ciencias del deporte.
«Me gusta practicar deporte. Practico fútbol y tenis, pero no me gusta la natación. Me gusta ir al cine. Me gustan las comedias, el drama y las películas de terror.»

Cristián
Argentina

Trabaja como abogado.
«Me gusta jugar tenis y me gusta salir y divertirme. Salgo con amigos a la noche y voy a cenar. Es buena vida.»

Eduardo
México

Estudia telecomunicaciones.
«Estudio japonés como hobby porque me gusta la cultura japonesa. Soy patinador (*skater*) sobre hielo. Me gustan los tangos y la música electrónica.»

Jahyr
Panamá

Estudia.
«Juego fútbol y me gusta ver fútbol y béisbol en la televisión. También voy al gimnasio. De música me gusta la salsa y también el merengue y el reggae.»

Suggestions (Act. D):
• Have students work in pairs to write the profiles.
• Assign *hombres* or *mujeres* to each student or pair so that there is an even distribution of both.

D. Lo mejor y lo peor Basándote en los ejemplos en la **Actividad C,** crea los siguientes perfiles.

■ un perfil del hombre perfecto / la mujer perfecta
■ un perfil de un hombre / una mujer horrible

• When students are done, select volunteers to write one of each profile on the board. Have the class discuss the profiles and make suggestions for changing them. Moderate the discussion and allow changes to be made when most of the class agrees.

Reciclaje

Review: The preterite and imperfect

PASO 1. Completa las conjugaciones del pretérito de los siguientes verbos.

hablar	hablé	hablaste	habló	hablamos	hablasteis	hablaron
aprender	aprendí	aprendiste	aprendió	aprendimos	aprendisteis	aprendieron
llegar	llegué	llegaste	llegó	llegamos	llegasteis	llegaron
ir/ser	fui	fuiste	fue	fuimos	fuisteis	fueron
decir	dije	dijiste	dijo	dijimos	dijisteis	dijeron
hacer	hice	hiciste	hizo	hicimos	hicisteis	hicieron
tener	tuve	tuviste	tuvo	tuvimos	tuvisteis	tuvieron
dormirse	me dormí	te dormiste	se durmió	nos dormimos	os dormisteis	se durmieron

PASO 2. Ahora completa las conjugaciones del imperfecto de los siguientes verbos.

amar	amaba	amabas	amaba	amábamos	amabais	amaban
comer	comía	comías	comía	comíamos	comíais	comían
salir	salía	salías	salía	salíamos	salíais	salían
irse	me iba	te ibas	se iba	nos íbamos	os ibais	se iban
ser	era	eras	era	éramos	erais	eran

16.2 Cuando llegaron a la iglesia, los invitados ya los esperaban.

Review: The preterite and imperfect together

Actividades prácticas

A. ¿Te acuerdas?

PASO 1. Dos amigas están hablando de cómo se conocieron por primera vez. Primero empareja lo que dice **Amiga 1** con la respuesta de **Amiga 2.** Luego completa las oraciones con el pretérito del verbo entre paréntesis.

AMIGA 1

1. _d_ ¿En qué clase te _conocí_ (conocer)?
2. _h_ Sí, claro. Y te _pregunté_ (preguntar) sobre la tarea, ¿no?
3. _b_ ¡Y me _dijiste_ (decir) que no! ¿Te acuerdas tú?
4. _a_ Sí, la recuerdo bien. Pero luego Uds. _hablaron_ (hablar).
5. _g_ ¡Ja, ja, ja, qué chistoso (*funny*)! ¿Por qué _pensaron_ (pensar) que yo era buena persona?
6. _f_ ¿Con solo una sonrisa (*smile*)? Y entonces, ¿_seguimos_ (seguir) con nuestra conversación?
7. _c_ ¿Y luego? Te _invité_ (invitar) a comer con mis amigos, ¿no?
8. _e_ ¿Y qué _comiste_ (comer) tú? Seguramente no te acuerdas.

AMIGA 2

a. Sí, y _decidimos_ (decidir) que parecías una buena persona.
b. Claro. Es que _hice_ (hacer) la tarea con otra amiga y ella me estaba mirando.
c. Lo recuerdas bien. _Fui_ (Ir) con Uds. a un restaurante.
d. Nosotras _nos conocimos_ (conocerse) en la clase de biología. ¿Te acuerdas?
e. No es cierto. Me acuerdo perfectamente: _Pedí_ (Pedir) las enchiladas verdes.
f. Pues, te _di_ (dar) la tarea y me lo _agradeciste_ (agradecer).
g. No sé. Creo que porque nos _sonreíste_ (sonreír).
h. Sí, me _pediste_ (pedir) permitirte ver mi tarea de la noche anterior.

narratives of their own using the two tenses. Full control of the two tenses in spontaneous speech won't develop in most students until later, but this series of activities will give them a good foundation for this. (*Continues*)

■ Answers to this activity are in Appendix 2 at the back of your book.

Se conocieron en la secundaria.

Note (Act. prácticas): The preterite and imperfect can be difficult not only because the preterite forms are complex, but also because using the two tenses together in narration requires a true understanding of the core meaning of each. The *Actividades prácticas* here guide students through each component of the knowledge required. *Acts. A* and *B* give them practice with each tense on its own in a meaningful context. *Act. C* heightens their awareness of the difference in meaning between the two, and *Act. D* requires them to choose between the two in concrete, meaningful situations. *Acts. E* and *F* give them a structured environment in which to create small

PASO 2. Explícale a un compañero o una compañera cómo conociste por primera vez a una persona importante en tu vida. Tu compañero/a debe hacerte preguntas para sacarte más detalles.

> **MODELO:** E1: Cuando conocí por primera vez a mi entrenador (*coach*) de fútbol, me cayó mal. Ahora es una de las personas más importantes de mi vida.
> E2: ¿Por qué te cayó mal? ¿Te acuerdas? ¿Te dijo algo?
> E1: Al contrario. No me dijo nada por dos meses. Pero luego me dijo que quería observarme primero.

Suggestion (Act. B, Paso 1):
• Have students work in groups to decide if the statements are true or false.
• Point out that since these sentences are in the imperfect, the beginning and end points of these actions are not important to the sentence context.

Expansion (Act. B, Paso 1):
For each of the true sentences, have students put them in the present tense and modify them so that they are true of our society: *En general, los jóvenes se casan cuando tienen entre 25 y 30 años.*

Note (Act. B): This activity gives students practice with a range of verbs in the imperfect, all used in an environment where the imperfect meaning is clear. *Act. A* and *Act. B* together give students a good foundation for using preterite and imperfect together, as they will need to do in *Acts. C-F.*

B. El matrimonio en la civilización inca

PASO 1. Los incas eran una de las grandes civilizaciones en América en la época prehispánica. Sus tradiciones del matrimonio eran parecidas a las europeas, pero no en todos los aspectos. Completa cada oración con el imperfecto del verbo entre paréntesis. Luego decide si cada oración es cierta o falsa para los incas en los tiempos prehispánicos. **¡Atención!** Tres de las oraciones son falsas.

¿Cierto o falso?

_C_ 1. En general, los jóvenes _se casaban_ (casarse) cuando _tenían_ (tener) 16 años.

_C_ 2. Antes de casarse formalmente, _vivían_ (vivir) juntos para ver si _eran_ (ser) compatibles.

_C_ 3. Los padres del novio _arreglaban_ (arreglar) el matrimonio con los padres de la novia.

_C_ 4. Una vez al año, el gobierno _hacía_ (hacer) una boda en cada pueblo para todos los que _querían_ (querer) casarse.

_F_ 5. Todos _iban_ (ir) a la iglesia católica del pueblo para asistir a la boda.

_F_ 6. La novia _se vestía_ (vestirse) de blanco.

_C_ 7. Después de la boda oficial, cada familia _hacía_ (hacer) su propia ceremonia en casa.

_F_ 8. Durante la boda, el novio _tenía_ (tener) que bailar un vals con la novia.

PASO 2. Ahora, en grupos de tres, creen tres oraciones, dos ciertas y una falsa, sobre el matrimonio en tiempos de sus abuelos. Luego lean sus oraciones a otro grupo para ver si ellos pueden decir cuál es la oración falsa.

C. Oraciones sobre el amor

PASO 1. Completa cada oración con el verbo en el pretérito o en el imperfecto.

Pretérito	**Imperfecto**
1. a. «Gerardo y Luz _se conocieron_ (conocerse) ese día.»	b. «Gerardo y Luz ya _se conocían_ (conocerse).»
2. a. «Gerardo _estuvo_ (estar) en Las Vegas el 21 de abril.»	b. «Luz ya _estaba_ (estar) en Las Vegas el 21 de abril.»
3. a. Gerardo dice: «Cuando éramos estudiantes, yo _me enamoré_ (enamorarse) de ti, y tú _te enamoraste_ (enamorarse) de mí después.»	b. Luz dice: «Cuando éramos estudiantes, yo _me enamoraba_ (enamorarse) de ti y tú _te enamorabas_ (enamorarse) de mí.»
4. a. «Ayer _se casaron_ (casarse) Luz y Gerardo.»	b. «Ayer _se casaban_ (casarse) Luz y Gerardo.»

Se conocen.

Se enamoran.

Se casan.

Suggestion (Act. C): Remind students that the preterite is used to portray an action as being completed, and the imperfect is used to portray an action as ongoing, when the beginning and endpoints are not important. Ask students how sentences 4.a. and b. would be expressed in English.

Note (Act. C): This activity allows students to really think about how sentences can mean different things depending on whether the preterite or imperfect is used.

PASO 2.   Ahora empareja cada oración del **Paso 1** con la situación más lógica.

SITUACIÓN

1. _b_ octubre 2013
   _a_ el 14 de septiembre de 2013: se hablan por primera vez en la clase de biología
2. _a_ en Las Vegas: 21 de abril
   _b_ en Las Vegas: 20, 21, 22, 23 de abril
3. _a_ el amor: primero Gerardo y luego Luz
   _b_ el amor: Gerardo y Luz, poco a poco y al mismo tiempo
4. _b_ Hoy no sabemos si están casados o no.
   _a_ Hoy están casados.

D. La pareja Perón

PASO 1.   Eva y Juan Perón son, sin duda, la pareja política más conocida en toda la historia de Latinoamérica. Se hicieron aún más famosos por la obra de teatro y la película *Evita*. Completa las siguientes oraciones sobre ellos con el imperfecto o el pretérito de los verbos entre paréntesis.

Juan y Eva Perón

1. Juan ___entró___ (entrar) al Colegio Militar en 1910, cuando Eva no ___vivía___ (vivir) todavía.
2. Eva ___nació___ (nacer) en 1919 en una zona rural, cuando Juan ya ___era___ (ser) militar (*soldier*).
3. Eva ___se fue___ (irse) a Buenos Aires en 1935 para trabajar como actriz, pero ella y Juan no _se conocían_ (conocerse) todavía. _Se conocieron_ (Conocerse) por primera vez en un concierto organizado por Juan en 1944.
4. Un poco después, Juan _se hizo_ (hacerse) vicepresidente, cuando ___tenía___ (tener) 48 años.
5. Eva y Juan _se casaron_ (casarse) en 1945 y al año siguiente, Juan _se hizo_ (hacerse) presidente de Argentina.
6. Eva _empezó_ (empezar) a hacerse muy famosa a nivel mundial por sus discursos (*speeches*) de un gran impacto emocional.
7. Eva _se murió_ (morirse) en 1952 cuando apenas (*barely*) ___tenía___ (tener) 32 años.
8. Juan ___siguió___ (seguir) como presidente hasta 1955 y después ___vivió___ (vivir) muchos años en el exilio.
9. Juan ___regresó___ (regresar) a Argentina en 1973 para asumir la presidencia de nuevo. _Se murió_ (morirse) en 1974.

PASO 2.   En parejas, hagan una cronología (o «línea de tiempo») de las vidas de Eva y Juan Perón basada en la información en el **Paso 1**. Empiecen en 1910 y terminen en 1974. En un lado de la línea, apunten cada evento o período de la vida de Eva, y en el otro lado, cada evento o período de la vida de Juan.

PASO 3.   Crea una cronología sobre tu propia vida con un mínimo de seis eventos o períodos, y explícasela a tu compañero / compañera. ¡Empieza con el evento más importante: «¡Nací»!

Suggestions (Act. D):
- Remind students that two preterite forms in combination usually show a *sequence* of actions, two imperfect forms show *simultaneous* or *overlapping* actions, and a preterite and imperfect together shown one action *interrupting* another.
- Ask students to think of other famous political couples (such as, Franklin and Eleanor Roosevelt, Bill and Hillary Clinton, Benigno and Corazón Aquino).

Note (Act. D): This activity gives students practice with sentences with two preterite verbs, two imperfect verbs, or one preterite and one imperfect.

Note (Act. E): This activity allows students to create their own sentences where an action in the preterite interrupts one in the imperfect.

Suggestions (Act. E):
• Tell students that they need to find actions that were ongoing (*lo que pasaba*) and other actions that interrupted them (*lo que pasó*). Give students some verbs that might help them come up with ideas: *hablar, tomar, comer, sentarse, quedarse dormido/a, caerse, olvidarse, toser* (cough).
• Have students work on this in pairs or groups of 3. When they finish, have them choose their most interesting event and write it on the board, or have them read their story out loud while another group acts it out silently, in the style of improv acting.

España

En España se celebra la nueva legislación a favor del matrimonio entre personas del mismo sexo.

Note (Act. F): This activity gives students further practice in using the preterite and imperfect together creatively to tell a story.

Suggestion (Act. F): Tell students that if they don't know how their parents met or if they don't feel comfortable telling the story, they can make up a story.

Expansion (Act. F): Ask students to do the same with regard to their grandparents. Not all students will be able to do this in detail, but they can say what they know. If students do not know how their grandparents met, they could tell the story of how a fictional couple met in the 1960s.

E. ¡Un desastre! Cuando uno trata de empezar una relación amorosa con otra persona, las cosas no siempre van muy bien. Usa tu imaginación para terminar la siguiente historia, creando cuatro incidentes desastrosos (*disastrous*) en una noche que iba a ser muy romántica. Para cada incidente, escribe lo que **pasaba** en ese momento y lo que **pasó**.

Salimos a cenar y luego...

	¿QUÉ PASABA?	¿QUÉ PASÓ?
1.	_____	_____
2.	_____	_____
3.	_____	_____
4.	_____	_____

F. ¿Cómo se conocieron tus padres? ¿Sabes cómo se conocieron tus padres? Cuéntale la historia a un compañero / una compañera e indiquen juntos si eso sería común hoy en día o no y por qué.

> **MODELO:** Mi papá vivía en Fullerton, California. Mi mamá fue a un baile allí con su prima, y allí se conocieron. Eso ya no es muy común ahora, porque ahora nadie va a bailes.

G. Cultura: El matrimonio entre personas del mismo sexo en España

PASO 1. Lee el texto sobre España.

El 3 de julio de 2005, España legalizó el matrimonio entre personas del mismo sexo (es decir, entre dos hombres o dos mujeres). Fue el tercer país del mundo en aprobar una ley[a] similar —después de los Países Bajos (Holanda) y Bélgica[b]— y el primer país en el mundo hispano. El proyecto de ley[c] fue apoyado[d] por el entonces presidente del gobierno, José Luis Rodríguez Zapatero, cumpliendo con[e] una promesa que había hecho durante su campaña electoral. El resultado final fue una reforma al Código Civil: la nueva versión declara que «El matrimonio tendrá los mismos requisitos y efectos cuando ambos contrayentes[f] sean del mismo o de diferente sexo».

Según las encuestas de 2004, un 66 por ciento de los españoles estaban a favor del matrimonio entre homosexuales. Sin embargo, la nueva ley no tenía el apoyo de los grupos más conservadores. El Partido Popular, que tenía la mayoría de los votos en el Senado, argumentó que la homosexualidad era una patología y que tendría un efecto negativo sobre los hijos de una pareja. Sin embargo, esos argumentos se rechazaron[g] y a pesar del veto del Senado, la ley sí fue aprobada por el Congreso, el presidente del gobierno y el rey Juan Carlos I.

Después de que la ley se ratificó, quedaban dos temas importantes por resolver. Uno era si en los matrimonios entre personas del mismo sexo la ley le daría residencia legal en España a un extranjero o una extranjera que se casara con un ciudadano español, incluso si viniera de un país donde el matrimonio homosexual todavía no era legal. Se determinó que sí, que los derechos de esa pareja, incluso la residencia de la persona extranjera, serían reconocidos dentro de España aunque el matrimonio no fuera legal en otros contextos. El otro asunto era «la adopción homoparental». Según la ley, si una pareja lesbiana tuviera un hijo o una hija, la madre no biológica tendría que hacer todos los trámites[h] formales de adopción para ser reconocida legalmente como la madre. Eso no era el caso entre las parejas heterosexuales: si una mujer con hijos se casara con un hombre, el padrastro se reconocería automáticamente como el padre legal de los hijos. Esta desigualdad se resolvió modificando la ley sobre la reproducción asistida, aplicando los mismos derechos legales a las familias homoparentales que tenían ya las familias heteroparentales.

[a]*law* [b]*Belgium* [c]*proyecto... bill* [d]*supported* [e]*cumpliendo... keeping* [f]*parties* [g]*se... were rejected* [h]*paperwork, legal processes*

PASO 2. Completa las oraciones conjugando el verbo más lógico de la lista en la forma adecuada del pretérito o el imperfecto. **¡Atención!** No repitas ningún verbo.

apoyar	dar	existir	legalizar	querer	ser
causar	declarar	hacer	presentar	reformar	

1. Cuando España ___legalizó___ el matrimonio entre personas del mismo sexo, ya ___era___ legal en los Países Bajos (Holanda) y Bélgica.

2. José Luis Rodríguez Zapatero __quería__ cumplir con una promesa que __hizo__ durante su campaña electoral.

3. El Congreso __reformó__ una ley que ya __existía__ en el Código Civil.

4. Muchos españoles ya __apoyaban__ el matrimonio entre homosexuales cuando el presidente del gobierno __presentó__ el proyecto de ley al Senado y el Congreso.

5. El Partido Popular __declaró__ que las relaciones homoparentales __causaban__ daño (*harm*) a los hijos.

6. La ley les __dio__ residencia legal y otros derechos a parejas de países que no habían legalizado el matrimonio homosexual.

PASO 3. En parejas, contesten las preguntas y explíquense las respuestas.

1. España y el resto del mundo hispano tienen una larga tradición católica, pero en general, hay una separación muy clara entre la religión y la política. ¿Piensas que eso tiene algo que ver (*something to do*) con el hecho de que (*the fact that*) algunos de estos países (Argentina, España, México, Uruguay) fueron de los primeros en el mundo en legalizar el matrimonio entre personas del mismo sexo?

2. Los cuatro países mencionados, en comparación al resto del mundo hispano, tienen un nivel de desarrollo y un nivel de educación relativamente altos. ¿Piensas que eso también tiene algo que ver?

3. En tu país, ¿la religión tiene mucha o poca influencia en la política? ¿Esto ha tenido un efecto en el debate sobre el matrimonio entre personas del mismo sexo o la adopción homoparental?

 ## Reciclaje

Review: Object pronouns

Empareja el término con la descripción. Luego completa cada oración con el pronombre de objeto directo (**lo, la** o **los**) o de objeto indirecto (**te, le**). La primera ya se ha hecho.

1. __b__ la pareja perfecta
2. __c__ tu amigo/a
3. __e__ el amor
4. __f__ el estado civil
5. __a__ tu esposo/a
6. __d__ el novio y la novia

a. __Le__ regalas algo cuando tienen un aniversario de boda.

b. Muchos *la* buscan, pero no todos *la* encuentran.

c. __Te__ habla con frecuencia para ver cómo estás.

d. __Los__ puedes ver en una boda. Son el centro de la atención.

e. Los casados a veces tienen que trabajar para mantener__lo__ en su matrimonio.

f. __Lo__ tienes que indicar en muchos formularios oficiales.

Note (Reciclaje): Object pronouns were introduced in the following *Estructura* sections: 5.2 Reflexive verbs; 6.3 Direct objects and direct object pronouns; 7.2 Indirect objects and indirect object pronouns; 8.3 Object pronoun placement with infinitives; 11.2 Commands with object pronouns; 12.1 The present perfect with object pronouns; 12.2 The present progressive with object pronouns.

■ Answers to this activity are in Appendix 2 at the back of your book.

16.3 Le pidió un divorcio porque ya no lo amaba.

Review: Object pronouns

Actividades prácticas

Script (Act. A): 1. ¿Dónde está mi novio? 2. ¿Cómo te mantienes en contacto con tus amigos? 3. ¿Cómo conoces a mis padres? 4. ¿Por qué está tan contenta tu novia? 5. ¿Dónde va a ser tu boda? 6. ¿Conoces a mi novia?

 A. Preguntas y respuestas Vas a escuchar seis preguntas. Escoge la mejor respuesta para cada una.

1. __b__ 2. __c__ 3. __a__ 4. __e__ 5. __d__ 6. __f__

a. Los conocí en una fiesta en tu casa el año pasado.

b. Lo vi en el parque con su hermana.

c. Les hablo por teléfono de vez en cuando y nos mandamos mensajes por Facebook.

d. La queremos tener en Acapulco, pero no sé si podemos ahorrar el dinero.

e. Le dieron un trabajo muy bueno en el banco.

f. Nunca la he visto. ¿Existe o es una fantasía tuya (*of yours*)?

■ The audio files for in-text listening activities are available in the eBook, within Connect activities, and on the Online Learning Center.

Note (Act. B): This activity reinforces students' awareness of the distinction between objects of prepositions and object pronouns.

B. Un gran problema

PASO 1. Lee esta carta que explica un problema. Luego completa las posibles soluciones al problema con un pronombre de la lista. ¡**Atención!** Algunos pronombres se usan más de una vez.

Pronombres preposicionales: él ella
Pronombres de objeto directo e indirecto: le lo me

Para: doctor@amor.com
De: Anónima
Asunto: Dudas

Doctor Amor:

Tengo un gran problema. Ya no quiero seguir con mi novio, pero no sé cómo romper la relación. Lo quería mucho y me parecía muy guapo, pero no sé qué pasó. Últimamente no lo aguanto (*I can't stand him*) y además, ahora me parece muy feo. Me sigue mandando mensajes constantemente, siempre quiere estar conmigo y les cuenta a sus amigos que está locamente enamorado de mí, pero la verdad es que ya no lo quiero en mi vida. ¿Qué hago? No es malo y no quiero lastimarlo (*hurt him*). En el archivo adjunto (*attached*), puse una lista de ideas.

—Anónima

POSIBLES SOLUCIONES:

1. Decir_le_ que solo quiero ser su amiga.
2. Decir_le_ que _lo_ odio y que ya no _lo_ quiero ver.
3. Decir_le_ que _lo_ siento mucho, que es muy buena persona, pero _me_ parece mejor si terminamos nuestra relación.
4. Ya no hablar_le_.
5. Invitar_lo_ a un restaurante muy caro, cenar allí con _él_, decir_le_ que voy al baño y luego desaparecer.
6. Presentar_lo_ a una amiga y esperar que él se enamore de _ella_.
7. Decir_le_ que siempre _lo_ voy a querer mucho, pero que quiero estar sola por un tiempo.
8. Empezar a vestir_me_ muy mal, para que piense que soy muy fea y que _me_ deje.
9. Presentar_le_ a una amiga y decir_le_ que _ella_ es mi novia y que ya no _me_ interesan los hombres.
10. Dar_le_ buenísimas recomendaciones como novio en Internet para que otras mujeres _lo_ busquen para salir con _él_.

PASO 2. En grupos, decidan cuál es la mejor solución de todas y cuál es la peor.

La mejor solución es el número: ____

La peor solución es el número: ____

Note (Act. C): This activity reinforces students' awareness of the distinction between object and reflexive pronouns.

Suggestion (Act. C): The noun *muxe* is usually masculine, though usage varies. Tell students to read the sentences carefully for clues to gender and number when choosing the pronoun.

PASO 3. Basándose en la mejor solución que escogieron en el **Paso 2**, escriban un guion (*script*) de lo que «Anónima» le puede decir a su novio.

C. Los muxes de Oaxaca

PASO 1. En el estado de Oaxaca en México, la cultura indígena de los zapotecos es muy fuerte. En esa cultura, existe la tradición del muxe (se pronuncia *MU-she*), un hombre que en muchos aspectos lleva la vida de una mujer. Completa las siguientes oraciones, utilizando un pronombre de objeto (**lo**, **los las**, **le** o **les**) o un pronombre reflexivo (**se**). Luego indica la oración falsa.

1. En general, a los muxes _los_ tratan con respeto en las comunidades zapotecas.
2. A muchos padres _les_ gusta tener un hijo muxe porque los hijos muxes no _los_ abandonan en tiempos difíciles.
3. Tienen una competencia de muxes cada año y al más bonito _le_ dan un premio.
4. Muchos muxes _se_ visten de mujeres, pero algunos _se_ visten de hombres.
5. A un muxe _lo_ escogieron como presidente del país en 2008.   falso
6. A muchos niños _les_ dan la opción de ser muxe cuando entran a la adolescencia.
7. A las personas muxes, mucha gente _las_ considera dotadas (*gifted*) de un talento artístico especial.
8. A muchos muxes, _los_ puedes ver de vez en cuando en las comunidades zapotecas vendiendo cosas en el mercado, haciendo artesanía o en otros trabajos tradicionales de mujeres.

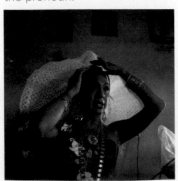

Un muxe de Oaxaca

PASO 2.   Si pudieras hablar con un muxe, ¿qué le preguntarías? En parejas, creen tres preguntas para ellos.

> **MODELO:**   ¿Uds. se casan?
> ¿Cómo los tratan los demás?

 D. Cómo pueden cuidarse bien el uno al otro   Si uno ama a su pareja y quiere cuidarla bien (mental, física y emocionalmente), ¿qué debe hacer? En grupos pequeños, creen una lista de por lo menos cinco ideas de cómo podrían cuidar a sus parejas y cómo ellos/ellas pueden cuidarlos a Uds. **¡Atención!** Escriban sus ideas en forma del infinitivo.

> **MODELO:**   Ayudarlo con la tarea.
> Prepararle comida.

 E. La amistad

PASO 1.   ¿Qué hace un buen amigo / una buena amiga? En grupos, creen una lista, basada en su experiencia, de las cosas que hacen los amigos / las amigas de verdad (*true*).

> **MODELO:**   Los amigos te piden ayuda cuando tienen problemas.

PASO 2.   ¿Son iguales las amistades entre los hombres y las amistades entre las mujeres? Creen una lista de algunas diferencias que Uds. han visto entre los hombres y las mujeres en cuanto a (*concerning*) la amistad.

> **MODELO:**   Una mujer les pide ayuda mucho a sus amigas. Un hombre no les pide ayuda tanto a sus amigos.

PASO 3.   Si encontraron diferencias entre los hombres y las mujeres en el **Paso 2,** ¿piensan que esas diferencias son comunes en todas las culturas?

Suggestion (Act. D): Tell the class that each student needs to contribute 2–4 ideas, none repeating those that other group members have listed. Have each group present their best ideas orally or on the board, and discuss the answers as a class.

Note (Act. E, Paso 2): There are no correct answers here. Students will have a variety of answers.

Suggestion (Act. E, Paso 3): It is sometimes claimed that in the Spanish-speaking world, friendship among men and among women tends to be tighter than in North America. In particular, men and women tend to each keep their own friends even after marriage (getting together frequently, going out for drinks or meals, etc.), whereas in North America, this is less common. If this is your experience or something you have observed, share it with students.

CONÉCTATE AL MUNDO HISPANO

En muchos países latinoamericanos, la industria televisora es un sector importante de la economía, gracias en parte al enorme éxito internacional de **las telenovelas.** En su temática (*topics*), las telenovelas son parecidas a los «soap operas» de los Estados Unidos, pero en otros aspectos, son parecidas a programas dramáticos, como *Game of Thrones.* En general, los programas se transmiten (*are broadcast*) por la noche y muchas veces tienen actores muy reconocidos. Atraen (*They attract*) a un público de hombres y mujeres de todas las edades y de todas las clases sociales. A veces parece que el país entero se detiene (*stops*) a la hora indicada para ver su «novela» favorita.

Los países que producen más telenovelas son Argentina, Brasil (en portugués, pero dobladas al español para exportar), Chile, Colombia, México y Venezuela. Pasan los programas no solo en Latinoamérica y España, sino también en otros países de Europa, en Asia y en el Medio Oriente (*Middle East*), con subtítulos, doblados, o hasta con otro equipo de actores. Dos de las telenovelas más famosas internacionalmente son *Los ricos también lloran,* una telenovela mexicana de 1979, y *Yo soy Betty, la fea,* una telenovela colombiana de 1999 a 2001. Esta última fue presentada en su versión original en más de treinta países e hicieron más de veinte versiones con nuevos actores para otros países. La versión norteamericana se llama *Ugly Betty* y estuvo en el aire de 2006 a 2010.

Reciclaje

Review: The present subjunctive

Completa las conjugaciones del presente de subjuntivo de los siguientes verbos.

amar	ame	am<u>es</u>	am<u>e</u>	am**emos**	am<u>éis</u>	am<u>en</u>
casarse	me case	<u>te</u> cas<u>es</u>	<u>se</u> cas<u>e</u>	nos cas**emos**	os cas**éis**	<u>se</u> cas<u>en</u>
volver	vuelva	<u>vuelv</u>**as**	<u>vuelv</u>a	<u>volv</u>**amos**	<u>volv</u>**áis**	<u>vuelv</u>**an**
hac<u>er</u>	hag<u>a</u>	hag**as**	hag<u>a</u>	hag**amos**	hag**áis**	hag<u>an</u>
ser	<u>se</u>a	se<u>as</u>	<u>sea</u>	se<u>amos</u>	<u>se</u>**áis**	se<u>an</u>
tener	tenga	teng<u>as</u>	<u>teng</u>a	teng<u>amos</u>	<u>teng</u>**áis**	teng<u>an</u>

■ Answers to this activity are in Appendix 2 at the back of your book.

Note (Act. A): It takes years for learners to be able to produce subjunctive forms spontaneously in conversation, so it is not reasonable to expect that here. It is reasonable, however, to expect students to be able to understand how subjunctive forms are conjugated and to grasp the basics of when the subjunctive (vs. the indicative) is used. That is the focus of the activities in this section.

Suggestion (Act. A): Remind students of a basic distinction between the indicative and the subjunctive: the indicative expresses things that you believe to be true, while the subjunctive expresses what you would want or hope to be true (volition) or what might not be true (disbelief and uncertainty). Give some examples with *pienso/sé/creo que* + indicative, *quiero/espero que* + subjunctive, and *no creo que* + subjunctive.

16.4   Espero que rompa con su novio antes de que se enamore de él.

Review: The present subjunctive

Note (Reciclaje): The present subjunctive was introduced in the following *Estructura* sections: 12.3 The subjunctive: Volition with regular verbs; 13.1 The subjunctive: Irregular verbs.

Actividades prácticas

A. Una telenovela   Las telenovelas son programas de televisión muy populares en Latinoamérica y otras partes del mundo. Se trata de una historia de amor, presentada de una forma sentimental y melodramática.

PASO 1.   Lee la siguiente versión muy exagerada de cómo hablan en las telenovelas. Usa los verbos de la lista para completar las oraciones. El primero ya está hecho. **¡Atención!** Algunos verbos están en el indicativo y otros en el subjuntivo.

| eres (2x) | se casa (2x) | sea (3x) | te cases |
| haya | se case | seas | te vayas |

MUJER: ¡Quiero que <u>te cases</u> conmigo! ¡Quiero que <u>seas</u>[1] mi esposo!

HOMBRE: ¿Estás loca? No quiero casarme contigo, porque <u>eres</u>[2] muy fea.

MUJER: Es posible que yo <u>sea</u>[3] un poco fea, pero ¡tú eres peor! No creo que <u>haya</u>[4] otro hombre más feo en todo el mundo.

HOMBRE: ¿Pero no entiendes? Me voy a casar con Angélica Antonieta. ¡Necesito que tú <u>te vayas</u>[5] de mi vida!

MUJER: No pienso que Angélica Antonieta <u>sea</u>[6] tan tonta. Ella dice que <u>se casa</u>[7] contigo solo para que la dejes en paz.

HOMBRE: ¡No es cierto! Ella me quiere mucho y hace todo para que yo <u>sea</u>[8] feliz. Si yo le digo a ella que <u>se case</u>[9] conmigo, entonces <u>se casa</u>[10] conmigo.

MUJER: ¡Qué idiota <u>eres</u>[11]!

PASO 2.   En parejas, escriban un diálogo de telenovela usando el **Paso 1** como modelo.

Suggestion (Act. A, Paso 2): Tell students that they can either write a dialogue together or take turns (where each students writes the lines for one character).

Suggestions (Act. A, Paso 1):
• Rather than going over the answers dryly, have pairs of students present their answers by doing a melodramatic, over-the-top reading of the dialogue.
• Before beginning the dialogue, remind students that the verb *decir* sometimes expresses a recommendation (with a meaning like *to order*), in which case it is followed by the subjunctive. When *decir* simply conveys information (with a meaning of *to say*), it is followed by the indicative in the dependent clause.

B. William Levy

PASO 1. William Levy es un actor y modelo cubano que inmigró a los Estados Unidos a los 15 años. Durante muchos años, fue uno de los galanes (*leading men*) más conocidos de las telenovelas, sobre todo de las telenovelas mexicanas. Aquí hay unas afirmaciones (*statements*) sobre él que pueden ser ciertas o falsas. Escribe cada afirmación en la categoría correcta para completar la oración. **¡Atención!** En dos de las categorías, tienes que cambiar al subjuntivo el verbo de la afirmación.

William Levy, actor cubano

AFIRMACIONES

Es originario de Cuba.

No puede conseguir una novia.

Vive en los Estados Unidos.

Habla bien el inglés y el español.

Muchas personas lo consideran feo.

Pasa mucho tiempo en diferentes países de Latinoamérica.

Hace ejercicio todos los días.

Es un gran ídolo de las telenovelas.

Se ve (*He looks*) mal sin camisa.

ES VERDAD QUE...	ES POSIBLE QUE...	NO CREO QUE...
es originario de Cuba.	hable bien el inglés y el español.	no pueda conseguir una novia.
vive en los Estados Unidos.	pase mucho tiempo en diferentes países de Latinoamérica.	muchas personas lo consideren feo.
es un gran ídolo de las telenovelas.	haga ejercicio todos los días.	se vea mal sin camisa.

 PASO 2. Crea una o dos oraciones más sobre Levy para cada una de las categorías. Luego en grupos pequeños, compartan sus oraciones para ver quien esta de acuerdo.

C. La Malinche y Hernán Cortés

La mujer indígena conocida como «Malintzín» o «La Malinche» fue intérprete (*interpreter*) y consejera (*advisor*) diplomática entre los españoles y los aztecas en los tiempos de la conquista de México. Su relación de amor con el conquistador español Hernán Cortés es muy conocida. Completa las siguientes oraciones con la forma adecuada del presente de indicativo o subjuntivo del verbo entre paréntesis. Luego escribe **M** si la persona que está hablando es La Malinche y **C** si es Cortés. Escribe **M/C** si los dos podrían haber dicho (*could have said*) la oración.

¿M, C o M/C?

1. __C__ «Yo nací en España. Hablo español, pero no hablo ninguna lengua indígena de México. Quiero que La Malinche __trabaje__ (trabajar) como mi intérprete.»
2. __M__ «Estoy aprendiendo el español, porque es necesario que lo __hable__ (hablar) bien.»
3. __C__ «La Malinche y yo vamos a tener un hijo. Quiero que __se llame__ (llamarse) Martín.»
4. __M__ «El hijo que tuve con Cortés ya nació. Dicen que __es__ (ser) el primer mestizo (*person of mixed race*) de México.»
5. __C__ «Ahora me quiero casar con una española. Le voy a decir a La Malinche que __se vaya__ (irse).»
6. __M__ «Ahora estoy casada con un noble español. No creo que Cortés y yo __volvamos__ (volver) a vernos nunca.»
7. __C__ «Ahora estoy casado con una española y tengo seis hijos con ella. Creo que ellos __van__ (ir) a estar bien, porque les __voy__ (ir) a dejar mucho dinero en mi testamento para que __tengan__ (tener) todo lo que necesitan.»
8. __M/C__ «Espero que la historia me __trate__ (tratar [*to treat*]) bien.»

D. ¿Cómo consigues novio/a?

PASO 1. ¿Qué le recomiendas a un amigo / una amiga que quiere conseguir novio/a? Escribe por lo menos tres ideas.

> **MODELO:** Yo te recomiendo que seas simpático/a, que te vistas siempre bien y que te bañes cada día.

PASO 2. Pregúntales a tres compañeros/as qué recomiendan ellos que uno haga para conseguir novio/a. Apunta las respuestas.

> **MODELO:** ¿Qué recomiendas que uno haga para conseguir novio o novia?

Suggestion (Act. D): Have each student choose the best answer of those he/she collected and write it on the board. Then have students work in small groups to do two things: check to make sure all the sentences on the board are grammatically correct, and choose the one that they think is the best suggestion. When they have made their choices, have them put a tally mark by their top choice.

Note (Act. D): This activity requires students to use the subjunctive conversationally and in a meaningful way, but it does not require them to produce it spontaneously. If they continue using Spanish, this spontaneous usage will come in a few years. Activities like this one keep them moving along this path of development.

¡Leamos!

Los jóvenes retrasan° su emancipación   *delay*

Antes de leer

Suggestion (Antes de leer, Paso 1): Tell students that the title of the article is the headline: *Los jóvenes retrasan su emancipación hasta la fecha de la boda, en el umbral de los treinta.*

Suggestion (Antes de leer): Prior to having students read the article, have them review adjectives of nationality in *Cap. 2*. Have them look at the first paragraph of the reading, fourth sentence. Ask them which country someone of each of the nationalities mentioned would be from (and allow them to give the country in English as they will not know most of the Spanish names): *británicos (Reino Unido de Gran Bretaña), daneses (Dinamarca), suecos (Suecia), alemanes (Alemania), vascos (País Vasco [España]), españoles (España), irlandeses (Irlanda), italianos (Italia).*

El siguiente artículo informa sobre un estudio europeo sobre una tendencia de los jóvenes, pero se concentra en Vitoria, una ciudad en el norte de España, como su punto de referencia.

PASO 1. Lee el titular (*headline*) del artículo y escoge la mejor respuesta para cada una de las siguientes preguntas.

1. Los jóvenes no se mudan de (*move out of*) la casa de los padres hasta...
   a. casarse.   b. empezar sus estudios universitarios.   c. tener 25 años.

2. La edad promedio (*average*) para casarse es:
   a. 25 años.   b. 30 años.   c. 32 años.

PASO 2. Ahora, lee el primer subtítulo y escoge los tres factores de la lista que, según el subtítulo, influyen en la decisión de los jóvenes de emanciparse más tarde.

☑ Es más cómodo vivir con los padres que independizarse.
☑ La familia se siente responsable de sus hijos.
☐ Los estudiantes universitarios europeos prefieren vivir con sus padres.
☑ Los precios de los pisos son muy altos.
☐ No hay muchas casas en Vitoria.

Have them look at the second subtitle. Ask them what countries someone would be from if described as *anglosajón*

A leer

(*Inglaterra*) or *escandinavo* (*Dinamarca, Noruega o Suecia*). Allow them to give the country in English.

PASO 1. Lee el artículo del *Diario de Noticias de Álava* e indica si cada afirmación se refiere principalmente a gente de países del **norte** o del **sur** de Europa.

Have them determine (using a map as needed) which are northern and which are southern European countries.

Los jóvenes retrasan su emancipación hasta la fecha de la boda, en el umbral[a] de los treinta

LA FAMILIA, LA ESCASEZ[b] DE PISOS DE RENTA BAJA Y LA **COMODIDAD** INFLUYEN EN ESTA DECISIÓN

Anglosajones y escandinavos se mudan antes para vivir solos, pero no ocurre lo mismo en los países de tradición católica

R. Ruiz De Gauna
Diario de Noticias de Álava

1 VITORIA. De casa de los padres al hogar conyugal. A diferencia de lo que pudiera parecer,[c] la frase sigue siendo válida. Y es que, a la hora de independizarse, Europa también camina a dos velocidades. Mientras los jóvenes británicos, daneses, suecos o alemanes se mudan de casa a los 25 años, como solteros, para vivir solos, los vascos, españoles, irlandeses e italianos se resisten a abandonar el nido familiar hasta fijar[d] la fecha de la boda. El matrimonio y la emancipación suelen[e] coincidir en el umbral de los 30.

2 ¿Por qué esas diferencias entre el norte y el sur de Europa? Básicamente son factores culturales, económicos e incluso institucionales los que condicionan la emancipación al matrimonio y hacen que esta se retrase, sin olvidar que por detrás de todos ellos subyacen[f] las raíces[g] del catolicismo.

3 En los países anglosajones y escandinavos, el Estado ejerce un papel activo y directo para garantizar el bienestar de sus ciudadanos. Rol que en los territorios de tradición católica asume la familia, entendiendo que son los padres los responsables del bienestar de sus hijos.

4 La otra cuerda que ata[h] a padres e hijos es la que se deriva del desempleo, la precariedad laboral y los bajos salarios —variables que se han acentuado con la crisis.

[a]*threshold* [b]*lack* [c]*pudiera... might seem* [d]*setting* [e]*tend to* [f]*underlie* [g]*roots* [h]*ata... ties*

5 Tras varios años en el mercado de trabajo, alaveses[i] y vascos,[j] en general, logran un empleo estable y mejor remunerado. Ha llegado la hora de mudarse a una vivienda propia y entonces se topan con[k] la cruda realidad: apenas[l] hay alquileres de renta baja y el precio de los pisos en propiedad es prohibitivo para afrontarlo con un único salario. Vitoria se mantiene entre las cinco ciudades con pisos libres más caros y casas de segunda mano que intentan venderse por encima de su valor real. ¿Solución? Casarse, y así poder sumar dos sueldos para afrontar la hipoteca.[m]

[i]people from the city of Álava (located in the Basque Country) [j]Basques (people from the Basque Country) [k]se... they bump into [l]barely [m]mortgage

	EL NORTE	EL SUR
1. Después de independizarse, viven con su esposo o esposa.	☐	☑
2. Después de independizarse, viven solos.	☑	☐
3. El Estado garantiza el bienestar.	☑	☐
4. La familia garantiza el bienestar.	☐	☑
5. Se emancipan a los 25 años.	☑	☐
6. Se emancipan a los 30 años.	☐	☑

PASO 2. Indica si cada factor que influye en el retraso (delay) de la emancipación es cultural o económico.

	FACTOR CULTURAL	FACTOR ECONÓMICO
1. bajos salarios	☐	☑
2. cierta independencia personal	☑	☐
3. el desempleo	☐	☑
4. la religión	☑	☐
5. la vivienda cara	☐	☑

Después de leer

PASO 1. Empareja el párrafo del informe con la idea principal que corresponda.

a. __5__ A pesar de tener un puesto de trabajo estable con un buen salario, es difícil poder pagar una vivienda cara. Al casarse, los jóvenes pueden unir dos salarios para pagar una vivienda.

b. __4__ Con la crisis económica es más difícil que los jóvenes encuentren trabajo estable y que ganen suficiente dinero para independizarse.

c. __3__ En el norte el gobierno ayuda a uno a independizarse, mientras que en el sur se supone que son los padres los responsables de sus hijos adultos solteros.

d. __1__ Los jóvenes del norte de Europa son más jóvenes cuando se mudan de la casa que los jóvenes del sur.

e. __2__ Varios factores influyen en el retraso de la emancipación de los jóvenes en el sur de Europa.

PASO 2. En grupos, respondan a la pregunta «Donde viven Uds., ¿cuáles son las razones para independizarse de los padres antes de casarse?» Escriban por lo menos cinco razones e intenten ponerlas en orden de prioridad.

Suggestion (Después de leer, Paso 1): Have students work in groups to do this activity as a puzzle. Make copies of the six summary statements and cut them in six pieces (one summary statement per piece). Give the statements to students, who must physically put them in order by matching them to the content of the reading. This will give them a visual summary of the article in order.

Videoscript (A escuchar): 1.

MAGNOLIA: Bueno, hace 38 años que estamos casados o sea que ya hace tiempo que nos conocemos. Eh... Yo creo que desde que nací que lo conozco. Ay... Bueno me parece que toda la vida he estado con él y lo conocí en Cuba y bueno, pues, seguimos juntos hasta ahora y hemos seguido en el trabajo también. Creo que... bueno, ya nos vamos a tener que morir juntos por lo que veo. **2.** *CLODY: Eh... Yo hace 25 años, 22, 23 años que me fui de turista a Israel... Pero tú sabes... John Lennon decía que la vida es lo que te sucede mientras estás ocupado haciendo otros planes y conocí a una sudafricana en la calle y me quedé y hoy volví a mostrarle dónde nací...* **3.** *VÍCTOR: Sí. Nos conocimos en... aquí en Barcelona. Ella estaba trabajando de trabajo doméstico, y bueno, tenía que pagarse sus estudios y tuve la suerte de que recaló en mi casa unos días y entonces, a raíz de vernos, nos empezamos a ver, pasó el tiempo y nos hicimos pareja, ¿vale? Yo había tenido otras parejas y estaba solo en ese momento. Y entonces ella también estaba sola y acabamos juntos.* **4.** *MARÍA ESTHER: —Jejeje... Muy interesante porque él me conoció primero y se flechó de mí, desde que estaba chiquilla, jejeje... Yo cuando lo conocí, para nada lo hacía en mi vida. Lo ex... Lo excluía totalmente, lo veía, y lo veía y me le escondía, no me gustaba, no me agradaba, me habló para novia y «ay no... yo con ese no porque es muy serio». Le di mucho la vuelta y después de algunos años no acordé cuando, este... me flechó. Jejeje... me flechó y aquí estoy, todavía considero, después de 22 años, enamorada de él. Sí... —Si, yo la conocí primero, yo tenía 14 años cuando la vi la primera vez, cuando la vi la primera vez en un colegio.* **5.** *MARÍA LUZ: Sí, nos conocimos cuando estábamos los dos estudiando en la universidad de Los Ángeles y éramos estudiantes allí por... él primer*

¡Escuchemos!

¿Cómo se conocieron?

Antes de escuchar

Indica si conoces a muchas (**M**) o pocas personas (**P**) que hayan conocido a su pareja de las siguientes maneras, o si no conoces a nadie (**N**) que lo haya hecho.

____ a través de (*through*) otra persona que conocía a los dos

____ a través de un grupo religioso

____ desde la niñez

____ en colegio (*high school*)

____ por Internet

____ en la calle

____ en otro país

____ en un autobús (u otro transporte)

____ en un bar o restaurante

____ en un lugar de trabajo

año y yo estaba estudiando inglés como segunda lengua porque no sabía como había llegado recién de Perú. Y ahí nos conocimos. Y nos casamos un año después. Y tenemos dos hijos, un niño y una niña. Que ahora mi hija tiene dos niños —dos nietos para nosotros. **6.** *ÓSCAR: Ah... Nos conocimos trabajando en una fábrica de ropa. Trabajábamos juntos y empezamos a salir como 6 meses antes de decidir ser novios y duramos 6 meses más y nos casamos. Yo tenía 19 años, ella tenía 24.*

¿Cuál es la manera más común de conocer a la pareja? Cuál es la menos común?

 A escuchar

Video track (A escuchar): This video clip can be found on the DVD to accompany *Conéctate: Cap. 16*, Track 4.

Mira y escucha el video en el que los participantes responden a la pregunta, «¿Cómo conoció Ud. a su pareja?». Luego escucha otra vez con pausas e indica quién dice cada una de las siguientes frases.

Magnolia, de Cuba

Clody, de Argentina

Víctor, de España

María Esther, de México

María Luz, de Perú

Óscar, de Costa Rica

1. _María Luz_ «Ahora mi hija tiene dos niños —dos nietos para nosotros.»

2. _María Esther_ «Aquí estoy, todavía (me) considero, después de 22 años, enamorada de él.»

3. _Clody_ «Conocí a una sudafricana en la calle y me quedé.»

4. _María Esther_ «Él me conoció primero y se flechó (se enamoró) de mí.»

5. _Víctor_ «Estaba solo en ese momento. Y entonces ella también estaba sola y acabamos juntos.»

6. _Magnolia_ «Hace treinta y ocho años que estamos casados.»

7. _Magnolia_ «Lo conocí en Cuba.»

8. _Clody_ «Me fui de turista a Israel.»

9. _Víctor_ «Nos conocimos en... aquí en Barcelona.»

10. _María Luz_ «Nos conocimos cuando estábamos los dos estudiando en la universidad.»

11. _Óscar_ «Nos conocimos trabajando en una fábrica de ropa.»

12. _Magnolia_ «Ya nos vamos a tener que morir juntos.»

13. _Óscar_ «Yo tenía 19 años, ella tenía 24.»

14. _Clody_ «La vida es lo que te sucede mientras estás ocupado haciendo otros planes.»

Después de escuchar

En una oración completa, describe el comienzo de una relación importante (puede ser relación tuya o la de otras personas).

> **MODELO:** Mi hermana conoció a su esposo cuando él compartía un apartamento con el novio (ahora ex novio) de ella.

Suggestion (Después de escuchar): Have students get together in small groups, then choose the best anecdote and present it to the class. The class can vote for their favorite.

¡Escribamos!

La emancipación de los jóvenes estadounidenses

En diferentes culturas, las costumbres asociadas con la emancipación varían mucho según la época histórica, la situación socioeconómica, las tradiciones familiares, la religión y la cultura popular. En esta actividad vas a comparar tu experiencia como joven con las experiencias descritas en la lectura de ¡Leamos!

Antes de escribir

Escoge dos temas de la lista y apunta algunos detalles relacionados con cada tema. Los detalles deben ilustrar lo que tienes en común con los jóvenes mencionados en la lectura «Los jóvenes retrasan su emancipación» y lo que no tienes en común con ellos.

TEMAS

la edad de la emancipación	la religión
el matrimonio	la situación económica
la posición política/social	

MODELO:	Semejanzas	Diferencias
el matrimonio	_como los vascos, españoles, irlandeses e italianos, mis amigos y yo solemos casarnos a los 30 años_	_no vivimos con los padres hasta casarnos; vivimos con grupos de amigos o con novios_

	Semejanzas	Diferencias
TEMA 1		
TEMA 2		

(Continues)

ESTRATEGIA

Comparing and contrasting

When comparing your situation to that of others, it is important to consider similarities as well as differences. Understanding what you have in common can help you better understand what you don't have in common, and any discussion can be made richer by looking at more than one side. If you contemplate different perspectives by comparing and contrasting them with your own, you will no doubt gain a better understanding of the situations of others as well as a new appreciation of your own.

CONÉCTATE AL MUNDO PROFESIONAL

In any kind of international business travel, knowing just a few polite fixed expressions and their associated cultural customs is a huge advantage for a professional who wants to fit in and succeed. With more advanced fluency, you will be able to do even more. Imagine a border conference in your professional area, such as a communicable diseases summit, a security meeting, a trade relations meeting, or an import/export trade show. It will be a place where many attendees will be able to participate in sessions and network with others in either Spanish or English. But if you are bilingual, you can do both, thus doubling your access, participation, and networking.

Expansion (Después de hablar): Have students do a chain activity in groups of 5–8 in which each student adds another element to the story of a fictitious first encounter with a professor. Model a way to start the story: *Fui a la oficina de mi profesora de inglés antes del primer día de clase. Cuando toqué a la puerta...* Then give students time to brainstorm a few elements before beginning the chain. Either have students add to the story in a specific order or encourage them to volunteer their elements at an appropriate moment in the story-building.

A escribir

Usando la información de **Antes de escribir,** escribe un ensayo de cuatro párrafos.

☐ En el primer párrafo, explica los dos temas.

☐ En el segundo párrafo, compara y contrasta tu experiencia de uno de los temas con la experiencia de los jóvenes de la lectura.

☐ En el tercer párrafo, compara y contrasta otro tema.

☐ En el último párrafo, concluye el ensayo con una afirmación sobre la comparación entre tú y los jóvenes españoles.

 ### Después de escribir

Revisa tu ensayo. Luego, en parejas, intercambien los ensayos para evaluarlos. Lee el ensayo de tu compañero/a y decide si ha incluido tanto semejanzas como diferencias con respecto a los dos temas. Lee de nuevo el ensayo con cuidado para revisar los siguientes puntos.

☐ ¿Concuerdan los sujetos y los verbos?

☐ ¿Concuerdan los sustantivos y los adjetivos?

☐ Cuando es apropiado, ¿ha usado las excepciones **mayor, menor, mejor** y **peor**?

☐ ¿Ha usado **que** con **más** y **menos**?

☐ ¿Ha usado **como** con las formas adecuadas de **tan** y **tanto**?

☐ ¿Tiene sentido la conclusión?

Después de revisar el ensayo de tu compañero/a, devuélveselo. Mira tu propio ensayo para ver los cambios que tu compañero/a te recomienda y haz las revisiones necesarias.

¡Hablemos!

Mis primeros días en la universidad

Antes de hablar

Usando el pasado (pretérito e imperfecto), escribe una descripción del comienzo de una relación en la universidad. Luego usa el presente para describir la relación en este momento.

MODELO: Estaba nerviosa el primer día. Luego conocí a mi compañera de cuarto y su familia me invitó a cenar con ellos. Fuimos a... Luego... Ahora somos muy buenas amigas.

 ### A hablar

En grupos de tres, comparen sus historias. Luego formen nuevos grupos de tres y cuenten todas las historias del primer grupo; tienen que contar sus propias historias en primera persona (**yo**) y las historias de los otros estudiantes en tercera persona (**él, ella**). Al final, deben saber nueve historias de los primeros días en la universidad.

Después de hablar

Cuéntale a tu profesor(a) la mejor historia y explícale por qué es la mejor.

Conéctate al cine

Película: *Machuca* (drama, Chile, 2002)
Director: Andrés Wood

Sinopsis:

Es 1973, Gonzalo tiene 11 años, es de una familia de clase media alta y asiste a una escuela privada. Cuando unos niños de los barrios pobres entran a la escuela, Gonzalo se hace amigo de Pedro («Peter») Machuca en su clase de inglés. Visita la casa de Pedro y conoce a su vecina, Silvana, una chica mayor y bastante coqueta (*flirtatious*). Los tres pasan tiempo juntos hasta que estalla el golpe de estado (*coup d'état*), lo que cambia sus vidas para siempre.

Escena (DVD, 01:06:30 to 01:10:02):

Gonzalo, Pedro y Silvana van al cine y luego van a la casa de Pedro. Pedro lee un libro de «El Llanero Solitario» (*The Lone Ranger*). Llega el padre de Pedro, borracho (*drunk*), y empieza a insultar a todos.

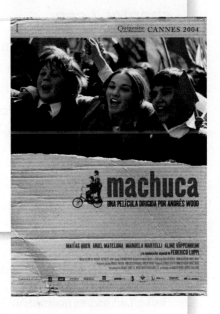

Antes de ver

Gonzalo y Pedro son amigos de clases sociales diferentes y de barrios diferentes. ¿Cuáles son algunas diferencias que se encuentran entre barrios y familias de diferentes niveles económicos? Indica tus respuestas y, en parejas, explíquense sus respuestas.

- ☐ las calles
- ☐ la comida
- ☐ las mascotas
- ☐ la seguridad
- ☐ las casas
- ☐ los estilos de vestirse
- ☐ los padres
- ☐ las tiendas

Suggestion (A ver): Turn subtitles off, if possible. Students won't understand everything, but they won't need to. Stop at the words *a veces sí mienten*.

A ver

PASO 1. Lee las **Expresiones útiles** y mira la escena. No trates de entender cada palabra, pero escucha con atención. Presta atención a las actitudes y perspectivas de los personajes.

PASO 2. Ahora indica quién diría cada declaración: Gonzalo, Pedro, Silvana o el padre de Pedro.

1. _____Pedro_____ Me gustaría esta película si hubiera más acción.
2. _____Gonzalo_____ Si Silvana fuera mi novia, aprendería a bailar con ella.
3. _____Silvana_____ Si los niños no estuvieran leyendo ese libro tonto, me estarían mirando.
4. _____Gonzalo_____ Viviría en un barrio como este si fuera pobre como ellos.
5. ___el padre de Pedro___ Si no hubiera racismo y represión social en mi país, mi hijo tendría las mismas oportunidades que su amigo.
6. _____Pedro_____ Si mis padres pudieran ver de cerca (*up close*) nuestra amistad, entenderían que las diferencias de clase social no importan (*don't matter*) entre amigos.
7. _Silvana / el padre de Pedro_ Si Pedro supiera lo que yo sé, no tendría tantas ilusiones sobre su amistad.
8. _____Silvana_____ Si este señor no estuviera borracho, no estaría diciéndonos la verdad.

Expresiones útiles

fome (*Chile*)	boring
tontería	nonsense
po (*Chile*)	**pues**
suelta	let go
empresa	business
papito	daddy
dueño	owner
adivina	take a guess
ni se va acordar de	won't even remember
curado	drunk (*adj., n.*)
mienten	lie

■ For copyright reasons, the feature-film clips referenced in **Conéctate al cine** have not been provided by the publisher. Each of these films is readily available through retailers or online rental sites such as Amazon, iTunes, or Netflix.

Después de ver

En parejas, contesten las siguientes preguntas.

Silvana dice que nunca ha visto una amistad entre un indio y un blanco. Luego dice que «los niños y los curados no mienten». ¿Por qué dice esto? ¿Estás de acuerdo con sus ideas? Explica.

VOCABULARIO

Now that I have completed the chapter, I can . . .

☐ discuss my marital status

☐ express sympathy and regret

☐ talk about personal relationships

☐ discuss personal relationships in the Spanish-speaking world

Comunicación

Lo siento mucho. / Cuánto lo siento.	I'm very sorry.
Mi/Nuestro más sentido pésame.	My/Our deepest condolences.
Te/Le/Les doy/damos el pésame.	My/Our condolences.
Te/Lo/La/Los/Las acompaño en el sentimiento/dolor.	You're in my thoughts. / I'm with you in your time of pain.
Te/Lo/La/Los/Las acompañamos en el sentimiento/dolor.	You're in our thoughts. / We're with you in your time of pain.

Los sustantivos

la amistad	friendship
el amor	love
la boda	wedding
la cita	date; appointment
la cita a ciegas	blind date
el divorcio	divorce
el estado civil	marital status
el hogar	home
el matrimonio	marriage
el nido familiar	parents' home (*lit.,* nest)
el noviazgo	relationship; engagement
el novio / la novia	boyfriend/girlfriend; fiancé/fiancée; groom/bride
la pareja	partner; couple
la relación	relationship
el/la viudo/a	widow

Los adjetivos

abierto/a	open
cariñoso/a	affectionate
casado/a	married
celoso/a	jealous
comprensivo/a	understanding
comprometido/a	engaged; in a serious relationship
divorciado/a	divorced
enamorado/a	in love
soltero/a	single
tolerante	tolerant
viudo/a	widowed

Cognados: en una relación

Los verbos

amar	to love
casarse (con)	to get married (to)
comprometerse	to get engaged; to commit (oneself)
conocerse (zc)	to meet (each other)
emanciparse	to become free/ independent
enamorarse (de)	to fall in love (with)
independizarse (c)	to become independent
mudarse	to move (*residence*)
querer (ie)	to want; to love
responsabilizarse (c)	to take responsibility
romper con	to break up with

PARA SABER MÁS

Capítulo 1

1.1 Singular nouns and articles

More about gender of nouns

1. Nouns with the endings **-ción / -sión** (frequently corresponding to the English *-tion / -sion*) and **-tad / -dad** (corresponding to English *-ty*) are generally feminine. Many of these words are cognates with English.

-ción / -sión	la nación (*nation*)
	la solución (*solution*)
	la comprensión (*comprehension*)
	la televisión (*television*)
-tad / -dad	la libertad (*liberty*)
	la ciudad (*city*)
	la universidad (*university*)

2. Nouns with the ending **-ma** are often masculine. Many of these words are cognates with English.

   el clima (*weather*)   el problema   el telegrama
   el idioma (*language*)   el programa   el tema (*theme, topic*)
   el poema   el sistema

3. Feminine nouns that begin with the stressed vowel a- use the singular definite article **el** instead of **la**. However, in the plural these feminine nouns do use the expected article **las.**

   el agua (*water*)   **las** aguas
   el águila (*eagle*)   **las** águilas
   el área   **las** áreas

Capítulo 2

2.1 Adjectives

Adjective placement

1. Descriptive adjectives in Spanish usually follow the noun that they modify.

   una mujer **alta**   un libro **blanco**   un estudiante **inteligente**

   Some descriptive adjectives, however, occasionally appear before the noun that they modify. **Bueno** and **malo** are two common adjectives that do this, but they are shortened to **buen** and **mal** in the masculine singular form in this case.

   un libro **bueno**   un **buen** libro
   un día **malo**   un **mal** día
   una mesa **buena**   una **buena** mesa
   una semana **mala**   una **mala** semana

2. Ordinal numbers generally come before the noun that they modify. The first three ordinal numbers are **primero/a** (*first*), **segundo/a** (*second*), and **tercero/a** (*third*). Of these three, **primero** and **tercero** are shortened to **primer** and **tercer**, respectively, when they precede masculine singular nouns. **Segundo/a** is never shortened.

   el **primer** día   la **segunda** vez
   la **primera** noche   el **tercer** café
   los **primeros** estudiantes   la **tercera** puerta
   el **segundo** libro

3. With some adjectives, there is a noticeable difference in meaning depending on their placement. If the adjective follows the noun, it has a literal meaning, but if it precedes the noun, it has a more figurative meaning. This difference is seen clearly in adjectives like **grande, pobre,** and **viejo.** Note that **grande** is shortened to **gran** when it precedes either a masculine or a feminine noun.

	Before the noun	After the noun
grande	una **gran** universidad *a great university*	una universidad **grande** *a big university*
pobre	un **pobre** hombre *a poor (unfortunate) man*	un hombre **pobre** *a poor man (without money)*
viejo	un **viejo** amigo *a friend for a long time*	un amigo **viejo** *a friend who is old*

In English, adjectives always precede the noun, so position cannot differentiate between the above two types of meanings. Context determines whether *an old friend* is intended to mean **un viejo amigo** or **un amigo viejo.**

2.2 The verbs *estar* and *ir*

Using *tener* to express states

The verb **tener** + *noun*, like **estar** + *adj.*, is often used to express states. **Tener** is used with **calor** (*heat*) and **frío** (*cold*) to say whether someone *is hot* or *is cold.*

¡Tengo calor!	*I'm hot!*
¿No **tienes frío**?	*Aren't you cold?*

To say that someone *is hungry* or *is thirsty*, use **hambre** (*f., hunger*) or **sed** (*f., thirst*).

Elena **tiene hambre.**	*Elena is hungry.*
Tengo mucha sed.	*I'm very thirsty.*

A variety of other states may be expressed using **tener,** such as **ganas** (*pl. desire*), **miedo** (*fear*), **prisa** (*haste*), **razón** (*f., reason*), and **sueño** (*sleepiness*).

Tengo ganas de un café.	*I feel like (having) a coffee.*
¿**Tienes miedo**?	*Are you afraid?*
El profesor **tiene prisa.**	*The teacher is in a hurry.*
El bebé **tiene sueño.**	*The baby is sleepy.*

With all of these expressions, you can use **mucho/a** or **muchos/as** to express a greater degree of these states.

Tengo **mucho sueño.**	*I'm very sleepy.*
Perdón, tengo **mucha prisa.**	*Sorry, I'm in a big hurry.*
¡Ud. **tiene mucha razón**!	*You are so right!*

2.3 The verb *gustar*

Nos gusta(n), os gusta(n), les gusta(n)

To say what *we* like, use **nos gusta** or **nos gustan.**

Nos gusta la música.	*We like music.*
Nos gustan las películas.	*We like movies.*

When addressing a group of people as **vosotros/vosotras,** use **os gusta** or **os gustan.**

¿**Os gustan** las clases de biología?	*Do you (pl.) like the biology classes?*

When addressing people as **Uds.,** or when saying what other people (more than one person) like, use **les gusta** or **les gustan.**

¿**Les gusta** el fútbol?	*Do you (pl.) like soccer?*
No **les gusta** la cerveza.	*They don't like beer.*
Les gustan los libros.	*They like books.*

Capítulo 3

3.3 Stem-changing verbs: *o → ue*

Additional *o → ue* verbs

1. Here are some other common verbs in Spanish that belong to the **o → ue** family.

contar	*to count; to tell*	¿**Cuento** de uno a diez en español? *Shall I (Do I) count from one to ten in Spanish?*
costar	*to cost*	¿Cuánto **cuesta** el libro? *How much does the book cost?*
encontrar	*to find*	¿Dónde **encuentras** buena comida en la universidad? *Where do you find good food at the university?*
mostrar	*to show*	El mapa **muestra** dónde está la universidad. *The map shows where the university is.*
recordar	*to remember*	No **recuerdo** cómo te llamas. *I don't remember what your name is.*
soler*	*to tend (to do something)*	Jaime **suele** llegar tarde al trabajo. *Jaime usually arrives / tends to arrive late to work.*
volver	*to return*	**Vuelvo** al mismo lugar cada año. *I return to the same place every year.*

2. The verb **jugar** (*to play*) follows the same pattern as the **o → ue** verbs, but it is the **u** that changes to **ue.**

Los niños **juegan** en el parque.	*The children play in the park.*
Jugamos fútbol a las cuatro.	*We play soccer at 4:00.*

3.4 Demonstrative adjectives

The demonstrative adjectives *aquel/aquella/aquellos/aquellas*

In addition to **este/esta/estos/estas** and **ese/esa/esos/esas,** Spanish has a third set of demonstrative adjectives used to indicate something very far away in time or space.

	SINGULAR		PLURAL	
masculino	**aquel** libro	*that book*	**aquellos** libros	*those books*
femenino	**aquella** clase	*that class*	**aquellas** clases	*those classes*

---

*The verb **soler** is very common in Spain, but less so in Latin America.

Aquel/aquella/aquellos/aquellas is similar to English *that,* but it refers to something that is particularly far away or that happened a long time ago.

No me gusta **aquel** libro.	*I don't like that book over there.*
Aquellas clases eran muy difíciles.	*Those classes (back then) were very difficult.*

Spanish thus makes a three-way distinction (**este libro** vs. **ese libro** vs. **aquel libro**) based on distance in time or space, while English makes only a two-way distinction (*this book* vs. *that book*).

Demonstrative pronouns

1. Demonstratives may appear without the noun when the noun has been previously mentioned or is otherwise obvious from the context. In this case, they are called **pronombres demostrativos** (*demonstrative pronouns*).

Esa clase es muy difícil pero **esta** es fácil.	*That class is very difficult but this one is easy.*
Ese es rojo y **este** es azul.	*That one* (masc. sing.) *is red and this one is blue.*
Aquellos son de Honduras.	*Those ones* (over there) *are from Honduras.*

Traditionally, demonstrative pronouns have been written with an accent mark (**ésta, ése,** and so on) to distinguish them from demonstrative adjectives. The accent mark is no longer required, but it is still common.

2. When a demonstrative pronoun refers to the situation in general or something else without a specific name, the neuter (genderless) forms **esto, eso,** and **aquello** are used.

¡**Esto** no me gusta!	*I don't like this* (situation in general)*!*
¿Qué es **eso**?	*What is that* (unknown object)*?*

Capítulo 4

4.1   Comparatives

Más de with numerals

In Spanish, when you want to express *more than* (or *less/fewer than*) followed by any number, use the construction **más de** (or **menos de**), followed by the number.

¡Elena tiene **más de** treinta primos!	*Elena has more than thirty cousins!*
Todos aquí tenemos **menos de** 25 años.	*All of us here are less than 25 years old.*

Comparatives of equality

1. To say that two people or things are the same with regard to some adjective, use **tan** + *adjective* + **como.**

José Luis es **tan alto como** Margarita.	*José Luis is as tall as Margarita.*
Mis hermanas son **tan inteligentes como** tú.	*My sisters are as smart as you.*

Notice that here the adjective agrees with the subject of the verb.

2. To do the same with regard to a noun, use **tanto** + *noun* + **como.**

Tengo **tantos primos como** tú.	*I have as many cousins as you.*
¿Tienes **tanta hambre como** yo?	*Are you as hungry as I am?*

Tanto agrees with the noun in number and gender, so it has four possible forms (**tanto/tanta/tantos/tantas**).

Superlatives

1. You have used **más** to compare one person or thing to another. When preceded by a definite article, **más** expresses the idea of *most*. To express the idea of *least,* use the definite article and **menos.**

María Elena es **la más alta** de todas mis hermanas.	*María Elena is the tallest of all my sisters.*
Jorge es **el más guapo** de la familia.	*Jorge is the best looking in the family.*
Rigoberto y Camila son **los menos atléticos** de todos mis primos.	*Rigoberto and Camila are the least athletic of all my cousins.*

This construction is known as the superlative (**el superlativo**). In English it is expressed with *most* or the ending *-est.*

2. When used with a noun, **más** + *adjective* usually follows the noun.

Carmen es **la abogada más famosa** de Panamá.	*Carmen is the most famous attorney in Panama.*
Marcos es **el estudiante más inteligente** de toda la universidad.	*Marcos is the most intelligent student in the whole university.*

When **mejor** and **peor** are used as superlatives, they usually precede the noun.

Mi primo es **el mejor médico** de la ciudad.	*My cousin is the best doctor in the city.*
Para mucha gente, el lunes es **el peor día** de la semana.	*For many people, Monday is the worst day of the week.*

Expressing things emphatically

1. It is very common in Spanish to attach the suffix **-ísimo** to adjectives to mean *extremely* or *very much.*

¡Elena tiene **muchísimos** primos!	*Elena really has a lot of cousins!*
Mi familia es **grandísima.**	*My family is extremely large.*

If the adjective ends in a consonant, **-ísimo** is simply added to the adjective.

facilísimo *extremely easy*   **dificilísimo** *extremely difficult*

If the adjective ends in a vowel, the vowel is dropped and **-ísimo** is added to the stem.

altísimo *extremely tall*   **delgadísimo** *extremely thin*   **feísimo** *extremely ugly*

When the stem ends in **c, g,** or **z** the spelling is adjusted to preserve the pronunciation of this final consonant. The **c** changes to **qu** (**rico** → **riquísimo**), **g** changes to **gu** (**largo** → **larguísimo**), and **z** changes to **c** (**feliz** → **felicísimo**).

Adjectives with **-ísimo** always agree with the noun they modify in number and gender: Elisa **está cansadísima.**, Tengo dos clases **larguísimas.**

2. In casual speech, there are many other ways to express the idea of *extremely.* One very common way is to use the prefix **super-.**

superfácil *extremely easy*   **superalto** *extremely tall*
supergrande *extremely big*

This prefix is common in the spoken language, but is not used in formal written Spanish. It is sometimes written as a separate word.

4.2 Stem-changing verbs: e → i

Additional e → i verbs

Here are some other common verbs in Spanish that belong to the e → i family.

conseguir	*to get, obtain*	¿Dónde **consigo** una foto de la familia real?
		Where can I get a picture of the royal family?
		Eva **consigue** los documentos del registro público.
		Eva obtains the documents from the public registry.
reír	*to laugh*	Mis papás **ríen** cuando ven la televisión.
		My parents laugh when they watch TV.
sonreír	*to smile*	Mi hermano **sonríe** mucho.
		My brother smiles a lot.

4.3 Stem-changing verbs: e → ie

Additional e → ie verbs

Here are some other common verbs in Spanish that belong to the e → ie family.

cerrar	*to close*	La profesora **cierra** la puerta a las ocho.
		The teacher closes the door at 8:00.
comenzar	*to begin*	El semestre **comienza** en enero.
		The semester begins in January.
entender	*to understand*	Mi mamá no **entiende** que ya no soy niña.
		My mom doesn't understand that I'm no longer a little girl.
perder	*to lose*	Cuando juego con mi hermano, siempre **pierdo.**
		When I play with my brother, I always lose.
preferir	*to prefer*	**Prefiero** caminar.
		I prefer to walk.

Capítulo 5

5.1 Verbs with irregular *yo* forms

More on *saber* and *conocer*

You saw that **saber** can mean *to know* (*a fact*), such as where someone lives or what they study. This can also include knowing an address or phone number, or knowing a poem or the words to a song.

¿**Sabes** el número de teléfono del hospital?   *Do you know the phone number of the hospital?*

Todos **sabemos** la letra de esa canción.   *We all know the words (lyrics) to that song.*

You saw that **conocer** means *to be familiar with* (*someone or something*). When used with reference to a song, for instance, the meaning is very different than **saber.**

¿**Conoces** esa canción?   *Do you know that song? (Are you familiar with it? / Have you heard it before?)*

More irregular verbs with *-zco*

You saw that the **yo** form of **conocer** is **conozco**. This is part of a larger pattern: verbs whose infinitive ends in **-cer** (or **-cir**) generally take **-zco** in the **yo** form, but are otherwise regular. Here are some other common verbs of this type.

agradecer	*to thank; to be grateful for*	**Agradezco** su presencia. *I am grateful for your presence (here).*
aparecer	*to appear*	No **aparezco** en la lista. *I don't appear on the list.*
conducir	*to drive*	**Conduzco** un auto muy viejo. *I drive a very old car.*
favorecer	*to favor; to be partial to*	**Favorezco** la idea de crear más parques. *I'm in favor of the idea of creating more parks.*
merecer	*to deserve*	¡**Merezco** una segunda oportunidad! *I deserve another chance!*
ofrecer	*to offer*	**Ofrezco** un apartamento en el centro. *I'm offering an apartment downtown.*
parecer	*to seem; to look*	**Parezco** tonto en esa foto. *I look stupid in that photo.*
pertenecer	*to belong*	**Pertenezco** a un grupo de estudiantes extranjeros. *I belong to a group of foreign students.*
reconocer	*to recognize*	No **reconozco** mi ciudad. *I don't recognize my city..*
traducir	*to translate*	No **traduzco** cuando leo en español. *I don't translate when I read in Spanish.*

5.2   Reflexive verbs

Additional reflexive verbs

Here are some other common reflexive verbs in Spanish. Note that the meanings of reflexive verbs do not necessarily express reflexive action.

alegrarse	*to be glad, happy*	**Me alegro** cuando veo a mis amigos. *I'm happy when I see my friends.*
atreverse (a)	*to dare (to do something)*	¿**Te atreves** a hablar con él? *Do you dare to speak with him?*
encontrarse	*to be found, located*	La librería **se encuentra** enfrente del museo. *The bookstore is located across from the museum.*
imaginarse	*to imagine*	**Me imagino** que la tienda del museo es muy grande. *I imagine that the museum store is very big.*
preguntarse	*to wonder, ask oneself*	**Me pregunto** si hay un cine en ese pueblo. *I wonder if there is a movie theater in that town.*
quedarse	*to stay*	¿**Te quedas** o te vas? *Are you staying or are you leaving?*
referirse (a)	*to refer (to)*	Cuando dicen «México», **se refieren** a la ciudad. *When they say "Mexico," they're referring to the city.*

The reciprocal meaning of reflexive verbs

Reflexive verbs with plural subjects can also have a *reciprocal* meaning, corresponding to the English expression *each other.*

Nos vemos los martes en la clase de química.	*We see each other on Tuesdays in chemistry class.*
Marta y Eduardo **se conocen** bien.	*Marta and Eduardo know each other well.*

The context generally makes it clear whether the intended meaning is reflexive or reciprocal. **Nos vemos,** for example, can have either a reflexive meaning (*we see ourselves*) or a reciprocal meaning (*we see each other*), but in the first example above, the reciprocal meaning is much more likely.

The infinitive after a preposition

Prepositional expressions like the following are a common way to show the relationship between two or more activities.

antes de	*before*	Antes de cenar, quiero bañarme.
		Before having dinner, I want to take a bath.
después de	*after*	Después de nadar, María va a estudiar.
		After swimming, María is going to study.
para	*for, in order to*	Para hablar con mis padres, tienes que hablar español.
		(In order) To speak with my parents, you have to speak Spanish.

In Spanish, the infinitive is used after prepositions. English sometimes uses *-ing* forms of the verb in these cases, but Spanish consistently uses the infinitive.

5.3   *Ser* and *estar* with adjectives

Ser and *estar* for location

1. To say where or when an event *occurs,* use the verb **ser.**

El concierto va a **ser** en el Teatro de la Ciudad.	*The concert will be at the City Theater.*
La fiesta **es** en la casa de Jaime.	*The party is at Jaime's house.*
El examen **es** mañana a las ocho.	*The exam is tomorrow at 8:00.*

2. Use **estar,** in contrast, to say where a person or thing is located.

La calle Torres **está** en el centro.	*Torres Street is downtown.*
Santiago **está** en Chile.	*Santiago is in Chile.*
Estamos en la casa de Jaime.	*We're at Jaime's house.*

In these cases with **estar,** the person or thing that is being described (a street, a city, or a group of people) is located at a particular place, but cannot be said to "occur" there.

Capítulo 6

6.1   The preterite: Regular verbs

Leer, creer, and *oír* in the preterite

The stem of the verbs **leer, creer,** and **oír** ends in a vowel (<u>lee</u>r, <u>cree</u>r, <u>oí</u>r). Verbs like these take the regular endings in the preterite with one small adjustment: the ending for the **él/ella, Ud.** form is **-yó** (instead of **-ió**) and the ending for the **ellos/ellas, Uds.** form is **-yeron** (instead of **-ieron**).

Marta **oyó** que hay un restaurante cubano en el centro.	*Marta heard that there is a Cuban restaurant downtown.*
¿Uds. **leyeron** el libro?	*Did you (pl.) read the book?*
Jaime **creyó** que Luis preparó la cena.	*Jaime thought that Luis prepared the dinner.*

Replacing the **i** with a **y** allows these verbs to avoid having three vowels in a row. For most verbs in Spanish, the stem ends in a consonant (for example, <u>trabaja</u>r, <u>aprende</u>r, and <u>escribi</u>r) and such an adjustment is not necessary.

Ver and *dar* in the preterite

1. For a few verbs in Spanish, the stem consists of a single consonant. The verb **ver** is of this type. Despite its very short stem, the preterite endings attach to **ver** in the usual way, and this verb is regular in the preterite.

Vi mucho pescado en el mercado.	*I saw a lot of fish in the market.*
¿**Viste** la carta?	*Did you see the menu?*
Jorge **vio** la torta.	*Jorge saw the cake.*
¿**Vieron** el restaurante salvadoreño?	*Did you (pl.) see the Salvadoran restaurant?*

Since **vi** and **vio** have only one syllable, a written accent mark is not used (in contrast to forms like **comí** and **comió**).

2. The verb **dar** also has a stem that consists of a single consonant, **d.** It too takes endings in the usual way, but in the preterite, it takes the endings of an **-er/-ir** verb.

Los cocineros **dieron** una clase sobre la comida japonesa.	*The cooks gave a class about Japanese food.*
Dimos una cena para los profesores.	*We gave a dinner for the teachers.*

As with **ver,** the one-syllable forms **di** and **dio** do not take an accent mark.

Capítulo 7

7.3   Pronouns after prepositions

Additional prepositions

1. The prepositions **entre, excepto,** and **según** are different from other prepositions because they are followed by **yo** and **tú** instead of by **mí** and **ti**.

Entre tú y yo, Juan es muy buena persona.	*Between you and me, Juan is a very good person.*
Según tú, vamos a tener un examen mañana.	*According to you, we are going to have an exam tomorrow.*

2. Expressions of location are also sometimes followed by pronouns. Some examples are **cerca de** (*close to*), **lejos de** (*far from*), **delante de** (*in front of*), **detrás de** (*behind*), and **enfrente de** (*across from*).

Vivo **cerca de** ti.	*I live close to you.*
¡Quiero estar muy **lejos de** él!	*I want to be very far from him!*
Robert estaba **delante de** mí.	*Robert was in front of me.*
Miriam estaba **detrás de** él.	*Miriam was behind him.*
Luz estaba **enfrente de** ellos.	*Luz was across from them.*

Stressed possessives

1. The preposition **de** may be used to express possession, as in **la casa de nosotros** (*our house*). Alternatively, a *stressed possessive* (**posesivo tónico**) may be used in place of the phrase with **de,** as in **la casa nuestra.** Here is the full set of stressed possessives.

STRESSED POSSESSIVES	
mío, mía, míos, mías	*my; mine*
tuyo, tuya, tuyos, tuyas	*your; yours* (inform.)
suyo, suya, suyos, suyas	*his, her, your; his, hers, yours* (form.)
nuestro, nuestra, nuestros, nuestras	*our; ours*
vuestro, vuestra, vuestros, vuestras	*your; yours* (inform., pl., Sp.)
suyo, suya, suyos, suyas	*their, your; theirs, yours* (pl.)

In form, stressed possessives are similar, but not identical, to unstressed possessive adjectives (see **Estructura 1.4**).

2. Stressed possessives are used *after* the noun or when the noun is somewhere else in the sentence (or not present at all). They agree in number and gender with the noun being referred to.

La casa de Uds. es verde, pero la casa **nuestra** es blanca.	*Your (pl.) house is green, but our house is white.*
Ese regalo es **mío.**	*That present is mine.*

3. When stressed possessives are used as pronouns, taking the place of the subject or object of the sentence, they have a definite article.

Aquí están mis libros. ¿Dónde están **los tuyos**?	*Here are my books. Where are yours?*
Tu coche es grande. **El mío** es chico.	*Your car is big. Mine is small.*
¿Te gustan tus tarjetas? A mí me gustan **las mías.**	*Do you like your cards? I like mine.*

However, when stressed possessives are used with the verb **ser** to describe the subject, they do not need the definite article.

Este regalo es de Ana. Es **suyo.**	*This gift is Ana's. It's hers.*
¿Esas computadoras son **tuyas**?	*Are those computers yours?*

In either case, all stressed possessives agree in both number and gender with the noun that they refer to.

Capítulo 8

8.1   More irregular preterite forms

Additional irregular preterite forms

The verb **conseguir** (*to obtain; to get*) has **seguir** as its root and is conjugated in the same way in the preterite. Likewise, **despedirse** (*to say good-bye; to take leave*) has **pedir** as its root and is conjugated in the same way.

Here are some other common verbs that change the stem vowel **e** to **i** in the preterite when conjugated in the **él/ella, Ud.** or **ellos/ellas, Uds.** forms.

divertirse (ie, i)	to have fun	Carmen **se divirtió** mucho en la fiesta.
		Carmen had a lot of fun at the party.
mentir (ie, i)	to lie	Carlos **mintió** cuando dijo que tenía 21 años.
		Carlos lied when he said he was 21.
preferir (ie, i)	to prefer	Marta **prefirió** comprar el vestido rojo.
		Marta preferred to buy the red dress.
reírse (í, i) (de)	to laugh (*at*)	Los niños **se rieron** de la corbata de su padre.
		The children laughed at their father's tie.
repetir (i, i)	to repeat	El profesor **repitió** la palabra tres veces.
		The teacher repeated the word three times.
sentirse (ie, i)	to feel	Catalina **se sintió** muy contenta cuando vio el anillo.
		Catalina felt very happy when she saw the ring.
sonreír (í, i)	to smile	El diseñador **sonrió** cuando mencionaron su ropa en la televisión.
		The designer smiled when they mentioned his clothes on television.
sugerir (ie, i)	to suggest	Ellas me **sugirieron** una falda más larga.
		They suggested a longer skirt for me.

8.2   The preterite and imperfect together

Comparison of meaning in preterite vs. imperfect

1. You have seen how the preterite can portray an action as having a clear end point. The preterite may also be used to show that an action has a clear beginning point.

   María se probó el abrigo y le **gustó** mucho.

   María tried on the coat and liked it a lot.

   Cuando vio la foto, Juan **entendió** que la camisa le quedaba mal.

   When he saw the picture, Juan understood that the shirt fit him poorly.

   Although the meanings of **gustar** and **entender** generally imply ongoing actions, in these sentences, there is a clear point when María begins to like the coat (when she tries it on) and when Juan's understanding begins (when he sees the picture).

2. The preterite forms of **conocer** and **saber** often refer in this way to the beginning point of knowing someone or something. With **conocer,** this is the point of meeting someone, and with **saber,** it is the point of finding something out. In the imperfect, in contrast, the simple state of knowing is referred to, without any specific beginning or ending point.

Pretérito	Imperfecto
Conocí a Francisco cuando éramos niños.	**Conocía** a Francisco cuando éramos niños.
I met Francisco when we were kids.	*I knew Francisco when we were kids.*
Elena **supo** que los zapatos eran caros.	Elena **sabía** que los zapatos eran caros.
Elena found out that the shoes were expensive.	*Elena knew that the shoes were expensive.*

In the preterite, **conocer** and **saber** are sometimes said to change their meaning, but in fact their meaning comes from what they mean normally, together with the regular meaning of the preterite tense.

3. The verbs **poder** and **querer** are similar. **Poder** in the preterite is often translated into English as *to manage to* and **querer** as *to try*. Both verbs in the preterite express an intention, but also communicate that an action took place: **pude** = *I was able to and actually did it;* **quise** = *I wanted to and actually tried*. Their preterite forms express the beginning or end point of being able and wanting, respectively, while the imperfect forms do not express any clear beginning or end points.

Pretérito	Imperfecto
Ayer **pude** comprar ese vestido negro.	Cuando yo trabajaba, **podía** comprar muchos vestidos.
I was able (I managed) to buy that black dress yesterday.	*When I worked, I could (I had the ability/means, though I may not have actually done it) buy a lot of dresses.*
Mario **quiso** hablar con Ana, pero ella no le hizo caso.	Mario **quería** hablar con Ana, pero nunca llegó.
Mario tried to speak with Ana, but she ignored him.	*Mario wanted (but didn't actually try) to speak with Ana, but she never arrived.*

When **poder** and **querer** are used in the negative preterite form, they are often translated as *to fail* (*to do something*) and *to refuse*, respectively.

No pude comprar ese vestido negro porque no traía dinero.

I wasn't able to (failed to) buy that black dress because I didn't have money with me.

Mario **no quiso** hablar con Ana porque estaba enojado todavía.

Mario didn't want to (refused to) speak with Ana because he was still mad.

8.3   Object pronoun placement with infinitives

Double object pronouns

1. Verbs often have both a direct and an indirect object, and both of these objects may be expressed as pronouns. In this case, the indirect object pronoun precedes the direct object pronoun.

Este sombrero es nuevo. **Me lo** dieron ayer.

This hat is new. They gave it to me yesterday.

¿Te gusta esta camisa? **¡Te la** regalo!

Do you like this shirt? I'll give it to you!

Necesito esos anillos. **¿Me los** pasas?

I need those rings. Will you pass them to me?

2. The indirect object pronouns **le** and **les** are not used together with direct object pronouns; the form **se** is used instead.

¿Te gustó la falda de María?
   Yo **se la regalé.**

*Did you like María's skirt? I gave
   it to her.*

¿La camisa de Jaime? **Se la** dieron
   por su cumpleaños.

*Jaime's shirt? They gave it to him for
   his birthday.*

A Ud., ¿qué le parece este abrigo?
   Se lo vendo barato.

What do you (form.) *think about this
   coat? I'll sell it to you cheap.*

3. When reflexive verbs are used with a direct object pronoun, the reflexive pronoun precedes the direct object pronoun.

¿Esa camisa? **Me la** probé pero no
   me quedó.

*That shirt? I tried it on, but it
   didn't fit.*

A mi hija le gusta mucho su suéter rojo.
   Se lo pone cada vez que sale.

*My daughter really likes her red sweater.
   She puts it on every time she goes out.*

You will see examples of reflexive verbs with indirect object pronouns in **Estructura 9.3.**

4. Just as with single object pronouns, double object pronouns may either both precede a conjugated verb or both follow and be attached to an infinitive. In the latter case, they are written as a single word with the infinitive, and an accent mark is written to preserve the stress.

¿Esa corbata? **Te la** quiero regalar.
   (Quiero regalár**tela.**)

That tie? I want to give it to you.

¿El suéter de Mario? **Se lo** voy a lavar.
   (Voy a lavár**selo.**)

*Mario's sweater? I'm going to wash
   it for him.*

¿El pelo? ¿**Te lo** vas a lavar hoy?
   (¿Vas a lavár**telo** hoy?)

*Your hair? Are you going to wash
   it today?*

The relative order of the two pronouns is always the same regardless of whether they precede or follow the verb.

Another use of *lo: Lo* + adjective

To express ideas like *the good thing* or *the bad part,* say **lo bueno** or **lo malo.** **Lo** may be combined in this way with the masculine singular form of any adjective.

Lo bueno de esos zapatos es que te
   quedan bien.

*The good thing about those shoes is
   that they fit you well.*

Lo malo de esa tienda es que es
   muy cara.

*The bad thing about that store is that
   it is very expensive.*

Lo difícil es encontrar un abrigo
   en mi talla.

*The hard part is finding a coat
   in my size.*

Capítulo 9

9.1   The prepositions *por* and *para*

Additional uses of *por* and *para*

1. The preposition **para** is often used to indicate the organization for which someone works.

Manuel empezó a trabajar **para los
   hoteles Hilton** el año pasado.

*Manuel began to work for Hilton
   hotels last year.*

Susana quiere trabajar **para la
   universidad** después de graduarse.

*Susana wants to work for the
   university after graduating.*

Para is also used to express a point of comparison.

Para un hotel tan barato,
   es muy bonito.

*For such an inexpensive hotel, it is
   very nice.*

Para un norteamericano, Jason sabe
   mucho de Latinoamérica.

*For an American, Jason knows a lot
   about Latin America.*

2. The preposition **por** may be used with units of measure to express a rate, like the English word *per.*

El hotel cuesta cien dólares **por noche.**	*The hotel costs $100 per night.*
El tren va a 120 kilómetros **por hora.**	*The train goes 120 kilometers per hour.*

Por may also be used with verbs of motion to show who or what you are going to pick up along the way.

Mañana paso **por ti** a las ocho.	*Tomorrow I'll come by for you at 8:00.*
Voy **por mi maleta.**	*I'm going for (to get) my suitcase.*

9.3   *Se* for unplanned events

Additional verbs with *se* for unplanned events

1. Some other reflexive verbs that are often used with indirect object pronouns are **irse** (*to go away*), **notarse** (*to be noticeable*), **quebrarse** (*to break*), and **quedarse** (*to stay behind*).

El tren **se me fue.**	*The train left without me.*
Elena dice que está muy nerviosa pero no **se le nota.**	*Elena says she is very nervous, but you can't tell (it isn't noticeable on her).*
¿**Se te quebró** algo?	*Did you break something?*
Las llaves **se me quedaron** dentro del coche.	*I left the keys inside the car.*

In each of these cases, the reflexive verb describes an unintentional action, and the indirect object expresses who is affected by this action.

2. The reflexive verb **hacerse** (*to be/get done*) has the special meaning of *to seem* or *to think* when it is combined with an indirect object pronoun.

Se me hace que el avión va a llegar tarde.	*It seems to me that the plane is going to arrive late.*
Dicen que Cancún es caro. ¿**Se te hace**?	*They say Cancun is expensive. Do you think so?*

Capítulo 10

10.1   The relative pronoun *que*

Que and additional relative pronouns

1. Unlike English *that,* the Spanish relative pronoun **que** is never omitted.

La impresora **que** compré ayer ya está en mi oficina.	*The printer (that) I bought yesterday is already in my office.*

2. Que is the most common relative pronoun and may refer either to people or to things. **Quien** (singular) or **quienes** (plural) should be used after a preposition when referring to people.

Ella es la ingeniera **con quien** hablé por teléfono.	*She is the engineer that I spoke with on the phone.*
El señor **a quien** te presenté es el gerente del banco.	*The man that I introduced you to is the bank manager.*
Los ejecutivos **de quienes** vimos una foto en el libro van a venir a la universidad.	*The executives that we saw a picture of in the book are going to come to the university.*

The preposition must always precede the relative pronoun in Spanish. Formal written English is the same (as in, *the engineer with whom I spoke*), but in spoken English, the preposition and the relative pronoun are often separated (as in, *the engineer that I spoke with*).

3. When used as relative pronouns, **que** and **quien/quienes** are not written with accent marks, but when used as question words, they are.

—¿**Qué** vas a leer?   *"What are you going to read?"*
—Voy a leer el libro **que** está   *"I'm going to read the book (that is)*
   en la mesa.   *on the table."*

—¿**A quién** viste en el trabajo?   *"Who did you see at work?"*
—Vi a la señora **con quien hablaste** ayer.   *"I saw the woman (that) you spoke*
                                                            with yesterday."

Lo que

Lo que is a very common expression in Spanish. **Lo** here is a pronoun, and **que** introduces the relative clause that follows. **Lo que quiero** thus literally means *that which I want,* but it is more naturally translated as *what I want.*

¡**Lo que** quiero es tener mucho   *What I want is to have a lot of*
   dinero y no tener que trabajar!   *money and not have to work!*
Me gusta **lo que** dijiste en la clase.   *I like what you said in class*
Es interesante **lo que** hacen   *What architects do is interesting.*
   los arquitectos.

Capítulo 11

11.1   The present perfect

Additional irregular past participles

Here are some other common verbs that have irregular past participles.

INFINITIVE	PAST PARTICIPLE		
abrir	abierto	Han **abierto** la puerta.	*They've opened the door.*
cubrir	cubierto	Hemos **cubierto** la mesa con un mantel.	*We've covered the table with a tablecloth.*
romper	roto	¿Has **roto** la lámpara?	*Have you broken the lamp?*
volver	vuelto	María se fue y no ha **vuelto.**	*María left and hasn't returned.*

Verbs whose root uses an irregular past participle will use that same irregular form.

des<u>cubrir</u> (*to discover*) → descubierto
re<u>volver</u> (*to stir*) → revuelto

Using the past participle as an adjective

Past participles may be used as adjectives, often with the verb **estar.** When they are used as adjectives, they agree in gender and number with the noun that they modify.

La lámpara **está rota.**   *The lamp is broken.*
Los platos ya **están lavados.**   *The dishes are already washed.*
La cocina **está cerrada.**   *The kitchen is closed.*

Using the past participle to form the passive

The past participle may also be used to indicate an action with the verb **ser,** creating a passive construction. The tense of the verb **ser** indicates whether the action is a past, present, or future event.

Las calles **son barridas** cada jueves.   *The streets are swept every Thursday.*
Esta casa **fue construida** en 1982.   *This house was built in 1982.*
El lavaplatos **va a ser instalado**   *The dishwasher is going to be*
   mañana.   *installed tomorrow.*

The person or thing that is doing the action may be expressed with the preposition **por.**

Los autos fueron lavados **por expertos.**   *The cars were washed by experts.*

The past perfect

The present perfect uses the verb **haber** in the present tense, followed by the past participle. The past perfect (**el pluscuamperfecto**) is the same but uses **haber** in the imperfect tense. It expresses the idea that you *had* already done something by the time some other event occurred.

Cuando llegó Ana, yo ya **había limpiado** la cocina.	*When Ana arrived, I had already cleaned the kitchen.*
Cuando yo te vi, ¿ya **habías barrido** el pasillo?	*When I saw you, had you already swept the hallway?*

11.2   Commands with object pronouns

Nosotros/as commands

1. To say what you want to do with other people as a group, you may use a **nosotros/as** command, equivalent to English sentences with *let's*. The **nosotros/as** command has the same form as the formal **Ud.** command (see **Estructura 10.3**), but with a **-mos** ending.

Limpiemos la casa.	*Let's clean the house.*
¡**Pongamos** la comida en la mesa!	*Let's put the food on the table!*
¡**Cenemos**!	*Let's have dinner!*

As with formal commands, **nosotros/as** commands use the vowel **e** in the ending for **-ar** verbs and the vowel **a** for **-er** and **-ir** verbs.

2. As with all other command forms, object pronouns (indirect, direct) and reflexive pronouns used in **nosotros/as** commands are attached to the end of positive commands and appear as a separate word before negative commands. An accent mark is added to the stressed syllable of a positive command when one or more object pronouns are attached.

Limpi**é**mos**la**.	*Let's clean it.*
¡No **lo** pongamos allí!	*Let's not put it there!*

When the reflexive pronoun **nos** is attached to a positive **nosotros/as** command, the final **-s** of the verb is dropped.

No nos levantemos a las ocho. Levantémo**nos** a las seis.	*Let's not get up at 8:00. Let's get up at 6:00.*
No nos sentemos en el sótano; sentémo**nos** en la sala.	*Let's not sit down in the basement; let's sit down in the living room.*

3. Unlike other verbs, **ir** uses its present tense form (**vamos**) for the positive **nosotros/as** command. With the reflexive **irse,** the final **-s** is dropped when **nos** is attached.

Vámo**nos**!	*Let's go/leave!*

4. It is also common to use **vamos a** + *infinitive* to express the idea of *let's*.

Vamos a limpiar la casa.	*Let's clean the house.*
¡**Vamos a levantarnos** temprano!	*Let's get up early!*

11.3   The present progressive

The past progressive

In the present progressive, **estar** is in the present tense. However, progressives may also be created with other tenses. It is especially common for **estar** to be in the imperfect.

Estaba limpiando la casa ayer a las ocho.	*I was cleaning the house yesterday at 8:00.*
¿**Estabas comiendo** cuando te llamé?	*Were you eating when I called you?*

Just as the present progressive describes an action in progress in the present, the past progressive describes an action in progress in the past.

Capítulo 12

12.2   The present progressive with object pronouns

The present progressive with double object pronouns

As you saw in **Para saber más 8.3,** verbs sometimes have two objects that are both expressed as pronouns. When the verb is in the present progressive, these object pronouns may either precede **estar** or be attached to the **-ndo** form of the verb, just as with single object pronouns. When attaching either one or two object pronouns to the **-ndo** form, a written accent mark is placed over the vowel where the stress normally falls.

¿La pelota? **Se la** está dando el entrenador. (Está dándo**sela** el entrenador.)	*The ball? The coach is giving it to him/her.*
¿Te gusta esta raqueta? ¡Mariana **me la** está vendiendo a muy buen precio! (¡Mariana está vendiéndo**mela** a muy buen precio!)	*Do you like this racket? Mariana is selling it to me at a really good price!*

The two pronouns must be together, either both before **estar** or both attached to the **-ndo** form.

12.3   The subjunctive: Volition with regular verbs

Additional expressions of volition

Here are some other common verbs and expressions that convey a recommendation, a piece of advice, or a desire, and which are therefore followed by the subjunctive after **que.**

aconsejar *to advise*	**Te aconsejo** que **hables** con tu médico.
	I advise you to speak to your doctor.
exigir *to demand*	**Nos están exigiendo** que **leamos** el libro para el lunes.
	They're demanding that we read the book by Monday.
insistir en	**¡Insisto** en que **juegues** tenis conmigo!
	I insist that you play tennis with me!
mandar *to order*	**Voy a mandar** que **caminen** un kilómetro al día.
	I'm going to order that they walk one kilometer a day.
permitir	**¿Permiten** que **andemos** en patineta aquí?
	Do they allow us to skateboard here?
preferir	**Prefieren** que **levantemos** pesas por la mañana.
	They prefer that we lift weights in the morning.
prohibir (í)	Nuestro profesor **nos prohíbe** que **hablemos** inglés en la clase.
	Our teacher prohibits (forbids) us from speaking English in class.
ser importante	**Es importante** que **duermas** bien todas las noches.
	It's important that you sleep well every night.
ser mejor	**Es mejor** que no **andes** en bicicleta en este clima.
	It's better that you don't ride bikes in this weather.
sugerir	**Te sugiero** que **comas** más fruta.
	I suggest that you eat more fruit.

Capítulo 13

13.1 The subjunctive: Irregular verbs

Additional irregular verbs in the subjunctive

1. In general, verbs that have an irregular stem for **yo** in the present indicative use this same stem in the present subjunctive. The verbs **conocer** (**conozco/conozca**) and **oír** (**oigo/oiga**) are common examples.

Quiero que **conozcas** a mi tía.	*I want you to meet my aunt.*
Es muy importante que Uds. **oigan** la canción de este pájaro.	*It is very important that you* (pl.) *listen to this bird's song.*

The person/number endings are regular for all verbs in the subjunctive.

2. Some verbs use a special stem for the present subjunctive. **Haber** (**haya**) and **saber** (**sepa**) are common examples of this type of verb.

Es necesario que **haya** un área especial para los pingüinos.	*It is necessary for there to be a special area for the penguins.*
Quiero que **sepas** que cerramos el parque a las siete.	*I want you to know that we close the park at 7:00.*

3. Verbs that change their stem in the present indicative (such as **poder** [o → ue] and **querer** [e → ie]) do the same in the present subjunctive.

Es importante que las tortugas **puedan** llegar a la playa sin problemas.	*It's important for the turtles to be able to get to the beach without problems.*
¡Quiero que me **quieras**!	*I want you to love me!*

4. Verbs of the **e → i** family, such as **pedir,** undergo this stem-change in all forms of the subjunctive, including the **nosotros** and **vosotros** forms, which do not undergo the change in the indicative.

No es necesario que **pidamos** ayuda. **Pedimos** ayuda de vez en cuando.	*It is not necessary for us to ask for help. We ask for help from time to time.*

Similarly, **-ir** verbs that have an **e → i** or **o → u** change in the preterite, such as **sentirse** or **dormir,** show this same change in the **nosotros** and **vosotros** forms of the present subjunctive. Their regular **e → ie** or **o → ue** change occurs in the other forms.

Es muy importante que **se sientan** / **nos sintamos** bien en la clase.	*It's very important that you* (pl.) */ we feel good in class.*
Los médicos recomiendan que **duerman**/ **durmamos** ocho horas cada noche.	*Doctors recommend that you* (pl.) */ we sleep eight hours every night.*

Present perfect subjunctive

The present perfect subjunctive (**el presente perfecto de subjuntivo**) is formed with the present subjunctive of **haber** and the past participle. It is used in the same contexts as the present subjunctive, but it portrays the event as having happened in the past when the main clause verb is in the present. The English equivalents in these cases may or may not use *have/has.*

Espero que **hayas podido** leer el libro.	*I hope that you have been* (were) *able to read the book.*
Ojalá que Arturo **haya escuchado** mis consejos.	*I hope that Arturo* (has) *listened to my advice.*
Es necesario que Uds. **hayan estudiado** antes de hacer el examen.	*It's necessary for you to have studied before taking the test.*

13.2 The subjunctive: Disbelief and uncertainty

The subjunctive in adjective clauses (after nonexistent and indefinite antecedents)

1. You saw in **Estructura 10.1** that the relative pronoun **que** introduces a clause (called a *relative clause* or *adjective clause*) that gives further information about a noun.

Hay tortugas **que viven en el mar.**   *There are turtles that live in the ocean.*

When the noun being described does not exist or is not known to exist, the relative clause appears in the subjunctive.

No hay ninguna tortuga que **viva** en la nieve. | *There is no turtle that lives in the snow.*
¿Aquí hay un parque que **tenga** muchos pájaros? | *Is there a park here that has a lot of birds?*

2. It is especially common to use the subjunctive in relative clauses when the noun being described does not refer to anyone or anything specific.

Los biólogos buscan un animal que **vuele.** | *The biologists are looking for an animal that flies.* (They don't have any particular animal in mind and there may not even be any.)

If you want to say that the biologists are looking for a specific animal, use the indicative.

Los biólogos buscan un animal que **vuela.** | *The biologists are looking for an animal that flies.* (Such an animal exists and they have this animal in mind.)

3. The use of the subjunctive in relative clauses is in keeping with the core meaning of the subjunctive: to express ideas that may not be true. To describe a noun that may not even exist, you thus use the subjunctive. Since the indicative expresses ideas that are thought to be true, you use it to describe a noun that you think exists.

The subjunctive: Emotion

The subjunctive is used after many verbs and expressions that convey an emotional reaction.

alegrarse *to be happy*	**Me alegro** de que **seas** uno de los mejores estudiantes. *I'm happy that you are one of the best students.*
gustar	**Me gusta** que **estés** en la clase conmigo. *I like it that you're in the class with me.*
lamentar *to regret*	**Lamento** que el sapo dorado ya no **exista.** *I regret that the golden toad doesn't exist anymore.*
molestar *to bother*	¿**Te molesta** que **te digan** «Susie»? *Does it bother you that they call you "Susie"?*
sentir *to be sorry*	**Siento** mucho que **hayan cortado** el árbol. *I'm very sorry that they (have) cut down the tree.*
ser bueno/malo	**Es bueno** que **tengan** un parque tan grande en la ciudad. *It's good that they have such a big park in the city.*

(Continued)

| ser una lástima *to be a shame* | **Es una lástima** que el bosque **esté** en tan malas condiciones.
It's a shame that the forest is in such bad condition. |
| temer | **Temo** que ya no **haya*** muchos pájaros en esta zona.
I'm afraid that there aren't many birds in this area anymore. |

The dependent clause uses the subjunctive and describes the situation that the person is reacting to in each of these cases.

13.3 The subjunctive: Purpose and contingency

The subjunctive in time clauses

1. Time clauses are introduced by words such as **cuando.** When the time clause refers to an event that has not yet happened, it is in the subjunctive.

| Marta se va a poner muy contenta cuando **vea** un cóndor en las montañas. | *Marta will become very happy when she sees a condor in the mountains.* (This hasn't happened yet.) |

When the time clause refers to something that happens regularly or that has already happened, it is in the indicative.

| Marta se pone muy contenta cuando **ve** un cóndor en las montañas. | *Marta becomes very happy when she sees a condor in the mountains. (This happens regularly.)* |

2. **Cuando** is the most common word to introduce a time clause, but some other common expressions are **antes de que, después de que,** and **hasta que.** They all use the subjunctive when describing an event that hasn't happened yet.

Quiero visitar el parque **antes de que** lo **cierren.**	*I want to visit the park before they close it.*
Vamos a hablar **después de que regreses** de tu viaje.	*Let's talk after you return from your trip.*
Tenemos que seguir trabajando **hasta que** las playas **estén** limpias.	*We have to keep working until the beaches are clean.*

Because **antes de que** always refers to an event that hasn't yet happened, it is always followed by the subjunctive.

3. The choice of subjunctive or indicative in time clauses follows from the core meaning of each. The subjunctive is to express ideas that may not be true, so you use the subjunctive in time clauses that refer to a future event. Since the event has not happened yet, there is a chance that it may never happen, and this uncertainty makes the subjunctive appropriate. The indicative is used to express facts or ideas thought to be true, so you use it in time clauses about something that happens regularly or has already happened.

The subjunctive: Additional expressions of contingency

Some other common expressions followed by the subjunctive are **a menos de que** (*unless*), **con tal de que** (*provided that*), and **sin que** (*without*).

Hay muchas hormigas cada año **a menos de que haga** mucho frío.	*There are lots of ants every year unless it is very cold.*
Voy a pasar el día en las montañas **con tal de que me acompañes.**	*I'm going to spend the day in the mountains provided that you accompany me.*
¿Puedes observar a los osos **sin que te vean**?	*Can you observe the bears without them seeing you?*

In all of these cases, the clause with the subjunctive expresses an event that may not happen.

---

*Recall that when **haber** is used to express existence, it is always singular.

Capítulo 14

14.1   The past subjunctive

Additional irregular past subjunctive forms

1. The stem of the past subjunctive is always the same as the stem of the preterite, even if the preterite stem is irregular. You have already seen some verbs with irregular past subjunctive forms. Here are more common verbs with irregular stems.

decir **(dij-)**	Queríamos que la actriz **dijera** algo interesante en la entrevista. *We wanted the actress to say something interesting in the interview.*
hacer **(hic-)**	Era importante que **hicieran** una película sobre la vida del general. *It was important that they make a movie about the life of the general.*
traer **(traj-)**	Recomendaban que **trajéramos** un diccionario. *They recommended that we bring a dictionary.*

Note that **decir** and **traer,** whose stems end in **-j,** drop the **i** in the past subjunctive ending. In **Estructura 6.2,** you saw this same adjustment with the **-ieron** ending of the preterite, as in **dijeron** and **trajeron.** In both cases, this small adjustment makes pronunciation of the verb forms easier.

2. As you saw in **Estructura 8.1,** some verbs change the stem vowel in the preterite. This change occurs in the past subjunctive also. Here are some common verbs in which stem vowel **e** changes to **i.**

mentir **(ie, i)**	Yo no quería que me **mintieran.** *I didn't want them to lie to me.*
pedir **(i, i)**	No era necesario que los músicos **pidieran** ayuda. *It wasn't necessary for the musicians to ask for help.*
seguir **(i, i)**	Era muy importante que los niños me **siguieran** en el museo. *It was very important that the children follow me in the museum.*
servir **(i, i)**	Arreglaron esta parte del edificio para que **sirviera** de biblioteca. *They fixed this part of the building so that it would serve as a library.*

3. Here are some common verbs in which the stem vowel **o** changes to **u.**

dormir **(ue, u)**	Con tanto ruido, era imposible que yo **durmiera** tarde. *With so much noise, it was impossible for me to sleep late.*
morir **(ue, u)**	No queríamos que la cantante **muriera** en la ópera. *We didn't want the singer to die in the opera.*

The past perfect subjunctive

The *past perfect subjunctive* (**el pluscuamperfecto de subjuntivo**) is formed with the past subjunctive of **haber (hubiera, hubieras, . . .)** followed by the past participle. It has the same basic meaning as the past perfect indicative (for example, **habían salido** [*they had left*]), but it is used in contexts where the subjunctive is required.

Yo esperaba que ya **hubieran salido.**	*I was hoping that they had already left.*
Nadie creía que **hubieras tocado** la guitarra tan bien.	*Nobody believed that you had played the guitar so well.*
Era imposible que **hubiéramos leído** todo el libro para el martes.	*It was impossible for us to have read the whole book by Tuesday.*

14.2   The future

Irregular future forms

The future tense endings are always regular, but some verbs have irregular stems. In addition to those that you have already seen, here are some other common verbs with irregular stems in the future.

querer	querr-	¿**Querrás** venir con nosotros al cine?
		Might you want to come with us to the movies?
saber	sabr-	¿**Sabrá** tocar el violín Gustavo?
		Does Gustavo perhaps know how to play the violin?
valer	valdr-	Ese libro **valdrá** mucho más en el futuro.
		That book will be worth a lot more in the future.

The future perfect

1. The future perfect is formed with **haber** in the future tense followed by the past participle. It is a common way to make conjectures about something that might have happened in the past.

   ¿**Habrán filmado** esa película en Lima?

   Might they have filmed that movie in Lima?

   ¿Borges **habrá entrado** a esta librería?

   Could Borges have entered this bookstore?

2. You may also use the future perfect to say what will have happened by a certain time.

   Para el 2 de julio, Marisela ya **habrá abierto** la galería.

   By July 2, Marisela will have already opened the gallery.

Capítulo 15

15.1   The conditional

Irregular conditional forms

Here are some additional common verbs with an irregular stem in the conditional.

querer	querr-	Yo **querría** acompañarte.
		I would like to go with (accompany) you.
saber	sabr-	Un guatemalteco **sabría** cómo se llama ese pájaro.
		A Guatemalan would know what that bird is called.
valer	valdr-	Mi teléfono **valdría** mucho, pero está roto.
		My phone would be worth a lot, but it's broken.

For many speakers, the conditional form of **querer** (**querría**) is rarely used and the past subjunctive form (**quisiera**) is used instead.

The conditional perfect

The conditional perfect is formed with **haber** in the conditional followed by the past participle. You use it to say what *would have* happened in the past.

Yo **habría viajado** a Uruguay el año pasado, pero no tenía suficiente dinero.

I would have traveled to Uruguay last year, but I didn't have enough money.

Habría sido buenísimo hablar con los indígenas de la zona en su lengua.

It would have been great to speak with the indigenous people of the area in their language.

15.2 *Si* clauses

The past perfect subjunctive in *si* clauses

1. When a **si** clause refers to a contrary-to-fact event in the past, use the past perfect subjunctive form of the verb (see **Para saber más 14.1**).

Si yo **hubiera sabido** que no tenías dinero, te habría prestado.	*If I had known that you didn't have money, I would have lent you some.*
Si Cristóbal Colón no **hubiera llegado** a América, el mundo sería muy diferente.	*If Christopher Columbus had not arrived in the Americas, the world would be very different.*

2. Many speakers also use this past subjunctive perfect form in place of the conditional perfect.

Hubiera sido buenísimo hablar con los indígenas de la zona en su lengua.	*It would have been great to speak with the indigenous people of that area in their language.*

APPENDIX 1: Verb Charts

A. REGULAR VERBS: SIMPLE TENSES

Infinitive Present Participle Past Participle	INDICATIVE					SUBJUNCTIVE		IMPERATIVE
	Present	Imperfect	Preterite	Future	Conditional	Present	Past	
hablar	hablo	hablaba	hablé	hablaré	hablaría	hable	hablara	habla / no hables
hablando	hablas	hablabas	hablaste	hablarás	hablarías	hables	hablaras	hable
hablado	habla	hablaba	habló	hablará	hablaría	hable	hablara	hablemos
	hablamos	hablábamos	hablamos	hablaremos	hablaríamos	hablemos	habláramos	hablad / no habléis
	habláis	hablabais	hablasteis	hablaréis	hablaríais	habléis	hablarais	hablen
	hablan	hablaban	hablaron	hablarán	hablarían	hablen	hablaran	
comer	como	comía	comí	comeré	comería	coma	comiera	come / no comas
comiendo	comes	comías	comiste	comerás	comerías	comas	comieras	coma
comido	come	comía	comió	comerá	comería	coma	comiera	comamos
	comemos	comíamos	comimos	comeremos	comeríamos	comamos	comiéramos	comed / no comáis
	coméis	comíais	comisteis	comeréis	comeríais	comáis	comierais	coman
	comen	comían	comieron	comerán	comerían	coman	comieran	
vivir	vivo	vivía	viví	viviré	viviría	viva	viviera	vive / no vivas
viviendo	vives	vivías	viviste	vivirás	vivirías	vivas	vivieras	viva
vivido	vive	vivía	vivió	vivirá	viviría	viva	viviera	vivamos
	vivimos	vivíamos	vivimos	viviremos	viviríamos	vivamos	viviéramos	vivid / no viváis
	vivís	vivíais	vivisteis	viviréis	viviríais	viváis	vivierais	vivan
	viven	vivían	vivieron	vivirán	vivirían	vivan	vivieran	

B. REGULAR VERBS: PERFECT TENSES

INDICATIVE

Present Perfect		Pluperfect		Preterite Perfect		Future Perfect		Conditional Perfect	
he	hablado	había	hablado	hube	hablado	habré	hablado	habría	hablado
has	comido	habías	comido	hubiste	comido	habrás	comido	habrías	comido
ha	vivido	había	vivido	hubo	vivido	habrá	vivido	habría	vivido
hemos		habíamos		hubimos		habremos		habríamos	
habéis		habíais		hubisteis		habréis		habríais	
han		habían		hubieron		habrán		habrían	

SUBJUNCTIVE

Present Perfect		Pluperfect	
haya	hablado	hubiera	hablado
hayas	comido	hubieras	comido
haya	vivido	hubiera	vivido
hayamos		hubiéramos	
hayáis		hubierais	
hayan		hubieran	

C. IRREGULAR VERBS

Infinitive / Present Participle / Past Participle	INDICATIVE Present	Imperfect	Preterite	Future	Conditional	SUBJUNCTIVE Present	Past	IMPERATIVE
andar	ando	andaba	anduve	andaré	andaría	ande	anduviera	
andando	andas	andabas	anduviste	andarás	andarías	andes	anduvieras	anda / no andes
andado	anda	andaba	anduvo	andará	andaría	ande	anduviera	ande
	andamos	andábamos	anduvimos	andaremos	andaríamos	andemos	anduviéramos	andemos
	andáis	andabais	anduvisteis	andaréis	andaríais	andéis	anduvierais	andad / no andéis
	andan	andaban	anduvieron	andarán	andarían	anden	anduvieran	anden
caber	quepo	cabía	cupe	cabré	cabría	quepa	cupiera	
cabiendo	cabes	cabías	cupiste	cabrás	cabrías	quepas	cupieras	cabe / no quepas
cabido	cabe	cabía	cupo	cabrá	cabría	quepa	cupiera	quepa
	cabemos	cabíamos	cupimos	cabremos	cabríamos	quepamos	cupiéramos	quepamos
	cabéis	cabíais	cupisteis	cabréis	cabríais	quepáis	cupierais	cabed / no quepáis
	caben	cabían	cupieron	cabrán	cabrían	quepan	cupieran	quepan
caer	caigo	caía	caí	caeré	caería	caiga	cayera	
cayendo	caes	caías	caíste	caerás	caerías	caigas	cayeras	cae / no caigas
caído	cae	caía	cayó	caerá	caería	caiga	cayera	caiga
	caemos	caíamos	caímos	caeremos	caeríamos	caigamos	cayéramos	caigamos
	caéis	caíais	caísteis	caeréis	caeríais	caigáis	cayerais	caed / no caigáis
	caen	caían	cayeron	caerán	caerían	caigan	cayeran	caigan

Infinitive / Present Participle / Past Participle	INDICATIVE					SUBJUNCTIVE		IMPERATIVE
	Present	Imperfect	Preterite	Future	Conditional	Present	Past	
dar dando dado	doy das da damos dais dan	daba dabas daba dábamos dabais daban	di diste dio dimos disteis dieron	daré darás dará daremos daréis darán	daría darías daría daríamos daríais darían	dé des dé demos deis den	diera dieras diera diéramos dierais dieran	da / no des dé demos dad / no deis den
decir diciendo dicho	digo dices dice decimos decís dicen	decía decías decía decíamos decíais decían	dije dijiste dijo dijimos dijisteis dijeron	diré dirás dirá diremos diréis dirán	diría dirías diría diríamos diríais dirían	diga digas diga digamos digáis digan	dijera dijeras dijera dijéramos dijerais dijeran	di / no digas diga digamos decid / no digáis digan
estar estando estado	estoy estás está estamos estáis están	estaba estabas estaba estábamos estabais estaban	estuve estuviste estuvo estuvimos estuvisteis estuvieron	estaré estarás estará estaremos estaréis estarán	estaría estarías estaría estaríamos estaríais estarían	esté estés esté estemos estéis estén	estuviera estuvieras estuviera estuviéramos estuvierais estuviera	está / no estés esté estemos estad / no estéis estén
haber habiendo habido	he has ha hemos habéis han	había habías había habíamos habíais habían	hube hubiste hubo hubimos hubisteis hubieron	habré habrás habrá habremos habréis habrán	habría habrías habría habríamos habríais habrían	haya hayas haya hayamos hayáis hayan	hubiera hubieras hubiera hubiéramos hubierais hubieran	
hacer haciendo hecho	hago haces hace hacemos hacéis hacen	hacía hacías hacía hacíamos hacíais hacían	hice hiciste hizo hicimos hicisteis hicieron	haré harás hará haremos haréis harán	haría harías haría haríamos haríais harían	haga hagas haga hagamos hagáis hagan	hiciera hicieras hiciera hiciéramos hicierais hicieran	haz / no hagas haga hagamos haced / no hagáis hagan

C. IRREGULAR VERBS (CONTINUED)

Infinitive / Present Participle / Past Participle	INDICATIVE					SUBJUNCTIVE		IMPERATIVE
	Present	Imperfect	Preterite	Future	Conditional	Present	Past	
ir / yendo / ido	voy	iba	fui	iré	iría	vaya	fuera	
	vas	ibas	fuiste	irás	irías	vayas	fueras	ve / no vayas
	va	iba	fue	irá	iría	vaya	fuera	vaya
	vamos	íbamos	fuimos	iremos	iríamos	vayamos	fuéramos	vayamos
	vais	ibais	fuisteis	iréis	iríais	vayáis	fuerais	id / no vayáis
	van	iban	fueron	irán	irían	vayan	fueran	vayan
oír / oyendo / oído	oigo	oía	oí	oiré	oiría	oiga	oyera	
	oyes	oías	oíste	oirás	oirías	oigas	oyeras	oye / no oigas
	oye	oía	oyó	oirá	oiría	oiga	oyera	oiga
	oímos	oíamos	oímos	oiremos	oiríamos	oigamos	oyéramos	oigamos
	oís	oíais	oísteis	oiréis	oiríais	oigáis	oyerais	oíd / no oigáis
	oyen	oían	oyeron	oirán	oirían	oigan	oyeran	oigan
poder / pudiendo / podido	puedo	podía	pude	podré	podría	pueda	pudiera	
	puedes	podías	pudiste	podrás	podrías	puedas	pudieras	
	puede	podía	pudo	podrá	podría	pueda	pudiera	
	podemos	podíamos	pudimos	podremos	podríamos	podamos	pudiéramos	
	podéis	podíais	pudisteis	podréis	podríais	podáis	pudierais	
	pueden	podían	pudieron	podrán	podrían	puedan	pudieran	
poner / poniendo / puesto	pongo	ponía	puse	pondré	pondría	ponga	pusiera	
	pones	ponías	pusiste	pondrás	pondrías	pongas	pusieras	pon / no pongas
	pone	ponía	puso	pondrá	pondría	ponga	pusiera	ponga
	ponemos	poníamos	pusimos	pondremos	pondríamos	pongamos	pusiéramos	pongamos
	ponéis	poníais	pusisteis	pondréis	pondríais	pongáis	pusierais	poned / no pongáis
	ponen	ponían	pusieron	pondrán	pondrían	pongan	pusieran	pongan
querer / queriendo / querido	quiero	quería	quise	querré	querría	quiera	quisiera	
	quieres	querías	quisiste	querrás	querrías	quieras	quisieras	quiere / no quieras
	quiere	quería	quiso	querrá	querría	quiera	quisiera	quiera
	queremos	queríamos	quisimos	querremos	querríamos	queramos	quisiéramos	queramos
	queréis	queríais	quisisteis	querréis	querríais	queráis	quisierais	quered / no queráis
	quieren	querían	quisieron	querrán	querrían	quieran	quisieran	quieran

C. IRREGULAR VERBS (CONTINUED)

Infinitive / Present Participle / Past Participle	INDICATIVE					SUBJUNCTIVE		IMPERATIVE
	Present	Imperfect	Preterite	Future	Conditional	Present	Past	
saber	sé	sabía	supe	sabré	sabría	sepa	supiera	sabe / no sepas
sabiendo	sabes	sabías	supiste	sabrás	sabrías	sepas	supieras	sepa
sabido	sabe	sabía	supo	sabrá	sabría	sepa	supiera	sepamos
	sabemos	sabíamos	supimos	sabremos	sabríamos	sepamos	supiéramos	sabed / no sepáis
	sabéis	sabíais	supisteis	sabréis	sabríais	sepáis	supierais	sepan
	saben	sabían	supieron	sabrán	sabrían	sepan	supieran	
salir	salgo	salía	salí	saldré	saldría	salga	saliera	sal / no salgas
saliendo	sales	salías	saliste	saldrás	saldrías	salgas	salieras	salga
salido	sale	salía	salió	saldrá	saldría	salga	saliera	salgamos
	salimos	salíamos	salimos	saldremos	saldríamos	salgamos	saliéramos	salid / no salgáis
	salís	salíais	salisteis	saldréis	saldríais	salgáis	salierais	salgan
	salen	salían	salieron	saldrán	saldrían	salgan	salieran	
ser	soy	era	fui	seré	sería	sea	fuera	sé / no seas
siendo	eres	eras	fuiste	serás	serías	seas	fueras	sea
sido	es	era	fue	será	sería	sea	fuera	seamos
	somos	éramos	fuimos	seremos	seríamos	seamos	fuéramos	sed / no seáis
	sois	erais	fuisteis	seréis	seríais	seáis	fuerais	sean
	son	eran	fueron	serán	serían	sean	fueran	
tener	tengo	tenía	tuve	tendré	tendría	tenga	tuviera	ten / no tengas
teniendo	tienes	tenías	tuviste	tendrás	tendrías	tengas	tuvieras	tenga
tenido	tiene	tenía	tuvo	tendrá	tendría	tenga	tuviera	tengamos
	tenemos	teníamos	tuvimos	tendremos	tendríamos	tengamos	tuviéramos	tened / no tengáis
	tenéis	teníais	tuvisteis	tendréis	tendríais	tengáis	tuvierais	tengan
	tienen	tenían	tuvieron	tendrán	tendrían	tengan	tuvieran	
traer	traigo	traía	traje	traeré	traería	traiga	trajera	trae / no traigas
trayendo	traes	traías	trajiste	traerás	traerías	traigas	trajeras	traiga
traído	trae	traía	trajo	traerá	traería	traiga	trajera	traigamos
	traemos	traíamos	trajimos	traeremos	traeríamos	traigamos	trajéramos	traed / no traigáis
	traéis	traíais	trajisteis	traeréis	traeríais	traigáis	trajerais	traigan
	traen	traían	trajeron	traerán	traerían	traigan	trajeran	

C. IRREGULAR VERBS (CONTINUED)

Infinitive / Present Participle / Past Participle	INDICATIVE					SUBJUNCTIVE		IMPERATIVE
	Present	Imperfect	Preterite	Future	Conditional	Present	Past	
valer / valiendo / valido	valgo	valía	valí	valdré	valdría	valga	valiera	
	vales	valías	valiste	valdrás	valdrías	valgas	valieras	vale / no valgas
	vale	valía	valió	valdrá	valdría	valga	valiera	valga
	valemos	valíamos	valimos	valdremos	valdríamos	valgamos	valiéramos	valgamos
	valéis	valíais	valisteis	valdréis	valdríais	valgáis	valierais	valed / no valgáis
	valen	valían	valieron	valdrán	valdrían	valgan	valieran	valgan
venir / viniendo / venido	vengo	venía	vine	vendré	vendría	venga	viniera	
	vienes	venías	viniste	vendrás	vendrías	vengas	vinieras	ven / no vengas
	viene	venía	vino	vendrá	vendría	venga	viniera	venga
	venimos	veníamos	vinimos	vendremos	vendríamos	vengamos	viniéramos	vengamos
	venís	veníais	vinisteis	vendréis	vendríais	vengáis	vinierais	venid / no vengáis
	vienen	venían	vinieron	vendrán	vendrían	vengan	vinieran	vengan
ver / viendo / visto	veo	veía	vi	veré	vería	vea	viera	
	ves	veías	viste	verás	verías	veas	vieras	ve / no veas
	ve	veía	vio	verá	vería	vea	viera	vea
	vemos	veíamos	vimos	veremos	veríamos	veamos	viéramos	veamos
	veis	veíais	visteis	veréis	veríais	veáis	vierais	ved / no veáis
	ven	veían	vieron	verán	verían	vean	vieran	vean

D. STEM-CHANGING AND SPELLING-CHANGE VERBS

Infinitive Present Participle Past Participle	INDICATIVE					SUBJUNCTIVE		IMPERATIVE
	Present	Imperfect	Preterite	Future	Conditional	Present	Past	
construir (y) construyendo construido	construyo construyes construye construimos construís construyen	construía construías construía construíamos construíais construían	construí construiste construyó construimos construisteis construyeron	construiré construirás construirá construiremos construiréis construirán	construiría construirías construiría construiríamos construiríais construirían	construya construyas construya construyamos construyáis construyan	construyera construyeras construyera construyéramos construyerais construyeran	construye / no construyas construya construyamos construid / no construyáis construyan
creer (y [3rd-pers. pret.]) creyendo creído	creo crees cree creemos creéis creen	creía creías creía creíamos creíais creían	creí creíste creyó creímos creísteis creyeron	creeré creerás creerá creeremos creeréis creerán	creería creerías creería creeríamos creeríais creerían	crea creas crea creamos creáis crean	creyera creyeras creyera creyéramos creyerais creyeran	cree / no creas crea creamos creed / no creáis crean
dormir (ue, u) durmiendo dormido	duermo duermes duerme dormimos dormís duermen	dormía dormías dormía dormíamos dormíais dormían	dormí dormiste durmió dormimos dormisteis durmieron	dormiré dormirás dormirá dormiremos dormiréis dormirán	dormiría dormirías dormiría dormiríamos dormiríais dormirían	duerma duermas duerma durmamos durmáis duerman	durmiera durmieras durmiera durmiéramos durmierais durmieran	duerme / no duermas duerma durmamos dormid / no durmáis duerman
pedir (i, i) pidiendo pedido	pido pides pide pedimos pedís piden	pedía pedías pedía pedíamos pedíais pedían	pedí pediste pidió pedimos pedisteis pidieron	pediré pedirás pedirá pediremos pediréis pedirán	pediría pedirías pediría pediríamos pediríais pedirían	pida pidas pida pidamos pidáis pidan	pidiera pidieras pidiera pidiéramos pidierais pidieran	pide / no pidas pida pidamos pedid / no pidáis pidan
pensar (ie) pensando pensado	pienso piensas piensa pensamos pensáis piensan	pensaba pensabas pensaba pensábamos pensabais pensaban	pensé pensaste pensó pensamos pensasteis pensaron	pensaré pensarás pensará pensaremos pensaréis pensarán	pensaría pensarías pensaría pensaríamos pensaríais pensarían	piense pienses piense pensemos penséis piensen	pensara pensaras pensara pensáramos pensarais pensaran	piensa / no pienses piense pensemos pensad / no penséis piensen

D. STEM-CHANGING AND SPELLING-CHANGE VERBS (CONTINUED)

Infinitive / Present Participle / Past Participle	INDICATIVE Present	Imperfect	Preterite	Future	Conditional	SUBJUNCTIVE Present	Past	IMPERATIVE
producir (zc, j) produciendo producido	produzco produces produce producimos producís producen	producía producías producía producíamos producíais producían	produje produjiste produjo produjimos produjisteis produjeron	produciré producirás producirá produciremos produciréis producirán	produciría producirías produciría produciríamos produciríais producirían	produzca produzcas produzca produzcamos produzcáis produzcan	produjera produjeras produjera produjéramos produjerais produjeran	produce / no produzcas produzca produzcamos producid / no produzcáis produzcan
reír (i, i) riendo reído	río ríes ríe reímos reís ríen	reía reías reía reíamos reíais reían	reí reíste rio reímos reísteis rieron	reiré reirás reirá reiremos reiréis reirán	reiría reirías reiría reiríamos reiríais reirían	ría rías ría riamos riáis rían	riera rieras riera riéramos rierais rieran	ríe / no rías ría riamos reíd / no riáis rían
seguir (i, i) (g) siguiendo seguido	sigo sigues sigue seguimos seguís siguen	seguía seguías seguía seguíamos seguíais seguían	seguí seguiste siguió seguimos seguisteis siguieron	seguiré seguirás seguirá seguiremos seguiréis seguirán	seguiría seguirías seguiría seguiríamos seguiríais seguirían	siga sigas siga sigamos sigáis sigan	siguiera siguieras siguiera siguiéramos siguierais siguieran	sigue / no sigas siga sigamos seguid / no sigáis sigan
sentir (ie, i) sintiendo sentido	siento sientes siente sentimos sentís sienten	sentía sentías sentía sentíamos sentíais sentían	sentí sentiste sintió sentimos sentisteis sintieron	sentiré sentirás sentirá sentiremos sentiréis sentirán	sentiría sentirías sentiría sentiríamos sentiríais sentirían	sienta sientas sienta sintamos sintáis sientan	sintiera sintieras sintiera sintiéramos sintierais sintieran	siente / no sientas sienta sintamos sentid / no sintáis sientan
volver (ue) volviendo vuelto	vuelvo vuelves vuelve volvemos volvéis vuelven	volvía volvías volvía volvíamos volvíais volvían	volví volviste volvió volvimos volvisteis volvieron	volveré volverás volverá volveremos volveréis volverán	volvería volverías volvería volveríamos volveríais volverían	vuelva vuelvas vuelva volvamos volváis vuelvan	volviera volvieras volviera volviéramos volvierais volvieran	vuelve / no vuelvas vuelva volvamos volved / no volváis vuelvan

APPENDIX 2

Answer key for *Reciclaje, Para empezar,* and *Actividades analíticas*

Capítulo 1

Estructura 1.1

Para empezar: un bolígrafo, una computadora, un diccionario, un libro
Actividades analíticas: 1. una, un, un, una 2. Sí

Estructura 1.2

Para empezar: 1. cinco 2. dos 3. dos 4. cuatro 5. tres 6. dos
Actividades analíticas: 1. **-s:** libro, mochila; **-es:** borrador, mujer 2. estudiantes, meses, universidades, bolígrafos 3. lápices, luces 4. el lápiz, las computadoras, los escritorios, la mochila; un gimnasio, unas sillas, una pizarra, unos bolígrafos

Estructura 1.3

Para empezar: 2. f 3. h 4. b 5. g 6. a 7. c 8. d
Actividades analíticas: 1. **él/ella, usted:** es, tiene; **ellos/ellas, ustedes:** son, tienen 3b. es, Tiene

Estructura 1.4

Para empezar: 1. d 2. b 3. a 4. c 5. e **Actividades analíticas:** 1. *my:* mi(s); *your:* tu(s); *our:* nuestro(s)/nuestra(s)

Capítulo 2

Estructura 2.1

Para empezar: 1. g 2. b 3. c 4. e 5. d 6. f 7. a 8. h
Actividades analíticas: 1. altos, alta

Estructura 2.2

Para empezar: 1. b 2. f 3. c 4. a 5. e 6. b, d 7. a, b, c
Actividades analíticas: 1. **tú:** estás, vas; **nosotros:** estamos, vamos 2. está, Va

Estructura 2.3

Para empezar: 1. Javier 2. Agustina 3. Pedro 4. nobody 5. Esther
Actividades analíticas: 1. **me gusta (singular):** la música, la biología; **me gustan (plural):** los deportes, los libros 2. Te gustan, Te gusta 3. le gustan, le gusta

Estructura 2.4

Actividades analíticas: 1. **-ar:** bailar, hablar, nadar, usar; **-er:** comer, correr, hacer, leer; **-ir:** dormir

Capítulo 3

Estructura 3.1

Reciclaje: 2. c 3. a 4. b 5. e; a. tiene b. vas c. es d. soy e. está
Para empezar: 1. Javier Bardem 2. Gael García Bernal 3. Gael García Bernal 4. Gael García Bernal, Javier Bardem 5. Gael García Bernal 6. Javier Bardem 7. Gael García Bernal, Javier Bardem 8. Gael García Bernal, Javier Bardem
Actividades analíticas: 1. **yo:** trabajo, leo, vivo; **tú:** trabajas, lees, vives 2. -o 3. -s

Estructura 3.2

Reciclaje: 1. son, falso 2. somos, cierto 3. van, falso 4. están, cierto *or* falso 5. tienen, cierto 6. vamos, falso

Para empezar: 1. 7 2. 2 3. 8 **Actividades analíticas:** 1. **cenar:** ceno, cenas, cenamos, cenan; **comer:** como, comes, comemos, comen; **vivir:** vivo, vives 2. -e, -á, -e 3. -mos, -is, -n 4. **bailar:** bailas, baila, bailamos, bailan; **correr:** corro, corre, corremos, corréis; **asistir:** asisto, asistes, asistimos, asistís

Estructura 3.3

Reciclaje: 1. ar 2. ar 3. er 4. ar 5. ir 6. er 7. ar 8. er 9. ar 10. ar
11. ar 12. ar **Para empezar:** pueden tomar café; pueden estudiar medicina;
pueden nadar; pueden leer en la biblioteca **Actividades analíticas:** 1. podemos,
pueden 2. nosotros/as: podemos; podéis 3. **yo:** almuerzo, duermo, sueño;
nosotros/as: almorzamos, dormimos, soñamos

Estructura 3.4

Reciclaje: 1. el 2. la 3. el 4. el 5. el 6. la 7. la 8. el 9. el 10. la 11. la
12. la *words related to time:* la noche, el día, el mes, la semana, la hora, la mañana
Para empezar: 1. Física 2. martes 3. Salud Pública 4. Química General, Química
Orgánica I 5. Química General 6. lunes, jueves **Actividades analíticas:** 2. *sing. m.*
ese; *sing. fem.* esa; *pl. m.* esos; *pl. f.* esas 3. este, estas, estos, esta

Capítulo 4

Estructura 4.1

Reciclaje: (*any order*) bonitas, jóvenes, delgadas, ricas **Para empezar:** 1. el rey
Felipe 2. la reina Letizia, la reina Sofía 3. el rey Juan Carlos 4. la reina
Sofía 5. el rey Felipe, el rey Juan Carlos 6. la princesa Sofía, la princesa Leonor
Actividades analíticas: 1. más 2. menos rica, menos alta, menos altos

Estructura 4.2

Para empezar: 1. «hola» 2. «diga» 3. «bueno» 4. «hola» 5. «aló»
Actividades analíticas: 1. dices, decimos, dicen 3. **tú:** sirves; **nosotros/as:**
servimos; **yo:** pido; **él/ella, Ud.:** pide; **ellos/ellas, Uds.:** piden

Estructura 4.3

Para empezar: 1. c 2. d 3. e 4. b 5. a **Actividades analíticas:**
1. queremos, quieren 2. **tú:** empiezas; **nosotros/as:** empezamos; **yo:** pienso;
él/ella, Ud.: piensa; **ellos/ellas, Uds.:** piensan

Estructura 4.4

Para empezar: 1. c 2. b, f 3. d, e 4. a 5. h 6. k 7. g 8. i 9. i, j
Actividades analíticas: 1. **ser:** es, son; **estar:** está, están 2. ...están en diferentes
países. 4. a. estar, location b. estar, quality that could change c. ser,
origin d. ser, identity

Capítulo 5

Estructura 5.1

Reciclaje: 1. Soy, ciudad 2. Voy, campo 3. Soy, campo 4. Estoy, ciudad
5. Tengo, campo 6. Estoy, ciudad **Para empezar:** 1. f, h 2. a, i
3. d 4. c, e 5. g, b 6. d **Actividades analíticas:** 1. hago, traigo, salgo
2. **yo:** tengo, digo; **tú:** vienes; **él/ella, Ud.** tiene, dice; **nosotros/as:** venimos; **ellos/
ellas, Uds.:** tienen, dicen 3. oigo, oye

Estructura 5.2

Reciclaje: 1. te llamas 2. Me llamo 3. se llama 4. Se llama 5. te llamas
6. Me llamo **Para empezar: BIBLIOTECA:** dormirse, sentarse; **GIMNASIO:** (*any four*)
afeitarse, bañarse, ducharse, maquillarse, peinarse, vestirse; **HOTEL:** *any*
Actividades analíticas: 1. -se 2. **yo:** me baño, me peino; **tú:** te afeitas, te peinas;
él/ella, Ud.: se baña; **nosotros/as:** nos bañamos, nos peinamos; **vosotros/as:** os
peináis; **ellos/ellas, Uds.:** se afeitan

Estructura 5.3

Reciclaje: 1. d 2. a 3. e 4. c 5. b; a. Es b. Está c. Son d. Somos e. Están
Para empezar: 1. cierto 2. falso 3. falso 4. cierto 5. falso 6. falso 7. falso
8. cierto 9. cierto 10. cierto **Actividades analíticas:** 1. ser, estar 4. a. location
b. change c. identity d. intrinsic quality e. origin

Estructura 5.4

Reciclaje: 1. Estos edificios 2. Esta tienda 3. Este muchacho 4. Estas chicas
5. Esta catedral **Para empezar:** 1. cierto 2. falso 3. cierto 4. cierto 5. cierto

6. falso   7. falso   8. cierto   9. cierto   10. falso   **Actividades analíticas:**   1. *first row:* algo, algunos, algunas; *second row:* nada, ningún, ninguna   2. a. algunas b. algunos c. ningún d. ninguna

Capítulo 6

Estructura 6.1

Reciclaje: un cocinero profesional: Cocina, Escribe, Trabaja, Aprende; **yo:** (No) Cocino, (No) Escribo, (No) Trabajo, (No) Aprendo   **Para empezar, Paso 1:**   1. i 2. f   3. h   5. c   7. d   8. g   9. e   **Paso 2:**   1. b   2. d   3. f   4. a   5. c   6. e **Actividades analíticas: yo:** trabajé, aprendí; **tú:** trabajaste, aprendiste; **él/ella, Ud.:** trabajó, aprendió, escribió   2. **yo:** -í; **tú:** -iste; **nosotros/as:** -amos; **vosotros/as:** -isteis; **ellos/ellas, Uds.:** -aron, -ieron

Estructura 6.2

Reciclaje: 1. Soy   2. hago   3. Digo   4. Voy   5. pongo   **Para empezar:** 1. estuvo mal   2. estuvo mal   3. estuvo bien   4. estuvo mal   5. estuvo mal   6. estuvo mal   7. estuvo mal   8. estuvo bien   9. estuvo mal   **Actividades analíticas:**   1. Primero fui a la casa equivocada (1), Fui muy educado (3) 2. **yo:** dije, hice, puse; **él/ella, Ud.:** estuvo; **tú:** -iste; **nosotros/as:** -imos

Estructura 6.3

Reciclaje: 1. el   2. la   3. la   4. el   5. la   6. el   7. las   8. los   9. la   10. la 11. el   12. el   13. las   14. los   15. la   16. las   17. el   18. los   19. la   20. el; **No se puede comer:** la cuchara, el cuchillo, la servilleta, las tazas, el tenedor **Para empezar:**   1. P   2. C   3. V   4. C   5. T   6. C   7. P   8. T **Actividades analíticas:**   1. b. la papa c. a mi hermano d. a Marisela   2. b. café, Ana lo toma por la mañana.; c. la fruta, Julián la compró ayer.   5. a. Lo invito a desayunar con nosotros. b. La llevamos a la fiesta.

Capítulo 7

Estructura 7.1

Reciclaje: REGULARMENTE: Hablo, Como, leo, Duermo, voy; **AYER:** Hablé, Comí, leí, Dormí, fui   **Para empezar:**   1. cierto   2. cierto   3. cierto   4. falso   5. cierto 6. cierto   7. falso   8. falso   **Actividades analíticas:**   2. **tú:** vivías; **nosotros/as:** comíamos, **ellos/ellas, Uds.:** hablaban, comían, vivían   3. **yo:** -ía; **tú:** -abas, -ías; **él/ella, Ud.:** -aba; **nosotros/as:** -ábamos; **vosotros/as:** -íais; **ellos/ellas, Uds.:** -aban, -ían

Estructura 7.2

Reciclaje: 1. la   2. lo   3. los   4. las   5. me   **Actividades analíticas:**   1. *sing.:* me, le; *pl:* les   2. his parents, her friends

Estructura 7.3

Reciclaje: 1. los papás   2. la mamá, Ella   3. el hermano, Él   4. el papá, Él   5. el hermano y yo, Nosotros   6. las abuelas, Ellas   **Actividades analíticas:**   1. mí

Capítulo 8

Estructura 8.1

Reciclaje, Paso 1:   Pasé, regresé, terminé; Estuve; ayudé; Fui, pasamos, Hicimos, comimos, bailamos; Trabajé   **Para empezar:**   1. B   2. H   3. H   4. B   5. H   6. H 7. B   **Actividades analíticas:**   1. **yo:** serví, vestí; **tú:** seguiste, serviste; **él/ella, Ud.:** pidió, sirvió, vistió; **nosotros/as:** pedimos, seguimos, vestimos; **ellos/ellas, Uds.:** pidieron, sirvieron, vistieron   2. **e → i verb forms:** pidió, pidieron; siguió, siguieron; sirvió, sirvieron; vistió, vistieron   3. **yo:** morí; **tú:** dormiste; **él/ella, Ud.:** murió; **nosotros/as:** morimos; **vosotros/as:** dormisteis; **ellos/ellas, Uds.:** durmieron 4. **o → u verb forms:** durmió, durmieron; murió, murieron

Estructura 8.2

Reciclaje: 1. llevabas   2. tenías   3. escogía   4. gustaba   5. lavaba   **Para empezar:**   1. cierto   2. falso   3. cierto   4. cierto   5. falso   6. cierto   7. cierto 8. falso   9. falso   10. cierto   **Actividades analíticas:**   2. 1, 5, 6, 8, 10   4. 7, 9

Estructura 8.3

Reciclaje: 1. d   2. e   3. f   4. b   5. a   6. c; a. Lo, b. Los c. Lo
d. Lo e. Le f. La   **Para empezar:** 1. e   2. b   3. a   4. d   5. c
Actividades analíticas: 3. a. Los voy a comprar. c. Lo/Las tengo que comprar.
d. La puedo comprar   4. a. Voy a comprarlos. b. Quiero comprarlos. c. Tengo que
comprarlo/las. d. Puedo comprarla.

Capítulo 9

Estructura 9.1

Reciclaje: 1. De México a Guadalajara   2. De México a Guatemala   4. De México
a Nueva York   5. De México a Santiago   6. De México a Madrid
Para empezar: 1. b   2. b   3. a   4. b   5. a   6. a   7. a   8. b
Actividades analíticas: 2. a. para Machu Picchu b. para las ocho c. para ir a
Machu Picchu, para evitar los grandes grupos de turistas d. para tus amigos, para
tu familia, para tu viaje   4. a. por el Valle Sagrado b. por la mañana c. por tren
d. por la gran cantidad de turistas

Estructura 9.2

Para empezar: 1. E   2. M   3. A   4. M   5. E   6. A   7. E   8. E   9. M   10. A
11. M   12. A   **Actividades analíticas:** 2. 4, 5, 9; The noun is plural.

Estructura 9.3

Para empezar: 7, 5, 2, 1, 9, 8, 6, 4, 3   **Actividades analíticas:** 1. un café, la tarjeta
de identificación, un café, el teléfono, el chaleco y los pantalones   2. Se me acabó
el dinero. Se me perdió el pasaporte.

Capítulo 10

Estructura 10.1

Reciclaje: EDIFICIOS / INFRAESTRUCTURA: los arquitectos comerciales y residenciales, los ingenieros civiles y estructurales, una agente de bienes raíces, **EDUCACIÓN:**
una profesora universitaria; **SALUD:** un médico especializado en cardiología, las
psicólogas clínicas; **SEGURIDAD:** un policía motorizado   **Para empezar:** 1. C   2. S
3. S   4. S   5. C   6. X   7. C   8. S   9. X   10. S   **Actividades analíticas:** 1. que
hizo muchos edificios muy famosos en Barcelona   2. sus hijos Carlos, Marco
Antonio y Patrick

Estructura 10.2

Reciclaje: 1. g   2. e   3. b   4. f   5. a   6. d   7. c   8. h; a. Escribes b. Haces
c. Tomas d. Cortas e. Aceptas, das f. Cuidas g. Apagas h. Llevas
Para empezar: 7. No te bañes el día de tu entrevista. ¡Eso te da buena
suerte!   **Actividades analíticas:** 1. piensa, aprende, pide; **él/ella, Ud.** form (third
person singular of the present indicative)   2. no hables, no comas   4. haz, pon,
sal, ten, ven   7. vístete; no te bañes, no te quedes

Estructura 10.3

Reciclaje: 1. ¿Necesita ayuda?   2. Es el nuevo gerente de la tienda.   3. ¿Sabe
cómo hacer esto?   4. ¿Dónde pone los documentos?   5. ¿Me puede ayudar en
algo, por favor?   6. ¿En qué le puedo ayudar?   7. Le voy a dejar el documento en
su escritorio.   8. ¿Se va después de la reunión?   **Para empezar:** 1. d   2. b   3. c
4. a   5. a   6. d   7. c   8. a   **Actividades analíticas:** 1. (no) use, (no) oprima; **-ar:**
usar, conectar, indicar, comprar; **-er:** poner; **-ir:** oprimir   2. (no) usen, (no) coman,
(no) opriman   3. *pos. form.:* after and attached to the verb, cómprela; *neg. form.:*
before the verb, no lo use

Capítulo 11

Estructura 11.1

Actividades analíticas: 1. he, hemos   2. lavado, comido, salido; trabajado,
aprendido, vivido   3. hecho, He hecho la cama. *I have made the bed.*; visto, He
visto una película.

Estructura 11.2

Reciclaje: 1. La, la 2. Los, los 3. Las, las 4. Lo, lo 5. La, la
Para empezar: 1. D 2. C 3. C 4. B, C 5. C 6. B 7. D 8. D 9. C, B 10. B, D 11. D 12. C **Actividades analíticas:** 1. Ponlos en tu dormitorio.; Ponte el pijama verde. 2. No le pongas más azúcar al café.; No te pongas el pijama verde. 3. **tú:** límpialo; **Ud.:** no lo limpie; **Uds.:** límpienlo, no lo limpien

Estructura 11.3

Reciclaje: 1. Es 2. Es 3. está 4. está 5. Está 6. es 7. Es 8. Está 9. Es 10. es **Para empezar:** 1. c 2. j 3. g 4. e 5. d 6. a 7. h 8. b 9. f 10. i **Actividades analíticas:** 1. *present participles:* cenando, estudiando, escribiendo; *infinitives:* cenar, estudiar, escribir; *present participles:* comiendo, saliendo, ayudando, viendo

Capítulo 12

Estructura 12.1

Reciclaje: 1. he caminado 2. he comido 3. he meditado / practicado yoga 4. he dormido 5. he hecho 6. he tomado **Para empezar:** 1. a 2. f 3. b 4. g 5. e 6. c 7. h 8. d **Actividades analíticas:** 1. reflexive, indirect object 2. I have had to do/make it., Have you been able to answer his/her question (for him/her)?, We have wanted to buy it for a long time.

Estructura 12.2

Reciclaje: 1. Están corriendo. 2. Están caminando. 3. Está nadando. 4. Están boxeando. 5. Está levantando pesas. 6. Está surfeando. 7. Está jugando tenis. 8. Está esquiando. **Para empezar:** 1. e 2. b 3. a 4. g 5. h 6. d 7. f 8. c **Actividades analíticas:** 1. le está dando, se está haciendo 2. está dándole, está haciéndose

Estructura 12.3

Reciclaje: 1. Tomen agua. 2. Practica yoga. 3. Levanten pesas. 4. Duerme más. 5. Come menos y haz más ejercicio. 6. Corran. **Para empezar:** La recomendación falsa: 7 **Actividades analíticas:** 1. *indicative:* comes, tomas, vives; *subjunctive:* busques, comas, compres, des, tomes, vivas 2. **-ar** verbs: -e-; **-er/-ir** verbs: -a- 3. **tomar:** tomes, tomemos, tomen; **comer:** comas, coma, comáis, coman; **vivir:** vivas, vivamos

Capítulo 13

Estructura 13.1

Reciclaje: 1. jaguar 2. Hago, pájaro 3. Tengo, tortuga 4. Soy, tortuga 5. Salgo, jaguar 6. Traigo, pájaro 7. estoy, jaguar 8. Digo, pájaro 9. Pongo, tortuga **Para empezar:** 1. cierto 2. cierto 3. cierto 4. falso 5. cierto 6. falso 7. cierto 8. falso 9. cierto **Actividades analíticas:** 1. **yo:** ponga, salga, traiga; **tú:** hagas, salgas, tengas; **él/ella, Ud.:** haga, ponga, salga, tenga, traiga; **nosotros/as:** pongamos, tengamos, traigamos; **vosotros/as:** hagáis, salgáis; **ellos/ellas, Uds.:** hagan, pongan, tengan 3. **yo:** sea; **tú:** vayas; **él/ella, Ud.:** vaya, sea; **nosotros/as:** seamos; **vosotros/as:** vayáis; **ellos/ellas, Uds.:** vayan, sean

Estructura 13.2

Reciclaje: 1. d 2. a 3. f 4. b 5. c 6. e **Para empezar:** 1. cierto 2. cierto 3. cierto 4. cierto 5. cierto 6. cierto 7. cierto 8. falso 9. cierto 10. falso **Actividades analíticas:** 1. esperar que..., no creer que..., es posible que..., no pensar que... 2. They all express the idea that what follows may not be true.

Estructura 13.3

Reciclaje: 1. c 2. e 3. d 4. f 5. a 6. b; a. por b. para c. para d. para e. por f. por **Para empezar:** 2. d 3. g 4. a 5. c 6. e 7. f **Actividades analíticas:** 1. subjunctive

Capítulo 14

Estructura 14.1

Reciclaje: 1. hagan 2. a favor del arte, es 3. cierren 4. a favor del arte, tenga
5. a favor del arte, participen 6. tiene **Para empezar:** 1. cierto 2. cierto
3. falso 4. cierto 5. cierto 6. cierto 7. cierto 8. cierto 9. cierto 10. falso
Actividades analíticas: 1. **yo:** viviera; **tú:** aprendieras; **él/ella, Ud.:** hablara;
nosotros/as: viviéramos; **ellos/ellas, Uds.:** hablaran, aprendieran 2. **tú:** -aras; **él/
ella, Ud.:** -iera; **nosotros/as:** -áramos; **ellos/ellas, Uds.:** –aran, -ieran

Estructura 14.2

Reciclaje: a. 3, ar b. 6, er, ar, ir c. er d. er e. 5, ar f. 4, ar g. 2, ar, ar
Para empezar: 1. e 2. h 3. g 4. a 5. d 6. f 7. b 8. c
Actividades analíticas: 2. **yo:** estaré; **tú:** serás; **él/ella, Ud.:** estará;
nosotros/as: viviremos; **ellos/ellas, Uds.:** serán

Capítulo 15

Estructura 15.1

Reciclaje: 1. b, Erradicaremos 2. e, Haremos 3. f, Resolveremos 4. a, Acabaremos
5. d, Mejoraremos 6. c, Conseguiremos **Para empezar:** 1. g 2. a 3. h 4. e
5. c 6. i 7. d 8. f 9. b *impossible:* f, h **Actividades analíticas:**
2. **yo:** pasaría, iría; **tú:** serías; **él/ella, Ud.:** iría; **nosotros/as:** pasaríamos, seríamos;
vosotros/as: iríais; **ellos/ellas, Uds.:** serían

Estructura 15.2

Reciclaje: *Querían que...:* los niños pudieran asistir a la escuela sin pagar; la
esclavitud ya no existiera; las mujeres tuvieran el derecho de votar; los trabajadores
descansaran dos días a la semana; toda la gente tuviera la libertad de practicar su
religión; *No querían que...:* creciera la desigualdad económica; hubiera guerras; la
corrupción estuviera presente en el sistema jurídico. **Para empezar:** **Paso 1.** a.
4 b. 2 c. 6 d. 5 e. 1 f. 3 **Paso 2.** Cierto **Actividades analíticas:** 1. b. fuera,
importarían c. funcionara, tendrían d. pudieran, funcionaría e. usara, sería f.
importara, ganaría 2. **Si...:** past subjunctive / imperfecto de subjuntivo;
Consecuencia: conditional/condicional

Capítulo 16

Estructura 16.1

Reciclaje: **caminar:** camina, caminan; **correr:** corro, corres, corre, corremos;
sacudir: sacudes, sacudimos, sacuden; **volver:** vuelves, vuelve, volvemos, volvéis,
vuelven; **pedir:** pido, pide, pedimos, pedís, piden; **pensar:** pienso, piensa, pensamos,
pensáis, piensan; **ser:** soy eres, somos, sois, son; **salir:** salgo, sale, salís, salen;
casarse: te casas, se casa, se casan

Estructura 16.2

Reciclaje: **Paso 1. hablar:** habló, hablaron; **aprender:** aprendí, aprendimos,
aprendieron; **llegar:** llegué, llegaste, llegamos, llegasteis; **ir/ser:** fui, fue, fuimos,
fueron; **decir:** dijiste, dijimos, dijeron; **hacer:** hice, hizo, hicimos, hicisteis, hicieron;
tener: tuve, tuviste, tuvo, tuvimos, tuvisteis, tuvieron; **dormirse:** me dormí, te
dormiste, se durmió, nos dormimos, se durmieron; **Paso 2. amar:** amaba, amaba,
amaban; **comer:** comías, comía, comíamos, comían; **salir:** salía, salía, salíamos,
salían; **irse:** me iba, te ibas, se iba, nos íbamos, se iban; **ser:** era, era, éramos, eran

Estructura 16.3

Reciclaje: 2. c 3. e 4. f 5. a 6. d; a. Le c. Te d. Los e. lo f. Lo

Estructura 16.4

Reciclaje: **amar:** ames, ama, améis, amen; **casarse:** te cases, se case, se casen;
volver: vuelvas, vuelva, volvamos, volváis, vuelvan; **hacer:** haga, haga, hagan; **ser:**
sea, seas, sea, seamos, seáis, sean; **tener:** tengas, tenga, tengamos, tengáis, tengan

VOCABULARIO

The following abbreviations are used:

adj. adjective	*inf.* infinitive	*poss.* possessive
adv. adverb	*inform.* informal	*p.p.* past participle
Arg. Argentina	*interj.* interjection	*P.R.* Puerto Rico
C.A. Central America	*inv.* invariable form	*prep.* preposition
Carib. Caribbean	*i.o.* indirect object	*pres. p.* present participle
conj. conjunction	*L.Am.* Latin America	*pron.* pronoun
def. art. definite article	*m.* masculine	*refl. pron.* reflexive pronoun
d.o. direct object	*Mex.* Mexico	*s.* singular
f. feminine	*n.* noun	*S.A.* South America
form. formal	*obj. (of prep.)* object (of a	*sl.* slang
gram. grammatical term	preposition)	*Sp.* Spain
ind. art. indefinite article	*pl.* plural	*sub. pron.* subject pronoun

Spanish-English Vocabulary

A

a to (1); at (*with time*); **a base de** based on; **a continuación** following; below; **a escondidas** secretly; **a favor (de)** in favor (of); **a fondo** in depth; **a la plancha** grilled (6); **a la(s)...** at . . . (*time of day*); **a largo plazo** long-term, in the long-term; **a lo largo de** along, throughout; **a mano** by hand; **a mano derecha** on the right; **a mano izquierda** on the left; **a partir de** as of, since; **a pesar de** in spite of, despite; **a pie** on foot; **¿a qué hora... ?** at what time . . . ? (3); **¿a qué se dedica?** what do you (*form. s.*) do (*occupation*)? (4); **¿a qué te dedicas?** what do you (*inform. s.*) do (*occupation*)? (4); **a raíz de** as a result of; **a sus órdenes** at your service; **a ver** let's see; **al aire libre** outdoors; **al ajillo** sautéed with garlic (6); **al cabo de** at the end of; **al contrario** on the contrary; **al final** in the end; **al igual que** just like; **es a la/las...** it's at . . . (3); **está/queda a la derecha** it's on the right/left (5); **está/queda al lado de...** it's beside . . . (5); **voy a/al +** *place* I'm going to . . . (2)

abajo below; underneath
abandonar to abandon
abarrotería grocery store
abarrotes: tienda de abarrotes grocery store
abastecedor *m.* grocery store
abastos: tienda de abastos grocery store
abatible moveable
abierto/a (*p.p. of* **abrir**) open (16)
abogado/a lawyer (4)
abolir to abolish
abono fertilizer

abordar to board (9)
abrazo hug, embrace; **dar** (*irreg.*) **un abrazo** to hug
abrigado/a bundled up
abrigo coat (8)
abril *m.* April (1)
abrir (*p.p.* **abierto**) to open (6)
absoluto/a absolute
abuelo/a grandfather/grandmother (4); *pl.* grandparents (4)
abulón *m.* (*pl.* **abulones**) abalone
abundar to abound, be plentiful
aburrido/a (*with* **estar**) bored (2); (*with* **ser**) boring (2); **¡qué aburrido!** how boring! (8)
acá *adv.* here
acabado impermeable waterproof finish
acabar to finish; to run out of; **acabar de +** *inf.* to have just (*done something*)
academia academy
académico/a academic
acampar to camp
acaso: por si acaso just in case
accesible accessible
acceso access
accesorio accessory (8)
accidente *m.* accident
acción *f.* action; **Día** (*m.*) **de Acción de Gracias** Thanksgiving; **película de acción** action movie
aceite *m.* oil (6); **aceite de oliva** olive oil
acentuar (ú) to accentuate
aceptar to accept
acerca de *prep.* about, concerning, regarding side dish (*food*)
acompañar to accompany; **te/le/les acompaño/acompañamos en el dolor** I'm/we're with you (*inform. s. / form. s. / form. pl.*) in your time of pain (16); **te/le/**

les acompaño/acompañamos en el sentimiento you're (*inform. s. / form. s. / form. pl.*) in my/our thoughts (16)
aconsejable advisable
aconsejar to advise
acontecimiento event, happening
acordarse (ue) (de) to remember (5)
acorde (con) in agreement (with)
acostarse (ue) to go to bed (5)
acostumbrado/a (a) accustomed, used (to)
actitud *f.* attitude
actividad *f.* activity
activista *m., f.* activist
activo/a active (2); **llevar una vida activa** to lead an active life
acto act
actor *m.* actor (14)
actriz *f.* (*pl.* **actrices**) actress (14)
actuación *f.* acting; performance
actual *adj.* current, present-day
actuar (actúo) to act (14)
acudir (a) to go (to)
acuerdo agreement; **(no) estar** (*irreg.*) **de acuerdo** to (dis)agree
adecuado/a appropriate
adelante forward; **¡adelante!** go for it! / let's go! / you can do it! (12)
además *adv.* moreover; **además de** *prep.* besides
adentro inside; **mar adentro** off-shore
adicional additional
adiós good-bye (1)
adivinanza riddle
adivinar to guess
adjetivo *gram.* adjective
adjuntar to attach (10)
administración *f.* administration; **administración de empresas** business

administration; **administración de negocios** business administration; **administración de restaurantes** restaurant management

administrar to manage

administrativo/a administrative; **asistente** (*m., f.*) **administrativo/a** administrative assistant (10)

admirar to admire

adolescencia adolescence

adolescente *m., f.* adolescent

¿adónde? where to? (2); **¿adónde va?** where are you (*form.*) going? (2); **¿adónde vas?** where are you (*inform.*) going? (2)

adopción *f.* adoption

adoptar to adopt

adquirir (ie) to acquire

adquisición *f.* acquisition

aduana customs (*at a border*); **agente** (*m., f.*) **de aduanas** customs agent

adulto/a *n., adj.* adult

aeróbico: hacer (*irreg.*) **ejercicio aeróbico** to do aerobics

aerolínea airline

aeropuerto airport (9)

afán *m.* desire, zeal

afectar to affect

afeitarse to shave (5)

aficionado/a fan (12); **ser** (*irreg.*) **aficionado/a (a)** to be a fan (of)

afirmación *f.* statement

afortunado/a lucky

africano/a *n., adj.* African

afrontar to face, confront

afro-uruguayo/a Afro-Uruguayan

afuera *adv.* outdoors

afueras *n. pl.* outskirts; suburbs (5)

agarrar to grab

agave *m.* agave

agavero: alambre (*m.*) **agavero** *dish which features an agave stock on a plate of rice with banana, chicken or beef, and melted cheese*

agencia agency; **agencia de prensa** press agency; **agencia de seguros** insurance agency; **agencia de talentos** talent agency; **agencia de viajes** travel agency

agente *m., f.* agent; **agente de aduanas** customs agent; **agente de bienes raíces** real estate agent (10); **agente de seguros** insurance agent (10); **agente de viajes** travel agent

agosto August (1)

agotador(a) exhausting

agotamiento exhaustion (13); depletion (13)

agotar to sell out; to exhaust; to deplete

agradable pleasant (9)

agradecer (zc) to thank; **te/le/les agradezco por** I appreciate that you, I thank you for (5)

agradecimiento thanks

agregar (gu) to add

agresivo/a aggressive

agrícola *adj. m., f.* agricultural

agricultor(a) farmer

agricultura agriculture

agroeconomista *m., f.* agroeconomist

agua *f.* (*but* **el agua**) water (6); **agua salada** salt water; **botella de agua** water bottle; **caída de agua** waterfall

aguacate *m.* avocado

aguacero rain shower; downpour

aguadulce *m. typical Costa Rican drink*

aguantar to withstand

ahí there

ahogar (gu) to drown

ahora now; **ahorita** right now

ahorrar to save (13); **ahorrar agua/ electricidad/dinero** to save water/ electricity/money (13)

aimara *m.* Aymara (*language*)

aire *m.* air (13); **al aire libre** outdoors; **contaminación** (*f.*) **del aire** air pollution

ají *m.* chili pepper

ajillo: al ajillo sautéed with garlic (6)

ala *f.* (*but* **el ala**) wing

alambre (*m.*) **agavero** *dish which features an agave stock on a plate of rice with banana, chicken or beef, and melted cheese*

alarmante alarming

alavés, alavesa *n., adj.* from Álava, Spain

albergar (gu) to shelter

albergue *m.* hotel

álbum *m.* album

alcance *m.* reach; **al alcance** within reach

alcanzar (c) to reach; to achieve

alcohólico/a alcoholic

alegrarse (de) to be happy (about)

alegre happy (2)

alegría happiness

alemán *m.* German (*language*)

alemán (*pl.* **alemanes**), **alemana** *n., adj.* German

Alemania Germany

alergia allergy (12); **tener** (*irreg.*) **alergia a** to be allergic to (12)

alérgico/a allergic

alfabetismo literacy

alfabetización *f.* literacy (15); teaching of literacy (15)

alfombra rug

algo something (5); anything

algodón *m.* cotton

alguien someone (5); anyone

algún (alguna/os/as) some (5); any; **algún día** someday; **alguna vez** once; ever; **de alguna manera** in some way; **en algún momento** at some point

aliada *m., f.* ally

alimentar(se) to feed

alimenticio/a food; **cadena alimenticia** food chain

alimento food, foodstuff

alineación *f.* alignment

alistarse to enlist

allá (way) over there

allí there

alma *f.* (*but* **el alma**) soul

almacén *m.* (*pl.* **almacenes**) warehouse; department store (5)

almacenamiento storage

almohada pillow

almorzar (ue) (c) to eat lunch (3)

almuerzo lunch; **preparar el almuerzo** to prepare lunch (4)

aló hello (*telephone greeting*)

alojamiento lodging

alojarse to lodge, stay (hotel)

alpinismo mountaineering; **hacer** (*irreg.*) **alpinismo** to do/go mountaineering/ mountain climbing (12)

alpinista *m., f.* mountain climber

alpino/a Alpine

alquilar to rent

alquiler *m.* rent

alrededor (de) around

altar *m.* altar

alterado/a altered

alternativa alternative

alternativo/a alternative (14)

altiplano high plateau

alto/a tall (2); **alta costura** haute couture; **en voz alta** out loud; **más alto que** taller than (4); **menos alto que** less tall than (4); **tacones** (*m. pl.*) **altos** high-heeled shoes

altura height (12)

alumno/a student

alzar (c) to raise, lift up

amable friendly

amanecer (zc) *m.* dawn

amante *m., f.* lover

amar to love (16)

amarillo yellow (2)

Amazonas *m. s.* Amazon (River)

ambicioso/a ambitious

ambiental environmental

ambiente *m.* atmosphere; environment; **medio ambiente** environment (13)

ambos/as both

amenazar (c) to threaten

americano/a American; **fútbol** (*m.*) **americano** football (12); **jugar (ue) (gu) fútbol americano** to play football (12)

amigo/a friend (1)

aminoácido amino acid

amistad *f.* friendship (16)

amo/a master/mistress; **amo/a de casa** homemaker

amor *m.* love (16); **canción** (*f.*) **de amor** love song; **Día** (*m.*) **del Amor** Valentine's Day

amplio/a broad

analfabetismo illiteracy (15)

analfabetización *f.* illiteracy

anaranjado/a orange (2)

ancho/a wide (8)

andar *irreg.* to walk; **¡ándale!** come on! *command inform. s.*; **¡ándele!** come on! *command form. s.*; **andar en bicicleta/bici** to ride a bicycle (2); **andar en patineta** to skateboard (12); **¿cómo anda?** how's it going (*inform. s.*)? (1)

andino/a Andean

anécdota anecdote

anexo attachment (10)

anglohablante *m., f.* English speaker

anglosajón (*pl.* **anglosajones**), **anglosajona** Anglo Saxon

angustia distress; worry

anhelar to long, yearn for

anidar to nest

anillo ring (8)

animación *f.* animation

animado/a lively (2)

animal *m.* animal (13); **animal doméstico** pet

¡ánimo! keep your spirits high! / give it all you've got! / don't give up! (12)

aniversario anniversary

anoche last night

anotación *f.* score

anotar to note

ansioso/a anxious (2)

Antártida Antarctica

antepasado/a ancestor

anterior before

antes *adv.* before (1); **antes de** *prep.* before (1); **antes (de) que** *conj.* before

antes *prep.* before; in front of

antibiótico antibiotic

anticipar to anticipate

antigüedad antiquity

antiguo/a old (5)

antillano/a Antillean (from the Antilles or West Indies)

antioxidante *m.* antioxidant

antipático/a disagreeable (2)

antojarse + *inf.* to feel like (*doing something*) (9); + *n.* to have a craving for (*something*) (9); **se me/te/le/nos/os/les antoja/antojó** + *inf.* I / you (*inform. s.*) / he, she, you (*form. s.*) / we / you (*inform. pl.*) / they, you (*form. pl.*) feel, feels / felt like + ([*doing*] something) (9); **se me/te/le/nos/os/les antoja/antojó** + *s. n.* I / you (*inform. s.*) / he, she, you (*form. s.*) / we / you (*inform. pl.*) / they, you (*form. pl.*) have, has / had a craving for (*something*); **se me/te/le/nos/os/les antojan/antojaron** + *pl. n.* I / you (*inform. s.*) / he, she, you (*form. s.*) / we / you (*inform. pl.*) / they, you (*form. pl.*) have, has / had a craving for (*something*)

antojito appetizer

antónimo antonym

antro nightclub

anunciar to announce

anuncio ad; commercial

añadir to add

año year (1); **Año Nuevo** New Year's (7); **año pasado** last year; **cumplir... años** to turn . . . years old (7); **¿cuántos años tienes?** how old are you (*inform.*)? (2); **¿cuántos años tiene?** how old are you (*form.*)? (2); **este año** this year; **tener** (*irreg.*)... **años** to be . . . years old; **tengo** + *number* + **años** I'm + *number* years old (2)

apagar (gu) to turn off

aparato appliance

aparcar (qu) to park

aparecer (zc) to appear

apartamento apartment (5)

aparte: aparte de in addition to; **hoja de papel aparte** separate sheet of paper

apellido last name; **mi apellido es** my last name is (1)

apenas barely

aperitivo appetizer

apetecer (zc) (*like* **gustar**) to appeal to

aplastar to flatten

aplicación *f.* application

aplicar (qu) to apply

apodo nickname

apoyar to support

apoyo support

apreciación *f.* appreciation

apreciar to appreciate

aprender (a) to learn (to) (6)

apretado/a tight (8)

apropiado/a appropriate

aprovechar to take advantage of

aproximadamente approximately

apuntar to write down; **apuntarse** to enroll; to add one's name to the list

apuntes *m. pl.* notes (*academic*)

apurarse to hurry

apuro hurry

aquel, aquella that ([way] over there)

aquello that ([way] over there)

aquellos/as those ([way] over there)

aquí here (2)

árabe *m.* Arabic (*language*); *n., adj. m., f.* Arab

árbol *m.* tree (5); **árbol de Navidad** Christmas tree; **copa de los árboles** top of the trees; **tala de árboles** tree cutting (13)

archivo document; file

arcilla clay

ardor *m.* ardor

área *f.* (*but* **el área**) area, region

arena sand

arepa *fried bread made of cornmeal*

argentino/a *n., adj.* Argentine (2)

argumentar to argue

argumento argument (*legal*); plot

arma *f.* (*but* **el arma**) weapon

armado/a armed

armario armoire, closet (11)

armonía harmony

aro hoop; ring

arqueológico/a archeological

arquitecto/a architect (10)

arquitectura architecture (1)

arrecife *m.* reef

arreglar to arrange

arroba @ (at, *in an email address*) (1)

arroz *m.* rice (6); **arroz con leche** rice pudding; **arroz graneado** *fried rice dish*

arruinar to ruin

arte *m.* (*but* **las artes**) art (14); **bellas artes** fine arts; **obra de arte** piece, work of art (14)

artesanal handcrafted; traditional

artesanía craft(s) (9)

artículo article

artificial artificial; **fuegos artificiales** fireworks (7)

artista *m., f.* artist

artístico/a artistic

asado barbecue, cookout

asado/a roast(ed) (6)

asamblea assembly

ascender (ie) to climb

ascensor *m.* elevator (9)

ascetismo asceticism

asegurar to assure

asequible accessible

asfalto asphalt

así thus; so; **así como** as well as; **así que** therefore, consequently, so

asiático/a Asian

asistente *m., f.* (**administrativo/a**) (administrative) assistant (10)

asistir (a) to attend (3); to go to (*a class, function*)

asma *m.* asthma (12)

asociación *f.* association

aspecto aspect; **tener** (*irreg.*) **buen aspecto** to look good

aspiración *f.* goal

aspiradora vacuum cleaner (11); **pasar la aspiradora** to vacuum (11)

asqueroso/a disgusting

astronauta *m., f.* astronaut

astronómico/a astronomical

asumir to assume

asunto matter; subject (10)

asustar to frighten

atacar (qu) to attack

atar to tie

atención *f.* attention; **poner** (*irreg.*) **atención** to pay attention; **prestar atención** to pay attention

atender (ie) (a) to serve, wait on; to care for

atentamente sincerely (10)

atlántico/a Atlantic; **océano Atlántico** Atlantic Ocean

atleta *m., f.* athlete (12)

atlético/a athletic

atletismo athleticism

atmósfera atmosphere (13)

atracción *f.* attraction (9)

atractivo attraction

atractivo/a attractive
atraer (*like* **traer**) to draw, attract
atrás *adv.* back, backward; behind
atrevido/a daring
atrocidad *f.* atrocity
atún *m.* tuna (6)
audífonos *pl.* headphones
aula *f.* (*but* **el aula**) classroom (1)
aumentar to increase
aumento increase; gain; **aumento de peso** weight gain
aun *adv.* even
aún *adv.* still, yet
aunque although
austral southern
autobús *m.* (*pl.* **autobuses**) bus (5)
autóctono/a indigenous
automático/a automatic
autónoma autonomous
autor(a) author; **violación** (*f.*) **de los derechos del autor** copyright violation
autoridad *f.* authority
autorización *f.* authorization
avanzar (c) to advance
avenida avenue (5)
aventura adventure; **turismo de aventura** adventure tourism
aventurero/a adventurous
averiguar to verify
avión *m.* (*pl.* **aviones**) airplane (9)
avisar to warn
¡ay! *interj.* ah!; oh!; ouch!
ayer yesterday
ayuda help
ayudar to help (13)
azotea roof terrace
azteca *n., adj. m., f.* Aztec
azúcar *m.* sugar (6)
azul blue (2)

B

bacalao codfish, cod
bahía bay
bailar to dance (2)
bailarín (*pl.* **bailarines**), **bailarina** dancer (14)
baile *m.* dance (14)
bajar to lower; to download (10); to go down; to get off (*transportation*); **bajar de peso** to lose weight (12); **baje (por esta calle)** go down (this street) (*command form. s.*) (5)
bajo/a short (2); **Países** (*m. pl.*) **Bajos** Netherlands; **planta baja** ground floor (11)
balada ballad
balcón *m.* (*pl.* **balcones**) balcony
ballena whale (13)
ballet *m.* ballet (14)
baloncesto basketball
balsa raft
banca bank
bancario/a banking

banco bank (5)
banda band (14)
bandeja tray, platter
bandera flag (2)
bañarse to bathe (oneself) (5); to take a bath
bañera bathtub (11)
baño bathroom (11); **cuarto de baño** bathroom (11); **traje** (*m.*) **de baño** bathing suit (8)
barato/a cheap (2)
bárbaro/a: ¡qué bárbaro! how cool! (8)
barca small boat
barranca ravine
barrer to sweep (11)
barrio neighborhood
basarse (en) to base one's ideas/opinions (on)
base *f.* base; **a base de** based on; **base de datos** data base
básico/a basic
básquetbol *m.* basketball; **jugar (ue) básquetbol** to play basketball (3)
bastante rather, sufficiently; enough
bastar to be enough
bastón *m.* (*pl.* **bastones**) cane, walking stick
basura trash; **correo basura** junk mail; **no tirar basura** no littering (*lit. do not throw trash*) (9); **sacar (qu) la basura** to take out the trash (11)
basurero/a trash collector
bata robe
batalla battle
batata sweet potato
batidora mixer; blender
bautizar (c) to baptize
bautizo baptism (7)
baya berry
bebé *m., f.* baby
beber to drink; **no beber y conducir** don't drink and drive (9)
bebida beverage; drink (6)
béisbol *m.* baseball (12); **jugar (ue) (gu) béisbol** to play baseball (12)
beisbolista *m., f.* baseball player
belga *n., adj. m., f.* Belgian
Bélgica Belgium
belleza beauty
bello/a pretty (2)
bendecido/a blessed
bendición *f.* blessing
benefactor(a) benefactor
beneficiar to benefit
beneficio benefit
berro watercress
besar to kiss
biblioteca library (1)
bici bike; **andar** (*irreg.*) **en bici** to ride a bike (2)
bicicleta bicycle; **andar** (*irreg.*) **en bicicleta** to ride a bicycle (2); **bicicleta de montaña** mountain bike (9); **correr en bicicleta** to ride a bicycle

bien *adv.* well; **(muy) bien** (very) well (1); **lo pasé bien** I had a good time (7); **(no) encontrarse bien** to (not) feel well (12); **pasarlo bien** to have a good time (7); **¡qué bien!** how cool! (8); **que le(s) vaya bien** have a good one / I hope things go well for you (*form. s., pl.*) (12)
bienes raíces *m. pl.* real estate; **agente** (*m., f.*) **de bienes raíces** real estate agent
bienestar *m.* well-being
bienvenida *n.* welcome; **dar** (*irreg.*) **la bienvenida** to welcome (11); **¡le damos la bienvenida a Ud.!** we welcome you (*form. s.*)! (11)
¡bienvenido/a(s)! *adj.* welcome! (11); **ser** (*irreg.*) **bienvenido/a/os/as** to be welcome (11); **usted es (siempre) bienvenido/a** you (*form. s.*) are always welcome (11)
bife *m.* steak
bilingüe bilingual
biodiversidad *f.* biodiversity
biografía biography
biología biology (1)
biólogo/a biologist
birria goat meal
bisabuelo/a great-grandfather/great-grandmother (4)
bisturí *m.* scalpel
bitácora digital blog
blanco/a white (2); **espacio en blanco** blank space; **línea en blanco** blank; **vino blanco** white wine (6)
blog *m.* blog
bloguear to blog
bloguero/a blogger (10)
bloqueador (*m.*) **solar** sunscreen
blusa blouse (8)
boca mouth (8)
bocado taste
boda wedding (7); **boda civil** civil ceremony (*wedding*)
bodega grocery store (*Carib.*)
bofetada slap; **dar** (*irreg.*) **una bofetada** to slap
bol *m.* bowl (6)
bola ball
boleto ticket (9)
boliche *m.* bowling
bolígrafo pen (1)
boliviano/a *n., adj.* Bolivian (2)
bolsa bag
bolsillo pocket
bolso purse (8)
bombero, mujer (*f.*) **bombero** firefighter (10)
bonito/a pretty (2); **¡qué bonita familia!** what a beautiful family! (4)
bordado/a embroidered
borracho/a drunk
borrador *m.* eraser (1)
bosque *m.* forest; **bosque tropical** rainforest (9)
bosquejo outline

botas boots

bote *m.* boat

botella bottle; **botella de agua** water bottle

botica pharmacy

botón *m.* (*pl.* **botones**) button

boxear to box (12)

boxeo boxing

boyante prosperous

brazo arm (8)

Bretaña: Gran Bretaña Great Britain

breve *adj.* brief

brindis *m. s., pl.* toast (7)

británico/a *n., adj.* British

brócoli *m.* broccoli (6)

bronce *m.* bronze

bucear to scuba dive

budista *n., adj. m., f.* Buddhist

buen, bueno/a good (2); **buen día** good morning (1); **¡buen provecho!** enjoy your meal! (6); **¡buena suerte!** good luck! (12); best of luck! (12); **buenas noches** good evening/night (1); **buenas tardes** good afternoon (1); **buenos días** good morning (1); **dar** (*irreg.*) **buena suerte** to bring good luck; **hace (muy) buen tiempo** the weather's (very) good (9); **pasar un buen rato** to have a good time; **¡qué buena idea!** what a good idea!; **¡que tenga(s) un buen día / fin de semana!** have (*form. s. / inform. s.*) a good day/weekend!; **¡que tenga(s) una buena tarde!** have (*form. s. / inform. s.*) a nice afternoon!; **sacar (qu) buenas notas** to get good grades; **tener** (*irreg.*) **buen aspecto** to look good; **tener** (*irreg.*) **buena/mala pinta** to have a good/bad appearance

bufanda scarf (8)

bus *m.* bus

buscador (*m.*) search engine (10)

buscar (qu) to look for (8)

búsqueda search

C

caballero gentleman

caballo horse; **montar a caballo** to ride a horse (3)

cabecera: médico/a de cabecera primary care physician

cabello hair

cabeza head (8)

cable *m.* cable

cabo: al cabo de at the end of; **llevarse a cabo** to carry out

cada *inv.* each, every; **cada vez más** increasingly

cadena chain; **cadena alimenticia** food chain

cadera hip (8)

caer *irreg.* to fall; **caer en** to fall on (*day of the week*); **caerse** to fall down (9)

café *m.* coffee; café, coffee shop; *adj.* brown (2)

cafeína caffeine

caída de agua waterfall

caja box

cajero/a cashier (10); teller

calamares *m. pl.* squid (6)

calavera skull

calcetines *m. pl.* socks (8)

calculadora calculator

calcular to calculate

cálculos figures

caldo broth, clear soup (6)

calendario calendar

calentamiento global global warming (13)

calidad *f.* quality

cálido/a warm, hot (9)

caliente hot

calificar (qu) (a) to qualify (for)

callado/a quiet

calle *f.* street (5); **baje/suba (por esta calle)** go down/up (this street) (*command form. s.*) (5)

calor *m.* heat; **hace calor** it's hot (9); **¡qué calor!** it's so hot! (4)

calvo/a bald

calzón *m.* underwear (8); **calzones** *pl.* underwear (8)

cama bed (11); **hacer** (*irreg.*) **la cama** to make the bed (11)

cámara camera

camarero/a waiter, waitress (6); server (6)

camarones *m. pl.* shrimp (6)

cambiar to change (12); **cambiar cheques** to cash checks

cambio change (12); **cambio climático** climate change

caminar to walk (3)

caminata *n.* walk, hike

camino road; path; **por el camino** on the way

camión *m.* bus

camisa shirt (8)

camiseta t-shirt (8)

campana: pantalones (*m. pl.*) **de campana** bell-bottom pants

campanada peal

campaña campaign

campeón (*pl.* **campeones**), **campeona** champion

campeonato championship

camping: hacer (*irreg.*) **camping** to go camping

campismo camping

campo field; countryside, rural area (5)

campus *m.* campus

Canadá *m.* Canada

canadiense *n., adj. m., f.* Canadian (2)

canal *m.* canal

canas: tener (*irreg.*) **canas** to have gray hair

cancelar to cancel

cáncer *m.* cancer

cancha (athletic) field, court

canción *f.* song (14); **canción de amor** love song

candidato/a candidate

candombé *m. Afro-Uruguayan music and dance*

canguro kangaroo

cano/a gray-haired

cansado/a tired (2)

cantante *m., f.* singer (14)

cantar to sing (3)

cantautor(a) singer-songwriter

cantidad *f.* quantity

canto singing

cañón *m.* (*pl.* **cañones**) canyon

caótico/a chaotic

capa layer

capacitado/a trained

capital *f.* capital city (5)

capitalismo capitalism

capitán (*pl.* **capitanes**), **capitana** captain

capítulo chapter

caqui: color caqui khaki

cara face (8); **lavarse la cara** to wash one's face (5); **¡qué cara!** what nerve!

característica characteristic

caracterizar (c) to characterize

caramelo candy

carbohidrato carbohydrate

carbón *m.* coal

carga cargo

cargador *m.* charger

cargar (gu) to charge; to load; **cargar con** to take on (responsibility)

cargo (political) office; **estar** (*irreg.*) **a cargo (de)** to be in charge (of)

Caribe *m.* Caribbean; **mar** (*m.*) **Caribe** Caribbean Sea

caribeño/a *n., adj.* Caribbean

cariño affection

cariñoso/a affectionate (16)

Carnaval *m.* Carnival (*the festivities in the days preceding Lent*) (7)

carne *f.* (red) meat (6); **carne de puerco** pork (6); **carne de res** beef (6)

carnicería butcher shop (5)

carnitas *Mexican dish made of roasted pork that is sautéed till browned*

caro/a expensive (2)

carpa tent

carrera major (field of study); career; race (12); **carrera de fondo** long-distance race; **¿cuál es tu carrera?** what's your major? (1); **¿cuál es tu correo electrónico?** what is your email (address)? **¿cuál es tu (dirección de) email?** what is your email (address)? (1); **¿cuál es tu número de teléfono?** what is your phone number? (1)

carretera highway (5)

carril *m.* lane

carta letter; menu (6)

casa house (2); **ama** (*f., but* **el ama**) **de casa** housewife (4)

casado/a married (16)

casamiento marriage

casarse (con) to get married (to) (16)

cascada waterfall

cáscara shell; peel

cascarón shell

casco helmet (12)

casi *inv.* almost

caso case; **en caso de que** *conj.* in case

casona mansion

casquete *m.* **(polar)** (polar) ice cap

castaño/a brown (2)

catador(a) taster

catarata waterfall (9)

catedral *f.* cathedral (5)

categoría category

categorizar (c) to categorize

catire fair-skinned, fair-haired (*Carib.*)

católico/a Catholic

catorce fourteen

causa cause (13)

causar to cause (13)

cauteloso/a cautious

caverna cavern

cazar (c) to hunt

cazatalentos *inv.* talent scout

cebolla onion (6)

celebración *f.* celebration

celebrar to celebrate (7)

celebridad *f.* celebrity

celeste heavenly; **color** (*m.*) **celeste** light blue

celos: tener (*irreg.*) **celos** to be jealous

celoso/a jealous (16)

celular: (teléfono) celular cell phone

cementerio cemetery

cena dinner; **preparar la cena** to prepare dinner (4)

cenar to eat dinner (3)

censura censorship

centenar *m.* hundred

centígrado/a *adj.* Celsius, centigrade

central central

centro center (5); downtown (5); **centro estudiantil** student center, student union

Centroamérica Central America

centroamericano/a *n., adj.* Central American

cepillarse los dientes to brush one's teeth (5)

cepillo de dientes toothbrush

cerca *adv.* near, nearby, close; **cerca de** close/near to (9)

cereal *m.* cereal

ceremonia ceremony

cerrar (ie) to close (6)

cerro hill

cerveza beer (6)

césped *m.* lawn, grass

ceviche *m. raw fish dish*

chacra small farm

chala husk

chamo kid

champán *m.* champagne (7)

champiñones *m. pl.* mushrooms (6)

chaqueta jacket (8)

charco puddle

charcutería delicatessen

charlar to chat

charrería horsemanship (*Mex.*)

chau good-bye (1); **chau chau** goodbye (1)

cheque *m.* check; **cambiar cheques** to cash checks; **cobrar un cheque** to cash a check

chévere cool; **¡qué chévere!** how cool! (8)

chicle *m.* gum

chico/a *n.* guy/girl; *adj.* small (2)

chido/a cool; **¡qué chido!** how cool! (8)

chilaquiles *m. pl. Mexican dish of fried tortilla pieces simmered in salsa or mole and served with cheese and sour cream*

chile *m.* chili pepper (6)

chileno/a *n., adj.* Chilean (2)

chillar to bawl

chimichurri *green sauce used for grilled meat (Arg.)*

chino/a *n.* Chinese person; *adj.* Chinese

chirimoya cherimoya fruit

chispa spark

chistoso/a funny

chivo goat

chocar (qu) con to run into; to bump against

chocolate *m.* chocolate

chofer *m., f.* driver (4)

chorizo sausage (6)

chulo/a cool (*Sp.*); **¡qué chulo!** how cool! (*Sp.*) (8)

chutar to shoot (*a soccer ball*) (*Sp.*)

ciclismo cycling; **hacer** (*irreg.*) **ciclismo de montaña** to go mountain biking (9)

ciclista *m., f.* cyclist

ciclón *m.* (*pl.* **ciclones**) hurricane

ciego/a *adj.* blind; **cita a ciegas** blind date (16)

cielo sky; heaven

cien one hundred (5)

ciencia science (1); **ciencias políticas** political science (1)

científico/a scientific

ciento one hundred (*used with* 101–199) (5); **por ciento** percent

cierto/a true

cigarrillo cigarette

cinco five; **cinco mil** five thousand (5)

cincuenta fifty; **son las ocho y cincuenta** it's 8:50 (3)

cine *m.* movies (2); movie theater (2); film (*in general*) (2)

cineasta *m., f.* filmmaker

cinematográfico/a *adj.* movie, film

cinta film, movie

cintura waist

cinturón *m.* (*pl.* **cinturones**) belt (8)

circuito circuit

circulación hallway

circular to circulate

círculo circle

circunstancia circumstance

ciruela plum

cirugía surgery

cirujano/a surgeon (10)

cita appointment; date (16); **cita a ciegas** blind date (16)

ciudad *f.* city (5)

ciudadano/a citizen

civil civil; **boda civil** civil ceremony (*wedding*); **estado civil** marital status (16); **guerra civil** civil war

civilización *f.* civilization

¡claro que sí! *interj.* of course! (6)

claro/a clear

clase *f.* class (*of students*) (1); class, course (*academic*) (1); **compañero/a de clase** classmate; **salón** (*m.*) **de clase** classroom (1)

clásico/a classic(al) (14)

clasificación *f.* classification

clave *n. f., adj.* key

clic: hacer clic to click

cliente *m., f.* customer

clima *m.* climate; weather

climático/a *adj.* climate; **cambio climático** climate change

climatización *f.* air conditioning

clínica clinic

clóset *m.* (*pl.* **closets**) closet

cobrar un cheque to cash a check

cobre *m.* copper

coche *m.* car (5)

cochi *Nahuatl word meaning* to sleep

cochinillo roast suckling pig (*dish*)

cocina kitchen (11); cuisine

cocinar to cook (3)

cocinero/a cook; chef

codiciado/a sought-after

codo elbow (8)

coger (j) to take (*transportation*) (*Sp.*); **coger a mano derecha/izquierda** to turn right/left (*Sp.*)

cognado *gram.* cognate

cohombro cucumber (*P.R.*)

coincidir to coincide

cola line (*of people*)

colaborar to collaborate

colar (ue) to strain (*liquid*)

colchón *m.* (*pl.* **colchones**) mattress

colección *f.* collection

coleccionar to collect

colectivo bus

colega *m., f.* co-worker, colleague

colegio high school

cólera cholera

colesterol cholesterol

colibrí *m.* (*pl.* **colibríes**) hummingbird

colina hill

collar *m.* necklace (8)

colmado small grocery store (*Carib.*)

colocar (qu) to place

colombiano *n., adj.* Colombian (2)

colonia colony; neighborhood (*Mex.*)

color *m.* color; **color caqui** khaki; **color celeste** light blue; **color verde oliva**

olive green; **¿de qué color es?** what color is it? (2)

columna column

com: punto com dot com (*in an email address*) (1)

comadre *f. godmother of one's child* (4); *mother of one's godchild*

comandante *m., f.* commander

comarca region

combatir to fight

combinación *f.* combination

combinar to combine

combustibles *(m. pl.)* **fósiles** fossil fuels

comedia comedy; **comedia musical** musical (*play*)

comedor dining room (11); dining hall

comentar (sobre) to comment (on)

comentario comment

comentarista *m., f.* news anchor

comenzar (ie) (c) to begin; **comenzar a +** *inf.* to begin to + *inf.*

comer to eat (3); **come/coma más** have some more (*command inform. s. / form. s.*) (11); **comer comida mexicana** to eat Mexican food (3); **dar** (*irreg.*) **de comer** to feed; **no dar** (*irreg.*) **de comer** don't feed (*animals*) (9)

comercialización *f.* commercialization

comercializar (c) to commercialize

comestibles *m. pl.* groceries, food (6); **comestibles empaquetados/enlatados** packaged/canned goods (6)

cometer to commit; **cometer un error** to make a mistake

cómico/a funny

comida food (3); (midday) meal (3); **comer comida mexicana** to eat Mexican food (3); **comida rápida** fast food

comienzo *n.* beginning

como like; as; **tal como** just as; **tan... como** as . . . as; **tanto como** as much as; **tanto/a/os/as... como** as much/many . . . as

¿cómo? how? (2); **¿cómo anda?** how's it going (*inform. s.*)? (1); **¿cómo está?** how are you (*form. s.*)? (1); **¿cómo estás?** how are you (*inform. s.*)? (1); **¿cómo se dice... ?** how do you say . . . ?; **¿cómo se escribe... ?** how do you spell . . . ? (1); **¿cómo se llama?** what is your name (*form. s.*)? (1); **¿cómo se llama él/ella?** what is his/her name? (1); **¿cómo te llamas?** what is your name (*inform. s.*)? (1)

¡cómo no! *interj. sure, no problem,* of course! (6)

comodidad *f.* comfort

cómodo/a comfortable

cómodamente comfortably

compacto: disco compacto (el CD) compact disc (CD)

compadre *m. godfather of one's child* (4); *father of one's godchild*

compañero/a companion; friend; classmate; **compañero/a de clase**

classmate; **compañero/a de cuarto** roommate

compañía company

comparación *f.* comparison

comparar to compare

compartir to share

competencia competition (12)

competición *f.* competition

competidor(a) competitor

competir (i, i) to compete

competitivo/a competitive

complacer (zc) to please

complejo *n.* complex

complejo/a *adj.* complex

complemento accessory

completar to complete

completo/a complete

complicar (qu) to complicate

componer (*like* **poner**) (*p.p.* **compuesto**) to compose (14)

composición *f.* composition

compositor(a) composer

compostador *m.* composter

comprar to buy (3)

compras: de compras shopping; **ir** (*irreg.*) **de compras** to go shopping (2)

comprender to understand

comprensión *f.* understanding

comprensivo/a understanding (16)

comprobar (ue) to prove

comprometerse to get engaged (16); to commit (*oneself*) (16)

comprometido/a engaged (16); in a serious relationship (16)

compromiso engagement; commitment

compuesto/a (*p.p. of* **componer**) **(de)** composed (of)

computación *f.* computer science

computadora computer (1); **(computadora) láptop/portátil** laptop (computer)

común common

comunicación *f.* communication; communications (*field of study*) (1)

comunicarse (qu) to communicate; **¿me puede comunicar con... ?** can you connect me with . . . ?

comunidad *f.* community

comunista *n., adj. m., f.* communist

comunitario/a community

con with (7); **con frecuencia** often; **¡con mucho gusto!** with pleasure! (6); (very) gladly; **con permiso** excuse me (8); **con tal de que** *conj.* provided that; **con vista a** with a view of; **¿me puede comunicar con... ?** can you connect me with . . . ?

concentrar(se) to concentrate

concepto concept

concha shell

conciencia conscience

concierto concert (14)

concluir (y) to conclude

conclusión *f.* conclusion

concordancia agreement

concreto: en concreto specifically; in particular

condición *f.* condition

condimento condiment (6)

cóndor *m.* condor

conducir *irreg.* to drive; **no beber y conducir** don't drink and drive (9)

conectar to connect; **conectarse** to get online (10)

conector *m.* connector

conejo rabbit

conexión *(f.)* **(inalámbrica)** (wireless) connection

conferencia conference

confesar (ie) to confess

confianza confidence; trust

conflicto conflict

confundir to confuse

congregarse (gu) to congregate

congreso conference

cónico/a conical

conjugar (gu) to conjugate

conjunto outfit (*clothes*)

conjuro spell

conmemorar to commemorate

conmigo with me (7)

Cono Sur Southern Cone

conocer (zc) to know, be acquainted, familiar with (5); to meet; **conocerse** to meet (each other) (16)

conocimiento knowledge

conquista conquest

conquistador(a) conqueror

consciente conscious; aware

consecuencia consequence (13)

consecutivo/a consecutive

conseguir (*like* **seguir**) to get (10)

consejero/a advisor

consejo (piece of) advice

conservación conservation

conservar to preserve, conserve (13); to keep (13)

consideración *f.* consideration

considerar to consider

consistir (en) to consist (of)

consola console

constipado/a congested

constitucional constitutional

construcción *f.* construction

construir (y) to build

consultar to consult

consumir to consume

consumo consumption

contacto contact; **lentes** (*m. pl.*) **de contacto** contact lenses; **mantenerse** (*like* **tener**) **en contacto con** to stay in touch with; **ponerse los lentes de contacto** to put on contacts (5)

contador(a) accountant

contagiar to infect

contaminación *f.* pollution (5); **contaminación del aire** air pollution

contaminar to pollute (13)

contar (ue) to tell, narrate; to count

contener (*like* **tener**) to contain
contenido content
contento/a happy (2); **ponerse** (*irreg.*) **contento/a** to become happy (5)
conteo count
contestar to answer
contexto context
contigo with you (*inform. s.*) (7)
continente *m.* continent
continuación: a continuación following; below
continuar (continúo) to continue
contra against; **en contra de** against
contraceptivo contraceptive
contrario: al contrario on the contrary; **lo contrario** the opposite
contrastante contrasting
contrastar to contrast
contratar to hire
contrayente *m., f.* party (*of a contract*)
control *m.* control
controlar to control
controversia controversy
controvertido/a controversial
conversación *f.* conversation
conversar to converse
convertir (ie, i) to convert; **convertirse en** to become
conyugal conjugal
cooperar to cooperate
copa drink (*alcoholic*); **copa de los árboles** canopy (of trees); **Copa Mundial** World Cup
copiar to copy
coqueto/a flirtatious
coraje *m.* anger, rage; **¡qué coraje!** how frustrating/annoying!
corazón *m.* heart
corbata tie (8)
cordillera mountain range
Corea Korea
coreano/a *n., adj.* Korean
coro choir
coronado/a crowned
corporación *f.* corporation
correcto/a correct
corredor(a) runner
correo mail; **correo basura** junk mail; **correo electrónico** email; **¿cuál es tu correo electrónico?** what is your email (address)?; **oficina de correos** post office
correr to run (3); **correr en bicicleta** to ride a bicycle; **correr en el parque** to run in the park (3)
corresponder to correspond
correspondiente corresponding
corrida de montaña mountain running
corrupción *f.* corruption (15)
corrupto/a corrupt
corsé *m.* corset
cortar to cut
Corte (*f.*) **Suprema** Supreme Court
cortés polite

corto/a short (*in length*) (2); **pantalones** (*m. pl.*) **cortos** shorts (8)
cosa thing (1)
cosecha harvest
cosido/a sewn
cosmetólogo/a cosmetologist (10)
costa coast
costal *m.* sack, bag
costar (ue) to cost
costarricense *n., adj. m., f.* Costa Rican (2)
costoso/a expensive
costumbre *f.* custom (7); habit (7)
costura sewing; **alta costura** haute couture
cotidiano/a daily
cráter *m.* crater
crear to create
creativo/a creative
crecer (zc) to grow
creencia belief
creer (y) (*p.p.* creído) to think; to believe (12); **creo que...** I think . . . (15)
crimen *m.* violent crime (15); **lugar** (*m.*) **del crimen** scene of the crime
criminal *m., f.* criminal
criollo/a creole; **pabellón** (*m.*) **criollo** *Venezuelan rice and beans dish*
crisis *f.* crisis (15)
cristiano/a Christian
criterio criterion
crítica criticism
criticar (qu) to criticize
crítico/a *n.* critic; *adj.* critical
cruce *m.* crossroads
crucero cruise; cruise ship
crudo/a raw; harsh
cruzar (c) to cross
cuaderno notebook (1)
cuadra (city) block (5)
cuadro square; **de cuadros** plaid
¿cuál(es)? what?; which? (2); **¿cuál es la fecha de hoy?** what is today's date? (1); **¿cuál es tu carrera?** what's your major? (1)
cualificado/a qualified
cualquier *adj.* any
cuando when; **de vez en cuando** once in a while
¿cuándo? when? (2)
cuanto: en cuanto as soon as; **en cuanto a** regarding
cuánto lo siento I'm very sorry (16)
¿cuánto/a(s)? how much? (1); how many (are there)? (1); **¿cuánto tiempo hace que** + *present tense*? how long have you (*done / been doing something*)? (13); **¿cuánto tiempo lleva(s)** + **-ndo** *form*? how long have you (*form. s. / inform. s.*) (*done / been doing something*)? (13); **¿cuántos años tienes?** how old are you (*inform. s.*)? (2)
cuarenta forty
Cuaresma Lent
cuarto room; one-fourth; quarter (*of an hour*); **compañero/a de cuarto**

roommate; **cuarto de baño** bathroom (11); **son las dos y cuarto** it's 2:15 (3)
cuatro four; **cuatro mil** four thousand (5)
cuatrocientos/as four hundred (5)
cubano/a *n., adj.* Cuban (2)
cubierto/a (*p.p. of* **cubrir**) covered
cubierto place setting (6)
cubrir (*p.p.* **cubierto**) to cover
cuchara spoon (6)
cuchillo knife (6)
cuello neck (8)
cuenta account; **darse** (*irreg.*) **cuenta de** to realize (13)
cuento story
cuerda string
cuerdo/a sensible; rational; sane
cuero leather
cuerpo body
cuestión *f.* issue
cuidador(a) curator
cuidar to take care of (13)
culantro coriander
culinario/a culinary
culpa fault; blame; **echar la culpa** to blame
cultivar to grow, raise (crop)
culto/a cultured; learned
cultura culture
cumbia *Colombian folk dance now popular throughout Latin America*
cumbre *f.* summit, peak
cumpleaños *s., pl.* birthday (7)
cumplir to achieve; **cumplir... años** to turn . . . years old (7)
cuñado/a brother-in-law / sister-in-law (4)
curado/a drunk (*sl.*)
curioso/a curious (2)
curita adhesive bandage
currículum *m.* resume, curriculum vitae (CV) (10)
curso course
cursor *m.* cursor
cuyo/a whose

D

danés (*pl.* **daneses**), **danesa** *n.* Danish person; *adj.* Danish
danza dance (14)
daño damage (13)
dar *irreg.* to give; **dar a luz** to give birth; **dar buena suerte** to bring good luck; **dar de comer** to feed; **dar el pésame** to give one's condolences; **dar la bienvenida** to welcome (11); **dar un abrazo** to hug; **dar un paseo** to take a walk (9); **dar un paso** to take a step; **dar una bofetada** to slap; **dar una fiesta** to throw a party; **darle vuelta a** to think about (*something*); **darse cuenta de** to realize (13); **darse la mano** to shake hands; **darse prisa** to hurry; **¡le damos la bienvenida a Ud.!** we welcome you (*form. s.*)! (11); **no dar de comer** don't feed (*animals*) (9); **te/le/les doy/damos el pésame** my/our condolences (16)

dato piece of information (12); *pl.* data; **base** (*f.*) **de datos** database; **tomar los datos** to take down information (*medical intake*) (12)

de of (1); from (1); **de alguna manera** in some way; **de compras** shopping; **de cuadros** plaid; **de dentro a fuera** inside out; **¿de dónde eres?** where are you from?; **de hecho** actually; **de la madrugada** in the early A.M. hours (3); **de la mañana** A.M.; in the morning (3); **de la misma manera** likewise; **de la noche** at night (3); **de la tarde** P.M.; in the afternoon/evening (3); **de lujo** luxury; **de madera** made of wood; **de nada** you're welcome (5); **de niño/a** as a child; **¿de parte de quién?** may I ask who's calling?; **¿de qué color es?** what color is it? (2); **¿de qué está hecho/a?** what is it made of?; **de repente** suddenly; **de verdad** really; **de vez en cuando** once in a while; **favor de** + *inf.* please + *inf.*

debajo de below (11)

debate *m.* debate

deber + *inf.* should, must, ought to (*do something*); **(no) debería** + *inf.* should (not) (*do something*) (13); **debo** + *inf.* I should (*do something*) (6)

debido a because of, due to; **debido a ello** due to this fact

débil weak (2)

década decade

decenas *pl.* tens

decente decent

decidir to decide

decir *irreg.* to say (4); to tell (4); **¿cómo se dice... ?** how do you say . . . ?

decisión *f.* decision; **tomar una decisión** to make a decision

declaración *f.* statement

declarar to state

decorar to decorate

dedicarse (qu) (a) to dedicate oneself (to); to work at (job); **¿a qué se dedica?** what do you (*form. s.*) do (*occupation*)? (4); **¿a qué te dedicas?** what do you (*inform. s.*) do (*occupation*)? (4)

dedo finger (8)

defecto de nacimiento birth defect

defender (ie) to defend

definitivamente definitely

deforestación *f.* deforestation

deforestar to deforest

degustación *f.* tasting

degustar to taste (*sample different items for flavor*)

dejar to leave; **dejar de** + *inf.* to stop (*doing something*); **dejar a la vista** to leave within view

del of the; from the

delante de in front of

delfín *m.* (*pl.* **delfines**) dolphin (13)

delgado/a thin (2)

delicado/a delicate

delincuencia crime

demanda demand (15)

demás the rest; **los/las demás** others; **todo lo demás** everything else

demasiado *adv.* too; too much

demasiado/a *adj.* too; *pl.* too many

democracia democracy (15)

democrático/a democratic

demostrar (ue) to show

demostrativo/a *gram.* demonstrative

denominación *f.* designation

denominado/a called

dentista *m., f.* dentist (10)

dentro inside; **de dentro a fuera** inside out; **dentro de** inside; within, in

departamento apartment

dependencia dependency

depender (de) to depend (on)

dependiente *m., f.* clerk

deporte sport (2); **hacer** (*irreg.*) **deportes** to play sports; **practicar (qu) un deporte** to play a sport (3)

deportista *m., f.* athlete

deportivo/a *adj.* sporting, sports

depositar to deposit

depresión *f.* depression (12)

derecha *n.* right side; **a la derecha (de)** to the right (of); **coger (j) a mano derecha** to turn right (*Sp.*); **doble/gire a la derecha** turn right (*command form. s.*) (5); **quedar a la derecha** to be on the right

derecho right (*prerogative*); law (*field of study*); *adv.* straight ahead; **derecho humano** human right (15); **siga derecho** go / keep going / continue straight (*command form. s.*) (5); **violación** (*f.*) **de los derechos del autor** copyright violation; **violar los derechos humanos** to violate human rights

derivarse (de) to derive (from)

dermatológico/a dermatological

derramar to spill

derretimiento melting

derrocar (qu) to overthrow

desaparecer (zc) to disappear

desarrollar to develop

desarrollo development (15)

desastre (*m.*) **natural** natural disaster (15)

desayunar to eat breakfast (3)

desayuno breakfast; **preparar el desayuno** to make/prepare breakfast (4)

descalzo/a barefoot

descansar to rest (11)

descarga download

descargar (gu) to download

descender (ie) (de) to descend (from)

describir to describe

descripción *f.* description

descubrir (*p.p.* **descubierto**) to discover

descuento discount (8)

descuido carelessness

desde *prep.* from; since; **desde hace** + *period of time* for + period of time

desear to wish; to want; **le(s) deseo mucha suerte** I wish you (*form. s., pl.*) luck (12)

desechable disposable

desecho (orgánico) (organic) waste

desempleo unemployment (15)

desencadenar to trigger; to unleash

deseo wish

desequilibrio imbalance

desesperación *f.* desperation

desfile *m.* parade (7); **desfile de moda** fashion show (8)

desgarrador(a) heartbreaking

desgraciadamente unfortunately

deshacer (*like* **hacer**) (*p.p.* **deshecho**) to dissolve; to undo

desierto desert

desigualdad *f.* inequality (15)

deslizar (c) to slide

desmayarse to faint

desordenado/a disorganized; messy

despacho office (1)

despedida farewell, good-bye (7); closing (*in a letter/email*) (10)

despejado/a clear (*weather*); **está despejado** it's clear (*sky*) (9)

despejarse to clear up (*weather*)

despensa pantry (11)

despertarse (ie) to wake up (5)

después *adv.* afterwards; **después (de)** after (1); **después (de) que** *conj.* after

destacado/a renowned

destilería distillery

destino destination

destreza skill

destrozado/a destroyed

destrucción *f.* destruction (13)

destruir (y) to destroy (13)

desventaja disadvantage

desviarse (me desvío) to change course

detallado/a detailed

detalle *m.* detail

detallista *m., f.* detail-oriented

detective *m., f.* detective

deteriorar to deteriorate

deterioro deterioration

determinar to determine

detrás de behind; **está/queda detrás de...** it's behind . . . (5)

deuda debt; **deuda externa** foreign debt (15)

devolver (*like* **volver**) (*p.p.* **devuelto**) to return

día *m.* day (1); **algún día** someday; **buen día** good morning (1); **buenos días** good morning (1); **Día de Acción de Gracias** Thanksgiving; **día de entre semana** weekday (3); **Día de la Independencia** Independence Day (7); **Día de las Madres** Mother's Day; **Día de Muertos** Day of the Dead (7); **Día de los Padres** Father's Day; **Día de los Reyes Magos** Three Kings' Day; Epiphany (Adoration of the Magi) (7); **Día de Todos los Santos** All Saints' Day; **Día del Amor** Valentine's Day; **día festivo** holiday; **días entre semana** weekdays; **hoy en**

día today; these days; **¡que tenga(s) un buen día!** have a nice day (*form. s. / inform. s.*)!; **son las doce del día** it's noon (3); **todo el día** all day (3); **todos los días** every day (3)
diagnóstico diagnosis
diálogo dialogue
diamante *m.* diamond
diario newspaper
diario/a daily; **rutina diaria** daily routine
dibujar to draw
dibujo drawing
diccionario dictionary (1)
dicho/a aforesaid
diciembre December (1)
dictadura dictatorship (15)
diecinueve nineteen
dieciocho eighteen
dieciséis sixteen
diecisiete seventeen
diente *m.* tooth; *pl.* teeth (8); **cepillarse los dientes** to brush one's teeth (5); **cepillo de dientes** toothbrush; **lavarse los dientes** to brush one's teeth
dieta diet; **estar** (*irreg.*) **a dieta** to be on a diet
dietética dietetics
diez ten; **son diez para las nueve** It's 8:50 (3); **son las nueve menos diez** it's 8:50 (3)
diferencia difference
diferente different (1)
difícil difficult (2); hard
dificultad *f.* difficulty
difunto/a *n., adj.* deceased
digestión *f.* digestion
digestivo/a digestive
digitalizado/a digitalized
dinero money; **ganar dinero** to make money; **sacar (qu) dinero** to withdraw money
dios *m. s.* god; **Dios** God
diplomático/a diplomatic
dirección *f.* address; *pl.* instructions; **¿cuál es tu (dirección de) email?** what is your email (address)? (1); **¿cuál es tu/su profesión?** what is your (*inform. s. / form. s.*) profession? (4)
directo/a direct (2)
director(a) de marketing director of marketing (10)
dirigir (j) to direct (14)
discapacitado/a disabled
disciplina discipline
disco record; **disco compacto** compact disc; **disco duro** hard drive
discriminación *f.* discrimination (15)
disculpar to excuse, pardon; **disculpa/ disculpe** excuse me (*command inform. s. / form. s.*) (3); **disculpen** excuse me (*command form. pl.*) (3)
discurso speech
diseñador(a) designer (8); **diseñador(a) gráfico/a** graphic designer (10)
diseñar to design

diseño design (1)
disfraz *m.* (*pl.* **disfraces**) costume (7)
disfrazado/a disguised
disfrutar de + *n.* to enjoy (*something*) (9)
dislocarse (qu) to dislocate
disminución *f.* decrease (13); reduction
disminuir (y) to diminish
disponer (*like* **poner**) (*p.p.* **dispuesto**) **de** to have available
disponible available
dispositivo device
dispuesto/a ready, prepared; willing; **estar** (*irreg.*) **dispuesto** to be ready/willing (10)
distancia distance
distinguir (distingo) to distinguish
distribuidor(a) distributor
distrito district
diversidad *f.* diversity
diversión *f.* fun
diverso/a diverse
divertido/a fun
divertirse (ie, i) to have fun (7); **¡diviértete!/ ¡diviérta(n)se!** have fun! (*command inform. s. / form. s., pl.*) (11); **me divertí mucho** I had a lot of fun (7)
dividir to divide
división *f.* division
divorciado/a divorced (16)
divorcio divorce (16)
doblar to turn; **doble a la derecha/ izquierda** turn (to the) right/left (*command form. s.*) (5); **no doblar** do not turn (9)
doble *m.* double; **doble ve, doble ve, doble ve** www (*in an email address*) (1); **triple doble ve** www (*in an email address*) (1)
doce twelve; **son las doce del día** it's noon (3); **son las doce de la noche** it's midnight (3)
doctor(a) doctor (4)
doctorado doctorate
documento document
dólar *m.* dollar
doler (ue) (*like* **gustar**) to hurt (12); to ache
dolor *m.* pain (12); **te/le/les acompaño/ acompañamos en el dolor** I'm/we're with you (*inform. s. / form. s. / form. pl.*) in your time of pain (16)
doméstico/a domestic; **animal** (*m.*) **doméstico** pet
dominante dominant
dominar to dominate
domingo Sunday (3); **Domingo de Pascua** Easter Sunday; **Domingo de Ramos** Palm Sunday
dominicano/a *n., adj.* Dominican (2); **República Dominicana** Dominican Republic
donar to donate
donde where
¿dónde? where? (2); **¿de dónde eres?** where are you (*inform. s.*) from? (1); **¿de dónde es usted?** where are you (*form. s.*) from? (1); **¿dónde está/queda... ?** where

is . . . ? (5); **¿dónde vive(s)?** where do you (*form. s. / inform. s.*) live? (1)
dormir (ue, u) to sleep (2); **dormirse** to fall asleep (5)
dormitorio bedroom (11)
dorso: nadar de dorso to do the backstroke
dos two; **dos mil** two thousand (5); **dos veces** twice (3); **son las dos y cuarto/ quince** it's 2:15 (3)
doscientos/as two hundred (5)
drama *m.* drama
dramático/a dramatic
drástico/a drastic
droga drug
ducha shower (11)
ducharse to take a shower (5)
duda doubt; **poner** (*irreg.*) **en duda** to call into question; **sin duda** without (any) doubt (14)
dueño/a owner (10)
dulce *adj.* sweet (6)
dulces *m. pl.* sweets; candy
duquesa duchess
duración *f.* length
durante during
durar to last
durazno peach
duro/a hard; **disco duro** hard drive
DVD *m.* DVD

E

e and (*used instead of* **y** *before words beginning with* **i** *or* **hi**) (1)
echar to throw; to add; **echar de menos** to miss; **echar la culpa** to blame
ecología ecology
ecológico/a ecological (13)
ecologista *m., f.* ecologist
economía economy; economics (1)
económico/a economic (15); economical (15)
ecoturismo ecotourism
ecuatoriano/a *n., adj.* Ecuadorian (2)
edad *f.* age
edificio building (5)
editar to edit; to publish
editor(a) editor
editorial *m.* editorial
edu: punto edu dot edu (*in an email address*) (1)
educación *f.* education
educado/a polite
educar (qu) to teach, educate
educativo/a educational
efecto effect
Egipto Egypt
egoísta *m., f.* selfish
egresado/a (de) graduate (of)
ejecutivo/a executive (10)
ejemplo example; **por ejemplo** for example
ejercer (z) to exercise
ejercicio exercise; **hacer** (*irreg.*) **ejercicio** to work out (2)

el *def. art. m. s.* the (1)

él *sub. pron.* he; *obj. of prep.* him

elaboración *f.* production

elaborar to manufacture, produce

elección *f.* election (15)

electricidad *f.* electricity

eléctrico/a electrical

electrodoméstico appliance (11)

electrónico/a electronic (14); **correo electrónico** email; **¿cuál es tu correo electrónico?** what is your e mail (address)?

elefante *m.* elephant

elegante elegant

elegir (i, i) (j) to choose; to elect

elemento element

eliminar to eliminate

élite *f.* elite

ella *sub. pron.* she; *obj. of prep.* her

ello: debido a ello due to this fact

ellos/as *sub. pron.* they; *obj. of prep.* them

elogiado/a praised

elogio praise

email *m.* email (10); **¿cuál es tu (dirección de) email?** what is your email (address)? (1); **escribir un email** to write an email (3)

emancipación *f.* emancipation

emancipar(se) to become free/ independent (16)

embarazo pregnancy

embarcar (qu) to embark

embargo: sin embargo nevertheless

emblemático/a emblematic

emigrante *m., f.* emigrant

emoción *f.* emotion; **¡qué emoción!** how exciting!

emocional emotional

emocionante exciting

empacar (qu) to pack

empaquetado/a packaged; **comestibles** (*m. pl.*) **empaquetados** packaged goods (6)

emparejar to match

empate *m.* tie (*score*)

empezar (ie) (c) to begin (4); to start; **empezar a** + *inf.* to begin to (*do something*) (4)

empleado/a employee (10)

empleo job; employment; **solicitar un empleo** to apply for a job (10)

emprender to undertake, start

empresa corporation; business; **administración** (*f.*) **de empresas** business administration

empresarial *adj.* business

empresario/a business person (10)

empujar to push; push (9)

en in (1); on (1); at (*a place*) (1); **caer** (*irreg.*) **en** to fall on (*day of the week*); **en algún momento** at some point; **en caso de que** (*conj.*) in case; **en concreto** specifically; in particular; **en contra de** against; **en el punto de mira** in the crosshairs; **en general** in general; **en mi opinión...** in my opinion . . . (15); **en**

negrita boldface; **en particular** in particular; **¿en qué puedo servirle(s)?** how may I help you (*form. s., pl.*)? (10); **en total** in all; **en una relación** together (16); in a relationship (16); **en voz alta** out loud; **está/queda en la esquina de... y...** it's on the corner of . . . and . . . (5)

enagua petticoat

enamorado/a (de) in love (with) (16)

enamorarse (de) to fall in love (with) (16)

encandilar to dazzle

encantado/a nice to meet you, enchanted (10)

encantar (*like* **gustar**) to like very much, love; to delight (7)

encender (ie) to turn on (*appliance*); to light

encerrar (ie) to enclose; to circle

encima de on top of (11)

enclavado/a nestled

encontrar (ue) to find; **(no) encontrarse bien** to (not) feel well (12)

encuentro encounter

encuesta survey

energía energy; **energía eólica** wind energy

enero January (1)

énfasis *m.* emphasis; **poner** (*irreg.*) **énfasis** to emphasize

enfermarse to get sick (12)

enfermedad *f.* illness (12)

enfermero/a nurse (10)

enfermo/a sick (2)

enfocado/a focused

enfocarse (qu) (en) to focus (on)

enfrentarse (a) to confront

enfrente de *prep.* in front of / facing; **está/ queda enfrente de...** it's facing / in front of . . . (5)

engañar to deceive

engordar to gain weight

¡enhorabuena! congratulations! (7)

enlace *m.* (web) link

enlatado/a canned; **comestibles** (*m. pl.*) **enlatados** canned goods (6)

enojado/a angry (2)

enorme enormous

ensalada salad (6); **ensalada mixta** tossed salad

ensayar to rehearse

ensayo rehearsal

enseñanza teaching

enseñar to teach (7); **enseñar a** + *inf.* to teach to (*do something*)

ensuciar to dirty

entablar to initiate

entender (ie) to understand

entonces so; then, next

entrada entrance

entrar to enter; **no entrar** do not enter (9)

entre *prep.* between; among; **entre semana** during the week; **días de entre semana** weekdays

entregar (gu) to turn in; to deliver

entrenador(a) coach (12); trainer (12)

entrenamiento training

entrenar to train

entretenimiento entertainment

entrevista interview (10)

entrevistar to interview (10)

entusiasmo enthusiasm

enviar (envío) to send (10)

eólico/a: energía eólica wind energy

episodio episode

época era

equilibrado/a balanced

equilibrio balance

equinoccio equinox

equipaje *m.* baggage (9) **recogida de equipaje** baggage claim (9)

equipo team (12); equipment (12)

equis *f.* × (*letter*)

equivocación: por equivocación by mistake

equivocado/a mistaken; wrong

erradicar (qu) to eradicate (15)

error *m.* mistake; **cometer un error** to make a mistake; **error ortográfico** spelling mistake

escala scale; layover; stop (9); **hacer** (*irreg.*) **escala** to have a layover; to make a stop (9)

escalada rock/mountain climbing

escalar to go rock climbing (9); to climb (9)

escalera stairs (11)

escalofríos chills

escándalo scandal

escandinavo/a Scandinavian

escanear to scan

escáner *m.* scanner (10)

escapar to escape

escasez *f.* shortage

escena scene

escenario setting; stage

escenografía set (*film*); scenery (*theater*)

escéptico/a skeptical

esclavitud (*f.*) **(infantil)** (child) slavery (15)

esclavo/a slave

escoger (j) to choose (7)

escolar *adj.* school

escondido/a hidden; **a escondidas** in secret

escribir (*p.p.* **escrito/a**) to write (3); **¿cómo se escribe... ?** how do you spell . . . ? (1)

escrito/a (*p.p. of* **escribir**) written

escritor(a) writer (10)

escritorio desk (1)

escritura writing

escuchar to listen (3)

escuela school (3); **escuela militar** military school; **escuela primaria** elementary school; **escuela privada** private school; **escuela secundaria** high school; **escuela tele-secundaria** distance high school

esculpir to sculpt

escultura sculpture (14)

ese/a *adj.* that (3)

esencial essential

esfuerzo force

eso that (*neuter*)

esos/as *adj.* those (3)

espacio space; **espacio en blanco** blank space

espalda back

España Spain

español *m.* Spanish (*language*)

español (*pl.* **españoles**), **española** *n.* Spaniard (2); *adj.* Spanish

espárragos *pl.* asparagus

especia spice

especial special

especialidad *f.* specialty

especialista *m., f.* specialist

especializarse (c) (en) to specialize (in); to major (in)

especie *f.* species (13); kind (13); **especie en peligro de extinción** endangered species

específico/a specific

espectacular spectacular

espectáculo show

espectador(a) spectator

espejo mirror (11)

esperanza hope

esperar to hope (for) (12); to wait (for) (9)

espíritu *m.* spirit

espiritual spiritual

esposo/a husband/wife (4)

espuma foam

esquí *m.* skiing (12)

esquiador(a) skier

esquiar (í) to ski (12)

esquina corner; **está/queda en la esquina de... y...** it's on the corner of . . . and . . . (5); **siga hasta llegar a** go / keep going until you (*command form. s.*) get to . . . (5)

establecer (zc) to establish

establecimiento establishment

establo barn; stable

estación *f.* station; season (1)

estacionar to park; **no estacionar** no parking (9)

estadio stadium (12)

estado state; **estado civil** marital status (16); **Estados Unidos** United States; **golpe** (*m.*) **de estado** coup d'état

estadounidense *n.* U.S. citizen, American; *adj.* of/from the United States of America (2)

estallar to erupt

estampilla stamp

estancia stay; living room

estar *irreg.* to be (2); **¿cómo está(s)?** how are you (*form. s. / inform. s.*)? (1); **¿de qué está hecho/a?** what is it made of?; **¿dónde está... ?** where is . . . ? (5); **está a la derecha/izquierda** it's on the right/left (5); **está al lado de / detrás de / enfrente de / en la esquina de... y ...** it's next to / behind / facing, in front of / on the corner of . . . and . . . (5); **está despejado** it's clear (*sky*) (9); **está lloviendo** it's raining (9); **está nevando** it's snowing (9); **está nublado** it's cloudy (9); **estar a cargo de** to be in charge of; **estar a dieta** to be on a diet; **estar dispuesto** to be ready/willing (10); **estar (pasado/a) de moda** to be (un)fashionable; **(no) estar de acuerdo** to (dis)agree

este/a *adj.* this (3); **baje/suba por esta calle** go down/up this street (*command form. s.*) (5)

estereotipo stereotype

estética aesthetics

estilo style

estimado/a dear (10)

estirarse to stretch

esto this (*neuter*)

estos/as these (3)

estómago stomach

estornudar to sneeze

estrategia strategy

estrecho/a narrow

estrella star (14)

estrés *m.* stress

estribillo chorus, refrain

estricto/a strict

estrofa verse

estructura structure

estudiante *m., f.* student

estudiantil *adj.* student; **centro estudiantil** student center, student union; **residencia (estudiantil)** dormitory (1)

estudiar to study (2); **¿qué estudias?** what do you study?; what's your major? (1)

estudio study

estufa stove (11)

estupendo/a stupendous (2); **¡qué estupendo!** how cool! (8)

étnico/a ethnic

Europa Europe

europeo/a European

evaluar to evaluate

evento event

evidencia evidence

evitar to avoid (6)

exacto/a exact

exagerado/a exaggerated

examen *m.* exam (1)

excelente excellent (2)

excesivo/a excessive

exclamación *f.* exclamation

excluir (y) to exclude

exclusivo/a exclusive

excremento excrement

excursión *f.* excursion; tour

excusa excuse

exigencia demand

exiliado/a exiled

exilio exile

existencia existence

existente existing

existir to exist

éxito success; **tener** (*irreg.*) **éxito** to be successful (12)

exitoso/a successful

exorcista *m., f.* exorcist

exótico/a exotic

expandir(se) to expand

expansión *f.* expansion

experiencia experience

experimentar to experience

experto/a expert

explicación *f.* explanation

explicar (qu) to explain

exploración *f.* exploration

explorar to explore

explotar to exploit; to develop (13)

exponer (*like* **poner**) to bring to light

exportador(a) exporter

exportar to export

exposición *f.* exposition

expresar to express

expresión *f.* expression

exquisito/a exquisite

extendido/a widespread

extensión *f.* extension

externo/a external; **deuda externa** foreign debt (15)

extinción *f.* extinction; **especie** (*f.*) **en peligro de extinción** endangered species

extinto/a extinct

extraer (*like* **traer**) to extract

extranjero: al extranjero abroad (9)

extraño/a strange

extremadamente extremely

extremo/a extreme

extrovertido/a extroverted

F

fábrica factory

fabricación *f.* production

fabuloso/a fabulous

fácil easy (2)

facilitar to facilitate

factor *m.* factor

factura bill

facultad *f.* school (*of a university*)

falda skirt (8)

fallar to fail

fallecer (zc) to die, pass away

fallo error, mistake

falso/a false

falta lack

faltar to be lacking

fama fame; reputation; **tener** (*irreg.*) **fama de** to be known for

familia family; **¡qué bonita familia!** what a beautiful family! (4)

familiar *n.* relative (4); *adj.* family; **nido familiar** parents' home (16); **planificación** (*f.*) **familiar** family planning

famoso/a famous

fantasía fantasy

fantástico/a fantastic

farmacia pharmacy

faro lighthouse

fascinado/a fascinated

fascinante fascinating

fascinar (*like* **gustar**) to fascinate (7); to like very much, love (7)

fauna fauna (13)

fauno faun

favor *m.* favor; **a favor (de)** in favor (of); **favor de no fumar** please don't smoke (9); **por favor** please

favorito/a favorite

fax *m.* fax

febrero February (1)

fecha date; **¿cuál es la fecha de hoy?** what is today's date? (1)

felicidad *f.* happiness; **¡felicidades!** congratulations! (7)

felicitación *f.* greeting; wish; **¡felicitaciones!** congratulations! (7)

felicitar to congratulate (7); **te felicito/ felicitamos** I/we congratulate you (7)

feliz (*pl.* **felices**) happy (2)

femenino/a feminine

fenomenal phenomenal; awesome; **¡qué fenomenal!** how cool! (8)

fenómeno phenomenon

feo/a ugly (2); **¡qué feo/a!** how ugly! (4)

feria fair

ferrocarril *m.* railroad

festival *m.* festival

festivo/a festive, celebratory; **día** (*m.*) **festivo** holiday

ficción *f.* fiction

fiebre *f.* fever (12); **tener** (*irreg.*) **fiebre** to have a temperature

fiesta party (2); **dar** (*irreg.*) **una fiesta** to throw a party; **hacer** (*irreg.*) **una fiesta** to throw a party; **irse** (*irreg.*) **de fiesta** to party

fiestero/a party-loving

figura figure

figurar to figure

fijarse to pay attention to

fijo/a fixed, set

fila row

filarmónico/a philharmonic

film *m.* movie

filmar to film

filmografía filmography

filosofía philosophy (1)

filtro filter

fin *m.* end; **fin de semana** weekend (3); **organización** (*f.*) **sin fines de lucro** nonprofit organization (15); **por fin** finally; **¡que tenga(s) un buen fin de semana!** have (*form. s. / inform. s.*) a nice weekend!

final *m.* end; **al final** in the end

finalmente finally

financiamiento financing

financiero/a financial

firma signature

firmar to sign

física physics (1)

flaco/a thin (2)

flamenco *music of Andalusia and southern Spain*

flan *m.* (baked) custard

flecharse to fall in love

flexibilidad *f.* flexibility

flor *f.* flower (7)

flora flora (13)

Florida: Pascua Florida Easter (7)

fluorescente fluorescent

fogata bonfire

folclor *m.* folklore

folclórico/a folk

folleto brochure

fomentar to encourage, promote

fondo background; bottom; fund; **a fondo** in depth; **carrera de fondo** long-distance race; **recaudar fondos** to raise funds

forma form; shape; **mantenerse** (*irreg.*) **en forma** to stay in shape (12); **ponerse** (*irreg.*) **en forma** to get in shape (12)

formación *f.* formation; (academic) training; education

formar to form

formato format

fórmula formula

formular to formulate

formulario form

fortalecer (zc) to strengthen

forzar (ue) (c) to force

fósil *m.* fossil; **combustibles** (*m. pl.*) **fósiles** fossil fuels

foto *f.* photo; **sacar (qu) fotos** to take photos

fotocopia photocopy

fotografía photograph

fotógrafo/a photographer (10)

fractura fracture

fracturarse to fracture

fragancia fragrance

francés *m.* French (*language*) (1)

francés (*pl.* **franceses**), **francesa** *n.* French person; *adj.* French

Francia France

franquear to go through

frase *f.* phrase; sentence

frecuencia frequency; **con frecuencia** often

frecuente often

fregadero kitchen sink (11)

frente *m.* front; forehead; *adv.* **frente a** facing

fresa strawberry (6)

frijoles *m. pl.* beans (6)

frío cold(ness); *adj.* cold; **hace frío** it's cold (9); **¡qué frío!** it's so cold! (4); **tener** (*irreg.*) **(mucho) frío** to be (very) cold

frito/a fried (6); **papas fritas** french fries

frontera border (15)

fronterizo/a *adj.* border

fruta fruit (6)

frutería fruit store (5)

frutilla strawberry (*Arg.*)

fuego fire; **fuegos artificiales** fireworks (7)

fuente *f.* fountain; source

fuera *adv.* outside; **de dentro a fuera** inside out

fuerte strong (2); heavy (*food*)

fuerza force; strength; **fuerzas militares** military forces

fumar to smoke; **favor de no fumar** please don't smoke (9)

función *f.* function

funcionamiento functioning

funcionar to function, work

fundación *f.* foundation

fundar to found

funeral *m.* funeral

fútbol *m.* soccer; **fútbol americano** football (12); **jugar (ue) (gu) fútbol** to play soccer (2); **jugar (ue) (gu) fútbol americano** to play football (12)

futbolista *m., f.* soccer player

futuro future

futuro/a future

G

gabinete *m.* cabinet

gafas *pl.* (*eye*) glasses

galán *m.* (*pl.* **galanes**) leading man

galería gallery

gallina hen

gallo rooster; **gallo pinto** *rice and beans dish of Nicaragua and Costa Rica;* **pico de gallo** *uncooked salsa made of chopped tomato, onion, and jalapeños*

galón *m.* (*pl.* **galones**) gallon

ganadería ranching

ganador(a) winner

ganar to win (12); **ganar dinero** to earn (*income*), to make money

ganas: tener (*irreg.*) **ganas de** + *inf.* to feel like (*doing something*); **¿tiene(s) ganas de** + *n./inf.*? do you (*form. s. / inform. s.*) feel like . . . ? (6)

garantía guarantee

garantizar (c) to guarantee

gasolina gasoline

gastar to spend (9)

gastronomía gastronomy

gastronómico/a gastronomic

gato/a cat (4)

gazpacho *cold tomato soup of southern Spain*

gel *m.* gel

generación *f.* generation; **generación de relevo** upcoming generation

generar to generate

género gender; genre, type (14)

generoso/a generous

genético/a genetic

gente *f.* people

geoglifo geoglyph

geografía geography

geográfico/a geographic

geométrico/a geometric

gerente *m., f.* manager (10)

gigante *adj. m., f.* gigantic

gimnasia gynastics

gimnasio gym(nasium) (1); **ir** (*irreg.*) **al gimnasio** to go to the gym (3)

gira tour

girar to turn; **gire a la derecha/izquierda** turn (to the) right/left (*command form. s.*) (5); **no girar** do not turn (9)

giratorio/a revolving

glaciar *m.* glaciar

glamoroso/a glamorous

global global; **calentamiento global** global warming (13); **Sistema** (*m.*) **de Posicionamiento Global (SPG)** Global Positioning System (GPS)

globalización *f.* globalization

gobernador(a) governor

gobernante *m., f.* leader, ruler

gobernar (ie) to govern

gobierno government

gol *m.* goal; **marcar (qu) un gol** to score a goal; **meter un gol** to score a goal

golazo: ¡qué golazo! what a goal!

golf *m.* golf

golfista *m., f.* golfer

golpe (*m.*) **de estado** coup d'état

gordo/a fat (2)

gorra (baseball) cap (8)

gorro knitted hat (8)

gracias thank you (1); **gracias por** + *n./inf.* thank you for (5); **Día** (*m.*) **de Acción de Gracias** Thanksgiving; **muchas/ muchísimas gracias** thank you very much (5); **no, gracias** no, thank you (6); **sí, gracias** yes, please (5)

gracioso/a funny (2)

grado degree (*temperature*)

graduación *f.* graduation (1)

graduarse (me gradúo) (de) to graduate (from)

gráfico/a graphic; **diseñador(a) gráfico/a** graphic designer (10)

gramática grammar

gran, grande large, big (2); great; **Gran Bretaña** Great Britain

graneado: arroz (*m.*) **graneado** *fried rice dish*

granizo hail

granja farm

grano grain

grappamiel *f. alcoholic beverage of Uruguay*

grasa fat

grasiento/a greasy

gratis *inv.* free (*of charge*)

grave serious (15)

gripe *f.* flu

gris gray (2)

gritar to shout

grupo group; band

guacamayo macaw

guagua bus (*Carib.*)

guanábana soursop

guantes *m. pl.* gloves (8)

guapo/a handsome; good-looking; **¡qué guapo/a!** how handsome/beautiful! (4)

guaraní *m. indigenous language of S.A.*

guardar to keep; to save

guatemalteco/a *n., adj.* Guatemalan (2)

guay: ¡qué guay! how cool! (8)

guayabera *lightweight shirt worn in tropical climates*

guerra war (15); **guerra civil** civil war

guía *m., f.* guide (9); **guía naturalista** nature guide (4)

guion script

guisado stew

guita dinero *sl.*

guitarra guitar; **tocar (qu) la guitarra** to play the guitar (2)

guitarrista guitarist

gustar to be pleasing; **¿le gusta(n)** + *noun(s)?* do you (*form.*) like + *noun(s)?* (2); **¿le gustaría** + *inf.?* would you (*form. s.*) like (*to do something*)? (9); **me gusta(n)** + *noun(s)* I like + *noun(s)* (2); **me gustaría** + *inf.* I would like (*to do something*) (9); **no me gusta(n)** + *noun(s)* I don't like + *noun(s)* **¿te gusta** + *activity?* do you (*inform. s.*) like + *inf.?* (2); **¿te gusta(n)** + *noun(s)?* do you (*Inform.*) like + *noun(s)?*

gusto like, preference; *pl.* likes; **¡con mucho gusto!** with pleasure! (6); **mucho gusto** nice to meet you (1)

H

haber *irreg.* (*inf. of* **hay**) there is, there are (1) **¿cuántos/as... (hay)?** how many... (are there)? (1); **no hay de qué** you're welcome (5); **(no) hay que** + *inf.* you (don't) have to / it's (not) necessary to (*do something*) (12)

hábil skillful

habilidad *f.* ability

habitación *f.* bedroom

habitante *m., f.* inhabitant

hábitat *m.* habitat

hábito habit

hablar to speak (2); to talk (3); **hablar por teléfono** to talk on the phone (3)

hacer *irreg.* (*p.p.* **hecho**) to do (3); to make (5); **¿cuánto tiempo hace que** + *present tense?* how long have you (*done / been doing something*)? (13); **desde hace** + *period of time* for + period of time; **hace** + *time expression* + **que** + *present tense* I've been (*doing something*) for + *time* (13); **hace** + *time expression* + **que no** + *present tense* it's been + *time* + since I've (*done something*) (13); **hace (muy) buen tiempo** the weather's (very) good (9); **hace (mucho) calor** it's (very) hot (*weather*) (9); **hace (mucho) frío** it's (very) cold (*weather*) (9); **hace (muy) mal tiempo** the weather's (very) bad (9); **hace (mucho) sol** it's (very) sunny (9); **hace** + *time expression* + **que** + *present tense* to have been (*doing something*) for (*time*); **hace** + *time expression* + **que** + *preterite* to have (done *something*) (*time*) ago; **hace (mucho) viento** it's (very) windy (9);

hacer alpinismo to do/go mountaineering/mountain climbing (12); **hacer camping** to go camping; **hacer ciclismo de montaña** to go mountain biking (9); **hacer clic** to click; **hacer deportes** to play sports; **hacer ejercicio aeróbico** to do aerobics; **hacer ejercicio** to work out (2); **hacer escala** to have a layover; to make a stop (9); **hacer escalada** to go rock climbing (9); **hacer kayak** to go kayaking; **hacer la cama** to make the bed (11); **hacer la maleta** to pack a suitcase (9); **hacer ruido** to be noisy; **hacer senderismo** to go hiking; **hacer snorkel** to go snorkeling (9); **hacer un recorrido** to take a trip / go on a tour (9); **hacer una fiesta** to throw a party; **hacerse de voluntario** to volunteer; **¿qué tiempo hace?** what's the weather like? (9)

hacia toward

hambre *f.* (*but* **el hambre**) hunger (15); **tener** (*irreg.*) **hambre** to be hungry

hamburguesa hamburger

harina flour (6)

hasta *adv.* until; even; *prep.* until; **hasta luego** see you later (1); **hasta mañana** see you tomorrow (1); **hasta pronto** see you soon (1); **hasta que** (*conj.*) until; **siga hasta llegar a...** go / keep going (*command form. s.*) until you get to . . . (5)

hechizo spell

hecho *n.* fact, event; **de hecho** actually

hecho/a (*p.p. of* **hacer**) made; **¿de qué está hecho/a?** what is it made of?

helado ice cream (6)

helicóptero helicopter

hembra female

hemisferio hemisphere

heredar to inherit

heredero/a heir

herencia inheritance

herida wound; injury

hermanastro/a stepbrother/stepsister (4)

hermano/a brother/sister (4); *pl.* siblings

hermoso/a pretty; beautiful

héroe *m.* hero

herramienta tool

hervor *m.* boil (*liquid*)

heteroparental *family made up of opposite-sex parents and their children*

hielo ice; **patinar sobre el hielo** to ice skate; **patinaje** (*m.*) **sobre el hielo** ice skating

hijastro/a stepson/stepdaughter (4)

hijo/a son/daughter (4); *pl.* children; **hijo/a único/a** only child (4)

hinchazón *f.* (*pl.* **hinchazones**) swelling

hipermercado large supermarket (6)

hipocondríaco/a hypochondriac

hipoteca mortgage

hipotético/a hypothetical

hispano/a Hispanic

hispanohablante *n. m., f.* Spanish-speaker; *adj. m., f.* Spanish-speaking

historia history (1)

histórico/a historical

hogar home (16); **sin hogar** homeless

hoja de papel sheet of paper (1)

hola hi; hello (1)

Holanda Holland

Hollywoodense *n., adj.* of or pertaining to Hollywood

hombre *m.* man (1)

hombro shoulder (8)

homenaje *m.* tribute

homoparental *family made up of same-sex parents and their children*

hondureño/a *n., adj.* Honduran (2)

hongos *m. pl. mushrooms* (6)

honor *m.* honor

hora hour; time; **¿a qué hora... ?** at what time? (3); **¿qué hora es?** what time is it? (3)

horario schedule

hormiga ant

hormiguero anthill

horno oven (11)

horrible horrible (2)

hospital *m.* hospital (5)

hotel *m.* hotel (9)

hoy today; **¿cuál es la fecha de hoy?** what is today's date? (1); **hoy en día** today; these days; **hoy es...** today is . . . (1)

huarache *m.* sandal

hueso bone

huevo egg (6); **huevos motuleños** *Yucatan dish of fried eggs over black beans and a fried tortilla*

huitlacoche *m.* corn smut

humanidad *f.* humanity; *pl.* humanities (1)

humanitarismo humanitarianism

humano/a human; **derecho humano** human right (15); **violar los derechos humanos** to violate human rights

humedad *f.* humidity

húmedo/a humid

humillar to humiliate

humorístico/a humorous

huracán *m.* (*pl.* **huracanes**) hurricane (13)

I

iceberg *m.* iceberg

idea idea (1); **¡qué buena idea!** what a good idea!

identidad *f.* identity

identificar(se) (qu) to identify (oneself)

idioma *m.* language

idiosincrasia idiosyncrasy

idiota *m.* idiot

iglesia church (5)

ignorar to ignore

igual same; igual; **al igual que** just like; **igual de** just as; **igual que** just like; **sin igual** unequaled

igualdad *f.* equality (15)

igualmente likewise (1)

ilegal illegal

ilegítimo/a illegitimate

ilógico/a illogical

iluminación lighting

ilusión *f.* dream; hope

imagen *f.* (*pl.* **imágenes**) image

imaginación *f.* imagination

imaginar to imagine

imaginario/a imaginary

imitar to imitate

impacto impact

impensado/a unexpected

imperfecto *gram.* imperfect

imperialismo imperialism

imperio empire

impermeable: acabado impermeable waterproof finish

imponer (*like* **poner**) (*p.p.* **impuesto**) to impose

importación *f.* importation

importancia importance

importante important

importar (*like* **gustar**) to matter (7); to be important to (7); **sin importar** regardless of

imposible impossible

impresión *f.* impression

impresionante impressive

impreso/a (*p.p. of* **imprimir**) printed

impresora printer (10)

imprimir (*p.p.* **impreso**) to print

impulsar to motivate

impureza impurity

inalámbrico/a wireless; **conexión** (*f.*) **inalámbrica** wireless connection

inauguración *f.* inauguration

inaugurado/a inaugurated

inca *n. m., f.* Inca; *adj. m., f.* Incan

incapacitado/a disabled

incidente *m.* incident

incienso incense

inclinarse (por) to lean (toward)

incluir (y) to include

incluso/a including

incorporar to incorporate

incrementar(se) to increase

indefinido/a indefinite

independencia independence; **Día** (*m.*) **de la Independencia** Independence Day (7)

independiente independent

independizarse (c) to become independent (16)

indicación *f.* indication; instruction

indicar (qu) to indicate

índice *m.* index; rate

indiferente indifferent

indígena *n. m., f.* native (indigenous) person (15); *adj. m., f.* indigenous

indigente indigent

indio/a *n., adj.* Indian

individuo individual

industrializarse (c) to industrialize

ineficaz ineffective

inesperado/a unexpected

infantil *adj.* child, children's; **esclavitud** (*f.*) **infantil** child slavery (15)

infección *f.* infection (12)

inferior inferior; lower

infierno hell

infinitivo *gram.* infinitive

inflable inflatable

inflar to inflate

influencia influence

influir (y) to influence

influyente influential

información *f.* information

informar to inform

informática computer science

informe *m.* report

infraestructura infrastructure (15)

ingeniería engineering (1)

ingeniero/a engineer (4)

Inglaterra England

inglés *m.* English (*language*) (1)

inglés (*pl.* **ingleses**), **inglesa** *n.* English person; *adj.* English

ingrediente *m.* ingredient

ingresos *pl.* income

iniciar to begin

inicio beginning

injusticia injustice

inmaduro/a immature

inmediatamente immediately

inmigración *f.* immigration

inmigrante *m., f.* immigrant (15)

inmigrar to immigrate

innovación *f.* innovation

innovador(a) innovative

inodoro toilet (11)

inseguridad *f.* insecurity

inseguro/a insecure

insistir (en) to insist (on)

insomnio insomnia (12)

inspeccionar to inspect

inspiración *f.* inspiration

inspirar to inspire

instalar to install

institucional institutional

instrucción *f.* instruction

instructor(a) instructor

instrumento instrument; **tocar (qu) un instrumento** to play an instrument

insultar to insult

integrar to integrate

inteligente intelligent (2)

intenso/a intense

intentar to try (to)

interacción *f.* interaction

intercambio exchange

interés *m.* (*pl.* **intereses**) interest

interesante interesting (2)

interesar (*like* **gustar**) to interest (7)

interior interior; **ropa interior** underwear (8)

internacional international; **relaciones** (*f. pl.*) **internacionales** international relations (1)

Internet *m.* Internet; **buscador** (*m.*) **de Internet** search engine; **conectarse al Internet** to connect to the Internet
interno/a internal
interpretar to interpret; **interpretar un papel** to play a role/part (14)
intérprete *m., f.* interpreter
interrumpir to interrupt
intersección *f.* intersection
íntimo/a intimate
intrínsico/a intrinsic
introducción *f.* introduction
introvertido/a introverted
inundación *f.* flood (13)
inundar(se) to flood
inventar to invent
inversión *f.* investment
inversionista *m., f.* investor
investigación *f.* research
invierno winter (1); **Juegos Olímpicos de invierno** Winter Olympics
invitación *f.* invitation
Invitado/a guest
invitar to invite (7); **invitar + a + *inf.*** to invite (*to do something*)
iPad *m.* iPad
ir *irreg.* to go (2); **ir a** | *inf.* to be going to (*do something*) (2); **ir al gimnasio** to go to the gym (3); **ir de compras** to go shopping (2); **ir de viaje** to go on a trip (9); **irse** to leave, to go away (5); **irse de fiesta** to party; **¿adónde va(s)?** where are you (*form. s. / inform. s.*) going? (2); **que le(s) vaya bien** have a good one / I hope things go well for you (*form. s., pl.*) (12); **voy a/al + *place*** I'm going to . . . (2)
irlandés (*pl.* **irlandeses**), **irlandesa** *n.* Irish person; *adj.* Irish
isla island
Italia Italy
italiano/a *n., adj.* Italian
itinerario itinerary
izquierda left; **a la izquierda** on the left; **a mano izquierda** on the left; **coger (j) a mano izquierda** to turn left (*Sp.*); **doble/gire a la izquierda** turn (to the) right/left (*command form. s.*) (5); **quedar a la izquierda** to be on the left

J

jaguar *m.* jaguar
jalar to pull; pull (9)
jalisciense *adj.* of or pertaining to Jalisco, Mex.
jamaicano/a *n., adj.* Jamaican
jamón *m.* ham (6)
Jánuca *m.* Hanukah (7)
japonés *m.* Japanese (*language*)
japonés (pl. **japoneses**), **japonesa** *n.* Japanese person; *adj.* Japanese
jarabe (*m.*) **para la tos** cough syrup
jardín *m.* (*pl.* **jardines**) garden (5)
jeans *m. pl.* jeans (8)
jefe/a boss (10)

jerarquía hierarchy
Jerusalén Jerusalem
jirafa giraffe
jitomate *m.* tomato (*Mex.*)
joven *n. m., f.* (*pl.* **jóvenes**) young person (1); *adj.* young (2)
joyería jewelry; jewelry store
joyero/a jeweler
jubilación *f.* retirement
judío/a *n.* Jewish person, Jew; *adj.* Jewish
juego game; **Juegos Olímpicos (de invierno/verano)** (Winter/Summer) Olympics (12)
jueves *m.* Thursday (3)
juez(a) *n.* judge (10)
jugador(a) player (12)
jugar (ue) (gu) to play (*a game, sport*) (2); **jugar básquetbol** to play basketball (3); **jugar béisbol** to play baseball (12); **jugar fútbol** to play soccer (2); **jugar fútbol americano** to play football (12); **jugar tenis** to play tennis (12); **jugar los videojuegos** to play video games (2); **jugar voleibol** to play volleyball (12)
jugo juice (6)
juicio trial
julio July (1)
junio June (1)
juntarse (con) to hang out (with); to get together (with)
junto a along with
juntos/as together
jurídico/a judicial
justicia justice; **sala de justicia** courtroom (10)
justificar (qu) to justify
justo/a fair (15)
juvenil young; youthful
juventud *f.* youth
juzgar (gu) to judge

K

kayak *m.* kayak; **hacer** (*irreg.*) **kayak** to go kayaking
kilo(gramo) kilo(gram) (1)
kilómetro kilometer
kiosko kiosk
koala *m.* koala
kuna *n. m., f.* member of the Kuna group; *adj. m., f.* of or pertaining to the Kuna indigenous group of Panama

L

la *def. art. f. s.* the (1); *d.o. pron. f. s.* you (*form.*), her, it (6)
laberinto labyrinth
labio lip (8)
laboral *adj.* work-related
lácteo/a *adj.* dairy; **productos lácteos** dairy products (6)
lado side; **al lado** beside; **al otro lado de** on the other side of; **de un lado al otro** from one side to the other; **dejar a un lado** to leave aside; **por otro lado** on

the other hand; **por un lado** on one hand
ladrón (*pl.* **ladrones**), **ladrona** thief
lago lake
lágrima tear
lamentablemente sadly, unfortunately
lamentar to regret
lamento lament; moan, cry
lámpara lamp (11)
lanzador(a) pitcher (*baseball*)
lanzar (c) to launch; to throw, pitch
lápiz *m.* (*pl.* **lápices**) pencil (1)
láptop: (computadora) láptop laptop (computer) (10)
largo/a long (2); **a largo plazo** long-term, in the long-term; **a lo largo de** along, throughout
largometraje *m.* feature film
las *def. art. f. pl.* the (1); *d.o. pron. f. pl.* they, you (*form.*) (6); **a la(s)...** at . . . (*time of day*)
lastimar(se) to injure (oneself)
Latinoamérica Latin America
latinoamericano/a *n., adj.* Latin American
lavabo bathroom sink (11)
lavadora washing machine (11)
lavandería laundromat
lavaplatos *m. s., pl.* dishwasher (11)
lavar to wash (4); **lavar el suelo** to wash the floor (11); **lavar la ropa** to wash clothes (4); **lavar los platos** to wash dishes (4); **lavarse la cara** to wash one's face (5); **lavarse las manos** to wash one's hands (5); **lavarse los dientes** to brush one's teeth
le *i.o. pron.* him, her, you (*form. s.*) (7); **¿en qué puedo servirle?** how may I help you? (10); **le acompaño/acompañamos en el dolor** I'm/we're with you in your time of pain (16); **le acompaño/acompañamos en el sentimiento** you're in my/our thoughts (16); **le agradezco por** I appreciate that you, I thank you for (5); **¡le damos la bienvenida a Ud.!** we welcome you! (11); **le deseo mucha suerte** I wish you luck (12); **le doy/damos el pésame** my/our condolences (16); **¿le gusta(n) + noun(s)?** do you (*form.*) like + noun(s)? (2); **¿le gustaría + inf.?** would you like (*to do something*)? (9); **que le vaya bien** have a good one / I hope things go well for you (12); **quiero presentarle a...** I'd like you to meet . . . (10); **se le antoja/antojó + inf. / s. n.** they, you feel/felt like ([*doing*] *something*) (9); **se le antojan/antojaron + inf. s. n.** they, you feel/felt like + *pl. n.* (9)
leche *f.* milk (6); **arroz** (*m.*) **con leche** rice pudding
lechuga lettuce (6)
lector(a) reader
lectura reading
leer (y) (*p.p.* leído) to read (2); **leer el periódico** to read the newspaper (3)

legalizar (c) to legalize
lejano/a distant
lejos (de) far (from) (9)
lema *m.* slogan
lengua tongue; language
lenguado sole (*fish*)
lenguaje *m.* language
lenteja lentil
lentes *m. pl.* (eye)glasses (8); **lentes de contacto** contact lenses; **ponerse** (*irreg.*) **los lentes / los lentes de contacto** to put on glasses/contacts (5)
lentillas contact lenses
lento/a slow (2)
león (*pl.* **leones**), **leonesa** lion; **león marino** sea lion (13)
leprosario leper colony
les *i.o. pron.* them, you (*form. pl.*) (7); **¿en qué puedo servirles?** how may I help you? (10); **les acompaño/acompañamos en el dolor** I'm/we're with you in your time of pain (16); **les acompaño/acompañamos en el sentimiento** you're in my/our thoughts (16); **les agradezco por** I appreciate that you, I thank you for (5); **les deseo mucha suerte** I wish you luck (12); **les doy/damos el pésame** my/our condolences (16); **que les vaya bien** have a good one / I hope things go well for you (12); **quiero presentarles a...** I'd like you to meet . . . (10); **se les antoja/antojó** + *inf.* / *s. n.* they/you feel/felt like ([*doing*] something) (9); **se les antojan/antojaron** + *inf. pl. n.* they/you feel/felt like + *pl. n.* (9)
letra letter (*of the alphabet*); lyrics
levantador(a) de pesas weightlifter
levantar to raise, lift; **levantar pesas** to lift weights (12); **levantarse** to get up (5); to stand up (5)
leve *adj.* light
ley *f.* law; **violar la ley** to break the law
libanés (*pl.* **libaneses**), **libanesa** *n.*, Lebanese person; *adj.* Lebanese
Líbano Lebanon
libertad *f.* freedom (15)
libre free; **al aire libre** outdoors; **tiempo libre** free time
librería bookstore (1)
libro book (1); **libro de texto** textbook
licenciado/a graduate; attorney
licenciatura degree (Bachelor's)
licopeno lycopene
licor *m.* liquor
licorería liquor store
líder *m., f.* leader
liga league
ligado/a tied, bound
ligero/a light
lima lime
limitar to limit
límite *m.* limit
limón *m.* (*pl.* **limones**) lemon (6); lime (6)
limpiar to clean (4)

limpio/a clean (2)
lince *m.* lynx
lindo/a pretty (2); **¡qué lindo/a!** how cute/pretty! (4)
línea line; **línea en blanco** blank (line)
lino linen
lío trouble, mess: **¡qué lío!** what a mess! (4)
líquido liquid
Lisboa Lisbon
lisina lysine
lista list
listo/a ready
literatura literature (14)
llamada (phone) call
llamar to call; **llamarse** to be called (1); **¿cómo se llama?** what is your name (*form. s.*)? (1); **¿cómo se llama él/ella?** what is his/her name? (1); **¿cómo te llamas?** what is your name (*inform. s.*)? (1); **me llamo** my name is (1); **se llama** his/her name is (1)
llanero/a plainsman, plainswoman
llanto sobbing, weeping
llanura plain
llave *f.* key (1)
llavero keychain
llegar (gu) to arrive (5); **siga hasta llegar a...** go / keep going (*command form. s.*) until you get to . . . (5)
llenar to fill
lleno/a full
llevar to wear (8); to bring (8); to carry; to take; **¿cuánto tiempo lleva(s)** + **-ndo** *form*? how long have you (*form. s. / inform. s.*) (*done / been doing something*)? (13); **llevar una vida activa** to lead an active life; **llevarse a cabo** to carry out; **llevo** + *time expression* + **-ndo** *form* I've been (*doing something*) for + *time* (13); **llevo** + *time expression* + **sin** + *inf.* I haven't (*done something* for + *time* (13)
llover (ue) to rain; **está lloviendo** it's raining (9); **llueve** it's raining (9)
lluvia rain
lluvioso/a rainy
lo *d.o. pron. m. s.* you (*form.*) (6); him; it (6); **cuánto lo siento** I'm very sorry (16); **lo contrario** the opposite; **lo siento** I'm sorry (7); condolences (7); **lo siento mucho** I'm very sorry (16)
lobo wolf
localidad *f.* locality
localizar (c) to locate
loco/a crazy
lógico/a logical
Londres London
loro parrot (13)
los *def. art. m. pl.* the (1); *d.o. pron. m.* they (6); *d.o. pron. m. pl.* you (*form. pl.*) (6)
lotería lottery; **sacar (qu) la lotería** to win the lottery
luchar to fight

lucir (zc) to wear, to dress up; to shine
lucrativo/a lucrative
lucro: organización (*f.*) **sin fines de lucro** nonprofit organization (15)
lúcuma lucuma (*fruit*)
luego then, afterward, next; **hasta luego** see you later (1)
lugar *m.* place (5); **lugar del crimen** scene of the crime
lujo: de lujo luxury
luna moon
lunes *m.* Monday (3)
luz *f.* (*pl.* **luces**) light; **dar** (*irreg.*) **a luz** to give birth

M

macerar to tenderize
macho male
madera wood; **de madera** made of wood
madrastra stepmother (4)
madre *f.* mother (4); **Día** (*m.*) **de las Madres** Mother's Day
madrina godmother
madrugada early morning; dawn; **de la madrugada** in the early morning hours (3)
madurez *f.* maturity
maestría Master's degree; **sacar (qu) una maestría** to get a Master's (degree)
maestro/a teacher (10)
mágico/a magic
mago: Día (*m.*) **de los Reyes Magos** Three Kings Day; Epiphany (Adoration of the Magi) (7)
maillot *m.* (sports) jersey
maíz *m.* corn (6)
mal *adv.* poorly; **lo pasé mal** I had a bad time (7); **(muy) mal** (very) bad (1); **pasarlo mal** to have a bad time (7)
mal, malo/a *adj.* bad (2); **hace (muy) mal tiempo** the weather's (very) bad (9); **¡qué malo!** that's terrible! (8); **sacar (qu) malas notas** to get bad grades; **tener** (*irreg.*) **mala pinta** to have a bad appearance; **verse** (*irreg.*) **mal** to look bad
maldición *f.* curse
maleta suitcase (9); **hacer** (*irreg.*) **la maleta** to pack a suitcase (9)
malgastar to waste (13)
mamá mother (4)
manchar to stain; **mancharse** to get dirty
mandar to order; to send (10)
mandato command
manejar to drive
manera way; **de la misma manera** likewise
manga sleeve
mango mango (6)
manifestación *f.* protest
manifiesto manifest
mano *f.* hand (8); **a mano** by hand; **a mano derecha/izquierda** on the right/left; **coger (j) a mano derecha/izquierda** to turn right/left (*Sp.*); **darse** (*irreg.*)

la mano to shake hands; **lavarse las manos** to wash one's hands

mantener (*like* **tener**) to maintain; **mantenerse en contacto (con)** to stay in touch (with); **mantenerse en forma** to stay in shape (12); **mantenerse sano** to stay healthy (12)

mantequilla butter (6)

manzana apple (6); city block (*Sp., S.A.*)

mañana tomorrow; morning; **de la mañana** in the morning, A.M. (3); **hasta mañana** see you tomorrow (1); **por la mañana** in the morning (3)

mapa *m.* map

mapuche *n. indigenous person of south-central Chile and southwestern Argentina*

mapuey *m.* tropical tuber

maquillarse to put on makeup (5)

máquina machine

mar *m.* sea (9); **mar adentro** off-shore

maracuyá passion fruit

maratón *m. (pl.* maratones*)* marathon

maravilloso/a marvelous (2)

marca brand (8)

marcar (qu) to mark; to score; **marcar un gol** to score a goal

margen *m. (pl.* **márgenes***)* margin

marido husband (4)

marino/a *adj.* sea; **león** (*m.*) **marino** sea lion (13)

mariposa butterfly

mariscos *m. pl.* seafood (6)

marítimo/a *adj.* maritime

marketing *m.* marketing

marrón brown (2)

Marruecos Morocco

martes *m.* Tuesday (3)

marzo March (1)

más more; **cada vez más** increasingly; **come/coma más** have some more (*command inform. s. / form. s.*) (11); **más alto que** taller than (4); **más de** + *number* more than + *number*; **más** + *adj.* **que** more (-er) + *adj.* than (4); **mi/nuestro más sentido pésame** my/our deepest condolences (16)

masa dough

máscara mask

mascota pet (4)

masculino/a masculine

masivo/a mass

máster *m.* Master's (program, degree)

masticar (qu) to chew

matar to kill

mate *m. strong tea of South America*

matemáticas *pl.* math (1)

materia subject (1)

material *m.* material

materno/a maternal

matrícula tuition

matricularse to enroll

matrimonio marriage (16)

máximo/a maximum

maya *n., adj. m., f.* Mayan

mayo May (1); **el primero de mayo** the first of May (1);

mayor older (4); oldest; greater; greatest

mayoría majority

mayormente principally

mayúscula capital (letter), uppercase

mazcora ear of corn; cob

me *d.o. pron.* me (6); *i.o. pron.* to/for me (7); *refl. pron.* myself; **me gusta(n)** + *noun(s)* I like + *noun(s)* (2); **me gustaría** + *inf.* I would like (*to do something* (9); **¿me puede comunicar con... ?** can you connect me with . . . ?; **no me gusta(n)** + *noun(s)* I don't like + *noun(s)* (2); **se me antoja/antojó** + *inf. / s. n.* I feel/felt like + ([*doing*] something) (9); **se me antojan/antojaron** + *pl. n.* I feel/felt like + *pl. n.* (9)

mearse *sl.* to wet/pee oneself

mecánico/a *n., adj.* mechanic

medialuna croissant

medianoche *f.* midnight; **es medianoche** it's midnight (3)

mediante through

medias *pl.* stockings

medicado/a medicated

medicina medicine

médico/a doctor (4); **médico/a de cabecera** general practitioner

la medida measurement (12)

medio *n.* medium; means; *pl.* mass media; **medio ambiente** environment (13); **medio de transporte** means of transportation

medio/a *adj.* half; middle; average; **en medio de** in the middle of (11); **es la una y media** it's 1:30 (3); **media naranja** better half; **y media** half past (*the hour*)

medioambiental environmental (13)

mediocampo mid-field

mediocre mediocre

mediodía *m.* noon; **es mediodía** it's noon (3);

medir (i, i) to measure (12)

meditar to meditate

Mediterráneo Mediterranean

medusa jellyfish

megaestrella superstar

mejillón *m.* mussel

mejor better (4); best

mejorar to improve; **mejorarse** to get better (12)

mellizo/a fraternal twin

melocotón *m.* peach

melodramático/a melodramatic

memoria memory; **tarjeta de memoria** memory card

memorizar (c) to memorize

mencionar to mention

menor younger (4); youngest; less; least

menos less; least; minus; **menos** + *adj.* + **que** less + *adj.* than (4); **menos alto que** less tall than (4)

mensaje *m.* message (10); **mensaje recordatorio** reminder

mensual monthly

mente *f.* mind

mentir (ie, i) to lie

menú *m.* menu

mercado (outdoor) market (5)

merendar (ie) to have a snack (6)

merienda snack (6)

merluza hake

mes *m.* month (1)

mesa table (1); **poner** (*irreg.*) **la mesa** to set the table (6)

mesita de noche nightstand (11)

mesoamericano/a *n., adj.* Meso-American

mestizo/a of mixed race (European and native American)

meta goal

metabólico/a metabolic

metal *m.* metal

meter to put, place; **meter un gol** to score a goal

metro subway (5); meter; **metro cuadrado** square meter

metrópoli *f.* metropolis

metropolitano/a metropolitan

mexicano/a *n., adj.* Mexican (2); **comer comida mexicana** to eat Mexican food (3)

mezcla mix

mezclar(se) to mix, blend

mí *obj. of prep.* me; **para mí** for me (7); for me (personally) (15)

mi(s) *poss. adj.* my (1); **en mi opinión...** in my opinion . . . (15); **mi más sentido pésame** my deepest condolences (16); **mi nombre/apellido es** my name/last name is (1)

micro bus (*C.A. and S.A.*)

microempresa micro-business

microfinanza micro-finance

micrófono microphone

microondas *m. s., pl.* microwave (11)

microproducto micro-product

miedo fear; **tener** (*irreg.*) **miedo** to be afraid

miedoso/a easily frightened

miel *f.* honey

miembro member

mientras while

miércoles *m.* Wednesday (3)

mil (one) thousand (5); **dos mil** two thousand (5); **tres mil** three thousand (5); **cuatro mil** four thousand (5); **cinco mil** five thousand (5); **seis mil** six thousand (5); **siete mil** seven thousand (5); **ocho mil** eight thousand (5); **nueve mil** nine thousand (5)

militar *n. m., f.* soldier; **escuela militar** military school; **fuerzas militares** military forces

milla mile

millón *m.* million

minería mining

minibús *m.* small bus

minifalda miniskirt
minimizar (c) to minimize
mínimo minimum
miniserie *f.* miniseries
minuto minute
mío/a(s) *poss. adj.* my; *poss. pron.* (of) mine
mira: en el punto de mira in the crosshairs
mirar to look at; to watch (3); **mirar la televisión** to watch television (3)
misa mass
misión *f.* mission
mismo/a same; **de la misma manera** likewise
misquito *indigenous group of Central America*
misterio mystery
misterioso/a mysterious
místico/a *n., adj.* mystic
mitad *f.* half
mixteco/a *n., adj.* Mixtec (*an indigenous group of Mex.*)
mixto/a mixed; **ensalada mixta** tossed salad
mochila backpack (1)
moda fashion; style; **desfile** (*m.*) **de moda** fashion show (8); **estar** (*irreg.*) **(pasado/a) de moda** to be (un)fashionable (8); **la última moda** the latest fashion
modalidades *f. pl.* manners
modelo model
módem *m.* (*pl.* **módems**) modem
moderado/a moderate
moderno/a modern (5)
modificar (qu) to modify
modistería dressmaker's shop
modo way; manner; means; **modo de transporte** means of transportation
mojar to wet
mola *embroidered panel used in the typical clothing of Kuna women in Panama*
molestar (*like* **gustar**) to bother (7)
molestia bother; **si no es molestia** if it's not a bother (6)
momento moment; **en algún momento** at some point
monarquía monarchy
monitor *m.* monitor
mono monkey (13)
montaña mountain (9); **hacer ciclismo de montaña** to go mountain biking (9)
montar to ride; **montar a caballo** to ride a horse (3); **montar en bicicleta** to ride a bicycle
montón: un montón a lot
monumento monument
morado/a purple (2)
morder (ue) to bite
moreno/a *n.* brunet(te); *adj.* dark brown (*hair, eyes*) (2)
moretón *m.* (*pl.* **moretones**) bruise
morir(se) (ue, u) (*p.p.* **muerto**) to die (8)
mosaico mosaic

mostrar (ue) to show
motivado/a motivated (2)
moto(cicleta) motorcycle
motuleño: huevos motuleños *Yucatan dish of fried eggs over black beans and a fried tortilla*
mover(se) (ue) to move (*motion*)
móvil *m.* cell phone
movimiento movement
muchacho/a boy, girl
mucho *adj.* much; a lot; *adv.* a lot; **me divertí mucho** I had a lot of fun (7)
mucho/a a lot (of); *pl.* many; **¡con mucho gusto!** with pleasure! (6); **le(s) deseo mucha suerte** I wish you (*form. s., pl.*) luck (12); **lo siento mucho** I'm very sorry (16); **¡mucha suerte!** good luck! (12); best of luck! (12); **muchas/muchísimas gracias** thank you very much (5); **mucho gusto** nice to meet you (1); **mucho tiempo** a long time (13)
mudarse to move (*residence*) (16)
mueble *m.* piece of furniture
muerte *f.* death
muerto/a (*p.p. of* **morir**) to die; **Día** (*m.*) **de Muertos** Day of the Dead (7)
mujer *f.* woman (1); wife (4); **mujer bombero** female firefighter (10); **mujer policía** policewoman
mulato/a mulatto
múltiples *pl.* multiple
multitud *f.* multitude
mundial *adj.* world; **Copa Mundial** World Cup
mundo world
municipalidad *f.* municipality
municipio municipality
muñeca wrist; doll
muñeco doll
mural *m.* mural
murga *typical song of Carnival celebrations in Uruguay and Arg.*
músculo muscle
museo museum (5)
música music (2); **música en vivo** live music (14)
músico *m., f.* musician
musulmán (*pl.* **musulmanes**), **musulmana** *n., adj.* Muslim
mutable changeable
mutuo/a mutual
muy very; **muy bien** very well (1); **muy mal** very bad (1)

N

nacer (zc) to be born (6)
nacimiento birth (7); **defecto de nacimiento** birth defect
nación *f.* nation; **Naciones Unidas** United Nations
nacional national
nacionalidad *f.* nationality
nacionalista *m., f.* nationalist
nacionalizado/a nationalized

nada nothing (5); not anything; **de nada** you're welcome (5)
nadar to swim (2); **nadar de dorso** to do the backstroke
nadie no one (5); nobody, not anybody
náhuatl *m.* Nahuatl (*language of the Aztecs*)
naranja orange (6); **media naranja** better half
narcotráfico drug trafficking (15)
nariz *f.* (*pl.* **narices**) nose (8)
narración *f.* narration
narrar to narrate
natación *f.* swimming (12)
nativo/a native
natural natural; **desastre** (*m.*) **natural** natural disaster (15); **recurso natural** natural resource (13)
naturaleza nature (9)
naturalista *adj.* nature; **guía** (*m., f.*) **naturalista** nature guide (4)
náuseas *pl.* nausea (12); **tener** (*irreg.*) **náuseas** to feel nauseous
náutico/a nautical
navegable navigable
navegador *m.* browser; **navegador web** web browser
navegante *m., f.* sailor
navegar (gu) to navigate
Navidad *f.* Christmas (7); **árbol** (*m.*) **de Navidad** Christmas tree
navideño/a *adj.* Christmas
necesario/a necessary
necesidad *f.* necessity
necesitar to need
negativo/a negative
negociar to negotiate
negocio business; **administración** (*f.*) **de negocios** business administration
negrita: en negrita boldface
negro/a black (2)
nervioso/a nervous (2)
nevar (ie) to snow; **está nevando** it's snowing (9); **nieva** it's snowing (9)
ni neither; nor; **ni... ni** neither . . . nor
nicaragüense *n., adj. m., f.* Nicaraguan (2)
nido nest; **nido familiar** parent's home (16)
nieto/a grandson, granddaughter (4)
ningún/ninguna none, no (not one, not any) (5)
niñez *f.* childhood
niño/a small child; boy/girl (2); **de niño/a** as a child
nivel *m.* level (15)
no no (1); **¡cómo no!** *interj.* of course! (6); **favor de no fumar** no smoking, please (9); **no beber y conducir** don't drink and drive (9); **no doblar** do not turn (9); **no encontrarse bien** to not feel well (12); **no entrar** do not enter (9); **no estacionar** no parking (9); **no fumar** no smoking (9); **no girar** do not turn (9); **no, gracias** no, thank you (6); **no hay de**

qué you're welcome (5); **no hay que +** *inf.* you don't have to / it's not necessary to (*do something*) (12); **no pasar** do not enter (9); **no pisar (el césped)** stay off / do not walk on (the grass) (9); **no puedo** I can't (8); **no tirar basura** don't litter (9); **no vale la pena** it's not worth it; **si no es molestia** if it's not a bother (6)

noble *m.* noble, aristocrat; *adj.* noble

noche *f.* night; **buenas noches** good evening/night (1); **de la noche** at night (3); **por la noche** at night (3); **son las doce de la noche** it's midnight (3); **toda la noche** all night (3) ; **todas las noches** every night (3)

Nochebuena Christmas Eve (7)

Nochevieja New Year's Eve (7)

nombrar to name

nombre *m.* name; **mi nombre es** my name is (1)

nominación *f.* nomination

nominar to nominate

nopalitos *pl. dish made with the leaves of prickly pears*

noreste *m.* northeast

normal normal

noroeste *m.* northwest

norte *m.* north

norteamericano/a *n., adj.* North American (2)

Noruega Norway

noruego/a *n., adj.* Norwegian

nos *d.o. pron.* us (6); *i.o. pron.* to/for us (7); *refl. pron.* ourselves; **se nos antoja/ antojó +** *inf.* / *s. n.* we feel/felt like + ([*doing*] *something*) (9); **se me/te/le/ nos/os/les antojan/antojaron +** *pl. n.* we feel/felt like + *pl. n.* (9)

nosotros/as *sub. pron.* we; *obj. of prep.* us

nota grade (*academic*); note; **nota de agradecimiento** thank-you note; **sacar (qu) buenas/malas notas** to get good/ back grades

notar to note

noticia piece of news; **noticias** news (15)

novecientos nine hundred

novecientos/as nine hundred (5)

novela novel

noveno/a ninth

noventa ninety

noviazgo relationship (4); engagement (16)

noviembre *m.* November (1)

novio/a boyfriend/girlfriend (4); fiancé(e) (16); groom/bride (16)

nublado/a cloudy; **está nublado** it's cloudy (9)

núcleo nucleus

nuera daughter-in-law (4)

nuestro/a(s) *poss. adj.* our (1); *poss. pron.* our, of ours; **nuestro más sentido pésame** my/our deepest condolences (16)

nueve nine; **nueve mil** nine thousand (5); **son diez para las nueve** it's 8:50 (3); **son las nueve menos diez** it's 8:50 (3)

nuevo/a new (2); **Año Nuevo** New Year's (7); **Nueva York** New York

nuez *f.* (*pl.* **nueces**) nut; walnut

número number; shoe size (8); **¿cuál es tu número de teléfono?** what is your phone number? (1); **un número a la vez, por favor** one number at a time, please (1)

nunca never (3)

nutrición *f.* nutrition

nutriente *m.* nutrient

nutritivo/a nutritious

O

o or (1)

objetivo/a objective

objeto object

obligación *f.* obligation (13)

obligar (gu) to force

obligatorio/a obligatory

obra work; **obra de arte** piece, work of art (14); **obra de teatro** play (14)

obrero/a worker, laborer

observación *f.* observation

observador(a) observer

observar to observe

obtener (*like* **tener**) to obtain

océano ocean; **océano Atlántico** Atlantic Ocean; **océano Pacífico** Pacific Ocean

ochenta eighty

ocho eight; **ocho mil** eight thousand (5); **son las ocho y cincuenta** it's 8:50 (3)

ochocientos/as eight hundred (5)

octavo/a eighth

octubre *m.* October (1); **el quince de octubre** October fifteenth (1)

ocupación *f.* occupation

ocupado/a busy

ocupar to occupy

ocurrir to occur

odiar to hate

oeste *m.* west

ofensivo/a offensive; **volante** (*m., f.*) **ofensivo/a** offensive midfielder

oferta supply (15); offer (15)

oficial official

oficina office (1); **oficina de correos** post office

oficio trade (*profession*)

ofrecer (zc) to offer

oír *irreg.* to hear (5); to listen to (*music, the radio*) (5); **oye...** listen . . . (*command inform. s.*); **oiga...** listen . . . (*command form. s.*); **oigan...** listen . . . (*command form. pl.*)

ojalá (que) I hope (that) (12)

ojo eye (8)

oleoducto oil pipeline

oler *irreg.* to smell

Olímpicos: Juegos (*pl.*) **Olímpicos (de Invierno/Verano)** (Winter/Summer) Olympics (12)

oliva olive; **aceite** (*m.*) **de oliva** olive oil; **color** (*m.*) **verde oliva** olive green

olla pot, pan

olor *m.* scent, odor

olvidar(se) to forget (9)

once eleven

onda wave

opción *f.* option

ópera opera (14)

operación *f.* operation

operático/a pertaining to opera

opinar to think; to have/express an opinion

opinión *f.* opinion; **en mi opinión...** in my opinion . . . (15)

oportunidad *f.* opportunity

oportuno/a opportune

optar (por) to opt (for)

optimista *m., f.* optimist; *adj.* optimistic (2)

opuesto/a opposite

oración *f.* sentence

orden *m.* order; *f.* order (*command, legal*); **a sus órdenes** at your (*form. s., pl.*) service

oreja ear (8)

orgánico/a organic; **desecho orgánico** organic waste

organismo organism; body

organización *f.* organization; **organización sin fines de lucro** nonprofit organization (15)

organizar (c) to organize

orgullo pride

orgulloso/a proud

oriental Oriental; Eastern

oriente *m.* east

origen *m.* origin

originario/a native

originarse to begin

orilla shore

oro gold

orquesta orchestra (14)

orquídea orchid

ortografía spelling

ortográfico/a *adj.* spelling; **error** (*m.*) **ortográfico** spelling mistake

os *d.o. pron.* (*Sp.*) you (*inform. pl.*) (6); *i.o. pron.* (*Sp.*) to/for you (*inform. pl.*) (7); *refl. pron.* (*Sp.*) yourselves (*inform. pl.*); **se os antoja/antojó +** *inf.* / *s. n.* you (*inform. pl.*) feel/felt like + ([*doing*] *something*) (9); **se os antojan/antojaron +** *pl. n.* you (*inform. pl.*) feel/felt like + *pl. n.* (9)

oscuro/a dark

oso (polar) (polar) bear (13)

ostra oyster

otoño autumn, fall (1)

otro/a other, another; **otra vez** again

ozono ozone

P

pabellón (*m.*) **criollo** *Venezuelan rice and beans dish*

paciencia patience

paciente *m., f.* patient

pacífico/a *adj.* Pacific; **océano Pacífico** Pacific Ocean

padecer (zc) to suffer
pádel *m.* paddle tennis
padrastro stepfather (4)
padre *m.* father (4); *pl.* parents (4); **Día** (*m.*) **de los Padres** Father's Day; **¡qué padre!** how cool! (8)
padrino godfather
pagar (gu) to pay
página page; **página web** web page (1)
país *m.* country (2); **Países Bajos** Netherlands; **País Vasco** Basque Country
paisaje *m.* scenery, landscape (9)
pájaro bird (13)
palabra word
palacio palace
palestino/a *n., adj.* Palestinian
paleta palette
pan *m.* bread (6); **pan tostado** toast
panadería bakery (6)
panameño/a *n., adj.* Panamanian (2)
panamericano/a Pan-American
panel (*m.*) **(solar)** (solar) panel
panorámico/a panoramic
pantalla screen (10)
pantalón *m.* pants; *pl.* pants (8); **pantalones cortos** shorts (8); **pantalones de campana** bell-bottoms
panteón *m.* mausoleum
papa potato (6); **papas fritas** french fries
papá *m.* father (4); *pl.* parents (4)
papel *m.* paper; role, part (*in a movie or play*) (14); **hoja de papel** sheet of paper (1); **interpretar un papel** to play a role/part (14)
paquete *m.* package
Paquistán *m.* Pakistan
paquistaní *n., adj. m., f.* Pakistani
par *m.* pair (*objects*)
para (intended) for (7); **para** + *inf.* in order to (*to do something*); **para mí** for me (7); for me (personally) (15); **para que** so that; **para servirle** at your (*form. s.*) service (10); **para ti** for you (*inform. s.*) (7); **servir (i, i) para** to be good at/for (*doing something*) (4); **son diez para las nueve** it's 8:50 (3)
paradisíaco/a idyllic
paradójico/a paradoxical
paraguas *m. s., pl.* umbrella (8)
paraguayo/a *n., adj.* Paraguayan (2)
parapente *m.* paragliding
parar to stop
parásito parasite
parecer (zc) (*like* **gustar**) to seem (7); **parecerse (a)** to resemble; **¿qué te/le parece(n)** + *n./inf.***?** how about (*inform. s. / form. s.*) . . . ? (6)
parecido/a (a) similar (to)
pared *f.* wall (11)
pareja pair; partner (16); couple (16)
pariente *m., f.* relative (4)
París Paris
parlamentario/a parliamentary

parlante *m., f.* loudspeaker
parlar to chatter
parque *m.* park (5); **correr en el parque** to run in the park (3)
párrafo paragraph
parrilla grill
parte *f.* part; **de parte de** from; on behalf of; **¿de parte de quién?** may I ask who's calling?
participante *m., f.* participant
participar to participate (13)
particular: en particular in particular
partido game (12); match (12)
partir: a partir de as of, since
pasado past; **estar** (*irreg.*) **pasado/a de moda** to be unfashionable (8)
pasado/a last; **año pasado** last year; **semana pasada** last week
pasaporte *m.* passport (9)
pasar to spend (*time*); to happen; **lo pasé bien/mal** I had a good/bad time (7); **no pasar** do not enter (9); **pasa/pase(n)** come in / go ahead (*command inform. s. / form. s., pl.*) (8); **pasar la aspiradora** to vacuum (11); **pasar por** to go through (9); **pasar un buen rato** to have a good time; **pasarlo bien/mal** to have a good/ bad time (7); **¿puedo pasar?** excuse me / may I pass by/enter? (8); **¿qué te/ le pasa?** what's happening with you? (*inform. s. / form. s.*) (1); what's the matter? (1)
pasatiempo pastime
Pascua Easter (7); **Domingo de Pascua** Easter Sunday; **Pascua de Resurrección** Easter (7); **Pascua Florida** Easter (7)
pasear to tale a walk, stroll; **sacar (qu) a pasear** to walk (*dog*)
paseo walk, trip (9); **dar** (*irreg.*) **un paseo** to take a walk (9)
pasillo hallway (11)
paso step; **dar** (*irreg.*) **un paso** to take a step
pasta pasta (6)
pastel *m.* pastry; cake
pastilla pill
patada kick
patata potato (*Sp.*)
paterno/a paternal
patinador(a) skater
patinaje *m.* skating (12); **patinaje sobre el hielo** ice skating
patinar to skate; **patinar sobre el hielo** to ice skate
patines *m. pl.* skates (12)
patineta skateboard (12); **andar** (*irreg.*) **en patineta** to skateboard (12)
patología disease
patrocinador(a) sponsor
patrocinar to sponsor
paz *f.* peace (15)
pecho chest (8)
pechuga breast
pedacito small piece

pedir (i, i) to ask for (4); to order (*food*) (6)
pedo *n.* fart
pedorrear to fart
peer (y) to fart
pegar (gu) to paste; **pegarse** to bump
peinarse to brush/comb one's hair (5)
película movie; film (2); **película de acción** action movie; **película de terror** horror film
peligro danger (13); **especie** (*f.*) **en peligro de extinción** endangered species
peligroso/a dangerous (15)
pelirrojo/a *n.* redhead (2); *adj.* redheaded (2)
pelo hair (2)
pelota ball (12)
pelotero/a baseball player
peluquería (hair) salon
pena embarrassment; shame; **(no) vale la pena** it's (not) worth it
peña *venue for musical and other artistic performances (S.A.)*
pendiente *m.* earring (8); *adj.* pending
pensamiento thought
pensar (ie) (en) to think (about) (12); **pensar** + *inf.* to intend, plan to (*do something*)
peor worse (4)
pepino cucumber (6)
pequeño/a small (2)
pera pear
percusionista *m., f.* percussionist
perdedor(a) loser
perder (ie) to lose; to miss
perdón sorry; excuse me; pardon me (8)
perdonar to forgive; **perdona/perdone(n)** sorry; excuse me; pardon me (*command inform. s. / form. s., pl.*) (8)
perejil *m.* parsley (6)
perezoso/a lazy (2)
perfeccionar to perfect
perfecto/a perfect
perfil *m.* profile
perfume *m.* perfume
perico parakeet
perímetro perimeter
periódico newspaper; **leer (y) el periódico** to read the newspaper (3)
periodista *m., f.* journalist (4)
periodo period (*of time*)
permiso permission; **con permiso** excuse me (8)
permitir to permit
pernoctar to spend the night
pero *conj.* but
perro dog (4)
perseguir (*like* **seguir**) to chase; to pursue
persona person; *pl.* people
personaje *m.* character (*in a movie, play or novel*) (14); celebrity, well-known person (14)
personalidad *f.* personality
perspectiva perspective
pertenecer (zc) (a) to belong (to)
pertenencias *pl.* belongings

peruano/a *n., adj.* Peruvian (2)

pesado/a boring; difficult; heavy; **¡qué pesado!** how annoying! (8)

pésame: dar (*irreg.*) **el pésame** to give one's condolences; **mi/nuestro más sentido pésame** my/our deepest condolences (16); **te/le/les doy/damos el pésame** my/our condolences (16)

pesar to weigh; **a pesar de** in spite of, despite

pesas weights (12); **levantar pesas** to lift weights (12)

pesca fishing

pescadería fish market (6)

pescado fish (*food*) (6)

pesero bus (*Mex.*)

pesimismo pessimism

pesimista *m., f.* pessimist; *adj.* pessimistic (2)

pésimo/a awful; **¡qué pésimo!** that's awful! (8)

peso weight; **aumento de peso** weight gain; **bajar de peso** to lose weight (12) **subir de peso** to gain weight (12)

petróleo petroleum, oil

petrolero/a *adj.* oil; petroleum

pez *m.* (*pl.* **peces**) fish (*animal*) (4)

pianista *m., f.* pianist

picadura bite; sting

picante spicy (6)

picar (qu) to bite; to chop, mince

pico peak; beak; **pico de gallo** *uncooked salsa made of chopped tomato, onion, and jalapeños*

pie *m.* foot (8); **a pie** on foot

piel *f.* skin (2)

pierna leg (8)

pijama *m.* pijama (8)

pimienta pepper (*spice*) (6)

pimiento pepper

pinchar to click (*computer, Sp.*)

pingüino penguin (13)

pinta appearance; **tener** (*irreg.*) **buena/mala pinta** to have a good/bad appearance

pintar to pain

pinto: gallo pinto *rice and beans dish of Nicaragua and Costa Rica*

pintor(a) painter (4)

pintura paint; painting (14)

piña pineapple (6)

pirámide *f.* pyramid

piraña piranha

pisar to step on; **no pisar (el césped)** stay off / do not walk on (the grass) (9)

piscina swimming pool (11)

piso floor, story (11); apartment (*Sp.*) (11); **primer/segundo/tercer piso** second/third/fourth floor (11)

pista clue

pitisalé *m.* salted meat of Dominican Republic and Haiti

pizarra chalkboard (1); whiteboard (1)

placer *m.* pleasure; **es un placer** nice to meet you (10); it's a pleasure (10)

plagio plagiarism

plan *m.* plan

plancha: a la plancha grilled (6)

planeación *f.* planning

planear to plan

planeta (*m.*) **(Tierra)** planet (Earth) (13)

planificación *f.* planning; **planificación familiar** family planning

planta plant; floor (11); **planta baja** ground floor (11); **primera/segunda/tercera planta** second/third/fourth floor (11)

plástico plastic

plata silver

plataforma platform

plátano banana (*Mex.*) (6); plantain

platillo dish

plato plate; dish; course (6); **lavar los platos** to wash dishes (4); **primer plato** first course (6); **segundo plato / plato principal** main course (6)

playa beach (2)

plaza plaza (5)

plazo: a largo plazo in the long run

pliegue *m.* pleat

pluma pen (1)

población *f.* population

pobre poor (2)

pobreza poverty (15)

poco/a few; (a) little; **un poco (de)** a little bit (of)

poder *n. m.* power

poder *irreg.* to be able, can (3); **¿en qué puedo servirle(s)?** how may I help you (*form. s., pl.*)? (10); **¿me puede comunicar con... ?** can you connect me with . . . ?; **no puedo** I can't (6); **¿puedo pasar?** excuse me; may I pass by/enter? (8); **sí, se puede** yes we can; it can be done (12)

poema *m.* poem

poesía poetry (14)

polar polar; **casquete** (*m.*) **polar** polar cap; **oso polar** polar bear

polémico/a controversial

policía *m., f.* police officer (4); *f.* police (*force*); **mujer** (*f.*) **policía** policewoman

polinesio/a Polynesian

política politics; policy

político/a *n.* politician (15); *adj.* political; **ciencias** (*pl.*) **políticas** political science; **proceso político** political process (15)

pollo chicken (6)

pólvora powder

pomelo grapefruit (*Sp., Arg.*)

poner *irreg.* (*p.p.* **puesto**) to put (5); to place; **poner atención** to pay attention; **poner en duda** to call into question; **poner énfasis** to emphasize; **poner la mesa** to set the table (6); **ponerse** to put on (*an article of clothing*) (5); **ponerse** + *adj.* to become/get + *adj.* (5); **ponerse contento/a** to become happy (5); **ponerse en forma** to get in shape (12); **ponerse los lentes / los**

lentes de contacto to put on glasses/contacts (5)

pop *adj.* pop (*music, culture*) (14)

popular popular (2)

popularizar (c) to make popular

por about; because of; through; for; by; **baje/suba por esta calle** go down/up this street (*command form. s.*) (5); **gracias por** + *n./inf.* thank you for (5); **por ejemplo** for example; **por equivocación** by mistake; **por favor** please; **por fin** finally; **por la mañana** in the morning (3); **por la noche** at night (3); **por la tarde** in the afternoon/evening (3); **por primera vez** the first time; **¿por qué?** why? (2); **por si acaso** just in case; **¡por supuesto!** of course! (6)

porcentaje *m.* percentage

porción *f.* portion; serving

porque because

portarse to behave

portátil: (computadora) portátil laptop (computer)

portero/a building manager; doorman

portuario/a *adj.* port

portugués *m.* Portuguese (*language*)

portugués (*pl.* **portugueses**), **portuguesa** *n., adj.* Portuguese

porvenir *m.* future

posada inn

posgrado graduate (study)

posibilidad *f.* possibility

posible possible

posición *f.* position

posicionamiento: Sistema (*m.*) **de Posicionamiento Global (SPG)** Global Positioning System (GPS)

positivo/a positive

posponer (*like* **poner**) (*p.p.* **pospuesto**) to postpone

posgrado (*or* **postgrado**) graduate (study)

postre *m.* dessert (6)

potencial potential

práctica practice

practicar (qu) to practice (3); **practicar yoga** to do yoga (3); **practicar un deporte** to play a sport (3)

práctico/a practical

precariedad *f.* uncertainty

precaución *f.* precaution

precio price

precioso/a pretty (2)

preciso/a precise

precolombino/a Pre-Columbian

predador *m.* predator

predicción *f.* prediction

predisposición *f.* predisposition

preferencia preference

preferido/a preferred; favorite

preferir (ie, i) to prefer

pregunta question

preguntar to ask (7)

prehispánico/a pre-Hispanic

premio prize

prenda (de ropa) item (of clothing) (8)
prender to turn on (*appliance*)
prensa: agencia de prensa press agency
preocupado/a worried
preocupar(se) to worry
preparación *f.* preparation; training
preparar (el desayuno / el almuerzo / la cena) to prepare (breakfast/lunch/ dinner) (4); **prepararse** to get ready, prepare oneself
preparativos *pl.* preparations
preposición *f. gram.* preposition
presentación *f.* presentation
presentador(a) presenter
presentar to present; to introduce; **quiero presentarle(s) a...** I'd like you (*form. s., pl.*) to meet . . . (10); **quiero presentarte a...** I'd like you (*inform. s.*) to meet . . . (10)
preservar to preserve
presidencia presidency
presidente, presidenta president
presión *f.* (blood) pressure (12)
prestar to lend; **prestar atención** to pay attention; **prestarse a** to lend oneself to
prestigioso/a prestigious
presupuesto budget
pretérito *gram.* preterite
prevención *f.* prevention
prevenir (*like* **venir**) to warn
previo/a previous, prior
prieto/a dark
primaria: escuela primaria elementary school
primavera spring (*season*) (1)
primer, primero/a first; **por primera vez** the first time; **primer piso / primera planta** second floor (11); **primer plato** first course (6); **primero de mayo** first of May (1)
primo/a cousin (4)
princesa princess
principal main; **plato principal** main course (*of a meal*) (6)
príncipe *m.* prince
principio *n.* beginning
prisa: darse (*irreg.*) **prisa** to hurry; **tener** (*irreg.*) **prisa** to be in a hurry
privado/a private; **escuela privada** private school
privatización *f.* privatization
privatizar (c) to privatize
privilegiado/a privileged
probador(a) tester
probar (ue) to try (6); to taste (6); **probarse** to try on (8)
problema *m.* problem; **problema social** social problem (15)
problemático/a problematic
proceloso/a stormy
procesar to process
procesión *f.* procession
proceso process; **proceso político** political process (15)
producción *f.* production

producir (*like* **conducir**) to produce
producto product; **productos lácteos** dairy products (6)
profesión *f.* profession (4); **¿cuál es tu/su profesión?** what is your (*inform. s. / form. s.*) profession? (4)
profesional profession
profesor(a) professor (1)
profundidad *f.* depth
profundo/a deep
progenitor(a) parent
programa *m.* program; area
programador(a) programmer (10)
progresar to progress
progresivo/a progressive
progreso progress
prohibir (prohíbo) to prohibit (13)
promedio average
prometedor(a) promising
prometer to promise
promoción *f.* promotion
promover (ue) to promote
pronombre *m. gram.* pronoun
pronóstico del tiempo weather forecast
pronto soon; **hasta pronto** see you soon (1)
propiedad *f.* property
propio/a own, one's own
proponer (*like* **poner**) (*p.p.* **propuesto**) to propose
propósito purpose
prosperidad *f.* prosperity
protagonista *m., f.* protagonist (14)
protección *f.* protection (13)
protector(a) protective
proteger (j) to protect (13)
proteína protein
protestar to protest
provecho: ¡buen provecho! enjoy your meal! (6)
proveer (y) (*p.p.* **proveído**) to provide
provincia province
provisión *f.* provision; *pl.* supplies
provocar (qu) to provoke
próximo/a next
proyecto project
proyector *m.* projector (1)
prueba quiz
psicología psychology (1)
psicólogo/a psychologist (4)
psiquiatra *m., f.* psychiatrist
pub *m.* pub, bar
publicar (qu) to publish
publicidad *f.* publicity
público/a public; audience (14); **transporte** (*m.*) **público** public transportation (5)
pueblo town (5)
puente *m.* bridge (5)
puerco pig; pork (6); **carne de puerco** *f.* pork (6)
puerta door (1)
puertorriqueño/a *n., adj.* Puerto Rican (2)
pues *conj.* well; since

puesto job (10); position; stand (5); **conseguir** (*like* **seguir**) **un puesto** to get a job/position (10)
pulmón *m.* lung
pulpa pulp
pulpería small grocery store
pulsera bracelet (8)
punto point; **en el punto de mira** in the crosshairs; **punto com** dot com (*in an email address*) (1) **punto edu** dot edu (*in an email address*) (1)
puñado handful
purificador(a) purifying
purificar(se) (qu) to purify (oneself)
puro/a pure; **¡pura vida!** cool! (8)

Q

que that, which; who; **hasta que** *conj.* until; **que le(s) vaya bien** have a good one / I hope things go well for you (*form. s., pl.*) (12); **¡que tenga(s) un buen día!** have (*form. s. / inform. s.*) a good day! (12); **¡que tenga(s) un buen fin de semana!** have (*form. s. / inform. s.*) a nice weekend!; **¡que tenga(s) una buena tarde!** have (*form. s. / inform. s.*) a nice afternoon!; **que yo sepa** as far as I know; **ya que** since
¿qué? what? (2); which?; **¿a qué hora... ?** at what time . . .? (3); **¿a qué se dedica?** what do you (*form. s.*) do (*occupation*)? (4); **¿a qué te dedicas?** what do you (*inform. s.*) do (*occupation*)? (4); **¿en qué puedo servirle(s)?** how may I help you (*form. s., pl.*)? (10); **¿qué estudias?** what do you study?; what's your major? (1); **¿qué hora es?** what time is it? (3); **¿qué tal?** how are you? (1); **¿qué te/le parece(n)** + *n./inf.*? how about (*inform. s. / form. s.*) . . . ? (6); **¿qué te pasa?** what's happening with you (*inform. s.*)?; what's the matter? (1); **¿qué tiempo hace?** what's the weather like? (9)
¡qué... ! what . . . !; **¡qué** + *adj.*! how + *adj.*! (4); **¡qué** + *adj.* + *n.*! what + *adj.* + *n.*! (4); **¡qué** + *n.*! how/what + *n.*! (4); **¡qué aburrido!** how boring! (8); **¡qué bárbaro!** how cool! (8), awesome!; **¡qué bien!** how cool! (8); **¡qué bonita familia!** what a beautiful family! (4); **¡qué buena idea!** what a good idea!; **¡qué calor!** it's so hot! (4); **¡qué cara!** what nerve!; **¡qué chévere!** how cool! (8); **¡qué chido!** how cool! (8); **¡qué chulo!** how cool! (8); **¡qué coraje!** how frustrating/annoying!; **¡qué emoción!** how exciting!; **¡qué estupendo!** how cool! (8); **¡qué fenomenal!** how cool! (8); **¡qué feo/a!** how ugly! (4); **¡qué frío!** it's so cold! (4); **¡qué golazo!** what a goal!; **¡qué guapo/a!** how handsome/beautiful! (4); **¡qué guay!** how cool! (8); **¡qué lindo/a!** how cute/pretty! (4); **¡qué lío!** what a mess! (4); **¡qué malo/a!** that's terrible!

(8); **¡qué padre!** how cool! (8); **¡qué pesado!** how annoying! (8); **¡qué pésimo!** that's awful! (8); **¡qué poca vergüenza!** what nerve!; **¡qué rabia!** how frustrating/annoying!; **¡qué rico/a!** how delicious!; **¡qué vergüenza!** how embarrassing!

quechua *m.* Quechua (*language*)

quedar to remain, to be left; to be located; **¿dónde queda... ?** where is . . . ? (5); **queda a la derecha/izquierda** it's on the right/left (5); **queda al lado de / detrás de / enfrente de / en la esquina de... y ...** it's next to / behind / facing, in front of / on the corner of . . . and . . . (5); **quedarle** to fit (8); **quedarse** to stay (5)

quehacer *m.* chore

queja complaint (12)

quejarse (de) to complain (about) (12)

quemadura *n.* burn; **quemadura de sol** sunburn (9)

quemar to burn

querer *irreg.* to want (4), **querer** + *Inf.* to want (*to do something*) (4); to love (16); **¿quiere(s)** + *n./inf.***?** Do you (*form. s. / Inform. s.*) want . . . ? (6); **quiero presentarle(s) a...** I'd like you (*form. s., pl.*) to meet . . . (10); **quisiera** + *inf.* I would like (*to do something*) (10)

querido/a dear; **ser** (*m.*) **querido** loved one

queso cheese (6)

quetzal *m.* quetzal bird

quiché *adj. m., f.* of or pertaining to the Quiche Mayan group of Guatemala

quichua *n. m., f.* Quechua

¿quién(es)? who? (2); whom?; **¿de parte de quién?** may I ask who's calling?

quieto/a calm, still

química chemistry (1)

quince fifteen; quarter (*of an hour*) (3); **el quince de octubre** October fifteenth (1); **son las dos y quince** it's 2:15 (3)

quinceañera *15th birthday celebration* (7); *young woman celebrating her fifteenth birthday*

quinientos/as five hundred (5)

quinta farm; country house

quinto/a fifth

quitar(se) to remove, take off

quizá(s) *adv.* perhaps, maybe (14)

R

rabia anger; fury; **¡qué rabia!** how frustrating/annoying!

racismo racism (15)

radio *f.* radio (*medium*)

raíz *f.* (*pl.* **raíces**) root; **a raíz de** as a result of; **bienes** (*m. pl.*) **raíces** real estate; **agente** (*m., f.*) **de bienes raíces** real estate agent

rama branch

ramo: Domingo de Ramos Palm Sunday

rana frog

rancho ranch

rango rank

rap *m.* rap music

rapanui *m. language of the Rapa Nui people of Easter Island*

rapero/a rapper

rapidez *f.* (*pl.* **rapideces**) speed

rápido *adv.* quickly

rápido/a fast (2); **comida rápida** fast food

raqueta racket (12)

rarámuri *m., f.* of or pertaining to the Tarahumara people of northwestern Mexico

raro/a strange

rascacielos *m. s., pl.* skyscraper (5)

rastafari *adj. m., f.* Rastafarian

ratificar (qu) to ratify

rato while, short time; **pasar un buen rato** to have a good time

ratón *m.* mouse

raza race

razón *f.* reason; **no tener** (*irreg.*) **razón** to be wrong; **tener** (*irreg.*) **razón** to be right

razonable reasonable

reacción *f.* reaction

reaccionar to react

real royal; real

realidad *f.* reality

realismo realism

realizar (c) to achieve, attain

rebaja sale (8); **estar** (*irreg.*) **de rebajas** on sale, at a reduced price

rebelde *m., f.* rebel

rebeldía rebellion

recalar en to end up at

recaudar fondos to raise funds

recepción *f.* reception (9)

receta recipe

rechazar (c) to reject

rechazo rejection

recibir to receive

reciclaje *m.* recycling (13)

reciclar to recycle (13)

recién *adj.* recent

recinto (universitario) campus

recipiente *m.* recipient

reclutar to recruit

recoger (j) to pick up (9)

recogida de equipaje baggage claim (9)

recolectar to gather; to harvest

recomendable recommendable

recomendación *f.* recommendation

recomendar (ie) to recommend (12)

reconocer (zc) to recognize

reconocido/a famous

reconocimiento recognition

reconstrucción *f.* reconstruction

récord *adj. m., f.* record

recordar (ue) to remember

recordatorio/a: mensaje (*m.*) **recordatorio** reminder

recorrer to traverse

recorrido tour; **hacer** (*irreg.*) **un recorrido** to take a trip / go on a tour (9)

recreación *f.* recreation

recrear to recreate

recto/a straight; **siga recto** go straight (*command form. s.*) (5)

recuerdo memory; souvenir (9)

recuperar to recuperate

recurrir to turn to; to resort to

recurso resource; **recurso natural** natural resource (13)

red *f.* network; Internet; **red social** social network

reducir (like **conducir**) to reduce

reelección *f.* reelection

reelegir (i, i) (j) to reelect

reescribir (*p.p.* **reescrito**) to rewrite

referencia reference

referéndum *m.* referendum

referirse (ie, i) (a) to refer (to)

reflejar to reflect

reforma reform

refrán *m.* saying, proverb

refresco soda (6)

refugio refuge

regalar to give (*a present*) (7)

regalo gift

regañar to scold

reggae *m.* reggae

reggaetón *m.* reggaeton

región *f.* region

registrarse to check in (9)

regla rule

regresar to return

regreso return

rehusar (rehúso) to refuse

reina queen

reintroducir (like **conducir**) to reintroduce

reírse (me río, i) (de) to laugh (about)

relación *f.* relationship (16); **en una relación** together (16); in a relationship (16); **relaciones internacionales** international relations (1)

relacionado/a (con) related (to)

relajante relaxing

relajar(se) to relax

relativamente relatively

relevo: generación (*f.*) **de relevo** upcoming generation

religión *f.* religion

religioso/a religious

relleno/a stuffed (*culin.*)

reloj *m.* clock (1); watch (1)

remoto/a remote

remover (ue) to stir

remunerado/a remunerated

renegar (ie) (gu) de to reject

renombre *m.* renown

renovación *f.* renovation

renovar (ue) to renovate

renta rent

rentar to rent

renunciar (a) to resign

repartir to deliver; to distribute

repelente *m.* repellent

repente: de repente suddenly

repetir (i, i) to repeat (4)

repleto/a full

reportaje *m.* report

reportar to report

representante *m., f.* representative; *adj.* representative

representar to represent

represión *f.* repression

reprochar to reproach

reproducción *f.* reproduction

reproducir (like **conducir**) to reproduce

reptil *m.* reptile

república republic; **República Dominicana** Dominican Republic

requerir (ie, i) to require

requisito requirement

res: carne de res *f.* beef (6)

resentido/a resentful; bitter

reserva reserve; reservation

reservado/a reserved (2)

resfriado *n.* cold (*illness*)

residencia residence; **residencia (estudiantil)** dormitory (1)

residente *m., f.* resident; *adj.* resident

residir to reside

residuo waste

resistencia resistance

resistir to resist

resolver (ue) (*p.p.* **resuelto**) to resolve; to achieve

respecto: al respecto on this/that matter

respetar to respect

respeto respect

respetuoso/a respectful

responder to respond

responsabilidad *f.* responsibility (13)

responsabilizarse (c) to take responsibility (16)

responsable responsible

respuesta answer

restar (*like* **gustar**) to remain, to be left

restaurante *m.* restaurant (5); **administración** (*f.*) **de restaurantes** restaurant management

resto rest

resultado result

resumen *m.* (*pl.* **resúmenes**) summary

resumir to summarize

resurrección *f.* resurrection; **Pascua de Resurrección** Easter (7)

retirarse to go away; to go to bed

reto challenge

retocado/a retouched

retrasar to delay

retraso delay

retrato portrait

reunión *f.* meeting

reunirse (me reúno) (con) to meet (with); to get together (with)

revelar to reveal

revisar to review

revisión *f.* revision

revista magazine

revolución *f.* revolution

rey *m.* king; **Día** (*m.*) **de los Reyes Magos** Three Kings Day; Epiphany (Adoration of the Magi) (7)

rico/a rich (2); delicious; **¡qué rico/a!** how delicious!

ridículo/a ridiculous

riesgo risk

río river

riqueza richness

risa laughter

ritmo rhythm

rito rite; ritual

ritual *m.* ritual

rival *m.* rival

robar to rob

rock rock (*music*) (14)

rocoso/a rocky

rodaje *m.* filming, shooting (*movie*)

rodar to film, shoot (*movie*)

rodeado/a (de) surrounded (by)

rodilla knee (8)

rodillera knee pad/guard

rojo/a red (2)

rol *m.* role

romance *m.* romance

romántico/a romantic

romper(se) (*p.p.* **roto**) to break (9); **romper con** to break up with (16)

ropa clothes, clothing; **ropa interior** underwear (8); **lavar la ropa** to wash clothes (4)

rosado/a pink (2)

rostro face

roto/a (*p.p. of* **romper**) broken

rubio/a blond (2)

rudo/a rough

ruido noise (5)

ruinas *pl.* ruins

rural rural (5)

ruso/a *n., adj.* Russian

ruta route

rutina (diaria) (daily) routine

S

sábado Saturday (3)

sabana savannah

saber *irreg.* to know (5); **saber** + *inf.* to know how to (*do something*); **que yo sepa** as far as I know

sabroso/a tasty

sacar (qu) to take out, withdraw; **sacar a pasear** to walk (*dog*); **sacar buenas/malas notas** to get good/bad grades; **sacar dinero** to withdraw money; **sacar fotos** to take photos; **sacar la basura** to take out the trash (11); **sacar la lotería** to win the lottery; **sacar una maestría / un doctorado** to get a master's/doctorate (degree)

saco suit jacket

sacudir to dust (11)

safari: ir (*irreg.*) **de safari** to go on a safari

sagrado/a sacred

sal *f.* salt (6)

sala living room; **sala de clase** classroom; **sala de justicia** courtroom

salado/a *adj.* salt, salty; **agua** (*f., but* **el agua**) **salada** salt water

salar *m.* salt flat

salario salary

salir *irreg.* to leave (*a place*) (5); to go out (5); **salir con** to date

salmón *m.* salmon

salón *m.* living room (11); **salón de clase** classroom (1)

salsa salsa; sauce (6)

saltar to jump

salto waterfall

salud *f.* health

saludable healthy

saludar to greet

saludo greeting (10)

salvadoreño/a *n., adj.* Salvadoran (2)

salvaje wild (13)

salvar to save, rescue (13)

san, santo/a *n.* saint; **Día** (*m.*) **de Todos los Santos** All Saints' Day; **Semana Santa** Holy Week (7)

sandalias sandals (8)

sándwich *m.* sandwich (6)

saneamiento sanitation

sangre *f.* blood (12)

sano/a healthy; **mantenerse** (*irreg.*) **sano** to stay healthy (12)

sapo toad (13)

satisfactorio/a satisfactory

se *refl. pron.* yourself (*form.*); himself/herself; itself; yourselves (*form. Sp.; inform./form. elsewhere*); themselves

secar(se) (qu) to dry (oneself)

sección *f.* section

seco/a dry

secretario/a secretary (10)

sector *m.* sector

secuela effect, consequence

secundario/a secondary; **escuela secundaria** high school

sed *f.* thirst; **tener** (*irreg.*) **sed** to be thirsty

sedentario/a sedentary

segmento segment

seguido/a one after the other

seguir (i, i) (g) to follow (4); to continue; to keep on going; **siga derecho/recto** go / keep going straight (*command form. s.*) (5); **siga hasta llegar a...** go / keep going (*command form. s.*) until you get to . . . (5)

según according to

segundo *n.* second

segundo/a second; **segundo piso / segunda planta** third floor (11); **segundo plato** main course (6)

seguridad *f.* safety (9); security (9)

seguro *n.* insurance; **agencia de seguros** insurance agency; **agente** (*m., f.*) **de seguros** insurance agent

seguro/a sure

seis six; **seis mil** six thousand (5)

seiscientos/as six hundred (5)

selección *f.* selection; team

seleccionar to select, choose

selva jungle (13)

semana week; **día** (*m.*) **de entre semana** weekday; **fin** (*m.*) **de semana** weekend (3); **¡que tenga(s) un buen fin de semana!** have (*form. s. / inform. s.*) a nice weekend!; **semana pasada** last week; **Semana Santa** Holy Week (7); **una vez a la semana** once a week

sembrar (ie) to sow, plant

semejante similar

semejanza similarity

semifinal *f.* semifinal

senado senate

sencillez *f.* simplicity

sencillo/a simple

senderismo: hacer (*irreg.*) **senderismo** to go hiking

sendero path

sentarse (ie) to sit down (5); **¡siéntate/ siénte(n)se!** sit down / have a seat (*command inform. s. / form. s., pl.*)! (11)

sentido *n.* sense

sentido/a *adj.* heartfelt; **mi/nuestro más sentido pésame** my/our deepest condolences (16)

sentimental emotional

sentimiento emotion, feeling; **te/le/les acompaño/acompañamos en el sentimiento** you're (*inform. s. / form. s. / form. pl.*) in my/our thoughts (16)

sentir (ie, i) to regret; to feel sorry; **cuánto lo siento** I'm very sorry (16); **lo siento** I'm sorry (7); my condolences (7); **sentirse** to feel (*an emotion*)

señal *f.* sign

señalar to mark; to point at

señor (Sr.) *m.* man; Mr.; sir

señora (Sra.) woman; Mrs.; ma'am

señorita (Srta.) young woman; Miss; Ms.

separar to separate

septiembre *m.* September (1)

sequía drought (13)

ser *m.* being; **ser querido** loved one

ser *irreg.* to be (1); **¿cuál es la fecha de hoy?** what is today's date? (1); **¿de dónde eres/es?** where are you (*inform. s. / form. s.*) from? (1); **¿de qué color es?** what color is it? (2); **eres** you are (*inform. s.*) (1); **es** he/she is / you (*inform. s.*) are (1); **es a la(s)...** it's at . . . (3); **es la una** it's 1:00 (3); **es la una y media/treinta** it's 1:30 (3); **es medianoche** it's midnight (3); **es mediodía** it's noon (3); **hoy es...** today is . . . (1); **mi nombre/apellido es** my name/ last name is (1); **¿qué hora es?** what time is it? (3); **ser aficionado/a (a)** to be a fan (of); **ser bienvenido/a/os/as** to be welcome (11); **si no es molestia** if it's not a bother (6); **somos** we are (1); **son** you (*form. pl.*) / they are; **son diez para las nueve** it's 8:50 (3); **son las doce del día** it's noon (3); **son las doce de la noche** it's midnight (3); **son las dos y cuarto/ quince** it's 2:15 (3); **son las ocho y cincuenta** it's 8:50 (3); **son las nueve menos diez** it's 8:50 (3); **soy** I am (1); **soy de...** I'm from . . . (1); **Ud. es (siempre) bienvenido/a** you (*form. s.*) are always welcome (11)

serie *f.* series

serio/a serious (2)

servicio service (9)

servilleta napkin (6)

servir (i, i) to serve (4); to be useful (4); to work (function) (4); **¿en qué puedo servirle(s)?** how may I help you (*form. s., pl.*)? (10); **para servirle** at your (*form. s.*) service (10); **servir para** to be good at/for (*doing something*) (4); **¡sírvete/ sírva(n)se!** help yourself (*command inform. s. / form. s., pl.*)! (11)

sesenta sixty

seteclentos/as seven hundred (5)

setenta seventy

sexo sex

shorts *m. pl.* shorts

si if; **si no es molestia** if it's not a bother (6)

sí yes (1); **¡claro que sí!** *interj.* sure, no problem, of course! (6); **sí, gracias** yes, please (5); **sí, se puede** yes, we can / yes, it can be done (12)

siempre always (3); **Ud. es (siempre) bienvenido/a** you (*form. s.*) are always welcome (11)

sierra mountain

siete seven; **siete mil** seven thousand (5)

siglo century

significado meaning

slgnlflcar (qu) to mean; to signify

siguiente following

silla chair (1)

sillón *m.* armchair (11)

simbólico/a symbolic

símbolo symbol

simpático/a nice (2)

simular to simulate

simultáneo/a simultaneous

sin without (7); **organización** (*f.*) **sin fines de lucro** nonprofit organization (15); **sin duda** without (any) doubt (14); **sin hogar** homeless; **sin unequaled**; **sin importar** regardless of

sincero/a sincere

sinfónica symphony

singular *m. gram.* singular

sino (but) rather; **sino que** *conj.* but (rather)

sinónimo synonym

síntoma *m.* symptom (12)

sistema *m.* system (13); **Sistema de Posicionamiento Global (SPG)** Global Positioning System (GPS)

sitio site; place; **sitio web** website

situación *f.* situation (13)

situado/a located

SMS *m.* text messaging (*abbrev. for Short Message Service*)

snorkel *m.* snorkeling (9); **hacer** (*irreg.*) **snorkel** to go snorkeling (9)

snowboard *m.* snowboard

sobre *prep.* about (7); on, above (7); on top of; over

sobremesa after-dinner conversation

sobresaliente outstanding

sobresalir (*like* **salir**) to stand out

sobrevivir to survive

sobrino/a nephew/niece (4)

social social; **problema** (*m.*) **social** social problem (15); **red** (*f.*) **social** social network; **trabajador(a) social** social worker (10)

sociedad *f.* society

socio/a member; partner

socioeconómico/a socioeconomic

soclología sociology

sociólogo/a sociologist (4)

sofá *m.* sofa (11)

sofisticado/a sophisticated

sol *m.* sun; **hace (mucho) sol** it's (very) sunny (9); **tomar el sol** to sunbathe (9); **quemadura de sol** sunburn (9)

solar solar; **bloqueador** (*m.*) **solar** sunscreen (9); **panel** (*m.*) **solar** solar panel

soldado soldier

soleado/a sunny

soledad *f.* solitude; loneliness

solemnidad *f.* solemnity

soler (ue) to tend (*to do something*)

solicitar (un empleo / un trabajo) to apply for (a job) (10)

sólido/a solid

solista *m., f.* soloist

solo *adv.* only

solo/a *adj.* alone (2)

soltar (ue) to let loose

soltero/a single (*not married*) (16)

solución *f.* solution

solucionar to solve, resolve

sombrero hat (8)

sombrilla parasol

someter to submit

sondeo poll

sonido sound

sonoro/a sonorous

sonreír(se) (*like* **reír**) to smile

sonrisa smile

soñar (ue) (con) to dream (about) (3)

sopa soup (6)

soportar to stand

sorprender to surprise

sorprendido/a surprised

sospecha suspicion

sospechoso/a suspect, suspicious

sostenible sustainable (13)

sótano basement (11)

su(s) *poss. adj.* his, her, its, your (*form. sing., pl.*), their (1)

suave soft

subir (a) to go up; to get on (*a vehicle*); to raise; to upload (10); **suba (por esta calle)** go up (this street) (*command form. s.*) (5); **subir de peso** to gain weight (12)

subjuntivo *gram.* subjunctive

subrayar to underline

subyacer (zc) to underlie

suceder to happen; to occur

sucesión *f.* succession

sucio/a dirty (2)

Sudáfrica South Africa

sudafricano/a *n., adj.* South African

Sudamérica South America

sudamericano/a *n., adj.* South American

sueco/a *n.* Swede; *adj.* Swedish

suegro/a father-in-law / mother-in-law (4)

sueldo salary

suelo floor; **lavar el suelo** to wash the floor (11)

sueño dream; **tener** (*irreg.*) **sueño** to be sleepy

suerte *f.* luck; **¡buena suerte!** good luck! (12); best of luck! (12); **dar** (*irreg.*) **buena suerte** to bring good luck; **le(s) deseo mucha suerte** I wish you (*form. s., pl.*) luck (12); **¡mucha suerte!** good luck! (12); best of luck! (12); **¡suerte (con todo)!** good luck (with everything)! (12)

suéter *m.* sweater (8)

suficiente enough

sufrimiento suffering

sufrir (de) to suffer (from) (12)

sugerencia suggestion

sugerir (ie, i) to suggest

sujetador *m.* bra (8)

sujeto *gram.* subject

sumar to add

sumergir (j) to immerse, submerge

suministrar to supply, provide

suministro supply

suntuoso/a sumptuous, luxurious

súper *m.* supermarket (2)

superficie *f.* surface

supermercado supermarket (2)

superstición *f.* superstition

supervisar to supervise

suponer(se) (*like* **poner**) (*p.p.* **supuesto**) to suppose

supremo/a supreme; **Corte** (*f.*) **Suprema** Supreme Court

suprimir to delete, erase

supuesto: ¡por supuesto! sure, no problem, of course! (6)

sur *m.* south

sureño/a southern

surfear to surf (12)

surfista *m., f.* surfer

surrealista *adj. m., f.* surreal

suscripción *f.* subscription

suspender to suspend

suspenso suspense

sustantivo *gram.* noun

suyo/a(s) *poss. adj.* your (*form.*); his, her, its, their; *poss. pron.* (of) your, his, her, it, their; (of) yours (*form.*), hers, its, theirs

T

tabla table, chart

tableta tablet (10)

tachar to cross out

tacones (*m. pl.*) **(altos)** high-heeled shoes (8)

tailandés (pl. **tailandeses**), **tailandesa** *n., adj.* Thai

tal such, such a; **con tal de que** *conj.* provided that; **¿qué tal?** how are you? (1); **tal como** just as; **tal vez** maybe, perhaps (14)

tala de árboles tree cutting (13)

talar to cut down

talento talent; **agencia de talentos** talent agency

talentoso/a talented

talla size (*clothing*) (8)

taller *m.* workshop

tamal *m.* tamale

tamaño size

también also

tampoco neither, not either

tan *adv.* so; as; **tan... como** as . . . as; **tan pronto como** as soon as

tanto/a *adj.* as much, so much; such a; *pl.* so many; as many; **tanto/a(s)... como** as much/many . . . as; **tanto como** as much as

tapar to cover

tapir *m.* tapir (*large mammal of C.A. and S.A.*)

taquillero/a: una película taquillera box-office success (*film*)

tarahumara *n., adj. m., f.* Tarahumara (see **rarámuri**)

tardar to delay; to be late

tarde *f.* afternoon; *adv.* late; **buenas tardes** good afternoon (1); **de la tarde** in the afternoon/evening (3); **por la tarde** in the afternoon/evening (3); **¡que tenga(s) una buena tarde!** have (*form. s. / inform. s.*) a nice afternoon!

tarea homework (1)

tarjeta card (7); **tarjeta de memoria** memory card

tasa rate; **tasa de natalidad** birthrate

taxi *m.* taxi (5)

taxonómico/a taxonomical

taza coffee cup (6); measuring cup (6)

te *d.o. pron.* you (*inform. s.*) (6); *i.o. pron.* to/for you (*inform. s.*) (7); *refl. pron.* yourself (*inform. s.*); **¿Cómo te llamas?** What's your name? (1); **quiero presentarte a...** I'd like you (*inform. s.*) to meet . . . (10); **te acompaño/ acompañamos en el dolor** I'm/we're with you in your time of pain (16); **te**

acompaño/acompañamos en el sentimiento you're in my/our thoughts (16); **¿te gusta(n)** + *noun*(s)? do you (*inform.*) like + *noun*(s)? (2); **te agradezco por** I appreciate that you/ I thank you for (5); **te doy/ damos el pésame** my/our condolences (16); **te felicito/felicitamos** I/we congratulate you (7); **¿te gustaría** + *inf.*? would you like (*to do something*)? (9)

té *m.* tea

teatro theater (5); **obra de teatro** play (14)

techo roof (11)

teclado keyboard (10)

técnico/a *n.* technician; *adj.* technical

tecnología technology

tecnológico/a technological

tejo *Colombian sport played by throwing a metal plate or disk at a target to try to hit paper triangles filled with gunpowder*

tela cloth, fabric

telecomunicaciones *f. pl.* telecommunication

telefónico/a *adj.* telephone

teléfono (móvil) (cellular) telephone **¿cuál es tu número de teléfono?** what is your phone number? (1); **hablar por teléfono** to talk on the phone (3)

telenovela soap opera

tele-secundaria: escuela tele-secundaria distance high school

televisión *f.* television (*medium*); **mirar la televisión** to watch television (3)

televisor *m.* television set (11)

temático/a themed

temer to fear

temperatura temperature (12)

templado/a temperate

temporada season

temprano *adv.* early

tendencia tendency; trend

tenedor *m.* fork (6)

tener *irreg.* to have (1); **¿cuántos años tiene(s)?** how old are you (*form. s. / inform. s.*)? (2); **no tener razón** to be wrong; **¡que tenga(s) un buen día** have (*form. s. / inform. s.*) a nice day!; **¡que tenga(s) un buen fin de semana!** have (*form. s. / inform. s.*) a nice weekend!; **¡que tenga(s) una buena tarde!** have (*form. s. / inform. s.*) a nice afternoon!; **tenemos** we have (1); **tener alergia a** to be allergic to; **tener buen aspecto** to look good; **tener buena/ mala pinta** to have a good/bad appearance; **tener celos** to be jealous; **tener éxito** to be successful (12); **tener fama de** to be known for; **tener fiebre** to have a temperature/fever; **tener ganas de** + *inf.* to feel like (*doing something*); **tener hambre** to be hungry; **tener miedo** to be afraid; **tener (mucho) frío** to be (very) cold; **tener náuseas** to feel nauseous; **tener prisa** to be in a hurry; **tener que** + *inf.* to have (*to do something*) (4); **tener razón** to be right; **tener sed** to be thirsty; **tener sueño** to be sleepy; **tener tos** to have a cough; **tener voz y voto** to have a say; **tengo** I have (1); **tengo** + *number* + **años** I'm + *number* + years old (2); **tiene** he/she has; you (*form s.*) have (1); **tienen** they/you (*form. pl.*) have (1); **tienes** you (*inform. s.*) have (1); **¿tiene(s) ganas de** + *n./inf.*? do you (*form. s. / inform. s.*) feel like . . . ? (6)

tenis *m.* tennis (12); *pl.* tennis shoes (8); **jugar (ue) (gu) tenis** to play tennis (12)

tenista *m., f.* tennis player

tequila *m.* tequila

tequilero/a *adj.* tequila

tercer(o/a) third; **tercera planta / tercer piso** fourth floor (11)

terminación *f. gram.* ending

terminar to finish

término term

termita termite

terraza terrace (11)

terreno land

territorio territory

terror *m.* terror; **película de terror** horror movie

terrorismo terrorism

testamento will

testigo *m., f.* witness

textear to text

textil *m.* textile

texto text; text message; **libro de texto** textbook

textura texture

ti *obj. of prep.* you (*inform. s.*); **para ti** for you (*inform. s.*) (7)

tibio/a lukewarm

tico/a *n., adj.* Costa Rican (*sl.*)

tiempo time; weather; **¿cuánto tiempo hace que** + *present tense*? how long have you (*done / been doing something*)? (13); **¿cuánto tiempo lleva(s)** + **-ndo** *form*? how long have you (*form. s. / inform. s.*) (*done / been doing something*)? (13); **hace (muy) buen/mal tiempo** the weather's (very) good/bad (9); **mucho tiempo** a long time (13); **¿qué tiempo hace?** what's the weather like? (9); **tiempo libre** free time

tienda store (5); **tienda de abarrotes** grocery store; **tienda de abastos** grocery store

tierra earth (13); soil (13); **planeta** (*m.*) **Tierra** planet Earth (13)

tímido/a shy

tinta ink

tinto: vino tinto red wine (6)

tío/a uncle/aunt (4); *pl.* uncles and aunts

típico/a typical

tipo type, kind

tirado/a stranded

tiranía tyranny (15)

tirar to throw (away) (8); **no tirar basura** no littering (*lit. do not throw trash*) (9)

tirolina zip line

titulado/a graduate

titular *m.* headline

título title

tobillo ankle; **torcerse (ue) (z, c) el tobillo** to sprain one's ankle

tocar (qu) to touch; **tocar la guitarra** to play the guitar (2); **tocar un instrumento** to play an instrument

todavía still; yet

todo *n.* everything; everyone (3); **todos/as** all of us/them/you (3); **todo lo demás** everything else

todo/a *adj.* all (3); every; **Día** (*m.*) **de Todos los Santos** All Saints' Day; **toda la noche** all night (3); **toda la vida** all my/your/his/her life; all our/your/their lives (13); **todo el día** all day (3); **todos los días** every day (3); **todas las noches** every night (3)

tolerancia tolerance

tolerante tolerant (16)

tomar to take (3); to drink (3); **tomar el sol** to sunbathe (9); **tomar los datos** to take down information (*medical intake*) (12); **tomar una decisión** to make a decision

tomate *m.* tomato (6)

tonto/a silly, foolish

toparse con to run into

topografía topography

torcerse (ue) (z) (el tobillo) to sprain (one's ankle)

torero/a bullfighter

tormenta storm (13)

toronja grapefruit (*L.Am.*)

torpe clumsy

torre *f.* tower (5)

torso torso (8)

torta cake (6); sandwich (*Mex.*)

tortilla potato omelet (*Sp.*); *thin unleavened cornmeal or flour pancake (Mex.)*

tortuga turtle (13)

tortuguero/a *adj.* turtle

tos *f.* cough (12); **jarabe** (*m.*) **para la tos** cough syrup; **tener** (*irreg.*) **tos** to have a cough

tostado/a toasted; **pan** (*m.*) **tostado** toast

tostar (ue) to toast

total total; **en total** in all

tour tour (9)

tóxico/a toxic

trabajador(a) *n.* worker; **trabajador(a) social** social worker (10); *adj.* hard-working (2)

trabajar to work (3)

trabajo work (2); job; **conseguir** (*like* **seguir**) **un trabajo** to get a job/position (10); **solicitar un trabajo** to apply for a job (10)

tradición *f.* tradition

tradicional traditional

traducción *f.* translation

traducir (*like* **conducir**) to translate

traer *irreg.* to bring (5); to carry (5)

tráfico traffic (5)

tragedia tragedy

traje *m.* suit (8); formal gown (8); **traje coctel** cocktail dress; **traje de baño** bathing suit (8)

trámite *m.* step; procedure

tranquilidad *f.* tranquility, peace, calm (5)

tranquilo/a tranquil (2), peaceful, calm

transbordador *m.* ferry

transecuatoriano/a trans-equatorial

transformar(se) to transform, change into

transición *f.* transition

tránsito traffic

transmitir to transmit

transnacional transnational

transparencia transparency

transportar to transport

transporte *m.* transportation (5); **medio/modo de transporte** means of transportation; **transporte público** public transportation (5)

tras *prep.* after

trasfondo background

trasladarse to move

traslado transfer

tratamiento treatment

tratar de + *inf.* to try to (*do something*)

trato agreement; contract

traumático/a traumatic

través: a través de across; through; throughout

trece thirteen

treinta thirty; **es la una y treinta** it's 1:30 (3); **y treinta** half past (*the hour*)

tremendo/a tremendous

tren *m.* train (9)

tres three; **tres mil** three thousand (5)

trescientos/as three hundred (5)

tribunal *m.* court (10)

tributo tribute

trigo wheat

trigueño/a light brown (2)

trilingüe trilingual

triple doble ve www (*in an email address*) (1)

triplicarse (qu) to triple

triste sad (2)

tristeza sadness

triunfo triumph

tropical tropical; **bosque** (*m.*) **tropical** rainforest (9)

trozo piece

tú *sub. pron.* you (*inform. s.*); **¿y tú?** and you (*inform. s.*)? (1)

tu(s) *poss. adj.* your (*inform. s.*) (1)

tumba tomb
turbulento/a turbulent
turismo tourism; **turismo de aventura** adventure tourism (9)
turista *m., f.* tourist
turístico/a *adj.* tourist
turnarse to take turns
turquesa turquoise
tuyo/a(s) *poss. adj.* your (*inform. s.*); *poss. pron.* of yours (*inform. s.*)
tzotzil *m. Mayan language spoken by the Tzotzil people*

U

u or (*used instead of* **o** *before words beginning with* **o** *or* **ho**) (1)
ubicación *f.* placement; location
último/a last, final; **la última moda** the latest fashion; **la última vez** the last time
ultramaratón *m.* ultra marathon
ultramaratonista *m., f.* ultra marathon runner
umbral *m.* threshold, beginning
un, uno/a one; *ind. art.* a, an (1); *pl.* some (1); **es la una** it's 1:00 (3); **es la una y media/treinta** it's 1:30 (3); **una vez** once (3); **una vez a la semana** once a week
único/a only; unique; **hijo/a único/a** only child
unidad *f.* unit
unido/a united; **Estados** (*pl.*) **Unidos** United States; **Naciones** (*f. pl.*) **Unidas** United Nations
unión *f.* union
unirse (a) to join
universidad *f.* university (1)
universitario/a *adj.* (of the) university; **recinto universitario** campus
urbano/a urban (5)
urgente urgent
uruguayo/a *n., adj.* Uruguayan (2)
usar to use (3); to wear (8); **usar la computadora** to use the computer (3)
USB: memoria USB memory card/stick (10)
uso use
usted (Ud.) *sub. pron.* you (*form. s.*); *obj.* (*of prep.*) you (*form. s.*); **¡le damos la bienvenida a Ud.!** we welcome you (*form. s.*)! (11); **Ud. es (siempre) bienvenido/a** you are always welcome (11); **¿y usted?** and you? (1)
ustedes (Uds.) *sub. pron.* you (*form. pl.*); *obj.* (*of prep.*) you (*form. pl.*)
usuario/a user
útil useful
utilidad *f.* usefulness, utility
utilizar (c) to use
uva grape

V

vacaciones *f. pl.* vacation

vacante *m.* opening
vainilla vanilla
valer *irreg.* to be worth; **(no) vale la pena** it's (not) worth it; **vale** OK (*Sp.*)
válido/a valid
valor *m.* value, worth
valorar to value, appreciate
vals *m.* waltz
vampírico/a *adj.* vampire
variación *f.* variation
variar (varío) to vary
variedad *f.* variety
varios/as several
varón *m.* son; boy; male
vasco/a *n., adj.* Basque; **País** (*m.*) **Vasco** Basque Country
vaso (drinking) glass (6)
ve: doble ve, doble ve, doble ve www (*in an email address*) (1); **triple doble ve** www (*in an email address*) (1)
vecindario neighborhood
vecino/a neighbor
vegetación *f.* vegetation
vegetariano/a vegetarian
vehículo vehicle
veinte twenty
veinticinco twenty-five
veinticuatro twenty-four
veintidós twenty-two
veintinueve twenty-nine
veintiocho twenty-eight
veintiséis twenty-six
veintitrés twenty-three
veintiún, veintiuno/a twenty-one
vela candle
velocidad *f.* speed
vencer (z) to defeat; to overcome
vendedor(a) vendor
vender to sell
veneno poison
venezolano/a *n., adj.* Venezuelan (2)
venir *irreg.* to come (5)
venta sale
ventaja advantage
ventana window (1)
ver *irreg.* (*p.p.* **visto**) to see (6); **a ver** let's see; **verse mal** to look bad
verano summer (1); **Juegos Olímpicos de Verano** Summer Olympics
verdad *f.* truth; **de verdad** really
verdadero/a true
verde green (2); **color** (*m.*) **verde oliva** olive green
verdulería greengrocer; vegetable market (6)
verdura vegetable (6)
vergüenza shame; embarrassment; **¡qué poca vergüenza!** what nerve!; **¡qué vergüenza!** how embarrassing!
vestido dress (8)
vestir (i, i) to dress (8); **vestirse** to get dressed (5)
vez *f.* (*pl.* **veces**) time (3); **a veces** sometimes, at times; **alguna vez** once;

ever; **cada vez más** increasingly; **de vez en cuando** once in a while; **dos veces** twice (3); **la última vez** the last time; **otra vez** again; **por primera vez** the first time; **tal vez** maybe, perhaps (14); **una vez** once (3); **una vez a la semana** once a week
viajar to travel (9)
viaje *m.* trip (9); **agencia de viajes** travel agency; **agente** (*m., f.*) **de viajes** travel agent; **ir de viaje** to go on a trip (9)
vicepresidente/a vice president
vida life; **llevar una vida activa** to lead an active life; **¡pura vida!** cool! (8); **toda la vida** all my/your/his/her life; all our/your/their lives (13)
videojuego videogame; **jugar (ue) (gu) los videojuegos** to play videogames (2)
videollamada video call
viejo/a old (2)
viento wind; **hace (mucho) viento** it's (very) windy (9)
viernes *m.* Friday (3)
vinagre *m.* vinegar (6)
vínculo tie, link
vino (blanco, tinto) (white, red) wine (6)
violación *f.* violation; **violación de los derechos del autor** copyright violation
violar to violate; **violar la ley** to break the law; **violar los derechos humanos** to violate human rights
violencia violence (15)
violento/a violent
virgen *m., f.* virgin
visión *f.* vision
visita visit (9)
visitante *m., f.* visitor
visitar to visit (9)
vista view (9); **con vista a** with a view of; **dejar a la vista** to leave within view
visto/a (*p.p. of* **ver**) seen
vitamina vitamin
viudo/a widowed (16); widower/widow (16)
vivienda housing
vivir to live (3); **¿dónde vive(s)?** where do you (*form. s. / inform. s.*) live? (1); **vivo en** + *place* I live in + *place* (1)
vocabulario vocabulary
vocalista *m., f.* vocalist
volante (*m., f.*) **ofensivo/a** offensive midfielder
volar (ue) to fly
volcán *m.* volcano
voleibol *m.* volleyball (12); **jugar (ue) (gu) voleibol** to play volleyball (12)
voluminoso/a voluminous
voluntariado volunteerism
voluntario volunteer; **hacerse** (*irreg.*) **de voluntario** to volunteer
volver (ue) (*p.p.* **vuelto**) to return (3)
vomitar to vomit (12)

vómito *n.* vomit

vomitona *adj.* vomiting

vorazmente voraciously

vos *sub. pron.* you (*inform. s. C.A., S.A.*)

vosotros/as *sub. pron.* you (*inform. pl. Sp.*); *obj. of prep.* you (*inform. pl. Sp.*)

votar to vote (15)

voto vote; **tener** (*irreg.*) **voz y voto** to have a say

voz *f.* (*pl.* **voces**) voice; **en voz alta** out loud; **tener** (*irreg.*) **voz y voto** to have a say

vuelo flight (9)

vuelta return; **darle** (*irreg.*) **vuelta a** to think about (*something*)

vuelto/a (*p.p. of* **volver**) returned

vuestro/a(s) *poss. adj.* your (*inform. pl. Sp.*) (1); *poss. pron.* your, of yours (*inform. pl. Sp.*)

W

web *m.* web; **navegador web** web browser; **página web** web page (1); **sitio web** website

WIFI *m.* WiFi

Y

y and (1); **¿y tú?** and you (*inform. s.*)? (1); **¿y usted?** and you (*form. s.*)? (1)

ya already; **ya no** no longer; **ya que** *conj.* since

yate *m.* yacht

yerno son-in-law (4)

yo *sub. pron.* I; **que yo sepa** as far as I know

yoga *m.* yoga; **practicar (qu) el yoga** to do yoga (3)

yogur *m.* yogurt (6)

York: Nueva York New York

yuca cassava, manioc

Z

zanahoria carrot

zapatería shoe store

zapatilla tennis shoe

zapato shoe (8)

zapoteca Zapotec

zona area; zone

zumo juice (*Sp.*)

CREDITS

PHOTO CREDITS

Front Matter

Page xix: © McGraw-Hill Education, Truth-Function, video photographer.

Chapter 1

Opener: © Orlando Sierra/AFP/Getty Images; p. 2: © McGraw-Hill Education, Truth-Function, video photographer; p. 3: © Jupiterimages/Getty Images; p. 4: © McGraw-Hill Education, Truth-Function, video photographer; p. 5 (Christopher): © Dennis Wise/Getty Images RF; p. 5 (Miranda): © Blend Images/Getty Images RF; p. 5 (Gloria): © Glow Images RF; p. 5 (Jason): © Purestock/SuperStock RF; p. 6 (1a): © Hill Street Studios/Blend Images RF; p. 6 (1b, 2b): © 2007, Mike Watson Images Limited/Glow Images RF; p. 6 (2a): © Purestock/SuperStock RF; p. 6 (3a): © BananaStock/PictureQuest RF; p. 6 (3b): © Kevin Peterson/Getty Images RF; p. 6 (4a): © Floresco Productions/agefotostock RF; p. 6 (4b): © Ariel Skelley/Blend Images RF; p. 6 (bottom left): © Chroma Press/Splash News/Corbis; p. 7 (top right): © GoGo Images Corporation/Alamy RF; p. 7 (Modelo): © Comstock Images/Getty Images RF; p. 7 (1): © 2009 Jupiterimages RF; p. 7 (2): © Terry Vine/Blend Images RF; p. 7 (3): © Realistic Reflections RF; p. 7 (4): © Image Source/PictureQuest RF; p. 7 (5): © PBNJ Productions/Blend Images RF; pp. 9, 11: © McGraw-Hill Education, Truth-Function, video photographer; p. 13 (a, b, f, g): © McGraw-Hill Education; p. 13 (c, d): © Nova Development RF; p. 13 (e): © Doug Ross/Getty Images RF; p. 16 (1): © Ingram Publishing RF; p. 16 (2-4): © McGraw-Hill Education; p. 18 (top left): © Ryan McVay/Getty Images RF; p. 18 (left): © Hola Images/Getty Images RF; p. 22: © Alexandra Wyman/WireImage/Getty Images; p. 23: © Jason Merritt/Getty Images; p. 25: © Allstar Picture Library/Alamy; p. 26 (Puerto Rico): © e-llustrations Inc/Alamy RF; p. 26 (los Estados Unidos): © Romantiche/Alamy RF; p. 26 (bottom): © Royalty-Free/Corbis; p. 28: © Comstock Images/Getty Images RF; p. 29 (top right): © Carmen Martinez Banus/E+/Getty Images RF; p. 29 (top left): © Walter Zerla/Blend Images RF; p. 29 (middle): © roevin/Getty Images RF; p. 29 (bottom right): © Brand X Pictures/Getty Images RF; p. 30: © Ryan McVay/Getty Images RF; p. 31: © McGraw-Hill Education, Truth-Function, video photographer; p. 32 (1): © C Squared Studios/Getty Images RF; p. 32 (2, 5): © McGraw-Hill Education; p. 32 (3): © Shakirov/Getty Images RF; p. 32 (4): © Susan LeVan/Getty Images RF; p. 34: © George Pimentel/WireImage/Getty Images.

Chapter 2

Opener: © altrendo images/Getty Images; pp. 38-40 (4): © McGraw-Hill Education, Truth-Function, video photographer; p. 40 (left): © Photodisc/Getty Images RF; p. 41: © McGraw-Hill Education, Truth-Function, video photographer; p. 42: © Michael DeYoung/Blend Images RF; p. 46 (1-8): © McGraw-Hill Education, Truth-Function, video photographer; p. 46 (bottom left): © Kevin Sanchez/Cole Group/Getty Images RF; p. 47 (flags): © Romantiche/Alamy RF; p. 47 (España): © Yuliyan Velchev/Alamy RF; p. 47 (Puerto Rico): © e-llustrations Inc/Alamy RF; p. 47 (bottom right): © David Levenson/Getty Images; p. 49: © Royalty-Free/Corbis; p. 50 (Panamá): © Romantiche/Alamy RF; p. 50 (bottom): Source: Dr. Edwin P. Ewing, Jr./CDC; pp. 51, 53: © Sam Edwards/agefotostock RF; p. 54: © McGraw-Hill Education, Truth-Function, video photographer; p. 56: © Foodcollection RF; p. 57: © Blend Images/SuperStock RF; p. 58: © UpperCut Images/SuperStock RF; p. 60: © McGraw-Hill Education, Truth-Function, video photographer; p. 62: © Picturehouse/courtesy Everett Collection.

Chapter 3

Opener: © National Geographic Image Collection/Alamy RF; pp. 66, 69: © McGraw-Hill Education, Truth-Function, video photographer; p. 70: © Esteban Mora Muñoz; p. 73 (Modelo, 1-3, 5-6): © McGraw-Hill Education; p. 73 (4): © McGraw-Hill Education/Elizabeth Cardany; p. 74: © McGraw-Hill Education, Truth-Function, video photographer; p. 75: © Denis Doyle/Bloomberg/Getty Images; p. 76 (left): © Andreas Rentz/Getty Images; p. 76 (right): © Larry Busacca/WireImage/Getty Images; p. 78 (Juanes): © Michael Kovac/WireImage/Getty Images; p. 78 (Shakira): © Morena Brengola/Getty Images; p. 78 (Camilo Villegas): © Fernando Vergara/AP Photo; p. 78 (Sofía Vergara): © Jeffrey Mayer/WireImage/Getty Images; p. 79: © Digital Vision/Getty Images RF; p. 81: © Lauren Nicole/Getty Images RF; p. 83 (Nicaragua, El Salvador): © Romantiche/Alamy RF; p. 83 (right): © Pixtal/agefotostock RF; p. 84: © Paul Bradbury/agefotostock RF; p. 90: © Valentin Ochoa/LatinContent/Getty Images; p. 92: © Norberto Lauria/Alamy RF; p. 95: © Reuters/Corbis.

Chapter 4

Opener: © Gregory Byerline/agefotostock; p. 99: © McGraw-Hill Education, Truth-Function, video photographer; p. 101 (Modelo): © PhotoAlto/PictureQuest RF; p. 101 (1): © Image Source RF; p. 101 (2): © Fairchild Photo Service/Condé Nast/Corbis; p. 101 (3): © Robert Harding/Robert Harding World Imagery/Corbis; p. 101 (4): © Chuck Burton/AP Photo; p. 101 (5): © Prisma Archivo/Alamy; p. 101 (6): © MedioImages/SuperStock RF; p. 103: © Anne Ackermann/Getty Images RF; p. 104: © McGraw-Hill Education, Truth-Function, video photographer; p. 107 (top): © Alexandre Meneghini/AP Photo; p. 107 (bottom): © Splash News/Newscom; p. 108 (top): © Fancy Collection/SuperStock RF; p. 108 (bottom): © Jeffrey Mayer/WireImage/Getty Images; p. 109: © McGraw-Hill Education, Truth-Function, video photographer; p. 110 (Guatemala): © Romantiche/Alamy RF; p. 110 (left): © Melba Photo Agency/PunchStock RF; p. 111: © McGraw-Hill Education, Truth-Function, video photographer; p. 113: © Foodcollection RF; p. 115: © BananaStock/PunchStock RF; p. 117 (top): © Tetra Images/Getty Images RF; p. 117 (right): © Digital Vision RF; p. 118: © Javier Lira/Notimex/Newscom; p. 119: © Digital Vision RF; p. 120 (top left): © Christian Kober/Getty Images; p. 120 (top right): © Christopher Herwig/Getty Images; p. 120 (bottom left): © fotoVoyager/Getty Images RF; p. 120 (bottom right): © Catherine Karnow/Corbis; p. 121: © Jim McIsaac/Getty Images; p. 122: © RubberBall Selects/Alamy RF; p. 123 (top right): © McGraw-Hill Education, Truth-Function, video photographer; p. 123 (bottom left): © Mike Marsland/WireImage/Getty Images; p. 125: © Laemmle/Zeller Films/courtesy Everett Collection.

Chapter 5

Opener: © Stefano Paterna/Alamy; p. 129: © McGraw-Hill Education, Truth-Function, video photographer; p. 130 (Modelo): © BananaStock/PictureQuest RF; p. 130 (1, 4): © I. Rozenbaum/PhotoAlto RF; p. 130 (2): © TRBfoto/Getty Images RF; p. 130 (3): © C. Zachariasen/PhotoAlto RF; p. 130 (5): © Purestock/SuperStock RF; p. 130 (6): © L. Mouton/PhotoAlto RF; p. 131: © Keith Brofsky/Getty Images RF; pp. 133, 134: © Facundo Santana/AP Photo; p. 137 (1-7): © McGraw-Hill Education, Truth-Function, video photographer; p. 137 (right): © S. Nicolas/Iconotec RF; p. 139: © Stockbyte/PunchStock RF; p. 142: © McGraw-Hill Education, Truth-Function, video photographer; p. 145: © Siri Stafford/Digital Vision/Getty Images RF; p. 147 (Modelo): © Digital Vision/Getty Images RF; p. 147 (1): © Elena Elisseeva/Getty Images RF; p. 147 (2, 4): © Purestock/SuperStock RF; p. 147 (3): © ERproductions Ltd/agefotostock RF; p. 147 (bottom right): © McGraw-Hill Education, Truth-Function, video photographer; p. 148: © Brand X Pictures/PunchStock RF; p. 149 (left): © Splash News/Newscom; p. 149 (middle): © Jewel Samad/AFP/Getty Images; p. 149 (right): © John Shearer/WireImage/Getty Images; p. 150: © Neil Julian/Alamy RF; p. 152: © Keith Brofsky/Getty Images RF; p. 153 (Paraguay): © Romantiche/Alamy RF; p. 153

(right): © mtcurado/Getty Images RF; p. 156: © Steven Lawton/FilmMagic/Getty Images; p. 159: © McGraw-Hill Education, Truth-Function, video photographer; p. 162: © Jason Merritt/FilmMagic/Getty Images.

Chapter 6

Opener: © Mira Zaki/agefotostock; p. 166: © McGraw-Hill Education, Truth-Function, video photographer; p. 168: © Bogdan Bratosin/Getty Images RF; p. 169 (top): © Danita Delimont/Alamy; p. 169 (middle): © Gise Bracco/Nick Albi; p. 169 (bottom): © David Martin-Warr/EA; p. 172 (Modelo, 1, 3): © Foodcollection RF; p. 172 (2): Source: NOAA/Department of Commerce; p. 172 (4): © McGraw-Hill Education; p. 172 (5): Source: Renee Comet/National Cancer Institute (NCI); p. 172 (6): © Iconotec/Glow Images RF; p. 173 (Selene, María, Víctor, Carolina): © McGraw-Hill Education, Truth-Function, video photographer; p. 173 (bottom): © Digital Vision/Getty Images RF; p. 175: © lynx/Iconotec/Glow Images RF; p. 177: © Toshifumi Kitamura/AFP/Getty Images; p. 180 (top left): © McGraw-Hill Education, Truth-Function, video photographer; p. 180 (bottom left): © monkeybusinessimages/Getty Images RF; p. 182: © Don Farrall/Getty Images RF; p. 183: © Pablo Corral V/Corbis; p. 187 (left): © cokemomo/123RF.com; p. 187 (right): © Ingram Publishing/SuperStock RF; p. 188: © Photodisc/Getty Images RF; p. 189 (Chile): © Romantiche/Alamy RF; p. 189 (top right): © David Frazier/Corbis RF; p. 190: © David Bleeker Photography/Alamy; p. 192 (ceviche): © Ildi.Food/Alamy RF; p. 192 (gallo pinto): © Jennifer Kirk; p. 192 (gazpacho): © Light Thru My Lens Photography/Getty Images RF; p. 192 (pico de gallo): © Raul Taborda/Alamy RF; p. 193: © Gandhi Emanuel Ponce Juárez; p. 195: © IMCINE/Album/Newscom.

Chapter 7

Opener: © Beowulf Sheehan/Getty Images; p. 199: © McGraw-Hill Education, Truth-Function, video photographer; p. 200: © Emma Lee/Life File/Getty Images RF; p. 201: © Dynamic Graphics Group/Creatas/Alamy RF; p. 204 (a): © Europa Press/Getty Images; p. 204 (b): © Luis Acosta/AFP/Getty Images; p. 204 (c): © Erin Patrice O'Brien/Getty Images; p. 204 (d): © Pablo Blazquez Dominguez/Getty Images; p. 204 (e): © Thinkstock RF; p. 204 (f): © Rodolfo Vanegas/LatinContent/Getty Images; p. 204 (g): © Arthur Tilley/Getty Images RF; p. 204 (h): © Jane Sweeney/Getty Images; p. 204 (i): © Roger Lemoyne/Getty Images; p. 206 (top left): © Zuma Press, Inc./Alamy; p. 206 (1-6): © McGraw-Hill Education, Truth-Function, video photographer; p. 207: © Brand X Pictures/PunchStock RF; p. 208: © Author's Image/PunchStock RF; p. 209: © Frank van den Bergh/Getty Images RF; p. 210: © Livia Corona/Getty Images; p. 211 (Uruguay): © Romantiche/Alamy RF; p. 211 (top right): © Jason Rothe/Alamy RF; p. 213: © John Dowland/Getty Images RF; p. 214: © C Squared Studios/Photodisc/Getty Images RF; p. 218: © Jules Frazier/Getty Images RF; p. 221: © McGraw-Hill Education, Truth-Function, video photographer; p. 224: © Kevin Winter/NCLR/Getty Images.

Chapter 8

Opener: © Miguel Tovar/LatinContent/Getty Images; p. 227: © McGraw-Hill Education, Truth-Function, video photographer; p. 228: © Keith Bedford/Reuters/Corbis; pp. 232, 233: © McGraw-Hill Education, Truth-Function, video photographer; p. 234: © McGraw-Hill Education/Ken Karp; p. 236: © McGraw-Hill Education, Truth-Function, video photographer; p. 237 (left): © Lipnitzki/Roger Viollet/Getty Images; p. 237 (right): © Charles Eshelman/FilmMagic/Getty Images; p. 239: © Gregorio Marrero/AP Photo; p. 240: © AB1 WENN Photos/Newscom; p. 242: © Vesna Andjic/Getty Images RF; p. 243: © Paul Bradbury/agefotostock RF; p. 244 (1): © Stock Montage/Getty Images; p. 244 (2): © Album/Oronoz/Newscom; p. 244 (3): © Interfoto/akg-images; p. 244 (4): © Bettmann/Corbis; p. 246: © Miguel Vidal/Reuters/Corbis; p. 247 (la República Dominicana, Cuba): © Romantiche/Alamy RF; p. 247 (Adolfo Sardina): © Gordon Parks/Time Life Pictures/Getty Images; p. 249: © Comstock Images RF; p. 250: © Kevin Winter/NCLR/Getty Images; p. 251: © Gary Gershoff/WireImage/Getty Images; p. 252: © McGraw-Hill Education/Barry Barker; p. 253: © McGraw-Hill Education, Truth-Function, video photographer; p. 256: © Photos 12/Alamy.

Chapter 9

Opener: © Dave Jepson/Alamy; p. 260: © McGraw-Hill Education, Truth-Function, video photographer; p. 264: © Jennifer Kirk; p. 265: © McGraw-Hill Education, Truth-Function, video photographer; p. 267 (Modelo): © Royalty-Free/Corbis; p. 267 (1): © Ingram Publishing/SuperStock RF; p. 267 (2): © Domino/Getty Images RF; p. 267 (3): © Comstock Images/Jupiterimages RF; p. 267 (4): © Glow Images/SuperStock RF; p. 269: © Design Pics/Keith Levit/Getty Images RF; p. 272: © Glow Images RF; p. 274: © Blend Images/SuperStock RF; p. 275 (top left): © MIXA/Alamy RF; p. 275 (right): © McGraw-Hill Education, Truth-Function, video photographer; p. 276: © IT Stock/PunchStock RF; p. 277 (Costa Rica): © Romantiche/Alamy RF; p. 277 (right): © Steve Bly/Getty Images RF; p. 281 (Modelo): © Royalty-Free/Corbis; p. 281 (1): © Ingram Publishing RF; p. 281 (2): © Ingram Publishing/SuperStock RF; p. 281 (3): © Chris Ryan/agefotostock RF; p. 281 (4): © trbfoto/Brand X Pictures/Jupiterimages RF; p. 281 (5): © Tom Grill/Getty Images RF; p. 282 (left): © Klaus Lang/Alamy RF; p. 282 (right): © Sean Sullivan/Getty Images RF; p. 282 (bottom left): © Digital Vision/PunchStock RF; p. 282 (bottom right): © tbkmedia.de/Alamy RF; p. 283: © Carlos S. Pereyra/agefotostock RF; p. 285: © McGraw-Hill Education, Truth-Function, video photographer; p. 289: © Paulo Ferreira/Album/SuperStock.

Chapter 10

Opener: © Zuma Press, Inc./Alamy; p. 293: © McGraw-Hill Education, Truth-Function, video photographer; p. 294: © Keith Brofsky/Getty Images RF; p. 297: © Somos/Veer/Getty Images RF; p. 300: © Pixtal/agefotostock RF; p. 304 (left): © Itar-Tass/Yuri Belinsky/Newscom; p. 304 (bottom left): © Jeremy Piper/AP Photo; p. 305: © Adrees Latif/Reuters; p. 307 (el Perú): © Romantiche/Alamy RF; p. 307 (right): © Jeff Greenberg 6 of 6/Alamy; p. 311: © Mike Kemp/Getty Images RF; p. 312: © Chris Ryan/agefotostock RF; p. 313: © CMCD/Getty Images RF; p. 317: © Royalty-Free/Corbis; p. 319: © McGraw-Hill Education, Truth-Function, video photographer; p. 322: © Lions Gate Films/courtesy Everett Collection.

Chapter 11

Opener: © Johnny Haglund/Lonely Planet Images/Getty Images; pp. 326, 333: © McGraw-Hill Education, Truth-Function, video photographer; p. 334: © James Woodson/Digital Vision/Getty Images RF; p. 335: © Jupiterimages RF; p. 338: © Brand X Pictures/PunchStock RF; p. 339 (left): © Abelardo Fonseca/La Nacion de Costa Rica/Newscom; p. 339 (right): © AFP/Getty Images; p. 341 (México): © Romantiche/Alamy RF; p. 341 (right): © Elías Martin del Campo; p. 343: © Daniel Diebel/Getty Images RF; p. 347: Source: Cade Martin/CDC; p. 349: © Frederik Vercruysse/dmva-architecten.be; pp. 351, 352: © McGraw-Hill Education, Truth-Function, video photographer; p. 354: © Kevin Winter/WireImage/Getty Images.

Chapter 12

Opener: © Mike Blake/Reuters/Corbis; p. 357: © McGraw-Hill Education, Truth-Function, video photographer; p. 361 (bicicleta): © Creative Crop/Digital Vision/Getty Images RF; p. 361 (alpinismo): © Fancy Photography/Veer RF; p. 361 (voleibol): © Fuse/Getty Images RF; p. 361 (patineta): © Stockdisc/PunchStock RF; p. 351 (béisbol): © Image Source/PunchStock RF; p. 361 (levantar pesas): © Radius Images/Corbis RF; p. 361 (boxear, esquiar): © Ingram Publishing/SuperStock RF; p. 361 (fútbol americano, patinar): © Comstock Images/Alamy RF; p. 361 (tenis): © Glow Images RF; p. 361 (surfear): © EpicStockMedia/Alamy RF; p. 362 (1): © Ingram Publishing/Alamy RF; p. 362 (2, 7): © Image Source/PunchStock RF; p. 362 (3): © McGraw-Hill Education/Mark Dierker; p. 362 (4): © Comstock Images/Alamy RF; p. 362 (5): © Ingram Publishing/SuperStock RF; p. 362 (6): © Don Tremain/Getty Images RF; p. 362 (8): © image100/Corbis RF; p. 362 (9): © Dana Hoff/Getty Images RF; p. 362 (10): © D. Hurst/Alamy RF; pp. 362 (bottom), 363 (top): © McGraw-Hill Education, Truth-Function, video photographer; p. 363 (right): © Steve Thomas/Alamy; p. 364 (1): © Blend Images/Ariel Skelley/Getty Images RF; p. 364 (2): © Thinkstock/Getty Images RF; p. 364 (3): © McGraw-Hill Education/Rick Brady; p. 364 (4): © BJI/Blue Jean Images/Getty Images RF; p. 368 (1): © Adam Gault/SPL/Getty

Images RF; p. 368 (2): © Sherrie Nickol/agefotostock RF; p. 368 (3): © Andres Rodriguez/Alamy RF; p. 368 (4): © dbimages/Alamy; p. 369: © Karen Wilson/ASP/Getty Images; p. 372 (Colombia, Venezuela): © Romantiche/Alamy RF; p. 372 (top left): © Tim de Waele/Corbis/Getty Images; p. 374: © Matthew Stockman/Getty Images; p. 375 (1): © Roy Hsu/Getty Images RF; p. 375 (2): © Steve Cole/Getty Images RF; p. 375 (3): © LM Productions/Getty Images RF; p. 375 (4): © Corbis/Jupiterimages RF; p. 375 (5, 7): © Ingram Publishing RF; p. 375 (6): © John Lund/Heather Hryciw/Blend Images RF; p. 375 (8): © Digital Vision/PunchStock RF; p. 376: © Richard Loader/Getty Images RF; p. 382: © Danita Delimont/Alamy; p. 384: © Caro/Alamy; p. 385 (left): © Lars A. Niki; p. 385 (middle): © PM Images/Getty Images RF; p. 385 (right): © Mark Andersen/Getty Images RF; p. 387: © Photos 12/Alamy.

Chapter 13

Opener: © Kuttig Travel 2/Alamy; p. 391: © McGraw-Hill Education, Truth-Function, video photographer; p. 396 (loro): © Ingram Publishing RF; p. 396 (mono): © Brand X Pictures/Getty Images RF; p. 396 (oso): © McGraw-Hill Education/Barry Barker; p. 396 (perezoso): © McGraw-Hill Education; p. 396 (sapo): © Corey Hochachka/Design Pics RF; p. 396 (tortuga): © Author's Image/PunchStock RF; p. 396 (ballena): © Purestock/Getty Images RF; p. 396 (delfin): © MedioImages/SuperStock RF; p. 396 (león marino): © Lissa Harrison; p. 396 (pingüino): © Guillen Photography/Wildlife/Ecuador/Galapagos/Alamy RF; p. 397: © McGraw-Hill Education, Truth-Function, video photographer; p. 399: © Melba Photo Agency/PunchStock RF; p. 400: © FAN Travelstock/Alamy RF; p. 401 (top right): © FabioFilzi/Getty Images RF; p. 401 (right): © Royalty-Free/Corbis; p. 402: Source: Charles H. Smith/U.S. Fish & Wildlife Service; p. 403: © Westend61/Getty Images RF; p. 404 (top left): © Steve St. John/Getty Images RF; p. 404 (top right): © Kevin Schafer/Alamy RF; p. 404 (left): © Richard Kemp/Getty Images; p. 404 (right): © Ammit/Alamy RF; p. 404 (bottom left): © Brand X Pictures/PunchStock RF; p. 405 (Ecuador, Bolivia): © Romantiche/Alamy RF; p. 405 (right): © Lissa Harrison; p. 406: Source: David Bowman/U.S. Fish & Wildlife Service; p. 410: © Glow Images RF; p. 411 (top right): © Jennifer Kirk; p. 411 (right): © Gerard Lacz/agefotostock; p. 412: © McGraw-Hill Education, Truth-Function, video photographer; p. 414 (Modelo): © Fuse/Jupiterimages RF; p. 414 (1): © Lane Oatey/Blue Jean Images/Getty Images RF; p. 414 (2, 5): © Sam Edwards/agefotostock RF; p. 414 (3): © Glow Images RF; p. 414 (4): © Brand X Pictures/Jupiterimages RF; p. 414 (6): © Purestock/SuperStock RF; p. 415: © Sayre Berman/Corbis.

Chapter 14

Opener: © Attila Kleb/Alamy; p. 419: © McGraw-Hill Education, Truth-Function, video photographer; p. 421: © Rodrigo Varela/Wireimage/Getty Images; p. 423: © Ingram Publishing/Fotosearch RF; p. 424: © McGraw-Hill Education, Truth-Function, video photographer; p. 426: © EPA European Pressphoto Agency B.V./Alamy; p. 428 (left): © Jack Manning/New York Times Co./Getty Images; p. 428 (right): © Wireimage/Getty Images; p. 429 (top right): © Mathew Imaging/WireImage/Getty Images; p. 429 (right): © Corbis; p. 431: © Francisco Goncalves/Getty Images; p. 434 (Argentina): © Romantiche/Alamy RF; p. 434 (bottom left): © Pascal Le Segretain/Getty Images; p. 436: © Jeff Vespa/THR/Getty Images; p. 438: © McGraw-Hill Education, Truth-Function, video photographer; p. 441: © Photos 12/Alamy.

Chapter 15

Opener: © EPA/Luis Galdamez/Newscom; p. 444: © McGraw-Hill Education, Truth-Function, video photographer; p. 446: © Corbis Premium RF/Alamy; p. 449: © McGraw-Hill Education, Truth-Function, video photographer; p. 450 (left): © Terry Vine/Blend Images RF; p. 450 (bottom left): © Monashee Frantz/agefotostock RF; p. 458 (Honduras): © Romantiche/Alamy RF; p. 458 (left): © Eduardo Verdugo/AP Photo; p. 460: © Hero/Corbis/Glow Images RF; pp. 463, 464: © McGraw-Hill Education, Truth-Function, video photographer; p. 467: © Victor Chavez/WireImage/Getty Images.

Chapter 16

Opener: © Melanie Stetson Freeman/The Christian Science Monitor/Getty Images; p. 470: © McGraw-Hill Education, Truth-Function, video photographer; p. 472: © Juice Images/Corbis RF; pp. 473, 474, 476:

© McGraw-Hill Education, Truth-Function, video photographer; p. 477: © Robert Daly/agefotostock RF; p. 478 (top): © PhotoAlto/SuperStock RF; p. 478 (middle): © Creatas/PunchStock RF; p. 478 (bottom): © Ned Frisk/Blend Images RF; p. 479: © Popperfoto/Getty Images; p. 480 (España): © Yuliyan Velchev/Alamy RF; p. 480 (left): © EPA European Pressphoto Agency B.V./Alamy; p. 482: © Eduardo Verdugo/AP Photo; p. 485: © Paul Fenton/Zuma Press, Inc./Alamy; p. 488: © McGraw-Hill Education, Truth-Function, video photographer; p. 491: © Photos 12/Alamy.

TEXT CREDITS:

Chapter 1 – page 34:

Source: Pacifika, "Docemeses," *Supermagique*, San Fancisco, CA: Six Degrees Records.

Chapter 3 – page 95:

Source: Celia Cruz y El General, "Ella tienefuego".

Chapter 3 page 90:

Source: Veronica García, "Presidencia (de la nación Argentina) para chicos, proyecto de la Secretaria de Medios de Comunicación," Secretaria de Medios de Comunicación. www.chicos.gov.ar.

Chapter 4 – page 122:

Excerpt from "Lo mejor de la vida: entre los 20 y los 30" October 7, 2008. Madrid, Spain: Multiprensa y Más, S.L. Copyright © 2008 by Multiprensa y Más. All rights reserved. Used with permission.

Chapter 5 – page 132:

Andrés Diplotti, "Paranoia," *Pulga Snob*. May 15, 2009. www.lapulgasnob.com. Copyright © 2009 by Andrés Diplotti. All rights reserved. Used with permission.

Chapter 5 – page 157:

Source: "Don Juan Manuel, "Padre, Hijo o Caballo?" *First Spanish Reader: A Beginner's Dual-LanguageBook* edited by Angel Flores. Toronto, NY: Dover Publications, 1964, pp. 2-3. Copyright © 1964 by Dover Publications."

Chapter 7 – page 220:

Domingo, Carmen, "Los ritos y conjuros de la Nochevieja," *El Nuevo Herald*, December 31, 2008. Copyright © 2008 by Miami Herald. All rights reserved. Used with permission.

Chapter 7 – page 224:

Source: Luis Fonsi, "Tu Amor".

Chapter 11 – pages 349-350:

"Casas para el siglo XXI: Pequeñas, flexibles y mutables," *El Buscador de Arquitectura*

Chapter 13 – pages 410-411:

Vicens, Toni and Tudurí, Carles, "Aventura y ecoturismoenPerú," *ViajesResponsables*. Copyright © by ViajesResponsables. All rights reserved. Used with permission.

Chapter 14 – pages 436-437:

Sánchez, Juan Luis, *Zoe Saldañaesunaestrella de cine bilingüe*, June 24, 2010. Copyright © 2010 by DeCine21. All rights reserved. Used with permission.

Chapter 15 – page 461:

Millán, José Antonio, "Malas y buenasnoticias," *El Pais*, November 3, 2010. Copyright © 2010 by El Pais. All rights reserved. Used with permission.

Chapter 16 – pages 486-487:

de Gauna, R. Ruiz, "Los jóvenesretrasansuemancipación hasta la fecha de la boda, en el umbral de los treinta," *Noticias de Álava*, May 9, 2009. Copyright © 2009 by Noticias de Álava. All rights reserved. Used with permission.

Note: There are two parts to this index. The Grammar Topics include a vocabulary list. The Cultural Topics index includes references to Spanish speaking nations as well as cultural features.

GRAMMAR TOPICS

a
  to clarify who is affected by unplanned events, 280
  emphasizing **gustar** and similar verbs, 217
  with indirect objects, 213
abbreviated words, 40
abrir, past participle, 507
adjective, opposites, 44
adjectives
  agreement in gender and number, 48
  cognates, 44
  colors, 44
  demonstrative, 88
  with **estar** or **ser**, 52
  hair color, eye color, and complexion, 45
  placement, 493–494
    changes in meaning, 494
  possessive, 27–28
  synonyms for frequently used, 44 See also descriptive adjectives
advice, literal translations versus fixed expressions, 5
afeitarse, 145
age, 38
ago, 179
al, 40
algo, 155
alguno/a/os/as, 155
alphabet, Spanish, 10, 10n
  i latina and **y griega**, 11n
  ll and **rr**, 10n
  w, 10
andar, uses, 347
años, expressing age, 38
antojarse, 279
aprender
  past participle, 337
  past subjunctive, 427
  preterite tense, 178–179
  tú commands, 309
aquel/aquella/aquellos/aquellas, 495–496
articles
  definite, 18
  gender, 493
  indefinite, 18
asistir, present tense, 81

asking questions, question words, 52
asking where someone is going, 40
auxiliary verbs
  estar in present progressive, 151, 346–347, 374
    See also **haber**
ayudar, present participle, 346

bailar, present tense, 81
bañarse, 145
to become, 152
body, parts of, 233
bueno, 108
  placement, 493
buscar, present subjunctive, 377

calendars, 75
capitalization
  days of the week, 75
  months, 14
cenar
  present progressive, 346
  present tense, 80
cognates
  adjectives, 44
  o → ue cognate pairs, 86
  true and false, 11
colors, 44
comer
  imperfect, 208
  past participle, 336
  present progressive, 346
  present subjunctive, 377
  present tense, 80
  tú commands, 309
  Ud./Uds. commands, 313
command forms, 309
  making polite invitations, 328
  nosotros/as commands, 508
  with object pronouns, 342–343, 508
  "opposite" vowel in, 309, 310, 311, 312
  subjunctive compared, 379
    See also **tú** commands;
  Ud./Uds. commands
comparatives, 108
  of equality, 496
  más de with numerals, 496
comprar, present subjunctive, 377

conditional perfect tense, 514
conditional tense, 452–453
  irregular forms, 514
congratulations, 202
conjecture, future, to express, 432
conocer
  irregular **yo** form, 141, 498
  preterite and imperfect forms, 503–504
  uses, 141, 498
contigo / conmigo, 217
contractions, **al**, 40
contrary-to-fact situations, 455–456
correr, present tense, 81
creer, preterite, 501
cuando, 512
cubrir, past participle, 507

daily routines, 71–72
dar
  indirect object pronouns, 213
  la bienvenida a, 326
  past subjunctive, 427
  present subjunctive, 377
  preterite, 501
dates, 16
days of the week, 75
deber, declining politely with, 168
debería + *infinitive*, 392
decir
  conditional tense, 452
  future, 433
  past participle, 337
  present subjunctive, 378, 400
  present tense, 111–112, 140, 378
  preterite tense, 182
  tú commands, 310
definite articles, 18
  plural, 21
  with superlatives, 497
demonstrative adjectives, 88
  aquel/aquella/aquellos/aquellas, 495–496
demonstrative pronouns, 496
descriptive adjectives, 43–44
  colors, 44
  placement, 493–494
  synonyms for frequently used, 44
de to express possession, 502

CULTURAL TOPICS

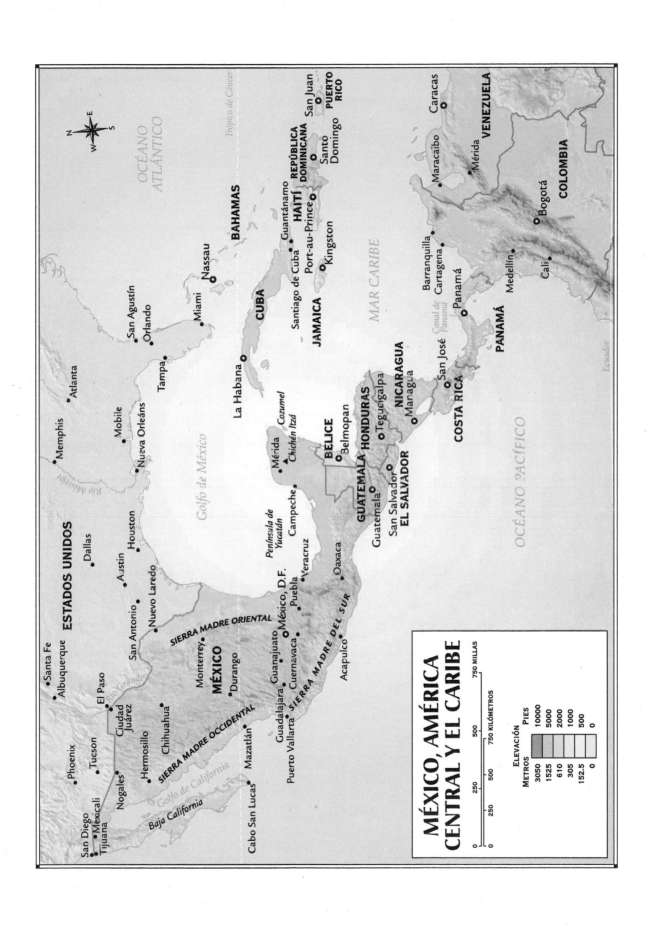

MÉXICO, AMÉRICA CENTRAL Y EL CARIBE

ESTADOS UNIDOS

San Diego
Tijuana
Mexicali
Nogales
Phoenix
Tucson
Santa Fe
Albuquerque
El Paso
Ciudad Juárez
Hermosillo
Chihuahua
Dallas
Austin
San Antonio
Nuevo Laredo
Monterrey
Durango
Memphis
Atlanta
Mobile
Nueva Orleáns
Houston
San Agustín
Orlando
Tampa
Miami
Nassau

MÉXICO

Mazatlán
Guadalajara
Puerto Vallarta
Guanajuato
México, D.F.
Cuernavaca
Puebla
Veracruz
Acapulco
Oaxaca
Campeche
Mérida
Chichén Itzá
Cozumel

Cabo San Lucas
Baja California
Golfo de California
Río Grande
Río Misisipí
Golfo de México
Península de Yucatán

SIERRA MADRE OCCIDENTAL
SIERRA MADRE ORIENTAL
SIERRA MADRE DEL SUR

OCÉANO ATLÁNTICO
Trópico de Cáncer

BAHAMAS
La Habana
CUBA
Santiago de Cuba
Guantánamo
HAITÍ
Port-au-Prince
REPÚBLICA DOMINICANA
Santo Domingo
San Juan
PUERTO RICO
JAMAICA
Kingston

MAR CARIBE

BELICE
Belmopan
GUATEMALA
Guatemala
HONDURAS
Tegucigalpa
EL SALVADOR
San Salvador
NICARAGUA
Managua
COSTA RICA
San José
PANAMÁ
Panamá
Canal de Panamá

OCÉANO PACÍFICO

Ecuador

VENEZUELA
Caracas
Maracaibo
Mérida
Barranquilla
Cartagena
Medellín
Bogotá
Cali
COLOMBIA

ELEVACIÓN

METROS	PIES
3050	10000
1525	5000
610	2000
305	1000
152.5	500
0	0

0   250   500   750 KILÓMETROS
0   250   500   750 MILLAS

AMÉRICA DEL SUR

NICARAGUA

COSTA
RICA

PANAMÁ

MAR CARIBE

Barranquilla

Maracaibo

Caracas

Río Orinoco

VENEZUELA

Medellín

Bogotá

Cali

COLOMBIA

Quito

ECUADOR

Guayaquil

OCÉANO
PACÍFICO

PERÚ

CORDILLERA DE LOS ANDES

Lima

Machu Picchu
Cuzco

Lago Titicaca

Arequipa

BOLIVIA

La Paz

Sucre

Antofagasta

CHILE

OCÉANO PACÍFICO

Isla Pinta

Isla Marchena

Isla San Salvador

Isla Santa Cruz

Isla
Isabela

Isla San
Cristóbal

Puerto
Baquerizo
Moreno

ISLAS
GALÁPAGOS
(ECUADOR)

0   100 MILLAS
0   100 KILÓMETROS

0   8 MILLAS
0   8 KILÓMETROS

Hanga Roa

Mataveri

Cabo Sur

Cabo
Cummings

OCÉANO
PACÍFICO

ISLA DE PASCUA
(CHILE)

Valparaíso

Santiago

ARGENTINA

Concepción

San Carlos de
Bariloche

Córdoba

Rosario

Buenos
Aires

PARAGUAY

Asunción

Río Paraná

URUGUAY

Montevideo

Río de la Plata

Bahía Blanca

GUYANA

Georgetown

Paramaribo

Cayenne

GUAYANA FRANCESA

SURINAM

Ecuador

OCÉANO
ATLÁNTICO

Manaus

Río Amazonas

Belém

BRASIL

Recife

Brasília

São Paulo

Puerto Iguazú

Rio de Janeiro

Trópico de
Capricornio

OCÉANO
ATLÁNTICO

OCÉANO
PACÍFICO

Punta Arenas

Estrecho de
Magallanes

Islas
Malvinas

Cabo de Hornos

Tierra del Fuego

AMÉRICA DEL SUR

0   250   500   750 MILLAS

0   250   500   750 KILÓMETROS

ELEVACIÓN

METROS	PIES
3050	10000
1525	5000
610	2000
305	1000
152.5	500
0	0